BAILEY'S METAPHYSICAL LEXICON

Volume 6

CREATE, ENHANCE, AND MAINTAIN HARMONY

JOSEPH A. BAILEY II MD FACS

Member of the clinical faculty at the UCR/UCLA Division of
Biomedical Sciences at the University of California, Riverside

ISBN: 1540796795
ISBN 13: 9781540796790
Library of Congress Control Number: 2016908784
CreateSpace Independent Publishing Platform
North Charleston, South Carolina

ABOUT THE COVER

Although Very Ancient Africans originated Lexicons, a beginning European Middle Ages' interest for them arose so as to order Greek and Latin literature. So, their starting to define words of one language in terms of another was spurred by culture pursuits of the C15-C16 Renaissance's peoples. The word "*Lexicon*" (Greek, 'Wordbook'), borrowed from Middle French in 1603, meant 'word legend'—concerning speech. The 1647 sense of vocabulary of a language or subject was expanded to 'words' in 1836. As a member of the family of Reference Books, Lexicon was deemed to be words of or belonging to a reference book. Its collection of articles, usually in alphabetical order, was also *Thematic*. Thematic is the arranging of words by themes or topics, usually accompanied by an index—e.g. Roget's Thesaurus. Thereafter, the study of the origin and meanings of words, a theoretical science, has been called *Lexicology*. *Lexicography* is the compilation of words (e.g. dictionaries) + books about things (e.g. encyclopedias), defining meanings + tracing etymologies of the words of a language. These comprised the Linguistic branch linking Semantics, an abstract discipline, with the tangible artifact, the Dictionary—whose making is the applied science. Meanwhile, "Lexicon," as a Classification term, has Dictionary, Wordbook, Glossary, Onomasticon, Gazetteer, Synonymicon, Thesaurus, Synonym Guides, Usage Guides, Concordances, and Encyclopedias as Class family members. An example is the German word for Encyclopedias, known as "Lexikons.

Since no Dictionary/Lexicon contains more than a fraction of all the words in a language, a major problem is to decide what vocabulary entries to include. Even though the largest unabridged English dictionary has more than 500,000 entries, Lexicographers have estimated ten times as many words could have been listed. Next Lexicographers decide each word's spellings (which vary over time and differ at a given time), capitalizations; etymology; and meanings (often conflicting). Hence, it is a fundamental error to use ancient European meanings of a word and apply that meaning to what goes on in today's times—or vice versa. Many borrowed words are derived from Indo-European via Middle English, Old English, and the Germanic Languages. Still, they all originated out of Very Ancient African words or word patterns during African Migrations starting c125,000 BC into the North and East into India, the Far East, the Near East, the South Pacific--and c45,000 BC into Europe.

Perhaps the pre-history of the European languages descended from the Ice-Age Cro-Magnons or from the mysterious Basques of North Spain and Southwest France. While Indo-European languages were developing in the late pre-historic times (10,000 BC to 4000 BC), German, Greek, and Latin were well-developed and mature by 100 BC. English, as a distinct spoken language, probably began early in the Christian era with the rude dialects of the Angles (from the Baltic Sea area), Saxons (modern Germany), Jutes, and Frisians. Throughout much of the ancient period, there were no authoritative references explaining what a word meant or how it was to be used in conversations. In business and the humanities, considerable confusion reigned because various groups used the same word to express different ideas; because the same idea was expressed in unrelated words; and because conquering tribes brought in their own words and meanings for the familiar ideas of the natives, in whatever culture. This meant the same word took on several meanings, some of which were often unrelated. As with old names changes, new words carried not only new meanings but also values and rules. These shaped and influenced how natives related to unfamiliar things.

After collapse of Roman authority around 410 AD, a group of primitive Germanic tribes (not to be confused with today's Germans), living along the North Sea Coast (between Germany and England), migrated from Jutland and Southern Denmark across the channel into Britain. They were settled by 449 AD—their today's descendants being Anglo-Saxons. These newcomers--the Angles, Saxons, and Jutes--spoke a mutually intelligible set of Germanic dialects which they called "*English*" but are now called "*Old English*" or "*Anglo-Saxon*."

During the Old English period (600 AD to 1100 AD), Middle English (1100 to 1500), and Modern English (1500 to the present) there was a revival of classical African and, to a much lesser extent, classical Greek and Roman. The Norman French 1066 invasion of England + Renaissance humanists introduced a host of more words. This involved great subjective processes in determining and arranging definitions by collecting citations to establish a word's many different meanings. For example, some *Lexicographers* distinguished 5 shades of meanings for a word but another, only 3. They proceed from the first meaning they recognized to the most recent—and being biased about that—or from the most common meaning of their culture, ignoring other cultures. Thus, Lexicon meanings given, rather than being about the truth, have always been opinions. Today, a *Lexicon* deals with classical or scriptural language (e.g. a Hebrew lexicon) or with a technical or factious (dissention) subject. Many embrace formal survey questionnaires and citation corpora use--both traditional, kept on cards, and electronic, stored in computer databases. Typically, European Dictionary/Lexicon makers only include Greek, Hebrew, Latin, Arabic, and non-African others + by-pass all words' "what it is" and focus on the word's "what it does" and "how it appears."

To set the record straight, my Metaphysical Lexicon reverses these standard European practices by: (1) spotlighting African words and using Outsider's terms to present contrast; (2) featuring African Tradition's knowledge soundness, by dealing with the "what it is" of a word and the nature of the word's creator; (3) de-emphasizing a word's "what it does" or the "how it appears"—for these merely reflect limitations of the human mind regarding creativity as well as in misperceptions. Despite African Tradition words always beginning with the Spiritual--and since the Spiritual is Unknowable--whenever available to me, herein, meanings are given in a Metaphysical sense. Such applies to all Ancient African derived Spiritual and Metaphysical denotative concepts, thoughts, and words. This is in marked contrast to Europeans who disregard the Spiritual and Metaphysical, substituting opinionated meanings within a Supernatural context for application in the Physical World.

For these reasons, anyone intensely desiring to know Truths of African Tradition is to absolutely avoid use of definitions, stories, or Denotative/Connotative meanings of a European Schematic or Supernatural nature. I have never seen a European give an accurate assessment of anything pertaining to Black History in general, and African Tradition in particular. Failure to adhere to this warning, guarantees an ever-increasing mental turmoil of confusion, conflict, and frustration. Still, one ought to know the European and Supernatural meanings and their etymology in order to help understand how Europeans are thinking about what they convey for application to self-defense, self-protection, and to go on a non-offensive offense. My 50+ years of research has been to find the truth as close as I can possibly get. That has required a tremendous amount of research in non-European written texts. One discovery is of African word meanings having an aura or atmospheric presence and to be in it enables me to "Feel" meanings. These meanings are always inside the Spiritual Elements of Unconditional Love, Truth, Reality, and the Natural--and anything 0.000001 degree off that flow is not African. On the one hand, this book includes--like all Lexicons--introspections, discussions of the nature, meaning, history, use of words, word elements + examinations of pre-existing works of reference and other sources. On the other hand, it does not follow any European guidelines for Lexicons, but rather mainly my impressions of African Tradition's Thought flow.

Cover Design is by Sharon Bingaman RN

PREFACE

The Mind grows by what feeds it—whether derived from Observation, Experience, Imagination, or Communication—as involved in persuading, informing, entertaining, expressing, sharing, teaching, instructing, educating, recreating (e.g. playing with words in figures of speech and figures of thought), or serving as a call to action. To approach "Spiritual Nourishment" wrapped in words, Ancient Africans selected Icon Images representing Essences of Divine Laws. Such *Laws refer to the Base Foundation of all Cosmic manifestations and denote a sequence of inherently related events that occur with unvarying uniformity under the same conditions.* Thus, Words of African Tradition pertain to what to do in order to fashion and experience infinite Beauty in a human's Private Self "ME/WE" world. As a boy, my Mother had me fetch books on the subjects of Mythology, Poetry, and related topics out of our small library so as to assist her in "Cross-Word" game struggles. As a result, I was introduced to the "ballpark" of Ancient African Words. But this made no conscious impression until in the mid-1970s when I had the urge to learn Black History, starting with Ancient Africa. Yet, no books in the library or anywhere—including my 46 sets of encyclopaedias—were beneficial because they were all written by Europeans with the intent to demean Black People. As a result of being nonplussed, I recalled my Mother's focus on Words and Mythology, and turned to those in order to gain insight as to where to begin my research. A key point was somehow learning that the ancient Greeks actually obtained their gods and goddesses from Africa.

Further pursuit along those lines opened up the wonderful world of Ancient Africans that had been deliberately hidden from today's world—no doubt because of envy of their super-brilliance. Next, I "stumbled" on true Black scholars of African History—not the Black Puppets taught by and caterers to Europeans—who made profound statements. One said people of today's world have never been taught the Truth about any ancient history. Thus, what is largely unknown is practically every worthwhile thing has come from our Ancient African Ancestors. Examples are: All Mathematics, Physics, Scientific Method, true Logic, Critical Thinking, Medicine and Surgery, and similar highly intellectual subjects. Millennia later, practically each of them spread throughout the Western world under the name of *"Greek creations"*. Despite being always presented in European textbooks as doing "everything" great in the world today, the fact is *that Greeks' work products were merely translations and transmissions of Ancient African intellectual property.* They laid out European plagiarism patterns persisting to the present--and to the point of their admiring it. This is what European Medieval and Modern "scholarship" is about. The African papyri of the Middle Kingdom (3348-3182 BC)—given by Europeans the European names of Moscow, Berlin, Kahun, and Rhind—have *proved to be plagiarized* by *Pythagoras, Archimedes, Thales, Plato, Eudoxus, Oenopides, Aristotle, Solon, Indocsus,* and other Greeks.

Realizing the truth of these statements made it clear to me that to become a student of Ancient African Philosophy Tradition requires ones mind be entirely open and totally dedicated to that pursuit--while putting "EVERYTHING" European "on-hold". As people are prone to do in learning something new, there can be no "Picking and Choosing" out of African and European Traditions' literature, including dictionaries—for they are like "oil and water". Oil does not dissolve in water because oil particles fail to divide into their separate molecules, but remain in much larger particles or globules that stick together. To mix anything European with anything African is the process of dilution and pollution of the Natural World's Spiritual Knowledge, as elaborated on by Ancient Africans. The fantasy of Europeans' Supernatural World has absolutely no way of getting to the Truth or to Wisdom. To disregard these points leads to more and more confusion, conflict, and ambiguity entanglements.

The gist reason is that African Tradition is all about the Spiritual Elements—i.e. Unconditional Love, Truth, Reality, and the Natural. Their evolution follows a Mathematical pattern inside the Processess of Observable

Nature because they have Correspondence with the Unseeable Esoteric. These process design "Knowings" and "Certainty." By contrast, Europeans' Supernatural Tradition is Anti-Spiritual Elements oriented. They define this Supernatural "Air Castle" as *not to be questioned for it is unnatural, unconquerable, unmovable, undeniable, unexplainable, incomparable, unimaginable, immeasurable, and unthinkable.* Also, Believers must accept their Supernatual God, Hell, and Devil based upon having "Faith," "Hope," and "Beliefs" as spewed by their military type authorities' say-so. Thus, by having no Thought Order, what is said they call "Non-Rational" thinking. Supernatural leaders add that this is "Superior" to anything pertaining to the Spiritual God of the Natural World. To follow Supernatural Beliefs and Opinions, anchored in an Indifference/Hate/Evil/Sadism mindset, is to be involved in a total "Sham/Scam". Its Inhumanity displays as Kill/Take/Destroy/Dominate/Oppress/Control.

Hence, a major purpose of this book is to present Ancient Africans' "whole Truth and nothing but the Truth" as best I can determine after 50 years of intense study. The bulk of the herein contents have come from my "Ambitious Black Isolated Individualists" and from "African Wisdom Tradition vs. European Knowledge" books. The rest is from 40 of my published books on the "Minds" of Black People—starting when Humankind first appeared 200,000 years ago. What anchored my insights into African Tradition was my "Ancient African Bible Messages" book. The overwhelming majority of the herein definitions are devised after going through up to 1000 books per word and extracting the theme of a given word on its different planes of existence. No other work does this! The point is to emphasize that since Black Americans and any people under European domination have never been taught the Truth about anything, it is ones obligation, duty, and responsibility to learn Truth on their own so as to be on the right track and going in the right direction towards a "Good Life" and "Heaven Afterlife."

This will take a great deal of work because following any Supernatural pattern makes it impossible to have a sound base on which one can build a sound Thought Structure. The Supernatural—being about the "here and now" in the Material world and based upon Fantasy--means its advocates do not know any Truths—do not want to know any Truths—do not want others to know any Truths—and do all they can to hide all Truths outright or by SEEMS right deception. Because of totally dedicating my retirement life to getting as close to the Truth as I possibly can, what I present in this book is a place to gather ideas for ones own research. This means going against the Crowd who, themselves, are led by Supernatural leaders without realizing their minds are controlled in military style to follow the leader—to be superficial and patterned thinkers—to stay "excited" by being addicted to Trinkets and Trivia—and to constantly stir up troubles to keep groups of humans fighting each other so as to never have time to focus on the real enemy all share. Elaboration on any subject included within this book can be found in any of my books listed in the back.

The author gives deep thanks to Sharon Bingaman RN for assisting with proof-reading, research, and critiques.

Joseph A. Bailey II, MD, FACS
12/2/16

A

ABILITY: During C8 AD, the ability to do things, as in the potent (the physical capacity to use an object) came into power. The Romance language shift factors led to its C13 English 'to make powerful'; then strengthen (1540); then powerhouse (1881); then 'supply with power' (1898). "*Capacity*" (the power to receive) includes power + Ability. "*Ability*"--the inherent power to do—i.e. improved with exercise implies a *Faculty* (an inherent quality within ones Selfhood) to perform acts in the 'here and now' without much training or education.

ABSTRACT: Abstract is an entity consisting of an Association of Ideas or Thoughts accompanying each other about one or a family of Metaphysical Things reduced to its/their essence.

ABSTRACTION: the "Big Picture" of a given like-kind Material Thing reduced to its Theme essence.

ABSTRACT/ABSTRACTION: An *Abstract* is one or an Association of Ideas or Thoughts about an individual's or a group's Primary Quality/Qualities (Intangible) which has been harmoniously meshed into its/their Metaphysical Essence (i.e. irreducible). Examples are Bonding and Caring. An *Abstraction* is an Association of Ideas or Thoughts concerning real "*Concrete*" Things which have been harmoniously meshed into its/their Metaphysical Essence (i.e. irreducible). The "Name" of a Concept—an Abstract--is like an algebraic or geometrical symbol—inasmuch as it "stands for" certain things not mentally pictured. It is like the figure "7" which stands for seven of anything.

ABSTRACT/ABSTRACTION CRITICAL THINKING: Inside the Whole of a Thing are an association of independent Things which interdependently work together for a common purpose. Thus, there is "Sameness" associated with "Uniqueness"—Unity among Diversity—Commonality within Multiplicity—Like-Kindness within Differences. The "Sameness," "Unity," "Commonality," and "Like-Kindness" are all Abstracts or Abstractions. These four are the inner similarity links present in a family of like-kind things together. To elaborate, a human "Family" is a group of people related by blood (Genetics), by marriage, or by adoption—all bearing the same family name. That *"Family Name" is an Abstraction* because it deals with what is in the Physical World. There is no family apart from the people. Apart from the Family, each person is Unique. Yet, as part of the family, that same person shares a Sameness that connects her/him to all others that make up the "Family" being considered. Thus, the word "Family," a symbol, has no independent existence, for there is no "Family" apart from the people in it. The web of relationships is the link connecting the Uniqueness of each member into the Sameness. The Material aspects of each family member's inner nature is an Abstraction while the Spiritual part is an Abstract. In a "Blood"-related family, both the Abstract and Abstraction ingredients make up the Family. Their shared "Genetics" of both a Spiritual and a Material nature makes for an Abstract/Abstraction combination. In the context of a family formed by marriage or by adoption but all bearing the same family name, the word "Family" is an Abstract but "Family," in reference to the people involved, is an Abstraction. So an *Abstract* is one or an Association of Ideas or Thoughts about an individual's or a group's *Primary Quality/Qualities (Intangible) which has been harmoniously meshed into its/their Metaphysical Essence (i.e. irreducible)*—e.g. "Family" exhibiting Bonding and Caring. *Abstract Thinking* is ones mind fashioning a "Virtual" (boundary-less) Contingent out of something in the Metaphysical (the Spiritual wrapped in the Ether) or Supernatural (e.g. cartoons) realms. Such virtual or Contingent Beings pertain to the Metaphysical and the infinite or to the Supernatural and the finite. An *Abstraction is about the "Big Picture" of a given like-kind Material Thing reduced to its Theme essence.* In bartering goods, Primitive Africans put stones into a sack to convey how much of something was owned or owed. This was an abstraction "figuring out" way to reduce object negotiation problems--a process embracing *"Forethought"* (doing all the necessary planning before taking "calculated" risks) by using Virtual or Contingent Being concepts. A "Virtual" or Contingent Being (a non-existent thing having a payload impact) pertaining to images residing in Objective and temporal dominions is an Association of Ideas or Thoughts concerning real *"Concrete" Things* which have been harmoniously meshed into its/their Metaphysical Essence (i.e. irreducible). *'Concreteness'* has no clear definition but often refers to: (1) an immediate experience of realities—whether of Unbounded, Partially Bounded, or Bounded physical objects themselves; (2) belonging to or standing for actual See-able or Physically realizable things (e.g. sensations); and (3) the degree of pictorial resemblance an Icon Image bears to its *referent* (real world counterpart). Example is the Family doing things together and helping each other in "Concrete" ways. *In summary,* ones ability to perceive Abstracts or Abstractions means one *cuts out all the material details so as to see the skeletal essence of the Thing, as close to the way it came into being as possible.* What is left is the Essence of the Things involved. That Essence *enables one to connect and unify Events and Things that may differ widely in form and external appearance.* The objective is to make Excellence Routine in whatever significant task is done and to have Self-Pride in your work products, even if no one else agrees or knows about it. This means being Selfish in accordance with the first Law of Nature—Self-Survival, Self-Protection, and Self-Preservation. But that Selfishness is in relation to ones Spiritual connections with all of God's creatures and creations—together constituting the "ME/WE". The purposes of life are first, for one to leave ones Lower (Animalistic) Self behind as one is striving to achieve ones Highest (Divinity) Self; second is to achieve ones Mission. Both of these demand that ones life is planned so as to Thrive. In the preparation for Thriving one keeps a record of ones struggles so as to share with interested "WE" members. Ones Mission is to help those most in Need, for no fault of their own. Otherwise, although people are important, that does not put them in a position of authority to guide your life. Instead, one is to be in charge and control of ones own life, of what one does, and of every situation.

ABYSS: (without bottom) is a bottomless gulf—unmeasurable and unfathomable; a symbolized realm of being out of the African Tradition cycle of life.

ACCIDENT PRONENESS: People who deliberately generate problems and guilt. Most participate in fearful or high risk activities for reasons other than to simply seek an exciting experience. Some reasons include: to get attention; escape something deemed to be worse; overcoming boredom; or to establish moral strength superiority by needlessly accepting hardships or failing to stop needless hardships. A fourth stance is taken by those having Splintered Selfhoods as a result of not being able to do what is natural for them in order to conform as well as those having dilemma conflicts featuring Good vs. Evil.

ACCOMMODATE: to hold without crowding and inconvenience, as in focusing on learning *Principles* (parts of the "what it is" of a Thing). This means one can figure out the various forms of "what it does" and "how it appears" using the Box Concept. See Self-Contained

ACCULTURATION: *Enculturation* is absorbing ones own culture while *Acculturation* is acquiring the culture of a new society (actually with the mutual interaction between two cultures, as with Europeans and Africans borrowing from each other's customs). Acculturation was automatic because when African Slaves stepped on board a European ship, they left all of the artifacts or physical objects of their culture behind them.

ADOPT: 1633, to chose to yourself--the meaning of opportunity or freedom of choice.

AFFECT SYMBOLIC IMAGERY (ASI). Mental Picture Stories heavily laden with Mental Images to convey Spiritual Elements Principles in a manner youth could most easily Internalize.

"AFFECT SYMBOLIC IMAGERY"—FOR TEACHING BLACK YOUTH: Very Ancient Africans used Affect Symbolic Imagery (ASI) to increase African youth's learning speed. Such was 2 to 50 times faster in complex subjects like Mathematics, Physics, Philosophy, Psychology, Spirituality perceptions, Art, Literature, and all other pedagogical (mental and physical development of children) engagements. *Affect* refers to ones "Feeling" (intuitive) Self and ones Emotive Self. *Symbolism* provides the *whole meaning of the Message* by disregarding limitations and boundaries of human thought. *Imagery* is the payload message conveyor vehicle. ASI works well for Black children by stimulating their Pure Emotions to do Metaphysically irrational and illogical thinking that enables experiencing naturally the wholistic meaning of the Message. Since this vital force is the most direct "Affect" experience of oneself, ASI-spurred thinking identifies one feeling as being with life. Because of being transported into an imagined situation, ASI touches the deepest emotions in ways one can see, hear, smell, taste, feel, and almost touch--as if one is an intimate part of it. Example: "The truth is real but cannot be touched, similar to the Sun whose rays warm your skin. Like the truth, you cannot see the sun because it is too bright. Nevertheless, you do not have to look at either to know they are shining. Yet, by proper positioning away from darkness, both the sun and the truth will find you." Note the *Imagery* is like a "mental movie"--scripted to open a path for touching the "Heart" by words and phrases intended to stimulate and attune all of ones senses to the colors, textures, shapes, movements, tastes, touches, sounds, scents and smells of the environment and what is in it. The orienting statement about ASI is that its *Compassion shares with all the same Spiritual Space* and confirms ones Spiritual connection with those involved. Here, Feelings do the orchestrating and Pure Emotions do the expressing. This entire *non-literary* African Supernatural entity is *outside the Physical Realm,* featuring personifications, metaphors, allegories, and analogies to suggest a picture, or an image, or to secure some other special effect. In African Tradition, *ASI* refers to *Spiritually oriented aspects of Metaphysical Knowledge explained by stories specializing in mental pictures--meaning they are imaginative presentations concerning the Spiritual Elements*. By 12,500 BC, Ancient Africans designed lessons that mainly appealed to the Right Brains of students—e.g. learning how to indicate relationships between different Cosmic planes of existence (e.g. the Spiritual, Metaphysical, and the Material), and writing in symbols on stone. Writing had been invented by Interior Africans at least by 77,000 BC and the Nubians had developed an alphabet consisting of 24 alphabetic symbols (representing vowels and consonants). Then, Ancient Egyptians increase the flexibility the alphabet, applications of ASI, and creative thinking by modifying the original Nubian alphabet into a sophisticated hieroglyphic system. The intent was for their Hieroglyphic System to take advantage of ASI's ability to convey *Mental Picture Stories heavily laden with Mental Images pertaining to Ma'at Spiritual Elements Principles* + develop their Right/Left brains + establish optimum mental condition for learning + improve civil records inventories, bills, and contracts in manners willing Receivers could most easily Internalize. This meant fashioning the 24 alphabetic symbols to communicate with their Left Brains. For their Right Brains, they created *Ideograms*, composed of non-alphabetical symbols possessing a literal or figurative meaning called "*Determinatives*". Determinatives stimulate the Right Brain because they generate wholistic mental images in thinking and meditating. By engaging both brains, African's Hieroglyphic System established an optimum mental Correspondence condition for learning and understanding the difficult and the Esoteric by all pupils.

This approach of *appealing to the Right Brain made easier understanding and retention (up to 500%) over the Left Brain*. They used the concept of Wholism with emotionally relevant mental items as the best way for their Black youth to learn decision making and problem solving. This carried further by Ancient Africans taking "liberties with letters of the alphabet and numbers". In African society, philosophical material was conveyed by ASI in Proverbs, Myths, Folktales, Folk Songs, Rituals, Beliefs, Customs, and Traditions--in African People's Art Symbols—and in their Sociopolitical institutions and practices. *Today's Black youth are taught just the opposite of what is best for them.* Ref: T. Owens Moore, Revisited; Bailey, Post Traumatic Distress Syndrome; Bailey, Teaching Black Youth. See Story-Telling; Griots

"AFFECT SYMBOLIC IMAGERY" INSIDE AFROCENTRIC MINDS: *The single most powerful teaching tool for Black youth is now, and always has been, Affect Symbolic Imagery (ASI).* ASI's origin dates to Very Ancient African Sages' discovery of hidden powers or determinations of life-shaping or life-changing creations from seeing involved Things' interrelationships with each other. ASI was formed by African Groits need to explain newly arriving African Tradition concepts to African People. Their style was like flashing a bulb to illuminate key Principles—*a style following alternate paths to Truth*—flashbulbs composed of *Figures of Communication* (FOC). All African FOC are Supernatural Fantasy Language—e.g. "Personification" (fashioning a "person" form to symbolize abstract or lifeless things). FOC tell stories, or present situations, meant to be taken at face value and to be understood in terms other than those actually described. Based upon the mind's inborn nature to form mental pictures, putting mental Images into words makes for *Surrealism* in Afrocentric minds—i.e. joined internal reality and unreality ideas--ideas projected externally—ideas that fuse with human-made pertinent external Things. Such Surreal FOC meshing of fantasy Mental Images with the realistic Message is done by *erasing boundaries* and *disregarding limitations of human thought* normally separating them. To this product, ASI "carves" features of "Style". *"Style"* is Art with, at its core and as its medium, the element of *"Play"*. Both enable Afrocentric minds to get through barriers of what is otherwise perceived to be difficult. FOC, a device of Style, spotlights *Thought* (a system of symbols standing apart from Reality) involved in comparisons between Things sharing an Essence when they all came into Being-hood. FOC enhances viewing something in terms of something else—typically as seeing similarities in the apparently dissimilar. By both Things having *Correspondence*, one can tell something about one Character as considered from the point of view of its Complementary Equal Character—a something otherwise Unknowable. The most distinctive Characteristic of those Characters' manifestations—e.g. a pattern, situations, structure, nature, acts, roles, processes, events—are what initially attract them for comparison. Despite both Things being Uniquely different, the Underlying shared Harmony sought and found is *the "This-ness of a That" or the "That-ness of a This."* "This-ness" is the Essence's "what it is" and Primary Qualities in the "here and now" as it came into existence. "That-ness" is the Thing's specificity, individuality, and 'here/now-ness'. The FOC consists of *Tenor* (the whole Disposition's meaning in context) and a *Vehicle* (the delivery device). *Synthesis* involving the Surreal gives a more varied toti-potence of powers than can be ascribed to either alone. *Totipotent* means capable of giving a *Sentiment* (a pertinent thought wrapped in a Pure Emotion) existence to any ray the Essence is capable of producing. As opposed to *European's Supernatural of the Non-Rational Serious Business Fantasy type*, African Tradition's Supernatural FOC is mystic in its childlike word-play. Hence, by being a partly ASI Message and yet having Qualities separable from the Message, ASI is basic to mentally *Visualizing* and extracting Messages out of what is Synthesized. The impact of the ASI Message displays as an explosive shock of recognition to Black youth's attentive minds. Still, its Quantitative Message is the most accessible, though not the only one. Because of its Toti-potency abilities to make unsuspected and novel connections, as noted in the progression of a dream, one can relate ASI Messages to oneself; to the Sender; to "ME/WE"; to others; or into uncontrollable, irrational, illogical, incongruous funny or horrible Fantasy realms of "Escape". When African Sages decided the most significant Knowledge was in need of a "telling" to the people, it was described, using FOC and Symbols, as *"Instructions"*. In contrast to FOC, *Symbols emphasize similarities with what they represent + generate their own meaning + follow their own discourse in elaborating on its Referent* (i.e. things to which ones words or Symbols refer). That is the purpose of Symbols in such FOC forms as a Metaphor extended beyond paragraph confines, like in Parables, Fables, or Allegory literary forms. *Instruction* is the piling of Knowledge into Receivers' minds through the vehicle of stylish informational Playful ASI surrounding the core message. By so doing and compared to what is like-kind in the FOC, the ASI message can go broader, deeper, and higher than words or thoughts alone. This is because ASI, FOC, and Symbols are sufficiently suggestive to *touch and awaken the Truths* already present in a human's Soul, "Heart," or "Head". Words cannot describe this desired message impact fully, except when wrapped in ASI. After that combination is "Felt," it fully penetrates into Receivers' *Mysticism Minds* (minds having the ability to intensely concentrate their Intellect Reasoning into their Pure Emotions). When skillfully disciplined, Mysticism Minds harmonize its irrational and incongruous ingredients so as to organize and illuminate the contained Spiritual Elements' ASI Message. *FOC delivers Knowledge in Supernatural Information form by embracing the involved mental ingredients and meshing the spotlighted messages with embellishments* so as to ease the sliding into an *Apprehension* (grabbing the "This-ness" through the senses, mind, and/or instincts) of what has heretofore defied clarity. Within the involved "big picture," ASI, Symbol, and FOC's powers fill transitional areas between what is and is not grasped by Apprehension. Each creatively does this with its own cup of fancy meanings--and in conjunction with its "dematerialized" boundaries--and without diluting or polluting the original message. This results in a striking and sudden fashioning of a connecting and meshing Link for two unlike appearing Things—even Things remote from one another in Character and yet have Correspondence through their "This-ness." That meshed Link consists of a Synthesis which makes for an easy apprehension—i.e. the grasping and taking hold of the "big picture" through the senses and the mind and/or the instinct. To enhance full understanding and appreciation for the ASI Message, African Griots (storytellers) used "*Personification*". The Goddess Ma'at is an example of having left an evolving and lasting Symbolic and ASI impression on all of today's world societies. This is what I have modeled in dealing with the Metaphysical subjects to which Black People are attuned as well as imitating the *Affect Symbolic Imagery* method of Ancient African Groits (storytellers). That method for delivering a story, which is absent information, is about invoking wonder experiences that make them care while suspending disbelief. The first impression is critical. It is the Caring to which the Receivers can relate. Its journey—perhaps having a normal beginning of "once upon a time" (which spotlights the dark)—slides into a middle. In that middle the character faces dramatic organized anticipation and uncertainty along with changing significant moments to which Receivers attach themselves into the actions or experiences of the characters in the images, while being the head of those characters--thus animating the art. As the end approaches, Receivers feel impactful changes within them. Together, these impart a significant meaning and they particularly remember what happens at the end. That end has the consequence of a "new normal" to help make meaning of their lives. That empowerment then tells them how to insert it into plans for the future. My style is based upon personal experiences and the "skeleton" of what I write about comes out of my struggling processes of daily living as it refers to my Mission in life. Besides, pertinent vignettes best suit the topic, mainly because of my not knowing any other sources. My hallmark is always to acquire Background ingredients by going into great depth derived from wide sources in order to find the truth as I know it to be about any subject of a particular interest.

"AFFECT SYMBOLIC IMAGERY" PREPARATION: Writing for others to read must be done early so as to get the superficial out of my system and allow meaningful profound thoughts to surface. There are various ways of writing with Order. Organization for understanding deals with the *Archery Pad "CPT" Concept*--the Core (bulls eye), the Periphery of the Core (e.g. the circles around the bulls eye); and the Transitional aspects (that which crosses several circles and heads to the bull's eye) of the subject in that order for busy people. For a complex subject, I start talking about what is not on the Archery Pad so that people will not get it confused with my points. I research the story of the key word in up to 1000 books and out of that fashion my own definition and story. Despite its narrow scope, that awareness of the original meaning and its developmental historical course immediately begins to illuminate paths into pertinent subject aspects. Then there is a search in children's and other simplified sources to get the clearest explanations of what is natural in Nature.

Or, Quotation books may give me an idea of how to better say something hard to describe. Once organized, things can be rearranged into specific relations for a given purpose. An example of rearranging numbers that are in order is the 3/7 Classification. The "Big Picture" is that the product looks like a funnel—starting big and getting to the narrow end of the funnel. See Story-Telling; Griots

AFRICAN LOGIC: *Ma'at applied to thinking by means of laws that establish Spiritual Elements' correspondence and connections between Principles for purposes of making Inferences of a Circumstantial Knowledge nature. See Logic*

AGE-SET SYSTEM: this concerned adolescences being initiated into what signified the beginning of adulthood. Kenyatta has nicely described how, on initiation day, the boys of the Gikuyu country in the central part of Kenya engaged in a race to a sacred tree in order to determine the leader of that particular age-set. An essential part of the ceremony was for each person to go through activities that represented the struggle between the spirit of childhood and that of adulthood. Similarly, in the female group, the girl who arrived at the sacred tree first became the leader of her age-group for life. Those leaders were simply the "spokes-person" for what the Age-Set (or age-group) had democratically decided. The male and female systems functioned independently but both systems were democratic. The community did the same and, at meetings, even children were allowed to expressed their opinions about community issues. Similarly, African Kings and Queens were simply in their positions for the purpose of carrying out the dictates of the people. From all Africans sharing the same Spiritual Elements philosophy inferred by mathematics as having come from the Spiritual Force called Sekhem, each had a Free Mind as to how to implement that philosophy and how each lived. See Mind Control

AGNOSTIC: *Agnostics*--there is no proof of God but do not deny the possibility. Most believe the Supernatural and/or the Spiritual home of God is unknowable, making it impossible to prove its existence or nonexistence; *Atheists*--nothing beyond sense perceptions is real--all else is imagination or insanity. If not denying God's existence, most are unsure

"AIR CASTLE": Thought structure having no real Base upon which it rests

ALCHEMY—AFRICAN SAGES CHEMISTRY OF NATURE: The original word "Alchemy" ("Chemi," parent name of Egypt or Kemet) means chemistry of Nature "from Egypt". Broadly, "Alchemy" is a philosophical system containing the beginning of all Science--originally dealing with Mysteries of Matter, Creation, and Right Life-seeking so as to harmonize humans wholistically with the Cosmos. Very Ancient Africans elaborated upon it with Astrology, Religion, Mysticism, Magic, and similar fields of study. As the keystone of Very Ancient African Sages' basic Physical Science studies of Matter, Motion, and Forces of Nature, Physics arose specifically to help Sage-Scientists follow steps within Nature's Processes and analyze each Effect. From Principles (ingrediences of unchanging Truth) arising from their priest astronomer's astro-mathematics, they inferred Circumstantial Truths (i.e. by God's observable manifestations having Correspondence with what is Esoteric and Un-observable) emanate from the One Cosmic Force, Sekhem—also called Atum, Amen, Aten— and symbolized by the Sun (Fiery). Ancient African Sages knew the *Sun's Physics as the factory for creating all Physical Matter and Energies*—the forces and building blocks of all Things in the Cosmos—the nexus of transformation of unshaped ingredients into shaped Matter (Amen, Metu Neter II:65). Three gods whom Atum (Atom) projected from Its body were Shu (Air); Tefnut (Moisture); and Geb (Earth). In creating Archetypes (African for "Seeds") for whatever is to appear throughout the Cosmos, there were the four "temperamental classes" of Fiery, Watery, Earthy, and Airy destined to appear within the Animal Kingdom Archetype. Since these four tie a vast number of types of "Sameness with Uniqueness" Creature and Creation Beings together across lines of genre and Kingdoms (e.g. Plant), this constituted a happening of Synthesis and Analogs (the holding together). Resultant African Physical Sciences conclusions led to Ancient African doctrines of the

Opposites (or Contraries); of the Change or Transmutation; and of the life and function of the Universe. These were presented under Matter's Four Qualities and Four Elements—Water, Fire, Air, and Earth--expressed by a diagram's outer and inner squares—with the implication of them being the four fundamental types of all manifestations (James, p80, 142; Amen, Metu Neter I:74). The diagram explains Fire's Qualities are hot/dry; Earth, dry/cold; Water, cold/wet; and Air, wet/hot—and each of these has significance. For example, Earth is the mud in which the lotus flower is rooted--and water, the surrounding support of its stalk. By specializing in the Transmutation of one kind of mental Vibrations into others, Ancient Africans Sages' Art of Hermetic Alchemy—i.e. named for the African Master Tehuti, whom Saleem (The Egyptian Book of Life p10) says lived around 50,509 BC--dealt with the *mastery of Mental Forces*. In other words, African Tradition Alchemy is the rotation of the Four Matter Elements in order to discover the processes of Nature and so being able to work with them. Such applies to humans by them being a manifestation of Nature and because of the Spark of God (off the Fiery Sun) present within the Soul of each--and felt by "Knowing Thyself". This God Spark gives them a "drop" of God's powers—e.g. those of Omnipotence (Unlimited and universal power); Omnipresence (everywhere simultaneously), and Omniscience--total knowledge of Cosmic Laws.

In modeling God's processes, humans' "Souls" have the power to transform potential Entities from their undifferentiated Subjective Virtual Image state into an Objective Being. To make these high level Metaphysical concepts understandable to students of true Hermeticism, African Sages spoke of it in terms of a mythological story. In this "*Philosopher's Stone*" legend, the transmuting Substance or Essence is found to be a black powder (?melanin) mystically identified with the Underworld form of the god Osiris and credited with magical properties. Thus, there grew up in Africa the belief that magical powers existed in fluxes and alloys. This signified the presumed production, by unperceived processes, of the Higher Qualities from the Lower that could be applicable to humans' Mental Forces. Hence, from using processes of purification and from knowing all about the black powder—itself equating to the various individualities of the lower mental qualities—one could infer how the Divinity of a human's Highest Self, along with life and power, could be transmuted into production. Such was behind Aten's Sun Fire (Divinity) study relative to Matter's Water, Air, and Earth. jabaileymd.com

ALCHEMY INSIDE & OUTSIDE AFRICA: Ancient Africans' Alchemy focus was on arriving at the mastery of Mental Forces to enable insights for paths to reach the Heaven Afterlife. They spotlighted the Melanin black complexion of Asar (Osiris) as symbolizing the unmanifest Deity in the profound *Darkness of Potentiality*. In the black body of the dead Asar, Ancient Africans visioned an Archetypal (primal, essential "Seed") Human Pattern. The keystone of this Divine Alchemy was to learn how to use Heavenly Energy to transmute (change from one form, nature, state into another + into each other) the black Earth of Ignorance into the gold of Wisdom. The process was, by "Knowing Thyself," to *involute*—i.e. unfold back to the center of the Sublime realm's foundational Cosmic Laws to thereby return to each human's pre-birth "First Wisdom" state. Following that unfolding, they could *evolute* (ascend outward like rays of the Sun) Spiritual Meanings which naturally manifest the involuted "Seeds" and their associated powers so as to learn principles of how the Lower Nature (Earth) gives birth to the Higher Nature (metaphorically called Gold). Cosmic Principles realized were that all of Nature's decomposition is re-composition; Death is transmutation, as in changing of bodies into light and light into bodies; nothing is ever finished; and nothing is ever isolated because it has reference to something else. Thus, each Cosmic Entity achieves meaning apart from that which neighbors it. Out of these Laws governing human Spiritual Evolution arose the strictest Harmony of African Tradition's beautiful Spiritual Philosophy. Its "*Philosopher's Stone*" concept implies the perfect and incorrupt God Substance—or "*Noble Tincture*"—and never to be found upon the imperfect Earth in its natural state. Still, its power was capable of purging all baser Mental Activities (or baser metals) of dross and turning them into the Spiritual

Elements flow (pure gold). So, African Alchemists' Art was to complete work of Perfection. Just prior to being borrowed outside of Africa, the Art of Hermetic (Tehuti) Alchemy dealt with mastery of Mental Forces by means of Transmutations of one kind of mental Vibrations into others. "The Art's" spread to China and India led to curiosity in finding out how to change ordinary rocks and minerals into precious metals. The greedy Greeks and Europeans transformed African's metaphoric descriptions of this being about gold and silver into "Fact"—similar to metaphoric stories they had copied out of the Ancient African Bible. Resultant European academic turbulence—later leading to world-wide misinformation, scams, and shams--occurred in the Christian era's early centuries when Greeks of Alexandria, Egypt pursued alchemic practices from a Material Elements aspect. For example, in the process of trying to transmute actual base metals into noble ones they believed they needed an imaginary modified substance—also called the *Philosopher's Stone*—because of its supposed linkage with the theories of Matter advanced by Ancient Egyptian philosophers. Their "*Hermetically Sealed*" concept consisted of placing "Mystical Metals" in mystical enclosures in hopes heightened forces would lead them into strange metamorphoses and transmutations. This was symbolical of Soul transfiguration beliefs under tutelage of their Supernatural god (Campbell, Hero p73). Note the switch from the Spiritual Cosmos whereby Truth is established by what is observable over to a Supernatural fantasy claimed to be unnatural, unconquerable, unmovable, undeniable, unexplainable, incomparable, unimaginable, immeasurable, and unthinkable. *These beliefs make it impossible to have any kind of Truth/Wisdom.* In Medieval times, the Philosopher's Stone—also called the "*Power of Projection*"—was the Magnum Opus (masterpiece) of Alchemists—meaning an object to be attained by them at all costs. Again borrowing and grossly modifying African Intellectual Property, it was an imagined stone said to consist of a powder or liquor formed of diverse metals, infused under a favorable constellation of the Stars. It was reputed not only to have the property of transmuting the baser metals into gold but also to possess the power of prolonging life indefinitely and curing most of the ills to which the body is heir--for through its agency could be distilled the "elixir of life." The "*Elixir*" (Arabic, "powder"; Greek root for "dry") was deemed a drug, essence, or tincture and applied to any alleged panacea or "cure-all." Later, it became synonymous with *Elixir Vitae*. This was the setting that opened doors for *Quacks* to rush in with "Sham/Scam" analysis of all sorts of things + solutions for people's personal problems.

ALGEBRA: "*Algebra*" ("al" "from Egypt"--"al-Kemit")—meant in Africa the reuniting of broken parts and was later defined by the Arabs as "restoration", including "bone setting." Note that the African originated Yin and Yang concepts are also about the union of separate parts. *Algebra,* a wordless thinking form of Arithmetic, is like those kinds of Thinking where pertinent mental ingredients put together are not words. Other substitution examples are: A + B x A − B; thinking in lines and angles and curves; thinking in Formulas, without words; thinking in musical note, as did the Mulatto Beethoven who was "stone-deaf." These are all Symbols and even the most difficult kind of thinking cannot be done without the use of some kind of Symbols. For Algebraic Thinking, instead of words or Numbers (figures), regardless of the plane of existence, the same Things put together or related are in Symbols. *Algebra* is partly analytic, for the solution of an algebraic equation means that unknown quantities or qualities become known. Three parts of Algebra are: (1) the comparision of things having Correspondence; (2) the reduction of those Things on both sides of the equation to its "That it is!" (its Primary Quality) or its "What it is! (its Primary Quantity) Essence state; and (3) representing each state by a Symbol. The Algebraic "Check and Balance" approach uses Pure Emotions = Intellect in a Mystical Mind manner. Creativity enables this to be endless. For example, it can assess Algebraic Words, like "Interestint"—which can mean something good or bad, depending upon the situation as well as on their repercussions. Another example is the "Present" = the past and future or is the equal sign between the Past and future. Still another is that 6/31/16 = 7/1/16 but June does not have 31 days in reality. African Tradition is built upon

Mathematical determinations for things and conveying those things in a reproducible order that starts from a sound Base. Non-Rational thinking of Europeans' Supernatural thinking starts from no sound base and is so scattered in presentation as to be confusing, incomplete, conflicting, and problematic because of the variety of ways their point can be interpreted. People whose Right Brains are undisciplined by their calculator type of Left Brain order are scatterned thinkers. In using the alphabet for illustrative purposes, scattered thinkers present their thoughts about something by starting with "X"—i.e. "That" or "It"—both unknowns to the Receiver but vivid in their own minds. Then they proceed, without orienting the Receiver to any specifics or even to the "ballpark" their ideas are in, to go in C, P, A, T, directions in conveying the information. A mathematical thinker starts with the "Big Picture"; then the definition of the keystone term to be discussed; then A, B, C, D, lay out of what is the message; and anticipates what might not have been clearly understood of the Principle being given by then providing an example or analogy in keeping with the Receiver's mindset and environmental familiarities—i.e. speak in the Receiver's language. An example of how Very Ancient Africans had applied valid non-syllogistic reasoning was, after developing Algebra, deducing from the usual algebraic equation, a = x + b—over to the solution x − a − b, in accordance with the postulate: *equals substracted from equals give equal results.*

ALGEBRA'S ANCIENT AFRICAN HISTORY: The concept of Algebra arose from Primitive Africans' method of Reasoning by Analogy--i.e. the comparing of two or more systems similar in structure and then taking the familiar in one to explain the unknown in the other. This feature introduced the concept of an "*Equation*" and "*Equate*" into an Equal Sign. The earliest known treatise on algebra is the Egyptian Rhind Papyrus (c.1700 BC). But in c.3000 BC Egyptians called it "aha Calculus" because "ahe" or "ahau" (a first dynasty pharaoh's name)--means mass, quantity, or heap (a pile of many things)—the forerunner of today's "Let X equal ….". In other words, both "X" and "Aha" represented an abstract term for the unknown in an equation. In the meantime, Very Ancient Africans had begun Algebra because of *a need to find an unknown or several unknowns from a few given factors in order to fashion Circumstantial Truths* (those of an Esoteric nature) drawn from Metaphysical Realms. One of the early formal applications concerned Cosmic Creations. The first of two situations concerning African Tradition's mythological concept of Cosmic Creation deals with Metaphysical Order; the second with *Metaphysical Disorder* (a break in the integrity of Ma'at). Ancient Africans conceived of the newly forming Cosmos as being surrounded on its outside by Disorder--existing at the beginning of time and thus present before humans appeared in the Cosmos. Metaphysical Disorder is amoral but has the potential to be cultivated by any human into a False Self and anti-Ma'at state. African Sages said God was situated in "The Other World" at the time of spilling metaphorical Waters into what would become the finite Cosmos. Those Waters, called the Ocean of Nun (OON), contained a special kind of Order. Its resting Energy and Matter, despite having no form and being undefined and undifferentiated, still were *not disordered*--a state called *CHAOS.* Imagine this OON--with its contents of the Spiritual Elements--flowing throughout the entire Cosmos, around and into every nook and cranny of each of God's creatures and creations. From the OON comes the etymology of Ma'at, suggesting an evolutionary order from a physical concept of straightness, evenness, levelness, correctness onward to embrace the Metaphysical concepts of Rightness of "Things"--Righteousness and Lawfulness of the Natural and Social Order (Karanga, p6, 374). The setting was realizing that things to the right and left of the "equal sign" and the Yin/Yang concepts (which were crystalized in the African Mythological Creation story) meant "Chaos" and "Order." Both are complimentary equals because each contains things involved in the other. Also, to discover the truth of one of the two opposites separated by an "equal sign" meant discovering Yin/Yang principles in the other. This Inductive and Deductive reasoning was the beginning of using symbols for unknowns. African Sages said the Material

World Order begins with *Divine Archetypes* ("Seeds") coming into Being as pre-figurements of something or someone to come afterwards--each containing a complete and pure complement of the Spiritual Elements. Its specific Genetic combination supplies everything for it to complete its purpose for being. A given *Divine Archetype* represents some Cosmic Entity, like the Animal Kingdom; or another "Seed" for the Plant Kingdom; or the Truth "Seed". In turn, each Archetype fashions eternal *Prototypes* (i.e. *Form-Ideas*) on lesser planes of existence--e.g. the phenomena of Matter or some Form of Truth--each having Certainty. To illustrate with the Tree Concept--from the Truth "Seed" evolves Truth *Prototype Patterns* in a certain Order--likened to Roots, a Trunk/Vines, Branches, Leaves, and Fruit Truths. Thus, it is evident that each Prototype gives rise to like-kind things which then branch. The reason is the Divine Archetype Seed of Truth conforms to the *Law of Holonomy* (i.e. the whole is inside the Seed; the whole is contained in each of the Seed's manifested parts; and the Seed is found throughout the whole). This Law makes applicable the *Law of Spiritual Creativity* (by itself, a Spiritual Element reproduces itself to become the thing it makes, regardless of its new form). As a result of these Laws, any off-spring branch of a Prototype Truth is like the African *Law of (Spiritual) Circularity*: the Spiritual offspring is proven by the parent and the Spiritual parent is proven by the Spiritual offspring--simply, the child copies the mother and the mother is the equivalent of the child—and the child's children are like its grandmother. To know the essence of one is to know the other--a concept of Algebra, like X = Y. Because the Prototype of the Archetype Tree is present on all planes of Cosmic Existence, *the X = Y concept illustrates the Law of Correspondence.* On an Earth World level it is an ongoing repetition of the nature of the original Thoughts manifesting in compatible behavior. See Unknowns

ALGEBRA BACKGROUND INGREDIENTS: The way any real thing in the Cosmos gets its Essence or "what it is" Background is from the God's Spiritual Elements forming the Ocean of Nun Cosmic Organism state of "Virtual" non-differentiated Creatures and Creations all in repose or Profound Peace. Once it is set in motion (e-motion), that motion causes Matter to assume the form implied in the Cosmos' Divine Consciousness. When a Thing in the Ocean of Nun comes into Being, it possesses the "what it is" or Essence composed of the Spiritual Elements (a "Sameness" with all others but in individualized "Uniqueness" combinations). That Essence is filled with *unrealized realities* capable of involuting (returning to the center) back into its Creator Source after evolving into actualization when the future for its proper placement within a human becomes the present in that human's Material Realm event. With any given human-to-be, that Essence goes through stages of development—similar to a fertilized ovum being a totipotent cell. Initially it starts out in a "That it is" state. Some parts remain in a Spiritual state. Other parts of that same organism are destined to be an Intangible "Thing" and still others continue the downward descent to be a Physical Thing.

After leaving the Subjective Realm to enter the Metaphysical, all "Cells" destined to be a part of a human's Selfhood receive Ether layered onto them. Ether enables it to possess a *Form* (etymologically meaning its image, impression) in the state of 'frozen energy' which vibrates in place. That Form's Spiritual part remains without Matter; its Metaphysical part, with some Ether, and its Physical part with enough layers to qualify that human-to-be a recognizable "*What it is*" Physical identity. The combination of the Animal Emotion's Spiritual "*That it is*" Primary Qualities and the "What it is" Primary Quantities fashions a specificity into a newborn human with its unmistakable individuality. The Essence's Nature in the Background of a human-to-be--which depends on no other thing for its existence--generates a "*That it is" Self Spiritual Identity* while the "what it is" aspect Individualizes that human from all other like-kind Things. Yet, the fact that all creatures have a Genetic "Sameness" gives them Correspondence with each other. Hence, the human exists as a combination of "That it is" and "What it is" aspects. The same applies to all God's creatures and creations. All share a "Sameness" (hidden) and each has "Uniqueness" (hidden + Seen). When maturing, every Entity becomes an increasing combination of Nature (its Essence + Character) and *Nurture* (i.e. the sum Effects of environmental influences and conditions acting on an organism). See Unknowns

ALGEBRAIC AFRICAN'S LAW OF OPPOSITES: "Is the glass half full or half empty?" Today, this expression pertains to the path one chooses to follow through life. To view the glass as half full is to see things optimistically or hopefully; to view it as half empty indicates one is pessimistic. Both describe habits of the mind--a disposition to take a positive or negative view of things--a Disposition containing an Intention to head in a direction compatible with ones views. Both optimism and pessimism operate in the realm of the Supernatural (what one makes up). In my life experiences it is better to be realistic or to straddle the Physical and Supernatural worlds by generating the expression of balance: "hoping for the best but preparing for the worst." However, Ancient Africans' Critical Thinking (CT) dealt only with the Metaphysical pertaining to African Cosmology. For example, they said the Law of Opposites and the Law of Complements exist before anything happens in the Objective Realm, including the Initiation and Manifestation of the Ether. In the Ancient African Bible, the Divine Light spoke a word that organized "Chaos" (the "material prima"--the forceful primordial state of undifferentiated universal existence) into a structured Cosmos. Thus, "Chaos" and "Order" are complimentary equals because each contains things involved in the other. *Complementary Equals*--mates independently doing different things--interdependently working better together to generate a dynamic *balance inside a harmonious whole*--and yet they contain the same "Genetics". Such is illustrated by the complementary female and male doing equally important things of different natures while going together in the same direction side-by-side, at the same pace, and at the same time to the same goal or destination. So, such occurs in the context of *Mathematics*--a science based on thinking in quantities.

In *Arithematic the quantities are displayed in Numbers*--with every number being expressed from the smallest to the biggest by using ten figures or digits (named for those on a human's hand (1, 2, 3, 4, 5, 6, 7, 8, 9, 0). In *Algebra* the quantities are expressed in numbers and in symbols to serve as a short-cut to difficult problems in Arithmetic. Though any letter of the alphabet can be used as symbols, in Algebra "X" stands for an unknown quantity; addition is shown by + as in Arithmetic; and subtraction is shown by -. When two symbols are put together, as *ab*, this implies they are to be multiplied. To put *a* on top of *b* means to divide *b* into *a*. To symbolize "Chaos" and "Order" as complimentary equals--both possess a "Uniqueness" and "Sameness" in a manner that makes them compatible mates. Thus, Very Ancient Africans separated the two by an "*equal sign*." This indicated that to discover the truth of one of the two opposites--i.e. in "Chaos" or in "Order"--is to discover "like-kind" principles in the other--both Qualities. Such was the basis of the *Law of Correspondence*--i.e. the harmonious fitting and agreement of the Spiritual Elements in every Cosmic off-spring--the "so above, so below" inference--the 'what is in' the microcosm is in the macrocosm, and vice versa. All of this occurs within the realm of Reality--a *profound concept for CT*. Existing below the Subjective Realm are Complementary Opposites--positive and negative aspects of qualities--and both enhance each other when viewed one way; or they can cancel each other when viewed in reverse. One opposite is balanced by another through the ceaseless interplay and transmutation of existence--the alternation of creation and destruction. The universal value of pairs of opposites--e.g. high/low, dry/wet, clear/dark--is demonstrated in their continued use not only in physical and material ways but also in psychological, intellectual, and spiritual matters. The circular impulse in a binary symbol leading to inversion of the expected order imparts a sense of cyclic movement to the entity in question. This *Inversion-Symbol* is a basic strand for explaining alternations of life/death, light/darkness, and appearance/disappearance--all making possible the continued existence of phenomena. Other examples of alternating Dualism include fire, although clear and bright in the sky (or in air), it leaves black traces on earth (i.e. a charred object). Rain, although black in the sky (as rain-clouds) becomes clear on earth. This weaving and unraveling of strands of all the pairs of opposites is the import of the Metaphysically positive/negative aspects of white/black working as a unity--white containing black; black containing white.

ALGEBRA'S OPERATIONS: The key to Algebra is the revealing of its *Mystery*—the clearing of ones incomplete Ignorance about it. For example, one may be aware of a "that it is" of a "Thing," but does not know its (Metaphysical or Physical) "what it is," "what it does," "how it appears," "how it is," "how it came about," or "where it is going." Any one of these may be a call for Algebra to determine how they are equal in two different appearing things. Suppose these Things are an apple tree and a grape vine. This means what is innate—the "what" has been designated to be the underground "seed" that gives rise to the above ground aspects. That "Seed," like the human heart, imparts the essential ingredients for all of its parts to have the existing or potential qualities, strength, and characteristics needed to manifest the inclination contained in the disposition of the "Genetics" making up the "Seed." The "Seed" nor its Essence nature has changed but the above ground aspects have been altered by Nurture. Since Operations are the *"What it Does"* with its *Properties* (i.e. what a thing has), *Algebra operates by using the Seeable or Known of a Thing to discover its Unknown or hidden "Uniqueness" and/or its hidden "Sameness."* The equal sign between the Known and Unknown indicates both have Correspondence. To determine their Common Ground, one always looks for what is *"Underlying"* everything else in search of the "What it is" of each Thing's essence when it came into Being—i.e. its "Seed". See Unknowns

ALGEBRAIC SYMBOLS: Because the underground "seed" gives rise to the above ground aspects and the above ground aspects are the result of a Nature and Nurture admix, they are placed inside a Symbol--an alternate idea way to convey that Thing's "what it is" and/or the "that it is". Thinking in Symbols was preferred by Ancient Africans because literal verbal functions of language--e.g. definitions, descriptions, names and narratives--were obstructions to acquiring Knowledge. Reasons for this are each, at best, is a hazy explanation of realities and they only give distorted pieces of Realities' dynamic multiple variables. A *Symbol* is a metaphorical vehicle for not only the Nature and Nurture admix of a Thing but also for the conception of the Essence's "what it is" and/or the what was the intension for the Essence's natural evolution. Though any letter of the alphabet can be used as symbols for the unknown, in Algebra, "X" stands for an unknown quantity. Since these same number quantities are expressed in Symbols, this serves as a short-cut to solving difficult problems in Arithmetic. For example, the problem is stated: "what is the number "X," if "X" + 5 = 8? The original Mathematical problem is now reduced to an equation involving an Unknown number. The content of the Symbol varies but that Symbol is the display of an Association of Ideas of whatever is the topic at hand. A definition of those contents cannot be precisely defined and actually is not required. Yet, those contents are known by their Primary Quality(s) and by the contexts in which they occur—the apple is good; it is a good day. The Primary Quality and the context enables most to understand the collected meanings being communicated even though one could not give an exact definition.

Letters from the beginning of the alphabet—a, b, c—represent numbers assumed to be known but not yet specified. Letters from the end of the alphabet—x, y, z—represent the unknown number. Easy equations involve only "X"—first Degree or Linear (one-dimensional) equations. Example: how fast to drive X miles to get to an apportment on time. Second Degree contain are "X2"—Quadratics (squared number). A two dimensional problem involves areas—how wide a sidewalk may be built around a rectangular lot of a certain sized with a certain amount of cement. Cubics are Third Degree. A three-dimensional problem concerns volume: how much metal is needed to build a million-gallon spherical oil tank. Quartics are Fourth Degree, as with complex scientific questions: find the constant reproduction rate at which a bacterium will spawn a given number of descendants in "N" generation (here "N" means any unspecified degree). See Unknowns

ALGEBRA LOOKS FOR WHAT?: For Algebra to clear ones incomplete (not complete) Ignorance about the relationship of the Symbols on both sides of the equation, the innate Essence or the acquired Theme of each is sought out in order to see if their Spiritual Essence or their Physical World Sets equate (e.g. like a nickel equals five pennies). Both the Abstract and Abstraction signify that within the "General" are the inner similarities with respect to their "what it is" ingredients. Those ingredients serve to link like-kind Things which share at least some of the same Properties. Since detecting the "What it is" of a Thing is Rational Thinking's starting point, one looks to see the inner workings of the factors inside and contributory to the issue at hand. Hence, to be assessed include: (1) what was each ingredient when it came into Being; (2) what was the Source of each ingredient—was it God-made (Reality) or Human-made (unreal); (3) what are the shaping factors of those ingredients; (4) are there mutual relationships and interdependence of the pertinent things with each other and the whole; (5) are those pertinent things harmonious or not; and (6) are all of its activities within and developing out of the Spiritual Elements and headed towards a Human Ideal Goal concerns. To perceive all the ingredient components underlying a given thing/event as being the whole is a form of Synthesis—and Order at its best! See Unknowns

ALGEBRAIC CORRESPONDENCE EQUATIONS: "*Keeping the Balance*" concepts of Ancient Africans and its focus on finding the unity underlying opposites -- i.e. discovering what the opposites have in common is an exercise in establishing Correspondence. A powerful Algebraic Equation related to Complementary Opposites is the *Thinker's Scale mindset* (a positive and a negative scale ruler separated by a zero), one is in the zero position and the opposites are represented by each arm. See Unknowns**.** I. SPIRITUAL ALGEBRAIC EQUATIONS *Spiritual Plane Equations*: If that Essence Seed is the Spiritual Elements on one side of the equation, then, on the other side, it represents Knowledge. An example is the Subjective Realm's *Chaos* is the forceful primordial state of undifferentiated universal existence which is ever ready to express itself in the Material Realms. When Chaos is called on to do this, two things happen. First, progressive Evolution means the Spiritual Elements express progressively thicker forms of matter. Second, it establishes Order--which was so important to Ancient Africans that its absence was explained as the Supreme Being's inability to find a place where It could stand in the world. Material World Order begins with *Divine Archetypes* ("Seeds") coming into Being as pre-figurements of something or someone to come afterwards--each containing a complete and pure complement of the Spiritual Elements. Its specific Genetic combination supplies everything for it to complete its purpose for being. A given *Divine Archetype* represents some Cosmic Entity, like the Animal Kingdom; or another "Seed" for the Plant Kingdom; or the Truth "Seed". In turn, each Archetype fashions eternal *Prototypes* (i.e. Form-Ideas) on lesser planes of existence--e.g. the phenomena of Matter or some Form Truth--each having Certainty. To illustrate with the Tree Concept--from the Truth "Seed" evolves Truth *Prototype Patterns* in a certain Order--likened to Roots, a Trunk/Vines, Branches, Leaves, and Fruit Truths. Its *Order* is the framing of Laws of Nature or Energy (the Spirit), and having nothing to do with Supernatural authoritative prohibitions or rules of conduct in the way Europeans are accustomed to considering Order. African Spiritual Order is explainable by certain laws known by both Subjective Science --i.e. Observation, Reflection, "Pure" Feelings, Productive Imagination, Contemplation, Inductive and Deductive Inferences, and Common Sense as well as Objective Science (e.g. astro-mathematics). Thus, it is evident that each Prototype gives rise to like-kind things which then branch. The reason is the Divine Archetype Seed of Truth conforms to the *Law of Holonomy* (i.e. the whole is inside the Seed; the whole is contained in each of the Seed's manifested parts; and the Seed is found throughout the whole). This Law makes applicable the *Law of Spiritual Creativity* (by itself, a Spiritual Element reproduces itself to become the thing it makes, regardless of its new form). On an Earth World level it is an ongoing repetition of the nature of the original Thoughts manifesting in compatible behavior. As a result of these Laws, any off-spring branch of a Prototype Truth is like the African *Law of (Spiritual) Circularity*: the

Spiritual offspring is proven by the parent and the Spiritual parent is proven by the Spiritual offspring--simply, the child copies the mother and the mother is the equivalent of the child. To know the essence of one is to know the other--a concept of Algebra, like X = Y. Because the Prototype of the Archetype Tree is present on all planes of Cosmic Existence, the X = Y concept illustrates the Law of Correspondence. African inferences allow for expanding beyond Ancient Africans' abilities to "prove" by direct evidence and yet Circumstantial Evidence was acceptable because all derived out of establishing Truth. So, based on the above laws, what develops within that context and then out of the Spiritual Elements would be part of the Spiritual Laws. In short, there is "Sameness" in every Archetype's offspring. Thus, each Truth + Unconditional Love, Reality, and the Natural, construct all Cosmic Real and Natural things. Form-Ideas (an African concept plagiarized by Plato) are self-realizable Divine ideas because they are patterns fixed in Nature. These "blueprints" that organize a structured Cosmos exist before anything happens in the Objective Realm, including the Initiation and Manifestation of the Ether. The Idea-Form giver of off-spring and their steadfast bonds internally link all things to which they give rise. Prototypes are made in their image and also display as resemblances of their Archetypes. Idea-Forms + Chaos--X = Y--enabled Ancient Africans to create the "equal sign" + the use of *symbols for unknowns (e.g. in algebra) + Inductive and deductive reasoning* + abstract Ma'at concepts of "Fairness," Justice," etc. + the *Principle of Polarity*. From this complex process, African Sages inferred metaphorical Beings symbolizing faculties of actual physical entities. Examples: Amon/Amaunet--i.e. hidden/concealed ones (Air/Wind); Nun/Naunet— i.e. Primeval Matter/Space; Huk/Hauket—i.e. Illimitable and the Boundless--Huh/Hauhet—i.e. Darkness/Obscurity. See Unknowns jabaileymd.com

ALGEBRAIC METAPHYSICAL-SPIRITUAL EQUATIONS: *Metaphysical-Spiritual Equations* start with Spiritual aspects of the Metaphysical. The Symbols carrying those Metaphysical Sets of the equation, by being metaphorical, enables their symbolic messages to disregard the limitations and boundaries of human thought so that its symbolic atmosphere conveys the like-kind ingredients which are capable of impacting aspects actually within the person touched by them. An example equates the bonding occurring between the mother and her newborn to using Algebraic Qualitative Mathematics in a conceptual relationships with Logic since both are permanent and unchanging. For example 2 + 2 = 4 which no amount of experience can ever change. The same holds for proofs in Mathematics and Logic. Thus, if the Good, which is unchanging and permanent, is to be known, it must be known by means of these unchanging and permanent conceptual relationships. The conceptualizing part is called the Mind. See Unknowns

ALGEBRAIC METAPHYSICAL-PHYSICAL EQUATIONS: Metaphysical-Physical Equations start with Material aspects of the Metaphysical. The "That it is" concerns sensations' "That is" existence, since it does have sufficient Ether to designate it as a "What it is. The Window of Right Living Inside Chaos illustrates this (see later). In deciding what to put inside that window, I called on a formula of Algebra where X = Y. The equal sign stood for Truth and Reality; the letter X represented my inner chaos from having to conform to prejudiced written/unwritten rules I disrespected; and Y symbolized being surrounded by overwhelming chaos. Inside the equal sign--i.e. the "window"--I placed Spiritual Element Standards to live by, applying them as a sound Selfhood foundation to *"Be Right," "Recognize Right," "Do Right," "Make Things Right," and "Defend the Right"*. While my Private Self lived safely inside the window, my Public Self operated normally in the world of chaos surrounding me except for one difference. My sound Selfhood foundation guided my dealing in the chaos of the medical-legal arena in a manner that I maintained my integrity. This is like having one foot inside the window and one foot in the chaos. One living in a chaotic environment can do the same. Let Sankofa stand for the equal sign while X and Y stand for whatever problems one ranks as the keystones. Sankofa is about discovering principles of African Tradition and applying them to ones present situation. Here, one internalizes the

Spiritual Elements of Unconditional Love, Truth, Reality, and the Natural. Its principles serve as the standard, tools, filter, and guides to establish a sound Selfhood.

These same principles are then used to pave a constructive path into a thriving future--a path whose goals are intended to benefit oneself, loved ones, and possibly others, including the yet unborn. *When ones Spiritual Element lifestyle is part of who one is, it is carried over by ones Public Self into ones underlying dealings with the outside world.* The way one fashions how to live and how to handle X and Y is ones own decision, independent of and uninfluenced by others' opinions to the contrary. One maintains a unity of harmony, connectedness, and balance in intimate relationships with non-Brute people. This may include "Friends of Brutes" who have a humaneness despite imitating Brutes' non-evil practices. One does what is needed to be part of the crowd so as to "belong" but always while remaining honorable. Still, the key is striving every day and in every way to be better and better. Though all this is hard, it is better than being fully exposed to the hostile world. See Unknowns

ALGEBRAIC PHYSICAL EQUATIONS: A comparison of Physical World Algebraic Sets is illustrated by a nickel equating to five pennies. One can have a mental picture of Titan, my dog, but not all dogs for they are in a given concept—like an algebraic or geometrical symbol in as much as "Dog" stands for" certain things not mentally pictured. It is like the figure "7" which "stands for" 7 of anything. Another example is the African Yoking Concept using oxen. See Unknowns; Yoke

ALGEBRAIC BIOLOGICAL "CHECK AND BALANCE" EQUATIONS: The Left Brain is relatively quiet from birth to around seven years old (for me it was around five). Then it becomes dominant for the perception and production of almost all aspects of non-emotional language skills (e.g. grammar, word production, spelling, reading, speaking and writing); the comprehension of the grammatical, syntactical, and descriptive components of language, including time sense, rhythm, musical scales, verbal concept formation, analytical reasoning, verbal memory. It does logical tasks, such as reasoning, analysis, and processing data like a calculator. When skillfully disciplined, it becomes extremely powerful. Together, the Right and Left Brains are "*Inseparable Harmonized Differences*"--like two sides of a coin separated by an Equal Sign--working mostly independently to interdependently first fashion a whole and then "Check and Balance" each other to perfect that whole. Ancient Africans utilized this concept as a mutually cooperative mind training control tool designed for temperance (i.e. exhibiting self-restraint) they called the *Middle Way*. "Check and Balance" is theoretically illustrated by the USA constitution separating the powers of the executive, legislative, and judicial branches and having each as "watch dogs" over the other two. For example, the Right Brain gathers from the subject or situation at hand its inner and outer similarities while the Left Brain gathers inner and outer differences of similar and dissimilar things and breaks them into pieces--the act of analysis. All are synthesized.

Ancient Africans perfected the Left Brain's discipline power so as to sharpen the Right Brain to serve as the vehicle for expansiveness into higher planes of existence regarding things like *Love, spirituality, compassion, peace, harmony, intuition, synthesis, nonaggression, and unity.* An undisciplined Right Brain is otherwise chaotic and accounts for chronic Juggling in life from failing to do the "Splitter" and the Precision Thinking contributed by the Left Brain. Hence mental entanglements occur from failure to separate what can be separated or from lumping together what is better left separated. Natural Right brain intuition has a creative (from "Pure Feelings") and non-creative part (e.g. the sixth sense; predominantly Ancient Brain Instincts). It, in conjunction with the Left Brain, organize all essences as well as existing bits and pieces into new forms, new arrangements, and new combinations, a key to Creative Thinking. As one matures, Mental Discipline arises more and more out of the world view of considering the deeper meanings of life and the temperament of what it takes to enjoy it and not waste it. See Unknowns

ALGEBRAIC COMPLEMENTARY OPPOSITES EQUATIONS: There is harmony in balanced natural complementary opposites--e.g. the sun/moon, man/woman, and night/day--with each pair being on both sides of the "Equal Sign". This equation converts the Mathematic Principle of Invention (1 +1 = 2) into the *Balanced Complementary Opposites* Concept of 1 + 1 = 3. For instance, though the man might be on the left of the equal sign and woman on the right, to be balanced complementary opposites means both are equally significant but in different ways. One hand washes the other. Hence, by independent things working together something greater happens than the sum of them working independently—and that is the Synthesis. Harmony occurs when these complementary opposites start going in the same direction, at the same time, at the same pace, toward the same goal. Or, they may deliberately each do different things as part of reaching the same goal—like a basketball team. Thus, there is always an equilibrium, despite at the same time, being unstable (if you zig, I zag). Alternation of this give and take creates rhythm, like the silence between the notes.

ALGEBRA AFRICAN DIALECTIC: In *African Dialectic Method*, Dialoguing by means of the was emphasized by Ancient Africans in order to get on the paths to "Know Thyself" (ramifications of the Law of Sympathy) and discover options for how to deal with the reconciliation of opposites by means of Middle Way synthesis--meaning finding the harmony in conflict. Behind this Dialectic approach is the belief that the human mind can be satisfied by nothing less than understanding the concept of the unchanging Spiritual, Subjective, and Objective Truth and realizing that *learning is a process of Recollection* because we are all born with all we need to know. A well-known law of dialectics is a *change in quantity beyond a certain point brings about a change in quality*, with its associated unique rules and character and characteristics. If that change is great enough and abrupt enough there is a transformation, called a *Revolution*, into its dialectical opposite. *Middle Way Synthesis* is finding the harmony in conflict--the essence of African Dialectic. Behind the Dialectic approach is the belief that the human mind can be satisfied by nothing less than understanding the concept of the unchanging Spiritual, Subjective, and Objective Truth and realizing that *learning is a process of Recollection*.

ALGEBRAIC COSMIC CREATION EQUATIONS: The Creation of the Cosmos consisted of differentiation (multiplicity) and activity so that the fundamental Dualities in the Cosmos are unity/multiplicity and inactivity/activity. Ancient Africans sort to understand these dualities and their manifestations in all areas of life and their roots in the foundation of life as well as how to resolve these apparent oppositions for they believed this understanding is the basis of Wisdom. Furthermore, since all things are integral parts of one Being encompassing the world, everything an individual wills to achieve must be in harmony with the will of the whole (God). This can be done only by intuiting the Will of God to know the who, which, what, when, where, why, and how of events that are to take place in people's lives so as to create, enhance, and maintain harmony. To help the people understand, African Sages presented this profound information as metaphorical stories in general and allegories in particular. See Unknowns

ALGEBRAIC MYSTICAL PSYCHOLOGY: Mystical Psychology deals with various levels of awareness and aspects of a given level inside Consciousness--levels and aspects well known to Ancient Africans. One of those aspects, the Ka, represents wholistic awareness and in the area of cognition (all the processes by which one acquires knowledge—including perceiving, thinking, remembering, wondering, imagining, generalizing, and judging) it stands for full knowledge and total intelligence. *Mystical spirituality* integrates and develops not only the intellect on one side of the Equal Sign but also the Pure Emotions to deal with practical life and the will-power capacity of ones Selfhood--all the while leading the soul to ultimate spiritual self-discovery. Both pave the way to discovering the transcendental reality of existence in a manner incapable of being done with words. This allows a balanced approach or "middle path" to a spiritual discipline needed for spiritual growth. Thus, mental balance is the way to achieve mental peace and serenity. See Unknowns

ALGEBRAIC CONTRARY OPPOSITES: If opposing religions agree—"X"--that both believe in the manifestations (Substance) of God—"Y," then this becomes their common ground to promote each other while maintaining their separate doctrines. If the problem is that one or both lack the Truth, such can be corrected. Find a common ground in the opposition and join them as a first step in bringing opposite sides together which are mutually necessary. To operate within the Law of Sympathy is to be powered by Spiritual Energy that keeps one on a balanced path through life--called the *Middle Way* by Ancient Africans. See Unknowns

"ALIVENESS": "Aliveness" is what replaces childhood "Excitement." The word "Aliveness" comes in from two roots by way of the word "life." One root derives from life in the sense of "Being In Life", the second root comes through the sense that Life was thought of as the body of the Divine Consciousness to which the Spirit is attached. "Aliveness" (African, life)--in the sense of "Being In Life" + Life as the body of the Divine Consciousness to which the Divine Spirit (a human's mind) is attached. The source of Aliveness is the Spiritual Energy Package springing from ones Divine Consciousness and its orchestration of a profound enjoyment of life. That Energy possesses the Essence for Aliveness's instinctual manifestations--as in vivaciously generating more and more mental and spiritual "doings". Example include the "Alive" human over-flowing with: (1) unending Creativity, Inventiveness, and Innovation just for fun or to problem-solve; (2) *Curiosity* with an eagerness to "see what's behind that" for "no reason," to learn, to discover; (3) an urge to prove/disprove a point so as to get to the Truth; (4) a drive to become and remain mentally free; (5) a peacefulness that displays as Nonaggression (as opposed to Aggressive, Passive, or Passive-Aggressive); (6) a natural stirring of Compassion (spiritual) as opposed to Sympathy (man-made); (7) Humor derived from non-harmful silly Imagination; and (8) and a healthy *Compulsion*--implying such self-discipline as to have "second nature" impulses to *"Be Right," "Recognize Right," "Do Right," "Make Things Right," and "Defend the Right"*. These essential ingredients enable "Alive" people to make great "ME/WE" contributions—and for no other reason than they are the Right thing to do, even when no one is looking. "Aliveness" comes from some new insight. That insight is, for me, is experiencing an entirely new way of thinking or looking at the common in an uncommon why or seeing the uncommon in a common way. To elaborate, "Aliveness" comes from *Perceiving* something in the sense of deeper understandings, more pointed meanings, having connected more interrelationships that provide a wider variety of implications and options; seeing *Inner Similarities in things with* dissimilar appearances; discerning uniqueness in similarities; and going into the Underlying in order to fashion interrelationships between dissimilar and similar things. The resultant new meanings increase my insights for determining the *Order and consistent Patterns underlying natural events; and that enables arriving at the Mystery's answer.* Every advancement expands ones Consciousness from the inside out and toward the Eternal. A sort of contentment comes from establishing *Order* that is essentially dependent on the existence of the interdependence (a type of Oneness) between independent things--a means of safeguarding their mutual dependence without any encroaching upon another. The "Aliveness" comes from these "Seeds" of insights causing a mushrooming expansion of my Sensory Consciousness which, in turn, expands my "ME/WE" Divine Consciousness. See Spiritual Energy Package

ALLEGORY: *Metaphors* (equates unlike things by implication), *Simile* (the abstract or suggestive aspect is directly expressed), *Allegories* (a hidden story within an obvious story), *Fables* (animals impersonating humans to impart a moral), *Personification* (making a lifeless or abstract thing alive), *Analogies* (explaining something unfamiliar by comparing it to something familiar), *Legend* (a story, above mere fiction, combining fact and personified spiritual concepts), and *Symbols* (symbolic messages disregard the limitations and boundaries of human thought in order to impart ideas of the indescribable).

ALLEGORY OF THE CAVE: To be spotlighted is the world Crowd being taught that they are in a "State"—in the sense that all individuals are to be subjected to authority rule as to make each human a non-entity. This is done for purposes of Mind Control. *Socrates' "Allegory of the Cave"* illustrates the "Illusion Life" people live as a result of a "State" Mind Control program. Its important for today's Black People stems from the same scenario being reproduced in many from the effects of African American slavery and the ongoing post-slavery racism. The story starts with prisoners chained in an underground cave and with their heads fixed in a straight ahead position. Thus, they can only see shadows cast on the wall in front of them and are unaware that between their backs and the fire are puppets, moved by a puppeteer along a walkway, that cause shadows of Reality outside the cave--the reverse of Truth (i.e. delusions). Being born into this situation and knowing nothing else, the prisoners are certain the shadows constitute "Truth." While some are being dragged out of the cave in order to face Reality, they do so with resistance shown by their "kicking and screaming." Once outside the cave they gradually acclimate by seeing more and more real things around them and by learning to distinguish the reality of the sun from the shadows it causes. They then declare shadows in the cave to be unreal. Upon re-entering the cave to inform the still chained prisoners what is Reality, they become aware of no longer being accustomed to the darkness or what is presented as "Real" in it. Also, the chained prisoners ridicule comments of the outside world reality. They fight against leaving their familiar darkness for fear of the unknown in the sunlight and not being able to cope. Of all of Maafa's (immeasurable catastrophes) resulting from African American slavery, the religious conversion of Black People from Knowing the Spiritual God over to Faith/Belief/Trust in a Supernatural God was the most devastating. Preparation for Scholarship practices is the opposite of Black youth's Socialization Mind Programming. This means the Black Diaspora that has any European influences have never been taught the Truth. So, struggling Black youth's answer is *Sankofa*: "We must go back and reclaim our past so we can move forward"; go back "so we can understand why and how we came to be who we are today"; go back to Ancient African Values to rebuilt our philosophy; go back in order to see and embrace a humanity for how to live in the present for the purpose of reaching the heaven Afterlife." This implies returning to the Certainty Truths of the Ancient African Bible, for they are the only Truths and "Right Living" ways that conform to African Tradition.

"ALL-OR-NONE"----"EITHER/OR": Major features of Superficial Thinkers are assessing situations, decisions, and solutions only in terms of "all-or-none" or "Either/Or" as well as failing to consider the past, the future, or anything outside themselves in the present. To say: "That's the best I can do," which it never is. Instead, the problem is these people are Patterned Thinkers and thus honor that because it belongs to them. They pride-fully build a lifestyle around it. One problem here is in using "emotions" as a substitute for sound thinking. This display of mental weakness considers an issue based upon how they "feel"--"if it feels right it must be true"--without genuinely seeking to understand it. The "Either/Or" partner, the *"All-or-None syndrome"* disregards different Cosmic planes of existence and *wipes out its boundaries*. An analogy for it in the Spiritual Plane is flipping up a light switch so as to cause the light to come on; or, flipping it down to cause the light to go off. "All-Or-None" is illustrated by a woman cannot be "a little bit pregnant"—either she is pregnant (a spiritual event) or she is not. In contrast to the Western world saying Supernatural love has degrees (e.g. Eros, Agape), Spiritual Love does not—thus one either show Love or not. The *All-Or-None* category is typical of the drama of Emotional People: "You always do the wrong thing" or "You never do the right thing". That complainer thereby fails to consider options between "All" (e.g. "always") and "None" (e.g. "never") and therefore this is not the truth. The overwhelming majority of people allow their Acquired Emotions (not to be confused with Feelings) to dictate how they think--and this is not a position for which emotions are suited. Emotions have no sense of fair-play and therefore do not see both sides of an issue in a proper perspective. Emotions block ones searching for Options. However, on Material planes are found a wide range between "All" and "None"—as in looking at the shades of grey between "black and white." By sharing similar principles, "All-Or-None" and "Either/Or" Syndromes are forms of incomplete and flawed thinking. For members of the Crowd this means there are only two Options for assessing anything--a limitation that comes from a lack of thought and/or a lack of exposure. Typically, Jugglers think in terms of "All-Or-None or Either/Or"; are full of opinions about any and everything; and cannot tolerate anyone disagreeing with them. They simply want to be right in order to protect their fragile self-esteem and the resultant lack interest in the truth leads them into more trouble. So when a mentee says: "If I didn't join the gang I would be killed," the mentor counters with: "let us explore options to determine the best answer and that may be anywhere within the wide range that is in-between "All-Or-None" or something other than Either/Or. Such is spotlighted by youth who arrogantly disagree with Elders; do not consider what Elders are saying; and believe Elders should do what youth suggests, despite lacking any track record of success. These flaws, when applied to serious business, is what creates, enhances, maintains, or prevents getting out of the Juggling Syndrome of life. The Thoughtful views "Either" as referring to both; each; only one; or any one. By itself, "Or" introduces an alternative. At some point in the Socratic Method a youth will resort to such "*Either/Or*" thinking. Then it is the mentor's job to point out the other options because the best answer may be that *Neither* of these may be the best option; or *Both* may apply; or *Combinations* need to be considered—maybe as a little bit of one and/or the other—and with or without something else. Or it could be that more reflecting and researching are needed to come up with many other options. Analysis opens new ways of looking at things and Flawed thinking deals with "All-Or-None or Either/Or" Sound, discerning thinking uncovers such options as: "Either this or that" or for "All of this and none of that." Something in the middle could be the category of things represented by static letters of the alphabet: "neither-nor"; "both-and"; "some of both"; "both alternating"; or "each having differing patterns, directions, pace, levels, rhythms, and goals complementing each other in yin/yang fashion." Correction is to train ones mind to instinctively leap to the thought of an "opposite" at the same time that it is considering any given quality. It thinks of this "Opposite"—not because of its "likeness" to the Thing—but because of its "Unlikeness" or Difference. Resultant Exploration concerns discovery and creating options in order for them to be Classified. Classification can be helpful for discernment or for categorizing complex issues, as in deciding on Methods of Classification. See Reciprocity; Compartmentalized Thinking

ALLIANCE: mutually helpful participants who are psychologically and philosophically disconnected from each other—and yet feature the sharing of common character traits, like the IHES mindset. *Liaisons* are people who support like-kind people but lacking close associations between them.

ALLURE: The sense of '*Attract*' in its ancient context embraces '*Alluring*' into something harmful by means of an enticing (exciting hope or desire) decoy possessing energetic twisting and squirming pleasurable motives or ideas of a fantasy nature. Alluring also conveys the idea of charm providing some prospect of pleasure or advantage done by purpose and endeavor. The feature of "Attract" is the drawing of "Like to Like."

ALLUSION SUPRANATURAL COMPETITION: Three favorite mind control tricks of con-artists are the manipulations and maneuverings of the triad: *Allusions, "Almost Good Enough," and "Seems" Right.* By these going in directions opposite to Certainty, they keep this triad secret from the World Crowd. The reason this triad topic came up was because I wanted to know more about the Supernatural in relation to European religion. Since boyhood I have heard White people mention their European Supernatural God and yet I have been unable to find a single discussion about it in any of my numerous books, including European Bibles. Then, I did a Google search and discovered countless references to the [European] Bible about its Supranatural God—without specifics except for interpretations alluding to that deity--as well as a number of other Supernatural beings, like angels, spirits, Satan and witches (Witch of Endor). *Allusions* (C16, playful reference) are roundabout, indirect, and suggestive indicators presented as: "by the way"; "or in passing"; "on second thought"; or "dropped in passing, as with little thought. In short, what or whom is alluded to is very lightly touched upon and without direct mention. Con-artists use allusions as tools to convince Receivers of certain deceptions. Allusions are extremely quick ways of expressing ones emotions as well as creating in listeners shades of those same emotions--but only when the listeners are already familiar with the setting that imparts an unspoken and shared understanding. The trick is to lead gullible Receivers to the gate and then let them make the connections. Within hyper-fearful Receivers, the triad (e.g. Allusions) can cause a Cascade of simultaneous Spirit, Body, and Mind destructive forces to various degrees—forces resembling a series of waterfalls pouring and spreading over steep rocks--disrupting humane Spiritual, Rational, and Physical networks in its path--networks which produce outputs serving as the in-put for the next component in each network. As seen in today's GUN addicts, the process follows a *"Slippery Slope"*—a 1900s metaphoric expression alluding to traversing a slick hillside and being in constant danger of falling. "You take away my gun, next it will be my dog"; or "If it is done, something else will happen or is likely to happen as a result; the something else, and then something else--right down the 'slippery slope' to a situation that is clearly undesirable. In European literature "Supernatural" manipulations and maneuverings are powerful mind control tools.

Although Enslaved Africans were brought to the Americas with mathematical Certainty that although the One Universal High Spiritual God could not be known, they did know God's existence based upon God's manifestations—i.e. by the Law of Correspondence. But being taught allusions to a European Supernatural God who punishes disobedient Slaves in a Supernatural Hell under the supervision of a Supernatural Devil was effective in switching many Enslaved to believing in the European Supernatural God. Since much of what was in the European Bible had been borrowed out of the Ancient African Bible, messages conveyed to the Enslaved could be fashioned in a manner so familiar to them as to "SEEM" right. What did not "jive" (e.g. to be good Slaves and antifeminism) had to be *accepted on "Belief" and "Faith."* Still, few lay out the meaning of the *"Supernatural"* (C15) which, by definition, *is anything that does not exist naturally.* Synonyms are *Paranormal* and *Preternatural* (limited to adjectives describing abilities appearing to exceed the bounds of possibility). See T-Scale

ALLUSIONS/ELUSIONS/ILLUSIONS/DELUSIONS: A feature of Deception is subtlety—and subtlety is about Nuances that go horizontally. Examples are exhibited by *Allusions*--a passing or casual reference; an incidental mention of something, whether directly or by implication, sort of like referring to the effect of the Halo of a full moon without mentioning the moon itself. An *Illusion* is something that deceives by producing a false impression. An *Elusion* (its adjective is *Elusive*) is an avoidance of something, a clever escape. A *Delusion* is accepting without question what is not real and not accepting what is real. The illusion that the sun goes around the earth is suggested by ones senses and to believe this is a delusion. The same is done by deceptive people (whether deliberately or out of ignorance) with the Spiritual Elements improperly presented. Such occurred with the cunning tricks devised by Europeans so as to take down the great nation of Africa and enslave its people. Evil deceptions appearing as Allusions, Illusions, Elusions, and Delusions are how Europeans now keep down Black People who remain victimized by them. In short, the thrower of a rock into a lake is the Source and the rock is the Cause of the splash (the effect) which then causes ripples (the Consequences). Any of these can be Illusions. "Throwers" of illusions are those who attempt to get people to believe the fantasy Effect presented is Reality. An analogy is the stripes of a Barber Pole do not move up or down as they appear but rather by rotating a single strip on the pole makes it look that way. The above have been examples of how evil *"Standing on the Chain Ring"* can generate illusions and delusions that "SEEM" right. To detect the several ways they are done is the job of CT. CT first assesses the "Source" and "Cause" aspects of the thrower in order to understand the perspective of the meanings of the resultant ripples. Then, CT recognizes them; defends against them; gets one off them; prevents one from getting on them; and/or takes advantage of them. Refn: Bailey, Word Stories Encyclopedia; Bailey, Word Stories of Ancient Africans.

"ALMOST" RIGHT: In the amazing European childhood fairytale of "Little Red Riding Hood," Mr. Wolf was attractive and friendly but yet he was not Red Riding Hood's friend. Being a con-artist, Mr. Wolf sent the poor child down the long scenic route to her grandmother's house. By taking the short cut, he got to the house first; ate the grandmother; coaxed the child into grandmother's house; and then ate her. Fallacies (Greek, "deceitful") are like Mr. Wolf--attractive on the outside but deceptively flawed (i.e. the "payload") where it is devastating. Suspected Fallacies alarm Critical Thinking (CT) into detecting, defending against, and maneuvering around Brute or ignorant people--especially those using "Subtle" tricks that SEEM right or are ALMOST right. It is hard for good people to think that those among the "best" in a given society would deliberately teach people how to be dishonorable. Nevertheless, that method is the rule rather than the exception. Ancient Greek Sophists (c460 BC) deceptions were not done to stir up a conflict situation by opposing what people believe. Instead, it was smoothly designed to subtly steer people toward staying focused on the "shiny trinket penny" (e.g. "Trinkets and Trivia) they put in ones face while ignoring or ridiculing the peoples treasures of Truth. "Payload" information *just a shade off the Truth-Track* is done by fashioning the misleading or fallacious so that its plausible *Subtlety* (evasive reasoning, superficial soundness) "SEEMS ALMOST" right. The Old English word *"Almost"* (all + most = 'for the most part') originally meant 'mostly all' or 'nearly all.' "Almost" and "Nearly" both mean within a small degree of--or within a short space of. Still, "Almost" is of smaller degree and/or of a shorter space than "Nearly." If one pulls the blanket over ones body on a cold night and is comfortable, except for one tiny uncovered area, one is closer to being completely covered ("Almost") than if one was "Nearly" covered. Yet, in either case, one might not get back to sleep until the cold draft is eliminated. It is CT's job to recognize mistakes and flaws in reasoning (commonly called *"Fallacies"*). The place for me to always start is with myself. From a long history of experience, I know it is easier to pick out flaws in other's thinking than in my own. But since I am not on top of my thinking game every moment of every day, there are *four categories for ordering my life--Necessary, Important, Desires, and "A lick and a Promise."* It is in this order that sharpness for thinking is required. The *Necessary is where I strive for 'Human Perfection.'* The 'Necessary' is anything of a life-maintenance (food, housing, safety, etc.), life-shaping (e.g. "How Shall I Live?") or life-changing (e.g. overcoming losses, lacks, and barriers) nature. Being the captain of my Selfhood vessel I cannot imagine letting anyone tell me what to think or do in these areas. Yet, I will listen to and assess the opinions of anyone--and the weight I give those opinions has nothing to do with their 'authority' status or recognized power or amount of money. I simply most respect the purity of Thought or Feelings. With Necessities, "Almost" is not good enough and it is my job to research and reflect on the subject until it is a *"Human Ideal."* In the category of "Important," there is a small space for "Almost." Often here, for any number of reasons, I lack the ingredients in the moment to arrive at a "Human Ideal." Thus, I put down all I know so it can *Marinate* (etymologically, 'dunk it in the sea') inside the matrix of my mind whereby "Like-Kind" thoughts out of memory and coming in from the outside world will support aspects of its evolution. *Matrix*--a nice word, implying to 'mother'--is a complete organism womb which imposes itself on, restricts the contents of, and places a boundary around a Thought or Creation. Meanwhile, it supplies nutrition, assists organization, and fashions orderly progression of development until the thought process or the creation is completed; or at least well along the way. Later, when I come back to the topic, its "wholism" aspects have been cleared of the fog--a fog otherwise likely to cause me to settle for "Almost." Next, some things have the potential possibility to be Important. But if its time has not come, then I will do the *"A lick and a Promise"* thing I learned as a boy. Aunt Cherry would say this when a little something had to be done but there was not time to do the job right--something like: "I'll take off the top dirt from the rug and promise to beat the rug tomorrow." Here, "Almost" is good enough. jabaileymd.com

ALTERNATE: "*Alter*" originated with "*Alternate*" (1385, in Chaucer's Troilus and Criseyde; other) something changed to other than what it was + "*Alternate*"—not ones first choice but the "other" or second choice, indicating a serious choice which must be made—there is no getting out of it—between two things. Choice implies more freedom, including making no choice at all. *Option* (sight, seeing) started out in Cawdrey's A Table Alphabetical (1604) as "to wish"; the "mood of wishing" (with longing and belonging); or "to desire." See Option; Adopt

AMAZED: (stunned) by being dulled through shock, as in being wide-eyed and open-mouthed while "*Bending*" (bring into a curve) Reality into Distortions or leaping into Fantasy (e.g. the Supernatural). When moderate or Extreme, there is an exit off reality's course as to stir so much disharmony, fear, and difficulty as to cause *Illusions* (seeing what is not there and not seeing what is there); *Hallucinations* (false images or beliefs having nothing to suggest it, outside a disordered mind); "*Delirium*" (temporary mental disturbance leading to believing ideas opposed to reality); *Delusions* (believing what is not real and not believing what is real); and *Misinterpretations* (wrong track, wrong plane of existence, and/or wrong direction). All disarray ones 'sureness' of any topic one thought one knew or will later know.

AMYGDALA BURN-OUT SYNDROME: Brain's *Amygdala*—a temporal lobe alarm center just under ones temples. It works with the frontal lobes' consciousness to increase the Fear Response alertness.

Moderate or Extreme Despair + Apathy + an inclination to "give up" on life with a "Don't Care" attitude. The Amygdala is a Limbic portion of the human brain which, when it loses its normal behavioral response to danger, is conceivably characterized by a mindset of Moderate or Extreme Despair and Apathy and perhaps to the extent of "giving up" (Bailey, Self-Protection Syndrome p85). This I long ago called the *Amygdala Burn-out Syndrome* and there is now confirmatory evidence of it being associated with fear and aggression as well as it being larger in those showing burnout from emotional distress. As a result, it is harder for them to deal with any new stressors. This leads their emotions to be out of control because they have weaker connections between the amygdala and the medial prefrontal cortex, a brain area associated with executive function. This makes them more susceptible to depression.

ANALOGY: *Metaphors* (equates unlike things by implication), *Simile* (the abstract or suggestive aspect is directly expressed), *Allegories* (a hidden story within an obvious story), *Fables* (animals impersonating humans to impart a moral), *Personification* (making a lifeless or abstract thing alive), *Analogies* (explaining something unfamiliar by comparing it to something familiar), *Legend* (a story, above mere fiction, combining fact and personified spiritual concepts), and *Symbols* (symbolic messages disregard the limitations and boundaries of human thought in order to impart ideas of the indescribable). To hold in one hand five long crooked sticks in their middle, all of them touch each other in ones palm and at this point these sticks share a Similarity (having likeness or resemblance in a general way simply because they are all touching. On either side of ones palm, the curves of two sticks cause them to touch each and that means they are Analogous--partially similar parts in dissimilar things--as in the partial similarity corresponding to where they are touching at a "*common point.*" This differs from Correspondence because the sticks do not have the same "Genetics" as, for example, one is real while the other is fabricated. The general *principle of Analogies is that: "If two things resemble each other in many Qualities, they can be used for further reasoning as Analogies on that basis.* Analogies possess the power to bring things to life by evoking images that illuminate the points of comparison the author is trying to make. Analogies have two parts: an original subject and a compared subject (what the original is being likened to). In comparing my love for my dog Titan to a gardenia, the original subject is my love while the compared subject is the gardenia so as to illuminate and express my love for both. The comparison can be either obvious (explicit) or implied (implicit). Emotive language often combines with visual imagery to present extremes of ideas and feelings, as seen in advertising. This is sort of like Ancient African ritual specialists who used ugly masks to personify things—like bringing into a mental picture existence the idea of a destructive evil spirit. By so doing the people could focus on that mask and then take the appropriate action. Primitive Africans *Reasoning by Analogy*--taking the familiar to explain the unknown. As Reasoning's simplest and most popular form, it is based upon the general *principle that: "If two things resemble each other in many points, they will probably resemble each other in more points.*

ANALYSIS: Analysis resolves the whole into its parts. Very Ancient African farmers, building on what Primitive (the first) Africans originated, tossed their wheat crop in the air so the wind would blow the chaff away from the wheat. Out of this separation was formulated concepts for formal Analytical (as the complimentary opposite of Synthesis), Abstract, and Abstraction Thinking used throughout the world ever since. Analysis was part of the original idea of African Logic's formulations—i.e. the putting statements of together correctly so as to arrive at new statements. However, this process required *"Analysis"* of the problem—i.e. subdividing the whole of a thing into its component parts in order to discover the general principles underlying its individual happenings--and prioritizing them so as to select the keystone. Specifically, Analysis involves the singling out of the characteristics and qualities of a Thing; concentrating the mind on one of these at a time in order to determine its potential possibilities, what it does, how it appears, and especially "what it is". Analysis is done to emphasize consistency of meaning and completeness before resorting to Synthesis. Resultant new deductions from Analysis and Synthesis could then be the basis for making other deductions on the way to establishing a logical train of thought for the opening up of important new information.

ANCESTORS--ANCIENT AFRICAN: The scope of our Ancestors includes: first, the *Nameless Dead,* signify fragments of former persons, who have lost any meaningful sense of self; have lost their names; and have lost the means by which they could be immortalized. Second, the *Living-Dead* are younger age-wise than the Nameless Dead but occupy a higher position with respect to moral function (Wiredu, African Philosophy p329). The "Living Dead" refer to lineage spirits remembered as individuals who maintain their vitality and active interest in their descendants. In African Tradition they are the most intimate divine spirits; the real rulers of the lineage; and owners of its property. African traditionalists believe their clan Ancestors charge each generation with the specific missions of ensuring the survival and continuation of the clan and facilitating the reemergence, development, and expansion of the national reality. Certain members of the clan, assigned to carrying out these missions, are chosen to reenter the physical and are then endowed with the necessary skills, talents, or personality features to facilitate the consummation of their tasks (Wells-Wilbon, *J. Black Studies 2010 40: 509-526*). In appreciation, *Ancestor Veneration* are engaged in by such rituals as libations inside or outside the Black Church and having home alters where communication is done directly with the Ancestors. Although they must be invited in and consulted on important occasions, there has never been any hint of *"Ancestor Worship"* as Europeans falsely advertize that Black People do. Whether celebrated among the Igbo of West Africa, the Bakongo of Central Africa, or elsewhere in Africa, Ancestor Veneration -- since ancient times -- has been a pivotal aspect of *African Harvest Festivals* (and this is where Thanks-Giving began). See Libations; Ancestor Veneration

ANCESTORS--LIVING-DEAD: They continue to make themselves known by doing whatever it takes to keep me "on-point". By 50 years of intense research into African Tradition, I am now in its flow and can immediately recognize any dilutions and pollutions in it. Such is exemplified by even the tiniest of deviations from the integrity of the Spiritual Elements. If one is off 0.000001 degree in going from here to the moon, one will wind up on Mars. As a result of being in the flow, I can write about a "string" in the "fishnet" of African Philosophy and have no idea where those concepts come from. Yet, in later comparing these concepts with established

African Knowledge, there is correspondence and what I wrote thereby expands my Sensory Consciousness. For example, in trying to gain insight into the Metaphysical meanings of "Essence," "Primary Qualities," and "Virtual" I awakened with the thought of "That it is"—a thought I would never have arrived at on my own. Such happens often. All Spiritual Entourage interactions come from keeping open ones inborn clairvoyance (Donkor African Spirituality, p145) for maintaining close rapport with ones Ancestral Spiritual counterparts in the Ancestral World. Real Self people are aware of an intimate connection with their Spiritual Entourage. This displays at birth with a bonding moment between the newborn and her/his mother. At eye contact, the infant declares its mother to be the ultimate in knowing when and how to care for all its needs because of her ability to see vital matter (Bailey, Ancient African Bible Messages). Thereafter, Real Self people cultivate their Pure Emotions through guidance by their Spiritual Entourage before the realization of what is happening make themselves known by successful results in dealing with Parents, Family, Relatives, Teachers, Mentors, and Peers. The more one refines ones Pure Emotions and Mysticism Intellect, what periodically flow out of being within the flow of the Divine Logos are statements of ones Conscience without thought (and are thereby Instincts). For example, in responding to a question, I told the person: "I do not deal with good or bad, but rather with the Truth in order to see things as they really are without judging." I had never thought of that prior to the response. Throughout the course of special ongoing episodes, Jann and I have a great relationship. Everyday he works along the lines I point out—and those are what are pointed out to me by my Spiritual Entourage. Then he performs those tasks I have distilled into basic problems without solution while I am asleep—apparently going anywhere in the Cosmos to get answers. When I awaken, he has organized it--the sorting, dissecting, prioritizing, and arranging of the evidence--before presenting it in a clear systematic shape to my mind. In total dedication to my Mission and from experiencing daily set-backs and frustrations, it is necessary for me to create my own gifts for my enjoyment. An example is seeing my books come from the publisher or spending great time, energy, and effort on a difficult topic and then writing a paper on it for which I feel great pride. See Libations

ANCESTOR VENERATION: practices and beliefs honoring the deceased. See Libations

ANCIENT AFRICAN BIBLE: The "Prt m Hru" (epitaph)--a name for Humankind's original Bible and dating to 60,000 BC (Seleem p 59, xiii), the "Book of Life"—says: *righteousness leads to spiritual realization; purification is acting with righteousness; and by learning about the nature of the Divine—acting, feeling, and thinking as the Divine—it is finally possible to become one with the Divine.* African concepts of the Divine Logos--*i.e. God's Universal Reason—of Thought and Creative Utterance and Power*—the Word—was presented in the world's first Bible (actually Spiritual Literature). Its need arose from the Spiritual Elements "Genetics" of Unconditional Love, Truth, Reality, and the Natural having such unique combinations of expression in each of God's Creatures and Creation as to call for standards, filters, guides, and measures. No matter the uniqueness in the sense of what each human does, how each appears, and in their orchestrating the Character and Personalities, there is a Common Sense and Logic way for each human to determine her/his lifetime as well as Afterlife Destiny. Since the tools for all forms of thinking come from Pure Emotions or Intellect, African Tradition's Spiritual Literature presented Principles—i.e. unchanging aspects of Wisdom—as to what gives rise to them and why they are the "contractors" for all Thoughts of African Tradition. In short, the point was to lay out *"The Way"* in a manner that could be understood by African people. The Ancient African Bible is the text(s) presenting mythological stories upon which a religion and its basic beliefs are based. Although this Spiritual Literature has been evolving since Human-kind first appeared 200,000 years ago in Africa's Ethiopia Afar beautiful, snow-capped Rwenzori ("rainmaker") Mountains, its contents are the ultimate human source for answering of all of today's Black People's most profound ways of getting their lives in order. This is called *Sankofa: (1)* return to African Tradition to learn Principles of how to; (2) Prepare in the present; (3) in order to go forward into a Thriving future--all staying within the boundaries of Ancient Africans' terminology defini-tions and descriptions. Its Language and Concepts are the only ones suitable to reflect, represent, and teach Afrocentric People. The word "Bible" (Greek, "the books") ultimately refers to Byblos, the Egyptian hieratic word for *Papyrus* -- the inner bark of Egyptian papyrus used to make "paper". Because the Egyptian word for paper was *pa-pe-ra* (the source of the English word, *paper*), ancient Greeks called it *papyrus*. Though a "paper" made book is how people of today's world think of a Bible, this is not how it originated. Rather, it was in the form of 40 or 50 strophes (stanzas like those of a poem) representing a text. The accumulation of the purist essence of the wisest thoughts and practices in Ancient African Tradition, before being penetrated by foreign powers, is what constitutes the Ancient African Bible. Its theme is to provide ways for every individual to reach the height of ones birth-gift potentials *for self-expression in order to pave a path that leads to the Heaven Afterlife.* Theme messages in this, the world's first text--*The Book of Life* (c60,000 BC)--includes the Practical and the Esoteric. The Practical is about paying honor and divine respect to the "Creator of all Humankind"; discussions of Judgment Day; and that the "West" (the Blessed!), the abode of those without fault. This context is by trans-forming ones consciousness from ones mortal Lower (animalistic) Self to ones enlightened immortal Highest (Divinity) Self--i.e. from human to divine. To these ends, Ancient African Bible message contents encompass collections of utterances intended to show how to purify the mind with wisdom about the neteru (gods and goddesses representing divine forces in the Cosmos); to practice rituals promoting Character integration; and paths to spiritual transformation by complete absorption into the Divine. Its contents consist of a distillation of the vast Spiritual Teaching Wisdom of prior African Sages, emphasizing ways to promote spiritual emancipa-tion, awakening, or resurrection (Ashby African Origin p454). African Sages synthesized all this information within the context of what was revealed to them by the Cosmic Mind and made Inference conclusions. One was that all of reality is connected into a Cosmic Unity--a concept serving to form the *Law of Sympathy* and the *Law of Ntuology* (all humans are interrelated through spiritual and human networks). Both imply an intimate connection between the living, the remotest of Ancestors, and the yet unborn. It follows that Spirit helpers and guides are assigned to each human to help one carry out ones task in life. To achieve the Right Living way of life, African Traditions' two forms of Thought are Poetic Spiritual Emotions/Feelings and Intellect. See Sun

ANCIENT AFRICAN MIGRATIONS: Human-kind first appeared 200,000 years ago in Ethiopia, Africa. From gathered bits and piece have emerged generally accepted prominent migration patterns out of Africa initially going North and East into India, the Far East, the Near East, and South Pacific. Around 125,000 BC a group of Africans moved northward towards the Nile and into the Levant (bordering the Mediterranean between Egypt and Turkey); another, c90,000 BC, across short sketches (major points) of sea along Asia's southern coast, then migrated into East Asia; then the Dravidians of South India, Pakistan and Iran; then c85,000 BC a group crossed the entrance of the Red Sea in the south and into the Arabian Peninsula to reach the Indian sub-continent, spreading to Indonesia and reaching southern China by 75,000 BC; then by 65,000 BC they had spread to Borneo, Australia, India, throughout Asia, Scandinavia, and close to the North Pole; then 45,000 BC into Europe; then 30,000 BC three separate migrations crossed land bridges the Bearing land bridge into Alaska and on down into North and then South America by 25,000 BC. Among these were Primitive African Shaman (priest/medicine men) who set the pattern for the evolving Amerindian Medicine man. Some of these migrations were by land, sea, and settlements gradually moving outward (Bailey, African Bible Messages). In the process, Primitive and Very Ancient Africans were making civilization and cul-tural advancements. Yet, areas in which they were living necessitated moving perhaps 10 to 100 miles away per year and in all directions. Each small migrating band of people for purposes of finding a better food and water supply meant it was more practical to simply memorized their history and other pertinent matters because they could only carry but so much on their travels. Prior to 12, 500 BC in Europe's Ice Age, the Mediterranean Sea was shallow and had land bridges in places.

ANECDOTES: For people in the West, the ancient Greeks had only two kinds of stories—those given out publically and the private unpublished juicy gossip "Anekdotos." Because anecdotes and testimonials were based only on reports of individual occurrences and had not been reviewed, tested, and accepted by authorities, they could not be adequate statistical evidence.

ANIMUS: "*animal spirit*" ("anima and animus" in Latin spiritual tradition)--possessing the functions of animating a human's life, especially the physical body. That "animal spirit" then activates the *inactive* Spiritual Energy which, in turn, activates the undifferentiated/unstructured potential Matter by adding an attribute of God--the Ether (i.e. Life's Force). See Life Force

ANOMALY: ("irregular")--marked deviation from the normal or average--referring to the resemblance of function between organs which are essentially different. In biology, Analogies denote the physiological similarities independent of morphological resemblance.

ANTHROPOLOGY: (the study of human development), the evolutionary tree's human branch, called Homo, is thought to have arisen from a group of ancient species called australopithecines. Said to be present 2 million years ago is Australopithecus sediba (aw-STRAL-oh-PITH-uh-kus se-DEE-bah, meaning "southern ape, wellspring"). It and an older South African species, A. africanus, appear more closely related to early humans than other australopithecines. An example is the famous African "Lucy" who has provided new insight about life for early human ancestors 3.18 million years ago. Its transitional features between humans and apes include: it both climbed in trees and walked upright; the ribs show the creature's upper trunk resembled an ape's, while the lower part looked more like a human's; the upper limb bones other than the hand and wrist look primitive, reflecting climbing ability, while earlier analysis of the hand had shown mixed traits; and the teeth also show a mix of human and primitive features. In addition, a mix of human and apelike traits in leg bones suggests A. sediba walked like no other known animal. Its heel was narrow like an ape's, which would seem to prevent walking upright, but the more humanlike knee, pelvis and hip show A. sediba did just that. Here is where environmental factors are influential. When people walk, they strike the ground with the heel first. Since that would be disastrous for A. sediba's narrow heel bone, the creature probably struck the ground first with the outside of the foot. In turn, the foot would react by rolling inward (called pronation). In people, chronic pronation can cause pain in the foot, knees, hip and back. But the bones of A. sediba show features that evidently prevented those pain problems--apparently adopting this gait as a kind of compromise for a body that had to climb trees proficiently as well as walk upright. As stated, Homo Sapiens Sapiens appeared 200,000 years ago in the area of Ethiopia's Afar, now known as the Cradle of Humankind. Since all human females' Mitochondrial DNA is traceable to an African female Ancestor, this identifies Africa as the home of the mitochondrial gene pool from which mankind arose. From a Spiritual perspective, the creation of the physical aspect of all living Beings derives from a Cosmic Gene Pool. The Cosmic intelligence activates certain aspects of its "Genetics" in order to produce customized and varied archetype Foundations to serve a specific role in the Cosmos (e.g. humans, animals, insects, and microorganisms). The DNA is what determines if two living Beings are compatible with each other for mating. Otherwise, they are of a different species.

Out of this Foundation arise visible structures with sufficient exterior and/or interior differences to allow for them to be put into a Classification. It has broad (e.g. Animals and Plants) Categories and their Subcategories -- e.g. Humans and Dogs are also Animal subcategories. Yet, all Foundations, regardless of their Cosmic sub-plane location, work in harmony as part of the Cosmic Organism's inherent intelligence reflecting the will of God. Similarly, the interior structure of each member in the Classification possesses wholism Coherence,

Consistency, Compatibility, Balance, and Harmony. Within a given human, it is said the Life Force of the human Soul engenders the impetus in the DNA to function (Ashby, African p422) in generating "Certain Sameness" features with other humans (and animals). Simultaneously, it activates certain other parts of cells, stimulates a certain cell, and inhibiting other parts to fashion unique features within that human. The way this comes about is an indwelling intelligence at the center of each human cell's DNA having programmed into it all of the infinite possible functions of life (similar to the Ocean of Nun). This fact allows for specialized duties (Uniqueness) within the world of cells of a given human. Thus, the only difference in an immune cell and a brain cell is that the DNA chooses to activate certain parts of a cell and inhibit other parts. Yet, they work in harmony because of the orchestration of the organism's inherent intelligence reflecting the will of God. Within this flow of DNA thought, I propose that Ancient Africans had developed their Brain/Mind DNA potential to perfection, as evidenced by their brilliant achievements admired, plagiarized, and copied to this day. Ancient Africans speak to the "Big Four" inner recess forms of awareness: (1) Ultimate Truths which originate from the realm of God and contain in all black structures (e.g. melanin) of Black People's physical make-up; (2) Ancestral Memories (called Epic Memories and termed "Collective Unconscious" by Ancient African Sages) generated by our brilliant Primitive (the first) Ancestors; (3) Religion/Spirituality; and (4) Acquired Spiritual Pains. African Tradition cultivates Types 1, 2, and 3 so as to avoid Type 4. Whereas Types 1, 2, and 3 could be inherently transmitted as part of ones Collective Unconscious (in the Omnibus Brain?), aspects of them were also likely transmitted to members of today's society via the Afrocentric Mystic Memory and culturally. What this means is the way each of us is at this time has been largely determined by our Ancient African Ancestors. Their DNA is in our DNA. But significant environmental alterations occurred to Enslaved Africans during African American slavery and those environmental alterations have passed down to particularly affect struggling Black Americans. Still, they contain DNA potential for greatness exemplified by our Ancient African Ancestors. To illustrate this point, some say the Ice Age caused people to be isolated and develop subspecies of Homo Sapiens. One of those was Neanderthals who, in turn, bred with anatomically modern humans who first entered Europe about 42,000 to 45,000 years ago. Evidence of this breeding is manifest in the DNA of people living today.

ANTHROPOMORPHISM: ('anthropos, man) is the act of endowing god with a human form and human attributes or qualities, like the acquired emotions of anger, wrath, fear, and jealousy.

A POSTERIORI: Derived from the experience of an object or quality whereas A Priori From Causes to Effects Reasoning is not derived from any sense experience. See A Priori

APPARITION: a sudden and unexpected appearance of some Being or object, usually implying a supposed Supernatural manifestation (e.g. a ghost). The Greek "*Chimaira*" means she-goat with the head of a lion, body of a goat, tail of a dragon, and capable of spitting fire. Those Chimera images are based upon some minor degree of reality--for obsessive-compulsive fulfillment. Since Chimera images are normal in children, this greatly enhances their abilities to absorb all aspects of Supernatural Predatory practices than most realize. Those who disbelieve in the Spiritual Realm (beyond paying "lip service") and instead believe all they see is physically and "mechanically" explainable, simply have information (not real) that crams the Immaterial (Spiritual) into the Tangible (Material).

APPEARANCE: C13 Old French (to show; to come in sight) is apparent and thus is opposed to actual reality. This means "Real" is to "Seem" as reality is to appearing--as the actual is to the possible--as Being is to Becoming--as "is" (i.e. Being) is to "is not" (i.e. non-Being). The formation of an Appearance of any Entity starts with the fully realized form of its Essence, called its *Pattern*. That Pattern possesses an Image on its outside and a Matrix on the inside. The "what it does" of that Essence is the making of a Virtual Image—called a *"That it is"*. To look at this from the outside in, when every ingredient of an Entity has been removed, the very least that can be thought of that Entity is its *"That it is"—meaning it constitutes the Cosmic Being of that Entity when it came into Being.* Within the *"That it is"* Form is imparted the "Genetics" which determines the capabilities and guidance for how it is to develop, for what it is to do, for how it is to grow, and for how it is to appear. In short, the *"That it is"* identifies the Spiritual undifferentiated and unformed but not disorganized Being by its Essence containing a Disposition and its specificity, individuality, and 'here/now-ness' aspects. This means the *"That it is"* refers to any Primary Quality (e.g. Spiritual Emotion) in any category because that Thing's essence lacks a Form-Body and thus is itself a virtual body (lacking boundaries). See SEEMS

APPETITIVE FACULTY: is about wanting, needing, craving, wishing, willing

APPRECIATIONS: Sitting on my favorite rock at the ocean's edge, I let my mind "Just Be" so as to begin my 81ˢᵗ birthday celebration. My attention focused on where the ocean meets the sky. Since Waves of ocean tides always harmonize my Selfhood with rhythms of Nature, my mind flowed into Nature's processes. Meanwhile, my Selfhood quieted as it settled into what is like the calm at the ocean's bottom. Since the ocean is the cradle of life, encompassing all of life's dim origins + receiving many transmutations of ends of life, my thoughts bathed in its obvious, forgotten, and hidden Truths. Natural Universe rhythms, as for all within and around Humanity, have Unconditional Love as its "Genetic" source. Nature's rhythms contain *aesthetic order*—and, by my becoming "One" with *the Cosmic Ocean,* I slid into discerning *invisible essences of Truths and Realities which otherwise I would be unable to see*—a discerning of the infinite in the finite as representing each imaged Thing's Beauty and Worth. That naturally led to "ME/WE" appreciations in the "here and now." Examples: I appreciate my good health--a career ideally suited for me—being enthusiastic about my Mission in life to help struggling people—my life's struggles and setbacks--having people to love and knowing they love me--my possessions that bring such pleasures as to not need to go anywhere else for a vacation--my integrity to remain honorable in the midst of dishonorableness all around me—my freedom from ever hating anybody, despite the world seeming to have gone mad by honoring hatred. No one has anything I want and I envy no one. Rather, I appreciate those who have been successful in a "ME/WE" manner—and I appreciate being able to help those willing to be better or 'less bad off'. From toddler-hood to now, I have appreciated my family and the wonderful all-Black community in which I was reared. They taught me to appreciate the fact that bad times were not any worse and that by having survived each made me stronger. But what is the meaning of Appreciate and what does it mean to be addicted to it? Note: to enter African Philosophy, *African Knowledge and European definitions/information for a given word are never, never to be mixed.* A European dictionary defines *'Addict'* (C16, "to be bound over to") as a self-generated chronic disharmony way of life—meaning one is literally sentenced to ones habit and thereby gives way to improper impulses to engage in adverse self-indulgences. However, the African equivalent is that Afrocentric people's *work of Spirituality is the subjection of their minds to the Divine Spirit so it can command the Life-Force in harmony with the Laws of Nature.* Within this context, a free flowing natural process of creating, enhancing, maintaining, defending, and protecting harmony as a way of life is a good addiction. The consequence of either definition is that Addictions arise from the awareness of something or the memory of something or the wishing for something so significant as for it to become an Icon Image one creates. It is then used for life as ones Standards, Guides, Measures, and Filters. European "*Appreciate*" definitions are: (C17) "setting a price on something"; estimating worth; esteem highly; Thankful; Gratitude. In African Tradition, each of these words is distinct—is Spiritually based—and is not about the Material. Instead, as opposed to Acquired Emotions (e.g. likes/dislikes), to *Appreciate* requires use of ones Pure Emotions. One enjoys Beautiful expressions out of Spiritual Elements' products within a given creation/creature--especially "ME/WE" displays. Such Appreciation may range from admiration--all the way over to being in awe and full of wonder for it "just being" the way it is and what it does. Personally, to see the infinite in the finite means to see my own Soul in a Thing. Since my Soul shares a "Sameness" of "Genetics" with all other like-kind Things, I can properly use my Pure Emotions for "Feeling" it. Those Feelings, said Ancient Africans, derive from ones Soul's Spiritual Elements being like a radar beacon "Trademark" and connecting with the infinite. They defined *Gratefulness* as recognition/enjoyment of the God Substance (Essence) naturally present in oneself as well as in any attribute received from other people. Appreciation and Gratefulness "Feelings" spur one to express *Thankfulness* to God for the ability to recognize and enjoy the Substance of God in real creatures and creations. *Gratitude* is Appreciation, Gratefulness, and Thankfulness for being made in God's Image + possessing *Selfhood Greatness* of incalculable magnitude and its provision of unlimited potential power directed toward achieving ones Mission in life. Appreciation is enjoying what you have as long as it is there. Supernatural, by contrast, have the motto that "Too much is never enough". jabaileymd.com

APPRECIATION TRIANGLE (EUROPEAN): The C17 European word "*Appreciate*" ("to appraise, set a price at") came from the idea of setting a price on something by means of making an estimate, even an unfavorable one. The first of its sides represented a "fair" estimated monetary appraisal: a second side represented a "feeling worth" appraisal; and the third side represented a "spiritual worth" appraisal. The "feeling worth" appraisal demanded the experts realize the sensitivity and delicate perceptions of viewers as a vital part of the experience of a given creative work. The spiritual worth was determined by the social common sense of the local people.

APPREND: lay hold of something in it, as through the senses, the mind, or via the instinct—with only a hint, at best, of understanding anything that it is about. Even then, it is uncertain that what has been apprehended is part of the Essence, or is given the right interpretation, or is the right part selected in order to form that Notion.

A PRIORI REASONING: A PRIORI (prior; 'seems right') Reasoning is any information, cognitive constituent, or knowledge prior to experience of the facts in question. Anything real is composed of a Universal Essence (or Form) that is prior to Matter. Hence, any reasoning from the general nature (or essence) of things is argument from that which is by nature prior—equivalent to Deductive Reasoning—going from Causes to Effects. A priori reasoning deals with what exists before and independent of experience. For example, an 'a priori' Symbol was present there before the first experience. To elaborate, what seems 'a priori' to one may nevertheless have been slowly acquired from experience in the long history of the human race and continually absorbed from the "Cultural Atmosphere". These concepts borrowed by ancient Greeks from African Sages and then confused, can somewhat be resolved by Ancient Africans "First Wisdom". This is Knowledge not derived from human experience but rather contains the Cosmic Organism's Universal Essence. By that essence also being within humans' Selfhoods (e.g. mind) makes possible Human experiences in time, space, substance, Cause, etc. When one has just washed clothes and sees it is going to rain, to then take the clothes off the outdoor clothesline is the acting from what has been learned through past experiences. A Priori Reasoning is carefully studying minute case details + ones education, training, and experience + relying on African Tradition's *Subjective Science* tools to make inferences in arriving at circumstantial evidence and judgments. A *Posteriori Reasoning* (argument from Effect to Cause) and A Priori Reasoning (from Cause to Effect)--starting with the definition formed or principles assumed and, without examination or analysis—and independently of experience, presumptively deducing consequences. Out of those consequences they then formed definitions and assumed principles to use as propositions to figure out what can be known by Reason alone. Based upon the mere examination of ideas of what appeared to them to be Self-Evident or what they presupposed by experience led to conclusions they classed as knowledge. Note that they demanded no appeal even to their "facts" of experience or to anything on a sound starting Base since what was Self-Evident to them was considered as antecedently necessary in order that experience in general be intelligible. Something under consideration was true or false by definition alone. carefully studying minute case details + my education, training, and experience +

relying on African Tradition's *Subjective Science* tools—i.e. Observation, Reflection, "Pure" Feelings, Productive Imagination, Contemplation, Inductive and Deductive Inferences, and Common Sense—to make inferences in arriving at circumstantial evidence and judgments

ARCHERY PAD CONCEPT: An Archery Pad is a useful way of classifying the complex subject of Knowledge, Information, and their associated components (e.g. the way these are conveyed by the various types of messengers). Being able to put these in priority order is crucial for sound Critical Thinking (CT) and assessing things to think about. The Archery Pad consists of a Bull's Eye in its center, the intended target for archers who shoot arrows at it. Rippling out from the "bull's eye" (space I) is 4 more transitional ringed spaces separated by 5 line circles to make a total of ten parts. Anything beyond the peripheral line circle (i.e. 5th line circle or 10th part) is off the archery pad. The Bull's Eye characterizes Knowledge whose Seed is the Spiritual Elements and which are known by Spiritual Knowledge/Certainty, for it can be thought of as the core for the Knowledge Tree. The single most important indicator of their presence is that they are right regardless of human opinions; they are Right when conveyed--Right when received--and Right when properly applied. The Circle around the Bull's Eye represents Common Sense. The first transitional ringed space surrounding the Bull's Eye is African Axioms; the Second, African Secular Knowledge—i. e. it is at the junction of Spiritual and the Secular; the Third, Second Ringed Space is the African Secular Information; and the Fourth Space is European Information. Off the Pad is Europeans' Supernatural. I call *Standing on the Chain Ring* the ringed Chain around the Bull's Eye. Scholars start their development toward Wisdom by recognizing they are operating out of European information because that is how they have been Socialized by the World society. This is like having a "Cloud" covering ones "Soul Sunshine"—i.e. ones birth gift Knowledge of the Cosmic Organism, including ones pre-birth Emotions. Others have been put in such mental turmoil as to be "Inside-Out" in their thinking patterns and therefore all over the Archery or off it completely. Those "Standing on the Chain Ring" may be likened to having a "Cloud" over their "Soul Sunshine" but with that "Cloud" having a silver-lining. Mainstream Black People possess African Secular Knowledge + African Secular Information + the Fourth Space's European Information. Their job is to shed any European Information that interferes with learning and understanding African Knowledge. Wise people with Knowledge have as their daily strivings to go deeper into the core of the Bull's Eye in order to perfect their Wisdom skills in activities of daily living.

ARCHERY PAD'S STANDING ON THE CHAIN: That ringed Chain indicates a transition between what is acceptable on its Bull's Eye side used by supreme thinkers while the opposite side characterizes Ordinary Thinkers. Thus, distinctions are Certainty/Beliefs, purity/impurity, perfect/imperfect, or Knowing vs. Faith. *Standing on the Chain* implies one has one foot in Knowledge and the other in Information. I think of the circle surrounding around the Bull's Eye as representing a ringed Chain, symbolizing a "Transition." One transition is "*Standing on the Chain Ring*" whereby several factors determine whether something is Knowledge or Information. "Standing on the Chain Ring" may be the result of first people do it voluntarily; second, they follow the crowd there; third is being pulled into it by ignorant people; and a fourth is by advertisers, con-artists, and Brutes for self-interest purposes. For others who do "pick and choose," so that it is difficult to determine what is their pattern. For any of these, one gets clues about people from how they have been socialized. "Standing on the Chain Ring" is a job for Critical Thinking (CT) to assess by recognition and a decision about its significance and the Source. For example, it is a powerful "SEEMS" right deception tool. Then decisions are made to defend against them; get one off them; prevent one from getting on them; and/or take advantage of them. If one is "Standing on the Chain Ring" and desires to advance into being a Scholar, one first determines ones Mission in life, for constitutes the Bull's Eye for daily living. In the process, the Spiritually Elements within that Bull's Eye is what one uses to fashion ones Philosophy of Life (POL). Both the POL and the Mission symbolize the Scholar archer. All of what one does in life is to be positioned on the arrow powered by ones Talent, the Scholar archer's Bow. African Tradition Mental preparation begins with being familiar with the types of Knowledge available for ones usage--an awareness guiding the bow's aim for shooting arrow. See Transition

ARCHETYPES: The Original Entities formed are called Archetypes and their offspring are called Prototypes. Principles are Unchanging Realities that are synthesized into the Great Ultimate Cosmic bottom "Oneness." Each Ultimate Cosmic Principle derived from "Oneness" is an Archetype Seed with its Archetype Essence (which is what God's Substance is called in the Cosmos). Archetypes—"Ideas" of the "Big Mind"--are in such Entity patterns as Music, Mathematics, Beauty, Goodness, Thought, Animals, Plants, and whatever category is represented in the Material World. Each Archetype is a Spiritual Principle whose nature is based on its assigned Vibration rate. Each Archetype Entity or Thing, upon being signaled by and then following a Divine Logos Plan, begins descending into Matter—starting with a first layer of Ether. At this point, its Spiritual aspects conform to the Material contents so as to maintain Harmony with all other of Nature's patterns of Universal Rhythms. In this state, African Sages referred to a given Archetype as an *Idea-Form or Form-Idea.*

ARGUMENT: A reason(s) offered for or against a presented point

ARYANS—ANCIENT: Europeans have hidden their true history and substituted it with delusions of grandeur (e.g. being "little gods") nonsense about their personal power (which they are not without the GUN—i.e. any superior killing device) so as to delude all peoples of the world. An important aspect of European history starts with Aryan nomadic tribes, who carried forth patterns of primitive Europeans, and served as a model for all subsequent European males. Despite not knowing where or when they originated, some say they were living in the grasslands of Eastern Europe, north of the Black and Caspian Seas perhaps 8000 years ago. Although inter-tribal warfare was an everyday occurrence, fighting would stop temporarily in order to form alliances with fellow tribesmen whenever threats by "out-siders" arose. This same pattern is seen today, most noticeably in the political arena. These horse-riding bands of tribes were not a genetic race but rather they spoke a common language. As part of a larger group now known as Indo-Europeans, their great migratory movements began in successive waves from central Asia, South Russia, and Turkestan during the 2nd millennium B.C. and spread throughout such places as Iran, Mesopotamia (Sumeria, Iraq), Persia, the Balkan Peninsula, and Asia Minor (an expanded Turkey). As each civilized city fell, these warring barbarians destroyed every bit of culture and civilization they encountered and could not use. Though a very dumb people, the Aryans' superiority in the development of weapons; in the use of tools for war; in their eagerness to fight, and in the ability to conquer--or subdue--peaceful people; and their pleasure from killing or causing pain and suffering--which they honored--led to their possession of a "sinful pride". They invaded India around 1700 B.C. and colonized the Punjab region of Northwest India; plundered the rich cities of the Indus valley civilizations; absorbed much of the culture; and considered themselves superior and noble compared to the Slaves they captured. While setting up caste systems (e.g. in India), they assumed positions of kings, priest, warriors, artisans, and traders. Part of the process was to impart the mental orientation of prejudices; the practices of discriminatory Caste System (the rigid and permanent separation of groups of people in society); and the self-declaration of being a superior people. By 550 BC, these savage and barbarian warriors were primarily living in Northwestern France, Southwest Germany, Bohemia (Czechoslovakia), and neighboring areas. They were known to be needlessly destructive, to chop up and drink the blood of the enemy they killed; to eat their dead fathers; and to grab hold of any trivial matter so as to fight friends--and without regard for their own lives or the lives of those close to them. Anyone not part of the in-group of these warriors became their slaves when conquered. As migrations of Aryans proceeded southward from their far northern European location they procreated several tribes. These tribes included Northern Eurasians (e.g. the Germanic), Slavic (e.g. Russian, Polish), Southern Europeans (e.g. Hellenic, Italic), Middle

Europeans (e.g., Gaelic, Welsh, Breton), and Middle East (e.g. Iran, Persian) tribes. While the Aryans were establishing social classes, they and other warriors (e.g. the Germanic peoples) were fighting battles everywhere in Eurasia. These warriors had a tremendous thirst for gold and other animalistic pleasures. Such was no better exhibited than by the Ukraine's Scythians of C7th to C3 BC. They lived in saddle, traveled light, and loved war--showing no mercy, being extremely cruel, and killing even their own kinsmen for minor violations.

ASHAMED/SHAME/EMBARRASSMENT: Ancient African Maxims are public declarations of basic moral principles--teaching the glory of Cosmic Order and Ma'at while infusing a spiritual consciousness into the social and political areas of society. This was based upon not discarding its traditions but in gathering the best of African Thought having occurred up to that time and simply building on it--often practicing or up-holding what originally seemed to be contradictory (which is the way I approach any difficult problems). The original essence of Ma'at and the Weighing of the Soul was laid out in Ancient Egyptian hieroglyphics. This summarized the wisdom recorded millennia earlier on temples, tombs, coffins, papyruses, and oral teachings pertaining to African Spiritual Literature. The purpose is to encourage spiritual liberation, awakening, or re-vivification from ordinary human consciousness and mortality to Cosmic Consciousness and immortality. It was drawn from 42 laws governing the way of living and Ma'at's Twelve Fundamental Virtues (Bailey, Ancient African Bible Messages). These and the Original Commandments out of the Osirian Drama--known as the *Negative Confessions or Declarations of Innocence or the 42 Admonitions of Ma'at*--are the guidelines for righteous thought, emotion, speech, and conduct as well as serving for the standard against which the soul of the dead will be judged (Karenga, Maat p234). Incidentally, it was from them that Moses, an Egyptian Priest, many millennia prior extracted the Ten Commandments. To get to the Heaven Afterlife one had to affirm they had not committed any violations of these 42 laws--e.g. no killing, violent or non-violent injury, robbery, negative emotions (e.g. hot-temperedness). Those living in strict adherence to Ma'at Principles are assured a just reward in the Afterlife. Since Sin proved to be closely associated with disharmony like foolishness and the disagreeable and since Guilt is linked with moral error, violations of any of the 42 laws reflects regret of ones errors and offenses. The regret is from aberrations which disturbed ones harmonious integration with the Cosmos--thus causing Shame. The correction for such foolishness is a better understanding--not repentance for sin--the pursuit of insights and the cultivation of self-restraint. Hence, Humans are not evil by nature nor sinfully corrupted. So, instead of Guilt (an inward sense of stain), there is Shame (the consciousness of fault of judgment in which one has displayed ones own ignorance, however worthy ones intent). When Europeans borrowed these concepts they made drastic changes from African Traditions' self-help orientation over to ways of controlling the people. Although the popular sense of the synonyms Disgrace, Ashame, Shame, and Guilt in Old English (450-1066) shared the core of "shy" and "Bashful" as a state of mind pertaining to needless failure causing disappointment and humiliation, its religious core of provoking abomination (loathing, disgust) was applied to people who violated European church doctrine. Added to this, if there was a design to deceive, the label of Shame was a Self-Esteem attack. By C17, such exposure was also for the purpose of covering "the sinner" in a cloud of shame with the intent to harm ones reputation. Thereafter, Shame went in the direction of having bad feelings about violating rules of decency. By the end of the European Middle Ages, when individualism and materialism were rising into prominence, the traditional vices became more desirable and respectable. As a result, Shame and Guilt not only separated in meaning but were less of a problem, thanks to the flexibility had been put into European morals. Also in C17, the original meaning of Embarrass ("put to shame"; to put behind bars; impede) was separated to signify ones reaction from one doing dishonorable acts. This created moral repugnant reactions from others, as manifested by others isolating the accused from all fellows. As a result of this combination, the accused would be hampered, endered (halt progress), and impeded in relation to what life-shaping path because of emotional confusion ("I don't know what to say or do") leading one to be perplexed--puzzled and worried as to how to act or decide. CONFUSION is a state in which the mental faculties are thrown into chaos so that the clear and distinct action of the different powers, as of perception, memory, reason, and will is lost. The embarrassed one finds it difficult to proceed. In short, Shame is the opposite of Belong.

ASSESSMENTS: in Medical training they involve: (1) Normal; (2) Effects of outside influences, ones condition, and ones choices in causing "normal variant" or abnormal behaviors or disease; (3) Diagnosis; (4) Treatment/Management; (5) Results.

ASSUMPTION: A statement accepted or supported as true without proof or demonstration, often serving as a belief or unstated premise.

ASSUMPTIONS--UNEXAMINED: The single most important reason people have distorted or false information and are absolutely resistant to change is because of Unexamined Assumptions. To "*Assume*" is to take the showing or appearance of something—taking for granted what is not proved and to adopt or undertake it voluntarily. *Assume, Affect, Feign, Pretend, Sham, and Simulate* all mean to put on a false appearance—whether out of ignorance or with a deliberate attempt to deceive. Whereas Axioms "are right," just below are Proven fragments of information (e.g. Human-Made facts derived by Science; realistic facts). Then come *Postulates* (what "seems right"). Information near the top of the leg is manipulated and maneuvered. For example, if an Axiom or a Postulate is available, the Sages used *Assumptions* (taking a position in realms of uncertainty). When the Assumption or, more properly, the *Proposition*, was shown to be true by logical analysis, African Sages applied the term known in English as *Theorem*—and with the understanding that it would be replaced as soon as better information became available. If the Proposition could not be proved and they were faced with having no idea how to step out of a confusing situation, all that was left was to try the best available suggestion—called *Guesses* (having no basis in fact but ranging from arbitrary to educated). "*Assumption*" was first used by European Supernaturals with reference to the reception of the Virgin Mary into heaven. As background, Ancient African Spiritual Literature says that from the Cosmic god Ra (the solar energy or life-force stored in physical bodies--same as kundalini of the Hindus; Chi of Chinese)--there were successive incarnations until the *Mythical Earth World Trinity*. This Trinity was the Ancestors of the Ancient Egyptians--consisting of the Father, the Son and the Black Virgin Mother appearing in the form of Osiris, Horus, and Isis (Diop, African Origins, p. 109, 194). All of this was recorded in Africa thousands of years before Christianity and served as a source for much of the European Bible. The family of Auset (Isis), Asar (Osiris, who had a decided Ethiopian appearance), and Horus was the forerunner of the hybrid Christian religion's Holy Trinity. However, in 200 AD, the European Church departed from Africans by issuing a Creed of Jesus Christ as "Conceived by the Holy Ghost" and "born of the Virgin Mary." In 431 AD, at the Council of Ephesus, Isis removable from the Divine Triad was to make for skin color compatibility by replacing her "black skin" with Europeans created "white skinned" Virgin Mary. Joseph Campbell, a world authority on religious mythology speaks of the Virgin Mary's Assumption into Heaven but, in the next paragraph, states that in a European temple there is a statue of the Black Madonna with the dark Christ on her knee. Then he makes the startling statement: "I do not understand the idea of the Black Madonna." How is it possible for him not to understand when it is no secret that the Virgin Mary is a European made-up version of the African Black Madonna? This is the type of context in which "Seed" images of Assumptions arise on false paths--"Seeds" called "*Speculations*" since they require many assumptions, and none capable of proof. Since very ancient times, apart from ongoing wars, Brutes have initiated non-violent measures of controlling others minds by introductions of *Assumptions because of their ability to generate an element of doubt* in Victims. The resultant uncertainty about what people "knew" is what galvanized chronic frustration, fear, confusion, Illusions, and

Delusions. Then Brutes would step in and reconcile all ambivalent attitudes, teaching with false fantasy stories containing such highly abstracted concepts as to create *Confusion*--stories that none-the-less "SEEMed" right--stories containing some familiar information the people had accepted--stories told in an interesting, imaged way. This combination leads people to simply "give-in" to these false and misleading stories, embrace them as true, and then defend them. Since what "SEEMs" right is presented as guiding Cosmic philosophies of Values, those *accepting them as basic Assumptions then form fixed Beliefs that give rise to emotions, attitudes, and character displays* of Values. When these Ethos Values become common characteristics of a group, at a given time period, thereafter they pervade that Crowd to actuate major patterns of thought and behaviors. *Then, as distorted or false deceptions of what is "Truth," they find their way into Propositions, Postulates, Premises, Presumptions, or simply Assumptions*—all within the category of *Presuppositions* (an unproven thing taken for granted or assumed). This spreads 'forever' as "*Destructive False Information.*" So, it is best *not to believe anything*!!! By philosophically arriving at absolute causes, using fundamental assumptions, is how individuals and cultures form Worldviews which serve as a "Skeleton" of organizing "How Shall I Live" and "How I Will Deal with people I deem to be 'For Me and Against Me.'" A *Society's Worldview* determines the way: (1) people are socialized to perceive, think, feel, and experience the world; (2) how both people and society define categories of Reality and structure it (*Cosmology*); (3) basic assumptions and beliefs (*Ethos*) about life, living, and people encountered; (4) ones Values systems (*Axiology*); (5) assumptions about life, the Cosmos, and the nature of Reality (*Ontology*); and (6) derive meanings of terms for practical use by means of using parent terms formed by Assumptions. jabaileymd.com

ASYMPTOTE: a line that continually approaches a curve but without ever actually reaching it.

ATHEISTS: *Agnostics*--there is no proof of God but do not deny the possibility. Most believe the Supernatural and/or the Spiritual home of God is unknowable, making it impossible to prove its existence or nonexistence. With *Atheists*--nothing beyond sense perceptions is real--all else is imagination or insanity. If not denying God's existence, most are unsure

ATMOSPHERES ASSOCIATED WITH KNOWLEDGE/INFORMATION: Many a flower is born to bloom and waste its fragrance on the desert air. The same happens to the budding gardenia if no one is in its atmosphere to appreciate its Elegance. Perhaps similar observations by Very Ancient African priest-astronomers (c20,000 BC) of the "flower fragrance" is what spurred them to search for "Lucky Stars" and then likened those Star's "Halos" to a "flower's fragrance". A reason for this assumption is that both the flower and the star make manifest Reality's radiance just as it is into the Atmosphere. One purpose for the search of "Lucky Stars" in particular was to mystically acquire God's messages designed to open and sharpen their minds to Truth and Unconditional Love while expanding their awareness of Reality and the Natural. They noted God appears in Nature as both the sun and moon as well as that both give off *Halos* (Nimbus, Aureole)--a luminous circle--a visual expression of irradiating physical forces and/or symbolized Intellectual or mystical Spiritual forces—forces that eventually expanded into the concept of "Astral" (starlight) body. Incidentally, African Mystics considered the Astral Body to be coexistent with the material body and yet, like the Soul, at times separable from the flesh (Walker, Woman's Dictionary p3). Nevertheless, African priest-astronomers inferred that metaphorically the "Cosmic Star" featured in the *"Star/Halo" Concept* symbolizes the Amenta (God's Cosmic home), while the Cosmos itself is its "Cosmic Halo"; that the Star represents the Substance of God and the Halo pertains to what radiates out of that Substance; that a human's Immaterial Soul is to a sky Star as the Astral Intangible "*Heart*" is to that Star's Halo. An effect of the Halo in its atmosphere making manifest Reality's radiance just as it is came from the substance of its Star being deemed an Icon. The inner character of that Icon carries the payload power of providing a "Feeling" sense of actual participation—a "Feeling" message delivering an inexpressible intellectual concept which the human "Heart" understands and embraces. Whereas each *Icon* bears some resemblance to the thing for which it is a sign, by being a Substance "Seed" Symbol leads Receivers to deem it as being "*Larger than Life*"—and with its own aura and atmosphere manifesting Reality's radiance just as it is. Using Qualitative Mathematics in association with measuring vibratory rates of radiations, Very Ancient African Sages gained insight into the Laws of Nature. Inferences from those Laws led to the Circumstantial Truth paths which would lead to the Heaven Afterlife.

Believing *"good"* people's minds and spirits ought to stay in contact with the Sublime, they built their temples on the topmost place of a sacred mountain. Besides being a strategic position for defending against animal and people attacks, the special *"high place"* was a sanctuary; a source of inspiration; and a sacred atmosphere for religious rites. Rituals inside a sacred space meant its atmosphere surrounded any human participating in a communal event. Each temple's location, presumed to be beyond the earth's normal atmosphere, was filled with "ether"--a subtle fluid of pre-matter consisting of a fine, flimsy, vapor mist. Since this Sublime location contained the highest concentration of Love, Goodness, Truth, and Beauty, they reasoned Spiritual "*Thought Cloud*" atmospheres were present (Ramacharaka, Fourteen Lessons, p 77)—Clouds possessed with Ancient African Sages' mystical values and traits uplifting to and supportive of Ma'at (Spiritual Elements) character. As a result of these *associations imparting Insights that formed a complex of transcendental Knowledge containing an aura around those who indulge in its products, they possessed a "Mystique."* Such Thoughts, by being a system of symbols derived from mosaic pieces of its Source, stand apart from Reality but yet convey the aura of its Source. One background to this concept came from the Ancient African Bible teachings that all forms of Matter are constantly throwing forth astral radiations in all directions (like a mind free of thought filth). Socialization of these Ma'at practices were passed along to the people. One method was by the collective Group Prayers which had the effect of transcending the upper boundaries of their minds to settle in the Sublime as a "*Mystic Memory Satellite.*" Then this "Thought Cloud" of Mystic Memories would resemble a space-located television satellite. Being above time and space, signals out of that satellite could radiate into any Afrocentric person anywhere in the world, regardless of ones age or time period throughout the ages (e.g. into the minds of today's Black Americans). An analogy from Astronomy is that a distant star may be destroyed and yet the light rays thrown off from it will continue on their journey. That same light may soon be seen by humans of the Earth years and years after the star itself has been destroyed. African Sages concluded the Astral Atmosphere, with its high degree of Ether, is charged with the vibrations of thinkers of many years past, and still possess sufficient vitality to affect those whose minds are now ready to receive them (Ramacharaka, Raja Yoga p283).

ATMOSPHERES--DESTRUCTIVE PSYCHIC SUPERNATURAL: Two broad categories of human Atmospheres are the Sublime (i.e. attributes of the Spiritual Elements) and the Supernatural. By being fantasized as above and beyond whatever is in the Natural World, the Supernatural necessarily deems itself to be superior to Unconditional Love, Truth, Reality, and the Natural and their Mathematical displays in the Natural World's Cosmos. Yet, without having a "Ground of Being," Supernatural thoughts are irrational/illogical and its Acquired Emotional processes are chaotic and fettered—both because they are cultivated from External World influences—both constituting *Non-Rational Thinking*. Whereas absorbing Sublime Atmosphere ingredients fills one with the "5Ss" of Safety, Security, Self-Confidence, Strength, and Stability, the opposite occurs from being socialized into or absorbing the Supernatural Atmosphere. That opposite has Conditional Love on one pole end and Indifference/Hate/Evil/Sadism (IHES) mindset on the other end. Similar Supernatural human minds have fantasized a Contingent Supernatual and Hell run by a Devil so as to intimidate those not going along with their anti-Spiritual Elements concepts. Those concepts spur Kill/Take/Destroy/Dominate/Oppress/Control (KTDDOC) practices derived from IHES mindsets. Apparently the *Devil and Hell are intended to* *punish Good People* within their own cult as well as the cult's feigned enemies! By the Supernatural being above the Spiritual source of the "5Ss" means all who absorb the Supernatural Atmosphere are Insecure, feel unsafe, lack self-confidence, are personally weak, and unstable. Since "misery loves company," the Supernatural cult is totally against any of their own who are non-joiners. Also, all must play the same IHES way so the cult can acquire "Scarce Desirables" from feigned enemies as well as be in an Atmosphere of safety and comfort. *Delusional Fears* (those made-up to serve self-interest purposes) are vital to have cult member "Individualists" without IHES mindsets—conform out of fear and share in the cult responsibility for doing some aspect of KTDDOC acts to feigned enemies. Leaders are the "Authorities" who know what is "Right". Even if what they do does not make Humanity sense, it nor they are to be questioned.

These leaders' daily living KTDDOC actions are self-evident conformities to their Devil's ways—the putting of restraints on the free actions of the Soul causing the employment of antagonistic imaginations. The fundamental process to *"Sham" the entire World Crowd* is first to put the blame on the Devil while second, presenting the Devil in a good light. Although saying their Devil is the "source" of their KTDDOC actions, their euphemisms dampen the unpleasant or disagreeable parts by saying this fallen angel is the strongest and fiercest Spirit that fought in Heaven. Such implies the Devil is not to be imagined as wholly bad. To this end, they write euphemistic things about the bad in not so bad terms: the Devil—gentleman "Prince of this World"; "Prince of Darkness" who tells the world there is no Afterlife; a purpose diverter. Milton's devils are admirable; Dante's devils stir pity; Goethe's devil suggests what a good thing has been wasted. Third, the leaders know that in order to *persuade* good and moral people to do evil, it is not necessary to first persuade them to become evil. Instead, it is only necessary to teach them their KTDDOC acts do good. So, religious leaders relay Scriptures saying all humans are equal in the sight of their Supernatural God—meaning each is divine and thus all are supposed to play their true function in life. Still, they add certain adjustments are to be made in Earth World society living in order to conform. This is because, they continue, Adam and Eve dammed all humans with Original Sin and thereby made all humans "inferior". Furthermore, since "everybody" knows their feigned enemies are crooks, they need to be enslaved and controlled by terror. Fourth, the cult needs no deep thinking or truth. Rather, simply accept the status quo without making changes. Since the cult's Supernatural God is too remote to be questioned, leaders say they are the messengers assigned to tell the people all they need to know. So, the cult's reward is to keep 'treadmill busy' with newest, bigger, better, stronger, faster Trinkets and Trivia—for that is the "Good Life"; to stay segregated so as to not be "contaminated"; to continue KTDDOC practices so as to stay superior over the feigned enemies; and to all share in some form of KTDDOC responsibility, for that generates "Excitement" and aids "social charm" with fellow cult members. jabaileymd.com

ATMOSPHERE SENSING: Extrasensory perception and precognition are examples of its irrefutable evidence being insufficient for wide-spread acceptance. This is because the conclusions cannot be reconciled with present information of the physical world—information disconnected from knowledge of the ancient world. In my life there have been things I see and "know" to be above the realm of Illusions. Similarly, there have been Things I could not see and yet "knew" that them to be an entity—what I call a "Sensed Atmosphere." However, such is quite different from the Atmosphere the ancient Greeks coined from "vapor" (air) and sphere. That "Physical atmosphere," in its C17 application, implied not to the envelope of air encompassing the Earth (as it does today), but to a mass of gas exhaled from and thus surrounding a planet. Then the denotation of the word moved forward with the development of meteorological knowledge which indicates that of its 20 or so gases, the two main ones are oxygen and nitrogen admixed with water vapor and dust particles. Our atmosphere is divided into layers, each different from the others--especially the troposphere, the stratosphere, and the ionosphere. Together they form a blanket several hundred miles thick and extending thousands of miles into space

(Tyson, p. 201). Regardless of its contents, there are outside factors radiating into and out of it. Of the several types of "Sensed Atmospheres" all are inside the "Physical Atmosphere." One type occurs at my regular study desk, meaning I can recall hazy information of years prior when writing at the same desk, compared to trying to recall it in any other location of my home. I have been to an empty prison where, upon entering the gate, could immediately feel the disharmony resulting from the conflicts that had no doubt been there when it was full of prisoners. I have been inside empty prison cells I could feel the hostility. Once, while in Jerusalem and walking toward the Wailing Wall my feel started burning. Someone called me and I turned around and went away from the wall—and my feet stopped burning. Then when I approached it the second time my feet began to burn again. After that I went back and forth several times and each time the same sequence occurred. This had nothing to do with intuition or insight—which many people inappropriately confuse with the "guessing" they are doing as *Instant Psychologist* to arrive at a decision or choice or solution ("I could tell as soon as I first met him that he was no good"). Rather, it is about being acutely aware of my "Pure" Feelings—not my emotions—that connect my Real Self to higher powers. Throughout my education, training, and experiences in practicing Orthopaedic surgery, to be sensitive to atmospheres within me, within others, and within my setting often made the difference in avoiding big trouble or defeats. This is not a topic that lends itself to clear explanations but perhaps some examples might convey the idea. We know there are many things in existence that we cannot see as, for example, the Electromagnetic Spectrum. We know that dogs can smell things beyond the capacities of humans, ranging from 20 to 200 times better. The point is that there are things around us of which we are not aware. As a boy I was around harmonious things—in doing gardening for home and for neighbors; in fishing at my favorite place; and in relationships with the wonderful people of my all-Black community. That, plus studying and applying Ancient African philosophy, enabled me to fashion a sense of harmony within myself. So aware was I of this sense that I could automatically determine disharmony in those who entered my atmosphere. The disturbances in me created by people in disharmony demanded that I react—either to help them or to get away from them. One repairman in my home that generated great inner turmoil in me, came back 6 months later and robbed my home. Throughout most of my life, whenever I felt disharmonious, relief would come from doing something to make the lives of others better—whether in a "hands-on" manner or by studying to benefit patients or struggling Black youth (despite them not being interested in what I had to offer).

ATTITUDES: consist of: (1) a Disposition (a Thought Structure comprised of a Predisposing cause with its prevailing trend). Part of the formation of a given disposition is the result of several prior judgments stemming from assessments and evaluations. (2) a Inclination which comes about by a Precipitating Cause with sufficient negative or positive energy to fill a Disposition with tension. This cause--whether driven by the mental actions of prior Judgments; by memory of past events; by a survival or self-protection or self-preservation mechanism; and/or by emotions out of control--mobilizes Will Power to pave a "leaning toward" what is preferred or a "leaning away from" what is undesirable. (3) a Intention--the decision, when pushed hard by Will Power from some Immediate Cause, to aim toward a specific action or a specific goal. In other words, an "Attitude" is a Mental Set (a selective process which determines the way one thinks or solves problems) that responds to something with a prepared reaction (e.g. rolling your eyes in disgust). Since this prepared mental and emotional make-up reaction is capable of displaying itself through the physical--a state called Temperament--it can be observed as a Body Language readiness to act. Similarly, a Temperament can trigger a hypersensitive Attitude.

ATTRACT: The sense of '*Attract*' in its ancient context embraces '*Alluring*' into something harmful by means of an enticing (exciting hope or desire) decoy possessing energetic twisting and squirming pleasurable motives or ideas of a fantasy nature. Alluring also conveys the idea of charm providing some prospect of pleasure or advantage done by purpose and endeavor. The feature of "Attract" is the drawing of "Like to Like."

AURAS SURROUNDING THOUGHT KNOWLEDGE: The process of expanding ones Consciousness is to unfold the mosaic pieces of the Spiritual Elements in the way a budding gardenia is likened to ones evolution into a Scholar, then flowering into Knowledge, and Fruiting into Wisdom. The feature of this process is that Wisdom is the ultimate in human elegance. Elegance embraces the association of Dignity and Simplicity being finely and skillfully made out of Sublime qualities--all immediately allowing one to be aware of things of worth and that it can be used with good taste and a dash of daring. Focusing on the Spiritually beautiful—because it vibrates with the same high frequency as with ones Soul's Spiritual Elements "Trademark"—operates under the Law of Attraction or Law of Vibration and thereby attracts beauty around them. Similarly, each mosaic piece of the Spiritual Elements has an aura or egg-shaped, aural energy field in a manner that a Star has a Halo aura. The story of this happening is out of the Ancient African Bible's origin of Aureole (Auras), Soph or Nu for undifferentiated Matter (feminine principle) and Ra or Aur (root of Aura, light) for Nun energy (masculine principle). These Canaanite names are given to the "Unmanifested and undifferentiated matter/energy in the Subjective realm--are the substance and energy underlying all forms and activities in the world— and are linked, like a halo, with all emanations of the body so as to viewed as Spiritual Symbols. By the *aura of each extending beyond their symbolism* meant they could be expressed in the mystical teachings of African Sages' Religious Mythology and Symbols. Together, they *describe the ultimate and transcendental reality which puts a given human being in touch with the ground of his/her own Being.* The essences nature of these Ancient Africans "Auras" concerned "*Breath*" as an emanation "flowing out from" them—i.e. the "Breath" proceeds from any substance (e.g. individual, animal, vegetable, and mineral substances). This is because all Cosmic entities are infused with an animating spirit (the reason why all things are in motion, as stated in laws of physics). Thus, the Earth's electromagnetic forces are always flowing through all things surrounding a human. It requires self-discipline + a focus on Ma'at living + maintaining a state of Peace to avoid being swept along by these subliminal (sub-lunar) forces. Such is aided by forming an Icon Image of a place of Peace so that ones Thoughts can refer to it at will. Such occurs because a THOUGHT is a system of symbols that stands apart from Reality. *Thoughts are things* and can be seen (like an aura) by the true psychic sight and felt by the Sensitives. There are a variety of theories of what produces thoughts. Evolutionists have claimed the animal ancestors of man had already been thinking to some degree and that the greater responsibilities of humans fashioned specialization of one aspect of Feelings. African and later Eastern philosophers speculated that thoughts resulted from certain vibratory activities in the brain/mind. Western scientists propose that thoughts were placed in the mind from the brains' neuro-chemical mechanisms. Just as "birds of a feather flock together," so do thoughts—and this creates a *Thought Atmosphere*. Thought Atmospheres can also contain Feeling Tones, as I have noticed while visiting places that were once emotionally charged (e.g. an empty prison). A Thought's power depends upon its ability to attract to itself other thoughts of a similar nature (and thus combine forces). The strength with which a Thought has been projected concerns the focus, and the amount of its Ether, Ch'I or Prana vitalizes the thought (Ramacharaka, Fourteen Lesson p78). Although part of the human brain is made of "Ether," it receives mental currents of "Ether" which flow through a person via Instincts under the term "*Feelings*." This is like a Cosmic Force sending Energy to the brain. That Energy goes through the brain/mind "committee" where it is admixed with what comes through the senses (seeing, hearing, smell, taste, touch) + perceptions (from reality, distortions, or fantasy) + memories. The brain thereby acts like a transmitter in changing the energy vibration rate to make that energy available to do whatever the "committee" dictates. For example, if ones aura is from love, it attracts loving things; if from anger, it attracts hateful and evil things. Whatever the source, the sound is given a mental organizing pattern whose shape determines the power of its *aura (i.e. its electromagnetic radiation)*. Yet, the aura's influence exerted upon the spirit--are not ordered by laws as it is with indwelling intelligence.

Rather, their electromagnetic energy which has the power of animating some part of ones animal spirit will, if unchecked, influence the physical body in some manner, create illness, unhappiness, and failure. Any who are led by ones emotions, cravings, and desires can never realize Knowledge (Amen, Metu Neter I: 98, 162, 298). Because philosophies in different cultures differ, miscommunications occur between unlike kinds of the prior mentioned five Thoughts--often stemming from the deliberate attempts to deceive and control by means of mixing "Auras" (African, light). This explains what is referred to as Psychic Phenomena, witchcraft (which Europeans call White and Black Magic), roots, radiaesthesia (manipulating auras), crystal healing, fetishes, etc. Mixing is used for the mystical expression resulting from a "soul to soul" interaction with others, as might occur in "the Call and Response" as well as for the purpose of Metaphors, Allegories, and Personifications.

AURA/ATMOSPHERIC KNOWING BY PARTICIPATION: African Sages said about the *Law of Attraction* associated with Auras and Atmospheres that humans attract to themselves Thought Vibrations corresponding in Nature—a correspondence with those which they are in the habit of entertaining. This is what fashions an Icon Thought into a system of symbols that, though standing apart from Reality, stills carries a payload in its symbolic vehicle in the form of *its symbolic atmosphere. It conveys like-kind energies of the same frequency that resonates with entities actually within the person touched by them.* The good or bad nature--e.g. optimistic/pessimistic, extroverted/introverted, or pleasant/ unpleasant--of the thoughts involved were said to fashion a readiness corresponding atmospheric mindset. Similarly, their forces were sufficiently significant to cause emotional reactions in those ready to enter the nature of the Icon Symbol's atmosphere. Whether from Thought Clouds or Auras' Law of Attraction radar "zeroing in" on something in the External World, chances are that the sensitivity of children enables them to absorb what is present in these atmospheres by means beyond human awareness. I have seen youth (including some very close around me) have a mindset about certain things or have learned certain things or have a certain way of doing things that are unique to their family, neighborhood, or culture. Yet, the amazing thing is these things were never shown or talked about by anyone around them. Well-established is Black people known to develop among themselves an *untaught particular way of silent communications that impart "know-how"* (Wiredu p6). Believed to be determined by their psychophysiology, such was a typical feature among Enslaved Africans. The congenial social interaction among the Enslaved on a given plantation relied heavily upon the unspoken principles of what it took to survive and endure. The Enslaved psychophysiology which fashioned a particular way of knowing by silent communication relied on them sharing the same Group Mind in a given situation. As a result, each understood what and what not to do and without any explanation needed--and for those who did not understand, no explanation was possible. "*Knowledge by Participation*" for cliques continued out of slavery to become part of every fragmented clique encompassed in the Black American Community Customs group of people. It is most obviously seen today among basketball team members who give "the Look" to the one with the ball and an entire pattern is set in motion. It is also seen on "the Streets" in the form of "the Talk" and "the Walk." A major problem with it is that Black American Community Customs people assume that Outsiders ought to know without explanation. That is why I have found them to be poor communicators to me—and that probably is true for examinations.

AWARE: C14 (vigilant, cautious, informed) meant to be watchful; be on ones guard, and take care.

"**AWE**": Fear (an emotion excited by threatening evil) + Fright (in actual presence of that which is terrible) + Pain + Distress + Terror (rendering one incapable of defense) + Dread + Apprehension + Fascination. Disasters are so shocking and known to create "Awe" in victims. Such occurred from the enslavement of free Africans in Africa and then brought to the Americas. Being overwhelmed by the most vicious captors who ever lived and with such formidable power that together, oddly enough, the effect could have had as its overlying or underlying sense something so extremely out of the realm of reality the reaction of "Awe" (fear, dread, terror, overwhelming reverence). An example of an "Awe" Effect comes from one being so stunned as to emit a spontaneous generation of a "Wow!" response. The "Over-Effect" can be in Sacred Awe encounters and/or in Terror caused Awe that eventually results in Extreme Despair. "Awe"—a glob of Quadridary Qualities--results from a layering of Realistic and/or Acquired Effects of Primary, Secondary, and/or Tertiary Qualities. Those Effects serve as a Cause to produce secondary Effects—called either a Realistic or an *Acquired After-Effect*—and these I call *Realistic* and *Acquired Tertiary Qualities* respectively. When ones Imagination adds to the *Tertiary Qualities, their Consequential Characteristics,* derived out of their Interchange, create a new mosaic Quality pattern. That pattern is placed on top of the entire "After-Effect" and "Over-Effect" combined happenings, to produce an "Awe" Effect. "Awe"--in the triangular family of "Awful" and "Awesome"--is a significant part of every human's Imaginative faculty. It results from the separation of the Essence of a thing from its Essentials to thereby enable those Essentials to "run wild." For people philosophically oriented to the Supernatural and its fantasy realm, the "running wild" is into *Phantasmagoric realms* featuring monsters, werewolves, 3-headed creatures, aliens, and the like—as amply exhibited on television and in movies. Natural World people, in the setting of "Awe," stand in wonder at—are shocked or startled by—and are overwhelmed with its sheer grandeur or manifested majesty. This may be from something imparting reactions of a Terror, Sublime, or Sacred nature. If what is perceived appears ominous and threatening, it causes *Dread*; if it is Sublime, one is filled with a Beauty and Lovely Sentiment; if it appears as Sacred, some experience fear--and others, a sense of inferiority, humility, and honor; and if mixed, it is experienced impersonally as an overwhelming "Glob" of Awe ingredients which "paralyzes". Regardless of type, when awed, one seems "so close and yet so far away". On the positive scale of "Awe" are many varied designs. One is the "Awe" part touched by vivid Poetry expressing itself in every possible shade of Pure and/or Acquired Emotions. Examples include: "Excitement, delight, sadness, disturbed, despair, silliness, and the like. The Primary, Secondary, and Tertiary Qualities inside "Awe" have the power to cause a change in other presented Things in that passage as well as to alter ones sensory perception of that Thing. Second, the resultant usual experience of "Awe" is for one to feel nicer and more pleasant—associates of overall health benefits linked to Vibratory Rhythms, as those in Nature. The beneficial effects of these Rhythms on the human body include reduced levels of *Cytokines*, a marker of inflammation linked to depression; lower blood pressure; and stronger immune systems. Third, I can vouch for the effects of being "Awed" by Nature, which I experience every day. Nature's rhythms contain *aesthetic order*—rhythms which are to the world of sound or Feelings as light is to the world of sight. To simply be in an "*Awe Atmosphere,*" that continually occurs in the Dance and Music Rhythms of Nature, is to be a participant in *the principal translators between dream or imagination and reality.* Thus, by my becoming "One" with the Cosmic Ocean of Nature, its Rhythms *shape and give new meaning* to ordinary or routine things. Such comes from my being slid into discerning *invisible essences of Truths and Realities which otherwise I would be unable to see*—a discerning of the infinite in the finite as representing each imaged Thing's Beauty and Worth. Simply being in Nature's flow is to be nowhere else mentally, except in the "here and now". Thus, the Real of a human goes on of itself into all aspects of Nature. This is because everything in Nature, in which every human is a part, depends on everything else. Since all Entities in Nature (e.g. Animals, Plants) are interconnected, to look out into Nature is to see oneself. That naturally leads to "ME/WE" appreciations in the "here and now." People aware of being involved in this *Awe Atmosphere* binds them together in a manner that dissolves the "ME" Individuality Self into an expanded "WE"—a now "Non-Self" in a 'far out' state of "Oneness". I have seen what might fit this description in the Black Church when members are "moved by the Spirit". It was associated with a palpable "Awe" sense of all exuding unity, compassion, generosity, and with good feelings.

"AWE ATMOSPHERES" FOR BLACK PEOPLE: The experience of "Awe" generates its own kind of Rhythm, depending upon the mindset of its source. That mindset fashions images with the same rhythm--images drawn together by a magnetic force—images that can be interchanged or admixed--images which affect both ones consciousness and ones unconscious. The result is an Icon Image which acts like either a "Lucky Star" or a "Disaster Star"—each with their respective "Halos" consisting of "Awe" ingredients. The principle for the operation of the "Lucky Star" and its Halo is similar to vibrations set up when energy is applied to a violin string. That process used with stringed instruments was how Very Ancient African Sages learned about Harmony. Whether dealing with a "Lucky Star" or a "Disaster Star," the Awed mindset's Icon Image acts like a transmitter that rhythmically radiates energy into space as electromagnetic waves, with off/on alternations. In African Tradition there has always been a flood of "Awe" experiences associated with the source of their never-ending Creativity in Arts and Style or in insights used in "That's It!" moments applicable in Science or otherwise in all aspects of life. Such Awe was recognizable as the sense of being in the presence of something vast or beyond human scale—that transcends current understanding of things. But the negative scale of "Awe" came into the minds of Black People upon encountering Europeans. Thereafter has been the recurring situation of Black People's tendency to accept and internalize the philosophies of these others at the expense of African Tradition's ultimate in Human Ideal Principles for Life Living. Maybe it is because in Africa the people had a homogeneous Spirituality Philosophy that was always shared as to what would be the best for the Highest (Divinity) Self of each other. Within this context, upon their earliest encounters, they-and no doubt Amerindians--could not conceive of Europeans being Supernatural aliens dedicated to doing just the opposite of the Spiritual Elements. Maybe, for them, it is because Material things never had priority over things of Worth.

Being introduced to these by Europeans generated "Awe" in Africans. Equated to the highly imaginative "Awe" experiences of the Enslaved was their "fish-netted" physical ominous (i.e. forecasting more evil) happenings. Perhaps this is what the unbounded horrors of enslavement in Africans in the Americas inspired—an Enslaved "Glob" sense beyond fear from the associated negative "Excitement" triggering their Sympathetic Nervous System and its orchestrating Emergency Brain's "Fight, Flight, and Fright" reactions. Perhaps "Awe" simultaneously activated the Parasympathetic Nervous System response "stay still and attentive" to absorb what is happening. That "stop-and-think" happening makes one more receptive to details and new information—and without judging it as good or bad. Associated with "Awe's" traits of *Dismay*, *Consternation*, and *Dread* served as constant *Alarms ('calls to arms')* to which these hapless victims could not respond. This Selfhood surrender is first a sudden loss of all meaning for whatever concerns reality. Second, a chronic mindset of "Awe" *lessens ones awareness of things "do-able" in reality and that is replaced by being less and less skeptical about things that cannot be done in the Supernatural*—an "abuse" fixator. Such was spurred by the STAY-IN-YOUR-PLACE brainwashing of the Enslaved that has continued to the present. The gist of its message is: "don't read"; "don't get an education"; "don't try to better yourself"; "don't be ambitious"; "don't trust each other or work together to fashion Black Power"; "don't be uppity" (i.e. do not be like a White man—and morally that is good advice!!); "stay in your place"—meaning Black people should "be about nothing"; "fight among yourselves"; and "spend your money foolishly." Learning would spoil the best nigger in the world; if you teach that nigger how to read the bible, there will be no keeping him; it would forever unfit him for the duties of a slave..." (3) From this Douglass realized that the Power Whites Have Over Blacks Comes From Keeping Blacks Ignorant. (4) Ignorance keeps the afflicted "Emotional" and thus (5) easily controlled: Don't forget you must pitch the old Black versus the young Black male. The 1712 letter of the slave owner Willie Lynch describes the process. You must use the dark-skinned slaves versus the light-skinned slaves and the light-skinned slaves against the dark-skinned slaves. You must also have your White servants and overseers distrust all Blacks, but it is necessary that your slaves trust and depend on us. They must love, respect, and trust only us. Gentlemen, these kits are your keys to control, use them. Have your wives and children use them, never miss opportunity. This has led to (6) the maintenance of Poverty by preventing the figuring out of ways to make money and by not having jobs available to earn a descent living. The combination of all that transpired with the Enslaved and following slavery as well as the products from being chronically "Awed" and their consequences have all lacked correspondence with reality. The Effect has been to keep most Black Americans minds in disarray. And that makes *products of "Awe" + Superstitions + the Supernatural consequences of "Awe's" products* able to be received by *Osmosis (i.e. brainwashing socialization)* throughout the time Black People have been in the Americas.

AXIOMS-AFRICAN METAPHYSICAL KNOWLEDGE: At their best, Axioms come from discovering a basic Spiritual Elements display on any plane of existence and thus cannot be broken down into smaller parts. These require no proof or explanations because "it is what it is" that can serve as "Seeds" of Knowledge or Principles for designing Knowledge. This means Ma'at philosophical "Seeds" or Principles are *Mathematically based upon vibrating Cosmic Laws*. They are verifiable because Correspondence is based on Ancient African Cosmic Laws which refer to the foundation of all Cosmic manifestations and denote a sequence of inherently related events that occur with unvarying uniformity under the same conditions—called *Correspondence*. Yet, Axioms embraced by humans can be positioned on the "T"-Scale. *Type A are Axioms* are statements admitted without proof. At the top are First Principles, "the truth of which it is not possible to prove. Just as African Tradition's Spiritual, Metaphysical, and Tangible Knowledge are above and beyond human conception (and thus any contrary input or opinions are meaningless), there is a similar realm having nothing to do with human's Belief or Faith. A human's *Spiritual, Pre-Birth,* or *Congenital Emotions*, for example, are not Tangible and thus do not have a Pattern (i.e. no Structure of Matter). By being more like an atmosphere, they are simply a "ballpark" type of awareness available to a human's perceptions. Still, they exist and are known by a human accepting its contents--with varying degrees of awareness, depth, scope, and meaning. So, when compared to Rational Patterns, they are Metaphysical representatives of the Spiritual Elements and yet not contrary to sound Reason—perhaps even approaching Certainty. These comment apply to *Type B--Indescribable Axioms* which are self-evident and indisputable truths which I call *Metaphysical Knowledge*. They have effects assumed to be so obvious and universally accepted as to need no proof (e.g. the beauty of flowers). Dealings drawn from the External World and/or Inner World regarding "what a thing is," "how a thing appears," and/or "What a thing does" require different assessments. Essential Knowledge has an essential relationship to existence. *Type C are Axioms* is that of Algebra applied either Quantitatively or Qualitatively (see Inference Leaps above). *Type D are Axioms* which Primitive Africans' *Subjective Scientific Method* remains of primary significance. An example is that if two equal qualities are added respectively to two equal qualities the sums will be equal. To be aware of how Spiritual Elements display its Earth World forms requires introducing Secular powers of thought as well as the powers of Observation and Perception. Observation and/or Experience—either furnishing Sensations" or "Ideas"—begin the operation of the human mind to deal with External World and/or Inner World things. *Type E Axioms* are like African Tradition's Certainty of Physical Realm Knowledge--"the Thing speaks for itself." This *Describable Axiom* form possesses observable aspects. Examples: the shortest distance between two points is a straight line; two straight lines can cross only at one point. These Describable and Indescribable Axioms statements have generally agreed human recognizable Truths that dominates in their Principles to the point that they are accepted as Truth, despite being unproven because they are without a need to be proved. See "T"-Scale

AXIOMS: *Describable Axioms* which possess observable aspects as, for instance, the shortest distance between two points is a straight line; two straight lines can cross only at one point. By contrast, *Indescribable Axioms* have effects assumed to be so obvious and universally accepted as to need no proof (e.g. the beauty of flowers). Inferred Essence Cosmic manifestations by Ancient African Sages have proven themselves to be "Right" in all ages, in all cultures that applied them properly, and in my daily applications.

BACKGROUND/FOREGROUND AS CONTRARY OPPOSITES: The Background of a human's Selfhood is Spiritually Pure at birth and contains Knowledge of the Spiritual Realm as well as ones Selfhood Greatness. This represents that human's "Soul Sunshine" which imparts everything one needs to have a thriving life and a sense of well-being. If and when problematic aspects of daily living arise in a child's life, that child is likely to develop "Clouds" over her/his "Soul Sunshine"—"Clouds with silver linings" or "Dark Clouds" in the world of Sunshine or "Clouds" that lead one into a "Dark World." Each of those are: (1) caused by a Trigger Event (e.g. causing Shame) or Trigger Person (e.g. abusiveness); (2) which causes a "Raw Nerve" which is protected at all costs; (3) which causes a loss of ones Selfhood Greatness and its "5Ss" (safety, security, self-confidence, strength, and stability); (4) which causes a Self-Declaration ("I will never..."—"I will always..."); (5) which leads to Self-Absorption and Selfhood Splintering; (6) which causes a False Self to thereafter orchestrate ones Selfhood; (7) which leads to some Defense Mechanism and/or some Coping Mechanism; (8) which drives one to "Bond" with anyone who supplies support or protection for ones "Raw Nerve" and/or supplies some desperate False Self needs and desires; (9) which leads one to "follow the crowd" or follow the leader into having a focus on External World things; (10) which causes the misperception that the "5Ss" will be regained by things in the External and that is the stimulus for striving for External World Illusions; (11) which automatically causes one to "Stop Caring" about anything or anybody else; and (12) which leads to one being chronically unhappy at not being ones Real Self.

This "Cloud" Pattern, which displays in ones "Foreground," causes people to think, feel, express, act, and react in every conceivable way—all self-defeating to varying degrees and in whether in an overt, tempered, masked, or concealed form. This causes a sense of being weak which they hide. On the one hand are the Aggressive who live by force (e.g. Satanists, Brutes, Bullies); who possess a "Superiority Complex" (donning a mask of self-confidence and greatness with a reality of arrogance and aggression to conceal a sense of deep inferiority); and who declare themselves "superior" so as to be against the Spiritual Elements and disregard all God's creatures and creations except those fellows with whom they compete in "the Game." On the other hand there are the Passive, Passive-Aggressive, or insincerely Nonaggressive who exhibit varying degrees of an Inferiority Complex. An inferiority Complex is about destruction of different foundational and prop elements of ones Self-Esteem by means of self-attacks on ones own thinking abilities, self-worth and/or self-value which generates chronic deep seated unhappiness. (Bailey, Self-Esteem). A primary way an inferiority complex shows is by destruction of either oneself and/or of what belongs to others or to nature. *Those with an inferiority complex attack in ways to tear others down; those with a superiority complex push others down* and stomp on them. In the process of the desire of all types to inflict pain, they will deny themselves benefits to hurt their victims—an "Un-noble" form of Stubbornness, like that seen in toddlers in the prime of the "Terrible Twos." When there is disharmony between ones Selfhood Background and Foreground presentation, the False Self of ones Background fashions and powers the standards, filters, guides, and measures for ones Foreground. The immaturity of the False Self leads one to be Emotional and therefore inconsistent and incompetent in handling the Necessary and the Important so as to instead focus entirely of engaging in ones Desires—whether that be "for" oneself; "with" others; or attacking others who are envied for "having it all together," for thriving in life, and/or for being happy. Others, whose False Selves are Fear-based, keep busy in trying to avoid being

"Exposed" to whatever might cause them to be abandoned or neglected. Thus, they give up advantages to which they are entitle and take on needless hardships—perhaps to get pity from others or as punishment for their self-imposed guilt. The "Clouds with a silver-lining" do "Almost" the right thing but are limited by incomplete Courage. Since they are most difficult to diagnose, insight might be gained by studying their family, and particularly their siblings.

BACKGROUND/FOREGROUND SELFHOOD DISHARMONY: For ones Background and Foreground to be in disharmony is like having ones boundless Selfhood features stuffed inside a container of Rigidity as a result of being controlled by Trigger Persons displaying "Conditional Love" ("we will love you only if you do what we tell you to do"--and "we want you to be free to be like us") or by being intimidating. Either way, one believes: "If I do not have them to fall back on I won't have anything or anybody at all." So, what this does is to empower other people to take the place of ones independence and self-reliance and thereby act as an agent for oneself. This state of permitting others to vote on behalf of oneself in a manner that votes against oneself is called False Self "Proxy" (short for "Procuracy"—originally one who collected the fruits of a benefice for another). A General Proxy authorizes the Trigger Person(s) to exercise a general discretion throughout ones life. By contrast, a Special Proxy limits the authority to some special proposal or resolution. An example is marriage by proxy, as when a soldier is overseas the "best man" can act as his proxy at the ceremony. Consequences of assigning a Proxy (e.g. ones in-group) include being locked into the status quo; having to ignore or tolerate the bad of the Proxy, as in abusiveness, dishonorableness); not free to be oneself or to disagree out of fear of the Proxy "going away"; and to fool oneself that by being agreeable or accepting of what the Proxy does "makes me an agreeable person." Instead, one is clinging to the Proxy in a manner that is like clutching on to air for support, mainly in case one is so desperate that one has the Proxy to fall back on. That automatically means one is "Bonded" to them and will not do anything to go against them "ever" and no matter what. That is what happened to many Enslaved African Americans and that "bonding" mindset has been culturally transmitted to most of their today's struggling descendants. To be self-absorbed prevents one from being Compassionate, which is about getting involved in "Right" things that are bigger than oneself. Eventually, trusted people in the Proxy are going to break ones trust. Some may react by making a defiant Self-Declaration of "I'm right" independence from anyone that deserves to be trusted and thus will do the opposite to what is recommended, even in simple things as going to the store in the proper direction. This rebellion applies to whether the other is inside or outside the Proxy. Yet, to "get along" with others, although ones Background if following the Self-Declaration, ones Foreground says all the nice and right things which are deceptive of how one really feels. But that position simply reinforces the need for maintaining the availability of the Proxy support. Again, her Foreground necessarily conforms to their biases and prejudices. This is a way of backing into disliking something simply because the Proxy does, despite that going against ones own morals. Otherwise, one wrongly believes one will be totally isolated by not showing total acceptance of the Proxy in every way—and that is a mindset that overrules having the complete Courage to do what one knows to be Right. Hypocrisy may range from being done unconsciously all the way over to being deliberately designed to mislead. Having a lack of awareness is the only way to satisfy two opposing urges and still maintain ones sense of fragile and flawed integrity and self-esteem. *Patterned Thinking* prevents these people from learning a general principle for correction—and they do not ask for help or ask what to do or even say what they are doing. To not appear weak, if they keep that situational story intact, they alter specific details. Or, if the true story is ignored, the details introduced are designed to favor them. Other examples include: (1) knowing a piece of something (partly wrong?) on one part of one plane of existence and believing that is 'everything'; (2) having faith in what one already believes is right and all there is to know; and (3) arrogantly judging unfavorably those who, by knowing other things, do not agree with their judgments. Each stops their learning and progress while believing one is separate from Nature/other people. I recall thinking Sandy was arrogant because she always dominated the conversation. Then, after spending time to know how she got that way made it clear that she was insecure. To hide this she talked as if she knew everything in order not to appear dumb to people.

BACKGROUND/FOREGROUND SELFHOOD HARMONY: In the 78th year of my life I began focusing on my perception of the Background of Black People, which is of a Spiritual and Metaphysical nature (in contrast to the Physical and Supernatural of Europeans). Since little truthful information is written about it, deep concentration was/is required to put pieces of the puzzle together. In the process, a realization was the importance of taking even a 30 second nap throughout the study period because it seemed to make me "Forget" the fatigue of the struggle needed for deep thinking. Could it be that Death is like this—the forgetting of ones present life in order to be reinvigorated for another form of life? By a nap removing the "Fatigue Cloud" enables me to switch from seeing only a part or all of one side of the coin over to the realization of every issue, like a coin, has more than one side. It is essential for Critical Thinking to know its "other side" to properly assess the full story or to begin opening my full human potential. Upon awakening from one such nap, my thoughts concerned: "what could cause Selfhood Background/Foreground Disharmony?" This thought was associated with the image of a "stick figure" "Clutching" to something unreal. The C13 word "*Clutch*" ("tight grasp") is the seizing for the sake of saving something. Clutching and Clinging are generated out of a perceived threatening, disturbing, or dangerous situation naturally leading to fear. One becomes chronically self-absorbed, filled with Doubts and inadequacies, and a neediness to both hide the losses and somehow replace them with a "superior" appearance. Practically everybody has something to which they cling, the nature and degree to which greatly determines how they live. Thus, those lacking the "5Ss" are fearful; "Don't Care; focus on gaining passive or aggressive power to control others; and have no awareness of the benefits of being personally free by operating out of their Real Selves. Since happiness is impossible from staying as is, they institute rigid rules as a way to feel less bad. As an Orthopaedic Surgeon it is automatic to think anatomically about ways of correcting disharmony. So, I thought of the human hand—the anatomical part capable of seizing and holding—that arises from the wrist with its 8 bones all wonderfully jointed. Beyond the wrist are 5 long metacarpal bones, covered by the soft tissue on the palm side and on the opposite top side. Each hand has 5 digits whose 4 fingers each contain proximal, middle, and distal phalanges while the thumb has only a proximal and distal phalanx. Each of these is a separate bone. The hands of "Clutchers," in playing a self-defeating game of life, are governed by one of the 14 bones in the digits—and all of what can be seen of life is within that narrow view. But suppose the Wrist symbolized the Cosmic Organism and its 8 bones represented all God's creatures and creations. Now suppose the digits represented different "racial" groups and the hands of a given "Clutcher" is around one of those digits. That Clutcher would have little or no clue as to who and what the other digits (i.e. other "racial" groups) are like but, instead, simply being limited to what the "Clutcher" could see or was told about them by others on that same digit. Thus, the discussion would be about "Us vs. Them" and "We are superior" because our digit moves differently. This means they fail to see how all digits are there to support and enhance each other. Actually, God's Plan was for all the "digits" to work together. To confine oneself to one digit generates disharmony in the Foreground. But suppose the "Clutcher" shifted positions in order to tenaciously grasp the Wrist bones and thereby have a complete view of Humanity. By being a vital part of it, Instincts expressing God's Will would let them know what Humanity is about. There would be an immediate shift from "Me/Us vs. Those people" over to "ME/WE" whereby all of us are in this together. In this way one can realize what one is missing and will stop selling short the other digits. To shed the disharmony is to free ones mind to see things as they really are; allow good things to attract other good things; and use those good things as "raw" ingredients for creativity. This would immediately reverse one being self-absorbed and selfhood splintered and thereby put one back on the path of the Spiritual Elements—a path allowing one to be happy and thrive because that is what results from the independent to interdependently work for a common purpose in life.

BAD: C13 "Bad" possibly began with a homophobic origin—derogatory terms (e.g. contemptible, worthless, moral depravity) for homosexuals (e.g. 'effeminate males'; hermaphrodites), with overtones of sodomy. This expanded to include "bad money drives out good"—based on the C16 concern that people tended to hang on to coins of a high intrinsic worth, like gold sovereigns, while being happier to spend those of a lower intrinsic worth but of equal face value. This gave rise to the sense that, as with eggs, things are either good or bad. Then a medical contribution referred to those who had a potential for abusive or destructive behavior toward oneself or others.

BAILEY FAMILY: PARIS SIMKINS: My great grandfather, Paris Simkins (1849-1930), a barber who taught himself and some Enslaved to read, became a lawyer, postmaster, landowner, licensed preacher, a South Carolina State legislator, and was very active in Civil Rights and voting. While playing with his infant son, he suddenly became aware of a KKK mob outside his home with the expressed intention of killing him because of being second in command of the State's Black militia. Calmly, while holding his son, Paris faced down the mob and preached a sermon, directing comments to each of them. That cause the KKK to back off and leave him unharmed. Upon his death, his children wrote *A Brief Narrative of the Life of Paris Simkins, ESQ., of Edgefield, S.C.* in a newspaper: "Nearly four score and ten years ago, within a little hut in Edgefield County, within a few miles of the Court house, was born a slave boy, Paris Simkins. He was loved by the old coachman of his master, who had by stealth learned to read. At a tender age, one night between mid-night and dawn his Mother, Charlotte Simkins, heard him running thru the grassy path, almost out of breath. He tapped lightly upon the door and called in a whisper, "mother, mother, get up and open the door, I have learned my A, B, C's.!" He and the old coachman had hid in the swamp and struggled with the alphabet all night, for it was against the law for a Slave to be taught to read. When the Civil War broke out he, a youth of less than twenty years, was taken along as a barber. He witnessed several battles, and was at the great battle of Gettysburg. After the din of the battles, he with another slave boy, ran and stumbled over the battle field from one wounded and dying soldier to another taking water to them and rendering whatever aid they could knowing that it was not for their cause that they were dying. When General M. C. Butler was wounded, he soon located him where he had been carried to a house nearby. There he hurried to him to be of whatever aid he could, for they were from the same town. General Butler was glad to see him and spoke very kindly to him. After the war he returned to Edgefield and opened a barber shop, and it was there that he battled with determination, with all odds against him, for an education. He studied every spare moment, and was assisted by the Rev. Mr. Luther R. Gwaltney and another learned scholar whose name cannot be recalled, for they took great interest in him. His barber shop was his classroom for he never attended school a day of his life. In after years we found in the home many college text books and asked him how came they here, then it was he told us the story of his life as very few know it. His children loved him and always regarded him with respect and reverence knowing the sorrows, disappointments and discouragements with which he has undergone. In 1868 he was married to Miss Mary Ann Nobles [Creek Indian/African wife--1850-1916], 16 children were born to them, eight of whom survive him--19 grand-children and 5 great-grand-children. He was married and baptized by his friend and counselor the Rev. Mr. Gwaltney and is the last of the original members of Macedonia Baptist Church. From early manhood to a ripe old age he was a great Sunday School and church worker. For many, many years he taught the Bible Class of his church. He arose to great prominence in his church, the community and his state. With the same determination, as in his apparently hopeless struggle for an education, so, also, in later years he resolved to become a lawyer. Day by day, step by step, only God knows how, he climbed upward to his goal. In 1872 he was elected to the Legislature of South Carolina and served four years. It was during this time that he had the privilege of entering the law class of the University of South Carolina, for a brief period, and from there he received his diploma. In 1885 in Columbia, S. C., he was admitted to the bar and became a lawyer of no mean ability. In the year of 1884 he drew up the Constitution and By-Laws of The Mutual Aid and Burial Society and was its first president. When in his community there was seen the need of a secret order of K. of P., he was advancing in age, but there being no one to take the lead and direct it he was again pressed into service. A life of service has he to lay down at his Master's feet. To the poor and distressed he was always a friend in need. One of his outstanding characteristics through life was faith in God. Never once was he known to falter in faith. On Friday, Sept. 24th, his children standing by his bed, realized that he was crossing "The Bar" asked if he had any pain; in a matter of fact way, so characteristic with him, he said, 'no, I have always prayed that I pass out without pain.' So as long as his words were audible he talked with God. And never had a pain. His children. Sept. 26th, 1930." jabaileymd.com

"BAILEY'S TEST": Acceptance for proceeding on with ones plans is to occur *only when all of a subject's components have been examined, researched, reflected upon, and tested// and one finds they "fit" with ones education, training, experience, instincts, intuition, insights, reason, common sense// and one is in its flow// and it "Feels Right"// and without friendship or hearsay input// and not dependent on traditions, customs, beliefs, faith, or "everybody" agreeing.*

BALANCE: equilibrium achieved through mediating opposing forces within and between individuals.

"BASE" OF THE COSMOS: The Verbum, *God's Inner Nature,* is that of Unconditional Love—the "Seed Essence" constituting the *Base upon which the Cosmos is situated. The "Seed's Essentials"* —*i.e.* the outward expression or effect of the ever concealed God Source--are Truth, Reality, and the Natural. Both the Seed Essence and that Seed's Essentials as well as their Spirit and Matter are within the "*Substance*" of the Verbum. Thus, the Spiritual Elements are the "Genetics" for all Cosmic Organism Creatures and Creations. This is what is meant by *Spiritual Correspondence*—the single most significant concept in African Tradition. Spiritual Correspondence is obviously demonstrable by the Human Family all having the same "Genetics" that was imparted in and distributed by the original African Ancestor dating to c200,000 BC. That *"Oneness" of the Cosmic Organism is at the basis for Cosmic Correspondence.* Genetic activities observed in the Known implies that the same ones are occurring in the Unknown, or Esoteric, realms. That Sample derived from the Known to explain the Unknown is called a "*Circumstance*" companion in African Tradition. This explains the profound path to Certainty as implied in the proverb: *As above, so below; as below, so above.*" Such is Supreme Thinking! It is vital to get oriented to African Tradition's Cosmic Base—that upon which all of the Cosmos arises. It started with the first Cosmic Force, called Sekhem, displaying the Ocean of Nun. This *Subjective realm* is also called "*Nothingness*"—the realm of Virtual (boundary-less) Being—which is the mother of all Being by it producing all Cosmic Organism Creatures and Creations. It is nameless, for it is greater than anything that can be named. It takes no action, in that it leaves Things alone. It supports all Things but does not take possession of them. It lets Things transform themselves. It does nothing and yet all Things are thereby done. In short, it is Nature transforming itself spontaneously by *Natural Order.* It is the source of the "*Voice of the Silence*" which: "says everything by not saying anything at all" while "it retains everything by giving away everything." Silence speaks the impossible--expresses the inexpressible and, in fact, is expressed inexpressibility. This is what happens when one practices being Quiet--itself a form of Meditation. For the mind to dwell in this realm is what Ancient Africans called Hetep (Profound Peace). This is the state of mind all pregnant mothers ought to be in for the best mental, physical, and spiritual health of their unborn.

BASE—SECULAR "HOME": imagine a skyscraper building sitting on a Base. Its most important part is not the Foundation, as most people think, but rather the Base upon which it rests. The word "*Base*" has so many complexities that the simplest definition serves the purpose—i.e. the bottom of something considered as its support; the part on which something rests. Most people think the Material—e.g. "The Rock"—is solid but nothing Material is solid or sound, for it is constantly changing. By contrast, the absolutely strongest Thing in the Cosmos is not anything Material. Rather, it is the Immaterial (Substance) which is part of the Cosmic Force, called Sekhem (the Spiritual God).

To build anything life-shaping or life-changing on anything in the External World is like doing it on Quicksand. By flowing upward under strong pressure (by coming from a higher level), the upward flowing water force is equal to the downward weight of the soil grains—and by the grains "floating" as thick liquid on top of the ground, that Quicksand will not support much superimposed weight.

BEAUTY: Since there is nothing to which any Spiritual Thing, like Beauty, can be compared, Ancient Africans devised Figures of Communication (FOC) to give bits and pieces concepts about each and all. Even then, those FOC are *Speculations—meaning they go in opposite directions within the Supernatural realm.* Even so, those FOC headed in the right direction and on the right plane of existence "Work" well for purposes of discussion—called *Poetic Speculation*—the pondering of each element on its every side; on every angle of every side; and on both sides of every angle—leads to insights. Yet, conclusions from Poetic Speculations (in the sense of inferred concepts from reflection) consist of thoughts about unrealistic things, since the human mind is not able to grasp its Spiritual nature. Ancient Africans considered Spiritual "Speculation" and Spiritual "Visions" as synonyms when "Speculate" and "Visions" blended and together reflections on the existence and nature of pertinent things present in the Cosmos, the psyche, and God to give what was compatible with their *Subjective Science.* Those tools—i.e. Observation, Reflection, "Pure" Feelings, Productive Imagination, Contemplation, Inductive and Deductive Inferences, and Common Sense—enabled the uncovered existing unities to be used as inferences for the making of new unities—entities useful in arriving at circumstantial evidence and judgments. By contrast, and what is worse than nothing, is Non-Rational Speculation. Here, ones mind acts impulsively--wandering at random and going no place in particular--as if the brain is idling between meaningful activity. This is the Old French sense ('spy out')—defined as to be filled with wide-ranging and conflicting appearances as to its meaning based upon *A Priori Reasoning*. Hence, Speculation contents start with a definition formed or principles assumed and proceeding--without examination or analysis—independently of experience so as to arrive at presumptively deduced consequences. Out of those consequences are formed definitions and assumed principles to use as propositions to figure out what can be known by Reason alone. But that Reason is like it is on a railroad train Roundhouse turntable. That turntable can change the direction of the train by turning it around to go back on the same tract or turn it to put it on another track so as to reach anywhere but the Truth or even what is more than mere guessing. My interpretation of the Ancient African process is that the Spiritual Elements Essences originally formed out of God's Androgynic plast to thereby constitute the Cosmic Organism "Genetics" for all of God' creations and creatures, including each human, were inside the Cosmic Circle of Wholism. The Spiritual Elements inside that Circle form an Interchange containing Dispositions—"blue-prints" of the Divine Plan + the Earth World equivalent of a *Temperament* (the type of reaction the aroused person takes). The nature of they Divine Plan is the "What and the Why" of assignments for each of God's creatures and creations. For example, in humans it is about *Ma'at "ME/WE" Life-Living.* What flows out of the Interchange is a fuzzy representation of the general meaning of each of the contributors concerning what it is about—what it probably does –what experiences it conveys--the state of its individual and collective association of Ideas—and/or how it might appear. Together there is a Creative Synthesis of Perfection—and that is Spiritual Beauty. So, Spiritual Beauty is the Spiritual Elements—independently and collectively—of Unconditional Love, Truth, Reality, and the Natural—flowing out of the Circle of Wholism in an illuminating manner. Thus, it illuminates whatever is associated with it. Beauty expands in all directions with each application of the Spiritual Elements. Nothing can be added, substracted, or changed without imparing the harmony and perfection of the whole. This is because anything Spiritually Beautiful is above any human in-put because the Beautiful derives its Perfection from itself—and asks nothing beyond itself, similar to Play and Dance. Hence, the correct assessment of a Beautiful thing is that it means only Beauty. The perception of Beauty is the experience of Happiness. A feature of the contents within the Circle is the operation of the *Law of Spiritual Creativity*--by itself, a Spiritual Element reproduces itself to become the thing it makes, regardless of its new form. Yet, their *Lofty words* used to refer to these components are invariably clumsy, inadequate, limited, and crude. This is because aspects in the Sublime can not be defined. Examples of words for "defining" aspects of the Sublime include: dignified, noble, exaltation, grandeur, elegant, graceful, majestic, magnificent, lofty, astounding, grand, ecstasy, imposing, stately, splendid, rapture, superb, marvelous, wonderful, terrific, magnanimous, supreme, transcendent, rapture, happiness, eminent, empyreal, celestial, heavenly, ideal, gorgeous, royal, perfection, and bliss.

BEGINNING: As with the *Beginning* of a physical body disease (from some bad germ going through various Cause stages) converting patients from normal to abnormal, a *Metaphysical Mindset Disease* (as from not using Spiritual Elements ingredients) does that also. Both result from an Immediate Cause being the match flame which lit a stick of dynamite and that explosion resulted in adverse evolving clinical manifestations.

BEING: When every other trait peculiar to a real "Thing" is removed, the "it is" represents the very least that can be thought of anything. That "it is," constituting its Cosmic Being aspect, remains. C13 Old French word "*Appearance*" (to show; to come in sight) is apparent and thus is opposed to actual reality. This means "Real" is to "Seem" as reality is to appearing--as the actual is to the possible--as Being is to Becoming--as "is" (i.e. Being) is to "is not" (i.e. non-Being). See Contingent Being

BELIEF: committing to Guesses or to Unproven Information with the hope those things are true. Thus, some Beliefs are closer to the truth than others. *Faith*: Beliefs + acceptance of the consequences of Beliefs. Opinions are matured Beliefs which makes choices from favored available options. The failure to consider all the options is often a way to keep from getting on track or a way to get off track.

Man-Made information consisting of a combination of things. An example is *Secular Faith:* This embraces Beliefs that may incorporate "Facts," "Opinions," "Assumptions," and/or "Superstitions." To have Secular Faith is to accept the consequences arising from everything having to do with its consequences. Belief and Faith are European inventions to control people's minds. Ones great Spiritual issue is whether to "Know" God exists or have "Faith/Belief." Ancient Africans said there was no point in having "Faith/Belief" because God and the Spiritual Elements remained unchanged regardless of people's thought. Rather, they proved God existed and the only thing for *people to have "Faith/Belief" in is their own self-efficacy to do the work to discover the requirements to live into and up to the ultimate unrealized Reality where Wisdom leads.* Any other type of Faith/Belief -- either made up or reflecting what one was told -- indicates one has not done the work required to "Know". Throughout history, Belief/Faith have been major manipulative tools for Religious people to control the minds of Believers. After all, the word "Religion" (ligare) means to tie, to bind, or to shackle.

"BEST/GREATEST/SUPERIOR" ARE UNEXAMINED ASSUMPTIONS: The Intent for the two forms of personal Standards—God-made and Human-made--concerns ones Character. Their Effects, Consequences, and Results may be beneficial, destructive, or Indifferent. *God-made Standards* are about Certainty, as exhibited in the Processes of Nature. Although they are independent of, and uninfluenced by human input, humans foolishly place their good, bad, or indifferent concepts on them for various good, intended good, self-interest, or evil purposes—any out of deliberateness or out of ignorance. *Happiness is a by-product of having a good intent and the doings to provide anonymous Selfless Service to any part of Humanity.* That process alone, when flowing spontaneously, is like the Star saying: "let me light my lamp" and without thoughts of helping to remove the darkness. But in Compassion situations, "Feelings" from ones Pure Emotions and "Thoughts" from ones Pure Intellect must be given to how to best relieve the darkness or at least make sufferers in the darkness more comfortable. Applications of Self-Love are to do the difficult, yet Necessary; to resist good advice with regret in order to do what is "Felt" to be Right; to sacrifice desires; and to stand against ferocious "Alligators" (e.g. losses, lacks, obstructions put up by Brutes). African Tradition's "Best," "Greatest," or "Superior" does not come by self-declaration or from ones own rewards. Instead, it follows *Spiritual Reciprocity*—i.e. "the reward of ones good Selfless Service acts consist in the fact that Receivers will act for her/him" in doing good, in the manner of a "Ripple Effect. This is one reason Europeans' "*Golden Rule*": "Do unto others as you would have them do unto you"--does not apply. Considerations given to such acts on a "Best/Greatest/Superior" positive scale do not exist because whatever is about the Spiritual Elements of Unconditional Love, Truth, Reality, and the Natural, either is what it is or it is not. In short, it is "All-or-None"—absent any "Best/Greatest/Superior's" relativity. *Human-made Standards* are never Certain. They are relative to what works for certain reasons; for something at that time; for personal goals; for what controls society or people's minds; and for biases and prejudices. Some come out of socializations; others out of ignorance from not knowing what constitutes positive scale "Best/Greatest/Superior". The socialized do not realize they are enslaved until they discover the gist concepts of *Racism*: cannot do the things they want because others prevent that from happening; are abused and forced to bear it; or compelled by GUN violence to suffer inhumanities. Effects, Consequences, and Results of Human-made Standards always involve the military leader, the troops, their Crowd followers and the Victims. The latter 3, by not living their Real Self natures, are Self-unrecognized forms of Slaves. Since none of the 4 have Virtues, none of these Slaves can be positive scale "Best/Greatest/Superior". So, they start using the leader as the standard and model the Troops in looking for negative scale ways to be "Best/Greatest/Superior". The most oppressed Victims adopt the leaders position that they ought to be Slaves and imitate treating each other as well as themselves just as their oppressors treat them. Reversing that mindset, regardless of where each is on the Destructive Scale, requires battling resistance of the defenseless' + overcoming perpetrators competitors. Perpetrators fight, even among their own, and fights fill them with childish "Excitement" of being "the "Best/Greatest/Superior" in life. Fettered Selfishness rules means there are no rules. Winning by any means necessary is the only thing. Despite the high cost, "Sick" pleasures come from leaving trails of pain, suffering, misery, poverty in others—---for demonstrations of who is "Best/Greatest/Superior" is for all to see. Leaders say: "too much is never enough" of what they are after and thus their "Best/Greatest/Superior" is measured by who has the most "Adult Toys."

Actually, "Best/Greatest/Superior" properly applies to competition with oneself—to be a little bit better today and in every way than yesterday. This comes from the "ME/WE" concept of serving the most needy—those who did not voluntarily cause their poverty situations—those whose cowardice perpetuates their own status quo enslavement—those who have no desire to escape from their chains--those who can neither help nor harm the Helping Hands—those who will never know the source of those Helping Hands. No human has been given the God-made power to set the "Best/Greatest/Superior" standards for being the master over any other human. jabaileymd.com

BIAS & PREJUDICE: C16 "*Bias*" (oblique line or curved path from which "Prejudice" derives) is simply a tendency, usually below ones awareness—to see only one side of the coin--to see facts in a certain way because of ones habits, wishes, desires, interests, values, or need to "save face." "*Prejudice*" (a Middle English term for harm or injury resulting from action or judgment) has a strict sense of preconceived favorable or unfavorable opinion or emotion without knowledge. Whereas "*Prejudice*" occurs when one does not know, or has not examined, or does not care about the truth and does not want to be confused by the facts, *Bias* is developed in viewing the facts and then "Picking and Choosing" only those facts which support ones point of view. What does matter is that when any situation is considered from different viewpoints it becomes clearer and easier to understand the one on the wrong side, if there ever is such a thing. People with Biases and Prejudices are primed to receive any rumor about a hated person or race and no matter how far off from the truth, it will SEEM right.

BIAS CONFIRMATION: The focus is not on what one knows or does not actually know but what one does not want to know or what one makes efforts to keep from knowing. It is worse to half know a subject and teach it than to be ignorant of that subject and not teach it. Like a hunting-nag the ignorant leap over what they cannot get through. But what is involved in this flawed attempt at Willful Ignorance is the reality of Confirmation Bias—the seeking and interpreting information that confirms existing beliefs or biases for or against something. Thus, instead of one being rational, logical, and objective, one operates only with information that upholds our ideas and ignoring the information that challenges ones existing beliefs. Such is also seen in how one gathers, interprets, and recalls information—always fashioning it in a manner that upholds their existing beliefs, biases, prejudices, opinions, and faith. As part of the "don't confuse me with the facts because my mind is already made up," they completely disregard contrary evidence with excuses like "the source is unreliable". Too much of what willful ignorance does is to take what one does not know much about and put it into a package called knowledge and present it as certainty. An ignorant person is ignorant of their ignorance and is very satisfied with that. Just as in the legal arena ignorance of a matter of fact may in general be alleged in avoidance of the consequences of acts and agreements, ignorance cannot be pleaded because the law says access to it is available.

BIBLICAL METAPHORS MIS-USED: Particularly in African Tradition Metaphors, the essential structure of religious language, are symbolic messages which disregard the limitations and boundaries of human thought in order to impart ideas of the indescribable. The vehicle by which this occurs is by means of Synthesis removing the boundaries from all Abstracts and Abstractions involved. This method, originated by Primitive (the first) Africans, enables people to become aware of spiritual powers and unity through the use of the "atmosphere" generated in metaphorical language and meanings. Whereas the Symbol, as a particular thing, stands for the general, a *Symbol Metaphor* is a Symbol energized by a metaphor to Metaphors convey a spiritual significance; transcend separation and duality; gain realizations of and ideas about the infinite; and serve as guiding living practices. This is a reason Ancient African Sages presented complex religious concepts--e.g. Unconditional Love, Truth, Reality, and the Natural--in writing the African Bible, for it was not possible to be conveyed in any other way. Metaphors convey a spiritual significance intended to transcend separation and duality -- not by the meanings in its words but by the "Heart-felt" atmosphere generated in those meanings which touch the soul. Thus, this approach constituted Spiritual Literature and not a mere made-up story. Just as the magnitude of Self-Love is too great for ones mind to grasp, using the metaphor of the Kingdom of God being who one is makes for some awareness of it. Similarly, to deprogram Obsessions can be through Images one entertains. For example, if one believes one is a failure which looks like a deflated balloon, the Image of Self-Greatness is conveyed by realizing how all powerful one was as baby, like a blown up balloon flowing freely in space. An African *Religious Symbol does not simply point to something else but rather contains a structure that awakens ones consciousness to a new awareness of the inner meaning of life and reality itself.* For example, when a metaphor speaks of gods, its symbolic "atmosphere" concerns entities actually within the person touched by them, and not referring to some invisible Being. The *Ausarian Drama* symbolizes an actual universal reference to the spiritual realm within ones inner life. It explains certain *fundamental aspects of human nature and conveys abstract or lifeless things* of great significance by means of Metaphors and Personifications (giving life to some non-feeling and unreal Being). They are selected to indicate the Kingdom of God is within each individual. They are the best way to affect memorization and understanding of what is beyond the human mind's ability to grasp. Once that "Seed" is embedded in the people's minds, it branches into such diverse aspects of daily life as tales, music, dancing, sculpture, and painting. But grave errors occurred from foreigners who did not understand that African Sages built all theological structures for African tradition upon "*Ultimate Wisdom*" metaphors. The most prominent situation came from those who decided to write their own Bible by coping from the Ancient African Bible but make profound alterations. Where as the Ancient African Bible focused on providing instruction on how to live "Right" in the present in order to reach the "Heaven Afterlife," the alterations were directed to controlling the people. Their first step to this end in fashioning the European Bible was to switch African Bible metaphors into "Delusional Facts"--the act of making non-truths for the European Bible out of the African Bible's God-revealed Truths. In other words, the now misinterpreted metaphors, which are Non-Truth Tools, were transformed into being falsely referred to as tangible facts and actual historical occurrences. For example, the European noted authority on Mythology, J. Campbell, says the *Garden of Eden* is a metaphor for humans' minds and thinking in terms of Opposites (e.g. man/woman, good/evil) being as holy as that of a god and what went on there is what is happening to humans right now. *The story of not eating the apple of the forbidden tree is an old folklore motif called "the one forbidden thing."* The innumerable scribe translators of this original Ethiopian Garden of Eden story made significant changes on their own (whether intentionally or out of ignorance) as well as under the direction of the European Religious authorities so as to thereafter take billions of Believers far away from the Spiritual Elements. Whether from listening to European religious leaders or from Believers reading on their own--in each instance there are further complicating misinterpretations having profound changes on life-shaping or life-changing decisions about "How Shall I live?" and "In What and Who shall I have Faith/Belief/Trust?" All life consequences go along with these decisions! See Metaphor

BINARY SYSTEM: A *Binary Number* system represents numbers having two as its base and using the digits 0 and 1. Yes/no, on/off, and positive/negative are all encounters of a binary nature. This System--persisting in what the Chinese called the *I-Ching* (Bynum, African Unconscious p182). See Yin/Yang

"**BLACK**": Designates African Traditions ultimate in Spiritual Perfection and so Ancient Africans proudly called themselves "Black People."

BLACK AMERICAN CUSTOMS: combination of African Tradition bits and pieces + European brainwashing + Enslaved Reactions to being Enslaved were gathered into Collage Patterns of Slave Survivals as a way to endure Life Living.

BLACK AFRICANS' BRAIN SWITCH ENSLAVEMENT: African Tradition says having the experience of Free Minds is the way to live life and nothing is more devastating than losing it. Because of this, the savage orientation of Europeans Warriors has always been just the opposite. To elaborate, in his book/movie entitled "*Roots,*" Alex Haley chronicled the life of Kunta Kinte in Gambia, West Africa. The story starts one day in 1750 when Kunta, a free African going about his normal thriving daily activities, was suddenly encased in a fishnet dropped on him. Kunta fought wildly and courageously against his African captors but was overwhelmed by their strength in numbers and by being clubbed unconscious. He awakened naked, chained, shackled, and aware of being permanently enslaved. But what I believe also happened, starting at the exact moment of the fishnet drop, was a series of very significant happenings to Kunta's physical body and his Quintaune Brain (i.e. Cortex, Limbic, and the Ancient Brain's Instinct, Omnibus, and Brute subdivisions). The instant switch from using his Thriving Brain (i.e. Cerebral Cortex and Limbic portions) for normal living over to his Instinct Brain ("fight, flight, or fright") was a happening that forever trapped his mind inside a mental vault. First, this immediate *Brain Switch* was destined for permanency throughout Kunta's life of enslavement, ensuring Selfhood problems because ones Emergency Instinct Survival Brain actions are only for temporary usage. It is what "Seeds" today's "Inside-out" mindsets in struggling Black Americans and accounts for their altered thinking patterns keeping them chained to poverty.

Second, at the same fishnet moment a host of biochemical factors were instantly released from Kunta's brain so as to instinctively prepare him physically for a desperate "fight or flight." It is medically established that under conditions of distress, brain hormones protectively release adrenaline (epinephrine) from the adrenal glands which, in turn, leads to a rapid release of glucose and fatty acids into the bloodstream. But the cumulative effects of these hormones -- particularly if prolonged -- are capable of damaging and killing cells anywhere in the Quintaune Brain, as in the hippocampus' memory and learning areas (Bailey, Self-Protection). It is difficult to predict which cells and what functions will be affected because the entire brain is like a tapestry of interwoven connections making it out of date to think of a single area in isolation as having one function exclusively.

BLACK ENSLAVED HORRIBLE MIDDLE PASSAGE: Enslaved Africans brought in from around African empires, included those of the Western Sudan Moslems. They and men, woman, and children from all over Africa ranged from the dignified, cultured, and refined in possession of noble character--to being quite intelligent and educated--to "normal"--to the problematic (e.g. bad characters, the disabled, the feeble). The moment of their capture was the formation of what would develop into "African-American cultures." The very earliest interactions of the newly captured Africans in Africa was that of were being shackled together in the coffles. Despair (hopeless hopelessness)--a Despair leading to submission--was easily achieved by the captors as a result of subjecting the Enslaved to long marches of often hundreds of miles while chained, barefoot, having inadequate clothing, and almost no food or water. All were transported to the African coast along the shore of the Gulf of Guinea. Here is where stood many trading posts or "factories" on the Grain Coast (Liberia), the Ivory Coast (now the Ivory Coast Republic), the Gold Coast (Ghana), and the Slave Coast (Nigeria, Dahomey and Benin, and Togo). After being placed in African barracoons (Enslaved holding areas on the West African coast) on the coast, the Enslaved awaited sale to European slave traders. Throughout this entire time they continued to receive every beyond conceivable mental, spiritual, and physical trauma. For example, African fellowship fragmentation started when they were forced to fight each other in the barracoons for tiny amounts of food and water. The brainwashing of Enslaved Africans in the barracoons began when they were prevented from using their languages. While packed into the dank barraccon "factory" dungeons--squeezed so tightly that they had no choice but to stand in their own feces and breath the stench in their poorly ventilated barred jails--Despair among all went further and further down in a bottomless pit. This resulted from becoming increasingly aware of the permanent separation from their kinsmen, tribesmen, or even speakers of the same language; left bewildered about their present and their future; stripped of all human rights or prerogatives of status or rank; and homogenized by a dehumanizing system that viewed them as faceless and largely interchangeable.

BLACK ENSLAVED ON SHIPS: There were established trade routes for slave ships sailing to Africa from a home port such as Lisbon, or Liverpool in Britain, or a city on the East Coast of the USA. A trade ship had a name, like a "Guinea-man," for the Gulf of Guinea on the West African coast. Ships would linger off the African coast, often for months, until it was "slaved," or filled up, with each Enslaved having a number and branded. When stowed, there was not sufficient room to put down the point of a stick between them. The hold below decks, where the Enslaved were packed, was not unlike a slaughterhouse. While taking its cargo across the horrific ocean to South America, the Caribbean, or the USA for sale, varied diseases, cruelty, death were ever present, making for extremely high mortality rates. The dead were thrown into the sea, and sharks grew accustomed to following the ships all the way across the ocean. All Enslaved were in the bottom of the ship, throwing up, having no strength to do much of anything and few knew how to swim. After the American slave ship Ascension left Newport, R.I., for Mozambique on October 15, 1791 with 276 Enslaved, 30 percent of whom were children, upon arrival in Havana, 62 were dead. The Ascension made similar runs from Rhode Island to Mozambique in 1795 and 1798, losing scores of Enslaved en route and delivering hundreds of Africans into bondage in Cuba and South America. The Portuguese slave ship São José Paquete de Africa that had left Mozambique Island four weeks earlier where the Portuguese had built an imposing fortress a century earlier and where the Enslaved would be gathered for the Brazil market.

It had a netting stretched out from the hull to catch slaves who jumped overboard, and a deck barricade built to guard against uprisings while heading along the East African coast with its cargo of 500 captives, bound for the rice and cotton plantations of northern Brazil, sank off the coast of South Africa in 1794. This occurred because it had been blown into treacherous waters near the Dutch settlement of Cape Town in southern Africa, and was impaled on rocks at 2 am and weighed down with cast iron ballast bars, trade goods (e.g. containers of wine, gun powder, olive oil and dry goods), and human cargo. Although torn apart in the swells, the captain, crew, and many of the Enslaved reached shore with a rescue line. Yet, 212 of the Enslaved drowned in the frigid water, and 11 more died in the next few days. On Dec. 5, 1801, a Spanish slave ship left Charleston, S.C., for Mozambique where it gathered 200 Enslaved. However, by the time it reached Montevideo, Uruguay, only 66 were still alive. On all of countless numbers of trips, the Enslaved resisted however they could, although they often were shackled or chained. Many jumped overboard to try to escape or commit suicide. Some refused to eat. But slave ships had a cruel device called the speculum oris that was used to wedge open the mouth for force-feeding. The Enslaved revolted often. For example, the Liverpool slave ship, Unity, had four insurrections in one voyage, causing the crew to retreat behind the deck barricade and fire on the Enslaved with muskets and deck guns loaded with grape shots. Such information is according to the Trans-Atlantic Slave Trade Database.

BLACK ENSLAVED MIDDLE PASSAGE TRIP: This trip from Africa to the Americas was the ultimate in evil, sadistic, and dehumanizing experiences in all of slavery—some trips last up to 4 months. Ships involved in the African American slave trade followed a triangular or three cornered trade pattern. Bound for the West Coast of Africa, empty ships would leave Europe; load up with West African Slaves; travel to America or to the West Indies -- called the Middle Passage; exchange Slaves for money, cotton, tobacco, rice, or sugar cane; and then return to Europe in order to sell the goods before repeating the voyage. Of the numerous ways designed to obtain Slaves, a simple and popular method was developed by the Englishman, John Hawkins (1532-1595). He would burn coastal villages and capture the villagers as they tried to escape. The preference was for "fit" Slave males, between ages 15 and 35. But half the Slaves were "unfortunates" in their own cultures: criminals, the mentally or physically handicapped, debtors, political prisoners, and outcasts. About 15 million Slaves (actual numbers are unknown) were shipped abroad but millions died in attempts at capture as well as died aboard ship. The conditions under which this occurred were on ships legally limited to carrying 150 to 350 people but actually carrying 600, 800 or more men, women, and children. Slaver captains anchored chiefly off the Guinea Coast for a month to a year awaiting their cargoes of the Enslaved. Captains of slavers were known either as *"tight packers" or "loose packers,"* depending upon how many Slaves they crammed into the space they had. The vast majority were greedy "Tight packers" who would have Slaves packed in like sardines in a can in order to transport the largest possible "cargo." When ready for another trip, the properly branded and chained Slaves were rowed out to the slave ships. Upon arrival on board ship, the Enslaved were stripped naked for the duration of the voyage; lying down amidst filth and dysentery; enduring almost unbearable heat or cold. Meanwhile, the Enslaved were wedged horizontally, spoon fashion, lying on top of each other in a 6 feet long, 16 inches wide and 18 inches high average space allowed per person. This was about the size of a coffin! Thus, it was impossible for positioned Slaves to even shift with any degree of ease (Alderman, p. 53-57). In the daytime, weather permitting, the Enslaved were brought on deck for exercise--called "*dancing the Slaves*" (forced jumping up and down). The excuse given by the captors for compelling, by the lash, to dance on deck was to straighten their limbs. Women and boys were repeatedly sexually abused. Many Slaves who survived blows to their heads became mentally ill--but most died. If bad weather or equatorial calms prolonged their journey, the twice daily ration was a cupful of water in a small pan--a pannikin. Along with this there was either boiled rice, millet, cornmeal (if they were from the Guinea coast), stewed yams (if they were from the Bight of Biafra, Nigeria); or starchy manioc or cassava flour or banana-like plantains (if they were from the River Congo region).

All portions were greatly reduced to starvation levels. This made dying either an easy or a desirable next step. Although it was always stifling, in a storm the gratings on each side of the ship were covered with tarpaulins so that great waves, breaking over the main deck at times, could not reach the 'tween' decks. This made the heat even greater; reduced the supply of air; and caused gasping for air. Slaves had to lie in their own waste while breathing noxious fumes in the unventilated, crammed space. Most would go mad from misery and suffocation or from being chained by the neck and legs. In their madness some killed others in the hope of gaining more room to breathe. Not having enough room to sit up or turn over, while in unbearable heat or cold, many Slaves died in this position. Some Slaves killed themselves by starving to death. Many were prevented from starving by being whipped, tortured with hot coal, or crews breaking their teeth so as to do force feeding. Men strangled those next to them; women drove nails into each other's brains. It was common to find a dead Slave and a living Slave chained together. Otherwise, all faced constant dangers from raids at ports by hostile tribes, threats of Slave mutiny, epidemics (of smallpox and dysentery resulting from filth), attacks by (French) pirates or enemy ships, maritime disasters, maltreatment, suicide (e.g. cutting their throats, jumping overboard, and, under the term and "fixed melancholy!" many died of a "broken heart"). "Trouble-maker Slaves were brought on deck and flogged to death or clubbed over the head and pitched over board. In desperate efforts to keep from drowning, Slaves who managed to cling to the taffrail at the stern of the ship would have their hands chopped off. So many bodies or sickly Africans were thrown overboard that sharks picked up ships off the coast of Africa and followed them to America. Death rates averaged 15% on the short end of a 21- to 90-day voyage but rose sharply on the long end, perhaps approaching 40%. On an average, about a third of the Slaves died on their walk to the African coast and another third died during the trip to the Americas or from the "*Seasoning*" that followed. Most of the Enslaved landed first in the West Indies (especially Jamaica) where they were "*seasoned*" or "broken-in" to their new Enslaved roles. Those not dropped off in the islands were shipped to the USA. The "Unfortunates" in the Americas were simply left to die. Despite the brutal capturing of Slaves and the horrible Middle Passage taking an unspeakable toll in misery and human life, an early White writer, reflecting the "sick" mentality of European slavers, described these Enslaved operations as "crusades" for bringing the savage brethren to civilization and Christianity for conversion. He gently decried the massacres but maintained such incidents were definitely outweighed by the fact that salvation was thus gained for the souls of the victims! (Bailey, Stopping The Violence)

BLACK ENSLAVED "SEASONING": "Seasoning of the Slaves" referred to getting prepared for the New World "Ordeal." The mindset of Europeans at this time was Human torture was spotlighted during the days of the Spanish Inquisition (discovering and punishing heretics). The Inquisition's original purpose in 1478 was to discover and punish those converted Jews and Muslims who where insincere in their Christian beliefs. From the view of Spanish royalty, the victims had *"twisted"* or *"distorted"* the behaviors of Christian doctrine into something wrongful (called a "Tort" in law). The concept of going away from the true direction or posture meant that parts of the whole were in disorder--that is, *"twisted away"* from its proper senses and direction. To reverse such distortion required torture by painfully twisting and stretching the victim's limbs on the rack. An extension of this idea was that right religious doctrines and facts could become *Distorted* ("bad twist") when people *"twisted"* them to suit themselves. Though the inhumane religious "Trials by Ordeals" were particularly prominent in the European Middle Ages, The Roman Catholic Church engaged in this from C13 to early C19. To a somewhat less degree torture questioning was also used in civil courts up to the C20, including witchcraft trials in New England (USA) colonial period. Apart from the huge numbers of the Enslaved who died during the "Middle Passage" from Africa to the Caribbean, more than twice that died during the brutal training period in the West Indies before they were shipped on to the American mainland. When Enslaved Africans neared the shores of the Americas the slaver ship crews prepared them for sale by washing, shaving all their body hair, and rubbing them with palm oil to disguise sores and wounds caused by conditions on board. The Enslaved were trained not to resist having all parts of their bodies examined--especially their reproductive organs, and sometimes were allotted a little rum to liven their spirits. The Enslaveds' New World "Ordeal"— called *Seasoning*—served to increase their sale price. Slaveholders and overseers called "Salt-Water" the newly imported Enslaved and "Country-Born" for the American born Enslaved. Upon arrival in the "New World," the ordeal of being *"Seasoned"* to be Ideal Slaves included severing any "Motherland" bonds with their African past, the "killing of their Spirits" which was devastating and 'Splintering' to the entire Selfhood of each; separation of their "God-Image Self" from their Divine Spirit to thereby cause each to become Self-Absorbed. The severing of equally great bonds by selling away family, Sippi, and acquaintance members on the auction blocks--while humiliated by being stripped naked to "inspect".

Fredrick Douglass describes being put up for sale at a slave auction. "We were all ranked together at the valuation. Men and women, young and old, married and single, were ranked with the horses, sheep, and swine." Here is what it means to be a slave and sold like any other commodity. Douglass concludes: "At that moment, I saw more clearly than ever the brutalizing effects of slavery upon both slave and slaveholder." Each one of these personal happenings vied for out-doing all the rest in causing unbearable Spiritual, Emotional, and Physical pains. There was total Selfhood destruction that ensured the lack of ever returning to a pre-Enslavement state or improving into a better state from reassembling the shattered Selfhood pieces. Perhaps by this time, since their Instinct Brains were ineffective, they were operating out of their Omnibus Brains (survival and enduring actions derived from compromised Thought). Because there is an in-born urge to bond with people, and because they could not count on the people they loved to be available, and because the only thing the Enslaved could count on in order to survive was the captors, they clinged to their captors. All the captors offered was barely enough food and shelter to survive—and although deficient to an ultimate degree, this constituted a *Physical Nature Needs bond* with the captors—one absent a Spiritual Human Nature Needs supply. To give a clue as to how Europeans think, immediately after landing, *Pest houses*--where the Enslaved arrived from Africa--endured a mandatory period of quarantine before entering USA soil--especially at Sullivan's Island, SC. Here is where smallpox, tuberculosis, and similar contagious disease victims were also isolated.

BLACK ENSLAVED "SPIRITS KILLED": Following the "Fishnet Moment," a third of the Enslaved died on their walk to the African coast. During the Horrible Middle Passage death rates averaged 15% on the short end of a 21-to 90-day voyage but rose sharply on the long end, perhaps approaching 40%. So many bodies or sickly Africans were thrown overboard that sharks picked up ships off the coast of Africa and followed them to the Americas. A third of the arrivals died from "*Seasoning*" or "broken-in" to their new Enslaved roles. In this process, the "Unfortunates" were simply left to die. At its mildest, Seasoning of the Enslaved can be analogized to prolonged and inhumane ways of "*breaking*" *horses* at "ordeal" camps. A young horse at first objects to carrying a rider's weight—bucking, rearing, and plunging in order to throw the rider off—until "Broken"—the allowing of being saddled, bridled, and mounted. However, "Seasoning" the Enslaved was even more harsh throughout its 1 to 3 years intended for the Enslaved to adjust to their new environment; horrendous working and living conditions; adopting new customs; and with machine-gun rapidity "little bang bullets" conveying the message of the Enslaved being subhuman. All of this was done in the setting of the Enslaved being in a terribly weakened by the trauma of the Middle Passage voyage and the addition of exposure to foreign diseases, inadequate nutrition, bad water, work exhaustion from being unaccustomed to the "sunrise-to-sunset gang labor," and cruelty were simply overwhelming. All of these practices (among countless others) continued during plantation life, following slavery, and up to today. There has been no change in these Satanist mindsets and the followers they orchestrate--and there never will be! Satanists' practices were/are designed to beat down the newly captured victims with endless layers of "Spirit Dismantling" until they *have no more fight for retaliation and are docile "forever."* "Seasoning" included the assignment of Christian names; learning a new language while forbidden to use their native tongues or to maintain any other cultural ties; and otherwise "educated" in the direction of being "good Slaves". By being totally dependent on these sadistic captors for their entire survival meant that the Enslaved were "Bonded" to them—what I call the *Evil Savior Syndrome.* The mindset of those who model the African god Set is that of Human torture--an orientation spotlighted during the Catholic Spanish Inquisition. Its 1478 purpose was to discover and punish Jews and Muslims deemed to be insincere in their Christian beliefs—heretics said to have *"twisted" or "distorted"* Christian doctrine to suit themselves. To reverse such distortion required torture by various practices and devices—one being "*The Rack*" These methods continue today but with a different appearance. Obviously, all of these episodes (among infinitely others of a "big bang" periodic display + of a daily cumulative micro-trauma nature) contributed to the "Killing of the Spirits" of the Enslaved. A human's Soul has its origin in the Cosmic Intelligence and thus consists of *Divine Consciousness* as its state of Being. The Divine aspect of that Divine Consciousness is God's Spirit within each human—and thus is eternal and independent of and uninfluenced by anything, including whatever evil a human does. Thus, a human's *Divine Spirit* inside that Divine Consciousness is comparable to a drop of God--like a drop from a boundless ocean--but all of God is in that drop. When ones Divine Spirit is "Killed," one has exchanged the truth of God for a lie—i.e. adopting a distrust of God' Goodness and even seeking after God. Such enables anti-Spiritual Elements—whether in the form of messages, objects, or entities—to be brought into the Conscious or Unconscious by ignorant and/or evil people so as to generate self-defeating Supernatural Icon Images. See The Rack

BLACK ENSLAVED INTRODUCED TO EUROPEAN RELIGIOUS BELIEFS: A first duty of King James VI of Scotland was to call for a Hampton Court Conference in January 1604 for "a new translation of the Bible, because those which were allowed in the reigns of Henry VIII, and Edward VI, were corrupt and not answerable to the truth of the Original." James said: "I wish some special pains were taken for a uniform translation, which should be done by the best learned men in both Universities, then reviewed by the Bishops, presented to the Privy Council, lastly ratified by the Royal authority, to be read in the whole Church, and none other…These translations are to be used when they agree better with the Text than the Bishops Bibles: Tyndale's, Matthew's, Coverdale's, Whitchurch's, Geneva." Since the atmosphere of this time concerned African enslavement by Europeans' in South America, do you think these men, randomly chosen, were God-inspired to re-re-rewrite the European Bible? At the time of its publication the King James Bible was the source for indoctrinating African American Slaves into obeying the slave owners and, of greatest importance, to have faith in the "White" Jesus. The obeying reward was being allowed to go to heaven and work in its kitchen for White people. Not believing all this was true, the Enslaved added aspects of African Religion and filled in gaps with what seemed to be the way the Bible should read. Following slavery the religious beliefs of most Black Folks have been fashioned by the King James Bible. Reasons for agonizing over bringing up the problems with this European Bible are several. One is Black People have used it as the only thing to hold on to in order to endure horrendous trials and tribulations. Especially in those times when they felt as if they lacked the strength, God's Word was a miracle worker. A second is that historically anytime anyone has asked the people to look differently at something they firmly believe in, that person is called bad names. Yet, I am a solid believer in God and God's Spirit Helpers and have difficulty seeing how the awesomeness of Nature does not lead everyone to that belief. Relying on them has been the secret of any successes I have had in life. I rely heavily on messages coming into me from having channels open to the Voice of the Silence. In turn, this enables me to keep a free mind; hate no one; and provide the truth as I see it to those who are not so sensitive as to get angry and "shut-down" mentally upon hearing something contrary to their beliefs. It is never my intention to persuade anyone to believe anything but rather to look at the familiar in a new way. Hence my comments are directed to those who are uncertain about what they believe; to those who have not thought of any other way to consider religion; and to those unaware of the Ancient African Bible. What will follow are only about a few but powerful things which have a great deal of influence on adversely affecting ones religious faith and trust and that I believe hamper thriving in life. This is not for people whose religious lives are working well or for those who say: "Don't mess with my religion." For those who open their Bible to a random page and find just the right message, I ask them to research Ancient African Spiritual Literature to see if they do not find that story or message predating the European Bible by thousands of years. Just as slavery modified the course of the Enslaveds' religious thinking, so has the European Bible. One setting for the comments to follow is in 1945 at Naj Hammadi (today's southern Egypt) 52 texts called the Gnostic Gospels spoke of Christianity's African rise. Another setting is the realization that what worked for the Enslaved is often not applicable today because one must do things to thrive for oneself and family as opposed to the Slaves' situation of needing to simply survive and endure. Still another setting is to "feel" the difference in hearing the fear-based messages of the European Bible and the Love-based messages of the Ancient African Bible. Which do you think would most likely be the Word of God?

BLACK HOLE: in African Mythology, if, in the "*Weighing of the Scales of Justice*" the "Heart" of the Deceased, it failed (i.e. too heavy to pass from being a bundle of ill-programmed behavioral responses) it travels to the *Places of Destruction*--a form of Purgatory purifier. This region was called a "*Black Hole*"--a *Nothingness*--a void where there is the absence of objects and where the "bad stuff" of ones Heart is concealed and securely hidden. The *goal of Auset's "Taut" is to deal with* the unperfected "Heart" and Soul of the deceased as it travels to the *Places of Destruction. It does not inflict suffering but rather brings about the complete elimination of evil-doers'* (i.e. enemies of Ausar) deeds by placing them into a Black Hole. As can be seen on this page, there are spaces between the words—spaces of "nothing". Yet, the "nothing" conveys meaning and reduces chaos in understanding what is read. To indicate *Nothingness's* meaning, Ancient Egyptians employed an empty space to indicate "*Exterminated*"—i.e. being absolutely "*Eliminated*". Since a Black Hole draws in everything and absorbs visible light never to release either, it is unable to betray the presence of its contents. This makes it a tangible Being, bound up with the *Void*--a state of "No Thing"—a realm of primeval darkness--the Ocean of Nun from which Cosmic Creation sprang.

BLACK PEOPLE--STRUGGLING: Struggling Black People's minds maintain the Enslaved mindset backdrop of *Fright*--essentially "frozen" negative emotions producing Selfhood "numbness"--similar to when an "anesthetic" takes away sensations from a part of ones body. All are about a lack of Courage to take charge and control of their own lives and, instead, wait hopefully for White people to come to their senses and "do the right thing." But that will never happen. There were innumerable causes of their negative emotions, including Spiritual pain, Emotional Pain, Despair, Shame, Rage, Depression, and Fear. Each played some part in generating a kaleidoscopic picture of mindsets, some of the common of which are the following.

A. Non-Sexual *Masochistic Minds* (Bailey, Special Minds) whereby victims invite or fail to prevent needless hardships.

B. *Encaged Minds,* reflecting a misarranged world view; a shattered ethos; the embracing of European system of values, and not realizing African Tradition is the best way to view reality.

C. *Special Minds* operate out of a primal self-preservation level and a broken spirit. For those so afflicted, a "make do" with poverty is good enough.

D. *Enslaved Minds* are those brainwashed by the evil Whites' dictates of "stay-in-your-place" and that has become a way of life.

E. *Despaired Minds*: *Mild Despair* (like Patience tolerated impatiently); *Slight Despair* (fear); *Moderate Despair* (a grandiose form of Funk); and *Extreme Despair* (despondency—a complex emotional attitude constituted of sorrow and sense of failure). Instead, the Enslaved *Extreme Despair*--a defect of spirit of an utter ruin inside a bottomless perdition (i.e. loss of the Soul) condition—stands alone by being far, far deeper, wider, and more devastating than European types. Whereas Fear, of all the base passions, is the most accused, to be entangled in the Extreme Despair woes of Spiritual Pain—a living "hell"--is to experience the very worst suffering. "Despair" (without hope), when Extreme, establishes a "no doubt" atmospheric effect of Certainty about the worst happening to them "forever". One Consequence is to so *wear out ones Courage* that ones *discontinued efforts* also *paralyze any desire to better a "ME/WE" situation.* One settles on *simply "Making Do".* Another is a chronic fury mindset of *Desperation*—i.e. a sense of always being cornered by predators, unable to run away, and, as a last resort, react with rash or frantic actions—as in taking reckless actions and venturing into any risks, regardless of consequences.

F. *Non-Thinking Minds* are those programmed into causing ones rational thinking skills to become atrophied or to not develop rational thinking skills in the first place. This is somewhat like individual cells in the body programmed to self-destruct and their residual remains provide nutrients to assist in birthing and enhancing new development. Its offshoots include Automatic, Impulsive, Patterned, Superficial, and "Off and On" Thinking.

BLACK HISTORY REWRITTEN BY SUPERNATURALS: To show the Supernaturals' racism Envy goes way back in history, when Romans came into existence, they were so awed with Black African brilliance as to say: "Ex Africa semper aliquid"--freely translated: "*There is always something new coming out of Africa.*" They, like the Greeks, proceeded to steal African creations and inventions and claim themselves as the originators—a process continuing to this day. Envy is dynamic hostility aimed maliciously at the real or supposed superiority of one(s) deemed to be "Inferiors." Envy consists of seeing thing never as they are within themselves but, instead, viewing them in their relations to oneself. Despite Bullies' Material Success--which is never enough to bring satisfaction--they are overwhelmed with Envy of their Victims. By Bullies never producing anything great in the world today is what keeps them as "inferiors" and being acutely aware of it. Besides, they are extremely sensitive to anyone pointing out even a hint of their "Inferiority" status. To illustrate, French Egyptologist Abbe Emile Amelineau was the first to discover and publish books in 1902 and 1916 that the Black Anu were the aboriginal Ancient

Egyptians. This scholastic courage cost him his reputation and research support at the hands of racists authorities and conventional Egyptologists. To this day his work is still ostracized and ridiculed by the world's conventional Egyptologists. In retaliation, this caused racists Egyptologists to engage in Phantasmagoric tales with writings for the world intended to wipe out truths about the super-brilliance of Black Africans. An elaborate one was in falsely claiming how Europeans came into ways to help settle Egypt. An example was a ship-load of Europeans had their vessel wrecked on the shores of Egypt and it was they who built all great products of the Egyptians before going back to Europe. A showering of racists Egyptologist in attempts to erase all records of Black Africans brilliance are various physical vandalisms on, say wall reliefs, to the extent that it justifies the vandals to present that the involved product's originators are a mystery. That paves the way for them to invent fantasy as to how the originators of these great works were fellow Supernatural cult members who happened on to Black African locations. An example of Ancient Egyptian culture, structure, and other aspects of destruction were by the Roman Empire. Two more examples are Herotodus and the Annu Egyptian High Priest Manethos who had available to them the 42 books of Tehuti. They lived and wrote their histories during the final Dynastic days of Egypt. Thereafter and throughout the Ages, there was deliberate books and records destruction of Ancient African works—and that is one reason why students cannot go to libraries to learn about the amazing Ancient Black African achievements. Instead, all this is available is the world-wide false impression that what is great today came from ancient Greeks who, in fact, were a semi-barbaric people. Africans Middle Kingdom (3348-3182 BC) papyri—given by Europeans the European names of Moscow, Berlin, Kahun, and Rhind—have now been *proved to be plagiarized* by *Pythagoras, Archimedes, Thales, Plato, Eudoxus, Oenopides, Aristotle, Solon, Indocsus,* and other Greeks who have left names on what is considered great in the world today. Practically all great things subsequently spread throughout the Western world under the name of "*Greek creations*" are merely translations and transmissions of Ancient African intellectual property. The *ancient Greeks, being at best mere transmitters and translators of African genius,* laid out a plagiarism pattern which has pervaded Europeans' character ever since--and to the point of their admiring it. This is what European Medieval (and modern) "scholarship" is about. No morals are associated with such racism Envy but, instead, there is Supernatural admiration for crimes carried out with daring. This is envied because it serves as a standard for Supernaturals to challenge themselves to succeed. This is like the worm always running to the choicest fruit. To deceitfully "win" gives them fodder to accuse others as inferior. Otherwise, to not accept the challenge equates to Bullies thinking they are going backwards. This is worse than all ills befalling them at every turn. Thus, because the envious are never satisfied and are more miserable upon seeing Victims with spotty happiness. Also, being aware of their Victims' brilliance, adding to their hard work to keep down is being dedicated to doing as much Blaming, Criticizing, and Fault-Finding as they can make stick as demeaning Stereotypes. See Bully

BLAME AND CRITICIZING: I do not believe in blaming and criticizing others but for some this is difficult for them to distinguish that from what they see me do. I will tell boys I am mentoring what I see that I believe to be self-defeating and I have no hesitation calling people down on evil things they do to hurt those who cannot help them or hurt them. To me those who blame and criticize have a personal problem and are trying to get relief by attacking others. I welcome constructive criticism for that is how I learn. I will evaluate destructive criticism to see if it has any truth but it rarely does from my perspective. I do not doubt that those who criticize me are annoyed by what I do but I think they should bring it to my attention and be willing to discuss it directly. Most will not face a discussion--for fear they will be proved wrong; for inexperience in direct encounters since they are accustomed to indirection; or because they feel superior by merely possessing blaming and criticizing thoughts. I prefer to stay away from people like that because of the bad atmosphere they bring into my space.

BLIND: "*Blind*" (Indo-European) was originally not so much 'sightlessness' as 'confusion' and 'obscurity'. Then the notion of someone wandering around in actual or mental darkness, not knowing where to go, naturally progressed to the 'inability to see. People "*blind to the obvious*," as in significant things like failing to see the "Elephant in the room" because of a huge "*Blindspot*" ('covered or hidden from sight') as to what they saw and heard have Private Selfhood problems.' Their obscurities to the eye—whether because of *what one does not want to see* and/or from being Socialized to be "*Blindfolded*" (Old English, 'to strike blind')—leaves them no choice but follow the stupidity of the Crowd or live in a "cave." As Sharon Bingaman states, this is what causes many people to come to the same point from different directions and still disagree. Some wear different colored lens and change the colors of those lens from time to time; some only see one side of the coin or part of only one side. By not seeing all the angles and sides and not sharing the same experiences explains why people cannot see another's point of view, not be able to appreciate the same things, or have conflicts about what is Beauty. What makes for these personal and interrelationship problems are multiple nuances and subtitles that are and are not made. See Dark vs. Light

BOOMERANG: an object resembling a bird or airplane, with a bend near the middle of its wings. When properly thrown, the leading edges of its "wings" (air foils) slice the air, thus providing a lifting force as it moves forward. Meanwhile, it is spinning end over end. This force from the leading wing experiences more lift than the retreating wing and the power process moves the boomerang in a circle and therefore back to the one who threw it (Bailey, Handling Bad Emotions).

BOUNDARIES ON THE BOUNDLESS: For practically all Ancient Africans, God was the model for boundlessness in wholism, completeness, integrity, freedom from all deficiencies, and power. However, prominent among Europeans has been plentiful disbelief in and substitutes for God. For example, the anthropomorphically derived deities of the Homeric pantheon were both ontologically (study of Reality and the essence of Being) and morally deficient. They differed from humans only in being "deathless." Similar binding of the boundless is typical of Europeans and devastating to the Spiritual Elements that are so vital to the philosophy of African Tradition. The following are a few examples. When the rock thrown into a lake causes a splash from which ripples arise, the first few symbolizes the Master Words. Critical Thinking (CT) first assesses the "Source" and "Cause" aspects of the thrower in order to understand the perspective of the meanings of the resultant words. For example, ideas of Europeans' religious meanings of Faith/Belief/Trust requires realizing Europeans essentially disregard Cosmic Spiritual Realms; operate out of a Fear Based philosophy of Life to justify Kill/Take/Destroy/Dominate/Oppress/Control; possess an Indifference/Hate/Evil/Sadism mindset and are obsessed to be in control of everybody and everything so as to be "little god kings and heroes. European males greatly despised being considered a coward or feminine. Two examples of their subtle brutish aggressions are placing restrictions on the Spiritually Magnificent (possession at once of greatness, splendor, and richness) and converting "Knowing" (with its certainty) over to Faith/Belief/Trust which SEEMS to be Right (with its element of doubt). A typical example of how Europeans put boundaries on the Spiritual Elements as a routine way to live is by converting Unconditional Love (called the inner Being of God in African Tradition) to *"Conditional" Love*. This serves as a means of control and/or punishment among their own "Troops": "If you don't do what I say I will not love you"; if you do not stop associating with Blacks you can no longer be "one of us." Instead, they attempt to get cult members and victims alike to believe their fantasy presented is Reality. An analogy is the illusion of the strips of a Barber Pole are not moving up or down but rather what is rotating is a single strip on the pole which makes it look that way. Thus, anything they consider saying will depend upon fellow Europeans might think about it and that prevents telling the truth. By being historically and philosophically aware of who these "throwers" of illusions are and the consequences of their words which cause a ripple effect, arms one to mentally defend against them. For example, historically Europeans have stolen Africans intellectual knowledge and renamed what they could not take away from Africa. A reason for renaming what they dishonorably acquire is sort of explained in the Encyclopaedia Britannica (1992, p 567): "...*men have seen in the ability to name an ability to control or to possess....*" They defined "*naming*" as applying a word to pick out and refer to a fellow human being, an animal, an object, or a class of such beings or objects. Despite disregarding the Spiritual realms, they can rename manipulation of anti-Spiritiual Elements actions as "love" and cause even the sophisticated to think this "love" (defined as an emotion) to SEEM right. Such is effective because it is popularized by the media and made to "SEEM" right until it becomes socialized into ones family. That allows it to be passed on and applied as "Right", causing more and worse conflicts among Black People who adopt these pervasive bad European practices. Another approach to bounding the magnificent is seen in what Europeans deem as patriotic. Examples are the *USA pledge of Allegiance* or the *salute to the flag* (1894)..."with liberty and justice for all" and the *American Creed* (1917)..."government of the people, by the people, for the people...." Though these are both magnificient statements, because it says that all people are "Equal" under God's eyes, still they have not applied to any USA citizens except to Euro-Americans. Great are the mental conflicts in the minds of Colored Peoples and even on the few humane White people who try to figure out and deal with restrictions placed on inequality. This spurs many of the excluded to act and react in "weird" ways. That happened to me when, during my medical training, I was "face-to-face" with overwhelming racism. Yet, at the scheduled end of the program I had made the bad things SEEM okay, accepted that, and considered staying on for additional punishment. Fortunately, my mind cleared so I could "Feel" what happened and do a CT assessment of first understanding the nature of Europeans. This enabled me to extract the lessons of where I got off my Goal-Track and figure out how to get back on it by returning to my philosophical fundamentals. One of those was to not allow anything to interfere with going straight ahead. Such shows how "Feelings" and CT join to detect certain problems; what is required for fixing them immediately; and then doing it.

BOUNDLESS SPIRITUALITY BINDING: A Shawnee Amerindian saying is: "*The Great Spirit knows no boundaries, nor will his red children acknowledge any.*" The C17 sense of one of the many 'faces' of "Bound" is to "form the edge (as where the river meets the land) or limit of; to enclose, to contain." A partner of this 'face' is the sense of bound in "the way of doing," based upon being under some obligation to follow the rules which limit the setting. The "big picture" of "Bound" is that there is a barrier obstructing a passage but that barrier is not necessarily impassable. To convert any Spiritual Boundlessness into the Bounded is a powerful way to have ones mind controlled. It also *"Constrains" and "Restrains" minds--C13 English words meaning to "hold tightly within"* by outward circumstances or by inner prompting. Both characterized slave owners' practices done to remold minds of Enslaved Africans brought to the Americas. For Black People this is like being born under a specific set of African Principles while bound to European laws--and those, similar to oil and water, do not mix! Resultant conflicts and differences meet to form every type of *Confusion (the keystone of mind control)*--especially when compared side by side so that the results are shadowy and vague. Confusion on Spiritual boundaries range from what happens to a bird with a clipped wing over to being cribbed and confined by doubts and fears. By generating shallows and miseries, Confusion leads one off the "Right" path so that ones thinking, feeling, expressing, and acting design vicious cycle decisions and solutions. So, how did bounded and confused minds in most of today's world come about? Much of the answer can be attributed to the art of ancient Greek government, which arose in tiny city-states to become the political mode of control over most of today's world. A building block of their philosophy was the necessity for Slaves. They believed Slaves to be like mechanical beings having the purpose of doing the ugly, horrible, uninteresting work of civilization's daily life, since otherwise culture and contemplation would be almost impossible. Hence, it was essential for them to put boundaries on the Spiritual Boundlessness of both the Slaves and Greek people. Since Free Minds are not controllable, Rules for fellow Greeks and for the Slaves--in the manner that "one size fits all"--were required so that all would conform to the behaviors and patterns the authorities dictated. Of course, this gave them free reign to also do violence to the African Spiritual Elements "Seeds"--Unconditional Love, Truth, Reality, and the Natural. Yet, what is absolutely fundamental for sound mental health in its application to "Right" daily living is that there cannot be the slightest or the tiniest of alteration in these "Seeds." *Sickle Cell Anemia* well illustrates the point. *Slavery, Racism, and bad information from ignorant people are orderly processes designed to put the minds of Black Americans into chaos that is self-defeating and that prevents rising above poverty of any type.* In applying these concepts to human interactions, one of the most terrible is Europeans placing boundaries, not simply on the greatness of Ancient Africans and today's Black Americans but legally and "scientifically" declaring they and their diaspora offspring have boundaries on their humanness--as when Euro-Americans considered the *Enslaved to be 3/5ths of a human.* The Enslaved who believed this were easily re-defined as to who they were; accepted this false definition; "lived down" to its evil label; built a lifestyle around it; and then socialized those wretched concepts onto their children and their children, thereby disabling them all up to today.

BOUNDING UNCONDITIONAL LOVE: European "Authorities" have placed into Confusion the Spiritual boundless African Tradition concepts by applying boundaries on them. That initiated and maintains devastating life shaping courses for countless numbers of the world's peoples. The very worst is the conversion of Unconditional Love (called the inner Being of God in African Tradition) to "Conditional" Love. Of the many concepts given to the Old English word "Love" (affectionate), a main one is "to find pleasing." It subsequently developed to 'praise'; be satisfied with; to trust; believe; beautiful (C13); and a strong liking. To put these highly confusing European versions into perspective, the setting in which their meanings originally arose--and thereafter traditionally applied almost interchangeably--was from ones Passion, Affection, Affect, Emotion, and similar senses. Early European scientists resorted to the imagery pervading Passions for Love, as in it possessing a magnetic attraction and repulsion (e.g. "the love of the iron for the loadstone"). Thereafter "love" between man/woman became the spotlighted feature in the "big picture" subject of Love--e.g. conjugal/illicit, normal/perverse, sexual/idyllic, infantile/adult, Romantic/Christian. Then these were grouped separately from friendship; familial ties (parental, fraternal, filial); self-love, love of fellow man, country, and God. Machiavelli (C15), in documenting worldly success, said being lovers of riches, fame, and power are the triad of seducers alienating the affections of men for truth, beauty, and goodness. Socrates, whom I believe was an African and well-schooled in African concepts, spoke of love's power in relation to wisdom and truth. On the European Ladder of Love, Plato's Symposium has different loves for its rungs--all of which Aristotle classified under the heading of Emotions.

Emotion (Latin 'e' or out + movere, to move) denotes a sentiment, meaning one literally moves out of ones mind as a result of stirred up Feelings. Many Europeans agree that both love and desire belong to the sphere of the emotions called the *Appetitive Faculty* (about wanting, needing, craving, wishing, willing) as well as to the Will, rather than to the sphere of perception and knowledge. European ancients had three distinct words for the main types of love: eros, philia, agape in Greek; amor, amicitia (or dilecto), and caritas in Latin. In order to indicate plainly that love is common to all three, *English Love equivalents are: sexual love (the love of desire generated by selfishness); love of friendship (predominantly altruistic motives from love preceding desire and determining its wishes, but making few demands); and love of charity* (not the same as Spiritual Instincts). *Agape* and *Caritas* are said to give the sense of a higher or selfless love. So the question is "how high?" because if it were Spiritual it would not be an Emotion. What is "Selfless Love" and for what purpose? Western literature is filled with Europeans willing to, and actually risking their lives without thought of "Self" in order to acquire gold or to

"Take" what belongs to other people. The love inside emotions implies, said Aquinas (C13), "perfection rather than imperfection since it flows from the act of Will to diffuse its own goodness among others." But let us look at inconsistencies in these 'love' concepts. The European Bible speaks of the multiplicity of loves in the history of mankind--of God/Mammon, perverse/pure, idolatry/vanity of misplaced love; every unnatural lust; every ecstasy of the spirit; every tie of friendship and fraternity; and all the hates which love engenders. They convey facts of European love even without going beyond that to definitions and doctrine. Whereas an emotional experience involves an awareness of widespread bodily commotion, to impart emotional "love" in degrees means one can determine how much of what kind of "love" to give and to whom and when. Since the Eurocentric literature views "love" as an Earth World Emotion, it is not only man-made but changeable for self-interest purposes and *having nothing to do with Spirituality*. Whatever is man-made is "Conditional"--implying that European type "love" depends upon certain circumstances: "I'll love you if you do…"; "I won't love you if you don't do…." Such "Gaps" present in "Conditional Love" means it is anti-Unconditional Love. "Gaps" are not permissible in African Tradition's philosophy of life because that means they lack integrity. "Conditional Loves" ensure one will not have a Free Mind or a happy life. jabaileymd.com

BOUNDING THE MAGNIFICENT: Let us say you consider your mother to be magnificent, as shown by your unconditional love for her. To use an analogy, just as the sun's rays go everywhere, indefinitely, and all the time, you say this about the magnificence of who your mother is, what she does, and how she appears to you. In the same way the sun is always in the sky, so is the presence of your unconditional love always there for your mother, no matter what she does. But suppose I told you the only reason you love your mother is because she took care of you as a baby. Would you believe me? The answer is "No" because you know there are no boundaries on the magnificence of your mother and your feelings for her. Now, if you were to substitute "Know" for your mother, you might see some similarities. To "Know" is like the sun's rays and to put any boundaries on the sun would mean this is not natural. But suppose some authority brought in people who all agreed that the sun has boundaries but other than that the sun is as great as ever. So what term would you use to refer to a sun with boundaries on it? Might you say: I "Believe" that is the sun; or I have "Faith" and "Trust in" that is the sun because it SEEMS like it. By getting many Enslaved to believe this meant they could define who the Enslaved were; have them "live down" to this evil label; and cause them to pass those witched concepts onto their children and children's children so that all continued to struggle as a way of life. Bounding the Magnicient has been done with the word "Black" -- a word indicating "Purity" because, said our Ancient African Ancestors, it embraces such African concepts as God -- the Absolute, the Potential, the Unknowable, the Un-manifest. Also, "Black" symbolizes resurrection and eternal life. Because *"Black" designates the African ultimate in spiritual perfection, it conveys the magnificent.* Hence, *Ancient Africans proudly called themselves "Black People."* Yet, Europeans have placed boundaries on it, wrongly regarding it (and white) as a distinct color. However, technically "black" is not a color but rather the absence of color. Pause for a moment to "Feel" the impact of "black" as a color as opposed to "black" as magnificent. Because "Purity" stimulates ones "Feelings" (instincts) as being a component of the magnificent of Beauty, one knows Purity when it is experienced. But suppose it is altered, even in the tiniest way as, for example, putting boundaries on "black" and calling it a color. Now "black" is no longer experienced as "Pure" magnificence but rather, at best, that it "SEEMS" pure. It is easy for one to be manipulated in this way. One reason is if one never knew the pre-existing purity concept of "Black" as magnificent, it would be wrongly thought of as "Pure" by a past/present kin and then become a family concept. Second, one can be so overwhelmed by the awe of the magnificient as to overlook the restrictions placed on it. This is what showers of advertisements on television and popular "buzz" words do. Third is being so lazy in not doing CT and/or researching as to willing accept anything said by Brutes (who are focused on controlling people) and the ignorant trying to pass themselves off intellectuals. Failing to appreciate distinctions between pure/impure, what is Right/what SEEMS right, good/bad--puts one on the anti-Spiritual Element path and makes one unable to distinguish the infinite (the Spiritual) from the finite (Earth World) or the treasures of African Tradition from the trinkets of European tradition. Such eases one into adopting the self-defeating European character, as is being displayed by far too many Black Americans today.

BOUNDARIES ON PERFECTION: Perfection is Ideal, Secular "Self-Made," "Spiritually-Made" (e.g. ones birth Selfhood Greatness) or simple the essence of Spiritual Existence. In African Tradition, *Spiritual Existence* is God as Perfect Wholism--symbolized as the *Black Dot*. Thus, "blackness" became the ultimate in spiritual perfection; a metaphor of the *Absolute* (beyond all mental concepts); and the identifier of the most important Egyptian god, Osiris, "Lord of the perfect Black." "*Spiritually-Made*" for Ancient Africans was based upon deeming God to be perfect, complete, and irreducible--with these traits passing into each human so as to embody a divine consciousness in a perfected (Enlightened) and immortal state (Ashby, African Origins, p. 408; Bynum, African Unconscious, p. 140, 290). They said that being Spiritual is living the Ideal--not the type lacking existence (since that is unable to be complete)--but rather from expressing the natural impulses derived from ones divine consciousness. Such formulates ones life within the mold of the Spiritual Elements. Humans were given all that is needed for the growth, realization, and perfection of the *Spiritual Ideal*. "*Perfect*" implies the final effect touches the highest level of ones divine consciousness (Soul) and elevates it above the Tangible world into the Sublime. To these ends, Ancient Africans devised perfect models, e.g. "Man, Know Thyself" for orientation so as to proceed along African Traditions' Tree of Life (see Amen, Tree of Life) for reaching the Afterlife and thereby avoiding reincarnation sufferings. To become perfect is to complete the spiritual vehicle needed to live forever as a divine being. *Human perfection* is about living an ideal life where every potential in ones Selfhood possession has been realized. This does not mean they are "perfect" in everything because that is not humanly possible. The "Weighing of Ma'at's feather" on Judgment Day is to merely "balance" it, not be lighter than it (Bailey, Ancient African Bible Messages). In activities of daily living, in order to reach ones full intellectual and Pure Feeling (not emotional) potential means reaching the state of Wisdom. One is motivated by a strong sense of purpose and governed by the right moral (right/wrong) and ethical (proper/improper) choices. To live perfectly requires Ma'at naturalness operating according to truth, reality, and rightness. Flowing in naturalness is what makes an ideal practical. Ma'at perfection flows in rhythm with what is natural for human beings. The Ma'at focus is having good relationships with and behaviors toward others (e.g. compassion, kindness, appreciation, non-aggression); being loving and lovable; and staying with Truth and Reality. To perform "win-win" activities is to be in the flow of perfect beauty. To appreciate each such experience means having a fulfillment moment. Each fulfilling moment represents a perfect moment and a perfect moment is a piece of Success in Life. Of course, the more frequent the fulfilling moments, the greater is ones life's successes. The place in ones "selfhood" where fulfillment occurs is in one's Real Self.

BOUNDARING "SELF-MADE PERFECTION: *European Secular "Self-Made" Perfection* for Plato consisted of the idea of the Good as the measure of the Being and essence in each thing. Biblically, it refers to conforming to a mature standard or pattern or has a state of sinless-ness. The perfectionist, in the pursuit of good ends, is to absolutely reject evil as well as reject the use of less-than-perfect means, even in extreme circumstances, to achieve a goal. The C13 English word "*Perfection*" means completely made, wholeness, or Integrity. What is Complete has all its parts, is fully developed, or is carried to its fulfillment. Criteria for the Secular "Self-Made" are for a thing to fulfill its nature in an unqualified state of excellence and faultlessness. Otherwise, European Secular Perfection has relativity. A complete day would be either 24 hours or the full hours of daylight, depending on how the word day is meant. Perfect has high quality and is free from defects or blemishes. For example, a perfect day would be a full day or a delightful or successful one; or, one that in some way had fulfilled the highest expectations. But what is so spiritually and religiously destructive is when this is applied to the Spiritual Elements and their products (e.g. humans). It is hard to seize the subtle damage to ones mind when presented with boundaries around Unconditional Love, Truth, Reality, and the Natural unless one has done the prior preparation of studying Ancient African Spiritual Literature needed for discerning it. See Salvation

BOUNDARIES ON UNCONDITIONAL LOVE: A powerful way of putting boundaries on the Spiritual Elements as a routine way to live is to convert African Tradition's Unconditional Love (called the inner Being of God in African Tradition) to "Conditional" Love. Of the many concepts given to the Old English word "Love" (affectionate), to find pleasing is primary. It subsequently developed to 'praise'; be satisfied with; to trust; believe; beautiful (C13); and a strong liking. To put this highly confusing European version into perspective, the setting in which these meanings originally arose -- and thereafter have traditionally been used almost interchangeably--was from ones Passion, Affection, Affect, Emotion, and similar senses. Early European scientists used the imagery pervading Passions for Love, as in it possessing a magnetic attraction and repulsion (e.g. "the love of the iron for the loadstone"). Thereafter "love" between man/woman became the spotlighted feature in the "big picture" subject of Love--e.g. conjugal/illicit, normal/perverse, sexual/idyllic, infantile/adult, Romantic/Christian. Then these were grouped separately from friendship; familial ties (parental, fraternal, filial); self-love, love of fellow man, country, God; love's power (e.g. Socrates, whom I believe was an African and well-schooled in African concepts, as in speaking of love of wisdom and truth); and Machiavelli in documenting worldly success being lovers of riches, fame, and power--the triad of seducers which alienates the affections of men for truth, beauty, and goodness. On the European ladder of love, Plato's Symposium has different loves for its rungs. Aristotle classifies different kinds of love. The European Bible speaks of the multiplicity of loves in the history of mankind--of God/mammon, perverse/pure, idolatry/vanity of misplaced love; every unnatural lust; every ecstasy of the spirit; every tie of friendship and fraternity; and all the hates which love engenders. They convey the facts of European love even when they do not go beyond that to definition and doctrine. European ancients had three distinct words for the main types of love: eros, philia, agape in Greek; amor, amicitia (or dilecto), and caritas in Latin. In order to indicate plainly that love is common to all three, English equivalents are: sexual love (the love of desire generated by selfishness); love of friendship (a predominance of altruistic motives from love preceding desire and determining its wishes; it makes few demands); and love of charity. *Agape* and *Caritas* are deemed by Europeans to give the sense of a higher or selfless love. So the question is "how high?" because if it were Spiritual it would not be an Emotion. *Emotion* (Latin 'e' or out + movere, to move) denotes a sentiment meaning one literally moves out of ones mind as a result of stirred up Feelings (which are Spiritual Instincts). What is "Selfless Love" and for what purpose? Western literature is filled with Europeans willing to and actually risking their lives without thought of "Self" in order to acquire gold or to "Take" what belongs to other people. There is agreement among Europeans that both love and desire belong to the *Appetitive Faculty* (which are about wanting, needing, craving, wishing, willing)--to the sphere of the emotions and the will rather than to the sphere of perception and knowledge. The love inside emotions implies, says Aquinas, "perfection rather than imperfection since it flows from the act of will to diffuse its own goodness among others" (note the inconsistencies in concepts). Whereas emotional experiences involve awareness of widespread bodily commotion, to impart emotional "love" in degrees is to determine how much of what kind of "love" to give and to whom--both concepts implied in the Western word *Sympathy*. Whatever is man-made is "Conditional" (implying that European type "love" depends upon certain circumstances) and that is anti-Unconditional Love. As with sympathy, "gaps" are present in "Conditional Love" -- meaning this is under a person's control. "Gaps" have never been permissible in the philosophy of life of African Tradition because that means they are not Spiritual. Hence, Black People only relate to Compassion and not "Sympathy." "Conditional Loves" ensure one cannot have a happy life. Europeans' emphasis on Individualism prevents "Oneness"-bonding of an African type with anyone and promotes fearing everybody. In European society the expression of hatred (e.g. fight, football) is more accepted than expressions of love. A lot of pretending is done: "Have a nice day" when one really does not care. If ones False Self is not sincere about anything, one discovers one cannot distinguish that False Self from ones other False Self -- like taking off a mask to reveal another mask on ones face. Now one has a wholeness of hollowness. A patriot believes in country and commitment but may do it without being loving to fellow countrymen. Rather it is done to personally gain the country's benefits. Such self-interest, for those who can feel guilt, means they cannot love themselves because guilt and self-love are incompatible. So an essential in life is to explore "Unconditional Love" for meaning and display. Despite disregarding the Spiritual, Brutes can manipulatively rename anti-Spiritual Elements actions as "love" and cause even the sophisticated to think this "love" (defined as an emotion) "SEEMS" right. Such is effective because it is popularized by the media and made to "SEEM" right. It then is socialized into ones family. The confusion of "Conditional Love" being presented as the aura of "Unconditional Love" serves as a means of control via intimidation of not having it and/or as punishment among their own people: "If you don't do what I say I will not love you"; "if you do not stop associating with Blacks you can no longer be one of us." That allows it to be passed on and spread widely as "Right," causing more and worse conflicts among Black People-- and many, in turn, adopt these pervasive bad practices. By being historically and philosophically aware of who these "throwers" of illusions are and the ripple effect consequences of their words, arms one to mentally defend against them. The consequences of these patterns of bounding the boundless and making organic things mechanical and believing in a Supernatural God, Hell, and Devil led to Delusions. See Sympathy

BOWLING PIN CONCEPT: Principles used to properly set ones Ultimate Legacy Goal so that ones Immediate, Short-Term, Intermediate, and Long-Term goals all head in that same direction

BOX CONCEPT: viewing matters so as inspect each side--the inside and outside details of every angle—inspecting the top and bottom and any wrappings--turning it in all directions--looking at it from underneath--seeing it from one view after another--holding it against the sky and imagining it in any material or even in glass--and think of all types of options based upon fashioning powerful meanings indirectly.

BRAIN: The Right Hemisphere of the brain has synonyms that include the Limbic, "the Imaginal"; "the Feeling"; "the Emotional" brain; and most commonly in lay language, the *Right Brain*. It is capable of its own independent train of thought beyond ones conscious awareness. The Right Brain's dominate activities are artistic, intuitive, spontaneous, imaginative, emotional, flowing in its patterns, and playful. It recognizes and distinguishes shapes and fragmented shapes (crucial to creativity) without being fooled by unimportant differences; thinks in images; is involved in memory; and has the creativity to bridge informational gaps (but the Left Brain is needed to grasp a good idea when it appears and logically works out the problems it presents). What makes this possible is the end-function of the Right brain which notes similarities between things below an appearance level; sees their relation to each other; and then harmoniously fits the parts--regardless of how remote in time or space--into a unified whole. This unifying of mutual relationships and perceiving their interdependence with each other and the whole expresses through abstract or metaphoric use of images contributes to complete forms of "flashes of insight" (Amen II: 104; Amen I:10, 18; Blakelee p47). But the right side pays attention to coherence and meaning; that is, your right brain tells you if it "feels" right. It normally passes through several stages of progress--e.g. that of a child; of an average person; and of a highly skilled person; and of Slave or diseased patterns (i.e. whereby one loses certain developed skills). The following discussion will assume the actions of a right-handed person. Type I: *The Right Brain of the Child (up to age 5)*: Right Brain is active from birth. Creativity, imagination, Aliveness, Curiosity, Loving, Lovable, Emotional expressions freely are basic Right Brain functions. As opposed to the latent (relatively inactive) Left Brain, the Right Brain is prominently active at birth (or before) and is manifested in a child-like manner. Throughout this course it is *Fantasy* oriented in its processing of information. While this fantasy orientation may seem a disadvantage, inside it there is a great deal of creativity. Creativity is instinctual mediated by the Cingulate Gyrus and Frontal Lobe. Gradually it becomes disciplined as the Left Brain begins to bring in its element of critical thinking and reasoning around ages 5 to 7. Nevertheless, in the expression of Emotions it is predisposed to the "negative" (e.g. anger, sadness, chronic anxiety, fearful mournful feelings); determines the emotional content of speech; plays a significant role in language (e.g. in comprehension of words); and notices tone of voice, facial expression, and body language. Since to the Right Brain words are relatively less important, it is about *Random Thinking* in contrast to sequential thinking. Compared to Left Brained people they are better at verbal fluency, speed, and attention to detail; can spot missing details on pictures; can memorize complex shapes; and have no concept of fair-play. When they read something very meaningful, they quickly forget what the title was or what the article was about. They may have had trouble learning to read using phonics. Type II: *The Right Brain of Average (or Maturing Normal)* Person: The emotions and feelings are very important to them and their lives are based on this. Their thinking is jumping. They tend to see things only from their point of view and not see things as they are. They like group activities and emphasize people relationships. They tend to follow the majority and the fashions and the trend. They only care about the concrete --tough, feel, see. They like group activities. Need to look good in front of others and care about how others see them. Their thinking patter is how to fit in. These individuals desire to change things--people, the environment, and whatever is the way it is--into the way they think things should be. This is because they believe their personal problems will be reduced by changing things or because they have a tinge of narcissism. They are not able to automatically conform to rules and believe rules and laws of Nature (as in returning to sports following an injury) are for everyone else but them. Typically they are very rigid in demanding others following rules but will excuse themselves for not doing so because this was never their intension and sometimes not being aware they did anything wrong. By desiring for things to be concrete, the Right Brain oriented person wants to see, feel, or touch the real object; and to see words in context, to see how the formula works. Type III: Beginning of Right Brain Discipline: *The Skilled Right Brain Neophytes: They are aware of their emotions and feelings and are able to control it to a certain degree. They start to search for spirituality. They try not to be confined by social rule. They have a certain degree of intuition and spiritual development. They can go beyond the ego's control.* By progressing above the stage of Type II, some of the added components of an Afrocentric healthy mind are to process from whole to parts, holistically by constructively using both its Left and Right brain hemispheres, but always orchestrated by the Right Brain. As stated, the Right Brain is responsible for having a God communication; for compassion; and for finding a place for all of God's creations so that they remain connected and respected. Whereas the Left Brain processes in a linear, sequential, logical manner, the Right Brain processes intuitively. In writing, it is the left brain that pays attention to mechanics such as spelling, agreement, and punctuation. But the right side pays attention to coherence and meaning; that is, your right brain tells you it "feels" right. These Right Brain individuals take a more symbolic and associational approach to information processing; concern themselves with aspects of intrapersonal reality; have a rather acute awareness of the perception of their own physiological state and body image; are less involved in the negotiation of their needs with the demands and constraints of the objective, external world; and when they learn new physical skills and perform them, they often do not remember having done the activities before (see Temporal lobe). With respect to inner vision these individuals are Neophytes who struggle to hold onto the flesh, a belief that the material world is real. There results a fear of the loss of the physical body. It is this mental fear that dreads the decay of the flesh. Neophytes are mental Slaves because they remain ignorant of their own historical Africanity (King p37). Type IV: *The Highly Developed or Skilled Right Brain Intelligences*: They have a Third Eye, inner vision and can see reality behind facade, illusion, and delusions of phenomenon world. They have ability to live in a spiritual world and not confined by society. Because of the Brainstem's Amenta nerve tract interacting with the *Hippocampal Limbic Cortex*, emotions, especially at sacred or "awe inspiring" times, can be signals that may expand consciousness to higher levels of expression (King in Bynum p153; see Locus Coeruleus, the Black Dot). With respect to inner vision these individuals are in the stage of Intelligence where there is the development of knowing that the physical body is but a doorway through which the soul interacts with the Eye of Heru and the Eye of Illumination. Their inner vision is awakened and moves like a river through the soul and has communication with and experiences the existence of many other worlds. Otherwise, they are adept at intuition, synthesis, gestalt; in sensory recall; in thinking in sensory images about things hard to put into words; in recognizing and manipulating complex visual patterns; in discerning disguised or fragmented shapes; in the copying of designs; in the discrimination of shapes e.g. picking out a camouflaged object; in understanding geometric properties; in reading faces; in being oriented to musical ability; in global holistic processing; in reading and expressing emotions; in perceiving the "whole" before noticing the parts; in grasping the concept of the whole from just a part; in imagistic coding; and in the recognition of complicated visual patterns and objects. The higher-level visual- spatial orientation, integration, processing, and memory seems to have some aspect of Right Brain styles and thereby spatial coding allows many things to be taken in at once; necessitating a suspension of the analytic process and leaving the time domain to the Left Brain. Examples include the recognition of faces (parietal region); route finding (sense of direction); an ability to figure things out in a nonlinear mode of association and based on multiple converging lines of information (which helps them understand metaphors and slang which may baffle a Left Brain oriented person); detecting new shades of nuance and meaning to color the incoming data; being inferential; effective in perceiving similarities based on broad qualitative features (e.g. recognizing everything one is wearing at a glance).

Type V: Super-Right Brain People: *Specialized (Highly Disciplined) Right Brain*: They have high wisdom the highest level of Human Beings -- Saints who are Enlightened and One with God and can fly in the sky. Can go to the Buddha level above Reincarnation. They Reincarnate just to help people. In the Ancient Egyptian Mystery System these are the Creators or Sons of Light--i.e. those who have attained true spiritual consciousness. This is a stage of Inner Vision in the advanced state--a highly disciplined form of introspection whereby one sees the hidden light. Although many of these features are present in young children, when mature, the Right brain is the vehicle for expansiveness into higher and multiple planes of existence regarding things like Love, spiritually, compassion, peace, harmony, intuition, wholism, synthesis, nonaggression, and unity. Their specialized Right Brains are associated with understanding abstract concepts. In the Right brain's process of unification, it notes similarities between things and their relation to each other and to the whole. For unification to happen requires synthesizing bits and pieces of Sublime or near Sublime information leading to insights and understanding (see Thought Ladder). At this lofty level, opposition can likely be resolved because of the Right Brain's component of compassion, spirituality orientation, and lack of any basis for the concept of the necessity of one side having power over others (Ani, p. 106). The *God Module* -- so named because of its association with spirituality, prayer, and religious experiences (also in Parietal and Frontal lobes)--seems to be related to direct divine spiritual encounters (Bynum, p. 123). Unconfirmed studies suggests that the God Module consists of specialized brain cells in the Right Brain's Temporal lobe. The Temporal lobe nearby to the

Hippocampus regions process signals from the eyes -- combining basic colors and shades into recognizable objects. These regions are the "what" visual pathways because of their role in determining what we are seeing. These cells have the capacity to get to the abstract concept of things. Otherwise, the Right Brain controls many abstract reasoning skills cultivates good relationships; leads to introversion, hence spiritual (the internalization of consciousness, which is opposed by the extroverting tendencies of the Left Brain) and on to the understanding of Self and thus to knowledge of how to function out of both sides of the brain. With respect to inner vision these individuals possess an awakened spiritual consciousness, the Eye of Heru, and have the capacity for travel and communication with the celestial family of Ancestors and spirits in the higher realms of mind and consciousness (King in Bynum p158). It is associated with Déjà vu. Type VI--Out of Control Right Brain: Very Emotional. Live by Emotion and constantly have tantrum like Terrible Two's. can not reason with them. No concept of fair play. Observation would suggest that the Limbic (Emotional) Brain arises out of the Ancient Brain and, if true, this might explain how and why that when people become enraged they seem to lose control of their senses (discussed elsewhere, based upon Le Doux's work). The hippocampus helps the brain learn and form new memories designed to inform the individual of how to avoid dangerous situations and how to recognize what situations are likely to be relatively safe. When one is in a potentially threatening situation, one calls on the hippocampus to bring into awareness the most common sense things to do and not do. The primary role of the Amygdala is instituting the fear response as a normal and immediate burst to physical danger -- a reaction affecting both the brain and the body. Biologically, fear is expressed by adrenaline. In turn, adrenaline affects the Amygdala's fear circuit to release warning messages to other brain areas in order to immediately prepare the body for "fight or flight" actions and reactions. The entire process is orchestrated by the autonomic nervous system (ANS) in general and the sympathetic portion of the ANS in particular. Type VII--Never Developed Right Brain and therefore stay at little kids stage. Enslaved or Disease-type Right Brain: A diseased Right Brain shows any variety of disturbances in the "normal" conditions mentioned in Types I - VI. In summary, to give a rough idea of the Right Brain function it does understanding of metaphors; facial recognition; attending to visual space; spatial perception; ability to "find way"; musical sense; forms memory consolidation; and proper form in drawings. Also, it is intuitive, spontaneous, emotional, nonverbal, visual, artistic, holistic, playful, diffuse, symbolic, physical. It is also divergent, sensuous, imaginative, metaphoric, horizontal, continuous, concrete, impulsive, free, existential, multiple, timeless, holistic, tacit, subjective, simultaneous (Springer p186). See Déjà vu; Omnibus Brain

BRAIN'S LEFT HEMISPHERE: The Left Hemisphere is dominant in right-handed individuals and in the literature it carries the names of Cartesian, serial, linear, deductive, segregative, and "outer culture" thinking. On an earth world level of understanding normal Left brain thinking is an essential process within all cognitive systems, including common sense. Mental processing for the Left Hemisphere is generally believed to include (among others) those numerical computations of exact calculations (like a step-by-step calculator and not flowing), analytical, and concrete (e.g. math). *Rational* Left Brain Thinking processes information piece by piece on its way to solving mathematic or working out problems in a science experiment. Both are done in a linear, sequential, and logical manner. *Emotional* Left Brain Thinking is positive and inherently cheerful and dominates in the overall coloring of mood. In writing, it is the Left Brain that pays attention to mechanics such as spelling, agreement, and punctuation. The Left Brain is the disciplinarian of the Right Brain's impulsive actions, Language skills, Skilled movement, and Analytical time sequence processing. It dominates in programming complex sequences of movement and in some aspects of awareness of ones own body. There are various planes of existence of Left Brain development. At the bottom is ordinary Left Brain thinking; next up is the Skilled; then the highly Skilled; then the Super-human Skilled. *Type I -- Childhood's*

Left Brain 5 to youth): There is reasoning and putting things together and spelling make sentence or paragraph. Understand meanings of words that are straight forward. Balance relationship with outside world. The Left Brain starts rising into significance around ages 5 to 7 and goes on to be mainly responsible for the Rational and Critical thinking that creates, enhances, or maintains equilibrium between the individual and the outside world. It engages in integrating language functions (parietal region); generally responds to the literal meaning of the words it hears and will not even notice the meaning of the inflection. Whereas the right hemisphere can express itself non-verbally by selecting the matching stimulus, the Left Brain expresses itself by verbally describing a stimulus. The left hemisphere deals with word choice, rules of grammar, and the meaning of words. In a practical situation, there will always be situations of conflict -- between strangers, between friends, between strangers and friends. To go with ones Left Brain in trying to solve such situations means one will be noting the differences between the involved parties, separating whole realities into parts. However, the Left Brain and the lower part of the spirit (the Sahu) are incapable of seeing beneath the surface (lacking in understanding) of things (Amen, Afrocentric Guide p28). *Type II -- Average Adults: Maturing Left Brains*: The learn grammar, vocabulary, linear reasoning. And comprehensible speech. Can see things as they are and adjust to environment change. Make a rule to follow. Concrete analysis. See difference between parts without making connections. Hard to go into abstract thinking. Unable to see common ground under the surface. Verbal Left Brain Thinking processes thoughts and ideas with word speech. The ability to form words seems to lie primarily in fashioning grammar, vocabulary, and the literal aspects of language. For most people the Left Brain is specialized for linguistic processing and for logical, descriptive analysis; in interpretation of the syntactic (grammatical), semantic (informational), and literal qualities of communication—i.e. one can understand both the grammar and content of this paragraph and allows one to convey this information to others, perhaps using a different form of expression (e.g. colloquial speech) while retaining the basic meaning and relating accurately to what has gone before. Also, one can make sense of this paragraph by analyzing the sequence of information and determining that it follows some orderly, purposeful course to a destination by way of a coherent meaning. Although many academic pursuits deal with symbols-such as letters, words, and mathematical notations--the Left Brain has no trouble processing symbols and, in fact, they tend to be comfortable with linguistic and mathematical endeavors while memorizing vocabulary words or math formulas. These individuals deal with things the way they are--i.e. with the reality they know to be. When Left Brain students are affected by the environment they usually adjust to it, starting by learning the rules and following them. In fact, if there are no rules for situations, they will probably make up rules to follow! Left brain students know the consequences of not turning in papers on time or of failing a test. *Type III -- Mature Left Brain: Step by step abstract thinking and analysis. Good at separate the complicated body into pieces to study. Put different parts of understanding to make a conclusion. Can see patterns in concrete and abstract world. Good at making comparisons, dividing, categorizing, can think like a high speed calculator with complex info put in order. Like to follow rules and have clear goals and complete things according to the plan. But they do not put much energy on morals or spirituality. Normal Adult Left Brains*: Linear (in a line) thinking is a process of thought following known cycles or step-by-step progression where a response to a step must be elicited before another step is taken--and it goes from beginning to end. The Left Brain processes information in a linear manner by processing things from part to whole; by taking pieces, lining them up, and arranging them in a straight forward orderly progression; and by drawing conclusions. It is segregative and analytic--i.e. unable to keep from separating things that belong together--e.g. women from men; food from healing; governors from governed; management from labor; producers from consumers; the races. It engages in comparisons; estimates; classifications; in time consciousness (e.g. an urge to arrive on time); in seeing outer interaction--the exchanges of affection, sensual pleasures, the sharing of responsibilities. Normal Left Brain thinking is done in a step-by-step manner—like a calculator—rapid, sequentially, and cumulatively manipulate precise numerical quantities and relationships; It sees things as "all-or-none" (instead of shades in between); perceives differences and operates most effectively within a consecutive, as opposed to a simultaneous, time frame. It is important in handling memory processes in general; in processing information based on reality; in focusing on rules and regulations; in being goal-oriented; in directing fact retrieval; in interpreting experiences in concrete materialistic terms. During the process of pursuing outcomes there is a strong sense of completion and a desire to do things right but in a non-spiritual manner. It is good at handling and remembering discrete, exact details and precise relationships over time. Since its thinking is dominated by syllogistic Cartesian logic it is unable to see the whole and thus incapable of establishing the truth of a logical premise. This eventually leads to the inability to clearly distinguish right from wrong. It is unable to abstract to the defining essence of the relationship which is selflessness and all that is implied by it (e.g. one cannot be selfless and vent anger). Social Left Brain Thinking is extroversion and in relating to people the result is to elevate friends into leadership positions. *Type IV--Skilled Left Brains Superb in logical thinking. Can handle concrete or abstract concepts, category, deduction, induction, definition, encyclopedia, put chaos into order. Skilled Left Brains: Sequential* (that which follows) designates a following in space, time, or thought and suggests that the things brought together are done so according to some logical system.--i.e. in some particular order or according to a plan in a manner in which things follow each other. Sequential Left Brain Thinking is like putting things in chronological order or in going from first to last; or in making a list or fashioning a master schedule or doing daily planning. One completes tasks in order and takes pleasure in checking them off when they are accomplished. Spelling involves sequencing and if one is Left-Brained, one is probability a good speller. The left brain is also at work in the linear and sequential processing of math and in following directions. Arithmetic is often associated with the Left Brain sequential processing and yet there is good evidence that mathematically gifted children tend to be left handed implying a Right-Brain dominance. This could reflect a difference between early mathematics which is often a repetitive rote learning, and more advanced mathematics which often requires high levels of visual-spatial reasoning and abstract thinking. *Type V -- Highly Skilled Left Brains: Harmoniously put Right and Left brain together rational and intuition and spiritual. Real genius who create what has never happened before. Explain the highly abstract e.g. music.* Although Words and logic are merely meaningful symbols of reality, they grasp the value of a good idea and works out the problems it presents. Meanings point to certain thing(s), as is typical of words. *Symbolic* Left Brain Thinking, common in many academic pursuits, processes symbols as pictures; likes to use letters, words and mathematical symbols; and tends to be comfortable with linguistic and mathematical endeavors. Left-brained students will probably just memorize vocabulary words or math formulas. Here there is the Genius stage where both the Left Brain "masculine" logical consciousness and the Right Brain "feminine" emotional consciousness produce a unified consciousness with an expansion and elevation of passion, logic, elevated neurogenesis of the Amenta nerve tract, and creativity (King in Bynum p182). *Type VI -- Super Left brain can calculate Super-human Left Brain thinking:* Ancient Dohgon (Dogon) of Africa, who trace their historical and genetic lineage to pre-dynastic Egypt (Bynum p108), are noted for hearing pure sound (as opposed to sound caused by vibrations). To do this they learned to perfect their Left brain "inner ear"-- the ear equivalent to an inner eye. As a result, they made astrological discoveries than have been verified only in the last fifty years. Professor Momoh-Sellu Sua Laye of The Dohgon University of Thought states that they were able to detect Pure Waves (different from vibratory waves which are subject to distortion) coming in from the Dark Universe, which they called the Cosmogonic Universe. An inner sound in the Left brain allowed them to use "Black Sight" of sonic mapping to see hidden stars that have only recently been proven by Western scientist. Perhaps this process began by means of Meditation which causes a shift of brain activity to the Left Brain. *Type VII -- Hitler Out of Control Left Brain Thinking*: Individuals in this group are "locked into their Left Brain thinking mode. Its associated flexibility in thought, action and ability to adapt to various life situations leads to Brute Brain and paranoid tendencies including fear. According to the psychiatrist Richard King (Bynum p133) the paradigm of White Supremacy/racism was born from a very great fear of melanin Blackness that pervades the Cosmos and of a melanin death/sleep. It represents a failure of growing up--a failure to evolve from a neophytic, strictly logical Left brain stage of consciousness to the second stage, a stage of intelligence with inner vision and dual cortical hemispheric integration. As a result, such individuals are incapable of ever being aware of the third stage of sons/daughters of light. Instead, what occurs is Left Brain Partnering with the Brute Brain--out of which spring modes of thinking patterns dominated by confrontation; lack of compassion and no spirituality; an intense desire to control; and the greedy acquisition of power. Such patterns make it impossible to understand or even see the whole related to Love, peace, and harmony. *In summary*, the Left Brain is heavily involved in speech; reading; writing; verbal memory consolidation; abstract categorizing; musical ability; fine manual sequences; seeing more than one thing at a time; left-right discrimination; detail in drawings. It is also positive, analytical, convergent, deductive, vertical, discrete, abstract, realistic, directed, differential, historical, explicit, objective, successive, intellectual, linear, explicit, sequential, verbal, concrete, rational, active, goal-oriented, and about intellect (Wonder p18; Springer p186).

BRAIN--RIGHT/LEFT BRAIN TEAMWORK: Left Brain handles information from the senses (*sight, hearing, smelling, touch, taste, meaning*); and Right Brain, handling the *emotional* (human energy package and will) and *spiritual* data, and helps fashion imagination and creativity with the Left Brain's arrangements and combinations so that they work as a "Check and Balance." The Right Brain takes it beyond to connect human consciousness with God's Consciousness.

BRAINWASHING BY EUROPEAN SLAVERS: Certainly mind control began at the "Fishnet Moment. Such constrains and restraints on victims' minds by enslavers was done by intention (so as to be in control), by ignorance, and/or by sheer evilness. Some Information imparted concerned serious business; some, the arrogant projection of Brutes' inner mental turmoil; and some, a means of entertainment. Since words are essential for thinking, for sharpening intellect, and for self-expression, after arriving in the Americas, slave owners limited the vocabulary of the Enslaved to perhaps a hundred or so words. The purpose of this "*Word Deprivation*" + not allowing the Enslaved to read, write, or count, was to maintain control over the Enslaved by keeping them mentally constrained. Furthermore, the captors' *selected and "channeled" the language of the Enslaved into restraints by determining the names for things; by determining the meanings and values of those things; and by determining the rules shaping and influencing how the Enslaved related to those things.* Being victims of "*Word Channeling*" and "*Word deprivation*" began a continuous episode of "*brain-washing*" (i.e. coercive persuasion or re-socialization). The deliberate aim of ongoing "brain-washing" was to fashion within the psyche of the Enslaved self-destructive restrained and constrained patterns of thinking and behaving that would be forever self-perpetuating. Both "Constraint" and "Restraint" were used by the captors for the purpose of making "Ideal" Slaves (total dedication to the captor). Examples of restraining the Enslaved included confining them to the plantation and enforcing Slave Codes as a means of holding them back from engaging in the actions of free persons. Reinforcing the bounding associated with *constraining* (draw tight, squeeze or press together) and *restraining* (bend back to keep under control through various hindrances) victims' minds is done to generate affliction, agony, anguish, torment, Grief (e.g. from loss, misfortune, or deep disappointment), and torture for purpose of hindering any thoughts of rebelling, for compelling an "Ideal Slave" way of life, and for coercing victims to worship them.

For most Slave children, the effects of the development of "compression" type mind enslaving patterns led to self-constraint that contributed to the slowing, stopping, and/or preventing of the development of Self-Esteem "props." Meanwhile, the captors' *Fetters* (e.g. arrogance, pride, greed, hatred, anger, lust, fear, lies, envy) stirred up disharmony among the exhausted Enslaved so that they would no longer be sure of anything. Such overwhelming confusion, with its Uncertainty, fashioned so much fear and difficulty as to cause Illusions and Delusions resulting in Despair--a mindset easing the most afflicted into looking for guidance. Meanwhile, the slave owners and White preachers took over "guiding" the Enslaved down a path leading away from being divine images of God. Numerous other "Real Self" and "Environmental Self" constraining methods were outlined in the Slave Codes and in the presumed 1712 speeches of Willie Lynch to fellow White slave owners. The enslavement Effects on victims is always of a profound nature which causes an infinite variety of mindset changes. For example some "lean" off the Truth-Track for Live Living and with the Effect being that of chronic nagging doubts; being Confused; losing ones way; entering dead-ends and "giving up". Some are put on a non-Truth-Track and always head away from the Spiritual Elements. Some convert to having "Inside-Out" minds whereby they reverse their survival, self-protection, and self-preservation and thereby enter the Indifference-Hate-Evil-Sadism (IHES) complex. They exhibited rage and aggression towards one another as a result of their fear of confronting their oppressors who both beat the "Spirit" (courage) out of their Ancestors and, simultaneously, the Enslaved Ancestors had to bond with the oppressors so as to be feed what it took to survive—the *Evil Savior Syndrome*. Regardless of the type of mindset, victims are always left with the invariable Consequences of Extreme Despair (i.e. hopeless hopelessness)--being in terrible poverty and with no concept of how to get out—and feeling so insecure, shamed, unimportant, powerless, and self-absorbed as to take every opportunity to "Escape" by addictions to anything that is self-defeating. They put up mental barriers around each of the "Raw Nerves" so as to hide the severe Spiritual Pains from themselves while putting up a "Front" to act like everything is "okay." This means their illiteracy stems, not from shunning reading and writing, but from being unable to unlearn the effects of their brainwashing in slavery and ongoing in the present. As a result, many simply "gave up" on who they were as individuals, including their own system of values, and drifted from day to day. The rest were forced to replace most of their values with those dictated by their captors. The transmitted patterns of "under-reactions" have led Blacks to "compensate" in a variety of ways, with the result that internal stress is increased and spontaneous expression is inhibited. And these remain controlled! Meanwhile, the slave owners drilled into the minds of the Enslaved four things of great importance. First, were Aryan European Bible examples, like White preachers saying evilness is a movement away from Europeans' virtues (and note these are not the same as the African Bible virtues for they carry one away from "Knowing" God and the Spiritual Elements). Within that context, a repetitious message imparted into the Enslaved was that if they did not believe what Whites said and did not work as hard as they could to make Whites rich, this was a sin against them and therefore a sin against God. Sinfulness meant believing in African Religions and therefore being under influence of the devil -- again the insertion of Doubt into "Knowing" about God and again instilling uncertainty of having done the Right things as part of African Tradition and within themselves. Second, to ignore the obvious inconsistencies in the religion they were being told to have Faith/Belief/Trust in; ignore the fact of them being enslaved and inhumanely treated; and ignore the fact that the European captors did not live the life they preached to be right. Third was to have Faith/Belief/Trust in whatever they were told to believe. Fourth, the Enslaved were to never question what European religious leaders told them, particularly not question what they said God told them to say. To ask how (e.g. what language) or under what circumstances God told things to the White man or why God did not talk with the Enslaved or why God would take the White man's side or why God was pictured as a White man with a long beard were grounds for severe punishment.

No doubt, some of the Enslaved knew in Africa those popularly known today as "crazy" who had done evil things in the name of God. Perhaps these Enslaved became confused as to how to distinguish those "crazy" people from the Europeans claiming they had been told by God to write the Bible and say it was the Word of God. Overtime, all of this evilness in the religious messages of Europeans took its toll -- an effect speeded along by the Enslaved increasingly believing they had been abandoned by their Ancestors and by God -- a belief necessitating generating their own beliefs about religion and God and combining them with the European Bible. Each of these beliefs set the atmosphere for not knowing anything and thus put the Enslaved in the mood to have religious beliefs. At the same time, in struggling to maintain mental sanity many went into Despair and Desperation. Both caused them to make peace with doom and not care what happened to them. Such made them ripe for accepting much European propaganda in spite of its obvious wickedness.

BRAND: to mark into a "sign" or "trademark"—as in branding cattle with a hot iron—to designate, in merchandizing oneself, as "I am the greatest!" in front of the cameras.

BREATH: an emanation "flowing out from" them—i.e. the "Breath" proceeds from any substance (e.g. individual, animal, vegetable, and mineral substances) because all Cosmic entities are infused with an animating spirit (the reason why all things are in motion, as stated in laws of physics). See Aura

"BROAD-STROKE" THINKING: an Umbrella idiom, embraces meanings of contrary (positive/negative) opposites. Further complications are from assigned connotations on different Cosmic planes—and any given concept is unique and operates under its own rules. Such a complexity accounts for it not being mentioned in hundreds of books (e.g. Oxford English Dictionary) I researched. On the positive scale, Broad-Strokes' Chinese Calligraphy's origin--an offshoot of Ancient Egyptians' hieroglyphic symbolism--is used to carry Sublime artistic and good taste whereby its decorative assessments involve *Metaphysical aphophasic (allusional) mental operations*. On a Physical World plane it refers to inclusiveness. Otherwise, Broad-Stroke's origin cannot be pin-pointed to time or place. Yet, it is in the family with "*Broad-Brush*" (sweeping general in scope, without giving details; crude, rough); "*Broad-Scale*" (shotgun); "*Broad-Gauge*" (concerned with wide policy rather than detail); and "*Tarred with the same brush*"—an expression of sheep farming where animal's sores were treated by the same brush sufficing to tar over all of them. Simultaneously, the brush was used to daub a special mark of ownership upon every fleece so that each sheep was identified as being a member of the same flock. In the early 1800s it was expanded to include uncomplimentary remarks pertaining to those humans having the same faults and bad qualities. "*Broad-Stroke*" is used here for an allusion of painting in the sense of making wide marks with a wide stroke by those habitually characterizing people, places, or things with such a huge brush as to whitewash distinctions among them. *Allusions* are extremely quick ways of expressing ones emotions as well as creating in listeners shades of those same emotions--but only when the in-group listeners are already familiar with the setting. Inherently, Allusions are about bias. See Patterned Thinking

"BRUTE" MINDSETS: Europeans are historically a warring people and, like children, project what they do onto on others. Projection is the turning a personal inferiority in morals, intelligence, or the like into a perceived moral, intellectual, or otherwise deficiency in someone else)--the hurling something "ugly" within ones own character onto a victim (a scapegoat) in order to make it seem as if it is the victim who has that "ugly" trait. For example, when the ancient Greeks encountered a foreign human language they could not understand, they said it sounded like the 'babbled' utterances of "no thought" out of the mouths of animals. Hence, they labeled these European foreigners as barbarians (Greek, barbarous, babble--so named from the Barbary Coast in northwest Africa). To the Greeks and their ancient Roman students the "Barbarians" were highly uncivilized and worse than beasts because they were wild, cruel, filthy, and inhuman in actions. Obviously, they, as is typical of Europeans today, failed to look at themselves and their ancestors. A spotlighted example was the Aryans of northern Europe who left a trail of dead people, dead animals, and destruction of anything they did not want--"for no reason." Later, the aspect of falsely assuming beasts lacked reasoning or even thinking abilities was expanded to characterize these dull, irrational, unreasonable, and unintelligent European barbarians—ideas incorporated into the C15 Latin word brutus ('stupid,' without speech). It was with this meaning of a human being having the quality of some non-human animal like wildness, viciousness, and stupidity—stressing degradation and extreme inhumanity--that 'Brute' reached English via French. The connotation of 'cruelty' in relation to "brute" began to appear in C17 in relation to how all Europeans having anything to do with the African American slave trade inhumanely treated Amerindians and the African American Slaves--and using religion as a deceptive excuse and justification of self-righteousness: "The White man's burden." Its sense applied to harmful, harsh, or destructive acts that inflict pain and suffering on others as well as to the Brutes' inhumane temperaments and attitudes lacking in sensitivity or compassion. Some estimate they have killed 740 million Black People and 100 million Amerindians. Back then and now, 'Brute,' as an adjective, means inhuman, irrational, and cruel. *"Brute" designates evil people doing evil things*--out of which have branched several words and concepts. As used here, the word "Brute" or "Brute Brain" encompasses all of the manifestations of a human being's Lower Self Nature (e.g. selfishness, arrogance, pride, greed, hatred, anger, lust)--or "Dark Side" or Sadistic tendencies or Evilness. The result is the establishment of evil atmospheres and evil forces in which all of the Enslaved had to operate. European Brutes are the most terrible people who have ever lived. *Transitional Brutes* are Brute Imitators who, in between brute actions, have a guilty conscious for the evil things they have done. They pay money to make amends. What Africans did not understand as they were being "depowered" by European brutes and what most Black Americans have never fully appreciated is that Brutes are not good people simply having many bad days. There is no such thing as them "waking up" and seeing the spiritual light. They are the way they are because of their philosophy of life. This causes them to consider themselves as "little gods" who are not accountable to any higher authority--and that includes God! *They are never going to change and it makes no sense to "turn the other cheek."* But it is foolish to fight them because fighting, destroying, and killing are what they do best. The Gun is their best and only friend. These savage people think differently, like the God Set who Ancient Africans represented as the worse but realistic part of human nature. They know nothing else but to dominate others and take what they have. Enslaved Africans dealt with them by knowing them thoroughly and then cleverly deceiving them.

BRUTE PRACTICES: Typical Brute practices are to be judgmental and tell others: "Do what I say, not as I do." This starts the generation of Confusion and Doubt. This is what religions teach when they do not impart the Knowledge for their congregation to fashion their own way to their desired destiny. In effect, such concepts imply the Spiritual God is their competition. They are left with having to cling to faith and beliefs in the presented dogmas and propaganda. It is these very Uncertainties which Brutes use as powerful tools to control people for self-interest purposes. Whereas one category of Competition leads to attacking others as a "show of force," another is to avoid competition. A European specialty has been to practically eliminate the world's access to African Spiritual Literature by means of deliberate destruction; terrible misinterpretations; rewriting history; plagiarizing claiming the majority and assigning the rest to non-African cultures; and so forth. Having no interest in being loved—perhaps having no idea what love is--they strive to be feared, most often in the form of implied power (meaning the problems his fellow Europeans can do) as an act to decrease the competition and to minimize their losses to fellow competitors. See Competition

BULLIES—SUPERNATURAL: "Bully" (1500, Dutch, 'sweetheart') originally meant "a fine, splendid fellow" (Shakespeare's Midsummer Night's Dream). But then it transformed into "swashbuckler" (gallant, boon companion); "hired tough" to do violence; "Pimp" who lives on the earnings of a prostitute (American

Revolution); and today, an "overbearing ruffian." All Bullies possess an Indifference/Hate/Evil/Sadism (IHES) mindset. *Type I* are the rich and powerful socialized into connecting with like-kind Networks, enabling them indulge in varied Kill/Take/Destroy/Dominate/Oppress/Control (KTDDOC) practices. Insecurities reign in competing against each other. *Type II*--though socialized to play roles of "Superiority" over others, become increasingly insecure with each challenge. *Type III,* developing sometime after birth an Inferiority Complex, desperately engage in ranging attempts to acquire a Superiority Complex—i.e. donning a mask of self-confidence and greatness with a reality of arrogance and aggression, so as to conceal a sense of deep inferiority and self-hate. Thus they, and Type II, for the sake of their own Bad self-image must degrade scapegoats. Both create fantasies about themselves and their Scapegoats using the motto: "How great we are, how bad they are". Type I does the same evils deeds for everybody not rich and powerful. All types are Selfhood-Unknown—meaning they are *disconnected from their birth gift of Spiritual Elements*—suppliers of ones Private Selfhood *"5Ss"*—i.e. Safety, Security, Sureness/Self-Confidence, Strength, and Stability. On one side of a Scale of Destruction is their Disconnections. They include discontinuity within ones "ME"; separation from their pre-birth "ME/WE" interrelationships; losing intimate contact with significant others; and lacking any concept of others' human existence. On the opposite Scale side are happenings from being *Selfhood Splintered.*

This means half of ones Selfhood becomes *Self-Absorbed* (viewing everything within ones world in relationship to oneself in a "me, me, me" manner) and the other half following dictates of External World influences and greedy pursuits of what is deemed to be "Scarce Desirable" Material things.

Type III, not feeling worthy or believing "I'm not good enough," may beam their disaster bully effects in a host of directions and involving a host of destruction of things. Most are "Street" type troublemakers—Evil humans who live by the "Law of Force", as in doing beatings, rapes, and killings. Type II males are likely to believe they have such flawed "man-hoods" as to make them grossly incompetent. By being part of a Evil humans Network cult, they demonstrate kakistocracy (defecating) type authority—i.e. rule by terrible self-made social laws—laws allowing lying, cheating, stealing, gossiping, and any form of KTDDOC as the norm. Type I are Shrewd in their greedy pursuits of riches and power. *Shrewd'*s etymology began as an ingredient of "Evil"—originally an Old English word meaning "uppity"--then "Bad"--then extreme moral wickedness. In 1280 AD, "Shrewd" signified evil, malicious, and dangerous before its euphemistic sense changed in 1520 to astute and cunning--and then to cleverness, scheming, and deception. *Euphemisms* are socially accepted indirect expressions substituting for harsh meanings contained in bad thoughts. To deal with being Self-Unknown, all engage in *Phantasmagoria*—i.e. *"Make-Believe"* displays, *featuring seeing reality in ways other than they are* regarding themselves and those whom they most envy. After acquiring the GUN from the Arabs in 1304 and developing it over the next 150 years, their top selected "enemy" was Black People because of historical envying their 200,000 years of world-shaping, world-changing, and world-maintenance achievements--achievements in who they are and in what they do. Such was above Bullies to achieve.

Extreme Envy is the beginning of hell on earth. It deals with ones Left Brain calculating emotional reasoning concerning comparisons related "for me or against me" Desires, and that is like being in an infinite abyss. This comes from envy always spotlighting ones consciousness of being inferior. Envy is so much about cowardice, inadequacy, and incompetency as for those owning it vigorously deny having it. Just as iron is eaten away by rust, so are the envious consumed by their own passions—so overwhelming/energy draining as to prevent them from cultivating their Rational minds. This leaves them with no choice but to do Non-Rational thinking—that which makes no sense. jabaileymd.com

BULLIES' ENVY DISPLAYS: Humans are born in intimate contact with their Inner "ME/WE" Spiritual World and to cultivate this guarantees having a truly "Good Life". Yet most, some time after birth, become disenchanted with themselves and choose intimate involvement in others' lives. By also adopting the External World's Material and non-Spiritual valuations put on Creatures and Things means never seeing either as they really are. Although at all humans' core is the Spiritual need for Unconditional Love, the afflicted search everywhere besides its Source to find it. *Type A people* follow their "*strong personality*" path—with its intense desires and vigorous preferences for indulging their Lower (Animalistic) Selves. Clamoring for "Make-Believe" treasures as their top priority leads them to try "Winning by any means necessary". Thus, they grow into a "numb, concreted" heart. But a law of Emotions says *to "numb" out one emotion is to "numb" out all*. The result is Spiritual Pain, generating the worst experiences humans can have. That can only display as a "*Not Caring*" attitude about anything except "me, me, me" + the urge to join a cult. They then stereotype cult members as "superior" and the rest as "inferiors," needing to be controlled. They hate seeing any degree of greatness produced by their self-declared "inferiors"—for besides *never having contributed anything to benefit any "ME/WE" thing, they are mentally incapable of doing so. Type B people,* being Non-Rational thinkers, react passively--"going along to get along" by being meek, humble, timid, and accepting things as they are. They are easily persuaded, cautious, and Slave-like submissive to the cult and relying on their leaders to tell them how to think, feel, say, and do whatever. Some momentary power comes from bullying the most defenseless "outsider group". Bullies shower Hate in their most envied "faceless" group. This is a "Weak" People's Crutch" to aid wallowing in the mire of facade "superiority." Yet, this addiction takes more and more applied inhumanities for them to get less and less of a momentary expansion of their own false spirits over their profoundly envied and so-called "inferior" Victims. The crushing realization of their own inferiority every time their feigned "Inferiors" are given voices of praise drives them to work hard with Type A and B people to ensure such voices of praise are never repeated. "Insurance" is for all cult members to try to convince themselves, their Victims, and others about: "how great they are and how bad the "Inferiors" are." By being Non-Rational thinkers—i.e. thinking unable to follow a Mathematical Pattern and thus make no sense—means they cannot solve any significant problems on their own. Hence, they try to salvage some parts of a meaningful self-image by generating overwhelming and constant problems for Victims. Their point is to slow the speed of their "*Envy eating their own hearts.*" Where there is Envy, there is Malice—and both are stronger than Greed. That Envy and Hatred gather emotional energy strength from each other by interdependently engaging their powers on the same Thing. So, of course, an all-out-effort is made to "keep down" Victims inside all types of poverty and do nothing contributory to their rising or even tiny bits of betterment. This is because when Bullies do not occupy the whole center of attention—falsely assuming their own well-being might be advanced by any benefits given to Victims--they feel themselves excluded. Such Envy is never able to see good/bad things in themselves as they really are but only in their relation to them. For example, "if you Inferior people have, then I, a Superior, don't and can't have that." Even success does not soften Bullies hearts, for Supernaturals never get enough of whatever they Desire—and never enjoy the unfair benefits they do have. Moderate Type A Bullies say insulting things about their Victims while all Type B Bullies speak depreciatively (disapproval, critical) + deprecating (belittle, deplore) about envied "Inferiors." Neither Type A or B envy the rich and powerful at the top of their cult but they do envy those fellow cult status members who are more successful. Both Type A and B are enraged—complete with evil passions--at undeniable Victim excellence—"sour-grapes" broadcasting a bad end for these "Super-humans". *Superseding a desire for their own well-being is for Bullies to ensure another's misery.* Admission is a self-insult by confessing their own inferiority--making Type A look weak and Type B look like a "nothing human" and thus Shameful. Hence, Bullies never confess anything and, instead, look for others to Blame/find fault/'put down'.

BULLIES CLASSIFYING SUPERNATURAL: The Supernatural cult and their Victims world-wide are never told the truth because that would destroy all they are about. A way of Mind Control is the presentation of confusing and conflicting information about anything significant. Once the public is entangled in this type of Non-Reasoning thinking, their minds are then shaped into *Imaginative appearance of the false being real; repeating it so loud and long as to cause Superficial thinkers to believe it is real and right; and thereafter using the Mass and Social Media to guide each such belief into becoming ones standard, filter, and guide for whatever requires assessment. Thus, the wrong becomes the "normal." This, a most powerful way to control the minds of Believers, is the essence of the meaning of "what SEEMS right".* Truth seekers have no choice but to resort to moral and knowledgable objective historians who have access to realistic knowledge for use in beginning ones own research. Meanwhile, they ought to avoid those unable to understand the Truth or will not expose them to sources of the Truth. Out of the false Believer cult comes different types of Bullies. *Mild Bullies* are cowards who abuses his strength by ill-treating the Weak. When there has been no harshness exchanged between the involved but they still engage in sniper activities while periodically being nice, that is one manifestation of Envy. This is a misplaced form of admiration. *Slight Bullies* are so unhappy with themselves as to apply the "misery loves company" practice of trying to impair others—hating, envying, and sabotaging Victims who block their light. Nor are they softened by their own success, for this pleasure is not as great as their distress as those they envy. Thus, for the sake of their own Bad self-image, they must: (1) degrade scapegoats; (2) play the role of being loudly arrogant, bluff, swagger, bluster, and coercive by threats. (3) maintain stirred up conflicts as a show of power; (4) continually disturb and subtly destroy scapegoats; (5) join with cult members to achieve a sense of "Winning" by any means necessary so as to reinforce their façade sense of being "superior".

Moderate Bullies, whether having unfair advantages or not, convey the impression of possessing what it takes to put Victims at unfair disadvantages so as to "undo," "take down," and keep down their feigned enemies. Their "bottom-line" means of gaining and maintaining control over Black People is by the GUN + an eagerness to kill + the actuality of killing (e.g. the "Killer" police).They are always quarrelsome, overbearing, badgers, who intimidate—more in a group in attacking the alone nonconformists, the smaller, or the comparatively weaker. All of this is done to conceal their lack of Higher Mind Intelligence. They are ignorant of the fact that they are not intelligent for several reasons. One reason for this reality is that humans Intelligence cannot occur in those who keep a foot forever on the throats of their scapegoats. Second, Warrior mindsets falsely believe they must follow their Acquired Emotions since non-rational thinking validates and justifies their reactions. Delusional Fears, Violence, Aversion, Adversion, Cruelty, Meanness, Rudeness, disguised Cowardice, Cunning, Shrewdness, Intemperance, Arrogance, Vanity, Deceit, Revenge, Jealousy, Malice, and Injustice.

Extreme Bullies are like irritated rattlesnakes in that they may or may not make violent "rattling" threats before Kill/Take/Destroy/Dominate/Oppress/Control (KTDDOC) types of strikes. All are dangerous because their harrassing of those they deem to be "inferiors" with realities overwhelming devastation. Their competition is with each other--meaning they have a Satanists standard to match—and the way this "Game" is played is to see who can be the richest, have the most power, be above the rules of society, and get the most people to serve them, regardless of how those people are treated. They implement Mind Control all who are vulnerable to them. One way of control is by rewarding Oreos to direct the desperately struggling Black People deeper into the status quo and simply "Make Do" as a way of life. A second to get all below them on the Social Ladder to become addicted to Individualized "Excitement" events and gadgets. In that way, addicts fail to learn to do any but Superficial thinking and which is done in Patterns laid out by the cult leaders. These Technology Trinkets effectively break up socializing, destroy addicts' brain cells, keep the gullible in the "here and now," and stamp out Manners. The advantage for leaders making "Excitement" addicts is that ensures maintaining stupidity--i.e. having eyes and cannot see--in the World Crowd. See Supernatural Bullies

C

CADUCEUS-AFRICAN: *African Caduceus* symbolized the three main channels of Life Force energy of the Serpent Power (Ashby, Book of Dead p124, 128)--the positive solar and negative lunar (the opposites of creation) from the external + the internal life forces which sustain the human body. If it operates in its higher energy-consciousness centers, one will have access to Cosmic Consciousness, Peace or bliss in ordinary human life. If its power were to be harnessed and transformed into spirit it would bring about ones spiritual evolution by "awakening" one to the deeper spiritual life existing in the unconscious depths of ones experience. Such is to "re-member"—i.e. put back together the consciousness of finite material aspect of ones life with the infinite collective and luminous life of the great Spiritual Being. The Serpent in the Ancient African Bible represents not evil—as in the European Bible, but instead the life force. Such is illustrated in the original medical caduceus of Africans.

CALL & RESPONSE: Response is of Ancient African origin was Griots (story-tellers) participatory audience communication—i.e. "*Call and the Response*"--characterized by the Griot sending out a "call" and the audience acknowledging the message. The audience responded while the speaker spoke--and not afterward--so as to make a fluid harmonious tone of participatory communication.

CALLING IN LIFE: a symbol of the admonition of the Conscience—a human's Divine Consciousness has that human's Conscience as its Character—a Character that is Ma'at oriented. A "*Calling*" possesses a Pattern inside ones Conscience having a virtual image on the outside and Matrix Disposition on the inside. The Virtual Image is ones Talent used within the context of ones Genius and contains the "What and Why" aspects for ones Talent. The Disposition includes whose Inclination is to urge that human's Private Selfhood to follow the Intention of its Genius and Talent Theme. Whereas the Cosmic Organism's Calling is to populate the Cosmic planes of existence, the Calling of a human's Genius with a Talent is to manifest "ME/WE" benefits of the Spiritual Elements. As a display of Human Nature, ones "Calling" in life has nothing to do with making money or other material world things. Instead, the high vibration rate of ones Spiritual Calling, by being an expression of that human's Spiritual Elements dominant Trait, is like a radar seeking its counterpart in the External World. Ones calling is always about what one has the talent to do; is never about what one cannot do if one has the will to do so; and is always about helping those who need help the most. It can be about making things better on the positive of the Thinker's Scale or making things less bad or at least keep things from getting worse. One originally heard this calling as a little child when one was naturally operating out of ones Real Self. Without putting forth any effort, one can hear ones Calling again -- in the form of vibrations and not words -- by clearing away all Acquired Emotional and Informational "junk" surrounding ones Real Self which form "Clouds" over ones "Soul Sunshine." A reason ones Calling never goes away is that it is part of ones Conscience—both being in the flow of Instincts. Instincts are a transition between the Will of God and ones Mind—and necessarily implying its operations are largely below the field of Consciousness. By contrast, the "*Habit Mind*" contains only what has been placed in the mind by acquired experiences, habits, and observation—and thereby becomes *Conditioned Reflexes*. This means the habit has been so often repeated as for the mind, by knowing it so well, as to carry it below the field of Consciousness and become "*Second Nature*," akin to Instinct. Today, a profession is considered an occupation requiring considerable specialized study and training in order to provide a special service. Some people stumble on these. Some have a spotlight shined on what they need to do and that is a Calling ("summons to a way of life"). The reason is that ones calling and the work involved in achieving it are connected to ones spirit and thus it flows out of that human without effort. When one is engaged in it one loses tract of time and one feels an urge to keep doing it without getting tire of it. One is not influenced by those who say that it cannot be done or it is not worth doing. One would rather work on it that to "take a break" or "party." By contrast, when one has to be pushed to do a job or desires to take short cuts or wants to quit early one can be sure that this is not ones calling. Neither is it when one follows the crowd and desires what everyone else wants as, for example, greedily pursuing money and possession. Some slowly figure out what they are here to do after a great deal of trial and error. This is ones mission—i.e. what one believes to be ones purpose in life. Nothing is more important for consuming ones time and efforts than a calling or a mission.

CAPACITY: During C8 AD, the ability to do things, as in the potent (the physical capacity to use an object) came into power. The Romance language shift factors led to its C13 English 'to make powerful'; then strengthen (1540); then powerhouse (1881); then 'supply with power' (1898). "*Capacity*" (the power to receive) includes power + Ability. "*Ability*"--the inherent power to do—i.e. improved with exercise implies a Faculty (an inherent quality within ones Selfhood) to perform acts in the 'here and now' without much training or education.

CARICATURE WEAKLINGS: victims are viewed as swollen shadows of their true reality.

CARING: In a plastic bag on the table of my study were unshelled peanuts. During the night they blew off and went under a chaise lounge chair. The next morning a squirrel had hopped a high netted fence covering the door and was shelling and eating the peanuts. This serves as an example for humans as to the taking of action on what is cared about--and to the extent of using sharpened faculties (in this case, smell) and ingenuity to overcome obstacles. Europeans use "Caring" (Latin, cura) in a manner that has degrees (ranging from mild to extreme Caring) with respect to the act of "careful looking after" in management and in supervision of any type. They also use it to characterize a special ability to do something accurately. For Ancient Africans "Caring" is a Spiritual Instinct--meaning it has "all-or-none" features. In other words, one either cares unconditionally or not at all, for there are no degrees. At the core of "Caring" is creating, enhancing, and maintaining safety and security as well as doing what it takes to prevent interference with safety and security. When "Caring" is effective it contributes to the enlarging of the Cosmic Organism. By contrast, not to "Care" damages the Cosmic Organism of which one is a part. Concepts contained in caring include the "*Charge*" (obligation, duty, and responsibility) and "Management" (regulation and order) involved in personal labor. A gardener has the care of a garden; a nurse has the charge of children; an overseer has the management of a farm. "*Obligation*" is a binding promise to take the steps necessary for caring. This means there is no problem too great to undertake managing--even if it has never been done before or the Mentor has never seen nor heard of it before. "*Duty*" is doing the tasks which have to be done without consideration of fame, money, or status. "*Responsibility*" is shouldering the consequences for anything not properly done or that is left undone but should have been done in accordance with ones obligation. Two of its features are: first, take care of other people's things better than if they were yours; second, stay in contact without needing something. As a boy, "Unconditional Caring" was the way of my all-Black community. What I saw happening everyday was people doing things to make each other's lives easier. Even in those situations where a man would hurt his wife's feelings she prepared his meals and did everything she would normally do--and vice versa. In other words, doing the "right" thing and being "right" with oneself took precedence over hurt feelings. These Black People did the task they promised to do (i.e. kept their word); did it in the suitable way the receiver wanted it done rather than how they thought it ought to be done; in the priority order the receiver thought best; and did it promptly and quickly. To do otherwise is to arrogantly say: "I know what's best and you don't." Or, if it was trying to help someone change, the practice was to figure out the core principle and give the receiver the single most important thing to start the process of change. For example, if the receiver was "down and out," the mentor might say the basic problem is that of a disconnection from ones *Unconditional Love Platter*--i.e. the instinct to Love; to spread Love; to be Loved; and to be Lovable. Step I in reestablishing the Love Flow is with Self-Love in general and vow not to do any harm to oneself in particular. Over the next 60 years I have noticed a terribly disturbing trend of people no longer caring about each other because they have become self-absorbed ("it's all about me!"). Another trend has been for people to talk about caring and deem simply talking about it to be good enough. Or, they might get started in a task and give up quickly before completion. Still another trend is to not work with someone to improve the struggles of Black youth simply because that someone was the cause of the hurt feeling. In other words, "Since I can't have my way I'm going to take my marbles and go home" (Sharon Bingaman). That is self-absorbed selfishness. This is a "Failure" of caring. Black People cannot self-improve without Unconditional Caring for each other.

CAUSE: *Predisposing Cause(s)* lay the foundation for a disease process to gain a foothold in ones body. As the first disease risk factors, they pave a way for a disease to occur within ones Selfhood. *Precipitating Causes* enhance the Predisposing Cause(s) by cultivating or maintaining the disease risk factors. The *Immediate Cause* is the agent instigating without delay--and with nothing in between it and the disease process. See SOBMER

CEREBELLUM: admits Spiritu currents for distribution into the spinal marrow, attracts the spiritual and life-giving substance.

CERTAINTY: The "T" Scale is concerned with the ranges of Certainty (100%) down to its opposite (zero). The *Unseen Absolutely Certain,* on the horizontal line, is illustrated by a "Thing's" essence of Being and it has no proof. *Seen Absolutely Certain* (i.e. Circumstantial Truths) is manifestations of Unseen Absolute Certainty. Example: Ancient African Sages devised paths leading to the indirect *Proof of God* by: mathematically figuring out Circumstantial Truths (like Spiritual Elements) + being aware of God's functions (qualities, powers, actions) + observing attributes (neteru) of God's domain in Nature (e.g. Instincts in all animals and humans) + Self-Knowledge + constant Reflection on how to overcome personal flaws + how to spread Ma'at. Circumstantial Evidence (e.g. observing attributes of God's domain in Nature, such as Instincts in all animals and humans) derived from Circumstantial Truths (God's manifestations in Nature) enabled inferring God's functions (qualities, powers, actions) giving rise to the Spiritual Elements (God's Substance) as the ultimate in solidness. Below this African level the European expression of Knowledge and particularly Information requires Proof. Mathematically, this is like a triangle with three equal sides—called an Equilateral or Equiangular Triangle whereby the sides and angles are equivalent and thus have Correspondence. This would be true even if a portion of that triangle could not be seen—and yet mathematically figured out. The "figured out" would be called Circumstantial but still have Certainty. See Proof; Scales

CHAOS--FAILURE TO EXAMINE WHAT UNDERLIES: In the beginning of "Poimandres" (the Vision of Hermes) the meditating African Sage Tehuti had a mystical vision of the first act of Cosmic Creation. This vision was borrowed by Europeans to serve as the basis for their "Big Bang" theory which says the creation of Matter and the World began with "gasses" encountering certain forces which then exploded. That explosion generated a great amount of heat that upon cooling down, formed such elements as hydrogen and helium which form atoms. Then they claimed life also came into being from a special chance combination of molecules—and later on brought consciousness and intelligence into existence (see Amen, MAAT 29 for elaboration). But what they failed to realize is that it had a numerical basis to it which can be understood through African Qualitative and Quantitative Mathematical Logic--thereby indicating a Cosmic Intelligence behind it. However, significant inconsistencies start with considering the C14 English word "*Etymology*" (Latin praeter- beyond, past + naturam, nature 1580—designating 'finding the underlying, literal, or true meaning of words'—that is applicable only to

Essence (i.e. what a Thing was when it came into Being-hood). First, they have failed to follow their own definition of finding the Underlying to get to true meanings. Second, their definition of Etymology suggests that all of their words are of a Supernatural nature. This is what prevents them from exploring behind what caused the Big Bang and thus they will never know what created the Energy, Matter, and Order that went into the stupendous explosion. Third, they could not explain—unlike all other explosions that display a random and chaotic form--why the explosion resulted in an Ordered Cosmos with its vital partners like radiant energy (e.g. light, gamma rays) and the lightest of elements (e.g. hydrogen, helium, and lithium)—themselves subdivided into leptons which combine to form larger ones, mesons, and these, to form baryons, and these, to form atoms, and these to form molecule. These building blocks of physical matter behave with such Order that their behaviors can be reduced to a Mathematically exact science. What Very Ancient African Sages' astro-mathematicians uncovered were fixed patterned processes of Nature underlying the seemingly randomized parts which, in turn, allowed for their scientific thinking (e.g. thermodynamics). The "Underlying" contents were discovered by them to consist of Nature's infinite *Foundation of Unified complexity and multiplicity Patterns*. From this—being what they could observe and measure—enabled them to infer the Circumstantial Truth that underlying each of these entities are a shared common parent--the Spiritual Elements Genetics. As a result, these Correspondences—the partner of Circumstantial Truths--*rest on the Ultimate of all Cosmic Orders—the Spiritual Elements of Unconditional Love, Truth, Reality, and the Natural. All Spiritual Elements are Orderly orchestrated by the boundless Force, called Sekhem by Ancient Africans.* The detection, assessments of what is detected, and the disposition is done by the human tools of the Instincts, Common Sense, Creativity, Reasoning, Knowledge, Logic, and Wisdom. These faculties can naturally develop from ones inborn Pure Emotions and Pure Intellect, Although it cannot be seen (it is hidden) its Presence is evident by the Intelligence and Power underlying the Cosmos. So, for Ancient Africans the creation of the Cosmos was not a physical event (like European's "Big Bang" concept) that just happened but rather was an orderly event pre-planned and executed according to a Divine Law or Order (Maa, to see, insight) that makes all forms and governs the Physical and Metaphysical Worlds. This Plan they called *Ma'at* (equated to Chinese Tao)—the law that governs all events in the world—electro-magnetic forces, quarks, gluons, atoms, molecules, chemical interaction, gravity, the diet of creatures, and human life. The Divine Law was said to come from the notion of a one Universal High Spiritual God, boundless and an incomprehensible intelligence and Energy. The point is for Black People to return to their "little child-like" Pure Emotions and Pure Intellect to examine the hidden underlying Assumptions used to create ones hidden Belief System. It is they which underlie all of ones daily living thoughts, emotions, expressions, and behavior conduct. After finding the deeper *Order and consistent* interconnecting *Patterns underlying natural events or disharmony, one will be back in the realm of the Spiritual Elements flow of Right Life Living for lifestyle fashioning.*

CHARACTER: the *Nature* ones Free Will choices "architect" to conform to ones selected self-recognized Identity. The combination of ones self-recognized Identity and the Nature corresponding to it thereby express a human's personal trademark-like individuality. See Nature; Self-Identity

CHARACTERISTIC: A Mosaic Image derived from the Interchange of its Essence parent and whose operation stands for the "what it is" Uniqueness of its Essentials family. It appears as a Notion

CHARGE: "*Charge*" is obligation, duty, and responsibility and "Management" (regulation and order) involved in personal labor. A gardener has the care of a garden; a nurse has the charge of children; an overseer has the management of a farm.

"CHECK AND BALANCE": The Left Brain is relatively quiet from birth to around seven years old (for me it was around five). Then it becomes dominant for the perception and production of almost all aspects of non-emotional language skills (e.g. grammar, word production, spelling, reading, speaking and writing); the comprehension of the grammatical, syntactical, and descriptive components of language, including time sense, rhythm, musical scales, verbal concept formation, analytical reasoning, verbal memory. It does logical tasks, such as reasoning, analysis, and processing data like a calculator. When skillfully disciplined, it becomes extremely powerful. Together, the Right and Left Brains are "*Inseparable Harmonized Differences*"--like two sides of a coin separated by an Equal Sign--working mostly independently to interdependently first fashion a whole and then "Check and Balance" each other to perfect that whole. Ancient Africans utilized this concept as a mutually cooperative mind training control tool designed for temperance (i.e. exhibiting self-restraint) they called the *Middle Way*. "Check and Balance" is theoretically illustrated by the USA constitution separating the powers of the executive, legislative, and judicial branches and having each as "watch dogs" over the other two. For example, the Right Brain gathers from the subject or situation at hand its inner and outer similarities while the Left Brain gathers inner and outer differences of similar and dissimilar things and breaks them into pieces--the act of analysis. All are synthesized. Ancient Africans perfected the Left Brain's discipline power so as to sharpen the Right Brain to serve as the vehicle for expansiveness into higher planes of existence regarding things like *Love, spirituality, compassion, peace, harmony, intuition, synthesis, nonaggression, and unity*. An undisciplined Right Brain is otherwise chaotic and accounts for chronic Juggling in life from failing to do the "Splitter" and the Precision Thinking contributed by the Left Brain. Hence mental entanglements occur from failure to separate what can be separated or from lumping together what is better left separated. Natural Right brain intuition has a creative (from "Pure Feelings") and non-creative part (e.g. the sixth sense; predominantly Ancient Brain Instincts). It, in conjunction with the Left Brain, organize all essences as well as existing bits and pieces into new forms, new arrangements, and new combinations, a key to Creative Thinking. As one matures, Mental Discipline arises more and more out of the world view of considering the deeper meanings of life and the temperament of what it takes to enjoy it and not waste it.

"**CHERRY-PICK**": pick the very best to suit ones self-interest, as test subjects get the desired results.

CHIMERA: In Greek mythology a Chimaera was an imaginary fire-breathing monster made up of grotesquely disparate parts—e.g. a lion in the fore part, goat in the middle, and a dragon behind—i.e. a chimera-like organism consists of two or more tissues of different genetic composition Then, in Indo-European folk-tales it possessed the quality of universality of a horrible, grotesque, fantastic beast. Since Hate is a trait of "Weak People" and since "Weak people" are Self-Unknown and since the Self-Unknown is about being in Fantasy realms, in order to have a tow-rope on which to hold throughout the course of their unstable and miserable lives, they create Chimaera out of scapegoats. In the process, they create a Chimaera of superiority to subdue the Icon Image of their inferiority. All of this is unstable inside an unsettled situation. "Killer" police treat Black People as if they are "Faceless monsters" (Bailey, Stopping The Violence; Bailey, Rekindling Black People's Genius). Perhaps this dates to early Europeans' "far out" Consciousness Occult Background—filled with "*Phantasmagoria*" (phantasm/ ghostly figures) fantasies. Pertinent here is Europeans' mythological "Faceless Ones"—i.e. mysterious and powerful monsters closely connected to the Old Gods and directly opposed to the Angels. A distinction of the Faceless is that they always attack in large numbers and attempt to swarm. Persisting from primitive European times to the present has been Delusional Fear mindset patterns associated with (among others) their "*Paracosms*". *Delusional Fears,* spurred by "Phantasmagoria" Contingent Beings, are the imagining of false, dangerous problems. They believe those to ever-threaten something significant to oneself. Out of these fears, their reactions to such Chimera patterns has been to fashion the villain into Icon Image-like Predators—forms that are something absurdly fantastic, wildly imaginary, vague--and what normal people would call foolish and grotesque. Then they would select scapegoats and make them into feigned enemies for purposes of fighting and destroying. Whenever people hate "Faceless" people, this means their own insecurities are threatened and their self-hatred is exposed. Both are confronted by displacing these into their victims and thereby making them into chimera (monsters). Since the created chimera follows their creators everywhere, the associated fantasy throws the entire picture of whatever involves the chimera into an Umbra--a complete and fully formed dark shadow. Hence, creators are unable to discern the face of one symbolizing the caricature or "Outsider" without it being distorted, if not "Faceless." See Paracosm; Chimera; Phantasm; Delusional Fears; False Self

CHRISTIANITY--VERY ANCIENT AFRICANS' ORIGIN: Although the ingredients of Christianity originated with Primitive Africans, its earliest recorded evidence of having begun in Africa comes out of Very Ancient African Spiritual Literature pertaining to *Esoteric Knowledge*. By this being derived from their Subjective and Objective Science implied they understood the core of fundamental inner most Principles in Physical, Metaphysical, and Spiritual Processes of Nature. Very Ancient African Sages' *Contemplation* on results of these inferences gave insights into the inner Truth lying hidden in the Esoteric--Truths revealing certain mysterious things about God--things belonging to God--and things revealed by God to humans. These were confirmed by God's Word Revelations to Tehuti—the African Master of all the world's Masters and Sages. Out of Tehuti's and other African Sages' well known revelations and astro-mathematic studies came insights into the latent powers of God that are present in humans. The earliest recording of this is from the "Prt m Hru": (epitaph)--a name for Humankind's original Bible and dating to 60,000 BC (Seleem p 59, xiii). A statement from this "Book of Life" says: righteousness leads to spiritual realization; purification is acting with righteousness; and by learning about the nature of the Divine—acting, feeling, and thinking as the Divine—it is finally possible to become one with the Divine. Before or after that, Ancient Africans thought in terms of a Messiah coming (some say the "anointed Messias"--a term meaning (K) Christos, or "Christ"); of a Madonna and her Child; of a Virgin Birth; and the Incarnation of the Spirit in flesh. *Ausares* is the African name given in order to indicate un-manifested aspects of God. Humans who achieved a spirituality-realized state were given the title "Ausar" (the God-Self dwelling in Humans). The same practice applied to the title of Christ. The word "Christ," says Diop (Civilization or Barbarism, p. 312), came from the Pharaonic Egyptian expression "kher sesheta": "he who watches over the Mysteries." Gadalla (The Ancient Egyptian Roots Of Christianity p65) adds the Greek Christos was a corrupted Ancient Egyptian word for "Christ," but with the consonants H RST. Since the Greeks could not pronounce the letter H, they substituted its sound with the letters Ch. The consonants of the name Christ are HRST, which means HeRu (Horus) and Son of ST (auST/Isis). Gadalla said the Jesus of history was Twt/Tut-Ankh-Amen, whose role as an Egyptian Pharaoh was (symbolically) to be the son of a Virgin Mother—Auset (Isis). This African origin of Christianity was common knowledge among Western scholars and their early Apostolic fathers of the Church. For example, St. Augustine (354-430) of Hippo (Algeria), who was quite familiar with Tehuti's works, said: "That which is called Christian religion existed among the ancients [i.e. Africans], and never did not exist, from the beginning of the human race until Christ came in the flesh, at which time the true religion which already existed began to be called Christianity" (Freke, Hermetica p20). All of this was supported (1836) by the renowned British, Sir Godfrey Higgins. He said in "The Anaclypsis, or an Inquiry into the Origin of Languages, Nations, and Religions" that people of the [European] Bible were Black; and in all early Catholic Churches of Europe: "the God Christ, as well as his mother, are described in their old pictures to be Black [people]; Jesus Christ, a Negro; and the African Origin of the Myths and Legends of the Garden of Eden. According to Darkwah ("Africans Who Wrote The Bible" p11), what Sir Higgins indirectly implied was that doctrines of the Ancient African Bible and original doctrines of the European Bible were both from Black People. His reasoning was that since Jesus was Black and his people wrote his story, then the people that conceived and wrote this story must also be Black. Hence, he continues: "the early Catholic Church knew, accepted, and acknowledged the Black ethnicity of the people of the Bible by portraying the God Christ and his mother as the Black People they originally were." Gadalla reinforces this by saying "Ancient Egyptian texts reveal irrefutable proof that the entire body of [European] Christian doctrine is simply a revamped and mutilated Egyptianism; the early Christian [Catholic] church accepted these ancient truths as the very tenets of [their] Christianity, but disavowed their origins". This plagiarizing of the Egyptian religion was noted by several brave European writers, including the world renowned British Egyptologist, Sir E. A. Wallis Budge. jabaileymd.com

CHRISTIANITY-- EUROPEAN'S EARLY DEVELOPMENT: Very Ancient Africans' "Prt m Hru"—the oldest of the world's highest Spiritual recordings (c60,000 BC)—contained in its African Spiritual Literature Christianity's original doctrines. But European Egyptologists renamed it "Book of the Dead" + selected the title: "The Book of Coming Forth by Day" to replace a chapter having nothing to do with the "Prt m Hru's" theme. The "Prt m Hru" assists humans to realize the purpose of their lives in the Cosmos--and has nothing to do with the dead or death. Instead, it pertains to African Christianity's focus (Amen, Nuk Au Neter p3-4) that includes: (1) the verifying of Human's divinity; (2) affirming the requirement for the realization of Divinity lives by Ma'at's Divine Law (the Spiritual Elements of Unconditional Love, Truth, Reality, and the Natural in action) so as to live a life free of Divine Ignorance (called "Sin" by Europeans); (3) humans, as Divine Beings, thus attain to an eternal existence with the freedom to leave Divine reality and enter Earth as she/he pleases or as God needs; and (4) the book's detailing of the faculties to be utilized in the work and how they are to be used. Historically, Europeans have always stolen African Tradition knowledge—including its civilization (social and technological) and cultural (Intellectual and Spiritual) developments and fashionings. After varying modifications, their process is to rename what they take + what they are unable to take away from Africans. A reason for renaming what they dishonorably acquire is sort of explained in the Encyclopaedia Britannica (1992, p 567): "...*men have seen in the ability to name an ability to control or to possess....*" They defined "*naming*" as applying a word to pick out and refer to a fellow human being, an animal, an object, or a class of such beings or objects. The consequences are that after a period of time people forget that what was renamed was attributed to the originator and that new name is assumed to be created by the one applying the present name." The Greeks ruled Egypt from 332 BC to 30 BC and adopted the Kamitic culture as fully as they could. They imitated the kingship, styling themselves Pharaohs (the Ptolemies); practiced the religion mixed in with their own customs; and thereby absorbed many Kamitic religious ideas which passed into Greek mythology (religion) and their form of Christianity. The Romans ruled Kamit from 27 BC to 641 AD. Incidentally, *B.C.E. (BC) means Before the Christian Era; C.E. (AD) is the Christian Era.* These added Christian designations have been used to force those who do not accept that there was a European God named "Jesus Christ," as Europeans claim, to still show respect. Like the Greeks, the Romans adopted many of the Kamitic religious, civilization, and cultural ideas. Such is shown by studying the various attributes of the African god Ausar—the Kamitic metaphorical Spiritual vehicle of human's divinity—for then one can see how closely Europeans' Jesus Christ corresponds to it. Support is given to this by noting the great number of European stories told about Jesus being present in African metaphorical literature thousands of years prior to what Europeans claim to be their Jesus' birth. For example, there were at least 16 myth crucified saviors before the European Jesus, starting with Horus, the Christ figure of Egypt. This is the same pattern used as the European Bible story of Adam and Eve being carved on an Ethiopian wall thousands of years prior + many teachings—e.g. the Sermon on the Mount, says Amen (Vol I: 117), being thousands of years older than Jesus. Also, Kamitic women and men attaining the realization of human-god Divinities had the title Ausar appended to their names: the Ausar Ani; the Ausar Unas. *Ausar meant the same as the Christ Jesus.* Beginning European Christianity cults in C1 AD were European influenced Black People who transposed African "Prt m Hru" + Egyptian concepts into budding European

Christianity. These Black "Founding Fathers" included Terullian (a Carthaginian, the First of church writers who made Latin the language of Christianity); St. Athanasius (293-373 AD, for whom the Athanasian Creed is named); Cyprian (a Carthaginian Bishop and martyr); and St. Augustine (one of the most famous "Fathers of the Church") who wrote and rewrote aspects of the original Ancient African Bible, perhaps changing some of the fundamental symbolism (see Bynum, African Unconscious p114 for details). Those first centuries of Christianity were evolved in Egyptian deserts and the new faith was spread by North African converts. [Main reference: Bailey, Ancient African Bible Messages] jabaileymd.com

CHRISTIANTY'S "ARYAN-IZING" OF EUROPEANS' EARLY BIBLE: From the beginning of their existence 45,000 years ago, Europeans have had a variety of gods developed in their own warrior image and possessing phantasmagoric mindsets (e.g. monsters). This was spotlighted by later Aryan nomadic tribes who carried forth primitive Europeans Supernatural patterns. In turn, these served as models for all subsequent European males to the present. Some say these warrior Aryans arose, perhaps 8000 years ago, out of the grasslands of Eastern Europe, north of the Black and Caspian Seas. After invading India c1700 BC and colonizing the Punjab region of Northwest India, they declared themselves to be superior and noble compared to the Slaves they captured. Meanwhile, in C8 BC, Egyptians' Book of Caverns, Purgatory was analogized to be like a cocoon where the damned enter, became non-Beings as a result of elimination of what is not about the Spiritual Elements, and then emerged as renewed beings, like a butterfly. Indo-European Aryans carried this concept through a long process to arrive at the fantasy of a Hell (Bailey, Post-Traumatic Distress Syndrome p158-168). Then cC6 BC, Satan appears in the Old Testament as an individual angel, subordinate to God, and thereafter gradually becomes the source of all evil as a result of disbelieving in God and acknowledging no law except of man. Aryans transformed the African god Seth/Pan, the God of Nature, into the phantasmagoric Red Angel of Evil, Lucifer, Satan (Set-Hen)--a red man with tail, horns, and hooves. Satan, Evil, and Dark became Europeans "*Dark Side*" trio--signifying misery, punishment, perdition or loss of the soul and Hell. In C2 BC, Romans applied the "numen" idea to indicate their divine Supernatural spirit. Perhaps this was the "Seed" idea for a later appearing Supernatural God. The Greek Ptolemy I found a council of Ancient Egyptian priests and priestesses in Memphis, Egypt, willing to please them. In C1 AD, these *Melchite Coptic Egyptians* formed the Coptic Branch of Christianity, using primarily concepts out of the Ancient African Bible.

"Copt" derives from the Arabic word Qubt, meaning "Egyptian". The *Melchite Coptic Egyptians* (those Hellenized into the Greek culture) gave Ptolemy I (also called Lagi and "Soter,") the name "Oserapis," and later Serapis c323 BC, eventually called Jesus Christ. They created a devotional ritual to him; spoke of him as "The savior and leader of souls to the light and receiving them again"; and fashioned new concepts from the African and Hebrew Bibles for their Church. The blending of African Christianity and European Christianity began to take hold in Egypt after the Evangelist, St. Mark's preaching in Alexandria AD 69. This was around the time ideas about the Gospels arose. The *Fall of African Christianity in Europe* came because of its own success. As a result of the new African Christianity faith being spread by North African converts, the budding European Christianity had to start stamping out the increasing power of the African Christianity Cult. At the Council of Niceae I (325 AD), Serapis was inserted into the Ancient Egyptian Divine Triad of Ausara (Osiris), the Father; Horus the Sun; and Auset (Isis, the Holy Cow Hathor), the Mother. Serapis replaced Horus and Isis.

Gradually, European Christianity became Aryan oriented, shedding its original Cosmic Spiritual Consciousness focus but retaining much of it. Constantine (285-337 AD) took information from the Ancient African Bible and modified it with existing pagan Roman Supernatural beliefs + individualizing the newly formed Jesus + adopting a Trinity—all opposed to African Christianity. To assist his purpose of controlling the people and suppressing the power of African Spiritual Literature, he declared Christianity to be the official Religion of the Roman Empire. Realizing the Ancient African religion to be superior and extremely attractive to the people, he ordered the closing of all Egyptian temples in an attempt to eradicate any and all competing Religious Systems. As part of replacing Kamitic antecedents with Christian myth and symbolism, in 391 AD, Theophilus of Alexandria, Egypt went on a destructive campaign of African Spiritual Literature. He destroyed the Serapeum Temple and the Great Library, including 500,000 *Ancient African Bible scrolls and manuscripts.* This is the pattern of any dominating power who has an inferior system they want the people to completely adopt. That is why it is almost impossible to find today readily available Ancient African Philosophies or the Ancient African Bible which gives metaphorical stories about Ma'at Principles. jabaileymd.com

CHRISTIANTY'S EUROPEANS BIBLE CONTROLLING POWERS: The Catholic Church acquired great power by eliminating Ancient Africans' all encompassing World Icon Image religion and replacing it with their own created white looking Messiah, Madonna and her child, and all deities of heaven. Now, the Church could control the "Savior's" image and messages by speaking for him. A resultant "Halo" effect was all people had to worship whatever the Church said and worship even the Church itself. In their evolving Aryan oriented Bible, they kept 'as is' certain Ancient African Bible Messages and modified others, like claiming ownership of virgin birth and incarnation of the spirit in flesh. Thereafter, all sorts of fashioned Bibles conformed to Europeans ideas of religion and their ruling Supernatural God. For example, during Queen Elizabeth I's reign, England had two main competing Holy Scripture versions. The 1560 anti-royal Geneva Bible, loved by Puritans and Calvanists, instituted the practice of numbering each verse. The other was the pro-royal but unpopular Bishop's Bible. To gain the advantages of both, a first duty of King James VI of Scotland, upon succeeding Elizabeth I in 1604, was to call forth a Hampton Court Conference for "a new translation of the Bible, because those which were allowed in the reigns of Henry VIII, and Edward VI, were corrupt and not answerable to the truth of the Original." James said: "I wish some special pains were taken for a uniform translation, which should be done by the best learned men in both Universities, then reviewed by the Bishops, presented to the Privy Council, lastly ratified by the Royal authority, to be read in the whole Church, and none other... These translations are to be used when they agree better with the Text than the Bishops Bibles: Tyndale's, Matthew's, Coverdale's, Whitchurch's, and Geneva." This era's atmosphere and its orientation concerned Europeans' enslavement of Africans to carry them to South America and to prepare a Bible to control upcoming Enslaved Africans. By there being no politics and religion gap, these ramdomly chosen writers added another re-re-rewrite of the European Bible. This King James Bible, authored by six subcommittees, out of which one prevailed, was published in 1611, revised in 1885 for its intended purpose--as a political and mind-controlling tool. It, the church, and the ministers--thought of as refuges from realities of life--focused on generating domination, fear, awe, and reverence. This persists today. The *powerful controlling tool* of spotlighting *Fear of God's wrath*—was so effective because average Europeans are fearful of *being seen* to be doing something wrong. Thus, they tend to go through life without ever expressing their Real Selves or their true feelings (National Geographic p54, Dec. 2011). By the mid-1600s, the King James Bible had replaced all competing Bibles and was the Bible of the English speaking world, readied to indoctrinate Enslaved Africans brought from all over Africa to the Americas. It *had no choice but to promote "Belief and Faith" in their White God and white Heaven.* This came from their awareness of *Africans "Knowing" their Real God existed*--and *when minds "Know," they cannot be controlled*!!! All Enslaved brilliantly organized Ultimate African Standard systems of thinking were shattered from exhaustion by beyond horrible Kill/Take/Destroy/Dominate/Oppress/Control deeds of enslavers. Brainwashing included Enslaved becoming children to Whites and love their White God more than they loved their own family or friends; that Whites were told the Word of God; that Whites were

God's messengers; Jesus had died to save them from Hell; and they were to completely and permanently forgive all Whites for all horrors used to convert them into being good enough to work in the kitchen of heaven so as to serve Whites. They were too 'beaten down' to resist. Reinforcements came from intimidation, the whip, and "Not to follow these dictates is a Sin punishable by the Devil's control and, at death, then go to Hell." As a result, most Enslaved bonded with the oppressors, and protected them as a child desires to protect its mother. Scattered variously were the Enslaved ways of coping with their horrible lives. Some became "Ideal Slaves"; some Mulatto House Slaves defended and adopted their European side; some stuck together; some went off on their own to either die or follow Isolated Individualists' path. The enslaves made each Enslaved fragment fight each other for "divide and conquer" purposes. It has been/remains vital to keep most Black People ignorant so as to remain Enslaved and thus always be at the mercy of Whites. jabaileymd.com

CIRCUMSPECTION THINKING: A more appropriate Ancient African term for the Western word "Reason" is "Circumspection." Unlike reasoning which deals with the logical consideration of the various ideas that can possibly affect a judgment, Circumspection is the coordination of the inputs from all of a human's Selfhood faculties. These involve syllogistic logical thoughts, creative visualizations, synthesis, analysis, observations, and intuition. These are the true foundations of Scientific Thinking (Amen, Metu Neter II: 102). By contrast, Europeans exclude synthesis, intuition, and creative visualizations. Circumspection embraces the watchful observation of danger and calculation of possible Consequences, but without the timidity implied in Caution. It views matters from all sides to make a prudent decision--looking far ahead and sacrificing the present to the future.

CIRCUMSPECTION: coordination of the inputs from all the mind's faculties—syllogistic logical thoughts; creative visualization; synthesis; analysis; observation through the senses; and intuition.

CIRCUMSPECTION REASONING: Unlike ordinary Reasoning which deals with the logical Pure Emotions and Intellect considerations of the various ideas that can possibly affect a judgment, *Circumspection is the coordination of the inputs from all of a human's Selfhood faculties. These--syllogistic logical thoughts, creative visualizations, synthesis, analysis, observations, and intuition--are the true foundations of Scientific Thinking* (Amen, Metu Neter II: 102). Ancient Africans said Mathematics is the one and only key to clear thinking, meaning, and communication. Thus, Mathematics was foundational to their Subjective Science (e.g. Observations) devising the *Law of Correspondence;* to verified their Physical World conclusion by their *Law of Spiritual Creativity*: by itself, a Spiritual Element reproduces itself to become the thing it makes, regardless of its different forms; and to do Circumstantial verifiable non-material Things inside a boundless realm with corresponding Seeable Material Things by the *Law of (Spiritual) Circularity or Reversibility*—i.e. Spiritual off-springs are proven by the parent and the Spiritual parent is proven by the offspring anywhere. Yet, the guidelines for both were staying within the flow of the Spiritual Elements and ensuring that all functions must be placed and maintained in their proper space and time—the African *Law of Equilibrium*. Following insights resulting from seeing interrelationships fashioned by Observation, Math, Truth, and Order, Ancient Africans discovered the essence of Correspondence between the Principles in Mathematics, Science (e.g. Physics), Philosophy, Logic, and Spirituality. Obviously then, all of these are related; are part of the same system; and although each has its individual obligations, duties, and responsibilities each reinforces all of the others. This Correspondence thinking is the feature of Circumspection (look around)--causing one to think abstractly, systematically, and rationally (i.e. step-by step) so as to see all sides of something, both aspects of each side of that something, and the angles present where the sides meet within that something. "Circumspection" uses the "Box Concept"— viewing matters so as inspect each side, angle, top, and bottom; turn it; look at it from underneath; see it from one view after another; hold it against the sky and imagine it in any material or even in glass; and think of all types of options based upon fashioning powerful meanings indirectly. Circumspection is the show of deliberateness and habitual carefulness--to be watchful observation of danger, cautious, and calculating with regard to all possible consequences by giving earnest attention to all significant circumstances and situation but without the timidity implied in Caution. One gives particular minute attention in considering all possible "what ifs" Consequences that could call for actions to be undertaken since the wicked are always alert. It views matters from all sides so as to make a prudent decision--looking far ahead and sacrificing the present to the future for ones destination of benefits for "ME/WE"—and figuring out how to move *forward in what is difficult while staying within the confines of the Spiritual Elements.*

This is Spiritually driven Courage which is always mixed with Circumspection related to a just cause so as to prevent rashness and foolishness. For Ancient Africans, Circumspection was the mental tool required to arrive at a proper Judgment. Prudence is about good judgment, foresight, and forethought, inclining to care and frugality in practical affairs. From considered calculated risks in the face of the dangers, one takes the first step, regardless of whether anyone knows or not what was involved or what was done—and still, in spite of having had clarity on both pain and pleasures—in spite of personal adverse consequences—in spite of obstacles and dangers and pressures—in spite of having to go against what displeases others--one does not shrink from facing necessary dangers. This is the basis of all human morality--a practical form of being true to ones Selfhood Greatness and a display of Character Integrity. Circumspection does not allow following the Crowd since it readily sees flaws Fettered opinions, like *Eugenics.* For example, a difference in dealing with humans and plants or animals is that humans on mating from choice and not because any scientific body have chosen suitable mates for them. This applies to Negative Eugenics which seeks to prevent the multiplication of the unfit as well as to Positive Eugenics—i.e. encourage multiplication of the fit. There is no human qualified to "play God" and decide sterilization, or with whom and how to live or die

CIRCUMSTANTIAL EQUIVALENCES REASONING: Let us return to the scenario of rivers, lakes, ponds, streams, and the ocean from which they arise. Despite each having a different name, they are all "equivalent" because each and all contain water from the same Ocean source—water that can do the same things no matter where located--water that in each varies in amount, in "what it does" and in "how it appears". Let us say that out of view and hidden from sight are the rivers that are outshoots of the ocean and the ocean itself. Yet, it is evident that the ocean and rivers are in existence, in the same way that one does not see a skyscraper's underground foundation and Base upon which it rests or in the way one does not see the gravity responsible for keeping Earth things from floating away. What applies to the Correspondence-Circumstantial connection is the *Law of (Spiritual) Circularity or Reversibility*: "the Spiritual offspring is proven by the parent and the Spiritual parent is proven by the offspring inside a boundless realm." This is how Un-seeable things of Worth are in relation to seeable things of Worth or Value. Still, the *consistent Patterns of the* Un-seeable "parent" is what gives the *Order to the underlying natural events of what is* the Seeable (the offspring). These Un-seeable Entities are Circumstantial because they have Correspondence with what is Seeable and with Spiritual Elements Genetics. Once the Circumstantial ("X") is established by the Seeable, although it is Un-seeable it can now be used to establish Correspondence with other Circumstantial Things ("Y") that are also established to exist and yet remain Un-seeable. Estimates about the Worth of ("X") and ("Y") can be made via Algebraic Qualitative Mathematical manipulations and maneuverings, as in the way Bartering is done in the physical world. Also, one can go deeper into the Esoteric Unknowns of both ("X") and ("Y") with the thinking tool of Reasoning by Analogy--taking of whatever is known in either ("X") or ("Y"). For example, when there is a known in ("X"), it becomes the offspring used to explore the unknown in ("Y"). Algebraic Qualitative Mathematics opens mental paths. Those paths allow ones in-born Pre-Birth Emotions and Intellect to generate assessments which give rise to Thoughts which are beyond comparison. The prioritization of those Thoughts provides the clearness and the Order to lay out paths that project further toward the "Rightness" of choices, decisions, and solutions. It was from such insights into Cosmic Rhythms discovered by Very Ancient Africans that laid the path leading to the exact science of Mathematics. Close observation of the Rhythms of the stars and planets was tightly woven into the internal structure of the Great Pyramid. And this was not confined to the Quantitative Mathematical aspects of the Earth, the cycles of Nature, or to the systems of the body.

Included were the stars, the planets, and the Constellations in such Qualitative Mathematical manners as the cycles of the Nile River reflected in the celestial river overhead—i.e. the Milky Way—being integrated into their Cosmic Religion. The reflection of the heavens on Earth gave rise to Tehuti's axiom: "as above, so below," as encoded in the sacred book of "What is in the Duat." The Pharaoh, at death, would make the great journey in his solar boat, becoming one with the immortals who had preceded him. Another example is that the three great Giza pyramids and the Sphinx are in exact alignment with the three stars of Orion Belt, known as the Duat, the Coffin Texts, the Book of Coming Forth by Day, the Book of Gates, and the oldest of them all, the Pyramid Texts (Bynum, African Unconscious p109). Ancient Africans' Qualitative Knowledge of the Good came from seeking the ultimate Principle on which all within their area of concern depended--examining the premises themselves—and deducing conclusions from premises through movement from the Physical or Metaphysical ("X") upward toward the Spiritual ("Y"). By being in the flow of the Spiritual Elements Patterns, one is able to gain Knowledge by "*Connaturality*" (connected by Nature). This, itself, is a Correspondence-Circumstance connection)--referring to what can be intuited in other persons or creatures. By all being spiritually co-natured with each other (i.e. the Law of Sympathy), one can have a "Subjective Plus" awareness of the other's Human Nature from knowing ones own Human Nature. This—called *Poetic Knowledge*—is acquired by union with attachments to the Thing by a "Oneness" in the Cosmic Organism Emotions—being imbedded into a fusion that cannot be reduced to anything more basic (Hodge p100, 208, 221). An example might be the bonding occurring between the mother and her newborn. The same principles applies by using Algebraic Qualitative Mathematics. Conceptual relationships, as in Mathematics and Logic, are permanent and unchanging. For example 2 + 2 = 4 implies that no amount of experience can ever change. The same holds for proofs in Mathematics and Logic. Thus, if the Good, which is unchanging and permanent, is to be known, it must be known by means of these unchanging and permanent conceptual relationships. The conceptualizing part is called the Mind. See Correspondence; Logos; Mathematics

CIRCUMSTANTIAL EVIDENCE: The C14 English word "*Consequence*" (to follow closely)--the off-spring of a Cause and Effect parents--carries such a peculiar birthing concept as to be placed in the "Kangaroo Pouch" category of words. It originally meant an inference or conclusion drawn from what possesses observable aspects for all or what was assumed to be so obvious and universally accepted as to need no proof (e.g. the beauty of flowers)--neither of which makes it "Right" or the truth. Yet, this beginning statement or proposition is a real, distorted, or false *Presupposition* (a thing taken for granted or assumed). In Logic, the first two syllogism propositions are called Premises. *Inferences* determine the unknown from the already known by reasoning from circumstances and observations to draw conclusions from evidence or Premises. *Circumstantial Evidence* indicating a Cosmic Truth is indicated when it demonstrates all aspects of the Spiritual Elements without Disharmony. "*Evidence*" is used in the sense of it being an indicator of where the truth lies and serves as a magnet to gather it.

CIRCUMSTANTIAL PROOF: Logic is "*Valid*" when it justifies the evidence given in support of it. It is "True" in a Physical Knowledge World sense if it expresses the facts as they are. Valid is the result of what integrates all and contradicts none of the relevant data It is present when an observed suspected Spiritual Elements ingredient or attribute reproduces itself in its own Essence Pattern and/or Image so as to become the Thing it makes.

CIRCUMSTANTIAL TRUTH: inferring from Known to an Un-Known or Unknowable Thing by that Thing's manifestations. *Circumstantial Truths are verified by Circumstantial Evidence* pertaining to Observable God-created Divine Forms for such things as in the Animal and Plant Kingdoms—from human experienced things as Thought and Mathematics--and such human "Felt" things like Music, Beauty, and Goodness. *Circumstantial Proof* comes when each reproduces itself in its own Essence Pattern and/or Image so as to become the Thing it makes. See Correspondence; Logos; Mathematics; Circumstantial; Inferences

CIVILITY: a congenial Deceptive tool to hide ones opposing true thoughts and emotions of what is presented). Its Alliances and Liaisons forms prevent cult members from being isolated from the Crowd. *Alliances* are mutually helpful participants who are psychologically and philosophically disconnected from each other—and yet feature the sharing of common character traits, like the IHES mindset. *Liaisons* are people who support like-kind people but lacking close associations between them.

CLASSIFICATION: A mental tool for putting "Things" derived from the same "Seed" with "family resemblances" or like-kind "Things" representing "brothers from different mothers" into arrangements or combinations that promote their better understanding and that assist with their prioritizing into a hierarchy of significance. Each entity is a "Class". Classification proceeds upon the principle that: *when many things resemble each other in a few basic qualities, they can be associated in a Class*. Patterned Thinking of Thinking Tools is essential for classifying anything. As essential as Classifying is for Critical Thinking the only one I was aware of in school was Taxonomy and that is not helpful. I classify something messy every day in preparation for Critical Thinking about it. If I go into a junky room I must put it in order before being able to do thoughtful work. Next is to put down all my thoughts to make room for new ones to come in so as to see as much of the "octopus" as possible. The original Classification Tool is African Tradition's *Planes of Existence*, as mentioned for "Beauty" in the A-Frame Ladder discussion. For me, this is the best way to start "classifying" any subject. The generic process is to start at the subject's beginning and determine the planes of existence it embraces. Planes of existence are a sort of "State" rather than a "Place." A portion of a space may be occupied by several planes at the same time. An analogy is a room filled with an assortment of rays, as the rays of the sun, the rays from a lamp, x-rays as well as magnetic and electric vibrations and waves. Another way of explaining this is by the second tool--the Tree Concept with its Seed, Roots, Trunk, Branches, Leaves, and Fruit subdivisions of a given subject. Those subdivisions are each a plane of existence and different things are going on at different parts of a given plane. For example, there may be bugs eating a Leaf or not enough water for a Root. Third is the *Thinker's Scale* (a negative and positive scale ruler separated by a zero. Most subjects have advantages (positives) and disadvantage (negatives) and the significance of each can be ranked on the proper scale. Those highest on the positive scale are the most important to cultivate and those lowest on the negative scale are the most important to defend against or eliminate or replace. Fourth is the Skyscraper Concept. Fifth is Outlining whereby a topic is put at the top of the page and subtopic categories are put below (and to be filled in when information about them become available. Others are the Table of Contents; Chronological; Alphabetical; Most to Least important; Least to Most Important; Easiest to most Difficult; most Difficult to Easiest; Custom (the way it has always been done). By combining "bits and pieces" of these Thought Tools enables me to generate new forms of classifications. In classifying anything the process starts by taking all the items involved and reducing them into principles (unchanging realities) and Events (changing realities). In turn, those Principles and Events are to be reduced into as few categories as possible. For example, of all the ways to make a living, there are only three fields of work: (1) making, handling, creating; or protecting things; (2) using words or music; and (3) leading and directing people or animals. In decision making and problem solving there are subtle differences in what is now being faced compared to how the "same" situation occurred in the past. For example, when treating war caused fractures, with each being unique and thus not available was written and Orthopaedic Surgeon had seen a likeness, I would see how that type of fracture was treated thousands of years ago and they update the principle with modern advancements to create a workable solution. The point which cannot be overemphasized is to respect every problem for its uniqueness and handle it by creating something workable after fully understanding the problem and doing the research. How similar and more common problems have been dealt with in the past provide clues as to what to consider. Then in proceeding to treat any decision and solution start with what is most practical in applying any Thinking Tool. For example, in teaching children, it may be most interesting to start with a "Leaf" (a situation occurring in their lives) before proceeding to the "Seed" or "Fruit."

CLASSIFYING: *Purposes* of a Classification are varied and include: (1) establishing Order; (2) enhancing Understanding; (3) Prioritizing so as to deal with the most important or the most pertinent; (4) for discernment or for categorizing complex issues, as in deciding on Methods of Classification; and (5) to Prepare for Change in order to acquire or maintain the "5Ss"--Safety, Security, Sureness, Strength, and Stability—mindset pertaining to the topic. What it does, even having very little information about the subject, is to provide a "skeleton" structure on to which I can properly place information coming into my awareness. Bringing in such order removes the cloud from my view of the "big picture" of what characterizes the scope and depth of my discussion. In the process of learning more, I am able to put the "skeleton" into better anatomical alignment which, in turn, may cause the rearranging or recombining of existing information. By so doing it helps me to find the Principles in the topic or to select off the "skeleton" what is most important to work on first. That Classification--a mental tool for putting "Entity/Things" derived from the same "Seed"—can form creative Classes into Orders like: (A) Chronological; (B) Alphabetical; (C) numerical order; (D) "Salad Mix" of "brothers from different mothers"; (E) Blending in the same space; (F) "family resemblances". This involved fashioning a topic into which these Orders could be placed. Bits and pieces can be taken out of one or more of these to fashion into various into arrangements, combinations, or new forms. Creative things could be done further, as by adding whatever evolved out of the product up to this point or by combining them with the thoughts they attracted. Then those thought products are placed into a "skeleton" classification (somewhat like a Table of Contents) and that could be elaborated into a discussion. This enables the items in a Class to be shifted about according to a plan but without altering the items themselves--the action of *Arranging*. One can then focus on one Class or subclass. The style of the discussion could be from: (a) the Most to Least important; (b) Least to Most Important; (c) Easiest to most Difficult; (d) most Difficult to Easiest; or (e) Custom (the way it has always been done); (f) Start to Finish; (h) Cause to Effect; or (I) Effect to Cause. Such enables the generation of new forms of classifications or insights.

CLING: Old English "*Cling*" (stick, adhere) suggests a close attachment--entwining, clutching, or hanging on. Its 'to hold dear': (1) is a chronic self-absorbed neediness and anxiety from being empty of the "5Ss"; (2) dependency to ones in-group (e.g. via cell phone) as well as to things (e.g. gadgets which mold them into having a "Flashing Lights" mentality, thereby maintaining the status quo); (3) is generated out of a dangerous situation naturally leading to fear; and (4) a lack of Courage. Practically everybody has something to which they cling, the nature and degree to which greatly determines how they live. *Clinging to Beliefs that SEEM right but one resists discovering the Truth for fear one will no longer have anything to hold on to. Clinging is the root of all of ones background daily living problems.* That Anxiety makes them envious of Real Self people to the point of doing what it takes to isolate them and throw stones at them--of various natures and with various impacts. Clinging is done for fear of abandonment and fear of being left on ones own while feeling worthless.

"CLOUDS" OVER THE SOUL: Un-Free Mind contains "Clouds" over its "Soul Sunshine." Type I: "*Clouds with a silver-lining*" are people least far away from the Spiritual Elements, maintaining some connection with African Philosophy so that the Sun rays can peep out from around the "Cloud's" borders. Type II. The *"Complete Cloud Cover"* group is totally confused and in a dream-like state—wandering away from the flow of the Spiritual Elements; Type III. The *"Complete Dark Cloud Cover"* generating a mindset of choosing not to Think and "Don't Care". Type IV: The *"Dark Supernatural World"* is the Enslaved "Inside-Out" mindsets from Supernatural's Indifference/Hate/Evil/Sadism complex net entanglements. Type V are the Common Sense" Black People I recognized as a boy in talking with ex-Slaves. They seemed to have no "Clouds" over their Souls but did not have well developed Intellect skills. Still they had great "Mother Wit" Knowledge (maturely drawing on realistic life experiences)--which I call *Common Sense*. Out of any of these groups, particularly Types I and V, come Isolated Individualists. The rest have an amazing "Sameness"—perhaps deriving as a Slave Survival of Black People being brainwashed into having intra-race "disconnections".

CLUTCH: C13 ("tight grasp") is the seizing for the sake of saving something; a claw developed into a swift, eager, tenacious grasping movement of fingers seizing for the sake of saving a situation (1525) and thence into a "tight grasp" of the whole hand. The result of being Clutched is to *"Cling"*--Old English, implying hanging on a tow-rope for "dear life" because of a lack of Courage. Clinging is done for fear of abandonment and fear of being left on ones own while feeling worthless. Clutching and Clinging are generated out of a perceived threatening, disturbing, or dangerous situation naturally leading to fear. One becomes chronically self-absorbed, filled with Doubts and inadequacies, and a neediness to both hide the losses and somehow replace them with a "superior" appearance. See Cling

CODEX GIGAS—"DEVIL'S BIBLE": world's largest surviving medieval manuscript, *Codex Gigas* (literally "giant book" in Latin) or the 'Devil's Bible'--some believe Satan himself is the book's scribe.

COGNITION: the widest system of mental activity processing--embracing attention, perception, learning, memory, language, step by step thinking as well as judgments expressive of these.

COIN CONCEPT: Like Nature exists all at once, so do both sides of a coin. The coin is the appearance (manifestation) of the Reality of the Law of Opposites. Thus, though not the same, Reality and the appearance cannot be separated. To try to make the appearance deviate from its Reality is artificial. The Spirit world (Reality) is in the Concrete World (the Event appearance) and they cannot be separated for that is a Principle (an unchanging Reality). One side of the coin contains the potential of the other side of the coin and what is in-between. If any of these three parts is not present the other two do not exist. No part stands by itself. The relation of the eye to the liver is an invisible interrelationship for it is part of the human organism. This means it is part of the human's homeostasis (self-balancing). One explores the nature of this balance by "Feeling" and not thinking. The same principle applies to the Cosmic Organism. Humans must follow these laws of Nature to maintain integrity for otherwise disorder occurs. If you want to create something find a thing that has its nature. Study its nature and go with it. Any problem is like a coin with its two sides. One side has "Certain Sameness" aspects, similar to other problems encountered in the past. The other side consists of "Unique" features (like no other). For elaboration, see Problematic Souls. The present day coin with its two sides is Symbol of Ancient Africans' Law of Opposites. It is fundamental to Critical Thinking (CT) to always consider both sides or both extremes; to be alert to when one side or one extreme is not being considered or not given its due or misrepresented; and to call out when the favored side is being exaggerated or its benefit fabricated. Violating one of these is understandably quite common among struggling Black People in particular because it is a Slave Survival. Enslaved Africans in Africa were brought together from all over Africa and it was necessary for them to overlook any differences existing among them because they shared the common cause of survival. This persisted throughout slavery and it was quite obvious to me as a boy in my all-Black community. Black People tolerated a tremendous amount of "slights" and "differences" present throughout the Black community because they needed each other. The same persists in many pockets of the Black community because all will be worse off if they call the police. This is "Normal" and practically everybody in a given Black community does it. But the self-defeating problem starts by the wrong assumption of because something is "Normal" and "everybody" is doing the same thing then that makes it "Right." The problem is that this mindset is an example of considering only one side of the coin and not being aware of the other side. The side in ones awareness has a range of "really dislike" certain things all the way over to "really like." And anywhere along this range there may be certain mixtures which vary in intensity and vary from day to day. One example is failing to see that ones "necessary" friends can be a big problem at times that one has to overlook and tolerate--but yet that hostility is suppressed or repressed. Still, the thought never crosses that person's mind to not be around them all the time for that could cause a private "panic" mindset. This is because many people today actually fear being alone and quiet. What might surprise them is to simply take time off and go to a wilderness park where there are few people and just be alone with Nature. That is often the best medicine one can get for their current problems. Another example is defending the bad things ones friend, Sandy, does, and particularly if the other side of the "Coin" is an "outsider" (whether White or Black). This simply soothes Sandy (as was so necessary during and after slavery, on up to this day. Soothing may not be the best thing to do for Sandy because that helps perpetuate Sandy's bad deeds. Yet, most people lack the courage to present the other side of the coin--e.g. scolding Sandy. To make excuses for Sandy is used as false justification to make excuses for ones own bad deeds (e.g. procrastination). Children pick up on these self-defeating ways and together this ensures the status quo. For whatever reason some people the other side of the coin also but do nothing--despite attempts to get them to act by rewards or punishment. For some this is due to them operating out of their Omnibus Brain (featuring "Fight, Flight, and Fright"). For some, it is due to "I'll Show You" stubbornness. Some fear leaving the familiar, no matter how self-defeating. Ancient Africans welcomed differing oppositions for each contributed to the truth. It is essential to know what one does because there are many annoying things about oneself that one overlooks and expects others to overlook--and if not the other gets blamed.

COIN GOOD SIDE/BAD SIDE CONCEPT: Space is essential to what it is in and they are like two sides of a coin—meaning one cannot be exclusively defined. Yet, there situations where good is on one side and bad is on the other. If a proven criminal by your observation who has done harm to another human then saves your life, this criminal is still to be held responsible for the crime and not prevent his discovery. But here you can do all you can to reduce the severity of the punishment

COIN"--UNEXAMINED "DISTORTED ONE-SIDED: The self-declaration of being the "Best/ Greatest/Superior" is the "Defense Mechanism" for the Dumbest people. "Dumb" (Old English, sensory or mental impairment) denotes the Indo-European confusion, stupefaction, or dizziness. In the Middle Ages it expanded to embrace unintelligent; then foolish from not understanding; and in today's "Dumbed Down" or Dim-Witted sense it means reducing the intellectual content so as to be accessible to the Crowd who are so compromised by Social Media. My focus is on the "Dumbness" associated with thinking in a "Distorted One-Sided Coin" manner. This idea was crystalized into being in C18 as an imaginary fourth player in whist or bridge with an exposed hand—hence the idea of 'a substitute for the real thing'—someone with nothing to say other that what is Non-Rational senselessness—a representative of a Real Self person—one which presents beliefs and opinions having little or no meaning but occupies, if not filling up space in the minds of others—lacking in power to speak any knowledge or wisdom—like a mute person who has never heard anything like it. They "SEEM" to be acting in their own interest when secretly they are hiding their Shame over being unable to think in a humane, sensible way and thereby acting as they deem to be what is the "Best/Greatest/ Superior" of the Crowd. In order to avoid looking like sheep being led to a slaughter, this Shame demands that they win and their only way of winning is to ignore the opposite position as well as down grade the ignored opposite person(s). Those are what produce the mental activity analogized to a "*Distorted One-Sided Coin*". "One-Sided" means considering only one group of people and making all others "invisible" with respect to what matters to them; a "Best/Greatest/Superior" unjust or unfair judgment as in there being absolutely no truth, proof, or even evidence—and, in fact, in the face of its contrariness. The model for such dumb displays is USA's Supernatural fantasy of Justice being "Blind, Deaf, and Dumb"—a fantasy because it caters, with distortions geared to "the Majority" on one side of the coin while failing to treat all other people on the coin's opposite side with equality under the law. Minorities are disregarded because in a Democritic Republic, the majority rules as a sacred birthright. The struggling and uneducated are too involved in poverty to know or care that USA justice works against them—simply moving them in ways that best serve the majority and rich. The poor have no money to pay for the proper advice they need.

Thus, all three serve as Scapegoats for the majority. Yet, their hidden grandeur is like the desert flower that wastes its fragrance on the lonely landscape. The majority dumbly acts as if it is dueling—a highly "civilized" institution among a savage people--with the defenseless others. Then they make their victories into virtues of revenge against "faceless" feigned enemies so as to convince themselves of their pride in being conquerors. What complicates the dumbness is its inability to admit the duelers inner weakest which drove them to project their "Dark Side" on to those uninvolved in any way. Nor can they explain the momentary satisfaction they get from it. Mind Control is made a reality by ensuring the Spiritual Elements of Unconditional Love, Truth, Reality, and the Natural are kept mute and, whenever feasible, ridiculed. Thus, the flood of prevailing information roars loud while its deep aspects are silent. The *Donkey Stick Concept* is about a stick holding a carrot in front of his face to give the false hope of reaching the carrot with the next step. That donkey could walk himself to death and never reach the carrot. Similar to this is the White Privileges of the majority, with the carrot representing hedonism. Their striving to achieve a hedonistic lifestyle and thereby achieve Happiness is like banging their heads into greater and greater degrees of dumbness. They are shrewd enough to win unfairly but dumb enough to think its important without knowing why or even when they have won—and they never do! Of most significant is good people who, from being unable to understand evils they see being done, hide their dumbness by ridiculing Victims with bad names. Even worse is able Black People who go overboard in "dumbing down"; then get trapped in the net of "following the crowd"; and wind up as Scholar "fish out of water," floundering down self-destructive paths. Experience has made clear to me how dumb, limited, narrow, and biased are most authorities/ experts.

COLLECTIVE UNCONSCIOUS: (Impersonal or Transpersonal Unconsciousness; Epic Memory) was said by Ancient Africans to represent repeatedly occurring primordial experiences in the course of generations + an explanation for instances of the Inheritance of Acquired Characteristics--a deep unconscious representation of experiences common to a human race for countless generations.

COLOR SPECTRUM: *Color Spectrum*--violet, indigo, blue, green, yellow, orange, red--each color, possessing its own place on the vibratory scale that reaches earth.

COLOR WHEEL—See Nuance

COMMON GROUND COSMOS PRINCIPLES: The word "*Human*" means "man" (Latin, homo) in the broad sense of men, boys, girls, and women. Ancient Africans considered a human's "Nature" to be those of God. This was based upon the Law of Sympathy that says all of God's creatures and creations are spiritually related no matter how remote in time or space. Because the essence of each came from God, that essence referred to Substance, defined as the Spirit of God within each of God's creatures and creations. This differs markedly from that of the Western world, which has no such foundational base. For example, C13 Europe's "*Nature*" implied the Essence of humans -- which is inferred from human qualities (Adler, The Great Ideas II: 517). Hence, "Human Nature" referred to bodily processes and the restorative powers of the body; then about 1380, to ones innate character or disposition; then in 1385, to ones inherent creative power or impulse; then to the human tendencies common in all societies; and then (1526), to the qualities present with the birth of humans. As knowledge about humans increased, "Nature" became impossible to define. Humans are of the same principle makeup as the Cosmos. For example, each human cell contains DNA which has programmed in it all of the infinite possible functions of life (similar to the Ocean of Nun). This fact allows for specialized duties within the world of cells. Thus, the only difference in an immune cell and a brain cell is the DNA chooses to activate certain parts of a cell and inhibit other parts. There is a non-energy and non-matter intelligence allowing this harmonious "Oneness" to happen which, in turn, is orchestrated by its Creator's knowing where everything is happening at once (much like DNA or the Mind). Thus the material realm is a symbol of the omnipresent, omnipotent, and omniscient Creator. This means one can know through symbolic imagery and rhythm, as is central to African worldview. Since human nature and the problems humans encounter do not change in their essence. In my interpretation of African Philosophy, there are four Natures of Man--Primary, Secondary, Tertiary, and Karma. "Primary" Human Nature constitutes the qualities and characteristics shared by all human beings -- independent of race, religion, creed, age, gender, time period, or culture. In general, Human Nature consists of needs, endowments (i.e. natural qualities), and mortality common to all the 37 billion people who have lived everywhere, in all societies, and in all ages. Those features, present thousands of years ago when the original humans came into being, are exactly the same in today's descendants. More specific human nature features include ones original and fundamental needs: ones propensities (in-born tendencies like your capacities, abilities, and language); and ones "Being" Aspects -- things like ones Real Self and its contents of life, Consciousness, a loving character, your purpose or mission in life, and constructive instinct selfishness (embracing a need for survival, self-preservation, self-protection, achievement, self-interest, and the desire of immortality). Included in the primary self-preservation urges are those for food, water, temperature control, elimination, reproduction, physical activity (e.g. a need to move and explore), and the experiences of emotions (e.g. pleasure, anger, fear, depression, and emotional pain) (Bailey, Managing Emotions). However, the expressions of Human Nature can be and are modified according to situations, circumstances, and the environment. By lacking moral overtones, folkways, in contrast to mores, were (and are) not considered vital to the welfare of the group. Typically they arose (and arise) from the *pursuit of pleasure and the avoidance of pain—the two non-spiritual fundamental guides of human nature.* Within these limitations, habits are acquired and imitated by others and retained as long as they provide satisfaction and pleasure. The basic problem is that today's education is geared to teaching only Supernatural (fantasy) propaganda within a Physical World context. The gist: the only things that exist are what can be observed or experienced. For those who doubt the existence of realistic Unseen forces, a superficial understanding of the *Electromagnetic Spectrum* clearly shows that only a tiny part of what exists is visible to humans. An analogy is the relatively small Seeable spectrum portion is like the part connecting both sides of a coin, say Arkansas in the USA. On the side heading westward from Arkansas toward the Pacific Ocean are subdivisions of infrared waves, microwaves, and, on the west coast, radio waves. On the side heading eastward from Arkansas to the Atlantic Ocean are ultraviolet rays, x-rays, gamma rays, and, on the east coast, cosmic rays. Yet, it is conceivable that undiscovered waves and rays could extend around the world. The point is that just because one cannot see something does not mean it does not exist. In fact, people have been programmed to "be blind to the elephant in the room." Similarly, since we cannot hear something does not mean it does not exist. For instance, dogs hear far more that humans are able to hear because their sensitivity is 20 to 200 times greater. Still, waves of light, rays, and sounds that one does not detect are in and around everyone and have profound effects, as does socialization. In focusing on Infrared light, the color spectrum—similar to that seen in the rainbow formed by sunlight passing through a prism—is illustrative. When the sun's white light passes through a drop of rain, the rays composing it are bent to different degrees and thereby forced apart. Upon reaching deep into each raindrop, these *primary colors of the spectrum* (the visible range of light) are separated rays--violet, indigo, blue, green, yellow, orange, red--reflecting back to ones eye—and of which only some are seen or noticed. The red light is warmer than the light passing through other colors. But if one were to hold a thermometer below the red where nothing is seen, the temperature would still be higher. This form of light "below the red"—i.e. infra (below)--is termed "*Infrared Light.*" To show its correspondence, similar to visible light, it is a kind of electromagnetic wave. Of the Seeable colors, red has the longest wavelength, and Infrared waves are even longer. Every object gives off some Infrared waves—detectible by a special film that produces a "Thermal Image" picture. Though Infrared cannot be seen, if strong enough, it can be "Felt" as heat. From this I suggest first that electromagnetic waves are like the Subjective Plane where all of God's Creatures and Creations come into existence; are interconnected like Infrared is connected to all of the electromagnetic waves giving rise to UnSeeable and Seeable colors; and that Compassion is the Cosmic Organism sharing of those interconnections. Second, out of the Cosmic Organism "Color" interconnections, the Infrared is like the "ME/WE" Compassion aspect possessed by all. However, if one is socialized to believe in humans being "Individualists" in machine-like fashion, instead of being part of the Cosmic Organism, then there can be no Knowing of Compassion. Yet, one never altogether forgets the Realities of its original Divine World home, which are held in the memory of even those on the White Supremacy Ladder. But the difference is that the Mild recognize it in their lives—like the rain Cloud that has a silver-lining. That Cloud interferes with the Humanity of the Mild because of their "*Un-willful Ignorance.*" Part of their programming to "be blind to the elephant in the room" is in not recognizing the Spiritual Elements Essences and their Primary Qualities in Colored Peoples who have not been afflicted by the Supernatural dogma. Neither do they recognize the "WE" portion of the "ME/WE" and thus do not see anybody as being *Individuated*—i.e. not taking note of Colored People's as each, possessing an Spark of God, as a Divine Being. The "me, me, me" shows in infinite ways—e.g. "pull up the anchor, I'm on board" and thinking their "bowel movements don't stink!" See *Electromagnetic Spectrum*

COMMON SENSE (AFRICAN): *Common Sense* is generally defined as the unified use of certain senses--regardless of their nature--and unified so many times by so many people that such use has become common. But this does not mean Common Sense is "right" or appropriate for the situation. Furthermore, it may now be out-of-date compared to when it originated. My concept came when I was a paperboy in Greensboro, North Carolina and talking with my several ex-Slave newspaper customers. The fact that had never been allowed to read, write, or count during and after slavery meant that the cultivation of their Intellect had been put "on-hold"—like the telephone's "call-waiting." Yet, in looking back, the profoundness of the concepts in their conversations gave me the impression of Common Sense being about the cultivation of pre-birth Emotions. In particular, my present idea of *Common Sense* is: *specialized Spiritual Feelings integrated with organized Thoughts arising out of the Spiritual Elements so as to give a practical understanding of the fundamentals of Right daily living.* To elaborate, in African Tradition Reality encompasses a range of states of Spiritual Energy/ Matter ranging in the unformed, hence imperceptible, Subjective Plane of existence all the way to the finite and restrictive Matter in the Physical Plane. All Entities in the Cosmos are like chain-linked divisions of the Spiritual Elements' "Genetics"—implying all of God's creatures and creations have Correspondence (by their Sameness Genetics) and are essentially One in Being. Thus, all "Beings" are in reality the percolation of one original Divine Consciousness through each separate Entity form (Amen, Metu Neter I:103). People who have cultivated their Pre-birth Emotions (i.e. Spiritual Feelings) are able to intuit these Cosmic Principles that give Order to existence—as occurs in the "First Wisdom" of newborn humans.

From the glob of Cosmic Principles they are able to create systems to integrate the lives of people with each other, the environment, and God. The Right Brain governs understanding and spirituality + is the symbol of omniscience and omnipresence of God within ones Soul + its natural intuition has a creative part (from "Pure Feelings"; Spiritual Emotions) and non-creative part (e.g. the sixth sense; predominantly Ancient Brain instincts). The core of the Right Brain is the "Ma'at" faculty which enables one to see the inner Qualitative factors that unify things based on the mutual relationships and interdependence of Things with each other and the whole. In other words, "Unity"--in Relational Right Brain thinking--denotes the abstract tie between what underlies a plurality of different Things in a Wholistic sense. That perception is called *Synthesis* which is likened to a mosaic assemblage of bits and pieces taken from different things in order form a mental image. This integrative (synthetical) ability depends upon a disciplined Right Brain capacity to think Abstractly or in Abstractions. An *Abstract* is one or an Association of Ideas or Thoughts about an individual's or a group's *Primary Quality/Qualities (Intangible) which have been harmoniously meshed into its/their Metaphysical Essence (i.e. irreducible)*. Examples are Bonding and Caring. An *Abstraction* is an Association of Ideas or Thoughts concerning real *"Concrete" Things* which have been harmoniously meshed into its/their Metaphysical Essence (i.e. irreducible) to enable one to see things as they really are. Ancient African Groits explained these Cosmic Principles and their Essences by means of *"Poetic Logic" Metaphors*. See Poetic; Knowledge; Wisdom; Logic

COMMON SENSE/KNOWLEDGE/WISDOM THINKING: The single most important concept in African Tradition is the Spiritual Elements of Unconditional Love, Truth, Reality, and the Natural. Next are Principles, Essences, Essentials, Foundations, and Fundamentals. All start out of their God origin with the Spiritual Elements forming a Cosmic Organism Interchange inside the Ocean of Nun—the source of which and upon which all God's creatures and creations are distinctively and individually composed. In humans, this composition concerns Divine, Spiritual, Psychic, Astral, Physiological, and Physical planes. Human minds do countless things with Common Sense, Knowledge, and Wisdom Ingredients. To be aware of these ingredients and how they can be manipulated gives a very crude sense of what goes on in ones Brain/Mind. That sense can assist one in decision making and problem solving of what is "tough," seemingly "Impossible," and of what is about major life-shaping, life-changing, and life-maintenance determinations. A background for understanding includes concepts about the categories of an Interchange, Mosaic, and Free Mind perspective. Because of the complexities involved with all of these, allow me to give a "Big Picture" of what this looks like in fashioning a career. In designing my medical career I combined the fields of Medical Genetics and Orthopaedic Surgery (the Interchange) in order to create, from the overlap, the new Orthopaedic Genetics field focused on Bony Birth Defects. This had a duel benefit. One was being a major part of my research and literature contributions on Dwarfisms; the other was invaluable in the Industrial Medicine aspect of my practice. In the process of developing this new field from the overlap, their ingredients inside the Interchange formed a Mosaic—i.e. 'bits and pieces' drawn from different associated things in order to fashion a unique creation. Put another way, from the Interchange formed by Medical Genetics and Orthopaedic Surgery I took bits and pieces from both as the ingredients for the Mosaic of the new Orthopaedic Genetics. That *Mosaic Inheritance* meant its independent ingredients from both contributors were in interdependent harmony. They also allowed for any given facet in that Mosaic team to independently dominate in pure form at appropriate points. This is because the various facets in the Mosaic possess had *Reciprocity* (equality within the domain of each aspect of the composite) as well as each produced outputs serving as in-puts into all other facets—and vice versa. To illustrate how the respective facets in each ingredient formed a composite that interdependently worked together for a new creation to arise out of what had evolved from the Interchange, the following Principles did not come complete by instant illumination. Instead, they resulted from continuous reflection—each successively revealing pertinent insights acquired in a fragment by fragment manner—seemingly to be like successive cellular developments. Out of that process I came to know that if I became disabled from doing Orthopaedic Surgery, I could go into the Radiology part of Orthopaedics, teach Genetics to Orthopaedic Surgeons, and/or teach Orthopaedic Surgical Bony aspects to Geneticists. This is about knowing clearly what one is about, realizing what is available concerning that Purpose, figuring out ways to use the ingredients in that process to the best advantages inside multiple options, and with no concerns about the difficulties and troubles involved in doing what has to be done in order to get what is of the "ME/WE" best.

COMPARISONS: *Complex Comparisons* involving two or more systems, based upon two or more things (e.g. analogous events), leading to the inference they are similar in structure; comparing two or more systems similar in structure and taking the familiar in one to explain the unknown in the other.

COMPETENCE: C14; (suitable; sufficient") means fitness, as acquired through education and experience; a sense of ability; the capacity to deal with a subject; to be proper; proved through competition; adequate means for living comfortably; sufficient to supply all the necessities and many of the lesser comforts; and a high output in work with a low input in energy that is a desired effect. Since then, it carried ideas of *Efficient* (do tasks quickly without wasted time, energy, effort compared with other options) and *Effective* (come up with the desired effect that satisfies the solution better than any alternative). These are what bring about *Efficacy*—the ongoing *Self-Empowerment* urging one to fashion an intended result that is headed towards ones ultimate Human Ideal goal.

COMPETITION IN LIFE OVERVIEW: As a tiny aspect of Nature's interrelatedness, all biological things are part of their eating society, living because they kill others. Predators aim to be the top eaters; Prey, to avoid being eaten. Such competition, in some form, is carried out by all Cosmic Creatures—each in a concentrated effort to maintain and enhance survival, self-preservation, and self-protection. Yet, there cannot be a successful in-group without an unsuccessful out-group--and that is the basis of competition in Nature. This, a Natural Spiritual Moral component in the Laws of Nature, is above the human mind's ability to understand—and that's the way it is!--and there is nothing any human can do about it. A dominant like-kind law in African Tradition—during the 155,000 years Africans were on Earth before Europeans began to appear--was Self-Competition. It was in the context of rising above ones Lower (animalistic) Self towards ones Highest (Divinity) Self. Next, as a result of early Interior Very Ancient Africans originating the sporting events known today as the Olympic Games, and formalized by Ancient Egyptian sports of 5200 BC, the concept of Competition expanded. Here emphasized was great determination on the part of one, or more than one, to achieve or win something, to shed something, or to make a record--concepts ancient Greeks took to form their Olympic games. Such a definition of "Competition" (Greek: "com," together, and "petere" seek, strive) enabled multiple offspring concepts to formulate a variety of etymologies--each opening different paths where competitions could apply. However, primitive Europeans introduced its placement on a vicious negative scale--a Competition about division, disunion, 'every man for himself,' and deeming any unlike them as rivals. Subsequently, because Western Warriors and Thinkers never honored the Subjective/Spiritual or Metaphysical Realms of the Natural Cosmos, they defined "Competition" as a "struggle against a rival to win." Note: this is an extremely narrow and flawed definition since world-wide it promotes only "me against you" delusions; focuses only on the objective (Physical) realm; always concerns a conflict struggle; demands at least a feigned enemy; and worst of all, sets inhumane standards for the World Crowd. For example, Unconditional Love (not an emotion!), by being Immaterial, is governed by the Law that the more of it you give away the more you have. By contrast, on the Concrete Plane of the material portion of the world, the more you give away the less you have. Nevertheless, these Warriors' inner world was about extreme tension or stress which drove them to be highly competitive; be clingers to anything deemed powerful (e.g. attachment to material possessions); cultivate an attitude of Indifference/Hate/Evil/Sadism (IHES) Complex ways of dealing with people; and be so greedily "ME, ME, ME" oriented as to constantly be on guard against victims' retaliation or revenge. Their Left Brain pursuits of worldly emotional excitement indulged their Fetters—e.g. extreme selfishness, greed, hatred, anger, egoism, fear, envy, jealousy, frustration, arrogance, pride, lust—all promoting a focus merely on analysis and excluding synthesis.

By contrast, African Tradition elevates Synthesis over Analysis since when humans' Right Brains orchestrate serious business thinking, it governs wholism (i.e. togetherness), understanding and spirituality. These are absent in Left Brain only people and thus their Analysis dominance fashions lifestyle concepts of an "I" (Individualism) society nature. Those features include: looking for differences in people (so as to form prejudices), individuality, uniqueness, advocating individual rights, separateness and independence, survival of the fittest, control over Nature, and being competitive (Nobles in Jones, Black Psychology p103). What naturally follows is unscrupulous arts and practices of achieving or maintaining advantages over others--ranging from mild to extreme—and acting like a "little god". Their IHES arts and practices to acquire "Scarce Desires" drives them to run over all things—holy, profane, clean, taboo, obscene, grave--and without shame, guilt, or regret. They are posters for absurdity and "Don't Care"—and such can clearly be seen in politicians (among endless others, regardless of marketplace type). Their dishonorableness aims for success through status symbols or displays of superiority over scapegoats; by outdoing or keeping one jump ahead of equal status competitors; and enjoy causing pain and suffering in the poor. jabaileymd.com

COMPETITION CLASSIFICATION: Out of ones chosen Philosophy of Life (POL) comes a lifestyle of how one thinks, feels, expresses, acts, and reacts. These, of course, are at the basis of ones success or failure in life's "Big Picture" of Competition. I define *Success as "getting what you really, really want and not getting what you really, really do not want"*. *Failure* is the reverse, originating from people disconnections. *Type I* is *Selfless Sacrificial Service*—as when one takes the task of a less able other—e.g. heroes who give up their lives from facing overwhelming competitive odds. *Type II* is *Private and Public Self success* which comes from living up to ones own Real Self nature. Ones "ME/WE" part engages in Selfless Service (competing with oneself to prudently help others now or later). *Type III* is *Private Self success* from Constructive Self-Competition—despite not being completely successful in External World "Creature Comforts". *Type IV* is Public Self "*Creature Comforts*" success but not success within ones Private Self. *Type V* lacks "Creature Comforts" + Private and Public Self success. *Type VI* is Miscellaneous situations. *Constructive Competition*: (1) "*Win*"—e.g. Types II & III—include: competing against ones own record for Personal Improvement; competing to establish a record above ones self-imposed limitations; finding the best against whom to practice; competing against ones own reluctance not to be involved; competing to simply experience the pleasure of being in the game; competing against the record of the top rival or against the all-time record or all-time champion. These are done for Spiritual and/or Material purposes--e.g. to become wealthy in worth (i.e. Spiritual Beauty) and/or rich in value (e.g. material things contributing to ones well-being)--so as to progress towards a goal. As a boy, I would teach myself discipline by seeing how long I could go without "scratching the bump that itched." One strives "everyday in every way to get better and better" (Couve), as by practicing to fashion skills and to remain honorable—even giving up an unfair advantage to do so. Self-Love does not allow any competition to do harm to oneself or others. (2) "*Win-Win*" was shown in Primitive Africans' hunting game where the men brought back food to feed the community while women did gardening. At a wedding ceremony, the bride and groom's candle (representing her and his character) lights a third candle to indicate a joining of their Spiritual Humanity to independently work interdependently toward a successful marriage. Hence, the "*Third*

Candle" Concept implies that the marriage is more important than the bride's or the groom's different ways of thinking--of their moods/emotions--of their different ways of expressions—or doing selfish behaviors. Their Complementary Equal strivings together fits like Yin/Yang symbols--an inseparable "We" working together for the same goal"—whether independently or interdependently—and without a competition "score-card" of who did more. Its "ME/WE" part is helping oneself now so as to later benefit the other. In both, the "We" and "ME/WE" go together toward the same goal. (3) "*Winner*" is what the Chinese Sun Tzu called "*Taking Whole*" so that it is "*Win-not Lose.*" It is playing "rough" for realistic or marketplace survival, self-protection, or self-preservation but without opponents necessarily losing. "Rough" is not the same as "dirty" (i.e. brute practices) but instead, for a special purpose, is doing things that are intimidating and respected, even though the opposition does not like them (Bailey, Black Americans in the Marketplace p200). *Destructive Competition,* according to African Tradition, is what is unnatural, as exhibited by humans intentionally doing harm to each other or to oneself--and for any reason. Type A are *Win-Lose.* Subtype A (1) is exhibited in all competitive Team or Individual Sports, if losing is not a learning lesson. Subtype A (2) is Mean Predator/Prey—i.e. hate-filled predators using scapegoats to feel superior. Subtype A (3) is "*The Game*" whereby the rich and powerful are dedicated to achieving status at the expense of the scapegoat poor. Type B is "*Win and Lose*"--striving together until envy or greed sets in (Love/Hate Relationship). Subtype C (1) "*Lose-Win*" is giving up ones Selfhood to be part of the Crowd. Subtype C (2) is being slave-like to another, as self-punishment or as imitating pursuers of Success (e.g. Oreos). Type D: *Loser*—e.g. Type V above--are drifters through life with Low Self-Esteem. Type E: *Lose-Lose* (e.g. feuds). Type F: *Chameleon False Self* people. jabaileymd.com

COMPETITION--SPIRITUAL CLASSIFICATION: This embraces: I. Selfless Service (competing with oneself to prudently help others); II. Win-Win (A) Striving with others--(B) Lifting others while Climbing--(C) Third Candle (Living in a harmonious realm); III. Winner--(A) Competing with oneself--(B) Competing against an outside standard; IV. Win-Not Lose (Taking Whole). The Cosmic Organism is the model for Type II. As an Isolated Individualist, my focus in daily living is on IIIA to strive for Perfection by ever increasing my Efficiency and Effectiveness. Typically, Isolated Individualists are introverts. The Introverts (a term quite confusing in European psychology) are those whose Inner World is more important than the External World because of being Introspective or from being "Withdrawn" as an "escape" or from a psychiatric problems (e.g. schizoid) whereby people express themselves in fantasy. The "Escape Withdrawn" are often passive, daydreamers, and avoiders of people while focusing their leisure on making contributions to Art, Science, or Philosophy. Introspective Introverts are most often seen in Isolated Individualists who feature Inner calm and an Intensity for "Aliveness." Thus, their Leisure is chosen within the setting of a disciplined contemplative, reserved, and sensitive self-assessment for how to best use what little leisure they have periodically. They do not have free and easy social contacts but are not self-centered, most having a "ME/WE" orientation.

COMPETITIVE--HISTORICAL "DARK SIDE'S": Predatory/Prey conflicts are a feature of the Physical part of the Cosmos. Sea animals fight by slamming, biting, or suction. Caterpillars' indirect fighting, when facing danger, is by spitting poison like a little snake. Since Humankind's very beginnings, there have been forms of competition battles in each of its embraced parts. All cultures, at some point and to some extent, have interpreted negative events as being inflicted upon them by malevolent, Supernatural spirits or forces. With Europeans appearance 45,000 years ago, a new lifestyle of Competition--called the "Dark Side" element--was introduced. It has subsequently spread and branched into so many forms worldwide as to now make "Dark Side" Competition an Umbrella Word. This means it acts like a mother hen with chicks under both wings--because so many different things of the same family are under its canopy. However, the concept of "Dark Side" Competition appeared in the Ancient African Biblical Mythology. The "good guy," Horus is portrayed as a falcon after he defeated the "bad guy" Seth in an aerial battle over good vs. evil. The mythological European Valkyries, Amazonian priestesses who ruled the gates of Death, brought the souls of the heroes killed in battle to the Hall of the Slain. After feasting, for amusement, they fought one another with savage fervor (similar especially to European warriors of the Middle Ages and on to today). Historically, Europeans have constantly been on some type of battlefield engaged in constant wars between losses and gains because of an insatiable greedy quest for the newer, the most, the bigger, the better, and the faster related to goods, material things, and adult toys. Such, as a challenge, a form of entertainment, and a display of power—are all to satisfy ego. They never get enough of fighting and "wins" carry nothing more than momentary hate-type pleasures—there is never peace or happiness. Such is driven by ones Brute Brain (part of the Ancient Brain) whose essence is characterized by the German word "Fight." Initially, "Fight" was a covering term meaning anything from sharp language to fisticuffs; then to battle and combat; and then embracing the general meaning "to contend or struggle for mastery." An early usage was as a Biblical phrase (1 Timothy 6:12): "Fight the good fight of faith, lay hold of eternal life." It expanded to include Imperialism--the process of a nation extending its territory by imposing its authority and thus gaining political and economic control of other areas. Europeans' imperialistic take-over of Africa and its people by means of the GUN was associated with exploitation, violence of unspeakable magnitude, and the worse of brutality ever known to Humankind. It began in 1433 with arrival of the first shipment of enslaved Africans and gold in Portugal. Its ending in 1870 was the beginning of the Colonial phase involving Africans. Meanwhile, European invasion of the Americas brought in Enslaved Africans to do the work of shaping the Americas into Europeans' cultural self-image. It also caused near total destruction of millions of Amerindians and their food supply. Increasing profits and increasing systematization of the economic infrastructure led to increased competition among European nations vying for power. Their competition and greed, with an emphasis on Africa, resulted in global devastation and inhumanity unequaled in world history. The first thing European enslavers did was to generate dissention among the Enslaved by starving them and causing them to fight each other for food. Then Europeans converted the mindset and behaviors of the Enslaved out of the realm of sound African Tradition into a realm of delusions. This was accomplished by brainwashing techniques; by breaking the spirits of the Enslaved; and by causing "Inside-Out" thinking. The point was to prevent them from ever recovering sufficiently to be a form of Competition to Europeans. Today, "Fight" continues to be about competition or conflict between two hostile forces, with or without direct physical contact. The nature of the worst of Competition is the Satanist "Evilness" which constantly attacks Spiritual Elements lifestyles. Whatever it touches, their anti-Spiritual Elements tactics and strategies--"by themselves, reproduce themselves so as to become the things they make." Their evilness generates Delusional Fear for victims. Perhaps their worst brainwashing mind control tool is the fantasy creation of Hell/Devil and burning forever in hell after death. jabaileymd.com

COMPETITORS' TEMPERAMENTS: An Attitude—i.e. a Disposition + a Temperament--fashions a mental position about a "Thing." A Temperament is an aroused physiological Sensory Consciousness reaction with a prevailing trend. Type I--Non-aggressive Spiritual Emotions' Temperaments are characterized by gentleness, kindness, compassion, and a "live and let live" win-win orientation toward life. To it, Ancient Africans joined the Spiritual Elements and evolved their self-assertion out of that. Type II Non-Aggressive/Acquired Emotional Assertiveness is an impure or "Misty" Type I. Type III--Aggressive Temperaments arrogantly go for Scarce Desirables in overt or tempered ways. Type IV, Passive-Aggressive Temperaments are masked or concealed Type III snipers. Type V--Passive Temperaments—compete by Conditional Love + guilt ("If you love me, you will not choose them"). Type I calmly and confidently pursues what rightfully belongs to them for purposes of their "ME/WE" Mission in life. For their Necessities, they get in proper position without pushing others away—as do good basketball rebounders—and avoid Attractive Distractions. To elaborate, throughout my education, training, and medical practice it was routine for racists to ensure that I started off in "the back"—far from where I needed to be. Yet, to not be left out of what belonged to my Mission, it was essential for me to "elbow my way" up to the front. In the process of persisting forward, I would always show good manners (e.g. "Excuse me, please") to those trying to block my way—but never being confrontational. I moved so quickly and silently that the racists did not have time to react. Type II, similarly working for the "ME/WE" team, is "Misty" because of its attached Acquired Emotions pertaining to a competitive spirit. Anticipating denial or objection, it "over-prepares" to handle both by Defense and Offense, as I also did. Types I & II can bring out the best in humans while Types III, IV, & V bring out the worst. The lives of all humans are typically faced with challenges, ranging in significance from mild to slight to moderate to extreme. Human Character is determined by how one reacts by going through hour-glass stricture challenges.

COMPULSIONS--"DARK SIDE": C15 "Compulsion" originally had the sense of "to use force"; to be driven; to compel, force, or coerce; and to drive together. The psychological sense of an uncontrollable impulse to be a certain way is first recorded in 1909 as, for example, a compressive desire for food for which one cannot refrain from eating. Then its idea went deeper, as in one being urged to do irrational behaviors though it serves no conscious purpose except removing the disquietude which would arise if it were not performed; next, more specific (e.g. denoting an act performed to relieve a fear connected with an obsession and dictated by ones subconscious); and finally, more complex (irresistible inner forces compelling outside actions--or even against the will of the individual performing it). Recently psychologists have defined Compulsions as a psychoneurotic reaction characterized by a persistent uncontrollable impulse to think certain thoughts (obsessions) or carry out certain actions (compulsions). Furthermore, when the Obsessive or Compulsive Personality is subjected to great stress, they may develop a full-blown neurosis. Some have concluded the actor, despite unable to modify his behavior, may fail to understand his act; insist it is absolutely necessary; and yet recognize its futility. According to my interpretations, today's Compulsions can be classified as follows: MILD Compulsions, when used to achieve goals without giving up, are on the positive scale and thereby contribute to strength of character and solid achievement. However, they are at a neutral point when they keep one under constant stimulated tension while causing one to become increasingly anxious by failing to achieve ones high goals all the time. SLIGHT Compulsions are at the beginning of the negative side since they cause one to act out of an inner drive to repeatedly perform an irrational and irresistible act. Perhaps this shows as an exaggerated sense of responsibility; an excessive need for perfection; an inability to relax; and an earnest, driven, humorless air. MODERATE Compulsions, like all neurotics, have strong feelings of inadequacy; display as a response to anxiety an impelling to perform some irrational act or a series of acts as a way of relieving anxiety; are excessively susceptible to guilt feelings; engage in *Reaction Formation* (going to the opposite extreme); and live under the belief of the world as a dangerous place. Because of their sense of inadequacy, at the bidding of another they may feel compelled to perform Compulsive behaviors against their own conscious wishes and judgment. The rigidity of their personalities makes them resistant to change and to impose their rigid standards on others. Their Obsessions and Compulsions nature keeps alive their drive to live inside a destructive/delusional IHES Complex world. EXTREME Compulsions characterize Brutes and their severe delusional IHES Complex. Because Fear and Distrust are the main controlling factors for European behavior, prominent Brute features are: (1) Serial Compulsions of all grades, as in carrying out sequences of acts or adhering rigidly to a certain order of brute behavior; (2) Compulsive Coercion -- the irresistible need to hold others in check by demanding devotion to routine or detail; and (3) Antisocial Compulsions -- the irresistible need to perform criminal acts. In one form or another Obsessions and Compulsions in their complete range are more common than is generally appreciated. What adds to these numbers are those who are so mentally weak as to be followers of Brutes.

Perhaps the importance of these Brute Followers is in moments of experiencing great guilt for what they have done, they may try to make symbolic amends. Could it be they who have named so many things (e.g. states, cities, streets, parks, etc.) after the very Amerindians whom they helped Brute Europeans slaughter in their own land. All of this is essential for Black People to understand so as to stop buying into the bad ways of European.

CONATIVE ELEMENT: The power for any natural tendency related to purposive behavior directed toward action or change--the power for impulse, desiring, striving, and resolving.

CON-ARTISTS: Confidence man ("Con-man" or "Con-Artist" for short), Swindlers, Cheaters, Deceivers, Tricksters, Defrauders, Beguilers, Quacks, Shark, Horse Trader, Card-sharp, Shyster, Land Pirate, and Land Shark are but a tiny few of the names used for plausible Deceivers. They cheat by faking for personal gain—whether putting themselves at an unfair advantage or putting Victims at an unfair disadvantage--and, to varying degrees, they usually succeed. Although they have been present throughout ancient cultures, they were most prominate among primitive Europeans with their Supernatural gods (e.g. Thor) made in their own image. Arbitrarily, let us pick up the story in Europeans' Biblical times with the Con-artist' presentation of metaphors copied out of the Ancient African Spiritual Literature and made into fact (Bailey, Ancient African Bible Messages). One of the countless stories is the serpent, disguised as the devil and pretending to be what he was not in his association with Adam and Eve. By smooth, hypocritical talk in saying what Eve wanted to hear—and by being emotional, Eve was able to be deceived by a serpent and both Eve and Adam were talked out of Paradise. In reality, the characters taking part in the original African Ethiopian mythological story were not Eve and Adam, but rather Aisha and Aish. Here, thousands of years prior to the formation of the European Bible, the point of the Serpent was to symbolize humans' Acquired Emotions and Sensations as being the essence of animalistic behaviors (Amen, Metu Neter VII: 51). Both combine humans' rational and artistic faculties and behaviors in the service of their sensual nature. Hence, there is no intelligence, morality, or spirituality in humans' Brain/Minds that generates them. Instead, they are human-made vehicles of the Life Force and their imposition of Force over Mind, Reasoning, and the Will is the cause of all that is wrong in the Universe. From this falsely presented fantasy story of the "Fall of Man," there was a Cascade of infinite magnitude that simultaneously served as Spirit, Body, and Mind destructive forces to various peoples of the world.

Those forces resembled a series of waterfalls pouring and spreading over steep rocks--disrupting humane Spiritual, Rational, and Physical networks in its path--networks which produce outputs serving as the in-put for the next component in each network while rippling in all directions. An example of a consequence of this story the making of a necessity for a Redemption to restore all humans from Adam and Eve having cursed the human race with "Original Sin"—supposedly as a result of God's wrath (itself an anthropomorphism concept). To make all of this work for controlling the minds of people, Europeans invented a Hell, Devil, and Supernatural God(s). Despite the false appearance of pleasantness and goodness, the European mythology authority Campbell (Thou Art p86) that the Garden of Eden [which is actually in Africa]; "…a world Flood; a Tower of Babel; an Abraham; and Exodus from Egypt; and edition of the Ten Commandments entrusted physically to Moses on the top of Mt. Sinai, followed by a second edition delivered to him after he had broken up the tablets of the first; a particular Virgin Birth, the End of the World--when taken as the message of truth, allows the symbols to be used as devices to control the people in churches and temples."

Practically every mythology in the world borrowed the African concept of the Virgin Birth to refer to a spiritual rather than an historical reality. The same, continues Campbell (Thou Art p7), applies to "the metaphor of the Promised Land, which in its denotation plots nothing but a piece of earthly geography to be taken by force." Meanwhile, a *Lexicographer's* con-artist trick concerned Alchemy—now wrongly deemed to be Arabic definite article (of "*Al*" which is like a prefix) and "*chemy*", a Greek stem (i.e. the word root or base).

But similar to so many misrepresented words, "*alchemy*" is an African word, with "chemy" (or Kemet) being the root for the original name of what is now called Egypt. One of its stories is that in the early centuries of the Christian Era, the Greeks of Alexandria, Egypt pursued the practice of trying to transmute base metals into noble ones but believed they needed an imaginary substance--called the *Philosopher's Stone*—because of its supposed linkage with the theories of matter advanced by the ancient philosophers. A deception from this was that the "Stone" possessed indefinite life prolonging and body curing powers. See Quacks; Alchemy

"CON-ARTIST" TRICKS: Ancient Africans determined God's Spiritual imperceptible Substance was not subject to the Qualities of Matter, making it Ideal, for its Infinite existence is, of course, in the Amenta Realm—a Realm higher that the Subjective Realm of the Finite Cosmos. Yet, the Substance imparted the Essence (i.e. a real Substance rather than Ideal) and its involuted Primary Quality Essentials into all Cosmic Creatures and Creations so as to constitute the ultimate nature or "soul" of a thing—regardless of whether that thing is Seeable or Un-Seeable. This is the purest and most fundamental part of anything. The Greek Pythagoras (582-500 BC), stealing these ideas from Africa, claimed this Celestial Essence—constituant elements of the Heavenly Bodies--was a fifth Essence, Ether, above the Four Matter Elements of Water, Fire, Air, and Earth and thus named it *Quintessence*. The *Quintessence* was extremely valued by Medieval Alchemists. They thought certain heavenly objects —called the *Philosopher's Stone* (consisting of diverse metals)--were symbolic forms of heavenly energy. Believing this heavenly energy was essential to the success of the transmutation of metals into gold and silver, they tried in vain to extract the Ether through chemical distillation. Actually, the only significant thing "distilled" was the word "*Essence*" out of the word *Quintessence* (Spence p322). Whereas of greatest importance to Africans was the Philosophers' Stone being about a Wholistic approach to medicine--i.e. attention to a patient's mind, body, and soul through magical spells, rituals, and practical herbal, sound, light, and muscial prescriptions, for Europeans it was a frenzy about getting rich—serving as a "hotbed" for producing Tricksters whose sole purpose was to deceive victims by any means necessary for personal gain. A particularly stimulating period (e.g. regarding the "Philosopher's Stone") for Con-artists was Europeans' Dark Ages and that, thereafter, became a way of life for most Europeans anywhere. A center stage spotlight was on "The Game" of C15 and C16 European "gentlemen". Arrogant Individualism drove their addictive obsession for Materialism to the point of them honoring the *Seven Deadly Sins*—pride (arrogance), covetousness (greed), lust, anger, gluttony, envy, and sloth (lazy). This combination displays as to Kill/Take/Destroy/Dominate/Control/Oppress (KTDDCO) those they feign to be "Against" them. The rules of these Brutes' "Games" were that there were no rules. Hence, any dishonorable acts were respected as a show of power. It had to be played with a "*Swagger*," as in being judgmental about everybody else plus the attitude of "the world belongs to me and I can push people around because the rules do not apply to me." Style included ostentatious appearances of being rich; being excessively wasteful; intimidating victims; acquiring endless numbers of "adult toys"; and one- ups-manship practices designed to outsmart competitors. Brute Europeans' trademark was (and is) aiming to live "the Good Life" of hedonism (i.e. pleasing the senses is the only "Good"). But to give the appearance of being "intelligent and deep thinkers" their pseudo-metaphysical topics were (and are) merely facades—Non-Rational thinking disguised in undefined or meaningless big words. Behind these presentations is the lack of a realistic Base beginning; opinions absent truth, wisdom, or constructive meaning; and on a course "going nowhere." The Renaissance "Gentlemen" financed the African American Slave Trade and came to the Americas' as "Southern Gentlemen" -- setting up local, state, and the federal governments so as to maintain their national dishonorableness to the present. Meanwhile, free use of every amoral/immoral KTDDCO measure imaginable to humankind was so admired by Europeans that these aspects of "The Game" trickled down to the masses of people who superficially imitated with the accoutrements of dress, possessions, and partying so as to appear rich -- a pattern persisting in full force throughout slavery and on to this day. During C18 and C19, Europeans' *Age of Reason* focused on understanding the universe and humankind through pure reason and logic. The idea was to holding everyone to fact and reason was the wellspring from which we got the scientific revolution, the Enlightenment, the rule of law, doctrines of universal human rights, the abolition of slavery, the emancipation of women, the civil rights movement, the concept of free speech and unprecedented material prosperity. European professionals--e.g. scientists, Physiognomists (those reading facial configurations or expressions in the belief they show qualities of mind or character), Astrologists, and others -- everywhere flowered in meeting the thirst the public had to take short cuts to the "Good Life." for "finding the hidden power within yourself" or for answers as to "why have you not been successful" or "I can analyze your personal assets and liabilities in order to bring light to your needs and conflicts."

CON-ARTISTS—RELIGIOUS: Foundational to Critical Thinking (CT) is to have a truthful or realistic "Big Picture" of the issue at hand (the entire perspective of a situation or issue, like the panoramic view an eagle gets while flying over a farm). "Confidence"-men/women are brutes who manifest in the categories of the Indifference-Hate-Evil-Sadist Complex and prey on the Naïve and Gullible, regardless of age, gender, or degree of intellectual sophistication in other areas of life. To buy into the Con-artist's entire program, is to enter the realm of Delusions. This was best worked out by the ancient Greek Sophists who taught it to the rich. Even worse were ancient Greeks scholars who took home from Africa what they learned from Ancient African Sages (e.g. profound African philosophy and mathematics); renamed it so as to plagiarize African intellectual property and practices; and destroyed almost all the original African source material. They did the same to African Christianity in converting it to European Christianity. During African American slavery, White religious con-artists, under pretense of using the King James Bible to bring Christianity and a higher civilization to Enslaved Africans, machine-gunned poisonous substances into their devastated minds. However, the real intention of Europeans was to implant seeds of self-destruction in the Enslaved so as to control them. Their purpose was greedy self-interest to enable the enslavers to live "the good life." From a wrong or false foundational base in presenting their evil religion to the Enslaved they would build true statements on top. For example, perhaps the most famous of the Beatitudes is Blessed are the meek: for they shall inherit the earth (Matt. 5:5)--modified to an Enslaved heavenly reward. CT must look at who said this and where did they get it from; when it was said and is that verified; what were the circumstances; and what are the various interpretations of it? As stated, it is recognized among European religious scholars that of all the many existing Gospels of Christ, only those of Matthew, Mark, Luke, and John were accepted for inclusion in the NT. And that the Roman Catholic Church took measures to ensure the questioning and inquisitions surrounding the authorship of this *pseudepigrapha* apocrypha literature would be minimized (i.e. writings falsely attributed to biblical characters or times). CT also looks at the philosophy of the culture and its flow of thought of the day in which meanings of words arose. What the ancient Greeks said is generally the way Europeans think about things to the present. For example, the ancient Greeks employed "meek" to describe a wild horse tamed to the bridle. In keeping with this, to many, "meekness" suggests the idea of passivity, humbly patient or docile, as under provocation from others; overly submissive or compliant; spiritless; tame; someone who is easily imposed upon because of spinelessness and weakness. Could this statement about the meek have reflected the interests of Christians when they were a small and powerless sect? European enslavers viewed Africans as meek for being victims of enslavement. Could the reason European preachers to the Enslaved emphasized meekness -- especially that "pushy people do not succeed in the end" -- to encourage a life absent any striving for improvement as being basic to their idea of "slave morality"? Is this not hiding your talents? Does that conform to the parable of the

Talents (Matt. 25: 14-30)? It is well-known "no striving" for the Enslaved was part of the European captors' "STAY-IN-YOUR-PLACE" admonition. A selling point to the Enslaved is supposedly Jesus declared Himself to be meek (Matthew 11:29). Certainly, the Europeans did not/do not buy into meekness even though claiming this message came from God. Does that make sense? Who decided to change "meekness" to mean the opposite of what the ancient Greeks said? Why is that? Who has benefitted from this double meaning? Is God's Word characterized by opposite meanings? What do you believe? Confused?

CON-ARTISTS--RELIGIOUS EXAMPLES: *Confidence man--*"Con-man" or "Con-Artist" for short--is a term for a plausible swindler who tries to deceive victims for personal gain. And he/she usually succeeds. By giving victims a wrong major premise so as to cater to their desires, a false foundational base results upon which true statements are built. They spotlight the above ground structure with the intension of getting victims to assume the false underground part is also true--the act of mis-representation. Or, what victims do is to see the nine things that are true but fail to see the tenth thing is false—or fail to see that the first thing onto which those nine things were laid was false and designed to give the con-artist the advantage. Many times victims desire for something to be true, even in the face of contrary evidence--a form of self-deception. These tactics know no racial or religious or age boundaries. Biblically, this story starts with the serpent associated with Adam and Eve. Despite the false appearance of pleasantness and goodness, the serpent pretended to be what he was not by hypocritically saying what Eve wanted to hear. The European missionaries who enticed Africans to give up their own superior religion and take on the "White man's" religion were con-artists. Fredrick Douglass (p. 310, 188, 344) said the darkest feature of slavery, and the most difficult to attack, was the religious slave owners and ministers of religion who used the Bible to justify their evilness. "I assert most unhesitatingly, that the religion of the South--as I have observed it and proved it--is a mere covering for the most horrid crimes; the justifier of the most appalling barbarity; a sanctifier of the most hateful frauds; and a secure shelter, under which the darkest, foulest, grossest, and most infernal abominations fester and flourish . . . There is not a nation on earth guilty of practices more shocking and bloody, than are the people of these United States, at this very hour."

The same applies to this day. Whereas religious hypocrites were at an extremely overt level of expression during slavery, there have been tempered, masked, and concealed forms--each with extreme, moderate, slight, and mild degrees--up to the present. They exist in all combinations. The sophisticated types have public support. It all starts with persuasion appealing to desires. In this way people's attitudes, rather than their reason, are most influenced. One method is to elaborate on their "prosperity gospel"--promising worshipers God will shower them with material blessings if they sacrifice by sending money to spread His word and save souls from damnation throughout the world. To give or send more than one can afford is presented as a "step of faith." "After all," they say, "God would not have trouble getting you the same amount of money in your time of need"--a typical con-artist statement that "seems right." A second approach is to show their power because of their claimed direct connection with God. Third is displaying great emotion by speaking in a sing-song voice and letting tears flow freely--whether from reading an audience member's "sob" story letter or recalling some childhood anecdote of God's help. A fourth is to not let the broadcast shut down for lack of money. They, too, show lack of compassion by persuading through religion ("when you give money to God, you are setting in motion the way to get it back and more"). These persuasive techniques are very effective. From 50 years old and over, there are increasing numbers of people who become increasingly lonely because their friends are moving away; older relatives are dying; the realization people built you up was to tear you down; feeling unappreciated and attacked; and in many other ways, losing contact with ones younger past and ones roots. Thus, these people need something to hold on to so as to keep from "going to pieces." Religion is such a major tow-rope. Of course, a certain amount of money is necessary to enable the minister to serve the spiritual needs of the people. But stay aware and keep things in balance.

"CON-JOBS" TODAY: When Religious conservatives get really worked up about abortion since their pastors tell them they will go Hell for voting for someone who is pro-choice. They also say voting for liberals is evil and to do so puts ones soul in mortal danger. Racist news disseminates more false information than truth and that is really sort after—blaming the Other; immigrants, the president, ethnic minorities, LGBT, women—while says people need to "take America back." Calvinism is one of the two major camps in modern Christian American theology and Predestination is part of Calvinist teachings. To many people it sounds like a horrible concept, but it explains part of why poor people vote for Republicans. In a nutshell, everything including the fate of your eternal soul was determined by God, and there is nothing you can do to change that. If you are poor, it is part of "God's plan" and it is not our duty as individuals or the government to help. If someone is rich, then they were chosen to be rich by God, and we should not punish them by making them pay more in taxes.

CON-ARTISTS: Confidence man ("Con-man" or "Con-Artist" for short), Swindlers, Cheaters, Deceivers, Tricksters, Defrauders, Beguilers, Quacks, Shark, Horse Trader, Card-sharp, Shyster, Land Pirate, and Land Shark are but a tiny few of the names used for plausible Deceivers. They cheat by faking for personal gain—whether putting themselves at an unfair advantage and/or putting Victims at an unfair disadvantage. And, to varying degrees, they usually succeed. Although present throughout ancient cultures, they were most prominent among primitive Europeans (who promoted Supernatural gods made in their own image) and with Greek Sophists's shrewd deceptions. Arbitrarily, let us pick up the story in Europeans' Biblical times and focus on Con-artists' presentations of metaphors copied out of the Ancient African Spiritual Literature and made into fact (Bailey, Ancient African Bible Messages). One of the countless stories is the serpent, disguised as the devil and pretending to be what he was not in his association with Adam and Eve. By the serpent's smooth, hypocritical talk in saying what Eve wanted to hear—and Eve, being emotional, was able to be deceived. She convinced Adam--and both were talked out of Paradise. These Eve and Adam characters, in the earlier devised African Ethiopian mythological story thousands of years prior to the formation of the European Bible, were originally named Aisha and Aish to convey the point of the Serpent symbolizing humans' Acquired Emotions and Sensations as being displays of animalistic behaviors (Amen, Metu Neter VII: 51). From this falsely presented fantasy story of the "Fall of Man" is humans' rational, artistic faculties, and behaviors combined in the service of their sensual nature. Hence, there is no intelligence, morality, or spirituality in humans' Brain/Minds that generates such fantasies. Instead, they are human-made vehicles for a false Life Force. Their imposition of Force over Mind, Reasoning, and the Will are the cause of all the varying wrongs in the peopled Universe. The result is a Cascade of infinite magnitude that simultaneously serves as Spirit, Body, and Mind destructive forces to various peoples of the world.

Those false forces resemble a series of waterfalls pouring and spreading over steep rocks--disrupting humane Spiritual, Rational, and Physical networks in its paths--networks which produce outputs serving as inputs for the next component in each network while also rippling in all directions. A consequence example of the Adam/Eve story was Europeans making Redemption necessary to restore all humans from them having cursed the human race with "Original Sin"—a supposed result of God's wrath (itself a false anthropomorphism concept). To make all of this work for controlling peoples' minds, Europeans invented a Hell, Devil, and Supernatural God(s). Besides the serpent's false appearance of pleasantness and goodness, the European mythology authority, Campbell (Thou Art p86) said the Garden of Eden [which is actually in Africa]; "…a world Flood; a Tower of Babel; an Abraham; an Exodus from Egypt; an edition of the Ten Commandments entrusted physically to Moses on the top of Mt. Sinai, followed by a second edition delivered to him after he had broken up the tablets of the first; a particular Virgin Birth, the End of the World--when taken as the message of truth, allows the symbols to be used as devices to control the people in churches and temples."

Practically every mythology in the world borrowed the African concept of the Virgin Birth to refer to a Supernatural rather than to a historical reality. The same, continues Campbell (Thou Art p7), applies to "the metaphor of the Promised Land, which in its denotation plots nothing but a piece of earthly geography to be taken by force." Meanwhile, a *Lexicographer's* con-artist trick concerned Alchemy—now wrongly deemed to be an Arabic definite article (of "*Al*" which is like a prefix) and "*chemy*", a Greek stem (i.e. the word root or base). But similar to so many misrepresented words, "*alchemy*" is an African word, with "chemy" (or Kemet) being the root for the original name of what is now called Egypt. One of its stories is that in the early centuries of the Christian Era, the Greeks of Alexandria, Egypt pursued the practice of trying to transmute base metals into noble ones but believed they needed an imaginary substance--called the *Philosopher's Stone*—because of its supposed linkage with theories of matter advanced by ancient European philosophers. From this, a deception was the "Stone" possessed indefinite life prolonging + body curing powers. *These teachings are "Shams!"* jabaileymd.com

"CON-ARTIST" TRICKS IN HISTORY: "Blue Blood"—called Quinta Essentia--was said by ancient Romans to be the sign of the god's aristocracy. This idea originated by Ancient Africans determining God's Spiritual imperceptible Substance was not subject to the Qualities of Matter, making it Ideal. The Greek Pythagoras (582-500 BC), stole this idea and wrongly claimed it to be the purest, most highly concentrated form of a nature of Essence. Aristotle later also wrongly said it was Celestial Essence—a constituent element of the Heavenly Bodies--a fifth Essence, Ether, above the Four Matter Elements of Water, Fire, Air, and Earth. He named it *Quintessence*. These misrepresentations were used by ancient European nobility to try instilling into their sons the gods immortal Blue Blood. They deeded a child well-born (i.e. born into a noble class) to automatically be a "Blue Blood". This was sealed by the custom of each noble Roman father placing his newborn child on his knee to proclaim the child genuine. For another reason, the *Quintessence* was extremely valued by Medieval Alchemists. In a never-ending frenzy to get rich, they thought certain heavenly objects—called the *Philosopher's Stone* (consisting of diverse metals)--were symbolic forms of heavenly energy. Believing this heavenly energy was essential to the success of the transmutation of metals into gold and silver, they tried in vain to extract the Ether through chemical distillation. But the only significant thing "distilled" from the *Quintessence* was the word "*Essence*" (Spence, Encyclopaedia of Occultism p322). Thereafter, everything involved in the Philosopher's Stone project became a "hot-bed" for varied types of Tricksters—each with a sole personal gain purpose to deceive victims by any means necessary and/or to disadvantage Victims. A particularly stimulating Con-artists period (e.g. regarding the "Philosopher's Stone") was Europeans' Dark Ages—powering a Con-artists lifestyle pattern for many anywhere. A center stage spotlight was on "The Game" of C15 and C16 European "gentlemen". Arrogant Individualism drove their addictive obsession for Materialism to the point of them honoring the *Seven Deadly Sins*—pride (arrogance), covetousness (greed), lust, anger, gluttony, envy, and sloth (lazy). This combination displays as to Kill/Take/Destroy/Dominate/Control/Oppress (KTDDCO) those they feign to be "Against" them. Brutes' "Game" rules were/are that there were/are no rules. Hence, any dishonorable acts were respected as a show of power. It had to be played with a "*Swagger,*" as in being judgmental about everybody except them + the attitude of "the world belongs to me + I can push people around because the rules do not apply to me." Style included ostentatious appearances of being rich; being excessively wasteful; intimidating victims; acquiring endless numbers of "adult toys"; and one-ups-manship practices designed to outsmart competitors. Brute Europeans' trademark was/is aiming to live "the Good Life" of hedonism (i.e. pleasing the senses is the only "Good"). But to give the appearance of being "intelligent and deep thinkers," their pseudo-metaphysical topics were/are merely facades—Non-Rational thinking disguised in undefined or meaningless big words. Behind such presentations are absent realistic Base beginnings; false truth opinions, no wisdom, no constructive meaning; and on a wrong course "going nowhere." The Renaissance "Gentlemen" financed the African American Slave Trade and came to the Americas' as "Southern Gentlemen"--setting up local, state, and the federal governments so as to maintain their national dishonorableness to the present. Meanwhile, free use of every amoral/immoral KTDDCO measure imaginable to humankind was so admired by Europeans that all aspects of "The Game" trickled down to the masses of people. Their superficial rich imitations were via accoutrements of dress, possessions, and partying--a pattern persisting in full force throughout slavery and on to this day. During C18/C19, Europeans' *Age of Reason* focused on universe and humankind understanding through pure reason/logic. European professionals--e.g. scientists, Physio-gnomists (reading facial configurations or expressions in the belief they show qualities of mind or character), Astrologists, and others--everywhere flowered. They met the public thirst to take short cuts to the "Good Life" for "finding the hidden power within yourself" or for answers as to "why have you not been successful" or "I can analyze your personal assets and liabilities in order to bring light to your needs and conflicts." Nothing has changed! jabaileymd.com

CON-ARTISTS' DECEPTIVE TRICKS: Racists European Egyptologists wrongly say *The Book of Life* is solely of Egyptian origin rather than it being a total African continent contribution. This is so they can falsely say "dark-skinned" Caucasions (e.g. their made up "Hamites") were the originators. They typically date profound African intellectual property and Egyptian Dynasties from perhaps 4,000 BC more or less forward. Perhaps the reason is so it conforms to the European Bible which says the Universe is 6000 years old. One reason this makes no sense is that for such conceptual thoughts to be present in the Book of Life or the Pyramid tombs in the first place meant they were already tens of thousands of years in evolutional development. (3) Historically it is seen and in the Encyclopaedia Britannica (1992, p 567) it explains why Europeans have renamed everything of great significance which belongs to other cultures. The greed concept says: *"You've got to name it to claim it,"* and *"...men have seen in the ability to name an ability to control or to possess...."* Such renaming has generated much confusion. Rather than following the order provided by African Sages pertaining to different African Biblical Texts, Europeans term them differently, depending upon where they were found or the name of the European who discovered them. This particularly applies to the situation of Ancient Egyptians often compiling an individualized Book of Life chapter at the death of a high status person. Because each is part of the collection occurring in different time periods, several texts -- most possessing the same concepts -- have their specific sequence placed in disarray by European renaming.

CON-ARTISTS' DAILY TRICKS: How one lives ones life is the biggest deal of ones lifetime. Good people cannot imagine how evil people think and evil people cannot conceive of why everybody does not think like them. Good people's main problems come from not recognizing the influence evil people have over their lives and some are so naïve as to deny that evil people exist. To this end, a January 6, 2014 news flash says: "The New York-based Satanic Temple formally submitted its application to a panel that oversees the Capitol grounds, including an artist's rendering that depicts Satan as Baphomet, a goat-headed figure with horns, wings and a long beard that's often used as a symbol of the occult. In the rendering, Satan is sitting in a pentagram-adorned throne with smiling children next to him. The statue will also have a functional purpose as a chair where people of all ages may sit on the lap of Satan for inspiration and contemplation…. Satan stands as the ultimate icon for the selfless revolt against tyranny, free & rational inquiry, and the responsible pursuit of happiness." Satanists have Intentional Deceptions of Good people as their objective in fashioning whatever would put themselves at an unfair advantage and Victims at an unfair disadvantage. They do this behind the scenes and win converts by Magical spells, charms, and tricks of "SEEMS" right. Many good but weak people absorb the "halo" effects of this evilness without being aware they have internalized some degree of it and are "dishing out" to others certain aspects of it. The bewitching influence of Satanists derives from getting the weak minded to believe they have extraordinary powers that "makes right" whatever they say and do. By contrast, the naïve are susceptible to their magic because it is a human nature trait to be fascinated by magic in general which, in turn, *holds the "magician" in awe because of the excitement of being mystified.* The success of any magician depends upon the fact that there are many things the eyes can see or the ears can hear, which the mind does not bother with. The Art of "SEEMS" right *Misdirection* lies in fooling people's minds by mental suggestions which divert their attention to what the Deceiver wants them to see and thereby steering their attention away from the secret evil actions so that they go unnoticed. This is the purpose of "Trinkets and Trivia" that get people so exicited to have "more, bigger, better, faster, greater power" as a way to hide their lack of the "5Ss". Instead, "Trinkets and Trivia" are made into Icon Images designed to make people dumber and dumber and more and more insecure. The "Trinkets" are "flashing Light" electronic gadgets (e.g. television, videos, smart-phones) which feed information that does not make anyone a better person.

The "Trivia" is about controlling spectators' attention by hired Deceivers' entertaining talk--diverting talk called "*Patter*"--so as to hold the Victims' attention; make the "Trinkets" more exciting; and hide the Deceivers' secret self-interest moves at the Victims' expense. For this to stay exciting, it is not necessary to change the product but rather to change the ways that product is presented. One way is to generate Supernatural realms that are mysterious and offer means of stepping into those realms, no matter how evil, for that is exciting and filled with awe and fascination. This means the Deceivers can tell the people anything and take advantage of their misunderstandings with "far-out" *sham science* wonders, using devices unlike anything people had ever seen and using complex meaningless words sounding "scientific." Such is easily accepted, even by those having sense enough to recognize the pretense. This is done in the same manner of the pretense of actors in plays who pretend to be pirates, kings, or whatever excites the fantasy aspects of the mind. *Fantasy is one of the human nature aspects which link people together and thus show a true respect for the fascinating art of magic*, no matter what its nature. Some of Deceivers' fundamental rules is never appeal to what is in the people's best interest because such an awareness would immediately stop the unfair advantages. The Decievers' path is eased by using the element of surprise and then "hit and run" with the new version of the same "Trinket" because "classic" products that endure would allow people to eventually see the damage done while they were being caught up in the excitement. To have "everybody" excited prevents insightful Critical Thinkers from being heard as to the damage it is causing.

CON-ARTISTS' TRICKS EXAMPLES: The "Big Bad" Wolf of "Little Red Riding Hood" fairy tale fame is a prototypical con-artist. After sending the poor child down the long scenic route to her grandmother's house, he took a short cut; got there first; ate the grandmother; coaxed the child into grandmother's house; and then ate her. The term "Con-Artist" (or Confidence man) refers to plausible swindlers whose success comes from the confidence shown in them by the trusting. Though their methods are endless, their objective is the same. They know the Bull's Eye Chain Ring has good and bad parts and present the bad wrapped inside the good box in order to deceive victims for their personal gain -- maybe create some degree of benefits so as to deflect the destruction they are doing out of sight. Con-artists use "what SEEMS right" to generate unfair advantages for themselves and unfair disadvantages for their victims. They select victims who are likely to get so emotionally caught up in what they want as to embrace what sounds right without looking behind the façade. The message is delivered with a persuasive slant to connotations their victims accept and have faith in. *Flattery* greases the path for victims to have faith in the con-artists and some are professional flatterers. Con-artists do not want victims to know what is being done and instead focus on "What it Is" -- the good feelings intended to provide victims with what they want. In this way, victims are engaged only with the Abstract -- i.e. nothing having to do with the thing's manifestations, its activities, its results, or what consequences proceed from it. This is an extremely common "snow job" practice of pseudo-intellectuals who victimize those who do not know how to do or detect CT. Their Sophists' Fallacy Methods include the following: *Trick* I. In disputes, make the worse seem the better cause. The attack is on the opponent as a person as well as what the opponent does -- whether on the opponent's strengths or weaknesses. *Trick* II. "*Deflection*"—a throwback trick to the ancient Greek Sophists and often used today by closet racists'. This pattern is typical of Whites in their advocating "how bad" Black People are. Deflection's intent is to hopefully ensure no one will notice the evil like-kind things Brutes do, as when the media steers a specific crime topic to appear as if it is "normal in Black culture" so as to distract one from noticing the "white color" crime. *Trick* III. Speak in a devious manner so that what is said in one direction actually implies something else going on in another direction. Brutes are trying to sell a bill of goods not in good people's best interest. Know what they are saying and realize they will not say what they intend to do. *Trick* IV. Brutes constantly send up smoke-screens, as in spotlighting the insignificant, to gain the advantages of deception while others have different concerns. *Trick* V. Dismiss the opponent's views by ridiculing them. *Trick* VI. Misinterpret the opponent's points so that the opponent appears to agree to something which the opponent also denies. *Trick* VII. THE 10% PAYLOAD of DESTRUCTION Method: *Trick* VIII. Act as if you did not just lose so as to disregard the reality of the situation. *Trick* IX. A *Slippery Slope* (also known as "thin edge of the wedge" or "the camel's nose") is a classic form of argument stating a relatively small first step leads to a chain of related events culminating in some significant effect, much like an object given a small push over the edge of a slope sliding all the way to the bottom. For example, what is considered abnormal behavior by Euro-Americans assessing a struggling Black person is likely to be vastly differently assessed by Afrocentric-grounded Black experts or by the Black community. For Europeans to then treat that Black person by European standards will be detrimental. Such is seen with IQ test that place Black students in "special education" and, in effect, ruin their lives. The Slippery Slope Concept is a price members of the Black community pay for the actions and reactions of their "Normal Variant" orientation (e.g. from Slave Survivals which worked for the Slaves but not in today's marketplace). This means the behaviors springing out of "Normal Variant" beliefs are usually of a Vicious Cycle or Slippery Slope nature -- i.e. one undesirable action will lead to a worse action, which will lead to a worse one still. An analogy for this course of action is the *Bowling Ball Concept* whereby the front pin sets off a domino reaction of knocking down all the pins to thereby get a strike. Vicious Cycle "strike" effects are like that of sliding down a Slippery Slope to some terrible disaster at the bottom.

Trick X. Fashioning permanent rules to favor Brutes whenever they get in power as, for example, "*Gerrymandering*." This means the changing of geographical boundaries of a legislative district in order to ensure that one political party will have a majority of voting supporters and keep that party in power.

Trick XI: Advertisers, politicians, con-artists, and anyone trying to be deceptive often give very good examples which "SEEM" right and "SEEM" connected with their general claim but are far off the track. To make this Trick palatable, they mix in Testimonials (getting one to believe in information given by friends or relatives in support of what one is claiming as truth or fact). Testimonials always raise the question of a *"conflict of interest"*. But closer examination and research shows a "crack" or gap between what is said and the truth. *Trick XII*: Evil lies or bad propaganda are mixed with obvious truths. *Trick XIII*: Con-artists follow the pattern of politicians who make waves in still waters and then sell the idea that they are the only ones who can save the ship from sinking if they can have their way.

Trick XIV: Those who declare themselves to be sophisticated to the ways of con-artists can be tricked into looking foolish if they are greedy. Here, con-artists permit themselves to be tricked into looking foolish so that the naïve greedy person assumes a superiority position and adopt an aggressive posture in hoping to get something for nothing. By no longer being aware or alert, they are easily exploited into acting in a fashion that injures themselves and/or others.

CONCEIVE: "*Vital*" (C14; 'life' and 'living') birthed "*Viable*" (C19; capable of life) and its wide range, even Mild. One example is the *Conceivable Impossible/Possible*: The C13 English word "Conceive" (com, take to oneself + conceiven, seed) originally meant in the womb; become pregnant; later, to take into the mind (perceive); absorb mentally. Whereas Absolutely Spiritually Impossible implies a conception which does not exist in the Spiritual Elements, conceivable things devised by humans may be distortions or Viable. Or, it may be "Fantasy," a *Conceivable Impossible* -- a parent word with multiple offspring (e.g. Fantastic, Fancy, & Phantom). All carry the idea of "to make visible" or "to bring to light" by means of imagining objects, symbols, or events not immediately present and thus in terms of imagery -- a utopian or otherwise unreal play of the mind. Fantasy, despite being impossible to bring into Reality, can still serve as a constructive means of fun (e.g. "what ifs") while, on the other hand, it can be quite destructive, as when used to generate fear and a call to delusional actions.

CONCEPT: (act of conceiving); mind act of forming an idea of a general Class of things—e.g. dog, humans

CONCRETE: *Concreteness* has no clear definition but often refers to: (1) an immediate experience of realities—whether of Unbounded, Partially Bounded, or Bounded physical objects themselves; (2) belonging to or standing for actual See-able or Physically realizable things (e.g. sensations); and (3) the degree of pictorial resemblance an Icon Image bears to its *referent* (real world counterpart). What is not "Concrete"—like psychic sensations and metaphysical axioms—can follow the same process but by substituting its Association of Ideas for what is Concrete. See Objective; Subjective

"**CONDITIONAL**": Applies to anything essential to the occurrence of something.

CONDITIONAL LOVE: Being socialized into an atmosphere of Conditional Love (CL) is to generate in the individual the sense of "I'm not good enough"--a mindset of personal incompleteness, unworthiness, and being unfit to deal with the problems of life--a mindset characterized by unrealistic Fear. So, how does this come about? European dictionaries say, first "*Definition*" is defined as 'to specify'; to limit; 'bring to an end'; 'set bounds to.' It necessarily includes--in order to give the exact meaning of a word or phrase or to delimit a problem or an undertaking--all that belongs to the object defined and excludes all that does not. Second, a definition can have varying aspects of a "*Description*" (including only some general features of the defined object); an *Explanation* (throwing light upon some point of special difficulty--as determined by who?); an *Exposition* (stating somewhat fully what is compactly given or only implied in the text); and/or an *Interpretation* (giving the doubtful or hidden meaning of the perplexing or confusing). After comparing all these aspects, critical thinking concludes European dictionaries do not abide by their own etymological (a C14 word meaning 'finding the underlying or true) definition of "Definition." Furthermore, an example of Europeans defining what they are incapable of knowing is "love"--defined as the intense, absorbing EMOTION a person feels for someone or something--e.g. affection, attachment, friendship, admire--of a 'desire' or an 'it is pleasing' nature. They define "*Feel*" in the sense of 'touching and handling'; perceive; experience as a sensation; a personal conviction; a state of intense receptivity or expressivity. In these definitions, both Emotions and Feelings are relative and inconsistent--enabling them to be used in any pleasing or disharmonious way, whenever, and for how long one sees fit. Hence, European's 'love' definition is *Conditional*--defined as depending on something else, not absolute; limited; 'set bounds to'. European Instrumentalism Thinkers crystallized the parameters of CL by saying that since 'love' is an emotion--it is something that can be made, divided, and bounded. Because their sole purpose was *to control the minds of the unsuspecting*, they said CL produces an all-or-none situation + a "for or against" mindset--a mindset characterized by CL's nature, which is to convey an aura of fear. Apart from Fear being part of human's First Law of Nature (Survival), Europeans are generally a "Second Nature" Fear-based people--a feature of ones False Self. At the moment one shifts to ones False Self, one will accept boundaries on Spiritual Boundlessness or split the Spiritually inseparable or make Conditional what is not, as Instrumentalism Thinkers do in converting these virtual products into artifacts (put together by assembling). Minds which buy into such artifacts are immediately controlled by ignorant or evil forces--a state whereby victims give up the mental tow-rope called the "5Ss"--safety, security, sureness, strength, and stability. Thus, CL has been/is being used as a manipulative tool--e.g. "if you love me then do…"; "I won't love you if you do…". As a tool, CL inspires selective hate (as with jealousy), anger, and fear as well as people's addictions to love passions. This provides an explanation for the Emotional Variation forms of "love/hate" relationships and the "love/displaced hate." With the latter, one loves the other without reservation but because of earlier life hostilities brought about by a third party, one desires to use "reenactments" to take out ones hostilities--not on the third party who caused it--but on the loved person within reach. Layering of old and new third party hostilities compound reenactments. For example, a boy may have been teased by females and then made a Self-Declaration to "get even" with all females. Later, he marries a woman he loves and yet imparts on her the "get even" revenge manifestations, even though she is not the cause of his intended object (see Bailey, Post Traumatic Distress Syndrome in Black People for details). Otherwise, CL has been/is being used repetitiously as a manipulative tool in every aspect of people's lives. Such is easily seen by assessing the CL *Fear Fashioned* approaches, methods, techniques, and manners used by all "authorities," advertisers, ignorant people, and evil groups for purposes of being in control of everybody unlike them and in every way. Or, it may be done to tear down people, or make people dislike themselves, or to keep people from doing things designed for their own benefits. jabaileymd.com

CONDITIONED RESPONSE: "*Conditioning*" is the slow and cumulative experience process of changing the (instinct) normal into the (acquired) unique; the process of acquiring, developing, educating, learning, or training new responses in an individual to influences of the environment. Conditioning "instructs" the mind to react in a certain way—the 'big picture' of which gives some benefits—positive or negative. "*Habit Mind*" contains only what has been placed in the mind by acquired experiences, habits, and observation—and thereby becomes *Conditioned Reflexes*. This means the habit has been so often repeated as for the mind, by knowing it so well, as to carry it below the field of Consciousness and become "*Second Nature*," akin to Instinct. Ones habitual, emotional, and sensory responses are not representative of ones newborn human nature. It begins with Recognition of a stimulus, forming a Disposition about it in the form of an Image; embellishing it with Imagination; committing it to Memory—some parts being of the Forgotten Imagination Memory type and other parts being of the Familiarity Memory type which are constantly repeated until its Icon nature spark increases so as to cause a pre-determine thoughtless reaction.

CONFUSION AND CONFLICT DECEPTION: Confusion by European writers about anything, including the European Bible, philosophy, word meanings, and the like is having different sources of information about names, places, people, as well as a chronology of events coming from different writers with different agendas causing biases. Since very ancient times Brutes have initiated non-violent measures of controlling others by the introduction of *assumptions because of their ability to generate an element of doubt* in victims. The resultant uncertainty about what people "knew" is what would gavanize chronic frustration, fear, confusion, Illusions, and Delusions. Then Brutes would step in and reconcile all ambivalent attitudes teaching with fantasy stories containing such highly abstracted concepts--stories that "SEEM" right -- stories containing some familiar information the people have accepted--stories told in an interesting way. This combination leads people to simply "give-in" to these false stories, embrace them as true, and then defend them. What Confusion does is to render clarity and certainty ineffectual by deliberate action or want of action. The African mythological god Set (Seth)--also deemed *"instigator of Confusion" and the Destroyer* -- was the Kamitic conception of evil. Ancient African's purpose for this Set metaphor is two-fold: First, rather than Set referring to some invisible Being, his symbolic "atmosphere" concerns *entities actually within the person* touched by them. Second, the personification of this symbolic "atmosphere" can expand the ramifications of what is being conveyed beyond the ability of words to do or to describe. To spotlight how confusion can be intentionally designed to convey the "Dark Side," the patterns of Set have been carried over into countless *Trickery* and *Deceit* fables of Africans. In perhaps the most famous Yoruba/Nigeria story about the god Èṣù, Eshu, a spirit of Confusion and Trickery, the setting concerns two inseparable friends who swore undying fidelity to one another and yet neglect to acknowledge the god Eshu. Since these two friends work on adjacent fields, one day Eshu walks on the dividing line between their fields, wearing a cap black on one side and red (or white) on the other. He saunters between the fields, exchanging pleasantries with both men. Afterwards, the two friends got to talking about the man with the cap, and fall into violent quarreling about the color of the man's hat, calling each other blind and crazy. The neighbors gather about, and then Eshu arrives and stops the fight. The friends explain their disagreement, and Eshu shows them the two-sided hat--all this to chastise the friends for not putting him first in their doings. The lesson of the tale is obvious, but just as interesting is where it places the god--namely, moving along the seam between two different worldviews. In this position he can confuse communication; spotlight the ambiguity of information or Secular Knowledge; and play with people's perspectives to thereby lead mortals to temptation and possibly into tribulation. In one of his innumerable roles as a master of exchange, or crossed purposes, of crossed speech, he delights in contradictions. With confusion or arguments, he is there. This Yoruba god also propels narratives of jealousy and power from confusion by occupying certain privileged places. He gives ideas and information--not the whole story -- but just enough to make the story happen. At one point, Shango the thunder god asks him, "Why don't you speak straightforwardly?" "I never do," Eshu responds. "I like to keep people from thinking by confusing them." Brutes' Confusion contains inconsistencies in life-shaping and life-changing issues--a pattern most applicable to information people receive today.

"CONFUSION DARK SIDE TOOLS": When it arrived into English in 1330, "*Confusion*" meant to defeat, frustrate; throw into disorder; and bewilder. Brutes purposely stir up Confusion (pour together; mix together; fail to distinguish) about all aspects of everything for purposes of controlling the confused. This is easily seen in any field of study of what is presented to Black People -- in school (e.g. mathematics, physics, philosophy, dictionaries); in the media; in the legal system; and especially in religion. A reason is so the Brutes have to be asked and that allows them to lead the people into self-defeating ends while simultaneously attacking the self-esteem of the confused. This makes them look superior, even though what they say makes no sense. By paying careful attention to information Europeans' peddled off as life-shaping knowledge, it will not take much effort to see it features "Confusion." The confused generate more Confusion by generating delusions. Confusion keeps people ignorant and prevents the learning of CT. Brutes entice people to be immersed in exciting trivia (e.g. game shows, movies, gadgets) so as to be unaware of what Brutes controlling them are doing. In this way, what one owns can be taken away; if one is down, one cannot rise; and one becomes so overwhelmed as to be filled with bad emotions expressed by self-destructive attacks on fellow victims within reach as to end up in jail or dead. Then severely afflicted victims willingly allow themselves to be led by the oppressors into a hard life -- and to the point of preaching for and living the oppressors' message. Things that can be confused are endless. For example, Confusion occurs when all the parts are present except an essential piece concerning the inner workings of the interrelationships (as a piece missing in a watch); when the obvious or the Base/Foundation is overlooked; when the Base/Foundation is faulty (as it being made of quicksand); when a part is suppressed by some covering (as occurs with the esoteric or hidden meanings in allegories) to make its true meaning too subtle to discern; or that which was already present is in a disguised form.

Such situations may display as a paradox or as "impossible" to solve or as too confusing and frustrating to proceed. Most remarkable is Ancient Africans' accurate Set metaphor description of each human being's Brute Brain and its anti-Spiritual Elements entities, whether rarely expressed or expressed as a Brute lifestyle. For the latter to occur it is essential for Brutes to disconnect from Actual Reality and then from Common Humanity so as to create an "Us" or Me" vs. "Them" or "You." By so doing, Brutes, primarily European males, see themselves as separate from, and enemies to, other human beings, especially those who are not like them. Brute methods embrace whatever conforms to the Seven Deadly Sins—pride (arrogance), covetousness (greed), lust, anger, gluttony, envy, and sloth (lazy) and the Fetters associated with them (e.g. "Me, Me" Individualism, hatred, fear, lies, and jealousy). Just as Ancient Africans described for Set, Brutes' philosophy of life is based only on Material Realms and the elevation of material things over people. Features are to get what they want by Kill/Take/Destroy means; be totally self-centered except for coming together to attack falsely perceived enemies; believe they are above societal rules; find "sick" pleasures in generating pain and suffering in others by first dehumanizing "Them" or "You" and treating them with no more regard than if they were flies needing to swatted; and believing "when you die, that's all there is." Brute ways of thinking and doing in designing certain scenarios are all for the intension of generating evil self-interest agendas in order for Brutes to gain unfair advantages while ensuring their victims have unfair disadvantages. Among themselves they play by a different set of rules which is about "anything goes."

Brutes fashion *Delusional Fear* (feigning being under attack to justify Kill/Take/Destroy) acts in order to gain benefits that belong to others. In other words, they create Delusional Fear to deliberately seize the opportunity to stir up false survival situations as a justification for attacking victims when no such real situation is present. With this background -- and note the exact duplication in European males with Set's animalism and fetters -- typically Set would start out by creating confusion in his victims' minds and then follow with a program of brute filled acts (e.g. Kill/Take/Destroy). To repeat, throughout European history the Set Character has been amazingly displayed by Brute males in obvious, tempered, masked, or concealed forms and in every field that affects people's lives. Besides their Kill/Take/Destroy purposes, another is to try to prove to themselves and their victims that they are superior -- the most outrageous delusion ever invented by mankind. In fact, they are just the opposite. I have noticed in researching thousands of words in up to 1000 books per word that whereas *Africans typically do not write about what they live (e.g. Love in action), Brutes do not write about the evil things they do.* The confusion Set generates entangles good people by: (1) allowing unwanted things to come inside to dilute and pollute the original contents of something simple; (2) allowing inside contents to go out of the simple so as to make it perplexing; (3) altering things to make for an inner weakness and thereby violating the integrity of a thing, as in stuffing metaphysical concepts inside the physical; (4) taking both sides of a given issue, depending on what best serves to be an advantage; (5) If Set was stumped or "exposed" he would retreat into a non-issue story so as to distract attention away from him; (6) If he was guilty, he blamed others for doing things of which he was guilty (called Projection); (7) Spotlighting only one side of the coin of something significant and disregarding its opposite (e.g. failing to speak of the bad complications or give the most important issue); (8) Only dealing with what something does or how it appears and never about what it is (so others cannot know it or be certain about anything); (9) Teaching the people to have Faith and Belief in them, not Know the Truth; and (10) writing laws in a confusing manner so that they can be interpreted according to biases that favor Brutes.

CONFUSION METHODS: Whereas Ancient Africans focused on the "What it is" of a Thing (i.e. the way the Thing is Known), Brutes avoid that and present only "What it does" and "How it appears"--both preventing Certainty. Since very ancient times, Brutes have spotlighted *assumptions because of their ability to generate an element of doubt* in victims. The resultant uncertainty about what people "knew/know" galvanizes chronic frustration, fear, confusion, Illusions, and Delusions. Then Brutes step in and reconcile all ambivalent attitudes--teaching with fantasy stories containing highly abstracted concepts--stories that "SEEM" right--stories containing some familiar information the people have accepted--stories told in an exciting visual media way. This combination leads people--because that is all they are aware of that exists--to simply "give-in" to these false and misleading stories, embrace them as true, and then defend them. The *Wheel Concept* helps order this complex subject. *Spoke 1* is *definitions* for a given thing being unrelated + in conflict + multiple versions. Thus, mixed dimensions reign in various groups using the same word to express different ideas or the same idea expressed in conflicting words. *Spoke 2: Informational gaps* caused by the ravages of time and Nature; by information deliberately destroyed, erased, rewritten, reassigned, or ignorantly misinterpreted; and by conquering tribes having brought in their own words and meanings for the familiar ideas of the natives. Spoke 3: *Misinterpretations* in the media, in museums, in educational magazines, and in all books and chapters in books; from layer by layer of addition, subtraction, and deviation changes in Word Stories between ancient and present time and/or due to time, erosions, corrosions, additions, and losses. Spoke 4: *lack of essential information*; faulty circumstantial evidence; the imposition of partition (wrong dividing or separating); "logic" and other statements lacking facts. Spoke 5: *structural weakness* violating the integrity of a thing--e.g. defective or incomplete in content, poor fit, mis-arrangements, improper combinations; inconsistencies; contradictions. Spoke 6: *incomparable*--the word Immaterial means there is nothing to which it--e.g. "Life," "Death," or "Consciousness"--can be compared. Spoke 7: *Bad Assumptions*--e.g. substituting "SEEMS" (information) for "what is"; grasping information as Knowing); equating familiar with Understanding; believing a piece is the complete scope of all there is to know about that situation. Spoke 8: *Modifications* from different systems of values.

Spoke 9: *Interchanging* near Synonyms--"dark"/"black"; Worth/Value/Values. Spoke 10: *obscure* ideas, nonsensical facts, meaningless ceremony to befuddle. Spoke 11: using technical jargon, This, That, There/Their without explaining. Spoke 12: *refusing facts*; biased *by viewing the facts and then selecting only those facts which support ones point of view*. Spoke 13: *Selective Planes of Existence*--e.g. focus only on the material. Spoke 14: *ethnocentric*--opinions related to oneself, ones subculture, ones society at large of "whatever benefits me"; failing to reconcile standards of different cultures--Brutes judging other cultures as heathen or superstitious for being "different." Spoke 15: *Disordered Thinking*. Spoke 16: *"guessing"* in reconciling ambivalent attitudes with highly abstracted formulations (what is taken out of physical aspects) in a way that contradictions or statements favor ones self-interest. Spoke 17: *Pseudo-intellectuals'* big words without definitions. Spoke 18: *lack of clarity* Camouflage what is already present in a disguised form; suppressing, misplacing, displacing, making murky, hazy to serve as perfect hiding places in the open for the devious. Spoke 19: *overlapping information* not distinguished. Spoke 20: *flaws*: (a) when one simply deals with only one stroke; (b) focuses on only one link; (c) only pays attention to the general idea within that one link; (d) ignores the details of each stroke; (e) connects or overlooks the interrelationships between the strokes and/or links; (f) fails to do a good job with the other links; or (g) ignores them completely. This means one has limited ideas--a set up conveying the wrong intension or message, for inefficiency, and for confusing the receiver. Spoke 21: *mis-directed*; placed on improper planes of existence; or headed in the wrong direction. Spoke 22: *Substituting* Connotations as definitions for Denotations. Spoke 23: *changing time lines* to redistribute African Intellectual property. Spoke 24: *failing to expose the truth*: Spoke 25: *giving bits and pieces of truth.* Such people think they are "right" but are actually on the wrong road. jabaileymd.com

CONFUSION AND CONFLICT WORDS: The chief merit of language is to clearly say what one means and to mean what what said. In African Tradition, words are chosen so as to be true to Nature's Processes so as to serve as a landmark. Thus, they used only a few sound words and thos when none other will answer the purpose. They could say extraordinary things using ordinary words. Clear and precise definition and the proper use of their names and denotations are expressive of their true and real nature. Anything short of that obstructs Understanding, convey false ideas, and lead to erroneous practices, as in "one size fits all". The thrower of a rock into a lake is the source and the rock is the cause of the splash (the effect) which then causes ripples (the consequences). If the subject is words, then the first few ripples are Master Words and the subsequent ripples are Servant Words. The ripples which are about the Master Words include those which shape ones life, those which change ones life, and those which have an effect on ones life. The ripples which are about the Servant Words include those which people use in daily conversation. Nevertheless, each ripple has its own rules which are discerned by Critical Thinking (CT). Those rules are determined by the thrower (the Source), the thrower's reason for throwing, and the type of rock thrown. Each word has three components CT considers: What it is; What it does; and How it appears. Regardless of the ripple chosen, CT assesses the thrower, the rock, and the components of each word. For example, the "Big Three" words Faith/Belief/Trust as applied to religion were devised by Europeans for the purpose of controlling people's minds for reasons to be explained. One way this was done was by making them incomprehensible so that the people were so confused that they selected out of the confusion "What SEEMS Right" in which to have Faith/Belief/Trust. To understand this requires knowing the history of these words and contrast them with the word "Know." Whereas "Know" carries the sense of certainty and puts one on the "Truth-Track," Faith/Belief/Trust, though SEEMING to be right, always have an element of doubt which can be progressively developed off the "Truth-Track" by mind controllers taking advantage of the confusion. Those who create new word ought to first define it so as to give it community status—i.e. say what it is"—its essence—presented as its Character, foreseeing to the degree possible the pernicious uses to which the term may be put later. Since the newborn word has no self-defense, it needs to be watched over and protected from encroaching and deforming connotations by demanding of others that they use it properly. Diagnosing is a system of accurate guessing in which the end-point achieved is a name. This name comes to assume the importance of being specific for a Thing whereas it is only an insecure and temporary conception.

CONFUSION COUNTER-ACTION: The word "Counteract" came into English in 1678 with the sense of adding up and rendering an account. Its spotlighted use was to generate Confusion in the Enslaved by rendering what they were Certain about from African Tradition into ineffectual thoughts and practices by deliberate action or want of action. Part of this was done by Spells, perhaps initiated in Africa by such alluring things as being *Enchanted, Beguiled, and/or Bewitched.* To know this and how such a mental barrier is constructed enables its management to do the reverse. Thus, since the essential aspect of a *Spell is the Habit of Expectation to which one has confidence,* to counteract Spells (or anything like Enchantment, Beguiled, and/or Bewitched) is to meet its effects by some direct force adequate to overcome the thing opposed, as a remedy counteracts a disease. Confusion has a cause. Somebody caused that Confusion out of ignorance or deliberately. The benefit of a deliberate cause is for Brutes to say: "since you do not know what to do, we can fix it." What is unspoken is a tremendously big price to pay for their "help" or about the bad consequences sure to result. The way to handle this is to reject the solution bearer and on ones own do the discerning to detect the keystone cause of the confusion. This is followed by researching how to handle it. One example is as outlined for a Spell. Most of such problems for me are resolved from studying the story of the word pertaining to the subject matter to see how it evolved and what its offshoot meanings were along the way. It is important to look at the subject in different ways. For example, the problem may be that the cause is in the stage of a Seed or Root of the Tree Concept; or at the stage of an idea in the Thought Evolution Concept; or, as presented in the Ancient Africa Bible where the pre-creation quality of existence is not so much one of chaos and confusion as it is an unbounded, not yet developed and thus unstructured or unordered unrealized potentiality for Reality. The problem may concern changing patterns in the subject's development. To get an idea of the Ancient African Bible being a *rolling corpus* or aggregate of sayings representing different moments in the life and history of the early Africans, allow me to use the *Prism Concept* as an analogy. Imagine that shining a white light through a Prism displays on the other side as visible rays of red, orange, yellow, green, blue, and violet colors and that each color represents a separate aspect of the Ancient African Bible. Yet, they are each related by having similar Spiritual Literature material. Suppose also that each ray appears in a successive sequence rather than altogether. Now also suppose that each ray is rolled up like a carpet and that over time it gradually unrolls. The beginning part of the rolled carpet follows the Tree Concept--originating with "Seed" ideas which sprouted into Roots, Trunk, Branches, Leaves, and Fruit philosophies and meanings.

When put together, the Ancient African Bible consists of an aggregate text consisting of accumulated spiritual concepts initially evolving into maturity. But then, outsiders bring in foreign concepts, traditions, and interpretations which, over time, dilute and pollute the original Ancient African Bible's basic principles. At some point there is a name change as, for example, now called the European Bible. Though it began out of the old core of the original Ancient African Bible's basic principles, or as I call it, a "Kernel gospel," Europeans expanded it to include new sayings and opinions that worked to align the new experiences of the European community with its own remembrances of its past. This expansion would not have been a conscious rewriting of the old African Traditions, as if a Christian sat down one day with a pen in hand and added new sayings and erased others. Rather, it would be the result of the seamless Europeans' community's memory. So, when faced with the confusing situation of whether the African or the European Bible is "the Word of God," how is it possible to distinguish them or even how is it possible to distinguish in the same Bible the earlier Kernel sayings from later ones that may have accrued during a later performance of the Kernel Gospel? How can later accretions added by foreigners from the earlier traditional material of the African Bible be identified and separated? The starting point for me is to first know the evolution of each using only the tiny few creditable authorities. Second come the identification and examination of sayings where there are obvious signs of secondary development: when interpretative clauses have been appended to older sentences; when sayings have been reshaped into rhetorical question-and-answer units; and when retrospective dialogues have reclaimed older sayings. Third, once these accretive units are identified, they can be examined in order to further identify vocabulary and themes characteristics of the accretive material. Fourth, only after the characteristic vocabulary and themes have been demarcated can they be used to expose additional accretions by searching the remaining sayings for their possession of Order, Regularity, Coherence, Consistency, Compatibility, Balance, Harmony, and Predictability to the cited vocabulary and themes. Those that exhibit these components are determined to be the oldest, the sayings which likely were part of the original Ancient African Bible Kernel. See Counter

COUNTER-ACTING CONFUSION BY BLACK STUDENTS: The spotlighted use of "Counteract" upon entering English in 1678 was for enslavers to make the Enslaved confused--to intentionally render their African Tradition Certainties into ineffectual beliefs, faith, thoughts, and practices. Compounding slavery laws against teaching the Enslaved to read, write, or count was the deliberate creation of *Vocabulary Deprivation* to about 100 words. The captors realized that keeping the Enslaved ignorant and "killing their spirits" were powerful "divide and conquer" methods. Subsequent Euro-Americans, to the present, followed this lead. Horace

Mann (1796-1859) was an important American education fashioner of today's USA educational system. Meanwhile, Whites' educational programs catered to the capitalistic elite so as to enable them to extend their riches; secure all valuable property; and maintain an impenetrable upper class. The idea is, by way of educational programs, for their youthful elite to remain *emotionally* excited about *Material Possessions*--acquiring them by any means necessary. Never allowing Black Americans in on these teachings has been a powerful ongoing source of confusion--adversely affecting their negotiations in the marketplace. Also, starting during slavery was the Satanists' practices of *Devious Euphemisms*, subtly adversely detrimental to Black students' struggles in the grossly inferior Euro-American educational system. For example, Satanists applied terms like 'slave master' and 'slave owner' so as to assert authority and status--while avoiding the accurate phrase 'slaver' in order not to be viewed as personally and professionally implicated by their immoral and sadistic actions. Continued *Devious Euphemisms* (among others) keep Black students from being on "the same page" in understanding meanings of concepts destined to be present on the examinations + not being able to get on track with the "White-in-group" meanings of words + their branches into all areas of life. These have the effect of compounding purposely generated Confusion.

I know this by comparing education presentations in my all-Black grade schools and at Morehouse College (Atlanta, Ga.)--both being infinitely better than any European teachings (e.g. the University of Michigan) which specialized in confusing "big words" (now known to be facades) + the boring European teaching + the non-pertinence of European subjects to my life. Such was so confusing and non-truthful that I flunked my senior year in high school. After that, I learned enough to pass European school tests and then pursue the Truth and what is meaningful in life using Ancient African Principles. Unfortunately, Black students get overwhelmed by all this confusion and that causes many to fail to recognize there is a problem with being on the "wrong" track of European ways. Others wrongly accept what "Seems" right as close enough to the truth for them to proceed on a path leading into increasing confusion. Despite being aware they are not taught the truth, they cling to the best of the presented doubtful. "Picking and choosing" as one goes along will only complicate an already difficult course in discerning good/evil. I am unaware of any European school system bothering to discover "right" ways to teach Black youth and those I have mentioned it to have not been interested. The best way to get over all of this confusion for Black students is for high level Black scholars to take control and be in charge of Black students' education. Common Sense confusion is cleared by having clarity about what is Important and Necessary and then discovering *Certainty* about it--or coming as close as possible. Ancient Africans said *Absolute Spiritual Certainty* refers to an essence state of Being of any God-made "Thing"--and it always contains Spiritual Elements. These have no degrees and are not subject to human opinions. Their power is in providing the *"5Ss" (safety, security, self-confidence, strength, and stability)*--what all human's seek. The highest form of Spiritual Certainty conceivable by the human mind is called *Knowledge.* Anything less is *Information. Defining key terms using only Afrocentric dictionaries is the only way to untangle confusion about Afrocentric life-shaping and life-changing words.* To untangle the Cultural Collage confusion, one must separate the useful from the bad information one has absorbed out of both White and Black cultures. Also, special attention to detail is needed to avoid baffling decisions that do not make sense and that lead to self-defeating solutions.

CONGREGATIVE THINKING: assembles a whole of things outwardly and perhaps inwardly different so that ones ones Analytical qualities can perceive the underlying differences of outwardly similar events. This enables Classification.

CONJECTURE: to put together the nearest available materials for a provisional opinion based upon insufficient evidence. Conjectures are put in the category of Hypothesis (a statement of what is deemed possible true, assumed, and reasoned upon as if certainly true, with a view of reaching truth not yet surely known); Suppose (temporarily assume a thing as true); and Likely. Nevertheless, Causes, Effects, and Conjuncts are best suited to Conjecture. See Definitions; Word Details; Conjectures; Postulates; Premise; Presume; Hypothesis

CONNOTATIONS: The variations people give to a specific etymology is called *Connotations*—variations under the category of Information. See Meaning Changes; Information; Etymology; Denotation; Word Details

CONSCIENCE IN HUMANS: The Image of God imparts in a human's Soul a Moral nature *Conscience*, meaning the presence and "Vibration Voice" (i.e. felt through Instincts and not by "words") of God. Furthermore, the seat of a human's Conscience is in the inmost sanctuary of a human's Soul. Ones "Self" is pure Divine Consciousness and Will—Immaterial entities. Their opposites are ones Divine Spirit, which is Energy and Matter. So, God's Wisdom and Spiritual Power are stored in Conscience part of the Divine Spirit (Amen Metu Neter IV: 58). Conscience is the Spiritual vehicle that conveys a human about the fundamental rights and wrongs in life. The righteousness aspects were installed within by the Cosmic Mind prior to ones birth on Earth. Thus, when Spiritually oriented people plan to do wrong or do it, their Consciousness involuntarily reacts—and not from an acquired reflex. Involuntary can be likened to the natural heartbeats or breathing—implying it is the objective within the subjectivity of ones mind. By being armed African Tradition's Ma'at Principles, it moves into position that justifies it being the Divine Judge of ones own Selfhood. It also deals with Divine judgments on problems of action formulated by the mind—actions within the context of ones purpose in life. Much of its work is deciding that certain things are disharmonious--from which one avoids or leaves--as well as things which are evil—from which one rebels by first awakening Wisdom. The Voice of Conscience, by drawing its ingredients from the Spiritual Elements, imparts the guidance to choose it whenever it is in conflict with ones in-born obligation, duty, and responsibility to stay in the flow of the Spiritual Elements. There can be no escape from the struggle, for that is the means to realize ones Highest (Divinity) Self on Earth. That is the indicator of what makes one a reliable moral agent—meaning the right of Private Selfhood judgment—to accept, modify, or disagree with certain established opinions. In short, one has the inner freedom to select for oneself what is right under that circumstance. It is not the place of humans to be in any position to judge others as Moral agents. A reason is that the same thing can be Right in one human and Wrong in another, or either at different times in the same human. But these do not apply to Supernatural people because they operate out of a human-made system that worships itself. Otherwise, for example, a young child does not have the same sense of responsibility as does a mature, developed adult. Spiritually oriented humans cast off many ideas of "Wrong" that were once held as a result of greater understanding of the core of the problem. That course is always towards the Spiritual Elements. This was the pattern of Ancient African Culture whereby there were no jails or policemen, no divorces, no teen pregnancies. Such is in marked contrast to the fear, restraint, and force required in Supernatural Non-Rational controlled societies. Most in this society have putrefying Consciences—meaning they have long since been dead.

CONSCIOUSNESS--SENSORY: Let us imagine ones Unconscious Mind is like a mouthpiece speaking into a Megaphone--representing a human's Sensory (Secular) Consciousness (SSC)--and the ingredients being spoken are Form-Bodies. The nature of the ingredients coming from the Unconscious is their "*What is*" (i.e. the Essence), as formulated by ones Character; the "*That is*" aspects include its specificity, individuality, and 'here-and-nowness'; and the "How it is"--its normal "Wild" reality--a state of Nature, undomesticated, unrestrained)--a state of mental activity free from any control by reason, by any aesthetic, or by moral preoccupation--a kind of absolute reality originally experienced and felt. The "*Form*" (etymologically meaning its image, impression) is the shape or contour given to the "Wild" reality and that constitutes the "Form-Body" of the structure entering into the SSC--an entering in a "peanut butter" type of fluid state. It is here that constitutes the real world of the Unconscious lying behind the artificial SSC world of ordinary objects known to ones normal awareness. Some say it is a reality above or within the surface of reality as a result of suspending the discipline of conscious and logical reason, esthetics, or morality in order to allow the expression of subconscious thought and feeling. Then impressions are produced through the startling juxtaposition of unexpected objects or themes in an atmosphere of fantasy's pervasive dreamlike quality or the juxtaposition of Images--which Freud said would reveal the true nature and content of the human Soul. This is so unclear as to be unacceptable to me. Does this refer to the Eternal Soul or to the Astral Soul? Where would the negativity come from? Rather, presumably present are SSC Astral Notions (also called Endocepts)--nondescript things incapable of being divided into parts or words--like a thought seed or element without a home. Their production manner comes from the Astral Body containing apparatus of sensory and motor conduction paths which convey vibrations from the brain and nerves to the Intellect Mind; and from the Intellect Mind to the brain and nerves (Gaskell 78).

What initially results from this interaction includes primitive organization of past experiences, perceptions, memory traces, and images of things and movements. The SSC 'big picture' is that it gathers, amplifies, matches, and synthesizes messages from the brain and/or outside world so that their monitored and interpreted messages can be revealed. SSC alone is competent to determine the meaning of the Images and to recognize their significance in the here and now--in the concrete reality of the present. Each *Experience* one has involves the process of registering a sensation (from direct acquaintance with it, hearsay, accepted authority), perception, or of some external fact or condition. In short, ones "normal" SSC state occurs via ones *sense perceptions, intellect, Images, Sensations, and Affections*. Hence, the mind's Imagination, Symbolic, and Reality experiences are inseparable from ones environment and ones speculative outlook. For all of this to happen means the SSC is a center of multidimensional processing for intellect, emotional and physical body experiences having variations in time and space. Different things occur on separate 'floors' of reality--without touching. SSC attention is looking at things as a spotlight. Once inside the SSC, the fluid is gradually removed from the "peanut butter" as part of reforming the entire peanut. Nevertheless, Consciousness is said to hold the key to the values of the unconscious, which is pure nature, capable of pouring out it gifts in profusion. Contributory to this is the SSC being a two-way street whose contents are arbitrary constructs of mind, as determined by habit and custom. In one direction the SSC is a connector of ones brain states with the outside world, whereby the state of affairs inside ones "head" goes through ones SSC megaphone to manifest in the outside world. At the mouthpiece level is Stage I of this reformation--equivalent to the beginning organization of some thought structure, whether logical, emotional, fantasy, and so forth. Here there is the organizing of vibrations into an awareness beam so as to understand its hidden rational meanings. Stage II, the next upward progression inside the megaphone of the evolving Form-Body, is equivalent to the pod of the peanut. Stage III is laying the husk on the peanut. Stage IV is the peanut and husk covered by their shell.

CONSCIOUSNESS IN NATURE'S PROCESSES: It is a human's Sensory Consciousness (Divine Will?) that is interposed between a human's Divine Consciousness and God's Consciousness. Thus, a substitute of an Ego for a human's Divine Consciousness disconnects that human from her/his God's Consciousness. The Supernatural is not part of Nature's Processes where these terms apply but are only used by the Afrocentric to help understand via alternative paths to the Truth. Europeans' Supernatural, by proposing their own image in a Contingent Being form of an Ego, leads one to be profoundly Confused from a Denial of Reality. Divine Immaterial Spirit is Divine Consciousness or Substance and consists of the nature of a human, called a human's "Self." Divine Sublime Spirit is God's Essence, not Substance, and denotes Will. Divine Metaphysical

Spirit is the Essentials of God's Essence and manifests as Energy and Matter. To elaborate on its Processes of Nature (1) *Source*: God's Immaterial Cosmic Mind messages—the *Substance*--are conveyed to ones Immaterial "Self"—i.e. ones Divine Consciousness--a Disposition indicating *What* it wants to manifest and *Why*. (2) *Essence*: Ones Will grasps God's Willing dictates to be manifest and institutes the initiation of the Disposition towards the Intensions of making happen all of its *What* and *Why* aspects in Image form. Yet, like ones Divine Consciousness, ones Divine Will is also devoid of energy. (3) *Essentials:* Ones Divine Spirit supplies the Spiritual Energy and the Ether Matter to create a Disposition Form. (4) Ones *Divine Spirit*, by knowing "How and When" to manifest the Inclinations, supplies *Energy (active) and Matter (passive)*. Ones Divine Spirit's power is composed of subtle electromagnetic energies—Ancient Africans called *"animal spirit"* ("anima and animus" in Latin spiritual tradition)--possessing the functions of animating a human's life, especially the physical body. That *"animal spirit"* then activates the *inactive* Spiritual Energy which, in turn, activates the undifferentiated/unstructured potential Matter by adding an attribute of God--the Ether (i.e. Life's Force). The Ether provides what is necessary to give shape or form to the Will's embryonic Image—the Pattern--and thereby starts an evolutionary process towards the Thing designated by the Disposition's 'blue-print'. (5) After ones Intangible Character receives the evolving contents, the Matrix of the Pattern supplies nourishment for the Form of the Pattern to entice the Inclination to orchestrate ones Tangible thoughts, emotions, expressions, and daily living deeds to conform to Ma'at principles. (6) Ones *Conscience*--the law giver that orchestrates ones Selfhood—determines the "Right" manner of ones manifested expressions. (7) The displayed product is a reflection of what has emanated out of an Interchange. See Essence Evolution; God's Substance; Human Birth; Essentials, Divine

CONSCIOUSNESS OF KNOWLEDGE/INFORMATION: Fundamental to African Tradition is that humans are made in the likeness of God, meaning God's traits reside in humans as their essential qualities. After establishing circumstantial proof of God by astro-mathematics, African Sages said there is only one Cosmic (formless) Consciousness ('to be aware, Know') dwelling in all living things. This makes all God's creations (e.g. the Cosmos) and creatures spiritually related--a realization basic to "Knowing Thyself" and to acquiring Wisdom. It is out of the Cosmic Subjective (Nun) Realm--consisting of Unconditioned Consciousness (the KA) and undifferentiated Energy/Matter--that the Objective Realm of the Cosmos arose. Since there are no things to be perceived in the Nun, then the KA (Consciousness) can only be conscious of being conscious. The KA, representing the body of the one universal high God, is "Nature's" Divine Archetype (Spiritual "Seed" for the universe). Ancient Africans believed this KA, by underlying and preceding every human principle, serves as the foundation for all ordinary and extraordinary Cosmic Entities. For example, the Humans Selfhood "coin" has Consciousness/Will representing one side of it and Energy/Substance, its other side. The "coin's" chain of command is: Consciousness then Wills (non-emotional driving force) Energy and Substance (Matter) into a Cosmic Organism. Those "Big Four" are responsible for and undergo branching so as to create things in every possible area of life as humans know it to be. Inside the Cosmic Organism are entities composed of Spiritual Elements and in infinite numbers, types, and complexities--each having a unique appearance and a unique function--each in perfect order--each independently working interdependently for evolution into a common Divine Plan. By containing a drop of God (same in quality but not in capacity), human's ability to know, to do, and to be are essentially unlimited (Amen, Meter Neter II:15). Human Consciousness, in contrast to animals, is a self-awareness of being alive with an identity (Ashby, Book of Dead, 343). A human's highest form of aware-ness is Cosmic Knowing. Above human' plane of Intuition faculties is that of Cosmic Knowing, occurring as a sudden flash in which all illusionary dividing lines between persons and things dissolve. One now fully, plainly, and completely "sees" there is One Great Life underlying all the countless forms and shapes of manifestation

(Ramacharaka, Raja Yoga p217). In short, one finds the consciousness of the Oneness of All. Rather than losing ones Individuality, one has an increased sense of power and strength and knowing (Ramacharaka, Gnani Yoga p 82). Whereas awareness of the manifestations of the KA is Knowledge, awareness of what comes through *Sensory (Secular) Consciousness* consists of Information (messages 'in-form'). Sensory Consciousness, popularly defined as the mind registering a sensation, perception, or state of affairs inside oneself or of some external fact or condition, occurs via ones sense perceptions or intellect. This is either on purpose or subliminally (an 1886 psychology term for below the threshold of consciousness). Those lacking control of their minds--as in doing negative Emotional, Automatic, Impulsive, Patterned, Superficial, and "Off and On" Thinking--are not fully awake and conscious, and thus are not their Real Selves. Information pushes people in the opposite direction of what it takes to have unlimited Selfhood Knowledge (i.e. operating out of their Divine Consciousness). Hence, following the crowd's flow into "Trinkets and Trivia" is to get further away from the "5Ss." Perhaps that is why the C14 Old English word "*Aware*" (vigilant, cautious, informed) meant to be watchful; be on ones guard, and take care. One can be aware in a waking or an asleep state. Yet, most are only partially Sensory Conscious or aware because of their inner world of problematic Emotions and mental turmoil. The struggling are in a coma; fail to claim their due; stay in the status quo; and simply "Make Do." Jabaileymd.com

CONSEQUENCES: The C14 English word "*Consequence*" (to follow closely)--the offspring of a Cause and Effect parents--carries such a peculiar birthing concept as to be placed in the "Kangaroo Pouch" category of words. It originally meant an inference or conclusion drawn from what possesses observable aspects for all or what was assumed to be so obvious and universally accepted as to need no proof (e.g. the beauty of flowers)--neither of which makes it "Right" or the truth. Yet, this beginning statement or proposition is a real, distorted, or false *Presupposition* (a thing taken for granted or assumed). In Logic, the first two syllogism propositions are called Premises. *Inferences* determine the unknown from the already known by reasoning from circumstances and observations to draw conclusions from evidence or Premises. Consequence is *the somethings which happen as a result of something happening* (Sharon Bingaman)-- the sequel; happenings from what sprang out of the Effects; whereas a Cause (e.g. trauma) gives rise to an Effect (Impairments), that Effect is pregnant with Consequences of the Cause. Those "Somethings," when gathered together, have an effect greater than the sum of each when added together--and termed ones *Disability* ('not able')—i.e. Larger than life.

CONSTRUCT: The C17 words Construct (pile up together), Construction, and Construe all mean to build. Constructive information is loved after it comes into Being and plays out well. However, in this area not much harm is done to others. The etymological root of the word "*Inform*" means to put the involved Essence ingredients into a Form or into a Mold. When it is fully realized, it is called a Pattern. That *Pattern* has an inside matrix (womb bringing energy nourishment to the ingredients) containing an Essence with its endowments and propensities fashioned into an Interchange possessed with a Disposition. That Essence is composed of Activity networks which account for the "what it does" of the new Form offspring. A given Pattern's *Shape* (a pattern of energy movement frozen in space) is an Image that possesses a specific power given to it by the nature of the Source of the ingredients—for good or bad. See Pattern; Information; Shape

CONTAIN: "*Contain*" denotes to have, or to be capable of having, within. "*Hold*" is to have the capacity to contain and to retain in the sense of what one actually has in it. An analogy is that a bookcase contains (i.e. actually has in it) 50 volumes, but holds (i.e. capable of containing) 100. Ones "*Contained*" (C14, behave in a certain or Ma'at way) Selfhood means that one is born with everything needed to have a contented and thriving life of a "ME/WE" nature. This includes Selfhood Greatness with its contents of the "5Ss" of Safety, Security, Sureness/Self-Confidence, Strength, and Stability. However, in the "*Self-Contained*" Selfhood sense, one is a complete and independent unit in and of oneself; not dependent on others; Self-Controlled;

self-sufficient--able to provide for oneself without the help of others; Self-Sustaining; Selfhood Order—having all Necessities for working in top condition, in their proper place, and working interdependently; powered by Spiritual Energy maneuvering and manipulating the Spiritual Elements in an "Aliveness" Selfhood condition; keeping to oneself; reserved; independent; and Continues.

CONTEMPLATION: "Contemplate," to devise solutions for Omens while in a state of Trance, originated with Primitive (the first of Humankind) African Shamans' Visions--as indicated by many rock paintings and engravings. Very Ancient African Sages devised *Primary Contemplation* as a way to make connections between the Cosmic Mind and ones Real Self nature--conveying all inner meanings which enable one to "know" certain things to be true, and without reference to the familiar intellectual processes. *Augurs* (ancient Roman priests) borrowed and applied African practices by marking out spaces in temples to "observe omens carefully" so as to predict the future. In C16, Europeans defined "Contemplate" as partial or complete identification of the observer with the object observed, while losing ones own personality. The African sense of *"Contemplate" is steadily holding all forces of life in the place of Silence.* When skillfully done so as to be "second nature," then one can see, hear, and know in a realm other than the phenomenal world of a higher power's existence. The more and longer this is done, the greater is the magnitude of clarity concerning the Essence of ones Soul while keeping the mind progressively more one-pointed. This was taught in Ancient Egyptian Mystery Schools (c12,000 BC) so Initiates could engage in the Mysteries of African Tradition's Spirituality leading to achieving Personal Freedom. The most important objective was/is *the deification of humans and teaching that the Soul of humans, if freed from bodily fetters, would enable them to be God-like; obtain the beatific vision; hold communion with the immortals; and see within the metaphorical gods in this life.* African Sages taught with gods and goddesses (Neteru). Yet, they made it clear that they are not realities but only windows into the transcendent—avenues by which ones mind and body energies may be channeled towards a higher, spiritual goal in life. In the process, a human's conventional "ME" and its boundary considerations are gradually eclipsed so as to become a "Non-Self." What occurs is "Dematerializing" the boundaries between the "ME" and the "ME/WE" *so that the symbolic messages are able to transform themselves inside the Union. Achieving a "ME/WE" union state is the Soul realizing its identity with the Infinite.* That inwardly luminous experience enables ones "Soul Sunshine" to have great Cosmos visioning.

CONTEMPLATION SECULAR: prolonged focused attention which enables one to become mentally one with the Spiritual Elements; internalizing assumed Truths

CONTEMPLATION—INTROSPECTIVE: an *Inner Exploring of "Know Thyself" nature.* This mindset is continuously examining the contents or qualities of ones own thoughts and feelings as well as ones mental experiences by means of repeatedly "thinking again" in focusing, pondering, or meditating on a significant life issue. *Problem or Situation specific Reflection* is consideration of some subject, idea, or purpose in the attempt to understand or accept it by viewing it in its true relations. This involves assessing, examining, and analyzing an issue's triad of "what it is," What it does," and "How it appears." Each of these is assessed for its obvious, hidden, and Base/Foundational features. If dealing with Cosmic Things, the idea is to prove or disprove that this matter has *Internal Unity.* Its Predictability is shaped by *Foresight* ("seeing" ahead and around corners), and therefore *Forethought"* ("figuring out" and planning ahead before taking calculated risks). See *Reflective Thinking*

CONTENT: *Content* implies one is quiet and placid, patient and undisturbed—despite having to curb or adjust desires to what is seen as possible, viable, and practical. There is no urge to communicate ones thoughts and feelings except to be social or to share. This is within the context of *"Satisfy"* (enough or sufficient)—meaning having enough to meet all one really, really wants—i.e. despite less than enough, there is all that ones restrained and submissive desires request. "*Contented*" means Happy from having a sense of "Aliveness" from the pursuit of what is in the Beauty of Worth.

CONTINGENT: an image of something either having no real existence or exists incompletely. *Contingencies* are very much like the grammatical *Subjunctive Mood* which expresses uncertainty or non-factuality through such key words as "can, possible, would be, or may." Within this context and despite doing violence to careful observations about the Universe, (1) the Cosmic Mechanical Artifacts concept (C19) has dominated Europeans' God concepts. Other European Supernatural God-related theories or substitutes located at different points around the stopwatch include: (2) quasi-mechanical believers who assume there is an element of spontaneity or freedom in all living organisms to account for the facts of observation; (3) Libertarians propose absolute freedom in a possible course of action, entirely uninfluenced by the past and the agent's character; (4) believers in the Ceramic Cosmic Creation (Potter God); (5) the "God is dead!" group saying the Cosmos is run by blind energy gyrations. (6) *Agnostics*--there is no proof of God but do not deny the possibility. Most believe the Supernatural and/or the Spiritual home of God is unknowable, making it impossible to prove its existence or nonexistence. (7) *Atheists*--nothing beyond sense perceptions is real--all else is imagination or insanity. If not denying God's existence, most are unsure and (8) some hope God is not;

CONTINGENT BEINGS: The nature of *Phantasmagoria* creations depends upon what rung of the metaphorical A-Frame Ladder one is mentally 'positioned' on. Some mental systems which affect behavior unconsciously are independent of and unrecognized by controlling people. "*Contingency*" (to touch on all sides) is broadly like looking at every possible aspect of a one-sided coin (e.g. "it may and also may not be"). To climb out of the unresolvable Controversies and the hopeless confusion of and conflicts in European Contingent Beings (CB) concepts--particularly in relation to God--my listing of issues includes: I. What is called Factual, like 'actual' and Necessity in the Possible and Impossible category—and yet what is claimed is neither necessary nor impossible; II. It might not have occurred if not for a real thing, like a shadow, from which is inferred the existence of a material thing and the light by which it is cast; III. Things determined by external causes--as in dependence of one state of affairs on another state of affairs. IV. Things that might not have occurred or might have been otherwise, as when a Cause (a Being that could not fail to have existed) gives rise to an Effect and Consequences; V. A CB happens to exist, but might not ever have existed at all because it does not contain within itself the reason for its own existence--and at some point it did not exist. VI. Whereas Necessity is true and Impossible is false in every possible world, Contingency is true in at least one possible world. VII. a CB can be imagined other than it is; VIII. a host of others. *Contingent entities* meaning they are made up in ones imagination but yet can have profound effects in daily living. The subject's complexity increases by trying to classify it. Examples: Europeans say Genuine Beings ("existential Beings"--actual or Potential)--are distinguished from Imaginary entities by their possession of "essential Being" with definable essences as reflections of the divine ideas. *Actual Beings* (with substance existing independently, such as humans, tree) differ from those existing in another--called *Accidents* (which can only exist in something else, like time, place). Both Actual and Accident Beings are distinguished from merely *Possible Beings*--and these are distinguished from *Beings deemed to be intrinsically impossible* and incoherent. Europeans say they are creatures in their mature and actualized state. My assessment is that CBs are imaginative and thus Supernatural (human-made fantasies)-- unrealities composed of a complex diversity of bits and pieces of the finite creatively organized into a coherent whole. The very identity of a CB takes the form of a distinction from something else and thus can have very little significance of its own. By reflecting the mindset of each ones human creator, it has a Disposition (a blue-print" with an Inclination to impart a specific Effect) that is implanted in the mind of those willing to receive it. That Effect has Consequences which creatively branch in all directions, signifying its dependence upon the nature of the temperament that formed it. However, it is apparent by inference that God emanates Intelligences throughout the Cosmos, which, despite lacking Matter, are composites of essences and existence. One of those is ones Archetype birth gift Talent--meaning it is Trademarked within ones Selfhood--which I call a Divine Archetype CB (DACB). That Trademark is unique because its specific shape has a specific vibration rate--a rate carrying a specific power capable of meshing with a similar vibrating type thing within the Cosmos--a thing capable of activating ones Mission or ones career. All vibrations generate sound waves and those of ones talents are in a dormant state at birth (Bailey, Word Stories Encyclopaedia p362). The awakening of ones Talent for the transformation into a DACB image is done by sound waves--waves from a something to which one is exposed in the environment--a "something" possessing a similar pattern, or vibration rate, with ones dormant Talent--a "something" capable of "Unlocking" the Talent's vault and activating its DACB. Thereafter, that DACB provides a standard, guide, and filter for the Talent's development--whether it starts as a totipotent CB (which can radiate in any direction) or a mature entity (which is cultivated out of its form). A *Probable* (provable) Potential Potency means the DACB has more points in favor of it maturing into reality than not. If one detects ones DACB at an *Unrealized Reality Possible* level of evolution, that implies its realization can happen. Yet, for one to believe any aspect of the above 8 mentioned CB of a one-sided coin nature, the chance of ones Talents being detected, or developed, or finding the proper niche for ones Talent is greatly diminished. Instead, what is essential is that appropriate special sound waves must be translated into the DACB image to serve as a matrix for the cultivation of the physical manifestations of ones Talent. See Phantasmagoria; Chimera

CONTINUE: C17, 'hang together' uninterrupted).

CONTINUITY: Unity running through Multiplicity--from all interdependently doing its independent things for the benefit of the whole in the *course* of their *Natural Processes*.

CONTRADICTIONS: Very Ancient African Sages believed in holding to contradictory views on the same subject at the same time. For example, simultaneously there were different creation events; different means employed by creator-gods in their creation; and differences in the condition of the primordial state at the beginning of creation. They tolerated great ambiguity, as with holding to at least three different means of creation simultaneously without concerning themselves with the contradictions. In fact they welcomed contradictions under the assumption that the Truth would lie at the point where the contradictions intersected. Together they went into creating new or evolving old cosmological systems -- and none became out of date because of each being considered a principle piece of the whole. Here, as in building a skyscraper, the uncomparable absolutely sound Base is Unconditional Love.

CONTRARY OPPOSITES: See Yin/Yang; Background/Foreground; Contradictions

CONUNDRUM: a riddle whose answer involves a Pun--"When is a door not a door?"; A: When it's ajar". See Puzzle; Enigma; Paradox; Problem; Mystery

CORRESPONDENCE—COSMIC "ANCHOR": Just as a ship's *Anchor* ('a crook or hook') exerts the power to hold a ship in place under varying extremes of conditions, so is the purpose of a human's Philosophy of Life (POL). That POL is based upon Cosmic Order that comes from a keystone African concept called Correspondence—of which there are several types. The source of all is God's "Seed"--consisting of Androgynic plast (called Protoplasm today)—a Substance plast which become Essences in the finite Cosmos—a plast comprised of the Spiritual Elements "Genetics" for all God's Creatures and Creations, including for each human. In that plast is what African Sages called the *Law of Holonomy*: the whole is inside the Seed; the whole is contained in each of the Seed's manifested parts; and the Seed is found throughout the whole. "Seed" represents "*Wholism*" ("Holism")—meaning as a whole living organism, it must be nourished inside a Matrix and its complexities cannot be understood by an analysis of the constituent parts alone. Yet, Unity of those inner factors—called *Principles*--means they share mutual relationships as well as are interdependent with each other and the whole.

Type I--*Direct Correspondence* displays as the *Law of Spiritual Circularity or Reversibility* whereby the parent and its offspring are interchangeable. Such is explained by Africans' *Law of Spiritual Creativity*: by itself, a Spiritual Element reproduces itself to become the thing it makes, regardless of its new form. Here, despite "A" being the parent, it IS "B, C, D" because the share the same "Genetic" combination Thus, despite subtle individual uniqueness, their "what it is" when it came into Beinghood as well as their "what it does" and "how it appears" share the same Essence with its Essentials of Character, Characteristics, Traits, and Features. Direct Correspondence is demonstrated by the Finite Cosmos being an image of the Amenta, God's home in "the Other World." It is also seen in the Soul of each human being an image of God—i.e. a Spark of the "Flame" of God. In the Earth World, these Laws are ongoing repetitions of Divine Archetype "Thought-Forces'" manifesting as correspondence and compatible Prototypes since the Animal Kingdom, Mineral Family and Plant "Queendom" are all "Genetically" related by God's Substance called Essence (i.e. their "What it is" when they came into Beinghood inside the Subjective realm). To elaborate, when the above 3 Laws are operating within the same Divine Archetype, say Animal Kingdom, this means Correspondence throughout.

The "Animal" Kingdom is the Genus that includes both humans and other animals. A "*Genus*" is a group of species alike in the broad features of their organization but different in their detail. To know one is to know the other--like X = Y--i.e. *the African Law of Correspondence*. A *Species* is a group of entities which reproduce their kind and are so nearly alike in all particulars as to indicate they may have sprung originally from the same parent stock—as did all "races" of humans. For example, all "races" or Species of people on Earth--each appearing quite differently from the rest but all sharing the same Underlying "Genetics"—have originally come from the same African Ancestors who lived 200,000 years ago when humans first appeared on Earth. Also, all prebirth humans are virtually joined in their Subjective plane home with other of God's Creatures and Creations in an unformed, undifferentiated, but not disorganized state called "ME/WE". Again, to know the ingredients in one is to know the other--like X = Y--i.e. *the African Law of Correspondence*.

Type II--Partial Direct Correspondence is discerning only some aspects that conform to the *Law of Spiritual Circularity or Reversibility*—as in: (1) seeing *Inner Similarities* in dissimilar things; (2) seeing *Inner Similarities* in Similar things; (3) discerning uniqueness in similarities; (4) discerning similarities in unique things; (5) discerning the uncommon in the common; (6) discerning the common in the uncommon; and (7) going into the Underlying of what is dissimilar in order to detect and fashion interrelationships between dissimilar and similar things or discover they share the same "Genetics". Here, although "A" IS not "B, C, D"—since they are either difference Essences (meaning the uniqueness of their Sameness is in different combinations) or are mere Attributes (i.e. unique Essentials) of Essences, they still all share the general class of family members to which they all belong (e.g. by having the same "Genetics"). Any one of A, B, C, and D is a specific and concrete example of the family (or genre) since their "Sameness" establishments make for Correspondence, in spite of their otherwise "Uniqueness" aspects. In spite of having different appearances and/or doing different things, the fact that they share the same "what it is" when they came into being means any one of them can serve as a Metaphor for attributes for which that family stands. *Metaphors* are a transfer of one sense of a Thing across dematerialized boundaries into another—i.e. something different in one Thing that means something of the same in something else. Resultant new meanings increase insights.

Type III--*Association Correspondence* occurs when certain aspects of Complete or *Partial Direct Correspondence* are meshed into harmonious associations of ideas, out which a "Big Picture" Abstraction emerges. In fitting the "Seed's" ingredient Essences into a Common Ground state, there are interrelationships from the essences being unified to each other and to ideas in a manner that they interpenetrate. This means *its old original elements have been put together to make a new, novel, and harmonious whole—i.e. a "Oneness or a Unity"—and therefore the new now shares a* Disposition's What and Why aspects. Any associate can serve as a Metaphor for attributes for which that family stands. Yet, all of this must conform to the Law of Correspondence so that resultant new meanings are able to increase insights.

Type IV—Inference Correspondence is using any Direct, *Partial Direct,* or *Association Correspondence* to enter into the Unknown part of the Cosmic Web as, for example, into the Esoteric. As long as this process modeled the Circle of Wholism, it was fundamental in leading Ancient African Sages to fashion Ma'at (Spiritual Elements) life-guides. The resultant new meanings from Types I, II, and III increase ones insights for determining the *Order and consistent Patterns underlying natural events.* That enables arriving at the Mystery's answer, even inside the Esoteric.

CORRESPONDENCE: Correspondence in African Tradition is the single most powerful thinking tool for acquiring Knowledge and for engaging in African Wisdom. Once I understood how it worked—and in conjunction with its Circumstantial partner, it opened a new world for how to approach subjects I had never seen nor heard of before. Correspondence refers to "Equivalent" Entities within the Cosmic Organism Family—meaning they have the "Sameness" of the Spiritual Elements Genetics—the "what it is" Essence--despite their "Uniqueness" in "what it does" and "how it appears." Type I "Equivalent" are those Family members engaged in the flow of the Spiritual Elements; Type II are those with one foot in and one foot out of the flow; Type III are completely out of the flow; and Type IV attack the flow and all that are in it—"Satanists" by definition. The "Sameness" is illustrated by all waves in the ocean having the same water content even though they are different in activity and form appearance. Put another way, Correspondence is based upon the general principle that "If two (or more) things share the same Genetics or have an Essence from the same Source when they came into Being (i.e. their "what it is"), then they are spiritually related, no matter how remote in time or space. This holds true despite being unlike in all other aspects, including external appearances. Type I are those creatures and creations that follow the Divine Plan of the same Divine Creator, for which the terms *Spiritual Correspondence* or *Real Self* (as with humans) are used. Types II and III are Secular *"False Selves"* while Type IV "Satanist" operate out of a Supernatural realm. Because they have adopted a non-spiritual or non-divine creator, Types II, III, and IV are not spotlighted in discussions on Correspondence, even though technically they are Family members. Ancient Africans said this adoption is done out of Ignorance because Evil does not exist per se.

Type I "Correspondence" is the keystone concept for "Knowing Thyself"--for "Knowing the Cosmos—and for "Knowing Thyself and the Cosmos" to have the same and equal Cosmic Genetics; to be Algebraic "Equivalent"—i.e. equal to the same thing and alike but not identical, as a dime is equivalent to 10 pennies. African Sages elaborated by saying such *Cosmic/Selfhood Wholeness* means all of its mutual ingredients are each enfolded (enclosed) within the Spiritual Elements—i.e. Unconditional Love, Truth, Reality, and the Natural. Each Element combination, fashioned into an Entity that conforms to God's Plan, does its own job—each interpenetrates all others so as to be throughout the whole—and each works in balance and interdependently as part of an interwoven flowing movement. This macrocosm ('big world') is present in each human, for example, as a microcosm ('little world'). This means all God-made things, regardless of their Type, have Underlying "Genetic Harmony" but how Genes in any Cosmic Organism is expressed is different. To elaborate, *Genomics* is an organism's complete set of genetic material including gene sequences, structure, and function; regulation of gene expression; and gene-environment interactions. DNA codes for genes are translated to create proteins, which can be associated with specific things. By understanding the regulation and function of the Laws involved regarding these genes (Seeds) associated with specific objects (protein equivalents) enabled

Ancient African Sages to eliminate confusion and thereby establish Certainty Laws of Nature. Putting these Certainty concepts into practical daily living were giant steps toward achieving Perfection and hence a sound Tradition. However, this concerned great attention to the details of how they lived, the human forerunner of *Epigenetics*—i.e. the development of an organism from an undifferentiated cell. Its two main stages are first, *Meiosis* whereby the mother's fertilized ovum's components separates into two equal halves while *staying within the same ovum. Next comes Mitosis*--the complete splitting of the ovum so that each half now has an individual existence. In the Cosmic Organism's demonstration of Correspondence with each human, *Meiosis equates to a newly conceived human being inside the Subjective Spiritual realm's Ocean of Nun while Mitosis is the state a human newborn enters the Earth World.* European Theoretical Physicists have just confirmed what Ancient Africans knew thousands of years ago—that there are two main features working interdependently to design individuality in each human. First is the information coded into all humans' DNA that make for a "Sameness" in Human Nature. Second is the way DNA folds itself that controls which genes are expressed inside a given human.

CONVENTIONAL: what is the result of human intervention, as by human laws and customs based upon Mechanics). See Gods--European

CORRESPONDENCE--SPIRITUAL: (have comparable elements)—*apply to two or more things that conform to one another or share certain characteristics.* Whereas the Spiritual Circumstantial surrounds the Physical, the Spiritual Correspondence embraces the Spiritual, Metaphysical, and Physical. The Law of Correspondence arose from the *Divine Logos--i.e. God's Universal Reason—Thought and Creative Utterance and Power—the Word—God's Germ Plasm* called Androgynic Plast. God's creatures began out of its Feminine/Masculine primeval Substance "Oneness." That "Oneness" is at the basis for all that is about Cosmic Correspondence. The Continuity of that Cosmic Correspondence provides: (1) a "Sameness" throughout the "Oneness" Pattern--regardless of its location in the Seen or the Unseen realms; (2) enables the realization of its Esoteric nature taken from any Sample at any location when compared with Spiritual Elements ("The Word") standards, guides, measures or "educated" Estimates, and filters; and (3) its Consistency and Compatibility give revelation insight into the nature of its Creator's attributes, based upon the nature of the Spiritual Elements work products. This *Verbum* (the "Word") is the smallest element expressible, which Ancient African Sages said consisted of the vibratory "*Genetics*"—i.e. *the Spiritual Elements of Unconditional Love, Truth, Reality, and the Natural.* This Verbum Essence is outwardly expressed as the Subjective Realm's Ocean of Nun's—having Correspondence with *Meiosis. Identical (monozygotic) Twins*--originating in the mother's fertilized ovum--separates and reproduces into two units while *staying within the same ovum*—called *Meiosis.* Next, the actual splitting of the ovum—called *Mitosis*--starts each Twin on a customized and unique existence. The Verbum Meiosis contains all God's creatures and creation in an unformed, undifferentiated, undivided, but not disorganized state. That means they are within the Interchange of the vibratory Spiritual Elements. An *Interchange* is the "*Common Ground*" (ingredients shared for beneficial mutual interaction) within the interlocking Spiritual Elements components. Within that "Common Ground" offspring of the Spiritual Elements are formed. The composition of each Entity is likened to a mosaic—an assemblage of small pieces of tile, marble, wood, glass, and stone that form an image or pattern with a payload Disposition. The image, say, of a given human has an Essence whose *Disposition Pattern* includes: (1) a Message (the "What" and "Why"); (2) its *Inclination*--a 'physical' "leaning toward" or "leaning" away from something; (3) an Intention--the decision of what one means to do with an aim toward a specific action or a specific goal; an earnest state of mind to reach the goal; and (4) a "Radar" effect from each mosaic piece that that forms a Spiritual Elements "Trademark" on that human's Soul so as to detect and draw to itself what is like-kind. In keeping with the Law of Attraction, one is able to determine if a Thing has Correspondence or not. Also present in the Essence of the human-to-be is *Endowments* (i.e. natural qualities) and *Propensities* (in-born tendencies, e.g. a human's capacities, abilities, and language) which operate some process of an Entity's Selfhood. At the proper moment, when it is time for the human-to-be to emanate (flow out) of the Interchange, it is a "Unique" package representing the start of a new human embryo. Simultaneously, a *Mitosis* type division of its "Seed" cell begins in a mathematically ordered fashion. That is because each piece of its Spiritual Elements' mosaic pattern, although working independently to contribute to every human Primary Quality, works interdependently to contribute to the making of a human whose Endowments are in harmony. What accounts for the "Uniqueness/Sameness" reality in all of God's creatures and creations is the DNA code in each human being determined in a Sequence (a succession when events viewed follow one another) the conveniently used letters G, A, C, and T. The order of these letters fashions which proteins are made in a human's cells. So, one with brown eyes results from ones DNA containing a particular series of letters encoding for a protein responsible for the dark pigment inside ones iris. Yet, even though all the cells in ones body starts out with the exact same DNA code, every organ has a very different function—a "Sameness/Uniqueness" concept. Obviously, ones stomach cells do not need brown eye protein, but they do need to produce digestive enzymes. Such happens by the way DNA is folded up inside ones cells. By every single body cell containing almost 7 feet of DNA (actually 2 meters; a meter = 39.37 inches), for that to fit inside it has to be tightly wrapped into a bundle--called a "Nucleosome" (nucleus, nut + soma, body--seen under the electron microscope as beadlike bodies on a string of DNA)--like a thread around a spool. How the DNA is wrapped up controls which genes are 'read' by the rest of the cell. For example, in contrast to those on the outside, genes all wrapped on the inside will not be expressed as proteins—and thereby explaining why different cells have the same DNA but different functions and appear at different times. For example, just as human genes are active at birth and others are delayed (like those that display secondary gender characteristics)--called *Congenital Tarda* genes. An example is the budding of a human's Intellect--slowly, between ages 5 and 12. Another Congenital Tarda is the development of secondary gender characteristics at puberty. Of course, all of ones *Genomics* 'nature' can be significantly affected by 'nurture.' See Divine Logos; Mathematics; Circumstantial

CORRESPONDENCE--AFRICAN LOGIC'S BOX-IN-A-BOX: As a Morehouse College student "chilling out" in a mixed male and female "bull session," one of the females was given a big box nicely wrapped and with a pretty bow. When she opened the box, there was a second box to open inside that big box—then a smaller box inside the second box—and so on until she got to a tiny box. Upon opening that final box she discovered an engagement ring. Thereafter, I called this the *"Box inside a box inside a box" Concept* which can be applied to many things. One is that the inner most box of a human represents a human's Soul. Another is that the tiny box can symbolize whatever gave rise to an Emotion. Still another is that it leads me to think of the somewhat similar Russian Nesting Dolls concept. These Nesting Dolls are separate and of decreasing size placed one inside the other—each a smaller figure of the same sort inside, which has, in turn, another figure inside of it, and so on to include 5 to dozens. This is called *Correspondence*—meaning each doll has the same "Genetics" as all the rest and yet the way that "Genetics" is packaged is different for each doll. Nothing has been for helpful for me to advance in conceptualizing things in the unknown or what is perplexing than observing the manifestations of the Ancient African concept of Correspondence. Correspondence present throughout the Cosmic Organism and throughout all Cosmic planes of existence means each entity made by God—and regardless at what level that entity is--has the same "Genetics" consisting of the Spiritual Elements. Elements means "First Principle"—meaning the simplest form of an entity when it came into being and out of which it, by itself, reproduced itself, to become the thing it makes. So, Spiritual Elements refer to God's inner nature of Unconditional Love and God's outer nature of Life in the form of whatever is "First Principle" Truth, Reality, and the Natural. These constitute Cosmic "Genetics." In other words, each God made thing has the same Base/Foundation "Genetics" in each of its offspring, regardless of what that offspring looks like and regardless of where that offspring is located within the Comic plane of existence. Despite the Uniqueness in each entity, the "Genetic Sameness" is what underlies the obvious and the hidden. An obvious observable "sameness" example is "Human Nature" while a hidden one embracing the entire Cosmic Organism is Instincts.

To illustrate this, all living organisms are able to detect changes within themselves (e.g. position, motion or static) and in their environment (of such things as light, temperature, sound, motion, and odor). Once detected, these changes must be analyzed and acted upon in order to preserve the integrity, well-being, and status quo of ones Selfhood. Humans have been given the ability to detect and make changes based upon Intellect—but that birth gift has to be cultivated out of its Ocean of Nun (Subjective Realm) potential possibility state. To understand Correspondence of say, Instincts, on any given plane of Cosmic existence means that gives insight into instincts of a less evolved or more complex nature. Hence, the African Tradition expression: "So above, so below; so below, so above." The entire "nesting" reaction types present throughout the Plant and Animal Kingdoms, including a human's Self, are orchestrated by Instincts. How humans are put together from representatives of all members of the Cosmic Organism can be analogized to Nesting Dolls.

To elaborate, let us say the Plant Kingdom was the first to come into existence following the creation of the Cosmos and thus represents Level--the most primitive form of Instincts. Plants engage in instinctual physiological-biochemical processes called *Photosynthesis*—i.e. using energy in the sun's light to feed themselves by synthesizing organic ingredients on the basis of mineral matter. Level II is the Plants/Animal transitions which possess some features of both Plants and Animals. An example is the *Venus Fly-trap*—operating in a manner that embrace Photosynthesis (to make its own food) + like animals' Reflexes (involuntary acts) to grab food from things that have fed on food. This heralds the Secular (Earth World) "First Principle" pertaining to the beginning of the Diffuse Nervous System category. It is the earliest form of communication through which will later develop a process consisting of a sensory process with a motor nerve meeting at a nerve center. Note that this "First Principle" is like the parent Spiritual "First Principle". Just as there are plants that act like animals, there are animals that look like plants. The more than a million different kinds of animals known range from microscopic in size to elephants and whales—living "everywhere" and under all types of conditions—and getting around naturally by flying, swimming, climbing, and walking. A *Species* is a group of animals that, while they may differ a great deal among themselves in appearance, are very closely related. One of the brilliant mental feats of Ancient Africans was their ability to not only discern the inner nature animals which makes for a Species but also to incorporate mathematics in order *to see the abstract unity and interdependence between all independent real things. As a result, they established Truth from their mathematically determined Spiritual Principles.* It is within a Species of any type that Ancient Africans derived the concept of *Classification*. The simpler forms of animal life is today called *Invertebrates*--Level III in evolution.

Protozoa (e.g. one cell creatures called *Monera* or Amoeba) are the simplest of all animals. Its cytoplasm (plasma substance) serves the functions of a Diffuse Nervous System. Its plasma can be easily molded—and I call this a *Form-Body* state because of its totipotent ability (a "jack of all trades" in an organism entity creation sense). When a stimulation excites the "inner stuff" all parts of the cell react. In more evolved Invertebrates the nerve cells are distributed throughout the organism—acting in a "fishnet" type pattern of communication. Higher Invertebrates introduce a *Central Nervous system* which coordinates information and permits almost instantaneous transmission of directs responses by way of electrical impulses along specialized nerve cells from one region of the body to another. Level IV: Vertebrates or 'backbones' (e.g. fishes, frogs, reptiles, birds) have a brain and spinal cord which carry impulses through nerves and together they make up the *Peripheral Nervous System*. Meanwhile, compared with Level I (Plants), there has also been evolution in the instinctually driven physiological-biochemical processes + Reflexes + a Mind which gives rise to Behaviors (among others). Featured at lower levels of Vertebrates are *Sensory-Perception* aspects—initially being an advanced regulator of behaviors in the direction of life. They form Percepts (which are also at a Form-Body state).

Level V: Mammals nourish their young on milk and are in the egg-laying and young born alive subclasses. They include those with claws, hoofs, swim, and graspers—monkeys, apes, and humans. All of Level IV is inside Mammals and are further developed. All of the Instincts are amazingly similar throughout the evolutionary scale—as, for example, the Reflex arc--and that allows for humans to better understand themselves in how they think, feel, express, and do things. This is especially true of Chimpanzees and Gorillas who are usually ranked next in intelligence—but that is debatable, especially in considering Porpoises and Dolphins. Mammals possess a *Pleasure-Pain System* appears that can develop into Notions. At higher stages there is the *Imaginative Faculty* which enable Notions to "ripen"—like into "Emotional Musical Notes." Still, in humans, this Emotional realm remains at an automatic Natural Instinct state. Level VI—RATIONAL: humans' Metaphysical birth gift abilities existing as Potential Possibilities. If one chooses to stay at Level V—operating Emotionally out of ones Omnibus and Old Mammalian Brains—then the Rational intellect that normally starts appearing around ages 5 to 7 will not be activated or even released out of their Potential Possibility "Genetic Vault." Otherwise, Rational intellect displays by making Concepts out of "raw" ingredients and puts those ingredients into order like one does in fitting the pieces of a puzzle together. Level VII: Ancient African Sages--the supreme thinkers of Humankind—and the masters of the masters. They thought in Principles (various forms of the Spiritual Elements) and used Spiritual Symbols (which, like "Musical Notes," are the closest things to vibrations) so as to minimize distortions and limitations of Words to the extent possible. "Full-circle" Correspondence between humans and Plants is shown by the Photosynthesis in humans by sunlight changing the provitamin ergosterol being changed into vitamin D but the ultraviolet rays in sunlight which is essential for children's bones to grow normally and to slow down the development of osteoporosis in senior adults. African Logic is directed to determining if the Known Sets Correspond to the Unknown Sets, as indicated by a balanced equation scale. *Sets* are a collection of like-kind Things (e.g. Objects, Essences, or an Association of Ideas) designated by some rule that indicates exactly which Things belong to the collection (e.g. steps on the ladders)—in both the Known and the Unknown Ladders which have Correspondence.

CORRESPONDENCE LAW: Cosmic "Oneness" is at the basis for Cosmic Correspondence as well as enabling the realization of a Sample of its Esoteric Creator. That Sample, called a Circumstance companion, enables the Esoteric Creator or its Esoteric realms to be known with Certainty because of the Law of Correspondence. Correspondence have equal Cosmic Genetics; equivalent——equal to the same thing—alike but not identical, as a dime is equivalent to 10 pennies

CORRESPONDENCE/CIRCUMSTANTIAL CRITICAL THINKING: Critical Thinking (CT) of a Correspondence/Circumstance nature is what enables one to arrive at Certainty in African Tradition. The foundation for and frame within which African Logic Thoughts exist is Qualitative Mathematics whose focus is on Essences of foundational Realities and their Principles. Essences are the "what it is" of a Thing in the form of a set of Primary Qualities (a Spiritual or Metaphysical Thing wrapped in Ether) that conjointly embody the nature of the Thing they qualify. They can be grasped intellectually or by Intuition (Feelings) so as to be able to express them in the definition of that Thing—a definition that is an Estimate of that Thing's ultimate realm—an Estimate based upon what the "Thing" is, what it does, and/or how it appears that has Correspondence with the Spiritual Elements, as known by its Effects on a human's Soul Spiritual Elements "Trademark." The thinking tool for this is Critical Thinking (CT). Having Cosmic Organism Knowledge as its standard, CT uses Common Sense, Rational Thinking, and Qualitative Mathematics to deal with Spiritual, Metaphysical, and Spiritual subjects so as to provide the ingredient for African Wisdom. CT establishes the Circumstantial Evidence and Circumstantial Proof that is the foundation of all Cosmic Organism manifestations—meaning each has Correspondence with all the other Cosmic Organism Entities because of each being made of the same "Genetic" (the "what it is") and are part of the Spiritual Elements flow (the "what it does") in spite of the Unique appearance of each. *Circumstantial Truths are verified by Circumstantial Evidence* pertaining to Observable God-created Divine Forms for such things as in the Animal and Plant Kingdoms—from human experienced things as Thought and Mathematics--and such human "Felt" things like Music, Beauty, and Goodness. *Circumstantial Proof* comes when each reproduces itself in its own Essence Pattern and/or Image so as to become the Thing it makes. Circumstantial Truths, Proofs, and Evidence have the same Vibratory Rhythm, as measured by Mathematics. Using Qualitative Mathematics in association with measuring vibratory rates of radiations, Very Ancient African Sages gained insight into the Laws of Nature. These are what reveal "*Esoteric Knowledge*"—i.e. the understanding of inner truths lying hidden within the core of fundamental Dispositions about foundational Realities. CT's use of Qualitative Mathematics involves making Estimates of like-kind Things of Worth (i.e. Essence Qualities) that have Correspondence and to thereby establish a Circumstantial Truth. Since these can only be determined by Mathematical measurement of Vibration Rhythms--implying that Cosmic Qualities have Mathematical Order.

Within this *Law of Correspondence* context, Mathematics can be defined as *quantitative* reasoning resulting from *assessments of Material World Entities which enable one to make Intuitive Inductions* (inferring general principles from particular facts present in the Cosmic Order) of a Celestial Order ("course" or "way") type. The conclusions from such Intuitive Inductions following the Processes of Nature led African Sages to match Observable Entities with Unseen Entities having Correspondence--then manipulate their situations and facts, laws, themes within those situations into organizing Principles of harmony—and finally maneuver those Principles into arriving at *qualitative Circumstantial Truths in Metaphysical or Esoteric Realms. Qualitative Mathematics is the process for knowing* Un-seeable *Divine* and *Spiritual Entities with Certainty—a process called Circumstantial Truth.* Inferences from those Laws led to the Circumstantial Truth paths which would lead to the Heaven Afterlife. From the result of having established the keystone or ultimate Principle on which all aspects of Correspondence/Circumstances depend, *Intuitive Inductions* (inferring general principles from particular facts present in the Cosmic Order) of a Celestial Order ("course" or "way") type enables Sages to generate organizing principles of harmony, situations for facts, laws, themes, and correspondences. From such broad knowledge were extracted Principles then organized into Truths and Order called Ma'at (Love in action). Ancient Africans inferred from Qualitative Mathematics (Hodge, Racism p100) that the origin of the Cosmic Organism containing all of God's creatures and creations is by the Spiritual Elements Genetics. In short, such Algebraic Qualitative Mathematics as a process leading to African type Knowledge.

CORRESPONDENCE--DISHARMONIOUS SECULAR: all God's Creatures and Creations have "Sameness" in their "Ground of Being"—i.e. the Spiritual Elements Genetics--which underlies their different manifestations—a "Sameness" called *Correspondence*. Hence, regardless of the plane of existence on which any one of those four operate and regardless of what combination, arrangement, or form any one of those four is in, these combinations, arrangements, or forms remain in parallel, in accord with, or match the Essences of its "Seed" Source or basic foundational Truth so as to maintain the integrity of the "family" in a connected, balanced, and harmoniously manner. As opposed to the Afrocentric way of using the word "Secular," the way of European literature is implied here. In early European Christian texts "Secular" referred to the "Temporal World" as opposed to the Spiritual World. "Secular" (C13 Latin; generation, age) meant "non-religious or non-sacred" when brought into English (C16). Today, it refers to public, ordinary, or everyday life of a non-religious nature or of "man-made" religions. On the negative connotation scale, "*Secularity*" is a degrading societal force characterized by the turning away from religion and living with the conviction that one can direct ones life without divine guidance. It also turns adherents towards hedonistic pleasure-seeking, un-tempered by moral restraints or ethics which come from religion. Thus, corruption and greed degrades the moral structure of the people, as with Individualism, seeking the "high-living Good Life," and self-gratification (Ashby, African p247). Within this context, as stated, Type I Correspondence pertain to those creatures and creations that follow the Divine Plan of the same Divine Creator. For these, the terms *Spiritual Correspondence* or *Real Self* (as with humans) are used. Types II and III are Secular *"False Selves"*—those off the Spiritual Elements path, while Type IV are "Satanist" who operate out of a Supernatural realm. Common to Types II, III, and IV is that they have adopted a non-spiritual or non-divine creator but yet maintain the Spiritual Elements Genetics of all God's creatures and creations. This combination makes for Disharmonious Correspondence within the Cosmic Organism Family members. The Correspondence makes for "Sameness" while the Disharmony makes for Uniqueness between each type and within each Type. For humans, Ancient Africans said this adoption of a non-divine creator is done out of Ignorance, not Evil per se. One such ignorant form of thinking is that of *Eugenics*—the science of being "well-born"—a Supernatural concept. As background, let us look at the effect of "Nurture on Nature." After birth, Environmental *"Nurture"* (what nourishes in the act of its cultivation and rearing into maturity) modifies a human's Nature (its Essence + Character). For example, prolonged distress can cause certain cells to be turned on and off—a process called *"Epigenetics."* Whatever simulates a human's Genomes assigns a second level of DNA information, complete with altered organic or "mechanical" cues. These cues, now encoded into certain DNA, affect how the DNA is folded and thereby alter how certain proteins are expressed and thereafter become equally important in a human's evolution as the original DNA code itself. Altered DNA ways include first changing the DNA letters and therefore its structure which differs the frequency of production of the involved protein. Second is by changing the mechanical cues that arrange the way a strand is folded and thus remove what protects and defends against disease. Just as a process causes a deviation from the successive formation and development of human body parts that do not pre-exist in the mother's fertilized egg, chances are that an equivalent process occurs in the mental development of a False Physical Self. Common non-organic daily living forces which cause human's Real Selves to adopt Types II, III, and IV mindsets are psychic alteration or a misdirected socialization.

Mindsets developing out of Psychic Trauma are typically Selfhood Insecurities and Self-Hate that serve as mental "Raw Nerves" which lead to an Inferiority Complex (self-attacks on thinking abilities, self-worth and/or self-value) or to a *Feigned Superiority Complex* (donning a self-confidence and self-greatness mask wrapped in an arrogance/aggression reality to conceal deep inferiority). Those Eugenically ('good birth') socialized to ridiculously believe they are superior—a dumb and stupid (blind to the obvious) self-declaration, as seen in "White Superiority." Their sham science of "what ought to be" is wrapped in delusional concepts of "what is"—based upon the un-transferrable information derived from stock and plant breeders which say that by allowing only the most perfect specimens to reproduce, certain weaknesses are done away with which strengthen the good points. Their flawed Eugenics thinking say it is a well-established fact that every living thing, whether plant or animal, receives its every characteristic from its ancestors, the most from those closest to it in point of time—the rest in ever-increasing degree from those further back. Meanwhile, they ignore the inferiority of all their ancestors. See Eugenics; Post Traumatic Distress Syndrome

CORRESPONDENCE/CIRCUMSTANCE PRACTICAL APPLICATIONS: To realize the Divine Logos is the Spiritual Elements which are in all creatures and creations is to know that what happens anywhere happens everywhere if there are no interferences. So that if someone has a lifestyle pattern, one can trace this back into his/her mind and draw a correlations that is a "Subjective Plus"—meaning it is more than simply

Subjective and thus use it to make calculated plans that follows in that pattern to enhance or defend/protect against. The same applies to those who say one thing and do another—there are subtle agendas brewing in such minds.

COSMOS FORMATION: Knowledge pre-existed humans but it was by means of Revelations of the Un-Seeable Cosmic Mind that manifestations of Knowledge can be known. *Revelations* are the ventriloquist of the Voice of the Silence which conveys Cosmic Knowledge in Symbol Messages. Those Symbols touched and awakened the Truths already present in a human's Soul. Revelations from God (c20,000 BC?) were given to African Sages. A specific recording (Freke, The Hermetica, p35; Chandler, Ancient Future p55) in the beginning of "Poimandres" (the Vision of Hermes) is that the African Sage Tehuti derived his Wisdom by intuiting God's Will from a dramatic mystical revelation while searching for Divine Truth. In seeking solitude and coming to a place of rest, he gave himself over to meditation. With an alert mind, yet still and empty, he hears God speaking to him. After asking to be shown the true nature of reality, suddenly everything begins to change before him—meaning that Tehuti witnesses the creation of the world. Revealed to Tehuti was the Physical world being temporal and with the underlying theme that what is above parallels what is below--the *Law of Correspondence*--what first exists in the Spiritual is later manifest in the physical. Thus, the Spiritual and the Material are interwoven and must be pursued together. Because Tehuti's divine revelation, which embodied the Word of God and Natural Laws, was verified as true by Subjective and Objective Sciences as well as by Correspondence, African Sages deemed Tehuti interpreter of all that was divine and the conveyor of the *"Word of God."* This vision was not meant to be understood intellectually but rather contemplated like images from a dream. Resultant interpretations guided African Sages' Subjective Science tools and Astro-Mathematics into conclusions used to make *Spiritual Inferences to arrive at Circumstantial Evidence* and judgments. These, in turn, verified African Sages' Revelations so as to arrive at Circumstantial Truths about Laws of Natures and concepts of God. Also, they concluded that God--the only Life which exists entirely in itself, from itself, and by itself is an Unknowable Life—the Absolute--"The All". The Absolute equates to God by residing within itself—wholly without change or variation. The "One" is God's inner nature of Unconditional Love. The "All" represents God's outer nature of Life—that part of Divine Life which discloses itself—appears or becomes visible—through its manifestations in the Cosmos. From these Revelations and derived Laws—each verifying the other--Ancient African Sages formulated the Spiritual Elements of Unconditional Love, Truth, Reality, and the Natural. Using their *Subjective Sciences* as well as their *Objective Science* (which Ancient Africans formalized, between 2000 and 1500 BCE, into today's recognized Scientific Method), African Mathematics led to the conclusion that the "Oneness" of Cosmic Origin in the Spiritual realm is the basis of *Order* throughout the Cosmos. According to Tehuti's Revelation, the Ocean of Nun is *to make all God's creatures and creations in a manner of each Involuting back into itself again.*

The ultimate purpose is to return again by Evolution after having accomplished the Mission for which they existed. That Mission for every human is for the growth and exaltation of the myriad Souls of Humanity. So, in the beginning out of the "Other World"—the Amenta--flowed the Ocean of Nun, from which all designated for the Phenomenal Universe would evolve. From the Universal Principle of Mind—i.e. the Great Ocean of "Mind-Stuff"--there is a "raying out" of all the Laws of Nature, all Qualities, all Potencies, and all Prototypes required for the Cosmos. Meanwhile, there first proceeded the Universal Principle of Spiritual Energy or Force and from that Energy, came the Principle of Matter in its disorganized, motionless state. The Laws of Nature compelled the Causes of the Great Involution (to wrap up; to cover; to hide; rolled up on itself). This involved the Spirit instituting Evolution to allow expression of all that came out of the "Mind-Stuff". Hence, the Spirit activated Intangible flimsy matter which, in turn, became increasingly more and more gross—like a snowball rolling down a hill and getting bigger and bigger. At Involution's grossest point, a moment's pause occurred in its spiral curving. This was followed by a reversal into Cosmic *Evolution*. Thereafter, the grossest forms of Matter began pairing down into refined forms while entering outer space.

COSMIC/HUMAN WEB: The uncreated/indestructible Background of the Cosmos in the Ocean of Nun lacks form, is undefined, undifferentiated, and limitless in expanse and in duration (i.e. infinite/eternal). Yet, it is not disordered. For descriptive purposes, its unfolding creations and development of all creatures and creations, as orchestrated by the Cosmic Mind located in its mystic Center can be analogized to a spider, sitting in its web to symbolize the center of the world, and two prominent features of its web. First is its creative power (as exemplified in the weaving of its web) and, second, is the spiral shape net form, converging towards a central point. Similarly, the Cosmic Web serves to link--with invisible strands of heredity and Spiritual Elements aura--all of God's creature and creations to each other of the past, present, and future. Each human is a thickened node in the web of Cosmic Forces--forces which repetitively and ever anew—forces which flow in and out of ones Selfhood. Hence, humans are part of an ecology involving plants, animals, climate, soil, as well as all kinds of radiant forces and chemicals. Nature--everywhere at once, wiggling back and forth, and with each of its ingredients possessing different dimensions and vibration rates--flows through webs of Cosmic structures while shifting through space and time: from ocean to cloud to rain to river to ocean. Throughout the Cosmic/ Human Web, the Spiritual Elements of Unconditional Love, Truth, Reality, and the Natural fashion "Genetic Harmony". The Background of the Cosmic/Human Web is the Divine Consciousness of the Cosmic Mind. That uncreated and indestructible Background in the finite Subjective Realm, called the Ocean of Nun, lacks form, is undefined, undifferentiated, and limitless in expanse and in duration--i.e. infinite/eternal from a human perspective. Yet, it is not disordered. For descriptive purposes, its unfolding creations and development of all creatures and creations, as orchestrated by the Cosmic Mind located in its mystic Center, can be analogized to a spider. That spider sits in its web to symbolize the center of the world the web's two prominent features. First is its creative power (as exemplified in the weaving of its web) and, second, is the spiral shape net form, converging towards a central point. Similarly, the Cosmic Web serves to link--with invisible strands of heredity and Spiritual Elements aura--all of God's creature and creations to each other of the past, present, and future. Each human is a thickened node in the web of Cosmic Forces--forces which repetitively and ever anew—forces which flow in and out of ones Selfhood. Hence, humans are part of an ecology involving plants, animals, climate, soil, as well as all kinds of radiant forces and chemicals. Nature--everywhere at once, wiggling back and forth. Each Web ingredients possesses different dimensions and vibration rates--flows throughout all webs of Cosmic structures—and is shifting through space and time: from ocean to cloud to rain to river to ocean. Each human's organ is packed with billions of cells and any given cell is a chemical factory—infinitely better as a chemist and physicist than all Nobel Prize laureates combined. Sustained activity inside each microcosm of a cell which, in turn, is within its given macrocosm organ, does its independent Mission to support health for any human's grand system. Meanwhile throughout this process, there is a constant and shifting balance of forces in which that human's hormones, ferments, enzymes, memories, ideas, emotions, and moods all play a part. Such is far, far above the human mind's ability to grasp or even categorize. Inside that human, the Cosmic Web extends into ones Soul—into countless networks of ones Brain/Mind—and into all aspects of ones body. Some networks embrace ones Thoughts, Feelings (Instincts), pre-birth Emotions, Acquired Emotions, and Memory.

By a human's associations of *networks being part of Cosmic Web harmony, they know when to fire together to carry out their common purposes. Simultaneously, from being Spiritually connected to ones* Mental, Physically, Selfhood Center + to all "Virtual" creatures and creations within the Cosmic Organism + those leaving and to be born into the Earth World, this Cosmic Web *constitutes the "ME/WE"*. The point is that to ruffle any web strand anywhere within a spider web is to disturb all of its webs everywhere. When one Selfhood part goes wrong, all team member parts of the "ME" and of the "WE" are affected. To thoroughly understand that *Order is essentially dependent on the existence of the interdependence (a type of Oneness) between independent things* and thoroughly know any one Pattern in this Web is to have insight into and an understanding of like-kind things regardless of their time, space, or plane of existence. This is because, by sharing the same "Genetics" of the Spiritual Elements, every part of the web has Correspondence with every other part. To see them all together in their web-like fashion is to experience an *expanding Consciousness—an expansion resulting from depicting the whole rather than its separated parts—an expansion that gives an understanding of the meaning of "ME/WE" relationships.* This understanding is the path to knowledge, even inside the Esoteric Unknown. For example, to "Know Thyself" and its "ME/WE" connections within the context of the Laws of Nature is to know that the *meaning behind both. Hence, their orchestrated order and harmony can be reduced to God* (a Big Mind).

COSMOLOGY: study of how God creates the world, provides a blue-print for living.

COUNTER: The Old French prefix "*Counter*" means: against, in opposition; in return (as in attack in return); and corresponding, as in counterpart (which though it is used as opposite it actually means duplicate, almost the opposite of opposite, as in complementary). See Confusion Counter-action

COURAGE: The foundation for preparation to become an Isolated Individualist is *Courage—the decision to* willingly *deal with problems one does not and would not ordinarily choose.* African Sages used the "Heart" as a metaphor for ones innermost instinct (Feelings) which gives rise to Courage--an inner strength and determination inspired by God. This implies Courage, Compassion, Wisdom, and Nobleness are exact expressions of ones Conscience. Ones Conscience is first orchestrated naturally by ones Soul--ones Real Self (Spiritual aspect) and is thus bound to Ma'at (i.e. Spiritual Elements in action) ideas urging one to obey the Divine Laws of ones Highest Self as a duty. To be ones Real Self and use ones Talents to create what is within ones Genius and realize that creation will necessitate ones suffering in a variety of uncertain ways is the exhibition of *Spiritual Courage.*

COURAGE FORMS: "The ultimate measure of a man is not where he stands in moments of comfort and convenience, but where he stands at times of challenge and controversy" (M. L. King, Jr.). Life shrinks or expands in proportion to ones Courage. That Courage may display completely in all things; completely in some things; incompletely in all or some things; or to some degree on one side of a coin while ignoring the rest. Nevertheless, Specialized Courage has many forms. Type I is Physical Courage which displays in the presence of danger. Type II is Social Courage, a willingness to go against the disapproval of fellows. Type III is Desperation Courage that manifests boldly for Survival, Self-Protection, or Self-Preservation. Type IV is "ME/WE" Courage that displays on behalf of the weak, unjustly oppressed. Type V is that in spite of ones terrible circumstances, one discovers, develops, and follows ones Talent to wherever it leads into the dark and hostile places of the stricture of the hour-glass. With persistence, one eventually emerges into the proper niche where that Talent can "flower" and "fruit." Type VI is having the Courage to stop clinging to whatever is ones mental "Raw Nerve" or anything self-defeating to ones Soul and/or to others. Type VII is the Courage to be ones Real Self. Type VIII is to acknowledge "the part I played in causing these problems" and then getting past ones Shame by admitting ones mistake as part of the process of making retributions and replacing them with Human Ideal Goals. Type IX is simply getting started on what seems to be an "Impossible" problem and make any errors portals of discovery to explore for doors leading to the "pot of gold." Type X is Scholar Courage which demands maintain ones Real Self course in spite of peers who choose to do otherwise. This means one necessarily becomes an Isolated Individualist and that has been the setting for my life. The Crowd is so insecure in their Selfhoods that they envy, like bullies, whatever anyone has the courage to do what they are afraid of doing. So they react aggressively (e.g. by physical attacks on the envied person or that person's work products) or passive-aggressively by "love/hate" displays (e.g. smile in your face while stabbing you in the back, or at least engaging in subtle sabotage (secret and systematic interference of the envied person's normal wholesome work products). It takes courage not to give into what the bullies want one to do and instead be about something having "ME/WE" benefits. My natural inclination has always been to by-pass what is popular and deal with significant things on which the spotlight never shines. Examples include my extensive research on Dwarfisms and on struggling Black People. To elaborate, when I found the African Tradition "Truth-Track", the Crowd had no interest in my discoveries. However, I stuck to what I knew to be right and foundational for reversing their "Inside-Out" thinking. Once in a "Hidden" Spiritual, Metaphysical, or Physical area, I explore that completely so as to get insights.

This Scholar Courage process started in grade school when it seemed to me that everybody knew things I did not know about what the teacher was saying. Because of my hypersensitive Curiosity—that had come being a gardener as a boy--I really, really wanted to know important things. Thus, I would go home--get out the encyclopaedias we bought for two dollars at a library's discarded book sale--and read everything available on and around the subject. In this way, I became an "*Overnight Expert*" by fashioning a "*Mental Skeleton*" onto which I arranged what I learn. For example, Spiritual aspects of the subject were placed on the "Heart" area of the Skeleton; Philosophical Theories, on the "Head" area; daily living "Tools" on the "Hands"; processes for doing the job, on the "Feet"; and so forth. The next day knew far more about yesterdays the subject than those who had said they "knew" it. This pattern was cultivated. Because I possessed a sense of Selfhood Greatness and knew how to do at least one thing so well as to give me Self-Confidence, I never hesitated to make teachers or others aware of what I did not know. To this day, it remains clearer than ever that "What is not fully understood is not possessed—and will not be until I become one with it." I explore the Unknown everyday and having no idea where it leads. But, as I gain new ideas or insights, I make the necessary corrections. Invariably, this takes me along paths away from the Crowd. Yet, the new ways of thinking and looking at things makes me feel "Alive"—i.e. wanting more and more.

COURAGE TO THINK: The foundation for preparation to become a Scholar is *Courage—the decision to* willingly *deal with problems one does not and would not ordinarily choose*. African Sages used the "*Heart*" *(Causal-Body)* as a metaphor for ones innermost instinct (Feelings) which gives rise to Courage--an inner strength and determination inspired by God. This implies Courage, Compassion, Wisdom, and Nobleness are exact expressions of ones Conscience. Ones Conscience is first orchestrated naturally by ones Soul--ones Real Self (Spiritual aspect) and is thus bound to Ma'at (i.e. Spiritual Elements in action) ideas urging one to obey the Divine Laws of ones Highest Self as a duty.

CREATIVITY: Creativity is an umbrella term—manifesting on different planes of Spiritual or Supernatural existence—either into a Purpose or into a Void. It deals with unrealized concepts for purposes of bringing them into reality, fantasy, or a surreal distortion of both a joined reality and fantasy. It deals with Realities by rearranging and/or recombining certain of their ingredients into new forms. It deals with cultivating ones birth gifts so as to elaborate on ones Real Self. It deals with the re-making, re-ordering, re-altering of ones Selfhood—either into to being an addict of the Crowd or into being a Self-Made person, following what one knows or believes to be Right. The *Self-Made* is about creating ones own obligations, duties, and responsibilities. For example, to recreate ones Selfhood to conform to the Cosmic Organism Unseen realm from within is to embrace forms which themselves become part of ones awareness of the Processes of Nature on the path to returning to ones Real Self or cultivating it. Creativity is like a human producing a rainbow that one can see but the sun that made it lies behind that production, like ones Subconscious that is part of the inner Spiritual world. Creative Thinking is on the Thinker's Scale (a positive and negative ruler separated by a zero). On the negative scale, it includes realizing there is no particular virtue in doing things the way they have always been done. All humans possess creativity, especially in one of the many areas of the endless numbers of humans' expressions. Type I creations are new to the Cosmos in the sense that the Thing that has been shall be again and the Thing done shall be done again; Type II are what is new to this Age of which had become antiquated; Type III is creating simply by living; and Type IV are new to the individual from relating things previously unrelated in ones experiences or awareness so as to thereby become novel. A feature of Type IV is that the individual craves to evolve what seems new in a "just so" manner that result in a product that is new (i.e. surprising), satisfying—even if it is inside a "Void", and somehow useful daily living applications. The "*Novel*" ('a new star') conveys an unusual little story that makes a curious and unfamiliar change at least in some respect—i.e. other than its usual course of what occurred prior to the change. A Novel creation is the result of ingenuity. *Ingenuity* is having a natural capacity of Intellectual power (a high degree of understanding) + a wear-house of ingredients, tools, approaches, methods, techniques, and manners to draw on) + cleverness in applying skill to devising or inventing what has resourceful qualities (i.e. using the thing to its greatest advantage). The result is that the "new star" has a halo consisting of radiations in all directions—analogous to the Novel opening new directions, new possibilities for thinking, choosing, deciding, or solutions. Harmonious Novelties are newly recognized Truths through which walks practical applications to daily living. Yet, the formless and boundless aspect of Novelty itself means it has no standards by which it can be rightfully judge. In the fourth grade, I wrote a poem: "The postman comes in rain or snow//and leaves a letter at my door//and then he goes on his way// but he will come back another day. My teacher had me read this to the class and then said that is not a good poem. My response was not about getting upset because learning was far more valuable. Instead, I said: "how do you know?" Flowing out of the Spiritual Elements Interchange are: *Gestalt State*—a totality that has, as a unified whole, properties which cannot be derived by summation from the parts and their relationships; "*Emergentism*"—the combination of elements--results in something new that was unpredictable from knowledge of those elements; and Conative *Ideo-motor Action*.

CREATIVITY OF THE SPIRITUAL ELEMENTS: A *principle of Creativity is that when several elemental components are organized or coordinated, the resulting synthesis has properties and characteristics fundamentally different in kind from those of the separate components viewed independently.* The secret of being endlessly creative is to be within and do imaginative thinking out of the Spiritual Elements. Such is fundamental for CT. Out of the Divine Essence comes Matter, which is Ordered by the principle of Unity, as well as Form, whose Principle is multiplicity since it has totipotency. Creation keeps within bounds the Universal Matter and Universal Form and offspring emanate from these.

CRITICAL THINKING: In African Tradition, *Critical Thinking* (CT) applies both to the Process of Nature as well as Intellect devised process of Reasoning for the purposes of: (1) determining what is and is not part of the Spiritual Elements; (2) helping to evolve what is in the Spiritual Elements flow; (3) quashing (to overthrow or make void) what is not real or is anti-Spiritual Elements oriented; (4) ever looking to create, enhance, and maintain harmony; (5) protect and defend against any disharmony in preparation to go on the offense with the least amount of harm to all concerned; (6) detect whatever is preventing harmony ; and (7) figure out ways to get around any losses, lacks, and/or obstructions keeping one from going "straight ahead." The Essences and Principles of gathered materials which qualitatively address the Spiritual and Metaphysical realms are then presented in a carefully organized flow of the Spiritual Elements. Scholars can make any subject great by means of CT by following pertinent natural processes of Nature. What this does is to show new ideas, information, or knowledge amid appearances as well as the way to become acquainted with patterns of the "impossible" by having insight into what has already happened in Nature's Processes.

CRITICAL THINKING PREPARATION: Critical Thinking (CT) is the tool for staying in or returning to the flow of the Divine Logos, developing "ME/WE" products out of it; preventing or defending outside forces attacking the Spiritual Elements; not allowing its owner to step outside it. Communication Components used by CT include: (1) the Source (where the communication comes from); (2) the Language; (3) the Message (the information transmitted by the source); (4) the Form (e.g. metaphors); (5) the Style of writing; (6) the Channel (the medium through which a message is sent, as in books, letters, song, radio, email, or movies); (7) the Messenger (the person sending or bringing the communication); (8) the Receiver (the one to whom the message is sent); (9) the Style of delivery; and (10) the Purpose. In other words, communication concerns who says or does what; and by what means to whom; and in what way. All of this, including "Self-Talk" is flawed, has no credibility for Serious Business, and is to be shed by CT. The only thing conveying Knowledge is the Voice of the Silence within oneself. Yet, it is a rare human who has not placed a "Cloud" of Emotional Junk, including Sentiments (thoughts wrapped in Emotions). All of these anti-knowledge factors and flaws start with human infants' transmitted processes of *Socialization* imposed by all members of the society of whom the infant is aware. Out of the false and flawed information each individual is brought up in a given cultural milieu conditioned to interpret reality in terms of the inadequate world-view to which one is exposed. A *world-view* is basic assumptions regarding ultimate things on which one organizes ones life. Actually it is a Paradigm--a "Becoming" world view--a theory building process of determining what is important/unimportant, reasonable/ unreasonable, legitimate/illegitimate, and possible/impossible so as to guide one in what to attend to—attend in what order—with what effort-- and what to ignore. This is a typical way of ordering and simplifying the perceptual world's stunning complexity of ones life. Yet, until late Senior years, its development continues by one making certain fundamental assumptions about the nature of the universe, of society, and of oneself. The usual pattern to which one is exposed is to be an "Instant Psychologist" who: (1) immediately *"Scrutinizing"* a person/thing/message, display "broad stroke" assumptions based (2) on a glance—and then (3) stupidly jump to conclusions. They wrongly believe that "glance" of the character behind ones face or appearance of a thing (e.g. a tough problem) tells them every important thing. Based on these emotional *misinterpretations,* judgments are made that a solution, candidate, or approach will/will not work. Worse yet is taking action on tinted "guesses." Delusions come from tinted begrudging emotions, an inability to do Rational Thinking, and from bad habits of allowing ones attention to be hi-jacked from the fire of "ought to do Necessities" by Attractive Distractions. Such happens in aiming only for the "gist" of what is of Life-Shaping or Life-Changing decision importance. This becomes a "Seed Habit" that sprouts like a grapevine into every facet of ones life. It theme is to immediately and automatically select one option—perhaps the emotionally stimulating-- without considering any others to think, feel, say, or do this or that. The "Seed Habit" is so comfortable and easy that when any new and difficult situation is faced, regardless of its life-shaping or life-changing importance, ones method is usually determined by the "way it has always been done". That implies bringing custom and habit to solve problems that require another way. In this "one-size-fits-all" manner, the same thing is done over and over from situation to situation and from generation to generation. If it was okay early on, it has now outgrown its place and is likely to become more and more self-defeating as it is repeated and/or handed down. This laziness stops thinking and its evolution. CT is ever on the alert to beware of any other (e.g. ancient Greeks) of any forms of Fallacy Thinking. Examples are those pieces of bad information uttered by those who have stolen and parroted Ancient African Knowledge. CT makes a distinction between the faulty and subjective aspects of the common people as opposed to those whose misinterpretations, deception in presenting what really happened, opinions, tastes, bias, and prejudices that are harmful. A self-assigned duty of CT Courage is to counteract whatever is not in the best interest of "ME/WE".)

CRITICAL THINKING--SCOPE AND DEPTH: The point of Detective CT is to explore deeply the scope and depth of the situation at hand. In using the INSIGHT SCOPE Tool: Phase I is "*Penetration*" (one looks just below the surface); Phase II, "*Perfusion*" (one sees just below the surface); Phase III, "*Permeation*" (spotlights nooks, crannies, and recesses below the surface); Phase IV, "*Pervasion*" (one sees and becomes part of the flow of the essence of what is on the surface as well as what is inside, surrounding, and outside the Essence of the topic, person, or thing viewed). Whenever the Insight Scope is used in assessing a situation of any kind, it is called CT. To elaborate, let us consider the emotionally charged subject of ones home being burglarized. Phase I, "Penetration": While shocked and in disbelief, one checks inside and outside the house for evidence and without touching anything. When one becomes aware of losses ones thoughts and emotions are in a "Glob" state (thoughts and emotions are interwoven and "stuck" together into a round mass resulting from being in a maze). One might feel violated; wondering how one is going to do without certain of the things most necessary for ones life's work (e.g. having ones computer stolen) or valuable of a monetary nature (a one of a kind antique) and/or that have such profound sentimental significance (as when the sterling silver set that belonged to ones great-grandmother or a guitar handed down through many generations of ones family). This is a superficial mindset. Phase II, "Perfusion": Whatever is done next about this situation is stepping into CT at a Mild level. Perhaps this is calling the police and while waiting making out a list and considering: "What am I going to do about all of this?" Phase III, "Permeation": One expands on the list of missing item by opening all doors and drawers to see what is missing by the empty spaces and the dust patterns only around where the pewter cups use to be. As part of starting the recovery process for the immediate situation one notifies the insurance company if the things were insured; buys essential things needed to bring some stability in ones life; and/or calls on relatives or friends to help with this or that. Phase IV, "Pervasion" (Extreme) arrives when one starts considering the situation on all planes of existence and uses Forethought and "Foresight" are fundamental to planning accordingly to get what one desires and help prevent what ones does not desire. The first thing I do is to declare an end to the "self-pity" by appreciating what I have left (e.g. my health; and that it was not worse) and whomever helped me. Philosophical Coping is how I deal with the loss -- thinking the things lost were what I had been clinging to and by losing these bonds provides a sense of freedom. After all, I could not take them with me when I died but rather only the good memories of them. Next, is the "Take Charge and Take Control" phase of constructive action. First is by seeing what is left and viewing the chaos as an opportunity to build something better, I determine how to improve on what was formerly present and make plans requiring the taking of some calculated risks. This elevated mindset helps me to better approach the tremendous problems needing to be solved related to things that improve my safety and the significant cost related to each. Second, regardless of my losses and their significance I refuse to live a life of chronic fear. This means not clinging to any anger or hatred. Third is prevention. There are simple things that can be put into effect, like stopping the newspaper and mail and not leaving an empty garbage container on the street. The police say chances are good that whomever did the robber has been there before and knocked on the door or have been inside the house. Fourth is Adjustments to the residuals. Like cracking an egg, a break in my safety atmosphere never goes away. Another is adjusting to the fact that the replacements will never work as well mechanically and will not fit in harmoniously. Still another is the time and expense in making future robberies more difficult (e.g. alarm systems; video cameras). Finally, is dealing with the Grief and mourning my losses.

CRITICAL THINKING--ALPHABET LEARNING: Knowing the exact meaning and being able to define it or characterize it in a Figure of Communication (e.g. Metaphor) lays out a path for how one learns and evolves thoughts. Living from the newborn stage to maturity in old age is much like how children to write. First they learn letters of the alphabet; next how to put those letters into words; then practice writing sentences, followed by paragraphs. At some point they learn about arranged/rearranged and combined/re-combined meanings in order to persuade, inform, entertain, express, share, teach, instruct, educate, or serve as a call to action. To learn otherwise is: (1) a process of maneuvering and manipulating a number of small independent acts into one or more new arrangements and/or combinations so as to arrive at a new order or a new form (e.g. learning to play a new piece on the piano); (2) performing a familiar act in a new situation (e.g. knowing how to focus a microscope makes it easier to learn how to focus a telescope—or learning how to use a computer makes it easier to instantly learn to use a car radio); (3) the stoppage of doing what is no longer needed (as in forgetting a friend's discontinued telephone number); or (4) not performing a familiar act in its usual setting because it is not worth it or not needed or not in ones best interest. The usages to which learning can apply include: 'learning how to learn' (e.g. taking information to assess and analyze so as to make corrections, and formulate a workable conclusion); correcting mistakes (e.g. spellings of words); classifying anything; predicting; decision making; problem solving; or forming habits. Learning any of these skills allows them to be transferrable to novel like-kind things. Fundamental to acquired learning is that one must be stimulated by a signal alerting one or more of the senses or by a stimulus to peak ones Curiosity. Start learning by correcting or replacing ones most firmly believed but unexamined assumptions (e.g. on religion). A person then reacts or responds to the stimulus. For instance, to hear a knock on the door (stimulus) causes one to take notice (response). Learning—the going from "nowhere" to "now here"--is the building of new relationships between stimuli and responses so as to design an usually long-lasting change. Much learning is the result of forming habits--pattern acting in a certain way under certain conditions. Approaches used for learning are by: volition; rewards or praise (i.e. *positive reinforcement*); *negative reinforcement* (using criticism or punishment as a way to learn not to do things); and fear. Whether the learning is for good or evil, certain features that enhance the learning process include: motivation; elimination of the non-favored response; discovery of the actual or seemingly most appropriate response; fixation of the desired or intended response so that it becomes "*Second Nature*" (acquired but deeply ingrained). This implies that a given mindset in how to respond has become a mild and possibly beneficial *Obsession* and a *Compulsion*. jabaileymd.com

CRITICAL THINKING—PRECISION: In the way a surgeon occasionally may have to use a sharp knife blade to cut between an artery and a nerve somewhere in the human body, Critical Thinking does the same in its mental activities. Historically, Ancient Africans used precision thinking to devise amazing concepts. For example, the Ancient African calendar, based on the cycle of the Sirius star's rise coincides with that of the sun every 1,461 years was in use in 4236 BC, the oldest date know with certainty in the history of man-kind (Diop, African Origin p91). Imagine the precision, at least before 20,000 BC it took to make this happen. Etymologically, the 15th century English word *"precise,"* in order to leave out extraneous matter, to *"cut off in front"*--cut close to the line of exactitude. This is not good enough in African Tradition, for the standard is Certainty of exactness. Without giving it a name, this was what I strove for as a boy because it was a fun thing to do. In my medical Genetics fellowship at Johns Hopkins, I undertook researching Dwarfs though no one had ever been able to make sense out of the subject. At the time there were 9 syndromes known in the world and I had all of that literature translated into English. All of that information was wrong, mainly because of the "broad-strokes" scientists were using. For example, at a conference 10 Achrondroplastic Dwarfs were presented and, because one had a parrot beaked nose instead of a puggy nose, I asked why. The answer was that this was a normal variation since there were no other obvious differences. By that answer not being good enough, I did a through evaluation. One of my advantages was that I could both read orthopaedic x-rays and examine patients, priding myself on doing both with great accuracy with respect to minute details. The result was that was my discernment paid off with discovering a new syndrome. When I published my classic book 4 years later, I reported on 116. Insight into this arena came from my having taken on the "Impossible" subject of Dwarfisms in my Medical Genetics Fellowship. When the "Little People" of America came to Johns Hopkins Hospital for us Fellows to medically evaluate, because I was the first and only orthopaedic surgeon they ever had meant having the opportunity to examine all 52 (whereas the medical Fellows could only examine 6). I heard about less than ideal treatment stories from them that caused me to want to focus on them as my Fellowship project. At the lunch table of all the Fellows I told them what I wanted to do and would that be a problem for any of them. Each indicated they had their own projects and none raised any objection. However, at the time I did not realize they were all interested in the subject because no one had ever been able to make sense out of the subject. A major problem they had was in not being able to read x-rays or do an examination from an orthopaedic perspective. By contrast, the radiologists who read the x-rays did not examine the patients. I could do both and that increased my discernment skills. Thus, I would travel up to 500 miles to examine a Dwarf and spend 4 days in a given hospital going through their x-rays in order to come up with 2 cases. It was amazing to discover that what a patient's x-rays looked like as a baby had no resemblance to that patient's x-ray appearance as an adult. Soon I my journal intended papers on different types of Dwarfs were being typed by all the typists in the hospitals typing pool and that riled up the other Fellows because they did not know how I could be getting all of that information. When I published my book on 116 Dwarfs that enraged those around the world who were working on the subject of Dwarfism. I had no idea as to why because it had never come up as an issue and because I simply thought the job of all physicians was to improve the lives of others. So I had to spend time handling the attacks but meanwhile I felt deeply content from having changed the world literature on the subject of Dwarfs and changed how they were surgically treated. It was never clear to me why people, in wanting to know a fundamental but somewhat obscure subject, like high level African Tradition type Critical Thinking (CT), would not pursue every little piece of detail possible to find and without constantly being on the look-out for "pearls" that give insights. Instead, most "pick and choose" what seems of interest to them--which to me, makes no sense. Emotional "likes" and judging material before studying it or disliking the writer or declaring it to be too hard or too boring have no place in precision CT. What requires even greater than ordinary sharp thinking is to do so inside Processes of Nature, as did Ancient Africans. Let us start with the Light and Dark and proceed the top thinking tools of Essences, Essential, Interchanges, Mosaics, Discernments, Nuances, Definitions and their Denotations and Connotations.

CRITICAL THINKING NUANCES: *Life literally occurs as a result of the union of Spirit and Matter*—the union of Heaven and Earth—the union of Male and Female Principle sexual symbols (i.e. a female oval surmounting a male cross) and all aspects of God. Such a union, which goes beyond the concepts of Duality, transforms one into an *androgynous* being—the union of opposites--the two becoming One. Put another way, the Ankh symbolizes the African originated (Bailey, Echoes p86) Yin/Yang-type balance between two Complementary Opposite forces of life—e.g. positive/negative, light/dark, long/short, male/female. When Duality is integrated within a higher context, its Binary System is based on the counterbalanced forces of two opposite poles--forces either symmetrical (i.e. identical in extent and intensity) or asymmetrical--either successive (day/night) or simultaneous (e.g. masculine/feminine in each human). Complementary (Yin/Yang) opposites mean both components are real; are identical in nature; and with both being equally significant but in different ways--like ocean waves. These criteria are the essentials to qualify as *Polar Opposites*. The point is that because all aspects of Cosmic Reality are underlay by the Principle of Duality (Amen, Metu Neter II:70), the job of CT is to re-establish Unity or at least discern what is blocking it. The setting for this task is to understand an African Law of Duality that says: (1) all real Things (Units, Wholes) are dual—or each Thing represents half or is a part of a larger Whole; (2) the Elements (halves) of a set of duality must be maintained in equilibrium with each other. In other words, the Cosmos is held together based upon the equilibrated dual nature of all Things (Wholes, Units). For example, males possess male and female hormones, making them dual in their nature. Yet, their dominating male hormones make them unbalanced in their perspective of life and social actions. So, a male must come together with a female in order for their gender essences to combined and thereby create a balanced perspective on life. Such a balance can only occur when a male's Higher (Divinity) Self is developed. In addition to generating such a balance, CT sees nuanced "bigger pictures." An example is that Humans are able to know their Highest (Divinity) Self by means of their Divine Consciousness (the Self)—which is connected to the Cosmic Mind. This is the means for "Knowing Thyself" to be Spiritually related to all of God's creatures and creations. A nuanced *Principle of Individuation of Being says humans are one in essence and origin but separate in physical substance and form* -- an *indivisible duality*. Thus, this faculty represents the oneness of the Universe and is the basic particle from which everything in existence originates. Located in a human's Subconscious, it prevents separating anything from oneself -- the first step in the process of "Knowing Thyself" on the way to experiencing the true self. Ones Selfhood Being is composed of an indivisible duality of the "Self" (Immaterial) and a "Not Self" or "Non-Self" (Material)—which is actually the "ME/WE" portion of ones Selfhood. One identifies with the "Self" because it is what perceives God's messages (i.e. ones Divine Consciousness) so that the Will acts voluntarily to make it happen. CT applies nuances in other ways. Within any given human: (1) the Unconscious and the Conscious appear as Complementary Opposites within a binary duality system by what underlies both--meaning they are the same but with different displays; (2) they are also a microcosm (i.e. a "little" world copy) of the Universal Soul's macrocosm (the Supreme world); (3) each has Spiritual (i.e. Highest Self) and Matter (Lower or animalistic Self) aspects; (4) the true reality of all 4 of these components resides only in their *Synthesis*--an assimilation of the higher with the lower--an assimilation that, when wisely used within a Ma'at context, one is able to ascend from ones Lower (animalistic) Self to ones Highest (divinity) Self--a "push-up" ascension measured by how duality is transcended. What leads to that assimilation is a series of nuanced decisions that change wayward meanings and thereby redirects one onto the "Right Life Living" path throughout life.

CRITICALLY THINKING PROBLEMATIC NUANCES: The beginning of Critical Thinking ends being foolish. Everything has at least two sides—e.g. Me/You, Us/Them. Each side has ingredients that are obvious and subtle. Weak, lazy, Crowd, Ignorant, and Brute thinkers see only their side and then only the obvious and not the subtleties. The result are the flip side of the truth and those Falsehoods are projected as "Facts." Because Nuances are hidden from normal perception, people are easily put on the wrong track with improper nuances. When children trust parents and then believes their lies, puts one on the wrong track. Connotations, allusions, implications of using one language to explain something in another--though not a lie, a *terminological inexactitude* also change the direction of Thoughts. A lie is like a snow-ball; the longer it is rolled, the larger it is—and, as I was told as a boy, the bigger the lie and the more often it is repeated, the more people will believe it. One reason is the naïve or lazy thinkers decide that since "everybody"—especially "authorities"--say so or does it, then that makes it SEEMS right. Despite lingering doubts, "Almost is okay." As perfected by ancient Greek Sophists, Nuanced "Payload" Fallacy information *just a shade off the Truth-Track* is done by fashioning the misleading or fallacious so that its plausible *Subtlety* (evasive reasoning, superficial soundness) "SEEMS ALMOST" right. In European literature, the almost ignored C18 word "*Nuance*" (shade, subtlety)—is undefined but carries the sense of imitating the showing of variations of shade, like a cloud. The implication is that Nuances" are really, really small differences between things. An example is putting a spin on a curve ball in baseball games (Sharon Bingaman). The orientation to this complex word "Nuance"--which defies European definition--is about the subtle blending of one color into another. Shade and shadow designate a partial darkness but shade implies no definite form or limit. These concepts can be used to help explain Problematic Nuances. As background, Nuances can be on all planes of Cosmic Existence and thus occur from different combinations of ingredients of the things involved and with different and unique patterns present inside each combination. A generic description is that Nuances are on the inside of an Interchange of different Primary Qualities—none being a thing of Substance or Essence. The pattern derived out of that Interchange is dependent upon the assemblage of small mosaic pieces from each Primary Quality. The picture those pieces form may be: Type I an overlap and interweaving—as with a kaleidoscope; Type II like ingredients from each that continually wash into one another, as do bands in a Rainbow washing into each other; Type III blended; Type IV mixed; Type V synthesized; or Type VI disconnected and chaotic in merely forming a design. To elaborate on the generic idea which serves as the setting for Problem Nuances, one example is seen by looking into a kaleidoscopic. Here ones sees overlapping mosaic colors, each mosaic of a different Primary Quality--all operating together in an interwoven manner. More complexity is seen in a Rainbow. Its Primary Colors are due to the bending and reflection of the sun's rays when those rays are shining on raindrops in the air. The white light of the sun is composed of all colors, each with different wave lengths, mixed together. But when this white light passes through a drop of rain, the rays composing it are bent to different degrees and thereby forced apart. When they reach deep into each raindrop, these *primary colors of the spectrum* (the visible range of light) are separated rays--violet, indigo, blue, green, yellow, orange, red--reflecting back to ones eye. Those Primary Colors, seen as bands, continually wash into one another. Generic features of these six types share the following, but in varying degrees and varying combinations: (1) when the Primary Qualities from which a given Type changes—e.g. Type I and II's continual appearances of changing colors—each combines into different color patterns; (2) each changing figure pattern possesses continually different and strikingly colorful geometric patterns; (3) the network within each pattern is *Interworking* together—meaning that as a result of having combined, one with another, the result is that the many different colors combine to produce a special interaction; (4) none of the Qualities are a thing of Substance, but rather an attribute (like rays of the sun); (5) each Primary Quality's mosaic operates together in an interwoven manner.

CRITICALLY ASSESSING NUANCED SITUATIONS: Regardless of a normal Thing's literal meaning, its implied Tone meaning is a standard against what variations are measured or estimated to categorize its manner of expression. That expression may be about an atmosphere, aura, shade, emotion, or savor (i.e. a specified taste, smell, or quality). A Tone may be an unseasoned normal taste, while an Undertone is its seasoning removed and an Overtone being seasoning added. This is a sliding standard, guide, filter, measure, or estimate for assessing Qualities. Some people take the tone of the company they are in and that may be good, sometimes good, or bad. Every tone of the songs of Enslaved Africans was a testimony against slavery. People who deal with only one side of a coin automatically mis-interpret their misperceptions of the reality they see, if they actually see reality or a distortion or fantasy. Upon deciding to judge a Thing, see it for what it is. When putting oneself in the other's place, allow for cumulative subtlities to see it though the different colored lens the other might have or is using. Problems arise from the attitude of Whites interviewing Black People or White teachers dealing with wanting to "Save" and "Convert" Black People on the one hand or discount them on the other. People who declare themselves to "superior" look at only the obvious on the side of the coin favoring them and miss all of the rest. That accounts for their bad manners and hatred. By contrast, the intelligent see all aspects of the "ME/WE". Whites fail to realize the ways of life are wrong for anybody else and that what they do to try to impose them on others generates many nuanced reactions in their victims. Still, Whites do not pay attention to those reactions or what they say or how they say it. The youth recognize lack of manners under the term "Disrespect"—are aware of what is missing that ought not to be—and that governs how they take the responses so as to formulate what to do. Being Thoughtful and mannerly cannot happen by broad-stroking or stereotyping or believing they have the answers for all people—none of whom they know anything about. Their aggressive movements are taken from bits and pieces drawn from only one side of the relationship coin.

CRITICAL PAYLOAD PROBLEMATIC NUANCES: Like a Halo from a Star, the Implicit is the Unique aura or atmosphere of a Thing's Essence (what it was when it came into Being-hood)—whether of Truth or not. Implicit Discernment enables that Unique Aura and/or Atmosphere to be distinguished from like-kind others. That area alone—the Implicit, Allusions, Nuances, Subtitles--is at least 25% of what is involved in communications of any type. Tools for that differentiation of Uniqueness is known by it being "Felt" by ones Soul Spiritual Elements "Trademark's" Radar Beacon; by "Thought Clouds"; by "Helping Hands" of ones Spiritual Entourage; by Intuition; by Common Sense (emphasizing ones Pure Emotions); and/or by Knowledge. "Tuned-in" Afrocentric People can know messages of their Ancient African Ancestor's "Thought Cloud" by means of the Afrocentric Mystic Memory implicit Vibration conveyance vehicle. By contrast, *Explicit Discernment* of an External World Thing is the acquiring of sensory inputs that enable that Thing to be distinguished from like-kind others. External or Explicit Discernments are done by some particular mark of differentiation which distinguishes it out of what has confusing or misleading appearances. These Discernments involve Nuances and Subtleties. They can be Altered by adding to or subtracting Primary or Secondary Qualities from what comprises the Natural or by multiplying or dividing what is naturally present.

Nuances in Things that are not Natural are like genetically engineered genetic mutations. These occur by the way Traits are changed in people. But what is true for all Nuances is that to *remove one or more mosaic pieces means either the original no longer exists or none of it exists or is greatly altered. Or, if some ingredient(s) is shaded, the "That-ness" is removed. This means that the Discerning can be only the "This-ness". But worst of all is* substituting false for what is accepted as normal and have it replace the Truth, then those involved head toward the Abyss, if they are not already there. Put another way, the more abnormal things that are substituted for ingredients of the Truth or the more normal things that are rearranged or recombined out of harmony, the harder anything is to discern. Even the tiniest deviation out of the Spiritual Elements means that it is not Harmonious and whatever is discerned may be so small in its degree of Disharmony as for people to accept "almost" as good enough—when "almost" will not get one into heaven. Outside influences (e.g. "everybody is doing it" or "everybody agrees" or "I don't want to appear disagreeable") makes the Weak and the Ignorant to step across the line and say: "It SEEMS right." For Weak and Ignorant people, Satanists do not have much trouble getting them to accept an attachment of the evil with the Spiritual Elements. This is especially true for Scattered Thinkers who have no concept of Mathematical Thinking. The countless somethings from the Supernatural Bible that were substituted for what was taken out of the Spiritual Bible has had devastating effects on the World Crowd.

CROWD: Old English word having the underlying sense of "pushing" or Pressing" (kin to 'Oppress') of a throng. It pertains to those under the influence of ignorant and/or Satanist leaders whose focal point is to control the minds of "The Crowd" and so occupy their minds with what is "Exciting" as for them not noticing they have an enslaved mind, orchestrated into a Trance--a state of heightened susceptibility to addictions, compulsions, and fetters--by "The Crowd". This means that everything any member thinks, feels, says, and does is "Programmed"--which besides establishing or removing behavior--it modifies physiological functions. *Programming* consists of supplying information in accordance with a cult code so as to be learned in a series of small, graded steps aimed to carry out approaches, methods, techniques, and manners to subtly achieve specific functions or solve Fad problems. The setting which maintains this "*being about nothing*" is the "here and now". Messages in each step delivered are of a Halo" whose nature represents what is like a Disaster Star. An obvious example is the Confederate Flag (a "Halo") representing the Satanist mental substance which formed it (the Disaster Star). The intent is to fashion Crowd mindsets that create, enhance, or maintain a life characterized by "*Fear*" concerning what might undergo a sudden terrible event unless the Socialized Rules are adhered to. Such "Halos" (e.g. demeaning racial stereotypes) are machine-gunned daily into the Crowd. The effect is each Crowd member exchanges his/her own independent thoughts so as to desperately seek, *always in vain*, the Crowd's animalistic emotionalism and concepts of the External World's self-fulfillments. These addictions convert each into a now "new False Self Me" caught up in the driven flow to express views and/ or commit acts of which one would otherwise be ashamed. These "Halos" are also absorbed by victims of the Crowd. These Halos of the Crowd and their victims cover their "Soul Sunshine" (i.e. the Spiritual Elements). However, a few have "Clouds with a Silver Lining" and they are susceptible to Self-Improvement. See Public

CROWDS FILLED WITH "MAKE-BELIEVE": The way to be liked by the Crowd is to cater to them; the way to be disliked by the Crowd is to not "go along" with them or to be virtuous or to not be excited. They are Non-Rational Thinkers and their notions are almost all adoptive. Their common prejudices contribute to order and quiet among them and unfair advantages are defended against over attempts at fair play. They value little that is the truth but all that is rumored—and it takes trickery to gain their approval. In the Supernatural realm, nothing is called make-believe when it is a permanent and universal modius operanda. Bonds which bring and keep Supernaturals together exist only in the mind for they are too self-absorbed to emerge from themselves so as to know fellows only in oneself. Out of professed European type love, friendship, politeness, deference, duty, obligation, and responsibility can come cheating and stealing from those very same people. This is because their philosophy of life is that they exist alone—called Individualism. All Supernatural leaders have delusions of grandeur and are totally focused on winning by any means necessary. Thus, they channel their followers to do the same. Money, being the best measuring stick of winning, overrules any of their feigned morals. For example, during African American slavery, as much as slave owners and neighbors were lynching Black males for alleged rapes of White women, those same owners had no problem with bringing White females to have babies by Black males so that those babies would increase their slavery profits. The idea is to always look to the leader for power—never looking within for personal strength. Leaders know that "make-believe" in the Crowd are like the blinders mill horses wear and without which they would not move. To this end, they have made the Crowd be responsible but without power, as seen in court eunuchs throughout the ages. Thus, Supernaturals have absolutely no interest in the Truth—do not know it; do not want to know it; do not want others to know it; and come down hard on those who seek it. What has always been accepted by everyone and is accepted now by the Crowd is almost certainly false. They are seduced by errors and flaws to the point of even turning aside evidence not to their taste--preferring to deify those flawed and who commit errors as their incompetence leads them to do. Whereas they can easily do without truth, no cult member is strong enough to do without illusions. Whoever can supply them with "Exciting Illusions" or "Exciting" anything of a fantasy or phantasmagoria (monster) nature is easily their master. The more violent, the most insane, the most delusive, and the most transient of what generates passions, the better. Whoever tries to temper the use of or to destroy their illusions is always their victim. What they call a sincere work is one that is endowed with enough qualities to appear to give reality to an illusion. For them, injustice for outsiders is relatively easy to bear because it is routine. What stings is justice for others and injustice for them. There are ever present delusions of contests open to the public. For example, Beauty contest are said to be for those who also show "goodness" in some manner and yet Whites decide the standards for both—making for a delusion. White Supremacists are geared to have victims do their work, or at least their "dirty" work with the attitude of: "And so we plow along, as the fly said to the ox." Supernatural people are geared to believe the nonsensical, like that to increase the size or quantity of anything is the way to change its quality. Supernaturals tend to hide the indelible stamp of their low life by feigning the possession of noble qualities. Conveyers of Supernatural leaders' messages never address any neutral or non-complimentary comments made about them—an indicator of the profound inner weakness they experience—a fundamental point to always keep in mind.

CROWD--BLACK PEOPLE: For the Enslaved during African American slavery, Illusions were beneficial to relieve suffering when nothing else could or would work. Still, during slavery there were countless "make-believes" implanted in their "spirit-removed" minds. By appealing to the Enslaved's perceptions (about qualities) than to ones logic, they were presented with "Fool's Goals"--an illusion of an object or concept or religion not being what it seems to be. To practice the "virtue" of European faith and Belief in the make-believe about Europeans' Supernatural God, Hell, and Devil, intimidation measures were used to get the Enslaved willing to suspend their sight and judgment; deny contrary evidence which they had brought from Africa; accept living with the unintelligible and with whatever was unable to be conceptualized or integrated into the rest of ones knowledge; and to not question what did not make sense—of which there was an overwhelming amount. The Enslaved were forced to induce trancelike illusions of understanding; to repress their rational and critical faculties; to hold their African derived mindsets as their guilt; to drown any questions that arose in protest; and to strangle any thrust of reason convulsively seeking to assert it proper function as the protector of their lives and cognitive integrity. It was not long before the Enslaved could not be convinced that what they are dealing with was "Fool's Goals". By that time, *Illusions, Hallucinations, Delusions* and misinterpretations were established. These prevented all from no longer being sure of anything they previously thought they knew. Following slavery, every ex-Slave on the way to getting a Free Mind felt richer with the shedding of each Illusion, Hallucination, and Delusion. What makes these self-defeating Beliefs powerful is disregarding ones integrity while inviting self-illusions that reinforce ones chosen Lower Self Identification. This is enhanced when Brutes can establish some type of rapport with their victims. That rapport--particularly if the Brutes keep spotlighting the victim's self-defeating behaviors and give encouraging and/or bad recognition to them--perpetuates the victims Enslaved Mind. Today's struggling Black People are haunted and influenced by "Dark Side" shadowy images which are merely Illusions, Hallucinations, and Delusions. Certain "make-believes" have been selected to be an Icon Image for one to model and cling to since to embrace any IHES is to be situated in the Self-Unknown and resorting to Supernatural ways of doing things. For example, one has no concept of there being any other way than to cling to what one is modeling. Being socialized into an IHES atmosphere is like being born into a dream—then awakening from that dream to enter into another dream. An analogy for that analogy is falling into the sea and trying to climb out into the air, only to drown. Both are like what the naïve struggle to do. Because of all of this being part of their slumbering as they go through life, they consent to being deceived by make-believe shows and cruelties they cannot imagine are real. Such, by being established on a purely illusory foundation, continues to confirm their daily life of routine and habit everywhere as "all there is". To be with the Crowd or with a gang, many members are so mentally advanced as to be painfully aware of members' "make-believes" clashing with their reality. Yet, they must accept it without complaint in order to continue receiving the benefits. Because enslavement was a shattering of the entire Selfhoods of the well-balanced Africans, the putting it back in piecemeal fashion have left Black Americans with mindsets that go in every direction of rays of a star. So many engaged in the *Vicious Cycle of Illusions*--believing what is falsely seen and thereafter seeing what one has falsely believed. Such has been culturally transmitted. Practically all struggling Black People have some degree of fearfulness of Supernaturals but some try to be servants in Supernatural camps and similarly oppose Black People. The overwhelming majority are closed like clams and will not allow their private Selfhoods to be known. Many also are either full of pity, looking for soothing; or are powerless, looking for the ability to display power at every opportunity. The majority have adopted and are fixed in European White Superiority ways but without the benefits Whites get. They want to lead despite being ill equipped to do so from an African Tradition perspective.

"CRYSTALS": Our Primitive, Very Ancient African, and Ancient African Ancestors had Common Sense which fashioned Wisdom. This Wisdom was created, enhanced, and maintained by the amassing of thoughts and experiences flowing in and arising out of the Spiritual Elements of Unconditional Love, Truth, Reality, and the Natural. After mathematically discovering certain Laws of Nature in 20,000 BC, one of their derived inferences was that humans were created to serve as the vehicle (Divine Consciousness and Will) through which God can come into the world and walk around God's creation, indulge in it, and assess it. This vehicle is the *Instinctive Lower (animalistic) Self* Faculty. It resides in the Life-Force division of a human's Selfhood Being, and is governed by unchangeable Laws to enable Humans to be in Harmony with the Cosmos. But the minds of humans must be programmed to harmonize with the Laws which govern the Cosmos—Laws deposited in a human's *Divine Spirit*—called, in African Tradition, the Ba, the Khu, and the Shekhem. In the Divine Spirit resides the Self's Divine Consciousness and Will + the Laws enabling the mind to think in harmony with the *Life-Force* (the faculty mediating with the world). Here, the Mind is intuitively informed of the Laws governing every situation in which one is involved. This means *Spiritual life is living according to Divine Laws* (Amen, Metu Neter III: 31). Since these Laws were mathematically derived, implying they are laid out from mathematical patterns of the Cosmos, this is *Metaphysical Mathematics*, meaning it is knowledge of permanent intellectual relationships. Yet, it is based upon stated, unproven premises or axioms and requires elaboration by use of illustrations and symbols belonging to the Physical World. By contrast, *Qualitative Mathematics* examines Premises to seek the ultimate Principle on which they all depend. Ancient Africans inferred from Qualitative Mathematics (Hodge, Racism p100) that the origin of the Cosmic Organism containing all of God's creatures and creations is by the Spiritual Elements Genetics. Thus, *each Entity has "Sameness" with Uniqueness,"* as demonstrated by Crystals. By exhibiting its material state as a transparency, *"Crystal"* is a word special for representing Things which illuminate Metaphysical aspects of the Laws of the Spiritual Elements. Here is a *manifestation of the conjunction of opposites in a paradoxical state*--meaning Matter 'exists' but it is as if it did not exist because one can see through it. Incredibly, Ancient African Sages apparently knew this and built their Logic thinking structures of Common Sense and Knowledge on Principles similar to how Crystals are put together.

What Crystals Are is a homogeneous portion of Matter which, like African Logic, follows a solid mathematical formulation. Understanding this is crucial for gaining clues as to the different thought patterns of Ancient Africans and today's struggling Black Americans (or any of those in the African Diaspora having been oppressed into submission and dominated by Europeans). Just as the *same basic elements are used in different types of Crystals, what makes them different is being arranged and combined uniquely.* Some crystals consist of certain kinds of atoms, called ions, carrying a positive or negative charge; some are made up of groups of atoms bonded to form molecules. *Thoughts are like Crystals.* Crystal shapes are built of many tiny crystal units of the very same shape. They start by the first particles coming close together and producing a unit cell--just like bricks are units making up a brick wall—and just like Percepts forming Ideas that produce Concepts and Thoughts. Other unit cells form on all sides of the first to start the process of growth. Similarly, *Memory* and *Apperceptions* (the result of bringing together a mass of ideas already in the mind to thereby form a new perception--a sort of synthesis of related memories in ones mind) are what make a Thought Structure grow. Both processes are like families coming together to create a unified village. By possessing an orderly and repeated atomic structure, they share certain general properties, as in having a sharp melting point (compared with the melting range of amorphous substances, e.g. glass). The same applies when any ingredients of African Logic having Correspondence ("equivalence") are brought together. An illustration of Correspondence, which allows Truthful Inferences to be made, is that although rivers, lakes, ponds, streams, and oceans have different names, what makes them "equivalent" is they all contain water. *This is Logical Thinking's pattern and method of African Tradition Scholarship.* jabaileymd.com

CUMULATIVE MICRO-TRAUMAS: See Racism

CURIOSITY: "Curious" (looking after) comes from C13 Latin noun 'cura'—meaning 'full of care' and eager to know, inquisitive. The sense of exciting curiosity related to odd and queer is first recorded in 1715. Chances are that curiosity is an instinct that is located in a human's Reptilian (Instinct) Brain and representing a faculty of ones mental tools which displays as an expression of the human spirit. This means that it is present naturally—like Love—and therefore any reduction in its presence results from an individual's choice to disconnect. Any reduction in curiosity as a way of life does harm to the persons mind in that it slows or stops ones creativity and causes one to become dull and bored and boring. It is also fundamental in the process of building Self-Esteem and represents the first step. What Curiosity does is to urge one to be interested in the unknown and that interest generates "Aliveness." Perhaps the process goes like this. Curiosity is the Motive that is stimulated by the fact that the "thing"--the unknown--"is simply there." This is what mountain climbers sometimes say as to why they choose to climb the highest mountain: "because its there!" What intensifies Curiosity's "Aliveness" energy is that the "thing" gives no clue as to what is in it, around it, on top of it, under it, or behind it. Nor is there any idea where exploring it will lead. Both of these make Curiosity dissatisfied. Understand that Curiosity is not interested in building on to something as occurs with "Technology progress" but rather to becoming satisfied from being exposed to what is available in the various unknowns it contains and unknowns with which that "thing" is associated. "Technology progress" means doing advanced work so as to learn or invent something that builds upon an established structure--which is still a "trial and error" achievement. While "Technology progress" adds to a design, curiosity opens up into a void into which things can be created. In other words, Curiosity activates the "Aliveness" energy (coming from ones life force) to "motor" (i.e. motivate) ones Selfhood "Energy Package"--i.e. being motivated sufficiently to be dedicated, committed, determined, persistent, and maintain motivation in order to persevere with a sense of urgency to completion.

Step I is curiosity pushing ones interest, attention, and concentration into the unknown (or new frontiers or the unfamiliar) which necessitates its exploration. While exploring the unknown one meets challenges (obstacles, detours, gaps) which causes one to devise mental tools to overcome lacks, losses, and things "just out of reach." These tools are used in trial and error fashion with set-backs and defeats checkered with *multiple small successes*-- from creativity; from figuring things out; or from "technology progress." The excitement of those multiple small successes causes one to better handle and emotionally control set-backs and defeats and therefore to keep going to the next stepping stone. Step II. As a result of multiple small successes, one experiences the birth of *Self-Trust*. This is an awareness that earned prior achievements over losses, lacks, or obstacles expand ones capacities and abilities. Step III. *Self-Reliance* is being aware of what is available for usage. Step IV. *Self-Respect* (properly ranking ones self-worth and self-value traits and honoring those which one has cultivated. Step V. *Self-Appreciation* is increasing ones esteem of ones spiritual essence. Step VI. *Self-Confidence* (sureness from empowerment). Step VII. *Self-Empowered*—sense of control, good direction, and inspiration. Step VIII. *Self-Efficacy* (workout")--belief in ones ability to meet challenge/problems never seen/heard before.

CURRICULUM--VERY ANCIENT AFRICANS: The Curriculum (C17, run a course) for Very Ancient African Scholars was designed to encourage them to learn to *discover the underling web of relationships operating in Nature* throughout the Cosmos. Its Mathematical nature was to help each student assume an obligation, duty, and responsibility for developing dormant Divine Life Forces within so as to be an Earthly embodiment of God's designing intelligence. By so doing, each Scholar's "Self"--i.e. the Consciousness/Will constituting a human's divinity--would be subjected *to the Divine Spirit in order to command the Life-Force in harmony with the Laws of Nature*. To this end, their most learned and wisest Sages formed *Houses of Truth* to discuss ways to make order out of chaos and then to educate, inform, and spread true understanding of knowledge and heritage of Nubian and Kemetic culture. Aligned with the kingship, over time these institutions gathered from all over Africa to create and preserve knowledge in written and pictorial form. *Elements* (a mass of moving essences) in the Book of Life, Pyramid Texts, Coffin Texts, Papyrus Texts as well as Temple Reliefs, Steles, Obelisks, and other monuments of Ancient Africa, when put together, constituted the sacred texts or Biblical teachings of African Mystical Spirituality. These writings--collectively known as *Medu Neter* ("the writings of God") or *Neter Medu* ("Divine Speech") Mdu Ntr, Medu Netcher, the Divine Words--were housed in Egyptian Cult Temples (Amen, Metu Neter III:4). To great temples, cultural centers were annexed. Their combined needs included *support services to a given temple in the form of libraries, medical services, cooking, magicians, artisans, scribes, and blacksmiths. As* Spiritual knowledge evolved, African Sages' early focus was on "Secrets" (referring to the operations of Nature). Ideas thus gained from Nature expanded to embrace the "*Mysteries*"—i.e. the existence and ways of God and the Spirit (the Energy/Material part of Being). Apart from crafts (e.g. sculpture, painting) used to embellish and decorate the temples, the topics Scholars pursued and taught in Houses of Life and Houses of Truth were widespread: dream interpretation, astronomy, astrology, geography, history, mathematics, music, liturgy (public worship), and Ifa-type divination used to elicit the hidden truth (Bynum, African Unconscious p226). By 20,000 BC, *Solfege*, the root of the Ifa System, used sets of syllables to represent musical relationships. This + creatively recombining symbols and sounds in disciplined states of meditation were part of a positive religious association to Trance states and being "possessed" by a luminous intelligence (called becoming "full of God"). *The lineage of combining and then recombining Symbols in states of unitative Conscious experiences is at the heart of some aspects of today's psychoanalysis.* Meanwhile, in order to learn its Principles, Scholars spent time studying common elements of Nature so each could be viewed from as many sides and angles as are in a box. So thorough was this study that Scholars learned how to recognize each Principle, no matter in what form it came and regardless of its plane of existence. That study would invariably cause them to see each element was interrelated to all other elements. Example: many of Water's qualities make it appear animated. Naturally occurring Water is always in motion; changing color in the light of the sun and stars; and is continually "speaking" with murmuring and roaring. This is a philosophical basis for understanding any form of Water (e.g. rain, sea, lakes, or rivers) is a natural phenomenon, displaying many forms. Each form reflects Cosmic and human ingredients; brings new life to dried out vegetation; refreshes humans and animals; heals the tired and the ill; and dissolves dirt. Emphasis was placed on seeing how all of these are interrelated by means of having Correspondence. But also stressed was to see both sides of a "coin" issue.

For example, humans judge Water to possess powers able to institute destructive forces (e.g. seaquakes, floods, storms). The point taught was that one must know how to handle both the good and bad sides of the Water issue. Its keystone pertained to extracting *the inner meaning of external appearances.* The more concentrated in exploring and discovering the completeness, simplicity, and clarity behind the obvious—all help expose the issue's Hidden Base/Foundation. Resultant insights gave the meaning of a drop of infinity being in finite bits/pieces. This leads to being "Awed" with the marvels of the simultaneous spiritual, intellectual, scientific, and philosophical connections which form Harmony "behind-the-obvious/hidden". jabaileymd.com

CUMULATIVE TRAUMA: *Cumulative Trauma* (Latin, cumulus, heap or piled—like cumulus clouds)--also called Continuing small Traumas, Micro-Aggressions, and Accumulative Micro-trauma--leaves multiple psychic 'little wounds' which in turn *erode* (wear away) and *corrode* (gnaw away) every mental, physical, emotional, spiritual, and soul aspect of a Victim's Selfhood. Those aspects, like having cracked an egg, could be so resistant to healing that the "yoke" continuously oozes out. This is particularly so in Victims with mental "Raw Nerves" resulted from a "Big Bang" trauma. That mental "Raw Nerve" acts as if it is set on fire an "*Inflamed*" or a-flamed—expressing like meteors in troubled areas of ones mind.

D

DARK vs. LIGHT COSMIC ASPECTS: Light and Dark have different aspects, depending upon the plane of existence in which one considers them. To over-simplify, on the Divine Plane, Ancient Africans said the all-Black Amenta (the Nun, the Void, Nothingness) contains the Cosmic Mind. Its total blackness, reflecting the Cosmic primordial state, corresponds to absolute darkness (Kekui)--itself "Light"—dazzling and blinding in its splendor. The undifferentiated dualism of "Light/Darkness" does not arise as a symbolic formula of morality until the primordial "Darkness" has been split up into Light and Dark. That split introduced *Involution* (how things get rolled up into being the way they are) and *Evolution* (how things can get out by unrolling back to their origin). Once activated by the powers of the Cosmic Mind, Ancient Africans said that out of the Cosmic Matter Principle comes the rarified, tenuous, subtle form called Ether. To begin the Cosmos, Ether then started Involution—i.e. producing forms of Matter less and less rarified so as to become progressively more gross. That Involution, in the sense of "to wrap up; to cover; to hide, wrapped up the all black Spiritual Elements that had come out of the Cosmic Mind so as to bring the ingredients comprising all of God's Creatures and Creations into entities with light needed for being in the Material realm (e.g. to physically see). But the dazzling and blinding light appearing as absolute darkness to human's perceptions was what was required for humans' "*Souls*" to have inner Self illumination in a human's Unconscious--comparable to its complementary opposite in the Amenta. This light is a symbolism corresponding to the *Color Spectrum*--violet, indigo, blue, green, yellow, orange, red--each color, possessing its own place on the vibratory scale that reaches earth. Thus light is the basic principle behind differentiation, creativity, hierarchal order, and spiritual strength--all in accordance with emanations from the "Soul" center. In turn, that human's Soul center is subjected *to the Divine Spirit in order to command the Life-Force in harmony with the Laws of Nature*. But in the setting of the Cosmos, humans limited knowledge would lead them to assess this situation by the standards they devised. In a Physics context, strictly what is black is absolutely destitute of color; what is dark is absolutely destitute of light. Darkness is equated with Matter. Anatomically, the profundity of each body is Matter and all Matter is dark. Philosophically, humans stand in the middle between the two realms of Spiritual Light and Darkness in a bad sense, left to ones own Free-Will. For those choosing Spiritual Light, that light is also life. Psychologically and Physiologically, for those who choose Darkness, by it being Illusions, the realm entered that of ones Lower (animalistic) Self—e.g. insecurity, shame from self-image problems, fear, rage, violence, sensuality, and fetters (e.g. "Me, Me, Me" Individualism, arrogance, pride, lies, selfishness, greed, lust, egoism, envy, jealousy, and frustration). A life-shaping Illusion is that the "Right Way" to live is by what is outside and detached from oneself. Hence, to be taught, one runs after others to tell one who one is, what one is to do, the goals of shrewdness, and teach ways of going about acquiring Material things. Such brings about Philosophical "Blindness." See Blind

DARK" SIDE OF EUROPEANS: Every human has the potential for the "Dark Side." Ancient African Sages were careful to lay out in their Spiritual literature the "Dark Side" of humans and, being of man-made nature the "Dark Side" has a wide range of manifestations. A "seed" idea for the term "Dark Side" came from the mindset of the god Set in African Spiritual Literature which remained within the world of his Lower Self fetters (e.g. greed or conceit) which are powered by receiving and not giving. As a result, this automatically interfered with the Love flow out of his Love Platter. This state of mind is filled with ones perceived personal power, completeness, and sufficiency apart from God. It is characterized by dealing with unreality in a deceptive manner and possessing fixed ideas in opposition to the truth (liar in wait). This delusional and ignorant mindset makes one vulnerable to more delusions and ignorance. For example, Seth gave gifts to others to help him obtain evil ends. In turn, Seth could be easily tricked by gifts that increased his possessions and appealed to this lecherous nature. Throughout history, a common approach of Brute Europeans' in taking over things of significance from Colored Peoples is to appear to be friendly while bearing gifts as preparation for using any means necessary to gain what is being silently sort. Whereas Ancient Africans said hateful thoughts and evil deeds came from ones ignorance of reality, Europeans tried to explain it by using the Devil--a distinction having a startling effect on an individual determining: "How shall I live?" Whereas the Greek 'diabolos' (Devil) means denouncer or calumniator, the Hebrew word "Satan" means "adversary" or "accuser." In the earliest sections of the Old Testament Satan is not an independent personage, nor even a maleficent being. Originally, Satan simply referred to an opponent appearing in black and not to a particular being. But subsequently Europeans generate concepts of Satan in all evil forms. Throughout European history people who possessed hateful thoughts and demonstrated evil deeds were thought to be possessed by demonic spirits, including the Devil. Around the 6th century BC Satan appears in the Old Testament as an individual angel, subordinate to God, and thereafter gradually becomes the source of all evil as a result of disbelieving in God and acknowledging no law except of man. Satan, evil, and dark (signifying misery, punishment, perdition or loss of the soul and hell) became the trio Europeans used to characterize the "Dark Side"--and with the justification of: "the "Devil made me do it." Still, the European ideas about Satan do not solve how evil got into the world--a world which God created and saw as 'very good." Yet, despite looking up the term "dark side" in over 1000 books—including those related to occultism, magic, witchcraft, druids, fairies, sorcery, Satan, Valhalla, Valkyries, spirits, mythology as well as books on word origins, slang, and on euphemisms, and the like—not one mentioned it as such. A little bit of information was found on the internet. Nevertheless, European psychologists have said Satan's many consciousness forms include Egotism (with its self-opinionated and puffed up personality) and its opposite, self-depreciation. In Jungian psychology, the "Dark Side" is called the shadow or "shadow aspect" of the unconscious mind and consists of repressed weaknesses, shortcomings, limitations, irrationality, and proneness to Projection (turning a personal inferiority into a perceived moral deficiency in someone else). The European taste for the "Dark Side" is readily evident by looking at the titles of television, video, and movies dealing with Satan, wickedness, demons, and the like. In my view the Dark Side of humans is denotative of the *full range of "indifference," hatefulness, evilness, and sadism.* That this complex is socialized into European males in general is indicated in their "True History" since appearing on earth--and not the nonsense presented in school textbooks and in the media about who they are.

DECEIVE/DECEPTION: Etymologically to "Deceive" (the quality of being false) someone is to "catch" or "ensnare" them. However, it came into English in C15 with the sense of concealing or perverting the Truth with the intention to mislead in any matter in which one has an end to gain. Deception per se is neither good nor bad. Rather these are determined by the intent and by the outcome. Any information that is the tiniest bit short of Spiritual Elements is deceptive and leads one further and further away from the Truth-Track. Much adversity is happening very rapidly to Brain/Minds of people today. This is compounded on what is the normal course for brain develop. The gray matter of the brain peaks just before puberty and is pruned back down throughout adolescence, with some of the most dramatic development happening in the frontal lobes, the seat of judgment and decision-making. The parts of the brain responsible for multitasking do not fully mature until age 16 or 17 years old. Also, teens have a neural excuse for "Me, Me, Me," self-centeredness. When considering an action that would affect others, teens were less likely than adults to use the medial prefrontal cortex, an area associated with empathy and guilt. This works against them having manners and empathy as well as by these no longer being taught at home or in practicing socializing. By age 20, they have adapted and remain in disarray, drawing on using their brains in ways that are not about Right Life Living. Here are examples: This has history behind it. Broom and Selznick (Sociology p88) said: "…the primitive peoples did not blindly accept the 'superior' culture of the Europeans even when defeated in combat. In art and drama the primitive peoples lampooned the white man and represented him as ignorant and destructive. Neither the manners nor the morals of the conquerors are objects for admiration as seen through the eyes of the primitive artist." Aristotle (384-322 BC) added: "The races that live in cold regions and those of Europe are full of courage and passion but somewhat lacking in skill and brainpower…." Poe (Black Spark White Fire p342) supported this comment by saying: "…that fair-headed northerners were not very bright. The stereotype of "dumb blonds" is evidently older than we think!" The truth of these three things—being dumb, destructive, and amoral--so bothered the barbaric Europeans that they tried to overcome them using a *Feigned Superiority Complex* (donning a self-confidence and self-greatness mask wrapped in an arrogance/aggression reality to conceal deep inferiority). Others are socialized to ridiculously believe they are superior—a dumb self-declaration. Deceive means to mislead by falsehood; lead into error; delude. In the Deceive Family is Deception, Trickery, Deceit, and Fraud—denoting misrepresentation or falsehood intended to mislead. Deception and Trickery are not always bad; a magician uses them both to entertain. Deception usually refers to the fact of misleading; Trickery, to the means; to profit from Deception. Deceit is always bad, and suggests a trait or quality. Fraud is the sale of property which one does not own.

DECEPTIONS' CLASSIFICATIONS: The subject of Deceptions is almost impossible to classify because so many things depend upon so many other things. Most people are *Unintentionally "Deceptive"* simply as part of their personalities. For example, Right Brain oriented people do not follow a reproducible pattern and may not see something best unseen for nine times in a row—causing the hider to feel safe. But on the tenth time, for unexplainable reasons, that person will examine every aspect of the Thing. Another deception wrongly affecting oneself and the other involve occurs when one gets the wrong impression and acts on it without every trying to find the truth. Yet, it may be useful to pick out certain categories to briefly discuss so as to give a sense of an overview. One can best avoid a snare if one knows how to set one. Yet, there is no way to completely prevent ever being deceived, and particularly when someone has what others desire. One reason is the reality of humans is there is no lie they will not believe under certain circumstances; no one who does not believe many lies; and most followers believe only lies. To separate people from what belongs to them is the career of the con-artists—they stay up late at night figuring out how this is to be done. What was unplanned but helpful for me was to never be attached to material things and never have a desire for the newest, the biggest, and the best. For example, a radio with an on/off knob on one side and a knob for tuning to get stations was good enough for me. Although there have been 5 home robberies in the last 5 years, the most valuable things taken were a sterling silver set belonging to my ex-slave great grand-parents and my Clown Doll collection from all over the world. Otherwise, I did not have much of a technological nature. In my Orthopaedic Surgical office practice, I chose to use any extra time I had to promote my skills for diagnosing and treating, rather than to whether I was being cheated or stolen from—and thus avoided "going over the books" every day.

"DEFLECTION"—draws attention away from ones own "Dark Side Sickness" by putting a floodlight on what is supposedly outrageous about happenings of ones Targeted Scapegoat(s)

DEFINITIONS: A definition is a worded statement that presents the Character in a Concept by differentiation and integration. The Character is its *Nature—i.e.* the gist of its original endowments or propensities. The Nature emphasizes the Character's Characteristics because it gives an instantaneous grasp of the Concept's mean—i.e. of the nature of its referents. Its words are visual-auditory symbols used to represent the Concept.

The meaning of a Concept consists of units which specify their referents. Inside units are such specific, particular aspects as properties, characteristics, traits, and features which distinguish from all other concepts. The hierarchical arrangement of the interdependence of those aspects is presented in Logical Order and highlighting the keystone characteristic to make the primary difference from look a-likes. Yet, its Character is part of a genus. To elaborate on the Integration (connectedness with a wider family) of a Genus, "Animal" is the genus that includes both humans and other animals. Hence, a "*Genus*" is a group of species alike in the broad features of their organization but different in their detail. A *Species* is a Family of 'like-kind' Class realities, like a group of animals that, differing in appearance, are very closely related. For example, a domestic cat is one species of "Cat". Thus, a Definition must include the "Genus"—i.e. the broad Classification category. See Denotations vs. Connotations; Word Details; Conjectures; Postulates; Premise; Presume

DEHUMANIZE: Conversion of humans' Image of God core into a machinelike imbrute—i.e. their rendering into a state of brutishness—impersonal--and unconcerned with human values.

DEMATERIALIZATION: *all limitations and boundaries of human thought are disregarded* + all differences are resolved by entering into the commonality which Underlies them. In this way unsuspected and novel connections can be made in seemingly unlike ingredients so as *to impart ideas of the indescribable.*

DENOTATIONS & CONNOTATIONS: Denotations vs. Connotations used in how terms can give a clue to type and level of thinking. *Denotations*--a word's primary, specific sense meaning when it came into being—provides knowledge about that word. Then the point is to assess that knowledge by the Source which gave rise to it. This tells "what it is." Those who give Beliefs, Opinions, or Faith and Hope aspects are called *Connotations* because each has totipotency. This means each person emphasizing them differently or placing them variously on difference planes of existence and they go off in many directions. A clear and profound illustration of this came when Pythagoras (480-411 BC), after spending 22 years in Egypt where he learned that "God is the measure of all things", returned home to Greece and eliminated the God element. He said: "Man is the measure of all things"—and not God. What he meant was that *things exist by virtue of how man perceives them to be.* Thus, the objective world is measured against man—and there is nothing outside man that determines "Being" or Truth. In this way, any given observation, definition, translation, interpretation of ones own ways or what others think, feel, say, and do comes out of that flawed thinker in any form of existence *by virtue of how that person perceives them to be.* Hence, definitions of the terms involved are fundamental and what is agreed on to accept has general world-wide agreement if one is to argue about the "what it is" Denotation of a thing as well as its similarities, dissimilarity, antecedents, consequences, and contradiction, cause, Effect, Consequences, and Results. However, to argue about those things using Connotation ends in total confusion and conflict. See Definitions; Word Details; Conjectures; Postulates; Premise; Presume

DELIBERATELY DECEPTIVE PEOPLE: *Deception Doers Classification* includes: (I) fools who deceive themselves, as by choosing to be their False Selves, believing that to be the false road to happiness—yet hoping to achieve a "little god" power status. Yet, that usually fails to deceive others for very long; (II) knaves (e.g. Brutes, Satanists), those who deceive others by malice added to falsehood, but not themselves; (III) Con-Artists; (IV) Supernatural cults, including religion and philosophers, who deceive both themselves and others. Features of Brutes or Satanists include: "Licking before biting"—like a shark; having the patience and shrewdness to go by steps, paying great attention to detail—and that is how they persuade good and wise people; withholding information or knowledge and even allowing the listener to be mistaken about what is vital; deliberately making confusing and conflicting what could be life-shaping or life-changing; smiling in your face while stabbing you in the back; (V) the Weak in Courage and in wise-ness or cleverness are strong in cunning--spending most of their lives attempting to display qualities they do not possess and gain applause they do not deserve; (VI) the Ignorant lack the insight as to the power of being knowledgeable about ways of Right Life Living. Then they struggle to prevent their ride from being so bumpy, as by such deceptive measures as thinking one thing and telling another. (VII) Combinations of False Self Deceptive Doers embrace the Selfhood Weak, Ignorant, Followers of the Crowd, Flexible Morals people, Brutes, and Satanists. All are False Self people from: (1) Psychic Trauma that is about hiding a "Raw Nerve" from themselves and from others; (2) Socialized; (3) Desperate; and/or (4) Brutes and Satanists. Psychic Traumatize people possess a profound sense of Insecurity, Shame, Guilt, and/or sense of an Inferiority Complex. So as to Deny they exist in ones own "Dark Side," to reflect that individual's manifestation of a hidden "Raw Nerve" causes each to take their personal mental turmoils and apply them the downward social assignments to selected Victims, Scapegoats, or Out-groups, without just cause. *Guilt* is experiencing a sense of blame and remorse or sorrow for immoral actions or for not living up to ones own internal standard. Simultaneously, because the nature of Guilt is to always find a victim, one has the urge to discharge these emotionally and/or spiritually painful experiences. On the one hand, the discharge can be done by Self-acknowledgement of the Guilt and "*paying*" (so as to ease ones conscience) for ones sin/offense, either by taking foolish chances in order to embrace fear and pain as punishment or by making retributions. Brutes who struggle to keep themselves from knowing the "real them" as well as Brutes who struggle to keep others from knowing the "real them" are often those groups of Europeans who felt so guilty about the evilness done to Native Americans as to name states, counties, streets, etc. after them.

If ones Guilt is not acknowledged within oneself, then that unresolved guilt will be projected onto a defenseless "*Scapegoat(s)*" who is then punished as a "stand-in" substitute. This means the punishment is done in a manner that one would punish oneself if one had the courage to inflict self-punishment for whatever evils one did. The degree of punishment inflicted on the scapegoat is determined by the degree of rage and fear making up parts of the punisher's mental turmoil. For example, if the punisher has a moderate or extreme degree of self-hate, then he/she will inflict cruel and inhumane punishment, using the excuse of "making an example of" the scapegoat in order to discourage others not to do the same type of thing. But because the punisher denies what he/she has done, this message does not apply to him/her -- and that is justification for him/her to keep doing it. This "Do as I say and not as I do" mindset pattern of punishing scapegoats for whatever evils occurred from their hands has been most prominently displayed throughout European history and especially projected onto Black People. The same applies to most of the above mentioned and following types.

DELUSIONAL FEARS: imagining of false, dangerous problems, spurred by "Phantasmagoria".

DECEPTION TOOLS: they used include Stereotypes, Projection, Deflection, and Reaction Formation—all from personal weaknesses kept hidden from others. A springboard for these is their sense that "evidently, I do not matter anymore." *Deflection,* as a deceptive device, is anything to draw attention away from ones evil deeds and ones own "Dark Side Sickness" by putting a floodlight on what is supposedly outrageous about happenings of ones Targeted Scapegoat(s). *Projection* is using ones own "Dark Side" internal ideas (reality) to paint out-group members as possessing them while those same projected ideas are fashioned to fuse with the corresponding human-made external (unreality) of fellow in-group cult members. Projection and Deflection are used by afflicted persons to distance themselves from their own rejected self-identies + distance themselves from their feigned enemies + keep fellow cult members at a distance from their "Raw Nerves" they are hiding. *Reaction Formation* (a reality/fantasy reversal)--e.g. saying about and to the victim: "you are the one causing the problem, not me!" Whether from nursing a "Raw Nerve" or having been Socialized into being devoted to the Supernatural, they cling to their supporting fantasy-made positions in the face of contrary evidence as a form of Self-Deception. For example, they do verbal or physically bad things, deny they did it, and cling to other fantasies that represent the situation. Then, as part of Deflection, they engage in *Reaction Formation.*

The contents in their *Projection* accusations are derived from fantasies which design feigned necessities—i.e. imaginary necessities. Such are the greatest cozenage (deceitful) things a predator does to his/her mind to break down any remote sense of moral "Right." Only mentally strong people are willing to face and record their mistakes, errors, or flaws in living for others to know. Europeans are not in that category. To hide by Deflection and Projection the "Dark Side" of themselves they desire to Deny, they come up with "tricks."

DECEPTION LABELING: *Stereotypes* which serve as a ready-made description to "hang on to" (e.g. "all men are…; all members of this race don't…") in order to prevent the thinking troubles stemming from being involved with the associated details. These are favorites of Brutes. For significant issues, when *Imaginative Concepts* are part of the Opinion or Belief information people grab for themselves or accept non-truths given or embrace what is derived from incompletely truthful sources, the conclusions constitute Stereotypes. Brute, Satanists, and other Creators intent on reducing their opponents into a state of being laid open to all types of ridicule, typically start the process with characterizing them into "*Caricature Weaklings*". This means victims are viewed as swollen shadows of their true reality. Besides inviting the most penetrating of criticisms capable of dismantling Selfhood, the spewed mockery and demeaning contradictions applied to this caricature are simply Projections of the creators' own "Dark Side". Nothing conveys a more inaccurate idea of a whole truth than a piece of truth put inside the caricature. Whenever people hate "Faceless" people, this means their own insecurities are threatened and their self-hatred is exposed. Both are confronted by displacing these into their victims and thereby making them into chimera (monsters). Since the created chimera follows their creators everywhere, the associated fantasy throws the entire picture of whatever involves the chimera into an Umbra--a complete and fully formed dark shadow. Hence, creators are unable to discern the face of one symbolizing the caricature or "Outsider" without it being distorted, if not "Faceless." Nor do they have the ability to see anything good in anything having any relationship to those victimized by the caricature. Segregating and shunning these "Outsiders" is a double-edged sword. On one side, it satisfies the creators' insecurity needs for being in control of people, having acceptance from, and a sense of belonging with, like-kind people, and gaining a feigned sense of power. On the other side, creators can never be happy or rise out of "Faceless Hatred" for the "Outsiders" because of their lifestyle overflowing with rage. *Victims' used Deceptions* to mislead the oppressor or predator, as did the Enslaved with masks and masquerades to display passivity. The mask may be of a camouflage or mimicry deceptive type. "Deflection"—a throwback trick to the ancient Greek Sophists and often used today by closet racists'. This pattern is typical of Whites in their advocating "how bad" Black People are. Deflection's intent is to hopefully ensure no one will notice the evil like-kind things Brutes do, as when the media steers a specific crime topic to appear as if it is "normal in Black culture" so as to distract one from noticing the "white color" crime. Politicians use Deflection Answers of the irrelevant type in order for people to not know what they really think about an issue. Other Victims are after Pity from others. An example is the manifestation of "*Accident Prone*". See Accident Prone

DEDUCTION: *Deduction conclusion* about a certain thing is reached by drawing out facts from a knowledge of the class to which it belongs

DEFINING MOMENTS: A "*Defining Moment*" is an Event (a changing reality) that, on the *Thinker's Scale* (a positive and a negative ruler separated by a zero), 'flips' on a Theme from Good to Bad, Bad-to-less-Bad, or Bad to Good. 'Flips" may occur with people, places, or things. The word "*Theme*" (C13, something put down) is in so many fields and with so many varied subjects as to often have incongruent associations of ideas. Definitions include: a unifying central or dominating idea; organization around a single topic; an emanating underlying aura or atmosphere (e.g. tone or attitude--implicit or explicit); whatever gives unity to a variety of examples; and shared essence properties (without saying the possible conflicting sources of those

Essences, as occurs between the African Tradition Spiritual and the European Supernatural). Since I think of "Skeletons" of the human body as being roughly the same and all else on it (e.g. fat, skin, muscles, blood vessels, and nerves) having more wide-spread unique variations, I liken a Theme to humans' "Skeletons" ('dried body'; mummy). Suppose there are an Association of Events that have the "Skeleton" as their Grand Central Station. Analogizing each Event to a subway means both with many railways miles, taking people from station to station, day and night. Any given subway may run underground, on top of the ground, or on elevated tracks. But suppose a subway train 'here and there' has an obstruction at some point that prevents, say 3, from not being able to get to Grand Central Station--until a repair crew, all at the same time, make the correction. A Defining Moment results when all trains are in normal "Skeleton" Interrelationship aspects. For this Physical World Mechanism, Nature's Organic model is *Nerve Cells*, which are always in touch with other nerve cells. Their Interrelationship point, where the Nerve Cells touch each other, is called a *Synapse*. The duty of a Synapse is to provide a means for an impulse arriving from some Messenger along a Nerve axon--and with sufficient focused power to leap across to a neighboring cell body. Once the ending of a nerve cell is stimulated, the process spreads towards the destination, like small waves—similar to happenings after a stone is thrown into a pond. Just as the human Nervous System has a *Web-like pattern*, correspondence is the Cosmic Organism's Web-like Subway of Associations. That Web-like system is each of all God's Creatures and Creations being interconnected. All independently act and interdependently interact in accordance with the God assigned identities of each. By being a "ME/WE" Web, what is done in any part of the Web affects the entire Web and its contents. Also like the well-functioning Subway System, when such happens in the Cosmos, there are beneficial Defining Moments. On Earth, when all things are working smoothly--whether on the positive or negative side of the Thinker's Scale--there will be Defining Moments. Most are beyond ones or a people's control; some can be somewhat influenced by one and/or other people; and some are under people's and/or ones control. Throughout my life, I have focused on only those 'Things' I can control. That means *making the best use of my Personal Power by Taking Charge and Control of my Selfhood--Take Charge and Control of all I do--Take Charge and Control of the situation I am in.* I avoid what I cannot control! This process is used on the positive scale to Create, Enhance, and Maintain Harmony; on the negative scale, to Protect, Defend, and when necessary, to go on 'soft' Offense to achieve my Mission. My invariable, seemingly inseparable contrary opposites or counterforces, are the Ignorant, Fools, Stupid, and Wicked people. They are dedicated to not controlling themselves while making an all-out effort to control others. So, *I must control cultivating 'winning' Ma'at Brain/Mind power.* Practice comes from perfecting *Focused Attention skills*, for then more power is given to mental acts of *holding neural circuits of my brain in place* so as to keep them steady in what they are doing. Maintaining sustained focus makes one mentally stronger; enhances my existing mental thinking capacities; and generates more tenacious mental (clinging) energy. That energy triggers more nerve structures to join the process of Focused Attention--similar to the way a crowd forms around a street magician. The greater the number of members in the crowd of neural circuits, the more power is available to make Creative paths to Good ends. Prolonged periods of *Concentration,* while gathering more clinging brain energy, gives decision and solution advantages over "smarter" people who do not concentrate. jabaileymd.com

DEFINING MOMENTS' DEFINITIONS: Grand Central Station in New York City--one of the busiest and most crowded railroad terminals in the world--has railroad tracks coming into it from all directions of the USA. A separate part is a circular garage--called the "*Roundhouse*"--where Locomotives are driven onto a huge turntable--like the kitchen table's "lazy Susan". On that turntable, workers do troubleshooting inspections, repairs, cleaning, and the attachment or removal of loaded or empty railway cars. Similar things happen at the Theme's "human skeleton" type Roundhouse of every decision and every solution of Serious

Business—whether of small or great impact. But a vital step in the process of Critical Thinking (CT) is that all pertinent mental ingredients are put on the "Skeletal-shaped Roundhouse". Here, troubleshooting inspections, repairs, cleaning, and the attachment of pertinent memories or information—or, removal of the non-pertinent because of being over or improperly loaded or because it is empty, useless, or handicapping. Such prepares for getting the "Big Picture" of the Problem or Situation, the Cause, and the Desired outcome readied for "arriving into the moment" that will produce a new Essence. This preparation is done by means of Circumspection Thinking. *Circumspection* coordinates train-like arriving inputs from all of a human's Selfhood faculties in order for them to independently do what will interdependently result in such things as: observations, critical analysis, Mathematical processes, creative visualizations, intuition, and synthesis. Part of the preparation is the mental erasing of boundaries + *disregarding limitations of human thought* normally separating whatever is involved so as to pave ways to proceed. To this end, child-like playful Imagination generates contributory Image forms, lightness of mood, and flexibility novel viewings. One looks to find the inner similarities of the involved components in order for each of them to be reduced to an Essence. Vital to this process of discovering inner similarities is to discern Essences, or at least their corresponding Essentials in the "Big Picture" of the issue at hand. The method for that is the application of the *Box Concept*—the viewing of all matters so as to inspect each side--the inside and outside details of every angle—inspecting the top and bottom and any wrappings--turning it in all directions--looking at it from underneath--seeing it from one view after another--holding it against the sky and imagining it in any material or even in glass--and thinking of all types of options based upon fashioning powerful meanings indirectly. What is gathered from Circumspection and Box Concept viewings are put into a CT sieve for *"Distillation"* (from 'Still'--distil, drop). This *Process,* learned in high school chemistry, is the separating of the ingredients of a liquid by boiling until it drips or trickles down in drops. After the resultant vapor is condensed, what is retained are the essential features or components of what was in the liquid—retentions already Synthesized. This entire process of *Synthesis,* likened to shuffling a pack of cards, *happens because the whole is greater than the sum of its parts.* So as to specifically select what is pertinent from that distillate and then cultivate that distillate with other mental ingredients by arranging/rearranging and combining/recombining and synthesizing all of it with organized thoughts into a *Common Sense* Product. As with Synthesis itself, the resulting Product has properties and characteristics fundamentally different in kind from those of the separate components originally viewed independently. As a result, one has gone *beyond existing awareness which* means transcending into another realm so as to engage in its *knowledge and Creativity* reality flow. That *Spiritual* Knowledge flow consists of *Essences made from the Spiritual Elements.— That alone has Cosmic Totipotency which enables endless Creativity,* in a manner emulating Nature. *Totipotent* means capable of giving a *Sentiment* (a pertinent thought wrapped in a Pure Emotion) existence to any ray the Essence is capable of producing. *Synthesis* involving the Surreal gives a more varied toti-potence of powers than can be ascribed to either alone. Any given Ray from the Essence may use its Creativity to fashion new Options or even new forms. But regardless of whatever new Entity that emanates, fashions in the Theme "Skeleton" a "Unity"--denoting the Abstract tie between what underlies a plurality of different Things in a Wholistic sense. Because that synthesized *whole is greater than the sum of its parts and is flowing in Infinite Unrealized Knowledge/ Creativity*, it equals a Defining Moment.

DEFINING MOMENTS' "ME/WE" SIGNIFICANCE: People who think for themselves, flourish in beneficial Defining Moments. One reason is they rise above what their culture has already defined for them and leave behind the boundaries of stereotypes and Patterned ways of doing things. Instead, each very significant moment popping up in their lives is viewed as a kaleidoscopic-type overlap of contributors to that moment. Examples are the situation itself, ones mindset readiness for this surprise, the participants involved in the situation, the environmental influences, the setting, and what all led up to the situation. Each of these has contents of significance and the slightest of kaleidoscope rotations changes the color combinations. So, to handle this, one must create an Interchange inside the voluntarily or pre-determined selected kaleidoscopic picture. Such a picture I suddenly stepped into on my first day as a freshman student at the University of Michigan. Immediately, I had to learn to be a self-sustaining *Isolated Individualist* on 3 fronts: (1) in pursuing my life's course to become a physician; (2) battle racist "alligators" along the way; and (3) find some way to continue my "ME/WE" orientation to life. For the latter, not being a learned position or having the time to do anything else, I simply *recorded "defining moments"* pertaining to overcoming overwhelming obstacles. This had several benefits for me: being a quick and secure way to release my pent-up emotions; and having me troubleshoot the mistakes I was making; how I was living as well as things to avoid, what to look out for, and proper directions to take. From Troubleshooting I became aware of flaws, like: (a) dealings with only one link in some interrelationship instead of stepping behind its origin to see where it came from and with what was it associated); (b) paying attention to only the general idea within a given link while overlooking how its particular aspects can be applied in a special way; (c) improperly linking things because they "SEEM" right (e.g. Spiritual and Supernatural ideas do not mix); (d) overlooking certain meanings in certain links (more often the right meaning was given in ancient times, but of which I was not aware); (e) failing to do a humanly perfect job with one or more of the links regarding arranging or combining them; (f) ignoring the obvious out of bias or trying to "conform" or to make myself "look good". Any of these (among countless others) causes one to have flawed or limited ideas. Frustration is then a set-up for inefficiency and ineffectiveness--a set-up for conveying the wrong intension or message--a set-up for confusing oneself and the receiver. While cultivating ways to have foundational "defining moments" lessons, I instituted ways to memorialize them for sharing with anyone interested. I asked other Black People who had good or bad Defining Moments to record every detail of what their course had been like so as to share in helping Black youth be successful in a hostile White society. This process, called the: "What's Behind That?" Self-Inquiry, starts with what happened? and progressively goes further and further back into the past in order to find the Keystone Cause. What caused the sudden change—what led up to that sudden change?—what was the slight additional weight straw that broke your overloaded back?--what was the Effect, Consequences, or Results of the happening on you and loved ones?—what was done?—what was the lesson learned and where was it applied in ones life?—what plan was put into place to ensure preventing repeats?—how are you now? During this process, mental "doors" are Opened so as to see what is behind each basic difference and explore its contents. Since it was clear how problematic it was for me not to know certain unchanging things and since I really disliked seeing the unnecessary duplication of mistakes, I was detailed in my recordings. The point was that maybe with my own children, I would have forgotten details of my struggles—and how I looked at them—and the right and wrong things I did to handle them. In short, all that happens at arriving at a bad Defining Moment and all that is required in recovering from it constitutes the best Selfhood advice the naïve can have. My "ME/WE" orientation demanded that I have available in detail what is needed in order to give youth insights for necessary preventions, handlings, and corrections. This is a way to overcome the Crowd's socialized "me, me, me, self-destructive habit and adopt the Thriving "ME/WE" attitude—an attitude of do what you do to climb while lifting the "WE" along the way.

DEFINING MOMENTS--SOLVING PROBLEMS INTO: Being appointed as an Independent Medical Examiner for the State of California meant the toughest of Industrial Injury cases were sent to me by judges. Since millions of dollars were riding on my decisions, the attorneys were "gunning" for me. On one case the medical records were almost as tall as me and I faltered for a moment, saying this is too much for me. Then I paused, went into my Selfhood Greatness mode, and said: "No one is better able to do this than you. They may do it differently, but not better." That was a profound defining moment and I never doubted myself again. An approach to handling these cases included never assuming I already knew enough about a subject to by-pass the need for further research on its keystone word meaning and its associated ideas. First, the best tools carried into all Tough Problems were how to eagerly and to immediately face and deal with any problem; work hard and do whatever work it took to handle it; and never "give up." I never approach a problem with the idea to use "how it has always been done"--nor discard out of date information since all it may need is a little something added to make it work. Second, all tough issues are carefully Analysized to make determinations leading to conclusions or formations. Both serve as a springboard by: (1) mentally seeing similarities in the dissimilar--uniqueness in similarities--the common in the uncommon--the uncommon in the common; (2) looking behind the obvious to see the consistent, permanent, stationary, and unchanging patterns/elements underlying natural events and the course of their Natural Processes; (3) going into the Underlying in order to fashion interrelationships between dissimilar and similar things; and (4) determining the interrelationships of the components involved and how they are unified into a harmonious pattern. That illuminates the 'what it is,' the way things are, why they are, how they are. To see these aspects together in their web-like interrelationships enables one to become aware of links connecting and meshing the Uniqueness of each member into the inner nature Sameness that makes the Cosmic Family a Unity-Web. Seeing interrelationships, key to creative solutions, designs a "Seed" that buds into a new start which, when cultivated in the proper matrix, may flower, bloom, and fruit. Since, on this adventure—not workable are pausing to engage in Attractive Distractions and forgetting; and "almost" is not good enough. To keep opening doors means surprising discoveries of unopened doors and which had not been opened previously. Opening each, gathering their contents and distilling them to their essence, enables awareness of even more aspects of associated things that have *Correspondence Interrelationships*. The resultant new meanings increase my insights for determining the *Order and consistent Patterns underlying natural events*. At that point, to get the most of what has been gathered, I learn more from constantly redoing my own work to *explore its Infinity Knowledge* than from bringing in outside material. In this way, a Knowledge Flow Interchange is created, out of which comes Mosaic pieces from each interwoven entity—and they form Image Pattern offspring. Despite its narrow scope, these bits and pieces of awareness of the original meanings of the associated ideas within the Common Ground Interchange and its developmental historical course, instantly begins to illuminate paths into pertinent subject aspects. But I always kept in mind there are interrelationships on other planes for dipping into those different planes and in different ways (equating to Classes of the theme of the Classification). Meanwhile, proceeding down this Unknown mental path will eventually lead to a "doorless room" which, when entered, one will find the Truth covered in the "rough". To do the troubleshooting inspections, in order to make repairs or adjustments, cleaning, and the attachment or removal of memory, associates, or "props," *enables arriving at the Mystery's answer*. The reason this works for any subject or problem is that the Cosmos is constructed Mathematically out of the Spiritual Elements and thus everything Real is connected and has Correspondence (a Sameness because of its Genetics, even though those Spiritual Elements Genes are in different combinations). Hence, if one knows well what is Seeable from having studied it thoroughly, the same Principles apply to what is UnSeen. An analogy is that if one can see half of a pearl necklace and cannot see the other half, one has a good idea of what the other half looks like—and this is Circumstantial.

DEFINING MOMENTS FOR BLACK SCHOLARS LIFE'S COURSE: Clark AFB USA medical facility was the closest to theViet Nam war "front-line". As a General Practioner, treating wounded soldiers led me to become an Orthopaedic Surgeon. But at that time Black People were not being accepted into this Southern dominated speciality. For reasons unknown to me, I was accepted at Hospital ABC and immediately gave my word of commitment. Then, ten days later I was accepted at one of the top residency programs in the world.

This created a dilemma because I had been reared to *always keep my word*. Based upon maintaining my integrity, I refused the top program. Hospital ABC made it so difficult for me that I had often wondered if it would not have been better for me to break my word and go with the top program. But in looking back years later, choosing Hospital ABC was a defining moment that put me on a beneficial path because struggling with countless varieties of problems, most from simply being Black in an all-White environment, forced me to solve each in silence. From then to now, my metaphorical tow-rope has been Ancient African Sages' teachings that *ones purpose in life* is to fulfill the Divine Plan *and to use the difficulties one has in life as a tool to force out the divine powers within ones Selfhood so they can be cultivated.* Tragedy is a tool for the living to gain wisdom, not a guide by which to live. Each on-going Defining Moment is a growing into discovering the survival core of strength within oneself that overrides very intense hurts and then drives one to instantly face/handle tough problems. Each of these had an effect on me, like the forging of steel by heating iron in a furnace so as to produce molten iron metal which could be pounded into a useful shape. Such is what prepared me for handling much greater problems later in life. Being in the Unknown and facing problems completely alone—and tough problems I had never seen or heard of before--required getting myself and keeping myself in good order. This enabled me to know what I could count on in myself and what around me was available when encountering "alligators." The paths inside the Unknowns had/have innumerable hour-glass shaped tunnels. Within each hour-glass stricture are always unique situations needing to be figured out for getting through—situations not allowing usage of previous solution patterns. As a result of having to observe closely every detail +learn how to arrange/rearrange and combine/recombine "bits and pieces" of facts and inferences in order to come up with creative solutions was a process that invariably made me stronger each time. What was constantly reinforced was to stay focused only on the goal, strive for Human Perfection, and proceed with a sense of Urgency. There was no time to rest or to do "normal" things or to be involved with the Crowd since it was quite clear that penalties for not staying "on-point" were heavy and ongoing prices that would completely stop my wholesome progress. From that moment of realization onward I had to intensify the depth of meeting problems head on and figure out ways to solve each—despite having little information, being unprepared and/or with no preconceived idea as to what to do. Of course, I made innumerable mistakes—and those mistakes would run in families, as a result of them having a mental flawed common ancestor. This taught me to go to the "Seed" of the Tree type ideas of an issue and learn that "Seed" thoroughly so as to stop that chain of mistakes. In the process, I learned to see things as they are--*extract teaching lessons from each mistake--and map out a plan to never allow that mistake and its family relatives to ever happen again.* I always liked silly humor because it kept my mind flexible inside a fun atmosphere of Serious Business. It really helps to have multiple projects in various stages of development because when I learn something for and from one, all of those specific aspects as well as new ways of viewing the ordinary—which I really enjoy--applies in several other areas. All broaden my sources and numbers of Options. I never was stopped because a problem was too difficult. Of what little I knew or guessed at, I would do the little something and/or write something and add to it over the weeks. I wanted to know every piece of information because even the weird stuff would one day be the answer for "Impossible" problems. Extremely beneficial is realizing the "dumbness" of most authorities and "experts." Thus, I never have to consider what they say and build on it. Instead, I get the "Big Picture" and branch off with its Essences into realms of my own novel ideas. Each Defining Moment problem, in looking back, was part of a plan.

DEFLECTION: a deceptive device, is anything to draw attention away from ones evil deeds and ones own "Dark Side Sickness" by putting a floodlight on what is supposedly outrageous about happenings of ones Targeted Scapegoat(s). *Projection* is using ones own "Dark Side" internal ideas (reality) to paint out-group members as possessing them while those same projected ideas are fashioned to fuse with the corresponding human-made external (unreality) of fellow in-group cult members. Projection and Deflection are used by afflicted persons to distance themselves from their own rejected self-identies + distance themselves from their feigned enemies + keep fellow cult members at a distance from their "Raw Nerves" they are hiding. See Deception

DÉJÀ VU: (French, "already seen") is an expression of familiarity that is unexpected—the sense of having already experienced the situation you are in for the first time or experienced the feeling, thoughts, places, dreams, meeting, and living in general. It is more common in women and children than in men—suggesting it is Right brain oriented.

DELIRUM: Amazed (stunned) by being dulled through shock, as in being wide-eyed and open-mouthed while "*Bending*" (bring into a curve) Reality into Distortions or leaping into Fantasy (e.g. the Supernatural). When moderate or Extreme, there is an exit off reality's course as to stir so much disharmony, fear, and difficulty as to cause *Illusions* (seeing what is not there and not seeing what is there); *Hallucinations* (false images or beliefs having nothing to suggest it, outside a disordered mind); "*Delirium*" (temporary mental disturbance leading to believing ideas opposed to reality); *Delusions* (believing what is not real and not believing what is real); and *Misinterpretations* (wrong track, wrong plane of existence, and/or wrong direction). All disarray ones 'sureness' of any topic one thought one knew or will later know.

DELUSIONAL INFORMATION: What is emphasized here is that *good thinkers look past how a word is defined and the connotation it is given in order to see what ones actions really are* and what effect they have within the context of the situation in which those actions are used. For example, some ideas contained in "Stubborn" are desirable all the time; some are bad; and some may be good or bad, depending upon the circumstances. A major problem with Mental Toughness is negative authoritative connotations have been allowed to cloud its true nature. An example of giving a bad connotation to a neutral concept is as follows. Every child has been mentally tough, especially during "the Terrible Two's." Although outsiders define such as *Stubbornness* -- a childish persistence going in the wrong direction -- its pattern is that of Mental Toughness, a mindset honored by Ancient Africans. Childhood stubbornness has many advantages. In fact, perhaps the purest childhood forms of focused attention -- apart from when one is in great pain or enraged -- is being stubborn. For Ancient Africans, ones duty in life was to discover methods for "yoking" to God and that was determined then to doggedly, almost stubbornly, stick to the settled purpose. Much of my own success has come from extending my childhood stubbornness into such things as stubbornly refusing to take short-cuts or to decide that something will not work until I have tried it. "I'll do it my way" is seen by many as stubborn but what it does is to cause me to think about all details of what I am going to do and to be creative in handling unexpected problems. However, in Europe, *"stubborn"* retained during and after Biblical times the ideas of a hard, obstinate attitude--and even that of rebelliousness. Both ideas, and especially those of a firm nature following an evil course, were thought of as beliefs antagonistic to God. Note that they focused only on the negative side of the coin of Persistence while ignoring the positive side. As a result, this generated the delusion that persistence, under the term "Stubborn" is always bad.

That delusion is a way to control ones mind, as when "authorities" tell their victims what is the best (i.e. non-stubborn) thing to do. A major job of Critical Thinking (CT) is to look at words which seem bad to people (e.g. selfishness, stubbornness), discover their essence (or denotation), and come up with a "big picture" and thus different view. A pertinent example is *Loyalty*, the partner of *Persistence*, which authorities present to the world as being "good." If ones philosophy of life leads one to honor anti-Spiritual Elements and their associated bad emotions, Loyalty holds both the emotional negative "glob" and stubbornness (or Persistence) together. Being loyal to a prime bad emotion (e.g. revenge) inside the glob implies "choosing and collecting" the traits of reliability, faithfulness, and cooperativeness -- all as part of forming a spirit of togetherness. But such loyalty is "*Un-Noble*" because it "glues" the bad emotion to these SEEMING virtues and both take off in the wrong and destructive directions. Whether good or "*Un-Noble*," Loyalty is inseparable from friendships or alliances with fellow destructive Evil people int the form of an unswerving and binding allegiance. Such is seen in "hate" groups and this means all of them are weak. Another group of "*Un-Noble*" Loyal and Persistent people are those who have lost their sense of Self-Greatness, self-trust, self-confidence, and self-loyalty. To justify their self-absorbed and Selfhood Splintered mindset they use the rationalization: "I'm too busy to get involved in trying to change." Actually they fear becoming overwhelmed in the unknown. Hence, despite being emotionally stimulated to start making self-improvements and to start achieving objectives leading to a beneficial goal, this False Self driven Emotional Energy enthusiasm quickly burns-out, causing them to become side-tracked by attractive distractions. These are causes of displayed *Poor Motivation* which, in turn, prevent them from rising above poverty. Under the excuse of staying with tradition, the bad habit of stubbornly clinging to the way things are is *a major factor in keeping Black youth from rising above mental, physical, spiritual, and social poverty.* It is not the nature of Spiritual Energy driving Spiritual Will-Power to "rebel" but rather to react to injustice, evil, and sadistic deeds causing pain, suffering, and disability. Here, stubbornness or Persistence denotes any expressed decisions and solutions to overcome or endure such inhumane things. These include what it takes for Survival (the first law of Nature and is thus Selfish), Self-Protection, and Self-Preservation -- each of which extends to others since all God's creatures and creations are spiritually related.

DENIAL: The C14 English word "Denial" ("refuse") has application on multiple planes of existence. Examples include: a conscious or sub-awareness erasure of the reality of what someone or oneself did or said and to erase true reality on the way to believing in delusions. Often spurring the Denial is to keep ones "Raw Nerve" from being exposed. Thus, one tries to camouflage ones Fears by means of a Superiority Complex. Ways this show are by Deflections, applying Stereotypes, and Projecting their "Dark Side" onto feigned scapegoats. At the basis of such SELF-DELUSIONS and Sham-Science is being Self-Unknown and thus wandering aimlessly in an abyss. Making up their Delusional world is an IHES mindset generating things like: (1) a *Superiority Complex* (donning a mask of self-confidence and greatness with a reality of arrogance and aggression to conceal a sense of deep inferiority) necessarily requiring (2) *Repression* (denial of being evil); (3) *Reaction Formation* (going to the opposite extreme of what one believes, as in being detached from God but speaking of being God-fearing); (4) "*Deflection*"—a throwback trick to the ancient Greek Sophists whereby Whites own evil and sadistic deeds are steered to appear as if it is "normal in their Victims' culture" and not in themselves; (5) *Projection* is Whites' reversal of the self-hate they experience by saying their Victims hate them; and (6) Denial for making all of their IHES mindset activities and their KTDDOC methods SEEM right to themselves and to their fellows. However, by that Denial pattern becoming fixed, it is a Self-Scam Lifestyle. Whatever causes them to stay Ignorant is what drives them to seek their Lifestyle and information for it from the External World. By ensuring this to be their only source, results in a vicious cycle of worsening Lifestyle. Since they make no effort to acquire Knowledge in order to self-improve, that is a sure indicator of them having great inner problems (e.g. insecurities). This necessitates selecting an Ego to orchestrate ones concept of oneself so as to be able to deem oneself as who one is not in order to avoid facing who one really is. The Self-Delusion continues by the "Self-Talk" (i.e. thinking) answers one gives oneself; or by not saying what one really feels, perhaps by saying one thing but thinking another or saying the extremes for the same situation in the same moment; or laughing when made uncomfortable by another who ought to have been "called out"; or for any reasons one cannot come to grips with ones true feelings. Self-Delusions are maintained by Denial. Having a protective Network to ensure there is no accountability for being dishonorable (e.g. lie, cheat, steal) is what fashions an "*Upside-Down*" opposite of the "Scarcity Syndrome". "*Upside-Down*" Privileges is the having of "too much" and "too easily," as to self-abuse by "trimming down," if not "shutting down," ones thinking every chance one gets. This is replaced with "*Impulsive Adventuring*" to see how much one can get away with—an "Exciting" form of self-entertainment. There is a historical track record of this. One instance is that as a result of Europeans giving birth to a "white Jesus" meant their necessity for tampering with historical names, events, and dates based upon denial of African history. To elaborate, although Ancient Egyptians had applied "Christ" to the divinities, Osiris, Anubis, and others, Europeans assigned "Christ" to Jesus only in the fourth century, and by religious contamination. Despite Europeans' Christianity claim to the contrary, the religion of Jesus had its origin from the Egyptians' Mystery Religions thousands of years prior to Jesus' birth (Freke, p. 15; Bynum, p. 172). Christianity was claimed by Europeans and termed "the White man's religion" as they rewrote history. Diop (African Origins p. 312) says: "Osiris is the god who, three thousand years before Christ, dies and rises from the dead to save men. He is humanity's god of redemption; he ascends to heaven to sit at the right hand of his father, the great god, Ra. He is the son of God."

Walker (Women's Encyclopedia, p. 749) added that after suffering, this god-man [Osiris] reigned eternally in heaven and served as the model for how men and women could be born again so as to inherit eternal life. Having the belief that no creature can attain a higher nature without ceasing to exist, Osiris' resurrection (death and rebirth) was about regeneration (Ashby, p. 566). Yet, Europeans' falsely attributed this metaphorical scenario solely to their "White Jesus" and presented it as "Fact." Another instance is Europeans always misrepresenting themselves as being great while deliberately omitting that what they have acquired is the result of stealing the intellectual property, discoveries, and inventions of Ancient Africans and Black Americans. Especially starting in ancient Greece, European Plagiarism ("to pluck") has continually demanded a denial of the truth of the brilliant African source + destroying all contrary evidence of their creations/inventions/discoveries. Europeans use their Bible to demean their Colored victims in every conceivable way through present day and ancient examples. Such can be seen when movies or television programs of Ancient Egyptians are presented. They are all so light-skinned as to look like White people. Presumably the deceptive reasoning goes like this. Since Egyptians today are light-skinned, it is natural for the non-thinking public to conceive of Ancient Egyptians as similarly light-skinned instead of their actual appearance of black-skinned with Negroid features. Often in documentaries they will use Black People as narrators so as to give the European lies an air of credibility. There is a trend for the producers of documentary religious programs to gravitate toward the truth -- perhaps up to 90%. But the 10% payload maintains White Supremacy. Another part of that 10% contains a series of lies. There is a tremendous effort to wipe out profound Ancient African knowledge in order to give credit to non-Africans or Europeans.

Examples of present day Denials are countless and are in the broad category of *seeing things that are morally wrong but acting like they do not exist*. This is the feature of "*White Privilege*" which, when denied, is so outrageously stupid as to not deserve discussion. Such a pseudo-Denial is willful ignorance at an infinite level--too gigantic to feign legitimate Denial unless the guilty is a "zombie." But this stupidity is an everyday occurrence. Many White people can see Big Foot, the Loch-ness monster, aliens, and Jesus in toast--but cannot see Racism or White Privilege that they either engage in or observe all around them. Most White people have "Righteous Indignation" in reacting to extremely racially biased news media, who do all they can to demean Black People and associate them with crimes. Apart from most of the time the situation is not as presented—and apart from the fact that Human-kind has known no greater vicious criminals in any area and about anything than by Europeans, White people say they do not understand the reason for Black People protesting about their "Killer" police. One recent report said 1100 unarmed Black People were killed by police in one month. There is Denial of the Cause of the problems Europeans are solely responsible for by enslaving free Africans, bringing them in chains to the Americas, working them into bad mental, physical, and spiritual health, and being forced to free them with providing anything but greater troubles, ensuring Blacks stay in poverty.

Following slavery, available jobs paying a livable wage have always been either non-existent or an ongoing problem for struggling Black Americans. Basically, the perpetuation of all of their problems originating in slavery and/or post-slavery racism can be attributed to an inability to earn money, causing many to give up + putting many in prisons for unjustifiable reasons + racism in every way possible. As a result, poverty living for most has been a necessity and with an inability to afford doing those things which enable them to thrive--things like critical and rational thinking which are expansive tools for thinking. Many "Escape" from their harsh existence by denying their problems and finding "trinkets and trivia" to be the most important. Whether White or Black, Denial of emotions causes conflict and stress from not recognizing ones shame, wrongness, or disgust. White people Denial's that Black People are human or that they do not exist determines White people get all the advantages. Yet, White people present themselves as being nonplussed by some Black People manifesting poverty in lifestyles. Amazingly, Whites never admit being the "seed" cause of this. White people then make up sham (IQ) test and other examinations to "prove" their vicious lies. A Final point is that those military Troops and followers of the military leaders will Deny themselves benefits from the government in order to Deny Black People those same benefits. And that is exactly what the Satanists leaders want since they gain even more of the pot of gold.

DENIAL IS KEYSTONE TO BADNESS--Spiritual Ignorance is the keystone to human Uncertainty at any of its levels and, in turn, that gives rise to most Bad and Evil information. The word "*Ignorance*" embraces: (1) to "ig-nore" and give selective attention to a part or to something else or to not know its significance; (2) the ignorance of not knowing a relevant, pertinent, or vital thing exits—and even worse, of not knowing that one does not know; (3) Ignorance from foolishly believing that all there is consists of what is in ones awareness; and (4) Denial of what is presented for ones Awareness but is not accepted or received. Reasons include deliberately doing so by disavowing thoughts, emotions, wishes, or needs; from intentionally misdirecting attention; or by being "blind to the obvious" as a result of socialization or out of laziness. "*Awareness*" means knowing the existence of the "that it is" of a "Thing" when it came into Being-hood—i.e. *its Primary Quality*--but not knowing its Ether laden Metaphysical or Physical "what it is," "what it does," "how it appears," "how it is," "how it came about," or "where it is going." African Sages said the ultimate in *Spiritual Ignorance* (to ignore and give selective attention to a part or to something else) is also the *greatest disease of the Soul—with both being the denial of God.* The most common way this comes about is by being *Self-Unknown—the keystone of both Ignorance and being Information* oriented. Self-Unknown persons result from: (1) having chosen to adopt a False Self (Ego) to orchestrate their "Life-Living"; (2) not knowing who their primitive ancestors were or where they came from; and (3) not knowing their most remote ancestral Cosmic Organism origin—i.e. the 'that they exist' or who they were or from where they came or when.

This particularly applies to European Brutes because they deliberately deny the reality of their ultimate African Ancestral origins. Since there is nothing in the Self-Unknown inner world realm or in any aspect of its mysteries to rationalize, an adopted self-identity is all they have to cling to being in existence. This causes their mindsets to be "upside down" and "inside out" while roaming in an abyss—an abyss they declare to be a Supernatural realm—a Surreal realm straddling the Fantasy Supernatural and the Physical World. They are so ashamed of this, as for it to fashion an "*Inflamed*" psychic "Raw Nerve"—one so ongoingly painful as to seem to act as if it is set on fire and remains ever aflamed. Philosophical and/or Psychic barriers are placed around ones "Raw Nerve". Further protection is provided by ones internal world defenses (e.g. Denial, Repression)

+ ones External World defenses (e.g. "Don't Care"; "Too busy"; Superficial Thinking) + ones "Escapes" from ones problems + the devising of methods to lessen the Spiritual and Emotional Pain generated by the "Raw Nerve." They hate this state of mind because of being alone, because of their distress resulting from the extremely severe nature of their Spiritual Pain, and because they are shut out from their Needy Wants. **Needy Wants** are Spiritual Human Nature Needs that are about *The Love Platter*--the instinct to Love freely; to expand the Courage in ones Conscience to spread Love regardless of how it is accepted or not; to receive being Loved unconditionally; and to be Lovable. Absence of the Love Platter's Unconditional Love is the worst experience humans can have and that drives them to seek relief in the External World. Its repercussions lead afflicted persons to distance themselves from their Real Self, whether to a Mild, Slight, Moderate, or Extreme level. By being in a Self-Unknown state and thereby anticipating denial or rejection by outsiders puts them in a hyper-alert state filled with rage and fear.

Hence, they are ever ready, from "over-preparation" in the use of the GUN (any killing device), to handle both by Defense and Offense even the slightest hint of attacking Expressions. Their Illogical and Irrational Non-Rational minds only think in "all-or-none" and "either/or" fashion and without a pattern. Thus, anyone not like them is deeded to be against them, thereby making it necessary to include killing, getting a group to fight their "enemy". Meanwhile, they are continually destructive; abusive and neglectful of others—no matter how bad off are those others; petty and vindictive--acting out like a child in the terrible two's when they do not get their way. They engage in self-contradiction, deception, denial, inconsistencies; ignoring relevant evidence; proceeding with their ways in the face of contrary evidence; jumping to conclusions; and thinking, feeling, saying, and doing things that do not make sense. They only know rationalizing, projecting, and stereotyping. This comes from being self-absorbed and Selfhood Splintered--viewing everything within ones world in relationship to oneself in a "me, me, me" manner. In the Physical World part, *Self-UnKnowers* become so envious of people not sharing their misery as for them to rise into a Bully mindset of Indifference/Hate/Evil/Sadism (IHES) complex. By possessing an IHES mindset leads them into Kill/Take/Destroy/Dominate/Oppress/Control (KTDDOC) Brute deeds. Meanwhile, the Self-UnKnowers must continually "Escape" as a consequence of denying who they are—a denial which shows by stopping loving and caring about others. A typical attitude is: "Since no one knows me or cares about who I am, I'll show them by not caring about them." This is followed by the destructive practice of believing in appearances, as opposed to operating inside Actual Reality and Truth. But feeling profound self-hatred, great personal weakness, and possessing an Inferiority Complex causes them to fear being alone in trying to carry out KTDDOC behaviors by themselves. Thus, they seek out like-kind mean and vicious others afflicted with similar insecurities of not knowing who they are. By so doing they experience themselves in terms of each other and together fashion a warrior dogma of shared values and beliefs which the entire cult lives up to and uses as standards, guides, filters, and measures for daily living. Those worst off are Satanists because of being "Inside-Out" in their relationship to God--meaning whatever the Spiritual Elements of Unconditional Love, Truth, Reality, and the Natural are about, these Brutes are against. Yet, since these think, feel, say, and do ways have been uninterrupted for thousands of years and have brought great "Scarce Desirables" Material benefits, the Satanists who have acquired the most are socialized into believing they are superior. Thus, their self-hatred, personal sense of weakness, and Inferiority Complex have been REPRESSED—meaning they are relegated to and maintained inside their Unconscious mind. Such Repression also occurs in the "generals" and others in this military cult while its equivalent in the form of Denial occurs in the Crowd directed by the military unit. This means both repressed thoughts and Denials are able to "do its own thing" without ones control and without ones awareness. Hence, many are sincere when they say: "I have no idea why I did that!" The repressed IHES contents do not go away but yet no longer have any restraints or a filter on what it displays. That allows denial of having done what is obvious. When confronted with what was done, one gets indignant with it being pointed out. Still, the Repressed mental activity ensures the same thing continues to happen over and over and that creates recurrent conflicts. "You are picking on me" and that generates resentment and revenge, usually subtle. A Fetter, like Hating "faceless" feigned enemies or someone or some group, will become fixed on that False Self's Sensory Consciousness Background and its hate messages are conveyed to the Sensory Consciousness Foreground to manifest as hate displays in the External World. As a result of ones Sensory Consciousness Background Acquisition of IHES Emotions, one builds a Lifestyle around them—a Lifestyle built on the fantasy belief of one being "superior."

A *Lifestyle* is ones characterizing behaving traits for daily living. The Lifestyle clamor of the Supernatural cult to gain these External World acquisitions and indulge their Lower (animalistic) Self Passions and Fetters causes them to: (1) immediately become and stay clutched to being self-absorbed; (2) shift to *Impulsive Superficial Reflections* about who one thinks one is and who one desires to become; (3) form an Icon Image of a Superiority Complex; (4) make an Icon Monster Image of scapegoats; and (5) focus on ways to improve on IHES and KTDDOC methods. All of this is done with Brute Non-rationalism (emotions orchestrated by Left Brain thinking) for the military unit. From the resultant patterns, varying degrees of these patterns are imitated by the unit's followers. These Mean people are always full of Distress and Fear and they pick on the most needy and defenseless. They enforce poverty by denying justice and jobs; deliberately making confusion out of what is certain; orchestrate conflict out of what has Harmony; degrade the victims; make the people and their property unsafe; present the appearance of "How great we are, and how bad you are; and otherwise demonstrating an intimidating conspiracy to do—and actually do KTDDOC actions to who scapegoats are, what they do, and stereotype world-wide how they appear. Consequences forming, arising out of, and accompanying the IHES complex are Tehuti's "Twelve Tormentors"–Ignorance; Grief; Intemperance (excessive indulgence of a natural appetite or passion); Incontinence (lacking a restraint, especially over the sexual appetite); Injustice; Avarice (greed); Falsehood; Envy; Guile (cunning, deceit); Anger/Rage; Rashness (impulsive, acting without due consideration); and Malice (desire to inflict harm). Under these 12 are many others but all begin to depart--although not immediately—from those who have subjected themselves *to the Divine Spirit in order to command the Life-Force in harmony with the Laws of Nature.* The twelve tormentors, Hermes said, prevents one from conceiving anything beautiful or good.

DENOTATIONS: See Meaning Changes; Information; Etymology; Connotations

DEPROGRAM: deprogramming is through replacement Human Ideal Images—using Imagination systematically and methodically.

DESPERATE: (C15, away from or without hope)—associated with Despair and Desperado—means one is so enraged as to become reckless. One becomes ones own enemy in the manner of a child so angry from having his/her favorite plaything taken away. In turn, the child reacts by throwing the rest of his/her toys into the fire. The rage of that child or of the Desperate expands with such forceful magnitude as for part of it to be turned inward. This is how Desperate people get into an "Inside-Out" mental state—a state causing them to exaggerate into overwhelming their misery and their weakness—a state where they see no way out, or around, or through the impasse—a state that is the end of the bottom. Then one becomes ones own executioner and revenges ones misfortunes on ones own head. The Desperate are acutely conscious of the hopelessness of their position and, in a sense, that is a freeing from personal responsibility--a "why bother to put out blossoms"--a disregard of fear. This means one cannot be "Scared Straight" since one feels one has nothing further to lose. From being imprisoned in a mindset of grandiose form of funk, they set themselves the impossible aim of being Happy. That mindset gives them the courage to "Don't Care" (which confirms ones desperation) about life or death—a Contingent state between Being but powerless bud, flower, and fruit because of a lack of an inner call--and Non-Being, wandering as a zombie—a state that gives a sense of victory. The Non-Being part means one cannot assess oneself. The Being part is unable to recognize in the Non-Being part what is the problem. Their methods include taking the easy way and avoiding struggle—by being addicted to the Crowd and to what excites the Crowd, using that as a port in a storm—staying on the "here and now" treadmill while demonstrating desperation noisily.

DESPOTISM: Oligarchy are control by some but not all people have political liberty and the equality of citizenship. Typically, European societies have historically been Oligarchies or Tyrannical Despotism (rulers governing without the people's consent)—perhaps checkered with Benevolent Depostism (dictators working for the good of the people).

DEVIL: The Devil reflects the mindsets that have created it—those who are serious and solemn—no fun or humor; through in devising ways to control the minds of people; profound in causing switches in Natural World philosophies over to Supernatural philosophies and thereby imparting a spirit of gravity; and absolute "coldness" in humanity by dehumanizing feigned enemies—promoting people act in atrocious ways to one another. By making up the fantasy of the Devil being a fallen angel means Satanists cannot imagine the Devil to be wholly bad. As a result, they write about the bad in not so bad terms. Milton's devils are admirable; Dante's devils stir pity; Goethe's devil suggest what a good thing has been wasted. Still, by Supernaturals never allowing themselves to take the blame for anything, the Devil serves as the direct inspirer of all of their human crimes. None of this is capable of being understood—and that is why confusion and conflict reign.

DEVIL--EUROPEANS CREATION: Of course, Europeans' Contingent (Fantasy) Hell had to be commanded by a self-made image of the European warrior. That took the form of a Contingent Being--another Fantasy--they called the Devil. That Devil is simply an Icon Image of the fundamental shrewdness, deception, and cunning expressions of Evil. Such includes inventions of names, slogans, concepts, Trinkets, and Trivia allowing one to gratify and cater to ones animal spirit--regardless of the prices paid by those involved. An Indifference/Hate/Evil/Sadism mindset, with practices of Kill/Take/Destroy/Oppress/Dominate, is the ultimate in a Devil Icon Image. Believers willfully and knowingly place their intellect and other faculties in the service and gratification of the Animal part of their Selfhoods while attacking the Spiritual Elements. This means they believe themselves to be superior to the powers of the Spiritual Force, Sekham. During European Biblical times, *Rebellion* (re, "anew" and bellum, "war") —a renewal of war and/or the subversion of the laws-- was a critical concept in the doctrine of Sin. But rebellion against Europeans' Supernatural God—in the form of conscious and willful disobedience--was a great sin because God was deemed to be the ultimate sovereign. Yet, *only those with a personal relationship with God—those following the practices featuring the Devil--could violate it.* The Old Testament concept of rebellion is said to be carried over into the NT--whether applied to struggles against an established secular authority (Ro. 13:2) or to a spiritual one (Heb 3). Thereafter, emphasis was more on secular aspects. Europeans used Set, as a rival to God, to orginate the name Satan, personified as the Devil (Amen, Metu Neter II:134). Whereas Greek 'diabolos' (Devil) means denouncer or calumniator, Hebrew's "Satan" means "adversary" or "accuser." Jews elaborated on Rebellion concepts by enlarging on the already developing philosophy of a Devil or a Satan (probably from the African god Set). In the earliest sections of the OT, Satan is not an independent personage, nor even a maleficent being. Originally, Satan simply referred to an opponent appearing in black and not to a particular Being. But subsequently, Europeans generated concepts of Satan in all evil forms. Throughout European history, people who possessed hateful thoughts and demonstrated evil deeds were thought to be possessed by demonic spirits, including the Devil. Around C6 BC, Satan appears in the OT as an individual angel, subordinate to God, and thereafter gradually becomes the source of all evil as a result of disbelieving in God and acknowledging no law except of man.

European Christians embraced the Devil concept as adopted in the OT (Ashby, Egyptian Mysteries III: 22). The African god Seth/Pan, the God of Nature, became transformed into the Red Angel of Evil, Lucifer, Satan (Set-Hen)--a red man with tail, horns, and hooves. Satan, Evil, and Dark (signifying misery, punishment, perdition or loss of the soul and Hell) became the trio Europeans used to characterize the *"Dark Side"* --and with the justification of: "the "Devil made me do it." Still, European ideas about Satan did not solve how evil got into the world--a world which they said God created and saw as 'very good." To address this idea of Evil, one approach was the borrowing and combining Ancient African Bible metaphors. First, thousands of years before organized Judeo-Christian religion is a mythological story of *Ausar (Osiris) and Auset (Isis) who symbolized the first fertile human couple assigned to beget humanity.* This was reassigned to the renamed *Adam and Eve* millennia later when the Hebrews borrowed this myth story and converted it to a "fact". This European Supernatural story, later in Genesis (Diop, Civilization or Barbarism, p. 311), declared Adam as "mankind's father". Thereafter, it was the European religious belief that the African god, Set, in the form of the Snake, presented a false appearance of pleasantness and goodness to Eve. By the serpent pretending to be what he was not by hypocritically saying what Eve wanted to hear, both Eve and Adam were talked out of Paradise. From this falsely presented "Fall of Man" African metaphor branched other European mythological stories. One was making necessary a Redemption to restore all humans from Adam and Eve having cursed the human race with "Original Sin"—supposedly as a result of God's wrath (itself an anthropomorphism concept). Another was that in Genesis (4: 25) one of Adam and Eve's son is named Seth (the African god Set) who replaces the brother Cain slew. jabaileymd.com

DEVIL & ADAM, EVE: By primitive Europeans declaring themselves to be in a Supernatural realm (above the Natural World)--led by Devil-type gods--and thereby being "superior" to all in the Natural World and its Spiritual God, automatically meant they were against everything pertaining to the Spiritual Elements of Unconditional Love, Truth, Reality, and the Natural. That philosophical mindset, by definition, made them Satanists. The later European Christian religion elaborated by making a refinement out of the Kamitic (Egyptian) symbol of the god "Set" and renamed him Satan. This historical pattern of stealing African Traditions' intellectual knowledge, converting its metaphors into "Facts," and renaming all African Spirituality aspects, was a routine practice eventually finding its way into the European Bible. A basic reason for the Renaming is sort of explained in the Encyclopaedia Britannica (1992, p 567): "...*men have seen in the ability to name an ability to control or to possess....*" They defined *"naming"* as applying a word to pick out and refer to a fellow human being, an animal, an object, or a class of such Beings or objects. The consequences are that after a period of time people forget that what was renamed was attributed to the originator and that the new name is assumed to be created by the one applying the present name. An equally powerful reason for "renaming" and making Supernatural "Facts" out of African mythology was to give an acceptable "SEEMS OKAY" background for mind control of the people as, for example, enabling European scholars to declare all humans to be born sinful. To illustrate, the characters taking part in the original African Ethiopian "Fall of Man" scene were not Eve and Adam, but rather Aisha and Aish--shown in the Garden of Eden with the tempting serpent and the fatal tree. In Genesis, the first book of the European Bible, God makes the earth, human males, rodents, animals, insects, plants and everything except a human female. When Adam, whom European Biblical writers declare was the first male, got bored with all the creations at his disposal, Eve, a woman, was created to simply be a help-mate—not having independent rights. The story continues with the Supernatural God making Eve out of a single rib of Adam--not the heart or brain. By being emotional, Eve was able to be deceived by a serpent, disguised as the devil. In turn, Eve then tempted Adam to go against God. In its original Ethiopian story, the serpent symbolizes the Emotions and sensations as the essence of animalistic behaviors—combining humans' rational and artistic faculties and behaviors in the service of their sensual nature. Hence, there is no intelligence, morality, or spirituality in the Brain/Minds that generate them. Instead, they are vehicles of the Life Force and their imposition of Force over mind, reasoning, and the Will is the cause of all that is wrong in the Universe. Amen (Metu Neter VII: 51) says the European Bible's purpose for this Adam and Eve story is to make humans better emotional creatures. Apart from that, by man giving birth to a female--(reversing Nature's laws of females giving birth)--and by Eve tempting Adam served European males' biblical anti-feminism and served the necessity for European males to be without blame for their self-interest concepts. Gen. 3's anthro-pomorphism orientation states God's wrath caused Adam's "Fall" and all humans thereafter would be cursed with "Original Sin."

Anthropomorphism ('anthropos, man) is the act of endowing god with a human form and human attributes or qualities, like the acquired emotions of anger, wrath, fear, and jealousy. Oddly, some of these (e.g. jealousy) are sins in the European Bible. All of this differs markedly from the Ancient African Bible's "Neter" or NTR--one of many African names that are equivalent to the Europeans' Supernatural "God". African Sages say that by being Unknowable, NTR is described as a Spiritual Force. Nevertheless, b*y creating God in his own image, the European male can then use God as a model for how to act as "little gods" with people.* Since the European Bible says Adam and Eve's actions 'forever' totally corrupted the whole nature of humans (Rom. 7:14, 15), this necessitated humans making *Redemption* (as determined by what standard?) in order to restore them to their original state. From this came an intimate association of *Faith* with sin, guilt, and fear. Also appearing from the moral of this story was the core meaning of the word "*Fail*"--being to deceive (as Satan did to Adam). So, to "Fail" is to fall short of having good success (as happened to Adam from engaging in sin). jabaileymd.com

DEVIL/SATAN MALES INTIMIDATED BY ANCIENT WOMEN: Throughout the Ages it was the norm for primitive European males to do warring any and everywhere, all the time—maintain their self-imaged Contingent Being leader Devil, personified as a standard, guide, and model—and brutally deal with, as infe-riors, anyone not like them—e.g. Women and Slaves. Naturally, they encountered all of the first civilizations outside Africa who were, of course, Black Africans. Examples were those of Sumer (Mesopotamia), Babylon, Canaan (Palestine), the Harappa Valley (Pakistan), India, and China. However, Imperialism, the subjection of one foreign nation by another, did not occur until the coming of the European Semites to Mesopotamia, starting with Sargon I of Akkad. Until then, the great powers of Kamit, Sumer, Kush, Harappa, Mohenjo, Daro, and Elam lived in relative peace--except for occasional skirmishes and quarrels over trade routes and similar commercial things. But there was never the setting out to plunder, destroy, kill, or subjugate another as has been the history of Europeans from their beginnings to the present. Neither did they go up north to enslave or exploit the militarily weak Caucasians (Amen, Metu Neter I: 130). As these warriors invaded and conquered peaceful nomadic societies, each of those societies was infinitely more civilized as, for example, the nation of Canaan--a matrilineal system (Amen, Afrocentric Guide p31). To elaborate, Canaanites came from Ethiopians and Egyptians who migrated out of the Nile Valley to settle Canaan, of which Jerusalem is one of its cities (Bynum, African Unconscious p211). It was from them that the semi-barbaric Greeks adapted the script—their alphabet c800 BC. Meanwhile, Aryans and Semites came down from Eurasia into Mesopotamia c2500 BC with a track record of Kill/Take/Destroy/Dominate/Oppress practices. But at this point, oppression attempts were rebelled against by resident women. One reason is they had observed liberated Black women being the spiritual and intellectual equal of men in Sumer, Canaan, India, Ethiopia, Crete, and Kamit (Ancient Egypt). Many were high priestesses, Queen Mothers, and governors. One European male relayed the following account of this clash: "In an earlier part of humanity on earth, we" lived in a matriarchal society. Then there was a shift and the patriarchal emerged. It was during this period that the devil was invented. Satan was a male invention. The "Evil one" was all a part of a male rebellion against the matriarchy, a period during which women ruled over everything from their emotions. They had all governmental posts, all religious positions of power, all places of influence in commerce, science, academia and healing. Men had no power. They had to justify their existence for they had very little importance beyond their ability to fertilize female eggs. What men had to do to gain control during the matriarchal period was not to convince women that men ought to be given more power over their lives, but to convince other men. Life was, after all going smoothly... so it was not easy for men who were powerless, to convince other powerless men to seek power. Until they discovered fear. Fear was the one thing women hadn't counted on. It began, this fear, with seeds of doubt, sown by the most disgruntled among the males. These were usually the least "desirable" of the men; the un-muscled, the unadorned, and hence, those to whom women paid the least attention. Their complaints were discounted as the ravings of rage born of sexual frustration. Still, the disgruntled men had to use the only tool they had. So they sought to grow fear from the seeds of doubt. What if the women were wrong? they asked. What if their way of running the world wasn't the best. What if it was, in fact, leading the whole society-all of the race-into sure and certain annihilation? This is something many men could not imagine. After all, didn't women have a direct line to the Goddess? Were they not, in fact, exact physical replicas of the Goddess? And was not the Goddess good? The teaching was so powerful, so pervasive, that men had no choice but to invent a devil, a Satan, to counteract the unlimited goodness of the Great Mother imagined and worshiped by the people of the matriarchy." The Great Mother he refers to was Africans' beginning Supreme Being since living things could only be made by females. Called the "Creatress" rather than a "Creator," she was embraced by all the original civilized cultures of Human-kind. [Ref: Bailey, Ancient African Metaphysical Glossary, Volume 5] jabaileymd. com

DEVIL/SATAN EUROPEANS' MINDSET SPREAD: A c2500 BC defining moment for European males was their encounter with resident women's rebelliousness to their dictatorial ways. To worsen matters, females were the most prominent divinities, including the Supreme Being. First, this situation shocked the males Astral Souls—their "Hearts"--the "deepest recesses of the human psyche"--the Selfhood Center where the most significant issues of ones life are determined"--the Center of thought, feelings, memory, and emotions--the place of ones moral and spiritual nature and Secular fetters (e.g. envy, hate). Second, this *Manhood Shock* affected not just European warriors but all European males, as those beginning to branch into formalized religion and other varied specialties of daily living. Third, it caused them to do defensive and self-protective things. This started with Myths emerging of Gods of enormous power--quarreling over and fighting for Goddesses of unspeakable beauty. Such competition led European males to the concept of a God of wrath and with such vindictive powers as to become the source of all fear. In order to be superior to everything that existed, they inverted the females' Spiritual God into the God Satan. By accepting this Contingent Being (a fantasy like a child's bogeyman) as an *Illusion* (deceiving by producing a false impression) it was easily and quickly exaggerated into *Delusions* (believing what is not real and not believing what is real). Fourth, for one to accept delusions and illusions—regardless of the combination—is to fashion a portion of ones mind into a Surrealist state. *Surrealism* (above, beneath, or beyond reality)—also called *A-dualism*—is the erasing of boundaries or the "*Dematerializing*" or the *disregard of the limitations of human thought* that normally separate Physical reality from Fantasy. The result of removing such boundaries between rationality and irrationality is mental imagery of Chance effects—a disordered or chaotic array of imagery, much like random sequences of events or recollections experienced in dreams or when one is "knocked silly." This mental joining of "the actual" and the "non-real" leads to an inability to distinguish Inner and External world realities or their true ingredients and/ or even their perceptual "raw materials". Effects of resultant Surrealism orchestrate a revolt against all restraints on logical reasoning, on standard morality (a "wipe-out"), and for males, create distortions of the female body. Fifth, these processes paved the way for European men to enter the "super-real" or Supernatural where they again self-declared to be "superior" over everything and everybody, including females. A peek at the mindsets used in abusive treatments of European and all women can be found throughout the European Bible—e.g. Deuteronomy 21: 10-14; Corinthians 11: 3, 7, 9; and 1 Timothy 2:11-14.

These European male practices modeled their concepts after the Devil—defined as "a deceiver" (Amen, An Afrocentric Guide To A Spiritual Union, p36). Such mind control of Women and Slaves was justified by men assuming empirically (numinous) unverifiable Satanic gods residing in their Unseen World generating "*Numinous Feelings*" in them. By European Satanist religious leaders promoting the Adam/Eve fantasy concept of everybody being born "sinful" served as a passage for the Roman state to survive by its ancient customs and manhood. To elaborate, although derived from an immediate and primary referent—i.e. a Thing outside the Self--numinous feelings are absorbed into Receivers so as to transform their belief into being "Super-human" with a Supernatural aura of omnipotence. By being Supernatural, nothing about them is explainable, for they follow no mathematically logical pattern. A theme of these Non-Rational mindsets include *Phantasmata* (sensory images received passively from some external object)—which have the peculiarity of the Receiver not being aware of them. In addition, they feature a "*double image*" whereby one image suggests or turns into a second and possibly a third image, either instantly or after some thought. "Dematerialization" continues by confusing similarity with identity—and thereby accounting for stereotypes. The associated excessive imagery filling ones mind from engaging freely in A-dualism leads to an inability to distinguish Inner and External world realities and thereby creates bizarre thoughts, images, and fantastic Beings. The mind abstracts universal qualities from these and uses them in making devastating judgments, as seen most dramatically today in the "Killer" police of unarmed Black People. [Research contributor: Joselyn Bailey MD] jabaileymd.com

DEVIL/SATAN EUROPEANS NUMINOUS EXPERIENCES: The ancient Roman word "*Numen*" meant a religious adopted custom sanctioned by law. It evolved out of shepherds and farmers seeing countless displays of power or forces in objects pertaining to a variety of phases of life--each by suggesting they were more than natural, were attributed to happenings coming from another world to inhabit, said animists, a natural object or phenomenon. To describe the powers in these objects and functions that inspired horror, or sacred thrill in the people affected, the Romans applied, in C2 BC, the "numen" idea to indicate a divine Supernatural power or spirit. This god's felt presence was believed to be of an occult power derived from that spirit's head nod ("nutus"). The head nod could: (1) awaken individuals to a mission; (2) signify approval of some thought in the individual's mind; (3) convey the insinuation— as an implication to discredit scapegoats; (4) convey an explanation for an attack to be done; (5) and stir the individual into a "call to action". Two primary aspects of the numinous "*Excitement*" effects were *Fear Emotions* of religious dread, "Awe," uncanniness, and/or religious fascination—each like being invested inside a surreal Unknown. The "*Awe*" state is an erasure of all meaning of everything--is filled with emotions embracing every fetter and hostility form—and is associated with a Contingent Being (e.g. a bogeyman). The "Excitement"--showing as fear, fright, pain, distress, terror, dread, apprehension--is generated by a threatening evil monster or a "Thing's" extremely grand character. *Fascination* by, attraction to, and prizing of the object which arouses the thrill in question creates both the desire to approach the object while sensing oneself to possess no value when considered in relation to this overwhelmingly powerful and prized object. These "Seed" ingredients design products which constitute *Superstitions*. Since the "Awed" now believe the Supernatural reigns, *superstitions become so firmly ingrained as for one to be totally resistant to being educated out of them*, no matter how utterly ones own reason may reject them. People so addicted to Supernatural stresses enter a Surreal state that expands their Supernatural universe, bringing them closer to the great secrets of fantasy life. This is like *"Escaping" into the reality of the Natural World but which they delusionally deem to be unreal.* Yet, many European psychiatrists call this a Psychotic realm since unreality does not exist in the External World. However, rather than Psychotic, I consider the problem as *Philosophical Disarray* causing Surreal mindsets whereby their inner reality is projected into and fuses with the External World. Such "Inside-Out" surrealism is intoxicating from admixed "Emotions" + ones sense of being filled up with the Supernatural Numen Satanist god's presence + sensing protection by the ever watchful un-beatable Supernatural power. This focused their energy into a kind of massive conspiracy urging the exhibition of crushing, invasive power for attack against any feigned outside evil forces. To prevent such feigned forces from entering into their own Selfhoods, they were spurred to act out of their own warrior influences, even to the death. Their Numinous thinking pattern was fashioned by how they used their imagination, dealt with their emotions, expressed themselves, acted, and reacted. To accept Adam/Eve making them sinful by nature provided justifications to define themselves according to their Lower (animal) Selves—essentially orchestrated by hostile minds, sensualism, emotionalism, and desires of the physical body. They were/are also obsessively and compulsively wed to the GUN (any killing device)--their sole source of power--and their eagerness to use it. That pattern of rampant evil and sadistic deeds (among others) caused Rome's ruin by rampant pursuits of the flesh and hostile in-fighting by all concerned. Yet, the Satanist religion continued in full-force and spread "everywhere," as in molding many of today's male mindsets. To elaborate, in the world's largest surviving medieval manuscript—the *Codex Gigas* (literally "giant book" in Latin) or the 'Devil's Bible'--some believe Satan himself is the book's scribe. To this end, it is said a monk sold his soul to the Devil in order to produce it. It contains a large illustration of the Devil pictured with a green face, talons, and horns, crouching in a squat, almost as if he were in a yoga pose. Nevertheless, the book was considered so exciting that many people imagined it was Satan inspired, along with Supernatural help. Otherwise, throughout the ages there have been numerous other pieces of art for which the Devil is rumored to have served as a muse. jabaileymd.com

DEVIL/SATAN EUROPEANS NUMINOUS MINDSET: A *Numinous Mindset* "big picture" gist is its possession of an absolutely unique way of viewing life that is almost like being made out of the same thinking conformity "cookie cutter." Included are an awareness of something mysterious, unconquerable, unmovable, undeniable, unexplainable, incomparible, unimaginable, immeasurable, unthinkable, terrible, beyond reason, awe-inspiring, adventurous, and rapidly headed away from happiness. Its superiority complex is unexplicable by established laws of human nature and is contrary to known reason or even to common sense. Nothing of what they want is ever enough and thus they can never be happy. A facade for their sense of unhappiness is *"act as if"* they have it all together and seek doing harm to others as a way of having some momentary sense of relief from their misery. The objective is to be rich like a king and have "little god" power and such respect out of being feared as to be enshrined in the "Hall of Infamy." In the background of their Selfhood are a myriad of Superstitions--beliefs about the occult in its negative range and beliefs in the existence of super-humans or Supernatural forces and Beings which they attempt to emulate. A speculative analysis of a *Numinous Mindset* in its "Bottomless Pit" (which Europeans call Hell), they are entangled with their mental self-created Phantasmagoric fantasy "enemy(s)". Inside its Contingent Interchange mosaic Indifference/Hate/Evil/Sadism aspects engaging in Evil (the behavior deeds of one who Hates) schemes directed toward feigned and "Faceless" enemies. The other side of that coin is hating themselves and hating being in that dreadful hollow Abyss which positions them beneath where they declared their victim(s) to be. That position is one of profound *Envy* that is powered by the hater's own *Inferiority*. Behind that sense of inferiority and numerous and complex *Fears*—e.g. of being isolated in a Self-Unknown state—of not being able to live up to their claimed state of "superiority" of those they envy and of actually feeling like cowards--of not being the Legends of their designed Icon Image and of not being who admirers say one is—of never having enough of "Scarce Desirables"—of never experiencing Happiness—of always being wary of attack by those they constantly attack--and so forth.

Behind those layers of Fears is ones hatred of ones own "*Dark Side*" and behind that is an extremely repressed awareness of the "*ME/WE*" *Spiritual Elements* sense of Belonging bathed in Love one had at birth of which, at best, they are vaguely aware. Those who are aware realize something Evil caused them to "Switch" from "ME/WE" to the "Dark Side" and that "something" was so hated as to become a metaphorical "Raw Nerve." A mental *"Raw Nerve"* results from a "Big Bang" trauma and/or Cumulative Micro-Traumas. Whatever caused the cause of the "Switch," it *dismantled the strength of their philosophy of life—of their psychological safety, security, self-confidence, or stability—and of their ability to recover alone inside the jungle in which the drift*. European religious traditions conceive of Evil as a "super-being" existing outside of humans and capable of even rivaling God. The existence of Satan as the center of Evil is part of the teaching of both the Old and New Testament. Examples of how they say Evil is allowed to enter into the Selfhood of humans includes: (1) one loses a sense of ones belief in the presence of ones chosen Supernatural God; (2) the "fall of man" (i.e. Adam and Eve); (3) whatever causes harm or deprives a Being of some good which is proper to that Being; (4) self-imposed Evil from a refusal to think and an inability to be reasonable; and (5) based upon their varied definitions of "Virtue," many European religions relate the problem of Evil to a movement away from their specifically self-defined "Virtues," under influences of a demon/devil. That enables them to say, without cross-cultural Sages' agreement, that Evil is a defect in moral purity and truth--whether in "Heart" or life--whether of commission or omission. Hence, Europeans *assign blame to an outside force which, of course, allows people with poor moral development to shirk responsibility for their actions*. These creations of a Hell and its military general, the Devil, derive out of the Satanists' "disease of their souls". They are for the purpose of being competitors with God as well as to exhibit the power to control the "Troops" and the Victims' minds. Both supposed powers provide the Satanist leaders with whatever they crave, along with "sick" pleasures from making people suffer so as to serve as verification for their "little god" self-concept.

DEVIL/SATAN MINDSET EUROPEANS NUMINOUS: By Satanists leaders personifying their own self-image as a Supernatural God and as the Devil, first meant that enemies would view them as unbeatable and therefore have "Awe" when in the Umbra of that Contingent Being's power. European psychologists have said Satan's many consciousness forms include *Egotism* (with its self-opinionated and puffed up personality) and its opposite, *self-depreciation*. Second, the personified Devil--ruling a Contingent Place—a Place inside an Abyss (a bottomless gulf)—was a mind control tool for the "Troops". One reason was so that the "Troops"— to keep from being destroyed--would realize the necessity for following Orders from superior but Unseeable powers. Another reason was for the "Troops" to willingly fight enemies since to accept the enemy would be to embrace all of the "Cowardly" experiences of having a malignant intrusion into them from the outside world. All of this persists to this day and their ramifications throughout history continue to cause great destructions. The formulation of feigned enemies for the "Troops" to attack by claiming them to be the "enemy" (like "The Negro Problem") and them being the heroes and martyrs (like "The White Man's Burden") invariably create powerful and malicious mental images on the minds of the World Crowd. Such works because the unfairly advantaged "ethnic" group of Europeans—by the sole means of the GUN--has the power to advertise the faulty conclusions and unfair disadvantages for those who do not. To illustrate in general, according to Campbell (Thou Art p86): "the denotation (i.e. the reference in time and space)--as in the beginning of the World; a Garden of Eden, with a serpent that spoke to Adam and Eve and in that Garden an incident resembling a Fall occurred making necessary a Redemption to restore humans; a world Flood; a Tower of Babel; an Abraham; and Exodus from Egypt; and edition of the Ten Commandments entrusted physically to Moses on the top of Mt. Sinai, followed by a second edition delivered to him after he had broken up the tablets of the first; a particular Virgin Birth, the End of the World--when taken as the message of truth, allows the symbols to be used as devices to control the people in churches and temples." Practically every mythology in the world borrowed the African concept of the Virgin Birth to refer to a spiritual rather than an historical reality. The same, continues Campbell (Thou Art p7), applies to "the metaphor of the Promised Land, which in its denotation plots nothing but a piece of earthly geography to be taken by force. Hence, the connotation of these symbols--powered by the rich aura of the metaphor in which its spiritual significance may be detected--is ignored altogether. For example, the connotation (i.e. its real meaning) of the Promised Land is of a spiritual place in the heart that can only be entered by contemplation." The Resurrection symbolizes how Christ's presence could be experienced in the present (Ani p140).

What mattered was not literal seeing but spiritual vision. In other words, whether in constructive or destructive mythology accepted as religion, the imagery and the rituals through which that imagery is integrated into an individual's life are presented authoritatively through parents or religious evangelization. Then, the individual is expected to experience the meanings and the sentiments intended, based upon what he/she is told. Among Ancient Africans there were no intermediaries between the individual and God (i.e. not preacher or minister telling the people how to live) and great preparation was done to experience meanings on ones own. Such spiritual aspects were part of everyday life--in the home, in the fields--and therefore symbolic images were innumerable--some commonly accepted by all the people and some personally accepted. Yet, the foundational "Elementary Ideas" which have symbolic representation remain constant and therefore detectable. This is regardless of the properness or improperness of the metaphor or the rightness or wrongness of its interpretation used by anyone throughout the ages. The images associated with them point past all meanings given--beyond all definitions and relationships--to that ineffable mystery that is just the existence--the Being of humans and the Cosmos. To give that mystery an exact meaning is to diminish the experience of its real depth. The idea is *to step behind the facade created by words in order to explore every aspect of the "Elementary Ideas."*

DIALECTIC: African Tradition's Critical philosophy—a rigorous logical method using argument and logical analysis to clarify and critique existing concepts on the way to discovering the truth. Ancient African Sages originated and emphasized Logic, teaching under the name *Dialectic*, as the highest form of abstract thinking known to mankind. African Logic means a moral discipline used to purge away a human's irrational tendencies (James p28) so as to reveal *"Esoteric Knowledge"*—i.e. understanding the inner truth lying hidden within the core of fundamental beliefs about foundational Realities. One of the uses of Dialectic was to study the causes and cures of infirmities in the light of Reason and Logic. Millennia before Greece came into existence, African Sages had popular evening lectures for *Exoterics* (the audience). For students allowed to attend the more abstruse (difficult to understand) morning lectures, the Sages stood behind a curtain when lecturing. Students not permitted to see the face of the Sage were called Exoteric Disciples. But those permitted to enter under the veil to see the Sage's face, were the Esoteric Disciples. Their extra duty was to pursue whatever it took to have insights about the hidden and its subtleties pertaining to and life-shaping/life-changing things "which seem to defy understanding." Also, they had to learn to be aware of the mysterious things about God; the things belonging to God; and the things revealed by God to humans. See Opposites

DIALECTIC DIALOGUE IN AFRICAN TRADITION: African Dialectic is the art of logically analyzing ideas themselves and in relation to the Spiritual Elements. It specializes in examining presuppositions underlying ones Belief System so as to get to the Base upon which a Thought Structure is built—whether on the Spiritual Elements or something else. It points out the conditions which all definitions must satisfy whatever their subject; investigates the general laws on which Processes of Nature are determined and the kind and degree of necessity to which they can attain. Much of this information came from the scientists who gave Greece its scientific fame—the ones persecuted and had to flee from Greece to take refuge in Egypt. This was because the Greeks were opposed to fixed meaning or the universality of moral law For example, Anexagoras, Socrates, Aristotle, and Plato received their training in Egypt. Aristotle (384-322 BC) recognized Egyptian priests could reach such high levels in theoretical and speculative sciences by being freed from daily material worries as a result of the state supporting them (Diop, Great African Thinkers p82). Socrates, in Greece, used African Dialectic so effectively that it is now called the Socratic Method in the West. In Ancient Egyptian Mystery Schools (?12,500 BC), *Dialectic* Education (c12,500 BC) represents the highest form of Abstract/ Abstraction thinking known to mankind. The *platform* of Egyptian priest-teachers was that self-cultivation is not about *teaching* (to show) or *instructing* (to build). Instead, since self-cultivation relates to Education (drawing out ones inner powers) then the best way to do this would come by questioning in order to bring out knowledge the student already possesses. By "*Education*" is meant reasoning by a Question/Answer process for the purpose of "drawing out the Knowledge already in you"—called *"First Wisdom" or "First Knowledge"*. *"First Wisdom"* is Cosmic Organism understanding by ones Spiritual Emotions and thus without the use of Thought. "First Wisdom" *Dialectics* is based on the African *Theory of Anamnesis*--that children are born with knowledge already in their Souls. Hence, it is of a Gestalt nature—i.e. referring to a unified and synthesized whole of the Spiritual Elements' Essence. Since *Gestalt* is above the ability to be analyzed, an idea of it can be gained from the aphorism: "*the whole is greater than the sum of its parts.*" Dialectic's reasoning by a Question/Answer process was spotlight student's opinions through questioning so as to arrive at the first principles of Cosmic Truth to serve as the base onto which the knowledge of the most pertinent and conforming intelligible realities can be erected. Along the path of dealing with the right choice there must be: (1) definition of key terms; (2) the statement of propositions or definitive declarative statements about the subject; (3) examination of the facts by analytic discussion to determine Principles by means of Deductive and Inductive reasoning; (4) identification of possible contradictions; and (4) the application of ideas in the manner of a dialogue by an exchange of arguments for and against each point raised. Through such Q/A contradictions and opposites are brought out in an effort to form a new synthesis or arrive at reliable or definitive knowledge. Behind this approach was the belief that the human mind can be satisfied by nothing less than understanding the concept of the unchanging Subjective, Spiritual, and Objective Truth and realizing that learning is a process of recollection.

Therefore, the proper form of education designed for self-cultivation is to "Know Thyself."

Then, from "Knowing Thyself" one has a foundation that serves as a means of acquiring knowledge about the Cosmos based upon the Egyptian Tehuti's (?5500 BC) Principle of Correspondence: "As above, so below; as below, so above." It embodies the truth of there always being conformity between the laws and phenomena of the various existence planes of Being and Life. Thus, once one "Knows Thyself," that constitutes the "known" from which African Sages could infer (by Deductive and Inductive reasoning) much that would otherwise be unknowable in unknown and unseen realms. Then one would proceed to live by proceeding through the Tree of Life. The approach is based on the use of antithesis--the pairing of contradictions to display the necessity of choice between them. Within the right choice the aim is to locate and account for the essences of all things of the subject at hand; see the common inner nature of seemingly unrelated essences; manipulate, maneuver, and synthesize the inner meanings of those essence principles so as to connect diverse things into a unified whole. The *method* these Sages used in Dialectic Education was to proceed with questions designed to be relentless criticisms and counter-criticisms of a subject during which internal contradictions and inconsistencies have ample opportunities to be unveiled by critical thinking (see Socratic Method). Perhaps a generic process went like this: Phase I—Starting by professing ignorance of the subject matter, the Sage lured his students into a display of supposed knowledge by carefully forming a series of questions. Students answered these as best they could. Out of the programmed questions and their answers came a fuller understanding of the subject. Phase II--the questioner then redirected the student to use the "*Splitter-Lumper*" (i.e. Analysis/Synthesis) method in answering the same questions in order to arrive at a more satisfactory view. Phase III consisted of the comparison of Phase I and II answers so that the inadequacy of the student's former opinions was clear to the student. Phase IV--students were required to test their best conclusions against reality and troubleshoot for contradictions. Phase V--once this Dialectic skill was perfected, the student was urged to "mull" over inner information and contemplate on it until he/she could behold the Forms themselves and thus grasp the First Principle of all knowledge. Hence, students were led--step by step—to conclusions the priest-teacher had reached before the class began. At least, such a dialogue helped students develop alternative explanations for future difficulties—"I'm no dishonorable person but I am ignorant of what is the right and decent thing to do under all circumstances." This process was preparation for the student to figure out a path to mysticism.

Another Dialectic Approach was: Step I is for a student to be clear of the Purpose to "Know Thyself." Recalling ones innate dormant inner Knowledge gives insight into ones inner world as well as in ones outer world. Step II is to gather the essence of metaphysical (away from the physical) and physical things out of ones daily living and apply them to Spiritual Knowings. Step III is making inferences about the essence of Step II and directing that to "climbing the ladder of thought". Step IV is to arrive at Spiritual Elements Principles applicable to daily living. Step II requires a profound understanding of Opposites one encounters within oneself and in the world. The idea is to go below or underneath all conflicts and confusions involved in those encounters in order to discover Harmony. One can then realize that prior to these conflicts and confusions there was no problem. Thus, one can choose to return to this state. I recall the day of the birth of one of my children where a comparable situation arose. Up to that moment in my life I was burdened with heavy responsibilities related to my family--to my Orthopaedic Surgical, Orthopaedic Medicine, and Orthopaedic Genetics practice—to my physical therapy business—to my 34 employees—to my parents—and to a host of other things. Seeing my child being born was like a transformation beginning for me—a transformation completed once I left the delivery room and drove up the mountain. Then I got out of the car; looked down on the smog capping the city; and had a "That's it!" revelation—i.e. to simply "Rise Above" the entire association of all my problems. Thereafter I prioritized my problems and handled each thoroughly, from top to bottom, one at a time. Step III's climbing of the thought ladder can be illustrated by an *African Dialectic* (dialogue) model as follows: X: "I do not want to suffer." Y: "you suffer because you desire." X: "How do I stop desiring?"; Y: "Do you want to stop desiring? -- and if you do, you must stop desiring not to desire"; X: "the answer is yes and no --I want to stop desiring to desire"; Y: "suffering comes from desiring more than you are going to get (and that causes anguish); X: "if I do not desire to get more than I can get then I cannot desire to succeed"; Y: "do not desire to succeed more than you can succeed"; X: "but I want to succeed"; Y: "do not desire to get more than you can successfully get." Notice that at each step X is taken to a higher rung of the thought ladder by Y. Y gets X to start looking at the hard facts of life. Then X is shown his appetite for things of success are about his own emotions. Hence, by X bringing in his emotions into the situation of his desire not to suffer are actually part of the hard facts of the situation. [I learned early to always look at the part I play in any problem]. Y tells X to accept his emotions and all that is in the situation as they are--and put boundaries on them by not desiring to accept any more than X can get—and accept the fact that his emotions are part of the world which seemed to be in opposition—then realize his emotions are part of what X has been calling the opposite—the attacker. X can now see how he, by being part of the problem, is not opposed to the situation of the problem. Now there is no problem and X is merely a witness -- a passive observer -- a watcher of the one being watched (i.e. X watching himself). Step IV is *"Thinking in Principles"* so as to model Wholism. Extracting Principles (i.e. an un-changing reality mosaic aspect of the Spiritual Elements "Seed") applicable to ones life. That Principle enables one to engage in the thoughtful aspects of the African *Law of Holonomy* (the whole is inside the Seed; the whole is contained in each of the Seed's manifested parts; and the Seed is found throughout the whole). By being clear concerning each mosaic piece in the context with the "Seed", that can be used as a model to compare every single thing one thinks, feels, says, and does in ones life. From this information, one can decide if ones life is going in the proper direction. If not, this calls for a Re-Ordering or Re-placement of ones Philosophy of Life (POL). By thoroughly knowing the contents of the Seed one determines *"What a Thing is"--the essence of Discernment.* From this one can make insightful distinctions so as to enter the "Hidden" and/or to enter perplexing parts of an "Impossible" Problem as well as to plan ones life. A Life's Plan requires determining self-applicable Human Ideal Goals and then using the mosaic pieces of the Principle discovered about oneself to fashion a POL structure. From that POL position, ones Talent and Mission in life become obvious as a natural flow. Then a prioritized Plans A, B, and C is made to connect where one is with ones Mission. Thereafter, ones Life Living follows that course.

DIALECTIC DIALOGUE--AFRO-EUROPEAN SOCRATIC METHOD: After borrowing the Dialectic Concept from Africans, ancient Greeks used this old name for Logic or the art of Reasoning for arriving at valid conclusions (not the same as the Truth which was Africans intent) by discussion and debate. Socrates used it by Questions and Answers to obtain philosophic clarity. Plato, starting with the familiar objects of sense, progressed by dividing and defining to the hopeful grasping of the basic and universal Principles of Reality he had gathered from Africans. Aristotle's idea was to establish probable Syllogism conclusions from Premises not self-evidently true. Kant, Hegel, and other European made even more changes. Today, Europeans use Dialectic to teach rules and methods of Reasoning as well as a systematic analysis of ideas to develop what they imply at sight. A background of Proverbs—e.g. "The unexamined life is not worth living"--doctrines and assumptions drawn out of Ancient African Traditions drove the foreground of questioning Socrates used in his method. These include: (1) virtue is knowledge; (2) no one does wrong willingly; (3) no one can harm a good man (because only ones soul can be harmed and only by oneself); (4) it is worse to do wrong than to suffer it; (5) virtue is necessary and sufficient for happiness; and (6) all virtues are somehow a unity (because such virtues as courage, self-control, piety, justice are really manifestations of a single knowledge of "Good" (whatever will bring true happiness). He believed contrary or different views would be shown to be untenable by the elenchus (i.e. his process of cross-examination). By means of tireless examination of basic principles (by questioning rather than by investigation and reflection) one can make corrective value-judgments and thereby act rightly. Like African Tradition, he insisted that social problems be addressed within the context of moral education, (which I assume he meant by having the agreement of Sages in all cultures determining the Standards and guide-lines, as opposed to fellow Greeks). The idea behind the Socratic Method was to carefully figure out a system designed to penetrate into the interior and recesses of a thought or idea by precision questioning--questions designed to prompt reflection. In turn, reflection would produce knowledge—or at least awareness of ones own ignorance. By focusing on virtues one would nourish and strengthen ones soul—an individual's chief business in life in African Tradition. Socrates used questions and answers, as opposed to lectures, to bring light-- point by point--to truths concerning virtue, justice, piety. He readily admitted awareness of his own ignorance and was intent on getting similar admissions from people who failed to recognize their ignorance. His typical method in dialogues was to challenge the use of a word which led to a consideration of cases. Questions and Answers would finally allow for the detachment of appropriate universal definitions from these cases. Definitions were discredited if they could be reduced to absurdity or shown to be either vague or inconsistent. The process was: (1)--a statement of the question; (2)--the answer to the question; (3)--exploration of objections to the answer; (4)—revised answers which evade these objections; and (6)--exploring objections to the revised answers. Successful dialogues reached an end when the answer stood up against all known objections. This was in contrast to the Sophists who utilized ambiguities of ordinary language and believed it was better to do evil than to suffer it. Socrates disagreed with, and thought to be vain, Pythagoras' (C5 BC) statement: "Man is the measure of all things"—and not God—a concept which shaped the entire Western world. What Pythagoras, the founder of the Sophists, meant was that things exist by virtue of how man perceives them to be. Therefore, the objective world is measured against man—and there is nothing outside man that determines being or truth. Without saying he disagreed, Socrates steered his young interlocutor (student) into understanding why it is false. By the end, neither of them had determined the truth but at least they agreed that Pythagoras was wrong. The Western world took Pythagoras' statement to imply that "ones needs and desires determine what counts in this world"; that the truth is the private concern of each individual; no one really knows what is outside him/herself; there is no truth apart from ones private feelings about things; and everyone is always right and no one can ever be wrong. These latter two went on to cause Western men to believe that they were little gods. This is clear today in how judgmental Europeans are when in fact they are "out of their league."

DIALECTIC SOCRATIC IRONY: In the marketplace, streets, and public resorts of Athens Socrates spent the greater part of his mature life looking particularly for two types of people. One type was those sincerely desiring to learn (e.g. students on the rise for which he would use Socratic Induction). A second type was young men who "knew it all" (and wanted to silence "the old man") or any pompous person with fixed opinions about everything. The reason was that people who think they have all the answers are not likely to make much of a search for the truth about anything. Their big egos generate delusions that they already know the truth. To persuade these men to seek an awareness of their own ignorance, he used the Socratic Irony Method. The "irony" was that he simulated ignorance in knowing what he was doing to destroy their faulty thought structure. The word "Irony" comes from the Greek eiron, meaning someone who hides under a false appearance or conceals facts or feelings by using some kind of pretense. In a Greek comedy, a character named Eiron, who, through cleverness and deception, triumphed over the bull Alazon (who did not understand the trickery in Eiron's assertions). In other words, Irony is a process of causing the opposite of what something appears to mean or appears to be. Socratic Irony has destruction of delusions as its first task—to convince men of their lack of knowledge by leading on the opponent to hopefully put them on the path in search for truth. Because he was only seeking the truth, Socrates had no settled philosophical views of his own. By so saying, he could counter the arguments of the most distinguished enemy scholars. Pleading his own ignorance in order not to intimidate the arrogant, Socrates would ask the benefit of his hearer's wisdom who, in turn, was usually only too ready to display his superior knowledge and intelligence. Socrates deflected criticism while moving his intricate arguments forward in small increments. He showed the way while being a trickster, speaking out of both sides of his mouth. As the searching questions continued it became obvious that the victim was utterly unable to give any coherent account of the practical details or the moral notions he professed to know all about. Nor did victims know the basic principles or purposes of their respective professions or why they practiced them or what they expected to achieve by them. Gently, Socrates would pile question after question upon the victim's responses until the foundations of the victim's thinking collapsed or until every premise of their thought had been thoroughly examined. He liked to think of himself as a ray fish that stings its victims into deeper reflection. He never takes center stage to make a display of his wit and presents at all times a model of decorum and refinement. Sometimes this procedure for pointing out mistakes in thinking while pretending ignorance—i.e.

the Socratic Irony--succeeded in achieving its aim to clear away rubbish of flaws, errors, mistakes, prejudices, and biases and thereby bring the serious inquirer into truth. For those mature enough to experience humility he would quietly convert them from critics (from having their ideas reduced to absurdity) to students. Since no one felt the need to best him, for he seemingly offered no challenge and thus no threat, there was no scarring them off. To show they were mentally receptive, before starting to work on one, a shoemaker would learn what a shoe is (the foundation) and what it is for (its foundational base). More often, however, by Socrates shrewd questioning as his victim undertook to explain their point and answer questions it became obvious even to them that their explanations were full of error. In such instances, the revelation of their ignorance simply drove victims to distraction and ended with Socrates making new enemies.

DIALECTIC SOCRATIC INDUCTION: Induction is the gathering of a number of related facts and putting them under a general law or truth. Socratic Induction, more positive in its function than Socratic Irony, consists of building up the meaning of a concept. It starts with a question: "What is justice?" The examination of what is just and unjust and the ways people use both leads to an inductive conclusion. Instead of telling students what to think, the mere asking of questions about what students believe they know produces facts, which, when arranged or combined, create a paradigm shift that allows them to see the old in new ways so that troubleshooting leads to a correction of their own errors. In the process, one must always be willing to rethink and reargue any question anyone might raise. All that is needed is knowledge of how the words in question are used as "Definitions." For example, Socrates directed questions showing how particular events or things varied in some respects or passed away. Then, he led students to discover something about them that were the same—that never varied—that never passed away. When satisfactorily answered, the student had arrived at the *definition* or its essential nature. To illustrate, although beautiful things differ from each other, each share the common element of beauty. Hence, the mind has the power to discover in facts (e.g. beautiful flowers) the abiding elements that remain (the concept of beauty) after the facts disappear. Beauty remains after the gardenia fades. In talking philosophy with people on the streets and to reduce the chance of semantic misinterpretations he stayed with homely examples drawn from everyday life. A deceptively simple question was to ask a carpenter how to make a table. The idea was to start spotlighting the need of the artist or craftsman or professional to know the rules of his craft and the limitations of his materials. From a thing used in ones job on the way to assessing that job, Socrates would ask searching questions about ethical problems and old beliefs so as to develop the meaning of concepts and to bring out knowledge already in a craftsman's or a student's mind. From this information he continued cross-examination with carefully designed questions. Along the way he would impart knowledge or evoke knowledge the person did not realize he possessed. Hence, the person activated his own rational powers to arrive at knowledge that had been dimly present in his mind since birth—a process resembling the way a midwife only assists at the birth of a baby. Once pupils paid attention to detail and begin to doubt some of their old beliefs, Socrates would then lead them to discover what is right. Efforts were made to step over to demonstrating the same need of knowledge and skill in the leading of the good life. The interlocutor was pressed to say what he thinks is the correct account of virtue of the particular virtue involved. The proposed account, which thereafter became common property between them, was then scrutinized for consistency with other beliefs firmly accepted by Socrates and/or by the interlocutor. Did they accept as virtuous those acts or objects that this definition would imply to be such? Does the definition agree with other beliefs about virtue or the virtue in question that they also hold. How do these fit with what a shoemaker, carpenter, or horse trainer does? Such an analogy shows the kind of powers and dispositions possessed by the just man and those other practitioners. If some account of justice had the effect of denying such analogies that was a mark against it. If no definition survives the test and inconsistencies persist, the examination continues. This uncovers ignorance where it existed unnoticed. When there was no further cross-examination, the answer was accepted as genuine knowledge of the subject. "Human excellence is a state of mind."

DIALECTIC SOCRATIC METHOD DIALOGUE: Allegories (a story within a story) are an African trademark. In Socrates' "*The Allegory of the Cave*" (Plato's Republic), we find a summary of what has happened to struggling Black Americans since the start of African American slavery. This story, a fictional dialogue between Socrates (Plato's teacher) and Plato's brother Glaucon, begins with the scenario in which what people take to be real would in fact be a combination of an *Illusion* (misinterpretations), a Delusion (false beliefs that cannot be modified by facts), or an *Hallucination* (perceptions of what does not exist)—all of which can cause behaviors which are senseless, if not absurd to those in contact with reality. Socrates asks Glaucon to imagine a cave inhabited by prisoners who have been chained and held immobile since childhood. Not only are their arms and legs held in place, but their heads are also fixed, which compels them to gaze at a wall straight ahead. Behind the prisoners is an enormous fire, and between the fire and the prisoners is a raised walkway, along which puppets of various animals, plants, and other things are moved. The puppets cast shadows on the wall, and the prisoners watch these shadows. There are also echoes off the wall from the noise produced from the walkway. Socrates asks: "Isn't it reasonable that the prisoners would take the shadows to be real things and the echoes to be real sounds, not just reflections of reality, since they are all they had ever seen. Wouldn't they praise as clever whoever could best guess which shadow would come next, as someone who understood the nature of the world? And wouldn't the whole of their society depend on the shadows on the wall?" Socrates, introducing something new to this scenario, says: "Suppose that a prisoner is freed and permitted to stand up (Socrates does not specify how). If someone were to show him the things that had cast the shadows, he would not recognize them for what they were and could not name them. He would believe the shadows on the wall to be more real than what he sees. Suppose further," Socrates says, "that the man was compelled to look at the fire: wouldn't he be struck blind and try to turn his gaze back toward the shadows, as toward what he can see clearly and hold to be real?" Once Glaucon understands, Socrates continues: "What if someone forcibly dragged such a man upward, out of the cave. Wouldn't the man be angry at the one doing this to him? And if dragged all the way out into the sunlight, wouldn't he be distressed and unable to see even one of the things now said to be true, viz. the shadows on the wall." After some time on the surface, however, Socrates suggests "that the freed prisoner would acclimate. Would he now see more and more things around him, until he could look upon the sun? Would he not understand that the sun is the "source of the seasons and the years, and is the steward of all things in the visible place, and is in a certain way the cause of all those things he and his companions had been seeing?" Socrates next asks Glaucon to consider the condition of this man. "Wouldn't he remember his first home, what passed for wisdom there, and his fellow prisoners, and then consider himself happy, and they pitiable? And wouldn't he disdain whatever honors, praises, and prizes were awarded there to the ones who guessed best which shadows followed which? Moreover, if he were to return there, wouldn't he be rather bad at their game, no longer being accustomed to the darkness? Wouldn't it be said of him that he went up and came back with his eyes corrupted, and that it's not even worth trying to go up? And if they were somehow able to get their hands on and kill the man who attempts to release and lead up, wouldn't they kill him?" Ancient African Logic CT is a Question/Answer process whose aim is to "Educate" (lead out the information already in a student) by exploring Abstracts and Abstractions; locate and account for the essences of all things; see the common inner nature of seemingly unrelated essences; and manipulate, maneuver, and synthesize the inner meanings of those essence principles so as to connect diverse things into a unified whole. Besides realizing *there is always an undiscovered logical coherence among the parts of a problem*, its basic logical structure (discussed by T. Obenga, in Wiredu p41 and in Bailey, Word Stories Originated by Ancient Africans), and its underlying base, they used Logic. Logic provided the rules related to equalities, differences, and similarities designed to lead to solutions embraced by the Spiritual Elements. For example, the rules show how to arrive at correct conclusions about things as well as their relationships to each other and to the whole so as to form Principles (unchanging Realities). This African art of Dialectic was later perfected by Socrates who, if not an African (which I suspect), had an African Spiritual education. Today, part of African Logic is popularly known as the Socratic Method. See Logic; Opposites

DIALECTIC--"THE MIDDLE WAY" (TYPE II): To align ones life to be in the flow of the Divine Logos and engaging in it as a way of life, just before arriving at the end of the path is what Ancient Africans termed: "Opening of the Way"; "The Way;" the "Doctrine of Moderation"; the "Middle Path" and "the Middle Way". The objective is to harmonize ones mental activities. "The Way" concerns the following of Ma'at to the heaven "Afterlife"—based upon the idea that: "As we believe, so we act. As we act, so goes our destiny" (Amen I: 143). Before being able to get on to the road to Wisdom ones belief system must be refashioned to conform to the indwelling intelligence present with ones Real Self. That Belief System has been like a Cloud over their "Soul Sunshine," blocking ones ability to see reality, meaning they switch over to being guided by their Acquired Emotions. That False Self make ones life increasingly more difficult and one becomes more and more insecure, emotionally hypersensitive, and unhappy to the point of needing "Addicting Escapes." Such an identification requires the removing of wrong belief impediments rather than evolving into it. The "Way" is a symbol for ones beliefs and ideas as conduits of the course of ones life. Reestablishing ones Soul Sunshine with a lifestyle of The Truth is a living, ongoing experience that is above human's ability to put into words. Thus, it was symbolized by the concept's originators, the Ancient Egyptians (Ap-Uat of the Pyramid Text—Pyramid of Unas I. 187). The Up-uat is depicted in the form of a wolf, but Anubis and Up-uat are often confounded in funery scenes because of having some connection with the funereal world (Budge, Book of the Dead p 182). This process is removing barriers to ones Real Self. Ways of doing this have been discussed in my book on: Selfhood Mastery. See Middle Path

DIGNITY'S ANCIENT AFRICAN ORIGIN: The Ancient African word "Dignity" derives from the Star Digitaria or Po Tolo—a "heavy" white "Embryological" dwarf Sirius B. Said to be associated with "Spirit Travel," it turns on its own axis. Being unable to be seen by the naked eye, it was only detected in the West by telescope in 1862 (Bynum, Dark Light Consciousness p306). This Po Tolo star itself makes a complete revolution about Sirius A in one year, elliptically orbiting it every 50 years, and simultaneously affecting Sirius A. To the Woyo people of Equatorial Africa and being the true center of the Dogon system (Diop, Civilization p314), it represented a bed-rock that was changeless overtime--and thereby indicating a *fixed point of eternal order*. Thousands of years later, in C13, the Dogon, who trace their lineage to pre-dynastic Egypt, incorporated these findings into myths and rituals—both based on a *Spiritual Metaphor*. Metaphors are like slang, and slang is having an eye for resemblances between two different things--a feat of association. Example: "the star basketball player is on fire" (i.e. shooting extremely well). Note that to use this Slang means ones imaginative thinking of it is transformed into symbolic messages which disregard limitations and boundaries of human thought. Spiritual Metaphors in African Tradition are Supernatural tools used to discover alternate ways to convey the idea of the "what it is" of a Spiritual Thing. Here, Po Tolo, as one fixed Cosmic Entity, represented a manifestation of God's power. That "what it is" Spiritual Thing constitutes a *Mythical Truth* which thereby allows inferring the "what it does" of that Spiritual entity as well as the various "how it appears" forms of both. So, since that Mythical Truth commanded such recognition as a result of its magnificence, this corresponded to humans' Soul Essence and their Essentials displays as presented in certain African Creation Mythology stories--stories revealed by God to Ancient African Sages as actual realities of life. Hence, equated to a mental picture of the Kingdom of God present within each individual was "Digitaria" (Po Tolo). When an African *Metaphor speaks of gods or God, its symbolic atmosphere conveys entities actually within the Receivers touched by them*—a symbolic atmosphere Ancient Africans referred to as "*Dignity.*" To elaborate on these intricacies, African Sages said the *Amenta* is the realm of the God Amen which gives rise to the Cosmos, while simultaneously being the Mind of God inside the finite manifestation of Cosmic Consciousness. Thus positioned, God created two fundamental divisions within the Realm of Cosmic Being—the "*Submerged*" (i.e. imperceptible, the Subjective--the Cosmic Consciousness) and the *Perceptible* (the Objective Realm which contains objects). The Subjective Realm—called the Ocean of Nun--contains no objects; consists of a dual nature of Consciousness/Will and Spiritual Energy and Matter in un-manifested and undifferentiated states—but not disorganized; and gives rise to the Metaphysical and Objective Realms (Amen, Metu Neter I:52). This *entirely dark* Ocean of Nun—called the "*Divine Blackness*"--is the reigning Divine Cosmic Principle of all real Cosmic things in Unseen and Seen realms. In it are infinite varieties of Potential Expressive Possibilities for the world of Reality (i.e. the Material Planes). The apparent *Darkness is itself light*—dazzling and blinding in its splendor—like the splendid Digitaria (Po Tolo Star). Throughout African history, "Black" had nothing to do with color and everything to do with the Essence giving Divine "color" to Black cultures. And that is why Ancient Africans were always so proud to call themselves a "Black" People—"Black" being a symbol conveying entities in African people's Soul, Body (e.g. Melanin), and Mind (when it has been subjected to the Divine Spirit so as to command the Life-Force in harmony with the Laws of Nature). When Subjective Realm "Things" are expressed as objects, the Objective Realm is present. The Objective Realm's two main planes of existence are the *Noumenal* (the metaphysical spirits of things, thoughts, images, and actual spirits) and *Phenomenal* (physical energy/matter). Thus, as a result of *Involution*, the image of God is present in human beings—and with the same attributes of God. These impart within each human the symbolic atmosphere of God--the symbolic atmosphere called Dignity. For people's "Heads/Hearts," African's Biblical Spiritual Metaphors create meaning, facilitate understanding, stimulate insights, link disparate ideas, and design simplified versions of complex systems in something explaining some other like-kind thing—as with Dignity stories. jabaileymd.com

DIGNITY IN AFRICAN TRADITION: At least a thousand years before the Jewish concept of humans being made in the image of God (Genesis 1, 27), African Sages said the sanctity of life is the central pillar inside each human's Character. By ones Character being a psychophysiological faculty—like the "Halo" from the Divine Consciousness comprising the core of ones Soul--Ma'at living affects all of ones Selfhood. The concept of humans possessing the same quality Spark of God but lacking the same quantity was first recorded as being introduced by the African Kheti in the "Sebait of Kheti." Being for his son Meritkara during the First Intermediate Period (c. 4188—3448 BC), Kheti's comments not only provide the earliest known concept of humans as the images of God, but it also poses them as God's offspring (Karenga, Ma'at, p. 318). By humans viewed as bearers of *Dignity* and *Divinity*--both *characterizing what it means to be human*—implied Dignity pertains to all parts of an individual created by God. In other words, since God's inner nature is Unconditional Love and outer nature is Life--and since each human is made in the image of God, Dignity is established in each person, including the ungodly. The African Tradition conviction that a human's Dignity is a natural endowment by God is summarize in the African maxim: "All persons are children of God; no one is a child of the earth." Each human's unique way of showing Dignity are in the categories of Spiritual Respect, Selfless Service, Compassion, Devotion to God, as well as having good behaviors toward and good relationships with fellow good people. Regardless of how these display by a given human, they are African Tradition expressions of Caring for the Dignity and feelings of others, deriving from ones "Heart" and properly balanced for each situation by ones "Head." So important was this that African Tradition's Ankh, representing the "sap of life" (meaning milk), signifies ones own Dignity (the Substance of God) and Divinity--both at the core of ones Selfhood Greatness. As a result, Ancient Africans said: first, "*The most natural way to live is by what spontaneously flows from ones Soul* Divine Consciousness--i.e. Dignity (ones God image) and Divinity"; second, by being of incalculable magnitude and powered by unlimited potential power, Dignity is what provides the symbolic atmosphere to each human newborn's *Selfhood Greatness.* The most direct way to know God, said Ancient Egyptians, is to study God's natural manifestations (Ashby, Egyptian Yoga, p. 50). By so doing, any human remains in the flow of the Divine Laws of Ma'at. So, to stay in that flow of the Ultimate Standard of African Right Life Living is called living by Ma'at Principles. It fashions the Spiritual Elements into attributes by ones Pure Emotions and Pure Intellect. The resultant 'big picture' of "*Living Right*" means one is a "ME/WE" enhancer of the Cosmic Organism. The foundational point about Dignity and each and all of its associated Worth type of Values—e.g. those comprising Integrity—is its presence in every individual, making it *incapable of being diminished.* Yet, violent attacks on people's Dignity from the Ignorant, Foolish, Stupid, and Wicked lead to *Shame Experiences* from ones eye seeing oneself, like in a shattered mirror, as multiple images of inadequacy. To do what it takes to cause "Defeated people" to see beyond their Shame gives a new perception that enables them to realize their own Dignity. Then, these assaults will roll off them, as happens with water running off a duck's back. Otherwise, when there are human-made alterations put into what constitutes Dignity, or any of its aspects, people doubt whether they possess Dignity or not—and doubt causes many to go in all sorts of wrong directions. One dictionary defines Dignity as: "The quality or state of deserving esteem or respect"; "Esteem"—to regard with respect; "Respect," to esteem; "Regard," to observe closely; and "Deserve," to earn. A second only says what Dignity does: "to infer a high rank, title, or office, especially in the church"; Dignify: "give a high sounding name". A third gives attributes: "bearing, conduct, or speech indicative of self-respect or appreciation of the formality or gravity of an occasion; degree of excellence, either in estimation or order of nature." Note: none say what Dignity actually is. African Tradition says: *Dignity is an in-born inherent Worthiness*—a human's Divine Background for Self-Worth—a Self-Meaning healthy birth gift of Self-Esteem because it conveys an implicit awareness of being a vital part of the Circle of Cosmic Wholism.

DISABILITY: the sum of the Consequences—i.e. the Result

DISCERNMENT: (C14, separate by sifting; seeing apart, as in the distance or through obscurity) is making out something in hazy, confusing, or misleading presentations, as those that imitate the showing of variations of shade like a cloud. These are about what the C18 word "*Nuance*" (shade, subtlety) implies with respect to making divisions between subtle variations, as with shades of an emotional reaction. Discernment embraces delicate and precise distinctions of meanings; utilizing only razor sharp determined thoughts; and having great depth of refinement in Manners. These design the characteristics of a Thing in order to gain ideas about its processes, values, meanings, and implications concerning what the thing is, what it does, and how it appears. Wisdom specializes in perfecting these skills so as to continually think in terms of making world-class products. The objective is to pick apart the good from the bad—the perfect from the imperfect— and the subtle in the obvious. Of particular importance is to see nuances that enable distinguishing similarities in the dissimilar--seeing uniqueness in similarities--selecting the common out of the uncommon or the uncommon out of the common—all being aided by intuition (derived from ones Soul Spiritual Elements "Trademark")—each so that all ingredients may be fairly judged or valued separately and as a whole. *Discrimination* (judge apart) so as to distinguish differences is what allows for the arranging/rearranging and combining/recombining so as to mesh into harmony the seemingly unconnected but corresponding things into new forms.

This process includes separating ones Pre-birth Emotions from ones Acquired Emotions. It also includes having a purity of Emotions from what one really likes as opposed to liking something because that is what one is supposed to do. Practice exercises are from deliberately forming challenge situations that enable "Feeling" the specialness and the considerable differences in the Thoughts and Feelings present. An example, is "feeling" the difference between being "Aware" of something and something accepted being "Internalized." Key to discerning is the Right Brain which is oriented to Spirituality (especially the Temporal Lobe) and to the control of behavior accordingly by its Imagination, Feelings, and Emotions aspects. At its best, Right Brain's ability to follow the process of noting similarities between things below an appearance level; see their relation to each other; synthesize its aspects; and creatively design bridging gaps by harmoniously fitting the parts--regardless of how remote in time or space--by taking acrobatic leaps which successfully unify pertinent things into a whole. The Right Brain gathers from the subject or situation at hand its inner and outer similarities while the Left Brain gathers inner and outer differences of similar and dissimilar things and breaks them into pieces--the act of analysis. Each Brain serves as a filter on the contents of the other so as to approach the Essence of what the gathered contents are about in relation to the topic. One application is that the Rational Thinking Process requires special attention in order of priority so as to reach a conclusion. All are synthesized. By being the Image faculty, trained Right Brains pick up a clue of the barely visible and generate inferences within the context of the Law of Correspondence to complete the "big picture." For example, if the one clue is the corner of a table, from prior experiences one has a good idea that the highest percentages of tables have four legs. Thus, one has an impression of what the other three corners look like so as to arrive at the conclusion of the hazy object being a table.

DISCERNMENTS CLASSIFIED: Discernments Classified are as follows: *Type I* Discernment: *In Spiritual realms*, when one has a compatible rhythm, one is able to discern *the "what it is" of some Unrealized Reality* as well as to be able to see in Realized Realities the *invisible essences of Truths and Realities others are unable to see*—both representing a Thing's Beauty. *Type II* Discernment: *In the Metaphysical*, by thoroughly knowing the contents of the Seed, one determines *"What a Thing is"--the essence of Discernment.* From this, one can make insightful distinctions so as to enter the "Hidden" and/or to enter perplexing parts of an "Impossible" Problem. Discerned "Roots" share a *consistent, permanent, stationary, and unchanging patterns/elements that have sprung from the same "Seed" of the Spiritual Elements. Type III Physical Discernment.* Analysis reduces a "Thing" to other facts or breaks it into its component parts in a manner that penetrates the Obvious and the Hidden of the problem or situation at hand so as to discern its consistent underlying pattern. A Visionary sees *invisible essences others are unable to see as a result of discerning similarities in the dissimilar as well as uniqueness in similarities.* This paves the way for the Truth to be presented, like a landscape to the eye. To become skilled in Discernment requires learning how to focus or anything and automatically assess it by the Box Concept. One might start with knowing the full story of a word. As you know, I may go through 1000 books to get that story. This enables understanding the subsequent course and how to make predictions based upon such foresight and forethought. For example, what confusion does is to stir up so much disharmony, fear, and difficulty as to cause *Illusions, Hallucinations, and eventually Delusions which explains this or that behavior.* Discernment (C14, separate by sifting) is the distinguishing of differences in the confusing or in misleading presentations to determine the characteristics of a Thing in order to gain ideas about its processes, values, meanings, and implications concerning what the thing is, what it does, and how it presents. To do that requires using not only ones vision but also other Selfhood means--e.g. the other senses of the 12 Senses--color, sound, smell, taste, balance, motion, direction, heat, cold, weight, tactility, and pressure + Measures and Estimates + Correspondence by using the familiar pattern to explain the unfamiliar + snapshots of a natural sequence (part of a continuous or connected series)—in a manner that mosaic pieces are extracted from certain ones so as to arrange and/or combine them in a certain manner. This process assesses the Obvious (for what has been overlooked); the Hidden (the masked and concealed covers of Deceptions); and the Base/Foundation (the type and source of the "Genetics" of what is being assessed). Typically there are opposites, similarities, or differences which lead from the Obvious to the Base/Foundation. To makes these discoveries, what one looks for is *similarities in the dissimilar--uniqueness in similarities--the common in the uncommon--the uncommon in the common.* The more something is studied and understood, some of the following happen in ones Feeling and Cognitive Systems: (1) one is better able to disregard the limitations and boundaries of human thought in order to impart ideas of the indescribable; (2) by endowing ones mind and feelings with both a meaning and a sense of participation inside that meaning enables one to create a mental picture of what one believes to be the source and the nature of the thing in existence; (3) one then sees the skeletal essence of the Thing, as close to the way it came into being as possible; (4) that essence possesses the power to transform ones thinking about the hidden and mysterious into a clear and orderly picture of a thing's origin; (5) provide paths to fashion ideas concerning incomprehensible subjects. In Spiritual and Metaphysical realms, because of the Law of Correspondence, these effects on ones Feeling and Cognitive Systems spotlight the Base/Foundation so as to enter the Cosmic Esoteric. Once there, *Contemplation eventually reveals certain of the mysterious things about God; the things belonging to God; and the things revealed by God to humans.* As each barrier to the secret knowledge is removed, the better ones spiritual evolution and the sharper ones inner vision for seeing what already existed. Insights into these are transferrable into every human because each human contains a spark of God and all of God is within that drop. Notice in each human the disposition of that human's sunshine rays--where they go--and into what--and for what. However, if a human's aura is not about the Spiritual Elements, notice where their rays go--and into what--and for what. Whether a human's life is chaotic and off the Spiritual Elements' Track or organized and on it, behind the obvious and the Hidden is great simplicity of the Spiritual Elements. The response to such discernment is to deal with people where they are so as to "Be With" them or, if necessary, to go on Offense or Defense. But the application of any of these is not easy. Historically, Discernment was foundational for skills in meaningful engagement in the ancient terms for *Foresight* (detecting and preparing for what is likely to happen in the future) and *Forethought* (careful planning to acquire yet unrealized beneficial realities) -- also called "*Providence*" (planning, doing, preparing, and perhaps expending largely to meet the future demand) and "*Prudence*". *Discernment* would draw out worthwhile information not easily seen or even being out of sight--so as to see and mark essential things. The Subtle form of Discerning requires *Penetration* (looking through, seeing beyond the surface) and *Perceiving* -- i.e. understand meanings and implications -- by the sight, or some other sense, or by the intellect so as to see a thing for what it really is under confusing or misleading appearances. *Discretion* is wise and proper discernment as to conduct, responsibility, or judgment from using good assessments, caution, and self-control.

DISCERNMENT APPLICATIONS: To discern or do precision thinking, as in "splitting hairs," is vital to every aspect of Thinking, and particularly to nuances. Yet, there is no insightful definition better than to recognize as separate and different by penetrating mind so as to apprehend. Addressed here are the Implicit and Explicit. NUANCED & SUBTLITY DISCERNMENTS: What blocks answers to solvable problem includes being blind to the obvious, failing to uncover the hidden, or not locating the underlying harmony. Here, the Mental Problem Solving tools of the *"Seven Ds"*: (1) *Discernment*; (2) *Distinguishing*; (3) *Demarcation*; (4) *Differentiation*; (5) *Discrimination*; (6) *Difference*; and (7) *Distinction and used in conjunction with the "5Ps"*: *Penetration, Permeation, Perceiving, Perfusion,* and *Permeating* as follows. (A) *Penetration* (looking through, seeing beyond the surface) to have clear and complete vision so see through and through into all details, allowing nothing to escape observation by means of apprehension by using the 12 Senses--color, sound, smell, taste, balance, motion, direction, heat, cold, weight, tactility, and pressure; (B) uncovering the hidden is by seeing things as with ones Pure Emotions + Intellect which thereby enable one to get past the covering layer and engage in "Subtle" investigation—i.e. 'going underneath the obvious' to do *Exploration of the Disharmony*; (C) mental *Permeation* spreads over the Underlying flowing contents, searching in it for snapshots of a natural sequence (part of a continuous or connected series) that hints at where to search out and discover the problem's conflicts and underlying opposites. (D) When snapshots are located and *Penetrated* so as to see through and through into all details, the *"Seven Ds"* are applied as a means to enter the interior of the Underlying with the intent of detecting any foundational Harmony. To the end of to *Perceiving,* in the sense of understanding meanings and implications, the Problem's innermost recesses and "nooks and crannies" are scanned.

DISCERNMENT DIFFERENTIATIONS: *Discernment* (C14, separate by sifting) is ones quickness, keenness, and accuracy of seeing into what is an identifying Essence (the Thing's existence entry) by detecting any aspect of its *Properties* (what a thing has)—any *Endowments* (i.e. natural qualities) or any *Propensities* (inborn tendencies, e.g. a human's capacities, abilities, and language) which operate some process of an Entity's Selfhood—*any of the Essentials (i.e. its Character, Characteristics, Traits, and Features)—any of its Disposition* (with its "What" and "Why" Message)—any Activity networks' "what it does" to suggest its Pattern and thus the Source of the Essence. In spite of what is Discerned being hazy, confusing, or misleading, it is more prominently *Distinguished* by recognizing and separating its most available Characteristics (i.e. the most outstanding Primary Quality in what is Discerned) and/or traits. The Distinguishing may be by *Demarcation* (separating done by setting boundaries); by *Differentiation* (separation done between similar things based on quantitative assessments--i.e. things touchable or measurable); or by *Discrimination* (separating done based upon qualities--e.g. sound, smell). Now, *Pervasion* (Latin, walk through) thoroughly "goes through" to Discern *Differences*--either external or internal—in order to make *Distinctions* which lie in the Character of the Things themselves and yet display as a Characteristic, a Trait—i.e. Characterizing Behaviors, or a Feature (what best illuminates the Identity of the Essence. Feature *Distinctions* are always external, as initially illustrated by Ancient African bricklayers who carved their trademark in each brick they made. Intents to harmonize underlying differences or contrary opposites means one searches for whatever *Permeates* throughout what has been Penetrated in order to get through to the realm underlying the Hidden. At that point, one mentally engages in *Perfusion* (pouring over) and *Permeating* (spreading or flowing) through or over or under or around the barrier at the entrance of the Distinctions to filter the pertinent. This is like *Distillation*—the process of vaporizing, condensing, and separating the involved ingredients into distillate products. Examples of such distillates are discovering the common in the uncommon; the uncommon in the common; *Inner Similarities in things with* dissimilar appearances; discerns uniqueness in similarities; detects interrelationships between dissimilar and similar things; or discovers that they share the same "Genetics". These establishments of "Sameness" makes for Correspondence, in spite of their otherwise "Uniqueness" aspects. All of these can generate new meanings and increase ones knowledge so as to (e) enable one to determine the *Order and consistent Patterns underlying natural events* and arrive at the Problem's Harmonious answer. The *"Seven Ds"* assessments have ever increasingly fine Nuances and Subtlety for determining questions of: "how far down that 'beneath' goes in order to make necessary Discernments".

DISCERNMENTS--IMPLICIT: To Discern in the Spiritual Un-seeable requires first an instant access to ones innate Spiritual Elements' "Trademark" of Unconditional Love, Truth, Reality and the Natural "stamped" on ones Soul. Second, the Trademark's "Radar Beacon" must connect harmoniously with a corresponding Thing. After Ancient Africans discovered all God's creatures/creations contained Melanin and Carbon, they inferred their properties and activities represented *a total Cosmic Correspondence exhibition*. From such correspondences' "Truths," extracted Principles—i.e. *Circumstances*—paved ways to Implicit (aura-like) Discernments (seeing subtleties) into veiled Cosmic Correspondence Harmony workings. In *Reasoning by Analogy (known to unknown),* as no human has seen Gravity or physical forces cause Matter to variously vibrate to produce sound, light, heat, and cold, like-kind *Circumstanced Implicit patterns of Principles* infer the Unknowable God is the Ultimate Creator of all Cosmic manifestations (Amen, Nuk Au Neter p87). Such *Certainty Principles*, said Ancient Africans, are applicable on all planes of Cosmic existence. On the *Sublime* plane are nuanced Ma'at Attributes (like rays of the Sun) of Spiritual Worth--channels to the highest of human excellence. Examples: Goodness, Wellness, Natural Order, and Perfection are Cosmically "One"--meaning Indivisible, Coherent, Complete, Ordered, and Whole. Their "ME/WE" Consequences include features of Humanity—e.g. *Non-Aggression*--gentle, kind, compassionate, affectionate, caring, helpful, sociable, Selfless Service, and humor. To implicitly discern each, so as to "Be With" them as "One," enables seeing the significance of their Worth for its own sake and from it simply having come into Being—a significance of Implicit (atmospheric) Beauty since therein resides the infinite and the eternal. The "Being With" Implicit experience is known by one having a total inside-out sense of the "5Ss"—Safety, Security, Sureness, Strength, and Stability—an experience lasting as long as one bathes in the experience—an experience, when prolonged, becomes a state of Contentment—a state designed from living a Calm and Peaceful life. On *Metaphysical and Physical Thought planes*, all forms of thinking are Symbolic or Implicit processes since they deal with representations of Things. Those representations of referents give thought processes their fundamental character and worth. "ME/WE" Thoughts emanate out of the setting of the Thing's Implicit Beauty--a Beauty significant for its own sake—a significance from simply having come into Being out of the Spiritual Elements—a Beauty discerned by "Feel". In short, Worth inside a Material thing requires *the art of seeing, feeling, hearing, touching, or tasting invisible essences pertaining to the Spiritual Elements.* Because of the *Cosmic Law of Creativity:* "by itself, any given Spiritual Element reproduces itself to become the thing it makes, regardless of its new form," all "ME/WE" thoughts provide both an implicit grasp for regarding things in a certain Spiritual Elements Cosmic Organism way. It also ensures "*Totipotency*" from the basic mind state out of which these "ME/WE" thoughts arise. Totipotent Thoughts are *symbolic messages which disregard the limitations and boundaries of ordinary human thought in order to impart implicit ideas of the indescribable that touch the "Heart" or "Head".* Their Implicit milieu Sensations, like smells of forming gardenia flowers, is vague, hazy, unformed, but not disorganized. This gives ones mind an *Awareness* (knowing its existence) of what is contained or included, though not expressed, in the Sensation.

As "seeds" without restraints or limitations, and by lacking any specific organization pattern, Totipotent Thoughts allow ones mind to be influenced to develop in various "ME/WE" beneficial ways--ways depending upon which molding "Source" exerts the most influence. Hence, they are capable of birthing into an Entity existence any Attribute residing in the property of its Essence parent. Since an Attribute is like a Sun ray, a "ME/WE" fashioned Worth Implicit Attribute is a *Sentiment Aura* (a Worth thought wrapped in Pure Emotions). Because Toti-potency of Worth Implicit thoughts are in an "Aliveness," Creative, and an unmaterialized state, they can make unsuspected and novel connections, as noted in the progression of a dream. One can relate the Message to oneself; to the Sender; to "ME/WE"; or to others. Since humans have Free Wills, they can be led astray by biasing filters implicit in the process of forming impressions. An example is producing implicit bias as a kind of unconscious prejudice. jabaileymd.com

DISCERNMENTS--EXPLICIT: Discerning the Real/False in Seeable/Un-seeable realms is both Implicit/Explicit. Like a Star's Halo, *Implicit is the undertone or overtone (Aura, Atmosphere) of a Thing's Essence* ('what it is' appearing in existence). *Implicit* (implied and understood by inference and without being stated) *or Explicit* (defined and 'unfolded' into clarity) *Discernments* enable the Essence or Character "*Identity*" to be distinguished from like-kind others. Tools for Implicit differentiations are known by it being "Felt," by ones Soul Spiritual Elements "Trademark's" Radar Beacon or, as well-known by me, of ones Spiritual Entourage's "Helping Hands". "Tuned-in" Afrocentric People can know messages of our Ancient African Ancestor's

"Thought Clouds" via the Afrocentric Mystic Memory--an implicit Vibration conveyance vehicle. By contrast, *Explicit Discernment* of an External World Thing is the acquiring of sensory inputs that enable that Thing to be distinguished from like-kind others—a distinguishing via a Thing's Primary Quality—a Quality of a particular mark of differentiation out of what is confusing or has misleading appearances. An analogy is the trademarks made on bricks by Ancient African bricklayers. The sensory inputs come from perceptions or apprehending by sight, intellect, instinct, or the 12 special senses: color, sound, smell, taste, balance, motion, direction, heat, cold, weight, tactility, and pressure. Explicit or Implicit subtle Discernments are in play when only *Apprehensions* are possible—i.e. one grasping or taking hold of an Idea, as through the senses, the mind, or the instinct—without full understanding or appreciation of any other of that Idea's aspects. While entering a human's senses, Discernments originate out of the ingredients of Sensations--whether from the outside world, out of ones memory, from "happenings" inside ones Selfhood, from ones interpretations of the monitored feedback one gets from outside influences, or from a combination. The acquiring of disorganized sensory inputs from Sensation are the "raw materials" in Discerning an External World Thing. The sensory inputs entering the mind's "committee" are organized into a *Stage I* form--a *Percept*. That Percept has a *Disposition* with a message intended to be brought into ones mind from its Source. Ones Imagination then gathers all incoming pertinent image items + qualities of sense perception + what it generates out of 'raw' materials + like-kind entities given in prior sense perceptions. They are arranged into an Icon Image conforming to the Receiver's interpretation—and that may/may not be what was intended. That new mental entity of organized Sensations constitutes a "Thing" when it comes into a mind's Being-hood so as to make ones mind aware of the nature of those sensations as something good or bad. *Creating an atmosphere of beauty and other forms of Worth* is Good to *woo children into Implicit and Explicit learning*. A "bad" Percept is like a threat, disturbance in harmony, or atmosphere of danger. *Stage II,* the Percept evolves into a beginning *Conceptual state*—a maturing Identity. It is heralded by the *Implicitness* (understood though not directly expressed) of the vague, hazy, organized Percept's Sensations. Ether added to Sensations begins molding ones mind into a sort of better awareness of what is contained or included, though not expressed, in the Sensation of the Percept—and that enhances Identity. However, the Implicit ("That it is" identity) is capable of being implied by inference and without being stated. Since Form I Percept is that of Primary Qualities, the Being of those "That's"--while in a "Glob" and Un-seeable state of activity--also includes the 'what it is doing'. Stage III is added Ether advancing the Implicit into a *Notion* –a recognizable "what it is"--an "*Entity*" with a specific nature hinting at the "Thing's" Seeable Identity and its specific attributes. Stage IV is more added Ether evolving into an "*Idea*" bud having: 1) awareness of specifics--e.g. properties, characteristics, traits, features; 2) an Explicit (clear, emphatic) "*Identity*" concept; and 3) forces shaped into a defined "Thing"—a shape imparting power to a patterned quantity of "frozen" energy. Stage V--a matured Idea is the formation of a "*Unit*" called a Concept. A *Concept* describes phenomenon (i.e. a phantom; to 'make visible'; a Contingent Being) lacking life and lacking reality. At this Entity's core is a Disposition of a '*payload' message* of the Conceptual *Essence's shared properties,* an *Inclination,* a *Temperament,* and an Attitude. Discernment's dull to sharp degrees are an awareness of Stage IV, then III, then II, then headed toward Stage I.

DISCRETION: wise and proper discernment as to conduct, responsibility, or judgment from using good assessments, caution, and self-control. Prudent Mentors give the same weight to the Mentees' past and future pains and pleasures as they give to their present ones for learning and planning purposes. See Discernment

DISCRETIZATION: Ancient African concept for *disjoining where things are coupled* so as to slow, stop, reverse disharmony; to prevent interferences to Harmony; to defend Harmony; and to create, enhance, and maintain Harmony. See Dissociation

DISGRACE: Although the popular sense of the synonyms Disgrace, Ashame, Shame, and Guilt in Old English (450-1066) shared the core of "shy" and "Bashful" as a state of mind pertaining to needless failure causing disappointment and humiliation, its religious core of provoking abomination (loathing, disgust) was applied to people who violated European church doctrine. Added to this, if there was a design to deceive, the label of Shame was a Self-Esteem attack. See Shame

DISHONORABLE: Ancient African introduced the formal concepts of "Dishonorable" (the opposite of the honorable) in the mythological story of the god Set. Dishonorable people are characterized by those who commit crimes of omissions (failing to do the right and descent thing) or commissions (doing things against the honorable). The latter includes crimes against property (e.g. "white collar" crimes); society; people; animals; or things. However, the determination of what is and what is not dishonorable is often hazy and controversial because of how they are defined, who defines them, what was done, and who interprets what was done and the intention behind it.Every wise youth in the Life Planning process needs to determine "How much is Enough?" of material things required for ones life. But what most fail to factor in is the rampant dishonorableness--perhaps as high as 95%--one will encounter. There is no exempt field. Honorableness (the absence of lying, cheating, and stealing) requires such personal self-discipline dishonorableness--lying, cheating, stealing--so as to unfairly acquire things and/or to unfairly gain power over others by means of intimidation and mind control. In this sense mind control is the takeover of one's systm of values through such means as propaganda, brainwashing, censorship, and advertisements. Because historically Black People in general are an honorable people, it would be difficult for them to believe the efforts a people go through to be dishonorable. Nor could they believe the skills taught to devise cheap tricks to fool the people have been (and are) no different than the teaching of Art, Music, or any other school course. For Black People to understand this pattern used by Greek Sophists (professional teachers for only those who could afford to pay) would help reduce the frequency and magnitude of being deceived by supposedly "play-fair" people. To illustrate, the ancient Greek Heraclitus said conflict, not harmony, was the true and proper state for maintaining Good—"strife is justice—and war is the father of all" (Asante, Egyptian Philosophies p41). He taught the use of political cunning, intrigue, and dishonorable acts. These concepts have been amply supported by countless European leaders (e.g. Machiavelli).

DISRESPECT: "the eating of ones self-esteem"

DISSOCIATION: The 1623 word "Dissociate" means to separate from companionship. European psychology says it is a pathological (e.g. insane) disconnect between various mental elements—Type I. Enslaved Black People's Dissociation was a disconnection of the most painful portion of their consciousness, with its memories of important personal events, from the remainder of their Selfhood and self-identity—Type II. This coping mechanism's purpose was for its resultant "*Excluded Self*" (the part related to the outside world and containing much of the Spiritual pain, emotional pain, rage, fear, and depression) to be disconnected and repressed from the "*Included Selfhood*" (the afflicted person's remaining Selfhood) for dealing with the horrors of daily living—Type III. Ongoing racism and the hostile conditions it imposes on Black People characterizes this type of "Dissociation" as a "normal variant". See *Discretization*

DIVIDE AND CONQUER: "*Divide and Conquer*"—to generate ignorant Crowds who shun thinking for themselves and who "go along to get along." This is what generates the essence of *Racism*—a competitive relationship between those in power who are focused on providing unfair advantages for themselves and unfair disadvantage for their scapegoat opponents.

DIVINATION: an Inductive method for obtaining knowledge of the unknown

DIVINE LOGOS: God's Universal Reason—Thought and Creative Utterance and Power. Divine Logos stands for itself contents--for its creatures and creation offspring throughout the Cosmos—and for designating the hidden aspects of how the work of the Cosmic Spiritual Force, Sekhem, is bound into Cosmic Correspondence Harmony.

DO: Old English "DO" (place, put) "to make" or "make ready" and later "to work" in the sense of labor—any work done by hand. In Medicine, this implied action with instruments upon the body—as in performing a surgical operation. This was expanded to include a series of coordinated individual and group acts that are part of a job routine; then the performance of mental or physical tasks in an orderly manner. Philosophically, the "Do" in the context of an operation came to mean a controlling agent, force, or principle making something and determining chiefly or wholly its constitution, development, well-being. For example, the Creative Cosmic Intelligence formed a set of principles for the regulation of the universe, as observed in its operations. In short, the *"What it Does" is the proper acts or operations of the substance or essence of a Thing when it came into Being—i.e. the Character of its "Nature".*

DONKEY STICK CONCEPT: *Donkey Stick Concept* is about a stick holding a carrot in front of his face to give the false hope of reaching the carrot with the next step. That donkey could walk himself to death and never reach the carrot.

DOUBLE CONSCIOUSNESS: The sense of being two people—one, the Self they know; the other, the Self they are told by others is the real one

"DOUBLES" OR "SHADOWS"--AFRICAN ESSENCES/ESSENTIAL: Concepts of a "Double" or "Shadow" in African Tradition are based upon Correspondence—in a sense of metaphorical African Macrocosm (Greek, 'world order') type concepts as being the Essence (e.g. the Amenta) and its Essentials (e.g. the Cosmos); in the *"Star/Halo" Concept* whereby the Star represents God's Essence and the Halo, the Star's Essentials; the human and animal Spiritual Essence and their "Shadow," called an Astral Body or Astral "Double"; the Cosmic Mind Substance inside the Human Mind's Divine Essence compared to the Astral Soul or Manas—the Essential "mind" faculty which make humans intelligent and moral beings; and Cosmic luminescence as the Cosmic Essence of God displayed as Essentials in the form of an Astral Light—the Essence's subtle aura visible (around humans and the globe); the artwork of the Ancient African Bible whereby the sun god Ra (Re), an Essence reflection of the Cosmic "Light," is shown as an Essential—i.e. a circle of light--a Halo signifying *Glory*, the radiant beauty of splendor and magnificence. The innate "What it is" of oneself, of life living, and the Cosmos that "Underlie" "how things appear" and "what things do"—i.e. the Knowledge of the Thing--reveals its unique Form in its plane of Metaphysics. An example of Entities in the Metaphysical and Physical planes of existence in the Foreground, using space as its Material Background means that Idea-Forms able to be seen in the Foreground because they use space as its Material Background. Yet, the Idea-Forms are Essentials for their Essences in the Unseen Background, just as the Immaterial is the Essence for the Seeable Material Background. Thus, the Divine Essence or Reality of humans is the Divine Consciousness (called by some the Infinite Spirit) meaning ones "Self" (i.e. ones Spark of God) in the Thought-Forms of their Souls. This Divine Essence (i.e. the Real "Self") is never born, never changes, and never dies—for it is "One" with Sekhem. All else of a human—i.e. the manifestations of Essentials--is what some call *"Personality"*—which changes and ceases to be. A human's Divine Essence, being composed of the Spiritual Elements, is like an Archetype—i.e. Seed resembling a box-in-a-box-inside-a-box containing contents of Prototypes. This means by its ever arranging/rearranging and combining/recombining its ingredients, it is endlessly Creative. Examples are each Prototype subdividing into endless sub-Classes and each sub-Classes has sub-sub-Classes. Yet, each of these has Essentials. It implies that African Tradition is built on the innate "What it is" of oneself, life living, and the Cosmos which always "Underlie" "how things appear" and "what things do". "Underlying" contents consist of Nature's infinite *Foundation of Unified complexity and multiplicity Patterns. These rest on the Ultimate* *of all Cosmic Orders—the Spiritual Elements of Unconditional Love, Truth, Reality, and the Natural—all Orderly orchestrated by the boundless Force, called Sekhem by Ancient Africans.* The detection, assessments of what is detected, and the disposition is done by the human tools of the Instincts, Common Sense, Creativity, Reasoning, Knowledge, Logic, and Wisdom. These faculties can naturally develop from ones inborn Pure Emotions and Pure Intellect, provided one does not exercise volition to do otherwise. Throughout any of these processes, vital to Thought Harmony inside Creative explorations of the Infinite "Underlyings" is *Critical Thinking— serving like* a protective, defending, and guiding "seeing eye" dog. These processes express ones innate *Selfhood Greatness*--derived from possessing a Spark of God + the supreme Ancient African "Genetics" + a "Unique" Talent to be a bridge to ones Mission in life. Proper use of these thinking faculties, while staying within Nature's Processes, makes one a "Non-Self" individual--meaning: "because we are, therefore I am"—and thus oriented to producing "ME/WE" benefits. Also addressed are Healing for and Protective Measures against the European mindsets and methods used to generate a massive Maafa (immeasurable catastrophes) on Black People. To summarize, the Substance of a Real Thing is from the Reality of God—likened to the "Lucky Star"- -and the Essentials are its Halo. "Substance" is the word that applies to the Spiritual Elements, whether from God's androgynic protoplast (out of the True Reality) or its display in Cosmos (a copy of the True Reality) as Essences. Substance is not about Primary Qualities, as are all Essentials are Primary Qualities. These Process Patterns are profound for Critical Thinking.

"DOUBLE" or "SHADOW" METAPHYSICAL SELF-IDENTITY: Whereas the Divine Consciousness is ones "Self-Identity" in Spiritual Realms, its Astral "Double" or "Shadow" counterpart is ones Intangible Metaphysical entity called a human's Character. During the Divine Consciousness Involution/Evolution process--the "bull's eye" process of a human's Selfhood--a *Metaphysical Identity* is added in a manner like the periphery around the bull's eye. It is like an "Idea-Form"—the Idea being the Spiritual and the Form being the Metaphysical. So, the Soul "Idea's" Form is called an *"Astral Soul"* or *Manas*—the "mind"--the mental faculty which makes humans intelligent in the Material World and its *Metaphysical Character*, moral beings. That Character, regardless of its Real Self or False nature, emits from its Essence a subtle aura—called an *Astral Light*—which is visible (around humans and the globe) only to clairvoyants. Nevertheless, to that Metaphysical portion of ones *"Being,"* the Divine Spirit, which activates Matter inside the Sublime, does so by what Ancient Africans called the *Ka*—i.e. the vital energy which is the former of an *"Ethereal Double"*. Thereafter in heading toward the Earth World, layer after layer of "Ether" (flimsy Matter) is placed on the Metaphysical Identity as the entire human evolves its *Propensities* (in-born tendencies, e.g. ones capacities, abilities, and language). So, for a human being, there is a Spiritual "what it is"—i.e. the Self—as well as a Metaphysical "what it is"—an Identity that serves as a "Double". Combined, both of these "what it is" means a human's Spiritual and Material reality upon coming into existence and represents the system of values and character behind Propensities—which are the Endowments empowering them. Whereas the Spiritual "Self" is a human's Divine Consciousness, the Metaphysical Astral "Double" represents a *Secular Sensory Consciousness* on one side and a *Secular Sensory Awareness* on the other side. Both sides of this Astral "Double" Coin will serve as a human newborn's Earth World Selfhood Foreground for interfacing with activities of daily living. These Metaphysical Primary Quality *Astral Attributes* of the Spiritual form of "Who one is" *do not exist independently of the "Self"*. Instead, they are orchestrated by the Self in Real Self humans or by the Ego in False Self humans. Either way, it carries an impactful 'payload' activating something good or bad in the "Heart" and/or "Head" of one possessing it as well as in the "Heart" and/or "Head" of the people or creatures touched by it.

E

ECLECTIC SUPERNATURAL RELIGIONS: The 1683 word *"Eclectic"* ('picking and choosing') referred to a group of ancient Greek philosophers. Though unattached to a particular school, they selected doctrines from every system of Thought. Their *Supernatural Realm--meaning what human's make up to put in it--*lends itself to selecting and using what seems best from various sources--but not following any definite pattern. And those sources, for European Religions, tend to be self-created or gross/wrong modifications of African borrowings. The story begins in 45,000 BC when Europeans, born into the harsh Ice Age, embraced a "here and now" focus in struggling for survival--with no concern for the future. They created Gods/Goddesses whose names in the original Indo-European languages include such Supernatural myth types as: 'The God of Thunder' (Scandinavian Thor, Celt Taranis, Slav Perun, Balt Perkunas)--represented as a man standing on a chariot, his weapons being lightning and an axe or a hammer, and his assistant is a wolf. *Atheism--*the type having no concept of a Spiritual God--characterized primitive and ancient European religions. People possessing hateful thoughts and demonstrating evil deeds were deemed to be possessed by demonic spirits, including the Devil. Satan appears C6 BC in the OT as an individual angel, subordinate to God. Thereafter, he gradually becomes the source of all evil. Followers, *disbelievers in God*, acknowledged no law/power except of evil men called Satanists. But how evil got into the world--a world which God created and saw as 'very good"--is not solved by their ideas about Satan. This changed when they borrowed the Adam and Eve metaphor from the Ancient African Bible, converted it to a Supernatural "Fact" so as to portray Satan as an angel + made up and described Hell + selected which factors are to determine 'right' faith/beliefs. In fashioning concepts of "Earth Beauty," the ancient Greeks confirmed they "borrowed" their gods/goddesses from Africans and then designed them to the highly Supernatural abstract and unreal nature taste of the Greek people. Greek philosophers like Plato (427?-347 BC) and Aristotle (384-322 BC) referred to gods as symbolizing special man-made ideals (unrealizable) for humans: the Greek Apollo (renamed from the African god Heru) symbolizes ideal Beauty; Athena (Isis in Africa), of ideal Wisdom; and Zeus (Amun in Africa) of ideal Power. Romans "borrowed" gods/goddesses from the Greeks directly and from Africans indirectly. The Roman's Venus (Beauty goddess) and Aphrodite in Greece was borrowed from Africa as a Ma'at and Isis composite, representing the Mother of all gods/goddesses. Isis and all images of her with the Infant, Horus, was worshipped in Italy (e.g. Genoa, Pisa, Padua) many centuries before the Christian era. Notre Dame in Paris was built on the remains of a Temple of Isis and *Paris' original name was Para Isidos, the Grove of Isis.* Cults of Isis continued worldwide when other gods/goddesses of antiquity had long been forgotten. Europeans' four Apocryphal gospels of *Matthew, Mark, Luke, and John (esoteric teachings of 125 AD) shunned the Jewish God and selected Jesus Christ instead. They, being the only sources of Jesus' life and teachings,* interpreted his supposed words through their own sociocultural and contextual circumstances. After completely disconnecting from the Ancient African Bible, modification Bibles were made to conform to Catholics' desires. Then, in C10 AD the European Bible arose from the Catholic Church. Meanwhile, passages put in them advocated justifications for such anti-loving aspects of living as slavery and sexism. The next Supernatural theories were on Ceramic Cosmic Creation (Potter God); Atheists, denying God's existence; Cosmic Mechanical Artifacts (C19) run by blind energy gyrations; and those (e.g. Nietzsche C19) saying "God is dead!" *Agnostics* believed the Supernatural and/or the Spiritual home of God is unknowable, making it impossible to prove its existence or nonexistence. Still others remain confused. During this process, ancient Europeans' made up concepts characterized the Supernatural as the home of Spiritual Beings (e.g. angels, demons, fairies, and dead ancestors); of "Super-humans"; of heaven; of hell for sinners; and where God dwells, making it easy to say what God says and looks like. Their Supernatural views--based on their faith, revelations (?), and the authority of Scripture they wrote--take the place of reason or proof. Be clear: *African and European "Supernatural" are not the same.* jabaileymd.com

EDUCATION: "*Education*" ("to lead out what is inside"); "*Teaching*" ("to show" so as to impart knowledge for learning); *Instructing* ("to build in or into"), or "*Training*" (active mind exercising in order to form habits)—in short, by study, reflection, and/or practice--depending upon the topic.

EFFECTIVE: "that which works"

EFFICIENT: "doing it quickly"

EGO: Narrowed focus of ones Consciousness to ones own Selfhood

"EITHER/OR" = "ALL-OR-NONE": Being born with pre-birth Emotions means one has a pure state of "Common Sense" (because everybody is born with all the Knowledge they need to have a thriving and "Good Life"). Naturally following in 5 to 12 year olds is intellect skills intended to elaborate on ones "Common Sense". However, when children are socialized to merely add acquired Emotions onto pre-birth Emotions instead of following the natural course of cultivating their Intellect, they then become Emotional People (EPs). The nature of that socialization is to have either an Inferiority Complex or a Superiority Complex—both meaning ones Real Self has been replaced by a False Self. After that, the game of life proceeds somewhat like *Billiards* ('playing stick' or 'cue') with its white cue ball and 15 colored balls racked in a triangle, with the 1-ball on the foot spot (the lead ball). The one pocketing the first 8 balls wins. That False Self then invites a "pool shark" (i.e. Rational thinkers) to play as an opponent—a "no contest." The "pool shark" goes first, making the break shot and causing the cue ball to strike and pocket the lead ball (i.e. EPs' Common Sense + Rational, Critical, and Creative Thinking). Hence, EPs are left with "Broad-Stroke Thinking" pool sticks to play the "SEEMS Right" and "Almost Right" balls that do not really fit into the side pockets. The reason it is such a struggle to pocket any of the other balls of the False Self is because Options, Accuracy, and Precision were lost when the Intellect ball was pocketed. As a result, EPs only have "Either/Or" and "All-or-None" assessments to work with and thus need to depend on others for ongoing help. A personal benefit of racism was that it forced me to become an "*Isolated Individualist*"—meaning there was no choice but to follow a path away from the crowd—a path filled with "alligators" constantly having to be handled—and becoming self-reliant and ever thoughtful and without taking short-cuts.

Thus, I did not jump on the train going through the External World (and headed over a cliff), as does "the crowd". Instead, I *thought about every little detail of everything* I did to devise "new ways" for almost every significant aspect of my life. By such being strange to "the crowd" means they pass judgment on things I do—and never asking me "Why did you do it that way?" Thus, much of my time with people is explaining what I did and why, in hopes of avoiding their invariably negative judgments. This is because "the Crowd" has problems with (and envies) people who do not do things they like or do things their way. By contrast, Thinkers appreciate those differences and learn from them. EPs typically consider things as "normal/abnormal"; "true/false"; "either this or that"; and "All-or-None." But much ranges between each pair--and such recognitions expand ones Options or insights. Those insights are useful for understanding complex things; for why people do "weird" things; for serious business decision making and/or problem solving to do or to not do something; for creativity; for Fun. EPs lack of intellect development makes them Incompetent, Inconsistent, Ill-Mannered, focused on being "Excited," and "Don't Care" about anything but the "ME" side of the "ME/WE" coin.

Much of this is due to getting away from Spiritual Values and knowledge and believing invention of names, slogans, concepts, and stereotypes that allow Lower Self people to gratify and cater to their animal spirits—regardless of the price they pay to their own and others' well-being. By thus expanding with "the Crowds'" "Either/Or" and "All-or-None" assessments focus in the Secular World and its Material (unstable) things of Value, means they are about *believing in nothing in particular*. What is substituted is "*Flexible Morals*," which do not work for those who know/live by laws of the one Universal High God's laws, called *Amen* in African Tradition. Divine Standards, relied on by Real Self people, are based upon things of Worth (i.e. Love experiences; things money cannot buy, like peace, harmony, and unity). Their absence of degrees, in contrast to the Secular, makes them solid & "all-or-none." Its Spiritual Elements standards are what everything in the universe is judged against. Yet, on Material planes are found wide ranges between "All" or "None" (e.g. the shades of grey between "black and white"). See Reciprocity

ELECTROMAGNETIC SPECTURUM: An analogy is the relatively small Seeable spectrum portion is like the part connecting both sides of a coin, say Arkansas in the USA. On the side heading westward from Arkansas toward the Pacific Ocean are subdivisions of infrared waves, microwaves, and, on the west coast, radio waves. On the side heading eastward from Arkansas to the Atlantic Ocean are ultraviolet rays, x-rays, gamma rays, and, on the east coast, cosmic rays. Yet, it is conceivable that undiscovered waves and rays could extend around the world.

EMANATION: a process guided by the Cosmic Mind's Intelligence under an immutable (unchanging) Law. Humans' Souls, as being a Spark of God, was likening this Emanation to a fire of God's flame being imparted to and caught up by each human's Soul as a trail of inflammable substance.

EMBARRASS: Although the popular sense of the synonyms Disgrace, Ashamed, Shame, and Guilt in Old English (450-1066) shared the core of "shy" and "Bashful" as a state of mind pertaining to needless failure causing disappointment and humiliation, its religious core of provoking abomination (loathing, disgust) was applied to people who violated European church doctrine. Added to this, if there was a design to deceive, the label of Shame was a Self-Esteem attack. By C17, such exposure was also for the purpose of covering "the sinner" in a cloud of shame with the intent to harm ones reputation. Thereafter, Shame went in the direction of having bad feelings about violating rules of decency. By the end of the European Middle Ages, when individualism and materialism were rising into prominence, the traditional vices became more desirable and respectable. As a result, Shame and Guilt not only separated in meaning but were less of a problem, thanks to the flexibility had been put into European morals. Also in C17, the original meaning of Embarrass ("put to shame"; to put behind bars; impede) was separated to signify ones reaction from one doing dishonorable acts.

EMERGENTISM: the combination of elements--results in something new that was unpredictable from knowledge of those elements

EMOTIONAL GLOB: Fear, Fright, Dismay, Consternation, Dread, "Awe," Fascination

EMOTIONS (PRE-BIRTH): (Spiritual Non-Rational or Congenital) Metaphysically irrational and illogical thinking, based on "Feelings" (intuiting). It is identified with being with life—i.e. the vital force and is the most direct experience of oneself in the form of 'Affect." The resultant tone and spirit of unity is like what the baby has for its mother before the ability to make distinctions is acquired.

EMOTIONS--PRE-BIRTH: The formation of an Interchange features a human's pre-birth Emotions being directly connected with Cosmic Knowledge. A way to sharpen ones thinking and creative skills is by perfecting ones Pre-Birth Emotions by means of practicing Predictions. For example, I often spend idle time in a car by predicting what drivers in front are going to do. Whatever helps improve predictions or gain insight into "Impossible" problems sharpen faculties in ones Brain/Mind that are extremely subtle in letting their owner know they are there. I suspect that these areas lie in the Interchange located in the small overlap space between ones Selfhood Center and the Cosmic Organisms' realm. That *interlocking of components* is what I call a human's Spiritual Emotions overlapping with its parent source. Thus, the Interchange is a "*Common Ground*"--a Zero complementary equal Relationship Point where like-kind things are mutually shared and exchanged to form a Mosaic. "Seeds" within that Mosaic consists of *the ingredients of each Knowledge component + the chosen ingredient pieces from each Useful piece of what is of concern, reduced to its essence Endowments and Propensities. These are what form and are from the core of what goes into the Common Ground* (ingredients shared for beneficial mutual interaction) within the *Interchange*. Out of this interchange flows a Non-rational (i.e. personal-social, and spiritual) awareness of how to do *Ma'at "ME/WE" Life-Living* and is always aimed at doing what is best for "ME/WE". The way to access the Interchange is by necessarily drawing on ones inner Self (i.e. Divine Consciousness) intuition. The "Sameness" of the essence ingredients of Knowledge present in the Mosaic at the core of the "Common Ground" Interchange can be developed by perfecting one own Spiritual Elements aspects so they enter into the Interlocking Rings. How such cultivation of this Interchange comes about is by "trial-and-error" continuous effort express Ones Unconditional Love. The standard for this determination is to have the resultant product in a state of Order, Regularity, Coherence, Consistency, Compatibility, Balance, Harmony, and Predictability. In dealing with Predictions, the more something is considered predictable, the more it seems to be determined by some Cause or Source. This may or may not be true but do not assume that what is not predictable is or is not determined. What one follows is a *Feature* of the Interchange--that something in whatever is detected is a Trait of the Essentials or within an Essential that is Vital (Necessary) to keep going "straight ahead" while "staying-on-point." The objective is to be a *Spiritual Elements Creator, Enhancer, Maintainer, Defender, and Protector*. This background led me into Truth pursuits.

EMOTIONS—ACQUIRED: A two-sided coin is a useful analogy for discussing the essence of the a human's Right and Left Brain that work interdependently to fashion sound Critical Thinking (CT). The Left Brain side figures things out for goals in efficient (done quickly) and effective (done right) manners. The Right Brain has the capability to penetrate the metaphysical (away from the world of Matter) to see interconnections and it operates in the "Here and Now." What made Ancient Africans such super-brilliant CT was their perfecting to a humanly possible ultimate degree their Right and Left Brains but with the highly disciplined Right Brain (done by the Left Brain) orchestrating their entire brains. For example, they fashioned their Left Brains to prioritize the most important things -- like selecting the Right Brain's urge to interconnect with people in a manner -- designed to have the greatest benefits for the most people over the longest period of time. By their Selfhood's being in harmonious order I suspect the Spiritual Chain of Command" went like this: (1) from God's Mind messages are conveyed to ones "Self" (ones Divine Consciousness which contains the "drop of God"); (2) through ones "Self," God's messages are conveyed to ones Divine Spirit (containing Energy/Matter); (3) through the Divine Spirit, God's messages are conveyed to ones Character; and (4) upon receiving these messages ones Character orchestrates ones Tangible thoughts, emotions, expressions, and deeds to conform to Ma'at Spiritual Element principles for daily living (i.e. Unconditional Love, Truth, Reality, and the Natural). **D**uring African American slavery the Enslaved brought over as an emotional inheritance a deep-seated aesthetic endowment (Alain Locke). But the European captors were dedicated to "Killing the Spirit" of the Enslaved--i.e. to disconnect the "Self" from ones Divine Spirit--in order to control the "*What*" and "*Why*" of everything involved in the lives of the Enslaved. Wherever this was successful meant the Enslaved "deprogrammed" their Left Brains so that an undisciplined Right Brain, with its Emotional dominance, would orchestrate. This was in keeping with the Maafa (immeasurable catastrophe) lives they were leading. Naturally, interpersonal interrelationships dominated as shared experiences needing "soothing" so as to endure. The hellishness of slavery, White terrorism, and racism and their devastating rippling effects emotionally welded Black Americans as others could never be, providing them with a Spiritual advantage. Since the "central control" of the Left Brain shifted from the Rational to the Omnibus ("Fight, Flight, Fright") part of the afflicted's brains, no thought was directed to anything outside the "Here and Now"; ones Emotions took "center stage"; and there was no need for or cultivation of CT.

My experiences, observations, and research strongly suggest this was a viable pattern among the Enslaved, as noted by this pattern being present today in many of the Enslaved's struggling descendants. In the process, of great importance has been for Black Americans to develop the power to convey emotions. Such is seen in the flavor of language; the flow of phrase; the accent of rhythm in prose, verse, and music; the color and tone of imagery, idioms, and Symbolism; in dance. "The Blues" is the expression of the emotional life of Black Americans. The point is that Emotions are a vital part of contributing to a happy and fulfilling life as long as they are disciplined by Spiritual Elements--and that is absolutely essential for becoming a skilled CT. To these ends the "Big Picture" is to return to the ways of our Ancestors. Switch back to using ones Rational Brain (this tells what is more important for serious business than ones emotions). The Omnibus Brain is not designed to do CT. Besides, it has obsessive-compulsive features intended to prevent the switch and only converting to operating out of Spiritual Energy will give one the motivation and persistence to make the "Brain Switch" and convert to CT.

EMOTIONS: *Emotion* (Latin 'e' or out + movere, to move) denotes a sentiment, meaning one literally moves out of ones mind as a result of stirred up Feelings. Five basic Emotions are Rage, Fear, Depression, Emotional Pain, and Pleasure

EMOTIONS DISCIPLINE: For Black People desiring to do skilled Critical Thinking (CT), understand everything has its proper place which means keeping the good (e.g. whatever is satisfying); shedding the bad (out of control bad emotions), and expanding the needed (e.g. CT). The discipline of Emotions starts with making the decision and putting into action the separating and shedding of ones bad emotions while cultivating ones good emotions. Because Emotions are normal and spontaneous they cannot be commanded to do anything. And to fight bad emotion is to pour energy into them and that energy gives them increasing power. Instead, the change of habit is to withdraw attention from them and that lack of energy causes them to wither and disappear. To enhance this one uses ones reason + ones Right Brain awareness that it is natural to engage in interconnections and thus it is normal for the Right Brain (with its Emotional faculty) to return to working as a team player with ones Left Brain. As one develops the use of ones Left Brain skills it automatically disciplines the Right Brain. Its display is in one no longer expecting things done in the way one has always done things and/or for people to be a certain way in order to relate closely to them. Just as discrimination is not good for different races, neither is it good for people within ones own Brain/race. To make these changes is to engage in a way of living that is a thriving process and that constitutes an initiation onto a Truth-Track that carries one through the mysteries of the mazes of life whereby one gains deeper and deeper understanding of the Spiritual Elements. To enter without an opinion of it being drudgery or fear of the unknown is a display that one has reconnected ones Right and Left Brains as independent team players focused interdependently on a shared goal to achieve a thriving course through life. To proceed down the "Truth-Track" necessarily develops an understanding of Cosmic Laws because of ones experiences of knowing for oneself. When one drinks iced water one knows it is cold. This is vastly different from *Beliefs* whereby one has a fervent hope that what they are doing is true and right--but Beliefs are not self-correcting because of the emotion contained within them (and emotions have no morals and are thus not self-correcting). *Facing head-on the mysteries of the mazes of life + the experience of handling them + the "knowings" from each experience + the desire to thrive (and not keep repeating the same mistakes as well as not procrastinating) + the understanding of all these parts and the "Why" of their necessity is what forms a sound and skilled CT.* One will then be able to compare ones old Ordinary Thinking

(OT) and bad emotions results and consequences (which were causing recurrent vicious cycles and thereby making life harder and harder) with ones new CT results and consequences (which started off hard, tedious, and boring but then caused life to get better and better). One will find that the absence of ones bad emotions relieves chronic tension; the need to run to others for "soothing"; the uselessness of "Escapes"; and the increasingly interesting adventure in pursuing how to thrive in life. CT causes one to see the benefits from doing unimportant things (e.g. untangling strings) so as to get a "flavor" of what to do when it is most needed. By generating an atmosphere of good Emotions and desiring to cultivate them might change ones entire outlook on life, including whom one chooses for friends and how to relate to them; or even carve out a Mission to help others get past their Bad Emotions and start enjoying life. In contrast to having to "Believe," one will see that CT operates out of "Knowing" and that works best for serious business. Then Belief and Faith separate so that faith is applied--not to outside things that others (including religion) says to accept without question--over to oneself. What is better than *Self-Efficacy* (knowing ones skills match the challenges, even those never seen nor heard of before) and having *self-faith in there being no alternative but to do it right*. The point: get rid of Acquired Emotions. BE IN, BUT NOT ABSORBED BY, THE EARTH WORLD. The *Metaphysical Window Concept* is a way to transition ones mind from constant chaos to one of calmness. A calm mindset is the best way to solve difficult problems in life. This concept arose early in my Orthopaedic surgical practice when it was necessary for me to get involved in the medical-legal arena. Apart from its interesting and challenging contents, what I really disliked was the Brute-centeredness of this arena, featuring Critical Thinking dishonorableness (e.g. telling lies; cheating deserving people out of everything because of being unable to defend themselves). The objective is to generate the confusion that enables one side to win by stomping on and destroying opponents and then celebrating making the loser suffer. "Everybody" is suspicious of everybody else. By arrogantly playing "the game" by their own rules and in defiance of the law which lacks "accountability teeth," they are free to do the least amount of worthwhile work that justifies over-charging. My Orthopaedic involvement enabled me to step into this chaotic amoral arena; be part of what is interesting; and then step back from it without having to sell my soul to the devil.

"EMPIRICAL": Very Ancient Africans instituted the *Pre-Scientific Method* by means of the Observation of the stars and planets and used mathematics to record the results of what they observed so as to begin the realm of formal research into the unknown. Then came the *Experimental Method* which was distinguished by the manipulation of items according to a hypothesis in such a manner that inferences could be made as to the causation of the observed changes that resulted. Outside Africa, Hippocrates (460?-377? BC)--a Greek physician who studied and borrowed the methods of the Egyptian Imhotep--set up a "Dogmatiki" (dogmatic) school. Its foundation for medical practice-- the Deductive Approach--was based upon certain reason-derived theories, logic, and statements of established authorities presented in the form of scientific dogmas or theoretical principles. Skeptical of theoretical explanations and accepted authoritarian methods, Serapion, a Greek in Alexandria, Egypt (c200-150 BC), contended that it is not necessary to obtain a knowledge of the nature and functions of the body in order to treat diseases and that rationality alone has no ability to provide insight into the nature of the world. Instead, he and a group of Greek physicians held that experience, skill, and an element of intuition is the surest and best guide for drawing conclusions and directing treatment and that medical practice be done by means of observation, of fact, and of experiment. Thereafter, the Empiricism Method concerned the collection and evaluation of data following experimentation and without formalized knowledge. However, overtime history showed that empiricism could not account for complex factors in the world. Those who tried to convince the public otherwise came to acquire in English (1621), mostly in medical contexts, a strong derogatory sense under the label of "Quacks." The "quack-salver" concept was extended to other activities to indicate ignorance or imposture and embraced by the term Empiricism in C17. Arguments for what Empiricism was and was not were hotly debated and part of the problem that "*Experience*" and "*Experiment*" shared a common Latin origin (to try, to put to the test). So, in the 16th century the main idea inside "Experience" veered off while carrying the meaning of becoming a conscious test or trial; then a consciousness of what has been tested or tried; then a consciousness of an effect or state; and eventually a knowledge derived from real events as well a from particular observation. "Experiment" simply meant a test or trial. At that point Empiricism switched from being a single view to a type of view with many different examples--making it appropriate to speak not just of empiricism but of empiricisms. Hence, the term Empiricism Theory referred to Knowledge and Skills based on trial-and-error experimentation and not training; "Empirical" were materials of scientific experiment; Empirical was about the primary scientific procedures being observation and experiment; and Empirical Data, information gathered through practical experience and not theoretical conjecture. In recent times, to make "empirical" appear to be "scientific" the Experimental Method has been admixed so that data are derived from the systematic manipulation of variables in an experiment--a process greatly simplified by means of a computer. This does not work for two main reason. One is the Extrapolation of most items involved in the Empirical Data process. *Extrapolation*—meaning an educated guess resulting from calculations from a fact(s) about what preceded that fact or is likely to follow it (Trueblood p98). Because each aspect in it is about an estimate, which derived in 1300 Europe from measurement (meaning partially bounded and meant to evaluate approximately, subject to conditions and experience). In other words, estimates cannot be accurate because they involve some degree of speculation. Speculation is a way of viewing ranges on a scale--with a mere guess at one end and a scientific type pondering on the other. Today, empirical data consists of that derived from the trials and errors of experiences and with no idea of what to expect going in. An empirical statement or theory is one which can be tested by some kind of evidence drawn from experience. To arrive at something empirically is to do it through status or statistics. For example, the Probability Distribution for the possible number of heads from four tosses of a fair coin having both a head and a tail can be calculated from experimentation and observation by allowing for the accumulation of empirical data. See Anecdotes

EMPIRICAL ASSESSMENT OF DATA COMPONENTS: The components that exist in the universe can be categorized as Immaterial, Intangible (a transition between the Immaterial and the Tangible), and Tangible. By being made of matter, the Tangible is subdivided into the concrete (the completely bounded), the partially bounded, and the unbounded. The Tangible lends itself to measurement in its most complete form in the concrete; less so with that inside the partially bounded; and even less so in the Unbounded Tangible category. According to Ancient Africans any matter contains the Immaterial and therefore accuracy demands that the assessment of any component involved in Empirical Data must include its spiritual and matter aspects. To elaborate, let us look at the components of how C17 Europeans appraised an item that would enter the marketplace for sale to a buyer. The C17 European word "*Appreciate*" ("to appraise, set a price at") came from the idea of setting a price on something by means of making an estimate, even an unfavorable one. Whereas a "True Price" was derived from "justly" evaluating everything capable of evaluation ("to find the value of"), an "Estimate" meant the assigning of a rough "price tag" evaluation to something based on certain conditions and experiences. However, for buying and selling in the marketplace an approximation of the exact value of the object was the best that could be had and, in fact, all that was needed. In this situation the best estimates came from experts who specialized in making them without emotions. Thus, for things of significance, such experts were sought to "evaluate truly" or "evaluate justly a material product that was created or produce to convey value (e.g. money significance) and/or Worth (significance beyond the realm of money). To make these determinations called for the use of the "*Appreciation Triangle*." See *Appreciation Triangle*

EMPIRICAL: Whereas the C3 BC school of Greek physicians who believed this way were called Empirics (Greek for Experience) what they deemed to be necessities (collected data that undergoes Induction) were called Empirical. The Greek word "Empiric" is composed of "em" or in and "peira," a trial, an experiment--literally one who is skilled or experienced. There writings, called the empeirika, have survived in a few sentences quoted by the C2 AD Greek anatomist and medical writer Galen. *Induction* (going from the specific to the general) was essential because from the body of ascertainable "facts" a conclusion is drawn rather than being deduced from some general theory. Today, a "Worldly Fact" is usually considered as a statement of perceived Secular Reality, verifiable by Observation and called *Empirical Science.* "Empirical" ('relating to experience') embraces all sciences called "Physical" and "Social"--e.g. chemistry, biology, psychology, physics, economics, and sociology. The street sign located near ones home is a worldly fact. This address is visible and real to any number of observers at any time. In addition, ones home address is recorded at the county seat and on many documents (e.g. utility bills). See Fact

EMPIRICAL SCIENCE: "Emperical" ('relating to experience') embraces all sciences called "Physical" and "Social"--e.g. chemistry, biology, psychology, physics, economics, and sociology. By contrast, *Formal Science* concerns Mathematic and formal Logic, asserting nothing about natural phenomena or experience.

EMPIRICISM METHOD: The Greek word "Empiric" is composed of "em" or in and "peira," a trial, an experiment--literally one who is skilled or experienced. There writings, called the Empeirika, have survived in a few sentences quoted by C2 AD Greek anatomist and medical writer Galen. The African derived form of *Induction* (going from the specific to the general) was essential because from the body of ascertainable "facts" a conclusion is drawn rather than being deduced from some general theory. Thereafter, the Empiricism Method concerned the collection and evaluation of data following experimentation and without formalized knowledge. However, overtime history showed Empiricism could not account for complex factors in the world. Those who tried to convince the public otherwise came to acquire--in English (1621) and mostly in medical contexts--a strong derogatory sense under the label of "*Quacks.*" The "*Quack-Salver*" concept was extended to other activities to indicate ignorance or imposture and was embraced by the term Empiricism in C17. Yet, it generated debate as to whether it was about "Experience" and "Experiment." At that point Empiricism switched from being a single view to a type of view with many different examples--making it appropriate to speak not just of Empiricism but of Empiricisms. Hence, the term Empiricism Theory referred to Knowledge and Skills based on trial-and-error experimentation and not training; "*Empiricals*" were materials of scientific experiment; *Empirical* was about the primary scientific procedures being observation and experiment; and *Empirical Data*, information gathered through practical experience and not theoretical conjecture. In recent times, to make "Empirical" appear to be "scientific" the Experimental Method has been admixed so that data are derived from the systematic manipulation of variables in an experiment--a process greatly simplified by means of a computer. This does not work for two main reasons. One is the Extrapolation of most items involved in the Empirical Data process. *Extrapolation*—meaning an educated guess resulting from calculations from a fact(s) about what preceded that fact or is likely to follow it (Trueblood p98). Because each aspect in Extrapolation is about an estimate, it is subject to certain conditions and experiences. In other words, estimates cannot be accurate because they involve some degree of speculation. *Speculation* is a way of viewing ranges on a scale--with a mere guess at one end and a scientific type pondering on the other. See Con-Artists

ENCULTURATION: *Enculturation* is absorbing ones own culture while *Acculturation* is acquiring the culture of a new society (actually with the mutual interaction between two cultures, as with Europeans and Africans borrowing from each other's customs). Acculturation was automatic because when African Slaves stepped on board a European ship, they left all of the artifacts or physical objects of their culture behind them.

ENDOWMENTS: Endowments are the system of Values and Character generating Propensities.

ENEMIES: Anti-Spiritual Elements oriented humans are not part of the "WE" because they are living in and operating out of an alternative realm. Since these False Self people got this way out of ignorance, feeling inadequate, or by choice, there are great problems generated for all concerned. Thus, the display of Unconditional Love can only be shown by the display of Spiritual *Courage—the decision to* willingly *deal with problems one does not and would not ordinarily choose.* Ma'at Laws and Unconditional Love cannot be shown through the daily giving of thanks, prayers, meditation, rites and rituals, reading scriptures, or the like—for these are only preparatory practices for the struggle (Amen, MAAT p84, 92, 77). Neither have anything to do with "Hope," doing nothing by leaving it in "God's hands" since the Law of Herukhuti: "*Know that God neither punishes nor rewards nor protects, that you will have the comfort of controlling these for yourself*". However, Ancient Africans said: "*Peace in the face of "Opposition" generates Spiritual Power and Wisdom*"—consisting of the Omnipresence, Omniscience, and Omnipotence mentioned above. Yet, these are not generated unless there is a genuine demand for them, as provided by trials and tribulations--adversities and difficulties—for them to flow from ones Divine Consciousness. What works for me is a concept borrowed from the Chinese Sun Tzu under the title of "*Taking Whole*"—i.e. playing "rough" but without opponents necessarily losing. "Rough" is not the same as "dirty" (i.e. brute practices) but instead is doing things that are intimidating and respected, even though the opposition does not like them. Neither will benefits come from not applying the knowledge to where it is appropriate. Skill techniques for resolving conflicts--with/without help, alone/in opposition with another(s)--must be cultivated by applying the Peaceful mindset comments discussed under Selfless Service. One cultivation is on the techniques that avoid any attacks on the opponent but rather on the bad things they do. A second is on self-discipline and self-control, as in maintaining a state of calmness. Both are needed to awaken the dormant pattern representing ones skill. Third, in spite of losses, lacks, and obstacles, keep going straight ahead. After going through a variety of racially hostile Orthopaedic Surgery training and practice experiences, in the mid-1970s it was time to focus on doing what I could to help struggling Black youth in teaching sessions. Despite innumerable attempts, in all sorts of ways, to enlist help from others on each rung of the social ladder, it became clear that White people were not interested in helping--and if so, they wanted to be in charge.

On the one hand, Black People who claimed to be interested would come to my home, have me give talks, teach classes, email from around the USA, and otherwise make promises of "let's do it!" On the other hand, at "doing something" crunch times, they were nowhere to be found. Some community leaders refused to get involved, despite me volunteering to pay for programs to benefit their own children and saying they could be in charge. Some were hostile for reasons unknown to me. The youth gave me no problems but typically I would only see them once. So, I continued as a "one-man band" to do all I could to help--by writing (40) books, medical journal articles, and a weekly column in Black newspapers for 25 years. On my website, 600+ thoroughly researched Black History articles (dating to events 200,000 years ago) were totally destroyed. Four other such total destructions —including someone breaking into my home and apart from someone secretly downloading my computer information—did not stop me from starting over. Despite losing over 1500 thoroughly researched articles on the "flowered, fruited, and devastated" Black Minds, the Self-Declaration to stay with my Mission until its completion was primary. There were no allowances for me to simply "give up" doing what I could to help my people—those who are struggling through no fault of their own. Powering this persistence was my awareness of the African Law that says: *the Divine Plan and to use the difficulties one has in life as a tool to force out the divine powers within ones Selfhood so they can be cultivated.* This has always been so motivating as to override my sense of having been beaten down. The point: Unconditional Love can only be known by its manifestations for it is beyond the mind's ability to grasp what it is. One manifestation is that one has a sense of well-being without any interferences and it takes great insight to discern the absence of problems. Those whose work is so well done as to have an absence of a significant problem are deserving of Appreciation. A second, *Unconditional Love is about persisting through losses, lacks, and obstacles--even walking alone--while paying a high price (money, time, energy, effort + by-passing pleasures, convenience, or respect) in order to provide Selfless Service. This is because "We are all One."*

ENEMIES--FEIGNED BLACK BY EUROPEAN MALES: Humans' common "Enemies" (C13, 'not a friend) are tyranny, poverty, disease, cults, and war. If these do not end in ones death, the next worst thing any of them do is to rob one of ones true sense of Selfhood Greatness. Human enemies are of many types. Group I is oneself—ones own unruly nature and the dark forces pent-up within oneself. These members minds are filled with illusions that are cast as fierce to behold monsters, demons, and other contingent Beings. One is not harmless who harms oneself and thus is to be carefully watched. Group II is ones envy of others because the others have what one wants and which one cannot get because of being incapable or unwilling to go after it. Group III is an injured, angered, person watching opportunities for revenge. Their anger may have come from the other knowing, with or without exposing, their flaws; saying truths that violate ones beliefs or from which one is hiding; or being a model of good living against which the unhappy compare themselves. Group IV is the desire of two or more competing people to have the same thing which only one can enjoy. Group V get "excitement" and a sense of importance and power from having enemies. Thus, they invent weak excuses for declaring hostility against victims. Group VI are socialized to be open to and seek out battle as a lifestyle. Their attitude is: "if you are not for me, you must be against me". Group VII are "little gods"—"do it my way or we fight because I'm entitled, not you". They are furious with those who excel them in anything they do, for that stomps on their self-declaration of being superior. Group VIII have such intense self-hatred as to dedicate themselves to Kill/Take/Destroy in hopes of getting some temporary tension relief. Group IX have such great fears and helplessness concerning death or other things as to displace that onto scapegoats. Group X are willfully incapable of demonstrating the Spiritual Elements of Unconditional Love, Truth, Reality, and the Natural. No Group possesses the ingredients to be a friend—and neither is one a friend who associates well with these Groups. Regardless of the reason for attacking another, to do evil to even an innocent by-stander makes that innocent person an enemy to the attacker—which may/may not be reciprocated. Enemies, by being ignorant or by embracing the Indifference/Hate/Evil/Sadism (IHES) Complex, operate out of their Lower (animalistic) Self. Their total focus is on self-aggrandizement (increasing the scope of ones power, influence, stature, riches, conquest, or reputation)--using methods that attack the body, mind, and spirit--by any means necessary. A spiritual attack example is for the enemy to create some Supernatural power, declare it to be *The Spiritual God*, and destructively apply it in physical realms. From observations, personal experiences, talking with thousands of victims throughout my education, training and Orthopaedic Surgical practice, and doing extensive research since college days on all types of subjects, I conclude the ten Groups in Supernatural cults always design Black People as feigned enemies--upon whom they use enemy methods—and at their own great loss. "*Feign*" (C13 contrive, false pretenses) means to invent a story, excuse, or allegation—hence make a pretense of an emotion or response so as to exhibit behavior entirely different from what is the real condition or situation. "Feigned enemies" are characterized as those easily exploited for self-interest gains—and who in no way attack, hinder, or interfere with the cult's hostile military or dogmatic set-up. This is a *Deflection* method illustrated by *Reaction Formation* (a reality/fantasy reversal)--e.g. saying about and to the victim: "you are the one causing the problem, not me!" The contents in their *Projection* accusations are derived from fantasies which design feigned necessities—i.e. imaginary necessities. Such are the greatest cozenage (deceitful) things a predator does to his/her mind to break down any remote sense of moral "Right." However, compared with those living out of their Higher Self inside the Natural Cosmos, Supernatural cult members have a totally different concept of "Right". Examples include a lust of conquest, a love of ease, a craving for power, and an obsession to be superior. The cozen's "wheeling and dealings" are infinitely worse when used as an excuse for generating an IHES Complex in order to Kill/Take/Destroy/Oppress their victims. Yet, such actions are complimented and even honored by Supernatural Cult fellows. jabaileymd.com

ENGRAMS: Neuronal patterns of an acquired skilled act of learning—i.e. permanent memories representing what has been learned

ENIGMA: one with a baffling or confusing hidden meaning, clear only to one who understands the allusion(s) therein. An Allusion--relying on suggestion and connotation by a causal or passing reference--is an extremely quick ways of expressing ones emotions to an in-group as well as creating in listeners shades of those same emotions--but only when the listeners are already familiar with the setting (e.g. history, literature, sayings, slang, people, events) alluded to--as, for example, family jokes. See Puzzle; Conundrum; Paradox; Problem; Mystery

ENTOURAGE: The Old French term "Entourage" refers to a group of attendants 'round about' their leader--a concept originating from Primitive (the first people) Africans who regarded animals as highly spiritual creatures. They believed the image of a given force of Nature conveyed by a given animal (or totem) characterizes a human and his/her kinship group. Calling this Nature force Ka, Ancient Africans said it represented the essence of Atum (God) who imparted it to humans. This shared nature with the divine--i.e. binding of all things of common origin from the single God source into an indestructible unity--became a fundamental tenet of Very Ancient African Maatian anthropology.

ENTOURAGE SPIRITUAL IN BLACK PEOPLE: Although I use myself as an example, the following Realities apply to the entire Human (Black) Family. The key is that one must be open to receiving them as family members, invite them into ones life, and remain as ones Real Self. False Self people equate their Acquired Emotions to the Pure Emotions of Real Self people by "acting as if" they are *Instant Psychologists*. From a glancing peek, they feign "complete and accurate scrutinizing" of a person/thing/message. Then they jump to conclusions which wrongly characterize what is behind the scrutinized face or behind its face or physical appearance. Based upon failing to see every important thing and emotionally *misinterpreting what they have glanced at,* wrong opinions are made--perhaps that a solution, candidate, or approach will/will not work. Worse yet is taking action on these "guesses" and getting others to follow. The result of those delusions lead to bad actions/reactions and to detrimental consequences for all involved. Nevertheless, since age five, I have been aware of my *Spiritual Entourage*—i.e. my inner world Living-Dead Spiritual Attendants. It started at age 5 when, sitting on my back porch counting my marbles, a "neon" like sign appeared in my mind that said: "Help Bright Black Boys." These SPIRIT ADVISORS inside my Spiritual Entourage were explained by Ancient Africans saying that by being created in the image of God, every human carries the potential for genius, *as orchestrated by a special attendant spirit allotted to that individual at birth.* That spirit forever watches over and shapes ones character and fortunes. As a boy I really enjoyed the Boy Scouts and camping out. Although I normally slept very soundly, when it was time for me to get ready to leave for a fishing trip at 4:00 a.m., I would be wide awake at 3:30 a.m. By Affect Symbolic Imagery, Ancient African Griots (story-tellers) informed African people about their SPIRIT SERVANTS in stories that were used outside Africa. An example, was made into Arabian Nights magical tales which supposedly were taken from the Persians by the Hindus and then from India by the Arabs. Characters within these tales included The Jinn--magical spirits created out of fire--some of whom were good and some evil. Because of the just mentioned Boy Scout experiences, I became aware of my genie, whom I named Jann. After leaving the warm, compassionate, and "ME/WE" members of my all-Black community to enter the University of Michigan as a freshman student, I was totally unprepared for the hostile environment of Europeans. On numerous occasions of being faced with problems I had never seen or heard of before, there arose "HELPING HANDS" in the form of certain thoughts entering my mind that were "totally out of the blue"—things I had never thought of before—thoughts that were simply the right things to do for a specific happening and occurring at exactly the right time—things which when carried out immediately got me out of trouble or kept me from getting into trouble. These "Helping Hands" appeared without my asking and often before I was aware of a problem. In was not long into my college matriculations that I was convinced of being cared for and guided by a Spiritual Entourage. As a test, I started calling on them for assistance in doing little things and they responded. On countless occasions during my education, medical training, and Orthopaedic Surgical practices there were "Impossible" problems needing solutions or something needing to be created in order to get past barriers. African Griots conveyed the ideas about *"Helping Hands"* as those Spiritual Helpers which, when allowed, guide the defense and self-protection to each human throughout life. Their Spiritual Metaphors were about gods, goddesses, and spirits destined to function as the vehicles to carry out God's dictates relating to the First Law of Nature—Survival, Self-Protection, and Self-Preservation. The deeper I proceeded into preparing to become an Orthopaedic Surgeon, the more intense in depth, frequency, and variety was having to deal with European racism. Some of these "alligators" included deceptive tricks, failing to open paths to what would be normal and uneventful progressions, and shutting down whatever was beneficial, being rejected and isolated, assigned the worst tasks, extra tasks, unrelated tasks, and task belonging to others. It was so discouraging and overwhelming that I had to constantly dismiss thoughts of "giving up." However, my boyhood community had prepared me by various members periodically telling me: "you have to succeed for your race"—a powerful "ME/WE" motivator. To simplify the complex concepts involved in "Motivation" by using Affect Symbolic Imagery, Ancient African Sages resorted to a *Personification* (making a lifeless or abstract thing come alive) named *"Mercurius Homunculus"* (the "little man" exerting Will Power). They said "Will," arising into being from the crude stuff in the Ocean of Nun (i.e. the "material prima" of the Subjective Realm), is powered by Spiritual Motivational Energy. A factor triggering *Motivational Action* (an energized movement) *within* Will was the result of a direct connection with the Spiritual Motive Force inside a given human's subconscious mind (which is part of the image of God's Mind).

EPIGENETICS: "Nurture on Nature." After birth, Environmental *"Nurture"* (what nourishes in the act of its cultivation and rearing into maturity) modifies a human's Nature (its Essence + Character). For example, prolonged distress can cause certain cells to be turned on and off—a process called *"Epigenetics."* See Correspondence-Disharmony Secular

EQUAL SIGN: The Algebraic "equal-sign" stands for Truth. From Primitive Africans use of pebbles as a means to have a symmetrical final result in the exchange of goods, bartering required an "equal sign" (=) between goods to its right and something to its left. That balance gradually led to abstract concepts of "Fairness" and Justice. Hence, in early Africa the "equal sign" became a keystone of math. What happen here is that both numbers and symbols (e.g. pebbles) were expressed in quantities and that is now called Algebra. The concept of the "equal sign" instituted the concept of the Law of Opposites by African Sages discerning that this is the means by which ones mind creates thoughts. They inferred Opposites to be the means by which the Cosmic Mind (God) brings into being and sustains Creation. Thus, each creation is composed of two opposite, but complementary forces, which, when synthesized, unite in a balance, and form a transcendental harmony (Order) that manifests in the human possessing it. To Very Ancient Africans--the inventors of algebra and all of its Abstracts and Abstraction--an essential to their discovery of and elaboration on Mathematics was a "Figure" concerning a numerical symbol. That "Figure" served as a "Sign" to say what something is or where something is. Its associated Symbol is the bridge that 'carries across' some message contained in that Sign or from where the process started around that Sign over to another place. The message is contained in the Figure of Speech.

EQUATION/EQUAL: "*Equation*"—meaning the *balancing of associations or identifications* of any two diverse Things; a statement of equality between *two mathematical expressions* (e.g. numbers, functions, magnitude, operations). By Algebra being an equation makes it easier to study relationships among like-kind Things—to generalize, abbreviate, and simplify (because its operations are concise). All of this is by reducing aspects of the situation to its essence (the "what it is" when it came into Being-hood)--then generalizing the solution + discovering general laws true for all that are on both sides of the equation. The reason is that the equation is like a balanced seesaw or a scale in balance. Its mid-part is a *Transition Zone* connecting completely different "kingdoms"--a "zone" typically filled with apparent chaos--a "zone" in which, said African Sages, *there is always an undiscovered logical coherence among the parts of a problem, its basic logical structure, and its underlying base.* "Equate" means to make comparable (as in meaning); to show relationship between (e.g. as in worth or value or significance). Of course these may vary depending the situation and the applications in different situations. The reason is that the equation is the "bull's eye" of the Truth—since the letters may stand for anything. This makes the equation like a balanced seesaw or a scale in balance.

EQUATION VERIFICATION: Equation Verification between two Knowns or between what is Known and Unknown comes from making an Inference out of any one of these four and then using the "*If-Then*" *Method* to see if there is a meshing correspondence between the beginning and the conclusion. Hence, "If so-and-so is correct, then it follows that thus-and-so is true"—a basic Algebraic balancing. Correspondence between a Known and Unknown makes the Conclusion Circumstantial. For example, Correspondence between the two at points (e, above) along the path from Beginning to End, the Conclusion about the Unknown would be a Circumstantial Truth. Circumstantial Truths are established when inside a boundless realm, *the Familiar (the "Seeable") explains the Unknown (the "Un-Seeable") because they are made of the same Spiritual Elements "Genetics" derived from the Mind of God.* Conclusions come from the "*Since-Then*" *Filter*. For example: "Since the Genetics of the Known consist of the Spiritual Elements, then they must be present in the Circumstantial Assumption pertaining to the Esoteric Unknown. Even if one can only get so far as Circumstantial Evidence (i.e. bits and pieces of the Spiritual Elements), Inferences can still be made within the Common Sense that applies to the standards, filters, guides, and measures of Spiritual Elements of Unconditional Love, Truth, Reality, and the Natural.

"ESOTERIC": Although humans were born with "First Wisdom," life living causes most, if not all, to escape ones understanding because it is buried. By "Knowing Thyself," there is a return to understanding the inner truth lying hidden; exposing its subtle meanings and forms; unfolding its intricacies of what defys fundamental thoughts/beliefs so as to see its message.

ESOTERIC KNOWLEDGE: "*Esoteric Knowledge*"—i.e. *understanding the inner truth lying hidden within the core of fundamental concepts about foundational Realities*--requires *Inference Leaping* by illogical, not logical Quantitative Thinking. Here, the word "Illogical" refers to Spiritual (pre-birth) Emotions which, by originating in their Cosmic Organism "home" and are thereby outside the realm of the later appearing Intellect's systematic processes.

ESSENCES: *Essences* are what a thing is when it comes into being; an "*Entity*"—i.e. a specific something constituting some aspect of that human's (or Thing's) *Endowments* (i.e. natural qualities) and/or *Propensities* (in-born tendencies, e.g. a human's capacities, abilities, and language) which operate some process of an Entity's Selfhood

ESSENCE & QUALITIES IN AFRICAN TRADITION: The following discussion on Essence and Essentials (Qualities) is foundational for understanding the "Home Base" of African Knowledge vs. Supernatural Information. As part of the design and order of the Cosmos and of all God-made Creatures and Creations, including each human, there is a Spiritual Elements Substance (Latin, sub, 'under'—Underlies--and stare, 'to stand') underlying all perceptible or visible manifestations in the Cosmos, called *Unconditional Love*. In African Tradition's Creation story of the Cosmos, the Amenta as well as the Nun (the Void, Nothingness) contains in its upper region the Cosmic Mind of God and the body of God. Springing from the Cosmic Mind, as the Substance of God, are the Spiritual Waters called the Ocean of Nun (Nu or Subjective or Body of God or Cosmic Hub or Tao by the Chinese) and its Intelligence. So, in African Tradition, *"Nature"* is the Cosmic Organism's Unconditional Love in action, powered by God's Laws; the home of God's Laws; & a Web-like system of interconnecting, independently acting, and interdependently interacting God manifestations in accordance with their God assigned identities—and that Correspondence gives insight into the Unknown. In the Spiritual Cosmic Realm, from the Cosmic Mind or from a human's Soul springs a continual manifestation of the Essence consisting of an Immaterial Actuality Virtual Image Idea. That Image contains a *Disposition*, within which is (among others) a "What and Why" message for what the Entity, in its mature state, is to do. At the proper time for it to undergo Involution, its next stop is into the realm of Ether. *Ether,* a quanta of Spiritual Energy and beginning Matter, constitutes the minimum amount needed for any Metaphysical or Physical entity to become involved in an interaction. In its natural, realistic, and most highly concentrated form, Ether is shiny, pure, upper air in the form of a subtle fluid of pre-matter consisting of a fine, flimsy, vapor mist of which "the Heavens," the lintel's (i.e. the Sublime) stars and planets, Nature, and natural laws are said to be made. The Immaterial Virtual Image Idea meets with Spiritual Energy and Ether (Matter) in the Astral part of the Metaphysical realm, is activated, and given Form to create a faint Notion of a Thing. That Form has a *Shape* (consisting of 'frozen' Energy and Ether) that gives it a specific Payload Power--a manifestation of Force, or Energy—while neither Substance/Essence are Force or Energy (Ramacharaka, Gnani Yoga 127-137). The Form is like putting paint on the Idea so as to be its "Double" or "Shadow". Similar to the Halo around the Sun, the Form (Halo) consists of Attributes (like rays of the Sun)—also called the Essentials of the Essence. *Essentials* consist of a "copied" Character, Characteristics, Traits, and Features. The Form's *Character* is the Identical "what it is" Copy of the Virtual Icon Idea. The most consistent Pattern(s) of the Operations of the Essentials in action is its *Trait(s)*. The most outstanding Trait(s) operation is its *Feature(s)*. The most outstanding Featured Trait of the Character is the Essence *"Trademark."* The *Traits and Features constitute the Characteristics* of the Essence because they represent and reflect the various changing and developing modes of the Soul's Disposition expressions within a given context of that Essence. However, there are no dynamic Characteristics in its Essence parent because that Essence parent lacks Energy and Ether. Still, the Essentials' *Characteristics represent the dormant counterparts of the "what it does" and how it appears" of its Essence* parent. The *"what it does"* depends upon *Properties* of the Essence to display an Entity's *"nature"*. The *Nature of a Thing—the "It is"*--is how each of its properties' operations manifest. The *Properties* consist of a Thing's *Endowments* (i.e. natural qualities) and *Propensities* (in-born tendencies, like a given human's capacities, abilities, and language). Put another way, the Essence's Virtual Icon Idea, with its Mind, is fashioned into a *Pattern* based on its Disposition's message. Outlining that Pattern with Ether gives Form to the Pattern. The Pattern has the Virtual Icon Idea on its outside and the Spiritual Energy nourishment in the matrix (womb) on its inside—and the product is an *Entity*. A human's every act undertaken involves a Moral Significance and Consequence—for every act deliberately conceived and purposed has its corresponding image in the mind— or Astral Soul. *Right acts* enhance *"who one is"* spiritually—i.e. ones *"Self"* (Spark of God) Soul--ones source of *wisdom. "Who one is" in ones Astral Soul is the pattern of ones Behaviors. "What one Does," if different from "Who one is," is who one is becoming.* jabaileymd.com

ESSENCE/ESSENTIALS MANIFESTATIONS: Ancient Africans, from discoveries about the Laws of Nature, inferred that God's inner nature is Unconditional Love and outer nature is Life, with its Truth, Reality, and Natural aspects. Both natures, as indivisible differences, are present in humans as part of their Divine Essence. These natures, whether manifested in the Cosmos or within human minds, are manifested as "Thought Forms"—Mental Creations in the Infinite Mind of the Cosmic Force, Sekhem. They are in the Subjective Realm as Archetypes. An Archetype relates to its many "Particular" offspring because they all have the same Spiritual Genetics and because Forms, by themselves, reproduce themselves, and become the Things it makes. Each Thing, by following a Divine Logos Principle, was given a *Number—i.e. an Intelligible Essence*—and that Essence gives each type of Thing its distinctive Essentials (e.g. its Character) which makes it display as "what it is." Out of that Number emanates a Form (also called an Idea, Number, Noumena, or Reality)—i.e. a Pattern with a Virtual Image on its outer side and a Matrix (womb providing nourishment) on its inside. That Form acquires a power based upon its *Shape* as it evolves into "Concrete" Things. Very Ancient Africans inferred these *Idea-Forms* to be self-realizable Divine Patterns fixed in Nature and with the capability to reproduce themselves in their own Essence Virtual Image (what it was when it came into Being-hood) so as to become the Thing it makes. The Pattern possesses an Icon Image on its outer side and a Matrix (womb bringing nourishment) on its inside. Since Ancient Africans considered Ether to be spiritual and equivalent to the Cosmic Psyche or "Soul," it was called *Quality* so as to avoid confusing it with the Divine Soul and Divine Mind of humans. When Ether was the *Cause* of the mental conception of a Thing (because the Thing is invested in at least flimsy Matter, like an idea in ones mind) and/or when Ether was the *Cause* of the existence of a Thing (like a Halo in the Spiritual Realm—or like taste, smell, hearing, and touch feeling in Secular realms) it was called a *Primary Quality*.

But when Ether simply played a *supporting* part for the conception or existence of something (e.g. color) already in "Being-hood," it was a *Secondary Quality*. The inside the Matrix of the Essence's *Thought Form* has Activity networks with a *predisposition to behave in a conforming manner to the Essence's Disposition*. The outer aspect of the Essence's Pattern constitutes its Perceptible Primary Qualities in the form of an Icon Image. It is the further descent into the Ether (the primary life-force) which fashioned the Virtual Primary Quality Image of the Essence into a visible display. These Essentials are a copy of the Essence, in the way the Cosmic Realm is a copy of the Amenta. These new layers of Ether enable the Characteristic of the Essences' Essentials to begin displaying a beginning physical Form—equivalent to a Notion. So, the seeable Characteristic—acting like a Symbol--is the "Form-Idea" of the Reality of its Essence parent. This Essential's outer Image with a inner Matrix—despite being a duplication of those for the Essence parent--constitute *the "what it does" and "how it appears" aspects of the Essence. The Character of the Essential reflects the Essence of its Essence parent; the Characteristic of the Essential enables the Essence to be known in appearance and shape; the Essential's Traits reflect the dictates of the Inclination of the Disposition in the form of* Characterizing Behaviors *performances dictated by its parent Essence of the Thing's*; and *Essentials' Perceptible* Primary Qualities, in the display of Features, spotlight the Identity of the Essence.

All of the *Essentials' Perceptible* Primary Qualities designate the unique appearance of Character, Characteristic, Trait, and Feature portions of the Essence parent, while carrying out the Essence's *"what it does" and "how it appears"*. They, too, are "nourished" by the Essence Matrix. An example would be that which has the shape of "roundness" or which is "hard". Those Image Qualities, orchestrated by their Thought-Forms, eventually enable one to see material objects as a unity—e.g. a chair, a star, a human—as opposed to a jumble of Qualities (e.g. a Thing's roundness, hardness, smoothness, color). By contrast, to see in back of the Essentials so as to become aware of the Essence and its Message of the Divine Disposition is how one serves ones Purpose in life. Its Essentials do help shape shape the*"what it does" and "how it appears" aspects of the Essence.* So, to Ancient Africans, Number was the key to Nature—a concept having incalculable consequences for the evolution of their Sciences, Art, Mathematics, Humanity, and Guidelines for Life-Living.

ESSENCES AND ESSENTIALS' EVOLUTION: An Essence's manifestations begin with a human's Divine Consciousness and *Divine Will.* Since both are devoid of energy, the Disposition derived from one Divine Consciousness is in a Virtual Image state. Yet, the Will, by means of Virtual Images, is the initiator of the intensions of all that happens in ones life. Will includes the process of asserting ones choice to do something.

DIVINE WILL: *To Will something to take place means it is going no further than declaring its Disposition, as a potential act, in the form of a Virtual Image.* Overall, the life's Mission of the Divine Will is to cause the evolution of ones Lower (animalistic) Self into ones Archetypal (Highest Divinity) Self. Within this dual expression of Truth-Wisdom, while the Archetypal (or "Seed") Perfect pre-exists in the Background, the actual life-living Principles involved are based upon wherever are the imperfections existing in a given human's Foreground. Upon receiving a Divine Disposition, Will carries the Disposition to the Mind. Up to this point both Energy and Matter have been resting in an inactive non-differentiated—but not disorganized form.

DIVINE SPIRIT: ones Divine Spirit sets the Disposition in motion (e-motion). This means the "Virtual Image" from the human Will acquires from the Divine Spirit both *the How and When* aspect for the Divine Disposition's *What and Why* + the Spiritual Energy. These enable the Will to yield the mental events involved in initiation of further mental actions (Amen, MAAT, p12).

HUMAN MIND: Upon receiving sufficient layerings of Ether Matter on the Will's Virtual Image, the Essentials contained in the Essence are activated so as to present a Percept of God's Plan to ones mind. When the Divine Disposition payload "What and Why" message enters ones mind as a Percept, it displays as a fully realized form of an Essence, called its *Pattern.*

PATTERN IN ONES MIND: The mature Essence's Pattern possesses an *Icon Image* on the outside and a *Matrix* (womb bringing nourishment to the offspring) on the inside. Both are realizations because of the endowments and propensities of the Substance and are orchestrated by the Disposition's Divine Logos force received from its Divine Source. The "How it appears" of the Patterns components are made known by the Essentials. Those Essentials are in the form of a "Trademarked" Individuality display of the Character of the Essence. Its Pattern consists of the Divine Spirit's Energy and Matter which imparted its Form. That Form, as a Primary Quality, means its movement is frozen in space. The *Shape of the* Form of the Pattern possesses a specific power given to it by Nature. The "*Womb*" or *Matrix* inside that Pattern is composed of Activity networks which account for the "what it does" aspects.

INTERCHANGE/MOSAICS INSIDE THE PATTERN: The arrangement of the *Properties* comprising those networks interlock in a manner (e.g. like the Olympic Rings) that form an Interchange. Emanating out of the Interchange are Qualities--each with a mosaic pattern extracted from and in harmony with all of the contributing Properties of the Essence. Since the Interchange is the core of the Essence—which Ancient Africans called the "That" of the Thing—what generates all of the Thing's active and passive Qualities is the "That's" underlying "Eye"—like the 'happenings' within the "Eye" of a storm.

MOSAIC PATTERN'S PERCEPT DISPOSITION: The Primary Qualities emanating as a Mosaic Pattern out of the Interchange represent the Disposition of the Essence: (1) *Inclination*--a 'physical' "leaning toward" or "leaning" away from something; (2) *Temperament*-—i.e. a mindset + its physiological Sensory Consciousness systems fashioning the type of reaction the aroused person takes to conform to the 'blue-print' of "the *what*" Concept Theme about a Thing or subject or individual/group with a prevailing emotional trend; (3) *Attitude* (C17, disposition, posture) a prevailing trend mindset about a Thing/subject/ individual/ group; and (4) *Intention*--the decision of what one means to do with an aim toward a specific action or a specific goal; an earnest state of mind to reach the goal. See Human Birth; God's Substance; Essentials Divine; Consciousness In Nature; Humans

ESSENCE: See "DOUBLES" OR "SHADOWS"

ESSENCE & ITS ESSENTIALS EVOLUTION: The "*Dome*" of the sky was considered by Primitive Africans to be the "house of God" to where they would ascend into a god-like plane of existence by remaining "yoked" to God. Such they considered to be within a human's control since the human is not simply a mind and body which will someday cease to exist (as many Europeans believe). Then, Very Ancient African "Hour-Priest" astronomers observed in the sky's "Imperishable Stars"--visible in the night sky at all times of the year--facts sufficient to infer that underlying and inside stars in the sky were messages of the Divine Will. The intent, which they eventually realized from studying these Lucky Stars, was to mystically acquire God's messages designed to open and sharpen their minds to Truth and Unconditional Love while expanding their awareness to Reality and the Natural. Though metaphorically stating these circumpolar stars were Souls of those who had achieved perfection in the Afterlife in order to serve as a means to maintain an Image connection with the Ancestors--they said the goal of all souls is not in the stars but rather in that abode absent changes or fluctuations, the Absolute (Ashby, Anunian Theology p116). The brightest Star for a given family, as indicated by prophesy, was determined to be the *Family Lucky Star*—i.e. the residence of their Living-Dead Ancestors deserving of eternal blessedness. That "*Lucky Star*"--to those whose "Hearts" were pure enough to see it--provided the inner Selfhood luminescence to guide them successfully through life. To them this was like being under the influence of their Lucky Star because it led the people to give trust to luck in taking those risks designed to bring ongoing happiness. To this end, Very Ancient African priest-astronomers (c20,000 BC) intent in studying the sky in general and looking for Lucky Stars in particular was to mystically acquire God's messages designed to open and sharpen their minds to Truth and Unconditional Love while expanding their awareness of Reality and the Natural. They noted God appears in Nature as both the sun and moon as well as that both give off Halos (Nimbus, Aureole)--a luminous circle--a visual expression of irradiating physical forces and/or symbolized Intellectual or mystical Spiritual forces. From this they inferred that metaphorically the "Cosmic Star" featured in the "*Star/Halo*" *Concept* symbolizes the Amenta (God's Cosmic home), while the Cosmos itself is its "Cosmic Halo"; that the Star represents the Substance of God and the Halo pertains to what radiates out of that Substance as an Essence; that a human's Immaterial Soul is to a sky Star as the Astral Intangible "Heart" is to that Star's Halo. An analogy would be the flower, Nature's "star" jewel, whose "halo" is its fragrance. This gave rise to the "Star/Halo" Concept—a "Double" that pervades profound African Tradition concepts. For example, whereas the "Ka" is a human's divine spirit or inner nature--an astral body received at birth containing ones mind, senses, emotional body, and creative power, the "AB" ("Ib") is ones Conscience, intellect, or Will. Yet, "Ib" (ib) means "Heart" and Mind and is used in sacred texts as Moral Conscience. As early as Ptahhotep's (?5000 BC) Sebait or Books of Wise Instruction containing Egyptian moral philosophy, the "Heart" had become the Moral Conscience and causing its owner to hear or not hear both rationally and emotionally—meaning moral responsiveness in a manner that benefitted Ma'at. For example, the Conscience decides certain things are evil and thereby stirs the sense of rebellion and awakens wisdom. The "*Heart*" was used in a figurative sense for the "deepest recesses of the human psyche" (and for them 'psyche' meant Soul). Furthermore, the "Heart" was believed to constitute a human's center--i.e. the place where issues of his/her life are determined"; the place of ones moral and spiritual nature; the home of the very "Subtle Mind." Whereas the Divine Consciousness is ones "Self-Identity" in Spiritual Realms—as derived from the Spark of God and is thus a human's Essence--its Astral "Double" counterpart is ones Intangible Metaphysical entity or Essentials (e.g. a human's Character). This *Astral Attribute* of "Who one is" in Cosmic Life Finite Realms, "what one does," or "How one appears"—do not exist independently. Yet, these Essentials of the Essence carry an impactful 'payload' activating something good or bad in the "Heart" (an Essential) of the one possessing it as well as by the people or creatures touched by it.

ESSENCES AND ESSENTIALS' PROCESSES & PROGRAMS: Once sufficient Ether has been added to the Pattern--and even though the Percept of the Character of the Essence is something of a specific nature and made of specific attributes—the Percept is barely perceptible. But as it evolves with the addition of more Ether, the *Characteristic* Quality fashions that Character into *a unique sensibility--possessing a unique Shape and a compatible Power that conforms to its specific Disposition. That sensibility" focusing is done by the *Trait's Quality* highlighting the Character's specific Individuality into an *enduring mainly emotional predisposition to behave in a certain way.* MOSAIC PATTERN'S NOTION DISPOSITION: The *Feature Quality* in the Pattern spotlights its Character to the point that the Percept now evolves into and appears as a *Notion*–a recognizable "what it is". The Divine Disposition is now a formed *"Entity"* with a specific nature, hinting at the "Thing's" Identity and its specific attributes. Added Ether and its associated energy is now able to initiate the Notion's Intention to enter Consciousness. All that is required for that to happen is the human's volition to generate the *Motivation* to do so--the urge to produce sufficient Desire energy within his/her Selfhood to proceed with the Disposition Plan. The Disposition's Inclination thoughts are in a state of coiled up *Potential* energy. *Whatever builds Attention and Desire builds Will Power to stay focused on the 'bull's eye' and its destination.* When activated the Disposition's Inclination, in spring-like fashion, carries its Imaged message impression. In order to head towards an *Intention,* the nature of the process uncoils its Potential energy and thereby supplies the "motive-power"-–a power possessing the capability to activate the Will and direct ones behaviors for all present and future thoughts and deeds about similar matters. The resultant powered impulse inside the Inclination steers the motives (the "why" of behaviors).Once the action of Intention is powered and under way inside the Unconscious, the Notion's "Ether Image" inside the Disposition Plan holds the hand of the Intention and leads the way by providing the standard, guide, filters, and measures needed for what the Intention is to do while proceeding on into Consciousness. MOSAIC PATTERN'S IDEA DISPOSITION: Meanwhile, from ingredients added by reflection and memory apperceptions, the Notion is budding into an "*Idea*" ('a becoming'; 'model'; form). An Idea: 1) is an awareness of specific, particular aspects--e.g. properties, characteristics, traits, features; 2) represents an explicit ('defined and unfolded' into clarity) concept of "*Identity*"; and 3) has a payload symbolizes into a mental picture whose shape possesses the hidden energy power to *touch and awaken the Truths already present in the "Trademark" of the Spiritual Elements stamped on each human's Soul.* MOSAIC PATTERN'S CONCEPT DISPOSITION: A matured Idea is the formation of a "Unit" called a Concept. A *Concept* describes phenomenon (i.e. a phantom, to 'make visible' a Contingent Being) lacking life and lacking reality but that is about a sort of better awareness of what is contained or included in the Character part of the prevailing Disposition, though not expressed because of of vague, hazy, remaining aspects. A human's "ME/WE" oriented mind has as its instinctual Goal the best that satisfies the Disposition Plan for the greatest benefit, for the greatest number of people (including oneself), and over the longest period of time. Here, one is using Spiritual Energy rather than Emotional Energy to drive the Process. The Goal selection is made by one Pure Emotions. Next, to decide upon the proper usage of the concept of the Divine Disposition, one resorts to ones Ma'at Intellect to select *What is to be done* to conform to the Character's either Familiar or Creative *Approaches* (ways a goal is reached), *Methods* (how to do the job),

Techniques (how tools are used in the approach and method) and *Manner* (the different ways a technique can be handled) for producing the Disposition's unique Product. From this, the engram established by Will and its Real or False Self orchestrator, is in place to direct ones behaviors for all present, future, and Ari (Karmitic) thoughts and deeds about similar matters. For example, inside the Ari conglomerate are Inclination thoughts in a state of coiled up *Potential* energy. Inclinations related to goodness will lead to good Karma (Ari) actions; bad ones to Bad (Ari) Karma actions.

ESSENCES--ABSENCE OF: The reason for this discussion is because I suspect that to understand how Supernatural people are is a key for Black People to free themselves from the societal trap many are in. To review, Spiritual Essences are the Spiritual Elements of Unconditional Love, Truth, Reality, and the Natural and their Primary Quality attributes. This reigned in Africa for 198,000 years of the 200,000 years humans have been on Earth—the alterations being the result of coming in contact with Europeans' Supernatural concepts. Those concepts began with the origin of primitive Europeans 45,000 years ago in the harsh land of living in northern Europe. The "Scarcity" of Human Nature Survival Needs led to a warring people who engaged in "*Philosophical Hallucinations*" in the form of attempts to gain superiority over others by Superstitious means. These Superstitions embraced beliefs about the occult in its negative range and beliefs in the existence of super-humans or Supernatural forces and Beings. The fact of them not realizing they are imagining fantasy things bind them in invisible chains by each one opening doors to new, bigger, and better ones. The effect is like that of kaleidoscopic patterns of Conditioned Reflexes consisting of fear, terror, or other emotions concerning oneself, others like them, and others unlike them. These tinted emotions compel one to believe in what one cannot prove or disprove to the satisfaction of ones senses. Such Superstitious beliefs are fixated by the encroachment of faith on the rights of reason and knowledge and maintained because one is unconscious of the narrow range of ones own experiences that are properly interpreted in a Natural World sense. Thus, their Supernatural interpretations done involuntarily and non-rationally automatically lead them to believe in Superstitions that derive from the Supernatural. They are socialized to believe this is truth. Superstitions are: (1) beliefs, dispositions, and tendencies of humans' weaknesses that cast its spell over the mind so as for them to ascribe to phenomena admitting of natural explanations from occult or Supernatural causes; (2) the making up of Supernatural things and using Magical Thinking to convert it into a facade reality; (3) switching things from the Supernatural world into the Natural world—or vice versa—and then acting on it in ways contrary to its original design—i.e. "Inside-Out" thinking; (4) always inspiring Indifference/Hate/Evil/Sadism mindsets; and (5) all engendered, preserved, and fostered by Fear. Superstitions are definite willfull beliefs contrary to Nature's Laws, to experience, and to Natural world common sense. Because Superstitions and Supernatural things are part of "Air Castles," they must be cling to because the idea of letting go means falling through a bottomless pit—clinging done in the face of contrary evidence. Superstitions have spread as counterfeits of religions, science, and all Social institutions. They are each the more dangerous because the afflicted are profoundly convinced they are freed from Superstitions—a mindset incongruous with intelligence. They *cannot see their Superstitions as springboards for most horrible crimes* for their own and for their feigned enemies. Both have their minds programmed into ignorance for exploitation by those who mislead by their amoral, hypocritical, facade Consciences as a result of their self-delusions and thoughts of grandeur of mind about being "right" and thus superior concerning what is incomprehensible. Misleading is by ensuring whatever is life-shaping and life-changing is incomprehensible, conflicting, and confusing. By socializing the naïve of all cultures into Supernatural patterns mean they cannot be wholly educated out of them or the associated fears implanted in their imaginations, no matter how utterly their reason may reject them. A cause is they have barriers removed from what fantasy things cannot be done and thus accept more fantasies of their leaders. Mindsets of the

Supernatural differ on each rung of the White Supremacy ladder—Type I: a few socialized to actually believe they are "little god" leaders; Type II: the Moderate and Slight with profoundly weak Selfhoods filled with fear, melancholy (fear and grief without a cause which torments one into bitterness), and inferiority; and Type III: the Mild "Un-willfully Ignorant." Type II conveniently project their "Dark Side" onto Colored Victims, using the dark skins to dramatize, based upon Superstitions, how sinister they are and that justifies attacking them. Such is accepted because "Dark goes with them and does not go with me"—a fantasy they need to refuse to see.

ESSENCES--AFRICAN vs. EUROPEAN NON-ESSENCES: *Happiness ("Aliveness Beauty")*, by resulting from right applications of Knowledge and Wisdom to ones Mission, is experienced as a *Metaphysical Idea-Form*. "Happiness" is like the "Immaterial Idea"; Knowledge, like the "Form". African Tradition *Essence* is *Knowledge* consisting of *Spiritual Elements' "Immaterial Ideas"* and their Inseparable Harmonized Complementary Equal Material *Primary Qualities* Attributes. *Wisdom* forms them into "ME/WE" beneficial products. In short, any *Immaterial Idea-Primary Quality Form association is foundational to developing Knowledge, Virtues, Wisdom, Happiness, and Thriving in life.* African Tradition *Essence Qualities* can be likened to a *Tripod* ('3 footed')--a 3-legged stand or support, as for a telescopic camera. The telescope's infinity range is analogized to the Cosmic Mind; the camera to the Cosmic Organism—i.e. all of God's Creatures and Creations; the tripod to Idea-Forms of what came from the telescope. All three of a Cosmic Essence are made of Spiritual Elements derived from the Cosmic Mind. A Spark of the Cosmic Substance/Essence of the Cosmic Mind forms each human's Soul, from which comes an Immaterial Idea reflecting God's Will. It joins Intangible Ether to birth an *Idea-Form*——the *"what it is"* individuated Entity Spiritual Elements attribute. Each Idea-Form travels down the tripod "legs" to become a distinct Entity somewhere in the Cosmos while the *"Form" initiates the "what it does" and the "how it appears"* aspects of that Entity. All of these different aspects have mutual *Continuity*—i.e. Unity running through Multiplicity in the *course* of their *Natural Processes*. Continuity means each part is interdependently doing its independent thing for the benefit of the whole. The Primary Quality in each Idea-Form is what enables the Immaterial Ideas to be expressed on the tripod as Characteristics, Traits, and Features. All Idea-Forms are interconnected, like strings on a tennis racket. By having a "*Sameness Continuity*," to know anything about one string—like its "Genetic" composition and its purpose—gives insight into all other strings. That, the concept of *Correspondence,* is what allowed Ancient Africans to take what they saw in Nature and infer those same Principles into the Un-seeable so as to know the Unknowable God by God's manifestations. Any philosophy standing outside Spiritual Elements Essences cannot possibly be Mathematical because it lacks Continuity. Since European history beginnings, there have been countless differing concepts about the Universe's orchestrator—and all with some degree of a Supernatural component. Dictionaries define "*Supernatural*" as: "Of or relating to existence outside the natural world; attributed to a power that seems to violate or go beyond natural forces." First, this means the Supernatural is not to be questioned for it is unconquerable, unmovable, undeniable, unexplainable, incomparable, unimaginable, immeasurable, and unthinkable. Second, by the Greek Pythagoras (582-500 BC) teaching European males that they were the "Measure of all things"—means *there could be no higher truth than what each White males determined it to be.* Third, by Europeans not believing in the Spiritual God or the Spiritual and Metaphysical realms implies there can be only human-made Universal Essences. When combining these 3, their 'big picture' can be likened to a *Dart Board* with innumerable God darts all over it as well as off it and in every direction. Because there are *no Supernatural Universal Essences*, there *can be no reality Primary Qualities*. Thus, the only alternatives are to make fantasy Primary and/or real, distorted, or fantasy Secondary and Tertiary Qualities for Supernatural/Physical World realms.

In usages of these Supernatural Qualities, all are simply made up to match how each Supernatural person mentally "measures" each Thing or Situation. This "*Distorted One-Sided Coin* situational viewing violates

Rational striving duties to see whole Essences in reality. Fantasy Primary Qualities are necessarily associated with false or unnatural problems—whether originated or perceived. Thus, in actuality, whatever solution is achieved is meaningless and worthless. Yet, Supernatural mindsets give significance to what is beyond ordinary in the Natural World by placing biased/prejudiced Secondary or Tertiary Qualities on such solutions. *Failing to recognize Victims' Spiritual Essences* using practices from Indifference/Hate/Evil/Sadism mindsets means *no Supernatural philosophy standard is violated.* They abdicate any responsibility for their terrible harms done--keeping a sense of having won. Yet, the absence of Idea-Forms means one lacks *Knowledge, Virtues, Wisdom, and Happiness.*

ESSENTIALS: Primary or Secondary Qualities that get unusual attention--are inside a given Essence and consist of Characteristics, Traits, and Features of Essences

ESSENTIALS DIVINE: Since a human's *Soul Substance is its Divine Logos*, that Substance's (whose nature is Divine Spirit) Essence emanates, upon entering the Sublime realm's of Ether, that human's Divine Essentials. The home of the Sublime is the Divine Spirit. The character of this human's Divine Spirit, by being a follower, takes orders from ones Divine Consciousness. When "installed" into the human mind prior to birth, that human's Divine Spirit was subjugated to the Cosmic Mind's Spirit *so as to enable it to draw on the power needed to command the Life-Force in harmony with the Laws of Nature.* Since the "substratum" of the entering Divine Essence is the Sublime *"Ether Substance,"* its Essential are thereby spotlighted as a fully formed Pattern. The inner aspect of the Pattern is its *Matrix* (womb which brings "nourishment" to the Pattern). Inside this Matrix are Activity networks with a *predisposition to behave in a certain way—the "what it does" performances of the Essence—i.e.* Characterizing Behaviors. The outer aspect of that Pattern constitutes its Perceptible Primary Qualities in the form of an *Image* of the Essence. Those *Perceptible* Primary Qualities are shaped into Character, Characteristic, Trait, and Feature portions. The Imperceptible part of the Divine Essence is its *Thought Form*—that which has the shape of "roundness" or which is "hard". Those Image Qualities, orchestrated by their Thought-Forms, eventually enable one to see material objects as a unity—e.g. a chair, a star, a human—as opposed to a jumble of Qualities (e.g. a Thing's roundness, hardness, smoothness, color). See God's Substance; Human Birth

ETHEREAL: Out of the "home" of the Cosmic Organism, come the descending of each of its Entities into the "Ether," called *"Ethereal"* in C17 because it was considered a Matter so fine as to border on the heavenly and thus maintaining its Spiritual purity and excellence. See Quentessence

ETHOS: guiding Values philosophy pervading people to actuate major thought/behaviors patterns.

ETYMOLOGY: C14 English word *"Etymology"*—designating 'finding the underlying, literal, or true meaning of words'—that is applicable only to Essence (i.e. what a Thing was when it came into Being-hood). Essence applies broadly to all Denotations. However, a vital next step is to determine the Source of that Essence. *If the Thing is Knowledge, it is derived from a Pure Spiritual Elements source; if it is Information, it is derived from a Human-made source.* The sense of Etymology has been used by European post-classical grammarians (referring to ancient Greeks) to point to the root from which a particular word's meaning is derived. These are called a word's *Denotations.* Modern etymology deals with a word's origin and history. The variations people give to a specific etymology is called *Connotations*—variations under the category of Information. Today, *Information* is a "catch-all" term referring to anything conveyed that affects the mind in non-Truth ways--affections with respect to sources related to aspects of the Life Triangle components—Nature, people, things, and ones Selfhood (e.g. the body, the mind, or spirit) (Bailey, Rational Thinking). The promoted overall definition of Information as that which *reduces or removes uncertainty as well as creates or enhances feelings of security* must be put into context and classified. Whereas *Knowledge* conveys the Spiritual Elements and its Certainty in whatever form and provides the "5Ss," *Information* is something less than knowledge—and to degrees ranging all the way down to its opposite. Information is awareness of what comes in from outside ones Selfhood--i.e. entering "in-form"—and then onto and through ones *Sensory (Secular) Consciousness.* Sensory Consciousness, popularly defined as the mind registering a sensation, perception, or state of affairs inside one-self or of some external fact or condition, occurs via ones sense perceptions or intellect. See Meaning Changes; Information

EUROPEANS--PRIMITIVE & ANCIENT: With respect to northern Europe, Geneticists say it was populated by the migration of a very small number of modern humans who left the center of the Great Lakes of eastern Africa about 50,000 years ago. Included among these migrators from Africa; These Grimaldi Negroids moved up through northern Africa into European places like Siberia to become, many believe, the Aurignacian foundations (c45,000 BC) of the various European "races." Evidence of this include cave paint-ings of animals in the Chauvet Cave in France (and elsewhere) 35,000 years ago and a carved stone figurine with a skirt of loose strings in Europe 25,000 years ago. Of greater importance is they brought with them their more advanced and inventive culture--things which ensured their survival—rafts, crude clothing, stone tools, weapons and traps, the wheel, pottery, the marked stick for measuring, and ways of making fire. After ice melt-ing deepened the Mediterranean Sea, Black Africans' Art became more isolated and readily distinguishable from European Art. Meanwhile, over the next 20,000 years they transformed into White people--e.g. Aryan, Alpine, and Slavic (Diop, African Origins p260; King, Africa p57; Bynum African Unconscious). During this Ice Age, the "Ice People" (e.g. Scandinavians, Germans, and Southern Russians) who lived in the region of the Baltic Sea encountered fierce weather in the Eurasian Steppes (vast treeless grasslands from the icy cold in winter). Today's European authorities are making a host of confusing and conflicting claims like what origi-nally happened is that newly arriving modern African Grimaldi Negroes slowly pushed their more ancient human-like predecessors out of existence. Either those new arrivals were swept aside by hunter-gatherers or themselves became so. Some of their comments pertain to African and Neanterhals matings 55,000 years ago; the Aurignacian age Goyet individual of 35,000 BC (who retreated to modern Spain and Portugal) and their 1000 year later successor, the Gravettians being of a completely different lineage. Nevertheless, Europeans call the birth of agriculture in 20,000 BC by African women and it finding its way into Europe as a critical transi-tion. This refers to the taking of European Homo Sapiens from scattered groups of hunter-gatherers to farming villages—called the Neolithic Revolution. Some say this geological epoch of the *Holocene* occurred c12,500 years ago when the Ice Age ended. This enabled small and mobile groups of hunter-gatherers to settle into non-nomadic societies, with the build up of villages. When families of Primitive Europeans began to settle down to live and work together as a given group they became Very Ancient Europeans. An illustrative example, according to the European scientist Spencer Wells, ancient Europeans [e.g. La Braña man with dark skin/blue eyes] adapted over 10,000 years to the much colder northern weather and low sunlight conditions with shorter limbs for heat conservation and lighter skin. Recent finding indicate a gene mutation contributed to light skin color in Europeans that was traceable to one individual of c10,000 BC. The key contributor in skin color dif-ferences between Europeans and West Africans consisted of one amino acid difference in one gene. Regardless of type, once such a "Seed" forms and survives it has even more branching effects. To illustrate, Light skin color provided an evolutionary advantage for people in northern climates. This is because people with light skin can absorb more vitamin D from sunlight which is not abundant at certain times of year at those latitudes. Sunlight and its ultraviolet rays transforms humans' provitamin ergosterol into vitamin D which helps build stronger bones, develop a stronger immune system, and may help fight cancer and heart disease. The barren-ness of those regions and the lack of riches within the soil all fashioned a setting of the necessity for basic survival (Asante, "Afrocentricity," p. 81) and striving for security. At that time, the Ice Age environment ensured the land was minimally productive of food and other such essentials required for survival. This had a profound philosophical effect on those struggling to survive—on how they thought—on what they felt the need to do—and on the religion they created. Thought patterns resulting from the resultant "Scarcity" of essentials dictated that individuals and their nomadic tribes rob and kill neighbors to acquire what they needed to live. *Scarcity* implies insufficient resources to supply everyone's needs and wants and the reaction to that is first: *Rapacious*--the robber instinct of "I'll get there first and take it all"; second, *"Covetous"*: "I'll want yours so I'll have some extra"; third, *"Defensive"*--using any means necessary to keep what one has and prevent others from having any. By these Eurasians also lacking other environmental advantages of necessities for life made it easy to develop a 'second nature' mindset of Scarcity. Realistic Scarcity initially led to survival in the world viewed as hostile to them by "any means necessary". Then, and up to the present, Europeans only source of power has been by the GUN—i.e. any device used to Kill/Take/Destroy/Dominate/Oppress/Control (KTDDOC). The various approaches, methods, and techniques associated with this allowed the Satanist leaders to have what is known today as "White Privilege: "the creation, enhancement, maintenance, defending, and protecting of unfair advantages for themselves and unfair disadvantages for their victims. But it was essential for Satanist leaders to control the minds of their Troops. This was done by creating "Desperation" among them by rejecting, abandoning, isolating, or killing those who did not conform. Conformity was carried out by Icon Images—a Supernatural (fantasy) God who would send violators to a Supernatural Hell that was ruled by a Supernatural Devil. All three, in a king-like capacity, are separated from the people—reside in a Supernatural realm—direct a Supernatural cult--and dictate Supernatural rules. Those rules and the Icon Images were made by the Satanist leaders in their own image. The overall attitude was to "stay in your place"; be ready to fight whenever there was a call to action; and otherwise "Be about nothing." Everyone was taught or learned the simple minded way of thinking alike—and as told how and what to think. In this manner, everybody knew what everybody else was thinking without having to say anything or with merely using "code" language. The "Desperation" could be relieved by accepting being controlled, not asking questions, worshiping all that is about the Supernatural, and becoming a "Zombie". It has always been essential for the troops and the victims to be made ignorant and stay ignorant by self-perpetuation. That self- perpetuation is to focus on always seeking whatever is "Exciting"—as in what is opposite to the best in the Natural World. This includes attacking the Spiritual Elements, causing pain and suffering, never being Happy but rather be full of hatred for "faceless" victims. A compatible Indifference/Hate/Evil/Sadism (IHES) mindset the one that makes for a "superior" people in the Supernatural. This ensures there will be no intellectual levels above innervations on what is stolen from Victims—no high level creativity—no humanity benefitting inventions—no discoveries of a "ME/WE" nature. Otherwise, staying "excited" is done by devoting life to Trinkets and Trivia and pursuing their animalistic passions (which are lower than any animal). By so doing, one avoid self-improvement and ridicule anyone who promotes it. This "Zombie-like" state is a tow-rope for the Troops and the Victims to hold on to and honor. This means they will absolutely never change because of their Self-Unknown state, their self-hatred—their inability to be happy or satisfied or at peace. Together, this IHES mindset and its associated practices became 'second nature' experiences that are clearly manifested today. 'Second nature' means that they produced imprints or impressions on the mind's "wax" (i.e. neuroplasticity). Plato called these "Memory Traces" or *Engrams*--i.e. the "Seed" of the *Scarcity Tree Concept*. Out of that came their religion and gods—both being within the confines of their channeled way of thinking within the context of "Scarcity" and Ice Age environment. By this, their mindsets, and their practices being about hostility meant they automatically created even worst Icon Images of their enemies. Put another way, their mindsets could be analogized to being a combination of "three heads"—a huge Fantasy head, a hypersensitive Emotional head, and a

Non-Rational Thinking head geared only to war. Such a "Three-Headed Brute" mindset has a Phantasmagoric (ghost and monster) orientation. See Ancient African Migration

EVIDENCE: it being an indicator of where the truth lies and serves as a magnet to gather it.

EVIL SAVIOR SYNDROME: In spite of Europeans' cruelty to the Enslaved in body, mind, emotions, and spirit + the inadequacy of the food, clothing, and shelter, many Enslaved bonded with the captors.

"EXCITEMENT:" as experienced by children—is to be stimulated by some "here and now" happening and then it immediately fades away.

"EXPERTS" & THEIR SUPERIORITY-- UNEXAMINED ASSUMPTIONS: Humans' Standards for "Best Living" come from their own minds and/or from the God they select to follow. The *Spiritual God worshipped in African Tradition is Knowable with Certainty by what is Seeable in Nature*. Others claim their God is Supernatural—either an individual or too remote to know about—either for bad or good. Out of a similar Supernatural pattern, humans' standards are used to designate "Experts". The Middle English root 'experiri' ('to try out') gave rise to *"Experience"* (trying out something for oneself); *"Experiment"* (a try out or test); and *"Expert"* (one who has successfully tried out or experienced something thoroughly). In 1384, "Expert" meant very skillful, experienced in, having experience of; in 1420, one wise through experience; and in 1868, *"Expertise,"* special Knowledge in appraising or reporting in any field. Today, Experts are deemed to show mastery or demonstrate extraordinary skill--with distinguished achievements--in execution, performance, or technique in a subject, art, or profession. In legal settings, an Expert—as I was in the Medico-Legal arena--is one selected to give opinions on points in issue on what one is peculiarly conversant and not within common knowledge. *Dictionary writers*—even those dealing with *lexicons* (vocabulary on a particular subject)--are called *Lexicographers (C17, about writing words), Etymologists, Glossarians, Philologians, Vocabulists, Wordsmiths*, and many others. They deal with such references as *dictionaries, glossaries, thesauruses, synonym guides, usage guides, concordances, or, as I do, Word Stories*. Two kinds of lexiography are: Alphabetical and *Thematic* (arranging words by themes or topics, usually with an index (e.g. Thesaurus). These may be books about words (e.g. dictionaries), about things (encyclopedias), or, like mine, mixtures. Hence, those setting up words for public use are called "Experts"—defined in European dictionaries as one who has special knowledge or skill—a *specialist* as a result of training, practice, or experience. While any of these may or may not be true, within their area of expertize it is extremely common for Experts to leave out words too complex for them. Or, the included information is not comprehensive from its beginning origin to the present. Or, only part of a word's "big picture" is present—thus giving incomplete information about the "umbrella" (all aspects) of a word on any plane of existence and/or on different planes of existence. Also, *what they do say is opinionated*. In the Supernatural: (1) there is no sound base on which to build a Thought Structure; (2) its eliminating the Spiritual--where Reality starts and where the Metaphysical makes it into Form; (3) it fits every word concept and meaning into Physical Planes of existence so as to be characterized by constant change; and (4) by the Greek Pythagoras (582-500 BC) teaching European males they were the "Measure of all things" and *there could be no higher truth than what each White male determined it to be. Thus, Unconditional Love, Truth, Reality, and the Natural concepts cannot exist*. Even in the simple relaying of factual historical information, original scribes' recordings and those, throughout the ages, who did subsequent transcribing, all engaged in *pseudepigraphic writings—i.e. stories falsely attributed to Biblical characters or times*. In the process, scribes typically altered original stories according to their own opinions. Of particular interest to me are *"Detour" Concepts* occurring in the course of a word's history. All of this gives me and scholars increased understanding of topics. That allows me to arrange "skeletal bones" in better order and research for missing ones. Note the Flaws: "Authorities" are spoken about in the form of: "Plato said or Decartes said"—but how do we know that is simply not their opinions, filled with bias and prejudices? Plato got his well-known information from African Sages but his presented non-African acquired information, by my assessment, makes no sense. Thus, no Base means either "Detours" are absent or, if present, are of questionable credibility. To what standards are "Authorities" and "Experts" held as, for example, those saying the world was flat? This was contrary to known Ancient African Knowledge. Or, based on his expertise on ancient documents and biblical genealogies, the Irish Archbishop James Ussher (1581–1656) estimated that our planet was created in the morning of October 23, 4004 BC. Now, Europeans know better. These are some reasons I avoid Europeans' opinions on anything since they are typically incomplete, weak, limited, facades, racially/ethnocentrically biased, conflicting, and/or mostly simply wrong! jabaileymd.com

EUGENICS: an ignorant form of thinking by Supernaturals pertaining to the science of being "well-born"; defined as the study of agencies under social control which may improve or impair the racial qualities of future generations either physically or mentally." It focuses on improving the human material, not the environment by preventing reproduction of those inferior or having undesirable traits. By contrast, it promotes mating and reproduction among those having desirable or superior traits. Such have been the practices of Europeans dealing with Colored Peoples.

EVIDENCE: "that which tends to show a thing to be true". See Circumstantial Evidence

"EVIDENCE/PROOF/TRUTH" UNEXAMINED ASSUMPTIONS: Since "Evidence" and "Proof" are words in daily usage by almost "everybody," it is assumed "everybody" knows what they mean—or at least can use dictionary definitions: *Evidence*: 1. "A thing or things helpful in forming a conclusion or judgment: evidence of a burglary. 2. Something indigative; an outward sign: evidence of grief. 3. Law. The documentary or oral statements and the material objects admissible as testimony in a court of law." Proof: "the evidence or argument that compels the mind to accept an assertion as true." All aspects within these two word definitions represent extremely bad thinking, as seen by their difficulty in understanding, their incompleteness, their dealing with examples of what they do and how they appear; their failure to say "what it is"; their limitation to the Physical Plane and completely omitting the Spiritual and Metaphysical planes of reality existence; their dependence upon; *things exist by virtue of how a human perceives them to be;* and there is nothing outside man that determines "Being" or Truth; what men wish to think or do determines *for them* what is true or right; and so forth. What such ambiguity does is to allow those in power, by having no objective standard that is agreed upon by the Sages of all cultures and of all ages--to *play by their own rules and declare that what they determine to be "right" for them does not apply to those who are not like them.* Furthermore, *what is "right" for those not like them is what they decide it to be.* Since whatever is presented by "Authorities" and "Experts" as "truth" of what constitutes Evidence and Proof, to accept this is to proceed based upon unexamined assumptions at every step leading up to the acceptance. To proceed onward is to be blindly led, as also programmed by Mind Control leaders, to conform in a series of small, graded steps to carry out approaches, methods, techniques, and manners that "SEEM" right so as to achieve specific functions and to solve spotlighted problems by what has nothing to do with Truth/Reality. In my book: "African Tradition Wisdom vs. European Information, I devoted 20 pages to discussing Evidence and Proof from an African Tradition vs. European Tradition perspective. In the early Western world, *"Evidence"*—an offspring of "Evident"—meant a distinction so clear to the eye that it impressed the mind with its luster or splendor. Such brilliantly shiny things--whether concerned with what was seen, heard, smelled, tasted, and/or touched--applied to deciding disputes. When present, they were deemed to be "Proof" under the belief that how something appeared was the same as saying what it was—a tremendously flawed thought. Note that this European way is a feature seen in children and immature thinkers. Both will select shiny trinkets over a dull appearing treasure. As a result, European Evidence has come to mean all the ways information can be presented to prove or disprove disputes. Yet, such Evidence cannot be relied upon to be true. One reason in the Western world is Proof and Evidence are supposed to relate to the objective but both are actually checkered with the subjective (e.g. opinions, tastes, bias, and prejudices) while ignoring the Spiritual origin of all Real Creatures and Creations. Regardless of the type of Evidence—whether good, bad, or indifferent—what makes this a "Guesstimate" thinking system is most people willingly accept what does not harmoniously fit because they want or do not want things to be a certain way or because they intensely desire to conform or because they are gullible and naïve or because of biases and prejudices. The problem is complicated when the dispute or issue involves more than one plane of existence. In African Tradition, generically, "*Evidence*" is Essence's Essentials display of *Character*--the Identical "what it is" Copy of the Virtual Icon Idea of the Essence Spiritual Elements contents. The most consistent Pattern(s) of the Operations of the Essentials in action is its *Trait(s)*. The most outstanding Trait(s) operation is its *Feature(s)*. The most outstanding Featured Trait of the Character is the Essence "*Trademark*"—meaning Evidence indicates where the Truth flow lies; serves as a magnet to gather it; and *by staying within the Spiritual Elements, that Evidence is capable of being used as a basis for Inferences serving as mediums for proof.* Then, the Observed, Inferred, Intuited, or Unknown having Circumstantial (e.g. as in reproducing its Spiritual Attributes to become the thing it makes) compatibility with established flowing Laws of Nature + all ingredients having Continuity (Unity running through Multiplicity) throughout all that is involved is Proof of Truth.

EVIL: a word packed with such destructive ideas as wicked, vile, sinful, depraved, inequity, injustice, wrong, and the violation of God's intention. It implies consequences like tragedy, distress, emotional pain, suffering, misery, and aging. What people think Evil is, what it does, how it appears, and when it began depends on how these have been defined and by whom. Among Very Ancient Africans, three basic sources and agents of evil believed to be realities in the Spirit World below the heavens (i.e. the Supernatural Realm) were evil magic, witchcraft, and sorcery. In Ancient African religion, including Kamit (Egypt), Evil and suffering were attributed to the failure to control the animal faculties of ones brain (e.g. the Brute Brain); the result of disruptive spirits (called Seban by Egyptians); to unrighteous living leading to SIN (a separation between oneself and God); and/or to the actions of people ignorant of the higher spiritual reality (anti-loving) within themselves--concepts still persisting in African Tradition. In general, African societies say God did not create whatever is evil; God does not ever engage in evil; and God has erected deities with independent free will existences that can either cause evil or are the agents of evil (Asante, African Intellectual Heritage, p. 302). Yet, there have been numerous African concepts of how evil manifests in every day life: (1) evil is whatever is contrary to Ma'at; (2) evil is not in the intrinsic nature of a deed but rather is in who does it to whom and from which level of status; (3) evil is a manifestation of chaos; (4) ignorance of ones true nature is the sure way to evil; (5) evil is anything causing a breakup of the family; (6) there is no such thing as good or evil; (7) evil comes from humans themselves; and (8) lesser spirits, not God, are the source and agents of evil. Whatever the cause, evil occurs on all planes of existence -- religious, moral, social, mental, physical, spiritual, and natural (e.g. earthquakes, famine). By contrast, the *Western* religious traditions relate the problem of evil to a movement away from virtue (originally meaning strength from magic power) under the influence of a demon (the devil) and thereby *assigning blame to an outside force which, of course, allows people with poor moral development to shirk responsibility for their actions.* In Biblical times, Satan, in Hebrew, meant adversary or enemy—a concept traditionally applied to the Devil, the personification of evil. He appears as the Serpent, a tempter of mankind in Gen. iii, I, and the existence of Satan as the center of evil is part of the teaching of both the Old and New Testament. Though having no concept of Satan or the devil, Ancient African Spiritual Literature's story of Horus and his brother Set conveys the idea that ignorance is responsible for "Dark Side" and brute behaviors. In other words, African Tradition never considered Set as a devil and never saw him as the source of evil itself (until the late Dynastic Period which was when the Jewish people were living in Egypt). The African concept of what orthodox Western religions call evil relates to an attraction to passion and to a movement away from virtue—and thereby retaining human responsibility. What fails to be emphasized is the Ancient Egyptian teaching that Satan is ultimately subject to God. Otherwise, if Satan were the true adversary of God this would mean God is not omnipotent because of a being capable of limiting God's power. By Africans believing one has control over ones Brute Brain means the fear of being possessed is a moot point (a matter of no importance). In my opinion, evil must be understood as the actions of people ignorant of the higher spiritual reality within themselves (egoism) based upon fear, pride, anger, hatred, greed, lust, envy, jealousy, etc. Evil people are cold and compassionless; planners and performers of deception; and manipulate whatever to gain power and control. African Sages say these destroy ones Soul while knowledge of ones Self (Aset) restores it to its true nature. Furthermore, the overcoming of such ignorance starts with getting "To Know Thyself" so as to re-establish the bonds of connection associated with all of God's creatures and creations--the Law of Sympathy.

EVILNESS--EUROPEAN: In European tradition, Evilness' scope, height, depth, consistency, variety, and magnitude of destructiveness are unequaled in the history of human-kind. Yet, in European literature it is extremely difficult to gain an idea of Evil's Moral (about Sin)"what it is" aspects. The relatively few books which mention Evil do so from "what it is associated with," "what it does," and "how it appears." No help comes from the etymology of the Old English word "Evil"--originally meaning "uppity"--then "Bad"--then extreme moral wickedness--then in 1280 AD, "*Shrewd*," signifying evil, malicious, and dangerous before its sense changed in 1520 to astute and cunning--and then to cleverness, scheming, and deception. None of these are to be confused with intelligence because they are of a patterned nature, perfected by *Innovation* (adding something new to what already exists and, in this situation, has been done for 45,000 years). Today's ruling European Evil concepts seem to be the choicest opinions of the most accepted "authorities." In general, these Evilness concepts are selectively attentive to what is in the Physical and the European versions of the Supernatural realms. What is "against a materialistic Good life" is often the standard to which Evil is compared and judged--especially for European males, and with no generally offered and acceptable justifying definitions, explanations, or reasons. Examples of how they say Evil is allowed to enter into the Selfhood of humans includes: (1) one loses a sense of ones belief in the presence of ones chosen Supernatural God; (2) the "fall of man" (i.e. Adam and Eve); (3) whatever causes harm or deprives a Being of some good which is proper to that Being; (4) self-imposed Evil from a refusal to think; and (5) based upon their varied definitions of "Virtue," many Western religions relate the problem of evil to a movement away from their specifically self-defined "Virtues," under influences of a demon/devil. That enables them to say, without cross-cultural Sages' agreement, that Evil is a defect in moral purity and truth--whether in heart or life--whether of commission or omission. By then assigning the blame to an outside force allows people with poor moral development to shirk responsibility for their evil actions. Though the African mythological god Set (who Europeans adopted as fact and made into a 'factual' Satan) was borrowed into the Judeo-Christian religion or philosophy as Lucifer (e.g. featuring a fall from Grace and moral deterioration after virtue), no help in pin-pointing can be found here since there is great confusion about how they represent Evil. Satan, Evil, and Dark (signifying misery, punishment, perdition or loss of the soul and hell) became the trio Europeans used to characterize the "*Dark Side*"--and with the justification of: "the Devil made me do it." Millennia later, Set became the basis of the Christian Satan--an evil Supernatural entity honored with a superhuman status; an opposing reality to God (a form of idolatry) and a user of blasphemy (false statements, problem creators, hypocrisy, or done out of "Me, Me" self-interest). In European literature, the "*Occult*" refers to the mysterious lying below the surface of things or beyond the ordinary range of ones information, perception, or understanding. Historically, it has been applied to the Magical Arts, witchcraft, astrology, alchemy, palmistry, and all aspects of the Supernatural (the made-up). Within these wide-ranging beliefs are concepts of Evil--essentially all deemed to be "Natural"--defined by them as what is beyond a human's control. That spanning range of Secular and Supernatural Evil--for which Europeans use the term "*Dark Side*"--embraces every degree of the IHES Complex--Indifference, Hate, Evilness, Sadism. The Indifference part is shown by those with one foot in the IHES Complex stream flow and the other foot on shore; those standing on the shore--the Hate part; those walking away from the shore and wandering into Evil Unknowns--called Brutes--the Secular Evil part. Satanists, do all they can to destroy the flow and dissipate the Stream while trapping all humans possible in their fishnet so as to perform Sadism acts. Those in the IHES Complex operate in the realms of *Illusions* (in attempts to affirm truth for deception, as opposed to Truth's operation through Reality to affirm itself) and Hallucinations. These fashion Delusions characterized by "Me, Me" Individualism--Evil "sick" pleasures--and Fetters--e.g. hatred, fear, lies, jealousy, egoism, anger, greed, lust, and envy.

EVOCATIVE: Possessing mystical powers able to evoke psychic forces of tremendous potency. This set in motion Sounds and Rhythms, both being vibrations transmitting energy under tension to turn on the Orisa (divinities)--both possessing *Evocative* (mystical) powers--both instinctive and therefore Natural--both designing Cosmic Unity from the Spiritual Elements. Hence, *Spiritual Natural pertains to the very essence of Being*. Natural vibrations (or rhythms) show as *Laws of Nature*.

EVOLUTION: going away from the center. The process is to *involute*--the process of getting involved by "Knowing Thyself" and thus the foundational Cosmic Laws by returning to a human's pre-birth "First Wisdom" state. Then comes Evolution of Spiritual Meanings which naturally manifest by the unfolding of its Involuted contents and their associated powers.

EXOTERIC: basic understanding of a given thing's mundane outer meaning

EXPERIMENT: "Experience" and "Experiment" shared a common Latin origin (to try, to put to the test). So, in the 16th century the main idea inside "Experience" veered off while carrying the meaning of becoming a conscious test or trial; then a consciousness of what has been tested or tried; then a consciousness of an effect or state; and eventually a knowledge derived from real events as well a from particular observation. "Experiment" simply meant a test or trial.

EXPERIENCE: C14 word "*Experience*" (try out) means being self-involved in something; actually observing phenomena; or undergoing special events—each to gain first-hand knowledge of a practical nature, as opposed to a speculative way of finding out about a thing. In this form of Knowing there is experience. Becoming one can be by Contemplation so as to perceive the inner unifying quality of the Thing as being compatible with ones Soul or experiencing its attributes—by "yoking" (to tie, unite) to it in the manner of a Circumstance

EXTRAPOLATION: an educated guess resulting from calculations from a fact(s) about what preceded that fact or is likely to follow it (Trueblood p98).

EXTROVERTING: Needing the External World for approval as well as gathering what is cherished in the External World as ones own standards, guides, measures, and filters.

F

FAÇADES: "Façade" (a false front; shape imposed on something) is a Thing intended to create a false impression—as of gentility. Its background concept originated in Africa by Ritual Specialists (c30,000 BC) using masks and masquerades to cure psychosomatic disease caused by disharmonious spirits. Primitive Africans resorted to all sorts of songs, dance, delusions, and dramatic tricks to either appease or control the spirits. Griots, skilled storytellers, employed their voice, hands, and bodies to best effect while mimicking the antics of the story's main character. As the story unfolded, the audience participated through interpolations (putting in new words and passages). This feature of hiding and displaying moods to influence or control nature, the gods, and human affairs + persuading, informing, entertaining, expressing, sharing, teaching, instructing, educating, recreating (e.g. playing with words in figures of speech and figures of thought), or serving as a call to action spread throughout the world. Of particular significance were the Etruscans who dominated Italy's northwestern coast from c900 to 300 BC. They brought all elements of Black Ethiopians' (Egyptian) civilization and culture to the Italian peninsula and then on to the Greeks. Africans' drama stage forefront aspect was expanded to include "Façade"—Italy's medieval architectural term signifying the external face of a building, especially applied to the principle front. Then European religious societies applied it to *Mystery Plays--initially* enacted by priests depicting events in the life, death, and resurrection of the African god Osiris with associated African myth stories. Later, called *Morality Plays*—they depicted out of the European Bible the miracles of Good triumphing over Evil. Vice, the opposite of Virtue, was a practical joker in the plays. In C17 French, Façade referred not only to the front part of a building but with little or nothing behind it. In C19 it was used in a figurative way for the face one puts on to meet people; then on the small "faces" or surfaces of a gem; then Hollywood extended this for stage sets when filming movies so as to resemble only the front of a real building; and from there, many variations of these. An example of a world-wide acceptable Façade is "Information"--always decorated frontispieces (facades) of Reality. Anything in Reality is multi-dimensional while Information is necessarily linear (one dimensional) in order for it to be conveyed to audiences. Any of its Sequences are *Linear*--meaning one word or image is followed by another and then another; or numbers are always strung out in a line and occur like stepping stones. To accept this "as is" means one is far, far from Reality. *Deceptive Facades* include: Type I--a False front with nothing behind it; Type II--a False Front with a sound Background; Type III--a False Front with an unsound Background. Whether good (e.g. entertainment), bad (e.g. evil deception), or indifferent, these are about *Hypocrisy* (false appearances of goodness, virtue)—a Greek word characterizing acting on the stage, as when one acts out the part(s) of a character in a play. Today, Hypocrisy implies the masking over of ones Real Self to thereby be in a different realm as one presents ones False Self while playing a role that pleases ones cult. An example of gross manipulating and maneuvering what is in the Foreground and the Background is re-writing history to falsely say: "how great we are and how bad you are." *Subtle alterations*—e.g. substitutions, additions, subtractions of a minor but payload degree can make the Message "SEEM" right or to be "Almost" right. A false front is to present what has a rich Background on all planes of existence as "All-or-None" and "Either/Or" when neither are the truth. Stereotypes may have two specks of checkered truths in either the Background and/or the Foreground but the presentation is that throughout both are "terrible". The psychological concept of *Projection* messes with the audience—said the Nazi Joseph Goebbels--by accusing them (or opponents) of what the Performers are projecting onto them but of which the Performers are guilty. Officially, Projection is stated as humans defending themselves against their own unconscious negative impulses or qualities by denying their existence in themselves while attributing them to others. It is a form of Dissociation, as when one asserts or believes in cooperation but behaves competitively; protects love but acts with hate; proclaims good-will but practices racism–all without being aware in part or in whole of ones inconsistency. A job of Critical Thinking is to first remove masks so as see the 'face'.

FACTS: African Logic, *"Facts" are truisms—i.e. in harmony with the reality at hand by conforming to the Spiritual Elements.* Whereas in African Tradition Knowledge is the basis of Science, Facts are the Western basis. Originally, as opposed to the sense of Knowledge, the Western concept of "Fact" meant anything that had been done or something that had occurred. By C16, Europeans' "Fact" referred to "truths" describing Reality as given by "experts." This led to the subdivisions of "Spiritual facts" (e.g. Nature) and "Worldly Facts" (e.g. a thing made by human's skill)--3 flaws in a row! Today, a "Worldly Fact" is usually considered as a statement of perceived Secular Reality, verifiable by Observation and called *Empirical Science*. See "Empirical" ('relating to experience')

FACULTY: "*Capacity*" (the power to receive) includes power + Ability. "*Ability*"--the inherent power to do—i.e. improved with exercise implies a FACULTY (an inherent quality within ones Selfhood) to perform acts in the 'here and now' without much training or education.

FAD: The world's society (e.g. school systems) is geared to Extroverts. Their craving for External World stimulation suggests an inability to be open to comprehending mysteries of Beauty, Primary Qualities, or Spiritual Essences. Being populators of the Crowd, such Worth is replaced with wallowing in Material things + wishing and hoping for endless amounts of "Scarce Desirables" + following "Fad" trends pertaining to items of *Value*. Measured material benefits depend upon how they are esteemed on the Ladder of Significance by the Public. This is what guides ones interpretations of the monitored feedback one gets from External World influences. "*Fad*"--a 'Hippie Era' term for something temporarily popular (like today's 'Flashing Light' gadgets)—means a "Trend" or "Craze" in any form of collective Crowd behavior that "comes and goes." In the process, Fad implies the Crowd's minds are excitingly entangled and encaged "inside-the-Crazed box". Absorption of these ways of thinking by socialization makes for Patterned and Superficial Thinkers—and the absence of profound explorations. An exhibition of this occurs in asking "Fad" people if their lives are better off by technology and its gadgets? Some start by asking: "better off than what"?—a stalling to consider if they may not have the newest, bigger, better, stronger, faster Trinkets—a thought making them terribly insecure. Other, almost endless questions follow, admixed with chatting about the latest and most wide-scoped Trivia. The result is simply "letting go" of the original question—and with no one having any more clarity than before. By contrast, that question--asked of Introverts in the Spiritual Elements flow and comfortably skilled in Contemplation—is instantly answered: "technology is of low priority."

FAITH: the union of beliefs and trust; trust in something that cannot be proven because it is Supernatural. *Beliefs*: This is committing oneself to Guesses or to Unproven Information with the hope those things are true. Thus, some Beliefs are closer to the truth than others. *Faith*: Beliefs + acceptance of the consequences of Beliefs. Opinions are matured Beliefs which makes choices from favored available options. The failure to consider all the options is often a way to keep from getting on track or a way to get off track.

FALLACY: Ancient Greek *Sophistry terms* are designed to subtly present "tainted" ideas, concepts, and thoughts about what is being done in a manner that is *just a shade off the Truth-Track*--called *Fallacies* (Greek, phelos, "deceitful"). This makes them plausible but misleading or fallacious presentations of information with the intent of deception.

FANTASTIC: parents for Fantastic are "Fantasy" and "imagination," both found in Chaucer's (1340?-1400) works--referring to "a mental image or reflection," or more particularly "an image of something which either has no real existence or does not exist." The sense of the unreal has survived inside the word "Fantastic."

FANTASY INFORMATION: Pre-feasible is the realm of *"Wishes"* (hoping for the unattainable or the non-existent). Next up is *Fantasy Information* (having no relationship with Truth). Some Fantasies are useful for humor and "Imagination Escapes" (e.g. Cinderella). Some are misleading, whether intentional or not. Some do great mental damage. Some Fantasies are useful for humor and "Imagination Escapes" (e.g. the Black Beauty fairytale). Some are misleading, whether intentional or not, and do great psychic or directional damage. *Man-Made "Pseudo-Truths"* -- what people call Facts (man-made), Beliefs, Opinions, Superstitions, and Faith--are distortions of Reality. Each has a range extending from approaching somewhere near to Cosmic Truths on one end of the scale all the way down to Guessing. Though Critical Thinking (CT) is against Possibilities, there are times when CT cannot do any better. Thus, CT uses the best available Man-Made Information until something better leads one into making modifications or replacements. *Secular Faith* embraces Beliefs that may incorporate "Facts," "Opinions," "Assumptions," and/or "Superstitions." And a taboo is to not question its internal conflicts. To have Secular Faith is to accept the consequences arising from everything having to do with its involvement.

FEAR IN EUROPEANS: Obviously, the system of Values of European society is opposite to the "We" societies of the Colored peoples of the world. Their typical "I" (Individualism) society features are: looking for differences in people, individuality, uniqueness, being competitive, advocating individual rights, separateness and independence, survival of the fittest, and control over Nature (Nobles in Jones, Black Psychology p103). These and similar features have been present throughout their history. For example, Machiavelli (1536-1603) did not invent a dishonorable way of practicing politics. He was simply describing how good politicians of his time went about their business--practicing international politics as a complex game of conspiracy and betrayal; being responsible for the mismanagement of banks; and accepting assassination as a form of succession. The reason this is important for Black people to know is because at the time of African American slavery African people were living in an honorable society where harmony and unity were foundational features. But in the Americas, European practices of dishonorableness persisted. Hence most Slaves failed to make the mindset conversion to self-protect because of unfamiliarity with a brute enemy. This failure made minds of Slaves quite vulnerable to being molded into self-defeating thoughts, feelings, expressions, and deeds culturally transmitted to today's descendants. Only by understanding this is there a chance for sound mental health in the afflicted. European mental health literature agrees Fear is Europeans' most common emotion. Medically it is known Fear automatically activates the Ancient Brain for a "fight or flight" response. Since their appearance on earth Europeans have been and remain a warring people and this, of course, generates fear in the predators and the prey. During their Ice Age beginnings in northern Europe, Fear was properly associated with *Survival*. A second form--*Self-Created Fear*--came from self-protection stemming from their ill-gotten gains and resultant worry about victims retaliating. A third form -- *Fear for Justification* -- is deliberately created to serve to justify attacks (mainly on Colored Peoples) so as to gain more possessions. A fourth is *"White Superiority"* Fear, taking the form of desiring to be isolated from and not diluted by those they try to keep down. Examples include Housing or school integration causing "White Flight." A fifth is Europeans' *Inter-Competition Fear*, as in "not being able to keep up with the Jones" (i.e. trying to match the lifestyle of ones more affluent neighbors or acquaintances). Among the richest Europeans this is called *"The Game."* The struggle for control is by the most powerful Brute people and their degree of destructiveness to people, animals, and Nature is of a Maafa magnitude (immeasurable catastrophe). These Brutes have a variety of names, such as the Illuminati, Power

Elite, the Knights Templar, and Free Masons. Even milder degrees of people like them are the enemy of not only Black People and all Colored Peoples of the world but also the Poor, Disabled, Women, and Elderly of all races. Fear, the shaper of European male's POL, thus controlled the force of their behavior. Behind the causes of the Self-Created Fear, Fear for Justification, the "White Superiority" Fear, and the *Inter-Competition Fear* is a profound sense of inadequacy, envy, an inferiority complex, and discontent (no matter how pleasurable their lifestyle seems to be). Money is made on--and the control of people is based upon--the manipulation of Fear. Hence, they constantly look for places where Fear can be applied. For example, since the 1980s a focus shift onto cultural issues has generated fear related to abortions, the role of religion in public life, and gun control. These issues divide Euro-Americans as well as along racial lines. As a result, Fear is a mass European addiction and its obsession/compulsion aspects serve as a kind of "sick" entertainment to make life interesting.

FEARS--DELUSIONAL: The "Three-Headed Brute" mindset has the resultant Effect of *Paracosms* being used to make "monster" mental images of their scapegoats. Such Phantasmagoria generates *Delusional Fears*—the imagining of false, dangerous problems and believing them to pose great problems to something significant to oneself. This Supernatural "out of this world" Fantasy thinking path's total focus on the *Scarcity Tree Concept* is characterized by ill-defined meanings. Examples include rapidly or strikingly changing scenes of real things, illusions, imagery fancies, deceptions, or distorted phantasy. Depending upon ones mood, figures supposedly seen or Icon Image fashioned monsters may increase or decrease in size, fade away, or pass into each other. Starting in primitive times and continuing to the present, "Phantasmagoria" contributed to the Occult Supernatural realm serving as an alarm to signal evil and sadistic *Evocative* (mystical) powers into action. Immediately these Evocative powers would focus on setting in motion whatever it took to destroy anything having the potential for good or whoever was standing in the way of ones desires or whatever was deemed to be a threatening or destructive "monster". Throughout the primitive European Ice Age of Scarcity there was an interweaving of Delusional Fears checkered with actuality aspects—as in seeing oneself as prey. Thus, partly to avoid allowing oneself to needlessly become prey, the Warriors developed the practice of preying on others before others had the chance to make them prey. By having a supportive "*Network*" to protect them from being accountable (because they do the same things) means they developed into adult bullies. In the process, the more cult members buy into Supernatural "Air Castle" codes of killing anybody not like them—just for "sport"--the greater the killing frequency and duration. For these "Faceless" enemy "monsters," the bullies designed an assortment of mental images having priority order. For example, "To get mine, I must take yours" requires killing or destroying those "monsters" having what they envy. As a result, it does not take much to pull the switch that evokes psychic forces of tremendous potency to display in the minds of "Killers" on seeing a hated scapegoat. At crunch time, their Phantasmagoria deludes their seeing enormous sized and strong scapegoat "monsters" rushing at them, in a constantly shifting and complex manner, to harm them. This moment symbolizes all of the "Killers" conjured Delusional Fears of nightmarish mirages of being destroyed by these 'monsters' and, of course, they "pull the trigger" to kill, even the unarmed.

FEASIBLE--capable of being done—is below Possible. PRE-FEASIBLE is the realm of *"Wishes"* (hoping for the unattainable or the non-existent)

FEATURE: The Mosaic markings from the Interchange of its Essence parent whose *Trademark Identity of the "How it appears" of its* Characteristics and Traits Essentials family.

FETTERS: extreme selfishness, greed, hatred, anger, egoism, fear, envy, jealousy, frustration, arrogance, pride, lust, conceit.

FETUS: Fetuses in the mother's womb have sense organs that respond to few stimuli, and then for only a short duration. Following birth, they learn to react to increasingly larger numbers of stimuli. Hence, they emerge gradually from their Inner World isolation while getting oriented to the External World. But in the process, even before their first birthday, babies are highly selective—discriminating in to whom they will pay attention. They select as a preference those of their "in-group" ("people like me")—wasting no time on those they deem unlikely to "deliver the goods." By age 11 months, they pay attention to those speaking the language familiar to them while ignoring foreign speakers. At the moment babies make those decisions, their brain waves detected, by electroencephalogram, indicate an "expectation to learn something new" pattern by "theta" oscillations in anticipatory moments.

Babies "Us vs. Them" judgments, resulting from an in-born drive for information, become ever more generalized and powerful with age —but without excluding "the Others". This is means that an infancy driven desire to learn new things makes them discriminating judges of who is worth listening to—heightened valuation of optimal informants being same group members. Assuming these stimuli are met in a satisfying manner, they crave more and more out-going activity and that stimulates them to activate their Imaginations and personally develop Fantasy in Play at two levels. First is using *Role Playing* to act out what they have developed with their imagination and this cultivates *a true respect for the fascinating art of Magic,* no matter what its nature. Some girls play "Dress Ups" and dramatize that scenario. By participating in such fantasy, they script being the "star" in settings as they desire. This puts their minds in a 'Supernatural box' that sprouted inside a 'Natural World Imagination box.' Second, they Play with their make-believe situation by *"Acting As If"* what they have fantasized is an actual and already existing reality. This develops a tool of *Fantasy for linking with other people's Fantasies.*

FIRST WISDOM: The original and Divine Intellect--consisting of Spiritual Realm and Cosmic Organism Knowledge from where each human newborn just derived.

"FIRST WISDOM" PRE-BIRTH COMMON SENSE: *"First Wisdom" or "First Knowledge" is possessed by human newborns* and is about Cosmic Organism understanding without the use of Thought. Its essence is the Spiritual Elements inside the Spiritual realm consisting of Unconditional Love, Truth, Reality, and the Natural. All God-made things in the Cosmos are made of these four, no matter what they look like and thus every human is "One" with them. By Type I being the *Pure Spiritual* form of the Spiritual Elements, it is derived from God's Mind in a "Pure" Immaterial state and displayed as Spiritual Feelings (Pre-Birth Emotions; Spiritual Emotions). When "First Wisdom" is in charge and control of ones Spiritual life, it also directs all of ones physiological functions, since they too are formed by the Cosmic Life-Force (Ether). To do this is to share the life of the Supreme Mind. By being inside the Spiritual/Subjective realm and thus lacking Energy and Matter means that Type I Knowledge is unformed and undifferentiated, but not disorganized. The human mind is imparted prior to birth with the power to know Intuitively (without observation or experience) and with Certainty all of the essence Laws of the Cosmos (or Laws of Nature). Those Spiritual Elements serve as a self-evident (i.e. needing no verification) Background for each human's Foreground Life Living decision and that is what maintains ones Selfhood Greatness. The Knowledge Base of the pre-birth Emotions within a newborn is composed of the Spark of God and therefore is the ultimate in providing a human's Private Selfhood the "5Ss"—Safety, Security, Sureness/Self-Confidence, Strength, and Stability. And nothing is more sound, solid and sure than these.

The closest human resemblance is knowing your mother loves you. That knowing, like pre-Birth Emotions, is without needing any defining items such as names, definitions, logical processes, or other mental activity for supporting evidence. The mind uses essences of Type I Knowledge to build paths for decisions and solutions. A way to discern it is by it not create problematic consequences when its fashioned solutions are in effect. In summary, without observation or experience, humans have the power to know all Laws of the Cosmos (or Laws of Nature) Intuitively (looking within to their Real Self Soul) and with Certainty. This means every human is

Selfhood Great and has all the power needed to thrive, be Happy, and achieve ones Mission as long as they stay with Spiritual Energy. It is up to each human to cultivate these birth gifts. "Mother Wit" Knowledge (maturely drawing on realistic life experiences) in African Tradition--is the ability to do what is best for Ma'at "Me/WE" Life Living. It features the Feeling Coin with Instincts following the Will of God on one side and, or the other side, a human's pre-birth Emotions being directly connected with Cosmic Knowledge. As the beginning stage of Wisdom, it implies a form of Talent in seeing things as they are; good judgment, sound discretion, and practical dealings in doing necessary and important things applied to the right time and place in common life. It resembles the instinct of animals in that it is diffused only within that very sphere. Still, within that boundary, it acts with vigor, uniformity, and correctness. Combined with Knowledge, it is *Wisdom*; with Method, it is *Power*; with Charity, it is *Beneficence*; with the Spiritual Elements, it is Virtue, Lifestyle, and Peace. In African Tradition, Common Sense is the perfection of ones pre-birth Emotions—as distinguished from ones Acquired Emotions. This is because the Wise know the relative Worth and Value of things and practice the art of knowing what to overlook in accommodating oneself to the world. Acquiring, enhancing, and maintaining Common Sense is done by being calm and quiet as a way of life; having a Free Mind and Pure Heart; always being alert to ones Ignorance; being diligent to conquer unrealistic fears; remaining inwardly separate from the Crowd while outwardly using the Crowd tools that work; listening twice as much as talking (since humans have 2 ears and one mouth); rememoring what has self-improvement significance; preventing making needless mistakes or wasting needless time, as by having an "in-door" mailbox and a readily available reference (e.g. ones self-created dictionary); unlearning wrong programming; know the proper boundaries of things involved; be clear about the distinction between good and evil; practice having word and deeds in accord. Although all Common Sense is applicable to various aspects of ones life, reflect on new connections so as to practice creativity and humor. Pure Emotions of First Wisdom does "ME/WE" sharing. Common sense so reflects a well-trained and disciplined mind as to have: (1) knowledge classified in order to reason from Cause to Effect; and (2) the ability to make "Right" urgent and emergency decisions out of its Philosophical Warehouses. The best is to be a *Spiritual Elements Creator, Enhancer, Maintainer, Defender, and Protector.* Part of assessment is by necessarily drawing on ones inner Self (i.e. Divine Consciousness) intuition. Out of this interchange flows a Non-rational (i.e. personal-social, and spiritual) awareness of how to do *Ma'at "ME/WE" Life-Living* and is always aimed at doing what is best for "ME/WE". This process is a mode of discursive thinking (proceeding to a conclusion by reason) of the essence of the aggregate of the best of human experiences--constantly accumulating, selecting, and reorganizing its own essential ingredients—always challenging the major premise of a life-shaping or life-changing argument--taking into account all important factors in a problem or situation—seeing each significant thing for what it is in reality and attaching to each its due weight--distilling the essence of what has been reflected upon--and associating that essence with ready and accurate perceptions of analogies in order to make it descriptive. Still, the conclusion is likely to possess elements of mental activity without the capability of having a reproducible end product. A display of Common Sense is to make a friend of a foe; carry ones enemy on ones back for use in consulting about ones flaws.

FISHNET MOMENT: Initiator of African American slavery by means of a fishnet being thrown over a free African in Africa to thereafter enslave him/her "forever"—set-off a cascade of simultaneous

FIVE or "5Ss"—Safety, Security, Sureness/Self-Confidence, Strength, and Stability

FLAMBOYANT: Originally an architectural term applied to a C15 and C16 French Gothic style, was characterized by wavy flame-like forms with shapes of flames conforming to the wavy flame-like tracery of the stonework in the windows of many Gothic cathedrals. The presents of these forms around some human (or thing) make ones "*Larger than Life*." However, the nature of those wavy forms has different ranges of significance, intensity, duration, presentations, and Effects. An analogy is the Stars in the sky. For eons, humankind has looked to the heavens and wondered at the lights in the sky. Ancient people, believing they could see shapes among the stars, identified both animals and people--and each had its own story. In transferring this concept, Mild "Flamboyance" is like the misconception that *stars twinkle*. Instead, the perception of twinkling stars is a result of atmospheric interference--an effect similar to what takes place on a hot summer day when one looks across hot pavement or a parking lot. Just as this rising air causes images to waver, it is also what causes the twinkling effect in stars. The lower a star is in the sky, the more it will twinkle because its light must pass through more of the atmosphere.

FLAWS: Flaws (a fissure or flake off a stone) include: (1) something missing from a loss or a lack; (2) weaknesses or limitations; (3) out of place, disordered, or improperly paired with something else; (4) malfunctioning or non-functioning (e.g. as in being off track); (5) being all right as it is but simply going in the wrong direction; (6) having an unclear goal or purpose; (7) containing insufficient motivational energy to sustain dedication, commitment, loyalty; (8) running from or avoiding facing an obstacle; (9) the right thing happening at the wrong time; (10) the wrong thing happening at the right time; and (11) the presence of something spoiling what is otherwise okay; (12) taking short-cuts that make for incompleteness or deformities. All of these flaws keep something from being complete, wholly efficient or effective, or desirable. Thus, a Flaw lacks integrity. When one spotlights a flaw within oneself or accepts one from the outside, that flaw has bad floodlight effects on ones Selfhood.

An Assessment is an evaluation of a Thing within the context of the competency of the appraiser—a competency that varies from one Thing to another. Using the Box Concept as an analogy, Assessment identifies what is beneficial/harmful and suggests what should be sought/avoided. It deals with (among others) Analysis, Classification, Correspondence, Details, the SOBMER method, Tools, What it is, Does, Appears, Worth, and Value. Medical training involves knowing five basic areas: (1) Normal; (2) Effects of outside influences, ones condition, and ones choices in causing "normal variant" or abnormal behaviors or disease; (3) Diagnosis; (4) Treatment/Management; (5) Results. the "What and Why" the *"Way Things Are" and the "Way Things Go" and the "Way Things Ought to Go."* anything by the SOBMER process—e.g. oneself, *people, experience, and the situation--is to see each for what it is.* This includes selecting the right tool for the job; gathering all that is needed to do the job; subdividing the information presented (history, definitions, clarity, consistency, coherence, and its suitability for readers; new insights; seeing common in the uncommon and the uncommon in the common; seeing the inner workings Organization. Always asking: *"How do you know that?" "How important is that?" "How do I know that?"*

FOCUS: nothing is better to *learn to do what one does not naturally do than the hard instruction involved in focusing and concentrating on the difficult, the unattractive, or the boring.*

FOCUSED MINDS: A Focused Mind is one trained not to allow reactions to interfere with its concentration. *Concentration* (Raja Yoga, 93) is a process of sustained Attention while collectively gathering more brain energy to apply to the Thing of focus. The more one clings to a focused mindset, Focusing Skills build on existing capacities while adding new neural circuits. A self-illustration of what concentration and focus are like is to recall the last angry moment when ones mind was totally focused on what is of no benefit. That situation had all of ones time, energy, and attention efforts. Scholars first show themselves with single-mindedness via Self-Limitation so as to go "Straight Ahead". Discernment is Focus' best starting tool. This means "zeroing in" on the "What it Is" of a problem or a situation before addressing the "What it Does" or the "How it Appears." Discernment is just barely being able to separate very, very slight differences in confusing things or in things having misleading appearances. Yet, the importance of Discernment is to "see"--apart from all other associated ingredients--the Essence of the "What it is". That is the Seed (the Law of Holonomy) which contains everything needed for understanding the whole evolution, even if all the other Associates cannot be distinguished. A fundamental is then to fashion as many Classes out of that family "Big Picture" so that as new thoughts and information arrive each can be put into its proper place. That gives Interrelationships. But its time in developing into maturity—maybe 3 years later—is like a pregnant women being in prolonged labor. The fact that a Class or place for it is already established means that I think about anything I see or come in contact with everyday might be an ingredient for that Class. I might think the job is complete 10 times only to discover that fundamental changes need to be made. Such is illustrated in my struggles to understand Essence and its Essential. It is always best to struggle alone with the problem since that leads into trouble that requires creativity and losses to come out of. Hence, my declaration is that to avoid ever going through that again, I will ensure it never happens.

FOREKNOWLEDGE: acquiring intuitively and instinctively an awareness of mosaic pieces of Principles related to the Laws of Nature.

FORESIGHT: detecting and preparing for what is likely to happen in the future. *Discernment* would draw out worthwhile information not easily seen or even being out of sight--so as to see and mark essential things. See Discernment; Discretion; Prudence

FORETHOUGHT: careful planning to acquire yet unrealized beneficial realities)--also called "*Providence*" (planning, doing, preparing, and perhaps expending largely to meet the future demand) and "*Prudence*". *Discernment* would draw out worthwhile information not easily seen or even being out of sight--so as to see and mark essential things. See *Discretion;* Discernment

FORMAL SCIENCE: concerns Mathematic and formal Logic, asserting nothing about natural phenomena or experience. None of its proofs rest on how facts actually stand.

FORM-BODY: a "*Totipotency*" (a putty-like condition able to be developed or reshaped into any new form

FORM-BODY STATE: The presumed state of a newborn's mind or traumatically whipped adult whereby their minds are completely susceptible to being molded by the one feeding it--the "Inside-Out" mindset

FOUNDATION: Any Spiritual Essence built upon a Spiritual Principle Base

FRAGILE BLACK BABIES SYNDROME

One of my important discoveries from 50 years of research into Black People's History has been problems affecting their babies from Acquired Emotional turmoil. Resultant chronic mental turmoil is of particular concern to pregnant women because Scientists in the field of Fetal Origins assert that their nine months of gestation constitute the most consequential period of human life. What happens then affects ones genes, the DNA inherited at conception to permanently influence a host of things in the developing fetus (e.g. the "wiring" of the brain and the functioning of organs such as the heart, liver, and pancreas). Environmental influences affecting the behavior of genes, without altering DNA, are called *Epigenetic Modifications*. The combination of parental genetic predisposition + intrauterine factors + ones childhood experiences (e.g. how one was treated), especially during the crucial first three years + ones kind of diet choices + the degree of exercise one does throughout ones lifetime account for ones ongoing health and lifestyle. Intrauterine factors of particular significance include the kind and quantity of nutrition the fetus receives (and poor prenatal nutrition is particularly damaging); the pollutants (e.g. from traffic, toxic water), drugs, and infections one was exposed to during gestation; the mother's health, stress level, and state of mind (e.g. moods) during the pregnancy; and beginning bonding. These shape ones susceptibility to all diseases (e.g. cancer, cardiovascular, allergies, asthma, hypertension, diabetes, obesity, mental illness, arthritis, osteoporosis, and cognitive decline); ones appetite and metabolism; ones intelligence and temperament. Of spotlighted concern to my research on the *Fragile Black Babies Syndrome* is that these research findings lend support to my proposition that a pregnant woman's mental state can shape her offspring's psyche and body.

To elaborate, as part of the Atlantic slave trade, at the moment the fishnet was thrown over the free African in Africa, each African immediately switched from using his/her Thriving Brain (neo-cortex) over to his/her Emergency Brain ("fight or flight"; Ancient Brain). Being thereafter in an ongoing survival mode, at no time during slavery was there an opportunity for the Enslaved to resume using their Thriving Brains. A major reason is that throughout African American slavery, the body of the Enslaved Black female was at the disposal of the slave owner, his sons, the plantation overseers, and any White males around. And they all took almost daily advantage of her body -- for their pleasure and for money gains by breeding of more children for enslavement. Even sons were forced to impregnate their mothers—the origin of "mother-f**. There were innumerable other Maafas (immeasurable catastrophes) of slavery (e.g. selling away family members; inhumane medical treatment and surgery without anesthesia) -- any and all of which took most Enslaved to the bottom of Despair of the "no doubt" hopelessness type. Chances are this accumulation of daily horrors generated an *"Atmosphere of Despair" Complex* (ADC) across the plantation and within each of the Enslaved. That this conglomeration (e.g. the Enslaved "fight or flight" Omnibus Brain effects) manifested on the in-utero fetuses of Black babies is suggested by the high rate of fragile babies born to Enslaved females as well as to their descendants' babies, on up to the present. Desperation of the Enslaved, springing out of Despair, as well as a daily struggle to survive led to a lifestyle which centered on being ever alert to possible or actual danger; having a readiness to run any risk; suppression of all emotions; and simply trying to actually survive the day--a situation pertaining to this day.

Hence, a "no choice" permanent Emergency Brain varied mental activities led each to fashion a "survival" mental and self-protective habit lifestyle. Pertinent to this discussion is that in the recorded cases of spontaneous abortion, stillbirths, and deaths in childbirth, those among Enslaved women were three times as high as among White women. Infant mortality was twice as high for Black babies as for White babies in the slave states. Meanwhile, their exposures to slavery's horrendous hellishness resulted in accommodative brain anatomy modifications. One was/is neuro-plasticity (ones brain can physically grow and change according to its exposures). A second is that the *Ancient Brain*'s Instinct, Omnibus (instincts with thought), and Brute subdivisions can be used selectively. Though each is quite different, they possess certain "Sameness" features. But, by their brains being part of the "Fight, Flight, Fright" nature, each had/have different self-defeating intents and displays. Examples include: some becoming Ideal Slaves/Oreos. Some resorted to imitating White people, as with Total Selfishness; Lack of Concern for others; treadmill Compulsions; Focus on the "Here and Now" excitement. Some were/are full of Despair—e.g. No Desire to Learn; No Self-Improvement efforts; problematic Morals. Most herd together to simply endure. All were constantly in a State of Survival Alertness; Resistant To Change; and brainwashed. All experienced excessive biochemical production of stress hormones causing accelerated Psychophysical destruction to themselves and to the fetuses of pregnant women. All engaged in Self-Protection patterns dominating daily living--whether realistic (for survival or self-preservation) or for Non-Sexual masochism to see how much pain they could take.

A third is that by the Omnibus Brain being intimately connected with the Autonomic Nervous System and hypothalamus, slavery's hellish daily experiences generated a Temperament in mothers of "Fight, Flight, Fright, or Funk" actions/reactions of a survival, self-preservation, and self-protective nature. In turn, each Temperament is either an aroused survival state of thoughts and emotions or one of depression. These characteristics are seen today in large numbers of struggling Black Americans. Acquired Emotions are well-known to physiologically affect hormonal glands and the nervous system. Not only does this occur in pregnant mothers, but their excessive resultant hormonal secretions into their wombs increasingly adversely sensitize the nervous systems of their in-utero fetuses. Each type of hormone is capable of damaging or killing certain brain cells of the developing fetus and presumably cells in the mother's womb. Excessive stress hormone output causes elevated heart rate and blood pressure. So, what is likely to have happened is that, prior to birth, each fetus perhaps possessed epigenetic modifications fashioning a predisposition for biochemical or nervous tissue sensitivity inherited from the parents; a hypersensitive nervous system shaped over a nine month period of gestation by hormones from the mother's traumatized psyche; and the mother's excessive stress hormone generated elevated heart rate and blood pressure. These are associated with (among others) later Poor Academia and the "Negro Diseases" which lead to early death in later years. Prevention is called Hetep by—i.e. maintaining a profound sense of peace under all circumstances.

FRAUD: gaining an unfair advantage over bodies of people) involved those aspects of "*Trickery*" (deliberately giving the wrong impression) that includes "*Deceit*" (the pursuit of personal gain at the expense of victims) and "*Manipulation*" (here meaning hypocritical dishonorableness).

FREE MASONS--AFRICAN BACKGROUND TO EUROPEANS: Freemasonry is an esoteric doctrine founded on the idea of God as the Architect of the Cosmos. This esoteric or understanding inner truths lying hidden about God, about things belonging to God, and about things revealed by God to humans is documented as having begun 77,000 years ago with the TWA (so-called Pygmies) of the Great Lakes region of Central Africa (Bailey, Ancient African Bible Messages, pvii). Such was displayed by their signs and symbols (Ben-Joc, Africa p508), like the "Cross" worn around their necks as jewelry and as amulets for protection. Sometime thereafter, Very Ancient African Sages said their "life force" arose from the spirit of God and it imparted the personal "Aliveness" needed for acquiring a pure spiritual essence as well as for communicating with Higher Powers. They enlarged the "Cross" into the Ankh, representing three elementary powers of creation: Emen-Ra; Reh, the sound which caused creation; and Water of Nu (Water of Chaos) (Saleem, Book of Life, p41). Later, this esoterically symbolized the Annu Khet or "Stream of Cosmic Life Energy" animating all life, emanating from the Godhead Annu (personified as Sun Goddesses). Ra, Giver of Light, Creator of the Mysteries, who resides in Amenta, was elaborated on in the world's first text--*The Book of Life* (60,000 BC). Theme messages in it include the Practical and the Esoteric. The Practical is about paying honor and divine respect to the "Creator of all Mankind"; discussions of Judgment Day; and that the "West" (the Blessed!) is the abode of those without fault. The Esoteric focuses on the five principle mysteries of Egyptian spiritual doctrines, namely: *Regeneration; Transfiguration (Transformation); Transubstantiation* (change one substance into another)*; Resurrection; and Ascension.* "*Mystery*" implies a secret religious/spiritual involvement whereby one sheds ignorance and replaces it with "*Wisdom*" (i.e. being able to intuit and apply the will of God to ones activities of daily living). Somewhere between 17,000 and 8,000 BC -- my guesstimate is 12,000 BC -- there arose an educational institution for teaching doctrines, technologies, and techniques required to establish a theocratic (governed by Religion/Spirituality) and prosperous society. Thus, there came the specializing in Mysteries under the title of the Egyptian Mystery Schools -- also called *Shetaut Neter* Egyptian Yoga, and the Book of Life. Started by the Demi-god Tehuti (Tchuti, Thoth), this school used Tehuti's 42 books as its curriculum. Foundational to Tehuti's teaching was a preoccupation with truth, justice, scholarship and honesty; the microcosm of the best of the entire African spiritual firmament; unified by science; verifiable by mathematically based logic; and powered by God's Spiritual Energy. One of Tethui's original hieroglyphic copies (written in stone) was located at On (Heliopolis, Annu) and another at the main campus in the Giza Plateau Complex where the *Spirituality of the Aten Path* (Path of Atannu) was taught -- both northeast of Memphis. These Schools were founded in the predynastic period on the aboriginal and esoteric Spirituality System called the Aten Path. Tehuti's books are said to have been gathered and crytalized from the Twa people (derogatorily called Pygmies by Europeans and who survive as Dogon people of Mali). In characterizing God, the Egyptian Tehuty, founder of the Egyptian Spiritual Mystery System and the original author of "The Book of Life" put it this way: "None of our thoughts are capable of conceiving God, nor any language of defining Him. That which is incorporeal, formless, invisible, cannot be grasped by our senses. That which is eternal cannot be measured by the short rules of time. Africans kept contents of the Mysteries a secret because only the most formidable minds were able to sustain its Spiritual Elements concepts. The idea of "Masonry" came because of the sacred character of the Mysteries—sacred because of the association with Divine inspiration. Thus, its symbols had to be scrupulously rendered in stone or in paintings on walls of the African temples, tombs, and palaces. This sacred work required knowledge and accuracy. Ancient African stonecutters whose Pictograms (picture symbols), cut on stone with chisels and hammers, were named hieroglyph "characters." The Very Ancient African priesthood and temple buildings connection led to the first carving: "Man, Know Thyself" to indicate *Introspective Contemplation* was the way to learn the whole of ones Body, Soul, and Spirit having Correspondence with the Cosmic Wholism Essence. See Ancient Greeks; Ancient Romans

FREE MASONS' AFRICAN ORIGIN: The Very Ancient African Spiritual Literature of eternal life have their roots in Mythology (Shetat)—the science of ultimate reality. Shetat means the purification of the natural in order to reach the real (Saleem, Book of Life p11). All matters relating to Earth and "Hereafter" life can only be understood through Mythology. God is, accordingly, ineffable (Unknowable). African Traditions' Cosmic concept of "*Mystery*"--implying a secret religious/spiritual involvement whereby one sheds ignorance and replaces it with "*Wisdom*"—was about Ancient African Sages mystical connections with "The Great Mind". These Mysteries provided insight into the divine knowledge to "See" the laws of Nature; to "Know" there are no separate organisms; to realize their "Sight" transcended time and space; and to possess the wisdom to penetrate all Cosmic Secrets. Thus, "The Eye" symbolizes divine consciousness embodied in a perfected (Enlightened) human (Ashby, African Origins, p. 408) who is thereafter immortal (Bynum, African Unconscious, p. 140, 290)--inseparable from Nature and the environment--and its proper utilization is a Spiritual or Sublime act. Nubians and their Egyptian offspring kept contents of the Mysteries a secret throughout the Per Ankhs or "Houses of Life" along the Nile because only the most formidable minds were able to sustain its Spiritual Elements concepts. By the "Eye" being 360 degrees implied Circumspection was required for the total learning processes of the Mysteries. *Circumspection,* the coordination of the inputs from all of a human's Selfhood faculties, is the discovery of insights into the underlying web of relationships in Nature comprising Divine Laws (Ma'at). Yet in later times, since only 22 of the 360 degrees of Circumspection insights were passed on to the Westerners, those first calling themselves Free Masons established 11 other Honorary Degrees. Since this moved the figure to 33, they were called "Christian Degrees". Ben-Jochannan (Africa, Mother of Western Civilization p417-19) says there is no such thing as "Christian Degrees" because "the entire 360 Degrees of the Africans' Mysteries and Secrets of the Grand Lodge of Thebes and Luxor were already completed before the existence of the first Haribu (Jew) much less before Jesus Christ—the Jew who became the God of the Christians. All of the above teachings were copied from the Pyramid and Coffin Texts of the African Mysteries System by the Hebrews. They are found in the Hebrew Torah and all of the European Versions of the Christian Holy Bible." Ben-Joc then gives references to include: Budge, Book Of Dead; James, Stolen Legacy; Churchward, Origin of Freemasonry, etc. He adds that Aristotle stole the African "Mystery" Spiritual property while he was in Egypt, most of which other Greek Philosophers did not know existed—and that very few of the alleged "Greek Philosophers" actually existed in reality, except for their names—and that traditional present day Masonic Symbols are in the African pyramids—e.g. the Ever-All-Seeing—Eye; Square of Life's Travails; Triangle of Heaven's Ladder; the 3, 5, and 7; the Inner Sanctorium; Double Pyramids; the so-called "Star of David" and so forth. These same symbols are in the Books of the Mysteries System and written in the Pyramid and Coffin Texts. The first Pyramid where this is seen was begun in Nubia but completed by the Egyptians.

Meanwhile, in Africa's Masonic lodges of Luxor, Abydos, Abu Simbel, and other Mystery Schools, the philosophical and science "Secrets" continued to be taught in a focused manner since at least as early as 12,500 BC. The original Grand Lodge of Luxor—built during the 3rd Dynasty (5046-4872 BC) –was 2,000 feet long and 1,000 feet wide. This oblong shape recurs as an Obelisk in many Masonic temples thereafter up to today. A lodge source of Africans' 42 Negative Confessions are where it is said Moses co-opted his Ten Commandments. Socrates, an advanced Initiate at a training center of the African Mysteries of Egypt, adhered to staying on the path of mastery which, among others, required Self-Knowledge, the basis of True Knowledge; the mastery of the Passions, to make room for the occupation of unlimited powers; search within ones Selfhood for the new powers taking possession of the Neophyte; unselfishness or sacrifice, justice and honesty as the cardinal virtue to develop a sense of Ma'at Values as an advanced stage of attainment. Such had to be accomplished before unlimited power could be bestowed upon the candidate (James, p88). See Ancient Greeks; Ancient Romans

FREE MASONS OUTSIDE AFRICA: "Egyptian Mythology is the root and foundation of Gnostic tradition, the Gospels, Islam, and all so-called 'divine' books—books written by men but declared to have been written by God. God's book is that of Nature and Creation" says Seleem (Book of Life p41). Africans' Mystery "Secrets" of how to acquire the rebirth of "*Wisdom*" so as to enter into a "new order of the world" through innumerable "points of light" was the Essence concept subsequently carried as a decoration in all modern Masonic lodges and retaining the same meaning (James, Stolen Legacy p90). It linked in trade and Spiritual practices with the Indus Valley civilizations of India in symbols and lineages of the Ureaus concerning knowledge of the Stars, the Soul, and the Heavens. Other African Mystery "Secrets" moved along the Mediterranean basin and into Europe implanted modified seeds that became Greco-Roman Mystery Schools. This was a *Transubstantiation* process—i.e. the change from the Spiritual God Substance of African Tradition over to the Supernatural God Substance of European Tradition. An arising illustration was the *Illuminati* ('the enlightened), perhaps of C2 Italian Gnostic origin. That name was assumed by or given to various groups of mystics which embraced many charlatans throughout its history. They claimed, either through direct divine inspiration or by means of mental exercise, to have special knowledge of the Supernatural god(s). In the early days of the European Christian Church the term was applied to people who had been baptized. However, the *elite, on whom self-declaring they had received a special divine knowledge (gnosis), used their purported gnosis, or illumination, to claim exemption from any type of prohibition and so indulged their passions without restraint.* See Ancient Greeks; Ancient Romans

FREEMASONS-- DARK & MIDDLE AGES: After the fall of Rome and the resulting "Dark Ages" the Mysteries survived in Europe and North Africa through Islamic scholars and Irish monks (Bynum, Dark Light Consciousness p13, 163). Instrumental in this progress was the formation of guilds or brotherhoods of cathedral masons. This was in keeping with Europeans plagiarizing all Ancient African "everything"—as with Ancient African stonecutters and painters. Such plagiarizing has continued to the present but was particularly emphasized throughout the European Middle Ages until the Age of Enlightenmens. During this time all things connected with writing were linked with the clergy. It was the occupation of scholar secretaries or clerks to either exactly copy the original manuscript ("*written by using a pen*") or to make certain alterations in it. In the process, they often misrepresented the intentions of the prior author. One of countless problems with this Western scholarly process throughout history and on to the present is similar to what occurred in the folktale of Henny Penny. While in the barnyard, *Henny Penny* was hit on the head with an acorn that fell out of the tree she was under. However, thinking it was a piece of the sky, she shouted to her friends: "the sky is falling." Her friends immediately ran to tell the king: "the sky is falling." Those friends, now elevated to the status of "scholars," were wrong because Henny Penny -- their authority source -- was wrong. The point is to not believe what scholars (or anybody) say about life-shaping things without personally examining the source. Yet, this was the way for European males to rise to success. Machiavelli (C15), in documenting worldly success, said being lovers of riches, fame, and power are the triad of seducers alienating the affections of men for truth, beauty, and goodness. He said that as the archetypal contest is between *virtue* and *fortuna,* between all that is manly, and all that is changeable, unpredictable, and capricious, a struggle between masculine rational control and effeminate irrationality. War is the supreme test of man, the energy force of manliness, of his physique, of his intellect, and particularly his character. Machiavelli's thoughts on the concepts of war and peace were summarized as "Necessity generates *virtue.* War is a condition of necessity that produces *virtue.* Without war a people become indolent, weak, and effeminate and lose their *virtu.* Here the concept of manliness as a gendered phenomenon, expressed as a male stereotype, was firmly introduced--"principle" referring not to a person but to an accepted professed man-made rule of action or conduct—and most were immoral. Now, let us look at the origin of this type of mindset. Meanwhile, Free-masonary used as symbols the working tools of operative masons—copies and modifications of those used in Ancient Africa. The apron, consisting of a square with a triangular flap, represented the descent of the divine Spirit into matter. The interlaced triangle symbolized man coming forth from God, passing through his pilgrimage in matter, and returning again to his divine source. The square in compasses showed the spiritual nature controlling the physical. The symbol of the cross had a similar meaning, the down-stroke representing spirit and the cross-bar matter. With declining membership, honorary luminaries were admitted and thereby reemerged into prominence in the Renaissance. Among these were the Naples cells of Illuminati, a rationalistic secret society. In C15, leaders of those elite had followers to pledge obedience to them as being their superiors. Various sub-sects were divided into: (1) the "novices," Minervals, and "lesser illuminati"; (2) "freemasons," "ordinary," "Scottish," and "Scottish knights"; and (3) the "mystery" class comprising two grades of "priest" and "regent" and of "magus" and "king." A "French prophets" sub-sect believed in a "light" communicated from a higher source, giving larger measure of exalted wisdom. C16 Rosicurcians combined mysteries of alchemy + esoteric principles of religion, claiming to be motivated by inner illumination, as also did by Joan of Arc). In C17 and C18 they adopted the rites and trappings of Ancient Africa and of chivalric brotherhoods.

After the 1717 first Grand Lodge in England there was opposition from European religions, despite containing many Christian aspects and concepts of White Superiority. In 1776, Weishaupt--remaining invisible as to be regarded by others as a god--established *Perfectibilists Deism*—the olden Freethinkers belief in a god(s) who, after creating the universe, relinquished control over life, influence on Nature, and gave no Supernatural orders. The Masonic Order based movement converted followers into blind instruments of his supreme will. It adopted the Jesuits organization (despite being opposed to their dogma), their system of espionage, and their maxim that the "*end justifies the means*". To blend philanthropy and mysticism, he took care to enlist in his ranks as many young men of riches and position as possible. Von Knigge, a master of most secret societies (e.g. Freemasonry), joined in 1780 and introduced expert occultist, mysticism, and the Supernatural into the workings of the brotherhood. Thereafter, an air of mystery pervaded all its doings—holding out hopes of the communication of deep occult secrets in the higher ranks. Within 5 years the power of the Illuminism became extraordinary in its proportions. Its members even had a hand in the affairs of the state—and several German princes found it to their interest to having dealings with the fraternity. The Roman Catholic Church repudiated the movement and, with the discovery of dishonorable acts, led Weishaupt into exile, the fire kindled by Illuminism burst into the French Revolution. It subsequently spread to the Americas as the Power Elite. See Ancient Greeks; Ancient Romans

FREEMASON--RENAISSANCE EVOLUTION: Renaissance European Scholars considered it a must to study the Hermetica (the works of the Egyptian Hermes, i.e. Tehuti) (Candy p8) and it was *acceptable for them to take information out of the Hermetica and claim it as their own.* Their scholarship was about being a learned person devoted to understanding and to being understood. Such European scholars were, in the "*Plato Dictionary*" (Stockhammer, p. 230), characterized as "*learning whatever he studies with facility and has a capacious and reliable memory...but no one will call a person wise on account of any of these erudite gifts.*" As early as the 1600s, Sir Francis Bacon was describing a construct that would later become recognized as critical thinking (Buckley, *American Journal of Evaluation*). In 1603, he listed a number of favorable mental traits such as a "desire to seek, patience to doubt, fondness to meditate, slowness to assert, readiness to reconsider, carefulness to dispose and set in order; and . . . [hatred for] every kind of imposture". These traits are not far from contemporary definitions of critical thinking. One of the earliest usages of the actual term appears to have been by John Dewey (1910) in How We Think, where he writes, "The essence of critical thinking is suspended judgment; and the essence of this suspense is inquiry to determine the nature of the problem before proceeding to attempts at its solution". More recently, especially in the 1980s, definitions of and debates on critical thinking have proliferated. Critical Thinking (CT) is broadly required to direct its skills both into ones Inner World and into the External World. The Inner World direction gives one an ability to challenge ones own presuppositions and examine ones own biases. In the External World, CT is required for what is established--for what is advancing—and for what is receding. Its starting point is doubting what does not conform to Spiritual Principles—for they are the guidelines. The declarations which best repay critical examination are those which for the longest period have remained unquestioned. An equally major problem is information of a near vintage generated for practical ends. In-between are illusions directing a way of life that are based on uncritical faith in things only understood by magic. Each discovery which sheds new light on each of these is a tacit criticism of things as they are—and that is why the wise are called fools. When information is advancing, CT is required for every aspect of what is being created or fashioned. What is receding is often because of some new technology promising more than it can deliver. Thus, the gullible readily leap to this new Thing, giving no thought to what is being left behind that not only still works but is likely to work better than its replacement. Furthermore, if that new technology is flawed, then what develops as a result of it is likely to be flawed.

This demands that CT have razor sharp discernments to see the exceptions. When CT is required to move Information or Knowledge forward, it is the proper selection of ingredients of the past that are indispensable soil of which improvement must grow. Of particular importance to me is always keeping note of the unusual so that it can be compared with the normal. An essential aspect of that is to be able to record it in brief and plain language. The way I discovered a new Disproportionate Short Statue Syndrome was that one of the 10 differed only by having a rather sharp-pointed nose which others had accepted as merely a variation from the other 9. See Ancient Greeks; Ancient Romans

FREE MINDS: The "*Big Picture*" is to be in charge and control of ones own life--in charge and control of everything of what one does--and in charge and control of the situation one is in.* Years ago, during a near drowning experience what was uppermost in my mind was to cling to my gloves by making tight fists. The Old English word "Cling" (stick, adhere) suggests a close attachment--entwining, clutching, or hanging on. Its 'to hold dear' is in the sense of suggesting anxiety or dependency to ones in-group (e.g. via cell phone) as well as to things (e.g. gadgets which molds them into having a "Flashing Lights" mentality and maintains the status quo). An equally common sense of "Cling" is done out of fear while in a situation of danger. A third is from a chronic self-absorbed neediness from being empty of the "5Ss"(safety, security, self-confidence, strength, and stability)--as contrasted with Self-Love which manifest by gift-giving because one is already full. There are many justifiable reasons Black Americans have had to make clinging part of their lives, as has occurred periodically in the "starving times" of Africa or during African American slavery. Clinging has continued through the metaphorical Struggling Tunnel that connects the "Slave Quarters" with today's inner cities. I suspect the reason many "Clingers" desire to know about Critical Thinking (CT) is the result of generational grieving for the loss of their mental freedom, snuffed out talents, and loss of possessions at the hands of Europeans. Contributory to this is being stuck in some type of poverty from which they would like to arise but have been unsuccessful in all they have tried. But many who desire to reverse their circumstances are looking for a "quick fix" where they can "Pick and Choose"--sort of like having CT in scattered compartments for the various roles in which it applies while mixing them with the various compartments to which they cling. Though that will not work, what can happen when one steps out of the open door of ones self-imposed mental cage is perfecting ones mental discipline to such a degree that two completely different and separate thinking styles are developed. That one step alone will enlarge ones self-trust, self-respect, self-reliance, self-confidence, and self-efficacy all at once -- and from inside out. This immediately puts one on the path to CT. However, for self-cultivation that heads toward thriving, ones present non-CT style for dealing with ones relationships and ways of occupying ones time must not be characterized by clinging. What both styles share in common is a "Free Mind"--i.e. a calm mind that sees things as they are without emotions and opinions attached. This is the best way to enter any tough situation with an eagerness to creatively handle all problems exactly as they are. Meanwhile, one is alert to and accounts for every consequence from each solution. A "Free Mind" possesses the "5Ss". This means one has a sense of *Self-Efficacy*--faith that ones skills are a match for challenging whatever problems one will face, even if those challenges (e.g. Unrealized Reality Impossibilities) have never been seen nor heard of before. A "Free Mind" is resistant to whimsical change or pressure except when confronted with better facts. A "Free Mind" is *Self-Reliant* (keeps ones word or promises to oneself). It best arises out of having a Purpose in life and that Mission will take one down a seldom traveled path. On this lonely path, which is taken in order to be true to oneself, there is no one ready, willing, or able to help or to do "soothing." Thus, there is no point in asking for help or waiting for any promised help; or depending on others to make ones decisions; or needing to rely on anybody to make things happen in ones dealings with the outside world. It does not take long for the Self-Reliant to know they can travel faster alone. Proceeding along naturally cultivates CT forever in little thing one does. One learns not to do anything without having a good reason. Nevertheless, this is not an "all-or-none" situation because it is equally important to use ones perfected non-CT style for dealing with people. However, the time, energy, and effort put into a CT or non-CT style will determine ones degree of success. A "Free" and self-reliant mind is expertly exhibited by Martial Artists. When faced with an opponent, they empty their minds in order to clearly see the situation and correctly intuit anticipated moves of the opponent. They have perfected *Involuntary Movement*--unconsciously, automatically, naturally, and coordinately moving on impulse as a result of pre-existing CT (e.g. mimicking postures of animals and the inherent intelligent ways and forces of water). This is a non-assertive mindset prepared for behavioral self-assertion that Self-Reliance would benefit from imitating.

FREE MINDS IN BLACK PEOPLE: Leaders of Black People must have *Free Minds*—i.e. that of ones birth or one re-acquired by shedding Emotional Junk and specialty training, as did Malcomb X who analyzed his experiences and attitudes as a follower in order to obtain new concepts of leadership. The way the Mind of animals came into existence was with no hesitation and with a clear conscious. It was above responding to all happening without action or reaction except to those that were threats, disturbances, or destruction of ones Selfhood—and for Jegna leaders who are "ME/WE" oriented. Because there was complete unity of mind and Nature meant that Mind was in Meditation. A Free Mind has nothing to cling to except whatever constitutes the Spiritual Elements. No delusions (i.e. no filth, clinging to conviction) leads to an empty mind, able to see things clearly and correctly. A *free mind* acts, not by motivation generated by past events or by fear or by desire, but rather it acts spontaneously--acting within the confines of the Spiritual Elements actions without motives because they are Natural and thus Instincts. Its Spiritual power is in continual conversion of the one into the many. Its mental power can convert the many into the one. A Free Mind finds a way to trust other people either completely but verifies; or trust people with certain things, being careful not to expose them to temptation. Free Minds are not vindictive. In going around a mountain and facing an on coming car with bright lights on, it does not flash it bright lights on because if it cannot see the other car it want the other car to see it. Free Minds forgive quickly--not because the perpetuator deserves it but because the victim deserves peace. Whereas emotions know no neutrality, inner freedom is a stable state Love is about what one can give because one is already full. Personally, free minds are so unattached to things that if others want to steal things, then they can have them as a way to "Buy the Peace" needed to keep going with is of top priority. A Free Mind does not view things of serious business with like/dislike but sees things for *what they are and how they are*—for both may provide new information that opens new paths. A Free Mind that assumes leadership does what one is called to do and this will lead to the lost of some "friends" but not those worth having. Knowing something accurately allows for the giving of directions to others. To know lets is self-reassuring—that one is okay as one is, meaning one can go forward into more difficult things without "what if" doubts. That "Okay-ness" embraces the gaining of benefits by doing something sort of okay or by doing nothing and realizing that, too, is okay. One then looks at things according to law or guidelines--without like/dislike or judging. In spare times, a Free Mind eagerly engages in the "inside of me" -- the world of inner imagination, fantasy, beauti-ful thoughts as well as things to shed, improve, or perfects. One exposes oneself to what one wants to be or thoughts to play with, as my exposure to jokes, wit, and humor—this helps see others as oneself. The art of leadership in large or small operations is first to follow the Spiritual Elements path, not the people's wishes. This leadership is born out of the understanding of the needs of those who would be affected by it—meaning being both a response and a stimulus. Different situations call for different leaders and/or different approaches by the same leader—the idea of serving by commanding. Within that context, focus is on arts of humanity dealings—working on people's behaviors, being compassionate but equally insisting they make a square facing toward their own problems. Freedom is not based upon everybody being the other's policeman. Public leader-ship is not likely to work if there is question about that leader's fitness—as in failing to stand behind, defend, and pay the price of the course of action that has been advocated to follow. Rather, leaders must be willing to squarely shoulder the obligation, duty, and responsibility—a triad in which most show deficiencies from being ill-prepared of from lack of Courage.

FUNDAMENTALS: The C15 English word Transition" originated from ancient Romans relating the word "*Fundamentals*" to the ground for burial. This implied "Fundamental" consisted of three parts: the foun-dation of stability below ground; the rest of the structure resting on the fundamentals above ground; and the connection between the two, called its *transitional* aspect and carrying the sense of to go through (something like the stricture of an hour-glass), go underneath, go around, or go over in bridge-like fashion to change from one place, state, condition, or circumstance to another. Ingredients for and which give birth to Patterns, Images, or starting points to help determine the structure or function of how the Essentials manifest for build-ing Specialty Essence Processes.

G

GARDEN OF EDEN: A precious gift of the Rift Valley, called *Khenthunnefer* ("Garden of Eden") by the earliest Africans, was located along the Nile River Valley. Plentiful food supply in all of its river basins and fresh lakes made it such a paradise during the Ice Age that it gave these Africans great leisure time from daily chores. Rock Art indicates they indulged their concept of Nature as being the home of God by devoting much time to its detailed study. This meant Primitive (the first) Africans necessarily cultivated *their Foreknowledge—i.e.* acquiring intuitively and instinctively an awareness of mosaic pieces of Principles related to the Laws of Nature. To deal with such hard to describe bits and pieces demanded the designing of concepts, symbols, or labels to stand for hazy isolated things in the real world and for the formation of thoughts and feelings about the things so named. While their foresight led them to deal with circumstances independent of them, their *Forethought* urged the careful planning for things more likely to be under their control. From such foresight came the word "*Visionary*"--an important Intuitive/Imaginative Faculty skill for visualizing the path and steps through which achievements occur. This is because *Vision--the art of being aware of invisible essences others are unable to see—led them to see the infinite in the finite* and thereby fashion Options of how to best handle problems. Such handling was by establishing connections of Cause to the Effects and then devising Solutions to fashion the Effects. In short, they were able to mentally walk through likely unrealized happenings to see beforehand possible obstacles, errors, flaws, requirements, desirable resources, and any contributing factors associated with the undertaking. How they built a Visionary foundation was derived out of acquiring knowledge of the Laws of Nature. That remains applicable to this day. Also, Geography continued to play a major role in Primitive Africans being able to pursue cherished things not biologically necessary for survival (e.g. exploring the world of the Unseen). These combined to lay out patterns of using Leisure to have plenty of focused time to seek Esoteric Knowledge. Those most focused were called Scholars and of Mild, Slight, Moderate, and Intense (Extreme) types. Eventually, African Extreme "*Scholar*" embraced: (1) Real Self people with (2) Selfhood Greatness + (3) an addiction to Learning + (4) driven to pursue their Mission + (5) who derive pleasure from striving for *self-improvement* perfection. These Scholars used inner vision into their own Souls' Divine Consciousness as the key to improving their higher order Thoughts. For Scholars of lesser intensity, upon entering into a Scholarship lifestyle, they had to decide how much to balance scholarship with practical experience; to what degree they would acquire information be pursued--and whether to use it for self-improvement or as ornaments. Yet, all Ancient African Scholars shared in common the awareness: (a) that each was a Selfhood Great master who drew on what was within in order for Selfhood mastery; (b) of mental strength demanding aloneness and quietness in Nature so as to become "One" with its Harmonizing Rhythms; (c) for creating a Selfhood life where a "vacation" could be had simply by residing in ones own Inner World; (d) of needing skill to really, really focus on seeing things as they are; and (e) everything and everybody being ones teacher, for any event has in it a lesson for what to do or not to do. These early African Scholars' duties included gathering information in order to form options which allowed them to select pertinent research subjects; or p*enetrate* beyond the surface of things so as to extract knowledge amidst attractive distracting appearances. As students of the world, these Scholars never cherished a love of luxury since that concerns Desire, not Truth. All Desires are a lack based on illusional 'Conditioned' "Likes/Dislikes". Instead, by hearing, observing, reading, experiencing, inquiring, reflecting, and answering inquires so as to pull "pearls" from the rubble,

African Scholars always wrestled with what reality channel might give best general "ME/WE" ends. Such was never done at the expense of sacrificing their Integrity, or seeking fame or status, or taking what is within others or belonging to others. Instead, Black Scholars saw Integrity like the North Polar Star which keeps its place and all stars turn towards it. They always chose not to set their minds for or against anything since they knew what was right would follow from their natural Inner Candle. the European noted authority on Mythology, J. Campbell, says the *Garden of Eden* is a metaphor for humans' minds and thinking in terms of Opposites (e.g. man/woman, good/evil) being as holy as that of a god and what went on there is what is happening to humans right now. *The story of not eating the apple of the forbidden tree is an old folklore motif called "the one forbidden thing."* The innumerable scribe translators of this original Ethiopian Garden of Eden story made significant changes on their own (whether intentionally or out of ignorance) + under direction of the European Religious authorities and thus take billions of Believers far away from the Spiritual Elements. Ref: Ben-jock, Black Bible p110; Bailey, Ancient African Bible Messages.jabaileymd.com

GENERIC: C17 (belonging to a kind or class) indicates nonspecific Information having indefinite usage. Crowd's trends flow deeper and deeper into "Trinkets and Trivia"—making members increasing dumber and also, by taking them further away from the "5Ss," they become so insecure as to be addicted to needing the Crowd to get through life. Perhaps that is why the C14 Old English word *"Aware"* (vigilant, cautious, and informed) meant to be watchful; be on ones guard, and take care. One can be aware in a waking or an asleep state. Yet, most are only partially Sensory Conscious or aware because of their inner world of problematic Emotions and mental turmoil. The struggling are in a "walking coma"; fail to claim their due; stay in the status quo; and simply "Make Do."

GENETICS: *"Genetics"* can be likened to picture patterns seen on floors or on walls and made of small pieces of tile, wood, glass, or stone called mosaics. As a boy, I often made designs out of soda bottle caps. In Genetics, those small pieces are called "Genes." Genes in a human are like mosaics. Genes are what parents pass on for the child to fashion the "What it Does" Patterns and the "How it Appears" Patterns for daily living. You and your brothers and sisters have the same Genetics because all of you come from the same parent. But when each of you was conceived, your parents' Genes were shuffled like a pack of cards. Those shuffled Genes were then arranged so as to deal each of you a different "hand"—like that of mosaic tile pieces arranged into a "just for me" pattern. The way these shuffled Genes work is like different combination locks. All of these locks operate with the same numbers shown on a disc and marked from 1 to 100. With a given lock, the only way to unlock it is with the right figures in the right order. This means the same pattern will not work for any lock other than the one it is made for—and that is how Gene displays work in you in relation to your family. The same idea is seen in music whereby from its 7 scale notes. Like Genes, a countless number of musical pieces result from using the same 7 notes in different combinations. Still, all brothers and sisters have many things similar to the mother that were passed through your Genes. Yet, gained from choices in daily living and history, different combinations of those same Genes enabled learning from the Patterns of What they Do and How they appear. This is how you could start getting connected with a brother or sister you have never seen. That is how Ancient Africans discovered using the Seeable is a way to gain insights into the Un-seeable. In stepping back to the world's first human being couple in Africa 200,000 years ago, that couple parented all of the people in the world. So, all of the 37 billion people who have ever lived have the same Genetics. Thus, *what makes for peoples' differences* stems from the Unique Genetic combination one has; what each human does in cultivating her/his Genetics in how they think and feel which, in turn, causes them to do what they do. They look different not only because of how their Genetics makes them look but also because of the environment (e.g. heat, cold) they are in. When you think more about you and people, you will have no trouble realizing that without the air, plants, animals, and ground you could not live. This is because all of these are connected, even though they look and act differently. Note, these understandings of yours means that you are Genetically connected to all humans, Animals, and Plants. You have established this awareness based upon what you can see. Then you applied Principles taken from that to enable you to know what you cannot see to be true. This *Correspondence—is the most powerful thinking concepts for Understanding and forming great Thoughts*. Its theme is about *"Uniqueness" in "Sameness" and about "Unity" in "Differences"*. This is a fundamental for *Creating* things. It has 3 parts: "What it is"—"What it Does"—and "How it Appears."

GENTLENESS: Gentle, like *Genteel*, goes back to Latin (gens, of the same race or clan). The same root word, Gentilis, was applied by the Latin Church Fathers to pagan Romans and is the source of *Gentile* (non-Jewish). By way of French, Gentle entered English in the 1200s and like all French words, was very quickly assimilated and combined with native English words and affixes. For example, almost as soon as its appearance Gentle was compounded with English elements to give gentle woman, gentleman, gentleness, and gently. But it has had different levels of meanings. One was in the spirit of "the gens" snobbishly applied to a family of high status. Second, out of the concept of Chivalry that had its origin (580 AD) from the colorful Black Arab lover-warrior-poet *Antar* (Antarah Ibn Shaddad), it referred to the "polite" society engaged in flattery. Third, and in the sense of the Mature, it refers to what was called *Thoughtfulness* in the South when I was a boy. Mother taught me Gentleness by taking me to Art Museums and having me listen constantly to Classical Music. One shows consideration for the feelings of others, not doing anything to hurt their feeling and doing nice little things "just for you." They always spoke to and spent time with me even though I had never seen me -- opening and closing the contact with a hug. As a way of life they are honorable, courteous; speak of things as they are; graceful; soothing; peaceable; elegant in behavior; pleasant in manners and sweet in disposition; kind; benevolent; standing tall in carriage, quiet, and careful as a result of always being under control. Their *Spiritual Gentleness* of the Mature is spirited strength not mistaken for being passivity or so relaxed as to turn to softness. The same applies to their Humility. Both can be likened, said by Lao-Zi and Daoism, to "The Ocean receiving all waters from hundreds of rivers because it is lower" and thereby gains the power of them all.

GENUS: group of species alike in the broad features of their organization but different in their detail. A *Species* is a group of entities which reproduce their kind and are so nearly alike in all particulars as to indicate they may have sprung originally from the same parent stock—as did all "races" of humans.

GESTALT: *Gestalt State*—a totality, as a unified whole, with properties not derivable by summation from the parts and their relationships.

GLOB: Personally meaningful emotions, feelings, thoughts, imagination, expectations, desires, symbols, and mysterious 'something' interwoven into a "sticky" tangled ball.

GLOSSARY: A *Glossary* (C14, a collection of glosses) has many meanings. One is a list of often difficult or specialized words with their definitions, often place at the back of a book. Second, an extensive commentary, often accompanying a text or publication. Third is encyclopedically specialized in which the close link between the concept and term is established by tradition or the coordinated effort of several experts in the subject concerned. They tend to be classified or thematic (based upon a theme) rather than alphabetical and are more concerned with meanings and concepts than with word forms; may relate to or result from the deliberate standardization of terms within a field.

GOD--SEKHAM, THE COSMIC FORCE IN AFRICAN TRADITION: One cannot travel the path to Wisdom until one is flowing in the path that leads to it. That path is based upon the Supreme Being a given human selects to know or believes will fashion it. For convenience, the selection choices are crudely limited to the Spiritual Force of African Tradition and the Supernatural Force of European tradition. Ancient

Africans' awareness that as representatives of the Spark or Image of God so as for this to characterize a human's Highest Divinity Self, inferred that it expresses as a Divine outpouring of life and form—the utterance of Creative or Spiritual Energy. That Spiritual Energy activates Matter and the Wisdom imparted by the Spark of God then aggregates the resultant diffuse Matter into Forms which conform to the Divine Plan. Hence, the Logo's three aspects in humans are Will, Wisdom, and Action for dealing with Life-Living Principles and Processes. Humans' minds are capable of making notches into their inner Logos and remain "Yoked"—i.e. staying connected to the Cosmic Force. To be "Yoked" is by humans' *work of Spirituality to subject their minds to the Divine Spirit so it can command the Life-Force in harmony with the Laws of Nature.* Such "yoking" thereby allow ones mind to Metaphysically express the "Word" or Verbum" Patterns of the ever concealed Logos—and that is what Ancient African Sages called *Logic.* The name "God" is European, carrying a Supernatural individual concept of their God, as in Jesus and God the Father. However, because of European indoctrination of Colored peoples of the World, "God" is also used in referring to the Spiritual Force of African Tradition. As a result, many people consider the two Forces to be interchangeable but they are vastly different. Further confusion is added by interchanging Europeans' Supernatural concepts with those of African Tradition. For example, the Substance Spirit is not to be confused with the Essence Spirit associated with Energy—to which that Energy adheres to the Essence Substance. That Substance Spirit is the Eternal Reality—the foundation of all Cosmic Organism Creatures and Creations. The "Seed Essence" derived from the Cosmic Substance is all Being--the only Cosmic Life which exists entirely in itself, from itself, by itself, and becomes the thing it makes. Anything placed beside it is a Contingent or non-Being. The ever concealed Cosmic Spiritual Force Source of the Substance is beyond human knowledge or conception, whether in the ordinary or the clairvoyant states—thus making that Force Unknowable. Yet, the Force's Essence manifestations through Cosmic Creative works makes it known as the Logos. Since *"The Word"—the Substance--*from the Cosmic Spiritual Force is *itself the Divine Presence, its power, and its manifestation,* the term Divine Logos stands for itself and for its contents + designates the hidden aspects of how the Cosmic Spiritual Force is bound into and works to produce Cosmic Correspondence Harmony. In African Tradition, because the Cosmic Spiritual Force, Sekham, is ineffable (unknowable), "The Word" or "The Name" for this Force cannot be specific. The Cosmos itself puts boundaries on the boundless Spiritual Force in order to enhance awareness of that Force's existence as Oneness of Will (what starts the evolutionary process), of Activity (creating Matter), and of ultimate Wisdom (aggregated diffuse Matter into Form). Yet, for convenience in discussions, African Sages assigned various words to this Cosmic Force. Prominent in African Tradition are Neter Neteru or Neter of Neters—with Neter symbolized as NTR. Other terms include Supreme Being, Sekhem, Amn, Amun, Pa Neter, Aset, Asar, Amen, Amon, Amonu, Amunu, Almighty Tu-SoS, the One Source, the Uncreated Creator, the Boundless, Neb-ertcher (who has no name or form), Ptah, and later the One Universal High God. All, the Sages said, are merely attempts of humans' limited minds to provide relative names, metaphors, and symbols. More recent African Sages agree that the word "God" is a poor substitute for what represents the Infinite Mind for which there is no name. To realize there can be no appropriate or specific name, any name or word of esteem, like God, is okay.

GOD SUBSTANCE: From what I can gather, with respect to God, Ancient Africans used "Substance" as that of the Divine Logos—i.e. the making of the Cosmos out of God's own "Substance". Emanating out of that God Substance is Spirit (Energy) and Matter. All particular Things result from the composition in varying degrees of these two. They added that God's inner nature is Unconditional Love and outer nature is Life, with its Truth, Reality, and Natural aspects. Both natures, as indivisible differences, are called its Essence. These natures in the Cosmos are manifested as "Thought Forms"—Mental Creations in the Infinite Mind of the Cosmic Force, Sekhem. "Thought Forms" are like containers or vehicles for the Essence (Infinite Spirit)

Reality in which they are mutually in each other. Thus, the Divine Essence or Reality of humans is the Infinite Spirit (i.e. the Spark of God) in the Thought-Forms of their Souls. This Divine Essence (i.e. the Real "Self") is never born, never changes, and never dies—for it is "One" with Sekhem. All else of a human is what some call "*Personality*"—which changes and ceases to be. Neither Substance nor Essence are Matter, for Matter is merely a manifestation of Force, or Energy. Substance nor Essence are Force or Energy because they cannot possess a Mind (Ramacharaka, Gnani Yoga 127-137). So, I infer, *God's Substance—a manifestation of the "Big Mind" or "Infinite Mind--is the Divine Logos,* having perceptible and imperceptibly manifested aspects—both aspects being inactive on the Spiritual (Subjective; Ocean of Nun) plane. See Human Substance; Humans' Spiritual Essences

GODS--EUROPEANS: The word "God" is a European invention whose etymology comes from a wide variety of sources. Examples: (1) Old English, the One, the Being, Deity; (2) Teutonic, a personal object of religious worship—applied to superhuman beings of heathen mythologies who exercise power over nature and humans + images of supernatural Beings or trees, pillars, etc., used as symbols. (3) Indo-European, that which is "invoked." Most everyone has ideas about their God—but no two are the same—none are complete—and perhaps only a rare few know how they arose. Primitive Europeans of 45,000 years ago created gods in their own image and that has remained the "skeleton" for all subsequent European gods in religion, philosophy, and other arears embraced by Europeans (Bailey, Stopping the Violence). There has been a constant conflict throughout the whole history of European Religious Thought about the various forms of their various gods. Some say the supreme question has been between Teleological and Mechanical Explanations for God and the Universe. Since 65% of all ancient Greek scholars studied at the feet of African Sages in Africa, they brought back concepts which they used to formulate Teleological Thought. However, by being a semi-barbaric people, even Greek scholars could not comprehend the extremely high knowledge of African Tradition discoveries about God's Correspondence nature. Plato and Aristotle laid out the extremely complex ideas about *Teleology (Gr. Goal)*--the oldest mode of explanation of human conduct. A crude over-simplification is that just as orchestral instruments combine to make symphonic music, Aristotle said every separate thing has its purpose to make the world whole and serve one complete purpose. The purpose found in Nature required a purposeful Designer. But he and others said this Intelligence exists either in the Natural world or outside it. Contrary to African Tradition, this European God's assumed Intelligence is separated from its creatures and creations. Cosmological Teleology would not fit with Cosmic Reality because it omits human's exercise of Free Will and makes no allowances for Play or Music. *Mechanical Explanations* set out by the ancient Greek Atomist, Democritus is crudely summarized as the universe works like a giant machine—all according to physical laws of Cause and Effect—and no living thing has a choice. What happens by immediately preceding conditions is illustrated by a baseball moving the way it does because it has been struck by a bat. By contrast, Teleology says that what happens is because of a goal yet to be achieved, as the motion of a baseball could be explained as a result of the batter's aim. *Vitalism* differs somewhat from Mechanism by their advocates' invention of a special Supernatural agent to explain Cosmic happenings. The ancient Roman "*Numinous Religion —i.e. being filled* up with a Supernatural Numen presence pertaining to something both with a value (e.g. the "excitement" of sought after Material "Things" and military victories) and an objective reality (e.g. the indulging of a human's animalistic desires)—gained from visual experiences. Of course, there are countless other explanations for God—e.g. in C17, "Nature" was substituted for "God". All four of these religious categories fail to satisfy each *Cosmic Wholism* requirement. For example, as vital parts to the Cosmic Wholism, all real creatures and creations are interconnected, interrelated, all interdependently do its independent things to benefit the whole, possess Continuity (Unity running through Multiplicity), and maintain their integrity. The Mechanical does not work because it fails to explain the Orderliness in Nature; the adaptations of part to part; or the interdependent growth of organic things from inside out. But to "*Invoke*" God is what most theories share in common—i.e. to petition for help or support; to appeal to or cite as authority; to call forth in Incantations (magic formula); Conjure (to effect, as by magic); to put into effect or operation. Invokes' significance implies European gods are separate from humans and what they do—whether in this world but especially in the Supernatural World; that Believers, by choice, are in control (i.e. in a superior position) of the gods appearances or disappearances; and these gods are anthropomorphic beings—meaning the ascription of human form and/or characteristics to a deity or to any Thing not human. Although these four have long ago been abandoned by experimental European biologists, their auras, atmospheres, patterns remain in full force today, even to the point of continued beliefs by many Europeans. jabaileymd.com

GOD—SPIRITUAL: *Omnipotent* (unlimited and universal power), *Omnipresent* (present everywhere simultaneously), *Omniscient* (having total knowledge of everything), and *Immanent* (entirely a Mind)

GODS—EUROPEANS CONFLICTS: From observation and research it is my opinion that the one Universal High God of African Tradition and the European God are not the same, despite being presented as the same by Europeans to Black People. The hub of Europeans' Religious Wheel concerns primary questions of God's existence while its spokes pertain mainly to problematic relations of the world and humans to the gods and/or their God. To illustrate, imagine standing a huge stopwatch on its edge; the hands of the timer point to zero at the top of the watch; and that the top of the watch symbolizes African Tradition's one Universal High God. Except for Zero, all other 359 degree positions of the hands of the watch represent European concepts about God. Perhaps the story starts with the origin of Europeans 45,000 years ago in a harsh environment and success for anyone depended (among others) on describing and handling whatever they encountered. These early ideas, which conform to aims of modern science, indicated some kind of order to which their observations conformed and belonged. By them being Material world oriented, the typical order sought consisted of artifact type laws (i.e. uniformities) governing the Thing because their most important laws first discovered and established were of Mechanics. Fruitfulness from Mechanical laws led to every other European science attempting to approximate to the Mechanical School. For example, Ancient Africans said *"Nature" is the God Substance the Cosmic Spirit impregnates into the essence of God's creatures and creations.* This Substance imparts the life giving elements for the physical development and spirit evolution of each. So, in African Tradition "Nature" is the Cosmic Organism in action--a system of interconnecting, independently acting, and interdependently interacting God manifestations in accordance with their God assigned identities, and powered by God's Laws. By contrast, although ancient Greeks learned these African concepts from studying in Africa, they changed it to say "Nature" includes everything there is. Greek Sophists contrasted the "natural" (what anything is originally) with the "*Conventional*" (i.e. what is the result of human intervention, as by human laws and customs based upon Mechanics). In this way, they made distinctions between the "Natural," "Humans," and the Super-humans. Owing partly to the influence of the Greek Plato and partly to the influence of European Christianity, the human body and mind were set sharply against one another. Thus, they separated "Nature" (i.e. "the world and the flesh") into material and mechanical parts of the universe only--a seemingly small distinction subsequently making a world of difference in shaping minds of the world's peoples. In the doubting of God, influential Atheist Europeans said nothing explains itself and all other explanations fall short of showing in any exhaustive way why anything is as it is, or why there is anything at all. By assuming nothing could come out of just nothing, they explained the course of Cosmic events out of a made-up 'blind force' Supernatural reality--itself not to be understood or explained in the normal way or at all. To account for the rest of the Universe being in the Supernatural meant embracing the concept of Contingencies.

Contingencies are very much like the grammatical *Subjunctive Mood* which expresses uncertainty or non-factuality through such key words as "can, possible, would be, or may." Within this context and despite doing violence to careful observations about the Universe, (1) the Cosmic Mechanical Artifacts concept (C19) has dominated. Other European Supernatural God-related theories or substitutes located at different points around the stopwatch include: (2) quasi-mechanical believers who assume there is an element of spontaneity or freedom in all living organisms to account for the facts of observation; (3) Libertarians propose absolute freedom in a possible course of action, entirely uninfluenced by the past and the agent's character; (4) believers in the Ceramic Cosmic Creation (Potter God); (5) the "God is dead!" group saying the Cosmos is run by blind energy gyrations. (6) *Agnostics*--there is no proof of God but do not deny the possibility. Most believe the Supernatural and/or the Spiritual home of God is unknowable, making it impossible to prove its existence or nonexistence. (7) *Atheists*--nothing beyond sense perceptions is real--all else is imagination or insanity. If not denying God's existence, most are unsure and (8) some hope God is not; (9) materialist Epicureans disbelieved in a Cosmic Order; (10) those declaring a Supernatural God with a white beard--sitting on a church throne surrounded by adoring angels at an alter--who tells certain humans the message to convey to the people; (11) Stoics believed in a world-soul controlling everything; (12) Theists are believers, relying on faith in a God who created humanity and the Cosmos. Meanwhile, a situation Europeans have set up is the distinguishing between the "Real" of Reality vs. the Ideal Being (purely conceptual). Here, the key is "Thing-hood" having its Being outside the mind, not merely in it. For example, by the objects of mathematics--such as numbers and figures--existing apart from the mind, those objects have reality without being "Ideal." But, if they have existence only as figments of the mind, they are "Ideal" beings. Some Europeans define "Ideal" as "God"--not in the name of an actual Being or Reality--but as the name for the highest Ideal of humans, as expressed by their anthropomorphic gods. So, this "Ideal" is a symbol for perfect Truth, Beauty, and Goodness--for the ideal of Happiness. Specifically, Apollo is the symbol of Beauty; Zeus of Power; Athena of Wisdom. Again, this is based upon ancient Greeks and the Western world adhering to the dictates of the Greek Pythagoras (480-411 BC) saying that: "man is the measure of all things." Note the different worlds separating African Ideals being God oriented (which is within each human) and European Ideals being self-determined, remote from humans, and operating within the realm of the Supernatural, outside the Spiritual. Such implies the Supernatural God is not seen as anything more than for some to hope for--explaining why many Europeans are greatly attracted to Satanism. As was done with the Supernatural gods, the personification of evil as a Supernatural Being--called Satan ('to oppose') in Hebrew religion appears at the time of the claimed Return from Exile (538 BC). At first, Satan is not presented as the adversary of Yahweh, but as one of God's heavenly court, and a zealous prosecutor of men before God (Job: 1-7). The separation of Satan from God, by which God was "cleansed" of darkness, had immense consequences—e.g. the starting point for the New Testament--the development of Satan as the antagonist of God--and a justification for why European slave owners carried a Bible in one hand and a whip in the other. To them and other "high class racists" all of this SEEMS right. Though there ought never be mixing of African and European elements, both elements must be known to be offensively and defensively prepared to not allow them to slow, stop, or reverse ones wholesome progress. Medieval authors spoke of a universal Magnetic fluid by which living Beings influence one another, much in the same way that they supposed the Planets influence plants, animals, and humans--adding that many respond to mere touch (because of a supposed magnetic fluid in the body), magnets, or the use of some simple means of appealing to the imagination. In the Middle Ages the Supernatural was the idea that finally turned Europeans' world into something like a wasteland, a land where people were living inauthentic lives, never doing a thing they truly wanted to because the Supernatural laws required them to live as directed by their clergy. This was because of the European

Bible's story of the Fall in the Garden causing believers to see Nature as corrupt--a myth which corrupted the whole world because every spontaneous act was thereafter deemed sinful and must not be yielded to. In a wasteland, people are fulfilling purposes that are not properly theirs but have been put upon them as inescapable laws. The C12 troubadour poetry of courtly love was a protest against this Supernatural justified violation of life's enjoyment in truth.

GRADE: implies some regular ladder of valuation and some inherent qualities for which something is placed higher or lower in the scale, depending upon a standard. The Standard for Information Grading is Knowledge of African Tradition. A "*Scale*" is a scheme or device by which some property may be measured or used for classifying the different types.

GRADING SCALE: Qualitative Mathematics fashions a rough scale is as follows: On a "Range of Numbers" Scale from 1 to 100, the beginning of Possible is at 1; the end of Certainty is at 100; and "Probable" is in between. Specifically, Low Possible – 1-20--a *Guess*; Medium Possible – 21-34--an *Educated Guess*; High Possible – 35-50--*Hypothesis*; Low Probable – 51-69--*Predominance of Evidence*; Medium Probable--70-89--*Clear and Convincing Evidence*; High Probable--90-96--*Beyond a Reasonable Doubt or Moral Certainty*; Reasonably Certain – 97-99--*Beyond a Shadow of Doubt or a Medical Fact*. Although Certain is 100 (absolute), Scientific Laws do not quite reach 100. This scale is extremely useful in understanding hypothesis and theories in the Scientific Method and as *Evidence* ("that which tends to show a thing to be true") in law.

GREASE: In C16, "Grease" related "to enriching" whatever was ordinary into something of abundance which people desired to possess.

GREAT: Old English 'large' (extension in more than one direction), stout, thick; expanded to include "Big" in a non-material sense and by 1200 AD, important, admirable, excellent, immense, infinite (no bounds can be set, as in God's mercy or ones hazy aspirations). In American English it came to mean splendid, wonderful, or grand. Great, used in the sense of important, imports or means much with reference to desired results. Greatness carries in it something that cannot be trifled with. In an African Tradition Spiritual context, every human is born with Selfhood Greatness. This mean every human possesses infinite Knowledge of the Cosmos, infinite Personal Power, and what every human seeks in life—the "5Ss" of Safety, Security, Sureness, Strength, and Stability. This is the basis of Courage to face the most difficult situations with a confidence that no one else is better able to handle them than is oneself. Courage opens ways for all other virtues to be expressed. Since every human is born with Selfhood Greatness, its cultivation is the first thing to work on in little children.

GREEK--ANCIENT RELIGIONS: Europeans of the Mediterranean are Euro-African. Crecian civilization was the offspring of the Egyptians, as proved by excavations on the island of Crete where the history of Greece began. Ancestors of the Cretans were natives of Africa, a branch of Western Ethiopians. This story starts when the Cretans, a group of highly advanced Eastern Black Africans called Keftiu by Ancient Egyptians, came from East Africa and occupied an island off the coast of Greece around 3000 BC. It is known today as the Aegean or Minoan civilization (Ashby, African Origins p254). The Cretans were present when a band of independent illiterate tribes (Bailey, Managing Emotions p1)—called Aryans (speaking a common language and using common customs) and later to be called the Greeks -- appeared in the Mediterranean region possibly around 1800 BC (Amen, Not Out of Greece p25). They allowed themselves to be subjected to the Cretans. Being highly advanced in architecture, sea navigation, and agriculture, the Cretans eventually passed these skills on to the Greeks. Also, they were the source of the Greek's first knowledge of boxing, gymnastics, music, astronomy, weights and measures, olive cultivation, and the *Olympics* (originally a Cretan religious festival, which began millennia before in Africa). Meanwhile, the name Greek and Hellenes derived from the Cretan religious customs. For example, "Greek" (graikoi), means worshippers of the Grey Goddess, or Crone;

and "Hellenes," from the "individual" (Hellen)—a priestess of the Cretan moon Goddess known as Helle, Hellenes, or Selene. Many of the Cretan religious influences, which make up a large part of Greek mythology, remained (underground) with the Greeks, even through the classical period. Yet, they survive in contemporary Western thought. Ancient Greeks used mythology to express their suppressed conscious thoughts. When the Cretan civilization was destroyed by a massive volcanic eruption around 1500 BC, the Greeks lost their source of culture and went into another "dark age" period. No substantial self-improvement occurred until they began developing significant contact with the Black Babylonians and the Black Egyptians around 700 BC. Even then, they were too barbaric to assimilate and retain the Egyptian influences. Up to this time there were no philosophies or any hint of scientific thought (Diop Great African Thinkers p232, 299). The Greeks had no alphabet prior to coming into contact with Ancient Egyptians and did not have any institutions in Greece. Ancient Greeks named all Black Africans as Ethiopians. The Greeks revered the Anu Kemetians (because they were so divinely filled with the god power of Ptah) to the extent of giving them the highly respected name Egypt. The two most important oracles of Greece -- Dodona and Delphos -- were Negroes. When Homer (850 BC) was born and finally became literate (because of the teachings the Africans gave him in Africa), he corroborated the evidence that Africans taught the Greeks. He added that even the gods of Europe, and Greece in particular, which was then called Pyrrhus, came from Ethiopia. To illustrate, first Athens is named for the African god Aten or Athen Ptah. Second, in Greek mythology Zeus--the Father of the Greek Gods and of Ethiopian ancestry-- mates with the fair Greek maiden, Io. They have a mulatto son, Epaphus, born in Egypt. The Greek Socrates (whom I suspect was an African; see Bailey, Word Stories Encyclopaedia) was a Ra-Athen Initiate-teacher. The *Greek city-states were the starting point of Western civilization* as it is known today. In ancient Greece and Rome the Supernatural included prodigies, portents, apparitions (ghost) of the dead, miraculous occurrences, intrusion of demonic agencies into normal affairs, and eclipses. The Greeks conceived of the world as full of spirits, of malefic characters in operation at all times, everywhere. The use of spells was a regular technique in Greek medical practice. Wounds were healed with incantations. Thessaly was the ancient home of Witchcraft. Spirits constituted, not subjective projections, but objective reality. Understandably, Ancient Greeks had no capabilities of understanding the rich culture of Ancient Egyptian. Whereas the Egyptian Tehuti possessed the complete knowledge of Cosmic Creation, Evolution, and Operation, the Greek Hermes' (the borrowed Tehuti) eyes could only see human emotions. All Greek gods and goddesses were similarly full of emotions without high spiritual substances -- possessing eternal bodies lacking a relation to the higher Spirit. The city-state civilization of the Ancient Greeks of which Europeans are so proud lasted only 400 years. Prior to the invasion of Egypt by Alexander the Greek in 332 BC, the Greeks had no alphabet of their own. Instead, they had adapted, around 800 BC, the script—the alphabet--of the Canaanites, an African people. In general, the Greeks were an illiterate people unable to read or write and therefore unable to record any data pertinent to their time and evolution as a people. Alexander forced the Greek language on the Ancient Egyptians, which caused them to apply an alphabet to the Greek language. This was the phonetic alphabet--called today hieratic-demotic. However, the Egyptians' first form of writing was the Medu Netcher--i.e. hieroglyphics (Williams p77). From this one can see the Greeks were in no mental state or educational level to create anything great as today's Westerners claim they did. The Greeks philosophical wisdom borrowed from Africa, underwent many modifications based upon the philosophy of the borrower. They accumulated knowledge for its own sake, as opposed to striving to reach the Afterlife. Ancient Greek "Wise" men were much concerned with the sun, the moon, planets ("wandering") and the stars; with living things; and how living things came into existence. But at no time did the Greeks come to know God and make it the core of Wisdom as did Africans. Very Ancient Africans discovery of vibrating musical strings that yield pleasing chords as a result of the pitch of notes depending on the rapidity of vibration as well as that the planets (spheres) move through space at different rates of motion was plagiarized by the Greeks it under the title of "The Harmony of the Spheres." Their various misconceptions (e.g. love) and plagiarisms spread into and throughout the Western world to be the source of much of today's delusions.

GREEKS' MANNERS: Since the *Greek city-states were the starting point of Western civilization* as it is known today, and since much of the "Bad Manners" seen in the world are a reflection of the Western world's standards and values, let us look at how a subtle but significant defining moment in the history of "Bad Manners" came about. This story starts when the Cretans, a group of highly advanced Eastern Black Africans called Keftiu by Ancient Egyptians, came from East Africa and occupied an island of the coast of Greece around 3000 BC. It is known today as the Aegean or Minoan civilization (Ashby, African Origins p254). The Cretans were present when a band of independent illiterate tribes (Bailey, Managing Emotions p1)—called Aryans (speaking a common language and using common customs) and later to be called the Greeks--appeared in the Mediterranean region possibly around 1800 BC (Amen, Not Out of Greece p25). They allowed themselves to be subjected to the Cretans. Being highly advanced in architecture, sea navigation, and agriculture, the Cretans eventually passed these skills on to the Greeks. Also, they were the source of the Greek's first knowledge of boxing, gymnastics, music, astronomy, weights and measures, olive cultivation, and the Olympics (originally a Cretan religious festival, which had originated in Africa). Meanwhile, the name Greek and Hellenes derived from the Cretan religious customs--"Greek" (graikoi), meaning worshippers of the Grey Goddess, or Crone and "Hellenes," from the "individual" (Hellen)—a priestess of the Cretan moon Goddess known as Helle, Hellenes, or Selene. Many of the Cretan religious influences, which make up a large part of Greek mythology, remained (underground) with the Greeks even through the classical period.

Yet, they survive in contemporary Western thought. When the Cretan civilization was destroyed by a massive volcanic eruption around 1500 BC, the Greeks lost their source of culture and went into another "dark age" period. No substantial self-improvement occurred until they began developing significant contact with the Black Babylonians and the Black Egyptians around 700 BC. Even then, they were too barbaric to assimilate and retain the Egyptian influences. Up to this time there were no philosophizes or any hint of scientific thought (Diop Great African Thinkers p232, 299). However, the Greeks had adapted, around 800 BC, the script—the alphabet--of the Canaanites, an African people. During the Classical Greek period (800-500 BC), Socrates (probably an African living in Greece) had the greatest impact. However, according to the Greek Proclus, Thales (650 BC) was the first Greek pupil of the Egyptians and that after his return he introduced science in Greece, particularly geometry. After teaching what he knew to his pupil Pythagoras, he advised him to go to Egypt in order to learn geometry, astronomy, etc. However, an Ancient Egyptian priest told the Greek Solon that *the Greeks were always children, young in spirit, possessing no true antique tradition.* Perhaps this referred to the Greeks' fragmented epistemology; their undeveloped spiritual consciousness; and their development of a strictly Left Brain approach, thereby losing the "intelligence-of-the-heart" (which Ancient Africans had mastered). R. King MD elaborates (African Origins of Biological Psychiatry p64) on how this went on to cause fears and jealousies of Black people's high achievements with an intense associated inferiority complex among the Greeks. See Free Masons

"**GROUND OF BEING**": The essence of a "Thing"—i.e. what that "Thing" was when it came into Being—the ultimate 'ancestor' that by itself, reproduces itself, to become the off-spring "Things" it makes—like ocean waves; or, the mental "home-base" from which ones deals with life.

GUESSES: People consider that at the bottom of the vertical line of Information are Guesses. '*Guessing*' ['no calculations'] is a C13 English word originally meaning to "take aim" by locking on to something in ones sights or fix on a particular figure without exact calculation. Later, it expanded to include "Estimate." This was a time when Propositions reigned but if the Proposition could not be proved, that meant being faced with having no idea how to step out of a confusing situation. Hence, all that was left was to try the best available suggestion—called *Guesses* (having no basis in fact but ranging from arbitrary to educated). In the process, people of a Supernatural orientation are unable to do Rational Thinking. Thus, from guessing the unseen from the Seen—i.e. Reasoning by Analogy—they do Non-Rational Thinking. Its associated tinted begrudging emotions generates Delusions as well as stereotyping—i.e. judging the whole piece by a specific pattern within an association of Unlike Things. Worse yet is taking action on tinted (flawed, biases, prejudices) "Guesses." Yet, some Guesses are better than others. To "Know" is to be inside the Bull's Eye and that is characterized as being accurate and precise about what is "Right." People who have never used a bow and arrow will most likely miss the archery pad altogether. They are equivalent to those whose Guesses are useless or detrimental. Those who hit any of the parts in between the Bull's Eye and off the pad, whether consistently or not, are equivalent to Believers. But archers who are blind-folded can draw on nuances that gives them a good chance of hitting the bull's eye. That is why an "Educated Guess" is better than "giving up" without trying from uncertainty.

GUILT: *Guilt* is experiencing a sense of blame and remorse or sorrow for immoral actions or for not living up to ones own internal standard. Simultaneously, because the nature of Guilt is to always find a victim, one has the urge to discharge these emotionally and/or spiritually painful experiences. Although the popular sense of the synonyms Disgrace, Ashame, Shame, and Guilt in Old English (450-1066) shared the core of "shy" and "Bashful" as a state of mind pertaining to needless failure causing disappointment and humiliation, its religious core of provoking abomination (loathing, disgust) was applied to people who violated European church doctrine. Added to this, if there was a design to deceive, the label of Shame was a Self-Esteem attack. By C17, such exposure was also for the purpose of covering "the sinner" in a cloud of shame with the intent to harm ones reputation. Thereafter, Shame went in the direction of having bad feelings about violating rules of decency. By the end of the European Middle Ages, when individualism and materialism were rising into prominence, the traditional vices became more desirable and respectable. As a result, Shame and Guilt not only separated in meaning but were less of a problem, thanks to the flexibility had been put into European morals. Also in C17, the original meaning of Embarrass ("put to shame"; to put behind bars; impede) was separated to signify ones reaction from one doing dishonorable acts.

"GUN" OF EUROPEANS: What led up to all of the Renaissance was the giant historical step which has had a profound bearing on today's World Crowd. It occurred after Europeans discovered *the GUN* invented by the Arabs in 1304. Savage European tribes rose to power from perfecting the GUN over the next 150 years. After arming ships and troops with the GUN, they raped the world's peaceful and rich Colored Peoples of their precious possessions-- simply "Taking everything of their interest and destroying the rest while eagerly leaving a trail of Killed humans and animals "for no reason". Such had been the pattern of their Aryan ancestors. That enabled Europeans to dominate the world and then continue to this day to adversely influence the world. Countless (30,000+) shiploads of gold, diamonds, ivory, copper, iron ore of Central American Indians were taken to Europe. That is how Europeans became rich! And that explains why they are married to the GUN so as to maintain dominance up to the present. By possessing the GUN and having their warring ships go around the world Killing peaceful people and Taking their riches led them to get involved in "The Game."

This came from Traditional European "Big Four" enslavement "Take-Down" methods of *penetration, conquest, occupation, and colonization.* Such was done out of profound envy of Black People's achievements in civilization (social and technological development) and civilization (intellectual and spiritual development) as opposed to none for Europeans. This caused Europeans to feel "invisible," shamed, and inferior. Their chance to reverse all of this came after Europeans discovered *the GUN* invented by the Arabs in 1304. Savage European tribes rose to power from perfecting the GUN over the next 150 years. After arming ships and troops with the GUN, they raped the world's peaceful and rich Colored Peoples of their precious possessions-- simply "Taking everything of their interest and Destroying the rest while eagerly leaving a trail of Killed humans and animals "for no reason". Countless (30,000+) shiploads of gold, diamonds, ivory, copper, iron ore of Central American Indians were taken to Europe. That is how Europeans became rich! And that explains why they are married to the GUN so as to maintain dominance up to the present. To emphasize their lethal "Bully" position, they proceeded to enslave the Africans with whom they were in unilateral competition. It started with nuanced penetrations by using Supernatural destructive Essential Qualities to over-ride Africans' Spiritual or Essence Qualities that "SEEMed" to be of the same nature. Then Europeans switched over to concealed (making façade promises), then masked (as in creating conflict among Africans), then tempered (e.g. enticing Africans to give them Slaves in exchange for guns), and then Overt (e.g. enslaving Africans themselves). Their Supernatural and Material world orientation have, since their onset on Earth 45,000 years ago, displayed every conceivable practice derived from an Indifferent/Hate/Evil/Sadism (IHES) mindset to the present.

H

"HABIT MIND": "*Habit Mind*" contains only what has been placed in the mind by acquired experiences, habits, and observation—and thereby becomes *Conditioned Reflexes*. This means the habit has been so often repeated as for the mind, by knowing it so well, as to carry it below the field of Consciousness and become "*Second Nature*," akin to Instinct. See Conditioned Responses

HALLUCINATIONS, ILLUSIONS, DELUSIONS: Reality is seeable only by those detached from anything that might alter the "What it is". Intermediate between Make-Believe and Reality is Surreal. What is *Surreal* attaches make-believe to reality. *Poetry* attaches emotions to an idea reduced to the essence of its active principle—its Trademark. Religion attaches Beliefs to an idea. Any of these may have "make-believe" as one of its components. But realistically, an *Idea-Form* attaches Ether to an Immaterial Idea. *Illusions* are false impressions of a person(s), place, or Thing—whether because of mis-interpretations of its Character, deceptions about its actions, or wrong appearances. The result of Illusions and Hallucinations are *Delusions*—i.e. believing what is not real and not believing what is real. Whereas the question of belief does not arise in Illusions or Hallucinations, Delusions are false beliefs about something real and held on to in spite of no proof, evidence, or good reason. All three indicate ones sensory experiences have no reality in the outside world. Yet, that unreality coupled with being fooled by ones senses forms what are like colored eyeglass lens that lead one to seeing what is unreal as well as what is unreal in misinterpreted ways—both with an element of doubt. That combination prevents one from no longer being sure of anything one previously thought one knew. When there are supporting outside influences that are overwhelming—e.g. constant displays of the same false images of God, or "everybody" saying it is true or false, or from the imagination of ones self-belief--most people believe delusions, even in spite of seeing contrary evidence. The worst Illusion is to accept how one is defined by others; the worst Hallucination is to see oneself as a "what it is" that does not exist; the worst Delusion is to believe one is what one thinks oneself to be from monitored feedback interpretation reflections gathered from one or more outside influences or sources, including oneself. For a Crowd addict to claim to have a Free Mind is make-believe. Illusions are beliefs when wish-fulfillments are prominent factors in ones motivations.

HALLUCINATIONS—SUPERNATURALS' PHILOSOPHY: Cultures and Societies set-up Standards that are relatively fixed—unchanging in Qualities, stationary in nature, and permanent in duration. African Tradition's "God-Made" Standards were Mathematically determined and that became the ultimate point from which they inferred the best way to live life that stayed within, evolved out of, and progressed towards the "Heaven Afterlife" characterized by Hetep (profound Peace) and Harmony with all of God's Creatures and Creations. African Sages said Spiritual Standards are the Spiritual Elements which: (1) fashion the filter, base, frame, and measures for channeling what is "Right" from the rest; (2) form Principles of Ma'at (Spiritual Elements Qualities in action) serve as guidelines (i.e. direction pointers); (3) are a fixed measure for comparing "Rightness" degrees of displays of human capabilities in thoughts, emotions, expressions, or deeds; and (4) impart an inspirational Spiritual Power influencing adherents in what to choose for goals and approaches to their solutions in "Impossible" situations. Sages of all cultures in all Ages agree that as long as one stays within those realms, Wisdom and Thriving lives will result. Yet, the Contrary Opposite Supernatural philosophical Standards inherently have so much variability as to make any Standards—by Natural World comparisons--be incomplete, limited, weak, poorly thought out, narrow in option considerations, and/or invaribly simply wrong! This is a shift from ones Real Self Pure Emotion and Pure Intellect development over to Acquired Emotions and Acquired Intellect--another aspect of Supernaturals' *Transubstantiation* which, for them, is the ultimate "Right" thing. Hence, Supernaturals: (1) ignore the Natural World's Spiritual Elements Essences used as Standards so as to thereby totally disregard there being any Standards in Natural World others; (2) self-declare themselves to be "little gods" and thus always right in think, feel, say, and do aspects; (3) attack the Spiritual Elements of Natural World people as part of their daily living "Excitement" adventures; (4) consider users of the Spiritual Elements to be chattel or machines; and (5) consider themselves as being "strong and invincible" by believing they are mechanical on the inside and the outside. Mechanical things malfunction but do not realize it and any negative thing hitting their outside is not noticed. So, either way they stay on their "Fettered ME" Supernatural course. That course embraces Lower Acquired Brute Qualities like animalistic sensuality/lust, Hate of even the "faceless," attachments to Things, Lies, Greed and its resultant Frustration, Indifference, False Pride, Chronic Anger/Rage, Egoism, Delusional Fears, Violence, Indifference, Aversion, Adversion, Cruelty/Sadism, Meanness, Rudeness, Cowardice, Cunning, Shrewdness, Intemperance, Arrogance, Vanity, Control, Domination, Deceit, Revenge, Jealousy, Envy, Malice, Injustice, Oppression, etc. These result from possessing a profound Inferiority, Self-Hatred, Insecurities, and Shame sense from being Inadequate or "Not Good Enough." These Flaws mold a deformed Self-Image and Self-Concept with all problems springing out of the Consequences of such mindsets. Typical reactions from choosing to enter such a Delusional World necessarily make one a "Me, Me, Me" Self-Absorbed Individualist. This means that for people unlike them, Supernatural people only recognize in them the Qualities they choose to apply to them. This, I designate as *Philosophical Hallucinations—i.e. perceptions of ones own "what it is" Fantasies as Standards for what does not exist + non-perceiving of Natural World "what it is" Standards in others that do exist.* This is a form of Phantasmagoric creations (fantastic sequences of haphazardly associative imagery) that are mentally maneuvered and manipulated to "SEEM" realistic. The errors of perception or the deliberate misperceptions go so far as to gather compelling supposed sensory impressions and make them into facts for presentation to ones "mind committee" as to determine the type of actions to take. Those actions are always about unfair advantages for oneself and unfair disadvantages for all others. When appropriate, there is *wilfull ignorance denial of facts* so obvious as for them to be like nonseeing "the elephant in the room". Whereas this is the result of philosophical socialization, European Psychologists variously define *Hallucinations* ("to wander in thought or speech," as in dreaming) as, without relevant stimulation, seeing, hearing, feeling, or smelling what does not exist in a compulsive mental disorder sense.

HALLUCINATION--SUPERNATURALS PHILOSOPHICAL DISPLAYS: As with anyone, including Supernaturals, there are: Type I Qualities one has; Type II Qualities one presents to fellows; Type III Qualities presented to enemies; and Qualities of reactions, Type IV to oneself, Type V, to fellows, and Type VI to enemies. An example of Type I is that by disregarding Spiritual Elements Standards causes Supernaturals to equate the God-made Spiritual Elements with their Indifference/Hate/Evil/Sadism as being on the same plane. Thus, they arrive at the belief that Love and Hate are opposites; that Love is an emotion; and that there are different types of Love. To elaborate, in African Tradition, Unconditional *Love* is the *perfect, permanent, stationary, enduring, eternal, and all powerful force emerging from God's mind.* By Unconditional Love being Spiritual means it cannot be compared with anything known to man. To disregard these Spiritual Standards is to put them on the same plane as the Supernatural and for Supernaturals to claim that *Love is the opposite of Hate.* This is wrong because Unconditional Love is God-made and Hate is man-made--and therefore they are in completely different realms, as the definition of Supernatural indicates. Hence, what is right is that the *opposite of Unconditional Love is its absence.* Since Supernaturals define "love" to be an Emotion and since those types of Emotions are "man-made," both Emotions and Western "love" have degrees. But this generates immediate confusion. For example, *Agape* and *Caritas* are deemed by Europeans to give the sense of a higher or "selfless love." So the question is "how high?" because if it were Spiritual it would not be an Emotion and it cannot be Spiritual because the Supernaturals do not believe in it.

Unconditional Love has no degrees because it represents the inner nature of the indivisible Cosmic God which similarly has no degrees. So both either are or are not internalized to orchestrate ones life. What does "selfless love" mean and for what purpose? Western literature is filled with Supernaturals willing to and actually risking their lives without thought of "Self" in order to acquire gold or to "Take" what belongs to Colored Peoples. That does not equate to the "ME/WE" Afrocentric type of Selfless Service. Other Supernatural forms of "love" include *Phila* (jen in Chinese), the kind involved in friendship. *Eros* and *Amor* are forms of "love" based on desire. By degrees of emotional "love" means one can determine how much of what kind of "love" to give and to whom and for how long. This characterizes concepts in the Western word *Sympathy*. Black people do not understand the concept of "Sympathy" because there is no sharing of a Spiritual Space, as there is with Afrocentric Compassion. Types II and III are similar because Supernaturals, by opting out of their natural Spiritual and its Astral attribute Intellect, have no Conscience and thus no moral judgment. Such "throwers" of self-interest emotions see nothing wrong with publicly insulting women, the disabled, or any unlike them. It is seen as the right thing to do because the throwers are self-protecting by attacking the Qualities they assume their feigned enemy has. Their self-interest of "little god" power comes from the destruction resulting from the impact of what they say—and of course there is no guilt. This is a Type IV reaction they give to themselves. Being "Individualists" indicate a display of how strong they are in the face of adversities from fellows and enemies. Type V is not to give honor to fellows because they are competitors. Besides, they see no standard achieved by a special deed of a fellow that deserves honoring. To outsmart fellows and to Type VI enemies is seen as giving themselves more benefits. This is justified as them been benevolent "little gods," by others benefitting from the money they have to spend in excess. Truth must be avoided because of their dedication to attack the Spiritual Elements. What is documented that makes them look bad calls for the defense mechanism of *willful ignorance denial of facts*. This is associated with *Projecting their "Dark Side" traits onto scapegoats so as to never be wrong*. By being Non-Rational thinkers, the real issues are avoided because there is no standard that makes them more important than talking incessantly about what has absolutely nothing to do with the issues. Those topics, in themselves, have no more than Trinket and Trivia significance but serve as a deflection to hide their profound dumbness. To reinforce their "little god" status, "manhood," and "superiority, they demean and refer to women as sex objects, as if they—like their feigned enemies—are dispensable mechanical beings whose use provides glitz and glamor.

HAPPINESS: a by-product of being who one really is and doing what one is here to do and conquering struggles.

HARMONY: *complete adaptation of each part to the whole, implying perfect adjustment of all conditions:* means all of what is present must be "involved" before it can be "evolved" + there is *complete adaptation of each part to the whole, implying perfect adjustment of all conditions* + being true on all planes--mental, physical, and spiritual + imparting an inner sense of Order and Balance. *Spiritual Harmony--any dynamic equilibrium of Spiritual Elements attributes*--is an experience of Worth (Beauty and Order)

HATE: It's original ancestral meaning was neutral (Indo-European, "strong feelings"); then "care, anxiety, grief" (ancient Greeks); then "love/hate" (Old Irish); and then strong dislike (Germanic). When "Hate" entered English in C14 it meant heinous. Original ancient synonyms for the word Hate included envy, sorrow, fear, and abhor. Today, "Hate" is considered to be an intense deep-seated dislike and strong aversion coupled with a strong malicious desire to harm or to destroy the object of ones emotions. By being man-made, "Hate" has relative degrees of thoughts, emotions, and tendencies to be destructive.

HEART: "*Heart*" composed of Spirit and Matter. Ancient Africans said the Astral System symbolizes the "deepest recesses of humans' psyche" + constitutes ones Selfhood Center. The Astral "Heart" is where issues of ones life are determined--the center of thought, feelings, memory, and emotions--the place of ones morals (Conscience), Spiritual nature, and Secular fetters (e.g. Brute Brain's envy, hate). This range makes a portion of the "Heart" accessible to heredity and also accessible to experience--both "carving" identifying good and/or bad marks in it. By constituting a mixture of the Spiritual and the Secular inside each human's Circle of Selfhood Wholism implies the "Heart" could be influenced by such factors as what is: (1) orchestrated naturally by the Real Self of ones Soul's Spark of God Star or "Soul Sunshine"; (2) controlled by ones 'head' contents (e.g. from ones philosophy of life); (3) the Free Will choice of being operated by ones Ego or False Self of a Secular nature; (4) operated by ones Supernatural Ego/False Self; or (5) by the Ether in the stars and planets and its astrological signs (hence the importance of finding ones "Lucky Star"). For any of these 5 reasons, what one chooses to allow for ones Astral Soul "carvings" are capable of being molders of ones "*Character*" (the manifested nature of its Source).

HELL--PRIMITIVE EUROPEANS PHANTASMAGORIA: Primitive African Shaman played a great role in formatting all Supernatural Imaginations of the world's cultures. Starting in Africa, Shaman were the particular guardians and reciters of incantations, chants, and traditions of African people. As Africans migrated all over the world, these Shaman aspects served as "Seeds" for every conceivable cultivation as it budded into every flowering society. To illustrate, African Shamans' "Seed" ideas were modified by primitive Europeans into all forms of Imaginary Beings residing in the Unseen--Fantasy Beings made in their own Warrior Image as, for example, the warrior god Thor—Contingent Beings representing the warriors' self-seeking interest pursuits. Those pursuits were symbolic animalistic characterizations—of Indifference/Hate/Evil/Sadism thoughts and practices--the lowest of human desires--the lowest compatible affections, emotions, and appetites. European warrior leaders worshipped their various self-made gods for purposes of being continually motivated to act on all that was significant to them--e.g. to acquire riches--to be ferocious in Kill/Take/Destroy/Dominate/Oppress practices—to be powerful ruling 'little gods'—to generate "Excitement" for the "here and now"—all of this without limit or satiety. By having self-declared occult powers over Nature, they applied brute force to harm enemies and to benefit themselves. This mindset persisted throughout all branching cultural transmissions into every European aspect of life—e.g. religion, society, government, business. The commonality of their Supernatural Beings diversified into various orders of angels, demons, fairies, dead ancestors, and of "Super-human" leaders believed to possess a numinous (Supernatural) aura of omnipotence. Of even greater significance was for leaders in the various fields of life to perfect their weapons (e.g. of mind control and/or of arms) for conquering others. Such reliance on, and skill in, using these forces left its terrible and lasting mark on the face of Europe--an ongoing savage status quo society + continent fragmentation into hundreds of small, independent states which transformed into compact, self-sufficient strong-holds that could be defended against conquest--a state persisting up to the Renaissance. Typically, upon settling among the conquered people, they adopted victims' customs, styles, and religions. Many of their gods were borrowed into their Christianity version of African Christianity. Yet, persistence of warring themes of their primitive religions did not die, even after the intensive efforts to convert these warriors into Christianity. In general, their concepts of warrior gods and their Indifference/Hate/Evil/Sadism mindsets remained selectively attentive to the "Scarce Desirables" in the Physical and the European philosophical versions of the Supernatural realms. And these were honored while Goodness was attacked. Furthermore, whatever was "against a materialistic

Good life" became the standard to which that deemed 'Evil' was compared and judged. Still, those assessments had no generally offered or acceptable justifying definitions, explanations, or reasons.

Meanwhile, out of African mythological stories brought to all foreign lands by migrating Africans, concepts extracted and fashioned by Europeans went in the direction of innovating mind control tools above humans' ability to contradict or to counteract. Thus, Supernatural "Air Castle" structures and Abyss-type "bottomless pits" were their perfect phantasmagoric (fantastic sequences of haphazardly associative imagery) creations that could be made to "SEEM" realistic. To this end, they drew on Very Ancient African perceptions of "Bad luck" stars being holes in the dome through which the fires of "a disaster" could be seen. For this "disaster" or "bad star" imagery they applied Hel (Hell)--the European goddess' name for the underworld and the dead--the spirit of evil. This was also in accord with the Indo-European root for *"inferior"* and *"infernal,"* carrying the idea of *"Hell,"* as well as of European leaders believing that by their "home" and gods being Supernatural thus made them "superior" and their enemies, "inferior." When later Europeans added "Complex" to "Inferior," that designated the twine-like braiding of bad thoughts and bad feelings into a *"mental hell"—a reflection of European warriors own mindsets.* [This series on Hell and the Devil/Satan is reproduced from Bailey, Post-Traumatic Distress Syndrome p158-166; Bailey, Ancient African Bible Messages; Bailey, Stopping the Violence; Bailey, African Knowledge vs. European Information] jabaileymd.com

HELL--ANCIENT EUROPEANS CREATION: An Ancient African mythological *Judgment Day* story said immediately upon death, the "Heart" of the Deceased enters Ausar's *Judgment Hall*--the region to which the Dead departed--a realm situated within the most profound depths called the Taut, Netherworld, Duat, Underworld, Dwat—and subsequently, by foreigners, as the "Other World," the "Underworld," the "place of departed spirits," "Sheol," "Jehannum," "Hades," and "Hell." However, these words have special and limited meanings and are not to be confused with Ausar's *Judgment Hall* inner most sanctuary--somewhat like a temple where Ausar (Greek, Osiris) is enthroned. To reach Ausar, by proceeding through gate after gate, the Deceased had to pass a test of her/his "Heart" on one side of a balance scale being equal in weight to Ma'at's feather on the opposite scale. Incidentally, this Scale is the origin of the *Symbol for Justice* in today's legal community. Throughout the *"Weighing of the Scales of Justice"* the "Heart" of the Deceased would be examined by Anubis and the deities. Standing nearby the scale would be a monster Devourer of the Dead--a beast with the head of a crocodile, the chest and forelegs of a leopard, and hind legs of a hippopotamus—a symbol for destroying records of the "Heart's" earthly bad emotional experiences (the Sahu)—i.e. the sinful part of the "Heart" (not the Soul). The weighed "Heart" passed the test by Living a Ma'at life (by the Spiritual Elements) which provided a "Light Heart"; it failed (i.e. too heavy to pass from being a bundle of ill-programmed behavioral responses) if its life's actions had been motivated by emotional (animal), rather than divinity Soul parts of ones spirit. It also failed by it having been so overly religious as to live by rules outside what it takes to be human. As a result of the "Heart" on the Scales being off kilt, it is immediately devoured by the monster Ammit (Amut, Aummaum). The "Heart's" offensive part proceeds into the home of bad monsters and Bad Spirits--the Taut, which possesses all characteristics of what is associated with the "Unseen," along with its dark, gloomy, pits of fire. What is left of the unperfected "Heart" and Soul which, because of vibrating at a rate too slow to enter the Heaven Afterlife, travels to the *Places of Destruction*--a form of Purgatory purifier. This region was called a *"Black Hole"*--a *Nothingness*--a void where there is the absence of objects and where the "bad stuff" of ones Heart is concealed and securely hidden. The *goal of Auset's "Taut" is to deal with* the unperfected "Heart" and Soul of the deceased as it travels to the *Places of Destruction. It does not inflict suffering but rather brings about the complete elimination of evil-doers'* (i.e. enemies of Ausar) deeds by placing them into a Black Hole. As can be seen on this page, there are spaces between the words—spaces of "nothing". Yet, the "nothing" conveys meaning and reduces chaos in understanding what is read. To indicate *Nothingness*'s meaning, Ancient Egyptians employed an empty space to indicate "*Exterminated*"—i.e. being absolutely "*Eliminated*". Since a Black Hole draws in everything and absorbs visible light never to release either, it is unable to betray the presence of its contents. This makes it a tangible Being, bound up with the *Void*--a state of "No Thing"—a realm of primeval darkness--the Ocean of Nun from which Cosmic Creation sprang. Satanist Brutes borrowed this Ancient Africans Purgatory mythology and converted it into the Fantasy they eventually called Hell—to be commanded by another Fantasy, they called Satan or the Devil. Both were then converted to "Fact". To elaborate, the name "Greek" and "Hellenes" derived from the Cretan religious customs of c1700 BC. For example, "Greek" (graikoi), means worshippers of the Grey Goddess, or Crone; and "Hellenes," from the "individual" (Hellen)—a priestess of the Cretan moon Goddess known as Helle, Hellenes, or Selene. Hell was adopted in the Hebrew Bible. Then came the name Amenti (hades) being used for the abode of the deceased damned. It was peopled with all types of fantastic creations. Such was initiated by *Melchite Coptic Egyptians* (Jews Hellenized into Greek culture). Giving Ptolemy I the name "Oserapis" and later Serapis c323 BC, they spoke of him as: "The savior and leader of souls to the light and receiving them again". Added was fashioning of new concepts from African and Hebrew Bibles for the new European Church. Since nothing about their Supernatural, including their God, could be "proved" or disproved, the Crowd was socialized to follow Orders in military style and accept these fantasies on "Belief" and "Faith."

HELL--EUROPEANS CONCEPTS: After establishing concepts for Hell, Europeans' descriptions of it have been extremely confusing and conflicting. Of the numerous Bible references of various types I reviewed, some do not mention Hell. Yet, since this sphere was mainly supposed to be found in the Underworld (Num. 16: 30; Matt. 11: 23), it was also called "the Pit" (Isa. 38. 18)—"the bottomless place (Luke 8. 31)—Abyss or the "lower parts" (of the world; Ps. 63: 10)—and Inferno. Some said it is the prison of evil spirits (Revelations); the original Chaos in the Greek Bible, imparting a tumbling sense inside an Abyss (Gen. i. 2); and a symbolized realm outside the cycle of life while in a state of emptiness, caged in hostile atmospheres. Some say it is a place; some say it is not (Isa. 66: 24). As a place, in the sense of future punishments, it is distinctly taught in the European Bible, more-so in the NT than in the OT. Some say it signifies the grave and the place of disembodied spirits—both good and bad. Sheol and Hades refer to Hell as a general dwelling place of souls after death (Gen. 37-35; Acts 2.27). Gehenna in the NT is a place where both soul and body could be destroyed. Jewish writings from the C3 BC onward speak of places of punishment by fire for evil spirits and the wicked dead (1 Enoch 18: 11-16). Revelations describes a lake that burns with fire and brimstone in which the wicked will be eternally punished (Rev. 19: 20; 20: 14-15; 21: 8). Some say it is used for the place of the departed spirits and for the place of tormenting the wicked after death. *Wicked* was defined as the violation of God's intention and how evil *Appears*--including displays that are vile, sinful, depraved--as inequity, injustice, and wrong. Some say Hell is on Earth, with agonies of the mind equaling, if not exceeding those of the body. . Some say the ever-lasting hell fire is not meant to be taken literally but rather, as a metaphor, it expresses endless remorse in eternity to come, when separated from God and all that is good. Thus, it is confined with all that are bad. There are many perennially debated questions. Is Hell about everlasting pain where sinners must dwell with devils—in darkness, fire, and chains? Are humans divinely predestined, some to eternal salvation and others to eternal damnation ("double predestination")? Or does "Hell" perhaps signify sheer annihilation?" Are all humans to be finally saved ("*Universalism*"), or only some? Does "Hell" signify an eternal state, or is it a temporally bounded purgatorial experience that might lead to eventual salvation? "*Eternal*" is used in the NT for "eternal"; for "the aeon, or age"; or for what stands above time and space. But what always catches my attention about European Supernatural (fantasy) subjects is that authors generally speak of how it is in non-European cultures but not about their own. For example, in speaking about Africa, one highly respected European "authority" says: "the idea of a hot hell is an afterthought…. With the Egyptians, Hell became a place of punishment by fire and not earlier than the seventeenth or eighteenth dynasty, when Typhon was transformed from a god into a devil. At whatever time this dread superstition was implanted in the minds of the poor ignorant masses, the scheme of a burning hell and souls tormented therein is purely Egyptian.

Ra (the Sun) became the Lord of the Furnace in Karr, the hell of the Pharaohs, and the sinner was threatened with misery "in the heat of infernal fires". None of this is true! It is entirely European!! The Ancient African Bible's discussion of Duat (Dwat) concerns the part of the Astral plane where the evil or un-righteous are punished. This is the realm of the Unconscious human mind and at the same time the realm of Cosmic Consciousness or the mind of God. My Mother told me: "the mind can make a heaven of Hell or a hell of Heaven" (Milton). In the C8 BC Egyptians' Book of Caverns, Purgatory was like a cocoon where the damned enter, became non-Beings as a result of elimination of what is not about the Spiritual Elements, and then emerged as renewed beings, like a butterfly. While inside the cocoon, they remain in a self-made "dream world". Its human counterpart, while on the Astral level of Consciousness and because of Ignorance, is being unconscious of the path needed to be on, in order to discover God. Thus, one must be born again into Physical realms (Reincarnation). The fire burning in the Duat rekindles the light of the world each day anew, purifying, and consuming—the Sun being symbolized by the mythological god Ra. [Bailey, Stopping The Violence].

HELPING HANDS: See Entourage

HERITABLE: "*Heritable*"—a term wrongly considered essentially synonymous with 'Genetic' and 'Inherited'--because it includes both. '*Inherited*' implies genes are transferred from parent to child while Mutations, along with the inherited genes, may result in new genes in a *zygote* (the union, yoking, fusion of the male spermatozoon and the female ovum to give a fertilized egg).

HETEP: ones pre-birth state of serenity or profound Peace

HIDE: (skin covering) withdraw or to withhold from sight or observation for various reasons.

HIDDEN: implies the internal structure of a problem or situation.

HIERARCHY: European history of ranking Information includes the C14 Greek/Latin word "*Hierarchy*" referred to the "sacred" or "holy" in the medieval categorizations of angels (e.g. the Cherubim and the Seraphim). Then, in C17 it was applied to the clergy and their grades and ranks—those at the top supposedly having the highest degree of authoritative Information. Yet, since their Information was based upon the Supernatural, it had nothing to do with that of the Natural World and thus was considered "Non-Rational" Information.

HOMOLOGOUS: derived from an animal of the same species but of different genotype. Still, in comparing the different animals, their Organs are analogous to one another, or are analogs, when they perform the same function, though being altogether different in structure. Examples are wings of a bird and the wings of an insect. Organs are *Homologous*, or Homologs, when they are constructed on the same plan; undergo a similar development; and bear the same relative position. And this is independent of either form or function.

HOMOLOGY--COSMIC: Cosmic *Homology*--i.e. a similarity in fundamental plans of the Cosmic structure, indicative of an evolutionary "Genetic Sameness" in all living forms.

HOLOCAUST: holocaust (etymologically, a 'complete burning' in the sense of an act of genocide so morally monstrous it is not only against the people themselves but also a crime against humanity).

HUMAN BIRTH: When the human is born to Earth, the Divine Spirit's *Disposition* and a Virtual Image are fundamental and foundational to the true meaning of the Essence Principles and Appearance for following the course of their nature. This is because the Disposition's *What* and *Why* aspects contained inside God's plan have been organized by the Mind. In the mind, all of the Essentials are fashioned into an Interchange, out of which mosaic bits and pieces come from all that is within the Essence and the Essential (see later). The cumulative Effect of these mosaic bits and pieces lead some aspect of the Disposition to "stand out" as an Icon Image. The message of that Icon Image contained in the Character has a payload Purpose and with the power imparted by the Shape of its Thought-Form. As a result, a human's Characteristics spotlight the Essence of the message and then Identifies those Traits and Features which best Distinguish the associated Characteristics. The objective is to emphasize the "What it is" aspects of the Disposition--the bull's eye of the Character, complete with its satellites. Put another way, The *Character of what is to appear* in ones mind and possibly the External World represents the Trademark payload of the Essence's Disposition. That Trademark is the nature of the Disposition of the Source. The *Characteristics* in the Endowments and Propensities of the Essence Properties are designated to best make known that Trademark's Nature. In turn, the Characteristics are enhanced in the form of Traits and Features in the way ones mind determines them to be. So, the Character is itself manifested by the Characteristics of that Disposition in the form of Traits and Features. These combine to give identity to the Character and expresses individuality—all in conformity with its Disposition—Inclination, Intention, Attitude, and Temperament. See God's Substance; Divine Essence; Divine Essentials

"HUMANE" EDUCATION IN AFRICAN TRADITION: When traced back far enough, Ancient Africans said all humans would be found to be Genetically and Spiritually related—both derived from God's Image in the Spiritual Elements. That Image refers to God's inner nature of Unconditional Love—a Cosmic Image orchestrator of all God's Creatures and Creations—the interlocking Virtual Entities called "ME/WE". This unifying feature of Unconditional Love—itself imparting Dignity—constitutes a Spiritual Space for its residents. Dignity is the qualifier for its possessor to deserve receiving whatever one would give to God. Since a human is part of God's entire Image—i.e. all of God is within each human--every human is a divine and a material Being. Contained in the *Storehouse* of this *Iconic Divine Image of God—i.e. ones Soul*--is the Essence of all Cosmic Knowledge. Each Essence, in the form of visual Images, represents a Ma'at Principle—Principles embracing Truth, Justice, Order, Righteousness, Balance, Reciprocity, and Harmony. Their Consequences—i.e. Effect happenings--are Respect, Selflessness, Sharing, Compassion, Devotion to God + promoting inner Peace, Social Harmony, and Contentment. Every human's duty is to complete the Cosmic Wholism Circle, carrying resultant Spiritual Elements off-spring into action and persisting in cultivating their evolution. Each Principle--an attribute of the Spiritual Elements comprising the Self's Image of God—are of three types. Type I is what *promotes the progression* of humans toward their Highest (Divinity) Self. Type II is what *prevents and/ or protects* threats, disturbances, or destruction of ones Highest (Divinity) Self—to which the term *Humane* is applied. Type III *brings relief* to effects of Type II--called *Compassion*—and broadly applied, *Humanity*. By sharing the same Spiritual Elements (e.g. Unconditional Love) space with all "WE," means if any "WE" goes through pain, misery, and suffering, then "ME" is instinctively moved, to the extent that is feasible, to do what can be done to alleviate it, its Effects, and its Consequences—or, if nothing else can be done, make the hurting as comfortable as possible. Thus, within the context of Ma'at Principles, Humane Education *in African Tradition is the foundational concept for "Culture"--meaning the formalized methods of cultivating—i.e. shaping behavior in a people in ways opposite to the animalistic influences of the older portions of the brain*, including the Brute Brain (Amen, Metu Neter II:97). Throughout Africa, as their overriding educational principle, Ancient Africans promoted Good Character building, and not the mere acquisition of Knowledge. They defined *Character* as the Selfhood's "what it is" or "Trademark" identifier. Such is determined by whether ones Real Self or False Self is orchestrating ones Selfhood. The ultimate intent was for every *African child's Divine Consciousness to manifest through that child's Conscience as its Real Self Character*—a Ma'at oriented Character. To this end, they said there is really no way in which Character can grow except by humanely interacting with good people. Their teaching theme to children was of ones Character being formed primarily through good relations with and good behavior directed toward other people. Of top priority was all internalizing *Good Manners* as "second nature"—*i.e. having a sensitivity to and showing care about others' feelings*. Although ones Real Self is present at birth, complete with its expressing Pure Emotions and its dormant Pure Intellect, the way ones Real Self is cultivated for Type I is: first, by straining what is allowed to enter into ones Selfhood—retaining only Spiritual Elements aspects for fashioning and discarding the rest.

Second, for Type II, carefully learn Brutish and Supernatural hatefilled and evil natures and features in order to devise Selfhood Armour for Survival, Self-Protection, Self-Preservation, and Defense. An African way, expressed by Sun Tzu in 3500 BC, is first to minimize or avoid gross or prolonged destruction by "winning or solving conflicts without aggression. Second, if confrontational conflict is unavoidable, resort to principles inside "*Taking Whole*"—i.e. victory over aggression—by effective ways to go on the Offense despite them. Third, is learning how to show Compassion for Type III. *Do you simply give them a fish? Or show them how to fish? Or take them to the lake so they can figure out how to fish? Or put them in contact with fishermen? Or take away the Attractive Distractions keeping them from fishing? Or give them a swift kick in the rear end to motivate them to start helping themselves? Or simply leave them alone so as to give them time to assess and learn from the flawed thinking that got them into their mess?* jabaileymd.com

HUMANITIES—NON-VERBAL: the arts of being directly aware of the origins of Cosmic Organism's Creatures and Creatures existence and connectedness, the Human-made Intellect believes these happen mechanically, by Supernatural forces, by accident, and so forth.

HUMANITY: *Moral values arising from human fellowship fashion ideas of Humanity*

HUMANITY" IN AFRICAN TRADITION: In Ancient Kamitic Tradition, the first step into *Humanity* is for each human to acknowledge her/his divine Self-Image from being a Spark of God. The second step is to stay in the flow of the Divine Laws of Ma'at. Ma'at means the Spiritual Elements of Unconditional Love, Truth, Reality, and the Natural in action. These two steps impart *Dignity* (the Selfhood Greatness one possesses at birth). Dignity consists of an obvious, real, and rising Sun type vivid Ma'at light. The sacredness of the gold-like Rays of Dignity open insights into such Spiritual Elements' attributes as natural Goodness, Decorum, Elegance and Gentleness. Its recognition produces an "awe" form of Spiritual Respect. The "awe's" *Reciprocity* urges one to do "ME/WE" sharing of Dignity. In any form of Thoughtfulness to others--particularly to the most needy, through no fault of their own--such sharing is transformed into symbolic messages. Those messages disregard limitations and boundaries of human thought in order to touch Receivers' appreciative "Hearts." The Essence of Dignity contains Ma'at Principles—i.e. Truth, Justice, Order, Righteousness, Balance, Reciprocity, and Harmony. Each human's unique way of showing these are in the categories of Spiritual Respect, Selfless Service, Compassion, Devotion to God. The result is the promotion of inner Peace, Social Harmony, and Contentment. Ma'at Principles, expressed in each individual's own style and in the form of a "collective," is called *Humanity*. Humanity has five main separate applications—each being about maintaining ones Integrity. *Integrity is living within African Tradition's Ultimate Standard Spiritual Elements* flow and making all of ones lifestyle think, feel, say, and behaviors from its ingredients. African Sages said *ones purpose in life* is to fulfill the Divine Plan. So, each *human's duty is to creatively use Ma'at Principles that contribute to Cosmic Organism Circle Wholism Harmony.*

First, is the *Spiritually Selfish Humanity* display of applying Ma'at Principles to oneself. Principle I is to do what *promotes the progression* of ones Selfhood toward being ones Highest (Divinity) Self, and thereby leave ones Lower (animalistic) Self behind. Principle II is to do what *prevents and/or protects* from threats, disturbances, or destruction of ones Highest (Divinity) Self. Principle III is to *bring relief* to effects of what is threatening, disturbing, or attacking ones Self-Esteem—whether from self-inside and/or External World influences. This is done, said African Sages, by using the difficulties one has in life as a tool to force out the divine powers within ones Selfhood so they can be cultivated. *"Tragedy is a tool for the living to gain wisdom, not a guide by which to live."* Second, when traced back far enough, Ancient Africans said all of God's Creatures, including humans, and Creations would be found to be *Genetically and Spiritually related*—since all are derived from God's Image and Spiritual Elements. Thus, Ma'at Principles also apply to this "ME/WE" Cosmic Organism. Principle I is what the "ME" does to *promote the progression* of willing humans toward their Highest (Divinity) Selves. Principle II is what the "ME" does to *prevent and/or protect the "WE"* from threats, disturbances, or destruction of ones Highest (Divinity) Self—to the extent feasible. Principle III is the "ME" *bringing relief* to the "WE. When done for non-self-imposed destructive effects by the "WE," this is *Compassion*—the feature of the *Humane* term. Third, when a human is on the *Ma'at Principles path* or is struggling in order to get on it, that human deserves Respect. *Respect* is the giving of Appreciation to such deserving humans as one would give to the Spirit of God. Respect does not mean liking or accepting everything one does. Still, if willing, they are to be helped. For them, *Unconditional Love* displays—as I define it--are *by paying a very high price to give them Selfless Service, and especially when they do not want it or refuse it.* Fourth, is similarly showing Compassion for those lazy people who have created their own problems. However, the best help for them is to be allowed to wallow in their own self-created problems until they are sincere in wanting to change. Sincerity is shown by demonstrating persistent self-help efforts. Fifth, are Satanists dedicated to attacking the Spiritual Elements and using their fantasy created Supernatural God, Hell, and Devil to control people's minds in order to achieve their ends. Ones Ma'at Principles dictate one must Courageously, by means other than confrontation, defend and protect whatever, or whomever, is threatening, disturbing, or attacking the Spiritual Elements. Then, to continue heading to ones goal, creative measures are used to get around Satanists' obstructions. In this way, one helps preserve Humanity or prevents, or slows, Humanity from further destruction. jabaileymd.com

HUMANITY IN AFRICAN TRADITION: Humanity's origin starts in the Subjective Realm and its processes are the "descent of the Divine Spirit into Matter whereby Cosmic Principles undergo Involution—i.e. the drawing inwards" —in order for it to Evolute—i.e. ascend outward like rays of the Sun. It is the process of increasing Perfection towards the interiors or the core of the Cosmic Organism. This is because interior things are nearer the Divine, and in themselves are purer. Humans get a sense of this by entering Selfhood states of the Sublime. By contrast, Exterior things are more remote from the Divine, and in themselves, grosser. Only when the mind is calm—i.e. free from Acquired Emotions that lead to "me, me, me" selfishness, cunning, and deliberate effort to do what is outside the Spiritual Elements can it be peaceful. One can then respond to things as they come up and then naturally maintain a balance between the internal and the external. This requires understanding the nature of Humanity. Then, rather than blaming, finding fault, and criticizing, one gains insight into how things developed—a mind elevation that frees one from all opposition between using oneself as the standard for how others ought to be. When one looks to see what is Underlying what is problematic, one enters into the infinite order of Nature—an infinite *Unified realm of complexity and multiplicity Patterns, like foams in ocean waves, called Continuity. Although these Patterns would otherwise escape ones daily living perception, by being in Nature's Continuity makes one aware of the Base upon which the Underground foundation rests—a realm of the highest of all Orders—the total Pattern of the Cosmos orchestrated by the boundless Force which Ancient Africans called Sekhem.* As a result, one is now able to re-form an awareness of a "Oneness" relationship with the problematic other. This means there is the sharing of a Cosmic Spiritual connection. Next, from that common ground, ones own Pure Emotions and its Pure Intellect Complementary Equal devises acceptable ways to troubleshoot and together alter or replace whatever is not harmonious in the best interest of warmth and spirituality of the "ME/WE". In a Compassion state as well as in "Knowing Thyself," there is Involution. In both instances, all boundaries of any type are *"Dematerialized"* + *all limitations and boundaries of human thought are disregarded* + all differences are resolved by entering into the commonality which Underlies them. In this way unsuspected and novel connections can be made in seemingly unlike ingredients so as *to impart ideas of the indescribable. What occurs in those* novel connections is the mind synthesizing the resultant ingredients into new insights. Those insights inside the shared "Oneness" in the same Spiritual Space is *Involution* (how things roll up into being the way they are).

HUMAN ESSENCES: Out of God's Substance (Essence) comes God's Spiritual Elements "Genetics"—i.e. Unconditional Love, Truth, Reality, and the Natural. Those Spiritual Elements constitute a human's Essence (a *"That it is"*)—a human's "Self" + its *Properties* they uniqueness of the doing of that human—i.e. the "what it does" + "how it appears". Together, the "That it is" + its Properties equals that human's "What it is". When God originally creates a human, that human is in the Meiosis Subjective Realm, residing in an inactive, unformed, undifferentiated, but not disorganized state. That virtual human is contained in the same "Cell"— the Circle of Wholism—along with all other of God's creatures and creations. All members of this Cosmic Organism are also of a similar undifferentiated and unformed virtual state of Meiosis within the same "Cell". Each member in that Meiosis Cell, although connected to all other members, individually possesses a non-atomic Monadic *"Elemental Essence"*—a term meaning each member contains Divine Sparks of God's Essence and Essentials. Once the time comes for a human-to-be to start the decent towards and into the Earth World, the Monadic *"Elemental Essence"* + its Monadic "Seed Essentials" which impart Spiritual Energy and Matter = the Divine Spirit of a human's Selfhood. Out of a human's non-atomic Monadic *"Elemental Essence,"* the previously implanted Seed Essence of God now begins to disclose itself by appearing in invisible and visible displays of that human's Selfhood. In this manner humans are able to participate in the Goodness, Unconditional Love, Being, Life, Wisdom, Reason, Power, and Justice aspects of the Substance of God because each human's Substance is the same, although in the proportion of a spark. Thus, to see these is to see God; to live these is to live up to ones Spark of God. The desire to self-express these is an Essential Attribute of the Absolute Beauty of Unconditional Love. The communication is by the "Voice of the Silence" which conveys Cosmic Knowledge in Symbolic Vibratory Messages. This Voice: (1) says everything needed by not saying anything at all; (2) retains everything of its Substance by giving away everything about it; (3) speaks the seemingly impossible to the part of one Soul that make it feasible; (4) expresses the inexpressible in a manner that is crystal clear; and (5) is expressed inexpressibility by direct reality. This enables one to realize that God is internal—within ones Selfhood—and there can be no external God. By God being infinite and eternal means there can be nothing opposite or anything to which God can be compared. Nature is but a fraction of the complete scope of God. There has never been any no proofs outside of Nature that go farther than to prove a God of Nature. Neither is there any no evidence any Supernatural God of which Europeans claim that can restore any disorders of Nature, as if there were such a thing. Whatever is the best of what can proved to be in oneself is proof of it being in God, since there is no other way a human can get it. Thus, the Spiritual God is part of the Cosmic Organism.

HUMANS' ESSENCE EVOLUTION: A prominent Ma'atian concept during Ancient Egypt's Old Kingdom (5660-4188 BC) was of humans modeling the Image of God—the archetypal beginning of a human's Selfhood containing the Spiritual Elements. The Image of God is a mind drop of the "Big Mind" of God signifies a projection of a Divine Ray or Spark which is a direct emanation of the Divine Logos of the Divine Nature on to the human Soul and constitutes the duality Feminine/Masculine Principles—making for a perfect Image of God. When those Principles are united with that human's Mind, they become the

Unconditional Love/Wisdom Principles—further aspects of the Image of God. The Unconditional Love/ Wisdom Principles at the core of the human Soul is intended to have domination over all manifestations of the ingredients of that human's the Monadic "*Elemental Essence*" + its Monadic "Seed Essentials". That Essence includes a human's *Endowments* (i.e. natural qualities—e.g. ones Genius, ones Talent) and *Propensities* (in-born tendencies, e.g. ones capacities, abilities, and language)—the *Nature of that human's Existence--the "what it is" that has a Cause and imparts an Effect as indicators of its Existence.* These Effects over which the Unconditional Love/Wisdom Principles have domination include a human's Pre-birth Emotions, Acquired Emotions, natural Genius Intellect, and entire Lower Self mental nature. So, the Monadic "*Elemental Essence*" in a human is like being one side of the two sides of a coin—with the Divine Will flowing with God's Will on the other. A human's Will (freedom to choose faculty) is a formless tool of action--a "Virtual" (boundless) "That it is" entity with power. Crudely, the process is presented as follows. Step I--Out of God's Divine Consciousness comes the "*What* and *Why*" eternal "Things" to benefit the "ME/WE" in the Cosmos. They are "Voice of the Silence" vibration messages contained in a Disposition and are always about Unity in the sense of "All for One and One for All". Step II—The Disposition messages from God's Divine Consciousness imparted into a human's Divine Consciousness (Monadic "*Elemental Essence*") flow into the human's Divine Will. Assuming the Will chooses to accept them, Step III--the Will integrates the message into a compatible Virtual Image abstract for making meaningful units for the mind to receive. As God's agent, the human Will institutes God's dictates by carrying the Virtual Image to that human's Conscience. Step IV: The Conscience is the Divine Judgment on problems of action formulated by the human's mind. For example, whenever there is a mental conflict with Duty, ones Conscience provides the standard, guide, filter, and measure for what ought to be chosen to follow the higher planes. It then either clears a way or provides a clear path for God's Disposition Message to proceed in the Will's formless Virtual Image (Immaterial) into the human's Divine Spirit (which is also in the human mind). Step V: The meeting of that Disposition deposit with the Divine Spirit activates both the dormant Spiritual Energy and Ether Matter. Layering of Ether Matter on the Will's Image provides such a Form as enable the human to recognize God's Plan as a barely perceptible--something of a specific nature and made of specific attributes present in the Message. These processes within the Divine Spirit activate the Essentials inside the human's Essence and thereby impart *life or health to the Thing*—both being biologic necessities.

HUMAN ESSENTIALS AND THEIR EVOLUTION: The Divine Spirit's activation of the Essentials inside a human's Essence are fundamental and foundational to the true meaning, Appearance, obligations, and duties of the Essence's Feminine/Masculine and Unconditional Love/Wisdom Principles. While flowing in the course of their Nature (original endowments or propensities), these Principles and their Realities within the Divine Spirit are in the Appearance form of Primary Qualities—making the Principle and the Appearance like two sides of a coin as they participate in worldly Events (an ever changing reality). Distinguishing ingredients inside that Essence are ones Character, Characteristics, Traits, and Features—all being part of a Thing on any plane of existence. For example, they evolve the designs of ones Thinking Type and degree—and that determines one Philosophy of Life (POL) formation. A POL first shapes ones Private Self components of: self-recognized *Self-Identity, Self-Meaning* (the Spiritual Self-Greatness standard against which one can compare ones Self-Respect); and *Self-Love* (ones self-anchor). These components are what fashion ones *Public Self Self-Esteem* components of Self-Concept (ones spotlighted qualities) and Self-Image. The point: CT must be quite aware of the Essentials when they came into Being-hood so as to be able to distinguish any alterations. That requires Implicit and Explicit Discernments. Verbal type Discernments used for Thinking include the *Distinguishing Separation tools of who, which, what, when, where, why, and how much.* Resultant Distinguishing forms are: Demarcation by boundaries; Discrimination by qualities; Differentiation by Quantities because of

Distinctive markings or Characteristics—regardless of whether Distinctions are by Differences (the obvious) or by Discernment (masked or concealed appearances). These Essence and Essential concepts are elaborated on in Bailey's Glossary

(1) CHARACTER: The Character of a flower is its perfume; of a drink, its flavor. The Character reflects the Disposition and nature of the Essence of its Source. This means it identifies and expresses the "what it is" individuality of its Essence parent—i.e. the standing out as a mark, like a personal Trade mark. It pertains to the Thing (e.g. a human) itself without regard to comparative considerations. For example, a human's Divine Consciousness has that human's Conscience as its Character—a Character that is Ma'at oriented. With respect to the Character of anything, what best displays the Substance of the Essence is the Trademark signifying the "what it is" of the Essence. That Trademark--composed of *a mosaic mixture of pieces* of the Properties of its Essence parent and *imparting it with a unique sensibility*--possesses a unique Shape + a specific Disposition + a compatible Power. The Power drives the *What is done* by the Character's *Approaches* (ways a goal is reached), *Methods* (how to do the job), *Techniques* (how tools are used in the approach and method) and *Manner* (the different ways a technique can be handled) for producing its unique Product. That Disposition has an *Inclination* (what turns the mind in a particular direction), Intention (a highlighted significance of what the conveyed meaning proposes); Attitude *(the posture of the mosaic mixture)*; and Temperament (the power approach).

Together they hint at what is meant by its Nature's "what it is". A human's Character buds out of the ingredients within that human's Essence and is of a crude nature. Yet, it is "marked" or "engraved" so as to further evolve: (a) in its in-born pattern by imitating Nature; (b) heredity; (c) by Socialization—i.e. modified and shaped by outside influences, like environmental factors and suggestion from others; (d) organic brain disturbances; and (e) by auto-suggestion, meaning deliberate self-training and reforming by means of focusing ones Will-power and attention on Human Ideal Goals in the process of Re-Ordering ones life. Regardless of its nature, ones Character is largely the result of the quality of Thoughts and mental activities held in the mind which, in turn, stem from the Icon mental pictures or philosophical standards serving as the Background for ones Foreground activities. The Icon Image represents the Essence Trademark giving the Character its identity and expressing individuality as a result of its Disposition—Inclination, Intention, Attitude, and Temperament. Ones *Character is judged by ones moral displays, if any, as well as their consequences* with respect to the inevitable losses, lacks, and obstructions which normally fill ones path in life—no matter the degree of magnitude or the numbers of the trial and tribulations one must face in life. [Ref: Yogi Ramacharaka, Raja Yoga p249 & Fourteen Lessons p84; Dumont, Master Mind p173-7, 49 & Personal Magnetism p104].

(2) CHARACTERISITICS: In-born *Characteristics* of a given individual or Thing are the Primary Qualities that serve as the most distinguishing ingredients of Essentials typical for that individual or Thing's Selfhood. The main *Characteristics are about Primary Qualities having the greatest Effects and Consequences.* Compared to Character, a Characteristic identifies and expresses individuality with more Distinctiveness ("stand-outish-ness")—i.e. standing out in relation to something else. So, what one responds to most readily is the Characteristic—a fragment of that Circle of Wholism which identifies and expresses individuality of the most Distinctive ("stand-outish-ness") part of the Whole. Such is regardless of whether that focus pertains to a person, place, thing, or situation. An illustration is with moths being attracted to light—the Characteristic of all that is involved there--even though they may burn themselves to death in contact with powerful electric bulbs. With flypaper, the fly reacts only to the sweetness Characteristic of the paper and not to the ensnaring stickiness. The effect of the Primary Quality marking of the Character of the Essence of the Thing gives it a specific Individuality and appears as a Notion. The marking in that Notion is a Mosaic Image derived from the Interchange of its Essence parent. It represents the Endowments and Propensities of the Essence

and together they are its nature whose operations stand for the Uniqueness "what it is" of its Essentials family. A Characteristic is the bull's eye of that nature—which, in turn, has satellites. To elaborate by an analogy to the military, the Characteristics are like those positioned on a descending chain of command. The President's ultimate command—equivalent to the Primary Quality of a Characteristic--is given to the Generals and Admirals in charge. In turn, those orders trickle down to lower ranking Generals and Admirals who, in turn, pass the orders down to Colonels, Captains, and so on down to those of the lowest ranks. This implies that Characteristics have satellites each of which is a Mosaic Image comprised of the Properties it acquired while in the womb of the Interchange of its Essence parent. Similarly, the bull's eye of the Character gives one an instantaneous "Gist" grasp of the concept's or the Thing's meaning—i.e. the nature of its referents. The operations of the Characteristic stand for and enhance the "what it is" Trademark Uniqueness of the Character representing its Essence family—a Uniqueness displaying either internally and/or externally. Whereas *Satellite Characteristics* are exhaustive and only designate isolated aspects of the Character of the Disposition, *Identifier Characteristics* are Foundations of Essentials because they most readily signify the Genus of the Thing.

(3) TRAITS: Traits *are Characterizing Behaviors*—i.e. a distinctive pattern pertaining to individuality behavior(s) and more-so than a Characteristic. They derive from Mosaic Images drawn from the Interchange of its Essence parent whose operation is "what it does" of the Characteristics, Traits, and Features family of a given Essence. It consists of a Contingent Disposition, Tendency, and/or Behaviors. *Traits*, a C16 English word (harness-strap for pulling), comes from Latin "tractus" (to draw) meaning a drawing out, pull, or a tract, or extension. The sense of a particular aspect of the mind or character as a distinguishing quality from 'making ones way' arrived in English in 1752; then a 'visible sign'; then a touch or "stroke of the pen or pencil in a picture" giving rise to a particular image in a mind or character. Here, Traits are abiding behavior patterns. For purposes of designing some type of Image, imagine the Quality characterizing a Trait is a supposed vision called a "Phantom." Its nature and its effect depend upon whether it is powered by Spiritual or Emotional Energy (high or low). Despite possessing no specific appearance, its image is simply a non-specific embodiment of something good, self-defeating, or evil arising out of ones "Heart" and has some sort of "pull and/or push" meaning to the Receiver's "Heart." This can have a mild, slight, moderate, or extreme effect on the Receiver's "Heart." abiding behavior patterns, are formed out of mosaic pieces of the Essence's endowments, propensities, Disposition Message, and the Image resulting from them. That Image consists of a matrix (womb bringing nourishment to the offspring) inside its parent Pattern which displays out of the endowments and propensities. The "Womb" inside that Pattern of the Essence is composed of Activity networks which account for the "what it does" of the new Form offspring. Inside that new form is an Interchange with a Disposition. A given Pattern's *Shape* (a pattern of energy movement frozen in space) possesses a specific power given to it by Nature. This is present regardless of the plane of existence of a Trait. *Spiritual* Traits are mosaic pieces of the Spiritual Elements inside the Subjective realm whose Shapes have the power to reproduce themselves to become the thing they make. *Metaphysical Patterns* are designs composed of mosaic pieces, each from a different Causative factor. While "running together" inside a given Metaphysical Pattern, some are capable of being observed or realized while others are not—and this constitutes a *Syndrome* (Bailey, Dictionary of Medical-Legal Terms p133). To the Shape of a given Syndrome, Nature gives its Pattern a specific power for action in space and time. For example, *Non-aggression* is a mentally healthy way of living life. Without attacking or running away, the "live and let live" orientation of Nonaggression includes the traits of gentleness, kindness, empathy, affection, helpfulness, and compassion. These African virtues are to be applied to every aspect of daily living –personal values, to family values, social values, cultural values, civic values, legal values, and spiritual values (Bailey, Self Esteem, p. 33). Traits are assessed by: "what they are"; "what they do" (fundamental for success);

and "how they appear." Their focus is mainly on what is done to Characterize. In the daily living, characterizing African Tradition Spiritual Trust is characterized by solidness, unchanging sameness, and enduring qualities, it has no flaws. Du Bois characterized "Sorrow Songs" as music of an unhappy people. *Spiritual Ignorance* is characterized by blindness to the fact of Cosmic Wholism. Traits are like Characteristics—both being symbols able to communicate with a deeper network—in the way of alphabetic characters being communicators with one Intellect and Emotional centers. Ancient Africans invented the 24 alphabet consisting of symbols (representing vowels and consonants) which communicated with the Left Brain while their Ideograms -- consisting of non-alphabetical symbols (possessing a literal or figurative meaning) communicated with the Right Brain. A human's Free Will choice of a Nature determines how they are expressed, thereby hinting at what is meant by the chosen Nature's "what it is" of one Character. Personal selections and reflections of ones interpretations of the monitored feedback one gets from outside influences so as to know how to assess ones own experiences and what standards to strive are made into values which one considers as ones own. These values, like Principles, order ones life and give it Character. Hence, a human's *Temperament consists of a mosaic mixture of pieces of that human's Essence of the birth gift Real Self or the after-birth acquired False Self—a choice associated with a unique sensibility.* Ones "*Temperament*" is ones tendencies contributing to the consistent patterns of how ones thinks, feels, expresses, and behaves out of the general nature of ones Shape/Patterns; ones reaction (Temperament) Sensitivity--i.e. how easy or how hard it is to arouse a person to action; as well as together with ones Character, constitute ones *Personality* (but there are many ways to define Personality). *That human's Attitude is the posture assumed by the chosen mosaic mixture.* All of these are a reflection of the mosaic interchange of Essentials.

(4) FEATURE: *Feature*—i.e. the *Special* something in a Character, Characteristic, or Trait arousing the most attention--the outstanding and special aspect of the Trait's work Product—the MVP (most valuable player or the most important Thing of the farm). Feature originally meant physical appearance, used chiefly in regard to Beauty. Now, it is more about generalized unusualness or striking-ness—embracing the keystone Characteristic and anything else prominent or peculiar about the Character of the Essence--whether it is a Quantity and/or Quality—whether it is an intent and/or deed—whether it is actual or a potential. For example, a distinctive feature of a triangle is that it has 3 sides. The Feature, as *the Icon Image of the Essence*—the "how it appears" of its Nature, contains its Essence Message. Thus, that Essence's Icon Image, with its Essence Message, constitute the "payload" effect—and this Notion is the most outstanding aspect of the Essence.

HUMAN NATURE: In C13 Europe, "*Nature*" implied the Essence of humans, as inferred from human qualities (Great Ideas II: 517) but omitted anything about the Spiritual aspects. Hence, "*Human Nature*" referred to bodily processes and the restorative powers of the body; then (1380) to ones innate character or disposition; then (1385) to ones inherent creative power or impulse; then to human tendencies common in all societies; and then (1526) to the qualities present with the birth of humans. As knowledge about humans increased, "*Nature*" became impossible for Europeans to define. For one to get entangled in this type of reasoning necessitates the *shaping of Imaginative concepts into the appearance of being real; believing it is right; using each such belief as ones standard, filter, and guide for whatever requires assessment; and declaring "everybody" agrees. This, a most powerful way to control the minds of Believers/naïve, is the essence of the meaning of "what SEEMS right".* Though initially one is unaware of the doubt in them, constant repetition of those flawed ideas are eventually programmed into ones Selfhood as a way of life. Thus, it is the job of Critical Thinking to question the major premise; recognize and dismantle each SEEMS; defend against them; shed them; prevent being fooled by them by finding sound answers; and/or take advantage of them.

HUMANS' SUBSTANCE: The *Divine Substance* of a human is the "Spark" of God implanted in that human's Soul when that human first came into Being-hood. This "Seed Substance" is the *"That it is"* (its

"Selfhood" identity and contains the Divine Substance's Sensory Consciousness Disposition + the Divine Substance "Genetics" which consists of *Properties* (what a Thing has) customized for that human-to-be. Essence existence when coming into Being-hood) + its *Properties* (what a Thing has). Both make it "*Such as it is*". It contains Properties consisting of Endowments, Properties, and Attributes which are responsible for the Essence's "what it does" and the "how it appears." That human's customized Attributes of the Substance + *Endowments* (i.e. natural Primary Qualities) + *Propensities* (in-born tendencies, e.g. a human's capacities, abilities, and language) will operate different processes of that human's Selfhood so as to make her/him "What it is". A human's Divine Essence is like an Archetype—i.e. Seed resembling a box-in-a-box-inside-a-box containing contents of Prototypes. In turn, each Prototype has sub-Classes and sub-Classes have sub-sub-Classes—and so on. This Pattern of Processes is a profound Principle for CT.

HUMANS' SPIRITUAL ESSENCES: a human's *Divine Essence consists of the nature of its Source.* That Source's *Divine Substance,* inside a human's Soul, emanates Divine Essences when it reaches the Sensory Consciousness of the Will. The Divine Essence (the "what it is" of ones Selfhood) itself is a Spark of the Divine Logos. *Spiritual Essences* are exhibited in and out of the Private Selves of humans and is manifest as a *Pattern with a Disposition. Dispositions (Substance)* are Spiritual Elements arranged into an innermost pattern of certain types of mental activities which imparts an embryonic readiness way to think, feel, express, and/or behave in a certain Ma'at (God's messages) manner. The Disposition's *Essentials* are: (a) the *Inclination* of the Disposition is a 'physical' "leaning toward" or "leaning" away from something; (b) the Intension; (c) the Attitude; and (d) the *Temperament.* Both the Attitude and Temperament are physiological Sensory Consciousness systems fashioning the type of reaction the aroused person takes. See Essentials; Human Birth

HUMANITY: *Humanity "Manners" of the Cosmic Organism*—as in having good behaviors toward and good relationships with all God's creatures and creations.

HYPOCRISY: "Hypocrisy" (false appearance of goodness, virtue) is a Greek word characterizing acting on the stage. In C13 it expanded to embrace pretense, especially in religious matters. It is a form of dissociation, as when one asserts or believes in cooperation but behaves competitively; protects love but acts with hate; proclaims good-will but practices racism–all without being aware in part or in whole of ones inconsistency. Although the general agreement is that hypocrisy simulates through behavior and by a general line of conduct of certain ideals or moral character which are foreign to ones nature, there is a fear based type which I recently discovered that explains my observation of over 45 years of Black History research of never finding a European who gave the true and honorable history of Black People in print. Instead, these authors range from being overwhelming liars (the vast majority) to those on every rung of the ladder that approaches the Truth. I recall one author who got near the top rung and another who actually told the truth about Africans being the creators of a world-wide expression used today. I admire him for having the courage to say: "It is surely a major linguistic irony…derived from the lips of a minority [Black Africans] which most other Americans still prefer to associate as little as possible." Almost none will even mention Ancient Africans as such but rather refer to them as "the ancients who invented this or that" so as to imply they might have been European. Chances are the "almost honorable" European authors are not racially prejudiced but, by lacking the sufficient Character "Substance" and releasing only a certain amount of Courage out of fear of being isolated from their European society in-group. Gene, a White male, grew up in a family where each member had the delusion of being "superior" over other people. Yet, Gene gave no clue of being racially prejudiced, periodically saying and doing various things to indicate his acceptance of all peoples of any ethnicity—complete with real Black friends. Gene's Character Background seemed to be as "clean" as it was at Gene's birth but at some point in childhood it was "Emotionally Tinged" by a Trigger Event which ridiculed his associations with minorities and followed with isolating Gene from the in-group. The effect of this *Ridicule* and *Isolation*—the Trigger Event--removed Gene's Selfhood Greatness and substituted insecurity concerning a fear of not Belonging. This mindset was so disturbing as for Gene to be ashamed of it, try to deny it, as well as repress it. *Repression* means that out of his Unconscious his Fear expressed itself in the External World without his conscious restraints or even his conscious awareness. Furthermore, Gene *Over-Compensated* (i.e. substituting an exaggerated effort to conceal a weakness) with the "Foreground" *Self-Declaration* of "I will do things my way no matter what others say"—and that made for *Contrary Opposites* battles between his Background and Foreground parts of his Selfhood. To "Belong" to his in-group of fellow White people became Gene's "*Raw Nerve*" and to preserve that was a "*Bonding*" with them—not so much because he liked them but rather because he so feared being abandoned. That *Fear of Abandonment* represented the feature in his now *False Self*. Thus, Gene built his life around this "Bonding" which included not doing what the in-group did not like and learning to say "Foreground" things that would ensure being liked, in spite of being incompatible with the "clean" part of his Background. Periodically, in front of any White people Gene was driven to "prove" he was like them by dealing with minorities the insulting or stereotypical way his in-group dealt with them. In a sense, most of Gene's thoughts, feelings, expressions, actions, and reactions "straddled the fence"—i.e. be undecided, not committed so as to be able to jump to either side when necessary to "save face" (avoid humiliation or embarrassment) so as to give the most acceptable outward appearances to his in-group. This "fence straddling" went so far as to prevent Gene from formulating a definite sound Philosophy of Life—perhaps partly out of Guilt. It prevented Gene from being a complete "Soul Mate" with his minority female "love of his life." Gene's Fear of Abandonment kept him self-absorbed so that he could not write books for teachers intended to help needy minority children without doing it from a European perspective so as to not be ridiculed by Europeans for doing so. Gene could not be his Real Self.

HYPOTHESIS: a general principle assumed as a "possible explanation" of a set or Class of facts.

"I AM!": consists of (1) My "What it is" when I first came into Being prior to being born into the Earth World; (2) My "What it does"; and (3) My "How does it appear". Where did I come from? Out of the Ancient African Bible, crystalized by Tehuti—the African Master of all Masters—I possess: (1) a Spark or Drop of God making up my Soul; (2) the same "Genetics" as carried by Ancient African Sages—in the way each ocean wave has the same contents of the ocean; and (3) a special Talent that makes me most unique. My *Spark of God means there has never been, is not now, or ever will be anyone greater than me.* My *Talent* is what no one has ever had—no one has it now—and no one will ever have it. My "Genetics" from our Ancient African Ancestors means these are the best the world has ever known.

ICE-BERG CONCEPT: most problems are in 6/8 to 7/8 of its mass, hidden underneath the water.

I-CHING: A *Binary Number* system represents numbers having two as its base and using the digits 0 and 1. Yes/no, on/off, and positive/negative are all encounters of a binary nature. This System--persisting in what the Chinese called the *I-Ching* (Bynum, African Unconscious p182). See Yin/Yang

ICON: An Icon of a Thing is a crystallization of that Thing's Essence as to the "What it is" when it came into Being—its Endowments and Propensities—the Essentials (i.e. its Character featured as Characteristics and Traits) contained in the Essence—all in the form of *a microcosm* (a "little world"). Its Schema Principles serve as standards, filters, guides, and measures to which one aspires to live, serves as model for living, or is the standard, measure, filter, and guide one is living in the course of ones life. Within this closed Icon figure is: (1) an association of independent things each doing its specific job); (2) each ingredient possesses interconnections which depend on all the others associated with the interconnections; (3) every ingredients therefore is interdependently contributing their independent products for the harmonious benefit of the whole. See Sign; Icon

IDEA-FORM: Ancient Africans said, while in "the Other World," God's Androgynic protoplast--the ultimate living Spiritual Elements' metabolic *Substance* in a Divine form--itself possesses a Cosmic metabolic nature. When it gives rise to protoplast/*Protoplasm* in every living and moving creature, it is called that Thing's Essence. In humans it is the Soul—the Spiritual center of that human's manifested Higher Self. To this Center and Source, the Essentials—the Primary Qualities—are attached. That God's Divine Essence or Reality of humans is the Infinite Spirit (i.e. the Spark of God) in the Virtual (boundary-less) sense of an Icon Image. That Virtual Icon Image contains a "What and Why" message for what Thing is to do. At the proper time for it to undergo Involution, it meets with Spiritual Energy and Ether (Matter) in Astral part of the Metaphysical realm. There, it is activated and given Form to create a Notion of a Thing. In this combined Idea and Form state, the Essence (Idea) with its Essentials (Form) is a Thought-Form or Idea-Forms of ones Soul. To elaborate, still the "Idea" consists of God's original Substance and a Cosmic Thing's (e.g. human to be) Essence—with both possessing a Mind. That Thing's Shape or Form consists of Energy and Matter—so called because they cannot possess a Mind. That Matter is merely a manifestation of Force, or Energy while Substance nor Essence are Force or Energy (Ramacharaka, Gnani Yoga 127-137). The Essentials are attributes and consist of a "Double" Character, Characteristics, Traits, and Features. The Traits and Features are the various changing and developing modes of the Soul's expressions within a given context of that Essence. Put another way, the Virtual Icon Idea is fashioned into a *Pattern* by its Disposition (its message). By outlining that Pattern with

Ether, gives Form to the Virtual Icon Idea—and the product is an Entity. The Pattern has the Virtual Icon Idea on the outside and the Spiritual Energy nourishment in the matrix (womb) on the inside of the Pattern. The Form is the Essentials of the Essence (i.e. the Virtual Icon Idea). That Form's Essential has the same Character as the Essence, but differing only by being an Ether-made Identical Copy. The Form's Character is also the Identical "what it is" Copy of the Virtual Icon Idea. The *Characteristics of the Character Copy consists of and contains the Attributes* of the "What it Does" (which is/are its Traits) and the "How it Appears". The "*what it does*" depends upon *Properties* of the Essence to display a Thing's "*nature*". The Nature of a Thing—the "It is"--is how each of its properties' operations manifest. The *Properties* consist of a Thing's *Endowments* (i.e. natural qualities) and *Propensities* (in-born tendencies, e.g. its capacities and abilities). The resultant behavior Pattern of ones operations is "*Who ones Essentials are*." So every act undertaken involves a Moral Significance and Consequence—for every act deliberately conceived and purposed has its corresponding image in the mind— or Astral Soul. In short, *"who one is" spiritually is ones "Self" (Spark of God) Soul. "Who one is" in the Astral Soul is the pattern of ones Behaviors. "What one Does," if different from "Who one is," is who one becomes.* The Thing's or ones behavior pattern having the most consistent impact is its *Trait*. The Thing's or ones behavior that is its most outstanding operation is its *Feature*. These Characteristics (i.e. Traits and Features) cannot have counterparts in the Essence because its Essence parent lacks Energy and Ether. Yet, the *Characteristics represent the dormant counterpart "what it does" and how it appears" of the Essence*. The most outstanding Featured Trait of the Character is the "*Trademark*."

Whereas from the human's Spark of God Soul come Immaterial Archetypes that remain in Spiritual realms, from a human's "*Metaphysical Astral Soul*" come Idea-Form Archetypes destined for display in the Physical (Phenomenal) Realms. These Astral Archetypes are within the "Astral Heart" and the "Astral Mind". Both display through a human's Sensory Consciousness, since it resides only on these Metaphysical Astral Soul Mental planes. Thus, all the various orders of Primary Qualities appear to the Personality part of ones Selfhood as fleeting states of Sensory Consciousness. Ancient Africans said the "*Heart*" is composed of Spirit and Matter which enables it to symbolize the "deepest recesses of the human psyche constituting ones Selfhood Center." The "Heart" is where the issues of ones life are determined--the center of thought, feelings, memory, and emotions--the place of ones moral (Conscience) and Spiritual nature and Secular fetters (e.g. envy, hate). By constituting a mixture of the Spiritual and the Secular inside each human's Circle of Selfhood Wholism implies that the "Heart" could be influenced by such factors as: (1) orchestrated naturally by the Real Self of ones Soul's Spark of God Star or "Soul Sunshine"; (2) controlled by ones 'head' contents (e.g. from ones philosophy of life) and the Free Will choice of being operated by ones Ego or False Self of a Secular nature; (3) operated by ones Ego or False Self of a Supernatural nature; or (4) by the Ether making up the stars and planets and its astrological signs (hence the importance of finding ones "Lucky Star"). This makes a portion of the "Heart" accessible to heredity and also accessible to experience--both "carving" identifying good/bad marks in it. For any of these 4 reasons, what one chooses to allow for ones Metaphysical Astral Soul "carvings" are capable of being molders of ones "*Character*." These may come about by ones Divine Consciousness or by ones Sensory Consciousness resides only on these Metaphysical Astral Soul Mental planes, all the various orders of Primary Qualities appear to the Personality part of ones Selfhood as fleeting states of Consciousness. To elaborate, there are 4 main order Types of Consciousness Qualities. Type I are the *Spiritual Higher Qualities* derived from human's Spark of God Soul in the state of Spiritual Elements Archetypes that lead one to remain in a Spiritual realm mindset. They are expressed as Unconditional Love, Truth, Reality, the Natural, Wisdom, Goodness, Justice, Perfection—as well as shown in Spiritual Selfishness, Selfless Service, Gentleness, Compassion, Kindness, Steadfastness, Patience, Reciprocity (--"the reward of one whose acts consist in the fact that one will act for her/him" in doing good). The display of these is done within the "ME/WE" realm, implying the "ME" goes out of its confined Selfhood so as to share oneself as a natural part of its Being with the "WE". The mere giving of oneself to be in union with another. is the way to realize ones individuality. Type II are *Secular Abstract mental Qualities*—e.g. Reason, Judgment, Dispassion, Balance, Breadth, Height, Depth, etc. Type III are the higher Natural Lower (animalistic) Self Qualities—Affection, Sociability, Friendship, Generosity, Courtesy, Courage, Prudence, Fairness, Truthfulness, Honorableness, Simplicity, etc. —all blending gradually into the Type I Higher Qualities. Type IV are the Lower Acquired Brute Qualities—e.g. Fetters like animalistic sensuality/lust, Hate of even the "faceless," attachments to Things, Lies, Greed and its resultant Frustration, Indifference, False Pride, Chronic Anger/Rage, Egoism, Delusional Fears, Violence, Indifference, Aversion, Adversion, Cruelty/Sadism, Meanness, Rudeness, Cowardice, Cunning, Shrewdness, Intemperance, Arrogance, Vanity, Oppression, Control, Dominate, Deceit, Revenge, Jealousy, Envy, Malice, Injustice, etc. These are the result of possessing a sense of Inferiority, Self-Hatred, Insecurities, feeling Shame from being Inadequate or "Not Good Enough," accepted Flaws that mold a deformed Self-Image and Self-Concept with all the problems springing out of the Consequences of such mindsets. Typical reactions from choosing to enter such a Delusional World necessarily make one a "Me, Me, Me" Self-Absorbed Individualist. At that cross-road, one may elect to remain Passive, become Passive-Aggressive, or be powered by extreme selfishness as arrogant "little gods". Type IV bind their Ego to them so that, for practical purposes, they will never change.

IDEA-FORMS CHARACTERIZE AFRICAN LOGIC: *Music (or Harmony)* means both the living practice of African *Philosophy* (i.e. the adjustment of human life into harmony with God) and the living practice of Mathematics (since African Philosophy is Mathematics put into words). Out of this, all African Logic is based. As background to understanding, nothing today's Europeans say about how great the ancient Greeks were is true. They were a semi-barbaric people whose brightest, except for Socrates, were on par with an average Crowd. Despite 65% of their scholars studying at the feet of African Sages, they had no idea what African Logic was about and, like the Crowd, only got a "gist" of what agrees with their preconceived biases, beliefs, opinions, and prejudices. This is easily provable by the superficiality of their Supernatural dissertations about their concepts, apart from the African Intellectual Property they stole. Examples are concepts pertaining to such things as Harmony, the Music of the Spheres, and Form-Ideas. Long before ancient Greeks came into existence, Very Ancient African Sages (c20,000 BC) discovered that vibrating musical strings yield pleasing chords. Of particular interest was first, the musical intervals known as Consonants and marked by four fixed strings on the seven-stringed lyre. These were explicable in terms of ratios of the numbers 1 through 4. Second, the division of a string into a third, fourth, and fifth gives different sounds (see Amen, Not Out of Greece p32 for details). Third, the lengths of those strings can be expressed in simple arithmetical numerical ratios. Thus, they associated these exact correlations between the lengths of the strings of a lyre and the notes they produce to conclude that Cosmic Forms could be symbolized by *Numbers. The realities equated to the Forms and were inferred to be made of Intelligible Essences.* By deeming God to be a "Big Mind," they inferred that each Intelligence Essence is derived from the Substance of the Spiritual Elements. The Pattern of a designated Essence made out of the Spiritual Elements contains a Divine Disposition with a "What/Why" Message intended for a Cosmic display. The Message Preparation meant *Involuting*--a process of the Message descending into Matter so as to generate the required limitations to begin Cosmic Evolution. Such an "*Involvement*" is by the Divine Will arranging all parts into a Spiritual Image on the face of the Pattern so as to direct its powers in keeping with the inclination and intension of the Divine Disposition. After the Involution has made the Message into a compatible *Virtual Image* abstract by fashioning meaningful units for the mind to receive, it is guided into a *Divine Spirit* realm (which, for a human, is in the mind) where Energy and Matter are layered on it. Now, it is able to Evolve—meaning the unfolding itself of all of what has been "Involved" of the Divine Message in preparation for its display in the Cosmos. This *Evolving* process does three things. First is to un-wrap the core Immaterial Message; second, from the original tremendously gross Tangible Matter also being unwrapped, is adding its simple elementary Matter discards onto the evolving ingredients; and third, combin-ing the unwrapped ingredients into more complex and intricate products of the Endowments and Propensities of the parent Essence—products of Character, Characteristics, Traits, and Features--fashioned into greater and greater definition. What led African Sages to infer this process started with using principles derived from the seven-stringed lyre to make the bold extrapolation, based upon the *Law of Correspondence,* that what held with the lyre music must hold in all cases. This brilliant African discovery of "*Harmony*" and its components: initi-ated a mathematical analysis of heavenly bodies and insights into their influence upon the Earth + humans' inner experiences and microcosm workings in the sense of being small versions of the workings of the mac-rocosmic Cosmos. Throughout this process, Very Ancient Africans fashioned the tool of Astro-Mathematics and then subdivided Mathematics into Numbers, Multitude, and Magnitude. In Astronomy, *Magnitude* is a number designating the apparent "Brightness' of a star (not its size) on a scale. The higher the number express-ing the magnitude, the fainter the star. African Sages *Multitude* consisted of two main subjects: the relation of a given part to itself (Arithmetic) and the relation of one part to other parts (Music). As a result, they saw the Cosmos as one glorious Harmonia, or mathematical-musical Organism--the concept of "Harmony" as it is known today.

IDEA-FORMS (FORM-IDEAS) APPLIED TO AFRICAN TRADITION: In typical African Tradition fashion, *each Principle relating to Nature's Processes stood on the shoulders of those preceding it and, in turn, provided shoulders for offspring Principles to follow.* At the Cosmic Base, African Sages realizing all Principles are at bottom "One"—and called the Great Ultimate Cosmic Principle derived from the Substance of the Cosmic Force. Since the Spark of God is instilled into each human prior to birth into the Earth World, that Image of God reproduces itself in the various forms of Spiritual Elements Attributes. Images from such at-tributes are instilled in all Cosmic Organism Creatures and Creations in their pre-Earth birth state while in the Subjective plane. But despite the Uniqueness in each, they share the same Spiritual Elements Genetics and thereby have *Correspondence.* While in the process of descending into Matter, they each undergo Involution until "Enough" wrapping up occurs. Then after a '*Moment's Pause,"* Evolution begins in an orderly fashion. For example, an Archetype (African for Seed) of a family of things (e.g. the Plant Kingdom) now begins to subdivide into Prototypes and, out of each, into various sub-classes and sub-sub-classes. One of the numerous things Plato did not understand was that an Archetype relates to its many "Particular" offspring because they all have the same Spiritual Genetics and because Forms, by themselves, reproduce themselves, and become the Things it makes. Each Thing, by following a Divine Logos Principle, is given a *Number—i.e. an Intelligible Essence*—which gives each type of Thing its distinctive Character and makes it what it is. Out of that Number emanates a Form (also called an Idea, Number, Noumena, or Reality)—i.e. a Pattern with a Virtual Image on its outer side and a Matrix (womb providing nourishment) on its inside. That Form acquires a power that is based upon its *Shape* as it evolves into "Concrete" Things. How the Thing appears or What it does must be *seen behind to discover What it is*, and that is in its unique Form—the plane of Metaphysics--the Knowledge of the Thing. So, Number was the key to Nature—a concept having incalculable consequences for Science. This implies the Metaphysical and Physical planes of existence are fashioned on the model of Immaterial Forms in the Foreground, using space as its Material Background. Ancient Africans considered Idea-Forces, represent-ing Numbers, to be the essence of Harmony and therefore that Harmony was thought to be the basis of the Cosmos and of humans. Though sound is perceptible only by contrast with silence--since these sounds are not heard because they were present at the birth of Humankind—and since this 'music' is actually a harmonic and/or mathematical and/or religious concept, African Sages trained their Left Brains to detect these sounds. This enabled them to arrive at awareness of the "*Music of the Spheres*"--also called "*Musica Universalis,*" literally Universal Music. The Corresponding essentials pertained to proportions in the movements of celestial bodies—the sun, moon, and planets--as a form of Music. Then, using Inductive Reasoning, they inferred: (1) the movement of the large celestial bodies must make sounds in their motion according to their different rates; (2) those sounds made by their simultaneous revolutions are concordant (agree); (3) their speeds, judged by their distances, are in the ratios of the musical concordances; (4) and the sound effects, by means of the relation of one part to other parts, are a form of *Music*. Since all things in Nature are harmoniously made, the different sounds must harmonize. In this way of Correspondence involving musical harmony, mathematics, and Spiritual aspects, *Music* (or Harmony) meant to Ancient Africans the living practice of *Philosophy* (i.e. the adjustment of human life into harmony with God) and the living practice of Mathematics--since philosophy is mathematics put into words. This led to a shift of focus on Matter onto its Form, geared to making Metaphysical inference conclusions. In transferring their conclusions about "Harmony" from vibrating strings, paved the way for Ancient Africans' reflections and inferences to fashion, through Musica Universalis, a connection between African derived Plain Geometry, Sacred Geometry, Cosmology, Astrology, Harmonics, and Music. They used these as tools for expanding meanings of Spiritual Truth, Goodness, and Beauty; power to change and continually grow towards ones Highest Self; for best developmental directions in applying knowledge to advance towards their Highest Selves and have a Masterpiece life. See African Logic

"IF-THEN" METHOD: "If so-and-so is correct, then it follows that thus-and-so is true"—a basic Algebraic balancing in order to determine if there is a state of Order, Regularity, Coherence, Consistency, Compatibility, Balance, Harmony, and Predictability within its own Being.

IGNORANCE: In Ancient African Spiritual Literature the bad acting mythological brother of Osiris was Set (or Seth), the god subsequently associated with foreign countries and with consorts coming from the Semitic pantheon. It was Set--the energy of uncontrolled egoism and brute force; the deity of the desert and murderous heat; and a symbol of the lower self--who caused the death of Osiris by chopping him into 14 pieces. The point of this mythology is to let humans know that the Set character is a normal brute part of each individual's Selfhood. However, Ancient African Sages never considered Set a devil or the source of evil itself. One reason is the traditional African World-view does not include a single deity which embodies the principle of evil or a devil. Instead, they explained Set's actions as one of extreme Spiritual ignorance. To elaborate, Ancient Africans believed humans are born with a sense of being connected to all God's creatures and creations in the universe--called the Law of Sympathy. But then almost all lose this awareness as a result of getting absorbed in activities inside the Material World. This shift ignores, causes to fade, and disconnects from what is instinctively known about the "5Ss" (safety, security, self-confidence, strength, and stability) Spiritual powers. As a result of this extreme form of Ignorance leading to a disconnection, what replaces it is *Spiritual Pain* (of a magnitude far worse than personal suffering and which leaves one chronically frustrated and intensely anxious). Such Ignorance causes the human mind to be fooled into believing its thoughts are its own and its memories and experiences constitute its unique existence. Ancient Africans believed that ultimately, *Spiritual Ignorance (ignoring the Spiritual) is a lack of knowledge of the Self.* Dilutions and pollutions of these concepts occurred outside Africa. For example, the Bible states Ignorance is lacking spiritual discernment to "see" and grasp divine revelation (Matt. 13: 13-15); in the New Testament, "ignorance is an inability to perceive or respond to spiritual truth." But during the European Dark Ages there was a sense change of "not to know." In C14, "Ignorance" (to not be acquainted with") was brought into English by Chaucer with the idea of "to have little or no knowledge." To this was added the realm of Delusions whenever one believes what dishonorable people say. Delusions reached their zenith as a result of African American Slaves' brainwashing by Europeans. These Delusions, designed to define the Slaves as subhuman, acted like hammers to shatter the Law of Sympathy and this instituted for many Slaves a separation from the Unconditional Love of African Tradition.

However, since the European captors were the most deluded and the most distanced from Unconditional Love (and hence in the greatest Spiritual Pain), they tried every evil and sadistic act conceivable in hopes of gaining momentary relief. By the afflicted looking on the Material World side for answers and ignoring the Spiritual side, the path of Spiritual Ignorance then and now has always followed a flawed "Value" orientation (i.e. material standards) throughout life--a deformed course powered by a philosophy of life limited in scope and extremely destructive to mankind. To hide/deny Spiritual Pain, Europeans display Arrogance--defined by Ancient Africans as the self-seeking passions of power, lust, and avarice or covetousness (envy leading to a greedy desire to possess what belongs to another). By also operating within their Lower Self, people possessing a *"Love/Hate"* disposition periodically visit the Hate Complex. The correction for Extreme (Spiritual) Ignorance is to return to the other side of the Material World in order to "see", bathe in, and internalize Spiritual powers previously ignored. In the process of reconnecting with the Law of Sympathy so as to be automatically powered by its "5Ss," one lets go of clinging to material things. *When one has nothing to cling to one is free--and life's struggle ends!*

ILLOGICAL: *"Esoteric Knowledge"*—*i.e. understanding the inner truth lying hidden within the core of fundamental concepts about foundational Realities*--requires *Inference Leaping* by illogical, not logical Quantitative Thinking. Here, the word Spiritual "Illogical" refers to Spiritual (pre-birth) Emotions which, by originating in their Cosmic Organism "home" and are thereby outside the realm of the later appearing Intellect's systematic processes. Secular Illogical means the thinking is not mathematical and thus not reproducible. Irrational has no pattern because of its infinite variability and ambiguity.

ILLUMINATI FREEMASONS: That the African "Eye of Horus" persisted in symbolizing divine consciousness embodied in a perfected (Enlightened) human to thereafter be immortal is memorialized on a USA dollar bill. Called the "all-seeing eye of God, it is positioned at the top of a Kemetic (Nubian/Egyptian) pyramid. The upper black capstone containing the Eye of Horus is separated to indicate that it takes a liberated, luminous spirit to see in all directions as a *Visionary* (*equating to a Prophetic Percept*). The lower pyramid base represents the material human body whose aspects flow upward into its Holy Spirit source. This and other symbols on the dollar bill and the Great Seal of the USA are clearly of African lineage, said the European, Campbell (Inner Reaches of Outer Space, p. 97). Today, the struggle for World control is by the most powerful Brute people and their degree of destructiveness to people, animals, and Nature is of a Maafa magnitude (immeasurable catastrophe). These Brutes have a variety of names, such as the Illuminati, Power Elite, the Knights Templar, and Free Masons. Even milder degrees of people like them are the enemy of not only Black People and all Colored Peoples of the world but also the Poor, Disabled, Women, and Elderly of all races. Expressed prejudiced comments against Jews and Colored Peoples include: "Let no stranger understand this craft of ours. Why should we make it free to the heathen and the foreigner?" Much circulates about Diabolic Occultism in it. Yet, there is much variation. See Free Masons

ILLUSION POSSSIBLITY: Personified into a fantasy reality--called a Contingent Being

IMAGE: The *most primitive unit of thought; a sort of mental pictorial representation of a specific event or object which shows 'highlights of the original;* a pattern of forms and figures endowed with unity, significance, a message having a 'payload,' and an obscureness from its remoteness to impart fascination.

IMAGERY: The mental representation of a sensory experience—visual (e.g. an elephant wearing pink slippers), auditory, gustatory, motor, olfactory, or tactile

IMAGE FAMILY: The Image family includes Images themselves have several subdivisions, like an Auditory Image--the forming of an image of a haunting tune; or a Tactile Image--a design, like a triangle pressed on a dog's back. In 1589 Image embraced "ornate descriptions or representations of images, as in Poetry, to distinguish it from "*Imagism*" (concrete imagery). *Creative Imagination* is the sequence of images, ideas, or constructs which proceeds under the guidance of a predetermination and according to a plan or goal. An intellectual *Fancy* (the power of inventing illustrative imagery) is a mental image or picture founded upon capricious (guidance by whims or fancies instead of reason) or whimsical (likes, dislikes) associations or resemblances. Fancy's adornments of Nature involve the act or power of forming pleasing, graceful, whimsical, or odd mental images; or of combining them with little regard to rational processes of construction. Out of Fancy and Imagination (the power of creating from within forms which themselves become a part of Nature) came such terms as Fairyland, Enchantments, Magic, Spells, and Wands. "*Imagining*"--the very height and life of Poetry--is a 1340 Old French word for fashioning a picture to oneself of an image or representation in ones mind of something as existing. "What it is" of an "Image" has variable concepts.

IMAGINATION AND EMOTIONS: There is a close connection between ones Imagination, the Ancient Brain, and the Old Mammalian Brain. These brain manifestations of emotions and sensual energies are expressions of the Ether life-force—a force of Nature. Thus, through Images and emotions one can arouse the forces of Nature within oneself and thereby affect the environment and other people. This means ones Imagination is a gateway to the forces of Nature and one ought to beware of its productive or destructive effects. Imagination and the normal human brain engaged in normal human mental activities work as a unit much of the time. However, Imagination is not part of the Instinct Brain but it is part of the Omnibus Brain in realistic, distorted, and fantasy forms as well as in the Brute Brain's distorted and fantasy forms (it has no realistic category). Most Emotional People (EPs) have Imagination in distorted and fantasy forms of the Omnibus Brain. When operational, Imagination is a coordinator of subtle physical forces that already exist (as in the ingredients of an Emotion) and that assists integration of the "building blocks". This is accomplished by organizing the power of the spirit involved. Such happens even if the goal is harmful or beneficial. But Imagination is not a "Creative Faculty" and therefore falls short of being able to be a problem solver. Rather, that is the job of Rational Thinking which reorganizes and coordinates the wayward shaping forces of the event or happening in question (Amen, Metu Neter I: 92; Amen, Tree of Life p188). To by-pass this means the imagination will create all sorts of harmful ends. Imagination is an initiating programming tool for ones subconscious by generating an Image. In the process of invoking and organizing these images, by being manipulated through the faculty of Imagination supplies them with energy through which one is motivated (i.e. provides emotive motor power—e, out +motion) to act in the world. Any image able to elicit an inner emotional reaction or strong expectation or anticipation believed to come to pass is a programming of ones Subconscious, thereby putting ones physiological processes in a state of readiness to make it happen for good or bad. A process is most likely to occur if one goes into a *Trance State*—one so engrossed that contact is lost with external happenings, as when one fails to hear, see, feel what is going on in ones space. In this manner people form Icon Images they use as Supernatural standards, guides, and filters for their lives—as in how things should go. Emotions arise by the images associated with them. Its images dictate how they are to think, feel, express, act, and react in a given "broad-stroke" type situation. They carry the power to funnel the flow of ones life-forces or emotions to the accomplishment of these happenings as well as the means of conditioning ones spirits to behave as visualized. In other words, *Deprogramming* is through replacement Human Ideal Images—using Imagination systematically and methodically. Superficial (or Surface) Thinking EPs' uncontrolled Imagination derives—not from the situation one finds oneself in or from things one is interacting with--but from a lack of Rational Thinking skills. This causes EPs to segregate things that belong together and lump together things that do not belong together (i.e. "Broad-Stroking"). This is suitable for their orientation to the External World and that justifies their substitution of happiness for pleasure; substituting the spiritual uplifting for the exciting; and the pursuit for information instead of for knowledge. Since these ideas and beliefs have been charged with Emotional Energy force which powers EPs, they have the power to influence ones life. Whether good or bad, ones Images can and do touch ones emotions in a manner that are accepted as "the truth."

IMAGINATION CREATING: The "Big Three" categories of the Mind are *Imagination* (synonymous with the Greek Phantasia, imaging), the *Symbolic, and Reality. Imaginary* differs because it exists only in someone's Imagination. *Imaginative* is a high degree of imagination, creativity, inventiveness, and originality. Ones powers to produce products are imaginative in the ability to form mental pictures. Imagination is not the obverse (other side) of Reality but affords, rather, a means *of adaptation to Reality. Imagination*--faculty of Imagining--to mentally form and manipulate new images into imagery and sensations not perceived through the Senses (e.g. sight, hearing)--is the *reworking* of the raw materials of sense, notions, percepts, ideas, images as well as the process of recombining memories of past experiences and previously formed images into novel, creative constructions. These may be primarily wishful, distortions, or largely reality-bound; involve future plans and projections; or be mental reviews of the past. Ones lifestyle has as its core Imagination and the Images it produces, for they give rise to ones Emotions and pursuits in life. Research is for the purpose of Creatively turning up what is already there. This might start from doubting the credibility, value, or worth of cherished practices. Thus, to create in this setting is to destroy a custom—i.e. the dividing of a whole in order to remove its disharmonious aspect. Such customs are under the spell of assumptions so familiar as to never be questioned, especially by those most intimately involved. To discover what everybody has seen and how they saw it, from which I extract Abstracts or Abstraction which give new meanings enabling me to think what nobody in the world has thought. To recall what has been seen is an image, more obscure than the mental comprehension of the thing when seeing it—itself an incomplete unreality. Imagination's reconciling of opposites or discordant and mediatory power means that it has go-between abilities so as to make differences dissolve, diffuse, and dissipate in order to re-create the remaining ingredients into agreement--perhaps of sameness, with difference; of the general with the concrete; or to idealize and unify. Imagination then incorporates the ideas within Reasons of the message with the Image to give rise to a system of Symbols, harmonious in themselves. These Symbols are one and the same as the ingredients from which they arose—i.e. sharing the same essence—and serving as the conductors of the messages contained in the Images and the directional and influential power of its Reason companion. Next, the Imagination of the individual blends or fuses—i.e. synthesizes--the Symbol so that the Symbol serves as the representative of the individual to thereby present a sense of novelty and freshness with the old and familiar aspects. This is a more than usual state of emotion, with more than usual order—implying the Synthesized entity enables judgments from an ever-awakened state that allows for putting one on the path to visions.

IMAGINATION--CLASSIFICATION: Imaginations' constructs can be divided into: (1) "*Simple*" (imagining something seen before); (2) "*Compound* (e.g. the act of conceiving a centaur from compounding the sight of a man and a horse); (3) *Reproductive* (taking the helter-skelter data of the senses and producing whole objects--completing the incompleteness of objects sensed); (4) *Productive* (the power through which the categories order the material of intuition to make possible an understanding of a unified world; (5) being the condition for novelty, as with *Fancy* (a compounded imagination); and (6) "*Constructive*" (the creating of its own world, shaping details into its own unity according to its own controlling plan). Except for a few things, all of ones actions are rehearsed in ones Imagination when confronted with a situation before enacting it. Imagination is the first of the programming tools of the Subconscious and is closely associated between the Ancient and Mammalian Brains and their manifestations of Emotions and Sensual energies—which are expression of the life-force. Its motivation is invoked and organized by payload images manipulated through the faculty of Imagination. A payload Image is able to elicit an emotional reaction in one. Ones strong expectation or anticipation is from a behavior pattern programmed into ones Subconscious. Images, Feelings (Instincts), and Emotions combine to "beget" thoughts and actions along a certain pattern, as to stay in a Poverty Status Quo or to Thrive in a "ME/WE" manner. *Emotions are invoked—not by the situations in which one is in or with which one is interacting—but by the Images associated with them* (Amen, Tree Of Life p188; MAAT p96). Out of ones chosen Lifestyle Pattern come Characteristics, Traits, and Features which conform to ones Character. These Images show how one should react or feel in a given situation; how one desires events to go; and are depictions of desired outcomes. They act as funnels that direct the flow of the forces of ones nature. One can be deprogrammed through the Image one entertains. Imagination is a coordinator of subtle physical shaping forces of the events of ones life and is not a creative faculty—regardless of whether it is harmful, undesirable, or beneficial. An analogy is the "Star" as a Thing's Essence, the "Halo" is its Essentials or Primary Qualities. A "Disaster Star" is a false Essence. The "Disaster Halo" may or may not have a "Disaster Star".

IMAGINATIONS--"LUCKY STAR": The "Lucky Star/Halo" Concept for Realistic Imaginations is featured in African Tradition. Realistic Imagination deals with "*Wholism*" ("Holism")—i.e. focuses on the whole although its complexities cannot be understood by an analysis of the constituent parts alone. The "whole" includes those living factors comprising an organism's Unity and sharing mutual relationships; with all ingredients being interconnected, interrelated, in Continuity (Unity running through Multiplicity) and all showing interdependence with each other and the whole; and each interdependently doing its independent things to benefit the whole. The perception of Concrete wholes is carried out by ones Realistic Imagination (Wisdom) and the perception of abstract wholes is carried out by Ma'at (Divine Laws—relations and interdependence between things). A self-improvement spiritual duty of each human in promoting ones ability to succeed in undertakings and life is the unification of ones African type Logical Intellect with the Divine Law. To this end, humans' *work of Spirituality is the subjection of their minds to the Divine Spirit so it can command the Life-Force in harmony with the Laws of Nature.* Such is perceived by *Intuiting*—being guided without precedents. Type I: Imagination's "Lucky Star" category acts by taking a Belief into a state of trance and elaborating upon it by using ones realistic Imagination to manipulate and coordinate the forces responsible for shaping the ingredients of happenings or events into a reality (Amen, Metu Neter I: 92, 152, 248). *Trance* occurs naturally when one concentrates on a imagined scene or thinks deeply—i.e. when one is so engrossed as to lose contact with external events—so focused as to fail to hear, see feel what is going on. When ones Thought ingredients are based upon the Spiritual Elements, the Creative part of ones Imagination arranges, combines, and synthesizes those ingredients into attributes of the Spiritual Elements. Ancient Africans said spiritual work is carried out through concentration on the Spiritual Elements derived Images while in a state of trance and from being powered by the Spiritual Energy Life Force. Whereas the "Lucky Star" is its Essence, the "Halo" is its Essentials. In other words, the Halo consists of Primary Qualities displaying as the Essences' Essentials of Characteristics, Traits, and Features. Despite those Essentials being part of the Realistic Essence, as Primary Qualities they are real--do not exist independently--and can be isolated only conceptually for the purpose of identification. Yet, by their independent exhibitions working interdependently, the result is the carrying of an impactful 'payload' activating something good in the "Heart" or the "Head" of the one(s) touched by it. Some Effects serve as a Cause and produce a secondary Effect—called a *Realistic After-Effect*—which I call *Realistic Tertiary Qualities*. Type II: To see the "Halo"—i.e. the reality of the Essence's Essentials or Primary Qualities—through tinted glasses is to introduce *Secondary Qualities* either into the Primary Qualities of the Halo or into a Fantasy. These Secondary Qualities--i.e. are not real--do not exist independently--and can be isolated only conceptually for the purpose of identification. Yet, by their independent exhibitions working interdependently, the result is the carrying of an impactful 'payload' activating something good or bad in the "Heart" or the "Head" of the one(s) touched by it. Some Effects serve as a Cause and produce a secondary Effect—called an *Acquired After-Effect*--which I call *Acquired Tertiary Qualities*. Type III: When ones Imagination makes an addition to Realistic or Acquired After-Effects that is independent of but influenced by the Primary and/or Secondary Qualities, the combined exhibitions work interdependently to produce an "*Over-Effect*". If this addition occurs just to a Star/Halo with its Primary Qualities, it produces a *Realistic "Over-Effect"* which is independent of and uninfluenced by the associated Primary Quality characteristics already present. If the addition occurs to a Halo Effect composed of Secondary Qualities, it produces an *Acquired "Over-Effect*. This Acquired "Over-Effect"--although surreal in and of itself as a result of being a Distorted Reality, is still independent of and uninfluenced by the associated Secondary Quality characteristics already present. Although neither the Realistic nor Acquired "Over-Effect" exist independently, each can be isolated conceptually for purposes of identification. An example of a Realistic Tertiary Quality is ones self-fashioned Depression overwhelming ones self-image. An example of an Acquired Tertiary Quality is an osmosis absorbed Depression from socialization that overwhelms ones self-image. An example of a Surreal Tertiary Quality is derived from Socialization and then complicated by ones own independent contributions of Depression overwhelming ones self-image. Type IV: What I call Quadriary Qualities result from a layering of those Realistic and/or Acquired Effects which serve as a Cause and produce a secondary Effect—called either a Realistic or an *Acquired After-Effect*—and these I call *Realistic* and *Acquired Tertiary Qualities* respectively. When ones Imagination adds to the *Tertiary Qualities, their Consequential Characteristics*, derived out of their Interchange, create a new mosaic Quality pattern. That pattern is placed on top of the entire "After-Effect" and "Over-Effect" combined happenings, to produce an "Awe" Effect-- what I call a Quadriary Quality.

IMAGINATIONS--"DISASTER STAR": "Disaster Star/Halo" Concepts of Imagination is the realm of all in the Supernatural and White Supremacy realms. It deals with fantasy parts presented as wholes, as is typical of Stereotypes. To separate the Essentials from its Essence so as to enable the Essentials to run "Wild" means those Essentials lose their Reality source and thereby enter the realm of Fantasy. In other words, *Fantasy focuses only on the dissociated Essentials* (i.e. those lacking a reality Essence) or *on human-made Essentials having nothing to do with the Spiritual Elements*). This is visualization of Fettered Emotionally or Animalistically Sensory aspects--both charged imagery of an untenable or self-defeating nature. Type IV: A "Disaster Star" is the use of the Imagination's Creative Power for what are beliefs short of Spiritual Elements contents but falsely presented as attributes of the Spiritual Elements. These facades constitute "SEEMs" right "Lucky Stars" used to manipulate and coordinate forces responsible for shaping the event under consideration into a false reality. Degrees of the "Disaster Consequences" depend upon how deep into harmful ends it is—going as far as Brute Imaginative products. Type V: A "Disaster Halo" is dissociated Essentials (i.e. those lacking a reality Essence) or on human-made Essentials--neither having anything to do with the Spiritual Elements, despite being presented as such. It is a Belief composed of creative Imagination *Secondary Qualities*.

IMAGINATIONS--"DISASTER STAR/HALO": The "Lucky Star/Halo" Concept for Realistic Imaginations, as discussed in Chapter VII, is featured in African Tradition. But let us now look more closely at "Disaster Star/Halo" Concepts of Imagination--the realm of all in the Supernatural and White Supremacy realms. To repeat, it deals with fantasy parts presented as wholes, as is typical of Stereotypes. To separate the Essentials from its Essence so as to enable the Essentials to run "Wild" means those Essentials lose their Reality source and thereby enter the realm of Fantasy. In other words, *Fantasy focuses only on the dissociated Essentials* (i.e. those lacking a reality Essence) or *on human-made Essentials having nothing to do with the Spiritual Elements*). This is visualization of Fettered Emotionally or Animalistically Sensory aspects--both charged imagery of an untenable or self-defeating nature. Type IV: A "Disaster Star" is the use of the Imagination's Creative Power for what are beliefs short of Spiritual Elements contents but falsely presented as attributes of the Spiritual Elements. These facades constitute "SEEMs" right "Lucky Stars" used to manipulate and coordinate the forces responsible for shaping the event under consideration into a false reality. The degree of the "Disaster Consequences" depends upon how deep into harmful ends it is—going as far as Brute Imaginative products. Type V: A "Disaster Halo" is dissociated Essentials (i.e. those lacking a reality Essence) or on human-made Essentials--neither having anything to do with the Spiritual Elements, despite being presented as such. It is a Belief composed of creative Imagination *Secondary Qualities*.

IMPAIRMENT & DISABILITY: Out of an Injury comes some type of *Impairment*—i.e. an *Effect* manifesting as a mild, slight, moderate, or extreme partial or complete disharmony or loss of *function of the body*. Evolving out of an Impairment are *Consequences*, defined by Sharon Bingaman as: *the somethings which happen as a result of something happening*. Those "Somethings," when gathered together, have an effect greater than the sum of each when added together--and termed ones *Disability* ('not able'). Thus, whereas a Cause (e.g. trauma) gives rise to an effect (impairments), that effect is pregnant with Consequences of the Cause and the sum of the Consequences is called Disability. To illustrate, people who decide to be their Real Selves and be non-joiners of the Crowd are deemed to be "weird" and deserving of some sort of penalty (e.g. rejected, isolated, hated). The Crowd's rule is: "You must play our game to avoid being penalized. To what is acceptable to us but only if you do it voluntarily." The reason for this rule is that insecure people need the Crowd and thus they must become conformists. Although each Crowd member may have been told by their religion that all humans are Divine as a result of being "made" in the Image of God, the Crowd's External World Satanist leaders contrary message takes precedents. Satanist leaders say all humans are equally inferior and thus must have their minds controlled. This concept—which accounts almost all Impairment and Disability of Colored Peoples of the world--was laid out by ancient Greeks. They believed Slaves to be like mechanical beings having the purpose of doing the ugly, horrible, uninteresting work of civilization's daily life, since otherwise culture and contemplation would be almost impossible. Hence, it was essential for them to put boundaries on the Spiritual Boundlessness of both the Slaves and Greek people. Since Free Minds are not controllable, Rules for fellow Greeks and for the Slaves--in the manner that "one size fits all"--were required so that all would conform to the behaviors and patterns the authorities dictated. History shows that Hatred is slavery's inevitable aftermath. To avoid such an aftermath, Western civilization has been intent on rearing a crop of humans who never had Free Minds. Thus, such Enslaved would be unable to know what they are missing by not being free. The goal is to fashion Ideal Slaves. The reason for the mind control of their own "Troops" is to carry out the leaders dictates to destroy any "outsiders" because they are to be feared for keeping the "Troops" from having their privileges. Mind control for the victims is done so they will be mindless followers on the order of Ideal Slaves. *Ideal Slaves* fear is so great as to not speak for the fallen and disabled, or even themselves; will fight those attempting to free or even help them; and will voluntarily advocate the enslavers' dictates to fellows who are free.

INCOMPETENCE: Ancient families seeking their Lucky Star, sort help in acquiring what would foretell the dictates of a family's fate and supposedly reveal the wishes of God. Yet, these families were always alert to the numerous Astrologists and others practicing *Divination*, for some Astrologers and Seers were less competent than others. The C14 word "*Competent*" (suitable; sufficient") means fitness, as acquired through education and experience; a sense of ability; the capacity to deal with a subject; to be proper; proved through competition; adequate means for living comfortably; sufficient to supply all the necessities and many of the lesser comforts; and a high output in work with a low input in energy that is a desired effect. Since then, it has carried the ideas of *Efficient* (do the task quickly without wasted time, energy, and effort compared with any other option) and *Effective* (come up with the desired effect that satisfies the solution better than any alternative). These are what bring about *Efficacy*—the ongoing *Self*-Empowerment urging one to fashion an intended result that is headed towards ones ultimate Human Ideal goal. By staying in the flow of the Spiritual Elements one is always in the infinity of Knowledge and that Knowledge is known without the necessity for proof, since it is a self-evident Process of Nature. This means an effortless learning that enlarges ones Consciousness beyond the boundaries-less bounds of Understanding. *Incompetence* means being insufficient for the purpose; inadequate; unequal to the occasion; unproved or inadequate fitness acquired through education and experience. From over a half century of intensive daily research on all types of subjects, throughout the ages, and in all cultures, I have been impressed with the degree of incompetence and false information or limitations by Supernatural fantasies of "experts" and "authorities." The "me, me, me" orientation of today's Crowd displays as "Don't Care" and with features: (1) *Incompetence* in what they are paid well to do--in what they are supposed to know (knowing only a small sample of what is available); (2) poor work products; (3) *Dishonorableness; (4) Thoughtlessness of others;* and (5) *Inconsistency* in what they promised or in their duty--substituting excuses. Thus, customers never know what things they depend on will be done, if at all. Whereas *to do something "consistently" is to do it repeatedly but always in the same manner*, it is the combined effect of inconsistency, with incompetence, prevent one from ever being in possession of the 'power-in-waiting.' This implies--that for getting out of trouble when it suddenly and unexpectedly arises--there is no system or expertise in the practical application of theoretical knowledge gained from the acquiring of correct lessons from experiences.

"INDIFFERENCE-HATE-EVIL-SADISM" COMPLEX: Ancient Africans devised a hierarchy of beliefs categorized into the "Loving/Good/Truth" Spiritual types and the "Indifference-Hate-Evil-Sadist" Complex (IHES). At the top of the IHES category is the great disease of the Soul--i.e. denial of God. This is followed by the destructive practice of believing in appearances, as opposed to operating inside Actual Reality. Arising out of and accompanying the IHES complex are the "Twelve Tormentors" (including envy), Spiritual Pain--and nothing good. Because there are no degrees in things of a Spiritual nature, by the IHES being of an Earth World nature it is not the opposite of the Spiritual. Whereas the absence of African type Love--i.e. Unconditional Love--is the opposite of Love, the degrees in the IHES Complex starts with Indifference and progresses to Hate; then Evilness; and the Sadism. Afflicted IHES individuals have "*Anhedonia*"--an inability to feel pleasure due to the dulling of their responsiveness to the brain's reward pathways (e.g. involving the Ventral Tegmental Area of the Midbrain, the Ventral Prefrontal Cortex). Hence, they are *never happy*! Many Brutes admit being "numb" (absence of feeling or interest) to their hatefulness and evil deeds. Nevertheless, the System of Hate starts developing within a person when there is an absence of or disconnection from Unconditional Love. "*INDIFFERENCE*" implies a settled or fixed lack of interest and attention to what ought to be cared about. In other words, Indifference is a dispositional quality (i.e. a Thought Structure with a prevailing trend) consisting of an immovable neutrality regarding things of worth and dignity. Thus, by the Indifferent lacking compassion or caring means they stay detached and aloof. "HATE's" original ancestral meaning was neutral (Indo-European, "strong feelings"); then "care, anxiety, grief" (ancient Greeks); then "love/hate" (Old Irish); and then strong dislike (Germanic). When "Hate" entered English in C14 it meant heinous. Original ancient synonyms for the word Hate included envy, sorrow, fear, and abhor. Today, "Hate" is considered to be an intense deep-seated dislike and strong aversion coupled with a strong malicious desire to harm or to destroy the object of ones emotions. By being man-made, "Hate" has relative degrees of thoughts, emotions, and tendencies to be destructive. "EVIL" is a word packed with such destructive ideas as wicked, vile, sinful, depraved, inequity, injustice, wrong, and the violation of God's intention. It implies consequences like tragedy, distress, emotional pain, suffering, misery, and aging. "SADISM"--defined as *aggression turned outward* during the Dark Ages--was the opposite of early Christianity's *Masochism as aggression turned inwards* (Psalm 73). Chronic FEAR and Distrust, by removing people from Unconditional Love, automatically drives one into the IHES Complex. This means a given individual's LOVE PLATTER (the instinct to Love; to spread Love; to be Loved; and to be Lovable) is shut down. Whenever there is a blockage to free flowing Love coming into ones Selfhood; or a blockage to Love circulating inside and around ones Selfhood; or a blockage to Love flowing outside of ones Selfhood there will be Spiritual Pain--the worst experience a human being can have. A blockage of any of these three channels will automatically cause a lack of the "5Ss"--Safety, Security, Self-Confidence, Strength, and Stability. That lack, in turn, leads to a state of total Self-Absorption in an attempt to gain even a moment of relief from Spiritual Pain. Those attempts, despite ones location inside the IHES Complex, manifest as destructive behaviors to oneself (Masochism) as well as to others (evilness and sadism). Brutes attempt to repress their Spiritual Pain by generating unfair advantages for themselves (the "Me, Me, Me" Syndrome) and inflicting unfair disadvantages on others. The nature of these destructive thoughts, emotions, expressions, and actions take the form of Obsessions and Compulsions.

INDIVIDUATION: becoming aware of ones Selfhood

INDUCTION: many facts about a certain thing are drawn in and put under a general law or truth.

INDUCTIVE REASONING: observing a number of things sharing the same property or quality and going beyond this observation to generalize that the same property or quality can be applied to all known or unknown things of like-kind--and therefore placed in one "big picture" category.

INFERRED: to conclude from evidence, or from premises, or by reasoning from circumstances

INFERENCES: reasoning from the known to the unknown; forming Judgments and Conclusions after a process of reasoning from premises or evidence

INFERENCES FOR LOGIC: After the kangaroo parents (Cause) give rise to the birth of their baby (an Event or Effect)-- and before that fetus reaches full development inside the mother's womb--that half fetus/half baby engages in a natural Consequence essential for its completion in order to evolve. That natural Consequence is for it to travel outside the womb so as to reside inside the mother's pouch on the front of her body. This illustrates the principle that while the Cause gives rise to an Effect, that Effect is pregnant with the contents of the Cause. Then that Effect delivers the Consequence(s). At least as early as 20,000 BC Very Ancient Africans used this principle concerning *observations of Nature's Tangible processes in order to make inferences about the unknown in Unseen planes.*" For example, they studied the stars in the sky and used all forms of Mathematics to establish God's manifestations as Circumstantial proof of God--manifestations featuring a "certain sameness" which qualified them to be Truths of Reality. Next, as a result of observing Space is what stands underneath those stars and constitutes the background which allows them to be seen, they inferred God is within that Space. Such processes helped African Sages understand certain Cosmic Laws (Causes) that establish Spiritual Elements' correspondence in all God made things. As a result of establishing mathematical connections between Principles to arrive at Effects from Causes, enabled them to make Inferences of a Circumstantial Knowledge nature. *Inference* is the act or process of deriving one judgment or proposition from another(s). Furthermore, the judgment or proposition so derived is also called an Inference. Science is essentially a matter of Observation, Inference, Verification, and Generalization. Only those which stay within the confines of the Divine Logos have creditability but others short of that can be used until corrections can be made. A "*Proposition*" is a judgment expressed in words, the judgment itself being the actual thought or belief in ones mind. Showing a valid inference drawn from a Proposition to be untrue is called "*Reduction to Absurdity.*" All *Beliefs* (what one does not know but still accepts as true--some adequately justified, some not) and all information consist of judgments. A *Judgment*--either of a perception or intuiting (being open to ones Divine Consciousness)--is a process of intellectual orientation from which humans learn from past success and failure experiences of ones own and of others. From fashioning approaches, methods, and techniques by assessing monitored feedback from interactions with the outside world and ones own inner world, those conclusions are retained in the form of ideas which may or may not be helpful in new like-kind situations. It was from such an Inference process, made precise through mathematics, that connections between things and events were felt and apprehended on an intellectual and Spiritual level and thereby designed in general ideas and/or laws of interconnection. No doubt, overcoming trial and error aspects, the Inference process rendered greater depth of insight, and an enormously increased range of foresight and forethought--all interconnected by "*why*" *and "wherefore," because" and "therefore." These constitute Inference and reasoning*, from which Ancient African Sages devised paths leading to the indirect *Proof of God* by: mathematically figuring out Circumstantial Truths (like Spiritual Elements) + being aware of God's functions (qualities, powers, actions) + observing attributes (neteru) of God's domain in Nature (e.g. Instincts in all animals and humans) + Self-Knowledge + constant Reflection on how to overcome personal flaws + how to spread Ma'at. Together, these convinced them of their human capabilities to "Know" the existence of the One Supreme Being. According to Ancient Africans, *Spiritual "Evidence"* is direct and/or circumstantial pieces of the Spiritual Elements arranged and combined into a pertinent "big picture" pattern constituting *Proof* of the topic at hand. Such an example of Spiritual Creativity enables branching in countless directions to explore Unknowns and arrive at *Inference Certainty* conclusions. The key to accurate *Inference Certainty* is compatibility with its tandem aspect--i.e. the known must have existence--not merely in thought, but in fact--and then go beyond the known to propose something specific in the unknown capable of having existence as part of its unrealized reality that remains inside and evolves out of the Spiritual Elements. Their resultant Ma'at Truth products--after undergoing maneuverings and manipulations from inferences--give explanations for everyday things applicable to "Right" daily living. And that is what makes for *Wisdom.* And this is how Ancient Africans set up their Tradition. jabaileymd.com

INFERENCES APPLICATIONS: In 20,000 BC African Priest-astronomers' study of the stars and their mathematical calculations led to the highest form of Truth--Metaphysical Knowledge. Out of this, they inferred Cosmic *Homology*--i.e. a similarity in fundamental plans of the Cosmic structure, indicative of an evolutionary "Genetic Sameness" in all living forms. An *Inference* is a probable conclusion (between 70 and 90 % chance of being right) toward which known facts, statements, or admissions point, but which they do not absolutely establish (Bailey, Medical-Legal Dictionary p81, 107). By contrast, *Imply* is to involve a necessary circumstance. The fact that a woman is living implies she was born. From this it is a natural development for it to mean to indicate or suggest something which is to be inferred without being expressly stated. Such is a feature of *Cartesian Logic* (named after Descartes d.1650) serves as a means to arrive at the best solution by considering all possible outcomes associated with a line of action (X). *Seven Questions*: "What happens if you do X?" "What happens if you do not do X?" "What would not happen if you did X?" "What would not happen if you did not do X?" "What would happen if you did X off and on equally?; or most of the time did X?; or rarely did X?" This covers all of the lines of scenarios associated with the line of action being contemplated and thus encouraging the confused one to evaluate all aspects and choose the most suitable answer. *Predictions* are Inferences when one attempts to determine what is currently unknown from what is already known. For example, one might say that "if and when" certain factors are combined in certain ways, the results are predictable—*Conditional Predictions.* In the European legal arena the *adjective* (a word that limits a word with color, as in a rotten apple) "Circumstantial", suggesting completeness of detail, has a special meaning. When combined with Evidence, the term "*Circumstantial Evidence*" concerns facts that "stand around" a crime. For each circumstance to be judged for its significance leaves much room for inferences to be made on either side of the Truth. Wrong convictions are more likely to result from false testimony than from false inferences based on circumstantial evidence. After all, in contrast to circumstantial evidence, witnesses can lie, be afraid, or be mistaken. Black People know inferences and false testimony made by Whites will go against them. Enslaved African Americans scrambled Europeans' inference patterns using Allegories ("to speak other")--saying something other than the exact thing meant. Furthermore, they were clever enough to have *more than one level of meaning at the same time.* At other times the in-group had to "READ BETWEEN THE LINES"--meaning to figure out what a fellow Enslaved was implying by inferring what was left unsaid. In Aesop's "The Fox and The Grapes" fable, besides accounting for how the fox acted, the inferred allegory message behind the story is that people tend to scoff at what they cannot attain. Bullies do that. To Create anything is to take bits and pieces out of Spiritual, Metaphysical, Supernatural, Physical realms and/or out of *Suppositions* (something taken for granted)--whether real, distorted, fantasy--and fashion it into new arrangements, combinations, or forms. The process of Thought to do this can be to select and fit compatible relationships from one thought to another in order to arrive at an effect and then proceed with reasoning performed correctly into the Unknown. Metaphysical Inference Certainty is arrived at by discovering what else must be true if the premises are true--and they will be true if ones Thoughts are inside and derived out of the Spiritual Elements. Yet, instead of doing "*Right" thinking on the "Right" Track*, alternatives are to do "*Right" thinking on the "Wrong" Track* or "*Wrong" thinking on the "Wrong" Tract* or "Wrong Thinking on the Right Track" or "Fantasy" Thinking on the Fun Track. In any of those tracks Inferences pertaining to Principles, or to flawed information or beliefs or opinions create something, and/or devise Options for choices. In my view--from 45 years of extensive research on countless subjects and going back tens of thousands of years and dealing with every culture--only African Logic gives "Right" thinking on the "Right" Track. I personally enjoy "Fantasy" Thinking on the Fun Track. I deal with nothing else. The other alternatives are needed for devising workable defenses and offenses. jabaileymd.com

INFERENCE IN AFRICAN TRADITION: A fundamental concept of arriving at Knowledge is contained in the word "Inference." The word "*Infer*" (C16 English) implies using reasoning to 'bring forward' into a conclusion that has followed a *Consequence* (something produced by a Cause or follows from a necessary connection or from a set of conditions) or a *Sequence* (i.e. what is part of a continuous or connected series). Children are a Consequence of the mating of their parents. Sequence is *Linear*-- meaning one word or image is followed by another and then another; or numbers are always strung out in a line and occur like stepping stones. Children follow in Sequence as a natural way to extend a family. The Theme of the parent/ children Consequence and Sequence *Continuity* (Unity running through Multiplicity) is based upon their shared "Genetics" (i.e. uninterrupted existence of germ plasm). However, applications of Inference within an African Tradition Spiritual and a European Secular context make for many Secular "look-alikes" of it in relation to the Spiritual. As laid out above, Satisfied from having discovered a celestial order by means of math, African Sages used this model to *Deductively* (making inferences from general truths to particular truths) build an earthly order for the benefit of kings, philosophers, and government officials. It was also used to organize principles of harmony, situations for facts, and intuitive *Inductions* (inferring general principles from particular Cosmic order facts). It is from this type of thinking and research that Ancient African Sages concluded that

God is unknowable but that God can be known through God's manifestations. That those manifestations are math based is evidenced on all planes of existence by all creatures and creations (including each human). See Mathematics; Logos; Correspondence; Circumstance; Critical Thinking

INFERENCES IN CRITICAL THINKING: Inference is the going from sound conclusion derived from African Reasoning to the Ma'at aspect of African Logic or from what evolves out of African Logic into Unrealized Realities. What keeps many Black students from being able to untangle concepts of Philosophical Thought is confusion about the definition of a keystone word; or not realizing that same word is used differently in African Tradition and by Europeans. To clearly understand the ways and ideas of Inferences provides insight into all forms of Critical Thinking (CT). To elaborate, in daily living everybody makes 'guesstimates' about things based upon 'hunches' or a shot in the dark' or a 'sneaking' suspicion'. In other words, one assesses where one is presently and, through a process of reasoning from what seems most likely, one arrives at a 'guesstimate' conclusion. More often than not the 'guesstimates' are rash, foolish, false, unjustified, or shallow inferences. However, when scientists and philosophers use this same process, it is called a "*Deduction*" if there is a sense of responsibility attached to their conclusion; or "*Inference*" if the situation is of a lighter nature. When Ancient Africans made inferences or Deductions they first established a Circumstantial Truth and used it, or the process of deriving it, to propose another. For example, by African Priest-Astronomers establishing Circumstantial Truths about the Stars and Planets, they connected the bits and pieces about them into patterns. Then they realized those patterns they saw in the sky were also present on Earth.

From those observations, *Inferences* could be made to go beyond the evidence given or known to deduce a conclusion. This came from manipulating/maneuvering links between Cause/Effect as well as the Known/Unknown so that those links could help predict Consequences. *Deduction is the use of Inference Reasoning to go from the General to the Particular*--e.g. about how humans should live according to the Math determined Laws of Nature: 'My deduction is that since all men die and I am a man I will die.' *Induction Reasoning goes from the Particular to the General* (e.g. about the Laws of Nature to which humans are a part)--i.e. from the known to the unknown. Instead of simply being curious about the Particular things they saw in daily life, rather than letting it go--as is typical of Ordinary Thinkers--Ancient Africans connected the relationships of aspects of each into wholistic patterns. Then they realized those patterns seen on Earth were also present in the sky. Again, knowing those links helped them predict Effects/Consequences. In other words, "*Induction*" concerns arriving at a general principle on the basis of probabilities suggested by experiment with, and observation of, a number of individual cases. Perhaps as early as 20,000 BC Africans called *inferring by Deduction and Induction the Law of Correspondence*--so above, so below; so below, so above. Examples: when you look, you must see; when you nibble, you must taste. That Law enables CT to make "What it is," "what it does," and "how it appears" inferences concerning probabilities in its Unseen state. Then further investigation is done so that each of them can be proven by their manifestations in the Seen world to establish Circumstantial Truths. Such occurs because, despite all the variations in the Cosmic Organism, they show interdependence to produce Beings with only a few principles in operation.

INFERENCE--SPIRITUAL: By inferring the Spiritual Elements established Cosmic Organism Spiritual Linkages binding all humans, African Sages' next inferred those spiritual linkages necessarily form connections between moral principles present in the Spiritual Elements, the Cosmos, and humans' interests (Coetzee, African Philosophy p. 401, 441). Moral values arising from human fellowship fashion ideas of humanity (Ani, Yurugu p. 352) and from which Inferences are applied to Metaphysical/Physical worlds. For example, people who live in Truth do Goodness because it naturally flows out of them and without thinking about it, or advertising it, or desiring recognition for it. Establishing "*Circumstantial*" ("stand around" the Spiritual

Elements) *Evidence*--suggesting completeness of detail--opens doors into the Unknown. Judging each circumstance for its significance leaves room for inferences to be made on either side of the Truth. Critical Thinking (CT) Inference reasoning from Circumstantial Evidence also enables combining it with *Subjective Science*--Observation; mental Reflection; "Pure" Feelings (not emotions); Productive Imagination; Contemplation; Inductive and Deductive Inferences; and Common Sense--to go beyond the known to propose something specific (e.g. a reasoned opinion drawn from evidence). The Principle of Correspondence + the accepted combination of concrete and Tangible inferences allowed for principles to be extracted and variously properly applied to the Spiritual Metaphysical Realms where the profound concepts of Ancient Africans lie. In turn, Ancient Africans spent their lives making inferences from Spiritual awareness and Metaphysical Knowledge to form inferences about the Immaterial realm of God. This is how they came up with Cosmic Laws, like that of Ma'at (Spiritual Elements in action). Early on, *Predictions* became Inferences when one attempted to determine what is currently unknown from what was already known. Circumstantial Evidence helped provide sensible explanations and make reasonable predictions. *Rational Predictions* were based upon facts used to make estimations or educated guesses. Of course, most were colored by the perceptions, biases, and prejudices of the individual. But typically, Ancient African inferences were from a scientific, especially statistical, analysis of known events. For example, one might say that "*if and when*" certain factors are combined in certain ways, the results are predictable—*Conditional Predictions*--and quantified according to the degree of probability of each. Then/now correct predictions are generally considered to be the test of validity of a scientific conclusion or law. An example of a Spiritual CT Inference occurred after Very Ancient Africans learned the pitch of notes depends on the rapidity of vibration--and also the planets move through space at different rates of motion. From putting this together, they inferred: (1) the movement of the large celestial bodies (e.g. planets, spheres) must make sounds in their motion according to their different rates; (2) those sounds made by their simultaneous revolutions are concordant; (3) their speeds, judged by their distances, are in the ratios of the musical concordances; (4) and the sound effects, by means of the relation of one part to other parts, are a form of *Music*. Since all things in Nature are harmoniously made, the different sounds must harmonize. Yet, these sounds are not heard because they have been with humans from the birth of mankind. Though sound is perceptible only by contrast with silence, African Sages trained the left hemisphere of their brains to detect these sounds. This African discovery of "*Harmony*" constituted the first step toward a mathematical analysis of the heavenly bodies (stars); of the influence of the heavenly bodies upon the Earth; and of the experiences in the inner Selfhood workings of humans. Though this had been present for thousands of years, all of it was plagiarized by ancient Greeks, particularly Pythagoras (570-495? BC) during his 23 year stay in Africa, who gave it the title of "*The Harmony of the Spheres*." Elaboration was done by Plato, the Bible's Book of Job ("the morning stars sang together"); Chaucer; Milton; Shakespeare (in the Merchant of Venice, V, i) and later hymn-writers (e.g. "This is My Father's World"). Ancient Egyptian Priests, inferring music vibrated at a certain rate, used music to cure disease as well as for healing of the mind, body, and spirit of individuals. That too has been plagiarized. An "Inference" ('to bear in') connotes selective judgment or opinion based upon a reasoning drawn from evidence or premises. It may range from a mere Guess to Truth, depending upon the creditability of those making the inferences and the nature of their evidence. A "*Premise*" -- applicable to European Logic -- is a statement accepted as a basis for further reasoning but it may be true, distorted, or fantasy. By contrast, African Logic, also called African Dialectic, reasons only from Truth or Circumstantial Truths.

Their main purpose for arriving at inferences was to reveal "*Esoteric Knowledge*"—i.e. understanding the inner truth lying hidden within the core of fundamental beliefs about foundational Realities for application in all aspects of the Cosmos. *Extrapolations* were used in their astro-mathematics to make estimates beyond the observation intervals they had just discovered. This was done to determine the value of a variable on the basis of its relationship with another variable to thereby project, extend, or expand the known into the unknown so as to arrive at probable reasonable conclusions about the unknown. More accurately, *Interpolations* were used to produce estimates between known observations. At the birth of those conclusions there was a probable correctness of between 70 and 90 % toward which known facts, statements, or admissions point, but which they do not absolutely establish (Bailey, Medical-Legal Dictionary p81, 107). Invariably they went about verifying their Inferences, particularly by putting them into practice and observing the results. For Ancient African Sages, their thousands of years of accumulated data showing correspondence, pointed to logical conclusions of Absolute Truth. To keep up with ongoing observations required the development of mathematics which, in turn, enabled precision and accurate scientific observations. Applying resultant laws of mathematics opened doors to reality that provided insight into Esoteric Sky Knowledge. Over thousands of years a formalized Reasoning, Critical Thinking, and Logic process was devised by African Sages, including the gathering of Facts and the manipulation (e.g. into varying combinations) and maneuvering (e.g. into new arrangements) of Circumstantial Evidence Truths.

INFERENCE IN AFRICAN QUANTITATIVE MATHEMATICS: *African Inferences follow a mathematical pattern* that provides a sound springboard. Step I starts by *looking behind the Obvious and the Hidden within a given aspect of a significant issue to see the consistent, permanent, stationary, and unchanging patterns or elements underlying natural events. Step II:* Then, to see in another given aspect of that same issue the *Inner Similarities between the dissimilar appearances of those two issues,* that establishes an interrelationship. Step III: To "Understand" is to see the interrelationships of the components involved and how they are unified into a harmonious pattern so as to become aware of the way things are and what they are. Step IV: that relationship brings the Order necessary for doing the manipulations and maneuverings leading to visualizing an *abstract unity*—a unity composed of an interdependence between all its independent entities and the parents of each entity. Step V: A Harmonious Pattern of Correspondence between the two involved aspects means the shared course of their *Natural Processes can be inferred.*

The Harmonious Pattern of the Correspondence springboard serves as a Base of "light" from which to take off into a "shadowed" Unrealized Reality or into an Unknown existence—with both having Correspondence with the Known. If dealing with an Unrealized Reality, then it must have existence in order for the realistic known Base to go beyond the known to thereby propose something specific in its Unrealized Reality Unknown. Since an Unknown or an Unrealized Reality must have existence as well as Correspondence, in African Tradition, that combination of "Equivalents" is called *"Circumstantial Truth"*—i.e. an extension of a Known Truth. But inferences drawn from Circumstantial Truths must follow the path of African Tradition Logic—*a path along which Inferences can Circumstantially evolve into Esoteric Unknowns—a path that expands ones insight above any human's abilities to prove by direct evidence.* This illuminating expansion of Knowledge from Known into Unknown realms is done by a Deducing Method—the "Equivalent" of going from General to Particular--called *Deductive Reasoning.*

To arrive at Circumstantial Truths and to expand Knowledge by Deductions requires that the springboard Base to launch toward Evidence, Proof, and/or Truth be a product of, and remains within, the Spiritual Elements. Such is present when all internal unchanging linkages throughout the process are maintained by means of Continuity (unity among multiplicity) between parts (e.g. continuous function; persistence of a quality, feature, element, unit, or time), Coherence, Consistency, Compatibility, Balance, and Harmony—linkages which persist in each link while formed together. The mathematical process followed by Deductive Reasoning enables creditable Judgments in both African Spiritual and Secular realms. An example of Spiritual

Inferences pertained to Africans Sages fashioning Laws of Nature and of the Unknowable God still being known by Correspondence manifestations. An example of the Secular is inferring from studies of Amerindian relics that some tribes had highly developed arts according to today's standards. In short, Infer and Deduce are reasoning processes to come to a conclusion based upon evidence, Proof, or Truth of what is "like-kind."

INFERENCE IN AFRICAN QUALITATIVE MATHEMATICS: *"Esoteric Knowledge"—i.e. understanding the inner truth lying hidden within the core of fundamental concepts about foundational Realities*--requires *Inference Leaping* by illogical, not logical Quantitative Thinking. Here, the word "Illogical" refers to Spiritual (pre-birth) Emotions which, by originating in their Cosmic Organism "home" and are thereby outside the realm of the later appearing Intellect's systematic processes. This is called Qualitative Mathematics because Spiritual Emotions have no fixed pattern and, instead, operate by "Inference Leaps" to arrive at an underlying order. That order conforms to the *Ancient African definition of a Law which refers to the foundation of all Cosmic manifestations and denotes a sequence of inherently related events—despite their apparent variability--that occur with unvarying uniformity under the same conditions.* So, the appearance of the starting point of a problem or situation is that of a *Paradox*, a term with great complexity. It is something seemingly self-contradictory on the surface but upon further investigation the inner aspects of the contradiction actually have harmonized linkages. Underlying those linkages is something *natural* and therefore coming out of Spiritual Elements. This includes hidden ones without obvious order--i.e. no human can pin it down. A match happens because Organic Patterns, besides being beautiful markings which never make an asthetic mistake, are each perfectly ordered--as evidenced by the resultant Thing's coherent, enduring, balanced, harmonious, connectedness, and unchanging elements or pattern. Thus, to assess the "Hidden" means knowing it by an intuitive insight and then assessing it as if one were examining all the sides and angles of a match box in order to discover its intimate esoteric (ingredient essences about a given form of reality) aspects. There is no other way to know it or describe it. So, to arrive at such knowledge requires inference leaping—a Right Brain process of Reasoning by relating ideas to each other—and that equates to the Left Brain's other abilities.

Together, this is a relatively overt mental process by which one reaches conclusions on the basis of Evidence. The Right Brain governs understanding and spirituality + is the symbol of omniscience and omnipresence of God within ones Soul + its natural intuition has a creative part (from "Pure Feelings"; Spiritual Emotions) and non-creative part (e.g. the sixth sense; predominantly Ancient Brain instincts). The core of the Right Brain is the "Ma'at" faculty which enables one to see the inner Qualitative factors that unify things based on the mutual relationships and interdependence of Things with each other and the whole. In other words, "Unity"--in Relational Right Brain thinking--denotes the abstract tie between what underlies a plurality of different Things in a Wholistic sense. That perception is called Synthesis. This reflects the Trained Right Brain's ability to follow the process of: (1) picking up a clue of the barely visible; (2) noting similarities between things below an appearance level; (3) seeing their relation to each other; (4) synthesizing its aspects; (5) creatively design bridging gaps by harmoniously fitting the parts--regardless of how remote in time or space--by taking acrobatic leaps which successfully unify pertinent things into a whole; and (6) generating out of this perception of the whole those inferences which stay within the context of the Law of Correspondence and thereby complete the "big picture." An example of (1) is that the Right Brain sees the corner of a table, then from prior experiences it has a good idea that the highest percentages of tables have four legs.

Thus, one has an impression of what the other three corners look like so as to arrive at the conclusion of the hazy object being a table with four legs. This unifying of mutual relationships and perceiving their interdependence with each other and the whole expresses through abstract or metaphoric means is by the use of images. The Right Brain's focus on and its manipulating images, symbols, and sensations stimulates its synthesis functions to produce new arrangements and/or new combinations to arrive at new forms. Both abstract and/or abstraction processes follow the same pattern—that of arriving at a conclusion or judgment through the maneuvering and manipulation of Symbols embodying those abstract or abstraction analogies. This ability to intuit the abstract or abstraction relations between things and the whole to which they belong means there is a tie with the like-kind Essences of different things. For example, it enables one to see through physical and emotional differences between people in order to discover how they are alike. This ability to perceive Abstracts or Abstractions enables one to connect and unify events and things that may differ widely in form and external appearance—the process called *Synthesis* (Amen II: 104; Amen I:10, 18).

Whatever is synthesized may be stable, as in Spiritual and Metaphysical Realms, or unstable, as in Supernatural or Physical Realms. Instability may pertain to those *meanings* created by incongruence and from unpredictable synthesis or by what is happening, similar to the changing colors in a kaleidoscope or in starry diamonds, or in golden clouds in the sky. Either effect can be used for what is appropriate to the situation. Some of the processes involved in these examples include the Right Brain unconsciously discerning and reshuffling ones past experiences in order to pull out pertinent pieces of information, most having been hidden in ones memory (Hippocampus). Then it and the Left Brain make new arrangements or new combinations out of the original extracted materials. Included may be the apperceptions from memory. All may engage in high level Synthesis of pertinent bits and pieces present on different planes of existence. These are fit together in various ways by manipulation and maneuvering to come up with options or new forms. This suggests inspiration or creativity has its source in the Unconscious--the well-spring of repressed emotions craving expression.

A *principle of Creativity is that when several elemental components are organized or coordinated, the resulting synthesis has properties and characteristics fundamentally different in kind from those of the separate components viewed independently.* Perhaps this Qualitative Mathematics method of "Inferential Leaps," coupled with the intuited Principles conveyed by Spiritual (pre-birth) Emotions, is how Ancient African Sages arrived at Evidence, Proofs, and Circumstantial Truths. They applied these aspects pertaining to God-created Divine Forms for such things as Music, Mathematics, Beauty, Goodness, and Thought--each containing an Archetype Seed with its Archetype Essence pattern. Chances are this process arose by Very Ancient Africans inferring *Idea-Forms* to be patterns fixed in Nature which reproduce themselves in their own image so as to become the Thing it makes. Also, despite being located anywhere in the Cosmos, all of the Archetype's Prototype offspring are in accordance with the Law of Correspondence and the Laws of Nature. As part of the process of manipulating Idea-Forms to successfully perform the highest levels of the Magic of Sacred Geometry, it was necessary to uncover Patterns obscured by their context; find hidden relationships between seemingly unrelated pieces of Patterns; and recognize a known principle in disguise so as to generate a match. A way this could have been done is by the *Right Brain converting corresponding ingredients into consistent, permanent, stationary, and unchanging patterns or elements.* The "Inference Leaping" Process is a way to approach solving any seemingly "IMPOSSIBLE PROBLEM" (Bailey, Leadership Critical Thinking).

INFERIORITY COMPLEXES: self-attacks on their thinking abilities, self-worth and/or self-value. An inferiority complex is a loss of Selfhood Greatness, characterized as a Self-Worth lacking the "5Ss" and largely based upon ones interpretations of the monitored feedback one gets from outside influences. There are varying degrees of destruction of different foundational and prop elements of ones Self-Esteem. A primary way it shows is by destruction of either oneself and/or of what belongs to others or to Nature. Ancient non-Mediterranean Europeans were burdened with an Inferiority Complex. An inferiority complex is an Icon reality for European males following their original contacts with Black cultures and civilization who had made startling discoveries and contributions to the world, in contrast to them. This led them to plagiarize African achievements. For example, during his 22 years in Egypt Pythagoras (480-411 BC) learned mathematics; the Egyptian Mystery System; obtained information about all the sciences; the idea of the omnipotence of the Number that governs the universe; the meta-psychosis or transmigration of souls; and the irrational numbers. All of which the claimed originated from him made Herodotus say that Pythagoras was nothing but a vulgar plagiarist of his Egyptian masters (Diop, Civilization p346). To illustrate a model way Europeans converted their inferiority complex to a superiority complex occurred when Pythagoras, upon his return from studying in Africa said: "*Man is the measure of all things*"--whereas he had learned in Africa that "God is the measure of all things." Some Europeans interpret this to mean the individual human being, rather than a god or an unchanging moral law, is the ultimate source of value. This does not seem reasonable to me because no doubt he learned in African that every human being, by being a "drop of God," possesses the divinity feature of God. Despite the divinity being dormant, it can manifest with the proper spiritual discipline. I would assume that since magic in its widest sense was native to the imagination of the Greeks in their theogony (origin of gods) and mythology that Pythagoras conceptualized each White males as being a god. Thus, to be a man-god meant each White male could be extremely judgmental and determine what is right and wrong for him to do as well as what is right and wrong for others to do. By being a man-god implied that what he did was right and what anyone else did that was not in agreement was wrong. These are exactly the traits exhibited by today's European male. Obviously, since the mass of people live out of their "Dark Side," Pythagoras' teaching put the Western world on a destructive downhill course. This course carries people further and further away from their Higher Selves and, by being disconnected from God, sanctions evilness to all concerned. Such was introduced to Enslaved Africans during African American slavery from a wide variety of European Brute tactics designed to create an "Ideal Slave manhood" image. This effort was to mold the Enslaved toward being weak-minded and mentally incompetent. In response, the Enslaved reacted in every conceivable mindset as, for example, the following. One is the Non-Sexual *Masochistic Mind* (Bailey, Special Minds) whereby victims invite or fail to prevent needless hardships. Second is an *Encaged Mind,* reflecting a mis-arranged world view; a shattered ethos; the embracing of Europeans' system of values, and not realizing African Tradition is the best way to view reality. Third, the *Special Mind* operates out of a primal self-preservation level and a broken spirit. For those so afflicted, a "make do" with poverty is good enough. Fourth, the *Enslaved Mind* is brainwashed by the evil Whites' dictates of "stay-in-your-place" and that has become a way of life. Fifth, a *Non-Thinking Mind* is one programmed into causing ones rational thinking skills to become atrophied or to not develop rational thinking skills in the first place. This is somewhat like individual cells in the body programmed to self-destruct and their residual remains provide nutrients to assist in birthing and enhancing new development.

INFORMATION: Latin word for "*Informare*" (to give form to; shape, fashion, describe) and it became popular in scholastic terminology. "Informare" meant the *function of Form when it perfects the matter united to it so as to constitute a specific body*. In another sense, "Inform" was viewed as the accidental giving of a "Being" and of a Life, as color gives "Being" (accidental) to a wall. In still another sense and coming out of "Classical" times, Inform was about telling or instructing people about something. Within this context, during the European C14--and under the spelling of enforme and informe--"Inform" referred to giving a character to; to imbue; to inspire; to fill, underlie, pervade, guide; and to teach, mold, train, educate, or instruct. The current meaning of 'provide with facts or new, to report, and to tell' is first recorded in 1384 in Chaucer's translation of Boethius' De Consolatione Philosophiae. But the confusing and conflicting means under the umbrella of the word "*Fact*" means it has no denotative meaning—only varying connotative meanings. In C14, "*Tell*" was designated as a general word meaning to make known by speech or writing. Inform then took on the compounded confusing sense of "to impart knowledge by communicating certain facts," separating it from "*Advise*"--an opinion suggesting a course of conduct be followed. By C15 the word "*Information*" was prominent in a legal setting. For accusations leading to calling the accused into court, a Constable (peace of-ficer) would begin evidence in court by means of "acting on information." Of course, that scenario branched into all the fields it touched. For example, an *Informed Consent* is the giving of full notice to that which is being consented to—whether in medicine or in other professions. Since then, "Information" has broadened to mean varied ideas and thoughts from sources inside and outside ones head.

INFORMATION GRADING SCALE: "*Grade*" implies some regular ladder of valuation and some in-herent qualities for which something is placed higher or lower in the scale, depending upon a standard. The Standard for Information Grading is Knowledge of African Tradition. A "*Scale*" is a scheme or device by which some property may be measured or used for classifying the different types. The Grade at the top of the Information Scale is what is "*Just Short of Certainty*." One candidate is a time honored Axiom. A step down is PROBABLE (after testing it has the appearance of truth but remaining room for doubt makes it SEEM or "likely" be true). Probable Opinions are like a *Rule of Thumb*--a rough and useful principle or method, based on experience rather than precisely accurate measures. What is "Likely" appeals to the reason as being worthy of belief because there are more points to favor believing than not believing. By using established past practices as a guideline for making a decision, "Probable" guides one in matters where one lacks Certainty. Next down is POSSIBLE (capable of happening, as in saying it is possible that it will rain today). FEASIBLE--capable of being done—is below Possible.

INHERITANCE: "*Heritable*"—a term wrongly considered essentially synonymous with 'Genetic' and 'Inherited'--because it includes both. '*Inherited*' implies genes are transferred from parent to child while Mutations, along with the inherited genes, may result in new genes in a *zygote* (the union, yoking, fusion of the male spermatozoon and the female ovum to give a fertilized egg).

INITATES: in Ancient Africa "*Pupil*" referred to those under a teacher's close supervision when partici-pating in higher religious education; "*Student,*" to those specializing in a branch of study in preparation for a profession; and *Scholar,* to "*giving oneself*" to learning intimate Spiritual Elements details concerning God's Laws. *Mortals* (Initiates, Neophytes), probationary pupils who had not yet realized the Inner Vision, were instructed in the Sages' doctrines. The *Intelligences*--advanced students from having attained Inner Vision by getting a glimpse of Cosmic Consciousness—had thus achieved the *Mysticism Mind*--minds having the ability to intensely concentrate their Intellect Reasoning into their Pure Emotions.

INNOVATION: adding something new to what already exists

"INSIDE-OUT": Victims who vote against themselves and their own

INSIGHTS: give understanding of the way things are

INSTRUCTION: "*Education*" ("to lead out what is inside"); "*Teaching*" ("to show" so as to impart knowl-edge for learning); *Instructing* ("to build in or into"), or "*Training*" (active mind exercising in order to form habits)—in short, by study, reflection, and/or practice--depending upon the topic.

INTELLIGENCE: Humans are composed of Spirit (in the sense of the Immaterial, meaning the Spiritual) and Matter—both being needed for proper dealings in the Earth World—both being needed to rise from ones Lower (animalistic) Self to ones Highest (Divinity) Self. Spiritual Intellect is Intuited while Metaphysical Intellect is developed. Ones Metaphysical Intellect—part of ones Astral Double—enables dealings with Earth World Living of an objective nature. Metaphysical Intellect is entertwined with ones *Secular Sensory Consciousness* serving as a Background on one side of a Matter Awareness Coin and a *Secular Sensory Awareness* on the other side, being about happenings in the Foreground of life living. Both sides of this Astral "Double" Coin will serve as a human newborn's Earth World Selfhood Sources (i.e. Background) in order to supply the think, feel, say, and do aspects related to the Foreground for interfacing with activities of daily living.

INTELLIGENCES: in Ancient Africa, "*Pupil*" referred to those under a teacher's close supervision when participating in higher religious education; "*Student*," to those specializing in a branch of study in preparation for a profession; and *Scholar*, to "*giving oneself*" to learning intimate Spiritual Elements details concerning God's Laws. *Mortals* (Initiates, Neophytes), probationary pupils who had not yet realized the Inner Vision, were instructed in the Sages' doctrines. The *Intelligences*--advanced students from having attained Inner Vision by getting a glimpse of Cosmic Consciousness—had thus achieved the *Mysticism Mind*--minds having the ability to intensely concentrate their Intellect Reasoning into their Pure Emotions.

INTELLECT HUMANS' SPIRITUAL: A *human's Spiritual Intellect* voluntarily has its mind *subjected to the Divine Spirit in order for it to command the Life-Force that is in harmony with the Laws of Nature*. This automatically means Spiritual Intellect operates inside the "ME/WE" whose Interchange contains the Cosmic Mind. Thus, Spiritual Intellect is in a state of "Oneness" with any situation or circumstance that is about the Spiritual Elements since that is the *only way that a Spiritual Elements Thing can be known*. It is this being in the flow of and the imparting of reality that establishes the true essence of Intellect. To apply it to and place it in each of God's creatures, said Ancient Africans, is to have a "Oneness" with God. Spiritual Intellect is *Intuited*—meaning having an immediate understanding of the Spiritual Elements' Truth without calling upon reason or feelings. One can intuit from the Ma'at faculty and then experience the urge to live by the Spiritual Elements—the Human Ideal in Life Living--according to the laws of ones indwelling Divine Consciousness. By seeking the Will of God through ones 'Self' (Divine Consciousness—a human's "First Wisdom") is simply to experience ones own true nature in relation to the "ME/WE". From resultant Insights, *Intuitive Inductions* (inferring general principles from particular facts present in the Cosmic Order) are done. This means making compatible imaginative leaps to discover unrealized realities--i.e. the *taking of Leaps from ingredients of Reality into realms dealing with corresponding Unrealized, Unseen, or Unseeable Realities*. The revealed Ma'at Principles are absorbed into ones mind to guide thinking and thereby be led "instinctively" to the apprehension of Truth for its application on any "Branch" of the "Truth Tree".

INTELLECT HUMANS' REAL SELF EARTHLY: A Real Self human's Matter or Metaphysical Being--representing ones Metaphysical "Shadow" Soul—is: (1) orchestrated naturally by the "Self" portion of ones Soul; (2) is controlled by ones 'head' contents when it is fashioned as a Ma'at philosophy of life; and (3) ones Free Will choices to decide and do whatever ones sees as best. False Self people choose what is outside the Spiritual Elements. As maturity proceeds, ones Intelligence grows from within outward and all parts grow simultaneously. For Real Self humans, their Spiritual Intelligence must be Intuited. The proper applications of these ingredients, when fashioned products come out of the Spiritual Elements, means one is always led to "*Be Right*," "*Recognize Right*," "*Do Right*," "*Make Things Right*," and "*Defend the Right*". Maintaining Soul Integrity always is the Right thing, regardless of the outcome. *Operating out of ones Divine Consciousness is what Knowledge and Wisdom are about*. The Real Self of ones Intellect and Sensory Consciousness enables the recognition of the uprightness and sacredness of Integrity. Because Spirit and Matter go together as indivisible Complementary Equals, there can be no breach between body and mind—between thought and action—between ones convictions and living. This displays as one who can be thoroughly depended upon; and will stand firm when others fail; is the best kind of friend—faithful and true; and is the adviser--honest and fearless. Integrity is the first step to true Selfhood Greatness. To live by ones convictions means that is done independent of and uninfluenced by the wishes, pleas, threats of one or all. This requires the Confidence of being Certain that one is right—the Courage to be true to ones existence and to the Spiritual Elements.

INTELLECTS--HUMANS' SPIRITUAL + ASTRAL/METAPHYSICAL: One of Humans' many Dualities is being made of a Divine Immaterial Spirit and Matter. Both are needed for proper Earth World think, feel, say, and do dealings + to rise from ones Lower (animalistic) Self to ones Highest (Divinity) Self. Ones "Self-Identity"—i.e. Divine Consciousness (Spark of God)—the Spiritual "who one is"—Intuits (inner Cosmic learning) *Spirit Intellect* from its Soul. From it emanates a Spiritual Elements' "What and Why" generated Immaterial Icon Image Essence message which, when joined with Energy and Ether, becomes activated. The activating Essentials are an identical Character copy of the Essence (the "what it is") as well as Characteristics, Traits, and Features—also content copies of the Essence (being dormant since it lacks Energy and Ether). When involved processes are put into action, that Spiritual/Mind Intellect plan is completed. The *Astral Intellect* differs from the *Soul's Background Spirit Intellect* by not existing independently + having to be developed + consisting of natural ethereal vital Energy and Ether (Metaphysical Matter) called the *Ka*. It is like an *invisible difference*s coin--representing a *Secular Sensory Consciousness* on one side and a *Secular Sensory Awareness* on the other. Its inseparably harmonized differences serve as a human newborn's *Selfhood Foreground* for interfacing with activities of daily living. This Real Self *Astral Attribute* of "Who one is" in Cosmic Life Finite Realms has a "*Heart*" composed of Spirit and Matter. Ancient Africans said the Astral System symbolizes the "deepest recesses of humans' psyche" + constitutes ones Selfhood Center. The Astral "Heart" is where issues of ones life are determined--the center of thought, feelings, memory, and emotions--the place of ones morals (Conscience), Spiritual nature, and Secular fetters (e.g. Brute Brain's envy, hate). This range makes a portion of the "Heart" accessible to heredity and also accessible to experience--both "carving" identifying good and/or bad marks in it.

By constituting a mixture of the Spiritual and the Secular inside each human's Circle of Selfhood Wholism implies the "Heart" could be influenced by such factors as what is: (1) orchestrated naturally by the Real Self of ones Soul's Spark of God Star or "Soul Sunshine"; (2) controlled by ones 'head' contents (e.g. from ones philosophy of life); (3) the Free Will choice of being operated by ones Ego or False Self of a Secular nature; (4) operated by ones Supernatural Ego/False Self; or (5) by the Ether in the stars and planets and its astrological signs (hence the importance of finding ones "Lucky Star"). For any of these 5 reasons, what one chooses to allow for ones Astral Soul "carvings" are capable of being molders of ones "*Character*" (the manifested nature of its Source). Within this Astral System's Sensory Consciousness all the various orders of Primary Qualities appear to the Personality part of ones Selfhood as fleeting states of Consciousness. To elaborate, there are 4 main order *Types of Consciousness Qualities*—Spiritual, Secular, the higher Natural Lower (animalistic) Self Qualities, and the Lower Acquired Brute Qualities. The Ka enables a volitional Free Will decision choice of one. Any *non-Spirit Intellect selection results in a False Self*. Regardless of the one chosen, that Quality category carries an impactful 'payload' activating something good or bad in the "Heart" and/or "Head" of one possessing it as well as in the "Heart" and/or "Head" of the people or creatures touched by it.

Supernatural people choose a False Self to manifest Brute Self Qualities. By automatically eliminating Spirit Intellect, it is impossible for them to arrive at any Knowledge or Wisdom, as defined in African Tradition (see Bailey, *African Tradition Wisdom vs. European Information* for detailed elaboration). Europeans define *Knowledge* as: "a result or product of knowing: information or understanding acquired through experience; practical ability or skill"; *Wisdom*, as: "the power of true and right discernment; also, conformity to the course of action dictated by such discernment". Note that both definitions are in keeping with the Greek Pythagoras (582-500 BC) teaching European males that they were the "Measure of all things"—and not the Spiritual God as he had been taught by Africans Sages. His evil point: *there could be no higher truth than what each White male determined it to be.* Also, by one choosing Astral Intellect means eliminating usage of ones Spirit Intellect. Thus, Supernaturals say all Cosmic Things become objects of Physical Realms—e.g. Supernatural Substance/ Essence consists of the Qualities possessed in things like rocks, wood, and water—not from the Spiritual Elements. jabaileymd.com

INTERCHANGE: The production of offspring out of the combined Genetics, as a fetus is produced from the meeting of the female's egg and the male's sperm inside their Interchange.

INTERCHANGES & MOSAICS: Ancestors of today's Olympic games were originated in Very Ancient Africa in association with the Spirituality aspect of their "ME/WE" constituting the indivisible "Sameness/Uniqueness interchange. This meant there was: "Me, You, Us, God—all connected by the Substance of God called the Spiritual Elements. This was the ancestor of Interlocking Olympic Rings symbolizing today's Olympic games which combine six colors [including the flag's white background] to reproduce the colors of all the nations. Nevertheless, a Southern Nigerian festival example is that of wrestling bouts being deemed "*Sympathetic Magic*" (practices based on all God's creations being related) for purposes of encouraging crops' growth. The god in charge of crops (among others) was Amun (Amon-Ra, Atom-Re, Amen) and these wrestling bouts were done in honor of the Spiritual God, Amen. Sports of Ancient Egypt in 5200 BC included foot races, long distance running, martial arts, playing ball, throwing sticks, and bowling. Added on were horse racing contests (?2000 BC) which were first held in Egypt. Meanwhile, the Cretans, called Keftiu by Ancient Egyptians, came from East Africa and occupied an island off the coast of Greece c3000 BC. The Cretans were present when a band of independent illiterate warring and intellectually dumb tribes (Bailey, Managing Emotions p1)—called Aryans (speaking a common language and using common customs) and later to be called the Greeks--appeared in the Mediterranean region, possibly c1800 BC (Amen, Not Out of Greece p25). These Aryans, allowing themselves to be subjected to the Cretans, were the source of the Greek's first knowledge of boxing, gymnastics, music, astronomy, weights and measures, olive cultivation, and the Olympics. Starting in ?884 BC, the Greeks then held athletic festivals every 4 years at Olympia in connection with rites honoring Zeus—the renamed god borrowed from Africans' Amen. A clue as to the mental sharpness of people pertains to the *Interchange*. Those Supernaturally oriented are automatically Superficial Thinkers and thus are "Blind to the Obvious"—i.e. never noticing the Interchange in the Interlocking Rings. Spiritually oriented Critical Thinkers notice and consider the significance of the Interchange in relation to a given problem. If also Deep Thinkers, they realize the profoundness of what can be symbolized inside the Interchange. So, what is an Interchange? If you pinch your index finger and thumb together on the right hand + pinch your index finger and thumb together on your left hand + have them pinching one inside the other, there will be a figure of "8" formed but with 3 circles. The middle circle or link connecting the two circles of the "8" is an Interchange. Since these four digits are interlocked into each other--note that their palm surfaces face each other. The space fashioned by their mutual facings is the same Interchange. Now, if one puts "sticker" polka-dots on each of ones four digits making up the Interchange, some dots will fall off into the Interchange. Each dot represents a Mosaic piece and all the pieces present in the Interchange's "Common Ground" space act like concrete Mosaics of small pieces of stone, glass, or wood of different colors that can be assembled and inlaid on a surface to form a picture or design.

A profound concept for Black Scholars is that the Spiritual Elements of Unconditional Love, Truth, Reality, and the Natural, emanating from the Cosmic Mind, form an Interchange. Each of these four have Spiritual and Matter components. This is done by their weaving or braiding in such a way as to keep them from untwisting by having different twists counterbalance each other. In Secular things, this may or may not occur. Weaving consists of 2 threads of yarn--one running lengthwise (the warp); the other running crosswise (the weft or woof). The weft is carried back/forth across the warp—going over some warp yarns and under others. In *Braiding*, 3 + yarns are twisted together like plaits of hair. Multiple Interchanges are in braids and weaves. The resultant Interchange formed by the Spiritual Elements means Mosaic bits and pieces of each one of the 4 aspects are given off inside the Interchange. By various assembling, they can be fashioned into a Pattern having an Icon Image constituting its outer aspects and nourished by a Matrix (i.e. the "womb" inside) so as to satisfy the issue at hand. That Icon Image contains the "What and Why" and as long as the nutrition consists of the Spiritual Elements, it will display in the Right manner in what one thinks, feels, says, and does. Any nutritional variants dilute and pollute these. Flowing out of the Spiritual Elements Interchange are: *Gestalt State*—a totality, as a unified whole, with properties not derivable by summation from the parts and their relationships; "*Emergentism*"—the combination of elements--results in something new that was unpredictable from knowledge of those elements; and Conative *Ideo-motor Action*.

INTUIT: to Intuit (i.e. learn from within) the Will of God in order to form "ME/WE" Order, Unity, and Harmony as expressions of "Life Living."

INTUITION: "Know Thyself" insight enables one to be aware of why things in the world are the way they are—aware of not being separate from what one does—aware that one can see the divine in everybody's eyes—aware that everybody plays an essential Cosmos part, even if ones does not like it--and aware one is part of the Cosmos 'doings' of the 'great happenings' of God--called the flow of Tao by the Chinese. Such enables *Mysticism*, the transcending of barriers so as to absorb an inexpressible—a vibratory essence--called *Intuition* (learning from within direct, immediate, and true "ME/WE" knowledge of the Cosmic Organism and its Laws of Humanity). These convey effortless flow of Ma'at Right ways to Think, Feel, Express, and Act/React.

INTUITIVE INDUCTION: inferring general principles from specific facts in the Cosmic Order

INTUITED: Meditating to gain insights above and beyond the realm of the mind's thoughts

INVENTIONS OF HISTORICAL BLACK SCHOLARS: Many people visiting my book display were interested in Ancient Africans' incredible inventions, Discoveries, and Creations superiority. *Gist:* Primitive Africans made the first "plastic" construction materials by mixing clay, sand, and water and molding it into articles (e.g. pottery) before drying them in the sun or baked until hard. Some were used for bartering. They improved on things designed by animals + invented and discovered things which ensured their survival—rafts, crude clothing, tools, weapons and traps, the wheel, pottery, the marked stick for measuring, and ways of making fire and smelting copper and iron. Enemas were devised by the Pygmies of the Ituri Forest; a loom for spinning cloth; coffee, from Ethiopia; and "Animal Tales"--Fables—for night entertainment. Resultant Principles underlying these inventions and discoveries remain fundamental to human existence. No one of the early inventions was the greatest, as each was important at the time—and *each invention stood on the shoulders of those preceding it and, in turn, provided shoulders for inventions to follow*. For example, without fire African's early metal industry could not have been born. When Africans started to live in villages and in larger settlements, more massive and more permanent structures were built—and some with brick. Those involved many new inventions. The earliest builders used rocks and dead trees. Tools were invented for cutting down trees used for bridges + for shaping and cutting stone. At first, these tools were themselves wood or stone but were later replaced by the discovery/invention of metal. Meanwhile, interior Africans invented writing and personal adornments, at least as early as 77,000 BC. Sometime later, Very Ancient Africans captured, tamed, and communicated with animals in the animals' language! Out of such communications, descendants of Primitive Africans--the Sans (Bushman as called by Europeans) of Kalahari--to this day engage in the "Click", "Whistle," and similar imitative language practices of animals. Agriculture and the plow's invention (?20,000 BC) required the invention of hoes and digging-sticks to plant, and sickles to reap. Circumcision, trephining (relieving brain pressure, Caesarean sections, the Scientific Method (1500 BC), Surgery (including inside the human brain and eyes) + being specialists in herbs for medicine were done by physicians. Ancient Nubians and Egyptians (c2600 BC) were heavily involved in tomb building and that led them to invent inclined planes to raise the great stone blocks of the pyramids into position—some blocks weighing 50 tons. Some blocks were even manufactured on the job site. To cut such large pieces of stone, shape them, and move them into position required many inventions. Daily time-keeping or the shadow-clock was invented around 1500 BC. Then was the clepsydra, or water clock (c1400 BC) to measure time by the flow of water from a small hole in a large container. Usually, an invention came as a result of key ideas after a long period of trial and error or sometimes from an accident. For example, although it had a long incubation period, an Egyptian knife (between 900 and 800 BC) is the world's oldest voluntary making of a "steeled" piece of iron (Diop, Civilization, p285). Since, from very early times, Africans engaged in traveling by sea, there were constant inventions on sea worthy vessels. To this end, the Ancient Egyptians had lamps for lighting, animal-powered gristmills and devices to lift water for irrigation. Their accurate calendar (4236 BC), recognized three seasons, each lasting four lunar months and based on the annual Nile flood, the sowing, and the harvesting. By 1800 BC, Black Egyptians had invented spoked wheels and a box, or wagon body for their vehicles. They used some of these in chariot races. When Romans came into existence, they were so awed with African brilliance as to say: "Ex Africa semper aliquid"--freely translated: "There is always something new coming out of Africa." In construction and architecture, Egyptian buildings made use of only two basic forms: the vertical post, or column, and the horizontal beam or lintel—which the Greeks later claimed + the Arch, which Romans also claimed as their own originals. Other inventions included all forms of Mathematics, bowling, chess, the alphabet, paper, wigs, door locks, toothpaste, glass, mascara, Physics, martial arts, Thanksgiving, books, schools, the Olympics, Spirituality, biochemical things like Melanin and Carbon, and infinite others. An equally infinite list applies to Creations and Discoveries. Hence, Ancient Africa was the world's mecca. jabaileymd.com

INVOLUTION: coming back to the center; "to wrap up; to cover; to hide the boundlessness of some aspect of the Spiritual Elements (e.g. Genius) in its descent process from Spiritual to Material realms. The process is to *involute*--the process of getting involved by "Knowing Thyself" and thus the foundational Cosmic Laws by returning to a human's pre-birth "First Wisdom" state. Then comes Evolution of Spiritual Meanings which naturally manifest by the unfolding of its Involuted contents and their associated powers.

ISOLATED INDIVIDUALIST: those who "live life my own way"

J

JAUDICED EYE: False Self biased/prejudicial viewings. Ancient Africans analogized a negative emotional nature to a "*Jaundiced eye*"—a term derived from ancient medicine's "yellow disease" (caused by liver or gallstone problems). It was thought jaundice sufferers saw everything in yellow tones--implying the False Self looks at something with a prejudiced view, usually in a rather negative or critical manner. Many seeds of this greenish-yellow color stream out from a diseased body to meet the Images of things. Besides, many are mingled in their own eyes which by their contact pain everything with lurid hues. The way they managed this was by replacing the jaundiced eye with a clear "Eye," and discarding one emotionally tinted glasses so as to see things for what they are.

JEGNA: *Jegna* (*Jegnoch*, plural form) is an Ethiopian term that best describes infinitely more than is covered by the Greek word "Mentor." What qualifies one to be a Jegna Leader for guiding struggling Black People is one with a track-record of demonstrating *the courage to protect African people, their culture, and their way of life.* These 'special people' have been tested in struggle or battle; have demonstrated extraordinary and unusual fearlessness; have shown and continue to show determination and courage to deal with the difficult; who continue to show diligence and dedication to their people; who produce exceptional, high-quality work. Jegna Leaders' spotlighted focus is on dedicating themselves to the protection, defense, nurturance, and development of African young while advancing Black People as a whole and their Community, and their stolen or lost culture (including intellectual property).

JOCKEY, LAWN: These Black faced "Footman" placed on lawns originated as tool for the Underground Railroad. A striped jockey shirt meant this was a place to swap horses. A Footman in a tailed coat meant overnight louging and food. A blue sailor's waistcoat meant the home owner could take you to a port and get you on a ship to Canada.

JOKES: mentally participating in a miniature circus

JUDGMENT: mental act of relating two concepts, accompanied by the belief or assertion of some objective or intrinsic relation between the two. For example, one can judge another by his/her foes as well as by his/her friends. See Circumspection

JUDGMENT DAY: (Psychostasis). If the "Heart" of the deceased weighed more than the *feather of Ma'at*, the two pans would be imperfectly balanced, indicating the deceased had been "too bad"; if reversed, the deceased had lived a rigid religious life by rules, implying one was "Too good". Balance was needed to proceed to the Heaven Afterlife.

JUDGMENT: inference reasoning from the known to the unknown; forming Judgments and Conclusions after a process of reasoning from premises or evidence

A *Judgment*--either of a perception or intuiting (being open to ones Divine Consciousness)--is a process of intellectual orientation from which humans learn from past success and failure experiences of ones own and of others to do Selections of the Superior: the putting of ideas together or separating them from one another when their certain agreement or disagreement is not perceived. Logic is "*Valid*" when it justifies the evidence given in support of it. It is "True" in a Physical Knowledge World sense if it expresses the facts as they are. Professional judgments (e.g. of medical, legal facts) are arrived at after weighing issues. Errors come from balancing probabilities

JUDGEMENT--QUALITATIVE: The mental act of relating two concepts, accompanied by the belief or assertion of some objective or intrinsic relation between the two.

JUSTICE: just (a balanced "ME/WE" scale)

K

"KEEPING THE BALANCE": Ancient Africans the focus was on finding the unity underlying opposites--to discover what the opposites have in common.

"KNOW THYSELF": "*Man, Know Thyself*" was written on Ancient African temple walls 14,000 years ago. It implies *discovering what is natural within oneself + what underlies what is natural* by awakening to there being no isolated center of action and instead one is part of the whole, doing what the Cosmos is doing. This exhortation, the fundamental principle imbued in the Spiritual Systems, was first developed in the far interiors of Africa--at the beginning of the Nile--at the base of the Mountain of the Moon (from pages 4 & 5 of the Declaration of Existence for the Spiritual Society of Amen-Ra...). Lest we forget, our African Ancestors, who defined "The Way," left instructions: "Know Thyself as Soul" carved in stone on the walls of temples and tombs. Remnants of these sacred teachings are the basis for the major religions of the Western World. In practicing this "ancient way", people experience balance, love and harmony within and this manifests in their outer world through the restoration and harmonizing of their male/female relationships, their families, and their communities. To bring forth this ancient way and teaching is to participate in the resurrection, restoration, and renaissance of African people worldwide. Such is a necessary step in the healing of The Human Family as a whole. So, it is that African Tradition is the beacon of light that restores to the world the Law of Oneness. In order to achieve *Mysticism* (Feeling interrelated with all creatures and thus having access to God), "Know Thyself" was taught in Egyptian Mystery Schools as ones vital pre-birth Cosmic Organism origin. Again, this required discovering *under-lying's and surroundings of what all is natural about* oneself so as to *discover what is natural within* oneself. Amazingly, Ancient African Sages said the Cosmos and a human female's single fertilized egg cell formation and reproduction had identical patterns. Before a cell actually reproduces itself into a *separate* state--called *Mitosis*--half of its ingredients move to opposite poles within the same cell—called *Meiosis*. Inside the Meiosis state, all God's creatures and creations are *Virtually joined*—each possessing God's Substance. Africans' Organic word "*Virtual*" originally meant an Essence ("what it is") when it came into existence—an immature, undefined, undifferentiated, unformed, patterned Being. It contains an *Ordered Disposition* (its "*what and why*" message) and the *Essentials* of a Character, Characteristics, Traits, and Features so as to fully display the Essence. Imagine each amorphous (i.e. without form) creature and creation being like a different colored pipe—each connected to the others so water (God's Substance) would run through them, all at the same time. Now suppose every pipe has a special position on a Web, thereby making it a Web of Associations of independent items working interdependently in accordance with God's plan. In short, each Web strand's interrelationships is like a link connecting each member's "*Uniqueness*" into God's plan. The Web of "*Sameness*" represents God's inner Spiritual Elements nature—the "Genetics" present in each of the Cosmic Organism Family. So, the "WE" pipes connected to the "ME" pipe fashion the "ME/WE"—and "forever." Since the water running through the pipes equates to Compassion, one feels Harmony when "ME/WE" is in Order or Disharmony when any of the Web is disturbed. Similarly, whatever out of the flow of the Cosmic Organism Rhythm the "ME" does or fails to do affects all Web strings. This crude idea of "Virtuals" in a Meiosis state transforms in human newborns into a "Non-Self" while remaining in the Earthly "ME/WE" Web. A "*Non-Self*" has the obligation/duty/responsibility to *discover and conform to the underlying web of relationships operating in Nature* throughout the Cosmos. As a result, its "ME" aspects are then able to transcend into the Sublime's reality flow—a natural flowing part of Cosmic Knowledge—a flow in which one recognizes ones own Being as a vital to the All (i.e. "Oneness" within the Cosmic Mind). Here, in the "ME/ WE" Sublime realm, Knowledge is known without proof.

Benefits from that Knowledge have nothing to do with Materialism characterizing ones Lower Self or with the European Supernatural. *Being in this infinity of Knowledge* allows one to discover new insights about any Spiritual Elements' attribute; see ones old blind-nesses to the obvious; and acquire new perspectives upon hearing old Wisdom over and over. Higher striving paths result from now being able to *see the Common in the Uncommon or see the Uncommon in the Common*. Every advancement expands ones Consciousness from the inside out and toward the Eternal. Thereafter, layers of coverings are removed from Esoteric Knowledge (i.e. "ME/WE" secrets) on the way to apprehending richer meanings in each new insight concerning ones Selfhood within the sum of the Cosmic Whole.

Each new meaning gives more in-depth understanding of Spiritual Elements Principles (pieces of Truth and its Unchanging Reality) which, in turn, peels away another top covering layer. This entire process is one of *Synthesis whereby the "ME/WE" whole is greater than the sum of its parts*. Such is illustrated each time I re-peat the study of a difficult topic by drawing on new sources for new ideas. Then, repeated reflections on the acquired ingredients + manipulating and maneuvering them into different arrangements and combinations gives wider scopes of understanding of the topic and asides associated with the topic. Most of these improve my insights into like-kind things—into Options—and into Creative handlings of problems never seen nor heard of before. The results "Feel" right in ones Selfhood Center--a "Feeling" known to be from ones Pure Emotions because it spurs "Aliveness"—a Spiritual Energy continually urging one to Self-Improve for "ME/ WE" purposes *and to develop "ME/WE" Harmonious products out of it*. "Knowing Thyself" is a primordial Experience of a human's ultimate attainment called "*Self-so-ness*." This means ones Personal Power encounters and interfuses with the 'WE' of the Cosmic Organism at a Primordial Substance (Ocean of Nun) plane of existence--an experience of Human Perfection called *Compassion*. This means that by inward intuiting of ones 'Self' (Divine Consciousness) so as to experience ones own true nature of "*Self-so-ness,*" one has harmonized ones body, mind, and spirit with ones Personal Power and thus become intimate with the Cosmic Organism. *What is under ones control in life is what fashions ones life and one must never make ones well-being dependent on what is beyond ones control. Everything in life is earned and there is no such thing as good or bad luck that happens by chance. What you sow, you reap.* Ancient Africans considered themselves as Divine Beings who were a "work in progress" (on their way to their Highest Self but with components of their Selfhood in various stages of development). Their "*Know Thyself*" starting point: *when one discovers what is natural within oneself and what underlies what is natural* about oneself, these same realizations can be discovered in the Cosmos—the Law of Correspondence. Such is from Correspondence being based on Ancient African Cosmic Laws about the foundation of all Cosmic manifestations. They denote a sequence of inherently related events occurring with unvarying uniformity under the same conditions.

Hence, *Correspondence* enables deriving "ME/WE" Ma'at philosophical principles that are *based upon vi-brating Cosmic Laws*. One can awaken to there being no isolated center of Cosmic action and instead realizing: (A) one is part of the whole--doing what the Cosmos is doing—i.e. being Spiritually connected to and interact-ing with all God's creatures and creations; (B) one is an essential being and an indispensable part of the Cosmos; (C) the essence of ones Selfhood, as with all God's creatures and creations, is the Spiritual Elements and thereby arriving at the conclusion: "I am the likeness of God"; (D) Cosmic Truth serves as the standard, guide, and filter for daily living as well as clears the "Cloud" covering ones awareness of ones Sacred Dream and Talent; and all of this conforms to *Mathematics*. Knowledge through the Soul is a realization of the identity of both the

Known Things and the Knower (or Knowing Mind) and the proper application of synthesized facts and figures to "ME/WE" benefits is Wisdom. Knowing is by the experience of a reality and by intuiting (i.e. learning from within) Intuiting what is Known includes the abstract general class (whole) to which the specific issues of life belong by it being intuitively perceived. What is extracted from that is Principles—like Unconditional Love is interwoven with having good relationships with and good behavior towards non-Brute people.

"KNOW THYSELF'S" TOOLS: Pause for a moment to realize what is within you that incompletely, wrongly, almost never is use or have "substituted out"—starting with only your Pure Emotions and Intellect. Is there a conflict of "whether I should go with my gut" or not?" There have been times you "went with your gut" or with your "Feelings" and have sometimes been right and sometimes wrong. "Sometimes" right is not good enough for Serious Business. The problem here is having a "*Salad Mix*" of what is in-born (always "right) and what is acquired (sometimes "right" and sometimes "wrong"). A "Salad (to salt) Mix" consists of like-kind but unrelated raw green leafy vegetables, often with other raw vegetables and/or chopped fruit, meat, fish, eggs, and the like. Each of these ingredients has a different external appearance, internal ingredients that have similarity in some aspects but not in others. Assess this by determining what all is involved in the "Salad Mix" and use the *Seven Questions of Inquiry* (who, which, what, when, where, why, and how) so as to discover the happenings of things present or past in order to reflect on them. The first major problem of most people is having "substituted out" their Pure Emotions for Acquired Emotions and that puts them on the "wrong track" and going in the "wrong direction." Pure Emotions are developed by fashioning all one does out of the Spiritual Elements of Unconditional Love, Truth, Reality, and the Natural for "ME/WE" usage + maintaining a mind-set of Calm at all times + not allowing oneself to get "Desperate" by Foresight, Forethought, and keeping ones "Needy Wants" (e.g. having Crowd-like "Things") to a minimum. The second major problem is failing to cultivate into a sharp skill ones inborn Intellect. Instead, it is usual to run from problems or take short-cuts or only get available information on a "need-to-know" basis or let others decide for you. Developing skillful thinking is like weight-lifting to get strong muscles —each time it is done, increase the amount of weight a tiny bit and be consistent. The setting for Sharp Minds is to take charge and control of ones Selfhood, of what one thinks, feels, says, and does—and of every situation one is in--meaning deciding not to be involved in what is not in your best interest. Sharp Minds are built up by thinking about every little thing you do to see where there are flaws or inefficiencies or how can it be better or even superb. Sharp Mind's intent is to know how to protect and defend against destructive forces while continuing to go "straight ahead" to a life of thriving and well-being. How these "ME/WE" benefits work is to become aware of who you were before being born into the Earth World. Our Ancient African Ancestors have laid this out very clearly by living "Proof" and with Mathematics in the Ancient African Spiritual Literature (also called the Ancient African Bible). Although the conspiracy to hide or erase this has been effective, it is available to hard working and persistent Scholars. And it is worth the time, energy and effort because ones entire life depends upon how one thinks and the ingredients used for thinking. The "gist" is that the Cosmos and all of God's creatures and creations began from the Divine Logos—"The Word" of God in the form of the Spiritual Elements—and that is part of the Background and Foreground of all real Things on the stage of life. Because, prior to birth, all humans are provided with inner Spiritual Illumination from "a kind of individualized fragment of the Supreme Being" means that a drop of God's Essence and power is "stamped" on each human's Soul like a "Trademark" with radar type actions. Ones Soul's Spiritual Elements "Trademark" is attracted to any Evidence of what is like-kind. Here, "*Evidence*" is used in the sense of it being an indicator of where the truth lies and serves as a magnet to gather it. Every human's Right brain Intuition, predominantly ones Ancient Brain instincts, has creative (from "Pure Emotions") parts which connect perceptions with awareness and intellect as well as a non-creative "*Sixth*

Sense" (giving snapshots of Reality) aspects. Both are closely associated with the soul--and its "what to do/not do" supersedes Reason. To be in the flow of Pure Intuition opens channels for one to receive guidance from ones Spiritual Entourage (e.g. wise Living-Dead Ancestors, Spiritual Servants that gather what is needed) + Afrocentric Mystic Memories from Ancient African "Thought Clouds" (see Bailey Glossary #5) + "Helping Hands" when one is alone and overwhelmed. The point: ones Pure Emotions and Intellect have right answers for Serious Business

KNOWING--"TRIAD OF SCOPE": The *Horizontal Bar* of the Cross Concept is called the "*Triad of Scope Knowing*" is: (1) What it is; (2) What it does; and (3) How it appears. To elaborate using Crystals, (1a) *What Crystals Are* is a homogenous portion of Matter which follows a solid mathematical formulation. Crystals start by the first particles which come close together and produce a unit cell, just like bricks are the unit making up a brick wall. Other unit cells form on all sides of the first to start the process of growth. This is like families coming together to create a unified village. By possessing an orderly and repeated atomic structure, they share certain general properties, as in having a sharp melting point (compared with the melting range of amorphous substances, e.g. glass). (2b) *What Crystals Do* includes reflecting and refracting light as well as behaving in many ways similar to those of matter endowed with life. In a suitable environment a crystal will "grow." If a broken crystal is placed in the proper solution it rapidly repairs the break, assuming soon again a perfect crystalline form. According to heat, electricity, and chemicals around them, Liquid Crystals switch colors like chameleons. Sprayed on the body, they can reveal what is going on inside. (3c) *How Crystals Appear* are with definite, regular shapes which identify them. They exhibit an outward form bounded by smooth, plane surfaces, symmetrically arranged and termed faces or "flats."SCOPE (1) WHAT IT IS--a thing's essence nature when it came into Being + its content potential (e.g. an apple seed contains the genetics for the entire apple tree) + its evolution pattern. Seed assessments avoid any dealings with its offspring (e.g. Roots, Trunk or Vines, Branches, Leaves, or Fruit) and looks for the Seed Source, health, or flaws in its genetic make-up. SCOPE (2) WHAT IT DOES in Events (changing realities) and the Event's influences on things inside and outside itself, as in Where and What is Being Done to it; Was Done; and Can be Done. Example: while and after the tree grows there are several environments that Tree experiences: rodents may be eating its roots or the soil may be poor; problematic weather and people carving their initials may adversely affect its trunk; animals may be eating its fruit buds or biting its apples. SCOPE (3) HOW IT APPEARS to ones Senses may be real, distorted, or fantasy—and, of course, the sharpness or dullness of ones senses varies from time to time. Who does the viewing?--for what reasons?--and with what bias or opinions are preferred--as an unripened apple is preferred by some; a ripe apple by others. Each of these (among others) determine conclusions, actions/inactions, effects, and consequences.

KNOWING--TRIAD PHASES OF DEPTH: The *Vertical Bar* of the Cross Concept is called the "*Triad of Depth Knowing*". It consists of: (4) the Obvious; (5) the Hidden (internal structure); (6) the Foundation (meaning the "Underlying" Foundation) and (7) the Base (i.e. the Source). The C14 word "*Depth*" (quality of being deep) refers to what is just below the surface all the way into an *Abyss* (without bottom), which is unmeasurable, unfathomable, and bottomless. Here, it refers to the native qualities of the mind that give rise to insight, judgment, profundity, reason, sagacity, sense, understanding, and wisdom--though each are capable of increase by cultivation. It starts with the Obvious, proceeds to uncover the Hidden, and thereby enters the Underlying—which is like what supports a skyscraper building. "*Underlying*" means what is innate—what has been designed by the Creator Source to give birth the underground "Seed" that gives rise to the Foundation ("Roots") and the above ground aspects that is available to be Discerned. That "Seed," like the human heart, imparts the essential ingredients for all of its emanating parts to have the existing or potential qualities, strength, and characteristics needed to manifest the inclination contained in the disposition of the

"Genetics" making up the "Seed." One enters the realm of Wisdom by seeking out the Underlying—initially equating to the Underground Foundation of a skyscraper building or the "Roots" of a Seed. That Wisdom part, in turn, connects with its Base—i.e. the Cosmic Organism (the "Seed") orchestrated by the Cosmic Mind (the Soil covering the "Seed"). That Cosmic Mind is the Source of the entire Thing. DEPTH (4) The *Obvious* -- Crystal sizes vary from hidden or too small to see without a magnifier or easily seen by all (e.g. snowflakes, sand grains, metals). Crystals having the same chemical composition and the same structure have equal angles between corresponding crystal faces.

DEPTH (5) The *Hidden* part of the entire internal structure is made of atoms, ions, and molecules fit together in an orderly, three-dimensional pattern (or unit cell) of definite shapes. When unit cells form on all sides of the first one and then are stacked together, they build the framework, or lattice -- like the steel girders making up the skeleton of a tall building. The result of the points and intersecting lines of this lattice (or internal structure or framework) is what gives the crystal its shape.

DEPTH (6) The Underground *Foundation*'s unit cells are composed of Ions which, in turn, derive from the un-demonstrable Ether. These unit cells are the basic building blocks of crystals. Just as in Science to arrive at truth without error, the foundation of Knowledge is in Mathematics. DEPTH (7) The Underground *Base* upon which the entire structure rests. The absolutely most sound Base of the Laws of Nature as well as of the Cosmos itself is that of Unconditional Love. On top of that Base are built attribute products of the Spiritual Elements. No matter how much "weight" is placed on top of that Base and no matter how great the magniture of the trials and tribulations (problems and difficulties) used as forces to try to disrupt it, that Base, nor the structure it supports, will be affected unless a human allows that damage to happen. Anything short of Unconditional Love serving as a Base will be like it is made of "Quicksand". In other words, at some point the entire structure will collapse when all of the Spiritual Elements attributes are added. Ancient African Sages used Symbols representing Spiritual Elements Principles for their thinking inside the Processes of Nature while the people used its Principles. Thus, there were no fixed Human-Patterns of Thought.

PHASE I--PROBLEMS WITH THE *OBVIOUS*

The word "*Obvious*" (1586) means that which is directly in the way on the path, presenting itself readily and so apparent, evident, or clear that it cannot be missed by ones instincts, senses, or emotions. It is inspected by sight, emotions, and/or Feelings to discover what is taken for granted or its subtlies. The steps for getting to a Secular Principle are to first see all that is in the Obvious. However, most people are partially or completely "*blind to the obvious*". The Indo-European word "*Blind*" applies in its original sense of not so much 'sightlessness' as 'confusion' and 'obscurity'. Then the notion of someone wandering around in actual or mental darkness, not knowing where to go, naturally progressed to the 'inability to see.' These concepts about "Blind" have been cunningly used by actors as well as by evil people--both orchestrate the audience by doing what it takes to deceptively change the Crowd's reality of who the Actors or evil people really are. Their intentionally deceptive methods ensure the audience ('lookers and listeners' or Crowd) remain ignorant about the obvious. They are highly skilled in the use of these deceptions to put the people into a Supernatural fantasy mindset where they are "*Blindfolded*" (Old English, 'to strike blind') to Reality. In other words, the illuded people have such a huge "*Blindspot*" ('covered or hidden from sight') as to what they saw, see, heard, and hear in the performance as to believe the proported Actors and Evil leaders' illusive acts are actually true. This happens because typically people who do what they are accustomed to and know already to be proper, so admire what is new and strange as to prefer that, although they do not know whether it is proper or not. This means they reflexively turn *a blind eye to what is real* ('pretending not to notice') and thus accept three things. First is not seeing the actor or evil person as is but instead as the exciting part the actor or evil person is playing. Second, accepting what is exciting, even though it may not be in their best interest. Third, giving up what they know to be proper because it has stood the test of time. Fourth, become so addicted to the excitement of the obviously "new and strange" + to the leaders generating that excitement + to the Crowd flowing with that excitement as to stay in that excitement flow wherever it leads and never return to reality and safety. As a result, the Crowd follows this into all Life Living patterns. To elaborate, any problematic or disharmonious situation is analogized by the Crowd's EPs (Emotional People) to be no more than a mere floating piece of ice, when in reality it is an Iceberg—meaning most of the problem is in the 6/8 to 7/8 of its mass, hidden underneath the water. They fail to see or acknowledge this *iceberg* of a problematic situation because of having made a habit of allowing others to make their decisions and protect them (e.g. overprotective parents or the Crowd). Much of this comes from having absorbed the bad habits of technology which makes for being addicted to the exciting and constantly seeking the next excitement on their Flashing Light gadget as soon as bordom sets in. This makes for an extremely short attention span. Each of these prevents them from sharpening their Critical Thinking skills by means of engaging in the struggle required to get through the stricture of the hour-glass. So weak do they become in problem solving as to be easily overwhelmed with problems. They ignore them with the excuse: "I'm too busy." Consequences of this Crowd way of Superficial/Supernatural Thinking are innumerable: (1) Almost all are incompetent in handling their private and workplace obligations, duties, and responsibilities. (2) The Crowd is socialized to not see the "*Spiritual Energy Package* in the room" because their socializer leaders (in the distant background) or the Crowd leaders (in the foreground) are intent on controlling their minds. Thus, it is to the leaders advantage for the Crowd not to think and to only see what they are told to see. Such is prominent in mind-controlling religions where one is not to question the evilness advocated and done (e.g. anti-feminism; or be a good Slave) but, instead, have "Faith and Belief." This serves to "dim the light of obviousness" on the "ugly" things they do. The leaders desire to get rid of their competition and therefore make them feigned enemies. Their "*Deflection*" *Method* both reinforces their Projections (putting their own "Dark Side" onto scapegoats) and generates Indifference/Hatred/Evil/Sadism practices towards those same scapegoats. An obvious example to which many victims are blind is the "Conditional Love" ("I/we won't love you if you do not do what I/we say") used to control minds of the European World Crowd. (3) EPs are "Glob" thinkers, meaning all of their thoughts and emotions about something are "Lumped" together. Here, the obvious is obviously not obvious for there is no space to distinguish thoughts from emotions and to do analysis in order to determine specifics. Hence, the tip of that Glob equates to an iceberg's tip but with the bulk of their mental turmoil below the surface. They are either unaware of the cause of those thoughts and emotions and/or are purposely biased. Biases see facts in a certain way because of ones habits, wishes, desires, interests, values, or need to "save face." "*Prejudice*" (a Middle English term for harm or injury resulting from action or judgment) has a strict sense of preconceived favorable or unfavorable opinion or emotion, without knowledge. Whereas *Bias* is developed in viewing the facts and then "Picking and Choosing" only those facts which support ones point of view, "*Prejudice*" occurs when one does not know, or has not examined, or does not care about the facts--and does not want to be confused by the facts. The process steps are positioned in the following order: *Prejudices of Ignorance* (all blindly adopted) are more easily removed than *Will-full Biases/Prejudices* (i.e. "Indifferent"—seeing what it pleases, not what is plain, and then passing that off as reasons to ignore facts and sensations. Associated with this is to not face the problem but instead substitute something else soothing or exciting. All of these are to self-protect from what one finds unpleasant so as to prevent or lessen high levels of stress one finds that the problematic produces when seeing things as they actually are. (4) Superficial Thinking is about "snapshot" thinking limited to the "here and now". Example: "I hope this works out" rather than going through the 9 Ps to give it the best chance of working and so clear instructions can be given to those involved. This means they are unable to put together the obvious concept: "Everything in your life is a reflection of a choice or decision you have made; If you want a different result, make a different choice or decision." Another example is: "your valuableness does not decrease based on others inability to see your worth." (5) *Mystery*--something incomprehensible to human understanding because it is in a Supernatural realm or has no coherence. Either prevent one from seeing the stated obvious.

PHASE II—PROBLEMS WITH THE HIDDEN

The Old English word "Hide" (skin covering) means to withdraw or to withhold from sight or observation for various reasons. The "Hidden" implies the internal structure of a problem or situation. Thus, it can only be entered by intense Curiosity, a flood of Questions, focused concentration, and trial-and-error explorations to discover what is behind the Obvious or the flaws covering the Hidden.Most broadly, hide is about what is covered by putting something over or around it--which may or may not imply intent by design, by accident, by some imperfection associated with something or in someone, or by unavoidable circumstances (e.g. clouds hiding the sun or a tall building hides what is behind it). The Problem: (1) the "Thing" may be visible, capable of being made visible, obscure (because of "dust in ones eyes" or its depth, or intricacy complexity, or being in a muddy pool, or defect of light) or invisible or *Ambiguous*—capable of being interpreted in two or more ways using denotative or connotative meanings; (2) the *location* of the Hidden may be via a place that *Screens* it (impling a concealment of someone or something in danger of being seen or known); is *Buried* (a hiding place under any mass or accumulation); is *Obstruse* (removed from the usual course of thought so as to make it remote); (3) the Presentation can be *Masked* from ordinary and easy perception and intelligence but only by unusual and difficult research; *Camouflaged* (to disguise, deceive by putting a whiff of smoke in ones face); *Tempered* (as with an understatement) within the *Occult* (whatever is mysterious, making one unable to see through and can only be illuminated by Spiritual, if realistic, or Supernatural, if a fantasy, perception); and of *Inclusion* (i.e. contained in something)—as an implied inclusion by inference. Problem examples include: (a) *Riddle*--an ambiguous statement with a hidden meaning to be guessed by ones mental acuteness; (b) *Conundrum*--a riddle whose answer involves a Pun--"When is a door not a door?"; A: When it's ajar"; (c) *Enigma*--one with a baffling or confusing hidden meaning, clear only to one who understands the allusion(s) therein. (d) *Paradox*--a view contradicting accepted opinion for seeming to be self-contradictory (even absurd).

But on closer inspection it contains a truth reconciling the conflicting opposites: "I never found the companion that was so companionable as solitude" (Thoreau); (e) *Puzzle*--a question or problem intricate enough to be perplexing; (f) *Mystery*--something incomprehensible to human understanding—e.g. Enigmatical words; (g) *Secret* (escaping sight without necessarily being hidden, like a code—e.g. Cryptic words have a hidden meaning); (h) an *Allusion* (hinted at but not stated); An Allusion--relying on suggestion and connotation by a causal or passing reference--is an extremely quick way of expressing ones emotions to an in-group as well as creating in listeners shades of those same emotions--but only when the listeners are already familiar with the setting (e.g. history, literature, sayings, slang, people, events) alluded to--as, for example, family jokes; (I) Allegory--the hidden story within an obvious story, though capable of being mentally seen and understood, passed unnoticed by those not highly Spiritually evolved. Similarly, Enslaved African Americans used Subliminal messages in Negro Spirituals as a signal or message embedded in another medium which the fellow Enslaved understood. Yet, the messages were designed to pass below the normal limits of the European mind's perception. This was called *Knowledge by Participation*.

PROCESS FOR DEALING WITH THE HIDDEN: Most of what causes something to be hidden is mentioned above and reasons for the hiding require *Trouble-Shooting* (a 1905 term for one who traces and corrects faults). It is applied to each part of the SOBMER Process (an acronym for Source, Origin, Beginning, Middle, End/Consequences, and Result). Within each of those 6 aspects there is a keystone. That keystone itself has "SOBMER" aspects. The purpose of each of these is to help penetrate the Obvious so as to enter into the Hidden and then explore the internal structure of the Hidden so as to discern the consistent underlying pattern of the problem or situation at hand. Inside this internal structure is something problematic: *Ambiguous;* a *Screen; a burial of the essence; an Obstruse concept; a Camouflage; a Tempered (i.e. non-spotlighted) pearl; a Masking; an Occult concept* dating back to Primitive Times*; the Pearl inside an Inclusion* (e.g. an Allegory); and *an Enigma* (a baffling or confusing meaning). Some clarifying answers cannot be known except by studying its Ancient African evolution or essence concepts. Some answers come from solving the easiest first and letting that serve as a key to open the next somewhat more difficult one—and so forth. Some cannot be clear until its original meaning is known—typically in Ancient African literature or in very old European texts (since they reproduced African Intellectual Property) or in the literature of those cultures which elaborated on Ancient African Philosophy (e.g. China, Tibet, India, and others of the Far East). Some are clarified by reviewing everything available on that subject with a free and fresh mind so as to enhance seeing more subtle interrelationships. Most answers come from realizing that the information presented by "experts" are flawed—because they copied flawed experts; because they do not understand the "Big Picture"; because of their ethnocentric biases and prejudices. The following are some things to be alert to for determining pertinent problematic issues and then locating *Essential* flaws in each issue.

Typical causes include: incomplete and/or inaccurate information gathering; a bad choice of information source; some flaw in what is available for study; or a misapplication in the label for the pattern of the conclusion. In troubleshooting one may find: (a) one is dealing with only one link in some interrelationship instead of stepping behind its origin to see where it came from and with what was it associated); (b) one pays attention to only the general idea within that one link while overlooking how its particular can be applied in a special way (that is why I like studying Wit, Jokes, Humor, and Silliness); (c) one improperly links things together because it "SEEMS" right (e.g. Spiritual and Supernatural ideas do not mix); (d) one overlooks certain meanings in certain links (more often the right meaning was given in ancient times); (e) one fails to do a good job with one or more of the links with respect to arranging or combining them ("almost" is not good enough; forgetting does not work); (f) one ignores the obvious completely because of bias or trying to "conform" or to make oneself "look good". Any of these (among countless others) causes one to have flawed or limited ideas and therefore frustration--a set-up for inefficiency and ineffectiveness--a set-up for conveying the wrong intension or message--a set-up for confusing oneself and the receiver. Chances are that these will not be detected as long as one uses a "snapshot" approach in assessing a subject, as opposed to being in the flow. Ancient Africans said that the first thing to do when faced with any complex problem is to put things in Order. To follow a previous well-worked out orderly process greatly aids Trouble-shooting—and that Process can be modified as ones Knowledge expands.

Step I--Clearly define the problem. This is what it takes to put chaotic things about a subject in order for purposes of beginning to understand that subject's triad of the Obvious, Hidden, and underlying Foundational essence. "Either/Or" and "All-or-None" have no place. Step II--Gather pertinent information about the subject before starting to select the keystone difficulty, put it into a Mental Skeletal form for assessment by examining and analyzing its triad. By European philosophy only dealing with the Supernatural and the Physical, and not the natural Spiritual or Metaphysical, means an incredible number of life-shaping and life-changing words are not mentioned in books; and if mentioned, are given no discussion; and if discussed, do "Concept Violence" to them causing one to be far away from the Truth-Track. European Dictionaries are of no benefit to me in delving into meanings of Spiritual, Metaphysical, or Supernatural words (e.g. "Awe"). All avoid the "*What it is*" essence of the thing when it came into being. Instead, they focus on describing the 'what it does'/'how it appears' aspects—which are merely opinions. To gain a "What it is" idea comes from first determining what it is not. I completely stopped using all European information in the 1980s and that skyrocketed my insights into African Sages hidden knowledge. To ensure accuracy I have looked up over 20,000 words using up to 1000 references for any given word. Hence, bad patterns of thinking by "experts" became obvious to me 30 years ago. Thus, except for 5 Black scholars who do "snapshot" discussions of African Tradition, I trust nothing anybody says. Even with those 5, what they say is placed in a "Holding Boot"-- ranging up to a year--while I try to verify what they present. The majority of the time, the best information I find is to gain ideas out of Quotation Books regarding that word. What I look for is a "Mental Movie" of African Tradition, starting when they came on Earth 200,000 years ago. Out of the gathered knowledge and information, separate them. With the Information, separate it into what is pertinent and non-pertinent. Then, prioritize the Pertinent information on the "T" Scale into Useful, Probably Useful, and Possibly Useful. Do not discard the non-pertinent or Possibly Useful since pieces of these may find a place as one progresses in perfecting ones Mental Skeleton. Finally, what remains of the gathered information and knowledge is *the ingredients of each Knowledge component + the chosen pieces from each Useful piece of an Informational component reduced to its essence. These ingredients form the core of what goes into the Common Ground* (ingredients shared for beneficial mutual interaction) within the *Interchange of these interlocking components*—as elaborated on later. Step III--Assess the Common Ground Components to gain broad metaphysical and physical realm concepts from gauging the good/bad, desirable/undesirable, Worth/Value of something or someone; and categorize resultant keystone issues into Pros/Cons. Instead of looking for answers, my interest is on the flow pattern of that knowledge and the best information. From that I extract what is pertinent in helping me to prove or disprove whatever is at issue at its essence. Rarely can any information in the Common Ground Components be used "as is." Any piece may be worthwhile when looked at in different ways and parts combined or subtracted to make a "fit" on a plane not previously considered. Within this context there are countless topics, many of which are totally new to me or are incompletely known. I never assume I already know enough about a subject to prevent the need for further research on its keystone word meaning and whatever is associated with it. Thus I gather information from "everywhere" and outline topic headings on separate pages so that as information comes in, it will have a place--like putting a paper in a file and placing that file in its proper alphabet location in the file cabinet. To fill that paper may take a year. Clues for each of these come from anywhere in general and nowhere in particular—like from something totally unrelated on radio or television. That is why I keep rewriting the same topic, for each time my mind will have more subject insight from seeing interrelationships. All key words have application on more than one plane of existence and separating a given word into its plane is the basis for classifying the concept within that word. The subclass selected is the one most pertinent to clearly defining the problem; putting boundaries on the topic under discussion; and laying out a stepping stone process to follow. The reason for researching the key topic word for its original etymological meaning—and on up to the present--is so as *to know what everybody in the world knows about that word*, regardless of subject. That is how I form a Secular Principle. It enables me to take off in new and varied thoughtful directions.

Step IV—ANALYSIS reduces a "Thing" to other facts or breaks it into its component parts in a manner that aids penetrating explorations of the Hidden of the problem or situation at hand so as to discern its consistent underlying pattern. Analysis singles out the characteristics and qualities of a Thing; concentrating the mind on one of these at a time in order to determine its potential possibilities, what it does, how it appears, and mainly "what it is". Analysis demands: A. *looking at things as they really are*; B. *avoid seeing only what is liked or familiar*;

C. ensuring not to be blind to the obvious—for any reason, as from trying not to see what one does not want to see; D. Avoid a like/dislike opinion about what has to be done but never avoid what is disliked if it has to be done. The essential of Analysis in Secular Principle determination or formation is: (1) mentally seeing similarities in the dissimilar--uniqueness in similarities--the common in the uncommon--the uncommon in the common; (2) looking behind the obvious to see the consistent, permanent, stationary, and unchanging patterns/elements underlying natural events and the course of their Natural Processes; (3) determine the interrelationships of the components involved and how they are unified into a harmonious pattern so as to become aware of the 'what it is,' the way things are, and why they are. Despite its narrow scope, these bits and pieces of awareness of the original meanings of the associated ideas within the Common Ground Interchange and its developmental historical course instantly begins to illuminate paths into pertinent subject aspects. Step V—MANIPULATE and MANEUVER: Instead of initially looking through Common Ground Components for answers to shed light on the Hidden, as in what is causing confusion and conflict, I often find a rich harvest in the flawed print or speech sources from which those components were gathered. Typically Flawed examples include them: being shoddy, weak, inadequate, limited, defective, incomplete; non-pertinent; not of keystone importance; facades; confusingly directed or headed; placed on improper planes of existence; improperly arranged or combined; deceiving; in conflict; evilly misinterpreted; racially/ethnocentrically biased; in conflict, and/or mostly simply wrong! By correcting whatever is wrong with any of these often gives me insights that help uncover what is causing the Hidden or at least heads me toward what could be Underlying it. This is the set-up for *Classification*--a mental tool for putting "Entity/Things" derived from the same "Seed" with Blending in the same space; "family resemblances"; or like-kind "Entity/Things" representing a "Salad Mix" of "brothers from different mothers" into arrangements, combinations, or new forms. Each promotes better Common Ground understanding--which assists Concept prioritizing into pertinent significance. Each "Entity/Things" is a "*Class*".

PHASE III--UNDERLYING PATTERN EXPLORATIONS

Humans are archetypes of what can be likened to a skyscraper building, whereby they can choose the level of life in which they prefer to operate. To elaborate, a decision to transcend into a "Non-Self" means slipping into the Foundation of what is Underlying their Public Displays. Europeans say a *Foundation* is a substantial supporting mass, resting on a Base and upon which the entire superstructure of something rests. In a finished skyscraper building, for example, the Foundation is usually below the surface of the ground and out of sight. To enter immediately Underground, ones mind enters into the infinite order of Nature—an infinite *Unified realm of complexity and multiplicity Patterns, like foams in ocean waves, called Continuity.* To get past the difficulties of the Hidden allows for arriving at the Foundation—*something on which to build.* In African Tradition, the Foundation for a Thought Structure requires Mathematical quantitative reasoning for looking behind or below the Obvious in order to uncover the Hidden. One can then see the consistent, permanent, stationary, and unchanging patterns/elements underlying natural events. The *"Underlying"* innate core of that Thought Structure is its "Roots" (Wisdom)—i.e. what has been born out of its underground "seed"—and by being indivisible difference, give birth to all that are about its above-ground aspects. That "Seed," to repeat, consists of *the ingredients of each Wisdom and Knowledge component. Out of what is Underlying are chosen pieces from each Useful piece of the above ground Informational components which are then reduced to its essence ingredients so as to enter into Wisdom. These essences are what form the core of what goes into the Common Ground* (ingredients shared for beneficial mutual interaction) within the *Interchange of these interlocking components.*

Put another way, the "Sameness" of the Essence ingredients of Knowledge and Useful Information constitutes the *"Common Ground" Interchange* which characterizes Interlocking Rings. The C14 word *Interchange* conveys the idea that: (1) the things inside that space are like overlapping mosaic colors seen in a kaleidoscope; (2) the slightest of rotating movements of the kaleidoscope results in the changing of different color combinations; (3) each color and each color overlap combination is uniquely shaped in forms; and (4) each form has contents of significance. At the 'Core' of the Interchange area—like the horny central part of an apple—is the central feature of a "Common Ground". Constituting the "*Common Ground*" is a Zero complementary equal Relationship Point where like-kind things are mutually shared and exchanged. The product may be a "salad" type mix or a "milk shake" type blend. Arriving at "Blend" was by Syntheses, implying the resultant product is in a state of Order, Regularity, Coherence, Consistency, Compatibility, Balance, Harmony, and Predictability.

PHASE III A: DISCERNING PRINCIPLES IN THE FOUNDATION

Physical World Knowledge forms of Secular Principles: A Secular Principle is a *human-made synthesized "Seed" derived from the ingredients of*: (1) seeing *Inner Similarities* in dissimilar things; (2) seeing *Inner Similarities* in Similar things; (3) discerning uniqueness in similarities; (4) discerning similarities in unique things; (5) discerning the uncommon in the common; (6) discerning the common in the uncommon; and (7) going into the Underlying of what is dissimilar in order to detect and fashion interrelationships between dissimilar and similar things or discover they share the same "Genetics". *Physical World Information form of Secular Principles*: My idea is to find out everything everybody else in the world knows about a given keystone word of a subject; organize it on its proper planes of existence. Then I extract the essence from the "Big Picture" of the findings as well as from the Principle essence of the given plane of existence that is the focus of my subject. From that, I formulate a novel path which enables me to Classify the subject and then select a Class for discussion. Of course, one of the most thorough methods I use is looking through up to 1000 books per word with said books involving all aspects of information and that would include, medical and law dictionaries, word finders, quotation books, philosophy, sociology, humor, religion, encyclopedias, slang, and the like. See Correspondence for elaboration

PHASE III B:—BASE FOR THE FOUNDATION

In African Tradition, the Base is Unconditional Love, out of which come Truth, Reality, and the Natural. Since the Base and Underground Foundation are like two sides of a coin, they are called the "Base/Foundation." Although the consistent Patterns discovered in the Foundation would otherwise escapes ones daily living perception, by being in Nature's Continuity makes one aware of the Base upon which the Underground foundation rests—a realm of the highest of all Orders—*the total Pattern of the Cosmos orchestrated by the boundless Force which Ancient Africans called Sekhem*. Here, one returns to the Cosmic Organism from which one originated prior to being born into the Earth World.

KNOWLEDGE IN AFRICAN TRADITION: Child-like Wonder and Curiosity—particularly about observations in Nature--are paths leading to the seed of any type of knowledge—i.e. direct perception of the "what it is" aspects of pre-birth Emotions' Reality. The "*What it Is*" of Knowledge is various arrangements and combinations of mosaic pieces of the Spiritual Elements—Unconditional Love, Truth, Reality, and the Natural. The resultant "package" is a potent and subtle distillation of experience—as a result of thinking, feeling, tasting, smelling and observing. Staying within and evolving out of these guides requires Integrity, is its own Proof, and imparts the Conviction of ones Private Selfhood of having the "5Ss"—Safety, Security, Sureness/Self-Confidence, Strength, and Stability. Since these must be experienced to be known, that experience indicates one is allowing ones birth gift of Selfhood Greatness to flower. The "*What it Does*" pertaining to Knowledge promote the creation, enhancement, and maintenance of "what is For Me" in life while defending and protecting from whatever is "Against Me." The more extensive ones knowledge of what has been done and what could be done, the greater will be ones power of knowing what to do. Tools for doing both are the rearrangement and recombining of pieces of the Spiritual Elements into unique forms is how ones Consciousness expands into new creations. Those pieces can be gained from every source—a pot, a bug, a dog, a fool, a chair, an enemy, a child at play. The "*How it Appears*" of Knowledge is like a flame lighting a piece of the "Darkness". To allow others to light their candle out of ones flame, instead of diminishing that flame, increases it from the wax drippings of the other's candles.

KNOWLEDGE ORIGIN IN AFRICAN TRADITION: Primitive (the first) Africans originated pre-Matter Knowledge by devising causes and reasons for what was going in the Unseen Realms. Then Very Ancient African priest-astronomers elaborated on Matter to gain insight into Knowledge of the Cosmos by a *Subjective Scientific Method*. Actually, this was initiated, not as a Superstition, but rather a Speculation derived from an image gained from their naked eyes (actually through *Astrocopy*, a reed). This Speculation started Science by "Tools" of Observation, Reflection, "Pure" Feelings, Productive Imagination, Contemplation, Inductive and Deductive Inferences, and Common Sense. In the process of studying every aspect of the objective Sky, the obtained pertinent knowledge ingredients were put in Order using their invention of Mathematics. Inferences from this process gave insight into the "Unseeable" or Subjective World. Its Spiritual value did not spring out of their Astrocopy image but rather from its power to suggest and support Sages inferred concepts about the Cosmos. To keep up with ongoing observations required the development of various forms of Mathematics which, in turn, enabled precision and accurate scientific observations. Applying resultant laws of Mathematics opened doors to reality that provided insight into Esoteric Sky Knowledge. Over thousands of years a formalized Reasoning, Critical Thinking, and Logic processes were devised by African Sages, including the gathering of Facts and the manipulation (e.g. into varying combinations) and maneuvering (e.g. into new arrangements) of Circumstantial Evidence Truths.

Ancient Egyptians formalized this and originated (between 2000 and 1500 BCE) a six step *Scientific Method* (Van Sertima). Its essence derived from both *Deductive* (going from the general to the specific) and *Inductive* (going from the specific to the general) Reasoning—starting with Observation--for the purpose of proving or disproving a point. In the process, Insights no doubt appeared suddenly as an understanding of the pattern for deciding or for solving a problem. Science advanced as a result of the advantages of Deductive and Inductive Reasoning. The Insights they provided consisted of answers serving as a "deposit" for idea withdrawals or for patterns used to solve similar problems in the present which, in turn, laid out a path for solving anticipated problems in the future. Then Ancient African Scientists and scholars built up bodies of knowledge by combining inductive methods, deductive methods, and mathematics--all used to this day throughout the world by scientists, engineers, doctors and all specialists. The original principles of greatest concern to Ancient Africans were of a scientific, Esoteric (knowledge beyond reason), and logical nature pertaining to higher planes of existence. They understood that *knowledge advances by finding how similarities and differences are related, harmonized, and synthesized*. The objective was to arrive at the Truth of Thought by Synthesis. Then they positioned facts and evidence on the proper rung of the Cosmic Ladder and maneuvered them according to the unique rules operating on a given rung. Some of their world-class discoveries *emerged from simple accurate observations spotlighting an understanding of the whole*. Principles on a given plane of existence were harmoniously fit to form the applicable solid Rational/Logical knowledge that was basic to the subject at hand (e.g. scientific and esoteric realms).

KNOWLEDGE--EXTERNAL WORLD COMPOSITION: Perhaps the world's first formal Intellectual Knowledge came from Very Ancient African priest-astronomers (c20,000 BC to 12,500 BC) exploring the

"*Order*" of the sky as a way to discover Truth. The necessity for having a better understanding of Vibrations throughout the Cosmos led to Mathematical discoveries. As a result, they discovered a fixed point in the sky's sacred space--a space conforming to African Sages' revelations concerning primordial aspects of the Cosmic Creation--a point essential for establishing natural order--a point useful as a central axis for all future orientation—the point of absolute finite reality. It was the Woyo (Equatorial Africa) and Dogons (Mali) who found this fixed point and named it the Po Tolo (Sirius B) Star (Diop, Civilization p314). In this example of following Nature's Mathematical Processes, many other things fell into place. For example, their measurements so matched the Celestial Order ("course or way") as to itself amount to a revelation regarding the organizing principles by which Ancient Africans recognized their own personal harmonies and harmonies in their environments. This came about from their instinctive *Cosmo-Logical Thinking which perceived Abstract general Classes (whole) to which specific issues of life belong.* Resultant Inferences from their accumulated and organized knowledge generated insights related to Ordered Rhythms "everywhere"--insights leading to Truths concerning the Earth's Events, the cycles of Nature, the stars, constellations, and human body organs independence that worked interdependently to establish health. My interpretation of African Sages processes of composing their acquired Knowledge—whether from Intuiting the Will of God or by using Subjective and Objective Sciences to discover aspects of the Spiritual Elements—consists of these Steps: *Step I* in the process of forming and displaying Knowledge is the Cosmic Mind's "*What and Why*" Message presented to a human's Divine Consciousness Spiritual Elements "Trademark". *Step II*, that Virtual Spiritual Image Message is an abstract of meaningful units integrated and arranged into a mosaic type Disposition for the mind to receive by ones Divine Will. *Step III*, ones Divine Will directs the Spiritual Image Disposition into the human mind's Divine Spirit whereby its deposit activates the Divine Spirit's Spiritual Energy and Matter. *Step IV* comes from the powers imparted by the Spiritual Energy and the Ether adding layers of Matter onto the Will's Image so as to fashion a barely perceptible Percept, enabling God's Divine Plan to be "Felt". *Step V*, a Percept's specific attributes—called Essences--has a specific nature or character in which are Essentials—all wrapped in Divine Desire. *Step VI*, inside ones Sensory Unconscious, the Percept's expansion into a Notion before manifesting as a Thought is done by adding that human's monitored feedback interpretations extracted out of other influences, like from ones memory, "committee" assessments, and External World impressions. *Step VII*, the Spiritual Disposition + its added influences are led into ones Sensory Consciousness, perhaps to display in the External World (Amen, Tree of Life p9; Amen, MAAT, 12; Amen, Metu Neter I:383-5 and IV:25-7). Vital parts of this process include: (1) the *What* and *Why* Divine Message of Step I which is inside a Disposition containing its Essence nature and an Inclination (or Divine Desire); (2) the Step II Virtual Spiritual Image being composed of meaningful units for the human mind to receive; (3) the Ether Matter layers of Step IV make for a Percept—and the more layers the more aware one is of the Disposition in the Percept; (4) the Percept has Essences which represent the *Disposition's Self-Identity—the "what it is" when it came into Being* (i.e. into existence).

(5) Essences—i.e. *Endowments* (i.e. natural qualities) and *Propensities* (in-born tendencies--e.g. ones capacities, abilities, language)--manifest by operations of *its Properties* (what a thing has) in forms of "*What it Does*"—and serves some processes of an Entity's Selfhood in the capacity of a Foundation; (6) Essentials--Characteristics, Traits, and Features of Essences--are potentials inside its Essence parent to support its attributes. By having *Secular Correspondence,* they need the mind's Sensory Consciousness interaction with Metaphysical, Physical, and Supernatural Things in the External World to manifest; and (7) the product of the Disposition which enters into the mind and maybe from there into the External World consists of a Mosaic thought, emotion, deed. See Knowledge; Knowledge (Cosmos Formation); Truths (Human); Knowledge Composition;

Knowledge Types; Circumstantial Knowledge; Circumstantial Algebraic Evidence/Proof/Truth; Inferences (African Tradition); Inferences (Secular); Great Mother; *Mythic Truths; Feeling True*

KNOWLEDGE BY THE THIRD EYE: Third Eye *is Instinctive Knowledge* whose instinctive faculty resides in the Life-Force division of Being (Amen, Metu Neter III:30). At least by c10,000 BC the Pyramid (Unas) Texts have been in existence and they referred to the "Eye" of humans associated with luminous "inner vision" apparently intimately associated with the Pineal Gland. This Third Eye—the Eye of Intuitional vision; of Heru (Horus); of Auraut; of Ureaus; of the Goddess' Brow; of Ajna chakra--is located at the top of the spinal column in the Mid-Brain, forming part of the floor of the third ventricle. It is associated with: the development of an expanded state of Consciousness; (2) is an organ of Spiritual and Psychic Perception where, and at no other point, the soul and body touch each other; (3) it and the Pituitary body are means for detecting vibrations subtler than science ordinarily recognizes; and (4) produces Melatonin, associated with the regulation of biorhythms, stimulating the brain to produce serotonin which regulates sleep patterns. The cerebellun attracts through the Pineal gland the spiritual and life-giving substance. Clairvoyance refers to the astral function of this "Third Eye" which enables distinguishing Spiritual Light, making the organ of Inner Vision, Spiritual Feelings, and the seat of Divine Knowledge. Originally, the Third Eye was a vague astral clairvoyant (Quaser) faculty of early humanity which, as evolution proceeded, was exchanged for the physical organs of sight. [Ref: Bynum, Dark Light Consciousness p110]. The Third Eye enables the seeing of Knowledge, which concerns itself first with the "what it is"—the Thing's essence when it came into Being. See First Wisdom; Correspondence/Circumstantial; Pineal Gland

"KNOWLEDGE"--MISLEADING FROM UNEXAMINED ASSUMPTIONS: It is natural to believe whatever one has been Socialized into and assumes it to be the "right" way for those things. Yet, only Critical Thinkers "double-check" to ensure how near to perfection is what they have absorbed by socialized osmosis. The reason is their 'best self' only comes from being on the right path with "right" Life Living ingredients. They know a society can be no better than those humans who formed it, and now comprise it. Also, by their Self-Seeking interests or gains--and not considering the welfare among their own and/or with "outsiders"— means they are "off-track." Self-Seeking leaders, to do *Mind Control*, create in the Crowd what is likened to members seeing themselves in the carnival's House of Mirrors. Here, there are "Fear" mirrors; Distorting Mirrors whereby one sees oneself as "Too Much" or "Too Little" or "Not Good Enough"; or "Shadow Selves" from "False Mirrors" imparting a beguiling appearance into each by receiving vital rays irregularly--thus similating a 1960s Disco dance hall "*Glitter Ball*" flashes. Any of these are absorbed when one gives up ones own inner Divine Consciousness "Soul Sunshine" birth gift so as to conform to ones society's teachings. An example of Mind Control using an unexamined assumption is the silent message that dictionaries give the "right" definition of a word. From 50 years of intense research, I know it is very rare to get the "right" definition for a life-shaping word. Since etymological story meanings of words are my hobby and from having published over 30,000 words in 5 dictionaries, it is clear that definitions given by wordsmiths are: opinions; limited by their living in a particular culture at a given time period; and the lack of world agreed upon standards. "*Etymology*" (C14, 'finding the underlying, literal, or true meaning of words') is applicable only to Essence (i.e. what a Thing was when it came into Being-hood) and to know that Source is vital. *If the Thing is Knowledge, it is derived from Pure Spiritual Elements.*

As attested to by world Sages of all Ages, Very Ancient Africans' Mathematically derived Knowledge came from Sky determinations of the Laws of Nature. By that Knowledge consisting of insights into harmonious relations between Cosmic parts of the Spiritual Elements--with each other and the whole--it was used as a path for Inferring certain conclusions for fashionings into African Tradition. Anything short of what all is involved in this process is merely *Information—meaning it is derived from a Human-made source which makes it relative, changeable, conflicting, and confusing.* Next, it is important to make *Informational definition* assessments by the *Seven Questions of Inquiry--who, which, what, when, where, why, and how* concerning each definition's formulation. Many of today's words came out of very ancient times—budding out of minds of "the savage who ascribes the mysteries of life and power to a supernatural source" and who are known to have displayed the pervasiveness of pre-logical factors characteristic of primitive mentalities. For the most part, ancient peoples could not read or write-- thus relying on stories told them. Particularly in Biblical times, these oral approaches were *Aggregative—i.e. adding details and new information to base information with each retelling*—like in the childhood game called "Whisper Down the Line" (or "Telephone"). Writings related to God require at least knowing the then prevailing concepts about that God, for there have been all sorts of Gods and non-Gods throughout the history of Supernatural adhering people. It was typical in Ancient and Medieval times for scribes to write in the voice of some authority—often unknown--in order to give it force and in fancy style.

Even the later writing processes were done by scribes oriented to oral recitations rather than to a literate orientation which dominates today's society. Those who did original recordings and then those who did subsequent transcribing throughout the ages, all engaged in *pseudepigraphic writings—i.e. stories falsely attributed to Biblical characters or times.* Also, *scribes typically altered the stories according to their own opinions.* The European term *Black Art* (Syn. Necromancy, conjuration, magic)—i.e. the art practiced by sorcerers and witches (usually for evil intents)--is a linguistic mistake having nothing to do with color. Medieval scribes wrongly substituted the Latin niger, black, for the necro (corpse) aspect of the Greco-Latin "Necromantia." Reasonable people are shocked when they read about how their Bibles were put together. Any resemblance to Reality and Truth is purely a coincidence. *Such is historical myth, not truth*! In short, *Knowledge is an experience of Reality and its Mysticism Mind.* jabaileymd.com

L

LAWS (AFRICAN TRADITION): *Ancient African Laws refer to the foundation of all Cosmic manifestations and denote a sequence of inherently related events that occur with unvarying uniformity under the same conditions. These Laws that govern Creation are stored in the Divine Spirit* and arranged in a particular format that graphically aids in the explanation of the 11 Principles, their functions, their relationship to each other and to the whole. Thus, the *work of Spirituality is the subjection of the mind to the Divine Spirit in order for it to command the Life-Force in harmony with the Laws.* TEuropeans define a Law as a rule of conduct or procedure established by custom, agreement, or authority. In *African Tradition, Laws* are the foundation of all manifestation and denote a sequence of inherently related events that occur with unvarying uniformity under the same conditions. Laws are objective, universal, consistent, and verifiable Principles—providing a sense of guarantee, security, and peace. Since the Laws governing Creation are stored in the Divine Spirit, the work of African Spirituality is the subjection of the mind to the Divine Spirit. The purpose is to command the Life-Force in harmony with the Laws. This definition applies to God's manifestations, to chemistry, physics, and biology, and to the 11 spheres of Spiritual influence operating in humans' Spirit and the Cosmos because of their relationship to energy—all based on observations of the behavior of the Spirit and the Life-force. Since African Laws are of Nature and Energy (the Spirit) they can be observed in a manner that governs ones life in an ordered function and in wellness. In other words, the quality of thinking, emotions, spiritually, and physical well-being are subject to immutable laws. To boil water requires applying laws of physics. To follow the 11 Laws Spiritual influence gives access to God's wisdom and Spiritual Power. As a result, all else that is needed or is important in life will follow (Amen, MAAT, p17-19, 55; Metu Neter III:124, 323, 327).

LAW OF ATTRACTION: the *What* and *Why* Divine Message of a human's Self is inside a Disposition—a Disposition containing its Essence nature and an Inclination (or Divine Desire). It is innate for a human's Divine Desire (i.e. the Inclination in the Divine Message) to spiritually connect and relate to the Spiritual Elements—a Divine Desire (a pre-birth Emotion), by always wanting to satisfy its Inclination, always operates by the mighty power of the *Mentative Law of Attraction*. A human's Spiritual Elements "Trademark" is like a radar sender and receptor for whatever is of like-kind and vibrates at the same rate. As a sender, its mighty power of influence manifests as the Law of Attraction which is constantly drawing towards ones "Trademark" the Things to which one is spiritually connected. Also, the Law of Attraction draws the human to those with whom one can Spiritually relate. In addition, Products of the Spiritual Elements have mosaic pieced that similarly have radar forms in keeping with the Law of Attraction. In this way it is able to determine Correspondence and detect or suspect like-kind Circumstances. Each Spiritual Elements, Shape/Pattern operates under the influence of the Law of Attraction--seeking its corresponding match from outside ones Soul as well as to maintain unity of ones Selfhood. Humans attract to themselves Thought Vibrations corresponding in Nature with those which they are in the habit of entertaining.

LAW OF AMEN: "you were made in the likeness of a peace that nothing can disturb. Reclaim your Peace that you may attain to your reasons for coming into existence—the enjoyment of life."

LAW OF HOLONOMY: the whole is inside the Seed; the whole is contained in each of the Seed's manifested parts; and the Seed is found throughout the whole.

LAWS OF NATURE: (1) Coherence (its hidden internal links and components being consistent with one another); (2) Consistency (standing firmly together within a state of harmony and balance with what makes sense); (3) Compatibility with Reality (practical); (4) Interconnectedness (everything real depends on every other real thing); (5) Order (sharing the "Oneness" of Cosmic Primordial Substance center); (6) Regularity (conforming to the prescribed standard or the established pattern for it kind); (7) Balance (rendering no favorites on either side but conforming to the Ultimate Standard); (8) Harmony (complete adaptation of each part to the Wholistic Circle); (9) Endurance (progressing inside/in tune with the Spiritual Elements); and (10) Predictability.

LAWS OF ANCIENT AFRICAN BIBLE: The Subjective Realm's *Chaos* is the forceful primordial state of undifferentiated universal existence which is ever ready to express itself in the Material Realms in an Orderly (i.e. Mathemetical) fashion. When Chaos is called on to do this, two things happen. First, progressive Evolution means the Spiritual Elements express progressively thicker forms of Matter. Second, it establishes Order--which was so important to Ancient Africans that its absence was explained as the Supreme Being's inability to find a place where It could stand in the world. Material World Order begins with *Divine Archetypes* ("Seeds") coming into Being as pre-figurements of something or someone to come afterwards--each containing a complete and pure complement of the Spiritual Elements. Its specific Genetic combination supplies everything for it to complete its purpose for being. A given *Divine Archetype* represents some Cosmic Entity, like the Animal Kingdom; or another "Seed" for the Plant Kingdom; or the Truth "Seed". In turn, each Archetype fashions eternal *Prototypes* (i.e. Form-Ideas) on lesser planes of existence--e.g. the phenomena of Matter or some Form Truth--each having Certainty. To illustrate with the Tree Concept--from the Truth "Seed" evolves Truth *Prototype Patterns* in a certain Order--likened to Roots, a Trunk/Vines, Branches, Leaves, and Fruit Truths. Its *Order* is the framing of Laws of Nature or Energy (the Spirit), and having nothing to do with Supernatural authoritative prohibitions or rules of conduct in the way Europeans are accustomed to considering Order. African Spiritual Order is explainable by certain Laws known by both Subjective Science--i.e. Observation, Reflection, "Pure" Feelings, Productive Imagination, Contemplation, Inductive and Deductive Inferences, and Common Sense as well as Objective Science (e.g. astro-mathematics). Thus, it is evident that each Prototype gives rise to like-kind things which then branch. The reason is the Divine Archetype Seed of Truth conforms to the *Law of Holonomy* (i.e. the whole is inside the Seed; the whole is contained in each of the Seed's manifested parts; and the Seed is found throughout the whole). This Law makes applicable the *Law of Spiritual Creativity* (by itself, a Spiritual Element reproduces itself to become the thing it makes, regardless of its new form). On an Earth World level it is an ongoing repetition of the nature of the original Thoughts manifesting in compatible behavior. As a result of these Laws, any off-spring branch of a Prototype Truth is like the African *Law of (Spiritual) Circularity*: the Spiritual offspring is proven by the parent and the Spiritual parent is proven by the Spiritual offspring--simply, the child copies the mother and the mother is the equivalent of the child. To know the essence of one is to know the other--a concept of Algebra, like X = Y. Because the Prototype of the Archetype Tree is present on all planes of Cosmic Existence, the X = Y concept illustrates the Qualitative Mathematics aspect of the Law of Correspondence. African inferences allow for expanding beyond Ancient Africans' abilities to "prove" this by direct evidence. And yet Circumstantial Evidence was acceptable because all derived out of established Truths which, in turn, establishes Truths. So, based on the above Laws, what develops within that context and then out of the Spiritual Elements would be part of the Spiritual Laws. In short, there is "Sameness" in every Archetype's offspring. Thus, each Truth + Unconditional Love, Reality, and the Natural, construct all Cosmic Real and Natural things. The Prototype *Form-Ideas* (an African concept plagiarized by Plato) are self-realizable Divine ideas because they are patterns fixed in Nature. These "blueprints" that organize a structured Cosmos exist before anything happens in the Objective Realm, including the Initiation and Manifestation of the Ether. The Idea-Form giver of off-spring and their steadfast bonds internally link all things to which they give rise. Prototypes are made in their image and also display as resemblances of their Archetypes. Idea-Forms + Chaos--X = Y--enabled Ancient Africans to create the "equal sign" + the use of *symbols for unknowns (e.g. in algebra)* + *Inductive and deductive reasoning* + abstract Ma'at concepts of "Fairness," Justice," etc. + the *Principle of Polarity*.

LAWS OF NATURE: Laws of Nature in its *Natural Processes*. Those processes it follows were derived out of the Cosmic Mind's establishment of the Essence Pattern of "Oneness"—a Pattern possessing: (1) Coherence (its hidden internal links and components being consistent with one another); (2) Consistency (standing firmly together within a state of harmony and balance with what makes sense); (3) Compatibility with Reality (practical); (4) Interconnectedness (everything real depends on every other real thing); (5) Order; (6) Regularity (conforming to the prescribed standard or the established pattern for it kind); (7) Balance (rendering no favorites on either side but conforming to the Ultimate Standard); (8) Harmony (complete adaptation of each part to the Wholistic Circle); (9) Endurance (progressing inside/in tune with the Spiritual Elements); and (10) Predictability. This means there is *Continuity* (Unity running through Multiplicity) from all of its components interdependently doing their independent things for the benefit of the whole. See Mathematics; Reasoning

LEADERSHIP BY BLACK SCHOLARS: The Old English word "*Leader*" as related to "Leadership" originally referred to "*Lead*" as to 'cause to go along ones way'; 'show the way'; guide; pass beyond. In 1570, it was the place in front and now, going ahead of in order to guide. In general, "Leaders" direct or conduct by preceding measures -- i.e. the action of showing the way to something or someone. To lead a horse to water is guiding the horse to follow without resistance. One who leads a band is a conductor. Some leading is by pushing, pulling, drawing, or dragging -- whether forward/backward, up/down, sideways, or side to side. Such applies to one leading oneself; by intentionally leading others; and/or by unintentionally leading others. Lead does not necessarily imply the exercise of force but one must be confident in public. A leader may draw out, as in moving someone or something to a new place or toward itself or in the direction of its own motion or natural inclination. The exertion of adequate pushing/pulling forces may range from mild to extreme. Or the drawing may be by forces of attraction--with motion involved or without motion. When in a position of leadership there is a "machine-gunning" rapidity of problems never seen or heard of before that hit almost daily. Despite having very little information and despite multiple variables, each problem is to be handled immediately--and with excellence--and in the face of opposition—and without help because no one understands the situation or what needs to be done. SII have chosen to go through life by their own developed ways of thinking and self-reliance. People with Selfhood Greatness know that with time, energy, and effort properly directed, they will be able to solve any problem. This Grit to eagerly take as a challenge to learn new ways of thinking supersedes the abilities of those said to be smarter. Setbacks and Defeats provide information that pave the way for trouble-shooting and going back to the "drawing board." Step I: there is never a thought of "I Can't." Never complain for that takes away your power. Know that there is no one better suited to do the job--since Experts do not brush their teeth any better that you. Instead, they do it differently. What is left from the disaster just experienced is an opportunity to build something better than before. Do the "9 Ps" process: Preparing to Prepare; Purpose; Plan; Planes of Existence; Preparation; Practice; Performance; Platform; and Post-Action Judgments, with post-action judgments at each step. Meet each problem faced with creativity—and not doing what has always worked before because this situation is new, despite its "sameness" features of old. Step II: use Spiritual Energy which generates "Aliveness". This means there are no limits. Emotional Energy burns out quickly and leads one to get involved in attractive distractions. That causes one to feel limited and putting a limit on any aspect of ones life causes it to spread everywhere. Step III: eliminate half of what you do daily and prioritize the rest into Necessary, Important, and Wants—and do them in that order. Step IV: have no opinion about what has to be done—no expectations—no fears—no dislikes. Step V: There is no place for short-cuts or sloppy work—even if no one will see it. The key is to "Over-Prepare." Do it perfectly—paying attention to all details—so as to have self-pride. It does not matter what others think. In everything thought, felt, expressed, and done, it ought to be better today than yesterday. Step VI: Know that you will have to travel alone—because you can move faster and because insecure people feel worse from being around those making progress. A sad oddity in today's culture is that besides there being a high price to pay for cultivating ones Self-Greatness, one must pay an equally ongoing high price for possessing Self-Greatness and its associated successes.

LEARNING: In the honorable society of Ancient Africans the people had "*Positive Learning*" as a way of life. This is like from learning how to drive a car enables one to drive a bus, tractor, or airplane with only a few adjustments. All of this changed for the Enslaved African American where there was "*Negative Learning*." By learning the pattern of no longer "Knowing" about God and instead switching to having Faith/Belief in God according to the evil brainwashing information imparted by Europeans made it easier to replace their "Positive Learning" as a way of life and in wide-spread aspects of their lives. The Enslaved were taught that "the highest knowledge of God is in not knowing -- one has to let go of trying to grasp with ones intellect -- that is why knowing you do not know is important and cannot know." This was in keeping with Ancient Africans but its European subtly was in representing only one side of the "God" coin. The other side is that one can Know God exists by God's manifestations. Still, a strong sense of God was brought in by Enslaved Africans from their African Tradition and that was so engrained as to persist through the hellishness of slavery and the post-slavery period. Only recently has it begun to start fading. Meanwhile, religion in the "*Negro Church*" setting during slavery was the main way of releasing pent up bad Emotions and experiencing a moment of pleasure. This combination of African Retention wrapped in the social benefits of the Church help account for the Emotionality that characterizes wide areas of Black religion. Whereas African Tradition uses the Supernatural as a Metaphysical Realm support to explain Spiritual Reality by means of Figures of Communication, Europeans are divided on its reality, significance, and usages. LEARNING is the process of acquiring refined knowledge attained through the process of the Learning Tools: LISTENING to wisdom teachings on the nature of reality (creation) and the nature of the Self. REFLECTING on those teachings--a process of analyzing events in terms of their grounds and implications so that judgments and principles could be formed and incorporated into daily living. Then MEDITATING on the meanings of the teachings. Reflection and Meditation (quieting the mind) are done until one returns to ones Real Self where there is a natural communication with Universal Energy—the realm of Wisdom. The Spiritual Energy in these Powers motivate one to start or to continue seeking to know what one does not know and would ordinarily believe one could never know. The most outstanding aspect of *Intuitional Knowledge*—by making one come "Alive"--is it opens new channels to the Spiritual Elements that ever undergo expansion. It also devises patterns of procedure that are transferrable to other areas. At the least, if one does not understand something or someone, gaining more details about how they got to be the way they are enables greater acceptance of the "That's the Way it is!" aspect, despite not accepting what it or they do. *Sensibilities Knowledge* comes from noticing resemblances and recurrences in the events which are within mental reach. When converted to Common Sense, it becomes plain and simple. That contributes to developing Wisdom.

LEARNING KNOWLEDGE PROCESS--When one has a sense of the infinity of knowledge about the Spiritual Elements, that carries one beyond the best of what one presently knows. As long as one stays in that flow and develops "ME/WE" products out of it, one will on the path to gaining as much meaning in ones life as is required to have a thriving and happy life. Both are realized by one continuing to unfold ones Private

Selfhood powers in the process of living productively by serving an end beyond oneself, as in providing things of Worth to others. Examples of Worth are Beauty, Goodness, Happiness, Wellness, and living in a Natural Order. This involves transcending the Crowd. Note that this process is very different from simply living a life based upon the meaning one gives to it. By staying in the flow of the Spiritual Elements one is always in the infinity of Knowledge and that Knowledge is known without the necessity for proof, since it is a self-evident Process of Nature. This means an effortless learning that enlarges ones Consciousness beyond the boundariless bounds of Understanding. Each time the subject comes up in any manner there are new Outer World sources to draw on. In addition, somewhere in the back of ones mind new Inner World ingredients have resulted from manipulating and maneuvering prior ingredients about the subject into different arrangements and combinations. With or without effort, what continues to happen in ones mind is the inner layers covering the core message of the Essence of the subject imparts new insights. Each new Insight enables the flowing out of richer meanings in each involved part of the subject as well as flowing out from the sum of the Whole. *To discover something new or even hear old wisdom over and over means the acquiring of a new perspective. This is the application of the Box Concept*--viewing matters so as inspect each side--the inside and outside details of every angle—inspecting the top and bottom and any wrappings--turning it in all directions--looking at it from underneath--seeing it from one view after another--holding it against the sky and imagining it in any material or even in glass--and thinking of all types of options based upon fashioning powerful meanings indirectly. Each of these new perspectives, insights, and meanings allows for the acquiring of more in-depth understanding of the Principles (pieces of the Truth or of the Unchanging Reality) which, in turn, peels away another top covering layer. Going beyond human recognizable knowledge means transcending into an ever increasing deeper realm of the Cosmos while, in the process, engaging in its reality flow—a flow that is a natural part of Cosmic Knowledge. The Effect of being in this flow is ones Experience of participation in Cosmic reality. The result is an ever widening of the scope of knowledge of the topic as well as all things associated with the topic. The various discovered principles can be prioritized into a Tree Concept of a Seed, Roots, Trunk, Branches, Leaves, and Fruit. By being aspects of the Spiritual Elements means that understanding and properly applying any one part of the Tree is the Truth and that is to be looked for in any subject. Yet, the Seed is what serves as the Base upon which the rest of the Tree arises. The Essence contained inside the Seed is the fixed and invariable meaning of every natural Thing. This entire process of *Synthesis happens because the whole is greater than the sum of its parts.* This Circumstantial route to the Spiritual Elements "Feels" right in ones Selfhood Center. This "Feeling" is known to be from ones Spiritual Emotions and not from ones Acquired Emotions because it spurs "Aliveness"—that Spiritual Energy which continually urges one to Self-Improve for "ME/WE" purposes. Acquired Emotions are Emotional Energy addicted to "Excitement" in the "here and now" and it provides nothing that is about self-improvement—being like running hard on a treadmill and going nowhere.

LEARNING BACKGROUND FUNDAMENTALS: Ancient Africans' term for "Learning" ('mathesis') came from astrological divination and meant 'Mother Wisdom' (the highest form of Common Sense). The Old English (725) word "Learn" (to get knowledge, be cultivated) carries the underlying notion of gaining experience by following along a track—a track that can be natural, acquired, or a natural one altered by an acquired superimposition. Broadly, learning is present whenever there is relatively permanent change in an organism's behavior resulting from its reaction to environmental influences. This may occur to the developing fetus in the mother's womb (Congenital Learning) or throughout ones lifetime following birth. "*Congenital*" *Learning* comes about by external influences (e.g. the mother's mood, dietary intake) that fashion a "track". That 'Learning Track' may affect the developing fetus in utero so that its behavior alterations are manifest in utero, at birth in the newborn, or as "Congenital Tarda" displays (congenital/developmental aspects present before or at birth but that do not flower until sometime after birth). To be distinguished from learning are changes in behavior derived from: (a) maturation from *Inheritance* (genetic parental derived predisposition transmissions)—i.e. normal growth and development which occurs as long as the organism is adequately nourished. A newborn's eyes, for example, cannot follow a moving object but by age 6 months she/he is able to be in control of head turning so as to follow the moving object; (b) from temporary changes such as sensory adaptation or fatigue and warming-up; and (c) miscellaneous factors, as from disease, injury, or by drugs. The complex subject of Natural Learning includes the *"Heritable"*—a term wrongly considered essentially synonymous with 'Genetic' and 'Inherited'--because it includes both. '*Inherited*' implies genes are transferred from parent to child while Mutations, along with the inherited genes, may result in new genes in a *zygote* (the union, yoking, fusion of the male spermatozoon and the female ovum to give a fertilized egg). This is the foundation upon which all "Genetic" learning of any organism rests. These, termed "Innate," are important for learning in that they are the paths for basic responses + being the started of basic drives for learning + fixing, at least within limits, possible levels of maximum performance. But to aid understanding, let us review two key definitions. First is a *Stimulus* (spur)—a 1684 word originally designating a goad used for driving cattle by pricking them. Today it means spurring to action or effort, as a needle against the skin or a signal acting on ones senses or a printed or spoken word serving as a call to action. Second, ways humans/animal react to a stimulus is called a *Response* (to answer)—i.e. something offered in return, almost as an obligation (hence 'Responsible'). Its Ancient African origin was Griots (story-tellers) participatory audience communication—i.e. "*Call and the Response*"--characterized by the Griot sending out a "call" and the audience acknowledging the message. The audience responded while the speaker spoke--and not afterward--so as to make a fluid harmonious tone of participatory communication. A stimulus response is an act, usually a movement—ranging from Mild (like the twitch of a muscle or the blink of an eyelid) all the way over to the Extreme (e.g. one 'jumping' from a door closing). Innate responses are termed *Reflex* ('turn or bend back') and may be brought about not only by the action of sense organs and the nervous system or by other means (e.g. images).

One innate example is respiration which is, in part, chemically controlled. Some responses are also subject to hormonal control. Type I Innate Responses—i.e. Instincts--are the somewhat undifferentiated mass activity involving a large number of muscles. Babies can be observed twisting, rolling, arching, and waving of the hands and feet. Type II are Reflexes—relatively simple responses to stimuli and are dependent on nerve pathways that develop with the normal growth of the organism. An *Unconditioned Reflex* occurs in the scenario where stimuli trigger responses without any learning. An example is reflexly pulling ones hand away when it touches a hot stove—an instinct reaction helping to keep one alive and healthy. Type III are more complex and integrated types of innate behaviors, as exemplified by combined Instincts and *Tropisms* (the movement of an organism or a part toward or away from an external stimulus, such as light, heat, or gravity). jabaileymd.com

LEARNING FUNDAMENTALS: The Innate aspects for Reflexes, Tropisms, Instincts, glandular secretions, and the like are important for learning since they constitute its raw materials. Part of an organism's Innate aspects includes various needs, drives, or urges—so as to acquire, to defend, or to avoid. Also, one will keep reacting to specific problematic stimuli until they are removed. Or, one immediately seeks to acquire food to satisfy hunger but, if not hungry, one does not do so. Learning is information or knowledge gained by "*Education*" ("to lead out what is inside"); "*Teaching*" ("to show" so as to impart knowledge for learning); *Instructing* ("to build in or into"), or "*Training*" (active mind exercising in order to form habits)—in short, by study, reflection, and/or practice--depending upon the topic. For example, *Motor Skills* such as riding a bicycle, can be learned without using words. *Mental Skills* such as playing board games or problem solving require thinking, learning from experience, and an assortment of things which are useful at times and then, to varying degrees (e.g. recognizing shapes, understanding numbers, reading). The core around which such learning occurs might be ones past experiences; the ingredients of Sensation out of ones memory; something going on inside ones Selfhood; something entering a human's senses from the outside world; ones interpretations of the monitored feedback one gets from outside influences; or a combination of these. Then relationships are seen that enable assessments of what is involved in light of ones own experiences. "Connections" are made to form significant meanings which pave the way to expansive learning and the setting of standards. It is more important to learn what not to learn. Part of knowledge is to be ignorant of what is not worth knowing. Just because the "Crowd" or even authorities say something is right does not make it so. They may be 'right' but on the wrong path or going in the wrong direction or what they say may be located on the wrong plane of existences. It is better to learn one thing well before going to the next thing. When learning is at a wisdom level, one has *Vision*.

LEARNING RESPONSES: As a boy living in Minnesota, following a heavy snow I would walk through it so as to admire the tracks I had just made. Sometimes I would walk backwards, being careful to step exactly in the same tracks I originally made. This is like the nervous system's tendency, when it has once acted in a certain manner, to duplicate that same manner again. Memory is but another phase of that same tendency. Like making tracks in the snow, *Engrams* are neuronal patterns of an acquired skilled act of learning—a process dependent on a Trance. A Learning Trance is a withdrawal from the External World while in a calm and peaceful mindset so that ones resultant total receptivity benefits programming of mental events. A Trance's aids an Engram with its physiological and emotional functions as part of becoming illogical and irrational memories (simply because they are outside the realm of Reason). That memory retains all that has ever been experienced and they serve as patterns for imitation or cultivation. Though memories may be difficult to recall from being repressed, they still exert powerful influences in shaping ones beliefs and behaviors. Meanwhile, they have been associated on the basis of external qualities and when those qualities are touched upon, they often give recall to prior experiences associated with them. Such causes Trance to accelerate learning 2 to 50 times enabled ancient Black nations to forge in cultures and civilizations far, far ahead of Western and Eastern nations (Amen, Metu Neter I:168). Trance also helps so to develop ones higher mental and spiritual faculties, thereby enabling the effective coping with and transcending of their emotional dysfunctions. For me, this boundary-less Spiritual Elements state is entered by totally focusing on the issue at hand and continuing to do so while constructing patterns made of dream-like intangibles. But it only works for "ME/WE" purposes. Since Normal people do "Life-Living" out of their Lower (animalistic) Self—e.g. desires, Secular passions, and appetites, both disciplined and undisciplined—and pursue "Emotional Excitement" (a childish trait), they have a False Self. While in a Trance state characterizing the child's high degree of receptivity and emotionality, the decision to enter ones False Self is to be attracted indiscriminately to and engage in imitation. All imitations of what is External to oneself is off the Real Self learning path. False Self people are in a perpetual state of Trance—as with habitual ways of thinking, emoting, desiring, and capabilities. These define ones Secular Self-Identity (i.e. "Personality"). One enters a Trance with each strong emotion, desire, sensation, "spaced out," in "suspense," "absent minded," or devotion to places or things. It is thus that one cultivates or reinforces negative behaviors since one is not mindful of what self-destructive thoughts one takes into the Trance. By being Self-Unknown and not having developed their Intellect within the stream of the Spiritual Elements, their indiscriminate imitation of the "crowd" + society's Trinkets and Trivia + Flashing Light gadgets destroys thinking skills. These keep them in the status quo—and showered with problems. Emotional mindsets fail them because to recall memories and the external qualities associated with them means emotional colors and exaggerations have been added to both. Hence, they misunderstand more than they understand. That means they deceive themselves in assembling their "Personality" (Secular Self-Identity) out of distorted or fantasy entities—most being other people's statements used to define oneself. The same applies to perceptions through the senses. A typical result is: "I'm not good enough"—and that wrongly refers to External World thinking limited to the Physical and Supernatural realm. Attempts to make life-changing habit changes fail because ones chronic tension, Emotional Energy, lack of analytical thinking skills, and being pervaded and possessed with ignorant information—most SEEMING alright--is antagonistic to change. The process of awakening to begin the journey to ones Highest Self is to "detrance" or "dehypnotize" ones Consciousness away from ones "Personality" in order to re-establish with ones Real Self ones Self-Identity (Amen, Metu Neter II:88). Half of what does in daily life is useless and should be eliminated. It takes volition to cultivate ones divine Self-Image, using reasoned understanding within the Spiritual Elements so as to fashion Selfhood *Order and consistent Patterns underlying ones behaviors*.

LEARNING--METAPHYSICAL: e.g. delving into the infinity of knowledge and going beyond knowledge) is looking past Materialism and its "Concreteness" to see what is boundary-less—and that helps explain why Black People are so Creative. Metaphysical Learning demands removal of rules and boundaries and replace that with Guidelines (where mistakes are allowed) while flowing in the Boundless (e.g. Spiritual Elements). Next, there is more than reading the profound statement and understanding what that means. It is like adding fluid to a dried sponge so it can get increasing pliable and less rigid. What to look for and extract is the Essence/Principle (the Unchanging Reality) in order for it to be explored according to the Box Concept. Once all of the meanings are spotlighted, wallow in each until they are internalized. Throughout this entire process leisure (the African definition of scholar) is needed to deal with each ingredient involved in the process. Such is always to be done completely while in its energy flow, so as to get every little detail out of it. Finish by Mulling on it—i.e. stay quiet so that ones Selfhood keeps combining and arranging ingredients into new forms that give new insights. That moments of pregnant insights will never appear again because of the situation being bathed and showered with its Thought Cloud of Spiritual Energy. The time spent doing this process, though seeming to take a long by those who live a "I'm too busy" life, will be paid back a thousand fold that lost time. One is in the automatic ways of doing things out of ones Philosophical Warehouse—what one uses to make Emergency Decisions when there is no time to think. I never look down on anyone for we are all part of the Cosmic Organism. Yet, I do not allow others Indifference/Hate/Evil/Sadism (IHES) to affect my life. Nor do I engage in IHES. It is from the setting of desiring those struggling through no fault of their own to succeed that I do my presentations.

LEGEND: *Metaphors* (equates unlike things by implication), *Simile* (the abstract or suggestive aspect is directly expressed), *Allegories* (a hidden story within an obvious story), *Fables* (animals impersonating humans to impart a moral), *Personification* (making a lifeless or abstract thing alive), *Analogies* (explaining something unfamiliar by comparing it to something familiar), *Legend* (a story, above mere fiction, combining fact and personified spiritual concepts), and *Symbols* (symbolic messages disregard the limitations and boundaries of human thought in order to impart ideas of the indescribable).

LIAISONS: that form of "*Civility*" (a congenial Deceptive tool to hide ones opposing true thoughts and emotions of what is presented) where people support like-kind people but lack close associations between them. *Alliances* are mutually helpful participants who are psychologically and philosophically disconnected from each other—and yet feature the sharing of common character traits, like the IHES mindset. Its Alliances and Liaisons forms prevent cult members from being isolated from the Crowd.

LIBATION: *Libations*--a practice built upon the Law of Sympathy inside the concept of Wholism—are performed as an act of pouring water. It denotes its transformation as it passes from the *Lunar Order* (the world of transient forms and feelings) to the *Solar Order* (the world of fixed forms and of reason). At this point the water now consists of the "Upper Ocean" (of Nun)--or vital fluid, suggesting universal life and ceaseless circulation through formation, regeneration, and purification. In the process, any words given are in the form of prayer, invocations, or instructions to the departed. These words are the bridge of communion and people's *witness* (to observe and testify to) that they recognize the departed as alive in the Other World. By performing rites and rituals, the performers transcend time, space, and limitation to connect not only with their fellow African people but also with their dead Ancestors who created those rites and rituals. The reason is that the performer(s) is a necessary part of the Afrocentric "Group Spirit." See Ancestors

LIFE FORCES: Very Ancient African Priest-astronomers' study of the Stars and their Mathematical calculations led to their inference of Cosmic *Homology*--i.e. a similarity in fundamental plans of the Cosmic structure, indicative of an evolutionary "Genetic Sameness" in all living forms. They inferred all of this was powered by what they called the "Cosmic Life Force"--the vital Substance/Essence of God's Creatures and Creations and symbolized by the Ankh. As a manifestation of the "Cosmic Life Force," Ancient Nubians and Ancient Egyptians concept of "the breath" gave rise to the word "*Spirituality*". Hence, Spirituality implies breathing the Essence of God. This Cosmic-Spirit, by being present in all embraced under the term Homology, implies resemblance in relationships between all of God's Creatures and Creations as well as it penetrates, pervades, and enlivens each and all. Also, whether in reference to all or to each, the Life Forces display simultaneously as independent and interdependent, self-assertive and integrative, as well as whole unto themselves. Yet, each and all are always a part of systems larger than themselves. In humans, the "Life Force" or transfigured "God-Image Spirit" provides inner spiritual illumination by being "a kind of individualized fragment of the Supreme Being." In other words, the presence of God's "Life Force" in each human--the image or Spark of God--forms that human's Highest or Divine Self called the "Eternal *Soul*." Similarly, just as God's Substance/Essence reflection underlying and surrounding each Star is called a Halo, so is there a Halo--called the Astral "Heart"--around human's Eternal Soul. Within a given human, Ancient Africans said the Life Force of the human's Eternal and Astral Soul engenders the impetus in the DNA to function (Asbhy, African p422) according to the messages within one or both Souls. Some functions pertain to the Spiritual Knowing (e.g. Survival urges). Some functions concern Human "Knowing" (e.g. Subconscious Knowing e.g. Epic Memory; Collective Unconscious). Some are Astral Body "Knowing", as seen in a human's fundamental abilities of Sensory Consciousness. These abilities include: Likes/Dislikes/Desires/Possession; Sense of action/reaction; Distinction/Perception/Sex attraction; and Thinking/imaging/imitating. To elaborate on one, as a Spiritual Life Force "Unconditional Love" has nothing against which it can be compared. Any attempts to compare it with anything known to humans only introduces illusional concepts of it. The Life Force in the Astral Body contains ones called the Ka by Ancient Kemetics. It embraces ones Astral Personality--which includes ones Emotions and Mind fashioning the patterns of habitual mental, emotional, and physical characteristics that distinguish an individual. This Divine Astral Personality, originally and naturally powered by ones Life Force, is the nature of ones Persona in African Tradition. The Persona's distinguishing features--ones conveyed image, the mental attributes characterizing the extent of ones Genius, and the disposition of ones Character, is called ones *Real Self 'Social Personality.'* Yet, humans have the choice of something else—and any such choice is ones *False Self*, orchestrated by ones chosen Ego type (e.g. aggressive, passive, passive-aggressive).

LIFE FORCE SPIRITUAL ESSENCES--AFRICAN TRADITION: Ancient African Sages said the "Soul of the Cosmos" or "Life Force" or the Cosmic KA--represents the body of the one universal high God in its diffused state throughout all Nature. It is God's Androgynic plast Substance, consisting of the Spiritual Elements "Genetics" for God' creatures, including each human, and constituting "Nature's" Divine Archetype. This implies the Life Force is both the continuity of Being and the shared essence of Being pertaining to the

Cosmic Force in relation to each Cosmic Organism Being. Hence, the Being of an Entity corresponds to the Divine Plan. In other words, the Entity's Ka originates from the one universal high God Atum and results from the transmission of the Essence of Atum's Being into humans (i.e. as a drop or spark of God). Ones Divine Spirit's power is composed of subtle electromagnetic energies—Ancient Africans called "*animal spirit*" ("anima and animus" in Latin spiritual tradition)--possessing the functions of animating a human's life, especially the physical body. That "animal spirit" then activates the *inactive* Spiritual Energy which, in turn, activates the undifferentiated/unstructured potential Matter by adding an attribute of God--the Ether (i.e. Life's Force). The Ether provides what is necessary to give shape or form to the Will's embryonic Image and thereby starts an evolutionary process towards the Thing designated by the Disposition's 'blue-print'. This concept of all humans possessing a shared nature or essence with the Divine Force became a fundamental tenet of Maatian anthropology and central to the concept of human potentiality and power. Involuted (wrapped up) in the "Genetics" of the Ka (Soul) is a "spirit moving force" which, as a Spark of God, is Collectively imparted into every human in the Cosmic Organism in an undifferentiated (but not disorganized) state constituting a creative power of continuous integration. That "Animal Spirit" ('Khaibit'), called Ether, permeates, animates, and informs all, from the smallest atom of Matter to humans. So, each human's Ka, or inner nature, is "Unique" and yet has a "Sameness" with all Humankind. An analogy is the "Sameness" Genetics of children of the same parents operate in different combinations, like "combination locks." The Life-Force is Spiritual Power what is required to carry out Spiritual Work and is called Ra, Kundalini, Shekina, Shekhem (Sekhem). The Ether portion is programmed for preservation of ones survival with instincts, curiosity, motivation, sense perceptions, sensuality, sensory/motor nervous powers, physiological functions, fighting, fleeing, and other motions. Yet, humans are born with ingredients to develop their Higher (Spiritual) Self mind to rise above their already developed Lower (animalistic Secular world) Self minds. The type and nature depends upon the close connection between the Imagination, the Ancient (Reptilian) and Mammalian Brains of a human, for their manifestation of Pure Emotions and sensual energies are all expressions of the Life-Force. Humans' Ancient Brain have three unique subdivisions. First, the *Instinct Brain,* powered by the Divine Plan, orchestrates what to do in emergencies and without thought. It is associated with the Fear and Rage "Alarm Centers" in accord with the Survival Law of Nature. Since the Instinct part of the human brain is made of "Ether," it receives mental currents of Cosmic "Ether" which flow through it under the term "*Feelings*" (vibrations from the Will of God). It also unconsciously does the constant work of repair, replacement, change, digestion, elimination, assimilation, and health maintenance. Second, similarly but to a somewhat lesser degree, is the queer storehouse called the *Omnibus Brain* (instincts with thought). Habits learned on the Intellectual plane are passed to the Omnibus Brain for automatic powering. Third, the anti-Spiritual Elements' *Brute Brain* accounts for evil and sadistic deeds. Emanations from each Ancient brain part also create Thoughts. A human Will partners with the brain's Cerebrum so its *Animating Electromagnetic Energies* can domination orchestrating ones physical body. Through the resultant images and Emotions one can arouse the forces of Nature within oneself and through these affect the environment and other people. The dominant Pure Emotion is Higher Self Enjoyment which, when partnered with Imagination, is the maintainer of one health and powers the factors that shape ones successes in life by energizing the Images that attract and organize all ingredients affecting ones destiny.

LIFE FORCE—SUPERNATURAL: The Cosmic Life-Force is Spiritual Power what is required to carry out Spiritual Work and is called Ra, Kundalini, Shekina, Shekhem, etc. Springing out of the Spiritual Life Force is pre-matter (also called *Universal Energy* or Ch'i, Ether, Prana) and Spiritual Energy is everything known to exist as forms on different planes of existence and with varying degrees of differentiation. The process is initially involution and eventually evolution into *Universal Matter.* It is outwardly expressed as the animal spirit--the Khaibit—the essence of living Beings which carries out the physiological and psychical functions of humans. Its integrity is chiefly governed by a special way of breathing (the breath's nutriment) and by the Law of Cycles (Amen, Tree of Life p205). It is the infinite complexity, yet perfect order of the world—and the infinite number of Things and types are evidences that the Cosmos is the product of an all knowing and all powerful Being. Although it cannot be seen (it is hidden) its Presence is evident by the Intelligence and Power underlying the Cosmos. One is born with a dynamic Lower (animalistic) Self and an unrealized Reality Higher (Divinity) Self. Under or over indulgence of ones Lower (animalistic) Self results in Supernatural Life-Force which is automatically about failure in life. The reason is a Supernatural Life-Force consist of Acquired Emotional Fettered Energy powered by undifferentiated Hatred. That Energy is also of an electromagnetic nature, having the power of animating some part of ones animal spirit will which, if unchecked, negatively influences the physical body to create illness, unhappiness, and failure. This is because these Endosomatic electric currents that a living organism produces serves as a continuously flowing source of stimulation for whatever part of the Ancient Brain that is dominating ones psychic movements of inclinations towards what is "For me" and away from what is "Against me". That principle acts as mediator of ones sense perceptions, Emotions, desires, sensations (Pleasure/Pain), and physiological functions—regardless of whether its nature is realistic, distorted, or fantasy. It begins out of ones *Omnibus Brain* which, despite being most valuable as a servant, is a tyrant when out of control in a lifestyle totally oriented to Materialism as the means to ones life's end. Thus, the *Omnibus Brain*, in conjunction with the adjacent Old Mammalian Brain, is the seat of the appetites, passions, desires, sensations, and emotions. This graduates into Indifference which, in turn leads to the anti-Spiritual Elements which characterizes the *Brute Brain's Hate, Evil, and Sadistic* deeds. The Brute Brain effects in the Material Earth world in the form of a Radar type action. Radar acts like a ball thrown against a wall that, in turn, will bound back into the space through which it came. The same happens when an electric current, heat, or sound (a wave of radiant energy), or ray of light strikes upon a surface—is turned back, or reflected. If a power source stimulates this to keep repeating, electric currents reverberate. The reverberation is cyclic, with each cycle mutually reinforcing the Cause and the Effect. When the reverberations is at a high level because of rapid rates of vibrations between ones Soul and the like-kind Thing it attracts in the External World or from a Perception formulated within ones Inner Vision World, an "Alarm" will go off—indicating a "That's It!" meshing. Conative power is in Mild, Slight, Moderate, and Extreme degrees—driven, said Ancient Africans by "animal spirits" ('Khaibit,' Ether). *Velleity* implies a Mild or weak desire or inclination so insignificant that one makes little or no attempt to realize it by actions. Such is present in non-racists Europeans who benefit by "White Privilege". To make this okay, they exercise Willful Ignorance—choosing a refusal to know—issuing from cowardice, pride, crowd addiction, laziness of mind, or "Me, Me, Me" self-interest. Its distinction from apathy is: "I don't know and I don't care!" Extreme or Brute conative power is conviction behind its absolutely deliberate Willful (Volitional) Ignorance--an active aversion to knowledge opposing their Confirmation Biases. European mental health specialists call this the "Dark Triad" of Personality—i.e. psychopathy [I substitute a Normal Variant Philosophy of life], narcissism, and Machiavellianism. It shares a propensity for callous exploitation and being a 'killer' is done at every opportunity for its sheer "sick" pleasures alone—particularly when there is direct physical contact.

LIFE FORCES--DISPLAYS OF EUROPEAN SUPERNATURAL: According to Ancient Africans, the Ka of no human is innately evil, even if it has inherited some evil qualities from past lives. It always comes to this life in a neutral state because the Soul, after ones death, passes through the *"River of Forgetfulness"* prior to birth and is born innocent. Yet, the Ka is not strong but, instead, is so subtle and delicate that its Spiritual nature can be easily overcome by anti-Spiritual Elements type habits, by behavioral attitudes, and by cultural pressures. For Europeans, "*Culture*" is the sum total of the ways built up by a society and passed on to following generations—or what is excellent in the Arts, or a specific stage in the expression of a society (Amen, Metu Neter II:97). By contrast, in African Tradition, "*Culture*" means the formalized methods of cultivating—i.e. shaping behavior in a people in ways opposite to the animalistic influences of the older portions of the brain, including the Brute Brain. If someone prevents the good qualities of ones Ka from being expressed—or suppresses them—one will become "sick" in all areas of think, feel, say, and deeds. These become "Raw Nerves" that are so personally painful as to devise all sorts of "Tricks" to hide them from oneself and from others—aiming to appear and be thought of as just the opposite. Just as the Imagination is the gateway to the forces of Nature for Real Self (Spiritual Life Force powered people), the Brute Brain orchestrates mindsets in the direction of *Monomania* (an obsession with one idea or subject that is thought about constantly). That process cultivates ones Lower Self "Animal Spirit" into what characterizes the "*Dark Side*". That path, in turn, leads these Non-Rational mindsets into the realm of *Teratological Beings*—a Greek term for Wonder or Monster. Historically, Supernatural thinkers have used Superstitious legends to explain any departure from normal, whether plant, animals, or humans. If a woman gave birth to a deformed child, it was believed she was being punished for some evil or that she had suffered a serious shock while pregnant. From this was formed Chimaeric symbols of complex evil, the most well known being the European Devil, particularly of a *Phantasmata* nature. The Phantasmagoric are sensory images received passively from some external object and have the peculiarity of the Receiver not being aware of them. They have been mentally imaged into Monsters after 4 major groups of abnormalities: (1) *Hemiterata*—e.g. giants and dwarfs; deformities of the head or stomach; albinism; club feet; curvature of the spine; (2) *Heterotaxics*—abnormal arrangement of body organs—e.g. the heart on the right side, the liver on the left; (3) *Hermaphrodites*—those having reproductive organs of both sexes; and (4) *Monsters*—i.e. disease acting upon the embryonic organism as a result of arrested development—manifested by rudimentary brain, arms, or legs; or fused legs, feet, eyes, and other organs. In Double Monsters there is a duplication of the principle parts of the body, such as two heads on one trunk or Siamese twins. However, the monsters Supernatural Brutes choose to design in the Image in which they would like to be seen is that of Super-powers that they can *use for how to act as "little gods" with people* on a whim. The Desire, driven by their Brute Brain fashioned Life-Force, is to be a *Super-human* who possesses such a special aura of omnipotence—i.e. all powerful from having unlimited and universal power deeds—as to have their cult contemporaries and posterity elevate them into a Legend-god status. The model for that *Devil Complex* is in the form of an Icon Image of the fundamental shrewdness, deception, and cunning expressions of Evil.

Indifference/Hate/Evil/Sadism + Kill/Take/Destroy/Dominate/Oppress/Control (KTDDOC) mindsets and practices are the ultimate in a Devil Icon Image. They have a monomania to be able to act out that character since they believe it is a natural and desirable part of their make-up and the best means for them to achieve "Success." It displays by their inventions of names, slogans, concepts, Trinkets, Trivia being viewed as *the ability to name, control, and possess it all.* This mental Icon Image is symbolized in reality by the GUN on the Extreme end—"Hoods" in the middle-range--and the greatly oversized tires on their trucks on the Mild end. The entire scale--displays allowing one to gratify and cater to ones animal spirit--regardless of the prices paid by those involved. By so doing, they see themselves as "superior"—above the law—and powerful based upon their ability to cause frustration, pain, suffering, and tragedy.

LIFESTYLE: ones characterizing behaving traits for daily living

LOGIC: Ma'at's mental wisdom processes involved in tying ones mind back to the Cosmic Organism with which it had originally been "One" and to which it belongs with by natural connectivity.

LOGIC—AFRICAN: *To begin Cosmos, Selfhood, or Thought Unity, African CT and Logic starts with the "What it is"—the aspect that gives rise to Knowledge of what is or is not Truth—while Western logic deals with the "What it does" and the "How it appears"—which are human-made judgements and therefore only Information.* African Tradition's story of Logic began with the brilliant Common Sense practices of Primitive (the first people) Africans. Out of their Reasoning by Analogy arose African Rational Thinking--later evolving into the world's first scientific method and Ma'at "fair-play" judgments--advances based on African astro-mathematics of c20,000 BC. Very Ancient African priest-astronomers, after developing Geometry (Qualitative Logic) and trigonometry (Quatitative Logic), advanced the abstract forms of Rational Thinking. A key conclusion was the Universe (meaning a One or Uni Verse--i.e. one statement) is Oneness and its Harmony is established and maintained by Cosmic Laws. By extracting Principles (unchanging realities) out of these Laws, they inferred that only through observing the Laws of the Universe can a human be One with it and with God (Amen, Metu Neter IV: 55). In the manner that all humans derived from one ultimate African Ancestor parent 200,000 years ago, from the ultimate Cosmic Creator (parent) have come all creatures and creations. This makes all Spiritually related (the Law of Sympathy) and thus Ancient Africans inferred the Law of Correspondence. It states that what first exists in the Spiritual Realm is later manifest on every plane of Material World existence--in accordance with God's "Genetics" of the Spiritual Element. This Law arose--in accordance with God's plan--from the Ocean of Nun's essence before its Spiritual Elements' "Genetics" reproduced itself in every later manifested plane of Cosmic existence in Mathematical Order. Having previously arrived at the concept of the Eternal Soul of each human consisting of a "Spark" of God, they likened the human Soul to a coin. On one side is a Self (the core of a human's "Being")--itself-subdivided into ones Divine Consciousness and ones Divine Will. On the other side is ones Divine Spirit (divided into *Spiritual Energy* and Matter). Ones Divine Consciousness (ones Soul or inner God's Mind) determines the "What" and the "Why" (i.e. what it is willing) of what the Cosmic God-Mind wants one to manifest. However, it relies on Will to determine How and When. Yet, the Will is merely an indication of a potential act, lacking the energy to carry out what has been willed--needing the Spirit's Energy for that. *'To Will' is to activate ones Divine Conscious.* African Sages used certain extracted Principles from Cosmic Laws to serve as Logical Reasoning vehicles. They inferred the essence of these Principles comprised a given human's divine Self-Image, which then transfers the essence of Cosmic Laws into ones Life-Force to ensure its harmony and vitality--Forces having the ability to successfully manifest in ones Will. So, it can be seen from this process that the original idea for *African Logic was to embrace the abilities to synthesize (think cosmologically)--to see the abstract unity and interdependence between all independent real things—to see the infinite in the finite--and to establish Truth from mathematically determined Spiritual Principles.*

LOGIC: (Greek, law, legal)—law applied to thinking—are rules that establish a legal connection with the establishment of the legitimacy between ideas—and that includes African Spirituality.

LOGIC--AFRICAN: The African word "Logic" originated from the Ancient African Bible's (e.g. Shabaka Text) description of the "Logos". Ancient Africans realized their minds are capable of making notches into their inner Divine Logos. This means that to be "Yoked" to the Cosmic Force is by humans' *work of Spirituality to subject their minds to the Divine Spirit so it can command the Life-Force in harmony with the Laws of Nature.* Such "yoking" thereby allow ones mind to Metaphysically express the "Word" or Verbum Patterns of the ever concealed Logos—and that is what Ancient African Sages called *Logic*. African Sages personified the Creator as Ptah who states the fundamental assumption that Mind or Thought is the source of everything. The idea is the myriad of created things "came into Being through that which the Heart (Mind) Thought and the Tongue (creative speech) commanded." This ontological potency of Speech appears also in other African cultures. The Luba's Creator, Maweja Nangila is said to have called forth humans "who, at the time of Creation bore an exact resemblance to him"—linking the Intellectual life with the Material (Karanga, MAAT p189). In other parts of Ancient Africa it was said that the essential state of the Supreme Being is Energy/Matter undifferentiated into Things. To create the Cosmos and have experiences, required God's Essence to be modified into human offspring to serve as the vehicle for transferring God's Divine Consciousness into, and realizing the fullness of God's own Being. That "*God is within you*" is expressed in many world scriptures so as to guide humans to understand themselves and for Right Life Living. This is because African Sages said: "Self-Knowledge is the beginning and end of all Knowledge" (Amen, Metu Neter I: 82). To this end, African Logic had as its fundamental nature the inquiry into the ideas that shape and influence the life of Humanity (Gyekye, African Philosophical Thought p50). Obviously, this involved the necessity for Critical Thinking's critical assessment aspects. For example, academic assessments by African Scholars would cause them to say: "I am learning scrolls," for the Learned knew the scrolls' (i.e. the Ancient African Bible) writings in hieroglyphics (Issa, Origin of Amen p52).

However, from misinterpretations, from incomplete and superficial research, and from shoddy analysis which have led European scholars to come to "strange" conclusions about African Spiritual Literature, their opinions are to be completely discounted. Nevertheless, the *theme of African Logic is that of the Divine Logos with respect to its God Essences and the Pattern and Course resulting from it.* The "*Seed Essence*" is that by which a Thing" is "what it is"—as distinguished from the Thing's *Essentials* (Endowments, Properties, and Attributes) and the Thing's Existence which is about the "what it does" and the "how it appears." God's "what it is" Essence "Genetics" is the Spiritual Elements—i.e. Unconditional Love, Truth, Reality, and the Natural. The *Pattern* is a mature Essence. God's Substance (Essence) which births the Cosmic Organism—i.e. all God's Creatures and Creations in their bonded "Virtual" *Meiosis* state (unseparated)--is activated by the Divine Spirit's Spiritual Energy/Matter (i.e. the Ether) Life Force. Once that Course is activated, Archetypes of the Cosmic Organism descend in a Mitosis form of an increasing heterogeneity through the various worlds. A *Monad* is the Divine Sparks of Creation containing God's Essence (Substance). The downward descent converts the Meiosis non-atomic Monadic "*Elemental Essence*" into a power possessing atomic "*Monadic Essence*" by the addition of Ether in the Sublime just below the Subjective Ocean of Nun realm. Further descent towards Earth causes the Essentials of the Essence within a given Entity (e.g. human) to differentiate according to the activated combination and arrangement of that Entity's Genetics, as is in keeping with the Divine Plan. That Entity's customized *Endowments* (i.e. natural qualities) and *Propensities* (in-born tendencies, e.g. a human's capacities, abilities, and language) will operate different processes of an Entity's Selfhood. Once a human has descended to Earth, her/his obligation, duty, and responsibility is the Selfhood fashioning into daily strivings so as to leave ones Lower (animalistic) Self behind. Simultaneously, there is ones evolving towards ones Highest (Divinity) Self. Such is done by consistently producing "ME/We" workable benefits + using life's difficulties for Self-Improvement + remaining Honorable (no cheating, stealing, or detrimental lying) + staying in the flow of, while developing out of, the Spiritual Elements. As these (among others) start increasing the high vibration rate of ones Soul back towards its newborn homogeneity rate level, one begins ones Selfhood *Cosmic Evolution* ascension. Such Ma'at Living is perfected as one enhances ones Spiritual Emotions, Intellect powers, and virtues to fashion Wisdom, Beauty, Harmony, and Unity within oneself and with all others with whom that can happen. When one achieves the high vibration rate of ones Soul as a lifestyle, reproducing the same rate of ones original creation, ones Life Cycle re-ascension heads towards returning to ones Divine Source so as to then enter the Heaven Afterlife. So, *African Logic is the Critical and Poetic Thinking that stays within the confines of the Course of the Divine Logos and uses its Essence to fashion work products for Ma'at Living (the Spiritual Elements in action).* As applied to daily living, the theme of African Logic is to "Keep Your Word"—the Word flowing out of a human's Real Self mindset that has been *subjected to the Divine Spirit so as to be able to command the Life-Forces that are Harmonized with the Laws of Nature.* To help in the understanding of why "Keeping your Word" is so important in African Tradition, let us go back to Ancient African Spiritual Literature relating to the creative act of using "The Word" of God (or Logos) in forming the Cosmos—i.e. an immanent (all Mind) reason. Ancient Africans said this creative act originated out of the grounding provided by the Spiritual Elements emanating out of the eternal mind of God (which the ancient Greeks elaborated on under the title *"The Logos"*). The Divine Logos occurred before the existence of the Cosmos--as a mental form of sound—and whose sounds set Cosmic Energy/Matter into motion, organizing its Essence into Patterns. These Patterns were derived from the Unconditional Love which provided the Form of Reality in which those Patterns could express their nature. Out of the Divine Logos Essence comes what is pertinent to African Logic—Poetic Logic and Reasoning Logic.

LOGIC—AFRICAN SCOPE: Three main approaches (which verify each other) Ancient African Sages used for determining Truth included: studying the Laws of Nature by means of the Music of the Spheres; astro-mathematics; and embracing what was revealed to them (see The Kybalion). Because these three demonstrated *Correspondence Continuity*—i.e. Unity in Multiplicity—as a result of sharing the same Spiritual Elements "Genetics," African Sages inferred the Great Ultimate Creator is both the sum total of all Principles and each Principle is part of its "Oneness." Practical applications from this complex process were mainly fashioning Principles used as the Base, Foundation, and "Skeletal" Outline for African Tradition. Because this Knowledge was at such an elevated intellectual level, African Griots (story-tellers) presented it to African people via the vehicle of Figures of Communication. This means they made up Affect Symbolic Imagery stories of metaphorical Beings who symbolized faculties of actual physical entities capable of meshing with inner realities present in humans' "Hearts" and "Heads". Examples: Amon/Amaunet--i.e. hidden/concealed ones (Air/Wind); Nun/Naunet—i.e. Primeval Matter/Space*;* Huk/Hauket—i.e. Illimitable and the Boundless--Huh/Hauhet—i.e. Darkness/Obscurity. Each of these, like mosaic pieces of the Cosmic Wholism, formed Things that depended for its meaning, its power to change, its ability to grow all it can, for the direction of its development, its fullness and sufficiency, upon a Life larger than its own. The resultant product was likened to a web of independent items working with an interdependence of each that is essential to the organization of the whole and a unity of its actions. The point was to get African people to realize that when ones Soul becomes identified with God, so as to vibrate at the ultra-high rate, it would hear and participate in the higher realms of living equating to the "Music of the Spheres" (James, p28, 140). African Griots elaborated on this type of Harmony by analogizing it to weaving—saying its like threads so intertwined as to create a single, coherent fabric held together on its own. Though this Knowledge had been accumulating for thousands of years in Africa, all of it was plagiarized by ancient Greeks, particularly Pythagoras (570-495? BC) during his 23 year stay in Africa. Pythagoras and the Western world's stealing of African Intellectual Property also included (among infinite others) semi-mystical, semi-mathematical philosophy, and systems of numerology. Yet, these thieves omitted the African core of Harmony—i.e. Ma'at Principles of displaying in action the Spiritual Elements of Unconditional Love, Truth, Reality and the Natural.

LOGIC IN AFRICAN TRADITION: African Logic is African Law applied to thinking and it only reasons from "what" is Truth or Circumstantial Truths. Its major process in making Truth prevail leads to a *Poetic Gestalt*—a unified whole--established by all ingredients within the processes being within and about the Spiritual Elements. The Gestalt process emphases seeing Things in whole or unities. A Tree is a unity, despite its roots, trunk, branches, and leaves. An animal is an organism, although it consists of body organs and cells. The perception of Unity occurs when a given figure is moving out of the Background into the Foreground and that is probable what happens with Infant babies and thus is innate. Whatever is experienced deeply and leads to the main response is part of the figure and Foreground. Hence, the figure, in contrast to the Background, seems to have a compelling or a releasing quality. Whatever is less strongly perceived and leads to weaker responses is part of the Background (Arieti, p41). Still, Character, Characteristic, Trait, and Feature aspects in the Background and Foreground and Figure are each part of the whole. Each overlaps—forms an interchange--and presents it *Nature* (its Essence + Character) in its operations. Each is influenced by *Nurture* (i.e. the sum Effects of environmental influences and conditions acting on an organism). But what one responds to is the Characteristic—a fragment of that Circle of Wholism which identifies and expresses individuality of the most Distinctive ("stand-out-ish-ness") part of the Whole. Such is regardless of whether that focus pertains to a person, place, thing, or situation. Otherwise, the rest of what is in the Foreground and all of the Background of the whole is disregarded. Such is seen in Nature, as with moths being attracted to light even though they may burn themselves to death in contact with powerful electric bulbs. With flypaper, the fly reacts only to the sweetness of the paper and not to the ensnaring stickiness. Such reactivity to a single part of the environment is often used to trick the Crowd or trick and kill insects or, I propose, for mind control. To elaborate, in the horrific brainwashing of the Enslaved, there was "Dedifferentiation" so that victims would see fragments of the whole, or parts, or only salient parts. Then, what one responds to is the Characteristic—that part of the whole with the most Distinctiveness because of standing out in relation to all else that is part of "Big Picture". They selected those parts which reflexively spurred them to make the choice of a "Fight, Flight, or Fright" reaction on each emergency occasion. And those types of patterns were culturally transmitted. As a result of a *Characteristic* of a "Big Picture" encounter identifies and expresses individuality of the most Distinctive ("stand-out-ish-ness") part of the Whole. That perception of a part is enlarged to be the equivalent of the perception of the whole—called "Closure."

An analogy is perceiving a crescent moon and doing *A-dualism* which makes it into a full moon perception. This is a faculty of the Imagination which permits a part to stand for the whole. Thus, the whole is not experienced at a sensory level but rather it is filled by ones memory, what is desired, what is feared, or what is its symbolized Icon Image meaning. An equivalent—which could be an altered form of Perceptual Closure--is those who think about doing something and then equating that to having already done it. All of these things cause many people to start running from these imagined unrealities and that running causes them to get scared. Other problems are situational as, for example, struggling Black American youth are overwhelmed with such substantial racially induced mental disorganization that all they have is an Oceanic sense of Ancient African Traditions—i.e. subtle and subliminal experiences of its mystical Spiritual Elements powers. These are some of the realities that call for African Logic. An example is that it refrains people from drawing conclusions which only SEEM to follow or that SEEM right. African Logic cares nothing for the opinions of the Great—nothing for the prejudices of the many—and nothing for the Supernatural or similar Superstitions. African Logic embraces the abilities to synthesize Cosmic Principles by thinking Cosmologically--to see the abstract unity and interdependence between all independent real things--and to establish Truth from mathematically determined Spiritual Principles. African Logic requires: (1) that humans properly be part of the Processes of Nature by *the subjection of their minds to the Divine Spirit in order for it to command the Life-Force in harmony with the Laws;* (2) carrying the topic at hand within pertinent African Laws in order for resultant Thought Structures to evolve out of those Laws; (3) building involved Thought Structures upon a Base of Unconditional Love (or the Spiritual Elements); and (4) following the Processes of Nature using its Mathematical Order. *Ancient African Laws refer to the foundation of all Cosmic manifestations and denote a sequence of inherently related events that occur with unvarying uniformity under the same conditions. These Laws that govern Creation are stored in the Divine*

Spirit and arranged in a particular format that graphically aids in the explanation of the African Tree of Life's 11 Principles, their functions, their relationship to each other and to the whole. This means the "Oneness" ('uni verse') and harmony of the Cosmos (world) are established and maintained by Laws. *African Logic is only built upon a solid Base—a Base carrying the Essence with a Disposition that maintains all meaningful life-shaping, life-changing, and life-maintaining choices, decisions, and solutions within the confines of the Spiritual Elements.* Out of that Base arises an underground foundation able to support all of the weight of whatever is built on top of it. Ancient Africans knew thousands of years back what Western science is just beginning to learn--that the *solidarity of things is just a mental illusion.* What make up atoms (which is 99.9% empty space) are protons and neutrons in the nucleus + a very small contribution from orbiting electrons + energy. Matter only appears solid because of the electrical charges of the atoms that repel one another. When humans are born to Earth, the *Essentials of their Essence are fundamental and foundational to the true meaning of the Essence Principles and Appearance for following the course of their nature in the flow of Natures Essences.* The Processes of Nature are motions and actions--as part of a series of operations or events leading to the achievement of specific results--conform to Cosmic Spiritual Laws governing the course of Nature. Rather than use reason, the "What it does" that characterizes thinking according to *Nature's Processes* is to "Feel" it in order to detect it, follow it, and avoid doing anything to interfere with it. To be in the flow of Nature's Processes is to automatically step into patterns of Circumstantial Evidence, Proof, and Truth--patterns comparable to the Direct Rational Pattern for which the words *Correspond* (have comparable elements or be "equivalence"). Only by conforming to these Cosmic Laws can a human be "One" with it and with God. Humans' Divine Spirits are that portion of their minds which contains God's Plan in the Essence. Such Essences are formed as a Virtual Image and a Disposition with Spiritual Energy/Matter. The Divine Spirit adds to the *What* and *Why* aspects contained inside God's plan its knowledge of the *How and When* so that can be refined by means of the mind's *Circumspection.*

Circumspection's job is to discern the issue's Premise and determine if it conforms to the processes and Laws of the Cosmos. Conformity/non-conformity to the Spiritual Elements of what is being assessed is called Ma'at, Dialectics, or African Logical Thinking. African Logic applied to thinking by means of Laws that establish Spiritual Elements' Correspondence are by means of connections between Principles. That is what gives rise to African Logic Inferences of a Circumstantial Knowledge nature. African Logic establishes that the ingredients of the topic at hand is of a Spiritual Elements nature because it has legitimacy (i.e. are parts of the Spiritual Elements) as well as Correspondence between all parts of those ingredients—as verified by the product being in a state of Order, Regularity, Coherence, Consistency, Compatibility, Balance, Harmony, and Predictability. Such African Logic enabled Ancient African Sages to conclude that God is unknowable but that God can be known through God's manifestations.

LOGIC (AFRICAN) STANDARDS: Within a Spiritual Element context the Principles of greatest concern to African Sages were in relationship to scientific information, esoteric (knowledge beyond reason) elements, and logical events (changing Realities) pertaining to higher planes of existence. For Ancient Africans, the objective of Logic was to arrive at the Truth of Thought by Synthesis. They understood Knowledge as similar to a "Seed" following a process like an apple tree developing from an apple "Seed". Advances in that process to achieve the standards for Logic are only by staying within and developing out of the Spiritual Elements--while finding how similarities and differences are related for harmonizing and synthesizing. African Logic means a moral discipline used to purge away a human's irrational tendencies (James p28) so as to reveal "*Esoteric Knowledge*"—i.e. understanding the inner truth lying hidden within the core of fundamental beliefs about foundational Realities. Those Esoteric Truth became the standard and guides for African Logic. Living by them is what designed Ancient Africans into the most brilliant CT of history. This was achieved by perfecting their Right and Left Brains. However, since they knew the God Module--the home of Intuitional Wisdom—perhaps located in the Right Brain's temporal lobe—they cultivated their Right Brains to orchestrate the Left. Such enabled them to locate and deeply explore Metaphysical realms. When there is Real Self purity of Intellect and Character, it is concerned with spirituality, prayer, and religious experiences.

Humans standards, guides, filters, measures, and estimates applied to the processes of decision making and problem solving of any type is to follow along the path which ties ones mind back to the Cosmic Organism with which it had originally been "One" and to which it belongs with by natural connectivity. This process is in keeping with the Greek etymological roots pertaining to "Legal" and "Logic" as a result of them trying to understand the meaning of Africans' Divine Logos. Thus, African Logic is part of, and not opposed to, religion or reason or philosophy or science (a word meaning knowledge, particularly of the Physical World). The "Big Picture" is that the Divine Logos, symbolized as the god Ra, the Holy Spirit, provides the words through which the Will of the Immaterial Self (Soul or Divine Consciousness) is manifest. The power of ones Will resides in Logical convictions and yet it must result from a Premise rooted in Truth (Divine Law) and Wisdom. Ones Wisdom faculty can sort conflicts that the Rational Intellect' syllogistic thought procedures cannot (Amen, Tree of Life p124, 154). Wisdom's approach is to solve the major conflicts based on their underlying fundamental dualities—noting for each its place in time and/or space (hierarchy). Here, Truth concerns the validation of a Premise that is operated on in Logical Thinking. This means the Ma'at system of thinking through which the truth or falsehood of a Premise used in reason is determined—and which Reasoning is incapable of doing. This is why a European conclusion may be: "Logical but not necessarily true." But such does not apply to African Logic because the foundation for and frame within which African Logic Thoughts exist is mathematical. As a result, what arises out of a given Ma'at oriented Mathematical Thought "Seed" is a thinking pattern which also follows *mathematical designs and in a layered manner (as do patterns of Nature)*. Contributing to the formation of this Ma'at Seed was Ancient Africans utilizing their perfected Right Brain faculties in order to cultivate both their Imaginations and Synthesizing skills for purposes of perceiving all the structural components underlying things and events (Amen, Metu Neter II:105). This discerning of the inner factors *that unify things, based on their mutual relationships and interdependence with each other and the whole,* involves Logic and Mathematics. To arrive at a conclusion, ones Intellect and Emotions design the ingredients of those things into a wholistic mode of thinking is called *Creative Synthesis. The resultant whole constitutes a Symbol containing an Image and a payload message needed for the application of the Conclusion.* So, unlike Logic, the creative aspect consists of assuming the Causes discovered but does not need to be established Principles to proceed along lines that could lead to the "Truth" because the objective is about Taste and Workability for the issue at hand.

LOGIC AFRICAN POETIC REASONING: The African word "Logic" means the mental wisdom processes arising out of a human being from being *"Yoked to the Cosmic Organism/God Source"* to thereby share Essences. Very Ancient Africans connected concepts about Yoga, the human mind (and its consciousness, subconscious, and unconscious aspects), the body, and ones spirit. The 'Roots' gathered for "yoking" humans to God's Consciousness were: the invention of agriculture + its plow (c20,000 BC) + the two oxen plowing together as a unit and fastened (i.e. "*yoked*") by a wooden frame + Egyptians' devised Yoga (c10,000 BC) Spiritual path practices to the heaven afterlife. One human "yoking" requirement was/is for ones mental activities to be halted in order for one to experience "Oneness" with God. "Yoking" occurs because God's Consciousness is Immaterial and thus indivisible--implying ones Divine Consciousness experiences are identical experiences of God's Consciousness. My greatest insight into African Tradition thinking came upon realizing the correspondence of all real things—e.g. the similarities within the Animal Kingdom; similarities between the Animal and Plant Kingdoms; similarities in my Thoughts (which are Unseen) and my displayed actions (which are

Seeable). I could then infer that such similarities are present between things in the Seeable World and in the Un-seeable World as well as similarities within the Un-seeable World. See Poetic Logic

LOGIC--AFRICAN APPLIED TO CIRCUMSTANCES: After African Common Sense was successful in establishing Correspondence between Seeable things and between Seeable things and Un-seeable things, having established proof of Truth within any Un-seeable thing meant that any truth in the Un-seeable is Circumstantial. One reason for the term Circumstantial was the Spiritual and Metaphysical Un-seeable are around and within all Seeable things made by God. This is because Ancient Africans defined *Circumstantial as meaning the Underlying of a Thing. So, "Underlying"* designates what is innate—i.e. what has been born as the potential or the present to impart the essential qualities, strength, and characteristics of the nature of a given work product overlying it—and yet those Essences of the Underlying remain hidden within. In order to *understand the Continuity--the Unity underlying the multiplicity of all Real Things in the Cosmos*—including any and all of God's creatures and creations when each came into Being—gives insight into Correspondence and Circumstance. Hence, because all Cosmic Organism Entities have the same Spiritual Elements "Genetics," to know any one of them is to have insight into all. A Thing *Known by such African Logic implies it can be equated to an Equivalent Thing Unknown, even if not exactly.* The thinking processes involved in arriving at "Circumstantial Truths" is that of *Inferences.* For example, Seeable "ME/WE" Good deeds equate to the Spiritual Elements. *So, by staying in this flow pattern while heading into the Unknown, at any point along the Course, there are correspondences which give insight into the Circumstantial. African Logic* reasons only from Known Truths or Circumstantial Truths into Unknown Truths or Circumstantial Truths. All that gives rise to Correspondence is to remain Orderly in its evolution by following Nature's Spiritual Elements Processes' natural Mathematical progressions. This implies that all aspects remain about the Spiritual Elements, stay within its flow, and evolve ingredients and concepts out of that flow. Perhaps African Sages following of Nature's Processes Pattern was like this: Step I is making Circumstantially derived Assumptions as to what is likely to have Correspondence. Step II--African Logic follows Nature's Processes pattern and deals with relations analogously in order to determine if there is Correspondence. This was done mainly in the African Mystery Schools. Foundational studies included the *Trivium* (Grammar, Dialectics or African logic, and Rhetoric) + the *Quadrivium* (Music, Arithmetic, Geometry, and Astronomy). Grammar, Rhetoric, and Logic were disciplines of a moral nature, by means of which the irrational tendencies of a human being were purged away (James, p. 28). Examples of possible analogy connections enable such to occur included those which made for a geometrical transformation; or of becoming aware of resemblances or similarities of interior detail; or paving the way to insights concerning a functional relation of congruity or of something equivalent.

Of necessity, purging required knowing their meanings by Intuition. To this end, an essential of African Logic teaching was the usage of both the Left and Right Brain in for students' reasoning. Yet, it was the perfection of having their Right Brains orchestrate that process in order for its intuitive faculties to lead one into deeper realms of the Cosmos and thus allows for creativity. Correspondence Verification of Inferences by African Logic is summarized as follows. All Ultimate Truths and Realities are connected into a Cosmic Unity by its Truth Sap; there are very few principles of Nature; and all Ultimate Truths always have a correspondence of Truth, regardless of the Cosmic Tree plane on which any Truth operates. "*Correspondence*" means all parts, in relation to each other, possess the same nature, and are in Harmony, Balance, and Order (in the form of hidden and unified connections). Hence, understanding growth Principles in a Tree enables understanding growth principles of Cosmic Truth. Interwoven with these Liberal Arts was a life of virtue. These were the studies for three primary types of African Dialect: Type I—the Law of Opposites, borrowed by Europeans and modified into the Thesis vs. Anti-thesis Concept. Yet, both are designed to arrive at Synthesis. ; Type II—"The Middle Way"; and Type III—a Dialogue or Conversation between teacher and student.

LOGIC—AFRICAN TEACHING: At least as early as 12,500 BC in the Egyptian Mystery Schools, where young men and women learned to become Egyptian priests, African Sages taught Asar's (Osiris) esoteric doctrines on how to "Know Thyself". Its essence was to achieve a concept of Wholism on the way to reaching a state of Mysticism. But students' starting point was to transcend their minds and senses so as to discover their Real Selves' infinite and eternal Divine Consciousness. Then, a mysticism type event would occur whereby one is able to transcend barriers on the way to absorbing the essence of the Cosmic Spirit--an essence inexpressible--an essence called *Intuition* (an immediate understanding of the truth without calling upon reason or feelings). Sages' teachings were mainly through the metaphorical Affect Symbolic Imagery of Myths. These provided a Cause and a vehicle for the Spiritual (Moral) messages to transcend the story itself and thereby impart Spiritual Truths beyond a student's rationality or experiences (Ashby, African Origins p43, 297). Yet, a Myth is like a head of lettuce, with each layer successively removed to enable one to get closer to the profound Essence layers of the mystery of life. The subjects, called the Seven Liberal Arts of the Ancient Egyptian Mystery Schools, were designed to liberate the soul. These Arts were the *Quadrivium* (Grammar, Arithmetic, Rhetoric, and Dialectic) and the *Trivium* (Geometry, Astronomy, and Music). Of necessity this requires knowing each of their meanings in-depth (James, Stolen Legacy p. 28). From their research of the Immaterial, the Intangible, and the Material by means of these Arts, Truths about each emerged. The focus of these Truths was to reach *Salvation*—i.e. the freeing of ones Soul from its bodily fetters (among others) by means of them having a Mystical Death so that Redemption and Rebirth could naturally occur. An analogy is to remove the Cloud covering ones "Soul Sunshine" (i.e. Divine Consciousness). Of the Seven Liberal Arts, Mathematics and Logic (originating in the African Kimetic texts) were particularly important in freeing the mind, in controlling wild thoughts, and in developing order. African Sages knew Intelligence is cultivated by discerning (reading what is not easy to read) the unique Laws of Sympathy (all God's creatures and creations are Spiritually related) and Nature. Grammar, Rhetoric, and Logic were African disciplines of a moral nature and by means of which a human's irrational tendencies are purged away. As a result, "*Esoteric Knowledge*" would be revealed—i.e. understanding the inner truth lying hidden within the core of fundamental Knowledge about foundational Realities. Geometry and Arithmetic helped provide understanding of the problems of ones "Being" and of a physical type. Music (or Harmony) meant the living practice of philosophy (i.e. the adjustment of human life into harmony with God). By reflecting on the discovered Cosmic Laws and extracting from them pertinent Principles that explain the Nature and Interaction of the forces influencing humans' lives—e.g. thinking, feelings, actions, and destiny—one had the ingredients to pave a Ma'at path for living. Living in accordance with these Principles enables one to live in harmony by gaining access to God's wisdom and spiritual power. Then, all else needed or of top importance in life will follow. All of this is in accord with humans' observations, common experiences, and reasoning powers—not Belief, Faith, or some Non-rational Supernatural agent. In short, the *Ancient African Bible (i.e. Spiritual Literature) connects Religion, Laws, and Science by means of Logic (the legitimacy of ideas)*. This stems from those unperceivable aspects or Laws of Nature which give evidence of its existence and proof of its reliability through the perceivable things in the world to which it is linked. Gravity is not perceivable and yet its existence has been proven through the mathematical relationships of the objects through which it operates. Though Energy cannot be perceived, its operations are understood through Mathematics, an equally abstract vehicle. The common denominator of all manifestations in the world is activity (i.e. vibrations) which, in turn, are governed by Laws that give to the world and to life its order, regularity, predictability, and so on. African Sages said Law, not Belief or Faith, is what must guide humans in physical, emotional, mental, and spiritual aspects of life. Any Belief or Faith contradicting these Laws--even in the face of "works," Grace, positive thinking, rituals, meditation, or prayers—because they do not enable one to "Know" and thereby live in accordance with what brings Salvation.

LOGIC--CULTIVATION OF POETIC: Ancient Africans said mathematics is the one and only key to clear thinking, meaning, and communication. Since African Logic and all laws for living were based upon mathematics, their process of mathematical reasoning was referred to as *Discourse*. When Discourse was put into words, it was called *Philosophy*. *Philosophy* in its truest application is properly a matter of pure Logic. Philosophy of Life (POL) is the standard, filter, and guide for how one lives ones life. Ancient African teachers used a question and answer method--called *Dialect*--to assess a student's POL. Its aim is to "*Educate*" (lead knowledge out of ones Soul) by exploring Abstracts and Abstractions; locate and account for the essences of all things; see the common inner nature of seemingly unrelated essences; and manipulate, maneuver, and synthesize the inner meanings of those essence principles so as to connect diverse things into a unified whole. In the Ancient Egyptian Mystery Schools (?12,500 BC), Dialectic consisted of an exercise designed to help students figure out the truth or to clarify an issue by recognizing and shedding what is false; by showing which aspects are wholly inconsistent with one another; and by determining aspects having a harmonious fit on higher planes of existence (Bailey, Supreme Thinking of Ancient Africans). Regardless of how hard the problem, Ancient Africans realized there is always an undiscovered logical coherence among the hidden parts of a problem and its basic logical structure. They started the search of the Unknown or the incomprehensible by assessing the underlying base of the problem, searching for Principles. Out of this process arose African *Critical philosophy*--a rigorous logical method using argument and logical *analysis to clarify and critique existing beliefs*--as all should do--on the way to discovering the truth.

With respect to the cultivation of Poetic Logic processes, the nature of its Logic's subject matter, whether using reasoning, analysis, or processing data, is general rather than concrete because it omits great numbers of individual differences--an omission highly necessary and superbly useful for handling great masses of facts and experiments. Spiritual Symbols do the same thing. *The C15 word "Symbol"* ("throwing them together" -- with "them" referring to two things, each with a story) and "*Parable*" ("throwing them side by side," referring to an Allegory-type deduced veiled story from an obvious story) were originally synonyms. Both were used in the comparative sense of *Identity* ("unchanging sameness") to prove (after scrutinizing for any contrasting features) the two parts of something matched. The principle which corresponds to this is discussed from "yoking" above. A variation concerned a coin applied when the bank vault contained half of a divide coin (the symbol) while the absent customer's half was not available to be seen (the mystery). When the Customer returned to claim her money, she proved her identity when her half of the coin matched the half in the bank vault. From this practice, one concept of a Symbol was a concrete (touchable) object (the half coin in the bank) yoked to its absent near twin (the customer's half, the token). Like an Icon, a Symbol is *a microcosm* (a "little world") of the "Macrocosm" it represents (i.e. a great world). The interrelatedness of the two might be signified by the outward and visible appearances resembling and/or by the Symbol carrying a crystalized gist of the inward and hidden meaning of the "Thing" it symbolizes. Mystique Thinking is learned in a similar manner. Hence, the qualities or the attributes' Characteristics, Features, and Traits are maneuvered and manipulated in a manner similar to "*Alphabet Learning*." Only after the alphabet is learned and internalized can one advance to putting words together where they await (in a Paradigm storage place) being meaningfully put together for communication. The degree to which speaking or writing is successful depends on the content, the words chosen, and the "polishing" of the communication. Logic helps determine which best word to speak--the *proper selection of which shortens the distance between the message of the messenger and the people's understanding of both.* Distinguishing Truth and Falsehood was by the Spiritual Elements and, within it, by possessing knowledge of relations between parts with each other and the whole. Its syllogistic logical and segregated thinking enables one to separate parts of a whole (usually mistaken for analysis); to focus on isolated parts (Amen Metu

Neter I:107); and devise options for a solution. Mathematics and logic (originating in the African Kimetic texts) were particularly important in freeing the mind, in controlling wild thoughts, and in developing order. Intelligence is cultivated by discerning (reading what is not easy to read) the unique laws of sympathy and Nature. Logic and Dialectic are disciplines of a moral nature, by means of which the irrational tendencies of a human being are purged away (James, p. 28). Such is necessary to have a mindset geared to achieving ones Highest (Divinity) Self.

To that end, Esoteric Knowledge is required. Insight required to enter the Esoteric realm concerns itself with the five principle mysteries of Ancient Egyptian spiritual doctrines, namely: *Regeneration; Transfiguration (Transformation); Transubstantiation* (change one substance into another)*; Resurrection; and Ascension* (see Seleem, Book of Life p41). Although all of these were imitated and modified by the Christians, Kabbalists, Masons and others based upon the objectives of a given culture's philosophy of life (POL), none are to be consulted because they are quite limited and often, "off-track". In African Tradition, necessary to carrying out these five Principles includes establishing harmony between God made things, like the Soul and body of a human. African Logic says all life-shaping and life-changing decisions based upon Spiritual Elements can have its source "Known" and thus by-pass the need to have "faith" in what one is told to believe. But the starting point is at the highest spiritual level—i.e. of the Ultimate Truths present in the Cosmic Consciousness.

Every human is born with this Knowledge. To stay in this flow while going through life imparts an awareness of ones birth gift of Selfhood Greatness with its "5S's" sense of Safety, Security, Sureness/Self-Confidence, Strength, and Stability for meeting any and every challenge of life. So, when one encounters any person, place, or thing, one has the capability, resulting from ones Soul's Spiritual Elements radar system, to instantly have a *"Feels True" Knowing* as to whether it is "For Me/WE or Against Me/WE". Such *"Feels True" Knowing* signals itself by one having a sense of Harmony or Disharmony, as opposed to a sense of "is it good or bad"—which may be from flawed assessments. Harmony meshes with the human Soul's Spiritual Elements "Trademark". At a practical Earth World level are reality, distortion, or fantasy Principles applied to daily life. Whatever is not in keeping with "ME/WE" is indicated by a sense of Disharmony. For example, I hired an electrician to work in my home and immediately experienced great disharmony upon meeting him. Then, 6 months later he came back and robbed my home of all kinds of treasures, including belongings from my Enslaved Ancestors. Another example is how the ancient Greeks "butchered" Fundamental Principles they learned in Africa and applied them to their imaginative Supernatural realms. The World-wide effects have generated ongoing disharmony to all of the World Crowd victims. But humans must be made aware of what to look for to survive and self-protect. This start by controlling ones Acquired Emotions. Learning not to scratch the bump that itches is a way to control emotions

LOGIC vs. REASONING IN AFRICAN TRADITION: African Logic (non-contradictory identification) is to African Reasoning (best Option) as Genius is to Talent. This means African Reasoning is proper when it stays within the confines of African Logic and has all of its Choices, Decisions, and Solutions arise out of it. All organized Rational thinking is a process of identification (distinguishing its unique mark) and integration that follows a Mathematical Pattern. Its starting point is the "what it is" of a situation—the keystone of Reasoning and the foundation upon which the remaining Thought Structure is put in order. They objective is prove or disprove a point. If the Source of the "what it is" has a Ma'at Character, then one follows that pattern which is in keeping with what is Harmonious. This means that from start to finish there must be residing in the Nature of the process within each and among all aspects: (1) Coherence (its hidden internal links and components being consistent with one another); (2) Consistency (standing firmly together within a state of harmony and balance with what makes sense); (3) Compatibility with Reality (practical);

(4) Interconnectedness (everything real depends on every other real thing); (5) Order (sharing the "Oneness" of Cosmic Primordial Substance center); (6) Regularity (conforming to the prescribed standard or the established pattern for it kind); (7) Balance (rendering no favorites on either side but conforming to the Ultimate Standard); (8) Endurance (progressing inside/in tune with the Spiritual Elements); (9) Predictability; and (10) "Workableness". Harmony is present when there is complete adaptation of each part to the Wholistic Circle. African Sages realized that reasoning per se contains nothing capable of determining the truth or falsehood of any Premise. That is why something can be *Logical but not necessarily true* (which Europeans apparently do not understand and therefore they do violence to the Spiritual Elements). Thus, African Sages based Reasoning on the foundation of Logical Thinking on Ma'at--the Spiritual Elements in action as a system of thinking. This system that stays within and evolves out of the Spiritual Elements serves as a standard, filter, measure, and guide through which the truth or falsehood of a Premise used in reasoning is determined. This follows a "tried and true" Pattern.

LOGIC WARNINGS ABOUT TODAY'S EUROPEANS: Europeans' scholarship, Common Sense, Reasoning, Critical Thinking, and Logic are not be used by Afrocentric People for any aspect of Life Living because they have no Truths, no Knowledge, and no Wisdom that conforms to the Spiritual Elements or anything stable and sound. Europeans have no way of arriving at the Truth about anything. This is because they pride what they have to say as being "Bold." The original European idea in the word "bold" dates to the Indo-European for swell, in the sense of being "puffed up." This probably stemmed from a bellows (associated with fools deemed to be "windbags) or referred to a belly or bell or bald. The basis for their "bold certainty" to everything about anything—even if they have never seen nor heard of it before (e.g. Black People's problems)—comes from their definition of the Supernatural. Like a boy hiding behind his mother's dress, they define Supernatural as that out of this world realm that is unconquerable, unmovable, undeniable, unexplainable, incomparable, unimaginable, immeasurable, and unthinkable. And this is the model for their thinking. It is out of that "bold" Base, built on an "Air" Base, that their conversations start. Prove this to your self by noting all statements which Europeans deem to be profound. Then note they are simply the opinion of someone they consider to be 'great.' Examples: "Aristotle said"; "Plato said"; "Descartes said"; "Hobbes said". If they use any non-African derived Base, it is a Material one. Africans have known for millennia that the *solidarity of the seemingly most Material things are just a mental illusion*. Yet, there are European church hymns—like "Rock of Ages"—which advocate the opposite. A rock is not sufficiently stable to support the Ages, no matter what is ones view in considering the "Ages" realistically. What makes up any Material's atoms is 99.9% empty space and Matter only appears solid because of the electrical charges of the atoms that repel one another. Matter is merely a very low form of vibratory energy. Neither do Europeans, for anything non-mechanical, follow a reproducible thinking process—i.e. a mathematical process—for how they arrive at anything they consider profound. They explain this by saying they do "Non-Rational" thinking which models their definition of the Supernatural. Yet, it is important to know Europeans' scholarship, Common Sense, Reasoning, Critical Thinking, and Logic in order to live in their world dominated institutions and marketplace. In European school systems, Afrocentric People must know enough of European propaganda in order to pass their tests so as to be able to resume the Right Life Living path for thriving and well-being. Since Europeans are oriented to Mind Control of the World Crowd, Unconditional Love, Truth, Reality, and the Natural do not matter to them. What they substitute for these obvious flaws of being unable to fashion anything that is "Right" and what is their primary concern is the *correctness of the pattern* of thought by analysis. Correct Greek logic may start with the right, the unreal, or the wrong assumption for a foundation. By contrast, African Logic always starts building a Thought Structure from a "real" or Truthful foundational base--and proceeds within the flow of the Spiritual Elements perspective—and adheres to African Tradition's emphasis on the Mathematical truth of thought by means of Synthesis. An additional contrast is that African logic emphasizes *what* one thinks to build a solid thoughtful structure, but Greek logic emphasizes *how* one thinks when one thinks correctly. This means they can have the right logic on the path to falsehood. The Greek way can and does lead their followers far off the path of the Truth. Most likely this comes from the authority's intention to control and discipline the people. Another problematic Greek and Christian argument is, despite advocating a sort of fantasy certainty, their foundational base is shaky. Examples: "For the religious to believe in and hope for what is said to be the promises of God is to seize faith". Or, "Hope moves the will to trust in eternal happiness and the all-good God." Note the essence of what these say is wrong because the assumption (major premise) they used to begin their arguments is wrong—and not because it does not make sense. In fact, it makes perfect sense to the naive. A job of Critical Thinking is to *find and always challenge the assumption lurking behind the (quite valid) conclusion.* Thus their major premises about what God says/does/thinks do not stand the test of Truth *because they have no way of knowing God/God's Mind.* So ask: "How do you know that?"

LOGIC—EUROPEAN's TERM CONCEPTS: Words associated with Supernatural--'anything beyond Nature' or cannot be explained by Common Sense experience or the Scientific Method--include: Magical, Miraculous, Preternatural, and Superhuman. Some European authorities say Supernatural is the same as Supra-natural. Others say Supernatural refers to the miracle, the revealed truths of religion—and adding: "but it does not exist—in contrast to the Unnatural." The Encyclopedia of [European] Philosophy (p2-520) defines "super-" or "supra-natural" as "the miracle, the revealed truths of religion. For the enlightened, all these are simply figments of the imagination, nonexistent, indeed at the bottom of priestly inventions designed to keep men ignorant of the ways of Reason and Nature." To paraphrase, it continued by saying the corruptions of religion, social structure, convention, and beneath the often misleading impressions of sense experience not properly organized by Reason, have led to the hypostatized conception of the beautiful and the good. "*Hypostatize*" means to transform a conceptual entity—a Contingent Being—a phantom—into or construe as self-subsistent substances—i.e. "unreal actuals". Nevertheless, European Superficial Logos Nature continued to uncover and develop creatively (not mechanically as Europeans say) the "talent" of producing life. Nature's works of art are endless, though indirect, depictions of the divine.

In this way, the created universe itself is an unfathomable Icon revealing God. The creative symbols of the divine *Logos* (defined by Europeans as a synergetic art involving the process of unifying ideas and forms within a single meaning) are means by which God's hidden presence is recognized--and they are scattered throughout creation Mystical life. "*Logic*" (the practice of drawing conclusions from premises) in arriving at beliefs. When the Sophists (c400 BC) perfected this "Logic," its users became very clever and shrewd in ways to *generate unfair advantages for themselves and unfair disadvantages for their victims.* Since God was not their standard, they said "*virtuous*" success came from material things (e.g. having money) and power over people. For the ancient Greeks, and subsequently for the Western world, Logic designates a specific branch of philosophy dealing with the study of principles of reasoning. Military Order Ladder. Ancient Greeks (e.g. Plato), after borrowing these and other high level thought processes from Africa, made drastic modifications--like dismissal of the Spiritual (i.e. Right Brain) aspects permeating African Thought. This placed them on anything but the Spiritual Elements Track. Nevertheless, they devised "logic" that "made sense" to them on whatever track it was on. All actions following those "logical" conclusions took them further and further away from the Spiritual Elements Track. It is amazing to read how they present the exact opposite position of all knowledge deriving from Greece. What all of this means is that although the ancient Greeks have been credited by the Western world as originating much of what is now important, the fact is that the *ancient Greeks were mere translators and transmitters of African Knowledge*. What they borrowed from African Wisdom was diluted and polluted, ancient *Greeks have been responsible for generating the seed of world wide delusions* of a profound degree. This continues to be perpetuated by the Western world to the present.

LOGOS: An awareness of both Quantitative and Qualitative Mathematics clearly indicates the Cosmos and the Laws of Nature are based upon Mathematical Order. This stems from the "Oneness" established by the Divine Logos—a "Oneness" that is the basis for Cosmic Correspondence. The Essence Pattern of that "Oneness" possess: (1) Coherence (its hidden internal links and components being consistent with one another its internal components are consistent with one another); (2) Consistency (standing firmly together within a state of harmony and balance with what makes sense); (3) Compatibility with Reality (practical); (4) Interconnectedness (everything real depends on every other real thing); (5) Order (sharing the "Oneness" of Cosmic Primordial Substance center); (6) Regularity (conforming to the prescribed standard or the established pattern for it kind); (7) Balance (rendering no favorites on either side but conforming to the Ultimate Standard); (8) Harmony (complete adaptation of each part to the Wholistic Circle); (9) Endurance (progressing inside/in tune with the Spiritual Elements); and (10) Predictability. This means there is *Continuity* (Unity running through Multiplicity) from all interdependently doing its independent things for the benefit of the whole in the *course* of their *Natural Processes*. That "Oneness" formed by the Divine Logos is at the basis for Cosmic Correspondence. The Continuity of that Cosmic Correspondence provides: (1) a "Sameness" throughout the "Oneness" Pattern--regardless of its location in the Seen or the Unseen realms; (2) enables the realization of its Esoteric nature taken from any Sample at any location when compared with Spiritual Elements ("The Word") standards, guides, measures or "educated" Estimates, and filters; and (3) its Consistency and Compatibility give revelation insight into the nature of its Creator's attributes, based upon the nature of the Spiritual Elements work products. Quantitative Mathematics is for exact Left Brain minds that demand all aspects of the Seeable be explained to them by means of definitions and axioms. This is because Matter can be observed to be in the most exact proportions—of number, weight, and measure—and that is the way to reason about them. Qualitative Mathematics is "Musical Reason" which deals with the Un-seeable origins of the Seeable Matter. Since that origin derives from the touchstone of the highest Cosmic excellence, its Essence is from more than the human mind can grasp. It is thought moving in the sphere of complete abstraction from any springboard of Quantitative Mathematics and deals with the relationship of concepts to the Divine Logos, without consideration of their relation to experience or to each other. Its conclusions are to what all things in the Cosmos conform. *This process was introduced by Very Ancient African's Subjective Science* tools—i.e. Observation, Reflection, "Pure" Feelings, Productive Imagination, Contemplation, Inductive and Deductive Inferences, and Common Sense—to make inferences in arriving at circumstantial evidence and judgments. Conclusions from these Inferences enabled their discovery of Qualitative Algebraic Mathematics which, in turn, enhanced Quantitative Mathematics.

LOVE PLATTER: The instinct to Love; to spread Love; to be Loved; and to be Lovable

M

MAAFA—THE BLACK HOLOCAUST: The term "Maafa" is a Kiswahili word for "disaster" or "massive death" or "catastrophic disaster" or "immeasurable catastrophe" or "great misfortune" or Holocaust (Greek, 'something which is burnt whole'). Etymologically, a *Holocaust* is a 'complete burning' and the word was originally used in English for a 'burnt offering'; a 'sacrifice completely consumed by fire' (Mark 12, 33, 'more than all whole burnt offerings and sacrifices); and in present day application, 'nuclear destruction' and 'mass murder.' Holocaust is not quite the same as '*Disaster*' (a bad configuration of the stars which generates 'bad luck'). Not all disasters or misfortunes are holocausts as, for example, a flood, a train wreck, or the collapse of a building. In an Afrocentric sense a holocaust is an act of genocide so morally monstrous it is not only against the people themselves but also a crime against humanity. According to Harris (in The Best of the Kemetic Voice, Vol. I p27), the most outstanding of the broadest categories of holocaust occurring in Black people include Islam, Christianity, slavery, colonialism, racism, and White supremacy. Among Afrocentric scholars, Maafa refers to the great suffering of Black people at the hands of Europeans--and most explicitly to the period from 1500s-1800s when Europeans hunted, captured, transported away from Africa, enslaved, dehumanized, objectified, sold, traded, destroyed African Tradition, and instituted self-destruction in African people (see Dona Richards, Let the Circle be Unbroken p12). This is a unique event of horrific and morally monstrous destruction of human life (where tens of millions of Black people were killed); of the horrible odyssey of the Middle Passage with all of its pathos and suffering; of humanity in Enslaved Africans by extracting them from their proud history and denying them their humanity; of destruction to physical African culture (cities, towns, villages; great works of art and literature; of human possibility (suppressing all but the survival instinct of African American slaves—an evil act whose ramifications have been culturally transmitted to today); of preventing the rising out of poverty for millions; and of brainwashing struggling Black people's manner of thinking into a self-defeating mindset. In short, Black people's cultural identity was cruelly derailed by the evil and sadistic acts of Europeans during African American Slavery. Following slavery Maafa has continued to refer to the fact of struggling enslavement; to the sustained attempts to dehumanize and control the minds of afflicted Black people; and to the on-going efforts to maintain Black people in a needless struggle. Ani (Yurugu pxxi) states: "the minds of African people are still crowded with the image of Europeans as superior beings. This is a condition which locks our will and freezes our spirit-force." John Henrik Clarke applies the term "the imprisonment of a people to image" and adds that we must "instill will into the African mind to reclaim itself." After 25 years of constant research on Black history and in personally evaluating thousands of Black patients and from living among and mentoring innumerable Black people, I strongly believe that the mental trauma suffered by the Enslaved was so profound—so repressed and suppressed—and so not talked about that it accounts for well over 90% of the problems of struggling Black Americans. Layered on this "Post-Traumatic Distress" Syndrome are additional components of Dissociation and Delusions. This process starts by honoring those involved in the Maafa (and it continues to this day) and handling the residual effects of the Maafa in each individual. Many Black scholars attribute the moral decay throughout the world to the evil and sadistic Europeans' enslavement of Africans—first in the form of African slavery taken into Europe and into the Americas and second, as Colonialism, beginning in Africa in 1870 and lasting into the 1960s.

The associated inhumanity has never been seen in human history. Both phases were characterized by the enslavement of Africans, raping African women; taking riches of the Americas and Africa back to Europe (whereby merchants, institutes, and kingdoms accumulated huge fortunes); either destroying or stealing the natives' cultural contributions; and engaging in an imperialistic system of absolute exploitation. Every gain, profit, and benefit realized by Europeans came at Black Peoples' expense. Following slavery, the victims were left in terrible mental and economic poverty from which most have not recovered. Continued European economic suppression of their victims has ensured the maintenance a struggle for day to day survival, causing Europeans to 'trash' the ways and "Being" of their victims and tell horrific lies about them. The combination of slavery and post-slavery features justify the term Black Peoples *Holocaust* (Greek, 'something which is burnt whole') of enslavement. The third phase, Globalization, features the control of money and power by the European male Power Elite--and at the expense of health care, education, and food production for the needy and disregard for the care of the planet's resources (Beckman, in Asante, Encyclopedia of Black Studies, p270).

This is done by dominating social, religious, economic, media, and education systems of peoples throughout the world by means of "the gun" (in the form of the most powerful and dangerous technologies). The majority of people contribute by allowing the amoral/immorality and inhumanity of Europeans to happen. Dr. Ani states: "We have been duped into believing that we are free and healthy, but we are still living in Maafa. Only by going through the pain and the grief can we find our way to Sankofa, an acceptance of our being, our spirit." Sankofa signifies the search for knowledge, starting with returning to the source and doing the intensive research so as detect and correct all associated problems. All of this is about "Depersonalizing" Black People. So, who is a "Person?" A Maafa (immeasurable catastrophe) is far, far worse than a Holocaust. (etymologically, a 'complete burning') because although the crime against humanity at the time of its occurrence is devastating, the spiritual, mental, social, financial, and Selfhood residual effects remain equally as bad for the afflicted but on different planes of existence.

MA'AT FACULTY: Kamitan (Egyptian) Sages said the *only purpose and goal of life* is to develop ones positive potential. When it has been completely and perfectly realized so that one has infinite wisdom, compassion, and "ME/WE" skills—i.e. Caring and beneficial things one does in recognizing one is connected to the Cosmic Organism of God's creatures and creations so as to create, enhance, maintain, defend, and protect Harmony. To these ends, a *human's Spiritual Intellect* voluntarily has its mind *subjected to the Divine Spirit in order for it to command the Life-Force that is in harmony with the Laws of Nature.* That is what transforms a human's "ME" Self into an expanded Self-Identity—called a "Non-Self". A "Non-Self" expands beyond ones own "ME" Selfhood Entity to mesh into the Cosmic "ME/WE". Then in situations involving the "ME/WE," it utilizes the Ma'at faculty--the mid function of the Right Brain. The *Ma'at faculty* communicates to the mind the workings of those forces which maintains order of a human's physiological and mental functions; perceives all structural components underlying Things and Events; enables one to see the inner factors that unify things; fashions the perception called *Synthesis* by integrating all mutual relationships and interdependence of Things with each other and the whole; and, thereby fashions that human's ability to see the whole. By the "Non-Self" having one "hand" in the Cosmic Mind and its Creatures and Creations and another "hand" in daily living settings, it has channels to the *Twelve Cardinal Virtues of African Tradition.* These--symbolizing the highest of human excellence—are: Propriety (be in accordance with the fitting and appropriate), Balance, Order, Truth, Harmony, Peace and Tranquility, Fellowship, Justice, Rightness, Straightness or Righteousness, and Reciprocity ("the reward of one whose acts consist in the fact that one will act for her/him" in doing good). By being in *harmony with the Laws of Nature means they are Intuited and spontaneously flow without thought or effort. To Intuit is to be* guided without precedents into ones own Divine Consciousness, so as to have an immediate understanding of the higher sources of the Spiritual Elements without calling upon reason or feelings. This is what enables one to live a Ma'at lifestyle—i.e. the Human Life Living Ideal in accordance with laws of ones indwelling Divine Consciousness—i.e. the "Soul Sunshine" of ones Private Self.

MA'AT PRINCIPLES FOR AFRICAN CRITICAL THINKING: Ma'at (pronounced "Ma aut"—derived from "Maa", the measure of a cubit)—is the central moral and spiritual theme in the Traditional African approach to life. Ma'at is the Spiritual Elements in action—i.e. Unconditional Love, Truth, Reality, and the Natural. Ma'at's origin dates to ?20,000 BC, following Very Ancient African priest-astronomers charting of the stars and planets by devising units of measurements (e.g. arithmetic and geometry) based upon the observed periodicity of astronomic events. These measurements so matched the Celestial Order as to itself amount to a revelation regarding the organizing principles by which Ancient Africans (e.g. the Dogon and Woyo) realized and recognized its own latent harmony. So wondrous were the cycles of Celestial Bodies--and their ever greater, more majestic, and infinitely widening cycles—that African Sages inferred laws by which gods came into being and then disappeared. These laws were "hooked" up to their new mathematical insights and into the earlier-known mystery of biological death and regeneration. Thought to arise from the lunar rhythm of the womb (i.e. the Great Mother) as a result of Cosmic Order, the goddess Ma'at emerged through a mathematical law. Besides being a model on how to Live Life, she crystallized the "Big Picture" Seed, Pattern, and Vision of Divine Cosmic Order. By putting pertinent mathematical connections into philosophical words, African Sages formulated Ma'at laws.

Ma'at was personified as holding the Ankh cross, a symbol of the heka Aung (i.e. magic power) in one hand and the Papyrus scepter (representing the book of Law) in the other. On her head rests the feather—her main symbol. She was next designated as the feminine counterpart of Tehuti (god-man of Wisdom)--and was viewed as a correspondent between the Earth and Celestial realms. In the Book of Ptah-hotep (?4599-4402 BC)—the oldest complete Sebait (or Books of Wise Instruction which also contained Ancient African Moral Philosophy)—the concept of Ma'at is introduced as an intimate link with the Ultimate Divine Plan Ideal. To this end, Ma'at's name became associated with the idea of Truth, Righteousness, and Order—with what concerns respect, levelness, genuineness, uprightness, and with the world steadfast and in equilibrium. This meant Ma'at became an unalterable connection of measurement for Social and Spiritual order—by the relationship between one human being and another—between humankind and the gods—and serving to bridge humankind and the Living Dead. All of this was an elaboration on the meaning that any human, by being *made in the Image of God,* was naturally imparted with *Dignity* (inherent worthiness incapable of being diminished).

The creation, enhancement, and maintenance of Dignity were comprised of the *Twelve African Cardinal Virtues*--pathways symbolizing the highest of human excellence—Propriety (be in accordance with the fitting and appropriate), Balance, Order, Truth, Harmony, Peace and Tranquility, Fellowship, Justice, Rightness, Straightness or Righteousness, and Reciprocity ("the reward of one whose acts consist in the fact that one will act for her/him" in doing good). Modeling a Rightness path of standards, filters, measures, and guides to a thriving, more meaningful and rewarding life, and Happiness was called "*The Way*" of Ma'at. These twelve were fashioned into 42 laws governing "the Way" of living—and also for criteria in the Hall of Justice to weigh and measure the deceased life's beliefs and actions on the "*Day of Judgment*". The Judgment included first the deceased having to pass the Negative Confessions or Declarations of Innocence or the 42 Admonitions of Ma'at. Next, the deceased's "Heart"/ab was placed on one Balance Scale pan and Ma'at's feather on the other--Truth's lightness being the standard against which initiates' Will (i.e. "Hearts") were weighed. This was followed by judging the Soul. The determination was based on living by a standard imposed by ones essential divine nature—i.e. staying within and living life out of the Spiritual Elements since one could not claim to have done Right Living if there had been inconsistency at every moral choice crossroad.

The original essence of Ma'at and the Weighing of the Soul was laid out in Ancient Egyptian hieroglyphics. This summarized the wisdom recorded millennia earlier on temples, tombs, coffins, papyruses, and oral teachings pertaining to African Spiritual Literature. The purpose was to encourage spiritual liberation, awakening, or revivification (give new life to) in order to elevate from ordinary human consciousness and mortality up to Cosmic Consciousness and immortality. Although Ancient Africans discovered and codified mechanical, physics, chemistry, and other academia, their focus was on the patterns governing people's day to day existence and spiritual development. Rightness' Twelve African Cardinal Virtues implied each human has an obligation, duty, and responsibility to pursue them as goals. This stemmed from defining the Divine and the Natural ingredients for Human Ideals as: social right relations with and interaction behaviors toward people—with personal behavior—with Nature—and with the Divine. To follow the Ma'at Way is the path to a successful life—preparing and qualifying one to cross the great abysm in the Afterlife so as to bathe in the divine powers at ones appropriate Ari (i.e. Karmatic) level. Because the supreme law governing humans' divinity is centered on a Free Will to choose, the knowledge of the law is conveyed to one in such a manner that allows one the freedom to follow or reject it. Ancient Africans said such happens via human's Ma'at faculty deeply buried in the Spirit of the mid-function of the Right Brain. It has the capability of communicating to ones mind the working of forces that maintain Order of ones physiological and mental functions. Ma'at itself is a projection of the forces that inter-relate the various functions of the body into a human's awareness. The perfect harmony existing between these various functions is Truth and Reality. One can intuit from this faculty and experience the urge to live by the Spiritual Elements—the Human Ideal in Life Living according to the laws of ones indwelling Divine Consciousness—i.e. the "Soul Sunshine" of ones Private Self. They defined *Intuiting* as seeking the Will of God through ones 'Self' (Divine Consciousness—a human's "First Wisdom") so as to experience ones own true nature. From resultant Insights, *Intuitive Inductions* (inferring general principles from particular facts present in the Cosmic Order) are done. This means making compatible imaginative leaps to discover unrealized realities--i.e. the taking of Leaps from facts of Reality into realms dealing with corresponding Unrealized Realities. The revealed Ma'at Principles are absorbed into ones mind to guide thinking and thereby be led "instinctively" to the apprehension of Truth for its application on any "Branch" of the "Truth Tree"--perhaps of a premise or to do what is Right, even if it puts one at a disadvantage and ones opponent at an advantage. One can thereby live in harmony with all things because all things in the Cosmos are functions within a system.

Examples include giving Unconditional Love without seeking anything in return or making available needed entities of life in spite of the needy refusing them. The components on the Cover indicate the major aspects of how to get out of a mindset of Violence and return to the Spiritual Elements stream in order to swim through the course of ones life. The Sankofa Process starts it by reviewing Ancient African *Wisdom* (derived from deep experiences and realizations about them) of Tehuti so as to extract pertinent principles to put ones present life in Order. The switch over process is spurred by a *Self-Declaration* ("Nothing will stop me from becoming my Highest Self"). However, all switching Self-Declarations demand paying a high price. At first, it seems things will get worse--but that worsening is simply the process of getting rid of all that is contributing to Violence applied to oneself and to others. To best solve ones major problems, ones skilled Critically Thinking Intellect partners with the Spiritual Emotions (i.e. Pre-Birth Emotions) emanating from ones "Heart." The ingredients needed to harmoniously fit together ones newly fashioned Human Ideal Goals into a workable plan is by Ma'at's 12 virtues. The correctness and effectiveness of ones time, energy, and efforts are determined by one gradually experiencing in ones Private Selfhood the essential "5Ss" (safety, security, self-confidence, strength, and stability) so as to move confidently into a thriving future and be happy in the process of simply doing Right Life Living. Since Ma'at is Spiritual, African "Logic" arose out of its "Religion"--both about applying connecting Ma'at Laws/Principles. *Ancient African Laws refer to the foundation of all Cosmic manifestations and denote a sequence of inherently related events that occur with unvarying uniformity under the same conditions. These Laws that govern Creation are stored in the Divine Spirit* and arranged in a particular format that graphically aids in the explanation of the African Tree of Life's 11 Principles, their functions, their relationship to each other and to the whole. Thus, the *work of Spirituality is the subjection of the mind to the Divine Spirit in order for it to command the Life-Force in harmony with the Laws.* In African Tradition, "Religion's" origin was guided by mathematical and scientific understanding of Cosmic Laws fitting to human behavior and humans' relationship to God. The African etymology of "Religion" (re, again, once more + ligion, to tie, unite, yoke--and logic, and the law) implied that on the basis of Logic and Law there was the reuniting of elements illegitimately separated previously (e.g. Soul from Will). *African Religion--the Ma'at system helping humans reunite with God--is a function of a human's Will rejoining and activating ones Divine Conscious.* Thus, in African Tradition, "*Religion*" is based on certain Knowledge--and not faith, belief, or mysticism, which are European inventions in their applications to God.

MA'AT--THOUGHT SYSTEM OF AFRICANS: The greatest geniuses the world has ever known were the Ancient Black African "man-gods" Tehuti and Imhotep. Their divinity genius was a spontaneous part of natural ability not requiring instruction or training for creation, invention, discovery, or expression--called Wisdom. As African Sages, Tehuti and Imhotep sought Principles (Spiritual Elements pieces) inside the Esoteric (exposing intricacies of defying fundamental thoughts/understandings)--inside the Scientific--and about logical events (ordered changing Realities) pertaining to higher planes of existence. They spoke of Cosmic Matter in Space acting like a balloon deflating (*Involution*--returning to the center) and inflating (Evolution--growth where things are set free to expand)--as Einstein embraced in modern times. Such integrating assessments of the Obvious, the Hidden, and the Essence of Things required thinking *in Symbols while manipulating Principles.* For example, the way they arrived at God being *Omnipotent* (unlimited and universal power), *Omnipresent* (present everywhere simultaneously), *Omniscient* (having total knowledge of everything), and *Immanent* (entirely a Mind) started with realizing the "Space" in the sky served as the background enabling humans to see the stars. To use a today's example, you are looking at this printed page and noticing the words while ignoring the white background upon which the black ink is printed. What one sees on this page is the result of having learned definite rules about its words--e.g. its letters of the alphabet which form the words and the message you get from assigning a meaning to them. But none of this would be possible if it were not for the blank white page on which the words are printed--a page called a Substance ('stands underneath'). So, "Things" of awareness from human's senses can only be known by its Opposite. Ancient Africans had no images of God for they considered God--the enabler of all Real Things--to be like a "blank" (unknowable). Imaging all God's manifestations is the only way to know God. But to see God as an image (e.g. one with a white beard) or as a "Sound" (God said…) or as a man is idolatry. Manifested Opposite pairs alternate between Yin (feminine--the Womb, the Void, the Negative, the Dark, the Nothingness--all beyond human's perception or conception) and the Yang (the Masculine--the image or sound of what can be known). Both are involved in interactions underlying and constituting the whole world of Forms ("the 10,000 things"). Although Cosmic Energy's distribution throughout the Cosmos is invariable, each Form features the sum of two equal amounts of energy--one positive and active in kind and the other negative and passive. Yet, their nature has varying proportions of these two modes of energy involved in their creation. Such multiplicities of creation as Forms are what energy takes on as it moves and interacts in different polarities or pairs of opposites. By being beyond any concepts of duality, it (e.g. Truth) operates out of singularity, not duality--proceeding to make manifest: (a) Tao (road, way, Truth, Right conduct); (b) the source of Laws and Being; and (c) the way or course of Nature, Destiny, Cosmic Order. This is because the Absolute (God's Substance) which underlies the Cosmos is made manifest and it inhabits every created thing. African Sages used knowledge of Opposites--the Yin-Yang binary--to form *African Logic*. First, they emphasized the *"Big Three"* of: (1) using pure and spontaneous expressions in addressing the Metaphysical and Supernatural; (2) Spiritual Elements presentations by means of a harmonious and unified spirit; and (3) maintaining a mystical expression aura by interacting "Soul to Soul" with others--as in the "Call and Response." Second, since planes of existence combinations are exemplified by a human, this example of Nature's Unity consists of parts so inseparable that none can, without fundamental damage, be separated from the others. Even sitting still or resting in the deepest of sleep, the atoms, molecules, cells, tissues, organs, and systems of the human body dance in astounding harmony and exchange ambient energies from air, water, food, and invisible electromagnetic radiation. Such *Unity of Action* is a complete, ordered structure of activities directed toward intended effects with each unit functional. When forming a Thought Structure requiring a premise Base, that Base, if Spiritual Elements compatible, it is in the *Ma'at System of Thought*.

MAGIC COMPONENTS: Elements of Magic include: (1) The Spell, with magical powers in the formula believed to have been handed down from Legends of the miraculous deeds of Ancestors and made effective by citing their names in Charms and Spells as part of the formula (and without variation). (2) Rite, a set of actions needed to convey the Spell to the object which it is desired to affect. (3) Condition of the Performer--avoiding taboos, certain foods, etc. Religions of Nature are those forms of Magic intended to work for constructive and destructive purposes. Most of those working either way contain elements of both magic and religion. Amulets, Talismans, Fetishes, Totems, Necromancy, and Taboos are all elements of both magic and religion. Depending upon the agreement or disagreement of a given magician, all Magic actions are able to influence Spirits, ghosts of the dead, demons, or gods by certain Rites, or at least that certain imagined powers in an object respond to certain actions. In ancient cultures, some Magicians specialized in the Supernatural by engaging in Divination--"Seers" or Fortune-tellers'--those attempting to discover future events by extraordinary or Supernatural means. To *Divine* has reference to the ancient Soothsayers' arts (as in Gen. xliv, 5, 15) and refers rather to instinct or intuition than to reading the future. *Divination* includes *Telepathy* (ESP affecting another); *Clairvoyance* (seeing objects far away and hidden); and *Precognition* (acquiring information about the future). *Natural Magic* (Sorcery, Juju use of roots, herbs, animal substance, etc.) and *Ceremonial Magic* require Words of Power and Symbols because of an intimacy with Imagination. *Conjuring* produces illusions involving the Supernatural. Foreign Magic found its way into Greek civilization. Here, all sorts of Prophecy, Astrology, Invocation of the gods, Psychomancy (a form of divination involving communication with the spirits of the dead), and Anthropomancy (a method of divination using the entrails of dead or dying men or women, often virgin female children, through sacrifice) were in constant use.

MAJOR PREMISE: the main fact assumed to be true and accepted as a fact, making no further inquiry concerning the truth of the same, in order to reason further by Deduction. See Premise

"MAKE-BELIEVE": As a baby, illusions are the first awareness and the first pleasure. That generates an Engram (permanent memory) for obsessive-compulsive fulfillment. *Obsessions* are a persistent uncontrollable impulse to think certain thoughts. *Compulsions* are uncontrollable impulses to be a certain way or carry out certain actions irresistibly and contrary to the inclination or will. Furthermore, there is something satisfying about being in make-believe and that automatically leads one into the Crowd unless one has the Selfhood Greatness to be oneself. To be well deceived is to be habituated in Illusions, Hallucinations, and Delusions without interruption so that these make-believes constitute ones Self-Absorbed lifestyle. Such a lifestyle cannot be enriched or have a Mission because it is Useless and Static—resistant to the Spiritual Elements because it, not they, are considered real. From these come ones sensations, emotions, desires, and aspirations, no matter how limited or self-defeating. As one grows older, ones make-believe world is supplanted by new make-believe ingredients which are equally convincing. Obsessed by this fairy tale, one spends ones life searching for a "magic" door to a fairyland of happiness. By never having seen an attractive reality keeps one preferring the make-believe in which one is familiar. Support for ones position comes from the unspoken Supernatural rule that when everyone is in the wrong, everyone is in the right. This means obvious errors slip through the cracks. Since Hallucinations are perceptions of what does not exist, this means ones sensory experience has no reality in the outside world. Rather, these false perceptions are only present in ones mind despite seeming to come from the external world. As an intern at Los Angeles County hospital, in the ward containing alcoholics, it was usual to see several patients picking at things in the air or swatting at imaginary things or trying to grab what was not there. Another type of example is seeing objects or hearing sounds as one is prone to do at a graveyard at night. The Illusional/hallucinational appearances can seem very real to the naïve--so real as to be misled by the well-intentioned and by con-artists who are persuasive in getting them to believe what does not exist—so real as to require much proof to realize they are not real. "Throwers" of historical and philosophical formal and informal teachings of "make-believe" about their feigned enemies lead the current Crowd to trend similar Illusions and Hallucinations about the same "enemies." Each represents Echos or ripples or memories which add layer after layer of Indifference/Hate/Evil/Sadism (IHES) of what does not exist and yet has a tremendous payload effect. These "throwers" of Illusions and Hallucinations are deliberate efforts to get the cult to believe the presented IHES fantasy to be Reality, so that the consequences of their words will cause never ending ripple + echoing effects. To buy into that is to be entrapped and encaged. Whenever these "throwers" are challenged, they become hostile and, in turn, aggressively brand and attack any deviants from the concepts they have accepted. A reinforcement for "make-believers" is that, in contrast to religion, there are no penalties imposed for having any of them; for doing or not doing them in any particular situation; and for not sharing them. They are satisfied with the "make-beliefs" of knowing what they want when, in reality, they are merely parroting what the Crowd tells them they are suppose to want. This is somewhat accounted for by them needing to believe they are unmanaged while actually they are being managed effectively. But gradually there are layers of turmoil added from one realizing one is not and never will be who one is or knows one could become. Gradually, ones becomes unfaithful to what one has been and to what one wished for in order to remain immortal. *"Make-Believe" is seeing reality in ways other than they are.* This concerns such categories consisting of "All-or-None," "Either/Or," Biases, Prejudices, stereotypes, Secondary and Tertiary Qualities and their Nuances. Any of these categories can be presented in Facades, "SEEMs" right, "Almost Right," and "Good Enough forms. To this end of making deceptions believable ones mind has to be turned "Inside-Out" by Illusions, Hallucinations, and Delusions. What dominates here is Implicit understandings—i.e. Unstated but understood via implied by inference; capable of being sensed, though not directly expressible. *Implicit*--like the smell of a newly forming flower bud--is vague, hazy, organized Sensations which give ones mind an awareness of what is contained or included, though not expressed, in the Sensation. Those Sensations mold ones mind into a sort of better awareness of what is contained or included, though not expressed, in the Sensation of the Percept

MANAGEMENT: "*Charge*" (obligation, duty, and responsibility) and "Management" (regulation and order) involved in personal labor. A gardener has the care of a garden; a nurse has the charge of children; an overseer has the management of a farm. *Manage* derivatively means handling. It connotes devising and contriving ways and means by which one gets something to fall into Order.

MANHOOD—EUROPEAN: What best characterizes European "Manhood's" historical 'big picture' is "Male Chauvinism" (1970s)—an attitude attributed to insensitive men from prejudices against woman and of excessive loyalty (or fanatical patriotism) to fellows in 'like-kind' male cults (nixing the "I'm my own man" concept). As exemplified by Nicolas Chauvin, a legendary French soldier enthusiastically and overzealously devoted to Napoleon, this prejudiced superiority 'airy' foundational belief in ones own cult constitutes

"Extraversion"—the deeming of External World 'Things' (e.g. social phenomena; the realm of 'changeableness') to be superior to ones own Inner World powers—a sign of weakness. Its extension is that European "Manhood" considers the best of the External World to be 'out of this world'—i.e. placed in a Supernatural World—and to which most European males desire not only to be part but a leader in it--or at least have special recognition or status in it. European "Manhood," unlike "Womanhood," is widely viewed as a status that is tenuous (it must be demonstrated) and elusive (it must be earned)--both by action and aggression so as to quell each male's doubts about his gender status to himself and to outsiders. A dominant belief is that since open expressions of emotions are a sign of femininity, they and even 'felt' emotions must be controlled to avoid being viewed as possessing a sense of inferiority and a weakened masculinity. Men are therefore expected to be consistently "individualistic," tough, calm, rational, and in control. In my view, the pivotal point of what constitutes "Manhood" in an individual or a group or a society is, in general, its *prevailing philosophy* and, in particular, the *chosen pattern of Thinking*. To elaborate, the European "Manhood" focus--the opposite of African Tradition--is on the structure rather than the content of "Manhood." Yet, it is full of contradictions, even from purely a European perspective.

One example is that the Supernatural is fantasy and thus cannot be about a standard if one uses the European definition of a *Standard*--what people's ideas are measured against of the "What it is" of the ultimate value of a "Thing"--the "what it does," and the "how it appears". Then that flawed assessment serves as a definition guide for solving problems + points out direction + places boundaries (e.g. time and space limits) + provides rules for performance and variations. Second, a criteria for European "Manhood" in self-declaring heir Supernatural "Air Castle" and the best of its contents are 'superior' can only be believed by their own "Non-Rational" thinking. The "Non-Rational"—Emotions admixed with Left Brain mental activities—derives out of the dogma of the Supernatural and those declarations are deemed to be 'superior' to the Natural Cosmos' Rational Thinking (i.e. Logic as originated in African Tradition). *Think about that!* Thus, "Non-Rational" Supernatural rules make it acceptable to follow a 'realistic' (?) analytical discourse that permits putting '*Boundaries on the Boundless*' (by the Supernatural said to be 'superior' prevents European philosophy from believing in the Natural Cosmos' Spiritual or Metaphysical realms). So, for example, nothing seems wrong with reducing *Organic life*—which naturally undergoes a "birth-growth-decay-death" process, followed by rebirth to another cycle--in terms of rational truth into precise *mechanical laws*. Natural Cosmos "Common Sense" is negated by "Non-Rational" Thinking. By definition, "Non-Rational" Thinking is not thought out--only sensed by emotions and evolved out of that with Left Brain thoughts. Its action course, outlined by the 'payload' message in its "Non-Rational" Disposition--complete with its inclination and intention--may be quite supportable on grounds of the "Air Castle" Supernatural's concepts of the rational or ethical (proper/improper) or moral (right/wrong)—grounds that are "6:30 opposites" by the clock to what is best for all in the Natural Cosmos. European patterns for living that springs out of "Non-Rational" Thinking, when compared with Natural Cosmos Logic—and without my judging either—impart mental Dispositions that, upon "playing them out", are "*Non Sequitur*" ('it does not follow'). Its contrariness to sound Logic or Reason makes it Irrational (i.e. absurd) and Illogical (i.e. false or foolish). It does not require Understanding one or more fundamentals of life or any topic essentials because its focus standard is: "what can it do for me and my goals." The European Ego requires one to view oneself in opposition to others as well as requires a ceaseless pursuit of power (i.e. control over objects such as people, Nature, material things) for its emotional satisfaction--all with the aid of flawed "science." By deeming people unlike them to be "Objects" Europeans justify imperialism by "saving" the world, "ordering" it, and going so "far out" from reality to convince themselves of their own magnanimity and altruism (based upon "the White man's burden"). Such Ego projection is a substitute for self-fulfillment.

European psychologists characterize European males as aggressive, assertive, ambitious, competitive, dominant, forceful, independent, self-reliant (Ani, Yurugu p308, 559), judgmental, scornful of others' interests and opinions, and possessing a superiority complex. Female traits such as affection, compassion, gentleness, love toward children, loyalty, sensitivity, sympathy, understanding, and warmth are liabilities for European males. A failure to experience such interdependence between humans is a Left Brain function mixed with the Right Brain's Acquired Emotions. Its aggressive readiness displays is a means of validating their precarious gender status. Naturally, for such 'high stakes" there was/is a constant struggle in "Manhood" quality and/or quantity displays of the most desirable aspects of life in order to achieve and maintain status. Hence, in activities of daily living, masculinity relative to femininity is precarious the higher one goes on the social status ladder. The worst of some type of Psychic Trauma imparts an inclination to be in a cult.

MANIPULATION: *Fraud* (gaining an unfair advantage over bodies of people) involved those aspects of "*Trickery*" (deliberately giving the wrong impression) that includes "*Deceit*" (the pursuit of personal gain at the expense of victims) and "*Manipulation*" (here hypocritical dishonorableness).

MANLINESS: Developing oneself out of ones Spiritual Elements ingredients and using those ingredients to discover, develop, and find just the right niche for ones birth gift Talent.

MANTRAS: You must know that events in life are not controlled by circumstances and natural born talents. One of the greatest achievements of ancient Egypt is, on one side, the knowledge that all events in the universe are the products of energy. This includes your way of thinking, emotions, talents, attitudes, your life path with the challenges and opportunities that occur in it. And on the other side is the knowledge of how to manipulate, and control the energies that are responsible for your talents, opportunities, health, wealth, and so on. In the same manner that western science has identified and learned to manipulate atoms (chemistry) and physical forces (electricity, magnetism, and the host of subatomic forces), the ancients identified the effects that different sounds exert on man's mental and psychological faculties. This is the science behind the use of mantras, or hekau, or words of power. Qigong is the world's only holistic exercise system. It clearly identifies and targets all of the physiological and energy systems that govern physical, mental and psychological functions and well being. Given that it is based on the same theoritical foundation of Chinese herbalism, diet, acupuncture, I Ching, and much more, the exercises can be prescribed in support of these other therapies and practices. Ra Qi gong is one of the only qigong systems that address all of the five energy organ systems that govern the functions of the body, mind and psyche; and incorporates all of the techniques (healing sounds, breathing, mudras, meditation and postures) for manipulating the subtle forces that govern our well being. The effectiveness of the system is seen in the rapid and permanent health improvements that it brings. Many practitioners have seen permanent improvements in probems with their joints, vitality and stamina, libido, mental clarity and much more following two to three days of practice.

MARINATE: ('dunk it in the sea') inside the matrix of ones mind whereby "Like-Kind" thoughts out of memory and those from the outside world support its evolution aspects. See Matrix; Options

MARKETPLACE--COMPETITVE "CUT-THROAT": The "Marketplace" is a special kind of arena for which Black People have never been adequately prepared to successfully compete. A mindset of *Ferocity* (1646, 'wild-eyed savage) and *Cunning* (C16 'skillfully deceitful') are essentials to enter this competitive struggle. Competition for Riches, Honor, Command, or other powers puts those striving for them on the path to Contention (rivalry contests), Enmity (deep seated hatred), and sophisticated "War." Some reasons for this Brute mindset include the desire to do something distinctive; to give some evidence of originality; to attract public attention; to secure patronage; to be feared; and to be above the law. The story of the Grappling Hook is a metaphor for the gains Brutes anticipate from being shrewd and cunning in the marketplace. Both are associated with the challenge of winning at any cost, the excitement from confusion and conflict; the mutual envy of equal status competitors; the dangers of adventure, the thrill of victory, and the agony of shame or defeat. A snapshot setting for this was the theme Aryans handed to their descendants, the Greeks and then to Medieval European males—i.e. that being a warrior and enslaving people were manly. Such unabated influence was elaborated on by the Italian Machiavelli (1469-1527) who said Western ruling Manhood is about using force and fraud in order to gain and maintain money and power. All of this has been orchestrated throughout European history by influential Supernatural powers so great as to keep Brute followers in awe and controlled. The essence cause for this awe and praise for ancient and Supernatural players has stemmed, not from the reverence of them for being dead, but from the vicious competition patterns they laid out. "Survival of the fittest" reigns because every man is against every other man. The Marketplace motto is: "What's mine is mine—what's yours is up for grabs." Despite its Rules being inside a box, variations on those Rules are made by the defending champion. There is a similarity of the alliances, liaisons, and flunky group entourage of each reigning champion. *Alliances* are mutually helpful participants who are psychologically and philosophically disconnected from each other—and yet feature the sharing of common character traits, like the Indifference/Hate/Evil/ Sadism (IHES) mindset. *Liaisons* are people who support like-kind people but without much of an association between them. This is for purposes of ensuring mutual understanding, unity of action, and especially prompt and effective network support so all can acquire a common goal. Such was clearly exhibited by *Apartheid*, a European policy of racial segregation practiced against non-Whites. Its scramble for Africa climaxed at the Berlin Conference of 1884-5 when 14 European nation leaders publicly proclaimed their hypocritical desire to redeem Africa from the grip of nefarious Arab slave traders. Britain emerged from the conference with 12 colonies in East, West, and southern Africa. France acquired a vast swath of territory in West and North Africa. Upstart Germany secured a handful of territories, of which it would be divested after World War I. Portugal, an empire in dotage (deterioration), obtained Mozambique and Angola to which it would cling until the late 1970s. Throughout this time European nations were fighting each other for dominance over Africans. All of this goes back to primitive European "I" Society (i.e. Individualism) tribes who constantly fought each other until they needed to join forces to fight a common enemy. This has been modelled in European society ever since as, for example, with the ancient Aryans (a group of tribes sharing a common language but not being of the same racial stock). Similarly, the theme of the Marketplace *Destructive Individualist*s is: "*I'll do as I please and at anybody else's expense.*" It is *essential for them to practice Separatism (i.e. discrimination) in order to have scapegoats.* One reason for these scapegoats is to have their cult members and the Crowd's influence spend their attention in attacking them. In this way, all cult members can achieve and maintain a sense of superiority while the Crowd becomes so involved as to not notice what the leaders are doing to control them. They, along with "everybody" one knows, can be bought at some price—and especially when it comes to money. Since, in Western tradition, what trickles down from the top pervades the Crowd, all forms of vicious competition (e.g. coliseum lions vs. people) are approved of by Europeans.

MATHEMATICS: Today, two broad subdivisions are *"Pure" Mathematics* (Algebra, Analysis, and Geometry) and *Applied Math* (e.g. Mechanics, Physics, Geodesy (Earth's size and shape), Geophysics, and Astronomy)--with each having several subcategories. See Reasoning; Laws of Nature

MATHEMATICS UNDERLIES NATURE'S & CRITICAL THINKING: An amazing insight of Very Ancient African priest-astronomers (?20,000 BC to 12,500 BC) was to explore the subject of "*Order*" as a way to discover Truth--and nothing was better ordered in Truth and Reality than stars and planets in the sky. The concept came from revelations in which African Sages said all things in the Cosmos began in order; shall end in order; and then begin again. The first tool for observing the visible appearances of the stars, planets, moon, and sun was the *Astroscope* (the reed of a plant). Its purpose was for *Divination*—an Inductive method for obtaining knowledge of the unknown. From this research came general concepts about *Cosmic Order*—like realizing the rhythms inside Order and the Vibrations making up Rhythms. Refined instruments allowed African Sages to chart stars and planets' orbits more deeply; to note how the earth responded to these orbits; and to devise units of measurements (e.g. arithmetic and geometry) based upon the observed periodicity of astronomic events. To record this data, they had to invent Pure Mathematics, the highest rung of human Rational Thought--the most original creation of humans--the non-empirical (not based on observation or experiment) Science par excellence--the queen of the Sciences--in order to deliver the key to those laws of Nature and the universe, both concealed by appearances. Most early mathematical discoveries derived from needing to have a better understanding of Vibrations. To these ends they searched to find a fixed point in the sky's sacred space--a space conforming to African Sages' revelations concerning primordial aspects of the Cosmic Creation--a point essential for establishing natural order--a point useful as a central axis for all future orientation—the point of absolute reality. Eventually, the Woyo (Equatorial Africa) and Dogons (Mali) found and named it the Po Tolo (Sirius B) Star (Diop, Civilization p314). Their measurements so matched the Celestial Order ("course or way") as to itself amount to a revelation regarding the organizing principles by which Ancient Africans recognized its own latent harmony. Inferences from all this knowledge generated insights related to Ordered Rhythms--insights leading to Truths concerning the earth, the cycles of Nature, the stars, constellations, and human body mechanics. Hence, devised math blended the heavens and the earth in a manner fashioning them into one unity. For example, the "X's" and "Y's" of mathematics--invented by Very Ancient Africans--became short-cut ways of manipulating symbols without thinking of the specific meanings they may be standing for (e.g. so many bushels of beans or the area of a platform). Those Circumstantial Truths--based on Nature giving to the shape of a given pattern a specific power--paved the way for inferring more laws. Such enabled them to realize that Spiritual Energy vibrations formed the Spiritual Elements of Unconditional Love, Truth, Reality, and the Natural of the Divine Logos--each in the form of vibration patterns. African Sages said the Spiritual Elements create and proceed according to strict mathematical rules--as all elements are being made of the same components and simply configured differently. Similarly, the progression from one Spiritual Elements "package" to the next Elements "package" also follows a strict mathematical pattern in which the underlying properties of each Element are repeated in the Element 8 places away. This cyclic or periodic return of qualities is the basis of arranging the elements into the Periodic Table of Elements. Again, although each element is different, their "Genetics" are the same, and their structures all follow the same pattern. Such are the *Law of Correspondence's* underlying principles--i.e. harmonious fitting and agreement of all Spiritual Elements in every Cosmic off-spring of a Divine Archetype (Seed). See Logos; Correspondence; Circumstance

MATHEMATICS--VERY ANCIENT AFRICANS DISCOVERED COSMIC: The Very Ancient African temples of learning, called "Houses of Life" is where Sages, Seers, and Priest-Astronomers gathered to discuss and explore Nature's "Order" for purposes of learning about what constitutes Circumstantial Truths concerning God's Laws. To keep up with ongoing observations required the development of mathematics. To this end, they invented a double three-dimensional compass to measure four dimensional times and space to enhance systematically watching the positions and motions of the stars and heavenly bodies over thousands of years. Within this process the Dogons (Mali) and Woyo people of Equatorial Africa discovered a fixed point, known today as the Po Tolo [Sirius B] star — Diop, Civilization p314; Bailey, Common Sense). That enabled their measurements to match the Celestial Order ("course or way") and its ever greater, more majestic, and infinitely widening cycles. As a result of their newly determined Sky Knowledge meant their mathematical formulas which were compatible with the Celestial Order both became sources to lay out patterns for Circumstantial

Evidence, Proof, and Truth. An example of applying the resultant Principles was in seeing the Correspondence required for blending the Heavens and the Earth into being one Unity. It became evidence that this amazing Harmony throughout the Cosmso whereby there was complete adaptation of each Part to the Whole had to come from a given "Mental Order" existing in the Celestial System (called *Catasterism*). In other words, the secret Harmony holding sway throughout the whole Cosmos had to necessarily be powered by Ordered Love, "Truth," Reality, and Natural—i.e. the Spiritual Elements--for every aspect within the Cosmic context. What could be determined as evolving out of the Spiritual Elements was the exhibition in the largest and smallest parts of the Cosmos, as in the Laws of Nature mentioned above. This meant there is *Continuity* (Unity running through Multiplicity) from all interdependently doing its independent things for the benefit of the whole in the *course* of their *Natural Processes*. A key point is that these Natural Processes are mathematically based and thus can be mathematically determined. Ancient African Sages recognized and interpreted the Celestial System as a moral planetary *"series"* capable of explaining things in the Spiritual, Metaphysical, Physical, Philosophical, Psychological worlds. Since each of these derives from the same Spiritual Elements "Genetics," together all could be likened to strings in a fishnet—each doing its independent duty but working interdependently for the benefit for all of God's creatures and creations. It was on this foundation that Ancient African Sages patterned their Logic and Thought Structures used throughout African society with such uniformity as to be now known as African Tradition. At every step of this process and done all over Africa, there was no distinguishing between learning and playing. Very Ancient African Sages believed in holding to contradictory views on the same subject at the same time. For example, simultaneously there were different creation events; different means employed by creator-gods in their creation; and differences in the condition of the primordial state at the beginning of creation. They tolerated great ambiquity, as with holding to at least three different means of creation simultaneously without concerning themselves with the contradictions. In fact they welcomed contradictions under the assumption that the Truth would lie at the point where the contradictions intersected. Together they went into creating new or evolving old cosmological systems -- and none became out of date because of each being considered a principle piece of the whole. Here, as in building a skyscraper, the uncomparable absolutely sound Base is Unconditional Love.

MATHEMATICS--COSMIC MYSTICISM COMMON SENSE DISCOVERED: Based upon observations of the seasons, behaviors in people, health of bodily processes, and practical experiences with a number of related things showing interdependence, indicated to Primitive Africans that Order is implicit (implied and understood despite it not being directly expressed). These awareness were interpreted by Very Ancient African priest-astronomers (c20,000 BC) and Seers as Order being essentially dependent on the existence of the interdependence (oneness or unity) between things. Then they astutely applied this concept to the Unseen realms of the Cosmos. They inferred that Order was what underlay all creative processes and thereby believing that to explore Nature's "Order" was the most practical way to discover Circumstantial Truths concerning God's Laws. The *Sexigesimal System* of numeration originated in Ancient Africa for the purpose of allowing for earth and heaven-like measurements in degrees. This was based upon the ideal reflector of the principle of time-- the female crocodile, who carries her eggs for 60 days and broods on them for 60 days. She has 60 vertebrae and 60 teeth and lives for 60 years. From inferences and astro-mathematics, African Sages discovered it takes 25,920 years to complete a cycle of the zodiac and that divided by 60 = 432—again the *Sexigesimal System*. This astro-mathematics method--called in traditional Chinese astronomy "Tian Gan" and "Di Zhi" (literately meaning Heaven number and Earth number)--links mathematics to philosophy and many natural phemonenon. Incidentally, the Chinese calendar is in a 60 years cycle. Then, they measured a healthy man as having a heartbeat of one per second and in a 24 hour day the heart beats 86,400 times which, divided by 2 = 43,200.

They inferred that matched the beat of the universe. Thus, taking ones pulse would indicate if one was in tune with the universe rhythm. Listening to the heart beat is a way to meditate and it was believed this is how messages of the Cosmos are passed to humans. Making inferences from all this was a way Ancient Africans discovered that the Order of the Cosmos was mathematically based (J. Campbell, Thou Art p44). Furthermore, they said, that underlying all manifestations in the Cosmos and in humans is an *"Ordered Program"*--a program which refers to the maintenance of unity in the midst of increasing creation (differentiation)—a program which conforms in a series of small, graded steps to carry out approaches, methods, techniques, and manners so as to achieve specific functions. Historically, African Sages have always made observations of the repeated patterns of the "Seeable" aspects of Nature. Examples: (1) Observations related to the hatching of eggs shows eggs of the potato bug hatch in 7 days; of the canary in 14 days; of the barnyard hen in 21 days; of ducks and geese in 28 days; of the mallard in 35 days; and of the parrot and the ostrich in 42 days. Notice, they are all divisible by seven, the number of days in a week! (2) There is mechanical harmony seen individually in animals and Nature. Examples: Since the body of an elephant is too large to survive on two legs, as opposed to any other quadruped, their four legs all bend forward in the same direction. These four fulcrums enable it to rise from the ground easily. By contrast, the horse rises from the ground on its two front legs first while a cow rises from the ground with its two hind legs first. (3) The waves of the sea roll in on shore twenty-six to the minute in all kinds of weather; (4) Examples of the order of Plants: Each tree grows upright. Each watermelon has an even number of stripes on the rind. Each orange has an even number of segments. Each ear of corn has an even number of rows. Each stalk of wheat has an even number of grains. Every bunch of bananas has on its lowest row an even number, and each row decreases by one, so that one row has an even number and the next row an odd number. All grains are found in even numbers on the stalks, and specified even numbers in thirty fold, sixty fold, and a hundred fold. Flowers blossom at certain specified times during the day. From these examples, it is easy to see reproducible processes among like-kind things that derive from the same Spiritual Elements Genetics; that the "Seed" of each reproduces itself in its own image to become the thing it makes; that the unique Pattern (defined as a fully realized form) in each has a similar specific power and periodicity; and that they have a life's course. Any two or more of these have Correspondence and the feature of each makes them mathematical processes.

MATHEMATICALLY DERIVED KNOWLEDGE: Since the Laws of Nature are Mathematically ordered, to follow Nature's Processes establishes Human Truths. Here, one deals with the conditions creating the problem and translates the relations existing in a problem into Mathematical Language. Since there are no expressions of the relations in a problem or situation, to follow the Mathematical Processes of Nature, one next Abstracts from the specific context of a Metaphysical or Physical realm problem or situation what is comparable to the numerical aspects and relations of Algebra. Then, one states their relations in Algebraic Symbols so as to obtain an Equation. After describing those Symbols, they are manipulated and maneuvered by formal applications of definitions and principles. Resultant Products of their Ingredients are combined or synthesized according to various rules or guidelines in order to yield new ingredients or ideas. The End Product—Algebraic Knowledge--is interpreted within the context of the Problem or Situation and without regard to their exact nature so as to fosters Knowledge and/or Information content.

MATHEMATICAL THINKING: African Tradition is built upon Mathematical determinations for things and conveying those things in a reproducible order that starts from a sound Base. Non-Rational thinking of Europeans' Supernatural thinking starts from no sound base and is so scattered in presentation as to be confusing, incomplete, conflicting, and problematic because of the variety of ways their point can be interpreted. People whose Right Brains are undisciplined by their calculator type of Left Brain order are scattered thinkers.

In using the alphabet for illustrative purposes, scattered thinkers present their thoughts about something by starting with "X"—i.e. "That" or "It"—both unknowns to the Receiver but vivid in their own minds. Then they proceed, without orienting the Receiver to any specifics or even to the "ballpark" their ideas are in, to go in C, P, A, T, directions in conveying the information. A mathematical thinker starts with the "Big Picture"; then the definition of the keystone term to be discussed; then A, B, C, D, lay out of what is the message; and anticipates what might not have been clearly understood of the Principle being given by then providing an example or analogy in keeping with the Receiver's mindset and environmental familiarities—i.e. speak in the Receiver's language. An example of how Very Ancient Africans had applied valid non-syllogistic reasoning was, after developing Algebra, deducing from the usual algebraic equation, $a = x + b$—over to the solution $x - a - b$, in accordance with the postulate: *equals subtracted from equals give equal results.*

MATRIX: a nice word, implying to 'mother'--is a complete organism womb which imposes itself on, restricts the contents of, and places a boundary around a Thought or Creation. Meanwhile, it supplies nutrition, assists organization, and fashions orderly progression of development until the thought process or the creation is completed; or at least well along the way. See Options; Marinate

MAXIMS: Ancient African Maxims are public declarations of basic moral principles--teaching the glory of Cosmic Order and Ma'at while infusing a spiritual consciousness into the social and political areas of society. This was based upon not discarding its traditions but in gathering the best of African Thought having occurred up to that time and simply building on it--often practicing or upholding what originally seemed to be contradictory (the way I approach any difficult problems). See Ashamed

MEANING CHANGES: An example of focusing and sharpening a given capability is that in Middle English the word "Pigeon" (a peeping chick) meant a young bird, especially a Dove. But as this definition "Genetics" was passed down over the years, Pigeons and Doves (means the bird's diving flight) became part of a larger group of "like-kind" family members who shared homologous (similar) features from a common ancestor. That group, called Columbidae, possesses the same part or organ which, in different family members within the group's 310 species, has every variety of form and function. Dove is now used for a smaller variety of Pigeon. Such shifts in meaning are usually slow and tendential rather than rapid and absolute. Early usages continue indefinitely alongside later changes that have become dominant, as was true of Pigeon and Dove in C16. In the process of change, terms may acquire further meanings within a set of words: the Pigeon is not a symbol of Peace and no one "dove-holes" information. See Etymology

MEANING IN UNEXAMINED WORD ASSUMPTIONS: A human's personal experiences with a "me, me, me" vs. "ME" vs. "ME/WE" mindset are very different—each having to be "felt" to know the difference. But "me, me, me" oriented people—those wanting what they want, when they want it, and by any means necessary--are incapable of knowing anything else. Upon being exposed to "Scarce Desirable" Material things, "me, me, me" people think in terms as that being only for them. Such causes people to proclaim their own rightness while denying all others the validity of their ways—leaving a trail of misery and killings. Such has never been a part of those involved in African Tradition. Colored Peoples who have followed Europeans' "me, me, me" trend have made a mess of their lives. The "ME" experience is about Spiritual Survival, Self-Preservation, and Self-Protection—all necessary before being able to see beyond themselves, except for situations involving Compassion (of which "me, me, me" people have no concept). They think in terms of "That which is," as illustrated by the word "Plop"—simply the sound made when a frog jumps into a pond without splashing. "ME/WE" people experience the African word "Yoga"—meaning a union or integration of ones "Self" (a human's Spark of God Divine Consciousness) with the Cosmic Organism (i.e. all of God's Creatures and Creations) to become a "Non-Self." Since this is a non-verbal realm, it can only be "Felt" in order to be a part of it. That implies *the subjection of their minds to the Divine Spirit so it can command the Life-Force in harmony with the Laws of Nature*. Then, whatever they see happening to anything in the outside world is the seeing of themselves. So, when "ME/WE" people think of themselves, they know that their personal reality goes on of itself inside, around, and outside themselves. This simplifies life by them never doing anything to harm themselves or the "WE" and never allowing harm to come to either, if at all possible—or at least keep it to a minimum. To elaborate with the word "Selfish," it was "me, me, me" oriented leaders that gave it its "*Distorted One-Sided Coin*" meaning as a Mind Control devise in order for them to gain unfair advantages and put Victims of their propaganda at an unfair disadvantage. Their theme is "Do as I say, not as I do." Such Fettered Lower Acquired Brute Selfishness embrace animalistic sensuality/lust, Hate of even the "faceless," attachments to Things, Lies, Greed and its resultant Frustration, Indifference, False Pride, Chronic Anger/Rage, Egoism, Delusional Fears, Violence, Indifference, Aversion, Adversion, Cruelty/Sadism, Meanness, Rudeness, Cowardice, Cunning, Shrewdness, Intemperance, Arrogance, Vanity, Oppression, Control, Dominate, Deceit, Revenge, Jealousy, Envy, Malice, and Injustice. It results either from being socialized into it and then being to weak to overcome it and/or from possessing a sense of Inferiority, Self-Hatred, Insecurities, feeling Shame from being Inadequate or "Not Good Enough," Imitators are attracted to this pattern because it is a "short-cut" to acquiring "Scarce Desirables". And that is "just fine" since they do not believe in Ari/Karma; are "Numb" to the evil they do; and the whole course of existing institutions foster it. They are unable to "Feel" that they are the most cheated of all humans, are at the lowest level of all humans, and the absence of the benefits of being loved, making being "Feared" a substitute. Hence, they are incapable of the "Feeling" experience of the *Unconditional Love Platter*--the instinct to Love themselves or others; to spread Love; to be Loved; and to be Lovable. For this to be free flowing requires Unconditional Love coming into ones Selfhood--from oneself, if from no one else—so that Love can circulate inside and around that Selfhood and continue flowing outside. By observing chickens, the "me, me, me" will discover that when chickens quit quarreling over their food, they find there is enough for all of them. "ME" Spiritual Selfishness is never about disregarding the welfare of others but rather it is a matter of timing as to when to help others and in what way. One is not able to teach life lessons until one has become wise. Helping in daily struggles, as by means of support or comfort, is useful but not taking over ones problems so as to make them weak. "ME/WE" people "Feel" the "All for one and one for all" concept.

"MECHANICAL ORGANISMS" OF EUROPEANS: Aristotle said the realm of Nature includes no more than the Material Universe—Celestial and terrestrial—while the rest is Supernaturally mechanical or machinelike—governed by laws of science of mechanics, or any similarly limited number of physical principles or laws. Based upon Aristotle's Supernatural concepts about the Universe of things happening naturally or by chance (absent a repetitive sequence of law), Europeans, like Newton, wrote treatises on: "Mechanics, demonstrated and applied to Nature." This was about explaining or interpreting all phenomena by means of physical forces and laws as, for example, the human body is magnificent mechanism. Thus, as with a machine, the operations are not purposively but with blind regularity patterns that do not vary.

MECHANICAL ICON IMAGES: Icon Myths are metaphors with which one tries to make sense of the world and which carry the power of Icon Images. An example of an Icon Myth is using the European Bible to generate concepts of the Cosmos being an Artifact (a made thing) in a mechanical sense. As part of the European concept that the Cosmos is an artifact and not run by the African God, Amun, they misapplied the Ancient Egyptians' creation of the Mythological story of humans and animals. It says *Khnum* (Egyptian, *molder;* Divine Potter), a ram-headed deity and potter-god, uses the mud of the Nile, heated to excess by the Sun, fermented and generated, without seeds, the races of men and animals (Gadalla p142). Then the resultant created bodies of children are removed from the potter's wheel and inserted into their mothers' bodies. Immediately upon the delivery of each baby, Khnum's consort, Heket, offers the "breath of life," symbolized by the *ankh*, to the nose of the clay figure to animate the clay effigy into a living soul so as to become a vibrant part of the divine order charged with numinous (Sublime) power. This breath represents the hidden or occult force underlying creation. But European Bible Passages leave no doubt about the belief in the concept of the Divine Potter as a fact. Genesis, 2:7 mentions the material used to make man is the same type of substance used by Khnum: "And the Lord God formed man of the dust of the ground, and breathed into his nostrils the breath of life; and man became a living soul." This was again echoed thousands of years later in Isaiah, 64:8: "Yet, O Lord, thou art our Father; we are the clay, and thou art our potter; we are all the work of thy hand." "Breathing into the nose of the clay figure to animate the clay effigy" conveys to Western people the idea of a 'made' Cosmos. Such separates from each other the things made (e.g. each human being) as well as separates those things made from the Maker (i.e. God). First and most important in this powerfully flawed concept is that believers in the Cosmos being put together as a Mechanical Artifact will see themselves as *Individualists*--meaning "survival of the fittest." Second, if they were made out of clay, then when they stop breathing they will return to clay--and that is all there is to their existence. The phrase: "ashes to ashes, dust to dust" comes from the funeral service in the *Book of Common Prayer*, and it is based on Genesis 3:19. That passage says that we begin and end as dust. Genesis 18:27 and Job 30:19 refer to dust and ashes as components of the human body. Third, they might believe God's will is imposed on them, thus wiping out their "Free Will." That implies boundaries on God's Unconditional Love in the form of not being "free" to follow what they believe is best. In some, this can generate resentment and rebellious acts which, in turn, can go in the direction of being aggressive Brutes and Satanists. The first aggressive move is because as "Individualists" since God has set in motion the workings of the Cosmos, God is not needed to tell them what to do. In their view, reality is simply blind unintelligible energy needing to be conquered and controlled. By being "little gods" they are quite capable of running the show and doing whatever they like--Kill/Take/Destroy/Dominate/Control--and never, never show any signs of weakness. They see Competition as the name of the Game--who can win the most adult toys. The Game is played like Billiards, with each Brute symbolizing the white cue ball powered by aggression. The idea is to roll it all over the "table" and bang into other balls (victims) so as to "pocket" them as well as to knock cue balls (opponents) off the table. The rules are that there are no rules--and Fetters reign supreme. Thus, all players are on hyper-alert to any danger coming from any direction by competitors or victims. There is no such thing as discussing in order to gain understanding. For this reason, their "tough guy" tyrant attitude always carries a sense of insecurity with the fear that "I might not have what it takes." Hence, each must be ever-ready to compete from a warrior's position: having various GUN types with an eagerness to use them as a way of bolstering their Icon Image of what represents "manliness"; always sitting with their backs to a wall; having "body guards" of various types (e.g. in-group members, being part of systems designed to "take down" any opponents); and beating down those whom they take advantage of so that those victims lack the spirit to fight back. Brutes are miserable people!

MECHANICAL (SUPERNATURAL): Since newborn humans start life thinking with Images, maybe primitive European Warriors' immature and mechanical thoughts were imaged. Examples: Armor was for *mental* and physical defense mechanisms; strategically assessing significant problems was done from an Adaptive mechanical perspective (e.g. if X happens, do Z); troubleshooting utilized a mechanical process to locate problems and for repairs by mechanical patterns. Both warring and dancing were done mechanically. By being solely oriented to the Physical realm (a mechanical tendency) meant it was an easy next step for these Warriors to extend their "structured" way of looking at things into the realms of their environment, their culture, themselves, their victims, their gods, their thriving, and the Supernatural—pursuing/fixing each mechanically. Such a mechanical association of concepts meant primitive Europeans' mechanical language was applied automatically, even to organic things; for mechanically solving anything; and to have a false sense of "all is well" from that one 'broken' thing having been properly handled mechanically. To elaborate, the Hylozoists, ancient Greek thinkers, were not conscious of any fundamental difference between mere matter vs. life and consciousness. To them, Nature (to be born) included everything that is or that ever came into Being. Later Sophist contrasted the "Natural" with the "*Conventional*—or that which anything is originally and what it is as the result of human intervention. They described as conventional law, custom, colors, and other secondary qualities, in contrast with matter and motion. Thus, the "Natural came to be contrasted with the "human" and the superhuman. Plato and Christianity set the body and mind sharply against one another and to identify "nature" or "the world and flesh" with the material part of the Universe only. This made "Nature" (i.e. the entire universe) opposite to the Supernatural.

From this arose identifying "Naturalism" with Materialism, thereby converting the Organic into "machines"—a conversion allowing "Killers" of "Faceless" people to believe their victims have no feelings. Other Ancient Europeans similarly expressed this Supernatural state in terms of a machine—a mechanization taking reason out of its earthly domain and converting it to "Non-Rational" (Emotions + Left Brain) decisions and solutions. Their Supernatural cult rules put '*Boundaries on the Boundless,*' including making mechanical the Cosmic Organism. The Greek Euripides(480-406 BC) illustrated this by saying: "The way of God is complex. He [a gender boundary on their God] is hard for us to predict. He moves the pieces and they come somehow into a kind of order"—implying a mechanical universe. Dumbness of the Machine Concept implies: (1) that humans do the same thing all the time without change, like fool-proof machines; (2) seeing themselves as mechanical justifies being "coldly" disconnected from fellow humans; (3) stereotyping "those people" as insignificant Chimera sub-humans to be feared; (4) doing inhumane things to them without any compassion; (5) makes those Mechanical Believers think they do not belong to anything + the External World is what is happening to them and that they have nothing to do with it.

MECHANICAL--EUROPEANS' COSMOS CONCEPTS: Whereas Ancient Africans said a human's body organs worked independently to interdependently produce wholistic health, ancient Greeks borrowed and changed this concept to the idea of an organ being a tool, implement, device, or contrivance--like that used in manual labor. In the post-classical period "*Organ*"--by now a word of "*Mechanics*"--implied an instrument that works with a bellows, like the coordinated structure of a church organ, to produce harmonious music. In C17, "*Organism*" designated a group of organs functioning as a whole. To it as well as to the new devices called "*Machines*" (a word formerly used of plots and intrigues or for any kind of erection) the ancient Greek word "Mechanic" was applied. Then the Greek prefix 'auto' (self, as in self-moved or automatic or spontaneous of ones own free will) became associated with things working by machinery. The 1748 Oxford Dictionary said: "the motions of the body are of two kinds, automatic and voluntary. The automatic motions are those which arise from the mechanism of the body in an evident manner. They are called *automatic* from their resemblance to the motions of automata, or machines, whose principle of motion is within themselves. Of this kind there are motions of the heart and peristaltic motion of the bowels." Otherwise, today anything man-made is considered mechanical, relating to, produced by, or dominated throughout by physical forces." A *mechanical process*" uses (or acts as if it is using) mechanisms or tools or devices. *Mechanically*, a "Structure" (made by constructing) is composed of a number of parts built piece by piece and held or put together in a particular way to form a pattern or shape. And a "book of logic and rules" comes with it, especially if applied to humans by Brutes. *Many illusions/delusions are from Europeans evaluating Organic Organisms as if they were* *mechanical and this faulty way of thinking is entrenched in the world's informational literature.* One faulty reasoning process is: Wild beasts are born creatures of instinct and they, not man (Error I), possess fundamental powers called "brute instinct" and "brute strength." Next, by thinking animals had no language implied any animal "utterances" lacked thought (Errors II & III). Finally, it was assumed all animal behaviors could be explained on purely mechanical principles (Error IV). Another example is *Logos*, meaning in usual analytic discourse all is stated in terms of rational truth so as to reduce life to precise mechanical laws. Third, philosophical and psychological vehicles for thoughts, feelings, and emotions in which something happens to ones mind are called *mechanisms*--as with the hierarchy of cognitive processes being termed a 'mental mechanism.' This kind of thinking made no sense to me in school and stifled my pursuit of knowledge and creativity. One reason is it misdirects seeing an organism in relation to its environment as well as their intimate relationships to each other. For example, humans breathe out carbon dioxide absorbed by plants; plants give up oxygen which is needed by humans. To see the Cosmos as a machine forces a narrowing of ones vision off the "Truth-Track." Hence, Reasoning is unable to see any "big picture" embracing foreground and background contents of any given thing because of it being unnecessary in patterned thinking for machines. On the one hand, to recognize a problem arising out of an organism is to realize likely disharmony throughout, which hampers 'its all at once' growth. On the other hand, in assessing a significant problem from a mechanical perspective, troubleshooting (e.g. if X happens, do Z) will locate that problem and its repair gives a false sense of "all is well." Those bounding themselves and others as mechanical (e.g. Brutes) justify the delusion of each human being "coldly" disconnected from fellow humans. For Brutes to view humans whom they deemed to be insignificant or fear or dislike to be mechanical removes any personal feelings about it--making killing them easy. Mechanically oriented societies lack a connectedness with the whole and can thus Kill/Take/Destroy/Dominate/Control at will. They also conceive of Cosmos Icon Mechanical Images (e.g. God idols, like Satan). Victims accepting the stereotype of mechanical beings, self-declare they are less than human and then "live down" to that image pattern in behaving. By contrast, African Traditions' Cosmic Humanity connection, like kin, is so deeply felt as for there to be no "unplugging" of and replacement of another. jabaileymd.com

MECHANICAL BOUNDERIES ON THE ORGANIC: Ancient Greeks borrowed the Ancient African concept of an anatomical organ as a structure of the body functioning as a unit with other organs for the specific and single purpose of producing health (i.e. wholism). They changed this concept to the idea of an organ being a tool or implement in the sense of it being a device or contrivance, as used in manual labor. In the post-classical period "Organ"--by now being a word of "*Mechanics*"--carried the sense of an instrument that works with a bellows, like the coordinated structure of a church organ, to produce harmonious music. "Organism" came into use in the 17th century to designate a group of organs functioning as a whole. To it as well as to the new devices called "*Machines*" (a word formerly used of plots and intrigues or for any kind of erection) the ancient Greek word "Mechanic" was applied. Then the Greek prefix 'auto' (self, as in self-moved or automatic or spontaneous of ones own free will) became associated with things working by machinery. The 1748 Oxford Dictionary said: "the motions of the body are of two kinds, automatic and voluntary. The automatic motions are those which arise from the mechanism of the body in an evident manner. They are called automatic from their resemblance to the motions of automata, or machines, whose principle of motion is within themselves. Of this kind there are motions of the heart and peristaltic motion of the bowels." Otherwise, today anything man-made is considered mechanical, relating to, produced by, or dominated throughout by physical forces. "A mechanical process" uses (or acts as if it is using) mechanisms or tools or devices. *Mechanically*, a "Structure" (made by constructing) is composed of a number of parts built piece by piece and held or put together in a particular way to form a pattern or shape. And a "book of reasons and rules" come with it, especially if it is applied to humans by Brutes. For Europeans, instruments are means, like patterns imposed on things by the mind, employed to attain an end--ends like knowledge or the resolution of a problematic situation. In C17 and C18, part of Europeans' anthropomorphism was to use their ways of doing things by resorting to mechanical patterns as an analogy for God's creations and creatures. The idea was that there is a code--a preordained pattern of God that one must use to discover the Cosmic Laws. A *Law*, they said, is a pre-existing pattern which things follow and that a Standard must be regular like a clock. From knowing this pattern one could understand the mysteries of Nature. These are some examples of Western man's *Instrumentalism* patterns, concerning their minds imposing on other things the way these men think things should be. This, in effect, isolates Instrumentalism thinkers from those very things (e.g. the world, or human beings unlike them being deemed subhuman) and that justified them declaring God died. Yet, this was not a problem because since natural laws operate in a mechanical Cause and Effect manner, no God was needed, for things could now operate on their own. One of their justifications was that shapes are made of material but things operate without matter.

Let us pause here to indicate a major job of Critical Thinking (CT) is to always challenge the major *premise* (a statement, applicable to European Logic, accepted as a basis for further reasoning but it may be true, distorted, or fantasy). For example, a rock falls because it obeys the law of gravity which precedes it. But since this is not necessarily so (as when it is in a vacuum), the rest of what follows--"if one eliminated all the other explanations about the rock and about gravity--one would be led to the truth." But also needed is an awareness of the basics, as in knowing Nature's rhythms pulsate and hence one is not to be deceived by its analogy to a clock. Many delusions occur from Europeans evaluating Organic Organisms as if they were mechanical and this faulty way of thinking is entrenched in the world's informational literature. One faulty reasoning process is Wild beasts are born creatures of instinct and they, not man (Error I), possessed fundamental powers called "brute instinct" and "brute strength." Next, by thinking animals lacked a language implied any animal "utterances" lacked thought (Error II). Finally, it was assumed all animal behaviors could be explained on purely mechanical principles (Error III). Another example is Logos, meaning in usual analytic discourse all is stated in terms of rational truth so as to reduce life to laws that are mechanical and precise. Third is philosophical and psychological vehicles are called mechanisms for thoughts, feelings, and emotions in which something happens to ones mind. For example, the hierarchy of cognitive processes is termed a mental mechanism. This kind of thinking made no sense to me in school and stifled my pursuit of knowledge and creativity. One reason is that both require seeing an organism in relation to its environment for they are intimately related to each other. For example, humans breathe out carbon dioxide absorbed by plants and plants give up oxygen which is needed by humans. To see the Cosmos as a machine forces a narrowing of ones vision in a manner not allowing Critical Thinking to see the "big picture" of what is in the foreground and the background of any given thing because that is not necessary for machines. On the one hand, to recognize a problem arising out of an organism is to realize there is disharmony throughout which hampers its growth all at once. On the other hand, in assessing a significant problem from a mechanical perspective, troubleshooting (e.g. if X happens, do Z) will locate that problem and its repair gives a false sense of "all is well." In applying this to those who see themselves as mechanical (e.g. Brutes) is to give them the false belief that they are "coldly" disconnected from fellow humans. This makes it easy for Brutes to view humans deemed insignificant or whom they fear or dislike to be replaced without any personal feelings about it. Such a mechanically oriented society has no sense of connectedness with the whole. When applied to Conditional Love, this "disconnection" belief is associated with Brutes believing knowledge is something consisting of the possession of true ideas or hypotheses as, for example, Material things are all that is important. They consider members of their in-group as "cogs in our machine." Furthermore, they believe in having patterns about such things (among others) as love that come about from Instrumentalism thinkers so as to be in control of all--a path which encourages them to become predominately Patterned Thinkers. One way this displays is their Conditional Love causing them to treat others like agents, like entities which exist for the purpose of bringing about some prescribed result. Their victims who are made to feel as if they are mechanical beings are easily stereotyped into accepting a demeaned status of being less than human and then "living down" to that pattern of behavior. By contrast, Unconditional Love has a natural humanity connection that, similar to a family, is so deeply felt as to be absent any ideas of "unplugging" and replacement of another (e.g. a family member). To bind anything Organic by the mechanical frees one to bind everything.

MEDITATION: inducing experiences of altered and higher states of Consciousness for Spiritual Elements achievements—by means of *transcending* (i.e. by over-reaching human mental limitations) into the Sublime magnitudes exceeding life.

NEEDY WANTS: Needy Wants are Spiritual Human Nature Needs that are about *The Love Platter*--the instinct to Love freely; to expand the Courage in ones Conscience to spread Love regardless of how it is accepted or not; to receive being Loved unconditionally; and to be Lovable.

MELANIN: After discovering "Blackness" is a Divine Principle of the Cosmos + "Black" being the producer of superior mental and physical organisms + inferring *Black to be ultimate in Spiritual Perfection--Ancient Africans proudly called themselves a "Black People."* Melanin ('black or dark brown' pigment), as the keystone orchestrator Element in the Cosmos, is in greatest abundance in the darkest skin-colored humans. One of its widely imparted and many benefits is Black People's mental processes (brain power) being controlled by the same Melanin chemicals which generate their superior physical (athletic, rhythmic dancing) abilities. Melanin enables Black infants to sit, stand, crawl and walk sooner than Whites. Melanin causes Black humans to demonstrate more advanced cognitive skills. Etymologically, "Black" is the meaning of the 'KAM' root of Chemistry—the study of life's building blocks which, themselves, are founded upon Carbon. Melanin is the black element present in all living Carbon matter and thus is part of living tissue of every part of a creature or creation throughout the Cosmos. Knowing Cosmos-wide atoms "marched" with the heavens, planets (e.g. the Sun, Moon, Earth), and their associated entities while being in order, in tune, in proper degree, in proper priority, and synchronized, led African Sages to many realizations. Example: Melanin has "*Black-Hole*" properties (like those found at the center of the galaxy). Thus, their profound conclusion was these properties and activities were an *exhibition of a total Cosmic Correspondence display*. That opened the gate for insights into the Esoteric Unknown. Melanin contributes to controlling all mental and physical body activities; helping in "ME/WE" human (i.e. Black) family connections; attracting "mystic memory" that assists learning from Ancient African Ancestors' Thought Clouds; and, the "Intuition" Nervous center in the Pineal Gland's Substantia Nigra connects one with God's Amenta. In turn, this is associated with memory, Inner vision, Intuition, Creative genius, and Spiritual Illumination. Each of these were discovered to be dependent upon the Pineal Gland's blood borne chemical messengers that control skin color. Such opened the hidden door to the darkness of the *Collective Unconscious* mind, allowing Ancient African priest-scientists to visualize knowledge from the mind's timeless Collective Unconscious memory banks [which I believe is located in the Omnibus Brain]. In short, the *Black Dot* (locus coeruleus) was said to be the trap doorway to Universal Knowledge of the conglomerate past, present, and future. These Principles are an ordered interrelated divine and social binding of all God's creatures and creations within a state of Cosmic Wholism Organism existence. Though one may be light-skinned, the concentration of Melanin in their organs or in their melanated centers could be almost as high as that of dark-skinned people. To summarize, Melanin has proved itself to be: (1) a foundational ingredient in the DNA of the genes and protector of the DNA nucleus; (2) centrally involved in controlling all mental and physical body activities; (3) granulated like "central computers," capable of analyzing and initiating body responses and reactions that by-pass the brain; and (4) associated with proper Central Nervous System (CNS) functioning--as refining it so that messages from the brain reach other areas of the body, which is done more rapidly in Black People than in others. Melanin itself is "sweet," having a pleasant aroma. Perhaps this is why "MERi is the Kamite (MER = MEL) name of Creation's Great BLAK Mamma, source of "MARy". It has the same root as MELon, MOLasses, MELody. That root is associated with the neuro-chemical basis for what is called "SOUL" in Black People. When truly experiencing "Soul Music" (i.e. by means of Spiritual Energy), one is participating in the Cosmic quintessential Spiritual aspects by being part of, and unified with, its rhythm. The result is a strong aesthetic emotional experience that imparts Insight—like one sensing the touching of some aspect of the Cosmic Metaphysical realm. Many Black People have this experience when deeply absorbed with "Soul Music"--i.e. "Soul Art" or "Soul Thinking" Knowledge. These, by being of a Pure *Emotional* nature mix (not Acquired Emotions), are the basis of having good relations with and good behaviors towards other good people. In short, abundant Melanin means that upon removing barriers, Black People can excel in all human areas. That scares people! See Pineal Gland; Third Eye jabaileymd.com

MEMORY: *not thinking but rather the passive flow of stored images.*

MENTAL DISCIPLINE: *Taking Charge and Control of ones life and making ones Selfhood efficient and effective*

METAPHOR: an African metaphor speaking of gods, means its symbolic "atmosphere" is about entities actually within persons' "Heart" touched by them, and not referring to some invisible Being.

METAPHYSICS (AFRICAN): real, distorted, or unreal entities, descriptions, meanings, and explanations related to all planes of Cosmic existence except the Physical Realm which stay within Spiritual Elements boundaries

"ME/WE" Cosmic Organism and that ones Mission is to "Lift while Climbing."

"ME/WE" PHILOSOPHY: "ME/WE" benefit productions are the ultimate Beauty in African Tradition of what Black people do as a lifestyle. Just as musical conductors set down notes to be played or sung, and then shepherd their musicians as to when and how to play corresponding musical sounds, an African Tradition Philosophy of Life (POL) takes a human's scattered best efforts and weaves "ME/WE" products. To appreciate this requires understanding Ancient African Origin concepts of all Real Cosmic Entities. In the way an apple Seed gives rise to roots, a trunk, branches, leaves, and fruit, so does the Cosmic Creator "Seed" produce all Cosmic Things. African Sages said God's "Seed" consists of Androgynic plast (called Protoplasm today)—a plast whose Essences are comprised of the Spiritual Elements "Genetics" for all God's creatures and creations, including for each human. When those "Genetics" descend into Cosmic Matter wrappings of Ether, the result resembles an organic "Cell"—like a mother's *Identical (monozygotic) Twins' "egg"*. After that single egg is fertilized, before the twins separate, they move to opposite poles while *staying within the same egg*—called *Meiosis*. Next, the egg splits--called *Mitosis*—to separate the Twins so as for each to struggle to survive on their own. Thereafter, each twin has a customized and unique existence leading to an individualized Character and Personality. Such is the result of their different experiences in their different existences within the same womb and then after birth. Note the important concept of both twins having Uniqueness despite their "Sameness" Genetics. The same Meiosis is featured in the Cosmic Organism's humans, Animals, Plants, and Minerals members residing in the same Cosmic "Cell" prior to being born. Within this Meiosis Cell they are joined in a *Virtual* state--a shared womb--called the Ocean of Nun. "Virtual" means they are all bonded, lack form, are undefined, undifferentiated, and yet are not *in disorder*. Inside this Cosmic -shared womb, each Entity has a *Unique "ME" self-identity*--while simultaneously having a "Sameness" by sharing a *wholistic "WE" Identity* with all of the other Entities. Hence, all in the shared womb are Spiritually related to each and every one of God's Creatures and Creations, no matter how remote in time or space or how different in appearance--termed the *Law of Sympathy*. That is what I mean by "ME/WE" in African Tradition. In the Meiosis state, each cell in each Entity and all cells in all Entities carry forth the Omnipotence (unlimited and universal power), Omnipresent (everywhere simultaneously), and Omniscient (total knowledge) instilled by the Creator God but in a drop proportion to that taken out of the infinite ocean of God. All G*enes in each Cell have a memory of where they came from.* Each Cell--while moving through a human's life, an African Group's Spirit, or the African Diaspora throughout the Ages--is orchestrated by a spirit force apart from its DNA Essence. Despite having the same Essence, the "Genetics" inside each Cell differs in combination and arrangement. That explains why people's Talents and Individuality are "Unique" and yet they have the "Same" Human Nature aspects. "*Survival*"—a Lower Self's "First Law of Nature"—is about self-protecting and self-preserving of all in the Animal and Plant Kingdoms, independent of any other Entity. However, at ones first opportunity to have a measure of strength and stability, ones Highest (Divinity) Self nature takes over and does what is best for the "ME/WE". Examples are by struggling to get out of destruction, disturbances, or threats; to help; and to "Lift the 'WE' while the 'ME' is climbing into a thriving life of well-being". Thus, every 'ME' act is for the intension to daily Self-Improve towards its Highest Self + to blend into Compassion's space with the truly Needy + to provide benefits in each 'WE' otherness encounter + to enhance the 'WE' as part of oneself. On Earth, after Necessities, ones "ME/WE" Mission in life is of top priority. An African Tradition POL—not an assumed Mission--enables ones 'Calling' to naturally flow into ones life. Such attracts worthy people. One does not give up who one is to fit with the Crowd—or allow them to define who one is and how to live. Ones "ME/WE" POL orches-trates ones "Being-hood" as an authoritative administrator governor—e.g. instructing, arranging, combining, and conditioning the nature of ones "ME/WE" molding. This process is like kneading dough into a uniform mixture by pressing, folding, and stretching ones Selfhood so as to achieve ones life's Mission. See Non-Self; Humanity jabaileymd.com

MENTAL "SAFE SPACES": reason-free zones where feelings outrank facts

MESSAGE ASSESSMENT: *Consequences* are the somethings which happen as a result of something hap-pening (Sharon Bingaman) are not the same as *Sequences* (which are like going up or down the rungs of the Vertical Ladder). The fate of each of these depends upon: (1) the Source of the Message; (2) the nature of the Message (its what, why, who, which, when, where, and how aspects); (3) the Messenger (the Sender); (4) the Receiver of the Message; and (5) the application of the Message. Bull's Eye Sources deliver Spiritual Elements messages; the further away from the Bull's Eye, the more confusing and conflicting the messages. This is why almost all communications coming from the Supernatural is disharmonious. Sloppy researchers—which may or may not be the Messenger--exhibit multiple sources and methods of errors in their collection of informa-tion. Then the messenger carries these and additional flaws that form the conclusions used as an Evidence, Proof, or Truth Base. Is the message resulting from that interpretation translated creditably? Was that message later altered by the messenger or altered by the messenger's bosses? To complicate matters, the Messengers, the Receivers, and/or application of the nature of the Message received are flawed. For example, the Messenger may improperly receive the Message or alter the Message out of Ignorance, Selfhood Weakness for self-benefit purposes of a limited nature, or from being Brutes and Satanists whose greed for power is to control people's minds. Receivers have agendas whereby they may be trying to act as if they are important, usually so as to hide some deficiency from the public and themselves. Thus, they may say one thing and think another and what they say is not what they are really after. The nature of their character must be understood in order to know how to deliver information. Or, people oriented to in-group connotations will not understand those who use denotative language or other connotation groups. Since this goes unspoken, it is the cause for many errors and mis-communications. Superficial: When you fail to look deeply into what is said or seen this is a plane of thinking that prevents one from hearing instruction or learning a lesson or benefitting from other's experiences. "*Today, we can create sources of information and searches that allow you to get an answer to everything you are wondering.*" I have experience with the commuter adding addresses or changing information or leaving out information. Between the time the European NT Bible started being written 70 years after Jesus' death and the present, hundreds of writers have contributed to innumerable Bibles within and throughout each age. The context in which these writers wrote their portions of the European Bible included ten basic parts of Communication: (1) the Source (where the communication comes from); (2) the Language; (3) the Message (the information transmitted by the source); (4) the Form (e.g. metaphors); (5) the Style of writing; (6) the Channel (the medium through which a message is sent, as in books, letters, song, radio, email, or movies); (7) the Messenger (the person sending or bringing the communication); (8) the Receiver (the one to whom the message is sent); (9) the Style of delivery; and (10) the Purpose. In other words, communication concerns who says or does what; and by what means to whom; and in what way. At each stage, social influences and personal tastes and beliefs led those writers to have such conflicting philosophies as for periodic groups of European religious leaders to sit down and make decisions as to which writers to accept for the Bible. Even without conflicts there were interpretation changes in fundamental ideas because of: (a) evolution of thought (and not always for the best); (b) changes in denotative and connotative meanings; (c) chance; (d) mistakes; (e) deliberateness; and (f) a combination of these within any given writer. *Knowing the source of information and if it is pure* or not is fundamental to Critical Thinking. Thus anything one is told or reads of a life-shaping or life-changing nature requires knowing where did the messenger get the message? How reliable is the source of that message? Did the messenger or translation change any of it? Has the meaning or style of description changed from back then to now? Most people's problems is that the do not go far enough. Maybe asking a question and stopping without further investigation by asking more questions related to the Seven Questions of Inquiry for what happened; how wide spread (so you can have an idea about boundaries); what is the damage; The point is to gain ideas helpful for setting up a plan as to what to do and what to avoid; to predict; to have a general sense of a problem so you can learn from how it was handled. This is vital. Or if they receive "heavy" information from someone, rather than trying to learn more, they back off and "disappear." Things are always going to break down at the most inconvenient times. For example, an electrical storm shut down my computer and my son, the Geek Squad, or the place I bought it (because I did not have the sales slip) would not fix it. So the maker of the monitor was called and knew what the problem was. This is an instance of why I have developed the practice of working with a sense of urgency. Have a back-up plan or use that time to get things under control and while waiting handle things that have been put off--perhaps putting things in order (and that can remind you of things helpful in your main project). Spend all the time available in making a decision and once it is made, stick with it and not let others persuade you to do something different. Even it does not come out right you will know how to troubleshoot. Properly instructing people who can help requires them being oriented to what you are trying to get done and to familiarize them with the situation. Some people need a long background discussion if they are totally unfamiliar with what you have in mind. Experts who are busy simply need to know the problem in one sentence and let them ask what else they want to know. Generally, like me, I just want a direct answer to my question. Do not make the mistake of thinking that because someone does not meet your standards in one thing that they are stupid in everything. Some people wind up where they are going and some do not. The concept of apportionment is very important to CT. There are many tools for different jobs and for the same job. Know what is of Keystone importance and when and where to apply it. That requires knowing oneself and those involved. People get the obvious story of an allegory but fail to get the feel or the new way of looking at something present in the deeper meaning that will allow them to discern or understand or avoid or incorporate or modify. Getting the gist of something is not good enough for serious business but is okay for many other things. I allot 3% to pursuing pleasure and that comes from Nature, enjoying some achievement, or my woman. Read Efficiency, Effectiveness, and What Achievement Balancing Looks like. Many problems arise from irritating other people by one repeatedly doing what was just asked not to do. Why are you so inflexible as to not change?--because that person is faceless? You would not do that to the president.

METAPHORS: equates unlike things by implication); *Simile (*the abstract or suggestive aspect is directly expressed), *Allegories* (a hidden story within an obvious story), *Fables* (animals impersonating humans to impart a moral), *Personification* (making a lifeless or abstract thing alive), *Analogies* (explaining something unfamiliar by comparing it to something familiar), *Legend* (a story, above mere fiction, combining fact and personified spiritual concepts), and *Symbols* (symbolic messages disregard the limitations and boundaries of human thought in order to impart ideas of the indescribable). *Metaphors* are a transfer of one sense across into another; something different that means something of the same in something else. A common definition is a *figure of speech* in which a term or phrase is applied to something to which it is not literally applicable and yet is done in order to suggest a resemblance. It permits one to say a great deal in a few words. Furthermore, it sets up in the mind of readers/listeners a creative process that leads them to amplify the idea -- and come to feel it as ones own -- and hence to accept it as a Belief (to hold dear). Metaphors evoke concomitant *affect symbolic imagery* (i.e. thinking in mental pictures which touch ones feelings) because mentally seeing it makes it more easily understandable. In turn, these images usually call up apperceptions and emotions that strengthen or enlarge upon the intended meaning.

METAPHYSICAL DISORDER: of a non-moral nature; implies to "go astray," become lost," stray from correct behavior by being beyond Ma'at boundaries to enter "Badness." It is of the nature of the influence of a "*Disaster Star,*" one clings to its think, feel, say, and do ways.

MICRO-AGGRESSIONS: A "*Satellite*" is properly an astronomical term originated by Very Ancient Africans for a small body which revolves around a planet, held in its position by the gravitational pull of the planet and deriving its light by reflection. An example is *Micro-Aggressions—also called Cumulative Trauma,* Continuing small Traumas, Micro-Aggressions, and Accumulative Micro-trauma. They leave multiple (psychic) 'little wounds' which in turn *erode* (wear away) and *corrode* (gnaw away) every mental, physical, emotional, spiritual, and soul aspect of a Victim's Selfhood. Those aspects, like having cracked an egg, could be so resistant to healing that the "yoke" continuously oozes out. This is particularly so in Victims with mental "Raw Nerves" resulted from a "Big Bang" trauma. That mental "Raw Nerve" acts as if it is set on fire an "*Inflamed*" or a-flamed—expressing like meteors in troubled areas of ones mind. To elaborate, whereby "obstruction of justice" is the euphemism used for European rich criminals, "violently resisting arrest" is applied to poor Black and Brown people for the same action. Daily Black People experience a host of racism insult that act like satellites but can have their own additional influence as a result of a 'big bang' or cumulative micro-trauma. See Racism

MICRO-TRAUMAS: *Cumulative Trauma* (Latin, cumulus, heap or piled—like cumulus clouds)--also called Continuing small Traumas, Micro-Aggressions, and Accumulative Micro-trauma--leaves multiple psychic 'little wounds' which in turn *erode* (wear away) and *corrode* (gnaw away) every mental, physical, emotional, spiritual, and soul aspect of a Victim's Selfhood. Those aspects, like having cracked an egg, could be so resistant to healing that the "yoke" continuously oozes out. This is particularly so in Victims with mental "Raw Nerves" resulted from a "Big Bang" trauma. That mental "Raw Nerve" acts as if it is set on fire an "*Inflamed*" or a-flamed—expressing like meteors in troubled areas of ones mind. See Racism

MIDDLE: The disease's *Middle* is whatever conditions the explosion caused inside ones Selfhood.

"MIDDLE PATH" FOR ANCIENT AFRICANS: An Ancient African Physician Thinking pattern for dealing with patients was: (1) Name the Disease (e.g. human suffering); (2) Find the Cause of the Disease (clutching to desire); (3) Determine the Core of Treatment (release of clutching); and (4) Provide the Prescription--called the Middle Way; Middle Path, Mean Doctrine, or *"Keeping the Balance"*—These are not about a mid-point in a straight line joining two extremes represented by points. The stimulus for "Keeping the Balance" came from the dominating African World-view concepts of *Di-unitality* (union of natural opposites) and Ntuology (all sets of God's creatures and creations are interrelated through spiritual and human networks--also called the Law of Sympathy). Because this is a complex but extremely significant concept, allow me to introduce it in a story form. Since, according to Diop (African Origin p287), the original Buddha was an Egyptian priest chased from Memphis by the persecutions of Cambyses (Persians) in 526 BC, the religion and philosophy of the Egyptians was spread into Asia. Examples included Confucius in China, Zoroaster in Iran, and Buddhism in the Far East. Ample contrary literature says Buddha was born in India. However, part of the problem is "Buddha" (the awakened one) represents a title and not an individual's name. Thus, there were many Buddhists throughout Asia and some made varying degrees of modifications in the original Middle Way concept of the Egyptians. To each modification some story was added to illustrate its "origin." The most common story concerns Siddhartha Gautama of India who used "Middle Way" to describe the character of the path it was said he discovered--a path leading to liberation--a path of moderation and therefore wisdom between the extremes of sensual indulgence and self-mortification (a feeling of shame, humiliation, or wounded pride from self-denial). Within this context *Wisdom* is defined as: right understanding, right thought, right speech, right action, right livelihood, right effort, right mindfulness and right concentration. His realization of the Middle Way occurred as he sat by a river and heard a lute player in a passing boat. At that point he understood the lute string must be tuned neither too tightly nor too loosely to produce a harmonious sound--i.e. the Middle Path. An extension of this concept concerns death: there being neither a permanent self nor complete annihilation of the 'person' at death but rather only the arising and ceasing of causally related phenomena. In another application: suppose a person asks: 'What is taken for and called darkness?' A reply: 'Light is the proximate cause and darkness is the contributory cause. When light is ended, then there is darkness. By the means of light, darkness manifests; by the means of darkness, light manifests. [Their] coming and going are mutually proximate causes and become the meaning of the Middle Way.' Buddha recognized extremes cause mental upsets because one extreme leads to another. Therefore, mental balance is the way to achieve mental peace and serenity, which will allow a balanced approach or "Middle Path" to a spiritual discipline needed for spiritual growth (Ashby, The Mystical Journey p108). For *"Keeping the Balance"* they used the *Dialectic Method*--a dialogue exercise emphasizing questioning so as to bring out knowledge within each opponent that neither opponent had considered.

"MIDDLE WAY" STEPS OF ANCIENT AFRICANS: In pursuing a solution for things opposite, and especially if they are in conflict, is first, a Middle Way synthesis. Here, the aim is to discover options for "Either this or that" or for "All of this and none of that." Something in the middle could be: "neither-nor"; "both-and"; "some of both"; "both alternating"; Complementary Equals and opposites like Yin/Yang; Homeostatic whirlpool; or "each having differing patterns, directions, pace, levels, rhythms, and goals complementing each other." Second, in certain situations resolution requires considering a position "over and above" the opposition. For example, although churches squabble over who is right, the seed from which their faith derives is supposed to be that of Unconditional Love--and going to this level may resolve the squabble. Third is the: "What is Behind That Piece of Information?" When opposing sides are questioned this way on every argument each presents, eventually there will be a natural connection between the opposites at the "seed" level from which the argument sprang.

"*The Middle Way*" embraces the Ma'at principles (Spiritual Elements in action) of ethical behavior cultivation and Selfless Service. Its focus is finding the unity underlying opposites--i.e. discovering what opposites have in common. Type I need each other—e.g. life/death, day/night, male/female--like the *two sides of a coin* whose Truth is in the middle. That Truth makes them Whole ('whole' = holy, joining mutually necessary opposites). Type II is a *Doctrine of Moderation*--a reminder to be moderate in all things, not the same as a Compromise. Type III is a *Balance Scale*, rather than extremes. When Ancient Africans were faced with two people in conflict, it became a community dispute calling for preparation for resolution. Since early African societies were initially without chiefs, family or clan matters were settled by the family council, each having its own elder or by any mutually acceptable elder (see Chancellor Williams, "The Destruction of Black Civilization," p 168).

Step A was to leave a glass or a bowl of water on the home alter at all times, as the presence of water anywhere signified a desire for peace, reconciliation, and focus where needed. Step B, neighbors rallied around both disputants and had each offer the other a gift. If that did not work to end the dispute, Step C was to call a *Moot Court* for all to listen to the opponents' arguments. Step D, all parties concerned (elders, litigants, witnesses, and spectators) sat very close to one another in a random and mixed fashion. Step E, the investigation by the disputants themselves had to avoid blame and, instead, spread out fault in the dispute to both parties and then, rather than searching for differences, find what they had in common. Thereafter, whatever matter remained unclear was not a problem. Out of this, proper vibrations returned to cause ones realization for existence to enable the community to have well-being. Step F, an Elder decided what *solution was in the best interest of the community*, as opposed to one disputant. The principle was to do what brought most harmony to the entire group and that was more important than solving the problem. The point was to reintegrate the guilty party or parties back into the community; restore normal social relations between the disputing parties; and resolve any left-over bits of anger. The ending of the proceeding involved the ritual of an apology to the victim in order to symbolize agreement with the sanctions imposed by the moot. These sanctions were not so severe that the losing party had grounds for a new grudge against the other party.

After being assessed a small fine, the guilty party would give the wronged party a token gift and then make a public apology as a way of bringing about healing to the entire community. Step G, Elders who interceded for community problems were given gifts and the disputing parties would then "make up." Type IV is *avoiding the Boomerang Effect*. Ancient Africans said that on lower levels of existence the extremes cause mental upsets because one extreme leads to another, and the mind loses its capacity for rational thought and the intuitional awareness which transcends thought itself. For example, when evil thoughts over-ride ones Loving nature, the evil *Boomerangs* back to the sender of evil in an Earth world setting and thereby arouses more hatred within the original sender. For example, in an Earth world situation, if ones hate—for whatever reason--leads to a desire for or an action of *vengeance,* that vengeance further enrages the trigger person (i.e. the recipient) and then boomerangs from that person as a counter-vengeance. Such is seen in Gang Wars. Thus, mental balance is the way to achieve mental peace and serenity--allowing the Self's transcendental vision to emerge in the mind (Ashby, African Origins p82). Such is illustrated by Martial Artists who, as a result of doing much work to achieve such a Free Mind, start solutions with an "empty" mind which allows one to instantly move in keeping with any ray of the sun. A Free Mind is devoid of prejudices or biases; no clinging to any Belief, like favoring of men over women, or vice versa; and no "shoulds". It is not in anyone's best interest to put another on the defensive and thereby get angry because that invites manifest resistance "just for spite." Insight comes into what is the appropriated balance, not in the sense of between the extremes, but rather the Middle Way. Wherever disharmony lies--on one side or the other or with oneself--it is handled in the least offensive manner. This enables one to reconcile differences and contradictions so as to see non-evil things as wholistic (whole, holy, healed). This is what heals the Spirit. Steps of "The Way" are my interpretations as follows. Step I: According to Ancient Africans, people are born ignorant. Most are thereafter victimized by a host of illusions, segregated thinking, and rationalization of acquired emotions due to the operation of ones lower faculties. These fashion ones *self-recognized Identity* (the accepted Character for recognizing "who I am")—and that may be ones Immaterial Real Self (the "who I am" in actuality, as present at birth) or ones External World False Self (the "who I am" as I chose to be sometime after birth). The combination of ones self-recognized Identity and the Nature corresponding to it thereby express a human's personal trademark-like individuality. The self-recognized Identity gives rise to ones mindset Disposition—the "*What it Does*" and "*Why it Does it*" as well as ones Nature. Thereafter, they tend to learn things that take them further away from the truth—things called Illusions and Delusions (believing what is not real and not believing what is real). Thinking in reality cannot happen if one is manifesting Acquired Emotional conditioning at the same time, as in exchanging "Excitement" for Inner Peace. Pleasures and Pains are Acquired Emotional conditioning state and not Primary Qualities in Things. The mid-C19 word "*Conditioning*" is the slow and cumulative experience process of changing the (instinct) normal into the (acquired) unique; the process of acquiring, developing, educating, learning, or training new responses in an individual to influences of the environment. Conditioning "instructs" the mind to react in a certain way—the 'big picture' of which gives some benefits—positive or negative. Ones habitual and emotional and sensory responses are not representative of ones human nature at ones birth. By contrast, ones pre-birth emotions, which are unconditioned, enables the transcending of ones conditioning—especially things feared, hated. Step II: CALM MIND. Preparation for Re-Ordering oneself is to have a Calm Mind since that enhances what is needed to arrive at starting the process heading to mental balance and overcoming mood swing extremes. This unshakable inner Peace is needed to bring forth factors shaping ones Highest (Divinity) Self—Unity, Wisdom, and Spiritual Power. The extremes cause mental upsets because one extreme leads to another and the mind loses the capacity for rational thought and intuitional awareness which transcends thought itself. Ancient Africans said that on lower levels of existence the extremes cause mental upsets because one extreme leads to another, and the mind loses its capacity for rational thought and the intuitional awareness which transcends thought itself. Therefore, mental balance is the way to achieve mental peace and serenity, which will allow the transcendental vision of the Self to emerge in the mind (Ashby, African Origins p82). In light of the identification with the indwelling intelligence that is at the center of ones mental and bodily processes, the best way to reshape ones belief system is with a Free Mind. Step III: Since *Inner Peace* is a manifestation of inner harmony and unity—both of which derive from operating out of "Pure" Emotions or Spiritual Feelings (which connect ones Real Self to the Sublime)--it serves as an alarm system to indicate whenever anti-harmony is encountered. Whatever is of an anti-harmony nature within ones Selfhood is gathered and divided into three groups. First is what is working in harmony with the flow of the Spiritual Elements. Second is those aspects of ones life that are noncontributory or useless and simply waste ones time with promoting any advancement in self-improvement. Third is the self-defeating or anti-Spiritual Elements aspects. "The Way" proceeds through three stages: (1) undergoing a *Mystical Death* of ones False Self; (2) proceeding into a *Spiritual Transformation*-- e.g. recognizing the Dignity (God's image) within all beings and having compassion for their pain and suffering, even if you detest what they do because they are one of God's creatures to which you are spiritually related; and (3) emerging into a *Rebirth*-- into knowing what Love really is and how to spread it is in order to do the most good—for the most people—over the longest period of time. The resultant Free Mind with its harmonious balance constitutes the *Inner Self Stability Platform* from which all choices, decisions, creations, and solutions spring forth. Step IV is Reconciling the Contraries—i.e. the theme of the Middle Way (bringing together opposites). Rather than being a compromise, the contraries are reconciled by the marriage of Spirit and Matter and using insight into ones own nature. All conclusion must be known by its opposite. Know pleasure by having an awareness of displeasure and not necessarily experiencing displeasure. A man who has lived a hard life alone can appreciate a good woman better than if he had had an easy life. It heals the split between the Self and the Cosmos. African Logic's method for dealing with this starts by knowing *a quality can only be recognized when compared to its Complementary or Contradictory Opposite* (Dumont, p194). To be aware of its contrast allows one to know what something is. Thus, a trained mind instinctively leaps to the thought of an "opposite" at the same time that it is considering any given quality. It thinks of this "Opposite"—not because of its "likeness" to the Thing—but because of its "Unlikeness" or Difference. This is extremely important because one can obtain a clearer and more distinct idea or mental image of anything if one, at the same time, thinks of its "opposite"—either its opposite quality, or a Thing whose qualities are markedly opposite to that of the Thing under consideration.

Step V: Handle Mood Swings from MISJUDGMENTS. A major problem of human thought is to judge a Primary Quality as good or bad in relation to what gave rise to it and then becoming conditioned to seeing that way. For example, Stubbornness is a quality people's *Intellect* think of as bad. Yet, when one lives in Integrity, there is its "right" *Wisdom* sense when applied to unwillingness to violate ones Real Self Identity. This is opposite sense of "Stubborn" is about Persistence in virtues—and that is highly prized as well as independent of and uninfluenced by any human's contrary opinion. The same applies to "Selfishness"—which is the first Law of Nature. It is absolutely necessary in order to produce "ME/WE" benefit. Yet, great confusion in people's minds who have been socialized to believe any "Selfishness" bad. The point: seeing things for what they are and without judging them will clear many problems of seeming conflict. Such an emphasizing of balance rather than spotlighting the extremes is what Ancient Africans termed "the *Middle Way*" or "Middle Path".

One of their methods for this occurred when a community was faced with dispute between two members, preparation for resolving began with leaving the glass or a bowl of water on the alter at all times, as the presence of water anywhere signified a desire for peace, reconciliation, and focus where needed. Next, neighbors rallied around both disputants and had each offer the other a gift. If that did not work to end the dispute, they called a *Moot Court* for all to listen to the opponents' arguments and decide what *solution was in the best interest of the community*, as opposed to one disputant. Out of all of this, the proper vibrations were set up to cause ones realization for existence so that the community might survive its well-being. Any Elders who were intercessors for community problems were given gifts and the disputing parties would then "make up." From such understanding ones acquires a new or more meaningful perspective of Justice apart from moral rectitude. Insight comes into what is the appropriated balance, not in the sense of between the extremes, but rather the Middle Way. This enables one to reconcile differences and contradictions so as to see non-evil things as wholistic (whole, holy, healed). This is what heals the Spirit. Step VI: Synthesize Differences in Corresponding Opposites. Foundational to African Tradition Synthesis is Imagination heading toward the formation of Symbols with a message, and from there to a new entity out of the previously existing ingredients that went into forming it. Yet, there are things in the Physical World that are truly synthesized. Hence, an expansion of *my definition of Synthesis is: the essence of abstract or abstraction ingredients coordinated into a whole—a whole whose combined product emerges by means other than through a mere summation of the elements involved—retaining the original ingredients*, like the egg and the sperm producing a fetus. The mental application that *ties externally unrelated* species through an abstraction is "Synthesis." It occurs when, say, the egg and the sperm join to produce a fetus. Out of that new and novel "Seed" product is the emergence, *by means other than through a mere summation of the elements originally involved, of a new and original Entity. Still, it is a Mosaic of all the "Genes" present in the parents.* The same principle applies to gaining new insights from research or reflection. Those insights may lead down new paths, or see common things in an uncommon way or see uncommon things in a common way. See Dialectic; Opposites

MINDS—HUMANS: Humans know themselves by what they see in Nature. By then knowing themselves, they can ascribed Intelligence as a glorious attribute—like from rays of the Sun in spite not being able to see the Sun. The operations and nature of what is observed in Nature and ones mind being able to observe and organize these ingredients from ones own Soul to determine that these aspects are above all error and imperfection in their nature. By extending this into all possible aspects of the Spiritual Elements and for that to be known by ones own moral nature—called Conscience—gives Sages the idea of a Divine Authority that presents a "Big Picture" characterized by God being at least a "Big Mind" Spiritual Force. Although this "Big Mind" operates on levels to which humans have no access, they human mind is a "Spark" of the "Big Mind." The difference is that in contrast to the human mind, the "Big Mind does not have to infer anything, for it Knows—it does not have to guess or wonder, for it sees all there is to see; it cannot make mistakes, for there can be nothing outside is own range. Each human's Spiritual Mind, in order to become a "Spark" of God's mind, has 3 aspects: (1) the aspect of it Being or Substance: (2) the aspect of Thought, with the sub-divisions of Reason, Feeling (Instinct), Pure Emotions, Desire, Will, etc.—on both Conscious and Subconscious planes; and (3) the aspect of Acting—called Mind Power. Whereas some parts of the human mind deal with the various levels of the Instinct Brain (i.e. Instinct, Omnibus, and Brute)—and some parts deal with Secular planes--the Spiritual aspect of the human mind is in direct contact, in Symbolic forms, with ones Higher Cosmic Consciousness. This consists of every humans "ME/WE" pre-birth Virtual (boundary-less) Cosmic residence orchestrated by God's "Big Mind". A human's Spiritual Mind purpose is to serve as a storehouse of ones "Self" (Soul, Divine Consciousness) Knowledge of itself. Real Self people's Ma'at (i.e. actioned Spiritual Elements) Divinity Principles unfold (become revealed) in their pursuit of Self-Knowing within the profound realm of "ME/WE"—all occurring through the filter of their moral nature, called *Conscience*. This gatekeeper Conscience imparts ideas of Divine authority and binds one to obey, unless one chooses otherwise. Yet, at birth, a human's mind is devoid of the Cosmic Laws' dynamic effects--the discovery of which is by Self-Absorption inside the "ME/WE" Spirituality realm. Here are all aspects of the Spiritual Elements—i.e. Unconditional Love, Truth, Reality, and the Natural. They are to be cultivated into natural spontaneous flows of Life Living. Within a human: (1) the Unconscious and the Conscious appear as complementary opposites within a binary duality system by what underlies both--meaning they are the same but with different displays; (2) by being a microcosm (i.e. a "little" world copy) of the Universal Soul's macrocosm (the Supreme world), the Creation and the Creator are one since the Creation is the passing of Creator Being into Becoming what is created; (3) each human's Unconscious and the Conscious have Spiritual (i.e. Highest Self) and Matter (Lower or animalistic Self) aspects; and (4) the Spiritual Unconscious and the Spiritual Conscious possess Spiritual Knowledge of the Cosmic Organism--Knowledge which operates in each human in an Unconscious manner. [Ref: Ramacharaka, Fourteen Lessons in Yogi Philosophy, p21; Atkinson, Mind Power p27, 82].

MINDSET: An attitude of readiness to respond in a certain way, based upon ones prior experiences or expectations of "what is best for me or against me"

MINDSETS FOR MA'AT AND AFRICAN LOGIC: Logic originated by Ancient Africans is Humankind's highest form of abstract thinking. The process has embraced African Logic Common Sense, Knowledge, Reason, Critical Thinking, and African Wisdom in dealing with all planes of existence. Thus, since all of these follow the Mathematical Laws of Nature in staying in the flow of and evolving work products out of, it is necessary for African Logic to use both Quantitative and Qualitative Mathematics. One reason Ancient Africans remain as the most brilliant Critical Thinkers (CT) of history was by their dedication to perfecting their Right and Left Brains (i.e. hemispheres of their individual brains). Yet, they designed their Right Brain orchestrating so as to thereby enable them to locate and deeply explore Metaphysical realms. Humans brains' *Frontal lobes*, an experience simulator (done in the head) allow for reasoning; abstract thinking; organizing behaviors over Time/Space; spotlight paths for attaining future goals; and impart initiative, creativity, and feelings of personal autonomy and identity. This is mainly because the right frontal lobe is an integrative region of the brain where emotional, logical, and perceptual data converge. They used much time, energy, and effort to Understand the smallest of details. *Understanding* means seeing *Inner Similarities* in dissimilar things: fashioning interrelationships; distinguishing the superficial from the profound; separating the Truth from its look-alikes; selecting what to analyze; and determining what to manipulate and maneuver into Options to connect Cause/Effect. They understood *knowledge advances by finding how similarities and differences are related, harmonized, and synthesized*. The objective was to arrive at the Truth of Thought by Synthesis. Then they positioned facts and evidence on the proper rungs of the Cosmic Ladder and maneuvered them according to the unique rules operating on a given rung. Principles on a given plane of existence were harmoniously fit to form knowledge. Although 65% of all ancient Greek philosophers known today were taught by African Sages, they chose to use only their Left Brains and let go of Right Brain usages because it was deemed feminine. This ensured their wallowing in Material realms; being shut out of Metaphysical realms; and veering further and further away from Spiritual Elements. Do what has to be done when you have energy on it.

MIND CONTROL--SUPERNATURAL'S MILITARY: The Military (C16, 'serve as a soldier) is a primitive European innovation as a result of their beginnings being in the harsh Ice Age of 45,000 BC. Organization of family members by its leader was needed to survive by Kill/Take/Destroy/Oppress/Dominate methods over neighbors. This pattern, which does not allow for thinking outside the physical, other than of a fantasy nature, became a way of life. It has persisted to the present. By contrast, Black Africans gave rise to humanity 200,000 years ago, being born into a paradise-like environment where food was plentiful. This allowed time to think of the Un-seeable which is now known to be about the Spiritual and Metaphysical realms of the Cosmos. In addition, an "easy living" type life promoted sociability. Until they came in contact with the warring Europeans perhaps around 1700 BC, Africans were a peaceful people. For example, there were no jails, no policemen, no rape, no divorces, or any of the negative things featured in today's world societies. Peaceful Ancient African Power resulted throughout the continent from their strong democracy. It was dedicated to preventing leaders from falling victims to the offerings of trinkets from foreigners or anyone intent on undermining African traditions. This meant Ancient Africans Democracy was incompatible with any dictatorship type of centralized or individual authority, like the *Age-Set System*.

Meanwhile, throughout ever-warring Europe, early systems of a military nature continued among the professional warriors and other citizens who banded together in semi-military style for mutual protection. Their organizational pattern was essentially the same, as most clearly exhibited by the USA military chain of command. It starts with the President being in charge of the Army, Navy, and Air Force. Their ultimate command has the intent of promoting acceptable conduct for their respective cults by means of formulating "Codifications". These are orderly and authoritative statements of the leading rules of law on a given subject which are designed to influence thoughts and actions of each military personnel positioned on each rung of the Military Ladder. Those Orders are given to the Generals and Admirals in charge so as to then trickle-down through the chain of command. After the Orders are received by lower ranking Generals and Admirals they, in turn, pass the orders down to Colonels, Captains, and so on to the lowest ranks, the "Troops." In the military chain of command, for example, a soldier's rank is supposedly determined by merit. Leaders at the top give orders but do not take them; the new recruit takes orders and does not give them. Those in between give and take orders. It takes 90 days to re-program the minds of the recruits by means of basic training. Tools for this include ruling with vehement terror (e.g. stockade or worse) with the complementary opposite of bragging with a swagger. The Military slogans and even militaristic terms that fell under the "Patriotism" guise have included: "Might is Right"—"Might till Right"—"Might is the measure of Right"--"Might by Sleight"—and "Might over-cometh Right." They see the reason of the strongest as always winning and that justice is determined by the interest of the strongest. There is no understanding of, or interest in, Natural World Humanity. Displayed to both "Troops" and victims is constant, proven intimidating 'take-down' power, so widely and strategically located as to defy accountability + an army of law-enforcement personnel to dominate all teaching, business, media, and political systems. Hence, in 'playing out' their deeply held beliefs to their logical conclusions is to be certain that it is about delusions--amoral, non-Caring relationships, arrogance, greed, and violence. "*Feigned enemies*" are characterized as those easily exploited for self-interest gains—and who in no way attack, hinder, or interfere with the cult's hostile military or dogmatic set-up. This is a *Deflection* method illustrated by *Reaction Formation* (a reality/fantasy reversal)--e.g. saying about and to the victim: "you are the one causing the problem, not me!" The contents in their *Projection* accusations are derived from fantasies which design feigned necessities—i.e. imaginary necessities. Such are the greatest cozenage (deceitful) things a predator does to his/her mind to break down any remote sense of moral "Right."

However, compared with those living out of their Higher Self inside the Natural Cosmos, Supernatural cult members have a totally different concept of "Right". Examples include a lust of conquest, a love of ease, a craving for power, and an obsession to be superior and rich. The cozen's "wheeling and dealings" are infinitely worse when used as an excuse for generating an IHES Complex in order to Kill/Take/Destroy/Oppress/Dominate their victims. Yet, such actions are complimented and even honored by Supernatural Cult fellows. However, the focus here is on non-military "Troops" who, of course, are products of their primitive European heritage. Back then, the first phase of those governing and using mind control development grew out of techniques which required victims to be exposed to massive psychological and physical trauma, usually beginning in infancy. When Europeans write of democracy, they say it began in ancient Athens under the regime of Pericles. Back then only 30,000 of Athen's population of 120,000 were citizens and the rest were women, artisans, and Slaves—none of whom were allowed to vote—and all were subject to the old occult mind control techniques. Therefore, this was an Oligarchy whereby some but not all people have political liberty and the equality of citizenship. Typically, European societies have historically been Oligarchies or Tyrannical Depostism (rulers governing without the people's consent)—perhaps checkered with Benevolent Despotism (dictators working for the good of the people). Each of these Cults are *Cynics* (potent, practical, evil minds), believing those unlike them (the weak) are innately depraved; that irrationality and cowardice are scapegoat's basic characteristics; that *fear is the most potent of human incentives*—and not Unconditional Love, as in African Tradition. Cults deal practically with the public by counting on their stupidity + appealing to their knavery (dark side) + ensuring their constant terror. In short, it was Ancient Africans who invented Democracy and not the Greeks. In no large nation have the people, as opposed to the leaders, ruled as those of Ancient Africans!!! A true Democracy was operational in Africa thousands of years before the Greeks came into existence! Furthermore, the ancient Greeks nor the United States has ever had a democracy!! Even the USA up to mid C20 did not have a democracy within its Republic since all natural rights of all citizens had not been secured--non-democratic practices continued. An effect was discussed in C17 when Thomas Hobbes said Supernatural mental processes featured *Non-Rational thinking patterns dictated by Supernatural Contingent Beings*. These patterns by a mechanically oriented society gave Non-Reason thinkers delusional superior power and false control. By lacking a sense of connectedness with the whole or with Natural World reasoning, there was no need to follow Natural Realm Logic (Bartmanski *J. Sociology, 2014*). Non-Reason follows a "*Pecking Order*" of *Opinions*—a "domestic-hen" type competition that establishes status assignments. For example, Satanist leaders dictate orders to Corporations, Religion, the Media, Sports, and so forth. Each hen is allowed to peck the hen below--except the bottom row hen (the Crowd) has to submit to being pecked but cannot do any pecking. As dictators, cult leaders seek to enslave people's minds while using the *Argument of Determinism* (pre-destination) and other measures to *destroy people's reliance on the validity of their own judgments and choices so as to accept the rule of force.* Since they can only rise in a precisely uncertain but compliant society inviting them to take over, cult dictators run from, or erase (as with African Knowledge), the confident resistant—those with intransigent conviction and moral certainty. Dictatorships hold total, unlimited power over victims—considering it moral to treat people as sacrificial animals and rule them by physical force. Their Military style applied to non-military Troops is an abrogation of rights—negating a human's right to life—and establishes the core of *Statism* (i.e. that ones life belongs to the state and the state can claim it at will). They ensure everybody knows the rules, stays inside "the box" fashioned by the Orders, and are alert to all the Troops "passing the test" of following the rules—a concept well-known to White children in kinder-garden. Any cult or Crowd member who does not conform to the Rules will be punished by Isolation ("go stand in the corner"). Those going against the Rules will be harshly attacked to bring about their career destruction. Such control is so effective worldwide that I have never seen a White historian who gave Black People credit for any of the things Europeans have stolen.

My "guesstimate" is that 40 % of Europeans are Satanists (Supernatural oriented attackers of the Spiritual Elements); 50% are Crowd followers of the Satanists but not actually Satanists themselves; and 10% have a Natural World humanity. A tiny percent of the Satanists are leaders of the rest—the lower ranking Generals and Admirals as well as the "Troops". Since these citizen "Troops" lack the basic qualifications that are explicitly spelled out for military "Troops," they require special types of mind control. The leaders cunningly appeal to these 'normal' people "Troops" to *accept delusions and illusions leading into and embracing* Supernatural phenomena. The leaders know that *the only requirements is for those presentations to not clash with any held Belief that one deems to be "For me or my well-being"--or that threaten any of ones System of Values so as to convey the concept of that being "Against me."* In other words, when one is having difficulty with a certain type of behavior, one is to commit or is committing, one can mold the behavior seen as being inhumane into behavior seen either as humane or "inhumane but necessary"—and this lays the groundwork for the mind control of those "Troops." A necessary part of this "Air Castle" Supernatural mental and "cut-throat" process is exhibited power by "*Oppressive Othering*" as, for example, making feigned enemy scapegoats into subhuman stereotypes, if not in actuality. This is an emotional micro-politics called "*Intimidation*" ('impress profoundly') as a show of strength to competitors and to frighten victims in order to convey that the oppressors are in control of their own emotions, in control of emotions of the enemy, and can crack emotions of competitors. "*Oppressive Othering*" *rules* include: never letting scapegoats know you are scared of them—and that is done by means of having 'the GUN' (whatever it takes to kill) + an eagerness to use the GUN + an instantly available support Warrior Network 'back-up' + a like-kind supportive Crowd. Others are to *never admit being wrong* about anything--and that anyone who disagrees is so wrong as needing to be eliminated; always look them 'dead in the eye'; never back down; never do anything to make it look like you are nervous--and just pretend and act like you are confident the whole time. All of this imparts a feigned superiority complex intended to reduce the aggressors' fears; bolster warriors self-confidence and pride; and justify defining themselves as Supernaturally, physically, and mentally ("Implicit Othering") powerful. The idea is to present the Icon Image of ones virtual self as so "invincible" that "nothing can hurt me"—thus, "men don't cry." *Mind Control—also called Brainwashing, Coercive Persuasion, Re-Programming, Re-Education, Brain-Sweeping, Thought Control, and Thought Reform*—is about instituting a Form-Body mindset. Since *Imagery is a first and natural display of the human mind's activity,* psychic trauma, mob hysteria, and electronic-based subliminal messages (e.g. through Flashing Light gadgets) can re-shape the brain's raw materials via ones imagination to manipulate the forces of those materials into conformity with the Re-programming message. The process is that the emerging of the Form-Body—like a Percept--is the beginning foundation of ones Awareness about the "Thing," but as an intermediary construct of the brain lacking any specificity. This means it carries no clear disposition or intention. Then, from a beginning exposure to what is to be Re-Programmed there is an associated impairment of autonomy to prior awareness of impressions or to assess experiences--an inability to freely think independently—a disruption of established thinking patterns—and a shift over to accepting the thinking in European flawed patterns. In the process, some say the brainwashed Sensory Consciousness of the mind is fragmented, enabling one or more fragments to be separately programmed to perform any function or activity that has been "installed." Because of the shattering of the neuronal connections, each fragment can do what it does independent of and uninfluenced by the other fragments. Furthermore, each of the various fragments possess *Reciprocity* (equality within the domain of each aspect of the composite) as well as each produces outputs serving as in-puts into all other fragments. Any given fragment is susceptible to being stimulated by specific cues—appearances, colors, sounds, words, or actions--known as Triggers that institute *Conditioned Responses.*

A "*Stimulus*" is anything that makes a living thing act—called a *Response or Reaction.* What is "*Conditioned*" is not natural but instead is developed by regular association of some physiological function with an unrelated outside event. A fixated Conditioned Response and their unfavorable nature leads some afflicted to "*Overcompensate*" —i.e. fashion behaviors that are more than is really required to make up for, or to offset some liability. What is installed by programmers aspects of the Supernatural requires "Belief and Faith" under penalty of punishment for not conforming. To avoid punishements, what is installed becomes a *Conditioned Reflex*—meaning fear, terror, or other emotions may compel one to believe in what one cannot prove or disprove to the satisfaction of ones senses. Such Supernatural Superstitious beliefs are fixated by the encroachment of Faith on the rights of reason and knowledge. Both are maintained because one is unconscious of the narrow range of ones own experiences as they are properly interpreted in a Natural World sense. Those Supernatural motivated experiences are accepted as normal by the Crowd—thereby promoting Supernatural interpretations to be done involuntarily and non-rationally which, in turn, automatically reinforces beliefs in Superstitions and the Supernatural ad infinitum. Believers are programmed to be right but are on the wrong track and thus cannot be confused by contrary facts. From that group, Social Rank may be determined by public confidence, by public usefulness, or by the powerful. If one is able, has ambition, and works hard, one may get to the ladder's top where External World success is present.

Still there is ongoing Mind control layerings in two main categories. First is what goes into the mind that should not and second, what is not allowed to go into ones mind but ought to (e.g. the Truth). Satanist messages are intentionally delusional as they "move" in the "Air Castle" flow of their Indifference/Hate/Evil/Sadism (IHES) Complex orientation—and thus lack soundness. So as to give the "Troops" something to "stand on" so as to design compatible behaviors out of these messages, *"SEEMS" Right Truth Deceptions* are used. The purposes are to appease the Spiritual Elements "Trademark" stamped on each human's Soul. Hence, *"SEEMS" Right Truth Deceptions* are those preventing detection of anything against ones System of Values. An example of these spotlighted acceptable ideas that hide Satanists' deceptions is the USA government saying Iran is a threat to it and the "Troops" but fails to say they have 91 military bases surrounding Iran. Another example is that the KKK says they wear hoods to indicate all of their member have equal status with each other. Yet, the truths they are hiding include: (1) those hoods were originally use to scare ex-Slaves at night and continue to be used to intimidate Black People today since they symbolized lynchings; (2) those hoods hide who they are so as to not be criticized by fellows or detected by any anti-racists organization; and (3) those hoods give them a bravado (false sense of superiority) by being part of the cult.

Next, it is necessary to maintain mind control of the "Troops" by designed Deflections that divert their attention from what is really going on. *Deflections* are deceptive devices of any kind that serve to draw attention away from whatever is trying to be kept hidden (e.g. evil deeds). Politicians use Deflection Answers of the irrelevant type in order for people to not know what they really think about an issue. Crowd examples are being addicted to Trinkets, Trivia, Flashing Light gadgets *to keep people "Excited"*—*to keep people from thinking*—and to maintain mind control using these and other types of camouflage or mimicry. This pattern is typical of Whites in their advocating "how bad" Black People are—using the Formal and Social Media to convey false statistics, false stereotypes, and false claims of what the "Troops" are told to reject and be disgusted about. Meanwhile, the media steers a specific crime topic to appear as if it is "normal in Black culture" so as to distract the Crowd from noticing the much greater magnitude of "white collar" crime. By generating such hostile mob emotions in the European Crowd, no one notices the evil like-kind things the Crowd and the Brutes are doing.

One of the countless effects of Europeans' Non-Rational thinking patterns dictated by Supernatural Contingent Beings is *Adualism*--an inability to distinguish that reality from a Believer's own realities or that of the mind and that of the external world. Then experiencing a wish becomes equivalent to its actualization (as in schizophrenia). This partially accounts for European Bible writers borrowing the Ancient African Bible's mythologies and metaphors and converting them to "Fact." One example of the effect of this deception is in European religious leaders saying *"Original Sin"* or *"Natural Depravity"* (Rom. 5) is based upon their belief that Adam is the human race representative. They falsely say he brought guilt and sin not only upon the supposed Adam but upon all his posterity. A second example is that by having substituted the False Self for the Real Self has led European leaders, like Hitler, to say Anglo-Saxonism is to be held as the foundation for English people to have descended from German Angles, Saxons, and Jutes--a mythical racial origin. This myth was based on a German myth of Germanic people having roots reaching back to Adam (see Genesis in the Bible) and thereby possessing a language and culture richer than, and independent from, any other.

Management: The point of the above discussed aspects is that they have world-wide life-shaping consequences. Although constant warring over the millennia have honed Europeans patterns of aggressiveness and use of violence, the Tree Concept crystalizes all of this. The "Root" causes for both the military and the non-military "Troop" leaders' enthusiasm date to primitive European Warrior "Seed". Its "Trunk" formed when Europeans discovered *the GUN* invented by the Arabs in 1304. These savage tribes rose to power from perfecting the GUN over the next 150 years. As the sole result of the GUN, they simply "Took and Killed" everything of their interest from the rich but peaceful Black Africans and other Colored peoples' of the world. And the rest of what was worthwhile they destroyed. Countless shiploads of gold, diamonds, ivory, copper, iron ore of Central American Indians were taken to Europe. That enabled Europeans to dominate the world and then continue to this day to adversely influence the world. That is how Europeans became rich! New World "Branches" came to the Americas in C16-C17 when convicts, released from European prisons, were sent to "oversee" Enslaved Africans on sea and on land + Renaissance "Gentlemen" enslavers. Along with them were the "Leaves," as in an assortment of "low life" European Indentured Servants (e.g. prostitutes, religious dissidents, and the wayward) + a conglomeration of religious fanatics (advocating hypocritical concepts of Christian dealings with "all God's children"). Greed, Envy and Inferiority Complexes all "Fruited" as they became filthy rich on backs of Black People's "Slave-labor."

To accept the Ancient African Bible's Spiritual Metaphors is to get in touch with ones own ground of Being. The European versions lead one away from that reality and daily exposures to them causes Conditioned Reflexes.

The *Discretive Method* concerns first disjoining the Bad Emotions' dilution and pollution from the purity of the Real Self Emotions. Second, disjoin ones Selfhood from being on the wrong path. Third, disjoin ones mindset that led to switching to a False Self. Starting here first, the foundational cause was ones false interpretation of a loss of ones Spiritual Human Nature Needs which, in turn, caused a loss of ones Selfhood Greatness and the "5Ss." This begins to be reversed by generating a congenial atmosphere and proceeding toward Diagnosis (by the "What's Behind That!" method). Finally, handle the "Raw Nerve" that formed at the moment of the original Trigger Event which initiated the Bad Emotions. What got one on the wrong path was a False Self Icon Image. [Reproduced from Bailey, Ancient African Bible Messages] See Brainwashing jabaileymd.com

MIND CONTROL BY SLAVE OWNERS: One ought to never confuse shrewdness with intelligence. "*Shrewd*" originally meant wicked, dangerous. Brutes who originally set up the world society had as their major objective the controlling of the people and to keep the people ignorant was the best way to exploit them. Shrewdly these Brutes knew people would remain ignorant when they are not given the tools for thinking; are told what to believe and not how to think; to ignore the obvious; and to have faith in whatever Brutes tell them to believe—and to never question it in order to avoid being punished by the Devil in Hell. *Both the Devil in Hell were made up by Brutes.* In moving in on the precious material of rich Africans, starting in C15, Brutes knew the importance of controlling Africans' religion and Spirituality in order to control Africans minds. At that time Africans had no concepts of Faith or Beliefs in God—strictly a European concept--because they "Knew" God existed. But Africans did have Faith/Belief in was themselves to discover the best ways to communicate directly with God because there were no "go-betweens," like ministers, to do this for them. When Enslaved Africans were brought to the Americas it was the shrewd task of Europeans to stop having them "Know" God exists and convert this to Faith/Belief. The method of "What SEEMS to be true" was used. *"SEEMS" right is the false impression of Being real* while repressing any persisting doubt of its Truthfulness by the "SEEMS" not "Feeling right." First, it was necessary to beat the Enslaved into Extreme Despair on the way to them becoming completely submissive. To Brutes, this showed their "little god" power as a way to demonstrate to victims that they controlled the Earth. But they would immediately and insincerely add, since the Enslaved believed in Sekhem, the Cosmic Force, that God (meaning the Brutes made-up Supernatural God) controlled the sky. Second, they spotlighted the wicked lie of their patriarchal God--which constitutes an idol (a specific image of who is pretended to do certain things). Third, Europeans said their made-up God had all the power which was used to preserve the dignity of humans, meaning humans must rely on what is outside themselves for anything good to happen to them. Europeans resorted to fantasy stories taken from metaphors of African Bible literature to convey principles to the Enslaved as a means of reinforcing their wicked mind conversion program. An example of making a metaphor of Ancient African Cosmos Creation Myths into fact is the Ancient Egyptians' Khnum, the potter-god. The mythological story is that Khnum fashions on the potter's wheel both humans and animals out of the clay, the silt of the Nile. Then the resultant created bodies of children were removed from the potter's wheel and inserted into their mothers' bodies. Immediately upon the delivery of each baby, Khnum's consort, Heket, offers the "breath of life," symbolized by the *ankh*, to the nose of the clay figure to animate the clay effigy. Europeans' use of their conversion of this metaphor into the false reality was to preach to the Enslaved that humans are made out of clay by an external force and that a human's breathe similarly requires a force outside them. Fourth, after this emotional word illustration of the European Supernatural God being separate from humans --as opposed to being within each human as Africans knew to be so for tens of thousands of years--focus turned to the absolute necessity for having Faith/Belief in the European Supernatural God—and to stop "Knowing" the Sekhem God. Slave owners elaborated by saying Faith/Belief in God is humans' only guarantee for Heaven Afterlife rewards and that has to be so to preserve law and order in the Cosmos. Thus, the Satanists, disguised as European Christians, said the Enslaved must base their thoughts and actions on their fantasy God's authority standards and certain ways of life must be authorized by this God the Brutes made in their own image. The slave owners declared themselves messengers for God's Word, pointing out to the Enslaved that they, as indicated by them being rulers of the Earth, were the only successful group of people. By contrast, as part of their Projection of who they knew themselves to be, the oppressors told the Enslaved that they were simply objects in the world (i.e. without a spirit) and therefore no more than chattel (like cattle and other moving property). This, of course, made them sub-human and anyone who lacks a personality (i.e. "depersonalized") is supposed to be a Slave and do what the White man says do. Fifth was to frighten the Enslaved by telling them that only the White man knew what was sinful. For example, if the Enslaved sinned, they and their loved ones would die in hell. Most Enslaved were susceptible to these "Bully" tactics because of being so beaten down.

MISCELLANEOUS: C17 (mix) is a collection brought together largely by chance. It may or may not be Heterogeneous. If the Things are alike in kind, but different in size, form, quality, or use and without special order or relation, it is miscellaneous. Miscellaneous information in that it may or may not be pertinent; or may or may not be applicable to the situation at hand or may or may not be neutral. If not immediately pertinent, it might become so at some future time. What may not be applicable are those family members standing outside the family because they are characterized by "too much" or "too little" of something significant. They "stand apart" from their "cousins" by lacking the unifying principles required for a syndrome; by the unique masks they wear; and by their distinguishing masquerades. What may seem "neutral" are *Misfits*. One may be unaware that what seems to be a "Misfits" actually possesses a magnitude of importance far greater than their numbers or their "insignificant" labels might suggest. One reason is a certain "misfit" may represent the "tip of the iceberg" related to a new syndrome or even relate to a new category of syndromes.

MISFIT: See Miscellaneous

MISINTERPRETATION: Amazed (stunned) by being dulled through shock, as in being wide-eyed and open-mouthed while "*Bending*" (bring into a curve) Reality into Distortions or leaping into Fantasy (e.g. the Supernatural). When moderate or Extreme, there is an exit off reality's course as to stir so much disharmony, fear, and difficulty as to cause *Illusions* (seeing what is not there and not seeing what is there); *Hallucinations* (false images or beliefs having nothing to suggest it, outside a disordered mind); "*Delirium*" (temporary mental disturbance leading to believing ideas opposed to reality); *Delusions* (believing what is not real and not believing what is real); and *Misinterpretations* (wrong track, wrong plane of existence, and/or wrong direction). All disarray ones 'sureness' of any topic one thought one knew or will later know.

MISSION IN LIFE: Ancient Africans said every human has a "*Mission*" ("let go, send"). Every human newborn has this "First Wisdom" of knowing her/his Mission but most lose it, starting around 18 months of age when they start coming under the influence of "The Crowd". Ones Mission originally has nothing to do with ones likes/dislikes but rather one is in keeping with ones Sacred Dream (known in early childhood) and ones Talent. A Mission is about continually being on the path to it or being involved in it—and not about being successful. It has no rewards; is extremely hard work; one gets stomped on and disrespected. Yet nothing else in life will provide the profound sense of Self-Pride and Contentment and Happiness. These promote Self-Love and an ongoing sense of "Aliveness"—that supersedes any "Excitement," for it sustains high interest intensity—making one eager to get up in the morning and stay up late simply to explore one detail. It makes one put aside favorites (e.g. watching movies or television). It does not matter how hard it is or how long it will take to get ready or the problems along the way. All that matters is to go "straight ahead" in fashioning a Masterpiece. Along the journey, one becomes "Alive"—and that differs from liking or being "Excited" about it. Age 5 was the first occasion in my recall of Calling, Purpose, and Mission in life meant an instinctual

Self-Declaration. While sitting on my back porch selecting my favorite marbles, it suddenly appeared in my mind--like a neon flashing light sign--to "Help Bright Black Boys." That authoritative message was instinctually accepted. A remarkable thing about this is that I was living in Minnesota where I saw no Black People at all. The moment a human makes their most powerful of Life-Shaping, Life-Changing, or Life-Maintaining decisions—those, for good or bad, destined to cause them to change their present path of their lives and thereafter guide them along a new path for the rest of their lives—means they have made a Supreme Self-Declaration (i.e. the "willed" to do it). There are two choices one will make—either to remain on the course of ones birth-hood state or to get off that course. In other words, a Self-Declaration determines if one stays with ones birth-gift of Selfhood Greatness or switches over to outside world Standards, Guides, Filters, and Measures for living life.

The very best decision one will ever make in life is to make the silent *Self-Declaration* to stay with ones dignified Self-Greatness because Selfhood Greatness is God imparted. This is such a vital decision that it needs elaboration. A Self-Declaration is needed to be true to oneself, especially while holding oneself in check during bad "earthquake" life moments. If a mistake is made or if one is headed down the wrong path, them immediately correct it rather than "giving into it." In the Soul of every human prior to birth into the Earth World is an Essence containing a Virtual Image on the outside of that Essence Pattern and a *Disposition* with its "What and Why" Purpose in Life on the inside that serves as ones Matrix for making ones Mission happen (e.g. ones Talent). Ones Purpose in Life, said Ancient Africans, has Earth world and Spiritual realm duties as well as duties to ones Selfhood and to Others. All four require maintaining a connection with ones Real Self and thereby with ones Divine Consciousness (i.e. ones Spark of God) because out of its Divine Love come the Spiritual Energy. That Energy, in the form of *"Aliveness,"* gives one the awareness of having supreme self-worth (dignity); the ability to appreciate moments of prefect beauty (inside and outside oneself); the awareness of what is ones Purpose(s) in life; and the urge and determination to complete what one is put on earth to do. One of the clues I had this early in life what possessing a *strong sense of Completion.* Also prior to a human's birth, and while in a Virtual Image state, one is Spiritually Connected to all of God's Creatures and Creations. In the center of all that bonding is an Interchange of them all and orchestrated by the Cosmic Mind. This forms an ever permanent "ME/WE" state which has as its theme *Selfless Service*--the vital aspect of ones purpose in life. See Purpose

MONAD: the Divine Sparks of Creation containing God's Essence (Substance). Its down descent converts the Meiosis non-atomic Monadic *"Elemental Essence"* into a power possessing atomic *"Monadic Essence"* by the addition of Ether in the Sublime just below the Subjective Ocean of Nun realm.

MONOMANIA: an obsession with one idea or subject that is thought about constantly.

MOOT COURT: when Africans had disputes, neighbors rallied around both disputants and had each offer the other a gift. If that did not work to end the dispute, they called a *Moot Court* for all to listen to the opponents' arguments and decide what *solution was in the best interest of the community*, as opposed to one disputant.

MORTALS: in Ancient Africa, *"Pupil"* referred to those under a teacher's close supervision when participating in higher religious education; *"Student,"* to those specializing in a branch of study in preparation for a profession; and *Scholar,* to *"giving oneself"* to learning intimate Spiritual Elements details concerning God's Laws. *Mortals* (Initiates, Neophytes), probationary pupils who had not yet realized the Inner Vision, were instructed in the Sages' doctrines. The *Intelligences*--advanced students from having attained Inner Vision by getting a glimpse of Cosmic Consciousness—had thus achieved the *Mysticism Mind*--minds having the ability to intensely concentrate their Intellect Reasoning into their Pure Emotions.

MOSAIC: creation of a complex whole pattern out of differences within Things of a Classification, as a good painting has different colors and shapes; a musical piece has different rhythms and tones. See Interchange

MOSES--UNEXAMINED "AUTHORITIES" ASSUMPTIONS: "*Authority*" (C13, capacity to produce, invent, counsel, degree, judge) originally began its meaning as synonymous with "Right" and "Power". Next, it developed along the lines of the creator's power to command, establish rules and precedents, make decisions, judge, and settle issues or disputes. Then it settled into one in whom is vested power to control, so as to exercise controlling power to impose her/his decision or opinions upon others. "*Power*" implies inherent potency, ability, capacity. Since Supernatural oriented cults are "military" in their organization, their Authorities assume *Mastery* status—i.e. ascendancy superiority power achieved to a Certainty degree—meaning delivered supremacy justifying *Dominance* (ruling over others) by rights to command and to enforce obedience. Hence, in European tradition, Authorities have *Pre-eminence*—i.e. standing out to comparatively put in the "background" other persons/things. Power sources may be a leader(s), the Crowd, a book, or institutions. This human-made thinking form concerns Europeans' psychotherapy category of "*One-Ups-man-ship/One Down*" position—an oppressive Mind Control for the "one(s) down"--a Thought Process doing violence to Truth/Reality. Note, without content change, stepping stones from a Belief, to an opinion, to a fact, to truth for everybody—all without any proof or verifications. So, a socialized but unexamined assumption simply accepted as "fact" by almost everybody is that "*Authorities" say the Truth*. But it is vital to know the mindsets of "Authorities"—what is their Standard for such Truth? Where did they get their information? How did they get to be "Authorities"? Even to accept for discussion that they were "Authorities," how do we know they were translated or quoted correctly? Still, there are some subject points of view other than those given by "Authorities". An example is the different versions of the well-known European Bible story of Moses and the Ten Commandments. Since contrasting points have been discussed in my book: "*Ancient African Bible Messages*," a story gist is Gadalla, an Egyptian Egyptologist, saying Moses' life and religion match precisely with those of the revolutionary Pharaoh of Egypt, Akhenaton (1367-1361 BC). This Egyptian King, after changing his name from Amenhotep IV, crystalized concepts of a monotheistic deity. Ben-joc says Moses was born in Goshen, Egypt according to the Torah or the Old Testament in the Book of Exodus. Some say Moses was the son of Bathia (daughter of Pharaoh Seti I and the Pharaoh himself) and spent his early youth at On (Heliopolis). *The myth about finding a baby in a basket in water was quite common at the time, especially in honoring national heroes.* In this situation, says Naiwu Osahon, the Moses' episode was concocted to allow his parents to look after him in the palace as their son and without its incestuous implications (for another version see J. Campbell, Thou Art p55). He was taught in the Grand Lodge of Djoser at Sakkara. Assuming he went to the lodge at age 7, he would not have come out until he was 47, since it took 40 years of training to make a priest in all of the disciplines. As with all great religious leaders of that time, Moses was an initiate of the Egyptian Mysteries, for it was the One Holy Catholic Religion of the remotest antiquity. If so, Moses came as nothing but a copy of the Egyptian priests and Teachings of *The Egyptian Mysteries System* in On where he was trained (as confirmed by the historian Josephus and by Philo). The Greek Historian Strabo confirmed Moses was an Egyptian priest who had issues with Egypt's institutions, as believing God was in all things and thus could not take the form of an animal or a person. Yet, he wrote of sons of Heru in Genesis. People Moses convinced emigrated freely to Jerusalem. Moses (esoterically Pharaoh Akanaten), a prince or priest (Exodus 2:16-19), wrote (c1350 BC) the Pentateuch, including Numbers, in Egyptian hieroglyphics, his native tongue, after leaving Egypt with Ten Commandments knowledge taken from the 42 laws of African Ma'at and the Pillars of Osiris. The African "*Book of Coming Forth by Day*" contained nearly word for word what Moses is said to have brought down directly from God. A recent article by top Jewish leaders said there was no parting of the Red Sea by Moses, as reported in the European Bible. *Such was the way, as their style, scribes wrote during that time—and not because they were lying.* Others say the Red Sea was a misinterpretation for the "Reed Sea" which had no waters to be parted and therefore no "pillar of fire." jabaileymd.com

MOTHER'S MONEY METHODS: Mother taught to me as boy, and I supplemented it by learning the hard way, include: WISE BUYING: "Buy only what is absolutely necessary." "*If you really need it, then pay cash.*" This helped me the most. After working hard to save the money to buy what "I simply could not do without," by the time I had saved the required money the "need" for the thing had often passed. If you learn about class and what is classy, many of those over-priced clothes can be bought relatively inexpensively in garment districts. The same applies to other accoutrements of daily living. WISE SAVINGS: Have an ultimate goal for the use of your money. For me, it was a college education. At home, we never threw away any food and made use of all broken and worn out things—rehabilitating them into new uses or for parts to repair other things. BE CREATIVE: Barter to get the best books and the best teachers. SAVING MONEY: When you get paid, "first pay yourself *30% of your paycheck* and put it in the bank (or someplace similar where it can make money for you"). Education accounts usually pay higher interests than other types of "Mattress" accounts. I never want to put my principle at risk. WISELY INVEST MONEY: do not invest in anything requiring all the money you have; and do not ever invest in anything you do not understand. HAVE EMERGENCY MONEY: Always have hidden and secret money available for emergencies and replace it immediately. Do not let anybody know you have it. Only in emergencies is it okay to spend more than you make. In traveling, I use to carry a money belt. WISE DEBTS: "Pay whatever it takes to obtain a *superior education* (i.e. developing your talents and skills) related to your career for this breaks the vicious cycle of poverty and is the way to rise above poverty. When the opportunity arises *"Buy your own home."* Start with one you can afford and replace it when you are able. This establishes you as a solid citizen. It is wise to buy a duplex and rent out one side to reliable people (and not friends). If you are handy, buy a "fixer-upper" and sell it later. STOP BEING CHEATED OUT OF MONEY: When it comes to money, the overwhelming majority of people cheat. Being hypocritical was normal for medieval knights while cheating, stealing, lying, and other sins were honored by C15 Europeans. There is no realm where you will not be cheated—the government, banks, attorneys, gasoline stations. Do not trust other people to handle your money. It is important to know how salespersons get paid. Do not have business charge you for cashing your check. Throughout my life anything of great material value have been stolen or destroyed or thrown away either by dishonorable or by ignorant people. People are always eager to "borrow" money and always have a "hard luck" story—as in facing eviction or death by somebody. I have fallen for this maybe 200 times because in one case it may be true. However, I have never been paid back and always lost the friendship of them and those I have helped the most in other ways. Such has happened so often and caused such deep emotional pain that in recent years I have developed the Prophylactic self-protective measure of *"Non-Attachment"*--meaning that I recognize Tangible losses as a fact of life and choose not to get so attached as to allow it to bother me any longer than six weeks. What I learned is to accept each of those situations as if they are presented to serve as a test. Then I handle each in a manner that makes me stronger.

MOTHER WIT: an archaic term for astrological divination was "mathesis", the "Learning"—literally *Mother wisdom* or *"Mother Wit"* (referring to the highest form of common sense).

MYSTICISM MINDS: in Ancient Africa, "*Pupil*" referred to those under a teacher's close supervision when participating in higher religious education; "*Student*," to those specializing in a branch of study in preparation for a profession; and *Scholar*, to "*giving oneself*" to learning intimate Spiritual Elements details concerning God's Laws. *Mortals* (Initiates, Neophytes), probationary pupils who had not yet realized the Inner Vision, were instructed in the Sages' doctrines. The *Intelligences*--advanced students from having attained Inner Vision by getting a glimpse of Cosmic Consciousness—had thus achieved the *Mysticism Mind*--minds having the ability to intensely concentrate their Intellect Reasoning into their Pure Emotions.

MYSTIQUE MENTAL TONES OF BLACK SCHOLARS: From their 200,000 years ago beginnings, Black People's Mystique Thinking has concerned mental manipulations and maneuverings of Qualities pertaining to Spiritual Matters. It started with Superstitions, then the Science of Superstitions, then Science of the Spiritual. Resultant *associations of Insights formed transcendental Knowledge Patterns. Their Mystique minds bathed in a Knowledge's aura and used its vibrational tones to extract Principles for Right Life Living.* By contrast, since their beginning 45,000 years ago, Europeans' Non-Rational Thinking, as they call it, has been derived from their Supernatural Mythical Fantasy. Whether referring to the Divine (The Ultimate), Spiritual, Metaphysical, Physical, or Supernatural realms, a real Entity's "*What it is*" consists of a "*That it is*" (its self-identity Essence existence when coming into Being-hood) + its *Properties* (what a Thing has). Both make it "*Such as it is*". In Metaphysical, Physical, or Supernatural realms, those Properties, when Ether is added, consist of Primary Qualities, acting like Tones—with or without Secondary and Tertiary Qualities. Entities with Primary Qualities include: Emotions, Sound, an Essence's Essentials (i.e. *Character, Characteristics, Traits, and Features*), Musical Notes, Symbols, and Dance. A *Species of Primary Qualities,* each with differing Properties, make for unique appearances among like-kind Entities. Yet, they are very closely related in Essence since they have the same Spiritual Elements "Genetics." Classes of, say, Emotions which form a Classification are like a given Family of 'like-kind' realities. Similarly, all are very closely related in the nature of their Essence but each gives individualized manifestations. The top Primary Quality in each Entity has a Character. Its *Disposition* has a "What" and "Why" Message received from its Source + an Inclination + an Intention + a Temperament + an Attitude—all combining to give it a Tone. A *Secular "Tone,"* pre-1300, meant a musical sound or note emitted by a stretched string—i.e. the character of sound. Then, among others, Tone was applied to a word or phrase able to be changed by nuances so as to alter its perception, meaning, or function; then, to a special stress or pitch accent given to one syllable in a word; then, as a style of Thought; then, a pervading conduct. Manipulations and maneuverings of the ingredients making up the "normal" or the "middle" Value of the Tone design an Overtone or Undertone—each used to fashion new paths or insights. Originally, *Undertone* was described as a low or subdued tone, perhaps from a tone of lower pitch or lower loudness (e.g. a whisper). *A mind's awareness required subtle discernment skills.* This expanded to include whatever is *Underlying* as, for example, an undercurrent of kindness or rage. Some Undertone nuanced messages are *Subliminal* (beneath ones aware sensory threshold)—i.e. a message flash at an "imperceptible shadow" level—implying it can be seen without being noticed. Others are *Apprehended* (C14; seizing)—i.e. mentally grasped but ranging from not being understood or even not being seen--all the way over to getting bits and pieces of understanding of it so as to form an idea of what will happen in the future. *Overtone* initially referred to one of the higher tones in a complex musical tone—recognized by implying, suggesting, or characterizing it. It is raised in quality or strength by such means as Figures of Communication (e.g. Figures of Speech and Affect Symbolic Imagery). Those, by spotlighting a sense impression in the Tone, create enough vividness in that fragmentary piece to illuminate its hidden relationships or patterns while "dematerializing" that thought's boundaries. The resultant *Vivid Imaging* enables ones mind to blend into the Tone--switch from Thought to Emotions--and impart the more intensely vibrational Energy of stirred-up Emotions. The final result is to carry the "middle" Tone "over the top"—as a strong, enthusiastic message 'moves' one. Such an occurrence is a *Synthesis*--an assimilation of different types of ingredients present in the "middle" Tone, in the predominating disposition, and in the condition of the mind—as in ones mood and ones mental frame. Involved ingredients interweave, forming an *Interchange*. Next, happenings of each mosaic piece join to generate a mosaic Icon Image. Within the integration of whatever fashioned a Synthesis, the whole is greater than the sum of its parts. If this process has remained inside of and developed its products from the Spiritual Elements, by using the work product and its attributes, one slowly ascends from ones Lower (animalistic) Self to ones Highest (divinity) Self. See Nuance jabaileymd.com

N

NATURAL: Both the words "Nature" and "Natural" derive from the ancient Latin term "natural," neutral, and eternity. In turn, those words derive from the Egyptian words "*Neter*" (God) and "*Neteru*" (God's manifestations). Natural means resulting from Nature, implying what is inborn or inherent as well as possesses Spiritual and Matter aspects. The African Tradition story of Natural began when Very Ancient Africans said God gave birth to the Cosmos through sound (the Word). This prime mover set in motion Natural "Genetic" Sounds and Rhythms, both being the ancestors of all subsequent vibrations--which represent Instincts--in God's creatures and creations. Natural is like an Idea-Form. Hence, the Natural, Truth, and *Real are the "What it is"* of a God-made Thing when it came into existence—the very Essence of Being. This existence originates in the *Subjective realm*--also called "*Nothingness*"—the realm of Virtual (boundary-less) Being—which is the mother of all Being by it producing all Cosmic Organism Creatures and Creations. The Natural is Interwoven with Unconditional Love, Truth, and Reality to form an Interchange. This Interchange is the source of the "*Voice of the Silence*"—i.e. the Ocean of Nun in the Subjective Plane. It: "says everything by not saying anything at all" while "it retains everything by giving away everything." Silence speaks the impossible--expresses the inexpressible and, in fact, is expressed inexpressibility. The Product is nameless, for it is greater than anything that can be named. It takes no action, in that it leaves Things alone.

It supports all Things but does not take possession of them. It lets Things transform themselves. It does nothing and yet all Things are thereby done. In short, it is Nature transforming itself spontaneously by *Natural Order*. These aspects of the Natural remain in all of its Archetypes, Prototypes, and specific Entities evolutions. The Form part of *The Natural is what that Thing does in its essence state*--before anything is added to it, as in what is fitted for Nature. So the Natural's manifestations is its Idea-Form in an acquired display following birth into the Earth World within the context of the Spiritual Elements. What is Real and Natural--whether in Nature or in humans--has no limitations, prohibitions, or rules of conduct because it (among other things) lacks boundaries and is infinite. Its features are being at ease, without inhibitions, facile, spontaneous (i.e. happenings of itself), and unconstrained. It connotes simplicity and directness. To illustrate, a *Spiritual Natural* is present when, following birth, one operates out of Selfhood Greatness—as indicated by a lack of self-consciousness. For example, the toddler starts real dancing because it feels the vibrations and naturally flows with the rhythm of the music. But when she becomes self-conscious--i.e. aware of people watching her dance, she tenses up and does not dance well. This is because she feels as if there are certain rules to follow which she is not doing right. However, if she undergoes training and gets rid of the flaws hampering her dance, she will return to her birth gift of an effortless Natural flowing dance which has no rules to follow--simply Guidelines characterizing Harmony. Still, this is *Secular Natural*. Anything else is Disharmony. The most direct way to know God, said Ancient Egyptians, is to study God's natural manifestations (Ashby, Egyptian Yoga, p. 50). *The most natural way to live is by what naturally flows out of ones Dignity (ones God image) and Divinity (from being a God drop).* Such is called living by Ma'at Principles—fashioning the Spiritual Elements into attributes by ones Pure Emotions and Pure Intellect so that the spontaneous flow of those attributes are like being Instinctive by nature. Attributes of ones Nature include its appetites and Inclinations derived out of the Spiritual Elements and display—among others —as "ME/WE"; Nonaggressive traits of gentleness, kindness, empathy, affection, helpfulness, and compassion; and Selfless Service. If one has gotten away from this and when one knows of no human guides having shown themselves wise, the best thing is to take control of oneself and model a like-kind Nature's pattern. In short, *"The Natural" is Spiritual Greatness displayed out of the* Nature of the Spiritual Elements transforming themselves spontaneously by *Natural Order.*

NATURE: *ones "Private Personal Properties" operations in life,* as ones self-recognized Identity fashions them to be, consists of *Endowments* (i.e. natural qualities—e.g. ones Genius, ones Talent) and *Propensities* (in-born tendencies, e.g. ones capacities, abilities, and language) inside Essences. Their distinguishing ingredients are ones: (1) in-born *Characteristics*--the distinguishing ingredients of Essentials that are typical for the Selfhood of that individual); (2) *Traits* (a distinctive behavior pattern pertaining to individuality and more-so than a Characteristic); and (3) *Feature*—i.e. the something in a Trait arousing the most attention. These three are what evolve the designs of ones Thinking Type and degree—and that determines one Philosophy of Life formation which first shapes ones Private Self components of: self-recognized *Self-Identity, Self-Meaning* (the Spiritual Self-Greatness standard against which one can compare ones Self-Respect); and *Self-Love* (ones self-anchor). These components are what fashion ones *Public Self Self-Esteem* components of Self-Concept (ones spotlighted qualities) and Self-Image. See Self-Identity; Character

NATURES' PROCESSES: *Nature's ingredients come from the Interchange of the Spiritual Elements and represent mosaics. Each mosaic is a Principle—all having "Sameness" from being composed of vibrations and yet each is "Unique" via its different vibratory rate.* Each Entity is an independent worker that interdependently works harmoniously to maintain a "seemingly" normal whole--and yet all are nuances in constant change. "Sameness/Uniqueness" + the Independent being Interdependent are Cosmic Wholism features—features accounting for Nuance changes in a Cosmos which apparently remains the same. *Nature's Processes embrace the independent workings of each pair of its Complementary Natural Opposites*—e.g. heat/cold, light/dark, black/white, and dull/sharp. Each pair is varying degrees of the *"same thing,"* as in *"heat"* and *"cold"*. They imply one Form with a variety of appearances + unique differing rates of vibration + varying degrees of interrelationships between the two poles of one "spoke"—i.e. changing but remaining the same. Since Heat is the energy of motion of molecules, when a substance is heated, its molecules all begin to move faster. This motion of molecules is a vibration in which each molecule wiggles backward and forward extremely fast. At the same time, it moves (if at all) only comparatively slowly from one locality to another. In heating ice, the single molecules escape, as liquid water flows away. Thus, one cannot distinguish where *"heat"* stops and *"cold"* begins because *"the extremes meet"* (The Kybalion p. 32). A living Nuance in action is the Butterfly's four life cycle stages. *Music comes closer to being about Reality because it by-passes words and thus it has to be grasped nonverbally and intuitively.*

NATURE--THINKING INSIDE ITS PROCESSES: Pseudo-intellectuals are so enamored with their unrealistic, confusing, and conflicting thinking as to use big and undefinable words to prevent exposing their dumbness. Their audience is the "Crowd," themselves eager to have their minds controlled because of being too weak to independently think for themselves. This is how *Human-Made Patterns of Thinking* are established—i.e. that which is erratic, illusory, and linear (one dimensional). For example, the Old English definitions of "Shade" and "Shadow" originated as one out of the setting of "Darkness". This refers to their comparative or obscurity aspects, owning to the interception of the rays of light—an interception caused by an opaque body between the space contemplated and the source of light. But this concept has multiple other applications that are so nondescript as to make it a struggle to find their common theme. In paintings, shade can result by closely repeated lines or by adding a darker or lighter pigment to a given hue or tint. Both types of shade make for subtlety in the sense of having an *Apprehension* of what is suggested—meaning a Notion so lacking in pertinent details that ones imagination fills in the gaps. A *"Notion"* is the earliest stage of a developing idea and possesses vague and partially formed Images. To *Apprehend* it is to lay hold of something in it, as through the senses, the mind, or via the instinct—with only a hint, at best, of understanding anything that it is about. Even then, it is uncertain that what has been apprehended is part of the Essence, or is given the right interpretation, or is the right part selected in order to form that Notion. To make matters worse, the resultant flawed and counterfeit thought is acted upon as if it is "truth" and that causes damage. By contrast, the finest forms of Truth Thinking follow the mathematical Processes of Nature. On its sound Base, sound structures are built. Nature is imaged by the human mind to be configured into *an underlying web of relationships operating* throughout the Cosmos. Nature consists, *on all planes of existence,* of a *complexity and multiplicity of Patterns*—some reproducible; others being new creations from moment to moment, like foams in ocean waves. Yet, the *Unification of these relationships and patterns make for* an infinite *Continuity and Harmony.* To thoroughly understand one of Nature's Patterns—or a piece of one--gives insight into the Esoteric (Unknown) Cosmic Circle of Things. Such occurs since they all possess the same Spiritual Elements "Genetic Harmony" wherever located within the Cosmic Organism Web. Hence, even though each Entity is "Unique," *being part of the Cosmic Web gives each Correspondence* with every other part of the Cosmic Circle of Wholeness. From operating by Ma'at Principles and Laws, all Knowledge of it is very few in number. To see all of these aspects together in their web-like interrelationships enables one to become aware of links connecting and meshing the Uniqueness of each member into the inner nature Sameness that makes up the Cosmic Family. These Processes are designated "*Circumstantial*" because by Nature existing "all over" at once means no part can be reasoned by direct demonstrations. To illustrate, an over-simplified profound Ancient African concept is the all-Black Amenta (the Nun, the Void, Nothingness) pertaining to the Cosmic Mind. Its total blackness, reflecting the Cosmic primordial state, corresponds to *Absolute Darkness (Kekui)--itself "Light"*—dazzling and blinding in its splendor from its super-rapid vibration rate. While it appears as Absolute Darkness to human's perceptions, in reality it is the Cause of a human's Unconsciousness becoming Self-Illuminated. To think inside Processes of Nature is important for discerning nuanced Causes of problems. Example: in a biological *Mutation* there can be rearrangements, re-combinations, substitutions, subtractions, additions, or multiplications of genes and chromosomes—perhaps in a single base pair in the DNA molecule or in a somatic cell. The effect can be a transmissible variation, as in a plant or animal. That can make for hardiness, for a disability, or for pre-mature death. Its Complementary Opposite is a *Suppressor Mutation* which corrects mutation effects at one point (locus) by a mutation at another locus. Or, for a human's "*Soul*" to have inner Self-illumination, its vibration must be comparable to its black complementary opposite residing in that Soul's Amenta. Or, Spiritual Shade differs from Secular Shade by no impositions between its source and its Effect + it is not about staying the same or getting darker but rather about lessening the darkness to perceive Shade.

NETER: "Neter" in this sense means "Pa Neter" (the one Universal High God) whereas "Neters," as part of "Neteru" indicate masculine High Gods (as extensions of the "Pa Neter" -- see Octopus Concept). "Neter" (masculine) and "Netert"/"Netrit" (feminine), though translated by some to mean "god" and "goddess," more directly mean principle or law. Both words therefore, refer to the natural laws governing Creation, rather than deities (which are extensions of God symbolizing natural laws). "Netert"/"Netrit" and "Neter" are very similar in meaning to the Yin and Yang of Chinese philosophy (Seleem. Egyptian Book of the Dead p11).

NEUTRAL: In 1471 "Neutral" meant on neither side in a quarrel; or in war (1549). In chemistry it meant having neither acid nor alkaline properties (1661) and in electricity being neither positive nor negative in charge (1837). In African Tradition it is having a balanced scale from the weights and measures being on each side of algebraic equal side.

NINE "Ps": what I call the *"9Ps": Preparing to Prepare; Purpose; Plan; Planes of Existence; Preparation; Practice; Performance; Platform; and Post-Action Judgments.* Each of these empower one on the path to success. The purpose of mastering pertinent tools is to reach a state of Empowerment. To be *Empowered* is to possess that which alters ones life by giving one a sense of control, a sense of direction toward a better life, and a sense of inspiration as one goes through the maze of life. African Tradition strongly emphasizes Empowerment--the opening up of ones capacities so as to make available a greater sense of power in order to become a Man-God as well as for handling problems of a particular nature. *Mastery* is a journey of continuous improvement towards a pertinent Human Ideal Goal. *Preparing* the mind includes being totally dedicated with a *Spiritual Energy Package* of dedication, commitment, loyalty, determination, persistence, and perseverance to not give up—to never succumb to attractive distractions--to always give ones best effort—to achieve the goal in the most efficient and effective manner--that goes to completion, no matter what. Each of these six is like the links in a chain and each is needed to complete any worthwhile task while driving away ones Emotional Energy powered Ego (*False Self*). One has no inhibitions on exploring the Unknown—no fear of failure or fear of success—no "I can't" locks and chains on ones capabilities. You are free when you honestly examine your Fears and mentally play them out by saying: "what would I do if it happens?" *Purpose* is the desired special work that displays ones great inner Truth and Talents compatible with what ones assesses to be the most important as a life's Mission. *Plan* is a blueprint for carrying out the Purpose. *Planes of Existence* include the Amenta, Subjective, Sublime, Noumenal, and Phenomenal *Intangible or Metaphysical Planes of the Ether* and Physical. Inside each are many sub-planes. The *Sublime* is made of pre-matter, is above time and space; has boundaries but beyond human perception; and contains the Cosmos highest concentration of Love, Goodness, Truth, and Beauty in Thought Clouds. Giving consideration to each plane within the "Big Picture" means a focus on wholism--what is most likely to be beneficial to the most people (including oneself) over the longest period of time. To this end the physical, mental, spiritual, social, financial, time and effort are all to be considered from the perspective of creating, enhancing, and maintaining them to their best advantage.

Preparation is getting tools ready to remove obstacles along the proposed planned path. Then other tools are collected needed to prepare that path toward having the present meet the future. Part of this is selecting Approaches A, B, and C. *Practice* concerns perfecting whatever is required in the *Approach* (the way a goal is reached), *Method* (how to do the job), *Technique* (how tools are used in the approach and method), and *Manner* (the different ways a technique can be handled). As much as possible, time and effort are spent doing for Approaches B and C the same things done for Plan A.

Performance is actually trying to achieve the future Subjective Unrealized Reality which is at the core of ones Purpose. *Platform* is mentally and physically doing bits and pieces of your Purpose before your future Subjective Unrealized Reality is actualized. *Post-Action Judgments* occur after each step of what you are doing in the present and consist of what is not good or a waste of time that can be eliminated or made more efficient; what is good about what you are doing but could be made better; and what is excellent that could be made into a habit routine that is faster to achieve and with fewer motions. An overall aspect is to handle the problems each of these planes contain that are likely to slow, stop, or reverse wholesome and wholistic progress. Critical Thinking (CT) orchestrates all of these. CT mindsets operate on different planes of existence. Some pertain to the Cosmos (Immaterial, Intangible, Tangible). Some pertain to ones Selfhood (the physical, mental, or spiritual). "Head" type CT concerns primarily the Left Brain figuring out things -- some of a material nature in mathematical fashion and some figuring out how to clear ones Selfhood of fetters so as to proceed from ones Lower (animalistic) Self towards ones Highest (divinity) Self. Ancient African art depicts this Left Brain-Right side of body as opposed to Right Brain/Left side of body as well as a person with two left hands as a giver (whereas right hands indicate taking). "Heart" type CT, as exhibited by the African Great Mother, concerns primarily Right Brain activities in whatever is related to the Spiritual Elements of African Tradition -- i.e. Unconditional Love, Truth, Reality, and the Natural. See Noumenal; Phenomenal

NON-RATIONAL THINKING: People with an Indifference/Hate/Evil/Sadism mindset that puts them in a Supernatural realm and leads them to Kill/Take/Destroy/Dominate/Control behaviors (KTDDC) are barred from any Intellectual or Pure Emotion thinking. Instead, they are Patterned Thinkers who simply manipulate and maneuver shrewd (wicked) well-established KTDDC acts. Some add innovations (adding something new to what already exists and, in the case of European, has been done since their primitive warrior beginnings 45,000 years ago). Europeans are Supernatural oriented and say their Thinking is *Non-Rational because their realm is unconquerable, unmovable, undeniable, unexplainable, incomparable, unimaginable, immeasurable, and unthinkable.* Thus, Non-Rational Thinking is haphazard, random, unordered, and usually unprepared to meet pop-up challenges. This is why they do not answer penetrating (or often any) questions but, instead, change the subject. In their versions of Common Sense, it is normal to say one thing one moment and then say or do its opposite the next. Hence, there are no Rational, Critical, Logical, Intellectual, or Wisdom European Thinkers using African Traditions. *No method exists in European logic to correct whatever is not true and there is no permanent, stationary, unchanging Truth standard that has a pin-point Essence.* Webster's and The American Heritage College Dictionaries define "Truth as, in general, such conformity to facts or reality"… but denoting "an abstraction that is purely ideal construction." The *Major Premise* of European Reasoning by Deduction means the main fact is assumed to be true in order to reason further by Deduction. Of course, if one does not know what a Thing is or where it is located, then any place one goes might be there or not but there is no way to prove it. By contrast, "Logic" in African Tradition always starts building a Thought Structure from a "real" or Truthful foundational base--meaning it conforms to the Spiritual Elements. The spotlighted key point: *Always Challenge the Major Premise*!!!

NON-SELF: When ones mind is put at rest, as in a state of Hetep, it becomes aware of itself and the Self itself emerges. As a result of surrendering the vehicle of ones mental faculties, one is carried into a "Non-Self" realm—meaning ones Self is in the Cosmic Organism Web—being at once a "no-Self," an "excessive Self," and an identical Self—each meshes and is shared with all God's creatures and creations as One Being. Here one recognizes ones own Being as a vital part of the All (i.e. the Oneness of God). *A sense of the infinity of knowledge is realized—and proceeds beyond knowledge about the Spiritual Elements in order to be in "oneness" with its flow and develop "ME/ WE" products out of it.* Here, Knowledge is known without proof and it has nothing to do with Materialism or the Supernatural. In pausing to explore more deeply, the *infinity of knowledge means that I can keep hearing the same thing over and over and gain something from it each time—means a learning that enlarges beyond Understanding-- means that seeing more of what I have been blind to expands my Consciousness inside the Infinite. Each time I repeat the study of a difficult topic by drawing on new sources and each time I reflect on these ingredients by manipulating and maneuvering them into different arrangements and combinations, the wider is the scope of my understanding of the topic and the things associated with the topic. With or without my effort, what continues to happen is the inner layers covering the core message of the Essence impart new insights. Each new Insight enables the flowing out of richer meanings in each involved part as well as from the sum of the Whole and the aura resulting from what is greater than the sum. Each of these new meanings allows for the acquiring of more in-depth understanding of the Principles (pieces of the Truth or of the Unchanging Reality inside the Spiritual Elements) which, in turn, peels away another top covering layer.* The way this is assessed is because it "Feels" right in ones Selfhood Center. This "Feeling" is known to be from ones Spiritual Emotions and not from ones Acquired Emotions because it spurs "Aliveness"—that Spiritual Energy which continually urges one to Self-Improve and stay dedicated for "ME/WE" purposes. Acquired Emotions are Emotional Energy that is addicted to "Excitement" in the "here and now" and it provides nothing that is about self-improvement or focus—being like running hard on a treadmill and going nowhere. *To discover something new or even hear old wisdom over and over means the acquiring of a new perspective.*

This is the application of the Box Concept--viewing matters so as inspect each side--the inside and outside details of every angle—inspecting the top and bottom and any wrappings--turning it in all directions--looking at it from underneath--seeing it from one view after another--holding it against the sky and imagining it in any material or even in glass--and thinking of all types of options based upon fashioning powerful meanings indirectly. This entire process of *Synthesis happens because the whole is greater than the sum of its parts. Going beyond knowledge* means transcending into another realm so as to engage in its reality flow—a flow unknown to me but a flow that is a natural part of Cosmic Knowledge. The Effect of being in this flow is my Experience of participation in its reality. In pursuing my Mission, I enter into the *infinity of knowledge realms whereby my own Selfhood Center has been grasped and meshed into the presence of "a Beyond"—as from the less into the more—as from the smallness into a vastness—as from the microcosm (little world) into the macrocosm (big world).* The Effect carries me from Unrest to a Rest as a result of an expansion of my Spiritual Consciousness. My objective is to permanently "live into" that "ME/WE" Web because what is done in any part of the Web affects the entire Web and its contents. None of what is profound can be fully understood by reading it rapidly. Each profound phrase (e.g. infinity of knowledge and going beyond knowledge) must be contemplated and wallowed in. To be aware of these profound thoughts or realizations (e.g. the existence of the Spiritual Elements) is a life-shaping and life-changing moment. But to start the process requires, not trying to acquire knowledge but to discover what is keeping one from not being in Knowledge and from not being able to know and why. The point is not to be well-rounded, as emphasized by Europeans, in order to fit into the Crowd—for this keeps ones mind in scatter and superficial in its thinking. Instead, strive for great focused Spiritual Elements depth so as to produce Good Character and Wisdom. See "ME/WE"; Non-Self

"NON-SELF" WISDOM: "ME/WE" benefit productions are the ultimate Beauty in African Tradition of what Black people do as a lifestyle. Just as musical conductors set down notes to be played or sung, and then shepherd their musicians as to when and how to play corresponding musical sounds, an African Tradition Philosophy of Life (POL) takes a human's scattered best efforts and weaves "ME/WE" products. To appreciate this requires understanding Ancient African Origin concepts of all Real Cosmic Entities. While inside the Subjective Realm, residing in interconnections with the Cosmic Organism prior to Earth World birth, each Creature was a "Non-Self." Imagine being connected to all Creatures and Creations by a pipe in shish ke-bab style--and each being nourished by God's Substance—and each on equal status with respect to Worth. So, the "WE" pipes connected to the "ME" pipe fashion the "ME/WE"—and "forever." Since the Substance is running like water through the pipes equates to the Spiritual Elements which convey the "5Ss" of Safety, Security, Sureness/Self-Confidence, Strength, and Stability, one feels Harmony when "ME/WE" is in Order or Disharmony when any of the Web is disturbed. This means all of ones Selfhood is part of an Interchange with all of God's Creatures and Creations as well as of the one Universal Spiritual High God. This is such a vital life-living concept as to urge me to describe it differently. In the way an apple Seed gives rise to roots, a trunk, branches, leaves, and fruit, so does the Cosmic Creator "Seed" produce all Cosmic Things. African Sages said God's "Seed" consists of Androgynic plast (called Protoplasm today)—a plast whose Essences are comprised of the Spiritual Elements "Genetics" for all God's creatures and creations, including for each human. When those "Genetics" descend into Cosmic Matter wrappings of Ether, the result resembles an organic "Cell"—like a mother's *Identical (monozygotic) Twins' "egg".* After that single egg is fertilized, before the twins separate, they move to opposite poles while *staying within the same egg*—called *Meiosis.* Next, the egg splits—called *Mitosis*—to separate the Twins so as for each to struggle to survive on their own. Thereafter, each twin has a customized and unique existence leading to an individualized Character and Personality. Such is the result of their different experiences in their different existences within the same womb and then after birth. Note the important concept of both twins having Uniqueness despite their "Sameness" Genetics. The same Meiosis is featured in the Cosmic Organism's humans, Animals, Plants, and Minerals members residing in the same Cosmic "Cell" prior to being born. Within this Meiosis Cell they are joined in a *Virtual* state--a shared womb--called the Ocean of Nun. "Virtual" means they are all bonded, lack form, are undefined, undifferentiated, and yet are not *in disorder*. Inside this Cosmic -shared womb, each Entity has a *Unique "ME" self-identity*--while simultaneously having a "Sameness" by sharing a *wholistic "WE" Identity* with all of the other Entities. Hence, all in the shared womb are Spiritually related to each and every one of God's Creatures and Creations, no matter how remote in time or space or how different in appearance--termed the *Law of Sympathy*.

That is what I mean by "ME/WE" in African Tradition. In the Meiosis state, each cell in each Entity and all cells in all Entities carry forth the Omnipotence (unlimited and universal power), Omnipresent (everywhere simultaneously), and Omniscient (total knowledge) instilled by the Creator God but in a drop proportion to that taken out of the infinite ocean of God. All G*enes in each Cell have a memory of where they came from.* Each Cell--while moving through a human's life, an African Group's Spirit, or the African Diaspora throughout the Ages--is orchestrated by a spirit force apart from its DNA Essence. Despite having the same Essence, the "Genetics" inside each Cell differs in combination and arrangement. That explains why people's Talents and Individuality are "Unique" and yet they have the "Same" Human Nature aspects.

"NON-SELF" IN DAILY LIVING: Following birth into the Earth World, there is a modification of the Cosmic Organism status because of the requirement for the First Law of Nature—i.e. Survival, Self-Preservation, and Self-Protection—rising to the top of Right Life Living. Such is true of all in the Animal and Plant Kingdoms, independent of any other Entity. Every human's daily living is about Necessities, the Important, and Desires. The *Necessities* must be done independent of an uninfluenced by any Social aspects. Necessities include taking care of Physical Human Nature Needs, ones Private Selfhood Needs, and ones Mission in Life. This implies that no one else controls how one carries out these duties, obligations, and responsibilities because all decision come from within ones Selfhood. One is solely responsible for Thriving, having a sense of well-being, and being successful by getting what one really, really wants and not getting what one really, really does not want. No excuses (anything but the truth) are acceptable. For problems, Wisdom finds a way or makes one. On Earth, after Necessities, ones "ME/WE" Mission in life is of top priority. An African Tradition Philosophy of Life (POL)—not an assumed Mission--enables ones 'Calling' to naturally flow into ones life. Such attracts worthy people. One does not give up who one is so as to fit with the Crowd—or allow them to define who one is and how to live. Ones "ME/WE" POL orchestrates ones "Being-hood" as an authoritative administrator governor—e.g. instructing, arranging, combining, and conditioning the nature of ones "ME/WE" molding. This process is like kneading dough into a uniform mixture by pressing, folding, and stretching ones Selfhood so as to achieve ones life's Mission. The Social, including ones family, can be part of the Important things that are part of daily living—particularly with respect to a portion of ones Spiritual Human Nature Needs, and with ones Desires. In all Necessities, the Important, and Desires it is always significant to make wise choices, decisions, and solutions using the Spiritual Energy of "Aliveness" (eager to make "unfoldings" happen). Such is done by making Fun out of Hard work and facing problems head on immediately. While maturing, one is not in a position to do life-shaping or life-changing teachings but, instead, one records what one is learning and all defining moments so they can be shared with others. This is a preparatory step into being a "Non-Self." Its perfection concerns *going out of the "ME" in non-First Law of Nature situations—sharing with the "ME" at every opportunity—and giving the best of the "ME" in all that is done whereby others might benefit.* The "WE" aspect concerns, whenever it is reasonable and feasible, the lessening of the trials and tribulations (troubles and difficulties) of those on the negative scale—pushing all who are willing onto the positive scale—and helping those already on the positive scale to go forward. A "ME/WE" attitude is that the "*good one does to another is done to ones Self*" because "*All is One and One is in All.*" Another is the African Tradition concept of *Reciprocity* Ma'at living. This means one is not directly rewarded for good acts but, instead, *receives rewards through and by characteristics, qualities, and affinities acquired by having done them and by those helped demonstrating a ripple effect of helping others*. The key point is that the highest ingredients in Wisdom entwines around all that is purest in the Spiritual Elements. Unconditional Love is the form most divine of the infinite. Also, because of it being the most divine, is the form most profoundly human. The result of Unconditional Love spotlighting Wisdom means ones mind is continually filled with new and the most exalted ideas. In this way, Wisdom could not be misused. The objective is to do the greatest good, for the greatest number, over the longest period of time. The result of Unconditional Love spotlighting Wisdom means ones mind is continually filled with new and the most exalted ideas. However, at ones first opportunity to have a measure of strength and stability, ones Highest (Divinity) Self nature takes over and does what is best for the "ME/WE". Examples are by struggling to get out of destruction, disturbances, or threats; to help; and to "Lift the 'WE' while the 'ME' is climbing into a thriving life of well-being". Thus, every 'ME' act is for the intension to daily Self-Improvement towards its Highest Self + to blend into Compassion's space with the truly Needy + to provide benefits in each 'WE' otherness encounter + to enhance the 'WE' as part of oneself. A "Non-Self" has the obligation, duty and responsibility to *discover and conform to the underlying harmonious web of relationships operating in Nature* throughout the Cosmos. A "Non-Self" type of "ME/WE" life is about experience being the mother of daily living Truths, from which Wisdom is gained by connecting the inner and outer worlds, with ones Inner World orchestrating so as to demonstrate correspondences. That is about Wisdom being displayed as Knowledge manifested by and through Logic, Common Sense, and Critical Thinking. The display is by connecting ones inner and outer worlds in a manner that *disregards the limitations and boundaries of ordinary human thought which might prevent ones Wisdom from drawing on all aspects of the Sublime Realm as needed*. As a result, ones "ME" aspects are then able to transcend into the Sublime's reality flow—a natural flowing part of Cosmic Knowledge—a flow in which one recognizes ones own Being as a vital to the All (i.e. "Oneness" within the Cosmic Mind). This means all of ones Selfhood is part of an Interchange with all of God's Creatures and Creations as well as of the one Universal Spiritual High God. In short, *realizing ones "Non-Self" Individuality is the very act of entering into union with those of the "WE."* Ones progress can be measured by the *decreasing ones Emotional Junk;* the *backing off of criticizing, blaming, and fault-finding; trading in of "all-or-none"/"either-or" rule-type thinking over to guidelines for decision making; knows the Worth and Value of things and its Source.*

"NORMAL VARIANT": It lies between Normal and Abnormal but is not sufficiently different from either to be called one or the other.

NOTHING: this Scale is the origin of the *Symbol for Justice* in today's legal community. Throughout the "*Weighing of the Scales of Justice*" the "Heart" of the Deceased would be examined by Anubis and the deities. Standing nearby the scale would be a monster Devourer of the Dead--a beast with the head of a crocodile, the chest and forelegs of a leopard, and hind legs of a hippopotamus—a symbol for destroying records of the "Heart's" earthly bad emotional experiences (the Sahu)—i.e. the sinful part of the "Heart" (not the Soul). The weighed "Heart" passed the test by Living a Ma'at life (by the Spiritual Elements) which provided a "Light Heart"; it failed (i.e. too heavy to pass from being a bundle of ill-programmed behavioral responses) if its life's actions had been motivated by emotional (animal), rather than divinity Soul parts of ones spirit. It also failed by it having been so overly religious as to live by rules outside what it takes to be human. As a result of the "Heart" on the Scales being off kilt, it is immediately devoured by the monster Ammit (Amut, Aummaum).

The "Heart's" offensive part proceeds into the home of bad monsters and Bad Spirits--the Taut, which possesses all characteristics of what is associated with the "Unseen," along with its dark, gloomy, pits of fire. What is left of the unperfected "Heart" and Soul which, because of vibrating at a rate too slow to enter the Heaven Afterlife, travels to the *Places of Destruction*--a form of Purgatory purifier. This region was called a *"Black Hole"*--a *Nothingness*--a void where there is the absence of objects and where the "bad stuff" of ones Heart is concealed and securely hidden. The *goal of Auset's "Taut" is to deal with* the unperfected "Heart" and Soul of the deceased as it travels to the *Places of Destruction. It does not inflict suffering but rather brings about the complete elimination of evil-doers'* (i.e. enemies of Ausar) deeds by placing them into a Black Hole. As can be seen on this page, there are spaces between the words—spaces of "nothing". Yet, the "nothing" conveys meaning and reduces chaos in understanding what is read. To indicate *Nothingness's* meaning, Ancient Egyptians employed an empty space to indicate *"Exterminated"*—i.e. being absolutely *"Eliminated"*. Since a Black Hole draws in everything and absorbs visible light never to release either, it is unable to betray the presence of its contents. This makes it a tangible Being, bound up with the *Void*--a state of "No Thing"—a realm of primeval darkness--the Ocean of Nun from which Cosmic Creation sprang. See Hell; Weighing of the Heart

NOTION: the earliest stage of a developing idea and possesses vague and partially formed Images.

NOUMENAL PLANE: all Metaphysical Objective reality—e.g. spirits of things, thoughts, images, + Ethereally denser *Phenomenal Plane* (physical Energy/Matter) whereby its ethereal bodies--the Astral ('Star') Plane--are not far apart from Material World's physical bodies because their vibrational frequencies are capable of being a synchronized link them (Amen Metu Neter I:55, 58). See *"9Ps"*

NUANCES IN AFRICAN TRADITION: The literature defines "Nuance" (1781, a shade of expression) as a fine or subtle variation, as in color, tone, or meaning—a gradation. Yet, in extensive literature I reviewed, there is silence on the "what it is" or "how it does what it does". This is significant because at least 25% of a human's choices, decisions, and solutions are the result of nuances. Nuances are about dynamic Undertones/ Overtones but differ from their "cousins" called Background/Foreground and Top/Bottom since both have *almost invariable and thus unnatural natures.* By contrast, Nuances wiggle, as do all naturally occurring Things. Understanding the Mystery of Nuances requires *shifting from Human-Made Patterns of Thinking* (e.g. in *Linear* fashion, which is one-dimensional) *over to Processes inside the Flowing Patterns that conform to Laws of Nature.* The "big picture" is that *Reality is composed of multiple variables*, each on different *Planes* of activity, but occupying the same space. Also, everything in each Plane of the Cosmos is happening at once (which makes them non-linear). This means there are innumerable variables in the atmosphere surrounding a person. Ones brain handles millions of these variables without the brain being conscious of more than three at any given time. An analogy is the many musical notes in a certain degree of vibration of the air occupy the same position in a "State" space. Yet, they do not conflict with each other in so far as space-filling qualities are concerned. One can hear them because they are made of vibratory energy, not matter. Despite the axiom of Physics that no two bodies of matter can occupy the same space at the same time, on other planes, the Laws of Nature differ. One is a Thing in motion is natural among wiggly others at rest—and none are Linear (i.e. not straight). In this "State" ('way of standing, condition, position') of vibratory energy, besides each variable wiggly wave-like entity, each possesses different dimensions and vibration rates. By all occupying the same space at any Cosmic point, one plane is within the other. In other words, every plane manifests in the same point of space at the same time. Note the *Principle of "Sameness" from being composed of vibrations and yet each is "Unique" via its different vibratory rate.* Each Entity is an independent worker that interdependently works harmoniously to maintain a "seemingly" normal whole--and yet all are nuances in constant change. "Sameness/Uniqueness" + the Independent being Interdependent are Cosmic Wholism features —features accounting for Nuance changes in a Cosmos which apparently remains the same. *Nature's Processes embrace the independent workings of each pair of its Complementary Natural Opposites*—e.g. heat/cold, light/dark, black/white, and dull/sharp. Each pair is varying degrees of the *"same thing,"* as in *"heat"* and "cold". They imply one Form with a variety of appearances + unique differing rates of vibration + varying degrees of interrelationships between the two poles of one "spoke"—i.e. changing but remaining the same. Since Heat is the energy of motion of molecules, when a substance is heated, its molecules all begin to move faster. This motion of molecules is a vibration in which each molecule wiggles backward and forward extremely fast. At the same time, it moves (if at all) only comparatively slowly from one locality to another. In heating ice, the single molecules escape, as liquid water flows away. Thus, one cannot distinguish where *"heat"* stops and *"cold"* begins because *"the extremes meet"* (The Kybalion p. 32). An example of a living Nuance in action is the Butterfly's four life cycle stages. *Each independent activity is a tiny, multiple, ongoing series of changes.* When each independent thing is accumulated, their harmonious meshing is in a completely new form. Also, Nuances are like knocking down an old house and building a slightly new styled one out of its old material. The *Metamorphosis* (changing forms) four stages are: egg, larva (caterpillar), pupa, and adult. A grown, transforming 'worm' caterpillar slowly spins a silk button--a soft nest cocoon—around itself + hooking itself to the button + hooking the button to a tree + shedding its grub skin. Different continuous series of tiny changes are each nuanced happenings which, together, make it a pupa. The pupa then stops moving or eating as nuanced inner independent activities interdependently work toward the transformation. With completion of growth, it emits a liquid to loosen the shell. The emerging beautiful butterfly, in a new form, goes off on a different course, with different requirements, to do a different purpose. These are the same features and consequences of a dynamic Nuance. jabaileymd.com

NUANCES: (C18, the finer points; shade, subtlety) imitates the showing of variations of shade like a cloud. It is applied to anything pertaining to subtle variations. Example include being able to discern a shade of an emotion; or delicate and precise distinctions of meaning; or a keenness or sharpness of thought; or depth of refinement in Manners. It is almost a human nature trait to select flowers for conveying the expression of its finest emotions and sentiments (thoughts wrapped in emotions)—selecting one color, or a combination of colors, to accentuate certain nuances—perhaps to generate a particular amount of a given color--so as to impart different effects of hues, saturation, and lightness or brightness. My seeking out nuances may be to detect the speaker's plane of existence in discussing something. Even more important is the nature of what is selected to talk about, for that gives me a clue of the interests and the priority of the interest of the people in that category. Even though babies view things, like their mothers, in globs, *Symbolism* is basic to the human mind. As Nuances develop, so do Symbols. So when Nuances become like *Symbols--in that when accumulated into a mental idea, that created idea is viewed as a whole greater than the sum of its parts--*that whole has a Disposition with a Message. Such occurs for expression whenever shades of meaning accrue to produce a complex idea. The resultant Metaphysical concept is converted into a symbol. Primary Qualities of God-made Essences or Secondary, Tertiary, or Quadriary Human-made Qualities from Essentials are responsible for the power impact of Nuances. Nuances are about the manipulation and maneuvering of Tones consisting of Primary Qualities. *Spiritual Nuances* are naturally Harmonious Primary Qualities, as with the Pure Emotions coming from the Unconditional Love of a mother for her baby. *Secular Nuances* may or may not be Disharmonious, depending upon their nature and how they are defined. The nature of Nuances is like lace and how its effects cause changes on all planes of existences. The effects of nuances are located on what underlies all subtle and obvious ingredients on both side of the coin—in a "ME/WE" context. Its final meaning can be in the 'here and now,' in the short-term, in the intermediate term, or in the long term. Perhaps the simplest image of Nuance is to say that is one is off course by 0.000001 degree in going from Earth to the Moon, one will wind up on Mars. A

Tone is a predominating disposition, mood, frame, or condition of the mind. Nuance is a fine or subtle variation—meaning a gradation in a Thing, like color, tone, meaning, as a result of insidious, secretly active ingredients. Fine distinctions may be about something Unknown but not necessarily Unknowable. Yet, those distinctions change ones Understanding or Meanings and therefore ones Course Direction. By being about Primary, Secondary, and Tertiaries, there can be no definition—only descriptions in different "ballparks." Nuances are Mutations of Thoughts or Emotions involving the act or process of changing by alteration or modification in form, structure, function, aura, or atmosphere. Such may come from rearrangements or re-combinations, as occurs when the sperm meets and fertilized the egg while undergoing exchanging and pairing up of genes and chromosomes. The consequence may be a "big bang" sudden change or micro-accumulations of bits and pieces which, like the straw that broke the camel's back, breaks down into subtle changes off ones normal path. As such variations occur in an animal or plant, transmissible to then create a new individual or new species. The same Principles apply to doing things in new ways, developing creative ideas. A Nuance is a series of bits and pieces of related which give a slight modification or alluded (implied by not expressed) to things that, when accumulated, can change a direction by its suggestion. For example, it may be a color upon which other colors have been imposed and thus that color is seen through them, such as red with a purplish tone. A Nuanced Tone of a Thing can be seen with the ordinary eye; with eyes supported by glasses; by means of a microscope; using a telescope; or via ones Mind's Eye. Each give subtle differences of perception. If a normal human body is equated to Tone, ones energy level is more intense in the mornings to give it gains in vitality—an Overtone. Yet, at bedtime ones energy level is low—an Undertone.

NUANCES ESSENCE CONTENT: A gist of the story of any God-made Entity upon coming into a "That it is" Being-hood is its possession of God's Substance (Essence). That Essence is the individual, real, and ultimate nature or "soul" of a Thing— which Ancient Africans called the *"That" of the Thing* because it generates all of that Thing's offspring active and passive Qualities regardless of its subsequent unseen reality or its eventual "object" state. Inside its "what it is" Identity are *Properties* (what a thing has) of: (1) an Essence composed of *Endowments* and *Propensities*; (2) *Essentials of a Character, Characteristics, Traits, and Features*; and (3) a *Disposition* with its "What" and "Why" Message received from its Source + an Inclination + an Intention + a Temperament + an Attitude. All of these are contained in an Immaterial (Virtual) Image—an Image that eventually descends into the Sublime where Ether is added to make for its Icon Primary Quality—an Image having the synonyms of *Essence and Ultimate*. All subsequently added Primary and Secondary Qualities + the Essence and the Essentials have the "Genetic Sameness"—regardless of their Divine, Spiritual, Sublime, Metaphysical, and Physical location. Primary Qualities symbolize the Essentials of a Thing's Essence, but it changes as Ether is added. The Essentials, starring its "Characteristic" (*the most outstanding Primary Quality*), make the Thing's "Uniqueness" distinguishable from like-kind Things. African *Nuances are gradual and silent transitions from one plane of existence overlap to another.* Such transitions from one plane's micro-family to another fashions an interlocking ring type pattern, similar to the Olympic Rings that have separate and together aspects. The together part results from overlapping to form an Interchange. Thus, out of "raw materials"—called mosaic pieces— from both micro-families there is assembled a unique attribute "That it is" Image possessing a unique *Disposition*. An actual microcosm analogy is a grub fashioning a cocoon to later emerge as a butterfly. From the Divine (Amenta realm of the Cosmic Mind) realm come the Spiritual Elements which emanate Archetype (African for 'Seed') Attributes (like a Star's Halo). These Ma'at Attributes are, like rays of the Sun's illumination, pathways to the highest of human excellence. Examples are: Propriety, Balance, Order, Truth, Harmony, Peace and Tranquility, Fellowship, Justice, Rightness, and Straightness or Righteousness, and Reciprocity. Their "ME/WE" Consequences are Respect, selflessness, sharing, compassion, devotion to

God as well as promoting inner peace, social harmony, and contentment. Ma'at (Spiritual Elements in action) Primary Qualities mean their "That's" Being also include the 'what it is doing' while in an Un-seeable state of activity. Hence, "ME/WE" Selfless Service represents "who one is" as inseparable from "what one does". Such does not happen with any other thing and that is how one can get a clue as to whether one is or is not in the flow of the Spiritual Elements of Unconditional Love, Truth, Reality, and the Natural. Human's Sensory Consciousness resides only on the Astral Soul or Manas—the "*Mind*"--one of the many Metaphysical Planes. By humans having a Free Will choice, coming out of the Mind can be a wide variety abstract mental Qualities (which some call *Manasic*) from Reason, Judgment, Dispassion, Balance, and Breadth of each. Humane Lower Self Qualities embrace Affection, Sociability, Friendship, Generosity, Courtesy, Courage, Prudence, Fairness, Truthfulness, and Simplicity. Brute features range from Slight to Extreme. Examples include "Me only" Selfishness, Indifference/Hate/Evil/Sadism, Aversion, Meanness, Anger, Rage, Rudeness, Lust, Cunning, Intemperance, Cruelty, and Deceit. Satanist engage in Arrogance, Vanity, Conceited Pride, Kill/Take/Destroy/Dominate/Oppress/Control practices, Revenge, Jealousy, Envy, Greed, Malice, Injustice, Cowardice, and all other "Dark Side" features and traits. Ones choice of a "That it is" determines the capabilities for how any one of them is to develop, for what it is to do, for how it is to grow, and for the impactful 'payload' it carries to activate something good and/or bad throughout the course of ones life. The mental faculty which make humans intelligent and moral by staying within the Spiritual Elements displays as a "ME/WE" or "Non-Self" that *by giving the best of the "ME" by* going *out of the "ME," to share the "ME"*. The very act of these nuance progressions use to enter into union with those of the *"WE" allows the realization of ones "Non-Self" Individuality*—i.e. one individually working for interdependent "ME/WE" benefits.

NUANCES--FORMS: The theme for African Tradition's Natural Nuances is Primary and Secondary Qualities. These Qualities all have "Genetic Sameness" throughout their Divine, Spiritual, Sublime, Metaphysical, and Physical or Secular Entities. Primary Qualities constitute the Essentials of a Thing's Essence. Starring its "Characteristics," the Essentials make the Thing's "Uniqueness" just what it is as distinguished from other Things. African *Nuances are gradual and silent transitions from one plane of existence to another*—transitions from one micro-family to another so as to fashion an interlocking ring type pattern, similar to the Olympic Rings that have separate and together aspects. The together part results from overlapping to form an Interchange. Thus, out of "raw materials"—called mosaic pieces— from both micro-families there is assembled a unique Virtual Image possessing a unique a *Disposition,* with its "What" and "Why" Message received from its Source + an Inclination + an Intention message. A correspondence to this happening is a grub fashioning a cocoon to later emerge as a butterfly. From the Divine (Amenta realm of the Cosmic Mind) realm come the Spiritual Elements which fashion a *Form I (a "That")*. Its Virtual Image consists of Primary Qualities having the synonyms of *Essence and Ultimate*. That Essence is the individual, real, and ultimate nature or "soul" of a Thing— which Ancient Africans called the *"That" of the Thing* because it generates all of that Thing's offspring active and passive Qualities regardless of its subsequent unseen reality or its eventual "object" state. The Form I Higher Primary Qualities emanate out of the Spiritual Elements Interchange and those mosaic pieces form such nuance Ma'at Attribute (which are like rays of the Sun) pathways to the highest of human excellence as: Propriety, Balance, Order, Truth, Harmony, Peace and Tranquility, Fellowship, Justice, Rightness, and Straightness or Righteousness, and Reciprocity. Their "ME/WE" Consequences are Respect, selflessness, sharing, compassion, devotion to God as well as promoting inner peace, social harmony, and contentment. So, Form I Primary Qualities mean "That's" Being also includes the 'what it is doing' while in an Un-seeable state of activity. Hence, "ME/WE" Selfless Service represents "who one is" as inseparable from "what one does"—in contrast to something short of that. *Form II (a "This-ness")*: When Form I's "That it is" descends into the *Sublime* plane, the nuance is its addition of the first layers of Ether so as to transform it into a "This-ness"—taking on the earliest stage of an "Object." A "This-ness" can be apprehended as a "*Vision*"—*equating to a Prophetic Percept. Form III (a "That-ness")* is activated when Form I's "That it is" becomes further layered with Ether Matter in the Metaphysical Plane means encountering many planes which are considered in various combination types. Each type has its own unique Virtual Image, possessing a unique a *Disposition*. Type 7 is Astral Soul or Manas—the "*Mind*"--the mental faculty which make humans intelligent and moral beings. Since *human's Sensory Consciousness resides only on the Mental Plane*, all of the various orders of Primary and Secondary Qualities appear as rather fleeting states of Sensory Consciousness. Coming out of the Mental Plane are such abstract mental Qualities (which some call *Manasic*) as: Reason, Judgment, Dispassion, Balance, and Breadth. The first of Lower Self Qualities are the higher natural, Affection, Sociability, Friendship, Generosity, Courtesy, Courage, Prudence, Fairness, Truthfulness, and Simplicity. Second is Brute features of Indifference/Hate/Evil/Sadism, Aversion, "Me only" Selfishness, Meanness, Anger, Rage, Rudeness, Cowardice, Lust, Cunning, Intemperance, Kill/Take/Destroy/Dominate/Oppress/Control, Cruelty, Arrogance, Vanity, Conceited Pride, Deceit, Revenge, Jealousy, Envy, Greed, Malice, Injustice, and all other "Dark Side" features and traits.

Form IV's Physical World's Secular "That it is" constitutes what Icon Images for "How Shall I Live?" humans bring into Existence. Ones choice of a "That it is" determines the capabilities for how any one of them is to develop, for what it is to do, for how it is to grow, and for the impactful 'payload' it carries to activate something good and/or bad throughout the course of ones life. To stay with "ME/WE" means to go *out of the "ME" to share the "ME" by giving the best of the "ME"*. The very act of these nuance progression to enter into union with those of the *"WE" allows the realization of ones "Non-Self" Individuality*—i.e. one individually working for interdependent "ME/WE" benefits.

NUANCE "SHADES" LANGUAGE: Whether "Shades" are Secular and Spiritual, they share in common being based upon vibrations inside a state of a Tone. I define "Tone" as *a wiggling vibrating motion within a natural and stable Primary Quality. Their Nuances are a barely discernable change of direction, purpose, and aura or atmosphere.* Though the vibrations remain the same, their speed rates change—either from a Cause of a tiny "big bang" or Cumulative micro-intrusions. Both can lead to a change or modification in form, pattern, function, appearance, or essence. *Human-made Secular patterns of Shade* are given varied terms. The "*Value*" of a color refers to its lightness or darkness. When a color is full strength it is of "normal" or "middle" Value. If it is lighter it is called a "*Tint*"; if darker, a "*Shade*." If a leaf is of light value, it is "a tint of green." If it is dark, it is a shade of green. The Value of a color is changed by adding either white or black to it. To make a color lighter (a tint) is to add white; to make a color darker (a shade) is to add black. The "*Intensity*" of a color refers to its brightness or dullness. A color cannot be made brighter than its full intensity (brightness) but it can be made duller by mixing some of the color's "opposite" color with it. For example, if a red is too intense (too bright), it can be dulled by adding a little of green, its Color Wheel opposite color. Overlapping colors—e.g. a kaleidoscope or rainbow--give a "*mongrel*" effect--either the equivalent of cross-breeding of dissimilar colors of a wide and long mixing or transiently. In either instance there is a change in Value and in Intensity of the involved colors. In standard *Human-Made Patterns of Thinking*, Shade is thought of in the sense of "*Shadow*," as in seeing things through a fog or from which light is more or less cut off. Some Shades are fixed, as in Paintings where a degree of color has been modified toward a darker range; or dynamic, as in getting dark little by little, pertaining to motions of the Sun; or getting deeper and deeper (as in leaving the Superficial behind). These types are commonly thought of as the keystones to understanding Nuances. Seeable "Shade" differences are "*Comprehended*" (understand and/or embrace fully)--implying understanding of the object of thought in its entire compass and extent. Such a situation occurs sitting in a partly dark place not in the sun, as in under a tree, so as to nuance benefit from being cooler in the shade. Some "Shades" are Things (e.g. dark eyeglasses); others require contributions to express their resulting nuances: "pull down the shades of the windows"—and the shutting out light inside may range from somewhat to complete. Some shades are for Effect: "I want to see the silks in all shades of blue's lightness and darkness." Some shades are appreciated only by its opposites: "let us focus on the dark part of the picture." Some shades are for exploring: "let us give it a shade of difference in its meaning." Some shades are to point out differences: "there is a significant shade of doubt in her faith." *Spiritual "Shade"* is the subtle blending of one thing into another, as is operating within Patterns of Nature. Examples include: (1) the washing of bands of one entity into the bands of another(s) entity—either at the same time; by giving and receiving mutually at the same time; or by alternating; (2) a *Estuary* occurs when two rivers run into each other and at that point where there would be a random mixing of the fresh and salty natures of their water contents the water contents would exchange places; (3) a "milk-shake" blending; (4) a "salad" type mix associated with checkered blending of ingredients; (5) a synthesis of different ingredients. Each "Shade" can only be Apprehended, as a mother's love, which one does not comprehend until later—i.e. mother's love is understood in ones later life), or never. What is apprehended is the "*This-ness*" of the Essence's "what it is" in the Darkness—i.e. its Primary Qualities as it came into existence. Although still discernable in the "here and now," what is not discernable in Shade is the Thing's "*That-ness*"—i.e. its specificity, individuality, or even Form. In Cosmic Plane, each change in direction, function, or plane of existence is a Nuance—whether descending into birth or ascending from Death. At each plane there is an overlapping and incongruous mixture of layers of Ether being added or subtracted. The more layers of Ether added the more obvious the "That it is" Thing becomes—and vice versa. Such tiny, multiple, ongoing series of nuance changes escape perception by those in totally focused on the Physical world because of alterations in the mental activities by interferences from the outside world.

NUANCED COLOR-SHADED UNDERTONES & OVERTONES: Color Wheels can be used as a microcosm (a little world) to explain other like-kind microcosms that model the Cosmic Wholism macrocosm (a giant world) and, in the process, aid in understanding nuanced undertones and overtones. Color has three characteristics—Hue, Value, and Intensity (i.e. brightness or dullness). Because of Hue, one is able to distinguish one color from another. The green of a leaf is its hue or name of the color. A *Color Wheel* is Hues arranged in a circle, based on red, yellow and blue. These Primary Qualities are called *Primary Colours* because its 3 pigment colours cannot be mixed or formed by any combination of other colours. All other colours are derived from these 3 hues. By mixing 2 of them gives 3 more—called *Secondary Colors or Hues*—orange (red and yellow); green (blue and yellow) and violet/purple (red and blue). *Tertiary hues* are obtained by combining their left and right neighbors of the Color Wheel. For example, yellow-green, a tertiary hue, is made by mixing yellow (a primary), and green (a secondary). The same applies to make yellow-orange, red-orange, red-purple, blue-purple, and blue-green. Varying a color's Primary Quality, even subtly, changes its Tint, hue, degree, or Shade. *Colour Harmony* means all of what is present must be "involved" before it can be "evolved" + there is *complete adaptation of each part to the whole, implying perfect adjustment of all conditions* + being true on all planes--mental, physical, and spiritual + imparting an inner sense of Order and Balance. *Spiritual Harmony--any dynamic equilibrium of Spiritual Elements attributes--*is an experience of Worth (Beauty and Order), as in *Nature's Artistry*—e.g. several variations of yellow-green in the leaves on a tree, and several variations of red-purple in the orchid. *Secular Harmony* is a dynamic equilibrium of: (1) *Analogous colours--*any 3 colours side by side on a 12 part colour wheel, such as yellow-green, yellow, and yellow-orange—and usually with one dominating; and (2) *Complementary Colours--*any two colours directly opposite each other—e.g. red and green, red-purple, or yellow-green. These opposing colours create maximum contrast and maximum stability.

Color Context concerns how a colour(s) behaves in relation to other colours and shapes so as to give different perceptions—*nuances*--of the same colour. Normally, extreme adaptive unity of what comprises Worth leads to under-stimulation of the Brain—or if ones mind is preoccupied, the Worth will be too bland for one to be engaged--or if ones mind has peripheral freedom—then vibrations of Worth are in an Undertone state. They, if one goes into a Trance or Meditative state, may go unnoticed or serve as a partially noticed Background. Overtones may come from a quiet mind experiencing the Worth; from colours exhibiting extreme complexity that leads to over-stimulation; or from ones mind being hyper-stimulated by the overly-done colours, as to avoid viewing the chaos. Extreme complexity of colour or a colour associated with a Conditioned Response may lead to such over-stimulation as for one to enter a Supernatural Overload mindset. This might be the entering of a *Surreal* state which straddles the real and fantasy; or one might be so awed as to slide into a phantasmagoric state (seeing ghosts or monsters). Such seemingly changes incoherent sensory images received passively from the outer world, like a Chimera phantom. Although the human brain rejects what it cannot organize or understand, a pre-conditioned response allows for a slippage into imagining these Phantasmata. Each of these changes of mindset are nuances. So, when a color is full in strength, its Tone is of "normal" or "middle" value. If it is lighter it is called a "*Tint*"—like an "*Overtone*"; if darker, a *Shade*—like an "*Undertone.*" Shade is keystone to Nuances—getting dark little by little; or getting deeper and deeper; or the barely perceptible lessening of the depth or dark. A Color's change to dullness in Intensity or to a lower Value or to a different hue means these are nuanced changes. Beige is a very pale brown color which takes its name from the French word for the color of natural wool. Though, on its own, it is a calm, neutral background--and, like chameleons, it takes on certain attributes of the stronger warm or cool colors it accompanies. Red similarly appears more brilliant against a black background and somewhat duller against the white background. In contrast with orange, red appears lifeless; in contrast with blue-green, it exhibits brilliance. A red square appears larger on black than on other background colours. Each subtle change relative to a Colour's Tone is a nuance of that colour. These principles apply to anything. jabaileymd.com

NUANCED INTERCHANGES FORMING "SHADE" SETTINGS: *Blending Differences* (different similarities) of many ingredients to create a stew, soup, drink, or sauce give nuances of a unique essence, flavor, and/or aroma. Such Synergy nuances come from independent ingredients working interdependently to create a whole that is greater than the sum of its individual ingredients. Blending of Differences is the *Weaving of an Interchange* where different notions, ideas, thoughts, and memories have nuanced differences which are not opposed to each other. Emanating out of the Interchange are Primary Qualities--each with a mosaic pattern extracted from and in harmony with all of the contributing Properties of the Essence. Mosaic pieces flowing from all contributions come together to form a Pattern--a fully formed Essence of energy movement frozen in space--with an Image on its outside + a Matrix (womb bringing nourishment to the offspring) on the inside + a *Shape* possessing a specific power given to it by Nature. The "Womb" is composed of Activity networks which account for the "what it does" aspects. The arrangement of the *Properties* comprising those networks interlock in a manner (e.g. like the Olympic Rings) that forms an Interchange. The Pattern's realizations spring from its endowments and propensities contained in its Substance, while being orchestrated by the Disposition's message received from its original Creator Source. The resultant "how it appears" payload products are "Trademarked" Individuality displays. It contributes its received payload to making the known more knowable and bringing about awareness of something unknown. Blending of Differences leads towards Wisdom, personal Wholeness, and Oneness with the Cosmic Organism. Since the Interchange is the core of the Essence—which Ancient Africans called the *"That" of the Thing*—what generates all of the Thing's active and passive Qualities is the "That's" underlying "Eye"—like the 'happenings' within the "Eye" of a storm.

By contrast, the *Union of Opposites* is of two types—Complementary Opposites and Contrary Opposites—both involving thinking inside Nature's Processes. *Complementary Opposites* are "Things" in the Shade that can only be known, with respect to a human's senses, by its Opposite—in this case, contrasting Qualities, one being the Background. *Disharmonious Contrary Opposites* are most likely to be about one or both being Supernatural and thus unreal. *Harmonious Contrary Opposites* may be observable self-evident things (e.g. day/night). Or, they may be about a "Shade" beyond human's comprehension, meaning its boundlessness cannot be known except by its manifestations from its observable *Corresponding Opposite*. Ancient Africans said God is Unknowable and yet can be known by God's manifestations. Here, knowing is by means of these observable unchanging and permanent conceptual relationships. However, *Problematic Complementary Opposites and Contrary Opposites* involve penetration into the Underlying realms of Nature and its Processes. Doing so—called *Transcending Duality*—is to discover which of their Natural displays they share in common. What Underlies is those big and little Patterns *operating in Nature*. Despite the complex, multiplicity Patterns on all planes of existence, they are configured into *an underlying web of relationships* throughout the Cosmos.

It may be that the oppositional problem is in a "*Normal Variant Category*—e.g. aspects are on different planes of existence and/or going in different directions. Extreme opposites of the same concept may indicate that neither was complete and that merging the two heads it towards completeness. Or the problem may be about aspects in the *Flawed Category*. These nuances of Patterns of Nature disharmony can be "Felt" because of ones Wisdom having the ability to discern and apprehend the various nuances—i.e. the *tiny, multiple, ongoing series of changes*--present in *each independent activity* when the resultant product is not in a state of Order, Regularity, Coherence, Consistency, Compatibility, Balance, Harmony, and/or Predictability. Flaws include ingredients being misinterpreted; being unreal, incomplete, limited, or mutated ingredients. If difficulties remain after making all obvious corrections, then the idea is to join what is shared in common and build a structure together on that. Meanwhile, irreconcilable differences are put aside. Humans are Spiritual Beings living in a Physical realm. Hence, their Animal Self nature attracts so as to create differences; their Highest Self attracts similarities in order to attract Synergy Unity Power.

NUANCE TONES: Spiritually, tone is harmony in the form of a Primary Quality. Secular Tone prior to 1300 meant a musical sound or note emitted by a stretched string—i.e. the character of sound; by 1669 it expanded to embrace the manner of speaking normally by means of healthy tissue; and thereafter, any sound regarding its quality, pitch, strength, source, or character. Then, tone was applied to a word or phrase that could be changed and serve as a nuanced change in meaning or function—later to a special stress or pitch accent given to one syllable in a word. I define *"Tone" as a vibrating wiggling motion within a natural and stable Primary Quality*. Today, Tone is used for many things, as a style of Thought or a pervading state of conduct. Detection of the infinite in the finite is by observing Order remaining throughout natural progression of what is being Appreciate. This Unity and Order are the Tone of Appreciation. A *Tone* is a prevailing Abstract (of non-material ingredients) or Abstraction (of material ingredients) impression of its Unity and Order Primary Qualities produced by explicit and/or implicit effects. Three aspects of Art Appreciation concern *Theme* (the subject matter, story, mood, or meaning); *Technique* (the way the art piece is created, as by large, sweeping, strokes of the brush); and *Form*, general appearance and style—the way colors, tones, spaces, lines, and textures are combined to create a design. "Tone" refers to the lightness and darkness of a color, and that is called the "*Value*" of a color. Color has three characteristics—Hue, Value, and Intensity (i.e. brightness or dullness). Because of Hue, one is able to distinguish one color from another. Hues can be arranged in a circle, known as a Color Wheel. When a color is full in strength it is of "normal" or "middle" value. If it is lighter it is called a "*Tint*"—like an "*Overtone*"; if darker, a *Shade*"—like an "*Undertone.*" Varying a color's Primary Quality changes Tint, hue, degree, or Shade of a particular color.

NUANCED UNDERTONES: Originally this was a low or subdued tone, as in an undercurrent of feelings. This is a tone of lower pitch or lower loudness (e.g. a whisper) or more subtle to discern than is the "normal" or the "middle" value of the Tone against which it is compared. A Color's change to dullness in Intensity or to a lower Value or to a different hue means these are nuanced changes. The green of a leaf is its hue or name of the color. There are three *Primary Hues*—red, yellow, and blue. By mixing two of the three gives three more—called *Secondary Hues*—orange (red and yellow); green (blue and yellow) and violet (red and blue). In addition to the six hues (Primary and Secondary), Tertiary hues are obtained by combining their neighbors (one from the left and one from the right of the Color Wheel. For example, yellow-green, a tertiary hue, is made by mixing yellow (a primary), and green (a secondary). In short, Undertone in color is a subdued color, as seen through and modifying another color. Similarly, there can be different shades of all material things—but not what is Spiritual. Some Undertone nuanced messages are subliminal—i.e. a message flash at an "imperceptible shadow" level. If it is slipped in as a hinting at the truth allusion, it is a beneficial for the resistant. Otherwise, Subliminal messages are problematic. The flash at an "imperceptible shadow" level is a Subliminal message. The 1886 word "*Subliminal*" (sub, under, beneath a limen or sensory threshold) implies it can be seen without being noticed. This is the point of Allegories in African Tradition--the hidden story within an obvious story which is capable of being mentally seen and understood but is not noticed by those who are un-evolved. Enslaved African Americans used Subliminal messages in Negro Spirituals as a signal or message embedded in another medium, designed to pass below the normal limits of the European mind's perception. Auras and Thought Clouds generate a subliminal (an 1886 psychology term for below the threshold of consciousness) atmosphere capable of being absorbed by the children so as to constitute their reality--a type of "sixth sense" known--whether consciously or hiding in sub-awareness realms. See Auras: Thought Clouds; Subawareness

NUANCED OVERTONES: Initially "overtone" referred to one of the higher tones in a complex musical tone—implying, suggesting, or characterizing. It is raised in quality or strength. This is about being "over the top"—as in a strong message. With color, the "normal" or "middle" tone is increased in "Value"—i.e. in Tint (lightness), or in Intensity (brightness). An upper partial tone of sound, so-called because it is heard with and above the fundamental tone produced by a musical instrument. One who fools himself most of all when he imagines people believe him. The aim of liars is simply to charm, to delight, to give pleasure—and they are the very basis of the Crowd and without lies people would perish of despair and boredom. What survives is the pleasantest to believe. But a lie which is part of a truth is the hardest to fight and the lie which is half a truth is the blackest of lies. Within any given human: (1) the Unconscious and the Conscious appear as complementary opposites within a binary duality system by what underlies both--meaning they are the same but with different displays; (2) they are also a microcosm (i.e. a "little" world copy) of the Universal Soul's macrocosm (the Supreme world); (3) each has Spiritual (i.e. Highest Self) and Matter (Lower or animalistic Self) aspects; (4) the true reality of all 4 of these components resides only in their *Synthesis*--an assimilation of the higher with the lower--an assimilation that, when wisely used within a Ma'at context, one is able to ascend from ones Lower (animalistic) Self to ones Highest (divinity) Self--a "push-up" ascension measured by how duality is transcended. Leading to that assimilation is a series of nuanced decisions that change wayward meanings and thereby redirects one onto the "Right Life Living" path throughout life.

NUANCE COIN CONCEPT: A coin's two sides are indivisible differences—meaning one side cannot be exclusively defined—meaning despite being inseparable, their independent duties are about different things--meaning both sides operate independently to interdependently achieve the same goal. What it is," "what it does," and "how it appears" each are situated around the others. All of this makes for Unity (the combination of parts so as to fashion a singleness and complete whole) and the presence of Order. Yet, fundamental to understanding all of its aspects requires seeing all obvious and all subtle ingredients on both sides of its *indivisible duality* coin. This principle applies indivisible things with more than two sides. To illustrate, a four-sided shape, or quadrilateral, is not always a square. It can also be a rectangle, an oblong, a parallelogram, a rhombus, a diamond, a kite, a trapezium or a delta (arrowhead/chevron). Sometimes it does not even have a name. A square is the only quadrilateral to have all four sides and all four angles the same, and in any four-sided shape, the sum of the 4 angles is always 360 degrees. To change these into various correspondence forms involves nuanced thinking. A Spiritual example is seen in the interconnected family of Appreciation, Gratefulness, Thankfulness, and Gratitude. Their Sameness "Genetic" understanding in the face of the Unique differences in each is like how identical twins possess the same "genetics" in their make-up and yet have significant differences in what they do and how they appear. That Principle applies to the duality of "sameness" and "uniqueness" present in every Cosmic Entity. Specifically this embraces all of the Cosmic Organism whereby all God's creatures and creations were bonded in their Virtual existence when they came into Being and before being born into the Earth World. See Coin Concept

NUANCES--PROBLEMATIC "SEEMS": The C12 word "SEEM" (be suitable) means appears to be; to look like--as in to exist; to be true or right; give the impression; to fit; to resemble. The essential point is that "SEEMS" implies what is not complete in maintaining or reestablishing wholesome Integrity—or does not correspond—or is not on the proper plane of existence—or is not in the same world realm, as something of the Supernatural realm has no place in the Spiritual realm. What is outside the human mind, as opposed to merely inside it, or what is merely inside the mind and not outside is what "SEEMS." When unsuspecting people are deceived by con-artists or when suspecting people are uncertain as to what is presented as having Integrity, one is faced with a Nuance situation—deliberately intended for the Deceiver to have a decided unfair advantage while simultaneously putting the Victim at a decided unfair disadvantage. The keystone of these Nuances are Primary Qualities that can be on any plane of Cosmic Existence. They maybe of an Ether, Color, or Supernatural type—each operating inside the respective Interchange of the Thing with Integrity and the "SEEMS" right situation. Nuances are seen depending upon changes within the Source (e.g. time of day of sunlight for a Rainbow); the changing of the Source (e.g. slightest rotating movements of the kaleidoscope causing the overlapping of colors); the degree of Synthesis; the amount of the Ingredients, as in the mixed or blended types; the color of the Lens of the viewer (meaning type of mood or nature of the emotions and their intensity, duration, and so forth as mentioned above).

NUANCES--SELF-DECEIVERS: *The Personal worst fraud is to deceive oneself, as by not keeping ones Word.* Each time that occurs it is a nuance which, in denying it matters, is the type of deception that *erodes* (wear away) and *corrodes* (gnaw away) ones Conscience, ones mental, physical, and emotional health of being Selfhood Great; and engaging in Illusions whereby nuances of destruction lead one to seeing what is not there and not seeing what is there. This winds up with being unable to trust oneself and that means one has nobody to trust at "crunch time." This means one has chosen to disguise who one is so as to avoid taking as much pains as is needed to be what one ought to be. A lack of self-trust removes the barriers of self-protection from attacking deceivers. Another self-deception is Adualism—what one wishes for goes through the Surrealism Filter and comes out believing the wish has been achieved. A variation is what one wishes one believes to be true or just because a belief works does not mean it is true. A sure self-deceptions is believing oneself is more clever than deceivers.

NUANCED PROBLEM SOLVINGS: The aspects of Nuances begin and end in mystery, just as each day lies between two nights. To gain an idea of the tremendous involvements a nuance had in getting one off track and the significance of shining a spotlight what it takes to reverse this and substitute Human Ideal nuances is as follows. The Effects of Nuance influences is like each particle of sand being an immensity; each leaf, a world; each insect an inexplicable compendium. The dim haze of such nuances add an enchantment to the pursuit of its destination. Fine distinctions may be about something Unknown but not necessarily Unknowable. Nuances deal with what is quite beyond the power of perception or what is presently difficult to understand. Hence, the process is to discern the insidious, secretly active ingredients; or to what realm beyond human experience to which it belongs. A place to start is with what is called the SUBTLE BODY: how one feels to oneself—as in achieving a success or experiencing some failure. The process of Nuance Corrections embraces what may seem at first to be insurmountable conflicts. But their basis is in the fundamental dualities underlying all that have Correspondence and thus can be solved. A reason is the existence of a unity underlying natural opposites—meaning those which behave independently and seemingly in disregard to its fellows at an appearance level. Yet, they are mutually necessary to each other at a deep level. At this Underlying level they are interdependently working together in a connected net to bring self-regulating Order, Truth, and Justice. But, to transcend the mind or to see what is underlying pairs of opposites is to lose the concept of duality and thereby experience the oneness of all real things in existence --i.e. the *Law of Sympathy* (see Ashby, Maat Philosophy p110). This enables one to transfer the process and the knowledge gained from going through the process and from the conclusion to be transferred to other areas of ones life. For example, death and life seem opposites but the ramifications of the dead can still live in life. Or, those considered enemies are actually necessary for ones well-being. Whatever is one fight against an enemy embraces what it takes to improve ones focus and certain dormant personal powers. Step I Nuance Corrections, said Ancient Africans, was to see all of the Obvious so as to discover the Hidden and then search for the *Order and consistent Patterns underlying natural events or disharmony or the Mystery's answer*. Step II is to locate and *discover what does not conform to the underlying web of relationships operating in Nature* throughout the Cosmos. Pay detailed attention to whether one completely conformed to where the entrance Nuance led or not. Take notice of what is plain in having caused one to enter, say, into a gang. Step III, if not, those subtle things causing one to be "half-hearted" in being involved are to be studied to locate the area of doubts. Step IV is discovering what one has always wanted to do or has recently caused insights of where or where not to be. See Racism; Critical Thinking; Vibrations

O

OBJECTIVE: One European dictionary defines "Objective" as: "Perceptible by the external senses". In my dictionary of Medical-Legal terms (p91), "*Objective*" has a perceptive origin outside the mind—whether of a Tangible, Intangible, *Objective Minus* ("what is there but is not" and "what is not there but is"), and *Subjective Plus* (because it "fits" or "works" implies the truth seems valid in advance of Proof). An example of Objective Minus is acquiring Knowledge of the existence of all quantifiable events that cannot be perceived through the senses by using African Qualitative Algebraic derived Logic as well as by Quantitative Logic. By contrast, "*Subjective*," as I use it, is based on psychological processes—i.e. dependent of any interpretations or likes/dislikes. Both Objective and Subjective are to be distinguished from "*Subjective Minus*"—it is untrue and not there because it is Contingent. See Concrete

OBJECTIVE MINUS: "*Objective Minus*" method. An example was Very Ancient Africans acquiring, from what is incapable of being perceived through the senses, astro-mathematical Knowledge of the existence of all quantifiable sky events via African Qualitative Algebraic derived Logic and by Quantitative African Logic. From Revelations and added Knowledge, they inferred each human is a Spark from the Flame of God. This provided humans with "*First Wisdom*" illumination. Out of this context flow came inferences capable of establishing Circumstantial Truths having Correspondence with Observable Truths. These resultant "*Objective Minus*" conclusions imply: "*what is there but is not*" and "*what is not there but is*". Example: "*To Know Truth You Must Live It.*"

OBLIGATION: "*Charge*" (obligation, duty, and responsibility) and "Management" (regulation and order) involved in personal labor. A gardener has the care of a garden; a nurse has the charge of children; an overseer has the management of a farm. "*Obligation*" is a binding promise to take the steps necessary for caring. This means there is no problem too great to undertake managing--even if it has never been done before or the Mentor has never seen nor heard of it before. "*Duty*" is doing the tasks which have to be done without consideration of fame, money, or status. "*Responsibility*" is shouldering the consequences for anything not properly done or that is left undone but should have been done in accordance with ones obligation. Two of its features are: first, take care of other people's things better than if they were yours; second, stay in contact without needing something.

OBSESSIONS--"DARK SIDE": In the earliest records of human history and in the magical rites and formulae of ancient religions much is said about persistent attacks on humans by an evil spirit from without. During that time the word "Obsession" meant literally "to sit at or opposite to," as in "sitting down before a fortress or the enemy." Just as an army can besiege a castle, ancient Europeans believed the devil or a demon from without could besiege or beset a person (as opposed to "*Possession*"--i.e. being inhabited by a demon). In other words people who believed in evil spirits considered an obsession to mean a state of siege by an evil spirit trying to take possession of a man's personality and action and which suppresses ones normal personality. A story quite involved concerns this belief accounting for all forms of insanity and crime (Spence, Encyc. Of Occultism, p299). Even Ancient Egyptians had their intoxicating drinks and recipes for witch's salves. The miracles of Jesus included casting out legions of possessing spirits (control by an evil spirit within). Attempts at similar actions during the European Middle Ages were appallingly inhumane. Meanwhile, there remained a host of stories arising out of superstitions about one being vexed by an evil spirit -- and these have continued into modern times. For example, a chaplain in General Cromwell's English 17th century army exorcised a soldier's devil by throwing the soldier into the water. Though the devil came to the surface, the soldier did not. By 1680 "Obsession" had been gradually taken out of the realm of superstition and demonology and transferred to psychology so as to replace obsessing or besieging demons with a preoccupying emotion or fixed idea that haunts, preoccupies, dominates, torments, or bedevils. It set out to show the human mind to be an incomparably delicate thing, peculiarly at the mercy of the perceptions of the senses and their multitudinous impressions on the brain -- a balance so easily shaken by a shock, a drug, a momentary excitement but more often by prolonged and intense concentration upon single groups of ideas. During the hallucinary epidemics of all European ages and countries the unvarying character of these beliefs included being connected with some dominant cause, train of thought, or religious sentiment prevalent at the time. Obsessional-Compulsive Reactions were considered a neurosis (e.g. hand-washing by Lady Macbeth). *A Neurosis* is a functional psychological disorder with no organic causes and whose origins in emotional conflict can often be understood as Anxiety, Fugue, Hysteria, Obsession, Compulsion, or Phobia (Statt, Dictionary of Psychology). However, examples of increasing layers of confused terminology included the Obsessive-Compulsive Disorder also being called Compulsive Personality Disorder, Obsessive Compulsive Personality Disorder, and Anxiety Disorder. Recently, Obsessive-Compulsive Disorder has been placed under the wing of a Personality Disorder. Such terminology turmoil indicates a lack of diagnostic clarity. Meanwhile, Europeans' reality of aggression for survival faded (?12,000 BC) into greed which caused obsessive fantasies of aggression. As today, Opportunist Warriors convinced themselves (Justification *Delusional Fear*) the innocent were forcing them to defend themselves and, through no fault of their own, they had to attack. Success in acquiring material things led them to be narcissistic (a pervasive pattern of grandiosity in fantasy or behavior and with an excessive need for admiration). After acquiring the GUN and "Killing and Taking" from Colored Peoples of the world, it became "The Game" to see who could acquire the most material possessions. As this flourished in 15th and 16th century Europe, the rules were that the *Seven Deadly Sins* (Pride; Wrath; Envy; Lust; Gluttony; Avarice [covetousness]; and Sloth did not matter -- and in fact they *were honored*. This pattern of *dishonorableness became a European Obsessive-Compulsive Disorder* which persists and is increasing daily in the world.

OBVIOUS: (1586) means that which is directly in the way on the path, presenting itself readily and so apparent, evident, or clear that it cannot be missed by ones instincts, senses, or emotions. It is inspected by sight, emotions, and/or Feelings to discover what is taken for granted or its subtlies.

OFF-KEY: When children sing 'on-key' their pitch sound matches the tone without being flat or sharp + matches intended interval of the melody or harmony written for the song. If they were to sing the wrong notes as indicated by the music or deviate from the correct tone or pitch, the result would be somewhat irregular, abnormal, or incongruous—a situation called "Off-Key" or "out of tune."

OLIGARCHIES: some but not all people have political liberty and the equality of citizenship. Typically, European societies have historically been Oligarchies or Despotism

OMNIBUS BRAIN: "Omnibus" originally (1829) meant a horse-drawn wagon containing "some of this and some of that" which, when applied to it being a subdivision of the Ancient Brain, is like fire-flies inside a jar. Ranging between its partners, the Instinct Brain (ultimate human Goodness) on one side and the Brute Brain (ultimate human Disorder) on the other, the Omnibus Brain is a bridge between them and containing all mental ingredients which feature human behavior. In this way, the Omnibus Brain contents and its Ethereal composition (the finest, thinnest, and most tenuous form of Matter) resembles the Cosmic Metaphysical realm. This *Intangible plane* of existence (i.e. the Cosmos' transition between energy and matter in the universe) consists of the *Noumenal Plane* (all Metaphysical Objective reality—e.g. spirits of things, thoughts, images, etc.) and the Ethereally denser *Phenomenal Plane* (physical Energy/Matter) whereby its ethereal bodies are not far apart from the Material World's physical bodies because their vibrational frequencies are capable of being a synchronized link them (Amen Metu Neter I:55, 58). One result is a human's *Astral Body* forms an exact ethereal (or "shadow") replica of a human's physical body and yet the two interpenetrate at all levels, including the brain and nerves. Whether bad or good, the Astral Body houses memory, dreams, all physical forces, sensations, desires, emotions, the mind, and motivations of an individual. The point is that although it means well, the Omnibus Brain is a queer storehouse. Type I category is Reality Wisdom, as in what derives from heredity by way of instincts. However, added to this is self-preservation and well-being acquired non-destructive information from other parts of the Triune (or Quintaune) brain used in actions and reactions--and that implies thoughts and varied emotions are involved. Type II is "Phenomena" (from phantom, to 'make visible')--by possessing no life of itself--have no reality in themselves. Hence, all such appearances are subject to constant change Nevertheless, some phenomena are products of the intellect. Type III is a mixture, as when some contents come from what unfolds within it and whose seeds were sown at the time of the primal impulse (which started life along the path) and branched to incorporate the Collective Unconscious and ones race memory.; some are preserved in the basic memory of the race; some springing from the intellect; and some represent the past experiences of ones race, even reaching back into the animal kingdom. No human has a sense experience from such a deep meaning of nature within ones Selfhood; nor from the actual experiences of instincts themselves (Ramacharaka, Fourteen Lessons, p 25). Type IV is "*Foolishness*" ('empty-headed') from being full of things received from a variety of sources coming from the External World or by the Supernatural (made-up, either of a neutral or of a Brute nature). Type V are Brute influenced Emotions. Historically, the Limbic (Emotional) Brain came into being by evolving out of the Ancient Brain and over-growing it like a cap, hence a "Limbus" (a border). It is called Old Mammalian because its highest development first appeared among Mammals and served as the major influence of their behavior. In humans, it is the seat of emotional communication, especially the drives of "Fight, Flight, Fright" mating, and seeking food. This older and more primitive Brain, compared with a human's Cerebral Cortex and Frontal Lobes, dominates a human's first 28 years of life, thus laying the foundation for beliefs, opinions, outlooks, and behaviors gathered from the External World. Those gatherings are primarily an animalistic type of excitements, most shrewdly designed by Satanists and put into every aspect of today's society life (e.g. religion and government). Regardless of their degree, those bad influences take effect in a toddler as early as 18 months old. What is accepted into children's minds range from insecurity, shame from self-image problems, fear, rage, violence, sensuality, and fetters (e.g. "Me, Me" Individualism, arrogance, pride, lies, selfishness, greed, lust, egoism, envy, jealousy, and frustration). At its worse are *Brute Imitators* of the Indifference/Hate/Evil/Sadism Complex. Since "everybody" is "caught-up" in these society trends and because most youth are no longer being taught to display Spiritual Elements, this dominant societal animalistic mindset is deemed normal. See Brain

ONTOLOGY: Reality and the nature of Being

OPINIONS: **C13** "Opinion" means "think," believe, suppose, choose, or adopt. These keywords indicate a split in how Opinions are used--i.e. what is in ones mindset vs. what one does with it. For this reason "Opinion" is an umbrella term with a range characterized by Uncertainty on its Scale A/B/C, Scale X/Z, and Scale J. In considering the "*T*" *Concept*, if the horizontal bar is Certainty, then close to it on the Scale A/B/C vertical bar is Category A--*Reasoned Educated Opinions*--what one embodies as ones understanding from what one thinks, believes, or infers of an issue as applicable to a state of facts submitted for that purpose. On the opposite end is Category C-- *Wish Opinions*--false statements, maintained in spite of evidence to the contrary. In the middle is Category B--*Ambiguous Opinions*, deemed to be a leap of the mind beyond the facts because all the facts are not in--and perhaps cannot be in. Thus, they cannot be said to be "right" or "wrong" since it is not subject to verification. On Scale X/Z, one end is Category X--the "*Opinionated*" ('hold the opinion that...'). This 17th century term suggesting that at its extreme means the Opinionated are not thoughtful; possess attitudes of purely personal prejudices; have deep personal issues (e.g. to feel important to hide a sense of powerlessness or to act superior by putting others down); and are obstinate or conceited (an exaggerated estimate of ones own abilities). On the other end of the scale is Category Z--*Sentiment Opinions*. Here, influencing opinions are *Sentiments* (thoughtful deliberations colored by emotions) which imply a more profound sense of emotional orientation than of thought or logic. This is shown by prior formulations of ideas, thoughts, feelings, preferences; by taste based upon a combination of "Facts," "Beliefs," Doubt, certitude, and probability; Distortions; sometimes "Superstitions"; and by estimates (whether discerning or not) and relatively authoritative judgments not likely to be factual. Each of these forms is seen on Category J--*Public Opinion* (prevailing ideas that many people hold in common). *No number of people, even if it is "everybody," who agree with something wrong can make that wrong into right.* This is a powerful reason for one to make ones own decisions, especially about life-shaping and life-changing issues, in the face of contrary opinions of people. Regardless of where Opinions are located on the scale--from close to Truth all the way down to guesses--the intensity of ones sureness at each point along the vertical bar can range from Mild, Slight, Moderate, and Extreme. Regardless of the intensity, Opinions necessarily have an opposite point of view because the contents of each is checkered with what is confused, obscure, contingent, and variable conclusions regarding matters in dispute or in what is under consideration. Examples of the bad which can arise out of such problematic opinions are those resulting in injury or detriment and those of a legal nature. People who lack Certainty are fond of saying: "I have a right to my opinions" (implying a right to persist in them), one does not have a right to be in conflict with Knowledge. After reading my Category A Opinion paper on the "Delusional American Justice System," one man told me he had a conflicting opinion about it. I asked if he had ever had any experience with the Justice System and he said "no." By contrast, much of my orthopaedic surgical career was involved in being an expert witness in Industrial Injury cases. Thus people who claim "my opinion is a good as yours" fail to realize some opinions have higher priority than others. Yet, even when Opinions are held with certainty, such certainty does not equate to fact or truth and thus remains open to challenge. Despite all of the points made in this discussion, the Western World makes no clear distinction between Knowledge, faith, and opinion because none are deemed to be certain--and if that was true, they would all be opinions--which they are not. Still, differences of opinions may be resolved by consensus or by compromise or by the majority rule. But the courageous never do this with Knowledge, for it has the properties of necessity and immutability (unchanging essence), of universality, clarity, and distinctness. Critical Thinkers do not have many opinions. My only interest in Opinions is during information gathering because they may give me a lead. [Ref: This long series is from Bailey, Leadership Critical Thinking In African Tradition]

OPPOSITES--AFRICAN DIALECTIC LAW (TYPE I): The African Sage, Tehuti's Principle of Polarity says: "Everything is Dual; everything has poles; everything has its pair of opposites; like and unlike are the same; opposites are identical in nature, but different in degree; extremes meet; all truths are but half-truths; all paradoxes may be reconciled." Here, Hermes was referring to what is Real—i.e. all of God's creatures and creations, and not about that which is man-made; to real things being made of complementary pairs; to each part being an element or principle of reality; and to all parts as interdependent and necessary to each other in a unified system (as is the androgynous Divine Being who is therefore able to reproduce itself). To elaborate, Ancient Africans said humans' nature arise out of the Primordial Substance of the Cosmos, consisting of God's androgynic protoplast—a "Oneness". Out of this "Oneness" emanates all God's creatures and creations.

Creatures become so by having a binary pattern comprising two opposite phases or aspects integrated within the higher "Oneness" context—phases or aspects that can be either symmetrical (i.e. identical in extent and intensity) or asymmetrical, successive, or simultaneous. Humans' natures are part heavenly and part earthly. Both are based on the counterbalanced forces of two opposite poles consisting of Complementary Opposites as, for example, Masculine and Feminine Principles—the illustration of successive or simultaneous aspects, meaning that on all planes both aspects are present in greater or less degree. The Masculine (the Spirit or Life side) manifestation is the active and positive aspect which acts on the Feminine (the Matter or Form side) or receptive part of ones nature. All of this occurs within the realm of Reality--a *profound concept for Critical Thinking*. See Nuanced

OPPOSITES: A human's Real Self Spiritual Nature ingredients consist of the Higher Mind derived from each ones gift at conception of a "Spark" of God. This "Spark" imparts a "Pure Heart" or "Soul Sunshine" and is at the core of every newborn's Selfhood Greatness. The ultimate in Knowledge is *"Knowing Thyself" and this can only be done when one discovers what is natural within oneself + what underlies what is natural*. Inside such discoveries are the African Law of Correspondence and the *Law of Complementary Opposites* because to "Know Thyself" is to know what is in the Cosmos--Africans' *Inductive and deductive reasoning beginnings*. There can be no deviations or flaws, especially since the essence of the conclusion is expressed through the abstract or metaphoric use of Images. The fundamental distinction in dealing with Opposites is to determine what does and does not (e.g. Type VII) have Correspondence. What seems to humans to be insurmountable conflicts have their basis in the fundamental dualities underlying all that have Correspondence and thus can be solved. A reason is the existence of a unity underlying natural opposites—meaning those which behave independently and seemingly in disregard to its fellows at an appearance level. Yet, they are mutually necessary to each other at a deep level. At this Underlying level they are interdependently working together in a connected net to bring self-regulating Order, Truth, and Justice. This enables one to transfer the process and the knowledge gained from going through the process and from the conclusion to be transferred to other areas of ones life. For example, death and life seem opposites but the ramifications of the dead can still live in life. Or, those considered enemies are actually necessary for ones well-being. Whatever is one fight against an enemy embraces what it takes to improve ones focus and certain dormant personal powers. Enemies, despite exaggeration, are likely to "tell it like is" about ones flaws—when no friend will say. What they say, even if not true, ought to generate a self-examination to correct any flaw or tendency toward a mentioned flaw or to get rid of the useless and ineffective or use the enemies point to better defend, protect or improve. Thus, without paying respect to enemies and using them as teachers as to what not to do, means getting weaker and weaker from "disuse" of ones powers within. Or, from the damage enemies do, that is an opportunity to break out of ones tendency to remain inside the status quo and build something better. See Nuances

OPPOSITES CLASSIFICATION: Duality underlies all aspects of whatever has Correspondence in Cosmos Creation and there are many types. The following are examples. Type I: God in "the Other World" and God's Creatures in the Cosmos are indivisible dualities. Roots are not created without the soil and a seed and none are produced without a Source. *Type II:* Cosmic Duality—what later Chinese called *Yin/Yang*--is based on the counterbalanced forces of two opposite poles--forces either symmetrical (i.e. identical in extent and intensity) or asymmetrical--either successive (day/night) or simultaneous (e.g. masculine/feminine in each human). It features a Circle of Wholism which speaks to its stability in maintaining order while the parts turn around one another as well as having no beginning or end. Like graduation day commencement, the end of one plane of existence simultaneously begins another plane. These *Cosmic Complementary Opposites* mean they are halves of a unit and thus complement (complete) each other; both Yin/Yang components are real;

Correspondence and thus can be solved. A reason is the existence of a unity underlying natural opposites—meaning those which behave independently and seemingly in disregard to its fellows at an appearance level. Yet, they are mutually necessary to each other at a deep level. At this Underlying level they are interdependently working together in a connected net to bring self-regulating Order, Truth, and Justice. This enables one to transfer the process and the knowledge gained from going through the process and from the conclusion to be transferred to other areas of ones life. For example, death and life seem opposites but the ramifications of the dead can still live in life. Or, those considered enemies are actually necessary for ones well-being. Whatever is one fight against an enemy embraces what it takes to improve ones focus and certain dormant personal powers. Enemies, despite exaggeration, are likely to "tell it like is" about ones flaws—when no friend will say. What they say, even if not true, ought to generate a self-examination to correct any flaw or tendency toward a mentioned flaw or to get rid of the useless and ineffective or use the enemies point to better defend, protect or improve. Thus, without paying respect to enemies and using them as teachers as to what not to do, means getting weaker and weaker from "disuse" of ones powers within. Or, from the damage enemies do, that is an opportunity to break out of ones tendency to remain inside the status quo and build something better.

OPPOSITES-- HANDLING OF BY AFRICAN LOGIC: The tools for arriving at or stay inside harmony to deal with problems from Complementary Opposites include knowledge of Spiritual Truth, Goodness, and Beauty. Preparation for engaging Ma'at Principles so as to converge into lofty knowledge is to be ones Real Self and to ensure one is freeing up ones true nature, acquire a "pure" heart and cultivate *Inner Peace*. These are done as a lifestyle in order to live in inner harmony and unity.

KEEP A PEACEFUL MIND: True conflicts arise when innate traits are contrasted with acquired traits. For instance, the *Law of Amen* concerns the profound Peace (i.e. Hetep, Nirvana), unity, eternity, and infinity (no boundaries) present in each human's original state. It states: "you were made in the likeness of a peace that nothing can disturb. Reclaim your Peace that you may attain to your reasons for coming into existence—the enjoyment of life." This unshakable inner Peace is needed to bring forth factors shaping ones Highest (Divinity) Self—Unity, Wisdom, and Spiritual Power.

"*Systematic Observing*" involves following a Box Analysis system—e.g. looking beside, in front of, above, and behind the Obvious--to see what is readily evident in the situation at hand. These pave a way into the Hidden where one seeks what is called "*Manifest*" when there are outward signs or actions which reveal the inward character of the assessed thing. Also important is looking at what is not done that carries power. For example, one side of "Manifestation" is action or pushing as a way to make things happen. Another side of "manifestation" is its in-action and non-doing, the Yin (female) power. The harmonious interaction and application of Yin power and Yang power are always emphasized--a concept essential in the "*The Middle Way*" of Chinese philosophy. It emphasizes balance rather than extremes. The extremes cause mental upsets because one extreme leads to another and the mind loses the capacity for rational thought and intuitional awareness which transcends thought itself. Thus, mental balance is the way to achieve mental peace and serenity since it enables the transcendental vision of the Self to emerge in the mind. SELECT THE RIGHT THINKING FACULTY: The Wisdom faculty, which embraces both Poetic Logic and Intellect, is able to sort out types of conflicts above the ability that other parts of the Intellect cannot. It does this by noting for each thing its hierarchal place in time and/or space. For example, Ancient Africans used the moon as the chief means through which the distribution of "antagonistic" phenomena were reckoned. Certain functions increased with the waxing moon, and decreased with the waning moon. Since this does not fit in with Syllogistic thought procedures, it was used by Tehuti as a major symbol of the functioning of the Wisdom faculty (Amen, Tree of Life p123). Step V: The blending of the metaphysical and the philosophical is the Law of Sympathy. The Synthesis of these concepts into "Wholism" means that all pertinent real things have a place; and each is in its proper place; and each is essential to the integrity of the whole; and together they become elevated into the highest plane of existence of which the human mind is capable of perceiving.

"**OPTIONS**": Every step in ones daily living involves selections from Options, which people call making a Choice, and which I called Alternatives as a boy. The ancient Greek word epiopsesthai ("to choose") refers to the opportunity to choose, perhaps among many things; "a *Choice* of preference." "*Alter*" originated with "*Alternate*" (1385, in Chaucer's Troilus and Criseyde; other) something changed to other than what it was + "*Alternate*"—not ones first choice but the "other" or second choice, indicating a serious choice which must be made—there is no getting out of it—between two things. Choice implies more freedom, including making no choice at all. *Option* (sight, seeing) started out in Cawdrey's A Table Alphabetical (1604) as "to wish"; the "mood of wishing" (with longing and belonging); or "to desire." It expanded in 1633 to embrace *Adopt* (to chose to yourself), Opinion, and the meaning of opportunity or freedom of choice. It was in this right or privilege of choosing sense that "Option" (choose) found its home in the stock market. In 1755 Option took on a special legal and commercial use of a privilege acquired--particularly in the commercial sense of the right to buy or sell something at certain prices within a certain time. This embraced the demanding or the payment of a premium or consideration within a specified time; and the carrying out of a transaction upon stipulated terms. Note that in exercising a free choice to buy created an association with that thing. Once the association was in place, the two were pulled into a given direction--much like going down a tunnel. After giving up the free choice to buy or not, there were choices possible but those choices were limited by being in a tunnel of association—i.e. "Choices inside a Tunnel Framework." The following story may help elaborate on this important concept. Alsace-Lorraine, a region in what is now northeastern France, has changed military hands many times down through the centuries. One such change occurred in 1871 when it was supposed to be turned over to Germany. Because many citizens of Alsace-Lorraine remained loyal to France they were given a free-will choice: to either stay as German citizens or emigrate to France. Once the free-will choice was made, they were bound to make all other choices within the frame of France or Germany, depending upon which one they chose—i.e. "Choices inside a Tunnel Framework." Incidentally, this opportunity to choose gave us the verb *Opt*, derived from the French opter, to choose. The idiomatic expression "keep ones options open" arose in the 1960s. In the process, Option came to be linked with opinion and therefore "to think." In everyday usage, to say that "a thing is at our option" or "it is our option" is to imply more freedom of choice than does the word choice itself. To speak of our having the option of choosing to do physical exercise or not means a free-will right of choice. The same is often true in making judgments. "Option" is defined today as the *power or liberty of selection* among many or choosing from choices; the right, the opportunity, or the actual freedom of choice; the privilege of choosing; and the power or liberty of selection. But as used here, *Options are workable possible answers*--like different colored marbles--offered for choice during decision-making or problem-solving or creating. All Options are not equal and this means they can be classified into the degrees of *Viable* (capable of life) as opposed to the degrees of Non-Viable. In deciding what is important for you to pursue, the first step is to determine if your options are viable regarding each of your chances for success and to what degree. *An option is viable if it is available to you and within your capabilities to reach. Non-viable options* are not available to you no matter what you do and are also beyond your reach. The same applies to what is not real or is gender or age incompatible or physically impossible. *Borderline options* are at the limit of your reach. *Flawed Options* in content or application--whether coming from oneself and/or from others—are assessed in various ways. Examples include them being shoddy, weak, inadequate, limited, defective, incomplete; non-pertinent; not of keystone importance; facades; confusingly directed or headed; placed on improper planes of existence;

improperly arranged or combined; deceiving; in conflict; evilly misinterpreted; racially/ethnocentrically bi-ased; in conflict; and/or mostly simply wrong! *Failure to consider all the options usually keeps one from getting on the "Truth-Track" or gets one off it.*

OPTION CONSIDERATIONS: Almost on par with still being able to hear my Mother's messages is that, each I faced a tough situation, of the "gong"-like sound of me telling myself to always have an "Alternative"—i.e. have another Option--another choice of Thing B or even C in case Thing A did not work out. Perhaps this engram arose from my family struggling to get through the Great Depression. Nothing was thrown away because some could be repaired or used for repairs. We would never eat all we had but saved some food in case there was not enough food for the next meal. The C16 word "Option" (choose) originally meant the right or privilege of choosing and later found its home in the stock market. "Option" is defined today as the *power or liberty of selection* among many or choosing from choices; the right, the opportunity, or the actual freedom of choice; and the privilege of choosing. *Choice* implies the opportunity to choose, perhaps among many things. But as used here, *Options are workable possible answers*--like different colored marbles--offered for choice dur-ing decision-making or problem-solving or creating. The nature of Options depends upon ones mindset. In African Tradition the mindset concerns Higher (divinity oriented) Self features, like Self-Improvement, "ME/ WE," and a striving to reach the Heaven Afterlife. In many other traditions the mindset nature concerns Lower (animalistic) Self features, like satisfying Fetters by any means necessary. These are usually choosing between pre-worked out patterns of history or adding Innovations. *Innovations* (alter, renew) add something new to what already exists as well as improve on any known machine, art, method, or system. The mindset of Creativity looks at common things in an uncommon way and uncommon things in a common way. The world's society (e.g. school systems) are geared to Extroverts because they crave External World stimulations that follow "Fad" trends. In the process, Fad implies that the Crowd's minds are excitingly entangled and encaged "inside-the-box". Fashioners of "the box" contents are usually either Ignorant and/or Evil (with the intent of controlling the Crowd's minds). As a result, options for the Superficial Thinking Crowd are encaged "Either/Or" thinking patterns—patterns which change in order to conform to the "here and now" Fad. By failing to consider the past, the future, or anything outside themselves in the present, they are limited to think-ing that the answer to something is an either this or that. By contrast, I am an Introvert who prefers to live in a quiet world and create daily out of Nature's Laws. This means thinking inside, around, and outside "the box" using Spiritual Energy, not the Emotional Energy of Crowd Extroverts. It is fun for me to play with ideas drawn from options taken out of (1, 2) "Either/Or" may be (3) *Neither*; (4) *Both*; (5) a little bit of one and/ or the other in different proportions; or (6, 7) *Combinations* of the first 5 with or without something else. By itself and for creating, "*Either*" can refer to both, each, only one, or any one at different times. By itself, "*Or*" introduces an alternative. Analysis of a situation might bring to light several pieces for consideration that when manipulated and maneuvered, lead to Options. Within this context is a reason for students giving "wrong" answers, as judged by "inside-the-box" only thoughtful teachers. Furthermore, those teachers may be limited in option flexibility by how they were socialized. Routinely, Europeans make examination questions calling for answers—and both are based upon their connotations. All of this is foreign to Black youth because of their orientation to African Tradition Survival definitions, concepts, and thinking styles—despite them having been diluted and polluted during and after slavery. To make matters worse, Black youth are taught European definitions, concepts, and thinking styles which, for me, made no sense. Such were given as city wide "IQ" tests when I was in grade school and high school. The results were evilly applied to put Black youth in "Special Education" classes which confined them to the status quo. There were many true/false and mul-tiple choice "IQ" examination questions that I always considered unfair—e.g. I could think of other options for that question or, the correct answer depended upon the circumstances or the setting of a given situation. If those questions had been made by members of the Black community, I would be amazed if any European would have passed. *A pervading "Me" attitude is: "Just because I do not know any other reasons mean none exist"; "Just because they do not do things my way means there is no better way."* I often learn new options or new directions or new ways of doing things by being quiet and listening or seeing how things play out; by reading detective stories; or by playing chess. Options are mental tools and the more Option tools one has, the greater the chance of choosing correctly; making something work; doing it better and faster; fixing something; or stopping the bad from happening. jabaileymd.com

OPTIONS: One morning at daily Family Talks I was tired of hearing my children doing blaming without any evidence. So that morning's project was to consider other possibilities for explaining the bad outcome. They came up with 13 options. Flexibility in creating Options (choices) is to have the courage to leave the Crowd in order to mentally "step-outside-the-box" and look at what is available in a new way. An example is to see the common in the uncommon or seeing the uncommon in the common. To remove biases and prejudices in order to see a "Thing" for what it is—and without an opinion—often converts what is bounded by humans into its naturally boundless state. People with an inferiority complex are afraid to look at reality because they may uncover what they work so hard to hide from themselves and from others or it may take away their Projection safety blanket cause them to realize they, themselves, are the problem. If a "Thing" can be analogized to a "Star" or the Sun, then that allows it to spray rays in all directions to thereby generate unlimited options. Following a given ray could lead to a new realm of thought that serves as the missing link. Or, with any given option images of various types can be created and, in turn, each image can then be extended into any type of Thought Patterns and Concepts. Certain of those patterns and concepts may be used as Symbols for Cosmic and daily living Laws, from which reasonable Assumptions can be inferred and representative models can be made. In applying each in a manner that maintains correspondence with the issue at hand, this may allow one to get "unstuck" and thereby proceed. In the process, new information or knowledge may necessitate revising the Assumption. Opening up options can also come from seeing "the elephant" on the Obvious that others do not or refuse to see. Or, it may come from uncovering the Hidden. Or, it may come from tracing the Seeable back to its Underlying or planted roots or seed. For unavoidable problems, Critical Thinking seeks to discern that problem in its earliest stages because to delay makes their solutions far more complicated. For example, my staff was to inform me immediately when a significant problem arose so that I could start containing it right away using the best of two options. CT Genius honors no established standards; devises its own guides, filters, and measures; is self-relying; and, like unconscious Beauty, lacks any intention to please.

Whereas ordinary people think the solution for a problem is "Either this or that" or "All-or-None," the Talent of CT sees 2 or 3 more viable options for solution. To elaborate with the *"The 3/7 Concept,"* if items 1, 2, and 3 are laid out in a vertical row, the combinations which can arise are 1 + 2; 1 + 3; 2 + 3; and 1 + 2 + 3. Then, out of these 7 options, bits and pieces from each can be extracted so as to be arranged/rearranged, combined/recombined to come up with even more options. Selected out of the conglomerate of options, CT might use 2 or 3 of them to develop 10 things for application to what CT's Vision is about or to what the situation calls for. A fundamental of Critical Thinking is to separate and prioritize the Options so as to deal with one at a time. The ideas and concepts inside Option I are arranged/rearranged and combined/recombined into various forms to see if anything fits to connect the problem with a workable solution. The same is done for Options II, III, IV, etc.

But a word of caution is that to choose only those which one understands or those which one likes or those which one thinks the public will like puts one in the situation of ignoring those capable of providing results beyond what one would could imagine. Thus, to avoid those which require a struggle to unfold or disregard those that go against ones belief system or to select those which might put someone else in the spotlight, especially a disliked person, means there is no chance of getting on new paths of discovery. The point is to get the best result no matter who gets the credit or no matter how much time, energy, and effort is required. Those that work best serve as candidates for moving on to the next stage. However, if no piece of the puzzle is found or if any of the Options do not give a workable connection, something has to be created to arrive at a workable solution. Then one considers each Option in detail to evaluate how well a given Option works to explain the conclusion or that can be the best workable solution. jabaileymd.com

OPTION TRICKSTERS: Every daily living aspect in ones life involves selections from Options--which people call making a *Choice*, and which I called *Alternatives* as a boy. "Option's" complex etymology is defined today as the *power or liberty of selection* among many or choosing from choices; the right, the opportunity, or the actual freedom of choice; the privilege of choosing; and the power or liberty of selection. But as used here, *Options are workable possible answers*--like different colored marbles for contest use--offered for choice during decision-making or problem-solving or creating. Since all Options are not equal, they can be classified into the degrees of *Viable* (capable of life) as opposed to the degrees of Non-Viable. In one deciding what is important to pursue, Step I is to determine if ones options are viable regarding each of ones chances for success and to what degree. *An option is viable if it is available to one and within ones capabilities to reach. Non-viable options* are unavailable to one, no matter what one does. The same applies to what is beyond ones desire to reach; what is not real; is gender or age incompatible; or physically or mentally cannot happen. *Borderline options* are at the limit of ones reach. *Flawed Options* in content or application--whether coming from oneself and/or from others—are assessed in various ways. *Failure to consider all the options usually keeps one from getting on the "Truth-Track" or will get one off it.* The most terrible example of this occurred to Enslaved Africans. Their *Certainty about Knowing the Spiritual Force called Sekhem* existed by provable observations of: (1) the *totality of harmonious interrelated large and small patterns present within all of Nature; (2)* Nature's *Reality which—despite being composed of multiple variables*, each on different *Planes* of activity in the Seeable and Un-seeable realms of the Cosmos--possesses Continuity (Unity running through Multiplicity), and maintains Integrity. *But since the slavers could not control Certainty Knowledge minds,* they "beat the spirits" out of the Enslaved and then brainwashed them until the Enslaved could not see things as they really are. No longer, after that, did Black People have the option of seeing themselves as part of Nature. This shattering of the Cosmic Wholism philosophy of African Tradition brought about separating them from their Spiritual God, from their Living-Dead Ancestors, from each other, and from oneself, causing "Selfhood Splintering." *Selfhood Splintering* means one part of ones Selfhood becomes Self-Absorbed (viewing everything within ones world in relationship to oneself) and the other follows dictates of External World influences. The slavers substituted their Supernatural 'white' God image for Sekhem and gave him anthropomorphic (i.e. an Egoism creation of God in the slavers' own image) features. Examples included attributing to this "Individualist" God such human characteristics as body, mind, spirit, power, sensitivity (e.g. a "jealous God," vengeful), and perception. Rules were for the Enslaved to "SEEM" to "Know" the White God as equating to their God, Sekhem. To this end, the Bible the slavers wrote, included much out of the Ancient African Bible—the one of African Tradition used by all as Principles for Right Life Living. To institute Mind Control, the slavers and their White Supremacist descendants have always generated conflicting and confusing definitions to explain life-shaping, life-changing, or other significant meanings. This forced Victims to have to come to them for explanations. Those explanations, from the Supernatural, were made to SEEM legitimate by big words--undefinable or Mind Controlled defined in various ways (e.g. Vitalism)—a mask for convincing arguments. Such was introduced to me as a freshman at the University of Michigan.

To buy into this meant Black People's religion, how to live, or what happens at Death could only be based upon Belief and Faith pertaining to what the Supernaturals say it is. There are no other options. Another trick Non-Rational and Superficial thinkers play with options is that when asked a question, these Deceivers will take off on a completely off-the-point course and continue talking incessantly so as to avoid hearing the retort of this not being about what was asked. Politicians typically respond this way to questions asked. A third is Deceivers not wanting to be confronted with options calling for them to deal with what amounts to contrary evidence. So, they refuse to see *an obvious truth, ignore the question,* or present so many options as to discourage others from asking further question. *Hence, they* are "never wrong" and thus avoid being shown up as looking dumb. jabaileymd.com

ORDER: *Order is essentially dependent on the existence of the interdependence (a type of Oneness) between independent things* and thoroughly know any one Pattern in this Web is to have insight into and an understanding of like-kind things regardless of their time, space, or plane of existence. This is because, by sharing the same "Genetics" of the Spiritual Elements, every part of the web has Correspondence with every other part. To see them all together in their web-like fashion is to experience an *expanding Consciousness—an expansion resulting from depicting the whole rather than its separated parts—an expansion that gives an understanding of the meaning of "ME/WE" relationships.* This understanding is the path to knowledge, even inside the Esoteric Unknown. *Order is the foundation of Understanding //Understanding paves the way to Wisdom (the ability to intuit the Will of God) //Wisdom finds ways to generate Unity of God's creatures and creations//Generating Unity makes one a Cosmos Enhancer.*

ORGANISM: In C17, "*Organism*" designated a group of organs functioning as a whole. Whereas Ancient Africans said a human's body organs worked independently to interdependently produce wholistic health, ancient Greeks borrowed and changed this concept to the idea of an organ being a tool, implement, device, or contrivance--like that used in manual labor. In the post-classical period "*Organ*"--by now a word of "*Mechanics*"--implied an instrument that works with a bellows, like the coordinated structure of a church organ, to produce harmonious music. See Mechanism

OSMOSIS (SOCIALIZED) LIFE-SHAPING ASSUMPTIONS: Ones Unintentional and Unconscious Assumptions may begin in the mother's womb, as if by some subtle Essence Aura received by socialized "Osmosis" ('a thrusting, an impulsion). This Aura, a Metaphysical presence of an always one-way active happening, is powered by a Human Nature urge to reproduce itself and become the thing it makes. Of whatever is being imparted through the mother's womb into the fetus, it follows the natural processes of penetration, perfusion, permeation, and pervasion. After birth, "*Socialization Osmosis*" happens via absorptions of "*Social Atmosphere and Social Aura*" + what children are directly taught and observe. Like a Star's Halo, *Aura* (electromagnetic energy in wave-lengths), Atmospheres, and Thought Clouds are Rhythms of the Star Source. Each Rhythm's unique Vibration rate imparts power in its *shape + conveys Elements having resonating rates with like-kind energies of the same frequency that Correspond to entities actually within the human touched by them.* That human's resultant 'what it is' *Essence gives a new Implicit meaning* as it comes into existence. Such *Subliminal* (1886, below Sensory Consciousness's threshold) "Osmosis" messages are readily absorbed by children's naturally (in the sense of relatively pure) receptive minds. Its entrance is into the non-creative part of a child's Intuitive Natural Right brain as "second nature" or "*Sixth Sense*"--whether consciously or hiding in sub-awareness realms. By this Ancient Brain portion lacking any protective faculties, what is interpreted constitutes the child's reality. For socialized Racist messages, Unexamined Assumptions of "Race" thereafter prevent one from knowing a fellow "unique" looking human simply as being "Genetically Cosmic Organismally" the "Same". For example, to meet a dark-skinned person and interpret what is seen with the socializing Crowd's concept of a Black American, carries with it certain assumptions characterizing features of all Black People--features not actually having been experienced in this person. To such "Assumers," these *Stereotypes are "more real" than the actual human.*

Osmotically "Sensed Auras, Atmospheres, and Thought Clouds" are part of and inside the Physical World realms—as verified by all Sages of all cultures throughout the Ages. To elaborate, Ancient Africans determined Melanin helps in "ME/WE" human (i.e. Black) family connections; in attracting the "*Afrocentric Mystic Memory*" that assists learning from our Ancient African Ancestors' Thought Clouds (Ramacharaka, Fourteen Lessons, p 77); and, the "Intuition" Nervous center in the Pineal Gland's Substantia Nigra connecting one with God's Amenta. From my personal experiences, which are common place, one type of "Sensing" of an Atmosphere occurs at my regular study desk--meaning I often recall hazy information of years prior when writing at that same desk. Such recall does not occur in any other location of my home. I have been to an empty prison where, upon entering the gate, I could immediately feel the disharmony resulting from the conflicts that had no doubt been there when it was full of prisoners. I have been to active prisons where I could feel the hostility as soon as I arrived outside the gate. Once, while in Jerusalem and walking toward the Wailing Wall my feel started burning. Someone called me and I turned around and went away from the wall—and my feet stopped burning. Then when I approached it the second time my feet began to burn again. After that I went back and forth several times and each time the same sequence occurred. Nevertheless, socialized Osmosis learning is so subtle as to defy being put into words and those who have absorbed Racists ideas go along with the prevailing terms their socializers have devised. In thinking about how children absorb the assumptions to which they are subjected, Sharon Bingaman RN proposes that all assumptions thrown out by adults into the atmosphere around them mean children do not questioned such Socialization. Perhaps children figure their trusted adults know more and are smarter than they and hence automatically allow these contents (assumptions) to be absorbed into their realm of thinking. If the assumptions come from one of their peers, children are likely to accept what is not already fixed in that mental slot. Then from the Mass Media, children will accept what SEEMs right. Around that they build a lifestyle. The resultant Beliefs are anti-Spiritual Elements Certainty-like. Those who never challenge what they have been socialized into can never properly develop the fullness of their Selfhoods. Hence, everybody loses!!! jabaileymd.com

OVER-PREPARATION: 'Prepare' (Old English) originally meant "Tools" (devices to do work), as in what contributes to getting a job done. "Be Prepared," the Boy Scout's motto, was very significant to me. One reason was that after the racists Scout leaders "lost" my 21 merit badges earned for my Eagle Scout Award, my parents threatened federal legal action against them and they then allowed me to earn them again. One learned lesson was to always remain in a state of readiness in mind and body for not only doing my obligations, duties, and responsibilities but also losses, lacks, and obstructions. Also, though I could no make it rain, what was under my control was to ensure that when rains came, it would nourish prepared soil. Meanwhile, for fun as a gardner I would challenge myself to do a job perfectly and quickly. That drove me to be so prepared for what might have to be done—which, of course, meant striving for perfection. This required a mild obsessive compulsive attitude--e.g. *the seeking of every little aspect of the topic*--and with a sense of urgency. Both orientations were stimulants to developing skilled Critical Thinking that transferred into learning everything available on the path to my Mission. That preparation included seeking the most sound Base I could find so as to build such a solid foundation that, upon being faced with chaos down the line, I would not have to go back to do repairs. In other words, I would anticipate what might possibly cause gaps or weaknesses in the foundation being built and ensured they were handled before going forward with what needed to be done. The reason for practicing doing things Efficiently (done quickly), Effectively (done right) was because it gave me Self-Pride and confidence. Because "success breeds success," the fun challenge led me to advance to higher and higher levels after each "victory." In the process, I found my chances of success happened best by specializing in being "Overly Prepared". Two unexpected bonuses were that "over-preparation paved the way for "Lucky Accidents" and that I could to happen and to remain "Calm, Cool, and Collected" in times of Trials and Tribulations. It was crystal clear to me that *Success is in the details*. Because Black Americans do not honor their own scholars and feel those scholars are not part of their Crowd and because it is not in Europeans best interest for Black People to be successful (which makes them fearful), both groups are in readiness to attack Black Scholars. For this reason I had to over-prepare for everything so as to be prepared to deal with both groups. It is not a matter of being good at something—for they will find some flaw in that. Rather, it is about being excellent and making excellence routine. That setting, to repeat, comes from being strong, staying strong, and doing strong whatever is necessary to do so as to handle every problem that pops up. Doing strong--i.e. what one does— gets one to the top while courage and preparation enable one to be strong. To be Brave—going out to deal with tough problems one does not choose—means these struggles one goes through is what keeps one staying strong. All of this starts with a commitment to complete the task, no matter what. This first step involves constant preparation--and in the same way superstar athletes get ready and stay ready for what has to be done. This has nothing to do with "Excitement" and instead has everything to do with working out of the "Aliveness" that comes with Spiritual Energy—and, as is widely advocated, not Emotional Energy. One must seek Knowledge in the way one looks for a needle in a haystack with a determination of not leaving until it is found. That is what separates those who succeed since Emotional People only want what is easy and requires no work. When one does not know what is available to know on ones own, ones questions are timid and thus one will receive confident answers from the ignorant or the evil. Stop right then to discover the answers from multiple sources. I use 30 different dictionaries for one word. In preparation to discuss a difficult subject I make it a policy to discover all I could on my own so as to be able to ask experts questions that are on the leading edge of new frontiers. As a boy, I would offer the expert some service (e.g. washing his car) in exchange for advice.

P

PARACOSMS: A detailed Imaginary World created inside ones mind: amazing illusionary details in ones self-created Imaginary World

PARADIGM: *In metaphysical realms it is an idea-form (model, blueprint, pattern). In the material world it is a category (which is also a pattern containing a model of a certain type and within that model is a blueprint of characteristics)*

PARADOX: a view contradicting accepted opinion for seeming to be self-contradictory (even absurd). But on closer inspection it contains a truth reconciling the conflicting opposites: "I never found the companion that was so companionable as solitude" (Thoreau). See Puzzle; Conundrum; Enigma; Paradox; Problem; Mystery

PARALOGIC: *Non-Rational thinking of the Left Brain and Emotions, passed off as "Logic"*

PATTERNED THINKING: To "*Broad-Stroke*" is the habit of Patterned Thinking characteristic of Emotional People (EPs) whereby one stereotypes people (e.g. "all men are…; all members of this race don't…"). Since EPs are unable to do skilled Critical Thinking, they are thus hampered in being able to see things as they are--and particularly when thin strokes are called for—situations of distortions and fantasy which generate, enhance, or maintain needless problems of a vicious cycle nature. Though easy to broad stroke all people of any race or gender as this/that, such is simply not so. Yet, it "SEEMS" right. Patterned Thinking prevents people from learning a general principle for correction or even thinking to solve any significant problem.

PENETRATION: The Subtle form of Discerning requires *Penetration* (looking through, seeing beyond the surface). *Discernment* would draw out worthwhile information not easily seen or even being out of sight-- so as to see and mark essential things. See *Discretion;* Discernment

PERCEPTION: organizing, interpreting for understanding + giving coherence, meaning and unity to sensory in-put

PERCOLATE: (C17, to 'strain thought' by drip or drain through small holes or spaces) could occur.

PERFECTION: Integrity within the "Seed" of a thing, as in the core of ones Selfhood. Such a Seed of perfection shows *Integrity* by being complete, whole, healthy, flawless, and not divided against itself or by outside forces. The "Self," as a drop of God, contains the Spiritual Elements of Unconditional Love, Truth, Reality, and the Natural in a state of Consistency. When one maintains the structure of ones divine nature in a whole, complete, and uninjured state, this state of existence represents *Human Perfection*. Critical Thinkers (CT) seek out and do the mind discipline games ordinary thinkers refuse to do. And this is how CT develop and how they think. Hence, The "Self" (ones true identity) is in an unalterable state of peace--called Hetep (Nirvana of Hinduism). For Europeans, "Masterpiece" denoted the masterly achievement of a product when done with extraordinary skill or when declared by authorities to be of outstanding artistic merit.

PERFECTION STRIVING: Through astro-mathematics African priest-astronomers confirmed God's existence and God's moral laws. One conclusion was that ones purpose in life is to constantly strive towards perfection by going from ones Lower (animalistic) Self to ones Highest (Divinity) Self. In elaborating they taught that at the core of a human's Being is an indivisible duality consisting of a "Self" (immaterial) and a "not Self" (or Divine Spirit which is intangible) (Amen, Nuk Au Neter, p32). The "Self," as "a kind of individualized fragment of the Supreme Being" contains no energy or matter in it that can give any kind of visible manifestation detectable by humans. This is like the old saying: "If a tree falls in the forest does it make a sound if there is nobody present to hear it?" What happens is that the tree falling sets off vibrations independent of anyone's presence but for there to be sound the vibrations must activate somebody's eardrums. Thus, although the "Self" (like God) does what it does, by way of the Divine Spirit what it does is known only through the effects it produces in the Selfhood's material side. In African Tradition what is completely made, whole, healthy, flawless, and not divided against itself or under the influence of outside forces is deemed to have Integrity and is therefore "Perfect." When a human's Divine Self and Divine Spirit are connected and work in harmony with the Divine Self orchestrating ones Selfhood that human has achieved "Perfection." Note the difference in the European concept of "Perfection." In general, its definition is the masterly achievement of a product when done with extraordinary skill or when declared by authorities to be of outstanding artistic merit. Up to C13, "*Skill*" referred to an ability acquired through patient practice; to "skill in performance acquired by experience, study, or observation." Since human perfection, in African Tradition, is when one has fully activated ones dormant Divinity, this is an individual's piece of work on oneself in bringing about what is naturally within and independent of and uninfluenced by any outside forces. This is not about "skill" but rather it concerns living a Ma'at life using the Spiritual Elements as its principles for decision making and problem solving. Perfection is known to be present when one is aware of ones "Self" (ones true identity) being in an unalterable state of peace--called Hetep (Nirvana of Hinduism)--at a deep level, despite being in the midst of chaos.

The process of striving for human Perfection is not in being ideally perfect, as indicated by African Sages saying the "Heart" of the deceased must "balance" Ma'at's feather from it reflecting an overall life of Goodness. If one was "Ideally Perfect" that would not reflect humanness. What is meant by striving for a lifestyle of overall Goodness is to go with the natural inclinations which are generated by ones Divine Self. Then develop them to the fullest--and that will not be following any established pattern but rather one is going with ones own natural flow. African Sages' taught that ones purpose in life is to fulfill *the Divine Plan and to use the difficulties one has in life as a tool to force out the divine powers within ones Selfhood so they can be cultivated.* Ones guiding model for designing ones tasks in life, said Ancient Africans, is studying the work the God spirit does in Nature. What one will find is *Consistency* and that is characterized by firmness, uniformity, and lasting durability of Integrity and Perfection--whether in spiritual or earth world realms. Some ways Consistency displays in humans include: (1) constancy with respect to compassion; (2) sound and stable information when CT is skillfully derived; (3) steadiness and "Rightness" when it comes to ones actions or the motives of those actions; and (4) resolution for ones firmness of purpose without being pulled away by attractive distractions. Then on the path to Goodness "The laws of God and Spiritual Elements are the first things the seeker will find." *The closer one gets to the Truth, the simpler is living.*

PERFORMING ARTS: the drama, dance, and music generally presented before an audience. Here, the activity of the artist forms a central feature of this creative visual art. In contrast to most other goals whereby one cultivates a reality, performing artists provide the means of recreating or creating some aspect of their act. In other words, he/she becomes a partner to the author of the art being performed. It is the artist who gives more clarity, more depth, and more breadth to the aim of the author's artistic work. The basic principle is *Stylization*

PERFUSE: Phase I is "Penetration" (one looks just below the surface); Phase II, "Perfusion" (one sees just below the surface); Phase III, "Permeation" (spotlights nooks, crannies, and recesses below the surface); Phase IV, "Pervasion" (one sees and becomes part of the flow of the essence of what is on the surface as well as what is inside, surrounding, and outside the Essence of the topic, person, or thing viewed).

PERIODICITY: return of a celestial body to a given point at an even rate in Cosmic Cycles

PERIPHERY: The C14 word "Periphery" (Greek, circumference, perimeter) originally referred to layers of atmosphere around the earth or part of a circle. However, I use the African Tradition meaning of Spiritual "Periphery" in the sense--not of having a small degree of significance because it is quite the opposite--but of it being likened to a Star--a Star containing the essence of Knowledge. Although it refers more vaguely to the outer edges of such Certainty, the essence can only be known by stepping inside the Star.

PERSONA": As a boy living in an all-Black community which exhibited Unconditional Love to each other and enjoying the benefits of that atmosphere, I was fascinated by its contraries. Specifically, as outrageously ridiculous as the low levels of animalist thinking/behaviors are displayed in causing pain, misery, and needless death, such powers always seem to win over Good people to their Satanist philosophy. Historically, although Ancient Africans had no concept of a Devil, Hell, Supernatural dictator realm, they personified the mythological god Set to be a purely physical Evil principle, unrelated to anything Spiritual. Set signified a power of the "Dark Side," Limitation, Confusion, Conflict, and a Self-adversary—meaning a denial of and a disconnection from God. Hence, African Sages saw these displays as a mask symbolizing Ignorance of God and deemed this to be the greatest disease of the Soul—a disease whose Self-Unknown mind course puts the afflicted on anti-Ma'at paths with Indifference/Hate/Evil/Sadism leading to Kill/Take/Destroy/Dominate/Control/Oppress. When people are "Depersonalized," this means the *"Person"* aspect of ones presentation demands wearing masks concerning the exact role one is ordered to play. That mask of Ignorance referred to the roles their incredibly painful Egos called for while their Real Selves were behind the mask. Meanwhile, the usage of masks and masquerades, originated among Primitive African Ritual Specialists around 30,000 BC, were used to cure patients of psychosomatic diseases caused by disharmonious spirits. This feature of hiding and displaying moods to influence or control Nature, the gods, and human affairs spread throughout the world. Of particular significance were the Etruscans who dominated Italy's northwestern coast from about 900 to 300 BC. They were a wealthy, sea-faring people—similar to the Egyptians (i.e. basically Black Ethiopians). They brought all major elements of Egyptian civilization and culture to the Italian peninsula and then on to the Greeks. Prior to Greece trade exchanges, the Etruscans had applied masks as a device for the theater (among others)—more like the manner in which masks had been used in Interior Africa and to a lesser degree in the way they were applied in the festival and religious practices of Ancient Egypt. In fact, Etruscan actors never appeared on stage without masks. The reason is that between 700 and 500 BC, when it was fashionable for Etruscans to attend outdoor plays, the open theater was vast—even larger than some of our modern stadiums. The theater seats for tens of thousands of people were a great distance from the stage. Not only was there trouble seeing the facial expressions of the actor, but there was trouble hearing what was said. To help overcome both of the audience's distance problems, an actor would make several masks the size of a large Disneyland type Mickey Mouse face and each mask contained a megaphone mouthpiece. The entire device was called a *Persona* (an Etruscan word)—so named because of the resonance of the voice sounding through the megaphone of this image. Over time, Persona embraced dramatic characters represented by an actor's mask—serving as the vehicle through which a word or idea (sound) is manifested. This came from the Ancient African concept of a Divine Persona Image at birth manifests as a Ka (Divine Essence Personality—likened to a boundless ocean) and its cultivation for "ME/WE" achievements requires it become a Kau—a word symbolizing branches of rivers off its ocean Ka—i.e. Personalities). Such implies a part of ones Selfhood—the *"Person"*--serves to convey ('per') a sound ('sona'). Its importance was/is African people could learn to manifest their Self-Identity through the use of Heka Aung (i.e. Metaphysical Sound Technology Magic Power) which are the Words of God coming out of ones Soul. In short, these *Mantras* or Words of Power represented ones Divine Self-Image--a reason that *"Keeping ones Word"*—doing what one says one will do--was essential to living a Ma'at (i.e. a displayed Spiritual

Elements) life. Yet, when voices sounding through the Persona is of a Contingent Being—an Ego—a False Self, it completely replaces ones Real Self (i.e. ones Self-Identity). Then ones contaminated mind, now devoid of contact with its sacred contents, spews forth features of ones imagination and from the External World. To reverse this requires outsmarting and out working *Set at all costs--and confront him with all means possible in harmony with Divine Law*. Confronting Ignorance demands artistically refined behaviors, based upon subtle sensibilities in selecting nuanced forms of words in how and when to use what relative to the involved.

PERSONIFICATION: making a lifeless or abstract thing come alive

PHANTASMAGORIA: Phantasmagoria is a crowd of Phantasms. Whereas *Phantasy* is imaginative visionary notions--*Phantasm* (Fantasm) is the fact that illusive supposed apparition or spector do appear to any sense or to the intellect. In other words, Phantasms are an illusive likeness of something that might be seen in a hideous dream, such as a supposed vision of an absent person, living or dead, that possesses an elusive likeness. Three human-made layers of Fantasy "wild" Essentials and no Essence from which they are birthed generate images made around a selected person(s), place, or thing which spurs the Imaginative faculty. "Wild" Essentials imply no conformity to rule or duty while being irregular in presentation and consistency—unripe. This combination of using Fantasy to construct wholes from parts having no existence and applying them to a selected subject gives "Over-Effect" uncontrollable products consisting of a shifting series of Phantasms, Illusions, or Deceptive appearances created by the imagination. This may be associated with a changing scene(s) made up of many fragments consisting of a fantastic series of Images, produced out of a mechanically oriented mental background. The Fantasy "wild" Essentials and no Essence have different subdivisions. They come, says Amen (Metu Neter I: 247) from the use of ones syllogistic logical intellectual faculty without the guidance of the Synthetical faculty (Ma'at). One type is symbolized in Greek mythology by the Hydra. For every head cut off from this monster, two grew in its place. He adds that this characterizes the majority of proposed logical solutions offered by dominant European logic patterns. When used in this way one can only focus on a part at a time, a proposed solution derived from a Phantasmagoria concept. That creates a number of unforeseen problems in other parts. Usually it is accompanied by another type out of the *Chimerical* faculty portion of ones out-of- control Imagination. It is responsible for visionary imaginativeness (e.g. monsters, or hybrid, or bogy—an evil or mischievous spirit, hobgoblin) to an excessive degree. See "Disaster Star/Halo" Imagination

PHANTASMAGORIC HISTORY: The Limbic Brain is like the middle scoop of a 3-scooped ice cream cone. In it runs a human's emotions and imagination for play (among others). The bottom scoop next to the cone is the Ancient (or Reptilian brain—the purely Physical oriented brain which has control over (among others) Fear and Aggression powered by negative reinforcements. Two others are the Instinct and Omnibus Brains. The top scoop is the Rational Brain which speaks the thinking language of thoughts and words. These 5 brains-in-one—Quintaune Brain are intricately interconnected but most of the time the emotions and imagination are dominating for they are stronger than thoughts. The God Module--the home of Intuitional Wisdom—perhaps located in the Right Brain's Temporal Lobe. When there is Real Self purity of Intellect and Character, it is concerned with spirituality, prayer, and religious experiences. However, children, in categorizing Creatures and Creations in order to make sense of the world, evolve into sort of stereotyping people according to Group Membership and then attributing to the members the human-made Stereotypes that have been associated with a given group—and not about Animus. Thereafter, arises the implication, in conjunction with socialization, of forming unconscious or subconscious opinions or prejudices about race, gender and ethnicity that subtly affect ones actions, favorably for cult members and unfavorably for Victims. The result is at least Implicit bias which is capable of being implied by inference and without being stated to members or to feigned enemies. To elaborate, Humans are born with spirituality free of all human-made religions -- i.e.

no one is born with a religion, which is a European invention. The spirituality of ones most remote Ancestors is transmitted, perhaps in the Omnibus portions of the Ancient Brain of a human, to all of their off-spring. By being so deeply embedded in the inner recesses of ones mind, one does not change ones established spirituality when one converts to another Religion/Spirituality system. Instead, they change the way they relate to the old established one. In other words, their spirituality stays the same and the only changes are the rituals in which it is packaged. In Supernatural oriented religions, this repressed Spirituality of the original Primitive Africans is in conflict with the absorbed Supernatural religion and that has a significant influence on ones Imagination. For example, dating to ancient non-African times, pre-philosophical common sense beliefs in God as a Supernatural Being were wide-spread. Regardless of type, each has been bound up with a number of other like-kind beliefs. Both of these involve complex stories embracing every conceivable Phantasmagoic creation version of God. *Phantasmagoria* is an association of non-descript images of a form, a person, a disembodied spirit, as in the raising or recalling of spirits of the dead. When it is regarded as the product of subjective processes appearing in the form of Illusion or Hallucination, it is called *Fantasm or Phantasm*. Or, if regarded as the product of Perception, it is an Apparition. An *Apparition* is a sudden and unexpected appearance of some Being or object, usually implying a supposed Supernatural manifestation (e.g. a ghost). These are distinguished from *Phantasy or Fantasy*—a form of creative imagination activity, where the images and trains of imagery are make-believe and synthesized into a unified story orchestrated by the nature of ones Ego. It may be from such causes as being unsatisfied about something; a substitute for courageous action; for preparing or paving the way for later action; for soothing. Another aspect is that of *Phantoms*, perhaps based upon images one forms about what is in the Unseen realms and in which certain emotions are layered on it. *Phantasmata* (sensory images received passively from some external object)—have the peculiarity of the Receiver not being aware of them. When any of these appear and leave such an impression as for it to be deemed "property" to which one stakes claim and calls it God, I call that *Phantasmagoric Hallucinations*. Into them, Believers can socialize children and others. Supernatural beliefs are in agreement that God cannot be part of Nature. Another, that the Supernatural God is Anthropomorphic—endowed with attributes which characterize man. Still, this description in ancient literature and in much of today's organized religion allows God is held to be capable of wrath, jealousy, vengeance, and displeasure. This is a crude attempt to envisage a Supernatural Being pictorially--termed Idolatry. There is the assumption that God responds to prayer, that "he" participates and influences human relations that "he" rewards and punishes. There are many variations on this—most prominent being those who internalize their own image so as to worship it. Others hold a purely impersonal or non-anthropomorphic belief in God, not interfering with the course "he" has fixed for it, and indifferent to human affairs. This view, originating in ancient philosophy, is now known as *Deism*. Regardless of the kind, the mind abstracts universal qualities from these and uses them in making judgments. Those judgments, in the setting of Life Living, spring out of "Non-Rational" Thinking patterns. Since those patterns lack internal unchanging linkages of Coherence, Consistency, Compatibility, Balance, and Harmony, when compared with Natural Cosmos Logic, they are *"Non Sequitur"* ('it does not follow'). Its contrariness to sound Logic or Reason makes it Irrational (i.e. absurd) and Illogical (i.e. false or foolish). This is in keeping with the Phantasmagoric Hallucinations of having been socialized into them since birth—and which is made to seem perfectly normal, since "everybody" does it. All of this is within the context of seeing all Cosmic Creatures and Creations as "mechanical". In today's newspaper, for example, there was the sentence of "cellular machinery of autophagy [Greek, self-eating]" concerning what goes on in humans bodies for self-protection. Another is *"Defense Mechanism"*—a fundamental badly devised psychological term meaning an unconscious mental process that lessens the anxiety associated with a situation or internal conflict and protects one from mental discomfort. It simply is *not true that anything organic is mechanistic*. Non-Rational Thinking does not require the Understanding of even one or more fundamentals of life or any topic fundamentals because its focus standard is to use methods that ensure getting all the benefits of: "what can it do for me and my goals." By deeming people unlike them to be "Objects," Supernaturals justify *Imperialism* (an extension of their territory by imposing its authority and domination to thereby gain mental, political, and economic control of other areas) by "saving" the world and "ordering" it. Their Hallucination goes so "far out" from reality to convince themselves of their own magnanimity and altruism (based upon "the White man's burden"). Such Ego projection is a substitute for self-fulfillment. See "Disaster Star/Halo" Imagination; Apparition; Chimera

PHANTASMAGORIA--CAUSES: Here, I pause to engage with Speculations about Supernatural Speculations. Since newborn humans start life thinking with Images, chances are that primitive Europeans, who were Warriors, began life the same way but yet those images reflected their Savage orientation. "*Savage*" (C13, someone who comes from the woods) derives from woodlands being anciently viewed as places of untamed nature, beyond the pale of civilized human society, and living in or belonging to a primitive condition of human life and society. The overtones of Savage are negative, suggesting violence, merciless, brutal, ferocious, fierce, rude, sadistic, ruthless, relentless, cruelty, and murderous attacking, especially with ones teeth and without restraint or pity. It is generally accepted that: "the savage ascribes the mysteries of life and power to a supernatural source" and their minds show pervasiveness of pre-logical factors in primitive mentality. These certainly explain much of what has been shown in the Americas to Colored Peoples. No doubt these Warriors' immature and mechanical thoughts were imaged into a Phantasmagoric mechanical setting reflective of their well-recognized Savage and non-Spiritual God mindsets. Examples of supportive early derived terms include: Armor being for *mental* and physical defense mechanisms; strategically assessing significant problems was done from an Adaptive mechanical perspective (e.g. if X happens, do Z); troubleshooting utilized a mechanical process to locate problems and for repairs by mechanical patterns. Both warring and dancing were done mechanically. By being solely oriented to the Physical realm (a mechanical tendency) meant it was an easy next step for these Warriors to extend their "*Structured*" (that which is constructed using related parts) way of looking at things into the realms of their environment, their culture, themselves, their victims, their gods and religion, their thriving, and their Supernatural philosophy—pursuing and fixing each mechanically. Such a mechanical association of concepts meant primitive Europeans' mechanical language was applied automatically, even to organic things; for mechanically solving anything; and to have a false sense of "all is well" from that one 'broken' thing having been properly handled mechanically. As today, it was "*Fear*" that first brought ideas of gods into primitive Europeans' minds—a fear leading them to "construct" gods out of their own warring appearance and imbue those Images with warrior thoughts, emotions, and deeds. Resultant Contingent Being gods were fantasized to make happen what they desired--Desires to satisfy their brutish animalist lifestyle. Hence, their 'constructed' gods symbolized gross immorality standards, filters, guides, and measures which Warriors eagerly imitated--like the deity Thor ('thunder')—for whom Thursday was named (Thor's Day). He was common to all early Germanic peoples—a great warrior represented as a red-bearded, middle-aged White man of enormous strength and an implacable foe to the harmful race of giants. The thunderbolt, representing his hammer, was his featured attribute--in the manner that the GUN is the supreme attribute—the absolute means of all power--for today's European males. Ancient Europeans expressed this Supernatural state in terms of a machine—a mechanization taking reason out of its earthly domain and converting it to "*Non-Rational*" (Fettered Emotions + Left Brain) decisions and solutions. Their Supernatural cult rules put '*Boundaries on the Boundless,*' including making mechanical the Cosmic Organism. The Greek Euripides(480-406 BC) illustrated this by saying: "The way of God is complex. He [a gender boundary on their God] is hard for us to predict. He moves the pieces and they come somehow into a kind of order"—implying a mechanical universe. To switch from history to A Priori speculation, when something mechanically malfunctions, then there is a Cause. According to Supernatural religion, Adam and Eve created Original Sin. So, when Phantasmagoric Images appear in a cult member's mind, perhaps this is taken as some malfunctioning of what is within their "Dark Side" constituting a Sin. Such would equate to sin from not following Supernatural rules, as evidenced by a Devil-like monster—an "Over-Effect" fantasy of ones sinful "Dark Side." Such a monster, whether being machine-like or not, is their self-assigned Devil--the opposite of how they have been programmed to think. Their Sins start being punished by not knowing what the monster is or how to deal with it. Perhaps in order to make some compatibility with how they mechanically think, out of all of the Fantasy, Warring, Savagery, and Supernatural ingredients are synthesized Phantasmagoric moving scenes of Phantasms crowds, places, and things. To spruce these into more vivid Icon Images, bits and pieces of mechanical-like characteristics are added to make it like a hot-rod car. By being a self-declared "superior" and by a Supernatural rule to always put ones flaws on other sources, one does not accept ones own Sin. Instead, the Cause of that Sin must be coming from some outside source. Those sources are deemed to already be a feigned enemy or one strikes out at any defenseless person close-by. Since "it can't be me" who is imperfect and since the cult thinks in an "all-or-none" and "either/or" fashion, then it must be "them." Furthermore, by having no Conscience or interest in the Truth, the fact that none of this is "right" is deceptively made so that their Sin "SEEMs" right to themselves, to the public, and to even many of their Victims. The entire scenario is given Tertiary and Quadriary Qualities that fashion an "Over-Effect" perception associated with the Projection of their Dark Side onto Victims. *Projection* is a hallucination because the sick ones attribute their sickness to the well. The sick ones then fantasize that they are well and have to bear the agonies of those they have deemed to be sick. Then they institute horrible punishments on Victims so as to "beat their own sin out of the Victims"—an "Exciting" "on the edge" Adventure for the Supernaturals. This accounts for the saying: the White man's burden" in reference to Black People, when in reality it is just the reverse—Black People are burdened with these White Supremacists. In all cross-cultural encounters, *Emotions are invoked—not by the situations in which one is in or with which one is interacting—but by the Images associated with them* (Amen, Tree Of Life p188). These Icon Images--depictions of desired outcomes--show how one is to think; how one should react or feel in a given situation; and how one desires events to go. Images come about for the most part, by rehearsing what one is pre-programmed to do on ones own and/or by outside influences or by rehearsing all of ones actions in ones Imagination when confronted with a situation before enacting it. They are made more vivid and reinforced by spending much time visualizing how to react in anticipated events as well as indulging in the fears, pains, or pleasures of what was real or imagined in the past. Then, they make these part of the anticipated situation. These Icon images have powers to influence others, based on certain Laws of Vibration + are likely to transpire in a physical event if they are accompanied with the conviction of their possible manifestation. Next, they manifest by beating down helpless Victims because of them being burdened with what the Supernatural people has projected onto them, or, whenever possible, simply killing the Victims—as shown by "Killer" police. By Osmosis (Socialization), Phantasmagoria also eases novices and children into the Supernatural. For example, children of the Supernatural are told incredibly fantasized fairy tales with a recurring theme of "you had better do what we say is the right track (i.e. the Supernatural rules) in order to avoid evil from happening to you." This is the same routine used to control people by using the fantasized Hell and Devil. The Religious deem this to be keeping a "pure heart," which they claim they exhibit. Effective tools are Mind Control Stories like Hansel and Gretel or Casper, the ghost—types which are not told to Colored children. Yet, Colored Peoples have been brainwashed into being influenced by the "Halo" of the Phantasmagoric "Disaster Star's" Supernatural

God, Hell, Devil, and Sin. This is most notable in religion whereby most have a hybrid of the Supernatural and the Spiritual—as with the Background mindset of a Spiritual God but a Foreground involvement with the Supernatural God—not realizing the "6:00" different (i.e. hands on the watch being opposites. Still, the brainwashed have accepted the Supernatural form of Sin and that if they do not follow the Supernatural rules they will go to Hell to be punished for doing wrong against the Supernatural rules—all being about Mind Control and nothing about Reality. Even Black People doubtful about it may cling to it in the event it is true. See "Disaster Star/Halo" Imagination

PHENOMENAL PLANES: The Noumenal Planes are all Metaphysical Objective reality—e.g. spirits of things, thoughts, images, etc. and the Ethereally denser *Phenomenal Plane* (physical Energy/Matter) whereby its ethereal bodies--the Astral ('Star') Plane--are not far apart from the Material World's physical bodies because their vibrational frequencies are capable of being a synchronized link them (Amen Metu Neter I:55, 58). See *"9Ps"*

PHILOSOPHICAL WAREHOUSE: assuming one has chosen to stay connected with ones *Divine Consciousness, it extends past Instincts to coordinate the affairs of ones life.* That is made possible by a human's *Philosophical Warehouse* which is stored in ones Unconscious—the deepest part of one Selfhood which one does not know. Meanwhile, it is "doing" (making happen by bringing its contents into focus) ones Conscious vitals to serve as a source for emergency decisions; as a source to do its involuntary and automated behavior activities; and to assist in coordinating ones life's affairs. Because all of God's creatures and creations are made of the same Spiritual Elements "Genetics" derived from the Mind of God, at any given point throughout the *Natural Processes courses in the Cosmos,* humans can discern the Truth in reality by using *the Familiar (the "Seeable") to explain the Unknown (the "Un-Seeable").* A benefit of this is that any decisions or solutions needing to be made, especially on the spur of the moment, will draw from a Philosophical Warehouse wherein are located a sound Base from which its Truths flow. What is taken out of that flow of African Tradition's philosophy is transferrable for application to any tough situation in daily living. The reason it works is that unifying what is underlying anything Real but in a chaotic state means there are *consistent, permanent, stationary, and unchanging patterns/elements.* The tool for this process is Reason, which is Intellect's star. Truth is both Evidence and Proof when it has Correspondence with established Laws of Nature. In making an emergency decision, be bold and strong. As soon as available, explain to others why the situation demanded fast action. Thanks those involved when things work out and give credit to them, as star players give credit to the team.

PHILOSOPHY: "Seba," an Ancient Egyptian word for "Wisdom," gave rise to the word "Philosophy". The "Philosophy" part of a philosophy of life originated by Ancient Africans came from Africans' Creation Mythology called the Ocean of Nun (Nu)—the Subjective Realm of the Cosmos. Its "Flame"—symbolizing the ultimate in Cosmic Wisdom--includes profound Peace (Hetep); *Omnipotence* (unlimited Universal power); *Omnipresence* (everywhere simultaneously), and *Omniscience*--total knowledge of everything—characterize the Being of the Cosmic Force, Sekham. The Nu, representing the Creator's Divine realm Wisdom, is where a Spark of the Image of God is implanted into each human's Soul prior to Earth World birth to thereafter reside as Wisdom. *Wisdom is in action when one fashions the Spiritual Elements into Tools* for guiding one through the maze of life; using them as Standards against which one can compare how one is thinking, feeling, expressing, and living; having them as diagnostic filters for determining when something is of a harmonious or disharmonious nature; framing all ones decisions; allowing them to be the force driving "Heart-to-Heart" communications; and focusing them on looking for all anti-Love Platter expressions or when one does not know what else to do. Its realization in humans by Meditation is called Enlightenment or Satori. This can only be done by: *subjection of ones mind to the Divine Spirit so it can command the Life-Force in harmony with Laws* *of Nature*; by one manifesting Peace during life's trials/tribulations (i.e. troubles/difficulties); and by experiencing Reality itself—i.e. that which conforms to the Spiritual Elements of Unconditional Love, Truth, Reality, and the Natural. Wisdom is oriented to *Ma'at (Spiritual Elements in action)* forms of Virtue. The cultivation of ones *Virtues* enhances ones entire Selfhood—as with fashioning Wisdom, Beauty, and Unity within oneself and with all others with whom that can happen. Ancient Africans taught that modeling Ma'at Virtues was "Right Life Living."

Since they considered *Virtue as the first and most important quality to be developed by all desiring self-improvement,* one of their messages was that Adversity is only overcome with Wisdom and Virtue. Both were personified and conveyed in Figures of Communication and Personification. For example, African Groits (storytellers) performed lecture teachings using Affect Symbolic Imagery in saying the *gods and goddesses (Neteru) are not realities but only windows into the transcendent—avenues by which ones mind and body energies may be channeled toward a higher, spiritual goal in life*—in other words, alternative paths to the Truth. Hence, one necessarily did "ME/WE" type Critical Thinking pertaining to whatever best served ones own Divine Self as well as promoted the well-being of other people—even if it involved "tough love." Each Virtue helps open and purify ones "Heart" so as to receive experiences as magnanimous. By so doing, the way is paved to thereby transcend into Higher (Divinity) Self realms (Ashby, Book of Life p114, 338). Divine Truths drawn from ones Pure Emotions are able to be cultivated into *Moral Virtues* and Spiritual Practices—like justice, magnificence, magnanimity, liberality, gentleness, prudence, and wisdom. These Virtues, by residing in the flow of the Laws of Nature, include being *True to oneself,*—as when a gardenia blooms all it can. Virtues provide noble impulses for Courageous deeds. Such a lifestyle takes great Courage in order to progress from ones Lower (animalistic) Self to ones Highest (Divinity) Self. Thus, *Courage is the supreme virtue because it is required for any other virtue to manifest and persist.* What spurs Courage is that it is simply the "Right" thing to do. It is out of preserving ones Real Self and its birth gift of Private Self Spiritual Wisdom and Virtues that one designs, in daily living, the setting for applying ones Pure Emotions and Pure Intellect. Both provide the best decisions and Solutions in handling whatever is needed within ones Inner and Outer Worlds. Instances are seen in Nature, in Real Self people, and in acts of helping those in true need from no deliberate causes of their own making. All Wisdom is oriented to the Worth realm of Wealth--e.g. Unconditional Love, Family, Goodness, Wellness, Natural Order, Perfection, Universal Truth, Reality, and handling what blocks "ME/WE" Well-being. These lead to Beauty, Harmony, and Happiness--but only when one knows the Human Ideals of Ma'at Good. African Groits started their storytelling by saying the right way of doing things was by perfecting *Prudence*—i.e. following, without error, a daily Ma'at course—for it enables one to judge rightly about an act of virtue. It is basic to the performance of all virtuous actions in everyday living. After being firmly established in Prudence, ones focus is expanded to include general alertness, circumspection, cautiousness, understanding, deliberation, wise planning, and providing for the future. These African virtues are to be applied to every aspect of daily living–e.g. personal values; family values; social, civic, legal, and cultural values; financial values; Selfless Service, and Spiritual values (Bailey, Self Esteem, p. 33). Such enables one to know what is best to know, then to do what is best to do. As a result of Right use of Knowledge applications and knowing how to "mine" that knowledge--like finding a needle in a haystack--one is always able to discover and perfect what it takes to *"Be Right," "Recognize Right," "Do Right," "Make Things Right," and "Defend the Right".* One always does what is Just, whether seen by others or not—and meets danger head-on that demands it—remains temperate—subdues desires—and lives modestly. *Yet, Unconditional Love displays are the highest Wisdom.* There are many types of Wisdom. However, while on ones Death Bed, living a Wise life is based upon what one would desire one would have done to live the "Good Life". *Wisdom comes from the cumulative effects of a series of small lessons concerning successes, set-backs, and failures causing the uplifting of ones Consciousness.* From these, applicable mosaic pieces are taken for synthesizing them into Guidelines for living a better life. This is repeated each time one assumes one has reached the best. Every mistake becomes a lesson to discover and correct what went wrong; to replace it with a Human Ideal; and to put a plan in place to ensure it never happens again. That brings about a change of meaning because, in the "Big Picture," each one of those was necessary for present progress as well as for foresight and forethought regarding Consequences of each action in progress. Part of the process is to use errors of others to correct ones own, or to do the preparation to prevent the bad from occurring/recurring. "Wise minds" discuss Wisdom—e.g. about *the Essence by which all things are steered through all Things.* Wise minds are masters of Guidelines and do not need to summon the collective judgments of the laws made by those in power. They do not act out of fear and thereby gain the power of doing what is discerned to be right and true. Of greatest personal significance is knowing how to grow old, one of the most difficult aspects in the great art of Right Life Living.

PHILOSOPHERS' STONE: The African idea of the *"Philosopher's Stone"* is it being that perfect and incorrupt God Substance—or "Noble Tincture"—never found upon the imperfect Earth in its natural state. Still, it is capable of purging all baser Mental Activities (or baser metals) of their dross (waste) and turn them into the Spiritual Elements flow (pure gold). See Alchemy

PHILOSOPHY OF LIFE—ANCIENT AFRICAN BIBLE: A human's pathways through the stricture of the hour-glass are determined by that human's selection of a Philosophy of Life (POL). African Tradition's POL is the highest of human excellence, being about Ma'at—i.e. the Spiritual Elements and their attributes in mental, physical, social, and spiritual action. After Very Ancient Africans (c20,000 BC) used astro-mathematics to determine certain Laws of Nature, they inferred Principles pertaining to Salvation for reaching the Heaven Afterlife. In African, Canaan (its Kabalistical teachings), and Black (Dravidian) India, *Salvation* could only occur from transcending the animal dictated behavior to allow a human's Divinity Self to act in harmony with Divine Law's guidance of her/his hard word conduct strivings to be free of the limitations of the physical world. It was each human's obligation, duty, and responsibility to be a model of the highest virtues—i.e. those applied to ones Selfhood as well as those that make for good relations with and behaviors toward fellow humans. *Virtue is the first and most important quality to be develop by all desiring self-improvement.* Most, like those of Manners could only be tested in a single situation--that of human interaction. *When displaying virtues supersede making money, then one would be on the right path in African, not European, Tradition.* To make these happen involves a process of disciplines or purification--both for the body and for the soul—both to enhance ones Spiritual Emotions, Intellect powers, and virtues to fashion Wisdom, Beauty, and Unity within oneself and with all others with whom that can happen. One saying was: "well-established patterns that Challenge, also provide opportunities to discover ones inner resources for use in overcoming troubles. Hence, growing discoveries within ones ones deeper Self would urge such spiritual aspirations as to seek a Sage to assist in self-discovery by cultivating virtue. That is the reason Sages created the 42 Ma'at Philosophy injunctions--10 borrowed ones are called the Ten Commandments in the European Bible (Bailey, Ancient African Bible Messages). One of the performed lecture teachings consisted of saying the *gods and goddesses (Neteru) are not realities but only windows into the transcendent—avenues by which ones mind and body energies may be channeled towards a higher, spiritual goal in life.* It was essential to live by virtues, as they would open and purify ones "Heart" in order to have magnanimous experiences paving the way to thereby transcend into Higher (Divinity) Self realms (Ashby, Book of Life p114, 338). Since the Spiritual Laws are "all-or-none," there could not be any lifestyle flaws in ones POL that would allow for "Flexible Morals"—i.e. putting virtues aside in self-interest situations. Hence, one necessarily did "ME/WE" type Critical Thinking pertaining to whatever best served ones own Divine Self as well as those of other people—even if it involved "tough love." What life means to each human is made into an association of Sets. *Sets* are a collection of like-kind Things (e.g. Objects, Essences, or an Association of Ideas) designated by some guideline that indicates exactly which Things belong to the collection. Insight into the best of these will only be gained from studying Ancient African Philosophy. One Set I have realized is that for people to get an idea of the path to their destination in life is a cascade of events. One is the feature of their Selfhood Greatness will put them in the right "ballpark" of where to discover their Talent and Mission. Both will be about the Spiritual Elements singularly, as in Unconditional Love, Truth, Reality, and the Natural or in some combination of them or in some attribute of one of them.

Such has played out in my life when my Mission in life occurred to my mind while sitting on the back porch counting my marbles. All humans are born with this Sacred (Secret) Dream which they keep hidden for fear of being laughed at. My POL was known to me in kinder-garden when I would run to help a fallen classmate, rather than join the other kids crowding around to laugh. It showed as Compassion, an attribute of Unconditional Love. The combination of my Compassion and my Mission message laid the path for me to go into Medicine in order to cultivate my Compassion so that it could teach me about the Unconditional Love demanded for my Mission. During this process, a key has been to maintain Integrity throughout a lifestyle of POL displays. For example, I passed up many opportunities to make illegal money because it simply was not right. Besides, to have gotten caught could have led me to jail. Supernatural people make a POL in their own image.

PHILOSOPHY OF LIFE IS A HUMAN'S LIFE ANCHOR: Just as a ship's *Anchor* ('a crook or hook') exerts the power to hold a ship in place under varying extremes of conditions, so is the purpose of a human's Philosophy of Life (POL). An assessment starting point for ones mode of thinking is to identify the most sound POL based upon its most sound source because this is the anchor on which ones various Standards are chosen for determining "How Shall I Live". The most Sound POL is that of African Tradition because it is Immaterial. That includes: perfect, permanent, stationary, unchanging, dynamic, undefined, undifferentiated, limitless in expanse/duration (i.e. infinite/eternal)--uncreated/indestructible), and the most powerful of all else. Those aspects are what a POL provide to use as a tow-rope to hold on to and remain stable through thick and thin—through the worst of the trials and tribulations (i.e. troubles and difficulties) one suffers by the limitations of youth--throughout adulthood; and, in old age, the pain of disease and death. The keystone of African Tradition type POL is the self-anchor bull's eye core of *Self-Love*. Self-Love is naturally associated with being aware of ones Private Selfhood Greatness—e.g. having the Spark of God as the Essence of who one is; carrying the "Genetics" of the most outstanding and super-brilliant Ancient African people who have ever lived; and having a Unique Talent which serves as the bridge from ones POL to ones Mission. Self-Love's bathing ones Private Selfhood Greatness gives birth to ones Public Selfhood Greatness. Their proper synthesis means one is in Charge and Control of ones Selfhood; what one thinks, feels, says, and does; and every situation one is in. To daily study African Philosophy is to ensure continual self-improvement, as in Humaneness and Thought. To elaborate, Philosophical Uncertainties are diluted and polluted ingredients running throughout in those choosing to operate their lives out of False Selfhoods. The same applies to Thought Structures. Such dilutions and pollutions are like flowing water underground, resulting in "*Quicksand*". To put this in perspective, imagine a skyscraper building sitting on a Base. Its most important part is not the Foundation, as most people think, but rather the Base upon which it rests. The word "*Base*" has so many complexities that the simplest definition serves the purpose—i.e. the bottom of something considered as its support; the part on which something rests. Again, in contrast to what many people think, the absolutely strongest Thing in the Cosmos is not anything Material. Rather, it is the Immaterial (Substance) which is part of the Cosmic Force, called Sekhem (the Spiritual God).

PICTURE FRAME AROUND A PUZZLE CONCEPT: an analogy for today's African American diversity is illustrated various Ancient African subcultures. Each of the 55 African countries display uniqueness in customs, language (2000+ spoken by the 660 million continental Africans), and styles of worshipping God in serial religions (even in the same region). Yet, all 55 pieces of this puzzle are bordered with a philosophy of life (POL) Frame shared more or less by almost all subcultures. This Frame's ingredients are essentially the same Ma'at living principles and core spiritual concepts absorbed by all African People: (1) the good of the Spiritual Elements; (2) the good of Children; and (3) the good of Immortality, the crown of existence. Tens of thousands of years ago they established a law of Physics, also applicable to the Spiritual, that ingredients of the Cosmos can neither be created nor destroyed. An inference from this was that *bodily death is not the end of a human's life since that human's Soul lives on in a different plane of existence.* Ones Soul, considered an indispensable bearer of ones Purpose of Being, is encoded—like a "trademark"--with that God assigned role. Contents in that "trademark" are like the "Soul's Sunshine" since it makes its owner acutely aware of what one must accomplish in the world, if one remains open to it. The messaged role is an unrealized reality when a human initially comes into Being. Its realization returns ones *Spiritual Personality* to Immortal existence following resurrection at death. Then one becomes an Ancestor able to be invoked by the living. If ones life is terminated prematurely, says Donkor (African Spirituality p40), the Soul returns to God while the Spirit awaits Reincarnation—the nature of waiting is a mystery. Otherwise, after death ones Selfhood remains in existence along with ones accumulated actions— i.e. the Sub-conscious impressions one formed while still alive. Those who choose anti-Spiritual Elements deeds in life do it to a mild, slight, moderate, extreme or Inside-Out, Upside Down" degree. These display as Indifference/Hate/Evil/Sadism (IHES) complex mindset impressions in oneself and with others. All are associated with mental agitation and fetters as ones "Me, Me, Me" focus is on External World Desires. Whenever one has done sufficient wrong to acquire negative Ari impressions, on Judgment Day (Psychostasis) the *Ari (Karma) Law* becomes applicable. It serves as the standard against which the deceased's Divine Will (Heart) is metaphorically weighed by means of the Divine Law. Such is symbolized by the feather of Ma'at. Ones "Heart" (a Soul partner) contents include the nature of ones sown "residues" of feelings, emotions, and desires present in ones Subconscious. They are weighed against Ma'at Cosmic Order. Specifically, Ari ("action") judgments are based upon the *intentions and deeds* as well as their degree of impact Effects and its Consequences. Whether good or bad, these are attached to a person's Life Living--the cumulative effects of which lead one to ones "fate," even beyond death. For example, even if I have shown a consistent pattern of compassion and yet have not always done my best to help someone in true need, this conglomerate of Unconscious impressions and flawed Compassion are what will be judged. But there is a different judged outcome if I persisted in showing Ma'at Compassion in spite of it being repeatedly rejected by those to whom it was directed. In short, it is my Karma (intent and deeds) which leads me to my current condition. If the deceased "Heart" is to proceed into the Heaven Afterlife, it has to be as light as the feather of the goddess Ma'at, as indicated by a balanced scale. This implies one lived a "Good Life"—one of Human Perfection (not ideally) with respect to intents and deeds as well as with Ma'at naturalness operating according to Unconditional Love, Truth, Reality, and Rightness. If the "Heart" weighs less than Ma'at's feather, this implies one did not conform to the Spiritual Elements because of being "overly Good". Such living by strict "Righteousness" rigid rules is "Unnatural" in ones humanity. If the "Heart" weighs more than the *feather of Ma'at,* the two pans would be imperfectly balanced, indicating the deceased had lived a life characterized by IHES deeds. The latter two weighings demand the deceased Soul be Reincarnated in Earth life until ones actions balance the scale. Such a series of Reincarnations will continue until one achieves a life of Goodness—as indicated by *ones Soul vibrating at the same high rate as when one was originally conceived.* See Engram; Second Nature; *Personality;* Karma; Judgment Day; Boomerang jabaileymd.com

PIGEON: (a peeping chick) meant a young bird, especially a Dove. Pigeons and Doves (means the bird's diving flight) became part of a larger group of "like-kind" family members who shared homologous (similar) features from a common ancestor. That group, called Columbidae, possesses the same part or organ which, in different family members within the group's 310 species, has every variety of form and function. Dove is now used for a smaller variety of Pigeon. Such shifts in meaning are usually slow and tendential rather than rapid and absolute. Early usages continue indefinitely alongside later changes that have become dominant, as was true of Pigeon and Dove in C16.

PINEAL GLAND: The Ancient African Bible's Pyramid (Unas) Texts part (c10,000 BC) said the Mind's Eye (i.e. Pineal Gland)—the 'Eye' of Intuitional vision; of Heru (Horus); of Auraut; of Ureaus; of the Goddess' Brow; of Ajna Chakra—has luminous "Inner Vision." Their Pineal Gland (meaning "pine cone-shaped") Knowledge was contributed to by observations of circadian rhythms, by bio-metabolism of human's bodies, and by anatomical studies which showed a string of glands along the spinal column (backbone), called "*Chakra*" Energy Centers. The gland at the top of a human's head (the sixth energy wheel) corresponds to the third eye of reptiles. More research showed the Mind, Body, and Soul all touch each other at only one single point—the Pineal Gland. It and the Pituitary body are means for detecting vibrations subtler than Science ordinarily recognizes. Since human Sensory Consciousness is governed by Light, Light coming through physical eyes hits the Pineal Gland—i.e. ones center of consciousness with "Inner Vision." That "hit" illuminates understanding via its Mind, Body, and Soul interrelationships--all being intimately associated with certain similar mental, but very subtle vibratory waves, which thereby expand ones state of awareness. An analogy is to liken the pineal gland's ability to receive and transmit messages to wireless telegraphy (Swami Panchadasl, Clairvoyance p46; Swami Vishita, Genuine Mediumship p45). The Pineal Gland--the size of a grain of puffed rice--is situated between and behind the eyebrows, anatomically positioned at the base of the Brain/top of the Spinal Cord junction and attached to the mid-brain (Emotional, Limbic, Old Mammalian). The nearby *Cerebellum, said to admit currents of Spirit for distribution into the spinal marrow, attracts the spiritual and life-giving substance.* This helps the Pineal Gland's association with a human's highest spiritual function. The Pineal Gland's role is to provide *Instinctive Knowledge* whose instinctive faculty resides in the Life-Force division of Being (Amen, Metu Neter III:30). That concerns itself first with the Thing's essence and with Ma'at's "ME/ WE" Wisdom, Goodness, Justice, and Perfection displays. The Pineal Gland produces *Melatonin,* which activates the Pituitary to release Melanocyte Stimulating Hormone. It is associated with regulating biorhythms and stimulating the brain to produce serotonin, a sleep pattern regulator. *Sleep*--a process dependent on daylight--is an altered state of Consciousness. One reason is that Melanin granules form a large neural network whose function is to absorb and decode 'electromagnetic waves' which constantly come into the human body as a force. An over-simplification is that an electric current, electricity in motion, is always accompanied by a magnetic force. Increase and change in the electromagnetic field has profound effects upon the brain's Melanin precursory (introductory) centers for forming and developing adrenaline, serotonin, and norepinephrine (a neurotransmitter peptide related to altered brain function and consciousness states). Meanwhile, Ancient Africans found Carbon to be the key atom in all living Cosmic Matter. Linkages with other carbon atoms form black melanin. Melanin, the chemical key to life, was the first chemical that could capture light and reproduce itself. Next found was the brain draped around black neuro-melanin. In turn, this was associated with Inner vision, Intuition, Creative genius, Spiritual Illumination, and high intelligence in Black People. All of these were discovered to be dependent upon Pineal Gland blood-borne chemical messengers that control skin color. Such opened hidden doors to the Collective Unconscious mind, allowing Ancient African priest-scientists to visualize knowledge from the timeless Collective Unconscious memory banks of the mind [which I believe is located in the Omnibus Brain]. Spiritual Visions, said Ancient Africans, occur through ones Pineal Gland brain fibers which, in turn, are connected with ones nostrils--as when taking in the air one breathes. The air one breathes keeps one in spiritual consciousness with Cosmic rhythms, thereby maintaining a personal relationship with ones Creator. One is supplied with all the spiritual necessities required at birth--necessities cultivated by intuitive or even visionary modes of apprehension. Such has the inherent power to be what it is (i.e. its true self) and, by itself, expresses its true self so as to display its true nature. When recognized as being of itself--without anything making it go and without being worked upon--it is a *Vision*, bringing "*That it is*" Pineal Waves into awareness.

PLAGIARISM OF AFRICAN KNOWLEDGE: Honorable Black scholars—like James (Stolen Legacy) and Diop (Civilization)—term "*A tradition of Plagiarism*" as what the ancients Greeks did and then passed on to Europeans. But proper Induction by means of the African Law of Correspondence, often called the Scientific Method of Proof (originated and formalized by Ancient Black Egyptians between 2000 and 1500 BCE), is always studious and searching. Nevertheless, European minds were not sufficiently evolved to correctly interpret what they stole. Also, Europeans were not able to destroy all the proof that math was invented and perfected by Black Africans, including the Egyptians. Besides being spotlighted as dishonorable by such honorable historians as the Greek Herodotus and Diodorus of Sicily (Bynum, African Unconscious), I am continue to be amazed at how some of the most influential authority and expert speakers and writers take their information directly out of Ancient African intellectual property and never mention the name of Africa. A persisting deceptive mechanism concerns dates that are manipulated by racist Europeans so that all prior great Black African achievements can be intermingled with time lines of when "White" nations were said to come into being. For example, Black contributions of around 12,500 to 5,500 BC are placed by most Egyptologists at 3000 BC in order to declare that non-Black nations were the true originators. What these dishonorable writers fail to understand is that their originator "favorites" were actually Black Africans in a new location. These "agendas" and practices of European males make "suspect" whatever they present about anything. Truth seeking Critical Thinkers are alarmed at this acceptance of the correctness of the reasoning pattern but knowingly being on the wrong path.

PLAGIARIZE--STOLEN AFRICAN LEGACY OF SUPER-BLACKS: If an ocean of a haystack flood symbolizes plagiarism of Black People's achievement by Europeans, what is presented here are a tiny number of straws. They give a sample of what qualities they value. Full discussions are in my 40 Black African Tradition Books, for they begin in ancient times. : Plagiarism ("to pluck") originally referred to a net for kidnapping children, with the kidnappers called "plagiarius". In 20,000 BC, the Ifa religion of the Yoruba devised a *Binary Number* system—with symbols used for forecasting—whose symbols subsequently becoming the basis of the machine language of today's complex computers. It was later plagiarized by ancient Greeks. Very Ancient Africans discovery that vibrating strings whose lengths can be expressed in simple arithmetical numerical ratios yield pleasing chords led to the concept of "Harmony" as we know it. This constituted the first step toward a mathematical analysis of the heavenly bodies (stars); of the influence of the heavenly bodies upon the Earth; and of the experiences in the inner Selfhood workings of humans. Though this had been present for thousands of years, all of it was plagiarized by ancient Greeks, particularly Pythagoras (570-495? BC) during his 23 year stay in Africa, who gave it the title of "*The Harmony of the Spheres.*" Elaboration was done by Plato, the European Bible's Book of Job ("the morning stars sang together"); Chaucer; Milton; Shakespeare (in the Merchant of Venice, V, i) and later hymn-writers (e.g. "This is My Father's World"). Yet, this *Vibration Principle* was from what African Sages fashioned original concepts of "*The Way*"--the *Divine Logos*--i.e. "The Word"--written in the Egyptian "Book of Coming Forth by Day," the oldest written text in the world (60,000 BC, Seleem, p 59, xiii). Europeans mislabeled it "The Book of the Dead"; St. John plagiarized "The Word" and put it into The Gospel of the European Bible. Ancient Egyptian Priests, inferring music vibrated at a certain rate, used music to cure disease as well as for healing of the mind, body, and spirit of individuals. That too has been plagiarized. *Form-Ideas* (an African concept plagiarized by Plato) are self-realizable Divine ideas because they are patterns fixed in Nature. These "blueprints" that organize a structured Cosmos exist before anything happens in the Objective Realm, including the Initiation and Manifestation of the Ether. The Idea-Form giver of off-spring and their steadfast bonds internally link all things to which they give rise. Perhaps the world's greatest general was the Black Hannibal of Carthage, Africa; the world's greatest story-teller was the Ethiopian Aesop, who lived in Greek, and the strongest man, the Black African Hercules. All of these, and countless others were plagiarized.

The Collective Unconscious (Impersonal or Transpersonal Unconsciousness; Epic Memory) was described thousands of years ago by Ancient Africans as representing primordial experiences that have repeatedly occurred in the course of generations. They also considered it to be an explanation for instances of the Inheritance of Acquired Characteristics--a deep unconscious representation of experiences common to a human race for countless generations. These concepts were recently plagiarized by the European Jung. Ancient Africans' way of teaching principles of Spiritual Philosophy (e.g. in myths) was to spotlight it on the Right Brain of students by means of African Dialectic--a borrowing into the Western world and plagiarized as the *Socratic Method*. Ancient Romans plagiarized Matet under the Roman name "Aurora" as well as her African Story: "Daybreak." *All* Mathematics basics, physics, scientific method, logic, critical thinking, and similar highly intellectual subjects were derived from their Ancient African Ancestors. The African papyri of the Middle Kingdom (3348-3182 BC)—given by Europeans the European names of Moscow, Berlin, Kahun, and Rhind—have now been *proved to be plagiarized* by *Pythagoras, Archimedes, Thales, Plato, Eudoxus, Oenopides, Aristotle, Solon, Indocsus,* and other Greeks who have left their names on what is considered great in the world today.

Practically all great things subsequently spread throughout the Western world under the name of "*Greek creations*" *are merely translations and transmissions of Ancient African intellectual property.* The *ancient Greeks, being at best mere transmitters and translators of African genius,* laid out a plagiarism pattern which has pervaded Europeans' character ever since--and to the point of their admiring it. This is what European Medieval (and modern) "scholarship" is about.

PLAGIARISM—BY EUROPEANS: R. King MD elaborates (African Origins of Biological Psychiatry p64) on how this went on to cause fears and jealousies of Black people's high achievements with an intense associated inferiority complex among the Greeks. The lowly cultured ancient Greeks were united, less by blood than by common education and ideals, were so "blinded" by peeking through the window of the Ancient African world that they (and the Romans) declared black skin to be associated with high intelligence. By being in extreme awe of Africans, Greek scholars so envied Africans' achievements as to take back to Greece what they learned and claim that brilliant intellectual property as their creations. The African papyri of the Middle Kingdom (3348-3182 BC)—given by Europeans the European names of Moscow, Berlin, Kahun, and Rhind—have now been *proved to be plagiarized* by *Pythagoras, Archimedes, Thales, Plato, Eudoxus, Oenopides, Aristotle, Solon, Indocsus,* and other Greeks who have left their names on what is considered great in the world today. Practically all great things subsequently spread throughout the Western world under the name of "*Greek creations*" *are merely translations and transmissions of Ancient African intellectual property.* Practically all dilutions, pollutions, and fantasy aspects of Ancient African Spiritual Literature have become Western societies' "second nature" (acquired but deeply ingrained character). This makes for "Inside-Out" delusional, "philosophical disarray" and anti-humanitarian and anti-Nature patterns of thoughts, emotions, expressions, and deeds. jabaileymd.com

PLAN: "BIG FOUR" Plan for Goals. First, "Where am I now?" Second, "Where do I want to go (i.e. the goal)?' Third, "How am I going to get there?" Fourth, "What am I going to do once I get there?"

PLAY OPENS MENTAL INNER RECESSES: A metaphor for how Instinct Play works is found in the expression: "To grease someone's palm" (i.e. to give someone money in exchange for a favor). In C16, "Grease" related "to enriching" whatever was ordinary into something of abundance which people desired to possess. Instinct Play is like the grease which enriches the status quo atmosphere so that from then on good things can happen. For example, it greases all the processes that lead to Motivation. Yet, for reasons stated, such an enrichment is unknown to struggling Black youth. Furthermore, they are not aware that Instinct Play is one of their Needy Wants because it passed right by them in childhood. Still, Instinct Play is so attractive that when Mentees are introduced to it Mentors can use it to woo them; to bond with them; to get them to drop their defenses; and to make for a willingness to follow the path that benefits everyone involved. Child-like play paves the way for Mentors to get to and then enter the inner recesses of each boy's mind where there is found the most secluded lacks, losses, and traumas present in each boy's tough life. Instinct Play greases the keys for easy insertion into the locks designed to unlock mental vaults. Then when the pegs of each key go under the tumblers, the effects of Instinct Play make it easier to force the tumblers out of the bolt so that all of what is locking the boys mental vaults can be more easily opened. What Instinct Play does in and of itself is to help struggling Black youth return to that time in their lives, no matter how short it was, when they enjoyed themselves in a mindless state; when they were open to the best of things in the world; and when they were full of awe and curiosity. These are essential features of the Common Humanity of Instinct Play. Reasons for the extensive discussions on Common Humanities have been three-fold. One is that struggling Black Americans have their own Common Humanity -- some with unique variations. Second, to connect with struggling Black youth it is essential to step into and interact inside their Common Humanity before any attempts are made to try to lead them into an Actual Reality Common Humanity. Third, struggling Black youth are only vaguely aware, if at all, that there was a Common Humanity they once enjoyed as children but from which they have drifted far way.

Up to this point the discussion has been about the "Hub" and "Spoke" problems of struggling Black youth; how these problems were programmed into their family line; the effects that programming had on any given youth; preparation for interacting with these youth so as to get them to receptive to desiring to stepping out of their Delusional World; locating the trigger issue within the youth in general and in a given youth in particular; what it takes to get to the trigger issue; and the duties of the youth to help in this regard. Let us explore what "Play" is all about so that information can be used to either make Mentees' problems less bad or to bring about beneficial change. Can you imagine that the inner recesses of a human's mind is like a collection of different colored animal sponges joined at their base and looking like one big sponge? Despite being animals, sponges never move around; have no sense organs; and capture food from the water around it by means of tiny openings all over the outside of the sponge. Sponges reproduce in a sexual manner and by budding cells growing out from the body. While feeding, a given sponge grows by taking on the features of a sieve, as cell masses change into canals connecting the exterior with its interior. As a result the mouths and tiny pores on the outside lead into a network of large and small tubes. Let us liken the inner recesses of the mind of a struggling Black youth to a big sponge consisting of a collection of green, brown, yellow, red, orange, and white sponges. Let us say the green sponge contains that youth's collective lifetime experiences; the brown, the collective unconscious of that youth's family line; the yellow, the collective unconscious of that youth's race Ancestors; the red, that youth's human race Ancestors; the orange, that youth's Karma or Soul Experiences; and the white, that filled with what is from God's mind. These sponges, along with other mental contributors from other parts of the brain, represent that youth's "Mind Committee"--any of which could be dominant at a certain time. Self-Mastery is allowing the right one to consistently dominate. The green sponge (a struggling Black youth's life experiences) is almost filled with delusions locked inside its inner recesses. Those delusions are the result of all that has happened to these youth directly and to their loved ones since slavery indirectly. Superimposed on this is that their life's game of chance is played so that the odds are rigged against them by those who "play hardball for keeps (playing aggressively, seriously, competitively, and with evilness) and by a lack of experience in how to deal with these types of problems. The resultant barriers placed around that green sponge are formidable. What I believe will unlock the entrance is to disconnect or detach or dissociate from those delusional contents. Since Instinct Play causes such a disconnection or detachment or dissociation from the inner recesses of the mind, it can thereby help a boy's mind, along with guidance of the Mentor, to become free. Once freed, the mind will be receptive to new and better information for self-improvement. One reason is that Instinct Play is the characteristic of all worthwhile human learning and human relationships. Inherently it has an interest in things in themselves and a playful, idle desire to know them as they are and what they do and how they appear -- and not because that knowledge directly or immediately helps in other aspects of life. This is what is desired to change the mental course these youth are on and to keep the channels open for continued self-cultivation.

POETIC: "*Poetic*" encapsulates an art of ambiguity in the Symbolic complexity and depth of self-expression + the interweaving of ones Intellect and Pure Feelings by imagination + the resulting aura derived from the mosaic pieces of the Spiritual Elements so as to achieve an embellished effect and imply its allegory consequences. Here, *Logic* is sentiments (thoughts wrapped in emotions) that appeal, via pre-birth Emotions, to the intellect of people under its influence. A way these Spiritual Feeling were honed by the Enslaved was out of the overwhelming cruelty they all faced daily. That necessitated having Compassion for their fellows being tortured—a Compassion that *is the direct perception of the "what it is" aspects of pre-birth Emotions' Reality*—called *Knowledge*. This Knowing occurs in the absence of Thought so as to see things the way they really are—i.e. One in Being--so as to provide the path to a complete awareness of the interrelatedness of all of the Enslaved by their God given "Sameness Genetics". Presumably my ex-Slave customers lived by African Tradition's staying within and evolving out of the Spiritual Elements. See Common Sense

POETIC AFRICAN LOGIC: Poetry in African Tradition is creative imaginative expressions of the Spiritual Elements in Metaphysical manners. "*Poetic*" encapsulates an art of ambiguity in the Symbolic complexity and depth of self-expression + interweaving of Intellect and Pure Emotions (Spiritual Feelings) + imagination + aura so as to achieve an embellished effect and imply its allegory consequences. *Logic*, as used here, is sentiments (thoughts wrapped in emotions) that appeal to the intellect of the people by way of Pure Emotions. Since African Logic is *Poetical Order*--the order of Art--it awakens ones reality-beyond-meaning so as to experience a non-thought, non-feeling interior impact. As used here, *Poetic Logic* is the "Check and Balance" of Pure Emotions (without Acquired Emotions) and ones Intellect that remains within and operates out of the Spiritual Elements (without External World oriented Thought Structures). The Intellect Reasoning deals with Matter which has to be organized to put it all involved into a Concept. All Concept formations require creating a method to guide the process. These methods may be non-reproducible or placed into a Patterned Tool for transfer into other situations. Such a Concept guide is Affect Symbolic Imagery (ASI) since it uses African (not European) Supernatural Language. This is concrete reasoning with ones Pure Emotions and Intellect within the context of the Supernatural aspects contained in *Figures of Communication* (FOC), generates a Surreal mindset. The payload of that impact causes one to become disengaged from ones mentality status quo and assume a mental order of creative Artful structured thinking.

Because ASI helps in revealing the truth more vividly than do most literal statements, it is the best way to expand the Scholar's Consciousness. The Surreal straddles Reality and Fantasy—a straddling that designs *symbolic messages which disregard the limitations and boundaries of human thought in order to impart ideas of the indescribable*—a straddling with carries the symbolic messages with it as it moves horizontally by means of presenting a presumed parallel Truth to illustrate what reverberates out of a Circumstantial Truth. Through these Symbols one enters emotionally into contact with ones deepest inner Self, with other Cosmic Organism creatures and creations, and with God. From replacing being mentally disengaged from the limitations of routine thought over to a Free Mind that is in the flow of the Processes of Nature, one is able to benefit from the awesome Wisdom and Power behind what it takes to manage the infinite complexity of the mind and life support functions. One is now operating out of an Intellect orchestrated by pre-birth Emotions and they lead to insights. The result is the illustration of the Feature of the Essence and its enhancement by elaborating on its Metaphysical aspects so as to provide certain Circumstantial Insights inside the Esoteric Unknown. Proper use of these insights enables one to now poetically synthesize all existing pertinent high quality aspects involved in the mental activity. By both being a "check and balance" on each other ensures these cultivated natural Endowments stay in the flow of the Spiritual Elements. This naturally means one is also in tune with the Cosmic Organism and stays within the Processes of Nature. That flowing Harmony establishes the settings for, and then having the proper relationships with and behaviors towards humans, animals, and God. Throughout this process, the FOC's Symbol structure generates new and varied awareness of the inner meaning of what is ordinarily overlooked or inadequately thought about or gives a new point of view or, at an extremely high level of Synthesis, *to see the abstract unity and interdependence between all independent real things--and to establish Truth from mathematically determined Spiritual Principles*. Each of these carries the potential for providing life-shaping or life-changing meanings or that pave the way for better dealings with Reality itself. By living its mathematical Principles, such poetic motions flowed into Africans' lifestyle of thinking and humor.

An analogy is an artist who gathers from ones inner and/or outer world Senses as well as from ones Memory of experiences and of reflections so as to "see" a glob of color—a glob which is easily integrated into ones thinking patterns. The resultant "oneness" of the artist's thinking patterns and the glob of color is an efficient and effective way to arrive at a meaningful work product. The keystone of this Poetic Reasoning is that by the artist (or creator) knowing its source and thus its "what it is" Essence and the nature of its "what it is," a Foundation is presented. Upon that Foundation the intended message can be built into a mathematically ordered Thought Structure. It is effective if the desired comparison conveys the details of the Sender message and its associations which thereby enhance the desired impact. Such is known by an apprehension of the "what it is" but about which one cannot get ones mind around. What attracts and influences the maintenance of *Poetical Order of Spiritual Elements "packages"* is that Poetic Logic gives off an Aura and an Atmosphere of what comes out of the Truth. Its Efficiency (done quickly) and Effectiveness (done right) is enhanced by its nature of being like a radar beacon-like whose corresponding vibrational force connects with the human's Soul's Spiritual Elements "Trademark". The meshing of those two awaken ones reality-beyond-meaning so as to cause one to experience a non-thought, non-feeling interior impact. A Philosophical or Logic example is Indescribable Spiritually based Axioms.

POETIC THINKING—it follows the pattern of Art

POETIC LOGIC ORIGIN: An illustration of the "Big Picture" of African Logic within the setting of Essence of the Divine Logos is the symbolized god Ra, the Holy Spirit, providing the words through which the Will of the Immaterial Self (Soul or Divine Consciousness) is manifest. According to the "Book of Knowing the Creations of Ra," the scenario pertaining to the Divine Logos' *Verbum—i.e.* the outward expression or effect of the ever concealed God Source Cause (James, Stolen Legacy p140)--illustrates Poetic Logic. Such an expressive sound was: "I brought into my mouth my own name, that is to say, a word of power, and I even came into Being" (meaning a transformation from the Subjective Realm of the Cosmos into an Objective Being). Ancient African Sages interpreted this to mean "*The Word" itself is the Divine Presence, its power, and its manifestation.* The Divine Presence, being transcendental of time and space, is beyond naming, images, or concepts--hence the reason for no pictures of God in African Tradition. From this mythical dogma, the idea of divine kingship became established. The birth of the Divine Child Horus was the reincarnation of Asar (Osiris), his father. In turn, Osiris was an incarnation of the High God Ra. *Asar, Aset and their child Horus was the original Holy Trinity* and that Ancient African Bible concept was stolen by Europeans converted into images of a European likeness. Nevertheless, both mythical dogmas from which the African Holy Trinity gave rise to the idea of divine kingship—i.e. each king being a symbol literally of the mythical and mystically Hermetic (i.e. Tehuti) order--a reflection of the original all-pervasive light--known as the *Horian Logos*--a light containing universal energy coming from God's mind and divine intelligence. It was about Divine Consciousness embodied in a perfected (Enlightened) human (Ashby, African Origins, p. 408) who, thereafter, was immortal (Bynam, African Unconscious, p. 140, 290). Poetic Logic is a product of the Cosmic Mind, as manifested inside the human mind by the Spiritual Elements and its offspring (e.g. Beauty). Its emphasizes FOC Symbolic Vehicles to convey thoughts about unrealistic things containing payload Messages concerning the Esoteric and the Mysteries—mostly dealing with real heavenly life-shaping concepts unable to be grasped completely or even partially by the human mind. Examples include things like the Unknown things about God; the things belonging to God; and the things revealed by God to humans; like realizations of and ideas about the infinite, the Eternal, the Unchanging Certainties; about insights for guiding living practices. FOC disregard the limitations and boundaries of human thought in order to insert Affect Symbolic Imagery (ASI). This is because it is natural for the human mind to readily receive and think in terms of mental pictures which fashion summaries and memories about the Thing at hand. Hence, Reasoning is greatly enhanced by Poetic Logic's pondering of each issue's aspect--on every angel and side; on each angle of each side; and on both sides of each angle. In persistent Truth seeking, a bonus is the by-products of Reflective Thinking providing corresponding inferred Patterns and Concepts.

POETIC LOGIC'S CIRCUMUNSTANTIAL TRUTHS IMPACT HUMAN SOULS: Humans' minds are incapable of ever knowing all or complete Truths of Sekhem, the Cosmic Spiritual Force. Yet, *by apprehending their minds were God given and also emitted vibrations,* even early Africans never doubted the power of their minds to grasp the ultimate Truths and Realities about the laws of Nature. This started when *Primitive Africans originated the Supernatural* by starting with Superstitions, their made-up stories to explain Spiritual, Metaphysical, and Physical realms evolved in to a Science that saw into realistic Spirituality. Thereafter, African Spirituality was considered as an Unseen Science. In the interim, Very Ancient African Sages came as close as is humanly possible by doing incredible things leading to Circumstantial Truths—and those Truths have stood the test of time. Ramifications of their processes led to Figures of Communications inside Metaphors, Allegories, Personifications, Similes, and the like. In turn, these were used as alternate Truth paths to the Unseen and Un-seeable.

POETIC SUPERNATURAL LANGUAGE CLASSES: What happens inside the human mind as a result of a mind absorbing Affect Symbolic Imagery includes the following Classes: *Metaphors* (equates unlike things by implication), *Simile (*the abstract or suggestive aspect is directly expressed), *Allegories* (a hidden story within an obvious story), *Fables* (animals impersonating humans to impart a moral), *Personification* (making a lifeless or abstract thing alive), *Analogies* (explaining something unfamiliar by comparing it to something familiar), *Legend* (a story, above mere fiction, combining fact and personified spiritual concepts), and *Symbols* (symbolic messages disregard the limitations and boundaries of human thought in order to impart ideas of the indescribable). All of these follow an acceptable path towards a Logical Reality in ways other than Reasoning. An example of Personification is Aesop's Fables, stories of animals simulating humans of wide ranging qualities for teaching children humor, tragedy, and morals. Aesop (620 BC)--the superstar of fables possessing a moral message--was an Ethiopian, and not Greek as Europeans advertise. For example, by Metaphors operating in Imaginary Supernatural Realms but within the context African Logic that pertains to Corresponding things, a great deal of flexibility is allowed for creative explanations.

POETIC NATURE OF FIGURES OF COMMUNICATION: The way Figures of Communication work is by ones mind blends into the thing and thereby switches from Thought to Feelings. Now one has eased into "the Zone" of Reality so that everything happening inside and outside ones Selfhood is experienced as a flowing harmony of which one is a part. At that point focusing gets easier and one gains a sense of control over what is being viewed. All of these Figures of Communication share in common: *(1) the comparing two quite different things that are similar in at least one essential characteristic to give an Underlying essence; (2) the Underlying essence leap barriers to straddle two or more planes of existences that can be extra-mundane (out of this reality world) or extra-territorial (above land and waters); (3) erases time and space to wipe out long ago so as to be in the 'here and now,' while still remaining far away; (4) can unite the invisible and the visible; (5) fashion concepts outside the boundaries of the ordinary use of words in order to explain some fundamental but unexplainable aspect of human nature; (6) endows the mind and the Sentiments (thoughtful deliberations colored by emotions) with a sense of participation in a field of meaning; (7) the transformation of the Sender's message into symbolic messages which disregard the limitations and boundaries of human thought; (8) convey the "Aliveness" contained in some abstract or lifeless thing; (9) provide paths for people to fashion ideas concerning incomprehensible subjects; (10) possess the power to transform ones thinking about the hidden and mysterious into a clear and orderly picture of a thing's origin; (11) speak the language of the Receiver--in words, meanings, tones, rhythm; (12) convey "larger than life" concepts--meaning larger than the sum scope of what they represent; and (13) able to link whatever touched the heart of the people with the mystical.*

POETIC ALTERNATE SUPERNATURAL TRUTH PATHS: The African Bible explains African Tradition's Supernatural Science that gives insight into Esoteric Spirituality. The process has always started out of their Spiritual Elements Philosophy of Life (POL) Base. Alternate routes of Truths into the Esoteric is conveyed by African Tradition's POL Knowledge with the focused message being the "what it is" while Poetic Logic aspects are use to elaborate on the "what it does," and the "how it appears" of the Thing's Essence. The method African Groits (storytellers) used to make this understandable to African people was to explain the higher level Circumstantial Truths by means of the "*Poetic Logic*" contained in Affect Symbolic Imagery (ASI). This is the use of Figures of Communication as the means to its attainment. Its African Metaphors specialize in shedding light on realism concepts that are either unknowable or that cannot be known by the human mind. Whether the payload is to be conveyed for establishing the familiar within areas of realism, distortion, and/or fantasy or to explore the difficult so as to stimulate paths into new realms for persuading, informing, entertaining, expressing, sharing, teaching, instructing, educating, training, or serving as a call to action, "*Poetic Logic*" is the key. *Such "Poetic Logic,"* by substituting out God, the Divine, or the Spiritual with Metaphysical sign replacements is simply a display of Qualitative Algebra. The feat of "Logic" is to use signs of the real to represent the real itself. That merely creates an alternate system of equivalence of binary opposites and of combinatory algebra which *features a form of concrete reasoning. That reasoning moves horizontally by means of presenting a presumed parallel Truth to illustrate what reverberates out of a Circumstantial Truth (i.e. a Sample of what is in the Esoteric).* Since Poetic Logic ingredients are an Association of Ideas or Thoughts about real "*Concrete*" *Things* having been harmoniously meshed into its/their Metaphysical Essence (i.e. irreducible), this combination of familiar experiences of reality and the perceiving of Abstracts or Abstractions of the Associated Ideas enables one to connect and unify Events and Things that may differ widely in form and external appearance. Within this context, 'Concreteness' has no clear definition but often refers to: (1) an immediate experience of realities—whether of Unbounded, Partially Bounded, or Bounded physical objects themselves; (2) belonging to or standing for actual See-able or Physically realizable things (e.g. sensations); and (3) the degree of pictorial resemblance an Icon Image bears to its *referent* (real world counterpart). An example is the Family doing things together and helping each other. The key point: *NOTHING OF A EUROPEAN NATURE HAS ANY PLACE IN AFRICAN POETIC LOGIC*!!!

POETIC LOGIC AFRICAN SUPERNATURAL METAPHORS: African Groits explained the higher level Circumstantial Truths by means of "*Poetic Logic*" Metaphors. By Metaphors operating inside Supernatural Realms allows for a great deal of flexibility in dealing with any issue, particularly concerning Axioms (self-evident Truths) above ones ability to put into words for others' understanding. Since there are flowers that resemble animals and humans, one might compare the shape of an orchid flower to being like a female organ and the only way to describe the beauty of it is by the metaphor of a pretty woman. However, one is unsatisfied from not being able to use anything but such limited English words as pretty, beautiful, attractive and these words are far less powerful than the true expression of these flowers. But note how the comparison between a flower and a woman are of a similar nature and in the same general "ballpark," as opposed to being in different "ballparks" because one concerns realism and the other, distortion or fantasy. This I call a Type I "*Poetic Logic*" Metaphor -- *a designed Symbol that activates unrealized Truths*. Type I is applicable for handling whatever Truths one cannot get ones mind around. Rather than trying to understand the Truth by putting boundaries on it, the idea is to convey its boundlessness with comparisons of grandeur by means of something else. Support can be added by Type II or "*Prop Poetic Logic*" (see Halo below) -- i.e. concrete reasoning that moves horizontally by means of presenting a presumed parallel Truth to illustrate what reverberates out of a Circumstantial Truth. It is effective if it conveys the desired comparison as well as the details and associative comparisons of the primary comparison in enhancing the desired effect. To elaborate, Ancient Africans resorted to Type I "Poetic Logic" Metaphors for several reasons. First was the well-established success of African Sages and Shaman entering a trance state by deep "pot-belly shaped" diaphragmatic breathing so as to withdraw the focal point of consciousness from their senses and induce a state in which their mental wakefulness would be as much as 2 to 50 times more than the norm (Amen, Metu Neter I:168). By so doing they would be "Inspired" (in + breath or spirit animation) into an "awakening by divine influence" in their Eternal Soul. Second, Type I "*Poetic Logic*" *Metaphors* convey an aura or the atmosphere of what comes out of the Truth about which one cannot get ones mind around. An example is Indescribable Axioms. Third, the tool for instituting the Cause of Type I "Poetic Logic" Metaphors is a *Word Designed Symbol*. This Symbol represents the aura or the atmosphere of the Indescribable Axiom. Because of the Spiritual Truths already dormant inside ones Selfhood, the appropriateness of the Word Designed Symbol comes from its ability to "ring true" and thereby awaken the dormant inner Selfhood Spiritual Truth.

In keeping with the Law of Opposites this Symbol must be of the same nature as the Spiritual Truth as well as having correspondence. Fourth is the Consequence. A feature of Afrocentric People is they know the Truth when they hear it. When one is open to higher inner spiritual guidance and is willingly led by the Spirit, some perception of Truth higher than the Intellect will be passed on to ones conscious mind—a Truth it has been able to work out for itself. Each exercise in Dialectic or in Trance cultivated and sharpened Ancient Africans' Intuition (meaning to "Learn from within") abilities. Such intuition is not the Spirit itself but is operating through one of its human owner's channels of communication. A consequence of this may cause one to take a stand because ones "conscience" says it is the "Right" thing to do. Yet one cannot put words on "Why." When put these four together, *the Cosmic "Spiritual Realm" is thought of as the "Aura" of God*. Thus, a "Spiritual Realm metaphor may cause the ringing of an inner Truth about God in someone's mind. A consequence of skilled *Dialectic* is abstracting the essence of things so as to get to Principles which can then be arranged/rearranged and combined/recombined in various ways. Next, each combination can be manipulated and maneuvered into creative workable solutions. Using this method is what enabled Black nations to forge civilizations and cultures far ahead of Eastern nations and far, far ahead of the West. Please pause to allow the Type I "*Poetic Logic*" *Metaphors* concept to "soak in." It is important in developing Spiritual Common Sense CT in a manner that keeps one from being stumped and unable to move forward.

POSSIBLE: PROBABLE (after testing it has the appearance of truth but remaining room for doubt makes it SEEM or "likely" be true). Next down is POSSIBLE (capable of happening, as in saying it is possible that it will rain today). FEASIBLE--capable of being done—is below Possible.

POST-TRAUMATIC DISTRESS SYNDROME: When community violence becomes a recurring part of day-to-day life for youth, the sense of safety and security needed for normal development can collapse or never fully develop. Additionally, when chronic violence and eminent danger replace safety in a child's world and are combined with cultural, social, and economic risk factors, the child becomes at risk for developing emotional and behavioral disorders such as post-traumatic Distress Syndrome (PTDS). Thus, the effects of violence are combined with the stress of living with institutionalized poverty, racism, and oppression. Despite these tremendous stressors, some children appear to be less affected than others. Children's experiences of violence depend on their families' ability to act as barriers to the violence and the quality of family relationships and other social support resources available. However, the buffering effect becomes less powerful as children mature. Episodes of chronic, enduring interpersonal violence put children at higher risk for developing hyper-sensitivity to the racial context—including blatant forms of discrimination, subtle innuendoes and slights from individual micro-aggressions, and institutional racism—all contributory to their self-assessments which to experiences of invisibility in daily life by blending into the Crowd as an addict. Brain scans of children and teenagers with PTDS show male/female structural differences in a part of the Insula-- called the anterior circular sulcus--a brain region detector of body cues. It processes emotions and empathy so as to help integrate feelings, actions, and several other brain functions but differences more prominent in females, possibly because they tend to be Right Brain dominant; are weaker in strength for self-defense; and are instinctually tuned to care themselves and their babies. The *Insula* normally changes during childhood and adolescence, with smaller insula volume typically seen as children and teenagers grow older. The afflicted may experience flashbacks of traumatic events; may avoid places, people and things that remind them of the trauma; and may suffer a variety of other problems, including social withdrawal and difficulty sleeping or concentrating.

PTDS' high levels of chronic Distress hormones causes delayed learning in toddlers; spur brains to develop too fast; accelerate cortical aging of the insula in girls; contribute to early puberty in girls; and play into differences between the sexes in regulating emotions—necessitating different forms of management. This is in keeping with my research on the Brain resulting from the "Brain Switch" at the moment the Fishnet was thrown over the free Africans in Africa to begin Enslavement. This switch was from each Enslaved immediately stop using their total brain for thinking over using only their Emergency Instinct (non-thoughtful) Brain. No Enslaved ever recovered back to using her/his entire brain. However, once the Enslaved accommodated to the horrors of slavery, they all settled into operating out of their Omnibus brain. The Omnibus brain is the thoughtful part of the Emergency "Fight, Flight, Fright" brain. This brain pattern usage was culturally transferred so as to account for today's displays of Poor Academia, the "Negro Diseases, the "Fragile Black Baby" Syndrome (from Mothers being hyperemotional and not always calm), and "Inside-Out" thinking (i.e. "voting against themselves"—protecting the oppressors—and clinging to being in the Status Quo, with no Courage to start self-improvement). A smaller percentage of Black People did recover their full thinking ability skills. Yet, most of them are socialized into both the bad Black Community Customs as well as the highly destructive Europeans Supernatural concepts (e.g. Non-Rational thinking rather than African Traditions' Mathematical thinking). Even though many of these Black People do "okay," they cannot break through to their full potential until they give up both the negative Black Community Customs (e.g. being "Me" oriented rather than "ME/ WE"? as well as to completely discard everything that is about Europeans Supernaturals "Anything"—especially getting rid of all Indifference, chronic Anger/Rage, Hate, and leanings toward Evil ways.

POSTULATES: *Postulates* are voluntarily accepted assumptions which, when agreed upon by the experts in a certain science, become its conventional basis. Presume implies some justification by way of practice or example or logical procedure. All three—Assume, Postulate, and Presume are in the family of "Guess," Think, Reckon, and Expect. *Postulates* are voluntarily accepted assumptions which, when agreed upon by the experts in a certain science, become its conventional basis. If a Postulate is in the Physical realm, it may or may not start from Truth. Still, it cannot start from Truth or Reality if it derives out of the Supernatural. See Definitions; Word Details; Conjectures; Postulates; Premise; Presume; Hypothesis

POTENCY: Originally, Aristotle distinguished three aspects of *Potency*: as a source of change; as a capacity of performing; and as a state in virtue of which things are unchanging by themselves.

POWER: Power implies inherent potency, ability, capacity. During C8 AD, the ability to do things, as in the potent (the physical capacity to use an object) came into power. The Romance language shift factors led to its C13 English 'to make powerful'; then strengthen (1540); then powerhouse (1881); then 'supply with power' (1898). Meanwhile, and particularly in C20, the meaning of "Power" extended in various directions -- e.g. numbers raised to the second power; horse-power; the powers among the orders of angels; and Black Power (1966). With respect to humans, "*Capacity*" (the power to receive) includes power + Ability. "*Ability*"--the inherent power to do—i.e. improved with exercise implies a Faculty (an inherent Selfhood Quality) to perform acts in the 'here and now' without much training or education. The idea of power within the Objective Realms embraces notions of integrity and extreme self-awareness, defensive concentration of forces, appropriation and domination of the environment, and effulgence. "*Power Function*"--statistical index of whether or not a given hypothesis should be rejected at a given level of risk when other related hypotheses are assumed as true. "*Power Test*" is a test used to measure the level of achievement an individual can reach. See Authority

PRE-FEASIBLE: the realm of *"Wishes"* (hoping for the unattainable or the non-existent)

PREMISE: A *"Premise"* is a statement accepted as a fact--making no further inquiry concerning the truth of the same; as a basis for further reasoning; and yet it may be true, distorted, or fantasy. European premises based on observation and give conclusions via Inductions (generalizations from observed specifics) cannot be true (because no human observation sees even all of the obvious) and yet are used to establish the premise for reasoning that will assume to be true. The African way of assigning a proposition to be used as a premise is first examined according to the African Laws of intra-relationships and inter-relationships. For example, one looks at a human's functions in the world, framed by her/his interrelationship with God, the environment and other creatures, which determine ones makeup (form/function relationship) in order to arrive at the proper proposition to be used as the premise in all logical thinking regarding humans. See Definitions; Word Details; Conjectures; Postulates; Premise; Presume; Hypothesis

PREPARE: (Old English) "Tools" (devices to do work), as in what contributes to getting a job done.

PRESUME: *Presume* implies some justification by way of practice or example or logical procedure. See Definitions; Word Details; Conjectures; Postulates; Premise; Presume; Hypothesis

PRESUPPOSITIONS: *Presuppositions,* under which these terms are encompassed, is a thing taken for granted or assumed. It is always best to assume that a Proposition, Postulate, Premise, Assumption, or Presumption is distorted, or false—based upon unexamined Assumptions and doubt.

From logical or non-rational evolutions of Presuppositions come Effects from being used in Creativity, Conclusions, Inferences, Actions, Consequences, and Results. How good are ones Presuppositions Bases depends upon the Source of the ingredients involved + the proper selection of the ingredients + the nature and soundness of the ingredients + the skill and method used to make up a workable definition from the Ingredient + how properly were the Units in each Concept maneuvered and manipulated to arrive at the resultant Presuppositions. The "Big Picture" Result either generates harmony or the chaos of mental disintegration. Invalid Concepts have integrated errors, contradictions, or false propositions and that makes for bad Effects and Consequences. All of this is flawed thinking in African Tradition for all thinking processes must stay within and evolve out of the Spiritual Element—and not be off to the tiniest of a degree. The doubt at the core of these "Guesses" blocks entering the African Divine Logos Path. See Denotations vs. Connotations; Word Details; Definitions; Hypothesis

PRIMORDIAL: present prior to the beginning of time/space--before anything was created--not caused or created by any circumstance state of existence. Since "Black"/"Dark" were made by God--and since "Black" is associated with God, "Black" symbolizes dawn, before sunrise, and the state of searching the un-manifest and each potential. Ancient Africans said this same Cosmic plane of existence resides in a human's mind. Here again, the Ocean of Nun state of absolute Darkness (Kekui)

PRIMORDIAL IMAGES: also called Dominants, Imago's, Mythological Images, Icon Behavior Patterns—i.e. root displays of the Cosmic Mind acting in fashioning patterns or being models for the production of *Prototypes*.

PRIMORDIAL SUBSTANCE: God's androgynic protoplast—the 'Oneness' foundation of potentiality from which all 'Things' emerge, called "the Path".

PRINCIPLE--AFRICAN TRADITION: "Principle" is a synonym for ingredients in Essence because it means foundation or bottom or beginning or essential or primary law or doctrine. a principle is a bottom or origin or essential upon which successive thoughts or facts spring. Principles are the basics at the starting gate for learning or teaching. *Principles of African Tradition give more general and specific information—in smaller packages—and at a faster rate than any other method of thinking. Principles are pieces of the Spiritual Elements in "Packages" and located on different planes of existence.* Principles derive from the Cosmic Genetics—i.e. Unconditional Love, Truth, Reality, and the Natural—and each Principle has this Spiritual Elements Essence. And that makes Principles unchanging realities. To "see" this, one must step behind ones Sensory (superficial) Consciousness so as to be bathed by the Spiritual Energy present in ones Divine Consciousness, a reflection of the Cosmic Consciousness. Then one realizes all of reality is connected into a Cosmic Unity—like a Cosmic Web. By serving as Elements, Principles basic differentiations are upon and of which all Entities are built up. This applies, as long as they stay within the Spiritual Elements, to *Absolute Unchanging Principles* in the Immaterial (Spiritual) Realm, *Relatively Fixed Principles* in the Intangible (Sublime) Realm, and Hum*an-made Principles* comprising the Tangible (Material World) Realm. Principles can be imaged in several ways. One is being derived out of the Truth-Tree. Thus, it has subdivisions of Seed, Root, Trunk, Branch, Leaf, and Fruit types—any present on any Cosmic Plane of Existence. Second is to liken Principles to strings in a fishnet—with the fishnet representing the Cosmic Spiritual Elements Web. Third, if that Cosmic Web's Interchange looked like a fishnet, a Principle would be one of its strings—a general Rightness for Life Living on which other "strings" depend—whether in Spiritual, Metaphysical, and/or Physical realms. There are very few principles in the Cosmos and they are capable of being combined/recombined and arranged/rearranged so as to create different forms on any plane of Cosmic Existence. That is the explanation for a human's five basic natures: (1) Spiritual Human Nature; (2) *"Primary" Physical Human Nature*--i.e. bodily processes and the restorative powers of the body; (3) *"Second" Nature,* consisting of what is absorbed from socialization; (4) *"Tertiary" Nature*--the "Self-Made I'll do it my way" person; and (5) Karma. As long as these operate out of ones Real Self, all of these have Correspondence.

Similarly, when all Principles have Correspondence with the Cosmic Web, and when one "knows" the truth of any of God's creatures or creations on any Earth World plane, then that truth can be used to explain the Unknown on a Spiritual plane -- or vice versa. In other words, to discover what something is on Earth gives a clue as to its corresponding thing in the Unseen Realm. That is the concept of Circumstance within the context of Correspondence—a way to comprehend the concept of *Wholism*. That is why Ancient Africans of 12,000 years back wrote on their temple walls: "Man, Know Thyself." From Divine Certainties, like-kind Divine Archetypes emanate Prototype off-spring. Within each Archetype are any given human's *Endowments* (i.e. natural qualities) and *Propensities* (in-born tendencies like ones capacities, abilities, and language). A human's Soul orchestrates ones Selfhood via Spiritual *Principles*--Archetypes derived from the Soul's Spiritual Elements Interchange. Spiritual Principles are pieces or immanent forms of the Spiritual Elements, in the way that a string is a vital part of its fishnet. *Immanent* implies each "string" is dwelling in and pervading and composed of each of the Spiritual Elements--meaning all represent indivisible differences arising out of and reproducing each other. Spiritual Principles are products of that Interchange which consists of a closed system of Divine Certainties erected upon an Unconditional Love Base. That Base can serve for the formation of ones Philosophy of Life (POL). Thus, Principles are both part of what forms the Spiritual Elements Interchange and what emanates out of them. A practical example is an idea evolving into a thought, like the way a Seed evolves into a flower.

PRINCIPLES: (unchanging realities) are ingredients within Essences and are of 3 main types: (1) Absolute Unchanging Principles are in the Immaterial (Spiritual) Realm; (2) Relatively Fixed Principles are in the Intangible (Sublime) Realm; and (3) Human-made Principles comprise the Tangible (Material World) Realm. To best understand these differences, it is vital to get oriented to African Tradition's Cosmic Base of the Interchange mentioned above, for that upon which all of the Cosmos arises and from which Principles derive. It started with the first Cosmic Force, called Sekhem, displaying the Ocean of Nun. This *Subjective realm* is also called "*Nothingness*"—the realm of Virtual (boundary-less) Being—which is the mother of all Being by it producing all Cosmic Organism Creatures and Creations. It is nameless, for it is greater than anything that can be named. It takes no action, in that it leaves Things alone. It supports all Things but does not take possession of them. It lets Things transform themselves. It does nothing and yet all Things are thereby done. Within it is an *Indivisible Quadriary present inside each of the Cosmic Creations and Creatures: (1) each Entity as a Spiritual Being; (2) each having separateness in manifestations in* their individual actions and appearances and with uniqueness in each; *and (3) all Entities and Ingredients united in interdependence* to serve the common goal of the Divine Plan. These 3 impart Correspondence between them all—meaning each Entity and Ingredient in the Cosmos contains mosaic pieces of the *Quadriary*. Thus, if a Principle is likened to a string in a tennis racket or a thread in a spider web, each would contain the *Quadriary*. An elaboration of 10 types of Principles were given in Bailey, Rekindling Black People's Genius. Whether in African or European Traditions (and the last 6 are most applicable to European CT), Principles are the 'raw ingredients' of Critical Thinking (CT). However, it is ones philosophy of life (POL) which best characterizes CT for ones POL, since it is about "What is For me and What is Against me." That is geared to promoting compatible positives and eliminating what are negatives. To briefly summarize those 10, *Essential Positive Principles* (Type IV) and *Essential Negative*

Principles (Type V) are human-made and can be interpreted in various ways. There is an element of flexibility in them in the face of new facts and better information. Type VI are *Mystery Principles* which people pursue and yet have no idea what they are. For example, they equate money with happiness and yet the acquiring of riches does not bring happiness. Type VII is the *Principle of Anti-Principle* which features "Me, Me, Me" people who do whatever it takes to acquire unfair advantages for themselves and unfair disadvantages for others.

They only follow the "here and now" without living life based upon Principles. Type VIII is *Hypocritical Principles. Hypocrisy* is a term meaning one acting out of the part of a character in a play—the masking over of ones Real Self or ones False Self which is in a different realm while playing a part for ones cult. Such is seen in politicians who claim: "I am my own man"!!!—as they await orders on how to vote. Whites who often complain the most about Black crime are criminals themselves. A random sampling of Whites showed 91% had committed fraud, consumer cheating, embezzlement, petty theft, and price-fixing—all of which cost the nation more than 3 times as much in lost property as such crimes as robbery or theft. Type IX—*Principles of Ignorance*. Whereas total *Ignorance* is not knowing that one does not know something at hand, a Secular *Mystery* is incomplete Ignorance in that one is aware of a "that it is" of a "Thing," but does not know its "what it is," "what it does," "how it appears," "how it is," "how it came about," or "where it is going." For either to be a principle means one does not desire to rise out of ignorance. By contrast, in African Tradition, "*Mysteries*" refer to the existence and ways of God and the Spirit (the material/energy part of being as opposed to the Self--the consciousness/will constituting a human's divinity). Adopting the motto: "what you don't know can't hurt you" means one can never know the whole mystery of Beauty or the sweetness of solitude or the profoundness of Thought. Type X—*Principles of Convenience* show most destructively in having "Flexible Morals." *When ones mind is in foundational chaos, one is self-absorbed with flexible morals to do what brings "Escapes."* This implies that people put virtues aside in self-interest situations, as in promising to pay back a rich person and then not do so because "the rich can afford it." Their problem is fearing not winning the battle without looking at what happens over the long haul. The truly moral will give up an advantage or take on a disadvantage in order to do the right thing so as to maintain Self-Greatness Certainty and be at Peace.

PRINCIPLES: (SPIRITUAL): a customized Mosaic inside the Cosmic Organism Interchange made into a unique pattern by pieces composed of varying proportions of the Spiritual Elements. Any Spiritual Principle can serve as a Base to underlie a given creature or creation.

PRIVATE SELFHOOD COMPONENTS: *Private Self* components "packaged" into such interlocking forms called: *Self-Greatness* (Spark of God), *Self-Knowing* ("Roots"--Cosmic Organism yoking), *Self-Faith* and *Self-Appreciation* (the "Trunk" whereby one esteems ones Substance and realizes the infinite inside ones finite body), and Branches and Leaves--ones Self-Trust (awareness of expanding capabilities; Keeping ones Word); Self-Curiosity (*discovers what is natural within oneself and what underlies what is natural* about oneself); Self-Empowerment (unlimited power from prior successes); Self-Respect (honoring ones earned self-worth and self-value traits); Self-Reliance (in charge and control of ones Selfhood, what one does, and the situation by knowing and using what is available); Self-Efficacy (believing one can get any unique job done; "I can do anything that is part of my Mission); and Self-Confidence (Sureness from empowerment). African Sages said a human's *Private Self Components,* orchestrated by its "First Wisdom" or First Knowledge, is in the birth gift flow of the Spiritual Elements. A human's *First Wisdom* is absolute true Intelligence which, upon properly developing its ingredients, is all one needs to handle the very toughest of life's problems. Ones four *Private Self Spiritual Self-Esteem* components are: *Self-Identity* (ones unchanging "sameness" concerning "Who I Am" and that imparts Self-Respect); *Self-Meaning* (the Spiritual Self-Greatness standard against which one can compare ones Self-Respect); and *Self-Love* ("ME/WE" as the Selfhood anchor which obeys Survival, Self-Protection,

Self-Preservation). Ones Private Self concerns Instinct Selfish acts of ones physical, mental, or spiritual survival, self-preservation, and self-protection (Bailey, Self-Protection Syndrome). These components are what fashion ones *Public Self Self-Esteem* components.

PROBABLE: after testing it has the appearance of truth but remaining room for doubt makes it SEEM or "likely" be true. Probable Opinions are like a *Rule of Thumb*--a rough and useful principle or method, based on experience rather than precisely accurate measures. What is "Likely" appeals to the reason as being worthy of belief because there are more points to favor believing than not believing. By using established past practices as a guideline for making a decision, "Probable" guides one in matters where one lacks Certainty. Next down is POSSIBLE (capable of happening, as in saying it is possible that it will rain today). FEASIBLE--capable of being done—is below Possible.

PROBABILITY: The more facts agreeing with the hypothesis, the greater the "Probability" degree

PROBLEM: C14 referred to a scholarly or scientific doubtful or difficult question proposed for an academic discussion, study, and scholarship, with an aim toward a solution. A *Problem* is a fact(s) lacking an acceptable explanation; is seemingly unusual; and fails to fit in with ones expectations or preconceptions. Features of the Viable Impossible include them being on the far end of the scale of problems because they are marked by being Complex, Involved, Intricate, and Intractable. Its subdivisions include: (1) *Riddle*--an ambiguous statement with a hidden meaning to be guessed by the mental acuteness; (2) *Conundrum*--a riddle whose answer involves a Pun--"When is a door not a door?"; A: When it's ajar"; (3) *Enigma*--one with a baffling or confusing hidden meaning, clear only to one who understands the allusion(s) therein. An Allusion--relying on suggestion and connotation by a causal or passing reference--is an extremely quick ways of expressing ones emotions to an in-group as well as creating in listeners shades of those same emotions--but only when the listeners are already familiar with the setting (e.g. history, literature, sayings, slang, people, events) alluded to--as, for example, family jokes; (4) *Paradox*--a view contradicting accepted opinion for seeming to be self-contradictory (even absurd). Closer inspection shows a truth reconciling the conflicting opposites: "I never found the companion that was so companionable as solitude" (Thoreau); (5) *Puzzle*--a question or problem intricate enough to be perplexing; (6) Mystery--something incomprehensible to human understanding.

PROCESS: (C14, go forward) a selection of ingredients that form into an organized set of operations for doing something. That set is a series of operations or events leading to achievement of a specific result. The way the series proceeds and is done can be: (1) mere doing; (2) doing with a purpose; (3) doing which follows a thought-out plan; and (4) idealizing doing which results from vivid imaging. Mathematical thinking which follows a Process--"advancing during a period of time." Throughout a flowing motion, a process is continuous activity consisting of a series of actions concerned with change--change of an organized or disorganized nature--change headed toward a goal or into a void--change capable of being categorized or not--change constructive or destructive. A given Process includes the first step of a *Purpose*--a selection of ingredients that formed into an organized set of operations for doing something.

PROFESSIONALISM: Egyptian temples of learning, called "*Per Ankh*" (life force) served not only as libraries and medical schools but also as temples, seminaries, and universities. African Sage teachers--by having explored the most hidden region of the Duat (Unconscious Mind) through Yoga and Meditation insisted students: (1) Listen to the wisdom teachings on the nature of reality (creation) and the nature of the self; (2) Reflect on those teachings and incorporating them into daily life; and (3) Meditate on the meaning of the teachings (Ashby, African Origins p. 458). By Sages no longer being caught up in the illusions of the world (information derived from the senses)—the loftiest goal of human life—they could teach Liberation, Heru-hood, Waking up (so as to see the reality beyond the physical world), Meeting Asar, Resurrection, Nirvana, Salvation. Salvation concerned the achievement of perfect obedience to God's Will so as to have Wisdom and preservation from evil (i.e. ignorance of God's Will). These would lead to union with God and a Soul released from a reincarnation need. Thus, anything Sages said was considered to be directly inspired by the Divine. One saying was: "well-established patterns that Challenge, also provide opportunities to discover ones inner resources for use in overcoming troubles. Hence, growing discoveries within ones deeper Self would urge such spiritual aspirations as to seek a Sage to assist in self-discovery by cultivating virtue. That is the reason Sages created the 42 Ma'at Philosophy injunctions--10 of which are called the Ten Commandments in the European Bible (Bailey, Ancient African Bible Messages). Then, for making fine distinctions to enhance good practical judgement required one seeing both sides of a problem, studying each side from various angles, and then analyzing each angle discovered for its advantages and disadvantages. In addition to arriving at such African scholarship, to fulfill the meaning of *Schools*—i.e. 'leisure used for education' and 'lecture-places'—they were also theaters. The performances in these theaters were exclusively of a religious nature since the Performing Arts, including Music, were held to be powerful and sacred endeavors. Because the whole purpose of these Schools was to impart spiritual teachings and evoke spiritual feelings, the most esoteric elements were performed in the temple's interior.

Otherwise, they were not allowed to be diluted and polluted by frivolous forms of entertainment since that only dealt with the "here and now" and without advancing one spiritually. Yet, when religious dramas (borrowed by Europeans under the title of "*Mystery Plays*") were performed outside in the temple's courtyard or between the pylons—they were the most important attraction of the festivals. Such were forerunners' of the African Ring Shout dances seen in today's diaspora. Spectators knew well the stories of the Myths being acted out and that was done to spur the messages aimed at promoting their meanings and purposes in life. One of the performed lecture teachings consisted of saying the *gods and goddesses (Neteru) are not realities but only windows into the transcendent—avenues by which ones mind and body energies may be channeled towards a higher, spiritual goal in life.* It was essential to live by virtues, as they would open and purify ones "Heart" in order to have magnanimous experiences paving the way to thereby transcend into Higher (Divinity) Self realms (Ashby, Book of Life p114, 338). Teaching were that Adversity is only overcome with wisdom and virtue—and *virtue is the first and most important quality to be develop by all desiring self-improvement.* Hence, one necessarily did "ME/WE" type Critical Thinking pertaining to whatever best served ones own Divine Self as well as those of other people—even if it involved "tough love." So, for ones Unconditional Love to serve the God spirit in others often required discipline, perhaps interpreted as harshness by the Receiver. But all situations required outward expressions of Nonaggression—i.e. cooperativeness shown by attempting to have good relations with and behaviors toward that fellow human. Such was exhibited by being compassionate, gentle, kind, affectionate, helpful, sociable, empathetic, gentle,—even if it went unrecognized or unappreciated. Thus, Selfless Service was given--without needing expecting, desiring to be thanked, rewarded, appreciated—and with the full realization that the friendship could be lost is Unconditional Love. *When displaying virtues supersede making money, then one has reached what it means to be Professional in African, not European, Tradition.* jabaileymd.com

PROGRAM—ORDERED: "Ordered Program"--refers to the maintenance of unity in the midst of increasing creation (differentiation)—a program which conforms in a series of small, graded steps to carry out approaches, methods, techniques, and manners so as to achieve specific functions.

PROGRAMMING: *Programming* consists of supplying information in accordance with a cult code so as to be learned in a series of small, graded steps aimed to carry out approaches, methods, techniques, and manners to subtly achieve specific functions or solve Fad problems.

PROJECTION: Hurling onto a scapegoat some "ugly" aspect taken out of ones own bad character in order to make it seem as if it is only the victim who has that "ugly" trait; the turning a personal inferiority in morals, intelligence, or the like into a perceived moral, intellectual, or otherwise deficiency in someone else)--the hurling something "ugly" within ones own character onto a victim (a scapegoat) in order to make it seem as if it is the victim who has that "ugly" trait. See Deflection

PROPOSITION: In European circles, when several units are put together in logical fashion, based upon the Disposition in the original Unit, a Proposition (or definitive declarative statements about a given subject) is formed. From the logical or non-rational evolution of Propositions come Effects. See Assumption; Theorem

PROOF: what is Probable. The C15 English word "*Proof*" meant tested value or power against something in order to establish something as complete, irresistible evidence; to demolish a point of contention; or to determine its position somewhere in-between the extremes. Proof, in turn, requires the presentation of Evidence that must be universally acceptable to all reasonable people--Evidence that cannot be argued away. *Evidence* is what tends to show a thing to be true. Proof may be present in Metaphysical or Objective Realms. That is how one can "KNOW" as opposed to "Believing." The world has been misled into believing that only European type Material World proof is valid and correct when that is not so. In fact, it is of an inferior quality compared to African Spiritual Proof. A job of Critical Thinking is to *find the assumption lurking behind the (quite valid) conclusion.* Europeans say mathematical proof is necessarily deductive. The series of Deductive arguments which lead to the Theorem is the "Proof." The expression of Knowledge requires Proof—the presentation of evidence that is universally acceptable to everyone—evidence that cannot be argued away. See Evidence; Scales

PROPENSITIES: propensities are a dispositional (a habitual mental tendency) appetite for "Good" as well as ones talents, capacities, abilities, and language.

PROPERTIES--SPIRITUAL SELVES vs. SUPERNATURAL CULTS: When humans first appeared on Earth in Africa 200,000 years ago, the subsequent 37 billion humans--past or present—have emanated from the same Underlying Essence "Genetics". *Essence* is the *"what it is" of a human and contains its "What and Why" Disposition* and its Essentials--the "what it does" and "how it appears" in doing its *"When and How" nature of operations.* The nature of an Essence is its *Character* and its displayed *Nature* is how each of its properties manifests its operations. The *Properties* consist of *Endowments* (i.e. natural qualities, like Human Nature) and *Propensities* (in-born tendencies, like a given human's capacities, abilities, and language). The Essence's Essentials are manifested in its Character (a "Sameness" offspring) as well as its Characteristic(s), Trait(s), and Feature(s). The *"What and Why" Disposition and Endowments* have an underlying "Sameness" of providing "ME/WE" and yet each manifests uniquely for each human. The Propensities come from the "Sameness" Cosmic Genetics but those "Genes" which are active and in customized combinations display Uniquely. The Essential's Character has the same nature as its Essence parent. How the Essence's Essentials Characteristic(s), Trait(s), and Feature(s) are presented to a human's Inner and Outer World realms is a matter of that human's choice. Options for selection are to allow ones Essence and its contents to flow naturally (like little children); to be orchestrated by Socialization or Brainwashing (like the Crowd and/or Victims); to be "Self-Made"; or a Combination. The "*Self-Made*" is in control and in charge of ones own "Mind Committee". It monitors and interprets the feedback extracted out of ones own Inner and Outer World realms of influence—whether by direct experiences, vicariously assessed experiences, ones memory, assessments, and External World impressions. If the "Self-Made" stay true to their Essence nature, they will remain in the flow of the Spiritual Elements and develop their think, feel, say, and do aspects of Life-Living out of it. In my case, this was aided by my wonderful all-Black community socializing me into African Tradition ways. European enslavers brainwashed Enslaved Africans out of African Tradition and then socialized most into inferior Supernatural ways.

The Supernaturals—those in opposition to the Spiritual Elements which, they say, makes them "superior"—have as their motto the well-known quotation in European sports and "games" of life: "*Winning isn't everything; it's the only thing*". And for them, the same is true of Socialization into a military style. Their only possible way of "winning" is by the GUN used in military fashion. The GUN permits Inhumanity displays of Indifference/Hate/Evil/Sadism (IHES) mindsets. Expressions of IHES are Kill/Take/Destroy/Dominate/Oppress/Control (KTDDOC)—all without accountability. If the "military" leaders and their Troops are likened to contents within a "Disaster Star," its "Halo" represents those under its influence—the "Slight" ones being closest to the "Disaster Star" and the "Mild"—the only salvageable ones--being farthest away. Within this White Superiority Ladder reigns what I call "*Civility*" (a congenial Deceptive tool to hide ones opposing true thoughts and emotions of what is presented). Its Alliances and Liaisons forms prevent cult members from being isolated from the Crowd. *Alliances* are mutually helpful participants who are psychologically and philosophically disconnected from each other—and yet feature the sharing of common character traits, like the IHES mindset. *Liaisons* are people who support like-kind people but lacking close associations between them.

This is for purposes of ensuring mutual understanding, unity of action, and especially prompt and effective network support so all can acquire a common goal. Such goals include greedily doing dishonorable things to acquire "Scarce Desirables". The common goal is to keep their most Envied feigned enemies in various forms of poverty while the perpetrators are exempt from prosecution or from having those same practices imposed on them. Their *Non-Rational thinking* (i.e. fettered IHES emotionally based) leads "Moderates" to "blame victims" and kill them whenever; "Slights" to say: "I do not want any public benefits for me to come if Blacks will benefit"; "Milds" to have reverse bias against "Slight" Whites; and "Extremes" to be against all in order to carry out the required forms of KTDDOC against any who do not comply—who have what they want—who prevent them from getting all they are after--or who oppose what they do.

PROPOSITION: *Propositions* set forth what is claimed to be truth in formal statements. Concepts are building blocks for propositions--definitive declarative statements about the subject. In European logic's practical application, Premises, like a *Postulate* or Proposition, it may or may not start from Truth if it is in the Physical realm and cannot start from Truth or Reality if it derives out of the Supernatural, the Divine, the Spiritual, or the Metaphysical. See Definitions; Word Details; Conjectures; Postulates; Premise; Presume; Hypothesis

PROTOTYPES: created Spiritual Elements manifestations which, in turn, create like-kind things; The Essence (with its Virtual Image and Disposition) is powered by Africans' *Law of Spiritual Creativity*, which says: by itself, a Spiritual Element reproduces itself to become the thing it makes, regardless of its new form. As the Entity descends on towards and, if so designated, into an Earth World level, this Law ensures an ongoing repetition of the original Idea-Form whose "Thought-Forces'" nature manifests as a compatible Prototype with each Archetype reproduction of becoming the Thing it makes. Ancient Africans considered Idea-Forces, representing Numbers, to be the essence of Harmony and therefore that Harmony was thought to be the basis of the Cosmos and of humans. Also, despite being located anywhere in the Cosmos, all of the Archetype's Prototype offspring are in accordance with the Law of Correspondence and the Laws of Nature. Thus, they were led to the inescapable conclusion that all of the harmonious independent Entity Patterns of the Cosmos—both gigantic and microscopic—both Seeable and Un-seeable--all working interdependently to maintain an orderly Cosmic Wholism had to be the product of the "Big Mind" of the Cosmic Force, Sekhem. The Truth of all of this being shown to be reproducible throughout the Cosmos makes it African Mathematical involved and I addressed its details in my book: African Tradition Wisdom vs. European Information. A simple display of it is the SOBMER Process

"PROVIDENCE": planning, doing, preparing, and perhaps expending largely to meet the future demand and "*Prudence*". Today, these are called *Foresight* (detecting and preparing for what is likely to happen in the future) and *Forethought* (careful planning to acquire yet unrealized beneficial realities). See *Discretion; Discernment; Perceiving*

PRUDENCE: watching, saving, guarding is a keystone—never engaging in the extremes—using the right thing at the right time—being oriented to "Aliveness" rather than "Excitement." If one cannot avoid striving for excitement, the Prudence will keep that from degenerating into folly and excess—the pavers of obsessions and compulsions as a means to escape some type of personal poverty. *Discernment* would draw out worthwhile information not easily seen or even being out of sight--so as to see and mark essential things. The Subtle form of Discerning requires *Penetration* (looking through, seeing beyond the surface) and *Perceiving* -- i.e. understand meanings and implications -- by the sight, or some other sense, or by the intellect so as to see a thing for what it really is under confusing or misleading appearances. *Discretion* is wise and proper discernment as to conduct, responsibility, or judgment from using good assessments, caution, and self-control.

PSEUDEPIGRAPHA: Ways of Oral Tradition--passing information down from "lip to ear"--had certain rules. In *Dialectic* (a dialogue between teacher and student to bring enlightenment to the student) profound things taught by the teacher were not usually written down by the teacher but instead by students often attributing to the teacher things never said by the teacher. Authors were not allowed to put their names on their works but instead to only attribute it to original sources or the spirit imparted to one. Pseudepigrapha was not considered dishonest back then, as it would be today. Unfortunately, identifying historical landmarks were not preserved. For example, the name of the Sage who originated a maxim might be replaced each time the story was told a century or more later -- and neither was the story written. Similar to recorded stories, oral stories were dramatically presented in order to make a point and not to be taken literally. Points were numerically listed for easy remembrance and elaboration.

PSEUDO-INTELLECTUALS: Pseudo-intellectual treat themselves to word devoid of meaning, as when starving people swallow clay to silence their empty stomachs. Those in a given area create a jargon that keeps them from being discovered that they do not know. Terminology is in the categories of being helpful in definitions and descriptions, or in the overflowing ragged category of being on the wrong track and misleading. The bad makes simple things complicated and the complicated is made incomprehensible so that chaos reigns. What derives from that is bursting with junk, written in a hopscotch style and checkered with uncontrollable parts that lead nowhere or that seethes in restless unintelligibility. A major problem with Europeans dealing with African Tradition concepts is they know no language but their own and that leads them into confusing African symbols with their own limited and low level thoughts so as to produce a monster. When there is no realistic explanation or when ideas fail, as for "Intelligence," they give it a name which immediately explains everything. Also, things are named of which one knows exists but that does not mean they are known because they are named. Some names are so clever or pleasing that people assume that means something all-embracing when in reality the word itself conveys but little. The vastness of the meanings of words and the guessing at what the reality is for which the name is associated prevents any attempts at researching which, in turn, then stifles all further curiosity about it. Rather that describe what can be known, the Greek idea is to describe what cannot be known. One Deceptive "SEEMs" Right Nuance is set up by "pseudo-intellects" using big words that have no meaningful definition that can be universally accepted—like "Objective" or "Concrete" Thought Bases—applied to debate realistic situations like an Unconditional Love Thought Base. Because of the element of doubt in the meaning of "Objective" or "Concrete" suspected by the naïve, because the Deceiver is speaking with such confident boldness, the naive might accept them as "close enough" to equate them to the Unconditional Love Base. That immediately switches the naïve from the "Truth-Track" over to the "Off-Track"—while Deceiver rapidly mention "exciting" or irritating things that shifts the naïve's mind to instantly focus on that.

The theme of that Fantasy is to assign "SEEMS" words to imply they are equivalent in meaning to Unconditional Love's soundness—so as to dissolve all of the substantial incompatible realities existing between them. A reinforcing nuance practice is to use vaguely defined words—if they are defined at all—to be in the the the misleading category of "Objective" or "Concrete" in order to "explain" what they mean. If that route is chosen, those words chosen to "simplify" their points are even more confusing and conflicting —a plot to cause one to "give up" trying to stay sharp and "give in" to the Deceiver. Another trick is to wrap their confused thoughts into likes/dislikes Emotions intended to elicit interpretations suitable to the Non-Rational's thinking power by getting the naïve to "play by unfamiliar rules." The point: Europeans' Proof and Evidence is falsely advertised to relate to the objective—which they falsely say is "the greatest". But since they have no way of knowing what the Truth is, their "Objective" is checkered with bits and pieces of what could be true, what is distorted, and the payload of what is fantasy. Regardless of the type of Evidence—whether good, bad, or indifferent—most people are willing to accept what does not harmoniously fit because they want things to be a certain way or because they intensely desire to conform to those in authority or because they are gullible and naïve or because of biases and prejudices. A Greek Formal Logic study will show most assumptions, particularly as used by Europeans today (e.g. Republicans), to be deliberately false in order to deceive people and play on their fears for self-interest purposes (e.g. to control their minds). They declare these as "Truth" and claim any who cannot get it to be "stupid" or need "Special Ed."

PSEUDO-TRUTHS: what people call Facts (human-made), Beliefs, Opinions, Superstitions, and Faith--are distortions of Reality.

PUBLIC: C15 "of the people." Overall they make up the Middle and Lower Classes—and are like sheep standing on hind-legs and whose judgment is like the results of playing the lottery. A special segment being the raw and partially developed humans who are most dangerous because of being most early influenced by Satanists leaders. Features of the Public is in being simple-minded in a Lower (animalistic) Self and Non-Rational thinking manner—always in the wrong, stupid, mean, selfish, spiteful, envious, and ungrateful—having neither shame nor gratitude—and always uncertain, like moving with the wind. They are taught by constant repetition of "Big Lies" told over a long period of time by those who know which "Public Piano Notes" to poke. After being habituated, take literally the things their Satanist leaders tell them; it only wants to hear what it has been orchestrated to want by undisclosed Satanist leaders; and having assigned people (e.g. the Media) to keep making up reassurances of their positions being right as well as to put barriers between them and what they should not see. Thus, willful ignorance rules. It has mob yearnings to be instructed, edified by "Excitement," pulled by the nose, and demands "either/or" certainties. They dislike the true and embrace the novel and charlatans. They act without thinking and consequently judge effects without attending to their causes. See Crowd

PUBLIC SELF COMPONENTS: Ones *Public Self Self-Esteem* components, arising out of ones Private Self Components, in turn, build: ones Public Self Components of Self-Concept (ones spotlighted qualities) and Self-Image (the "big picture" of oneself (Bailey, Self-Esteem). These are the springboard for handling life's most difficult trials and tribulations. Possessing Self-Trust in ones own unique ways of doing things while always remaining within and expressing out of the Spiritual Elements is an illustration of the Spiritual "Sameness/Uniqueness" Characteristic which Ancient Africans called Ma'at living—the form of Right Living that heads one to the Heaven Afterlife.

PUPIL: Ancient African "*Pupils*" referred to those under a teacher's close supervision when participating in higher religious education; "*Student,*" to those specializing in a branch of study in preparation for a profession; and *Scholar,* to "*giving oneself*" to learning intimate Spiritual Elements details concerning God's Laws.

Mortals (Initiates, Neophytes), probationary pupils who had not yet realized the Inner Vision, were instructed in the Sages' doctrines. The *Intelligences*--advanced students from having attained Inner Vision by getting a glimpse of Cosmic Consciousness—had thus achieved the *Mysticism Mind*--minds having the ability to intensely concentrate their Intellect Reasoning into their Pure Emotions.

PURPOSE IN LIFE OF PRIVATE SELF: one must fulfill *the Divine Plan of returning to ones Creator and use the difficulties one has in life as a tool to force out the divine powers within ones Selfhood so they can be cultivated to* evolve (go away from the center) in order to involute (come back to the center). In other words, every human's purpose in life is to advance from ones Lower (animalistic) Self (evoluting ones state of consciousness so as to surpass itself) in order to achieve ones Highest (Divinity) Self.

PURPOSE IN LIFE: *Purpose*--a selection of ingredients that formed into an organized set of operations for doing something. Its story has always been associated with the personal power and its surrounding aspects. "*Purpose*" (put forward; declare) is roughly the same as ones Calling in life. Ones Mission is to provide Selfless Service based upon ones Talent. That Talent is in one of four or some mixture of the four Spiritual Elements. The Selfless Service is done so as to conform to the goal of divine growth for both the "ME" and the "WE". Anything short of this, at its best, only provides for a somewhat satisfying life. "*Satisfaction*," as opposed to something being perfect and wonderful, implies ones work products, serves ones purpose as much in degree and in progress as one could reasonably advance them. The effect of having filled a particular need or expressed a specific work product achieved sort of what was desired while using fair achievement means. In reflecting, even if possible, one would not change much of what happened. Yet, the degree to which could improve being happy about it would be to approach utilizing ones full birth gift potential Endowments and Propensities. For that to happen requires superb Selfhood Order. The way Selfhood ordering is done is to "Know Thyself" (see Bailey, Ancient African Bible Messages for elaboration). Failing to get to "Know Thyself" is self-neglect in self-understanding and that means one is asleep in doing activities of daily living. The longer one sleeps the more one is directed away from oneself. The further one drifts away from ones Real Self and the Truth it provides, the more blind one is to ones own delusions and living in a Delusional world. One drifts helplessly, says Rand (Lexicon, p. 398), "at the mercy of any chance stimulus or any whim of the moment. He can enjoy nothing. He spends his life searching for some value which he will never find . . . The man without a purpose is a man who drifts at the mercy of random feelings or unidentified urges and is capable of any evil, because he is totally out of control of his own life . . . The man who has no purpose, but has to act, acts to destroy others. That is not the same thing as a productive or creative purpose." Still, one remains vaguely aware of not fulfilling ones purpose in life -- an awareness generating a continuous low grade dissatisfaction with oneself (see Seleem, Book of Life p23 for elaboration). To force oneself to face oneself is a fundamental part of the awakening process. But typically such people develop a superiority complex, as with missionaries, with a holy attitude, going over to poor countries for the intent of persuading them to adopt their Supernatural God and to break up all of their eon aged traditions. A favorite saying in the Black Community is that missionaries went to Africa with their Bible and eventually the Africans had their Bible and the visitors had their land. In African Tradition ones Purpose in life is selected out of the work the God-Spirit does in Nature. Ones Earth world purpose, continued African Sages, is about self-fulfillment by discovering and developing ones talents and skills and then finding the best niche where they can be shared with the universe for the benefit of all concerned. Ones Spiritual purpose is inner and outer directed. See Mission; Calling

PUZZLE: A *Problem* is a fact(s) lacking an acceptable explanation; is seemingly unusual; and fails to fit in with ones expectations or preconceptions. Features of the Viable Impossible include them being on the far end of the scale of problems because they are marked by being Complex, Involved, Intricate, and Intractable. Its subdivisions include: See Riddle; Conundrum; Enigma; Paradox; Problem

PYTHAGORAS: Sophists ('wisdom-bearer') of C5 BC were self-declared wise-men who were unscrupulous distorters of facts. Following the Persian Wars, they travelled about Greece as purveyors of popular education. For pay, they taught "practical wisdom" deemed to be essential--how to 'get along' in the world and without certain knowledge; how to win disputes; how to speak well and convincingly in statesmanship by using grammar, rhetoric, literature; and the generalship of doing whatever promised to offer worldly success by tricking victims. They were identified with the households of the well-to-do and the powerful, specializing in the arts of eloquence and persuasion as a preparation for careers in the law courts and on the public platform. Their almost sole interest was on pleasure, pain, and the pathe (states of emotions) and, as a consequence, neglected argument and proof. Their underlying theory developed from two foundational Sophists' concepts. First was the Italian Sophist Gorgias (c483-375) who was indifferent to both the sufferings and the happiness of other people. He proclaimed: "Nothing exists, and if it did, no one could know it; and if they knew it, they could not communicate it." Second, Pythagoras (a Sophist), upon his return from studying 23 years in Africa said: "*Man is the measure of all things*--of things that are that they are, and of things that are not that they are not." He advised everyone to "measure" matters according to his own nature and needs, since man alone, and not God (as he had learned in Africa), was the measure of all things. He also insisted on sensation as the only source of knowledge, with any sensation being true as long as it is perceived. Sophists agreed with him in despairing of the possibility of reaching truth and that the detached pursuit of absolute truth had been proved to be a wild-goose chase, saying knowledge in the strict sense was unattainable. Thus, man should not bother to seek what he can never find. Although these "SEEMS right" statements are obviously false to followers of the Ancient African Bible, the Sophists began dismantling the Spiritual Elements. This is how most Westerners think! Obviously, since the mass of people live out of their "Dark Side," Pythagoras' teaching put the Western world on a destructive downhill course. This course carries people further and further away from their Higher Selves and, by being disconnected from God, sanctions evilness to all concerned. To elaborate, apparently Magic in its widest sense was native to the imagination of the Greeks in their *theogony* (origin of gods) and mythology. This meant Pythagoras conceptualized each White male as being a god--a misinterpretation of what African Sages state is the way to earn ones Highest Self divinity. Nevertheless, this short-cut to becoming a man-god implied each White male could be extremely judgmental of all others except himself; determine what is right/wrong for him to do as well as what is right/wrong for others to do; and conclude that what he did was right and what anyone else did that was not in agreement was wrong. These were all based on opinions. What Pythagoras and Gorgias' statements mean to Europeans continue to be debated. Group I: They did not mean to advocate the anarchy of an excessive individualism but to put forward the view that man is the greatest being of whom there is real knowledge. Therefore, standards of behavior cannot be found in some arbitrary, external code--but rather in the needs and desires that man is known to have. In other words, man's view of morals was relative, not absolute; that morality should adapt itself to the needs and customs of the time and contain no law rooted in the nature of things--and thus binding in all circumstances. In short, it was acceptable to say: "this moral principle is "out of date" or "hardly for people like us"--"we decide right!" Europeans interpret this as man, not God nor an unchanging moral law, is the ultimate source of value. Group II says it means no one really knows what is outside oneself--for each one, the appearance of things is different; what is true for one is not true for another and thus everyone is always right while no one can ever be wrong. Group III denies truth apart from ones private emotions about things--or if there is, it cannot be discovered. Since one answer is as good as another as far as right or wrong is concerned, man might just as well concentrate on a policy of self-interest according to his own opinion. These three are exhibited in today's White society and its Colored puppets.

Q

QUACKS: The word "Quack" comes from those in C17 sounding like a duck when boasting about the wonderfulness of their remedies. Yet, the crystallization of their con-artists ways dates to the European Dark Ages from attempts to be successful in carrying out "Philosopher's Stone" experiments. For example, Deceitful scientists devised an "elixir" (Arabic, "powder" or Greek root for "dry") deemed to be a drug, essence, or tincture with the capabilities of a panacea or "cure-all" for anything wrong. These self-styled con-artist "psychologists"–of course with no formal training—promised to analyze (break down) a client's mind into its component elements and improve their personality in 12 easy lectures. Quacks continued to flowered within C18-C19 European *Age of Reason*—the Age which focused on understanding the universe and humankind through pure reason and logic as outlined by ancient Greeks. In turn, Quacks picked up tricks from ways of deceiving taught by ancient Greek Sophists (c460 BC) and carried them forth. These con-artists tactics and victim responses have never known any racial, religious, gender, or age boundaries. Prime tools of European Enslavers were/ are *hypocricy and being Dissemblers--keeping* evil purposes from being discovered--as sending their missionaries to entice Africans to give up their own superior religion and take on the "White man's" flawed religion were con-artists. When Europeans invaded and slaughtered the Amerindians while enslaving Africans, they also brought to the Americas greedy enslavers, countless convicts, prostitutes, religious dissidents, and the wayward—all bringing Kill/Take/Destroy/Dominate/Control/Oppress (KTDDCO) practices + Indifference/ Hate/Evil/Sadism mindsets that engage in superficial and military patterned thinking. This savage evil lifestyle exposed Enslaved Africans, Amerindians, and all free people of the world to their terrible amoral and horrible practices. Because of the violence Europeans recklessly use in dealing with terminology, White males saying they co-partner with God or are messengers for God are both classic con-artists tricks. To accept this makes it easier to believe their anthropomorphism descriptions; the Word of God is in the bible they wrote; and the need to fear God Fredrick Douglass (p. 310, 188, 344) said the darkest feature of slavery, and the most difficult to attack, was the religious slaveowners and ministers of religion who used the Bible to justify their evilness. He continued: "I assert most unhesitatingly, that the religion of the South -- as I have observed it and proved it -- is a mere covering for the most horrid crimes; the justifier of the most appalling barbarity; a sanctifier of the most hateful frauds; and a secure shelter, under which the darkest, foulest, grossest, and most infernal abominations fester and flourish . . . There is not a nation on earth guilty of practices more shocking and bloody, than are the people of these United States, at this very hour." Meanwhile, the British made so much money and gained so much power from African American slavery as to begin the1700s *Industrial Revolution*. The great changes in the lives and works of people world-wide came from huge marketplaces demand for entrepreneurship and employment. Along with more and more unsophisticated people moving rural areas into the towns came Quacks, Charlatans, and opportunists with scams to get rich off deceptive advertising, showmanship, and products. Despite its wide-spread nature, today's dishonorableness is even more pervasive in USA marketplace businesses. Nevertheless, con-artists--admixed with the skilled work products from mechanical, construction, handicraft, and similar outdoor occupations -- also found a business "home" in the squares of those towns. The deception leading to *Fraud* (gaining an unfair advantage over bodies of people) involved those aspects of "*Trickery*" (deliberately giving the wrong impression) that includes "*Deceit*" (the pursuit of personal gain at the expense of victims) and "*Manipulation*" (here meaning hypocritical dishonorableness). Whether people acquire Deceptions on their own or are implanted by Brutes, they are inside an anti-Spiritual Element way of thinking and thus the consequences cause great harm to all involved. What is certain is people inside a Delusional World will never get on the "Truth-Track." This range of deceitfulness is under the umbrella of the word "Fallacy." Typically, like the Wolf con-artist in the story of "Little Red Riding Hood," fallacies look good and frequently are very persuasive when first presented to our common sense.

QUALITATIVE MATHEMATICAL INTELLECT REASONING: This is Reasoning in which Pure Emotions are a "check and balance" on the Intellect involving Algebra, the mathematical tool initiating the acquisition of knowledge. It is based upon the *Principle of Correspondence*--meaning the Original Cosmic "Seed" has a universal application and manifestation on the various planes of the material, mental, and spiritual realms. For that reason, the "what it is" of every Archetype Seed for a specific kind of Thing (e.g. the Animal Kingdom or the Plant Kingdom) is present in every Seed in the "Seeable" and the "Un-seeable" world. For example, whatever Cosmic Essence is within the Archetype "Seed" for the Animal Kingdom will be found in every human. This Ancient African concept is phrased as: "so above, so below; so below, so above"--implying that if one knows something thoroughly about a given chain-linked Thing along the course of that chain connecting the Archetype "Seed" for the Animal Kingdom to any given human, then one automatically knows a great deal about its "Unseen" or "Unknown" chain-links because all of the links are like-kind counterparts of each other. Qualitative Correspondence is based upon all God's creatures and creations (e.g. Laws of Nature) all sharing the same Spiritual Elements "Genetics," despite each Entity having unique or customized duty displays.

"QUALITIES" DEFINITIONS IN AFRICAN TRADITION: Ancient African Philosophy, drawing its Essence ingredients from observable Nature, is founded on Sekhem, the Cosmic Force's Spiritual Elements. Emanated as *Substance* and formed as *Divine Spark Essences,* each is the Ultimate Cosmic and Human Certainty. "Essence" is the "What it was" + "*That it is*" (its specificity, individuality, and 'here/nowness') when that pre-birth human came into Being-hood. "Essence" (Eu, water--partly in the sense of a "seat") symbolizes the Egyptian Coptic name for Deity--as with Ausar (Osiris) and Auset (Greek Isis; "endowed with spirit"). Deity implies the most basic and indivisible aspect of each human's "to be in Being" state, meaning humans are Spiritual Beings. "Humans as Gods" were represented by Tehuti, the African Master of all Masters of the Ages, being depicted as the Ibis--a wading bird related to the stork and the heron. *Wading* is a metaphor for the intuited spiritual learning required to walk into and on through whatever offers resistance, impedes, or makes movement difficult. To this end, "Water's Qualities" tools are first illustrated by Water unresistingly accepting the lowest level and settling into the lowest places, rather than seeking the highest levels. Second, water demonstrates *getting its way by yielding*--avoiding confrontation by going around whatever gets in its way, taking the path of least resistance, and, in the process, wearing down everything of resistance in its path while eroding the hardest substance. Third, flowing water always penetrates crevices, slows to fill deep places, and is persistent in continuing to flow onward. Fourth, water maintains integrity by holding to its true nature and by following the natural forces in the Cosmos. Fifth, water has great flexibility, as seen in its liquid, gas, solid, cold, and moist states. In a similar manner, *Pure Intellect* uses the mind and its capacities to cut (wade) through the myriad of thoughts and concepts (water-ocean of consciousness) in order to get to the truth. The Spiritual Elements in the Cosmic Natural World display its Water attribute as Qualities directed by its Essence Disposition. The *Spiritual Elements are the Essence "Home Base"*—out of which African Tradition emanated an Underlying Foundation, Frame, and Ingredients for all of its Thought Structures/Deeds. Whereas Spiritual Elements Essences are inside each of God's Creatures and Creations, the "Home Base" for each is Unconditional Love. This naturally displays as *Spiritual Higher Qualities,* derived from human's "Spark of

God" Soul. Real Self people who cultivate this are in the flow state of Spiritual Elements Archetypes. That ensures one remains in a Spiritual Essence mindset.

QUALITIES—PRIMARY: *Any Primary Quality is foundational to developing Knowledge or Wisdom; the rest, for Information.* Starting when a Thing comes into Being, its Essence evolves by becoming entwined in the Cosmic Ether--and that makes each involved aspect a *Primary Quality*. Examples are the Halo of a Star in Spiritual/Metaphysical Realms—or like taste, smell, hearing, and touch sensations in Secular (Physical) realms. For example, Sensations do not indicate a "what" but, instead, a "That is" existence. The Primary Quality has the power to produce insensible concepts about the "That it is"--like bulk, texture, motion, solidity, extension (size), figure, motion or rest, and number. A Trademark of a Thing is composed of customized Primary Qualities. Primary Qualities *can only be recognized when compared to its Complementary or Contradictory Opposite* while Secondary Qualities have no specific distinction. Secular Qualities have human-made sources which determine the Essence of the Thing. Africans *Primary Qualities* are expressed as Wisdom, Goodness, Justice, and Perfection. Attributes from these Primary Qualities are put into action as Spiritual Selfishness, Selfless Service, Gentleness, Compassion, Kindness, Steadfastness, Patience, and Reciprocity ("the reward of one whose acts consist in the fact that one will act for her/him" in doing good). The display of these is within the "ME/WE" realm, implying ones "ME" goes out of its confined Selfhood so as to share oneself as a natural part of its Being with the "WE". The mere giving of oneself to be in union with another is the way to realize ones *Individuality*. Effort is needed for *Secular Primary Qualities displays. Consisting of Metaphysical Abstracts + Physical Abstractions,* ones mind fashions "Virtual" (boundary-less) Contingents out of like-kind Entities. Here, all non-relevant parts are cut out so as to see the Entity's "Skeletal Essence" as close as possible to the way it came into being. By perceiving Abstracts and Abstractions and *reducing them to their Theme* enables one to connect and unify events and things differing widely in form and external appearance--as far as seeming to be Contrary Opposites—as long as the attributes share an Essence. Secular Primary Qualities—e.g. Reason, Judgment, Dispassion, Balance, Breadth, Height, Depth--*can best be--or only be--recognized when compared to its Complementary or Contradictory Opposite.* There are no specific distinctions for Secondary and Tertiary Qualities recognition. Resultant conclusions pave ways, via Virtual/Contingent Being concepts, to have reasonable "*Fore-Sight*" (probable developments) that enable "*Forethought*" (doing all the necessary planning before taking "calculated" risks) to be instituted. Such is the intuitive intellectual basis of Unconditional Love, as symbolized by the Goddess Ma'at Principles (Amen, Metu Neter I: 88). Realizing foundational Cosmic Principles are few means this Circumspection thinking made for Ancient African brilliance.

"QUALITIES" CLASSIFICATION IN AFRICAN TRADITION: Since all *Spiritual Elements--constituting Spiritual Essences--*in African Tradition have Unconditional Love aspects underlying each Un-seeable and Seeable Cosmos manifestation, Ancient African Sages used it as their Thought Structure "Home Base" concerning anything. Those Spiritual Elements, being interwoven into an Interchange, emanate mosaics. When used like a skyscraper building's Base for thinking, those mosaics also constitute Divine Essences for Thought Structures. Similarly, Essences emanate out of a Real Self Soul--i.e. its Divine Consciousness derived from the Spark of God implanted in that human pre-birth. Whenever an Essence's Virtual (boundary-less) Icon Image meshes with Ether, it takes on an *Idea-Form* reality in the Metaphysical Mind. However, since the Spiritual Elements consist of the Immaterial, to avoid confusing the Soul's Essence Idea Image with its onlayed Essential Astral Soul's Image Ether equivalent, the Essentials were called Qualities by Ancient Africans. When the Divine Plan spurred the Immaterial Image to *Involute* (gather all its mosaics), that *Spiritual Primary Quality* entered the Sublime to acquire Ether for that Spiritual Entity. Ether enables the Idea-Form to have a mental conception—a *Precept.* The *Sublime* ("just under the lintel"--like the cross-piece of a door underneath which people walk) is an *Intangible* transitional plane between the Heavens (the Immaterial) and the Metaphysical planes. Because the Sublime is in the upper portion of the Finite Cosmos, it retains in heavy concentrations the harmonious Spiritual Elements features of the Subjective realm's Ocean of Nun and of "the Heavens." Hence, the internally unified Sublime Idea-Forms show interdependence, with mosaic interpenetrations in constant creations of itself. Its unity features embrace the Intangible forms of "Oneness" (unified diversity) Indivisibleness, Wholeness, Completeness, and Perfection. Whatever is unified in the Sublime has a complete nature of "Being" and, by being undivided in itself, is separated from all Tangible human-made Entities.

But upon the Idea-Form's ("*what it is*") further descent into Matter, the Ether as the *Cause* of the existence of an Entity acquires the term *Metaphysical Primary Quality*. This is like a Sun's Ingredients, Disposition, and Message in its Halo. When Ether causes Tangible Unbounded, Semi-bounded, or Concrete Things—that is a *Secular Primary Quality*. Examples: taste, smell, hearing, and touch feeling—extension, figure, motion, rest—solidity and number--respectively. Yet, Ether as simply a *supporting* part of the conception or existence of something already in "Being-hood," means it is a *Secondary Quality*. Examples: colors, heat, cold, and cartoons--to which may be appropriately added colors, sounds, tastes, and smells to what is in like-kind. Secondary Qualities are image or senses embellishments—e.g. about for nuances to be directly experienced by ones senses or by having power impacts to produce certain subtle changes in a directional course of perception or thought. Such may ease the slide into an apprehension of what has heretofore defied clarity; serve to make something into an overtone or undertone; or present or emphasize meanings for purposes of persuading, informing, entertaining, expressing, sharing, demonstrating, or serving as a call to action for whatever reasons. Also, it aids "*Education*" ("to lead out what is inside"), "*Teaching*" ("to show" for learning), *Instructing* ("to build in or into"), or "*Training*" (active mind exercising in order to form habits).

Tertiary Qualities, like Secondary Qualities, deal with the "*what it does*" and/or "*how it appears*"—and if any have an Essence (a "*what it is*"), that implies intrinsic Properties independent of Environment. They have the power to cause a change in another object as well as to alter ones sensory perception of an object. Examples: the power of aqua regia (nitro-hydrochloric acid) to dissolve gold and platinum as well as the sun to melt wax or produce a suntan. Since C19, economic, aesthetic, and other qualities (e.g. fragility) called *Supervenience* or *Consequential Characteristics* are said to have characteristics come along on top of a situation of, or in addition to, certain other characteristics. *Any Primary Quality is foundational to developing Knowledge or Wisdom; the rest, for Information.* Of the Primary Quality Virtues, *Courage* is highest esteemed because it is what enables paths to all others. Metaphysical or Secular Primary Qualities are independent of any human's perception or opinion about them. Those + seeing them "as is" are criteria for being Unconditional Love, Truth, Reality and the Natural. jabaileymd.com

QUALITIES ON A "T"-SCALE: a "T-Scale" deals with "All-or-None" and "Either/Or"—in the sense of it is Spiritual (e.g. Cosmic Laws or Principles) or it is not--applies only to the Spiritual realms--not the Material realms, since anything containing Matter is relative. The "T"-SCALE Concept symbolizes one Ladder is placed horizontally on top to symbolize Knowledge and, extending down from its middle, a Vertical Ladder that embraces the scope of Information. The junction between the Horizontal and Vertical Ladder connection implies that at the top of the vertical ladder is the very highest level of Information. Yet, the two Ladders cannot mesh because each of the rungs of the Vertical Ladder are constantly changing, meaning by being "relative" it is engaged in contant Change. Because the Vertical Ladder has rungs going from its top down to the ground, there are different things happening at each rung which cause different degrees of Change at different times. The reason for all this change is that each rung is involved in the process of a Cause, Effect, and Consequences. By contrast, the Horizontal ladder is about "All-or-None" in the way that a woman is either pregnant or she is not. Thus, Knowledge (the Spiritual) Ladder is without rungs and without change—meaning Knowledge is Certainty and does not change. Note that different things, governed by different rules, are operating at each ladder and on each rung of the vertical ladder. Whatever is Absolute is "all-or-none" and it "Either is" or it is not—both being present in full force or not at all. This is similar to turning on a light switch and having the room lit up and then turning the switch off and the room goes dark. Whatever is Absolute does not change. It cannot be limited by another authority and it is free. It cannot be explained on a more basic level. Flawed thinking deals with "all-or-none" or "Either/or." Sound, discerning thinking uncovers such options as: "Either this or that" or for "All of this and none of that." Middle categories of things represented by static letters of the alphabet: "neither-nor"; "both-and"; "some of both"; "both alternating"; or "each having differing patterns, directions, pace, levels, rhythms, and goals complementing each other in yin/yang fashion."

QUALITIES FOR KNOWLEDGE vs. INFORMATION THOUGHTS: Since, in African Tradition, Unconditional Love aspects of the Spiritual Elements contents underlie all perceptible or visible manifestations in the Cosmos, Ancient Africans used it as the "Home Base" for all of their Thought Structures. The Spiritual Elements—constituting Spiritual Essences--are interwoven into an Interchange. Out of that Interchange emanates mosaics which themselves, when used as a Base for thinking, also constitute the Divine Essence of that Thought Structure. All Divine Essences emanate out of a Real Self human's Soul—from its Divine Consciousness which is derived from the pre-birth implanted Spark of God. Whenever an Essence meshes with Ether, it takes on a Idea-Form reality. However, since the Spiritual Elements consist of the Immaterial, to avoid confusing its Essence Virtual (boundary-less) Icon Image of the "Self's" Soul Divinity Consciousness with its Essential Astral Soul and Metaphysical Mind Ether Icon Image equivalent, the Essentials were called Qualities by Ancient Africans. When spurred to Involve according to the Divine Plan, what Ancient Africans called a *Spiritual Primary Quality* consisted of an Essence Virtual (boundary-less) Icon Image entering the Sublime. Spiritual Courage is highest esteemed of the Primary Qualities because it is what enables paths to all others. The *Sublime* ("just under the lintel"--like the cross-piece of a door underneath which people walk) is an Intangible transitional plane between the Heavens (the Immaterial) and the Metaphysical planes. Because the Sublime is in the upper portion of the Finite Cosmos it retains the harmonious Unconditional Love features of the Nun and of "the Heavens." This is in spite of the added Ether being the *Cause* of the mental conception of that Spiritual Entity. Hence, internally unified Sublime Idea-Forms show interdependence + interpenetration + unity features embracing Intangible forms of "Oneness" (unified diversity) Indivisibleness, Wholeness, Completeness, + Perfection.

Whatever is unified in the Sublime has a complete nature of "Being" and, by being undivided in itself, is separated from all that is human-made in Tangible realms. But upon a further descent into Matter, when Ether was the *Cause* of the existence of a Metaphysical Thing or Entity--like a Sun's message in its Halo (detectable as ones "Lucky Star" by Very Ancient Africans)—it was a *Metaphysical Primary Quality*. When Ether was the cause of the existence of Tangible Unbounded, Simi-bounded, or Concrete Things like taste, smell, hearing, and touch feeling—or extension, figure, motion, rest—or solidity and number respectively—each was termed a Secular *Primary Quality*. Any of these are foundational to developing Knowledge or Wisdom. Here, Primary Qualities are independent of any perceiver or opinion about them and thus are pare of Reality and the Natural. Yet, whenever Ether was just simply a *supporting* part of the conception or existence of something already in "Being-hood," it was a *Secondary Quality*. Examples include colors, heat, cold, cartoons. They may consist of adding colors, sounds, tastes, smells to what already exists in like-kind.

QUALITIES—SECONDARY: *Secondary Qualities are embellishments that can be about nuances directly experienced that affects ones senses or having the power to produce certain images* or senses that subtly change a directional course of perception or thought—perhaps by easing the slide into an apprehension of what has heretofore defied clarity; serve to make something into an overtone or undertone; present or emphasize meanings for purposes of persuading, informing, entertaining, expressing, sharing, "*Education*" ("to lead out what is inside") over "*Teaching*" ("to show" so as to impart knowledge for learning), *Instructing* ("to build in or into"), or "*Training*" (active mind exercising in order to form habits), demonstrating, or serving as a call to action for whatever reasons.

QUALITIES—TERTIARY: *Tertiary Qualities,* like Secondary Qualities, deal with the "what it does" or "how it appears"—and if any have an Essence (a "what it is"), that implies intrinsic Properties independent of Environment. They have the power to cause a change in another object as well as to alter a sensory perception of an object. Examples are the power of aqua regia (nitrohydrochoric acid) to dissolve gold and platinum as well as the sun to melt wax or produce a suntan. Since C19, economic, aesthetic, and other qualities (e.g. fragility) called Supervenience or Consequential Characteristics are said to have characteristics come along on top of a situation of or in addition to certain other characteristics. An example is Depression goes over Self-Image.

QUALITIES—QUADRIARY: the four numbered series of a Thing has different names—e.g. Quaternary and Tetramorph (mystic plane). The "Driary," like the "Ternary," is the number connected with the realization of the idea; the Quadriary, like the Quatery, is the number connected with the realization of the Idea. What I call Quadriary Qualities (see Imagination—Lucky Stars) is the result of a layering of Realistic and/or Acquired Effects which serve as a Cause and produce a secondary Effect—called either a Realistic or an *Acquired After-Effect*—and these I call *Realistic* and *Acquired Tertiary Qualities* respectively. When ones Imagination adds to the *Tertiary Qualities, their Consequential Characteristics,* derived out of their Interchange, they create a new mosaic Quality pattern. That pattern is placed on top of the entire "After-Effect" and "Over-Effect" combined happenings, to produce an "Awe" Effect--what I call a Quadriary Quality. However, its origin is from the Cosmos' *Subjective realm*--also called "*Nothingness*"—the realm of Virtual (boundary-less) Being—the mother of all Being by it producing all Cosmic Organism Creatures and Creations. It is nameless, for it is greater than anything that can be named. It takes no action, in that it leaves Things alone. It supports all Things but does not take possession of them. It lets Things transform themselves. It does nothing and yet all Things are thereby done. An *Indivisible Quadriary is present inside each of the contained Cosmic Creations and Creatures: (1) each Entity as a Spiritual Being; (2) each Entity has separateness in manifestations in* its individual actions and appearances and with uniqueness in each; *(3) all Entities and Ingredients are united in interdependence* to serve the common goal; and (4) the Divine Plan Message Disposition of that Common Goal is the instilled sense of Humanity present in all. That Disposition's Message is the "Voice of the Silence."

So, there first three are the "*Driary*"--the number connected with the realization of the idea. These 3 impart Correspondence between them all—meaning each Entity and Ingredient in the Cosmos contains mosaic pieces of the *Quadriary.* The *Quadriary* is the number connected with the realization of the Idea. The "After-Effect" and "Over-Effect" combined happenings and brought about by the fourth so as to produce an "Awe" Effect is the Disposition Message. The resultant "After-Effect" and "Over-Effect" Constituting the "Awe" Effect in the *Indivisible Quadriary* is the Cosmic "Voice of the Silence"—the Feeling Instincts in each Cosmic Entity. The Cosmic Mind Voice "says everything by not saying anything at all"--"retains everything by giving away everything"—"speaks the impossible and expresses the inexpressible in a manner that is expressed inexpressibility." Thus, if a Principle is likened to a string in a tennis racket or a thread in a spider web, each would contain the *Quadriary.*

QUALITIES--SUPERNATURAL CULT: In the earliest evolution of humans, their animal brains properly programmed them handle living their part in the Animal Kingdom regarding social organization and survival through the forces of the rule of might and of the fittest. During primitive Europeans journey through life, those with the most physical and weapon might engaged in predatory hunting of animal and human prey. Subsequently, rather than engage in transubstantiation (i.e. the change of their animalistic Essence for higher levels of Humanity) the simply changed, somewhat, the appearance of how they did things in the political, economic, financial, and social worlds. This implies their animal brains continued to be programmed to give a physically aggressive response to delusion fears for self-interest purposes—responses inadequate for what requires intelligence, morals, humane, and Spiritual problem-solving. Thus, "My way or violence and war" have remained the chief means of resolving social and international conflicts. These conflicts are basically about gaining "Scarce Desirables" (e.g. money)—based on general agreement of the value of their qualities absent any Essences to use as standards. For example, Money is power and god to Europeans because money is a measure of how rich they think they are—translation "how outstanding I am and therefore I out-do you". Thus, money is put in various contingent forms so as to give one the illusion of being rich as well as they believe in it bringing more power, status. By lacking a concept of how much is "Enough," there is an overwhelming need to grab all of the "Scarce Desirable" they can get. It does not matter that money is not real but only a form of statistic, like inches are to a ruler, displayed as simply printed paper, the illusion of it prevents *virtues from superseding making money.* Nor does it matter that money is a reflection of what is seen in the mirror of envied people. Absent money, there is nothing to measure inwardly or produced outwardly that would give Self Unknown Supernaturals a sense of pride.

But whereas *Characteristics* normally identify the Character of a Thing and use its Attributes to distinguish it from other things, because nothing is known about the Fantasy Supernatural, there can be no distinguishable Qualities of any type. If *Primary Qualities are considered to be Attributes of a Thing's Essence*, by dealing only in Qualities without Essence means there is no alternative to stereotyping, no matter how unlike individual Black People are. But at the root, they are Projecting their concepts of themselves onto Black People. They must constantly advertise that they possess good qualities without specifying what they are except that "Because I said so"; know everything without ever having been taught anything; and Winning has nothing to do with quality, just the final score of the degree of pain and suffering caused or how much illegal things they have gotten away with. Supernatural pseudo-quality is illustrated by practically all magnificent things subsequently spread throughout the Western world under the name of *"Greek creations" which are merely translations and transmissions of Ancient African Intellectual Property.* Type III are the higher Natural Lower (animalistic) Self Qualities—Affection, Sociability, Friendship, Generosity, Courtesy, Courage, Prudence, Fairness, Truthfulness, Honorableness, Simplicity, etc.—all blending gradually into the Type I Higher Qualities.

Type IV are the Lower Acquired Brute Qualities—e.g. Fetters like animalistic sensuality/lust, Hate of even the "faceless," attachments to Things, Lies, Greed and its resultant Frustration, Indifference, False Pride, Chronic Anger/Rage, Egoism, Delusional Fears, Violence, Indifference, Aversion, Adversion, Cruelty/Sadism, Meanness, Rudeness, Cowardice, Cunning, Shrewdness, Intemperance, Arrogance, Vanity, Oppression, Control, Dominate, Deceit, Revenge, Jealousy, Envy, Malice, Injustice, etc. These are the result of possessing a sense of Inferiority, Self-Hatred, Insecurities, feeling Shame from being Inadequate or "Not Good Enough," accepted Flaws that mold a deformed Self-Image and Self-Concept with all the problems springing out of the Consequences of such mindsets. Typical reactions from choosing to enter such a Delusional World necessarily make one a "Me, Me, Me" Self-Absorbed Individualist. At that cross-road, one may elect to remain Passive, become Passive-Aggressive, or be powered by extreme selfishness as arrogant "little gods". A feature of Type IV is to bind ones Ego to them so that, for practical purposes, they will never change.

QUALITY STANDARDS FOR SUPERNATURALS': A "Standard" (C12, English--stand fast and firm) is a *something* (e.g. a Truth, a Symbol, a thought, a feeling, a pillar) to determine what level is required to do a task. Among others, it forms: (1) a "skeletal home Base" for a Metaphysical or Physical structure to be built on or around; (2) possesses and may convey a quality, sense, quantity; (3) serves as a measurement against which something is compared and measured for its degree of accuracy or conformity to what is expected socially or practically; (4) be a filter, model, rule, or guide to learn what is "right" or agreed upon with reference to procedure as to how to do things—levels to be attained—or that idealizes what is the best end product; (5) a fixed unit for standardizing like-kind things; (6) a "rule of thumb" for making estimates of what is not measurable; (7) a model for reproduction; (8) a definition guide for solving problems and pointing out directions; (9) places boundaries (e.g. time and space limits); and (10) provides rules for performance and variations. Any of these may have application on any plane of existence in the Natural World or determined usages in Supernatural realms; to Essences and/or their Essentials (Qualities) in real, distorted, or fantasy situations; for Good, Neutral, or Evil; range from internal to external (e.g. inside-out)—top to bottom (high to low)--or vice versa. Some may be attainable while others are unattainable by being impossible to achieve or because of real or false limitations of an individual; or because of limitations placed by outside forces.

Some Standards may be flexible while others are rigid. *"Evidence" is fulfilled by the presence of the thing in question conforming to the criteria. "Proof" is the meeting of the Qualities of the Standard.* Standards are Mathematical when they lend themselves to being Reproducible, as seen in the Natural World's Correspondence between Unseen and Seeable aspects of Nature. Ancient Africans proved all God's Creatures and Creations are made of the same Spiritual Elements "Genetics". Thus, proving Melanin/Carbon in the Seeable, enables inferring it Unknown. By definition, Supernaturals are against any Natural World Standards or Essences, meaning they disregard, among others, the Spiritual Elements and their attributes (Qualities) as well as disregard the Spiritual (i.e. ones Divine Consciousness) and Astral (containing human Conscience as its Character) Intellects of Natural World humans. As the "Form" part of an Idea-Form, *Character* identifies and expresses the "what it is" individuality of its Immaterial Idea Essence parent derived from that human's Divine Consciousness.

In other words, Character is a "stand-in" for that Essence in Real Self humans. *Conscience* is the Spiritual vehicle that conveys to a human about life's fundamental rights and wrongs. So, when one plans to do wrong, ones Consciousness involuntarily reacts instinctively as a filter—and not from an acquired reflex. Character and Conscience, dormant in their original state, become activated by Ether which thereafter engages both in matters of living. The Conscience's filter is what qualifies for acceptance or not. *Qualify* means to give or attribute Qualities to—signifying all applicable qualities or all qualities it embraces for acceptance into ones Selfhood. By contrast, Supernaturals who self-declare to be in a remote and unknowable Supernatural abyss means they are orchestrated by the Ego they select to rule their False Self. Hence, a Supernatural *Character* identifies and expresses the "what it is" individuality as determined by ones Ego. This is a profound example of *Transubstantiation*—the changing from ones Real Self Natural World Substance into a Supernatural association of Philosophical Qualities that are in exact opposition to ones Real Self.

The Effects of this *Transubstantiation* are in realms of how Supernaturals see themselves and how to live life; see others like and unlike them; and react to others like and unlike them. Obviously, this affects every aspect of their lives as well as the lives under their influence. There is disarray in the Qualities of all involved because there is no standard by which the others can use to determine anything about the relationships and actions caused by Supernaturals. Supernaturals believe that they are "little gods" and whatever they do is superior to what anyone else does—and without having any concept of what Natural World people have as standards. Those that follow Supernaturals have admiration and they are locked so as to never change. The Victims are filled with "Awe" of someone being so out of the world—and they do not consider what has happened to them.

QUALITY THINKING EFFECTS OF SUPERNATURALS: A profound speaker in African Tradition is one who can extraordinary things by using plain and simple words. Those words clear and precise definition and are taken out of a family of like-kind and similar meaning words. But the specific "home" of that community of words corresponds to the community words of the Receivers. Such is done by specifying its Essential character—the "what it is" nature when it came into Beinghood) as close to its Essence reality as is possible. That denotation paves the way to more than one of its application possibilities as well as how its character may appear in different situations. Let us now focus on how Quality nuance changes affect word and mental interpretations for worse, or rarely for better. With the Supernatural oriented, a given defined word also provides a specific "home" within its world community of words but for mind control purposes. The word and its meaning does not necessarily relate to the Receiver because of the intent to confuse the mind so Quality description can be substituted. This set the stage for Receivers to be deluded. The process can start by it not being in the language of Receivers—as when White teachers use words of their culture to convey something to Colored children. Since cross-cultures do not use a word's meaning in the same way, attempts overcome the disharmonious fit by means of Connotations leads to further mental encroachments on, and typically even deformed aspects of Understanding. Compared with White students socialized into those Connotations for a word, Colored students are worse off because of their imperfect or even untrue ideas. More often than realized there is an intention to create falsities so as to reestablish a "SEEMS" right meaning by adding Qualities to assist in the description. Since each of those Qualities are interpreted differently by each mind, all sorts of erroneous misunderstandings and practices can and do result—practices leading one far from the Spiritual Elements. A second problem is things defying definition and whatever their Quality oriented label given that "explains everything," they follow the course of Connotations. So do a wilderness of like-kind things with a similar theme being walled off with a specific Quality symbolizing word. Such is further complicated by dealing with that word as if it is a Stereotype—i.e. the painting a group/things with the same paint on the same brush so that one sort of treatment may serve for all in order to avoid mental work—"all X people look alike and act alike"; or with varied meanings of a word under one definition—meanings improperly applying to different Cosmic planes of existence because each concept is unique and operates under its own rules—e.g. "*Success*" (which then tends be thought of in Quality word context. Pseudo-intellectuals strain to use "big words" to hide their lack of clarity about it and to hopefully shame the Receiver into not wanting to admit a lack of understanding. That Receiver, instead, often uses some Quality image for getting a "handle" on that "big word." Pseudo-Intellectuals also believe that knowing a great many names creates the façade of them appearing to know a good many things. This is associated with the mouthing of hard words "proves" one understands hard things. People greedy for any explanation rather than accepting their ignorance treat themselves to words devoid of meaning, like those who swallow clay to silence their empty stomachs. Words of Quality are often invented because of an absence of ideas on the subject. *Just because known things are named, does not mean they are known.* In medicine, a Diagnosis is a system of reasonable assumptions and guesses in which the end-point achieved is a name. That name comes to assume the status of a specific entity rather than the most part simply insecure and supposedly temporary conception to serve as a starting point for treatment. By so doing, it tends to stifle further questions and curiosity to discover more. Some ancient words have such descriptive meanings and, despite being wrong or misleading (Achondroplasia), they are retained so as to further mislead the novice. It vastness of acceptance prevents any attempt to a precise definition. Some prefer not to use a dull word to describe what they see in favor of using a better sounding to describe what they cannot see in the same thing. Sociologists, financial experts, and law have a jargon that is all their own. It keeps hidden quality concepts that prevents them from being pin-pointed and enables them give an interpretation to what is ambiguous that is always in their favor.

QUALITIES OF AFRICAN vs. EUROPEAN TRADITIONS: In contrast to African Tradition's definitions for Qualities discussed, Europeans definitions are greatly confusing, are in conflict, and no general agreement on any one. Besides, 'big words" without having adequate definitions are used to cover disharmonies or ignorance. Switching to algebraic symbols usually have the same effect. The same thing may be presented in different ways: "That is water"; "That is H20". For the same word, the European definitions are almost never the same for an African one. Because they are merely "authority" Opinions, each is like a *"Delusional One-Sided Coin"*. Hence, in European literature a product and its usages are to be assessed as having Quality in one, both, or neither and the nature of the involved Quality depends upon its Source. A problem with even certain comments that seem alright is that no background and setting are provided. Also, the assumptions of the science of centuries back may not be correct or more may be known. For example, one European text says: "Primary qualities are properties common to and inseparable from all matter"—but without commenting on the Metaphysical or the Spiritual. The crucial point is the absence of a sound Essence from which these Qualities derive. That is what makes the Delusional and one-sided in formulation and, when used among people, in conclusion. In none of the numerous European sources I reviewed did I see a definition of Quality. However, a useful one offered by Sharon Bingaman RN. is: " *A Quality is an Attribute of Something". Mine is: Quality is the "What it does" and "How it appears" of the "What it is" of a Thing.* The realties of both extend beyond the Supernatural. In African Tradition, the "what is is" constitutes an Entity's Essence—which either be out of the Spiritual Elements or out of the Imagination, called Figures of Communication (FOC). African FOC, in the form of Contingent Beings (e.g. gods and goddesses) serve to provide Secondary Qualities to explain aspects of Divine, Spiritual, Metaphysical, and Secular realities. Regardless of the type of Qualities or their plane of existence source, they share the following: (1) a bodiless presence; (2) interacting in relationship to the whole of its Essence parent and to other associated components; (3) can be experienced by its proper content properties of some characteristic, trait, and/or feature; and (4) is capable of being put into feelings, emotions, thoughts, and perhaps crudely into words. Since a bodiless presence--described as the "*That*" of the Form of what a Thing or Entity is, whatever active and passive qualities are overlying it, regardless of what they are doing, and how they appear means they are Attributes. In turn, its "That it is" determines the capabilities for how any one of them is to develop, for what it is to do, for how it is to grow, and for the impactful 'payload' it carries to activate something good and/or bad. Thus, the "*That" is the Character* and the *Attributes are the Characteristics*. Yet, Divine, Spiritual, Metaphysical, and Secular Qualities share the following: (1) a bodiless presence; (2) interacting in relationship to the whole of its Essence parent and to other associated components; (3) can be experienced by its proper content properties of some characteristic, trait or feature; and (4) is capable of being put into feelings, emotions, thoughts, and perhaps crudely into words. Since a bodiless presence--described as the "*That*" of the Form of what a Thing is, whatever active and passive qualities is overlying it are doing and how they appear means they are Attributes. In turn, its "That it is" determines the capabilities for how any one of them is to develop, for what it is to do, for how it is to grow, and for the impactful 'payload' it carries to activate something good and/or bad. Thus, the "*That" is the Character* and the *Attributes are the Characteristics*.

QUALITATIVE MATHEMATICS: The *Qualitative Mathematics* applied to the Physical World dealt with things of Worth which, in being like Metaphors (operating inside Supernatural Realms), allow for a great deal of flexibility in dealing with any issue, Qualitative Mathematics examines Premises to seek the ultimate Principle on which they all depend.

Law of Correspondence. That Law enables humans, using *Metaphysical Knowledge within the context of* of *Qualitative Mathematics,* to know Unseeable *Divine* and *Spiritual Entities with Certainty. This is called Circumstantial Evidence.* Using Qualitative Mathematics in association with measuring vibratory rates of radiations, Very Ancient African Sages gained insight into the Laws of Nature. Inferences from those Laws led to the Circumstantial Truth paths which would lead to the Heaven Afterlife. CT's use of Qualitative Mathematics involves making Estimates of like-kind Things of Worth (i.e. Essence Qualities) that have Correspondence and to thereby establish a Circumstantial Truth. *Subjective Science* tools—i.e. Observation, Reflection, "Pure" Feelings, Productive Imagination, Contemplation, Inductive and Deductive Inferences, and Common Sense— to make inferences in arriving at circumstantial evidence and judgments. These enable Qualitative Algebraic Mathematics which, in turn, enable Quantitative Mathematics. Quantitative Reasoning is thinking that follows the manner in which the processes occur in Nature. An example is to perceive God's (Sekhem) presence by displays of Intelligence manifested throughout all creatures and creations having Correspondence. This is the Intelligence behind all the Laws of Nature which can be understood through African Qualitative Algebraic derived Logic as well as by Quantitative Logic. Both forms of African Logic enables acquiring Knowledge of the existence of all quantifiable events that cannot be perceived through the senses. See Inference

QUINARY: a group of five elements—represented formally by the pentagon, the five-pointed star, and the square with its central point.

R

RACISM = NUANCED CUMULATIVE MICRO-TRAUMAS: Armed with a Supernatural (Fantasy) God, Devil, and Hell, Satanist Europeans have engaged in Kill/Take/Destroy/Dominate/Oppress/Mind Control (KTDDOMC) using the strategies of "Big Bang," "Shot-Gun," and Nuanced Cumulative Micro-Traumas (NCMT). Each of these are aspects of "Racism"—*the actions of Brutes and their followers to adversely affect one life.* Traditional European "Big Four" historical enslavement "Take-Down" methods of *penetration, conquest, occupation, colonization* (C. Williams, Destruction of Black Civilization p257; Irwin, *Race and Justice, 2012*) are "*Shrewdly*" (wicked, evil, malicious, dangerous) well-worked out patterns. *Phase I*: The process starts either as a "Big Bang" war conquering or by nuanced forced *Penetration* deceptive invasion by "missionary" or "diplomatic" types. *Phase II*: The *Conquest Phase* is setting up the situations that enable the colonizers' racist ideology to carry out *their intent to conquer the world* so as to obtain "valuable economic resources," indulge their lust of conquest, a love of ease as "little gods," a craving for power, have a triumph with glory, and an obsession to be superior. This is done by launching systematic assaults on native cultures, where indigenous languages, religions, worldviews, and ways of life are destroyed, distorted, and generally denounced as being primitive, evil, and savage. Victims are shunned, denounced, alienated from symbolic and material resources as well as constructed in zoological terms as being more like animals than civilized people. *Phase III*: *Occupation* consists of troops moving in to establish their government--stabilized by a racial or ethnic minority (i.e. foreigners)--premised on the belief that the indigenous people lacked a decent, moral, and civilized society. Parts of the process included casting indigenous people as needing governing and control by members of their superior culture. Phase IV, *Colonization*, is the set up of a rigid social caste system in which the oppressors receive the lion's share of privileges within the colonial society. The point: to so beat down Victims as to leave them forever devastated-- fighting each other to survive in any of their moral, cultural, financial, health, and physical environment poverties. Consequences include alienation among/within Victims' rampant conflict and competition.

"*Shot-gun*" daily racism attacks come with "machine-gun" rapidity. They include the "Killer" police's war on Black People; the government doing all it can to keep Black People from rising out of their various poverties; and the Marketplace staying closed to jobs for the struggling. The result is by recklessly generating prison records on struggling Black males so as to hamper them for life in such areas as being hired for good paying jobs; by failing to create safe schools; and by failing to present educational materials relevant to the lives of Black youth. Flowing through all of these forms of Racism is NCMT. Its *Cumulative Trauma* (Latin, cumulus, heap or piled—like cumulus clouds)--also called Continuing small Traumas, Micro-Aggressions, and Accumulative Micro-trauma--leaves multiple psychic 'little wounds' which in turn *erode* (wear away) and *corrode* (gnaw away) every mental, physical, emotional, spiritual, and soul aspect of a Victim's Selfhood. Those aspects, like having cracked an egg, could be so resistant to healing that the "yoke" continuously oozes out. This is particularly so in Victims with mental "Raw Nerves" resulted from a "Big Bang" trauma. That mental "Raw Nerve" acts as if it is set on fire an "*Inflamed*" or a-flamed—expressing like meteors in troubled areas of ones mind.

NCMT forms of include Institutional (Social Oppression) Racism so enforced in embedded social life as to not easily be identified as oppression and does not require conscious prejudice or overt acts of discrimination (e.g. the USA legal system is anti-Black People). These have generated environments where resultant composite bad thoughts are so powerful as to overwhelm and maintain control over its residents' minds, and from developing a hopeless sense that life will not get any better for them. What is ever persistent for the most struggling is daily survival, slum housing, underemployment/or unemployment, many single working mothers, inferior and wrong education, lack of police protection, police brutality, grossly inadequate sanitation services, crime, delinquency, exceptionally high disease and infant mortality rates, isolation from mainstream American life, a "Grand Canyon" sized gap in riches, chronic outrage, chronic prostitution, vice, and anything destructive to human existence (McPherson, "Blacks in America," pp. 188, 396).

RACISTS TYPES: three levels of Racism are: individual, institutional, and cultural. Type I are Overt Racists—Whites who say so, confessing their horrible racial sins inflicted on those unlike them and even denouncing less advanced White people. The term for this is "Virtue Signaling"— a way of dumb savages communicating how enlightened they are. Kill/Take/Destroy/Dominate/Oppress/Control (KTDDOC) practices are what they engage in. Type II are Tempered Racists who are partners in the background and partially "up-front" in doing certain KTDDOC deeds. Type III are Masked Racists. They do like being called Racists or being berated about how "their" country is racist. They complain that those using the "everything is about race" crowd is using race as a cudgel to silence critics and have their way. Yet, they are demonstrate clear Racism when it gets personal. Type IV is Concealed Racists in that they do not feel superior to those unlike them but they do most of the racist practices that have been socialized into them without their awareness. Examples are feeling "entitled" over other races; seeing other races as "Invisible"

RAW NERVE: A mental "Raw Nerve" results from a "Big Bang" trauma and/or Cumulative Micro-Traumas. Either or both dismantle the strength of ones philosophy of life and/or of ones psychological safety, security, self-confidence, or stability. One or more of these constituted the cause of the "Switch." The mental "Raw Nerve" acts as if it is "Inflamed" (set on fire or set aflame).

RATIONAL QUANTITATIVE MATHEMATICAL THINKING: Here, Pure Emotions are used to help guide ones Intellect by determining humanitarian aspects. To pursue Reasoning by Analogy past its usefulness is to enter along the lines of logical thought into Inductive Reasoning (i.e. inference from particular Informational "Facts" to general Informational "Laws") and Deductive Reasoning (inference from general Informational "truths" to particular Informational "truths"). Reasoning is more about suiting itself to the ways of the world and knowing what to do next than knowing what to do in the ultimate. It is a solid and entire Thought Structure, of which every piece keeps it place and bears its own mark. Great Reasoning prevents needing to do desperate thing where it would be needed the most. Reasoning (or Inference), lying at the heart of higher-order thinking, is a means of acquiring information from general truisms or beliefs—or, it is gaining knowledge from general principles. Reason is the only objective means of communication and of understanding between humans. Reasoning is thus an equally Right Brain dominant activity, as the Left Brain cannot relate ideas to each other. *Reason is the relatively overt mental processes by which one reaches conclusions on the basis of Evidence.* All Reasoning begins in perplexity, hesitation, and doubt. *Its process involves Analysis, Comparisons, Classification, Synthesis, and Conception.* As one progresses and is compelled to confront unique challenges, when correctly reasoning, one dissociates from the content (or experience) that initiated it so as to focus only on it; to weigh ones actions in terms of long-range consequences for ones own life or otherwise; and to determine what else must be true if the premises are true. There are many forms of Reasoning: In African Tradition, *Metaphysical Reasoning* is done to explain Spiritual Concepts in direct

Principle Language, Symbolic Language, or African Supernatural Language as, for example, Metaphors. African Secular Reasoning deals with Physical world aspects. *When the stepping stones lead to Seeable destinations, that type is called Quantitative Reasoning.*

RATIONAL THINKING's TEN STEPS:

Step I--Clearly define the problem

Step II--Gather pertinent information

Step III--Assess the gathered information and categorize the keystone issues into Pros/Cons

Step IV--Analyze the assessed information, including grading each Pro and Con by means of Measurements for quantitative items (e.g. things seen) and Estimates for qualitative aspects (i.e. things one cannot see)

Step V--Manipulate the analysis into cause and effect; gather all factors for both

Step VI--Maneuver creatively around obstacles so as to arrive at the Truth.

Step VII--by using this insight, one can now Poetically synthesize all existing pertinent high quality aspects involved in the mental activity. A well-known Dialectic law is a *change in quantity beyond a certain point brings about a change in quality.* Or, it gives a different perspective on existing qualities. Either way, pertinent changes are made in that Thing's unique rules and character to thereby bring about changes in the characteristics and the circumstances in which that Thing operates. If changes are great enough and abrupt enough, a *Revolution* transformation into a different mindset occurs. Out of this new mindset comes a higher level insight which carries a *Vision.* A Vision is the art of seeing invisible and unifying essences concerning quantities and qualities underlying the obvious and the hidden that others are unable to see or that they themselves, until now, have been unable to see. This Vision enables one to fashion Options of how to best handle problems by establishing connections of Cause to the Effects and then devising Solutions to handle the Effects.

Step VIII--Prioritized top 3 Options are for Judgments to make them into Plans A, B and C

Step IX--Troubleshoot the Plans A, B, and C

Step X--Post-action judgments of a "check and balance" nature are made after each mental and physical action. Here, one looks for any flaw, weakness, limitation, how can it be made better, what can be eliminated, how to make excellence routine) and follow that with Mulling ("Just Be") whereby one simply gets quiet and not think about anything. In this way glimpses of the peaks of what has been synthesized from the process show themselves quickly before disappearing forever. The point is to take advantage of that opportunity since that one thing along can represent the success path.

REACTION FORMATION: a reality/fantasy reversal)--e.g. saying about and to the victim: "you are the one causing the problem, not me!" Whether from nursing a "Raw Nerve" or having been Socialized into being devoted to the Supernatural, they cling to their supporting fantasy-made positions in the face of contrary evidence as a form of Self-Deception. For example, they do verbal or physically bad things, deny they did it, and cling to other fantasies that represent the situation. Then, as part of Deflection, they engage in Reaction Formation. See Deception; Deflection; Projection

REALITY: *Laws of Nature's Pattern of Flow* can start with Reality—i.e. that which is true, enduring, perfect, stationary, eternal, and permanent. At its origin, Reality is an Immaterial vital part of the Spiritual Elements—being interwoven into an Interchange with Unconditional Love, Truth, and the Natural. As Reality descends toward the Earth World, it meets with the Ether in the Sublime to become an Essence-Form—like an Archetype Entity giving rise to Prototype Entities and then to specific Entities (e.g. a given human). Thereafter, Reality also embraces Matter aspects. All Reality Entities—in their "what it is" state—are indescribable systems of wiggles and vibrations. During the continued descent towards Earth those Forms become layered with different planes of Existence. Regardless of its Cosmic Level, each Essence-Form (i.e. composed of multiple variables of Entities and Plane) occupy the same space. That space in any given segment of the total of Reality is called a "*State*" ('way of standing, condition, position'). To illustrate, in this "State" of vibratory energy, each variable wave-like Entity is not only wiggly (and not straight) but each Entity possesses different dimensions and vibration rates. By all different dimensions and vibration rates occupying the same space at any point in the Cosmos, one plane is within the other. In short, every plane manifests in the same point of space at the same time. Each Entity's Uniqueness depends upon its vibration rate and location in the range of Energy-Matter states--from unformed, hence imperceptible, to the finite and restrictive physical world matter. The ability to perceive and deal with any of these aspects of Reality as it is in actuality demands seeing the Real the way it is when it came into Being-hood—not what one would like/dislike for it to be. The transition from an Entity's original absolute un-differentiation in the Subjective Realm to Earthly existence is a graduated progression designed to maintain a connection at each and every step—between the qualities of Subjective Being in accordance with the Divine Plan.

Despite the axiom of physics that no two bodies of matter can occupy the same space at the same time, the Laws of Nature on each unique plane differ. For example, the more of the Spiritual Elements one gives away, the more one has. However, the more material things given away, the less one has. To understand this Mystery, one must *shift from Human-Made Patterns of Thinking over to the Laws of Nature's Patterns of Flow.* Yet, at each descent progression step there is an equilibrium between Being and Doing; Life and Living; the No-thingness of Subjective Being and the infinite numbers of Things on Earth; the infiniteness and eternalness of the Subjective Realm and the finiteness in time and space of the Objective Realm. [Ref: Amen, Metu Neter I: 54, 103]. By contrast, Supernatural "Seems right" is about altering Reality with beliefs, opinions, or "magic/miracles". This process starts by people being socialized to believe Spiritual and Cosmic Principles or Supernatural information about Reality demands them to translate what is presented from their linear recitations in spoken or written words. The fact that they are linear (since Reality is not that way) and that they are words (which are only Symbols of the gist of what each word describes) and the fact that they are translated by a human whose understanding of Reality is altered—both in the interpretation and in choosing the words to convey them to Receivers who, themselves, interpret them. Obviously, these multiple steps each take one further and further away from the Truth. The World is not the same as it is described.

But we are taught to be hung-up or what is described. For example, people fail to appreciate that images of oneself tend to come from descriptions given by outside influences (parents, friends, the Crowd) about who one is, what role one is to play. Words can never provide thoughts that come into the same world as to who one really is and what is ones Mission in life. Instead, these truths come from "Feeling" the involved Reality—a Reality that comes about by "Knowing Thyself" and "Feeling" the answers—as a child does who never learned to talk. Such explanatory descriptions cannot be done with Music or the Fine Arts for both have to be grasped intuitively. What could be said about musical notes of significance, have too many variables to convey any comprehension. This problem is eliminated by "Feeling" what is listened to and then using what is gained on an instrument. When that is "Felt," there is only the "here and now"—no past or future (which never comes)—no knowing/knower differences. Supernatural descriptions of the Laws of Nature define it as observed regularities, as determined by clocks and rulers which measure rates of change. Still, it is a fallacy to think the sun rises because it is 6:00 am. There are countless other fallacies which are like taking the piece of a Halo and saying it caused the Star. Similarly, most people believe money makes for prosperity but money is simply a measure of it. The reverse is likely to be true—that doing what it takes to become prosperous is what enables one to acquire money. People say the Law rules things but rules come from the mindsets of those who make laws. To be under Supernatural jurisdiction means the imposers of it are extremely insecure. It is presented as an "inside-out" statement that goes unquestioned: "you are required to do this voluntarily". Such is very military: "I want you, you, and you to volunteer" and to refuse is to be punished. Humans' God-given differences are to conform so as to not be threatening to the purpose of the leaders. Conformity means all the people are deemed inferior by the leader and the threat terror controls their minds.

REASON: Primitive Africans observed numbers all around them in everyday life—one sun, two halves of an apple, three animals—some things were too many to count using their fingers. Thus, they represented large numbers by pebbles, knots on a rope, or notches on a stick or bone. They learned to add at least as early as 77,000 years ago. Stones were put in an animal skin bag to convey how much of something was owned. Europeans borrowed this concept in C13 as the Latin word for "stone" to characterize "Reason" (calculate). Mathematical "colorblind," unbiased, nonprejudiced Logic. Reason is the only objective means of communication and of understanding between humans. It holds normal people to everybody to equal standards of Measures and Estimates so as to bring them to consensus, appeal to their Sensory Conscious and Conscience, and keep them under social control. Personally, Reason is the tool that brings workable solutions for *reconciling oneself to daily problems or existence difficulties + to fashioning offenses and defenses against losses, lacks, obstructions, opponents + for self-protection, self-preservation, and survival + designing ways to thrive.* To engage in Reason means reality is the objective standard and frame of reference. It carries ones Thoughts beyond the realm of mere Experience and, in contrast to Faith, allows for corrections. This enables learning leading to Knowledge and how to preserve and make Knowledge grow in areas of Art, Science, and Humanity without limit—but only if properly used on the right track and going in the right direction. Reasoning requires such close examination and such attention to detail as make the conclusions reproducible by anyone following that path. So, if the conclusion is disharmonious, Troubleshooting can be done to make the necessary changes. Still, Reasoning is not to be completely trusted because practically all of it is influenced by Emotions, Bias, Prejudices, and/or past experiences. See Age of Reason in Con-Artists' Tricks

REASONING: Reasoning in African Tradition is the process of staying within and generating objective standards and frames of reference out of the flow of the Spiritual Elements—i.e. following the Processes of Nature. *All such Reasoning begins in perplexity, hesitation, and doubt. Its process involves Analysis, Comparisons, Classification, Synthesis, and Conception.* As one progresses and is compelled to confront unique challenges, when correctly reasoning, one dissociates from the content (or experience) that initiated it so as to focus only on it; to weigh ones actions in terms of long-range consequences for ones own life or otherwise; and to determine what else must be true if the presuppositions are true. See Mathematics; Laws of Nature

REASONING BY ANALOGY INTO MYSTICISM COMMON SENSE: To hold in one hand five long crooked sticks in their middle, all of them touch each other in ones palm and at this point these sticks share a Similarity (having likeness or resemblance in a general way simply because they are all touching. On either side of ones palm, the curves of two sticks cause them to touch each and that means they are Analogous--partially similar parts in dissimilar things--as in the partial similarity corresponding to where they are touching at a *"common point."* This differs from Correspondence because the sticks do not have the same "Genetics" as, for example, one is real while the other is fabricated. The general *principle of Analogies is that: "If two things resemble each other in many Qualities, they can be used for further reasoning as Analogies on that basis.* Analogies possess the power to bring things to life by evoking images that illuminate the points of comparison the author is trying to make. Analogies have two parts: an original subject and a compared subject (what the original is being likened to). In comparing my love for my dog Titan to a gardenia, the original subject is my love while the compared subject is the gardenia so as to illuminate and express my love for both. The comparison can be either obvious (explicit) or implied (implicit). Emotive language often combines with visual imagery to present extremes of ideas and feelings, as seen in advertising. This is sort of like Ancient African ritual specialists who used ugly masks to personify things—like bringing into a mental picture existence the idea of a destructive evil spirit. By so doing the people could focus on that mask and then take the appropriate action. Primitive Africans *Reasoning by Analogy*--taking the familiar to explain the unknown. This, the simplest and most popular form of Reasoning, is based upon the general *principle that: "If two things resemble each other in many points, they will probably resemble each other in more points.* Reasoning by Analogy was a starting point to deal with difficult situations never seen nor heard of before. It was through this process of "win-win" that Primitive Africans advanced to imagining more realistically what *Abstracts* could be existing in the *"Invisible" Realm.* Their early hypothetical proposition was those of gods, goddesses, and Spirits acting as Magicians producing magic out of the hat or out of nothing.

Notice here that although this may not be the Truth, it helped them get started with looking into the "Impossible"--and that is the way to get started in dealing with any problem you have no idea how to handle. What they used here is what they saw in their daily lives and simply connected the known with the unknown. Thus, they speculated that these Spirit Magicians transformed the way everything is by continually turning something into something else--day into night, child into an old man, rain-water into wine, and grass into milk. This began their concepts called *Metaphors* (something explaining some other like-kind thing). As Primitive African forms of Magic evolved over the ages, greater discoveries about the Unseen came from *Reasoning by Analogy*--i.e. comparing solved and familiar problems as a starting point to deal with difficult situations never seen nor heard of before. While this process is very useful for ordinary purposes, one must stay on guard against errors in judgments in such reasoning. For example, many people have been poisoned by toadstools by false analogous reasoning that because mushrooms are edible, then toad-stools, which resemble them, must also be fit for food. Obviously, false analogous reasoning is extremely destructive in stereotyping people and then acting on it, as with "Killer" police killing unarmed Black People.

Since Reasoning is a process that looks at an idea in relationship with others in order to determine the credibility of conclusions and judgments, it is a Right Brain dominant activity. This follows the process of: (1) picking up a clue of the barely visible; (2) noting similarities between things below an appearance level; (3) seeing their relation to each other; (4) synthesizing its aspects; (5) creatively design bridging gaps by harmoniously fitting the parts--regardless of how remote in time or space--by taking acrobatic leaps which successfully unify pertinent things into a whole; and (6) generating out of this perception of the whole those inferences which stay within the context of the Law of Correspondence and thereby complete the "big picture." This unifying of mutual relationships and perceiving their interdependence with each other and the whole expresses through abstract or metaphoric means is by the use of images. The Left Brain cannot relate ideas to each other.

REASONING IN AFRICAN TRADITION: African Rational Thinking is a mathematical process characterized by stepping stones used to progress to a destination or to somewhere Unknown but always within the flow of the Divine Logos. To elaborate, its *Reasoning is a mental process that follows a Mathematical pattern in keeping with the Laws of Nature + deal with all subject matter the way that it really is. As a result, the conclusions are therefore Reproducible + open channels to Creative Concepts + generates a path for Inferences to be made into the Unknown.* This is the process I developed while in the medical-legal arena of my Orthopaedic Surgical practice where conflict and disagreements raged with very significant cases. It was typical for attorneys to verbally attack doctors and for doctors to attack doctors in written reports. My role was within the context of being an Independent Medical Examiner for the State of California and dealing with the very toughest of cases because of special training in Medical Genetics. Yet, amazingly, I never was aware of having been attacked by anyone, including doctors. The fashioning of proper Stepping Stones and making each step sound by dealing with it in the Box Concept is the key. *Stepping Stones* are a bridge to a destination—serving as a means to progress or advance. As divided links of a chain, they are breaks to facilitate the advance to the next level. But to rest on one before going to the next, that one must be sound and solid enough to support what is resting on it—and particularly when used as a springboard to go to the next "stone." Black Scholars who rise on the stepping-stones of their discarded False Selves for higher realms, take off from the stepping stone Truths of prior Black Afrocentric Scholars. Their Right Life Living is verified by being in the Spiritual Elements flow. Thereafter, they must discriminate between the pertinent within that flow as opposed to more attractive choices outside it—by selecting here and there the significant stepping-stones which will lead across difficulties to new understandings. The one placing the last stone and steps across to stand on the gong of achievement will get the credit. Yet, the wise know and honor those whose patient hard work, integrity, and devotion to exact observation have made the last step possible. An assessment of this process has been given in my book: Leadership Critical Thinking. Whatever enters the mind through Reason can and must be corrected. When the stepping stones lead to the Un-Seeable generating Esoteric Unknowns that put them in the categories of the Circumstantial which has a Certainty even more than what is Demonstrable. It is Circumstantial Reason that has been the indispensable agent in everything making Ancient Africans Supreme. It enabled them to learn from the Esoteric, to build Thought Structures Knowledge and preserve it; to build up Arts, Sciences, Civilizations (social and technological development), Cultural (Intellectual and Spiritual development), and all that is great in the world today—and all without limit. By contrast, those using its Non-Rational and non-Spiritual Elements ingredients have made these the enemy of all constructive activities. For the in-between of extremes, its Reasoning products are untrustworthy since practically all is influenced by Acquired Emotions, biases, prejudices, and misinterpreted or wrongly applied experiences.

REASONING ALGEBRAICALLY: "*Algebra*" ("al" "from Egypt"--"al-Kemit")—meant in Africa the re-uniting of broken parts and was later defined by the Arabs as "restoration", including "bone setting." Note that the African originated Yin and Yang concepts are also about the union of separate parts. *Algebra,* a wordless thinking form of Arithmetic, is like those kinds of Thinking where pertinent mental ingredients put together are not words. Other substitution examples are: A + B x A – B; thinking in lines and angles and curves; thinking in Formulas, without words; thinking in musical note, as did the Mulatto Beethoven who was "stone-deaf." These are all Symbols and even the most difficult kind of thinking cannot be done without the use of some kind of Symbols. For Algebraic Thinking, instead of words or Numbers (figures), regardless of the plane of existence, the same Things put together or related are in Symbols. *Algebra* is partly analytic, for the solution of an algebraic equation means that unknown quantities or qualities become known. Three parts of Algebra are: (1) the comparision of things having Correspondence; (2) the reduction of those Things on both sides of the equation to its "That it is!" (its Primary Quality) or its "What it is! (its Primary Quantity) Essence state; and (3) representing each state by a Symbol. The Algebraic "Check and Balance" approach uses Pure Emotions = Intellect in a Mystical Mind manner. Creativity enables this to be endless. For example, it can assess Algebraic Words, like "Interestint"—which can mean something good or bad, depending upon the situation as well as on their repercussions. Another example is the "Present" = the past and future or is the equal sign between the Past and future. Still another is that 6/31/16 = 7/1/16 but June does not have 31 days in reality.

REASONING--INDUCTIVE/DEDUCTIVE: Obviously, sound Deductive and Inductive Reasoning was wide-spread in Africa many millennia before the Western world falsely claimed that Sir Francis Bacon (1561-1626) "discovered" it. Keep in mind that Renaissance European Scholars considered it a must to study the Hermetica (the works of the Egyptian Hermes) (Candy p8) and it was acceptable for them to take information out of the Hermetica and claim it as their own—just as the ancient Greeks had done with Ancient African knowledge. Hence, note carefully the distinctions between African and European Inductive and Deductive Thinking.

REASONING BY AFRICAN DEDUCTION--For Very Ancient Africans as part of their astro-mathematics in 20,000 BC and as part of assessing their findings in order to get solid information, devised Deductive (using a general truth to form a particular truth) and Inductive Reasoning (using a specific truth to infer a general truth). Then, after being satisfied from having discovered a Celestial Order by means of mathematics, they used this model to *Deductively* make inferences from these broad conclusions to build an Earthy order of particular truths to serve as standards, filters, guides, measures, and estimates for the benefit of kings, philosophers, and African people. An image helpful for me in remembering *Deduction is that it is like looking at a funnel from the top down.* By contrast, *Induction is like looking at a funnel from the narrow bottom up toward* the wide top. Deductive and Inductive Reasoning are always one and the same process but their difference is in the starting point and in the direction in which one proceeds. Thus, in a sense they are Algebraic. Recall the first two situations concerning African Tradition's mythological concept of Cosmic Creation dealt with Metaphysical Order and with Metaphysical Disorder (a break in the integrity of Ma'at). The "equal sign" and Yin/Yang mean "Chaos" and "Order" are complimentary equals because each contains things involved in the other. Also, to discover the truth of one of the two opposites separated by an "equal sign" is to discover Yin/Yang principles in the other. This was the beginning of *using symbols for unknowns and of Inductive and deductive reasoning.* The essence is that the Scientific Method includes both Deductive and Inductive Reasoning—starting with Observation--for the purpose of proving or disproving a point. In the process of Deductive Reasoning going from the general to specific facts and Inductive Reasoning reverses this by observing particular objects and then proceeding to draw general conclusions, Insights often result suddenly as an understanding of the pattern for deciding or for solving a problem. The advantages of Deductive and Inductive Reasoning and of Insights are that the answers they provide become a "deposit" for idea withdrawals or a pattern for solving similar problems in the future. Ancient African philosophers knew that Induction and Deduction are interdependent in the mind's quest for knowledge—and one is incomplete without the other. Yet, each had areas of strengths and weaknesses. For example, "Speculation" occurs when one starts off trying to acquire knowledge by resorting to Deduction rather than with Induction. The reason is that one must then assume or hypothesize—i.e. reason from the absence of observation and evidence—which is avoided if one starts with Induction. Another example is illustrated by those Religions who intentionally keep Spiritual Element Knowledge sufficiently secret from most people as for the people to be unaware of its existence (Amen, Metu Neter III: 126). Then those people can be told anything short of the Truth. Other Religions produce similar effects by approaching the acquiring of concepts about Religion using *Deduction* (a general truism) rather than with *Induction* (a specific truism). By so doing, they embrace an inevitable element of Doubt because of having to assume or *Hypothesize*—i.e. reason from the absence of observation and evidence. This means "*Deductive Speculation*" is only a theoretical scheme, insufficiently checked or tested by practice, and that makes it a "SEEMS" Right Belief until verified or determined not to be Truth. Such is avoided if one starts with Induction. By thus being forced to rely on Secular Faith/Belief/Trust, adherents are channeled into what SEEMS right or true. Resultant *Secular Confidence* eagerly practices religion but lacking naturalness or rightness "Subtleties"; by following its rigid human devised rules; by clinging to those rules; and by defending those rules.

REASONING BY INDUCTION--AFRICAN: In ancient times, Divination was an Inductive method for obtaining knowledge of the unknown; for gaining insight into the future by means of Omens or Portents—i.e. a prophecy of something important; and a means to foretell the dictates of fate and reveal the wishes of the Gods in order to enhance Prediction accuracy. Occult Predictions, when verbalized, are statements about an event not yet observed, detailing what will be found when it is observed--like disorder follows a predictable orderly pattern. To this end, people and those of the Spirit World were said to be in constant communion. A later but still archaic term for astrological divination was "mathesis", the "Learning"—literally *Mother wisdom* (Walker, Women's Encyclopedia, p71) or "*Mother Wit*" (referring to the highest form of common sense). Spiritual Common Sense and its Critical Thinking—the primary tools which gave rise to recognizing and utilizing the Spiritual Elements and its network off-springs--was claimed to derive out of possessing knowledge of the Laws of Nature. Out of this scenario, Very Ancient Africans developed concepts about humans' abilities to gain control over their minds. They knew thought generate a form energy of intensely high vibrations which can be projected in vibratory waves to affect brains of others within its field of influence. This process of mental transmission is called Induction—i.e. "mind over mind"—the beginnings of *Parapsychology* as well as organized *Inductive Thinking*. *Induction is like looking at a funnel from the narrow bottom up toward* the wide top. Beginning without knowledge, it proceeds from logical connections between a category and its members—or a thing and its properties and modalities—to a general statement.

Because of the combined importance of stimulating minds, Algebra was combined with Inductive Thinking—within the setting of being in the flow of the Divine Logos. In other words, *Inductive Reason* began by being grounded upon Africans' intuiting the underlying uniformity of Nature—i.e. *it having consistent, permanent, stationary, and unchanging patterns/elements underlying natural events* as these flow in the *course* of their *Natural Processes*. Both African originated processes of Inductive Reasoning start with Known bits and pieces of the Truth in order to establish what is in the Unknown—i.e. the entire Truths or Principles which, in turn, are used to discover a general law. One considers a number of particular or specific items to develop more inclusive (or general) conceptions. From resultant Insights, *Intuitive Inductions* (inferring general principles from particular facts present in the Cosmic Order) are done. This means making compatible imaginative leaps to discover unrealized realities--i.e. the taking of Leaps from facts of Reality into realms dealing with corresponding Unrealized Realities.

Because of this power of humans' Right to penetrate intelligibly to the inner heart of things, it becomes possible to make the leap into saying this happens "all" the time or "every" time to a certain nature or class of things, even though this has not been observed in every possible member of that class. This is as close to the truth as humans can get. It is because of this type of inductive thinking that *Inductive Classifications* can be made. But whereas these "leaps" are orchestrated by humans' Pure Emotions, *Intellect Inductions* are by means of the African Law of Correspondence, often called the *Scientific Method of Proof* (originated and formalized by Ancient Black Egyptians between 2000 and 1500 BCE)--always studious and searching. Inductive Reasoning is observing a number of things sharing the same property or quality and going beyond this observation to generalize that the same property or quality can be applied to all known or unknown things of like-kind--and therefore placed in one "big picture" category. This is what Very Ancient Africans astronomers did from studying the stars and planets. A reasoned *structuring of the rhythm of the universe* emerged from them inventing Mathematics to seeing interrelationships. Another way this Induction Thinking showed was by Ancient Africans discovery of *Music (or Harmony)*. This implies both the living practice of African *Philosophy* (i.e. the adjustment of human life into harmony with God) and the living practice of Mathematics (since African Philosophy is Mathematics put into words), out of which all African Logic is based.

This brilliant African discovery of "*Harmony*" and its components, besides being the first step toward a mathematical analysis of the heavenly bodies (stars), gave insights into the influence of the heavenly bodies upon the Earth; of inner human experiences; and of the inner Selfhood workings of humans, as a microcosm, being small versions of the workings of the macrocosmic Cosmos. As a result of these reflections and inferences, African Sages fashioned, through Musica Universalis, a connection between African derived plain Geometry, Sacred Geometry, Cosmology, Astrology, Harmonics, and Music. They concluded that when ones Soul becomes identified with God by means of Ma'at practices, it hears and participates in "the Music of the Spheres" (James, p28, 140). Still, what one perceives as Harmony is any arrangement of forms, combination of colors, or other qualities which induce pleasurable feeling tones in observers. These Universal Music necessities induce proportions in celestial body movements—the sun, moon, and planets—in musical form. This 'music' is not literally audible but is, instead, a harmonic and/or mathematical and/or religious concept. Then, using Inductive reasoning, they inferred: (1) the movement of the large celestial bodies must make sounds in their motion according to their different rates; (2) those sounds made by their simultaneous revolutions are concordant (agree); (3) their speeds, judged by their distances, are in the ratios of the musical concordances; (4) and the sound effects, by means of the relation of one part to other parts, are a form of *Music*. Since all things in Nature are harmoniously made, the different sounds must harmonize. Yet, these sounds are not heard because they were present at the birth of Humankind

REASONING-TOTEM: Suppose that saying one category (e.g. Sharon, a human female) is the same as a concept from a different category (e.g. Titan, a dog) can enable one to have a different point of view to give a clearer and more complete understanding of the things being compared. Such can capture complex associations and relationships of different parts of the entities involved which are not ordinarily able to be consciously understood or logically appreciated. For example, Sharon and Titan might be *associated by the gathering of like-kind ideas about both* and meshing them into an Association of Ideas. Then, the essence of some aspect of Sharon might be represented in "Titan" features or described in "Titan" terms ("she fights like a bulldog"). Regardless of the nature of the comparison, it invites reflection on the ways in which these different categories might have shared common characteristics or underlying systems of definition logic. Algebraic Reasoning also can be parsed so as to highlight in Sharon and Titan some *unlike feature in their otherwise equivalences*, as through the differences in the "what it is" identity of the parts involved. Or, there can be highlighted in Sharon and Titan *certain similarities in their differences* (e.g. what each does and how each appears)--but not using a sharp and provocative contrast, as would be clearly visualized from using images of Sharon and Titan as they really are. Sharon would not like it if he said she looked like a dog. Instead, the spotlight is on the features shared by unlike things which come together to interdependently form a harmonious invisible Association of Ideas—"Sharon and Titan are my friends". Out of this Association one can gain an intuitive grasp of the relationship of Sharon and Titan. Very Ancient Africans used this type of Algebraic Reasoning in Totemic Systems, there is an equivalence, or correspondence—as in sharing a Ka (Persona)--between these two orders of difference. It is like a line that continually approaches a curve but without ever actually reaching it (called 'Asymptote). This implies the Totemic System remains open to the interplay of *Consequences* (the sequel: happenings from what sprang out of the Effects) and changing relationships brought about by the introduction of additional experiential, experimental, or conceptual information into the whole entity. Note: *Sequence differs from Consequence by not arising from the Effects*. Despite no proof, the 'payload' from the Association of Ideas possesses the power to bring the Totemic System to life by evoking images that illuminate the points of comparison one is trying to make. Totems can raise the questions related to the different ways in which "shared meaning" can be constructed and construed. In the totemic system, the comparing and contrasting allows for different assessment systems. Depending upon the type of equivalence one is looking for (e.g. something of worth and/or of value), the ways in which *Idea Associations may be categorized is chronologically, logically, conveniently, or in a correspondence of the elements that are the theme of the group*. For example, one can borrow the logical properties of an Order--i.e. the system of similarities/differences of this order--to express and understand another. In this way totemism is rather more than a question of content or simple analogy between two orders, but can be regarded as a method of Critical Thinking.

REBELLIONS OF ENSLAVED AFRICANS AMERICANS (by Sharon Bingaman, RN): Rebellion when talking about Enslaved African Americans? Absolutely. But let us take a minute to look at the word *rebellion*.so that we are clear on the meaning. According to Joseph A. Bailey, II, MD, in his book *Word Stories of African American Slavery,* the word is "derived from Latin –re, "anew" and bellum, "war"-a renewal of war. Rebellion is the subversion of the laws; Revolution is that of Tyrants. In Europe, "stubborn" retained during and after Biblical times the idea of a hard, obstinate attitude—and even that of rebelliousness. Both ideas, and especially those of a firm nature following an evil course, were thought of as beliefs antagonistic to God. Can your Real Self be about rebelling? Perhaps out of injustice. This term denotes any expressed resistance to a recognized authority—perhaps to a well-organized civil revolt against the government or perhaps to a domestic dispute between parents and children. Regardless of the cause, the intent is exactly the same where defiance of authority is involved." We can also classify rebellion as mild, slight, moderate and extreme. I am sure that we have all heard the question asked many times-'Why didn't the Slaves try to fight back" or "It must not have been too bad or they would have tried to escape." Well, just because the Truth was kept hidden and we were never taught, doesn't mean acts of rebellion by the Enslaved didn't happen. There were rebellions by African Americans taking place on many levels and in many areas of the country. The Enslaved fought back, not only physically but in other ways that showed them as heroes despite living their lives every day under the agony and horrors of the most evil and inhumane systems ever devised by man. Let's take a look at some of the ways the Enslaved were able to construct mild, slight, and moderate acts of sabotage in everyday life. They did whatever they could with whatever they had and they were very creative and brave. They knew they could be whipped and tortured severely or killed for their actions The Slave owners were motivated by a desire for money and power and this overruled any other problem that were generated by the Enslaved. This was the weak spot the Enslaved targeted, doing anything that would eat into the pocketbooks of the slave owners. The Enslaved would slow the pace of their work down-not so much that it was too obvious or they would get whipped more often - but just enough to make a difference in the overall production of the plantation. These tactics are examples of "Selfhood Armor". That the Enslaved used-an inner avengement (e.g. "White man you can enslave my body but you cannot enslave the rest of me.") They would break or hide a tool when possible and then time would be spent having to get a replacement tool or extra money to repair the broken one or buy a new one. Or they could play into the fixed idea that the overseer had of Black people as ignorant and lazy and pretend not to understand simple instructions to do a task and make that overseer spend precious time with repeated explanations.

Fences could be torn down or crops handled so badly they would not be fit for the marketplace. You can see that with "Time as Money" on the plantation these scenes playing out across the land would be very disruptive to the Whites sense of money and control. Taking something, like food, from the plantation owner or misplacing items was another form of sabotage. The idea was to strike back by disrupting the status quo of the plantation in every way they could, no matter how small it seemed. Plantation owners became ever more terrified of the Enslaved, in and out of their homes, as word of rebellions elsewhere spread. The slave owners would constantly be looking over their shoulder in fright as to what could happen next to them. They had food tasters to check the food before they ate or drank anything. The Enslaved resisted in every way they could, proving their strength and determination time after time. The female Enslaved had their own extreme form of resistance. Those who were of child-bearing age would make that decision that is so gut-wrenching for women. So strong was their love for the unborn baby and wanting to spare them from a life of misery and suffering, that they chose to abort their babies or kill them after birth to save them from a life of slavery knowing that child would also add to the riches of the owner. Many of the Enslaved with African knowledge of plant ingredients used it to poison the plantation owners and their families along with the livestock. Spitting into the food they prepared for the owner and family was also a way of feeling as though they were fighting back in some way. Another means of rebelling was the burning of barns and owner's homes. The "Selfhood Armor" and "Slave Resistance" worked well for the Enslaved but became self-defeating when culturally transferred out of slavery and on into today's struggling descendants. Another extreme form of rebellion by the Enslaved was running away when they knew the price to be paid if they were caught. That price could include having body parts chopped off, being tied naked to a tree during the winter or having each limb tied to a different horse and being pulled apart. Overriding all of this was the chance of being free. And don't let anyone tell you that the Enslaved did not put up much of a fight against slavery. There is documented evidence of more than two hundred and fifty rebellions or attempted rebellions of ten or more Enslaved From 1739 to 1858 there were many rebellions which the government called the Indian Wars involving the "Seminoles". Seminole was a term used to mislead and hide the fact that African Americans were involved in battles for freedom for over 100 years. The Seminoles were a mix of Black Africans and Native Americans who were allied against white oppression.   There was Dade's Rebellion, the Stono Rebellion, Gabriel's Conspiracy, Nat Turner Rebellion to name a few. The *Haitian Rebellion* of 1791 was a huge, successful, Black rebellion where the Enslaved fought valiantly, in Haiti, against the plantation system and slavery. It was an organized rebellion that saw Black slaves kill thousands of whites and burned many sugar plantations. But not only did they fight ferociously against Slavery, they fought and won against the well-armed and fortified forces of France's Napoleon Bonaparte. What courage it took to go up against that enemy with only the simplest of weapons, not enough food, clothing and no supplies! To add to that victory, the Enslaved were also able to fight back the British troops that came to the island. After a series of defeats, the British withdraw from Haiti. It struck panic in the hearts of white plantation owners for two reasons. One because it reversed the belief about the inferiority of Black people and their ability to achieve and sustain freedom as the formerly Enslaved were able to establish the second independent country in the Americas after the United States. And the second reason was because it threatened their comfortable and profitable way of life. The success of the Haitian Rebellion inspired many more rebellions when the Enslaved realized it could be done. The plantation owners of the USA organized police patrols, complicated slave -owner approved travel by the Enslaved, allowed gatherings of African Americans only if a white person was present and carried out increased inspections of slave quarters. An example of White folks being terrified by the Enslaved was the South Carolina legislature passing the Security Act in 1739 requiring all white men carry firearms to church on Sundays! Taking into account the repeated acts of defiance taking place all around them, on and off their plantations, even a rumor would send the plantation owners into a state of paranoid frenzy. The end of slavery came about not only because the Union won the Civil War but because White society could not continue to stand against the repeated and deadly attacks on every front by Black men working together for a common goal and that Free Black men would no longer tolerate it. We can look to our Ancestors with pride for the fact that they battled Slavery by every means available to them, keeping their culture, with its traditions, music, words and beliefs, alive in the face of repeated, systematic, if not complete destruction, devised to erase every trace of them. Remember the proverb that says the history of the hunt will not change until the lion learns to write? Well, get out there, find the truth and share it!

RECEIVERS—METAPHYSICAL: C13; "Receive" ('take it back') referred to persons buying and selling stolen goods. In African Tradition it refers to "re-yoking" with laws of the Cosmic Mind.

RECIPROCITY: Absolute "Either/Or" and *"All-or-None"* apply only in the Natural Spiritual World--e.g. either exhibiting all of Unconditional Love (God-Made) or not. Supernatural believers promote their superiority by doing the opposite. In the Supernatural Physical World, either something is *"For me"* or *"Against me."* By disregarding the Spiritual and Metaphysical planes of existence, it thus fits for Supernaturals to say: "Love and Hate" are opposites—because, they say, both are human-made relative emotions. To illustrate, *"Reciprocity"* is in Ancient Africans' *Twelve Cardinal Virtues*--pathways symbolizing the highest of human excellence. Others are: Propriety (be in accordance with the fitting and appropriate), Balance, Order, Truth, Harmony, Peace and Tranquility, Fellowship, Justice, Rightness, and Straightness or Righteousness. *Reciprocity is defined* as: *"the rewards from ones "Gifts" come by unknown Receivers doing "ME/WE" acts for the Giver in doing Good"*. This is African Tradition's way to determine ones *degree of "ME/WE" success*. To elaborate, one is not to expect to be directly rewarded for good acts. Instead, one *receives rewards through and by the characteristics, qualities, and affinities acquired by having done them + by those helped, in turn demonstrating a "ripple-helping-others" effect. Selfless Service is best provided anonymously* because this relieves Receivers from feeling obligations to respond in kind (i.e. Reciprocity), especially if unable to do so. The *Givers' pleasure comes from making the Gift and supplying it*, as opposed to the receiver wanting it or accepting it or using it or benefitting from it. The *Law of Causality* pertains to a relationship between entities and their actions but does not specify the kind of causal processes operative in any particular entity. Nor does it imply the same kinds of causal processes are operative in all entities. Yet, in the Consequences of the Giver (a generous Heart) and the Receiver relationship, there could exist a similarity of Spiritual Elements Feelings experienced: Appreciation, Respect, Selflessness, Sharing, Compassion, Gentleness, Kindness, and Helpfulness. These promote a Nonaggressive Atmosphere of inner peace, social harmony, and contentment. The quite different Supernatural sense was used by Hammurabi (1792-1750 BC) with the Babylonians. Since they had an Inequality social system, *Extremism* reigned—exploitation of the oppressed. Despite some laws being rather progressive, others were quite brutal—as in the phrase, *"an eye for an eye."* This signified equality within the domain of every aspect of the composite, depending upon the status of the involved person.

In Hammurabi's recorded words: "If a man has destroyed the eye of a man of the gentleman class, they shall destroy his eye .... If he has destroyed the eye of a commoner ... he shall pay one mina of silver. If he has destroyed the eye of a gentleman's slave ... he shall pay half the slave's price." The phrase "an eye for an eye" represents what many view as a harsh sense of vengeful justice--an alternating receiving and returning Reciprocity. Hence, the first determines the second and then the second determines the first--in a feud manner. Hammurabi's concept has been carried on to this day, with modifications off the theme of: "A blow is repaid by its like, to every action there is a similar response"—in short, "An Eye for an Eye" in retaliation—a Bible justification. A variant is attacking someone close to the intended (e.g. a family member) for revenge. An *"All-or-None"* variant is those "Individualists" who "Give" within liaisons and alliances so as to receive— otherwise they do not "Give". Such "Giving" of service is seen as an unspoken rule in urgency situations so as to receive help when they need it. Its story prominently occurred when Aryans of 2000 BC would stop daily fighting each other whenever they faced a common threat. They then joined forces to fight that common enemy. Similarly, in today's "civility" politics, Republican opponents, obviously hostile to one another at one moment, come together in the next moment to agree on plans designed to defeat a Democrat. By far, the most common *"All-or-None"* variant is seen in "me, me, me" oriented people who expect to be given what they want, when they want it, and for that to endlessly continue. Yet, despite giving nothing in return, they vociferously complain if there is anything they dislike about it. "All-or-None" and "Either/Or"—by being terms of opposition—are *"Make-Believe" when applied to almost all things in the Physical World because of leading people to see reality in ways other than they are—then make false conclusions—then take wrong actions of destruction.* jabaileymd.com

RECIPROCITY--AFRICAN: *"the rewards from ones "Gifts" come by unknown Receivers doing "ME/WE" acts for the Giver in doing Good".*

REFERENT: the Thing to which ones words refer or the Thing described—e.g. a real-world counter-part or the invisible features which gave rise to the Notion. It is the proper defining characteristic of the concept. A fundamental Characteristic is the one on which all other satellites depend—i.e. without it the others would not be possible-- or it explains the greatest number of others. A *Metaphysical Referent* is the total of the Spiritual Elements of which one is aware and that has a harmonious bearing. From that total one selects the keystone Characteristic to suit the issue at hand—the one that determines other Characteristics and distinguishes the Disposition of an Entity from all the others. It is Epistemological by means of its ability to Classify, condense, and integrate an ever-growing body of Knowledge. If one is clinging, ask what is referent or fact that gave rise to this concept and what distinguishes it from all other concepts.

REFLECTION: C15 (turn ones thoughts back) is connected with casting back light rays. When waves of any kind travelling in one medium arrive at another in which their velocity is different because of an unfree mind, part of their energy is, in general, turned back into the first medium.

REFLECTIVE THINKING: (C15, turn ones thoughts back) is connected with casting back light rays. When waves of any kind travel in one medium and arrive at another in which their velocity is different, part of their energy is, in general, turned back into the first medium. This is termed Reflection. If one looks in a mirror, one can see Images behind oneself--a sort of copy of oneself. If ones stands between two mirrors facing each other, there will be no end to the number of images one can see. Ones Genius is greatly enhanced by *Reflective Thinking*. This is like mirrors in ones mind that throw-back Images, experiences, thoughts, and emotions of ones own life, as well as the lives of others and of Nature. In this state, the mind is not on the stretch but is, at times, in passivity. Meanwhile, it is continuously introspective in order to discover something satisfying to the mind which was not there at the beginning of the search. This is achieved by examining ones own heart, mind, and Conscience. Looking back over what has been done so as to extract the essence meanings to serve as ingredients for dealing with further experiences. Such is especially true for what to do in a flash and for summing up what was done during the day so that in the morning one will know what has to be done. Thus, the Self-respecting do not peep at their reflection in carnival mirrors of their minds or see themselves as others see them. Instead, starting out in a meditative state, the Reflective mind has returned into itself to take notice of ones mind--its own operations and their manner--the acts of ones mind itself--and on its contents, so as to see the operations for purposes of understanding oneself. It takes the middle ground between the convenience of doubting everything and believing everything. In the process of being in the middle ground, Reflection encompasses intellectually the discovery of the multiplicity of things by: (1) selecting a difficulty; (2) defining it; (3) assessing, examining, and analyzing an issue's triad: the obvious, hidden, and Base/foundational aspects; (4) establishing hypotheses; (5)testing the hypotheses and rejecting the illogical; (6) discovering the Oneness behind or underlying all those of pertinence; (7) verification; and (8) extracting wisdom from principles discovered. These necessitate intense inquiry into the nature of ones Real Self; studying African Sages teachings; and putting ones insights from both into practice as a way to know their meaning and proper customized application (Ashby, African Origins p459). With respect to the issue at hand, the deeper one goes down, the more intense is the clarity about what is going on in ones inner or Unconscious world. Perhaps the inner fabric of ones life looks like the weaving pattern consisting of the interdependent woof (the transverse thread or yarn) drawn through the warp (the lengthwise or longitudinal thread in a roll). That inner world serves as a

Background of a tremendous amount of experience giving rise to ones thoughts related to ones Material Body (the dense formal part) and ones *Subtle Body* (how one feels to oneself—as when achieving some success or experiencing some failure).

REFLECTIVE THINKING--AFRICAN: African *Reflective Thinking about things of the world follow the Flow of Nature's Processes. It is the expression of the ability to recognize the quantifiable by following Natures processes so as to discover what is already present naturally.* This means that mathematical patterns underlie the creation of Physical Matter. Put the "Big Picture" in perspective by analyzing ones own interpretations; comparing and contrasting ones reading/thoughts with readings/thoughts of others; and attempting to arrive at conclusions based on Probability. See *Introspective Contemplation*

REINCARNATION: In African Tradition, the One God, Aten, is symbolized by the Sun--while the mythological God, Ra, is the Sun's rising attributes—i.e. as it transforms from the undifferentiated Subjective into an Objective Being. Upon the Sun's return ("sets") to its original unformed state in the Subjective, it is Temu. Such organized multiplicity of Unity is an unnamed One Being--a Cosmic Force conveniently called Sekhem. In short, the Supreme Being is ever coming into existence as Things in the Cosmos and returning to its essential undifferentiated state—i.e. *Reincarnations*. The "Inside-Out" Selfhood Reversal concept starts with pre-humans in the Subjective Realm being instilled with all of the Cosmic Laws of Nature—i.e. "First Wisdom"—and vibrating at the same rate as of the Creator God. This is to be ones primary intentions and deeds fashioned while living life while in the setting of the Ancient African concept of *Ari ("action")* which was said to be attached to a person in a manner that leads one to ones "fate," even beyond death. This Ari concept was carried by Africans into India (then called Dravidians) under today's popular term, Karma, as well as by African Buddhist into China and from there into Japan (as a feature of Zen). Ari is set up by the LAW OF HERUKHUTI: "Know that God neither punishes nor rewards nor protects, that you will have the comfort of controlling these for yourself" (Amen, Maat p93). Ari derives from the African Law of Ma'at in general and that portion called the *Law of Sympathy* (all God's creatures and creations are spiritually related no matter how remote in time or space and thus things can act on one another at a distance because of them being secretly linked together by invisible bonds) in particular. An extension of this is the LAW OF NTUOLOGY: Spiritual and human networks interrelate all humans. The standard for judging how one lives inside ones Earth World Destiny is *ones primary intentions and deeds fashioned while living life.* The LAW OF MA'AT has the Principle of Justice as one of its features--meaning, in one sense, that the just (fair) consequences of a human's actions must be tied into her/his level of spiritual evolution. So, stealing by those struggling to live or by the ignorant who do not know any better is not judged the same as it is for Brutes (the evil) or for Satanists (those doing the opposite of the Spiritual Elements as a way of life). Yet, the ultimate goal is the same--i.e. ones Redemption. The consequences are greater on those who choose to needlessly generate losses, lacks, or obstructions in the Spiritual Rights (i.e. God's Rights) of others. The spirit underlying all these laws is that all actions done to others react upon the doer, as demonstrated by the Twa (San) people. Called "Negroes, Bantus, Pygmies, Nilotes" and other derogatory names by Europeans, the San (Twas, *Twi,* pronounced Twii, as if the *i* were double) had a well documented presence in South Africa as hunter-gatherers more than 100,000 years back. They are credited with the origin of the human family as a whole as is known today and survived as the Dogon people of Mali. Their Affect Symbolic Imagery demonstration of what Ari is like was by their invention of the *Boomerang,* an object resembling a bird or airplane, with a bend near the middle of its wings. When properly thrown, the leading edges of its "wings" (air foils) slice the air, thus providing a lifting force as it moves forward. Meanwhile, it is spinning end over end. This force from the leading wing experiences more lift than the retreating wing and the power process moves the boomerang in a circle and therefore back to the one who threw it (Bailey, Handling Bad Emotions). This is why I never cast ill-will towards others. The Boomerang principle of Ari present in the Law of Ma'at states: "the good one does to another is done to oneself, because we are One in essence"--i.e. part of the same Cosmic Organism which operates by the Law of Sympathy. This is justice which rewards oneself. Because on an Earth World level there is an ongoing repetition of the nature of ones original Thoughts manifesting in a compatible behavior, it follows that the same law of Oneness indicates that: "the wrong one does to another is done to oneself." One will set up ones own circumstances that lead to punishment--and that is justice. From these Circumstantial Truths came the African concept of *Reincarnation* (the means for perfecting ones Spirit)--that all unrighteous people will eventually reap the ill actions they inflict on others. Some bad deeds or acts are so bad that they must be paid for in several incarnations before the "echo" fades away. Birth, death, and birth would continue until one completely learned of the illusoriness of the desires, worldly attainments, and actions. Such bad karma is based on Ancient Africans' system of Yoga/Religion/Spirituality lacking any death--only a transformation of ones thoughts, action, and innermost consciousness--a transformation of a purgatory nature located, not in another world, but in ones next life on earth. Right handling of this gives wisdom and power.

Of course, people who believe that "when you're dead you're dead" and come to earth only once, will not be persuaded otherwise. Yet, ones beliefs about ones fate does not affect the reality happenings of ones fate. But if they could objectively look at all aspects of this belief throughout its course (e.g. "why do anything good?"), they will soon discover that their philosophy of life (POL) is flawed and inconsistent. By contrast, African Tradition POL has Order, Regularity, Coherence, Consistency, Compatibility, Balance, Harmony, and Predictability--all indicating it is ultimately Right. Regardless of ones beliefs, one has the free choice of continuing to follow ones Karma of past thoughts and actions or of resisting them. Only through a *Purified heart*—i.e. ones conscious and unconscious mind—achieved by Karma reparations—is it possible to go to a higher plane of existence in intuitive (above thought) understanding and wisdom (discerning between the real and the unreal) about the nature of ones own existence (Ashby, Yoga p90, 181). The Base idea for each human in African Tradition is to wind up where one started--i.e. back with ones original Creator. That can only be done by one living life in such a Ma'at manner that ones Soul vibration will be able to mesh with that of the Creator God. There are no excuses for not doing so. Thus people reincarnate until ready to get serious about Salvation. In African Tradition, *Salvation* is the achievement of perfect obedience to God's will so as to have wisdom and preservation from evil and destruction. Since the natural progression of all real things is that of the Primal Circle, the Soul of each human being progresses from its God source through several lives as it eventually circles back to its God source and reaches it once one has lived perfectly. Also, *Ari ("action") was intentions and deeds* attached to and leading one to ones "fate," even beyond death--the concept of Karma in India.

RENAMING: Historically, Europeans have stolen Africans intellectual knowledge and renamed what they could not away from Africa. To illustrate, the European concept: *"You've got to name it to claim it"* has been and continues to be used to steal Black history (among others). Its reason is sort of explained in the Encyclopaedia Britannica (1992, p 567): "...*men have seen in the ability to name an ability to control or to possess....*" They defined *"naming"* as applying a word to pick out and refer to a fellow human being, an animal, an object, or a class of such beings or objects. Renaming, done to Africa itself, was originally named "Alkebu-Lan." All Enslaved Africans were renamed, which contributed to them being Self-Unknowing. Renaming was done to all that was sacred to Amerindians for at 10,000 years as, for example Mount Mckinley in Alaska for the American president who had never been to Alaska.

RELIGION: Ancient African Sages proved God's existence with Certainty by means of Circumstantial Truth--i.e. by God's manifestations, even though God is unknowable. They defined "*Religion*" ("re," again, once more + the root "ligion") from the Egyptian concept of "to yoke," as yoking oneself to God. Once yoking was done, for the purpose of maintaining a connection or reconnecting with the Cosmic Creator and remaining so as a way of life, they used rites and rituals within certain rules. One is type of religion (Amen, Metu Neter III: 126) is from the Ancient African Bible which provides Knowledge of how to reach the Heaven Afterlife. The second came about by Europeans getting an African Coptic sect to copy much of the Ancient African Bible. Then Europeans modified it by *withholding African Knowledge and the means to Heaven Afterlife attainment in order to leave its adherents to rely on Secular Faith/Belief/Trust in the way they presented it.* Of course, the purpose was to control the people's minds by having them rely on what SEEMS right or true. For example, they added the stories of "turn the other cheek" and "be meek," neither of which is in the African Bible. Neither do Brutes adhere to either.

RE-ORDERING: First, find the Right way—that there is African Tradition since it is Nature and Mathematically based. Second, make a decision about it—select a philosophy of life--and formulate Human Ideal goals that work by being custom-made just for you. You need a Philosophy of Life to develop principles for problems as they arise. Some places in dealing with Brutes does not allow the Spiritual Elements. Third, map out a course with stepping stones to arrive at your Human Ideal Goals.

Fourth, you have built a lifestyle around this and it adversely affects all aspects of your life. Discover each by completely spotlighting them—handle each—and plan to put in place what ensures they will never be allowed to happen again. Fifth, put the Human Ideal into daily operation, and without exception or without taking "breaks." Do not rush to end an insight since it is in the most productive time of a Thought Cloud.

RESPONSE: of Ancient African origin was African Griots (story-tellers) participatory audience communication—i.e. "*Call and the Response*"--characterized by the Griot sending out a "call" and the audience acknowledging the message. The audience responded while the speaker spoke--and not afterward--so as to make a fluid harmonious tone of participatory communication.

RESPONSIBILITY: "*Charge*" (obligation, duty, and responsibility). "*Obligation*" is a binding promise to take the steps necessary for caring. This means there is no problem too great to undertake managing--even if it has never been done before or the Mentor has never seen nor heard of it before. "*Duty*" is doing the tasks which have to be done without consideration of fame, money, or status. "*Responsibility*" is shouldering the consequences for anything not properly done or that is left undone but should have been done in accordance with ones obligation. Two features are: first, take care of other people's things better than if they were yours; second, stay in contact without needing something.

REVELALTION: See "The Word"

RIDDLE: an ambiguous statement with a hidden meaning to be guessed by the mental acuteness. See Puzzle; Conundrum; Enigma; Paradox; Problem; Mystery

RIGHTEOUSNESS: a human's "Soul's Sunshine" orchestrates all of its Selfhood faculties through that human's higher mind and Lower (animalistic) Self nature so as to create, enhance, maintain, defend, and protect its liberated and perfected Soul from ones Lower (animalistic) Self. Ones own moral nature—called *Conscience*--extends this into all possible attributes of ones Spiritual Elements products—i.e. those of Think, Feel, Say, and Do activities of daily living

RITES: Rites are more about the "Why" that gives rise to the social ceremony while Rituals are more about symbolic meanings expressed in physical drama and impact in the performance of the ceremony.

ROMANS—ANCIENT: Based upon observation of Etruscan pottery molded in the forms of Negro heads, the earliest known natives of Italy were Negroes. They interbred with barbaric Europeans from the North which made their offspring somewhat less barbaric than their Northern European ancestors. The influence of Africans on the spirituality of the ancient Roman world before Christ had expressed itself in the popular cults of Isis and Ausar (Osiris). In Rome these cults had numerous followers in every strata of society -- from the common man to the emperor. Roman tombs of the rich and noble were carved with the symbols of Osiris. The Roman goddess Diana was the same (from African borrowing) as the Greek Artemis which was the same (from African borrowing) as the Black African Bast--all of whom were painted black. The goddess Bast was painted black because the Africans knew the Madonna and Son as their very own Isis and her Black son Horus. Walker states (p233): "Roman towns all over Europe habitually called the local mother goddess Diana (who was painted black), as later Christian towns were to call her Madonna." The cult of the European Virgin Mary is thought to have sprung from the cult of Diana. However, both ancient Greeks and Romans thought the only way to subdue an enemy was to club, murder, maim, or bludgeon him into submission. Even with their own criminals, the Romans divided and punished only the "dispensable" ones (e.g. the poor, the Enslaved). Given the same crime as the "Indispensable", the "Dispensable" were put to death in public displays, as in coliseums where they were pitted against hungry beasts.

Similarly, the Christians were placed on the stage grounds so that 45,000 spectators could watch them being eaten by hungry wild beasts. Apart from punishment by death, public physical torture was dominant in attempts to control the people. For example, Jesus was said to be crucified and physically tortured until he slowly died. When these brutes became aware of the Coptic Egyptians they were impressed with their peaceful, docile, orderly, obedient, passive, and revering of their leader. Besides Roman leaders being envious, they knew *people who embrace man-made religions are easy to control and are easily led*. In addition, they were aware that Africans did not worship the Pharaoh because his only role was to keep "Cosmic Order" or "Cosmic Balance." Instead, the people worshipped the unseen universal Spiritual Consciousness. The Greeks and Romans wanted to be a part of that worship, but with themselves being worshipped. This began their thoughts and preparation for taking over the power of the Ancient African Bible messages by establishing their own religion and being in charge of all power that was African. Idolatry flourished by forming a specific image of God whom no human had ever seen (the definition of an idol). This was proof of them being atheists, despite them carrying a Bible in one hand. ." To illustrate instances of the *Inheritance of Acquired Characteristics* displaying as a deep unconscious representation of experiences common to Supernaturals since ancient times, let us look at the ancient Romans, considered a beacon of civilization in a dark world. One of them said: "Rome is the seat of virtue, empire, and dignity," ruled by laws so just that they could "surpass the libraries of all the philosophers." Although it is typical for people to use their concepts, standards, and ways of doing things in dealing with other cultures and even their own culture of the distant past, such is fraught with misinterpretations, say, of definitions of "virtue," humanity, and "dignity". The setting was that the Roman Emperor Domitian borrowed the Greek notions of *arête* and combined it with the Roman concept of *virtus*. *Arete*, of high value in Greek culture, was translated as "virtue" but likely meant reaching ones highest human potential or the pursuit of excellence. Let us see how these "virtues" displayed. One example is that if a Roman husband discovered his wife was having an "affair" with a Slave or a male prostitute, he could murder him. If it was a citizen, he would have to talk to his father-in-law. Fathers, in Rome, could legally murder their daughter's lovers. If a woman caught her husband having an affair, pretty much the only thing she could legally do was cry about it. However, it was against the law for women to cry at any funeral. Second, if one did something slightly bad, one was only beheaded; if moderately bad, one would be taken to the roof of the prison and thrown off; if one killed ones own father, one was blindfolded and by being unworthy of light, taken to a field outside of the town, stripped naked, and beaten with rods to within an inch of ones life. After that one was put in a sack containing a serpent, dog, ape, and rooster. This was followed by all being sewn in there together and sack was thrown into the sea. Third, Roman ladies all had naturally black hair and any natural blondes were deemed barbarians, especially the Gauls. Since prostitutes were not allowed to be associated with the dignity of a proper Roman woman, they had to dye their hair blond to make themselves look like barbarians. Yet, Roman women who were jealous of all these blonde barbarians started dying their hair blonde. Other chopped off hair of Slaves so as to make them into wigs—the point being for high-class ladies to be indistinguishable from prostitutes [notice how the same is practiced today]. Fourth, committing suicide was considered prudent thinking, as for kings who kept poison on hand in the event of things turning bad. Sick people were encouraged to drink hemlock to put an end to their suffering. For economic reasons, Soldiers, Slaves, and Prisoners were not allowed to commit suicide. If Criminals were "allowed to quit," the state could no seize their property; if a Slave did, the owner was entitled to a full refund. Fifth, Roman fathers had legal rights to temporarily sell their kids—three sales per child. Over 3 times meant an unfit father and the child would have to finish the indenturement as a Slave and then be legally emancipated for his parents. Sixth, Romans' "usuacpio" were laws on how long one could possess something before it became ones property. If you held onto anything long enough, it could become legally yours, including people. By this applying to African Intellectual and other properties meant the Romans are credited with most advancements they did not deserve. Wives, legally, became their husbands' property if they stayed in his house for one straight year. But if she really wanted her freedom, she could have it—as long as she left her house for 3 continuous days each year. Seventh, early on, Rome had no limit to what a father could do to his family as, for example, abuse—ranging from spankings to murder—even when they were grown. Daughters remained fearful of their fathers, even after marriage and sons only earned independence when their fathers died. For the most part, rights to murder ended in C1 BC. In time, Rome relaxed these laws a little bit. The right to murder family members ended in the first century BC—retained only if sons had been convicted of a crime. See Free Masons

ROUGH: Chinese Sun Tzu under the title of *"Taking Whole"*—i.e. playing "rough" but without opponents necessarily losing. "Rough" is not the same as "dirty" (i.e. brute practices) but instead is doing things that are intimidating and respected, even though the opposition does not like them.

RULE OF THUMB: PROBABLE (after testing it has the appearance of truth but remaining room for doubt makes it SEEM or "likely" be true). Probable Opinions are like a *Rule of Thumb*--a rough and useful principle or method, based on experience rather than precisely accurate measures. What is "Likely" appeals to the reason as being worthy of belief because there are more points to favor believing than not believing. By using established past practices as a guideline for making a decision, "Probable" guides one in matters where one lacks Certainty.

RITUALS: whereas *Rites* (more about the "Why" giving rise to the social ceremony), *Rituals* (more about symbolic meanings expressed in physical drama and impacted in the performance of the ceremony). Ancient Africans Rites and Rituals--based upon Ancient African (Bible) Spiritual Literature Principles--were inside a sacred space, meaning its atmosphere surrounded any human participating in a communal event. Such was to signify a sort of *"Religious"* practice serving as a symbol to stay with or re-yoke to the Cosmic Creator as a way of life. That *Unity among Diversity* became African Tradition's theme.

S

SADISM: *aggression turned outward* during the Dark Ages--was the opposite of early Christianity's *Masochism as aggression turned inwards* (Psalm 73). Sadistic practices originated in antiquity, particularly in the form of floggings or torture of animals, captives, Slaves, servants, children, wives, and concubines—practices notably seen and preserved most strongly among European males in totalitarian, militaristic, and patriarchal cultures--practices the Church during Biblical times deemed to be evil and the work of Satan. Psalm 73, in depicting the character of arrogant sadists says: From their callous hearts come iniquity; the evil conceits of their minds know no limits. They scoff, and speak with malice; in their arrogance they threaten oppression. Their mouths lay claim to heaven, and their tongues take possession of the earth. Let us pick up this wide-spread and complex story of Sadism in C7 when Europeans--calling Ancient Africans' four vehicles of evil, "Black" Magic, Witches, Wizards (male 'witches' or 'warlocks'), and Sorcerers (Bailey, Freeing Enslaved Minds)--fashioned practices known as Satanism (a word meaning "the opposition" to Christianity; "he who opposes"). Beneath the emblem of Baphomet, the horned god, they engaged in indulgences of the flesh and of the senses. The patterns thereby developed have not changed much since then. The witches and black magicians under the banner of Satanism came (and continue to come) from a variety of social class backgrounds and possess all shades of political opinions. The inhumane religious "Trials by Ordeals" were particularly prominent in the European Middle Ages. The C13 to early C19 Roman Catholic Church used questioning by torture in the *Inquisitions* (discovering and punishing heretics). Torture was also used in civil courts up to C20, including witchcraft trials in colonial (USA) New England (Bailey, Special Minds). What grabbed my attention about the subject of Sadism came from my readings of European practices whereby they not only would kill babies, women, and men everywhere they went but would also chop them up! What would be going on in a mind so warped that it would get "sick" pleasure from seeing or causing other living things to suffer to such an extreme degree— and having an urge to destroy them after they were dead? European authorities say Sadistic people do not feel what they do is wrong; may find their deeds to be socially maladaptive and therefore disruptive; and the most common trait of nearly all Satanic novices is a high level of general anxiety related to a feeling of inadequacy and to low self-esteem—which, historically, is actually an inferiority complex. An *Inferiority Complex* is about destruction of different foundational and prop elements of ones Self-Esteem and it shows by destruction of oneself, others, and/or of what belongs to others or to Nature (Bailey, Self-Esteem). Even though sadism was not part of African culture up to the time of contact with Europeans -- and is not now--what Europeans did to African Slaves was so vicious as to cause some Slaves to retaliate by showing various sadistic acts. Perhaps Psychologists might account for this by saying people exposed early to violence or neglect come to expect it as a way of life. Also, any Sadism that could be seen in Black Americans is a reflective response to what Europeans have done to them as individuals and as a people. This was an example of "copycatting" as opposed to voluntary acting out of a brute mind. European Psychologists say Sadistic Personality Disorder may represent a subtype of Antisocial Disorder since both share in an exploitative and guiltless interpersonal style. Ancient Africans' believed Sadism is either caused by or the result of Spiritual pain and the attempt to get relief from this. What I would add is sadism, by being socialized into European males and backed up by the GUN, gives them the power to get away with whatever they choose to do. By having a fascination with all that is within the "Dark Side," they find pleasure in "Killing and Taking" to the point of it being an obsession and compulsion.

Sadism is generated by the Ignorant mindset that adores the IHES applied to the KTDDOC run through kaleidoscopic War operations alternatives

SAGE MIND: The *Sage mind—meaning a God-human*--being in harmony with the Divine and living in a manner that upholds the world is achieved by successfully return its newborn state.

SALVATION: In African Tradition, *Salvation* is the achievement of perfect obedience to God's will so as to have wisdom and preservation from evil and destruction. Since the natural progression of all real things is that of the Primal Circle, the Soul of each human being progresses from its God source through several lives as it eventually circles back to its God source and reaches it once one has lived perfectly. Also, *Ari ("action") was intentions and deeds* attached to and leading one to ones "fate," even beyond death--the concept of Karma in India.

SATELLITE: A *"Satellite"* is properly an astronomical term originated by Very Ancient Africans for a small body which revolves around a planet, held in its position by the gravitational pull of the planet and deriving its light by reflection. An example is *Micro-Aggressions.* To elaborate, whereby "obstruction of justice" is the euphemism used for European rich criminals, "violently resisting arrest" is applied to poor Black and Brown people for the same action. On a daily basis Black People experience a host of racism insult that act like satellites but can have their own additional influence as a result of a 'big bang' or cumulative micro-trauma.

SANKOFA: (1) go back to Ancient African philosophy to extract its principles; (2) apply those principles to fashion a Free Mind so as to replace or correct today's Black People's problems; and (3) use African Tradition's entirely new ways of designing solutions to go forward into the future.

SAVAGE: (C13, someone who comes from the woods) derives from woodlands being anciently viewed as places of untamed nature, beyond the pale of civilized human society, and living in or belonging to a primitive condition of human life and society. The overtones of Savage are negative, suggesting violence, merciless, brutal, ferocious, fierce, rude, sadistic, ruthless, relentless, cruelty, and murderous attacking, especially with ones teeth and without restraint or pity. It is generally accepted that: "the savage ascribes the mysteries of life and power to a supernatural source" and their minds show pervasiveness of pre-logical factors in primitive mentality. See Phantasmagoria; Brute

SCALE: *"Grade"* implies some regular ladder of valuation and some inherent qualities for which something is placed higher or lower in the scale, depending upon a standard. The Standard for Information Grading is Knowledge of African Tradition. A *"Scale"* is a scheme or device by which some property may be measured or used for classifying the different types.

SCALES/LEVELS: *Mild* (or Minimal) ranging from 1 to 24 on a ruler; *Slight* spans 25 to 49; *Moderate* is 50 to 74; *Extreme* is 75 to 99. There are 4 categories with respect to consistency: Occasional (1 to 24% of the time); Intermittent (25-49% of the time); Prolonged (50-74% of the time); Constant (75 to 99% of the time). *Proof* is associated with what is "Likely" (having aspects which make something Probable) or Probable. The first of two rough criteria useful for *grading PROOF* is the *SCALE OF CERTAINTY:* (1) "Barely viable" means a 1 to 4% chance of happening or possessing "rightness"; (2) *Low Possible*, a 5 to 9% chance; (3) *Medium Possible*, a 10 to 24% chance; (4) *High Possible*, a 25 to 49% chance; (5) *Low Probable*, a 50 to 74% chance; (6) *Medium Probable*, a 75 to 94% chance; and (7) *High Probable*, a 95 to 99% chance. (8) Certain is 100%. (9) Sound *Premises*, together with their necessary conclusion(s) constitute a Demonstration -- the highest form of proof and approaches certainty. But it cannot be applied outside of pure mathematics or other strictly *Deductive Reasoning* (reason from reasoning from given premises to their necessary conclusion). A second grading system useful for Proof is: (A) *Predominance of Evidence* means something has a 60% chance of being true; (B) *Clear and Convincing evidence* is 80%; (C) *Beyond Reasonable Doubt* is 95% -- *Moral*

Certainty is a conviction resting on such evidence as puts a matter beyond reasonable doubt, while not so irresistible as demonstration. (D) *Beyond a shadow of doubt* is 98% (Bailey, Medical-Legal Dictionary p81, 107). *Moral Certainty* does not require absolute certainty because much of it is based upon Faith (meaning rational justifications are transcended so as to arrive at a state of freedom), which makes it theoretical or speculative. Any form of Faith lacking a Certainty Base/Foundation does not naturally produce Trust. Hence, both are Secular. On one end of the Moral Certainty scale is the sense of the SEEMS right feeling of certainty. Those this varies with different individuals, proof carries universal conviction--called *Practical Certainty* (that degree of conviction sufficient for acting on a belief). Wisdom is its own proof Philosophers of science say that proof is impossible, the highest accolade being a long-running failure to refute. We can also look at the amount of research and debate that it generates.

SCALE OF DURATION: (A) temporary, (B) long-term, or (C) indefinitely. As a result of long and terribly painful ongoing experiences with Europeans (C), most Black People and Amerindians today are very leery of anyone bearing gifts. *Quantities*: Abraham Lincoln's statement that: (1) "You can fool all the people some of the time and (2) some of the people all of the time, but you cannot fool all of the people all of the time" may not be completely true in the last part. (3) It seems to me the World Crowd is fooled all of the time by Satanist leaders. (4) In practice, the shrewd fool just the right people some of the time. *Recurrence Rates* can be: (a) continuous; (b) almost continuous; (c) off and on at regular intervals; (d) *Periodic*, or occurring at regular intervals of varying lengths); (e) *Intermittent*, or occupying at intervals that which constitutes about half of the total time but recurrences are more or less regular; (f) *Occasional*, or occurring at infrequent and irregular intervals; and (g) Rare.

SCAPEGOATS: Scarecrows are mechanized formed set-ups to create fear in birds on the prey. Scapegoats (Scape, an archaic form of Escape) are unformed mechanized set-ups symbolizing what cultures customize to perch on for relieving their tension when things go wrong. Scapegoating is the defense mechanism act of blaming a convenient, innocent, and defenseless person or group for ones own frustrations, grievances, guilt, or inadequacies. It is a deliberate propaganda form in Supernatural-run governments. Society people and governments use it for "Hiding" in order to avoid scrutiny of their own "Dark Side." Scapegoats' story in the European Bible (Lev. 16: 8-22) describes an ancient Day of Atonement ritual practice of Jews on Yom Kippur where the high priest was required to bring 2 goats before the altar of the tabernacle. By lot, one was selected for Jehovah. The other was for Azazel, presumably a demon, and on whom the sins of the people were transferred for release (or allowed to "escape") to go to Azazel's place in the wilderness. In other words, *Scapegoats are those made to falsely bear the guilty party's blame and to suffer in their place.* The purpose is to carry the sins away and thereby relieve the community of further responsibility of doing needed improvement. The scapegoat has always had the mysterious power of un-leasing human's ferocious pleasure in torturing, corrupting, and befouling (i.e. casting aspersions upon; speak badly of so as to dirty their Dignity and Humanity). Supernaturals apply these practices out of an assortment of Fears. Their Fears are the *most potent of human incentives.* They hold Black people--their feigned enemies and assigned scapegoats--up as if they were a *Mirror.* In that Mirror they see and then try to beat away their own "Dark Side" + their profound self-hatred + their overwhelming envy of their scapegoats + their personal insecurities. First, this is part of the 'big picture" of Supernaturals being too immature to take responsibility for the generation of their own sins and acknowledge the horrendous damage from their Indifference/Hate/Evil/Sadism mindsets. Some other Non-Rational thinking involved are: second, *Displacement* a common coping mechanism involving transferring predators hostile feelings or bad actions from themselves to a less frightening one (e.g. scapegoats, an animal, vegetable, body part, relative, mate, child, or whatever is close by). Third is the process called *Projection*--using ones own "Dark Side" internal ideas (reality) to paint "out-group" members with a "Broad-Stroke" brush (i.e. Stereotyping). Meanwhile, those same ideas are fashioned to fuse with the corresponding human-made external (unreality) of fellows—i.e. in-group cult members. Fourth, "*Deflection*"—a throwback trick to the ancient Greek Sophists of predators using *Deceptions* to mislead both themselves into believing they are innocent of their countless evils + mislead Victims into believing they were the cause of their attack and their present problems. Brutes and their imitators' Deflection intent is to hopefully ensure no one will notice the evil like-kind things Brutes do. Examples: the media steers a specific crime topic to appear as if it is "normal in Black culture" so as to distract one from noticing the "white collar" crimes. Politicians are highly skilled in giving Deflection Answers of the irrelevant type. For this reason, Supernaturals very rarely, if ever, mention in speaking or in print who they really are or what evil they do. Fifth, *Distancing* is *Selfhood Splintering*—the Public Self being so Insensitive to others as to be "machine-like". Meanwhile the Private Self is hypersensitive--with strong fettered Emotions and reactions to whatever prevents them from getting what they want, when they want it, and an endless supply of it. The Envy of their scapegoats is for an assortment of things the bullies can never achieve. Nevertheless, Distancing is followed by efforts to switch from a self-hated, low self-esteem, and associated Inferiority Complex all the way over to a Superiority Complex. This process is so internalized and so automatic as for False Self-expressions to flow out of ones Selfhood as "*Second Nature*"--a 1390s term alluding to such frequent repeating of something as to make it seem inborn (like a Human Nature trait). Their cult's "authorities" capitalize on this by putting these inside rigid rules. "Second nature's" obvious power of what results from that design, without ones awareness, makes for deeply ingrained inhumane thoughts and *Conditioned Response* behavior patterns. Intelligence cannot develop in those who keep a foot on the throats of their scapegoats. jabaileymd.com

SCHOLARS: Somewhere between the pre-20,000 BC Very Ancient African learning temples called "Per Ankh" (Life Force) and the 12,500 BC Egyptian Mystery ('Secret') Religions and Schools, young men/women learned to become African priests/priestesses. Selections were made, as crystalized in the African Sage proverb: "*when the student is ready, the Master will appear.*" The associated terms "*Scholar,*" "*Pupil,*" "*Student,*" School, Scholarly, Scholarship, and Scholastic each share "Leisure's" ('permission') root. That root embraces having the freedom to do as one likes in Nature and with a Free Mind to do the explorations needed to advance toward priesthood. Leisure's base for effectiveness is *Inner Peace,* a manifestation of inner harmony and unity—both derived from operating out of "Pure" Emotions (which connect ones Real Self to the Sublime)—both serving as a "*Radar Beacon*" (a receiver-transmitter) that sends out a code signal so as to appropriately react in Harmony or, upon encountering anti-harmony forces, as an alarm (which, incidentally, has "saved" me from countless bad problems). "*Pupil*" referred to those under a teacher's close supervision when participating in higher religious education; "*Student,*" to those specializing in a branch of study in preparation for a profession; and *Scholar,* to "*giving oneself*" to learning intimate Spiritual Elements details concerning God's Laws. *Mortals* (Initiates, Neophytes), probationary pupils who had not yet realized the Inner Vision, were instructed in the Sages' doctrines. The *Intelligences*--advanced students from having attained Inner Vision by getting a glimpse of Cosmic Consciousness—had thus achieved the *Mysticism Mind*--minds having the ability to intensely concentrate their Intellect Reasoning into their Pure Emotions. They were assigned tasks of following "*The Way*" of African Tradition's Divine Logos—i.e. to stay in harmony with, while engaged in, and developing out of Esoteric Ma'at Principles (the Spiritual Elements in action). *Esoteric Knowledge* is understanding the inner truth lying hidden in the observable or what defies understanding of core fundamental Ma'at concepts because it is *knowledge beyond reason.* In African Tradition, *each human is to discover his/her own way to Mysticism* so as to reach the Afterlife—i.e. look behind the Hidden or concealed so as to encounter the mysterious things about God; the things belonging to God; and the things revealed by God to humans. *Approaches* (ways a goal is reached), *Methods* (how to do the job), *Techniques* (how tools are used in the approach and method) and *Manner* (the different ways a technique can be handled) African Sages used to introduce Africans to Esoteric Knowledge were of four main types: (1) "*Education*" ("to lead out what is inside"); (2) "*Teaching*"--"to show" lessons which make students aware of information and experiences so as to impart knowledge for learning; (3) *Instructing* ("to build in or into"--similar to but broader, deeper, and higher than "directions" or guidance)--to prepare or equip students by building knowledge in an orderly, step-by-step manner--the process like that of Common Sense, Rational, Critical, Creative, and Logical thinking; and (4) "*Training*" (active mind exercising in order to form habits) by demonstration. "*Education*" had top priority and for this they resorted to *African Dialectic* (later renamed by Europeans the "Socratic Method"). This was about asking questions for the purpose of drawing out ones in-born "*First Wisdom*" (all that is about the Cosmic Organism) so as to unfold knowledge in the Neophytes' minds. Next, said the Sages, because *anytime one is faced with a complex subject, the first thing to do is put it in Order*, Initiates were taught to lay up their knowledge in a natural and regular way. The questions asked were in general conversation forms. Following in priority were the "*Instructions*"--including how to Meditate to quiet the mind. This aided ones focus on thoughts and ideas of wise Elders or Sages, especially as to how, when, and where to pursue Ma'at. Regardless of method, the point was to maintain focus on and manipulate the discovered knowledge until all of its Principles were fully understood. Understanding was best when Principles' Essences could be recognized in altered forms and when Mortals became "One" with it. When applied to practices of a Ma'at nature, this represented *Wisdom*. The basic idea was for Scholars to weigh and balance all aspects in the "Big Picture" and how they interacted with each other. The objective was for every Scholar *to be in charge and control of ones Selfhood--of what one thinks, feels, says, and does—and of the situation one is in.* jabaileymd.com

SCHOLARSHIP: The word "*Scholar*" (leisure)--derived from the Ancient Black Egyptian Mystery Religions of ?12,000 BC--embraced: (1) remaining in or returning to the Real Self of ones birth and thereby enable ones (2) Selfhood Greatness to be cultivated by an (3) addiction to Ma'at Learning in order to satisfy ones Spiritually Energy driven pursue (4) to ones "ME/WE" Mission and thereby achieve (5) a Happy Life. These Ancient Africans had other thinking structures to solve specific types of unrelated problems as, for example, in discussing the Immaterial Realms (God's world), geometry, and the calculation of the calendar. The objective was for each African initiate to learn African Scholarship--to derive pleasure from striving for perfection to *self-improve*. Such occurred from paying careful attention to details concerning how see things as they are (without an opinion); to weigh, balance, and learn skills of mental discrimination; to make fine distinctions needed to display good practical judgement; and to arrive at proper conclusions by seeing both sides of a problem, studying each side from various angles, and then analyzing each angle discovered for its advantages and disadvantages. These focused on how to see all of the Obvious as a means of discovering the Hidden—so as to then uncover the Underlying *Order and consistent Patterns underlying natural events or disharmony or the Mystery's answer.* Scholars use inner vision into their Soul's Divine Consciousness as the key to improving higher order thought. Yet, from the earliest of times and all over Africa, their Subjective Sciences tools, in relation to Nature's Correspondence, produced such accuracy and precision as for any African scholar anywhere in Africa to use those finding as building blocks. Their skills of Observation, Reflection, "Pure" Feelings, Productive Imagination were from an unbiased and unprejudiced position to see things as they are in reality. Then, the resultant thought products were Contemplated on (thoughtfully dissolving into and identifying with Universal Truths) so as to establish a platform for Inductive (Inferring general principles from particular facts) and Deductive (making inferences from general truths to particular truths) Reasoning. Out of those conclusions, Inferences were made within the Common Sense that applied to Principles and Laws based upon the Spiritual Elements. Much before 7000 BC, Interior African physicians began the story of professionalism by stressing the necessity for having a free flow of ultimate honorableness out of their Selfhood core as well as comprehensive competence, the likes of which are practically unknown today. Under the direction of an esteemed elder physician, medical students underwent long years in the forest studying plants, herbs, and berries. We know of the world-famous medical meccas of the Ancient Egyptians from medical documents (e.g. the Ebers, the Berlin, the Edwin Smith Surgical Papyrus) which illustrate the techniques of operations and details of prescribed cures. Well established prior to 2600 BC, the world admired everything about African Medicine and Surgery--the operations, the surgical tools, the physician's ingenuity, and the good sense in using medications. Their professionalism represented the highest flowering of civilization, culture, and the finest values (that which determines constructive life-shaping choices, decisions, and solutions) contained in universal and personal *Humanity* (i.e. integrity dealings with all people as if they are family members). To this end, each professional--whether in medicine, law, or otherwise--required a special fitness in a designed scholarship occupation.

Professionalism in any form of scholarship was expected for the Salvation of all Ancient Africans. The theme was that Knowing comes out of Ancient African Wisdom as well as out of Nature. Scholars' duties were to gather information in order to form options allowing them to select the greatest subject to research as well as use those options which make a subject great by extracting knowledge amidst appearances. The reason is that *scholars do not give "Opinions"* (as do Superficial Thinkers) for they will keep quiet until their research enables them to "Know." Desires for personal benefits were never done at the expense of sacrificing their Integrity or seeking fame or taking what is in others or belongs to others. Instead, they were like the North Polar Star which keeps its place and all stars turn towards it. They always choose not to set their minds for or against anything since they knew that what is Right would follow from their natural inner candle.

SECOND NATURE: So frequently repeating something as to make it like its Human Nature. "*Habit Mind*" contains only what has been placed in the mind by acquired experiences, habits, and observation—and thereby becomes *Conditioned Reflexes*. This means the habit has been so often repeated as for the mind, by knowing it so well, as to carry it below the field of Consciousness and become "*Second Nature*," akin to Instinct. See Sixth Sense

SECULAR: (C13 Latin; generation, age) meant "non-religious or non-sacred" when brought into English (C16). Today, it refers to public, ordinary, or everyday life of a non-religious nature or of "man-made" religions. On the negative connotation scale, "*Secularity*" is a degrading societal force characterized by the turning away from religion and living with the conviction that one can direct ones life without divine guidance. See Correspondence—Disaster Star

"SEEDS"--SUBSTANCE & ESSENCE LIFE-SHAPING: For Critical Thinking inside the Processes of Nature, the fundamental organizing Metaphysical Principle is that there is a family that, like a box-in-a-box-inside-a-box, passes down it "Genetics" to offspring. It starts with a Source, out of which emanates a Substance, out of which emanates an Essence, out which emanates Essentials, out of which emanates Particular Things. Any given term used to designate an aspect of this at any given point within the Cosmos has the same Essence "Genetics" meaning. All in this family remains "*Like-Kind*" in the sense of sharing the "Sameness" of the Divine Logos "Genetics" (i.e. the Spiritual Elements) but with each family member being "Unique" in accordance with how those "Genetics" manifest out of their customize patterns of activated "Genes". This means there are Unique Subtleties in design and function present in the DNA in all the cells when comparing one genetically related (i.e. having the same parents) family member with another. An analogy is the human body's various "organs" being are specialized for certain functions, featuring a division of labor. Yet, each is dependent upon all others for its necessities of life in order to create health. Although any Genetically related member of that human's family has the same organs, each organ and its functions is uniquely operating as it ought to for the best health of that particular family member. The problem with European literature is it uses the same term for different aspects in the Process but gives that same term different meanings based upon ones own interpretation of what it means to conform to ones thoughts about it. From then on, they are "experts on the obvious". Such ridiculousness is to be picked up by CT; rearrange the presented thoughts onto their proper planes of existence; and apply the proper term before proceeding with Reasoning. The proper term's meaning takes on the "Uniqueness" of the displayed Essentials of its Essence parent's location wherever that is inside the Cosmos. For example, there are Essences on every plane of Cosmic existence. But no word is layered with more confusion than that of "Essence." For this to have proper application it must be properly applied on its various planes of existence and for that to happen one must know what happens on each plane and what the same word means in its unique form on each plane. So much of my present insights into the "what it is" has come from exhausting searches leading to eliminations of "what it is not". Confucius said "Ren of human being is Love". "Ren" is the core part of "seed." Every seed, animal seed or plant seed has a core part, so has the spiritual seed.

SEEMS: C13 English word "SEEM" (Old Norse, conforming or fitting in the sense of 'becoming') conveyed the impression of appearing to be real. However, the C13 Old French word "*Appearance*" (to show; to come in sight) is apparent and thus is opposed to actual reality. This means "Real" is to "Seem" as reality is to appearing—or as the actual is to the possible--as Being is to Becoming--as "is" (i.e. Being) is to "is not" (i.e. non-Being).

"SEEMS" RIGHT: C12 ('to be suitable to the appearance of Reality') implies what is not complete in forming, maintaining, or re-establishing wholesome Integrity. Problems include: the part presented and the hidden do not correspond; parts are not on the proper plane of existence nor on the right track; are going in the wrong direction; and a Supernatural thing is substituted for a Spiritual thing. When unsuspecting people are deceived by con-artists or when suspecting people are uncertain as to the presented having Integrity, there is a Nuance situation involved—either out of ignorance; allusions; embellishments to persuade; intended deflections away from reality; and/or to deliberately trick. European literature overflows with all of these as a step below the Truth and decorating it to "SEEM" Right. The invariable intent and usual result is to generate a self-interest unfair advantage while simultaneously putting Victims at great unfair disadvantages. To illustrate, Dr. Samuel Cartwright (University of Louisiana), coined the "disease" words to 'scientifically' explain why Enslaved Africans frequently broke and wasted things--*Dysaethesia Aethiopiea*; and "to run away" from the plantation--"*Drapetomania*". Typical of European shams, "SEEMs" right validity starts with its etymology. Example: "*Drapetomania*" (Greek "drapeto," runaway slave + "mania," mad/crazy) defined: "Before Negroes run away, unless they are frightened or panic-struck, they become sulky and dissatisfied," usually handled by "whipping the devil out of them." For claims dumb Whites make that slavery is such a happy life and so "natural" to Negroes, their runaway tendencies and resistances could only be viewed as "a disease peculiar to Negroes". He concluded with the "scientific" prognosis: the endemic neural disease of "Drapetomania" is likely to cause permanent sequellae. Obviously, a neurological disease was not the problem and there were numerous other reasons for running away--such as not being allowed to marry. If these White pseudo-intellectuals were not so dangerous, they would be laughable (Bailey, Word Stories Surrounding African American Slavery). "SEEMs" right is done to enhance the "Troops" *esprit de corps* (team spirit)—a Supernatural military term used to spur a singleness of purpose so as to stir up "Killer" police and Citizen Patrols to embrace the ardor, enthusiasm, vivacity, and pride in group effort, group standards, and group achievement. For this to work, first is to *persuade* good and moral Troop supporters to do evil. It is not necessary to force them but to simply impress on their minds, by contrived images, that they are doing good when they kill feigned enemies. Second, Non-Rational thinking is necessary for all the Troops—equated to remaining ignorant and superficial. Such is done by teaching all, starting in grade school, the Supernatural codes conforming to what is on the wrong track, either using the right or wrong process of reasoning. Third is diverting anyone from "Knowing Thyself"; from intermingling and gaining cross-cultural understanding; and to prevent any competition from Spiritual sources so that none can obtain any Truth. To elaborate, European philosophers say Nature's Processes are due to Laws of *Mechanics* related to motions of bodies. Its corollary, *Materialism*, asserts all change is rearrangement of bodies resulting from bodies impacting one another. For Mechanics to explain any growing thing, they say one must look behind it to discover its *Teleographical* goal of what it is seeking. In this Supernatural's military controlled setting, such deceptive "SEEMS" right are accepted because "*the leader said so.*"

What "SEEMS" right is made so confusing and conflicting as to simply be accepted on "Faith and Belief"—both European inventions. *Deception Insurance* is provided by using 'big words' to keep the essences of what "SEEMS" from being clarified or analogized because it is founded upon quicksand and built with hot air. Military minds have an unlimited capacity for taking deception from authorities and deceiving themselves into believing they are the receivers' own "truths." Those whose great insecurities make them Weak characters are indiscriminate in their eagerness to be active participants in the Supernatural conspiracy that says: "how great we are and how bad they are". Non-Rational thinkers easily get locked into such "far out" fantasies because it is designed for easy "getting along by going along." At no time do the Troops demand any background of how things came to be and by whom. In reality, this fantasy is like a ravening wolf in sheep's clothing. jabaileymd.com

SELF-CONTAINMENT: when geared to Self-Improvement, one is in the flow of the Spiritual Elements and develop all that they do out of it. Within this context, they are "Self-Made" and "Self-Styled" by following what they Intuit out of their own Divine Consciousness. This has nothing to do with disregarding those who provided the shoulder on which one stands to progress in the world. "*Contain*" (C13, hold with or together, accommodate) and "Content" are doublets meaning to restrain in the sense of controlling or limiting desire so that it does not exceed what one has or is. *Content* implies one is quiet and placid, patient and undisturbed—despite having to curb or adjust desires to what is seen as possible, viable, and practical. There is no urge to communicate ones thoughts and feelings except to be social or to share. This is within the context of "*Satisfy*" (enough or sufficient)—meaning having enough to meet all one really, really wants—i.e. despite less than enough, there is all that ones restrained and submissive desires request. "*Contented*" means Happy from having a sense of "Aliveness" from the pursuit of what is in the Beauty of Worth. "*Contain*" denotes to have, or to be capable of having, within. "*Hold*" is to have the capacity to contain and to retain in the sense of what one actually has in it. An analogy is that a bookcase contains (i.e. actually has in it) 50 volumes, but holds (i.e. capable of containing) 100. Ones "*Contained*" (C14, behave in a certain or Ma'at way) Selfhood means that one is born with everything needed to have a contented and thriving life of a "ME/WE" nature. This includes Selfhood Greatness with its contents of the "5Ss" of Safety, Security, Sureness/Self-Confidence, Strength, and Stability. However, in the "*Self-Contained*" Selfhood sense, one is a complete and independent unit in and of oneself; not dependent on others; Self-Controlled; self-sufficient--able to provide for oneself without the help of others; Self-Sustaining; Selfhood Order—having all Necessities for working in top condition, in their proper place, and working interdependently; powered by Spiritual Energy maneuvering and manipulating the Spiritual Elements in an "Aliveness" Selfhood condition; keeping to oneself; reserved; independent; and *Continues* (i.e. C17, 'hang together' uninterrupted). One has a healthy Self-Esteem; is *Self-Assured*--confidence in ones own abilities in a awaiting Self-Command (having all of ones faculties and powers fully in a state of readiness); *Self-Reliant* ("under control") on ones abilities, motivation, resources, and judgment; *Self-Composed*—having ones Emotions under calm control; *Self-Restraint*--to bend back to keep under control through various hindrances; *Self-Confidence*—is in unaided charge and control of who one is, what one does, and the situation one is in on ones own; *Self-Sacrifice*—putting aside present pleasure for future gains; *Self-Pride*—doing things perfectly so as to feel good about the product. See Accommodate; Self-Reliance; Selfhood Greatness

SELF-CONTROL: Self-Control (the restraining or regulating of ones own actions that otherwise would be expressed).

SELF-DECLARATION: C14 "Declare" (to make thoroughly clear), when used here, is a self-command (i.e. a declarative mood statement): "You will do as I say!"—to cause a change of course to come into existence from an authoritative utterance. It requires a Self-Declaration to engage in what it takes to achieve any Necessary Task—and with the biggest to be in reaching ones in-born Genius and Talent potential. Europeans call this "Self-Actualization" or "Self-Realization." Rather, the answer is within your Private Self and it has been there since birth in the form of your Selfhood Greatness. All it takes to set what you really, really want in action is to make a Self-Declaration to get it as well as a Self-Declaration to not get what you really, really do not want. A Self-Declaration within the context of Selfhood Greatness means no one is now, ever has been, or ever will be greater than you. Others may know things you do not but you know things they do not. So they are not better or worse than you but simply different. You have your mission to follow which is not the same as their mission. They do not know any more about how you should live your life than you—and they are struggling to live their life. To ask them what to do is like the 'blind leading the blind'. Thus, I do not humble myself to anyone except those who are struggling and have no idea what to do. I do not see any European that is or ever has been superior to me. So when I deal the hostile ones I simply keep Quiet and follow directions. A Self-Declaration automatically causes you to not run from any problem but rather to face it head on because that is an opportunity to use the difficulties in that situation as a tool to force out the divine powers within your Selfhood Greatness so they can be cultivated to solve the problems at hand as well as the increasingly more difficult problems as you swim further down the stream to your destination. My Self-Declaration was one of stubbornness which meant I would *always be in charge and control of my Selfhood--of what I did--and the situation I was in*. I refused to let anyone make me so angry as to break my Self-Declaration. For this collection of traits, characteristics, and features to occur demands one have a sense of Selfhood Greatness. I never hope, expect, fear, anything from the uncertain events of the future. Nor do I or refuse to face "impossible" problems because simply getting started may change a point of viewing that thing or I may see an opening or I might stumble on information that gives an insight or I can count on my Spiritual Entourage to lend a "Helping Hand" whenever I am on a "ME/WE" mission. There can be no neglect or abandonment of the toughest issues (which makes you weak and prevents the 'struggle' necessary to get through the stricture of the hour-glass) or inconsistency—for these make useless the accumulated information up to that point. Self-Declaration is an absolute promise to oneself to follow a given course. That tranquilizes the mind because of its steady purpose derived from what the Soul focuses its intellectual eye. A Volitional ('I will') mental decision—i.e. a *Self-Declaration*—which activates Conative (underlying motivation) power to drive how one acts on the Disposition's thoughts and Emotions. To hold on to a vivid goal is done by a volitional act of Self-Declaration of "I will do this and not let anything stop me"; a promise to oneself to follow a given course, despite troubles and difficulties; "I will do these things, come hell or high water". To determine what qualifies as ingredients for progress is whatever is perfectly inside the Spiritual Elements. "Almost" or "Good Enough" will not work—even if it is 0.000001 degree off. It does not matter how difficult it is to acquire the Right Message or how much one does not want to do it. In studying for my Orthopaedic Surgery Board Examination I needed to go to certain Orthopaedic conferences where they made it clear they did not want me there. And though I really did not want to be around all that hostility, I went anyway because I had, earlier in my life, made the Self-Declaration of not allowing anything to prevent me from becoming an Orthopaedic Surgeon. For that same reason, I was silence White Orthopaedic Surgeons would metaphorically trip me and cause me to fall down stairs. I simply got up, put a band-aid on my wounds, and walked away showing no emotions and saying nothing.

SELF-DISCIPLINE: Self-Discipline (training the mind for a mental and/or physical purpose in order to have mental and physical strength and toughness)

SELF-ESTEEM: healthy is *Self-Assured*--confidence in ones own abilities in a awaiting Self-Command (having all of ones faculties and powers fully in a state of readiness); *Self-Reliant* ("under control") on ones abilities, motivation, resources, and judgment; *Self-Composed*—having ones Emotions under calm control; *Self-Restraint*--to bend back to keep under control through various hindrances; *Self-Confidence*—is in unaided charge and control of who one is, what one does, and the situation one is in on ones own; *Self-Sacrifice*—putting aside present pleasure for future gains; *Self-Pride*—doing things perfectly so as to feel good about the product. See Accommodate; Self-Reliance; Selfhood Greatness

SELF-ESTEEM FEATURES: The most outstanding Trait(s) operation is its *Feature(s)*. The *Traits and Features constitute the Characteristics* of the Essence because they represent and reflect the various changing and developing modes of the Soul's Disposition expressions within a given context of that Essence. *Features* are about "what it is"—pure; polluted; diluted—in its nature; what it does—seen to have an admirable impact or be absorbed; how it appears—be what is typical or common in a Character or prominent in comparison by distinguishing. Self-Esteem's most outstanding Featured Trait of the Character is the Essence "*Trademark*"—and that is: (1)Self-Love. Other features include: (2) Self-Knowing (3) Self-Trust (awareness of expanding capabilities); (4) sense of Self-Greatness (5) Self-Appreciation (esteem of ones God's Substance); (6) Self-Respect (honoring ones earned self-worth and self-value traits); (7) Self-Confidence (sureness from empowerment); (8) Self-Efficacy (believing one can get any unique job done); (9) Self-Empowerment (sense of control, a good direction, and inspiration); and (10) Self-Reliance.

SELF-IDENTITY: Ones self-recognized Identity (the "who I am" as a Real Self or False Self) gives rise to ones mindset Disposition—the "*What it Does*" and "*Why it Does it*" as well as ones Nature. See Character; Nature

SELF-LOVE: ones Selfhood anchor. One engages in *Self-Love*—never doing harm to ones "ME" or "ME/WE" self and not accepting it from anyone, if at all possible—including not allowing it for the "WE". The *keystone is to Not Do Anything That Does Me No Good*—like being angry or hating. My focus is always on things of Worth (Spiritually Beautify thoughts, feelings, expressions, and actions). I have never been attached to Material Things and that is fortunate because people have stolen gigantic things from me all of my life. People have an incomplete assumption about certain key words—like God, Stubborn, and Selfishness without ever researching to find out what is as close to the Truth as is possible at that time. *Spiritual Selfishness* is an instinctual part of the first law of Nature—Survival, Well-Being seeking, and Thriving. One is capable of Survival, Self-Defense, Self-Protection, Self-Preservation, and countering with Offense of the "Take Whole" type under all kinds of situations; Self-Denial—delayed gratification via Self-Sacrifice. The implication is that one does not allow ones Emotions to ruin whatever is of "ME/WE" benefits. These are Necessities before doing for others what would keep one in the Status Quo. Self-Love is extended naturally into a Non-Self state involved in "ME/WE" where there is Selfless Service. See Unconditional Love

SELF-MEANING: Spiritual Self-Greatness standard against which one compare ones Self-Respect.

SELFLESS SERVICE: A display of positive scale Unconditional Love is also the exhibiting *Selfless Service* for the "WE"—the "giving seeking nothing in return." This is based upon the *Laws of Ma'at: "the good one does to another is done to oneself because the "ME" and the "WE" are "One" in Essence" and therefore "the wrong one does to another is done to oneself"*. In a "ME/WE" setting, "what I give to you I have given to myself; the good I do for you, I have done for myself. If one does Ma'at living, one is *not rewarded for good acts but receives reward through and by characteristics, qualities, and affinities acquired by having done them*. This Process of Nature is derived from the inner nature of the One Universal High Spiritual God and deemed to be an active moral regard associated with good deeds, not bounded by any degrees. My *description of Unconditional Love* in general human terms as well as in Self-Love in particular is *"Paying a price to perform Selfless Service."* It has six parts. First, preparation for it starts with a Free Mind (that of ones birth or acquired by shedding Emotional Junk). Second is having a life's goal of striving to reach ones Highest Self. Third is to *provide Selfless Service to those desiring to be* lifted up. Fourth is to protect oneself and others who accept being part of the Cosmic Organism family from enemies—and even it there is rejection and attacks by those being helped. Fifth, while on the path to these goals, *persist through losses, lacks, and obstacles--even walking alone--while paying a high price (money, time, energy, effort + by-passing pleasures, convenience, or respect) to achieve ones lifetime goal*. Sixth, there is absolutely no thought given to or efforts made to receive in return any money, fame, status, or other benefits. None of this is about sex or affection since both can be about "Doing For but not Connecting With." Preparation for it starts with realizing the individuality of each human and each situation for which the self-centered "Golden Rule" of "do unto others as you would have them do unto you" does not apply. Instead, to deal with the involved uniqueness begins with a focus on the "Oneness" of oneself with all other creatures (Omnipresence). Approximating this "Oneness" is by creating, enhancing, and maintaining Peace by taking every opportunity to be in solitude, quiet, meditation, and serene environments. That understanding gives insight into how to assess the Underlying aspects of Complementary or Contrary Opposites—their shaping factors, their manifestations, their roots in the foundation of Life Living, and their resolution. Those applicable to humans are Omnipresence—as in a "ME/WE" feeling of Oneness as a "Non-Self" with all of God's Creatures and Creations; Omniscience—intuiting (Spiritual Elements awareness without thinking) paths to Knowledge and Wisdom. It takes knowing how an individual's present state evolved; that individuals reaction to the present situation; how full is that human's plate and with what kind of "food"; and what limitations that human has embraced. From that, decide: *Do you simply give them a fish? Or show them how to fish? Or take them to the lake so they can figure out how to fish? Or put them in contact with fishermen? Or take away the Attractive Distractions keeping them from fishing? Or give them a swift kick in the rear end to motivate them to start helping themselves? Or simply leave them alone so as to give them time to assess and learn from the flawed thinking that got them into their mess?*

SELFHOOD ARMOUR: defense mechanism to minimize hurts from others ("I won't allow you to touch me"). To avenge the hell to which they were being subjected, the Enslaved applied: First, *Selfhood Armor* is inner avengement (e.g. "White man, you may enslave my body but you cannot enslave the rest of me"). Second, their outer avengement was called *Slave Resistance* (e.g. procrastination, moving and working slowly). Both Selfhood Armor and Slave Resistance worked well for the Slaves but became *Self-Defeating Habits* when culturally transferred out of slavery and on into today's struggling descendants. Another way this shows is Black boys have so much game they do not use.

SELFHOOD GREATNESS: Before humans knew themselves in the Earth World, when originally created each Selfhood had instilled what makes for permanent Selfhood Greatness: (1) infinite power from possessing the Spark of God which makes each not a drop out of the infinite ocean of the one Universal High Spiritual God but rather the entire God ocean in a drop—so as to possess Spiritual Wisdom; (2) the supreme Ancient African "Genetics" with Earth World Wisdom which imparts intuitions into the world's finest Approaches, Methods, and Techniques for handling problems of daily living; and (3) a "Unique" Talent, powered by Pure Intellect to orchestrate ones life and Pure Emotions to enjoy life—all serving as a bridge to ones Mission in life. Proper use of these thinking faculties, while staying within Nature's Processes, makes one a "Non-Self" individual--meaning: "because we are, therefore I am". The point for all of these is to rise from ones Lower (animalistic) Self to ones Highest (Divinity) Self while producing "ME/WE" benefits so as to Thrive in life. In addition, each human is surrounded and helped by a Spiritual Entourage in the form of advice and "Helping Hands". Ones Immaterial "Self" (i.e. its Spiritual part, dominated by ones "Soul Sunshine") is ones Self-Identity derived from the Spark of God implanted before each human's birth into the Earth World. "*Identity*" means 'sameness' as the source of itself and thus the same as itself. The nature of a human's Self-Identity is fashioned in the image of the Spiritual Elements Essence of God's Substance. Thus, the Star of ones Selfhood is Unconditional Love and its associates are Life with its Truth, Reality, and Natural attributes. On one side of the "Soul" is a human's *Divine Consciousness* (which is Immaterial and contains an Image of God's Mind) + ones Divine *Will* (which is transitional between the Immaterial and the Intangible). The opposite side of the "Soul Coin" contains ones *Divine Spirit*—the Intangible, itself subdivided into the pre-Matter called the Ether + Spiritual Energy. Whereas ones "Self" (Divine Consciousness) knows *What* it wants to manifest (i.e. what it is Willing) and *Why*, ones Divine *Spirit knows How and When* (Amen, Maat p10). From the Divine Spirit ones Self thereafter undergoes evolution. To stay in this flow while going through life imparts an awareness of ones birth gift of Selfhood Greatness with its sense of Safety, Security, Sureness/Self-Confidence, Strength, and Stability for meeting any and every challenge of life. Humans are composed of Spirit (in the sense of the Immaterial, meaning the Spiritual) and Matter—both being needed for proper dealings in the Earth World. A *human's Spiritual Intellect* voluntarily has its mind *subjected to the Divine Spirit in order for it to command the Life-Force that is in harmony with the Laws of Nature.* Ones Spiritual Intellect is Intuited while Metaphysical Intellect is developed. Ones Metaphysical Intellect—part of ones Astral Double—enables dealings with Earth World Living of an objective nature. Metaphysical Intellect is entertwined with ones *Secular Sensory Consciousness* serving as a Background on one side of a Matter Awareness Coin and a *Secular Sensory Awareness* on the other side, being about happenings in the Foreground of life living. Both sides of this Astral "Double" Coin will serve as a human newborn's Earth World Selfhood Sources (i.e. Background) in order to supply the think, feel, say, and do aspects related to the Foreground for interfacing with activities of daily living. The Real Self of ones Intellect and Sensory Consciousness enables the recognition of the uprightness and sacredness of Integrity.

SELFHOOD GREATNESS ICON SYMBOL: A mindset of Selfhood Greatness is present in every newborn. Its acquisition by those who have chosen to "Cloud it out" *is done by means of the subjection of ones mind to the Divine Spirit so as to enable it to draw on the power needed to command the Life-Force in harmony with the Laws of Nature.* An achievement of a mindset of Selfhood Greatness is indicated when *ones Soul will vibrate at the same high rate as when one was originally conceived.* The components of Selfhood Greatness are first that the same Divine Creative power sustainer of life vital forces flowing out of the Cosmic Mind is identically imparted as a Spark of God into ones Soul. Since the Cosmic Spiritual Force called God cannot be grasped by form, the "likeness" image cannot be referring to arms, legs, torso, or head. Instead, it is about God's inner nature of Unconditional Love with its intertwined Truth, Reality, and the Natural. They are what impart a human with Dignity. Second, added to the 'Spark of God' aspect of the Ka of oneself while inside the Cosmic

Organism was and remains the supreme brilliance of "Ancient African Ancestors' Genetics". Third is that within the core of ones birth gift Genius is a specific and unique Talent that no one has ever had, no one has now, and no one will ever have. That Talent is intended to bridge where one is over to ones Mission in life. These are the source of ones Character, Self-Worth, and Self-Esteem and the maintenance of ones Integrity to ever strive to "Be Right," "Recognize Right," "Do Right," "Make Things Right," and "Defend the Right." Inside that Icon Symbol is the "5Ss" birth gift of Selfhood Greatness, with its sense of Safety, Security, Sureness/Self-Confidence, Strength, and Stability for meeting any and every challenge of life. This is what enables Do-ers to get thriving things done. Selfhood Greatness is a radiant "ME/WE" selfishness of the Soul which desires the best in all things—in values of matter and spirit—a Soul that seeks above all else to achieve its own moral perfection—valuing nothing higher than the Spark of God within itself. One never accepts any code of non-Spiritual Elements; never fails to practice the virtues one knows to be Right; never accepts an unearned guilt and never earns any—or never leaves it uncorrected; never resigns oneself passively to any flaws in ones character; and never accepts the role of a sacrificial Being. Productive work is the process by which ones mind sustains ones life. The keystone job of any striving to Re-Order their Selfhoods is to customize a Selfhood Greatness Icon Image that invariably stays within and evolves out of the Spiritual Element. Then back that up with a Self-Declaration and always live by it—and without exceptions.

SELFHOOD INTEGRITY: Doing what it takes to "Be Right," "Recognize Right," "Do Right," "Make Things Right," and "Defend the Right"

SELFHOOD PURITY: every human newborn operating out of its "pre-birth Emotions".

SELFHOOD SPLINTERING: one part becomes Self-Absorbed (viewing everything within ones world in relationship to oneself); the other follows dictates of External World influences. An integrated Selfhood has its thoughts, feelings, expressions, and deeds in harmony because it is operationg out of a Base of Love and a frame of Truth. Such is done without effort or even awareness of doing it. This is because one lives as if one is perpetually in "the Zone," similar to what top athletes periodically experience. These athletes have no idea what they did until they see a video replay and, by being unable to break down what they did they are not likely to be good teachers. The point of this analogy is that Truth and Reality "just are" and no matter what, neither can be defined, stated, or even pinned down. This is a fact which does not deter Europeans and constituting another reason why they are so dangerous to use as a source of the truth. They have no idea that they do not know the truth, even when it is in front of them. That they give definitions to what is undefinable and use that false information to "straighten things out" is indicated by such things as how they define "Love" and "Intelligence." Both are impossible to define. Yet, presenting these ridiculous notions as "the truth" and taking actions on them adds to everybody's Delusional World. That they do the same defining for the unknowable is shown by their anthropromorphic concepts of God. Many Europeans consider God as a White man with a long white beard who says what only Europeans can hear; who has aspects of their brute character (e.g. vindictiveness); and whose "message" gives them the absurd sense of being "superior." This implies those not like them are "inferior." To accept the label of inferiority, as has been done by many Black People, is to be disconnected/splintered from all Truth and Reality--and thereby be carried a long, long way from the "Truth-Track." Management is to stop believing anything Europeans say about anything! Another large source leading to self-defeating delusions (believing what is not real and not believing what is real) is self-induce Selfhood Splintering. One cause is from a "Big Bang" psycho-trauma or cumulative psycho-microtraumatic layers leading one to dissociate (disconnect) ones painful part from ones Selfhood. Usually this separation is done out of the necessity to take care of business; to get through the moment; and as an "Escape" from ones trials and tribulations. By having no time to handle grief, they become chronic jugglers who need all their energy to focus on "Here and Now" problems. Dissociation, as "*Selfhood Armor*," minimizes hurts from others ("I won't allow you to touch me"). Whereas this defense mechanism is useful for its intended purpose, it is a double-edged sword by causing one to lose a sense of enjoyment and richness in living. Besides, ones feelings are right up front and are as sensitive as an inflamed nerve--a sensitivy coming from extremely painful memories--a sensitivity causing one to be stubbornly self-absorbed. One way a Splintered Selfhood manifests is by the habit of saying one thing to people while feeling something entirely different--a manifestation which scatters focus and therefore weakens ones personal power. Another bad habit is not observing and listening to what is going on in the outside world. Periodically I meet people who have commented how one of my articles had meant so much to them. However, when I ask for which article or the "what" of the subject, they invariably say they have no idea. It always intrigued me as to how that could be. *Four stages of relationship involvement*. First is being "Aware" of the thing existing but it remains blank. Second is being "Introduced" but all one knows is that it has a faceless form. Third is getting "Familiar"--knowing it from association. Fourth is an "Intimate" involvement. Splintered Selfhoods are compulsively "Familiar"/"Intimate" (go over and over) with imaginative information about the "Here and Now" but only "Aware" or "Introduced" to self-improvement information. That "closed mindedness," with its narrow scope in dealing with life, keeps them from knowing the Truth about what is most important.

SELFHOOD TRANSFORMATION: The three parts for going from ones Lower Self (animal nature) to ones Highest Self are: Mystical Dying of the mortal part of ones Soul (the Ka); Regeneration by "re-yoking" ones Selfhood to God; and Rebirth by living and spreading Ma'at Principles (Unconditional Love and Truth).

SELF-IMPROVEMENT: starts with Curiosity for Self-love's how. That ignites educating oneself on what one did not even know one did not know but is vital to know. Truth originates in a minority of one, and that truth breaks a custom. It is by intuition that discoveries are made. To proceed starts by having the Courage imagine, discover, and institute the other side of safety so as to enter the unknown of what has been proven safe by your Ancient African Ancestors. Ships are safe in harbor but that is not what ships are for. My greatest discoveries have been made by not following instructions; by going off the main road; by trying the untried. Stokely Carmichael said in 1967 that "Black Power" is a call for Black People to unite, to recognize their heritage, to build a sense of community; and reject the racist institutions and values of this society." What Selfhood Correction is about is to bring out the best within—and that requires learning to love what is a very difficult struggle.

SELF-MADE: in control and in charge of ones own "Mind Committee". It monitors and interprets the feedback extracted out of ones own Inner and Outer World realms of influence—whether by direct experiences, vicariously assessed experiences, ones memory, assessments, and External World impressions. If the "Self-Made" stay true to their Essence nature, they will remain in the flow of the Spiritual Elements and develop their think, feel, say, and do aspects of Life-Living out of it.

SELF-UNKNOWN-STEPPING INSIDE ITS MYSTERY: Pertinent here is that those socialized by False Self people have no loss of Natural Cosmos standards, guides, filters, and measures because of being unaware that they exist—and thus is unsought. In other words, the loss of which is Unknown is not a loss at all. If this socialization is incomplete, there is ongoing turmoil with trying to figure out what is behind the dim Unknown.(e.g. superior)having a range of endearments that could go as high as "Superior" its most significant contents. Human newborns know their Cosmic Organism connections with all God's creatures and creations—and therefore the Cosmic Mind Creator whose attributes are in each—and therefore eternal living checkered with transformations from one plane of existence to another so that a human creature never dies into non-existence. This "Life-Living" path leads to a "ME/WE" thriving and happy life. To live out of the birth-gift of ones Real Self is to be completely "Alive" to ones Spiritual Elements (Unconditional Love, Truth, Reality, and the Natural) essence. This means ones inherent Wisdom has two categories of "Life-Living" Instinct Tools. First is ones *Spiritual* intuitive realization of ones own Being/Spirit lying beyond ones thoughts. Its instinct tools enable assessments of mysterious "Things" in Unseen Realms of existence—e.g. what it is, what belongs to it, what is revealed by it, what it does, and how it appears. Resultant conclusions serve as then knowing how to fashion harmonious 'big picture' relationships to the common things of life. Second is the *Collective Unconscious* (Supra-conscious, Universal Spirit, Impersonal or Transpersonal Unconsciousness; Epic Memory) acquired inheritance 'instinct' tools. As described by Ancient Africans, its memory bank contents of depository forms of Archetypes (African, Seed) are of ones most remote Ancestors' Spiritual experiences and wisdom—those representing the Cosmic Organism's reality, stability, absoluteness, universality, and permanent Truths for all time—those serving as the foundation for Earth World "Right Living" inside a connected and unified Wholism. When tuned into them, they are conceived as *Primordial Images*—also called Dominants, Imago's, Mythological Images, Icon Behavior Patterns—i.e. root displays of the Cosmic Mind acting in fashioning patterns or being models for the production of *Prototypes* (created Spiritual Elements manifestations which, in turn, create like-kind things). In other words, in Real Self people, both the Archetypes and Prototypes each, by themselves, reproduce themselves, to become the thing each makes so as to help shape how one thinks, feels, expresses, acts, and reacts in accordance with the Cosmic Organism. This Spiritual Archetype which imparts a Cosmic Mind Disposition into ones Conscience, enables it to assess the good or bad presentation of every deed or temper in life as being in harmony or in disharmony. Similarly, though every human's Collective Unconscious exists whether perceived by a given human or not and its manifestations are responsible for what occurs in the material world, both it and ones Spiritual Archetypes effects can be "Clouded" out by ones Free Will choice to do so. The trade-off for giving up ones complete "Aliveness" inherent in being ones Real Self is to step into a "blankness"—a mystery—an Unknown. This means ones understanding of profound answers to profound questions is buried, in a manner simulating being in a coma—a state of profound unconsciousness from which one is, in that mindset, incapable of being aroused. An ancient idea of a self-induced state leading into Self-Unknowing was that of an overpowering mental mighty wave force rolling into ones mental thinking paths--sending its power through, around, over, and under the mind so as to envelop and overwhelm all sides and thus burying everything along the way. Hence, the over-spreading hurricane-like force; the crushing weight; and the cutting off of the mind's thinking supply lines suffocated and made useless ones mind—like a "zombie." An early alternative cause for Self-Unknowing was bad energy pumping into ones mind and swelling up into the shape of a bowl to such an extent that the bowl would turn upside down and/or inside-out. These would prevent ones mind from seeing the sun's brightness and thereafter one would look over everything in a gloomy way. Being overturned covered up any bright and clear thinking. So, what is stepping into ones Self-Unknown? Since the living human mind is never inactive, perhaps one sees or experiences: (1) *Hallucinations* (wander in mind)—creations from existing, visible objects and incorporating other memories to form frightening Contingent Beings that seem real; (2) *Illusions*—misinterpretations of sense-impressions; (3) a *Kaleidoscope or variety of colors*—produced by, say, a type of people—and, hence, producing a symmetrical set of images that trigger self-induced "*Situational Epilepsy*" type mental disturbance as, for example, in the Brute Brain. Such Effects generate a sense of being among uncertainties, doubts, mysteries unprovoked by fact or reason and a craving to understand the nonexistent that is both within and without of oneself. Consequences may be resultant Supernatural voices or visions that inspire doing something dangerous to oneself and/or to others.

SELF-UNKNOWING MAKES BULLIES: Ones *Real Self* provides Spiritual Elements type Wisdom which imparts a *real* Self-Identity. But a *False Self* "Clouds" over ones birth-gift "Soul Sunshine," causing one to lose contact with who one is as a human. That philosophically puts one outside the Natural Cosmos +

establishes a Self-Unknowing + causes a loss of courage and the "5Ss" (which only comes from having a true sense of Selfhood Greatness). Resultant self-doubt automatically places boundaries on ones own Self-Trust in times of threats, disturbances, or destructions. Not knowing who one is *disconnects one from all there is in ones environment and in the Cosmos*—a disconnection making for a "me vs. everything else" mindset—a mindset of overflowing Hate-full-ness. Such Supernatural mindsets that now think "Inside-Out" see no alternative but to be aggressive against "everything else" before "everything else" can push me around." For example, if "Black" is "everything else," then I must fight "Black" and win before "Black" attacks me. By Self-Unknowing originally being rooted in an occult mythological context, all of this is serious business and for which there is no time to relax from "war" or to have "silly" fun. Because an "Inside-Out" mindset operates out of a fantasy "Air Castle," it fashions Delusions (believing what is not real and not believing what is real). Thus, all of its thinking patterns are confused, in conflict, and follow no order. To get through life they fashion "*Simultaneous opposites*" to live by—meaning hypocrisy seems natural, even if one contradicts oneself in the same breath—as done by politicians. These are the ingredients of Bullies. The word "*Bully*" originally meant a fine, good friend, sweetheart—and perhaps a swaggering fellow, as in Shakesphere's "Bully Bottom" in A Midsummer Night's Dream. Later it took the meaning of a hired and overbearing ruffian as well as those who show bravdo—"Bullyboy"—but are actually cowards who abuse their strength by ill-treating the Weak. Today, a "Bully is considered as a swaggering, quarrelsome, person who terrorizes weaker or peaceful people. One example is the souteneur, a man who lives on the earnings of a prostitute. Subsequent terms applied include intimidator, domineering, a coercer, a strong man, a tormentor, evildoer, combatant, and the like. With children, it is associated with those who do cruel teasing intended to frighten; for teens to bully is to engage in noisy threatening talk to intimidate others for self-interest purposes or actually hurting those who are smaller and less strong. With adults, one persuaded to institutue violence as a thug. Organized thugs—like European Hate groups (e.g. KKK, Skinheads, Killer police)—do what it takes to make victims submissive, compliant, or subdured by inspiring fear from using victims' own fears or weaknesses or deperate needy wants against them as a psychological weapon. This is followed by Brutes filling victims' minds with terrible consequences for non-compliance. When victims are so terribly "beaten down" as to have "Inside-Out" mindsets (i.e. the reversal of their Survival and Self-Protection instincts), they become intimidated through their own shyness, cowardice, sense of inadequacy, or fear of embarrassment. Examples of the countless ways these may show is by not asking questions, not returning telephone calls or emails, and attacking those trying to help them. Instead, they "Escape." They can only extend guarded trust to like-kind people who do not like each other. Together, Bullies who are part of a cult create in their own image a Contingent god (e.g. "bogeyman") who embodies their beliefs. So as to have some semblance of order, they all act in conformity to their cult. Hence, these "Individualists" are always in the dilemma of having to act out of conformity—a situation calling for partial trust in ones cult members and the cult's doctrines—but staying suspicious of both. Such is exhibited by all of today's Republicans voting to repeal the law of Obamacare—and doing it 60+ times—and with no power to change this law. They give up all independent thought so as to blend into each other's ways of think, feel, say, and do expressions, for these unhappy people are all they have. Their power is exerted, not by personal power, but rather by the GUN. This is the composition of the hypocritical state of each saying: "I am my own man"!!! Such "Inside-Out" thinking is simplified by all cult members seeing things in definite "Either/Or" and "All-or-None" terms; simultaneously "oppose/favor not just one but all"; believing there is no "Right" way other than what they think, feel, say, and do. From being mad with life's history as well as hating themselves and "everyone else", their presumed remedy is to select an enemy and destroy it so as to get momentary relief from causing misery to others. Many Europeans look at dark-skinned people and their achievements with extreme envy. Then they engage in

Reaction Formation—the converting of something extremely desired but wholly unattainable into something discredited and despised. The world's top tennis player, the Black Serena Williams, always receives a barrage of hateful insults. That *Envy Insults* are a pattern of Self-Unknowing people is illustrated by the Italian Vespucci (1451-1512) who gave his name of Amerigo to the New World as America. He borrowed labels of Jews as the ultimate racist metaphor for greed, cunning, super-human sexual powers, and malevolent Christ-killer. He then assigned such labels—e.g. savages, infidels, and cannibals--to Amerindians and Africans, including the cultured Moors in Spain and Portugal. Europeans (e.g. Freyre) who wrote/write about slavery in romantic and racist statements but disguised as liberal and enlightened scholarship have typically and stupidly implied: (1) Enslaved Africans took to slavery "like birds take to the air"; (2) the Enslaved were happy because they kept their music, dance, and song alive; and (3) they could be civilized by whips, chains, and forced labor and racism. To expose such "Inside-Out" thinking, Frobenius (1550) said: "Africans and Mexican Indians were civilized to the marrow of their bones—the idea of the barbaric Negro is a European invention."

SENSES: 12 special senses: color, sound, smell, taste, balance, motion, direction, heat, cold, weight, tactility, and pressure.

SENSORY CONSCIOUSNESS: See Consciousness

SETS: When Associations of Ideas are compared on both sides of the equation, they are called Sets. Sets are an Association of Ideas or a collection of like-kind Things (e.g. Objects, Essences) sharing some defining property(s). In short, it is the Thing's "what it is" Seed and serves as a harmonious connecting link for the Thing's "what it does" and its "how it appears." Sets have varying degrees of complexity carried within a Symbol's contents. Type I--a *Combined Set* is a Being's "what it is" unified with the 'what it is doing' as a result of its Essence. It is this "That it is" *Being is unified with 'what it is doing'* which enables the grasping of a Percept of a *Primary Quality*. Such is because --by its own nature of being a bodiless presence--it otherwise cannot be grasped explicitly by the mind because it is not clear, definite, or in detail. Type II--a *Complex Set* has the Thing's Nature/Nurture admix of the sum of all prior experiences one has accepted to be real—together with the Causes which produced them—including all that has happened and/or is happening to generate Effects and their Consequences—as well as all of the Results that have happened and all anticipated as being capable of happening. Type III--*Circumstantial "Sets"*—are a collection of like-kind Things (e.g. steps on the ladders). Here, both the Known and the Unknown sides of the equation have Correspondence. The path of African Algebra for Circumstantial Problems follows a process of reasoning based upon Algebraic Principles. Originally, this was based upon correlating their pertinent accumulated Experiences and newly discovered Knowledge so as to integrate it into Harmony and thus Human-made Truths. To this end, they decided to create a pertinent "Set" of what is Known—i.e. their Human-made Truths--in the See-able Realms and try to discover like-kind "Sets" in the Un-Seen Cosmic Realm. Thus, using the Known to discover a Correspondence Unknown focused on comparable *Algebraic Sets* ingredients. SETS are an Association of Ideas or a collection of like-kind Things (e.g. Objects, Essences) sharing some defining property(s) designated by some rule that indicates exactly which Things belong to the collection (e.g. rungs or steps on a ladder or different colored eggs for an Easter basket). A Set has a *Theme* which arises from the *shared essence properties* of an Association of Ideas or a collection of like-kind Things or of a given Thing(s). Arising from the common origin of what is gathered, that theme remains as a unifying central or dominating idea (or thesis), motif, field, principle melody. In short, it is the Thing's "what it is" Seed and serves as a harmonious connecting link for the Thing's "what it does" and its "how it appears." A Theme has an inherent Disposition (i.e. the What and Why of *a 'payload' message,* with an inclination ready for an intentional direction). It is fashioned for use as a discourse, discussion, sermon, pleasure, intimidation, or life's course.

SEVEN DEADLY SINS: pride (arrogance), covetousness (greed), lust, anger, gluttony, envy, sloth (lazy)

SEVEN QUESTIONS OF INQUIRY: who, which, what, when, where, why, and how

Symbols create a whole greater than the sum of its parts,

SEX: In African Tradition, the One God, Aten, is symbolized by the Sun--while the mythological God, Ra, is the Sun's rising attributes—i.e. as it transforms from the undifferentiated Subjective into an Objective Being. Sexual arousal is an expression of the Life-Force-Ra. At least as late as 77,000 BC the Twa of Central Africa wore a Cross, later called the Ankh, to symbolize several things--including the Union of Opposites. This means *Life literally occurs as a result of the union of Spirit and Matter*—the union of Heaven and Earth—the union of Male and Female Principle sexual symbols (i.e. a female oval surmounting a male cross) and all aspects of God. Such a union, which goes beyond the concepts of Duality, transforms one into an *androgynous* being—the union of opposites--the two becoming One. Arising out of this was the mythology in Egyptian Spiritual Literature, thousands of years before Jesus or the formulation of the European Bible, that Chaos was personified by the Goddess Neith, (Nut, Nepte, Nuk, the Egyptian Minerva), anterior to all gods--the Great Mother and the Immaculate Virgin, or female God from whom all things proceeded. She was characterized as the only God, without form and sex—the "Father-Mother"--who gave birth to itself and without fecundation (fertilization). A comparable mythology (if not the same) was Het-Heru being the female counterpart of the "deity" Ra and her sexual arousal and consummation led to her becoming the mother of the deities in the Spiritual mold form of Icon Images. Nevertheless, the Black Great Mother was adored world-wide under the form of a Virgin Mother who gave birth to God. To indicate a post-virgin birth moment of bliss, Ancient Egyptians depicted the original Madonna and child—Auset (Isis) with the sun-child Horus at her breast. Put another way, the Ankh symbolizes the African originated (Bailey, Echoes p86) Yin/Yang-type balance between the two forces of life—positive/negative, light/dark, long/short, male/female. If there is no unity or Oneness, the Ankh still expresses Reconciliation of Opposites or the integration of active and passive Qualities. The "Ankh Cross"--with the loop at the top (female) and the cross at the bottom (male)--was borrowed by Europeans but the loop was removed for anti-feminism reasons. During Biblical times, Biblical stories were being spun about David and Solomon concerning a star having nothing to do with the Jewish people. The Star's earliest appearance outside of Africa was in India's Indus Valley civilization (3000 BC), later symbolizing divine sexual energy and the union of the male and female elements in creation. Thus, the word "Sex" is rooted in mathematics, meaning "six" and its Spirituality in association with intercourse was extensively elaborated on in India. Its concept reached Judaism via the eastern Tantric influences on medieval Jewish cabalists. About a century ago the Star was officially regarded as Jewish (Chandler, Ancient Future p69).

SEXIGESIMAL SYSTEM: numeration originated in Ancient Africa for the purpose of allowing for earth and heaven-like measurements in degrees. See Mathematics—Cosmic Mysticism

"SHAM" SCIENCE HALLUCINATIONS: The gist of one C17 story of "Sham" was a lady of ill-repute who presented herself as a virgin, to which this was attested to by being in a maiden organization. Those who discovered the façade called it a "Shame" or "Sham" in some English dialects. Today, "Sham" means to assume or present a counterfeit appearance; feign; pretend to be; delude; deceive; imposture; one who simulates a certain character. Sham people—under such names as Quack-Salvers or "Doctors of Fools," Witches, Wizards, Alchemists, Mineralists, Mountebanks, Empirics, Charlatans, Idolatresses, Cast-Apothecaries, Health-Food Specialists, Old Wives, and Barbers--are interwoven with the best of societies back into ancient times. Whether advocating faith in Miracles, Relics, Recipes, or whatever—whether in religion, law, politics, or government, all have had the generating of *Hallucinations* as their aim in order to act on their awareness that humans are dupable. "Dupable" is founded on the preference of seeking those who might be able to cure their disorder, although unable to explain or be fair to all than to have the disorder explained but is unable to cure it. For "Sham" people, the aim is for money—an aim powered by whatever is amoral—and they study the methods of other Sham artist so as learn more "Tricks". Most "Victims" are unaware; some are willing and eager, as for cures of something bad in health or for ease or to deal with Superstitions; a few are naively humane, as in con-artists claiming they had been duped so as to again undeserved humanity benefits from others. This is seen today in many so-called charitable organization who use public donations for self-interest purposes. The even more evil type use religion or medicines or lack of proper sanitation to make sound people sick and sick people so adversely affected as to kill (e.g. gang wars resulting from the effects of overwhelming poverty).

Those who "Sham" themselves ensure they do not allow anyone to get close for fear they may be exposed. They make up the majority who do not respond to what is sent or presented. When people are Self-unknown and declare themselves to be "superior" by being in the Occult Supernatural, this causes them to believe they are above societal and humanity rules. That allows them to think they are entitled to get off with credit and not be held to proof. Supernaturals' Egos require viewing themselves in opposition to others + engaging in a ceaseless pursuit of power (i.e. control over people, places, Nature, and material things) for their animalistic Acquired Emotional satisfaction. Much of this comes with the aid of flawed or "Sham Science." For example, biologists such as Linnaeus (1707-78), Baffon, and Blumenback (1806) separated mankind into races on the basis of biological differences. In 1758, Linnaeus declared humans could be divided into races--white (European), red (Native American), Black (African) and yellow (Asian)--attributing various demeaning Personality traits to all except for Whites. Meanwhile, scientists used the sham concepts of race to justify slavery (e.g. by painting Africans as inferior) + refining ascriptions of different mental characteristics to each "race"—again deeming Europeans to be "lively" and "inventive" + arguing over whether God created the races separately or whether they diverged from a common creationist origin. In 1850s, a world famous American scientists, Samuel Morton, joined as a phrenologist such historical *Humbug-Dealers* as fortune-tellers, crystal gazers, astrologers, numerologists, gypsy tea-readers, and palmists in collecting world-wide skulls to attempt demonstrations of those of European ancestry having the world's biggest heads and thus being intellectually superior. Controversy remains as to whether Morton cheated or made a statistical error, but his conclusions are still debunked.

Other Sham practices range from deceptive nuances leading to what "SEEMs" right—as by Sophisms--over to the most vile of horrorable cruelties. To maintain control over their own cult, they generate storms and then offer to provide solutions for a high price. The "Excitement" associated with being able to "Dupe" spurs their phantasmagoria to make them so big in life as to be unable to repress emotions of just how tiny they are compare to Real Self people. Part of this involve self-declaring "How Great I Am and how inferior everybody else is". Hence, they claim to be an "Alpha male," brilliant, rich, super-sexual skills, and having the best of everything. They surround themselves with those like them and are secretly in competition with each of them.

SHAME: Although the popular sense of the synonyms Disgrace, Ashamed, Shame, and Guilt in Old English (450-1066) shared the core of "shy" and "Bashful" as a state of mind pertaining to needless failure causing disappointment and humiliation, its religious core of provoking abomination (loathing, disgust) was applied to people who violated European church doctrine. Added to this, if there was a design to deceive, the label of Shame was a Self-Esteem attack. By C17, such exposure was also for the purpose of covering "the sinner" in a cloud of shame with the intent to harm ones reputation. Thereafter, Shame went in the direction of having bad feelings about violating rules of decency. By the end of the European Middle Ages, when individualism and materialism were rising into prominence, the traditional vices became more desirable and respectable. As a result, Shame and Guilt not only separated in meaning but were less of a problem, thanks to the flexibility had been put into European morals. Also in C17, the original meaning of Embarrass ("put to shame"; to put behind bars; impede) was separated to signify ones reaction from one doing dishonorable acts.

SHREWD: In 1280 AD, "Shrewd" signified evil, malicious, and dangerous before its euphemistic sense changed in 1520 to astute and cunning--and then to cleverness, scheming, and deception.

SIGN: that which induces one to think about something other than itself. A Symbol is *about* the System Concept under consideration. It is distinguished from a *"Sign"*—that which actually *suggests* the thing it represents. Signs are a distinctive mark by which a thing may be recognized or its presence known. In contrast to Symbols which have totipotency, Signs do not contain the richness present of Symbols because of being more demarcated. See Symbol; Icon

SIMILE: *Metaphors* (equates unlike things by implication), *Simile* (the abstract or suggestive aspect is directly expressed), *Allegories* (a hidden story within an obvious story), *Fables* (animals impersonating humans to impart a moral), *Personification* (making a lifeless or abstract thing alive), *Analogies* (explaining something unfamiliar by comparing it to something familiar), *Legend* (a story, above mere fiction, combining fact and personified spiritual concepts), and *Symbols* (symbolic messages disregard the limitations and boundaries of human thought in order to impart ideas of the indescribable).

SIXTH SENSE: Every human's Right brain Intuition, predominantly ones Ancient Brain instincts, has creative (from "Pure Emotions") parts which connect perceptions with awareness and intellect as well as a non-creative *"Sixth Sense"* (giving snapshots of Reality) aspects. *Subliminal* (1886, below Sensory Consciousness's threshold) "Osmosis" messages are readily absorbed by children's naturally (in the sense of relatively pure) receptive minds. Its entrance is into the non-creative part of a child's Intuitive Natural Right brain as "second nature" or *"Sixth Sense"*--whether consciously or hiding in sub-awareness realms. By this Ancient Brain portion lacking any protective faculties, what is interpreted constitutes the child's reality. See Second Nature

SKILL: Up to C13, "Skill" referred to an ability acquired through patient practice; to "skill in performance acquired by experience, study, or observation."

SLAVE SURVIVALS: ways enabling the Enslave to survive and endure by "Making Do". Reasons for them are now faded but doing them—which are always on the negative scale--are self-defeating outside the Black Community, and particularly defeating in the marketplace.

SLAVERY TURNS ASIDE AFRICAN SCHOLARSHIP: As stated Ancient Africans had used Subjective Sciences to establish Correspondences between all of God's creatures and creations—established this by Metaphysical (Quantitative) Mathematics—and arrived at Esoteric Unknowns by Qualitative Mathematics (which examines Metaphysical Mathematically established Premises to seek the ultimate Principle on which they all depend) to thereby arrive at Circumstantial Truths. Since this entire process remained within and arose out of the Spiritual Elements, the Inferences made from them concerning the Esoteric (e.g. the origin of the Cosmic Organism containing all of God's creatures and creations is by the Same Spiritual Elements Genetics) and Laws for daily living remained within the flow of the Spiritual Elements. These were applied to establish African Traditions, as demonstrated by Ancient Africans staying focused on the Heaven Afterlife and building their lifestyle around it. African Sages established African Logic based upon how atoms and molecules were put together. However, this African Logic pattern for thinking was shattered by the enslavement of Africans brought to the Americas. At the *"Fishnet Moment" of the enslavement of free Africans* for transportation to the Americas there was an instant "Brain Switch" in each victim. This *"Brain Switch"* set-off a cascade of simultaneous mental, physical, spiritual, and social destructive forces to various degrees—forces resembling a series of waterfalls pouring and spreading over steep rocks--disrupting human nature networks in its path--networks which produce output destructions serving as the in-put for the next component in each network—in-puts and out-puts heavily salted with bitterness which caused Despair and Desperation. This process generated an ongoing avalanche to the thinking processes of most Enslaved. The immediate result was the switch from using their Thriving Brain (i.e. the Cerebral Cortex and the Limbic portions) for normal living over to their Instinct or "Emergency" Brain for the "fight, flight, and fright" actions and reactions in which each was engaged. Examples of the shattering were Spiritual, Intellectual, Emotional, Social, Physical Selfhood aspects; Right and Left Brain Discipline and thus a loss of self-discipline; and the explosion of the awareness of ones own Selfhood Greatness. All of these factors were about ones humanity degradation associated with the loss of ones sense of the "5Ss" of Private Selfhood Safety, Security, Sureness, Strength, and Stability. These introduced the reality of anguish of every aspect of their Selfhoods, like no other to the point of denying even bits of the Truth. Neither were they able to know the worst and that + being over-powered meant they could do no self-protection. The setting in which they lived was that of forced toil and work so the oppressors could eat and get rich.

Extreme Despair was a Metaphysical Disease that *underlay and unified all of their countless Emotional Maafas* (Kiswahili, Great Disasters on all planes of existence), serving in its cultural transmission as *the Consciousness Background out of which many of today's descendants think, feel, express, act, and react.* No doubt, all Enslaved in Extreme Despair stemming from Maafa effects—whether of Mild, Slight, Moderate, or Extreme degree—all shared a "*double-whammy*" (i.e. two simultaneous Maafas) inside their Abyss from the ever worsening and never ending Indifference/Hate/Evil/Sadism displays of amoral European captors. By being completely defenseless, all resolved to a "*Hopeless Hopelessness*" state. The first "whammy" concerned their whole sound past desirable Life Living experiences having sunk to great dimness in their bottomless Sensory Consciousness. Second, masks/masquerades for survival and enduring had to display to the Satanist captors eventually became, for many, their "Faces and Personalities"—meaning allowing the enslavers to define who they were and what role they were to "forever" play. Other Enslaved shattered into a multitude of mindset and social roles so as to adapt to their horrible enslavements. For example, some decided their best chance of surviving was to "join the enemy camp" as Ideal Slaves by opposing fellows and adopted European thoughts. Nevertheless, what underlay this variety was "Inside-Out/Upside Down" Thought patterns. Although the typical historical effects of Maafa suffering make for a lifestyle of weakness and helplessness in the context of adaptation and existence in the dark, yet most of the Enslaved maintained remarkable strength.

SLIPPERY SLOPE: *Slippery Slope*"—a 1900s metaphoric expression alluding to traversing a slick hillside and being in constant danger of falling. See Allusion

SOBMER PROCESS MENTAL SKELETON: Critical Thinking (CT) embraces established Mental Skeleton Outlines and Processes for Assessments of difficult situations and problems. One, the SOBMER Process—an acronym for a Source, an Origin, a Beginning, a Middle, an End, and a Result--is a way to provide a crude 'stepping stone' order through an extremely complex subject, made even more difficult since at each step multiple things were/are going on at the same time. PROCESS: (C14, go forward) a selection of ingredients that form into an organized set of operations for doing something. That set is a series of operations or events leading to achievement of a specific result. The way the series proceeds and is done can be: (1) mere doing; (2) doing with a purpose; (3) doing which follows a thought-out plan; and (4) idealizing doing which results from vivid imaging. As the fashioner of an Outline of a plan, a Process shows the parts of a discourse in some sort of skeletal form pertaining to *Order* (like rungs on a ladder). If the purpose is for decision making and problem solving, the selected parts of what are to become stepping stones can be arranged variously--like some sort of 'Body Skeletal" Organization--like rungs on a ladder going from the Earth to the Heavens—like alphabetically arrange stepping stones ordered from start to finish. However, if the purpose is to persuade, inform, entertain, express, share, teach, instruct, educate, or serve as a call to action, the arrangement may be from the most important or most interesting to the least—or reverse this--or alternate these. Ingredients for Ordering the SOBMER Process started when I was a USA Military Captain in charge of the Outpatient Department for 10,000 troops at Clark Air Force Base in the Philippines. There as well as in my Orthopaedic Surgical, Orthopaedic Medicine, and Orthopaedic Genetics practice over a 45 year period, I saw as many patients as would fill the Rose Bowl Stadium. What stood out in dealing with any patient's massive and complex medical problems--and transferrable to the subject of Black-On-Black Violence--are the four *Causes--Pre-existing, Pre-disposing, Precipitating, and Immediate*--related to any disease/disability process. The disharmonious Source(s) and Causes lead to a *Beginning, Middle, End/Ending, and Result*—each productive of plentiful Consequences. This "SOBMER" process is the single best "skeleton" mental tool for a crude understanding of what has led to struggling Black People—where they came from to where they are, to the way they are, and to why they are so today. Amazingly, the Source of today's Results of African American slavery was written over 10,000 years ago in the Ancient African Bible mythological saga of Ausar (Osiris). Because of the Brute Brain mindset of Set (*Pre-existing Cause*), Ausar's brother, Osiris was tricked and captured by malevolent forces; chopped up (characteristic of Satanists); placed in a casket; transported down river to the sea, then across it in a wooden prison; came to live as a pillar (tamarisk tree) and then supported an alien kingdom. This same pattern is what happened to free Africans in Africa. *Predisposing Cause(s)* lay the foundation for a disease process to gain a foothold in ones body.

As the first disease risk factors, they pave a way for a disease to occur within ones Selfhood. *Precipitating Causes* enhance the Predisposing Cause(s) by cultivating or maintaining the disease risk factors. The *Immediate Cause* is the agent instigating without delay--and with nothing in between it and the disease process. As with the *Beginning* of a physical body disease (from some bad germ going through various Cause stages) converting patients from normal to abnormal, a *Metaphysical Mindset Disease* (as from not using Spiritual Elements ingredients) does that also. Both result from an Immediate Cause being the match flame which lit a stick of dynamite and that explosion resulted in adverse evolving clinical manifestations. The disease's *Middle* course is whatever conditions the explosion caused inside ones Selfhood. Starting in slavery and continuing to the present, the Satanists' mindsets, actions, and goals—symbolized as a "Disaster Star"--has been to fashion Ideal Slaves. Enslavement itself shatters awareness of ones own Selfhood Greatness--a humanity degradation associated with the loss of ones sense of the "5Ss." The "Halo" effects of this Disaster Star on victims are characterized by the features inside such words as "*Turbulence*" (troubled, tumbling, erratic, chaotic, and confused). The driving force of human generated violence is a whirl of uncontrolled and unnatural emotions which, of course, is a reflection of the state of that human's mindset. Not only was this the intention of Satanists but their victim "beat down" practices were of such a nature as to burn this evilness into the Selfhoods of Black People "forever." Most affected have been victims in such overwhelming Despair as to find no more fight for retaliation now or in the future--to possess so much loss of Courage as to be docile "forever"--and to have minds so "Inside-Out" as to not speak for the fallen and disabled, or even themselves. Struggling Black People's Metaphysical Disease of Despair has no *End* in sight, meaning they are still in the Middle of the process. What prevents the process of heading to "the End" is those with "*Inside-Out*" mindsets--i.e. minds controlled by the Satanists to such an extent as to lack an Instinct for Survival, Self-Protection, and Self-Preservation. They block their own passageways to healing by fighting those attempting to free them; to even help them out of the status quo; while voluntarily advocating the dictates of the enslavers/today's Satanists and oppressors for fellow Black People to follow. Such "Inside-Out" mindsets are from an assortment of destructive Brain/Mind reactions--e.g. an organic brain disorder, a philosophical Disarray; a psychiatric or psychological problem; an Icon fantasy or distorted perception; and/or from a sense of helplessness causing Supernatural Bonding with Satanist Europeans. Or, the Cause may be from an actual situation involving survival, self-protection, or self-preservation and knowing nothing else to do. The *Effects* on most Black Americans is a *Maafa*--(Kiswahili for The Great Disaster on the order of an immeasurable catastrophe--which is far, far worse than a Holocaust (etymologically, a 'complete burning'). Superseding the devastation of crime against humanity and the Selfhood pain and suffering--its spiritual, mental, social, financial, and Selfhood residual effects are on different planes of existence, and typically involving multiple planes for those struggling the most. The harshness of the victims' lives urge them into such Consequences as Escapes at every opportunity. That becomes an obsession so as to avoid coming face-to-face with the serious trials, tribulations, and serious business of their lives. A Maafa makes one self-absorbed and struggling to find any degree of the "5Ss"--safety, security, self-confidence, strength, and stability. By such a Maafa induced mindset operating inside a "bottomless" pit and with no one showing them the way out prevents ones visualization for formulating solutions to rise out of ones various forms of poverty. As a result, struggling Black People experience every conceivable type of Poverty—the Result.

SOBMER'S "WHAT IT DOES" TREE: The Tree of "What a Thing Does" is characterized by assessing it by the "SOBMER" PROCESS--an acronym for Source, Origin, Beginning, Middle, End, Effect/Consequences, and Result aspects of that problem. It is a useful CT mental "skeleton" tool for organizing chaotic information by setting up a plan for the "Big Picture" of the problem. Featured in that is to see what part of the Rational Thinking Process requires special attention in order of priority so as to reach a conclusion; for Trouble-shooting in proceeding toward a solution; as a "Check and Balance" before putting the plan into action; and to be a means for Post-Action Judgments serving to determine the flaws in what was done; how to correct or replace those flaws; what was neutral that interfered with efficiency and effectiveness; how the good results could have been made better; and how to make the excellent routine.

CAUSATION

SOURCE: The "SOBMER" PROCESS starts with the principle that events or products have a Source (the creation of the 'creator' which has a Disposition) and that is equivalent to the SEED. *Source*--that which furnishes a first and continuous supply -- the Creator of the Process requires that CT determine what or who it is; the intent and the power of the Source to carry out that intent; for what Purpose; and possible Effects, Consequences, and Results. The initial spotlight is whether the Source is God-made (i.e. of the Spiritual Elements) or Human-made. If God-made, the stepping stones are to create, enhance, or maintain Harmony. If Human-made, where on the Thinker's Scale (a positive and negative ruler separated by a zero) are they located? If on the negative scale, the stepping stones are to defend against the anti-Spiritual Element attacks and figure out assertive ways to get around the blocks, losses, and lacks. If Human-made on the positive scale the idea is to look for flaws in going along in a cooperative manner. Regardless of the Source, what Origin it gives rise to has a Disposition—complete with an Intension and an Inclination.

ORIGIN: Origin, equivalent to the "Roots" of the Tree created by the Source, is that portion of understanding a plan, problem, and/or proposed solutions an initiator or motivating principle preceding the action of a Process. It brings about changes that produce activity and serve as the 'rising' of various Causes. Together, the Causes of that Origin will fashion the *Process* (i.e. the selected parts of what is to come. That Process is arranged in some sort of 'Skeletal Organization—like bones of the human body or like rungs on a ladder going from the Earth to the Heavens or like stepping stones ordered from start to finish). Each Cause is the initiator or motivating principle and specifics about the "why" of happenings arising from the Origin. The first of three staggered Causes is the:

Predisposing Cause— Predisposing Cause(s) trigger the initial internal reaction which is what puts the "Disposition" contained in the situation on a path for its potential evolution. *Predisposing Cause(s)* lay the foundation for a disease process to gain a foothold in ones body. As the first disease risk factors, they pave a way for a disease to occur within ones Selfhood.

Precipitating Cause--it adds conditions on internal reaction; is what fertilizes the "Disposition" and enables it to grow. *Precipitating Causes* enhance the Predisposing Cause(s) by cultivating or maintaining the disease risk factors.

Immediate Cause is the spark activating the Inclination process of the Disposition to begin its Intention. The *Immediate Cause* is the agent instigating without delay--and with nothing in between it and the disease process—i.e. the Proximate Cause that opens the starting gate for external actions. In other words, an Immediate Cause is like the stick of dynamite instituting an explosion which causes a flame, equating to setting in motion adverse evolving clinical manifestations.

EVENT

When happenings of a deliberate action, speech, or choice could or cannot be foreseen and/or were/are affected by conditions beyond human control, the happenings out of that are called an *Event*. In other words, the "*Event*" (i.e. changing realities) bringing about a Cause may be something that occurs or some change that takes place. To say something changes might mean it is the outcome of certain conditions—i.e. of a Cause.

BEGINNING: This is taking the first step to set a Process or Operation into action along the lines of the way in which the Disposition's Inclination is to be done. What follows from the Immediate Cause is the initiation of an observable evolution to carry out the Intention of the Disposition. The Beginning (the first part, point, degree, or start of external actions) is equivalent to the "Trunk" in the Tree Concept. As with the *Beginning* of a physical body disease (e.g. from some bad germ going through various Cause stages) converting patients from normal to abnormal, a *Metaphysical Mindset Disease* (as from not using Spiritual Elements ingredients) does that also.

MIDDLE: As the center of the Process, the Middle (i.e. the greatest activity of external actions) dynamics are in the midst of moving the Process along with speed and force—forming many "Branches" which are part of the Tree Concept. The "Branches" of the disease's *Middle* course is whatever conditions the explosion from the Immediate Cause led to inside ones Selfhood.

END: Limit, Bound, and Confined are ideas charactering the *End* of the dynamic activity of the Tree Concept. In other words, the End implies the Process has stopped moving or is moving very, very slowly—or one withdraws attention from it. Along the way of the Process of the situation, things have been done to upset the status quo and what is upset leads to Effects (what is done) and eventually to Results (the Origin's "Big Picture" outcome).

EFFECTS: "What happened" or "What is going to happen" concerns those factors in the complex Process of a situation or event that necessarily follow the Origin and its Causes as well as be definitely attributed to its operation. Effects—the "Leaves"--pertain to the degree of success in one or more areas and/or not successful in the targeted goal or some other aspects. These are deemed to be followed by rewards or punishment respectively. Some Effects serve as a Cause and produce a secondary Effect—called an *After-Effect*. Some drugs are avoided because of their harmful Aftereffects.

CONSEQUENCES, happenings directly derived from Effects, embrace any condition, situation, or event that may be traced back to an original Cause, Origin, or Source through a more or less complicated chain throughout the Process. Sharon Bingaman puts it this way: *Consequences are the somethings which happen as a result of something happening.* Whereas *Subsequence* (i.e. what follows after in succession) is like the vine growing out of a grape seed or like the blood following where the knife is driven, Consequences consist of variable branches—some being about gaining support; some generating loses, lacks, or obstacles; some concerned with experiencing rebounds. For example, war's Consequence branches include the pain and misery for the innocent; the lies that live on and propagate in the process; the undying hatred it has aroused; and some form of success for the rulers who took over. Just as the dimensions of the tree are not regulated by the size of the seed, so are the consequences of things not always predictable or proportionate to the apparent magnitude of those events which produced them. For example, the applause of one adult may change a child's life forever. Many people's repentance is not so much regret for the ill they did but from fear of the ill they may get in consequence. The courageous seek and tell the truth, knowing and accepting the consequences may be substantial. What one does with the Consequences determines the nature of the "Fruit."

RESULTS: It takes a long time to determine the sum of the good, bad, or neutral aspects of the Effects and Consequences, collectively called Results. It may be the last in a series of Effects or Consequences directly traceable to a given Origin. To elaborate, the Effect of a blow on the head may be a concussion of the brain; the Consequence, shattered health; the Result, the retirement of the injured from playing all contact sports. In this sense, Results shift one onto a new path which serves as the beginning of a circle since they initiate a beginning for a new course of some life's Process. All Results tell a great deal about the Source which produced that "fruit" while what one does with that "Fruit" constitute the final Effects of the "Fruit" of the Tree Concept.

Very Ancient African Sages insightful achievements of arriving at Spiritual Seed-Principle-Symbols (Bailey, Mentoring Minds) came about by starting where they were and, in the process of evolving discoveries, each Sage would ask at each step: "And where did that come from or what gave rise to that or what is the meaning of that?" Seed-Principle-Symbols are building blocks of African Philosophy and therefore constitute the foundation of the philosophy of African Tradition. Principles are present: (1) in the broad sense (see Principles); (2) within these broad realms; (3) within planes of existence of each of these broad realms; and (4) on any given portion of one plane of existence in a given broad realm. Regardless of which of these four one is dealing with each component of the Tree Concept (i.e. Seed Roots, Trunk, Branches, Leaves, and Fruit) contains a SOBMER Process--a Source, an Origin, a Beginning, a Middle, an End, and a Result—and this is an ordering (organizing) process. In short, Principles can be combined/recombined and arranged/rearranged to maintain a correspondence of Truth, regardless of the plane of existence on which it operates and regardless of what form it is in.

SOCIALIZATION: Socialization is a process through which members are prepared to participate in society through the understanding of that society's philosophy, symbols, and language in a taken for granted manner--i.e. "that's the way it is." There is no attempt made to explain the "what it is and why". Instead, one is put into a role, which may constantly change or have new aspects added, as in getting married or having a baby. This is associated with a sense of Attachment and Bonding--particularly from the Nurturing behaviors by parents regarding the degree of support in helping the child develop social competence. There are countless and profound changes in Black American tradition, in society, in the family, and in neighborhoods which prevent Afrocentric Scholarship. A major one is that as a result of the Enslaved not being allowed to read, write, or count meant they have never honored Black scholars. This is a socialization issue. The way people live their lives reflects their System of Values—their Philosophy of Life (POL). In early human history, how one lived was determined by the individual or the family. Subsequently, forced or non-forced processes of acquiring culture—both Formal (structured) and Informal (imitation and experimentation) Socialization--has dominated. Their forms of thinking are the tools for carrying out their way of life. Of foundational importance is that African Tradition strives for "ME/WE" Human Ideals within the Natural World to reach the "Heaven Afterlife" while Europeans strive for "me, me, me" Ideals within a Supernatural World. Black Americans, by being forced into an incompatible European society, range between the two POLs. Because Supernatural oriented people are directly opposed to the best in the Natural World, they have, from their beginnings, fashioned a "SEEMS" right substitute. Its idea is to allow people to feel they are part of the Spiritual Elements of the Natural World while checkering that POL with nuanced dilutions and pollutions that change the direction of their natural course—a change from them having a chance to realize their Selfhood Greatness over to having their minds controlled and dictated to. This begins with *Socialization*--a system of ideas, habits, customs, traditions, symbols, speech, media, government, military police force that all teach one how to act. By this being a "*State*"--one that demands the subjection of the minority to the majority, it is *a "Dehumanization" conversion into a "Personalization" system.* The "*Person*" aspect is for the majority public is commanded to wear masks that concern the exact role one is ordered to play. To get people to believe and have faith in them being a "cog in a machine system" is a Formal/Informal continuing process. The Troops a State designed personal identity and learn the "State's" norms, values, behavior, and social skills--each appropriate to his/her social position. This mechanical organization is based upon Rules analogous to walking a tight-rope—"one slip and one falls". The idea is to put trust in this System of Organization and suppress ones individuality. Recognition for conforming comes from the crowd—a "fitting in" that is the only way to acquire Power. Such socialization is grossly inferior to the in-born Powers present in each human. Thus, its "SEEMS" right POL puts one on the wrong track of what is real and natural, but simultaneously tries to pass off this illusion and make it into a Delusion by means of feigned "Soul Mate *Alliances/Liaisons." Alliances* are mutually helpful participants who are psychologically and philosophically disconnected from and may even hate each other. Yet, they feature the sharing of common character traits, like the Indifference/Hate/Evil/Sadism (IHES) mindset. *Liaisons* are people who support like-kind people but without much of an association between them. This is for purposes of ensuring mutual understanding, unity of action, and especially prompt and effective network support so all can acquire a common goal against feigned enemies. This is what Socialization tries to pass off as how it is in Reality and life. To cement this strangers call each other by their first names. But what its deception is modeling are those two or more humans who are "plugged-in" to each other. This means they have such a mental goal synthesis as to display "osmosis"—(i.e. "wordless understanding") to cover each other's "inner world Selfhood nakedness". Although Supernatural Socialization is merely a "SEEMs" Right it is an illusion, the "State's" Supernatural military police punishment ensures these "Person" roles will be enforced. Fear and Repression lead the Troops to accept the Commands as the "real deal." The Troops remain ready "Take Down" and/or "Keep Down" the feigned Enemies by means of IHES minds and practices. The Ultimate starting point to Kill/Take/Destroy/ Dominate/Control/Oppress is with the Victims' religion—substituting a Supernatural one. An acceptance of that serves as the "greased" slide that carries them into every realm and institution of mental enslavement. All of "Dark Side" features and applicable stereotypical labels earned by the Majority—those who control by the GUN—are projected onto the "Enemies" to keep those "Enemies" ignorant, poor, and so beaten down in Spirit as for them to Delusionally bond with their "Evil Saviors"--and to the extent of not having Courage to do otherwise. As a result, Satanists are free to do whatever they do to control the Crowd's minds and stay rich. See Crowd; Public

SOCIALIZATION WOMBS OF PHILOSOPHY: Inside a "Womb" (Icelandic, belly) is an Immature offspring possessing Potential or Latent powers of the unrealized Realities of those "Genetics" acquired from its parents. The womb of a given society is called Socialization. Just as the womb of animals or humans is where the young are conceived and nourished until birth, so does the wide womb of a society conceive in its offspring its unique philosophy and nourish it. Then, after the offspring is delivered "naked," society dresses it with its power and Energy of position so that its philosophy will reproduce itself and mold the offspring to display that philosophy as the offspring buds, flowers, and fruits throughout the womb of life. The parents of the off-spring may either be of the Spiritual (Natural) Cosmos--the highest levels of which are treasures of the Spiritual Elements and wisdom--or of the Supernatural realm--the highest levels of which are "shinny penny" type trinkets and trivia. This results in philosophies of life that are like oil and water--there is no chance of them blending, even with "picking and choosing." Example: Whereas Ancient Africans said each human reflects the image of God as well as that human's body organs work independently to interdependently produce wholistic health, ancient Greeks borrowed and changed this concept. Not only did they not deal with the former but their idea was of an organ being a tool, implement, device, or contrivance--like that used in manual labor. This Greek concept pervades most of the minds of today's society--as illustrated by those who operate as Individualists unconnected with Cosmic Humanity. A manifestation of this is doing what indicates that "Black lives do not matter" to them. The Supernatural society is un-phased by the "dusty" treasures because, by having no concept of the Spiritual Elements, it is possessed with clutching tightly to what is not real. Yet, the "shiny penny" can bewitch the naïve in the Spiritual realm to join the Supernatural ranks and thereafter be confused and lost. An illustration of the philosophy of the societal womb of the Supernatural is the powerful Icon Image planted by the folktales of the early C19 German Grimm brothers who authored what continue to be shown in movies and on television. Some examples include: "Hansel and Gretel," "Little Red Riding Hood," "Rumpelstiltskin," "Snow White and the Seven Dwarfs". Let us look at how these stories for children spotlight the "Dark Side" of the Supernatural. In "Cinderella" the evil stepsisters cut off their toes and heels trying to make the slipper fit and later have their eyes pecked out by doves; in "The Goose Maid" a false bride is stripped naked, thrown into a barrel filled with nails and dragged through the streets; in "Snow White" the wicked queen dies after being forced to dance in red-hot iron shoes; in "The Six Swans" an evil mother-in-law is burned at the stake. Even the love stories contain violence. The princess in "The Frog King" turns her amphibian companion into a human not by kissing it, but instead by hurling it against a wall in frustration. Other tales have similarly gory episodes. In the horrific "The Robber Bridegroom," some bandits drag a maiden into their underground hideout, force her to drink wine until her heart bursts, rip off her clothes and then hack her body into pieces. These Icon Images might play out in today's world. The situation with Cinderella might be to look pretty as the way to get a "prince" and that is all it takes to "live happily ever after." What about Cinderella's untapped talents that could make the lives of other people better and thereby bring her true happiness. Cinderella's sisters did their own form of plastic surgery based upon some pre-established model as determined by the taste of someone or an in-group. Certainly, there is a clamoring today for plastic surgery, as if human parts are like machine parts. The "choppin up" of humans is well featured in society, as in Europeans doing that to Amerindians after stripping them of their treasures; or to Enslaved Africans as punishment; or to lynched Black Americans. All Supernatural mindsets in Grimm's tales are readily seen today (e.g. mass killings; killings of unarmed Black People because of a host of Supernatural and Superstitious concepts about "black"). A life womb socialization example is little children dressed in KKK garments and fed its philosophical doctrine. Merit is for self-declared "good-people" to assess their unexamined assumptions and beliefs.

SOCIALIZATION PHILOSOPHY PATHS: The "Womb" of a Spiritual Society is exemplified by Ancient Africans. Their focus was on turning out offspring possessing and bonding with internal unchanging linkages of Coherence, Consistency, Compatibility, Balance, and Harmony. Their laying the foundation for or producing the products used by today's world was so brilliant as for its record and people to be wiped out--by the Supernatural law of "eliminate the competition." A prime former of today's Western Socialization Philosophy was that of the ancient Greek itinerant teachers called Sophists ('specious reasoning'). They were originally celebrated for the wisdom and rhetorical skill but eventually became intellectually suspect. Their reasoning style seems sound but is actually misleading--known in C14-18 as "hoodwinking" people (i.e. conceal ones true motives by deceiving or swindling or elaborately feigning good intentions so as to gain an end). Malcomb X used the term "bamboozle" to characterize what Europeans particularly do to Black People, as in presenting themselves as knowing what they are talking about and being truthful and honorable about it. Naïve good people simply cannot imagine such a low level of inhumanity--despite its long, prominent, and destructive history up to the present. Thus, when it is heard today, as from Right Wing Republicans, the naïve find it plausible but if one strains hard enough one will see it makes no sense--is of a Supernatural Indifference/ Hate/Evil/Sadism nature--and presented in such forms as cunning practicing upon fear. For such hypocrites, who still recognize they have a Conscience, to live with themselves they devise "Flexible Morals"--adopt morals for judging others and as a façade while disregarding them otherwise in situations of self-interest. Everything about the "shinny penny" Supernatural is based upon opinion generated out of the Imagination--and that is fundamental to understand when assessing information in any field and about anything produced by people with a Supernatural philosophy. By them not knowing any other way, they present their "shadows" as the truth and ridicule the sunlight from which the "shadows" derive as being wrong and unreal. The points they are attempting to make are always in a persuasive manner--wrapped in "shinny penny" things like "documentary" movies or television programs; in the setting of everybody involved with their point being happy and sexy; in being "Sham Scientific"--"doctors/scientists agree" or "research shows...". The idea is to make those who are not in the "in-group" to feel as if something is wrong with them and that to "follow their crowd" is the way to be "cool" and "popular." All of this is associated with either ridiculing the opposition or wiping out all traces of what they have to say because of an inability to compete. The implanted "Seeds" which spring into forms and patterns for living, each with "Germs" of its parents' like-kind qualities, cannot avoid being manifested in all aspects of the off-springs life. Meanwhile they are continually busy to ensure their victims are bitters. What do good people say about those who are hypocrites while doing horrible destruction in the back and who fear speaking up for what they think is right?

SOCIALIZATION INTO "SEEMS" RIGHT: *Socialization* is a society's series of events which form a recognizable pattern that recurs often enough for one to observe the pattern over and over again in different members of the same society so as to bind the minds of that society together and uphold its order. The result is a culture's Group Mind and Ethos Common Sense imposed on newborns; "delivered" to incomers; and "handed over" to be culturally transmitted from generation to generation. Humans are born into a societal "Womb" and nourished by that society's Philosophy of Life (POL). Since African Tradition POL is based upon the Spiritual Elements, is derived from the Laws of Nature, and follows a Mathematical process, it is the standard, guide, filter, and measure for Right Living. Evidence for this is African people having lived in peace for 198,000 of the 200,000 years humans have been on earth. By contrast, following the appearance of Europeans 45,000 years ago, disharmony and turmoil has been the setting wherever they were/are. To be Socialized into European "Womb" means that the way of living is one of SEEMS Right to its offspring—in what is done, the way it is done, and how people are who do it. Whether taught or discovered in dictionaries, the European practice is: the propounding of theories based upon biased or prejudiced opinions, beliefs, and faith--and making generalizations around them so as to serve as mind control of others so as to serve their own self-interest. All of what is conveyed is based upon many assumptions for which proof is not possible—especially since most are thoughts about unrealistic things--contingent or virtual beings." To absorb those assumptions means one is forever afflicted with the *Immanent*—i.e. what dwells in or pervades one mind without necessarily being a part of it—and yet being governed by that programmed Patterned Thinking. This implies each offspring carries a primitive European Warrior mindset into dealing with all outsiders. Hence, if whatever they have been socialized to say—a form of Patterned Thinking—is represented as a Disaster Star, then its Halo has a subtle "disaster" effect on the Speaker and the Receiver. Some Europeans have a Sun generated (the Sun representing African POL) silver-lining around the "Cloud" covering their Soul Sunshine and are thus capable of switching out of the Supernatural realm back to the Spiritually oriented Cosmos.

SOPHISTS' ANCIENT GREEK PHILOSOPHY: Sophists ('wisdom-bearer') of C5 BC were self-declared wise-men who were unscrupulous distorters of facts. Following the Persian Wars, they travelled about Greece as purveyors of popular education. For pay, they taught "practical wisdom" deemed to be essential--how to 'get along' in the world and without certain knowledge; how to win disputes; how to speak well and convincingly in statesmanship by using grammar, rhetoric, literature; and the generalship of doing whatever promised to offer worldly success by tricking victims. They were identified with the households of the well-to-do and the powerful, specializing in the arts of eloquence and persuasion as a preparation for careers in the law courts and on the public platform. Their almost sole interest was on pleasure, pain, and the pathe (states of emotions) and, as a consequence, neglected argument and proof. Their underlying theory developed from two foundational Sophists' concepts. First was the Italian Sophist Gorgias (c483-375) who was indifferent to both the sufferings and the happiness of other people. He proclaimed: "Nothing exists, and if it did, no one could know it; and if they knew it, they could not communicate it." Second, Pythagoras (a Sophist), upon his return from studying 23 years in Africa said: "*Man is the measure of all things*--of things that are that they are, and of things that are not that they are not." He advised everyone to "measure" matters according to his own nature and needs, since man alone, and not God (as he had learned in Africa), was the measure of all things. He also insisted on sensation as the only source of knowledge, with any sensation being true as long as it is perceived. Sophists agreed with him in despairing of the possibility of reaching truth and that the detached pursuit of absolute truth had been proved to be a wild-goose chase, saying knowledge in the strict sense was unattainable. Thus, man should not bother to seek what he can never find. Although these "SEEMS right" statements are obviously false to followers of the Ancient African Bible, the Sophists began dismantling the Spiritual Elements. This is how most Westerners think!

SOPHISTS' THINKING FALLACIES: The Greek Sophists Philosophers (c 460 BC) pride-fully developed devious ways of speaking, as in leading victims in one direction while actually implying something else going in another direction. Or, "in disputes, make the worse seem the better cause." Among their rhetoric, Emotive language was called "Loaded Language" or "High-Inference Language" or "Expressive Language" because they used words that attempted to influence listeners or readers by appealing to their emotions in order to entertain, impress, or persuade individuals or a group for self-gain. Their numerous methods of deceit meant preying on the human's weakness as, for example, to act immediately based upon an emotional response and *without* a considered judgment--as seen in today's advertisements. The Sophists characteristically had a great understanding of what words were "Loaded" and what phrases have strong emotional overtones or connotations to strongly evoke the desired positive or negative reactions beyond their literal meaning. These professional teachers for only those who could afford it would teach government leaders such things as: "virtuous" success comes from having money and power over people; or reject democratic laws in favor of the natural rights of those with the power. The bottom line was (and is): "Winning is the only thing" and to this end the attack is on the opponent as a person; on what the opponent does; dismiss the opponent's views by ridiculing them and/or misinterpret them so that the opponent appears to agree to something which the opponent also denies. Another feature is that if the Con-artist makes ten points in a persuasive presentation to their victims, nine will be correct (so as to gain the victims confidence) but the tenth one is the "big bang" which is designed to be a winner for the con-artist and a big loser for the victim. Such is clearly seen with attorneys whose motto is: "I build up my case while I tear down yours." This has nothing to do with the truth. Attorneys are good at giving plenty of rhetoric and "stacking the cards" (i.e. arrange the cards secretly and dishonestly in ones own favor and/or against ones opponent). Generally, however the flawed argument con-artists seems to be is sound but is rotten in reality. Instead, what they say turns out to be falsities of great magnitude and, by careful listening, what they say does not make sense. Prove this to yourself by analyzing advertisements. The pattern of the Sophists way is to try to sell you a bill of goods that is not worth it or is not in your best interest. They constantly send up smoke-screens, as in spotlighting the insignificant, so as to gain the advantages of deception. Similarly, their today's European imitators (present "everywhere" and in every field) are dishonorable people who dislike the sound of Truth. An example of closet racists' "*Deflection*"—a throwback trick to the ancient Greek Sophist--is seen by the media steering a specific crime topic to appear as if it is "normal in Black culture." This pattern is typical of Whites in their advocating "how bad" Black people are. The intended effect of "Deflection" is to hopefully ensure no one will notice the evil-like kind things the finger-pointing White people do.

Because Black people in general are an honorable people, most would find it inconceivable to discover how Europeans perfect their skills in being dishonorable and devising cheap tricks to fool and seriously cause hardships. This process of *Sophistry* (plausible but misleading or fallacious presentation of information with the intent of deception) is what caused the decline of the world dominating civilization of Africans to herald African American slavery. Those Africans were also deceived into embracing the false belief that what Europeans said they could offer and appeared to offer was somehow better than what they already possessed; what has stood the test of tens of thousands of years; and what has worked brilliantly throughout African history. Europeans have no intentions--now or in the future--of benefitting Black People!

SOUL MUSIC: No doubt music in Black people is the most powerful catalyst of spiritual expression, whether it be in rhythm, dance, or singing. The reason, according to Dona Richards (in Asante, African Culture p224), is those doing it at a "soul" level or at the level of "Being" are participating in the quintessential (purist) spiritual aspects of the Cosmos. From my observations and compared with other ethnic groups, music experienced in the Astral Body is more prominent in Black People; has a more profound effect; and stems from a love of life (historically present in Black People). As opposed to being animated by an intelligent life, the Astral Body (which embraces the human mind and emotions) possesses a kind of life sufficient to convey an understanding of its own existence and wants. Since the presumed Astral term "Soul" likely refers to individuals touched at an Astral Body level, allow me to speculate on what happens there. Observation suggests a given "Soul" Music piece takes the "deeply touched" musician and the avid musical listener directly and immediately beyond themselves into a realm of Aliveness. Here, each individual is connected to perhaps a Cosmic Rhythm, Metaphysical Vibration, or Life Pulse. Being triggered by the same "Soul" Music piece is a symbolic imagery derived from memory (e.g. of a happy, sad, or thoughtful nature) and it joins the connection (like an Apperception). The resultant multiple connections generate mental symbolic forms of a Metaphysical notion or Object image nature. Those mental forms are orchestrated by the Astral Body so that whatever is displayed as being in the past (e.g. memories) is experienced in the "here and now"--as opposed to being a memory in the physical body realm and a "present" happening in the Astral Body. Such occurs because the Astral Body is transitional between Time and Space (like "The Ether") and thus knows no separation between the past and present occurring within it. To elaborate, a "*Spiritual Octopus*," it is above time and space. Therefore the past, present, and future are one and the same. To illustrate, if you look through a knot hole in a fence and see only the head of the octopus, what is kept out of your sight are the tentacles positioned behind and the tentacles positioned in front. Thus, what you see in the present is based on--and includes--the past (the hind tentacles of the octopus you cannot see) as well as the future (the front tentacles of the octopus you cannot see) because the present is simultaneously extending into the future. This "*Spiritual Octopus*" Concept enables the musician or the listener to be an intimate part of the "movie" of the present "Soul" Music (i.e. combining all aspects of its past with the "here and now") and thereby transforming all components of ones Selfhood into harmony operating as a unit. Hence, "Soul" Music is unity music--uniting one with the inherent intelligence of the Cosmos--uniting the past and present as if they are different phases of the same present scenario--uniting ones Selfhood to head toward total liberation--uniting one with the truth of Black Existence and the Black Experience. In other words, "Soul" Music creates subjective cultural patterns or structures for Black People's expressions and actions in a manner making each part of the Group Ethos. But simultaneously, each individual is having a unique and uplifting "Soul" Music experience. The great jazz musician Charlie Parker (1920-1955), in "Hear Me Talkin' to Ya," put it this way: "Music is your own experience, your thoughts, your wisdom. It you don't live it, it won't come out of your horn."

SOUL SUNSHINE: In African Tradition, the One God, Aten, is symbolized by the Sun and the mythological God, Ra, is the Sun's attributes when it rises—i.e. when it is transformed from undifferentiated Subjective to Objective Being. When the Sun returns ("sets") to its original undifferentiated state in the Subjective, it is Temu. All of this is an unnamed One Being deemed to be a Cosmic Force which, for convenience, is called Sekhem. This is because the Supreme Being is ever coming into existence as Things in the Cosmos and returning to its essential undifferentiated state. By being a Spark of God, the Spiritual aspect of each human, which brightens ones Subconscious—the "Soul Sunshine"--is ultimately destined to do the same. Ancient African Sages knew the Physics of the Sun being the factory for creating all physical Matter and Energies—the forces and building blocks of all Things in the Cosmos—the nexus of transformation of unshaped into shaped Matter (Amen, Metu Neter II:65). The way to a human's Soul source of the "Soul Sunshine"—the Divine Self—was represented by the Sun and the Moon (Asar who symbolizes the Mind) forming Ra's eyes, both being passageways to the Soul. Asar is Consciousness dwelling in an inert and dead body--a death-like cessation of all activities except for ones Divine Consciousness--experienced as great peace and relaxation. This realm of the Setting Sun—the Beautiful West—the Amenta—is returned to when one succeeds in cultivating an *intuitive Intellect which understands the nature of Creation and the Oneness of all things in the "One Hidden God."* Humans see moonlight because of the light of the Sun shining on the moon and then reflecting onto the Earth. Hence, the Mind shines with awareness because the light of Universal Consciousness (God) is reflecting in it. Thus, humans can exist, think, be aware, awake since their Underlying Divine Consciousness supports these. An analogy is water sustained in a glass because the glass is holding and supporting it. From the Sun, Aten extend rays that terminate with hands which bestow Ankhs (Life Force) to all Creation. Such is an abstract of the transcendental nature of the Divine as a Principle, as opposed to a Personality like that for Europeans. The "Prt m Hru" (epitaph)--a name for Humankind's original Bible and dating to 60,000 BC (Seleem p 59, xiii), the "Book of Life"—says: *righteousness leads to spiritual realization; purification is acting with righteousness; and by learning about the nature of the Divine—acting, feeling, and thinking as the Divine—it is finally possible to become one with the Divine.* The divine Universal Soul in its manifested aspect—the ever-burning light—the personified Sun—is a web of Associations. That Web-like system is one of all God's Creatures and Creations being interconnected while both independently act and interdependently interact God's manifestations in accordance with the God assigned identities of each. That *Correspondence* gives insight into the *Circumstantial Unknown*—meaning a "ME/WE" Web because what is done in any part of the Web affects the entire Web and its contents. Hence, on any plane of Cosmic existence or on any one plane--and regardless of the appearances or functions of what all is being considered in a given God-made situation--it can be analogized to the Tree Concept. Whereas the Underground "Seed" is the *Essence*, the Underground "Roots" and All of the above ground aspects—Trunk, Branches, Leaves, and Fruit--are merely *Essentials of the Essence*. Nevertheless, despite those above ground aspects—some seemingly having no relationship to each other--those *underlying possess a web of relationships that are a Unified realm of complexity and multiplicity Patterns*. Certain Patterns operate in Nature and thus throughout the Cosmos in the macro-Cosmic Solar System. Other Patterns are operating in the micro-Cosmic Atom System. Yet, all of these large and small Patterns possess a *consistent, permanent, stationary, and unchanging state of Continuity (unity among apparent diversity)*. But still, Underlying these Underground Patterns are their shared in common *Home Base* consisting of movingly displayed Spiritual Elements Essences.

In short, the Cosmic Web's Spiritual Elements' *Essence* of Unconditional Love, Truth, Reality, and the Natural, manifests as independently working systems inside Cosmic Harmony. This knowledge enabled Ancient Africans to apply Mathematics to the Metaphysical, mainly using Qualitative Algebra to gain Principles from all planes of Cosmic existence and their relationships. Understanding these Mathematical Principles is the way they developed their dormant Divine Life Forces within, so as to be an Earthly embodiment of God's designing intelligence. Thus, they subjected their "*Self's*" (Spark of God Soul, constituting a human's divinity)--the Consciousness/Will--*to the Divine Spirit in order to command the Life-Force in harmony with the Laws of Nature*. Thereafter, whatever flowed out of the "ME" of a human was of a Cosmic Organism Rhythm nature which, in turn, would similarly affect all "WE" Web strings--a "ME/WE" Concept of Unity by that human's Non-Self.

A "Non-Self" has the obligation/duty/responsibility to *discover and conform to the underlying web of relationships operating in Nature* throughout the Cosmos. As a result, its "ME" aspects are then able to transcend into the Sublime's reality flow—a natural flowing part of Cosmic Knowledge—a flow in which one recognizes ones own Being as a vital to the All (i.e. "Oneness" within the Cosmic Mind). Here, in the "ME/WE" Sublime realm, Knowledge is known without proof. Benefits from that Knowledge have nothing to do with Materialism characterizing ones Lower Self or with the European Supernatural. *Being in this infinity of Knowledge* allows one to discover new insights about any Spiritual Elements' attribute; see ones old blind-nesses to the obvious; and acquire new perspectives upon hearing old Wisdom over and over. Hence, even though each Entity is "Unique," *being part of the Cosmic Web gives each Correspondence* with every other part of the Cosmic Circle of Wholeness. From operating by Ma'at Principles and Laws, all Knowledge of them are very few in number. To see all of these aspects together in their web-like interrelationships enables one to become aware of links connecting and meshing the Uniqueness of each member into the inner nature Sameness that makes up the Cosmic Family. These Processes are designated "*Circumstantial*" because by Nature existing "all over" at once means no part can be reasoned by direct demonstrations and some are hidden.

This entire process starts with the Spark from God's Sun symbol—with its Halo constituting the Cosmos. That Spark is imparted into a human to display as a "Soul Sunshine" Halo. Just as with the macro-Cosmic Solar System, with its Sun at its center and the planets orbiting around it, so is each human an image of that. In both instances there is an identical Correspondence web pattern of Associations with all God's Creatures and Creations—even down to the microcosmic atom, with the nucleus at its core, orbited by protons, electrons, and neutrons. Everything from the greatest Sun to the tiniest atom is in vibration. Each has a unique vibration rate--as seen in the circling of the planets around the Sun; the rise and fall of the sea; or the ebb and flow of the tide. By following the above mentioned Sun and Moon avenues, energies of the mind and body may be channeled towards a higher, spiritual goal in life (Ashby, Book Of Dead p130, 139, 167, 234). Resultant Spiritual Enlightenment—freedom from ones Lower (animalistic) Self demons--leads to freedom while alive and after death. The Sun's Rays equate to the Psycho-Spiritual Virtues Ancient Africans said must be cultivated in a 7 fold manner: (1) Righteousness; (2) Sex urge control; (3) Selfless Service; (4) Unconditional Love; (5) Silence, Introspectiveness, Self-Discipline; (6) Divine Vision; and (7) Transcendence into "Non-Self" Regardless of the aspect in life, one is to remain in the *moving Essences of the Spiritual Elements and develop all Think, Feel, Say, and Do aspects of life out of their Attributes.* These provide *the "5Ss"—Safety, Security, Sureness/Self-Confidence, Strength, and Stability—to a human's Private Self. See Speculation; Hallucination*

SOURCE: the furnisher of a first and continuous supply of whatever. Questions for assessing the integrity of the Source include: "Where did the information come from?"; "Why did it come?; "Is it concerned with what is "Right?"; or Honorable and correct?; or Honorable and incorrect?; or Dishonorable and intended to control the people for self-interest purposes?

SPECIES: A "*Genus*" is a group of species alike in the broad features of their organization but different in their detail. A *Species* is a group of entities which reproduce their kind and are so nearly alike in all particulars as to indicate they may have sprung originally from the same parent stock—as did all "races" of humans.

SPECULATION: Although the Old French word "*Speculation*" ('spy out') has wide-ranging and conflict-ing meanings, its dominant dictionary sense is the propounding of theories and making generalizations around them--both based upon many assumptions for which proof is not possible. In taking advantage of this confu-sion, attorneys in the Medico-Legal courtroom tried to trick me: "Doctor, didn't you arrive at your conclusions by speculation?" When this first happened in my capacity as an Independent Medical Examiner for the state of California, I said "yes!" Smugly, in his closing argument he told the judge my opinions were on the 'Guessing' ['no calculations'] end of the "Speculation Scale"—implying my opinions were merely Fantasy ('unreal'—only in my imagination). Actually, it was *A Priori* (prior; 'seems right') *reasoning, dealing with what exists before and independent of experience--and* from *Causes to Effects Reasoning as well as* A *Posteriori Reasoning* (going from Effect to Cause) —and again independently of experience. Either way, the process starts with the definition formed or principles assumed, without examination or analysis, and presumptively deducing consequences. Hence, I said my A Priori and A *Posteriori* Reasoning is carefully studying minute case details + meshed with my education, training, and experience + relying on African Tradition's *Subjective Science* tools—i.e. Observation, Reflection, "Pure" Feelings, Productive Imagination, Contemplation, Inductive and Deductive Inferences, and Common Sense—to make inferences in arriving at circumstantial evidence and judgments. This highly abstract Thinking method had been developed during my specialized training in Medical Genetics and Birth Defects at Johns Hopkins Hospital in Baltimore, Md. What makes "*Speculate*" so interesting is it can go in opposite directions in the assessment of something. And both form concepts of "SEEMS" true. In the direction of *a priori reasoning* (inferred concepts from reflection), it pertains to pondering the different aspects of a subject and evolving ideas or theories by mental re-examination of the subject. Such *Reflections* are mental activities which develop mental pictures around an imageless notion (a quality) typically made into ideas to express ones interpretation about that speculative notion. By contrast, in Speculation's Fantasy direction there is an unreal mental image or reflection giving an appearance of the "Fantastic" in a "*Contingent Being.*" Although it is an image of something having no real existence, some people's imaginations go out of control to create a fantastic magical Supernatural world of happenings and outside the common sense views of society. The dangerous ones, stemming from "*Phantasmagoria*" (phantasm/ ghostly figures) Fantasies, are *Delusional Religious Fanatics.* Each creation happens in ones mind by wishing to have that quality, impression, appearance, or message arise. Still, most believe it to be so. Or, if the situation is reversed and these four are real, there is denial of their existence (i.e. being blind to them). Both can SEEM right, saying they apply to what is sensible and changeable all the way over to what is Immaterial and absolutely immutable (unchange-able). No doubt, there exists combinations of a priori reasoning within a "*Contingent Being*" and that raises the question: "Where is the "SEEMS" true (an appearance form of thinking) located on the scale between the true/real and untrue/unreal?" Since European concepts of "Being" (even Supernatural Contingents) are part of European concepts of Knowledge, anything else is the subject matter of Opinion. Europeans say Opinion is between pure Being and absolute not-Being, intermediate between Knowledge and Ignorance where things fluxuate--i.e. the sphere of the Becoming containing the many and the variable. Nevertheless, the concept of a "Contingent Being" is very useful in applying it to established concepts contained within the category of Information. See Fantasy; Hallucination

SPIRIT ADVISORS: inside my Spiritual Entourage were explained by Ancient Africans saying that by being created in the image of God, every human carries the potential for genius, *as orchestrated by a special attendant spirit allotted to that individual at birth*. That spirit forever watches over and shapes ones character and fortunes. As a boy I really enjoyed the Boy Scouts and camping out. Although I normally slept very soundly, when it was time for me to get ready to leave for a fishing trip at 4:00 a.m., I would be wide awake at 3:30 a.m.

SPIRIT SERVANTS: By Affect Symbolic Imagery, Ancient African Griots (story-tellers) informed African people about them in stories.

SPIRITUAL ELEMENTS: Truth, Reality, Unconditional Love, and the Natural -- means that each, of itself, and by itself, becomes the off-spring it reproduces.

SPIRITUAL ENERGY PACKAGE: when one is Self-Propelled, this displays as: Dedication (selecting what is cared about); Commitment (becoming one with what is cared about); Loyal (sticking like glue to a Goal and Purpose no matter what); Determination (setting limits within which one will act); Persistence (holding fast to ones Purpose and Goal); and Perseverance (continuing ruthlessly in the face of opposing forces, set-backs, and momentary failures--to not give up—to never succumb to attractive distractions--to always give ones best effort—and to achieve the goal in the most efficient and effective manner). The manifestation of ones Spiritual Energy Package is the basis for ones personal power. These are just as applicable to Necessary and Important tasks as they are to Desires. I enjoy indulging Self-Expressions of being Creative about anything, as in learning new "pretzel" ways of solving problems. An example is to see how the opposite of what is standard practice can possibly used to solve "impossible" problems, for this is "Mental Self-Fertilization." Similar pleasures come from seeing how different words share similar underlying meanings and then coining new words (e.g. Quadriary Qualities).

SPIRITUAL EVOLUTION: Humans' "Souls" (Higher Divinity Self; Divine Soul-Consciousness in African Tradition)--while variously and confusingly called in non-African literature the personified alter ego; the first division of the Spirit--have the power to transform potential Entities from their undifferentiated Subjective Virtual Image state into an Objective Being. Such is done by coordinating the process, via the Will and carried out by the Spirit, of physical Spiritual Energy fashioning Matter into a physical Entity or Event. Each human's Spiritual "Soul Sunshine" aspect—i.e. a Spark of God--brightens ones Subconscious so as to guide ones ultimate Destiny to do the same. Thus, similar to the Supreme Being's manifestations, the human Soul is ever bringing its Spiritual Elements Image into existence and returning an assortment of Things projected into the Cosmos back to their essential undifferentiated state. Ancient Africans' Alchemy focus was on arriving at the mastery of Mental Forces to enable insights for paths to reach the Heaven Afterlife. They spotlighted the melanin black complexion of Asar (Osiris) as symbolizing the unmanifest Deity in the profound Darkness of Potentiality. In the black body of the dead Asar, Ancient Africans visioned an Archetypal (primal, essential "Seed") Human Pattern. The keystone of this Divine Alchemy was to learn how to use Heavenly Energy to transmute (change from one form, nature, state into another + into each other) the black Earth of Ignorance into the gold of Wisdom. The process is to *involute*--the process of getting involved by "Knowing

Thyself" and thus the foundational Cosmic Laws by returning to a human's pre-birth "First Wisdom" state. Then comes Evolution of Spiritual Meanings which naturally manifest by the unfolding of its Involuted contents and their associated powers. In short, the Lower Nature (Earth) gives birth to the Higher Nature (Gold). This is based upon the Cosmic Principle that all of Nature's decomposition is re-composition. Death is transmutation, as in changing of bodies into light and light into bodies. Yet, nothing is ever finished and nothing is ever isolated because it has reference to something else and each achieves meaning apart from that which neighbors it. Such is the beautiful African Tradition Spiritual Philosophy in strictest Harmony with the Laws govering human Spiritual Evolution.

SPIRITUALITY: : *purpose of African Religion or Spirituality is to construct ones mind to reflect the Divine attributes of ones Self Genius;* discovering practices for achieving and living inside the Spiritual Elements.

Spirituality, they said, is ones own means of discovery of practices for achieving and living inside the Spiritual Elements. Still, there was the Ancient African Bible for the people's use to convey Spiritual Elements knowledge and the means to attain their own devised forms of Religion and Spirituality. This established philosophical principles 'sameness' in no matter how customized were ones other choices. As a result of the combination of the 'uniqueness' and 'sameness' aspects one could achieve *"Feels True" Knowing* which, in turn, imparts the "5Ss" of safety, security, sureness/self-confidence, strength, and stability.

STANDARD DEFINITION: See Quality Standards for Supernaturals

STANDARDS: Standards pervade every aspect of ones life and those selected determine ones degree of success. Before one can do anything worthwhile for oneself in the outside world and before trying to "Lift others as you Climb," Ancient Africans said to put ones own life in order. Ordering starts by selecting African philosophy of life Standards which are so powerful as to provide an overflow of the "5Ss" as well as have the ability to defeat anything posing to destroy them. A *Standard is something* (e.g. a Truth, a Symbol, a thought, a feeling, a pillar) to determine what is required to do a task; which forms a "skeleton" around which a structure is built; conveying or possessing a quality, sense, quantity or measurement against which something is compared and measured as a means of determining its degree of accuracy or conformity; to learn what is "right" as to how to do things; and that idealizes what is the best end product. Standards are: (1) "God-Made" (based upon circumstantial evidence as is typical of African Tradition in striving to achieve the Truth); (2) "Man-Made" objectives devised by the agreement of experts as, for example power, fame, pleasure, riches); or (3) Man-Made Estimate Ranges (for what cannot be measured or that deal with Sentiments (thoughts wrapped in emotions or feelings). All three have application on different planes of existence and thus there can be double-standards for a given plane ("don't do as I do, do as I say"). For others, the rules for a given Standard may vary on different planes (e.g. money), as in ranging from the Spiritual to the Objective or ranging from internal to external--or vice versa. Some may be attainable while others are unattainable because they are impossible to achieve; because of limitations of an individual; or because of limitations placed by outside forces. Some Standards may be flexible while others are rigid. African Traditions' *four basic Standards* are: First is considering *God as the spiritual source* for Order and Stability in all real creatures and creations. Second is *Mathematics* ("the discipline which brings order to the mind") being the source of order for worldly matters. Mathematical demonstration has always been regarded as a method of knowledge satisfying the highest standards of truth. A *Standard* (what people's math ideas are measured against) serves as a definition guide for solving problems and pointing out directions; places boundaries (e.g. time and space limits); and provides rules for performance and variations. Third, *Ma'at* (Love in action) is deemed as the principle for interpersonal relationships. Fourth is an individual's *Real Self Divinity* being the source of all of ones Private and Public Self matters. Since Ancient Africans recognized different planes of existence in the universe, they devised Standards specific to each plane.

Examples: Whereas those of the Spiritual world use Love as its standard, for the Intangible plane it is Beauty, Goodness, and Truth as models of excellence which derives from ones Real Self. For the Unbounded Tangible Plane of a Feeling nature, the Standard is harmony and unity springing out of Maat while for the Partially Bounded Plane it is health. For the Concrete Tangible planes, it is proper measurements by mathematics or honorable estimates. Despite differences, they are all related to and are part of the big picture of Good Living and Humaneness. Each represents the frame in which right decisions and right actions are made. Thus, they represent points of stability against which things can be compared or measured. They also represent guiding lights for what is correct, worthy, and valuable in any type of choice, decision, or solution. *"Criticism"* is the term given to any deviation from the agreed upon Standard (Criteria) for judging well (Critically). Skills needed for proper selections of Standards include: (1) Deciding justly and without emotions; (2) Possessing a sensitivity and a delicate perception of the matter at hand; (3) Taking into account each pleasant and/or unpleasant Quality; (4) Adapting to the changing natures of Quantities.

STAR TWINKLING: the perception of twinkling stars is a result of atmospheric interference--an effect similar to what takes place on a hot summer day when one looks across hot pavement or a parking lot. Just as this rising air causes images to waver, it is also what causes the twinkling effect in stars. The lower a star is in the sky, the more it will twinkle because its light must pass through more of the atmosphere.

"STAY-IN-YOUR-PLACE": Such include: "don't read"; "don't get an education"; "don't try to better yourself"; "don't be ambitious"; "don't be uppity" (i.e. do not be like a White man—and morally that is good advice!!); "stay in your place"—meaning Black people should "be about nothing"; "fight among yourselves"; and "spend your money foolishly."

STEPPING STONES: *Stepping Stones* are a bridge to a destination—serving as a means to progress or advance. As divided links of a chain, they are breaks to facilitate the advance to the next level. But to rest on one before going to the next, that one must be sound and solid enough to support what is resting on it—and particularly when used as a springboard to go to the next "stone." Black Scholars who rise on the stepping-stones of their discarded False Selves for higher realms, take off from the stepping stone Truths of prior Black Afrocentric Scholars.

STEREOTYPING'S SELFHOOD BACKGROUND: Revelations to Ancient African Sages were that out of God's Androgynic plast Substance emanate the Spiritual Elements of Unconditional Love, Truth, Reality, and the Natural—the Essence "Genetics" for God' creatures, including each human. Thus, all have "Sameness" in their "Ground of Being" which underlies their different manifestations—a "Sameness" called *Correspondence*. So, although "Genetically" related to the Mineral and Plant "Queendoms" by God's Substance called Essence (i.e. their "What it is"), the "Animal" Kingdom is the Genus that includes both humans and other animals. A *"Genus"* is a group of species alike in the broad features of their organization but different in their detail. A *Species* is a group of entities which reproduce their kind and are so nearly alike in all particulars as to indicate they may have sprung originally from the same parent stock—as did all "races" of humans. For example, all "races" or Species of people on Earth--each appearing quite differently from the rest but all sharing the same Underlying "Genetics"—have originally come from the same African Ancestors who lived 200,000 years ago when humans first appeared on Earth. Also, all pre-birth humans are joined in their Subjective plane home with other of God's Creatures and Creations in an unformed, undifferentiated, but not disorganized state called "ME/WE". Hence, despite each doing customized Earth living, all interdependently carry out God's Plan. An analogy is they are like shining through a prism a white light (in the Subjective Realm) to give rise to *primary colors of the spectrum on earth—each Creature and Creation being like a visible* violet, indigo, blue, green, yellow, orange, red beam. Some "Genetic Sameness" aspects are altered by gene difference combinations and by Earth environment. Such a transition between Underlying Internal "Sameness" altered into External Differences is a Species Animal *Primary Qualities* Essentials (e.g. Human Nature). Still, their underlying "Genetics" ensure they are of the same nature with their own Essence and the Essence of their Species. *The Essentials of the Essence consist of a like-kind Character, Characteristics, Traits, and Features.*

The Essence/Essentials Pattern of the shared Spiritual Elements instilled in each human while in the Subjective Plane is according to God's Plan. Broadly, all humans 2 main individuality distinguishers from each other are first, Mosaic Essence-Essentials Uniqueness in each. This customized Essence Uniqueness is illustrated by the Talent within every human's Essence. By manifesting out of the Essential of its parent Essence, no other human has ever had that Talent in the past, does not have it now, and will never have it. In other words, even though all God's Creatures and Creations have the same Underlying "Genetic" Essence, the unique combination of a given human's Essence (like that of a Combination Lock) + its displayed unique Essentials, constitute that human's Individuality.

A second individuality factor is ones mindset arrived at by normal living—i.e. powered by a natural flow, from environmental influences, or from being a "Self-Made" individualist. A different category is Mind Control by coercion or socialization which causes *Selfhood Splintering*—i.e. one part being Self-Absorbed (viewing everything within ones world in relationship to oneself); the other follows dictates of External World influences. Here, White Supremacists ignore, reject, or fail to consider the Essence of their Scapegoats because they do not believe all humans (as well as the other of God's Creatures and Creations) come from the same Spiritual God. Instead, they have their own Supernatural God(s) or "Mechanical Organism" (an oxymoron) god concept of where humans originate. Since those concepts are Fantasy based, Believers are Self-Unknown, in turmoil inside an abyss type disconnection from their natural "ME/WE" Spiritual God source. The resultant mindset is Indifference/Hate/Evil/Sadism (IHES). Resultant profound Selfhood pain drives them to engage in Kill/Take/Destroy/Dominate/Oppress/Control practices to get "Excitement"—their only source of "relief." When people stereotype other humans, they separate their shared and same Underlying "Genetic" Essence from each other; pass judgment on their own and the Scapegoats; and institute inhumane actions. Some IHESs mentally grasp a Scapegoat's Essential aspect—i.e. the reproduced Character of the Essence parent--a Characteristic(s)--a Trait(s)—and/or a Feature(s) in order to make it demeaning in all other scapegoats. Some simply disrespect Scapegoats' Essence. jabaileymd.com

STEREOTYPES: Infants, by lacking discernment or speech abilities, over-simplify a person, place, thing, or situation--assessing it only a "*is it for me or against me*" perspective. Even before their first birthday, babies are highly selective—discriminating as to whom they will pay attention--preferring those of their "in-group" ("people like me")—wasting no time on those they deem unlikely to "deliver the goods." By age 11 months, they focus on those speaking a language familiar to them while ignoring foreign speakers. At the defining moment babies make those decisions, their brain waves indicate an "expectation to learn something new". As detected in anticipatory moments by electroencephalogram, it is a "theta" oscillation wave pattern--a state of very deep relaxation since brain waves are slowed to a frequency of 4-7 cycles per second—a state for retaining memories and feelings. In this state, one is able to create any and everything so as to instantly change ones views of reality by governing the Subconscious lying between ones Conscious and Unconscious—a state directing Knowledge, Beliefs, and behaviors inspired to be Spiritual. As normal development proceeds, Babies "Us vs. Them" judgments, resulting from an *in-born drive for information*, become ever more generalized and powerful with age —but without excluding "the Others". Infancy driven desires to learn new things makes them discriminating judges of who is worth listening to, with heightened valuations of optimal informants being same group members—with damage from poor quality information. Children, in categorizing Creatures and Creations in order to make sense of the world, evolve into sort of stereotyping people according to Group Membership. Then they attribute to members those human-made acceptable or indifference Stereotypes into which they have been socialized. If socialized into a cultural atmosphere consisting of Spiritual Elements, children respect the Social Harmony, Humanity, and Dignity present in all humans and demonstrate Respect by means of possessing Good Manners. Such was "normal" in my all-Black community as a boy, where the focus was of "ME/WE".

But, if children are socialized into a culture consisting of Selfhood weak people, savages or Brutes with a "Dark Side," Non-Rational Patterned and Superficial thinkers, or people who crave fear, then children absorb the Indifference/Hate/Evil/Sadism atmosphere by "Osmosis". The nature of their Personalities conform to the nature of their socializing culture. Some children are put on the "Anti-Humanity" path and follow its flow so that by "going along, they get along" with their in-group. Those who do/do not get pleasure from horror films may gain stereotypical images from them within the setting of Fear—to Mild, Slight, Moderate, and Extreme degrees. Some become "daredevil" risk-takers. Otherwise, all perceived Fear sources—whether realistic, distorted, or fantasized--are stereotyped and hated to varying degrees. The fearful react by becoming more inflexible and dogmatic about what they believe; internalize the values of their presumed protectors, while shrinking behind them; and make a panicky retreat into *Self-Absorption*--viewing everything within ones world in relationship to oneself and also following dictates of the Crowd and other External World influences. Such is associated with ones now activated Brain's *Amygdala*—a temporal lobe alarm center just under ones temples. It works with the frontal lobes' consciousness to increase the Fear Response alertness.

The degree to which ones alarm center pours out hormones and neurotransmitters is largely contributed to by ones immediate society—but Crowd's concepts are never real. Fears educated into humans are like a disease—every fearful hint is feared it will materialize. This weakens their resolve to go on in spite of unrealistic dangers assumed to be from even faintly resembling fixed Imaged Stereotypes. A self-fulling prophesy is to imagine exact realizations of the feared—then "they die a thousand deaths." Yet, some are so susceptible to the pleasurable relief coming from realizing their Fears were not real as to deliberately seek it out—putting themselves at dangerous risks to get a rush. Hence, many generate the fine spurs of (self-interest) Delusional Fears. Example: "Killer" police's feigned and unarmed enemies are fantasized in scary scenes to dramatically come out the winner + getting the "rush" from killing someone else. They are pre-armed with an excuse acceptable to their Network—"I feared for my life"—for which they are excessively rewarded. jabaileymd.com

STIMULUS: *Stimulus* (spur)—a 1684 word originally designating a goad used for driving cattle by pricking them. Today it means spurring to action or effort, as a needle against the skin or a signal acting on ones senses or a printed or spoken word serving as a call to action. Second, ways humans/animal react to a stimulus is called a *Response* (to answer)—i.e. something offered in return, almost as an obligation (hence 'Responsible'). Its Ancient African origin was Griots (story-tellers) participatory audience communication—i.e. "*Call and the Response*"--characterized by the Griot sending out a "call" and the audience acknowledging the message. The audience responded while the speaker spoke--and not afterward--so as to make a fluid harmonious tone of participatory communication. A stimulus response is an act, usually a movement—ranging from Mild (like the twitch of a muscle or the blink of an eyelid) all the way over to the Extreme (e.g. one 'jumping' from a door closing). Innate responses are termed *Reflex* ('turn or bend back') and may be brought about not only by the action of sense organs and the nervous system or by other means (e.g. images).

STORIES OF WORDS FOR BLACK CHILDREN: The metaphysically oriented Ancient African children learned best by Affect Symbolic Imagery (ASI) stories laying alternative paths to the teachers' keystone points. Since Ancient Africans were the most wise and intellectually brilliant people in Humankind, I have done my best to model in my 5 published Word Stories volumes how they taught their youth. The process can be analogized to the structure of a feather's long main stem. To stretch one of its two opposing webs along its length will show, on each web, several hundred barbs. Each barb, growing from the shaft, is itself like a tiny feather. Pressing the barbs together causes them to stick to each other as before, and the whole web will be formed again. This happens because the barbs lock themselves together by thousands of hooks, all being microscopically tiny. Once their attention is captured, children's minds (being like one of the webs), work similarly upon hearing ASI stories (the other web). A reason is children live the truism that *the only way a Thing can be known is to b*ecome *one with it.* The power of their Play to mesh with ASI causes them to shift interest from themselves over to a realm of Fancy. Here, each sense overflows with vitality + "Aliveness"—eagerness to see what is coming next. Their Imaginations spontaneously engage in creating "arriving into the moment." While play imitates the feather in Image form, lightness, and flexibility, it is erasing boundaries + *disregarding limitations of human thought* normally separating children's thoughts from the ASI message so as to form an Interchange. Out of that Interchange emanates offspring mosaic-like Symbols featuring parallel similarities with what they represent. Those wide ranging similarities—coupled with like-kind ingredients residing in children's memories—stick on to the barbs of both webs of the feather. There, they undergo an assemblage + a checkered *synthesis of those mosaic pieces so as to produce a unique Essence.* The resultant *Pattern* of that Essence has a virtual Image on the outside and a matrix (womb bringing nourishment to the offspring) on the inside. It is around the created Image that children design *a unitary new meaning for what the Word story is about—a "fed" meaning which serves as an alternate path to the reality* of the ultimate message of the Word Story. So, a fun way to "hook" children on Words is by telling its story in an ASI manner. Ancient African Griots (story-tellers) used the beautiful mythological African story of "*Daybreak*" to help the masses understand concepts contained in "Maturity" (Bailey, Common Sense). However, this story is wrongly attributed to the Romans because plagiarizing African stories and intellectual knowledge was typical of both ancient Greeks and Romans. The process began with the Greeks saying they derived most of their gods and goddesses from Ancient Egypt (Ashby, African Origin p. 261). Then Romans borrowed those same gods and goddesses from the Greeks--and renamed them for various usages. For example, the Egyptian Goddess *Matet* was renamed "Aurora" (also called Matuta) by the Romans. Nevertheless, Matet would daily stain her fingers red with henna for religious ceremonies—as was a routine practice of Egyptian priestesses. Every morning, so the Roman story goes, *Aurora* (actually Matet) arose before daybreak from her couch on the Eastern Ocean and climbed on a golden chariot drawn by white horses. While riding up into the sky, she would proclaim the rising of the day to the mortals as well as to the immortals. Her trip, in association with the Sun, grew in warmth as the day got older. Together, Matet and the Sun flew across the heavens. Within this dawn-to-sunset journey are many African concepts related to "Maturity." Since this ASI model carries children to a point just short of the conclusion, let them fill in conclusion options with roaming discussions. In this way, youth learn true history + how profoundly envious people stole African Intellectual Property + Critical Thinking + beautiful myths + how word stories led to various meanings in words and formed synonyms from nuance changes in a word's evolution. Or, for diagnostic purposes, they can create Word Stories to serve as a complete outlet for their negative emotions and thoughts. Have them select like-kind ideas out of synonyms and fashion stories from them. Next, do this for "distant relative" words taken from a wide variety of sources to see how they compare in their essence. Each group could arrange and combine the essences in order for stories to head in various directions. Each new direction leads into Unknowns and each Unknown can be made into a game. See Affect Symbolic Imagery; Story-Telling; Griots jabaileymd.com

STORYTELLING FOR BLACK YOUTH: "*Storytelling*" arose out of all of Primitive Africans' daily activities and imaginations about things in the Seen and Unseen Worlds--about the interweave of Superstitions,

Magic, Astrology, Subjective Science, Philosophy, and Medicine as they were perfecting concepts of Mythology and Religion. Each of these went through a similar process. Storytelling itself is the art of captivation--the ability to grab and hold the attention of Receivers in order to transmit pertinent Essences using Primary, Secondary, and/or Tertiary Qualities in the vehicle of Thoughts, Ideas, or Concepts. Human minds are already prepared for stories since Folklore, Legends, Myths, Fairy Tales, and/or Fables have followed practically all childhoods through the ages. Most children have a healthy, wholesome, and instinctive enjoyment for stories that are fantastic, marvelous, and manifestly unreal—for these stimulate the Imagination to enter new realms. It is typical for youth and adults to communicate for such purposes as to persuade, inform, entertain, express, share, teach, instruct, educate, or serve as a call to action for decision making, problem solving, pleasure, and/ or self-improvement. However, there are all sorts of storytellers. For example, Story-telling is very different from being a Scholar or one trying to change the world. Some are storytellers having nothing to do with the Truth—like television simulating a circus or carnivals so as to kill boredom. Great storytellers are benefitted by other people associating them with higher status. See Affect Symbolic Imagery; Story-Telling; Groits

Organization of Presentation: The weaving of a narrative has many options. *The Order can be: Alphabetical, Chronological, Historical, Anatomical, or by Numbers*; along a hierarchal or serial or prioritized arrangements; of the most important first and least important last; Least to Most Important; most Difficult to Easiest; Custom (the way it has always been done); by Entitlement, by Attitude, by Preference, by Position (as with the Bowling Pin Concept); by age, by skill, by grade, by order, by rank, by character. Or its Organization may be by intensity or degree (e.g. Mild, Slight, Moderate, and Extreme) or depth, height, scope—especially when the conclusion is to lead to Value Judgments of Sensations, Beauty, Goodness, Truth, Harmony, or Evil. Other arrangement approaches may be: Theoretical to Practical; Most to Least important; Easiest to most Difficult; Start to Finish—i.e. sequential of how things will appear; Cause to Effect; most important things of interest first or simplest first and progressing to the most important—or Arranging any of these in reverse order (e.g. Effect to Cause). But for the masses, I start with which of those is most interesting or ways to build suspense and thus keep their interest.

Weaving the Narrative: I look up all words I am not sure about or to get ancient meanings or meanings from synonyms in at least 30 dictionaries on all fields—regular, sociology, psychology, philosophy, etc. Being orderly--chronologically, spatially, anatomically, hierarchy of importance or reverse importance—or from other arrangements means all involved ingredients must each be doing their separate things and yet show their interdependence with all the others—like all the strings in the fishnet. In turn, whatever hierarchy is chosen enables the logical integration of all like-kind concepts that may lead to the conclusion of sound information or knowledge. In the process, some new insights may appear. From both Order and Understanding, analysis will open new realms which thereby spotlight possibilities for determining more and more Options for thought.

Writing the Story: The Principle is "*to tell them what you are going to tell them; then tell them; then tell them what you told them.*" Proven workable preconceived patterns are the simplest method of bringing about order. If this is ones first big paper and one has no idea how to start, review ones own life to realize one has lived a life of chronological order by cultural development and evolution. Simply following that pattern from babyhood to the present is a way to get started on an approach. What this chronological ordering of gathered information does, even if it is not the final choice, is to provide a frame for the subject's discussion. For example, in doing a historical review of a subject, its defining moments are presented in chronological order. In a presentation of bull's eye information for a complex subject, the complexity may lead me to select one aspect while simultaneously being aware of what is above, below, and around it in chronological order; or where it ranks on the priority scale; or how many Planes of Existence does the topic cover and which Plane demands focus for the subject at hand. Each of these have to be fitted in so that there is a continuous flow of thought. This hierarchy is very useful for troubleshooting in preparing to take the first step; in problems caused along the path of the process; and as a Post-Action Judgment to see where things could be improved over what happened. For a very difficult subject, it is important to keep rewriting the same topic, for each time ones mind will have more subject insight from seeing more interrelationships or one will have picked up from television or conversation a better way to say something.

Different rules are needed for whatever is dynamic or static. In writing, an inductive order is for paragraphs to be organized with the details at the beginning and in the middle, and with an ending summary or generalization, usually the topic sentence. Typically, a *Topic Sentence* (one summarizing the central idea of a paragraph) is introductory. A paragraph laid out in Deductive order makes a well-known reasonable structure by moving from a general statement to the particular details which support or explain it. It proves coherence by grouping details to show to which part of the generalization (usually the topic sentence) they are most relevant. When details are scattered throughout the paragraph, the result is incoherence.

Review and Refining: It may help to start with a quote that gives a gist of what will be discussed. Review it 20 times: (1) are the thoughts and emotions clearly presented?; (2) is the subject covered like a net?; (3) is it written in an enticing or reasonable manner?; (4) is anything left out or not needed? This requires giving great thought to each line for its flavor; for the mental pictures it conveys; for the chances of it being misunderstood or not understood. (5) Is it saying what you think, as opposed to preaching (i.e. what you Ought to do). People relate better to the former than to "shoulds." See Story-Telling; Griots; Affect Symbolic Imagery

STRUCTURE: constructed using related ingredients arranged and/or combined into a form.

STRUGGLE: Perhaps the "str-" part of the C14 English word "Struggle" refers the time, energy, and effort involved in the flawed processes in the "Surviving," the "Striving," the "Strength," and the Spiritual Energy Package necessary to Thrive and have a sense of Well-Being. Upon making the determination to pursue the Divine, there arises "the struggle"--a holy war against ignorance, illusions, and delusions within ones consciousness. The "STRUGGLE" through this stricture of the hour-glass makes you strong and builds self-confidence by improving your thinking skills. Nothing builds the strength of your Self-Esteem better than knowing how to do Rational, Creative, Critical, and Common Sense Thinking. It even went so far as for me to give up advantages in order to do the Right thing. All of this requires Courage, Keeping your Word, and Mental Toughness. This is about having such great Self-Love as to not allow yourself to do harm to yourself and if you discover you are doing harm, you will stop immediately. The core is optimism *struggle which can be analogized to being trapped in a net while chained inside a prison cell, half filled with water while upside down and then trying to survive without any help.* What constantly sharpens ones Critical Thinking decision making and problem solving skills is eagerly facing and handling Struggles—not warfare. When there is no struggle, there is no progress. People presently want crops without plowing up the ground—want rain without thunder or lightning—want water while polluting all its sources. The absence of struggle makes one weak and lose creativity to solve problems. That makes it progressively easier to give in to the wrong side of the eternal struggle between Good and Evil. Those looking for the easy way or the "quick fix" or to do as little as possible are the ones who will stay in the status quo and always remain unhappy with themselves.

"STUPID: "Stupid's" (Latin "stupere") varied etymologies give wide ranging meanings and words—e.g. Stupefy, Stupor, and Stupendous. Its origin was to be "*Amazed*" (stunned) by being dulled through shock, as in being wide-eyed and open-mouthed. In C16 it embraced the "slow-witted, foolish," dull, not intelligent, and 'dead-alive' senses. Later came "*Selective Stupidity*," as in "having eyes and cannot see"—the source of "*blindness to the elephant in the room*"—the idea referred to here. It provides *Excuses* (anything but the Truth) for "*Bending*" (bring into a curve) Reality into Distortions or leaping into Fantasy (e.g. the Supernatural). Any exit off this course stirs so much disharmony, fear, and difficulty (which, for some is *Guilt from Shame* or being inadequate in thinking abilities) as to cause *Illusions* (seeing what is not there and not seeing what is there); *Hallucinations* (false images or beliefs having nothing to suggest it, outside a disordered mind); "*Delirium*" (temporary mental disturbance leading to believing ideas opposed to reality); *Delusions* (believing what is not real and not believing what is real); and *Misinterpretations* (wrong track, wrong plane of existence, and/or wrong direction). All disarray ones 'sureness' of any topic one thought one knew or will later know. A benefit of "going along to get along" with the Crowd is members knowing how hard life is by being stupid and alone. The Weak-minded get necessary relief from "being on the edge" of "going crazy." Others gain self-esteem assurance from Crowd people more stupid than they. Stupidity is honored since, no matter how stupid the Crowd, what they do works for them. This is despite such being outside of Humanity and shattering ones Individuality. Clear examples show by the incredible degrees of Incompetency, everywhere! Stupid provides excuses to get mere Information and for not doing hard work to gain Knowledge or to self-improve. These give permission for an Indifference/ Hate/Evil/Sadistic (IHES) mindset to reproduce itself in behaviors--all justified by them being wrapped in Willful Ignorance and because "everybody" does it. To by-pass Courage is to "Escape" from Reality, as their role models have done. There is too much inner turmoil to leave the Crowd and then to take on the hard work of being Self-Reliant in discovering and developing ones Talent for application to ones Mission.

Besides, for good reason, they dread competition. By avoiding thinking skills—always using the excuse of: "*I'm too busy*"—they *complain,* as Supernaturals, *of people not relating to them*—people using hard and big words in obscure sentences are "boring." The same applies to books. Instead, Stupid is easy—e.g. enabling one to assess a situation without the taskmaster of Spiritual Elements Essences to consider. The Crowd's "noise" and "commotion"--like the empty wagon making greater sounds than when full--is well suited since the *Stupid cannot tolerate Quiet.* The Crowd makes things easy with preconceived fixed notions to insert according to wishes, while ignoring or rejecting any contrary signs, implicit indicators, or contrary facts. Thus, thoroughly Stupid or IHES things done have Crowd backing as being "noble," since it follows their patterns. Increasing stupidity equates to increasing Crowd loyalty. These *"Wax-heads" must avoid the hot Sun of the Truth* and Reality.

A Crowd favorite is *Stereotyping* persons, places, things, styles, or events—i.e. gist definitions, oversimplified and thrust into tight pigeon-holes which give no adjustment or individualizing "wiggle room". The Crowd is "*Conditioned*" not to research to 'know' but to "believe and have faith" in what is read or told them—biases/ prejudices *"Framed" with "Non-Essence" Secondary/Tertiary Qualities.* Then, these fantasies are "*Halo Effect*" painted—i.e. the picking out of one or two characteristics, traits, or features--based on *Unexamined Assumptions* one has been socialized into--for broad-stroking general identifying images. These false images and how such people are likely to behave, one might be told, are to be associated with, say, dark skin color. Stereotypes serve White Supremacists well in their Mind Controlling business of *shaping Stupid people's thoughts with "Sound Bites*" of ready cues having instant recognition. The Mass Media "Re-Enforcer" is focused on generating entertaining "Excitement" by Trinkets (e.g. Flashing Light Gadgets), Trivia (e.g. gossip, rumors), and whatever keeps one as a Superficial Thinker--and thus "Stupid"—i.e. having eyes and cannot see the "what it is"). [This series on White Supremacists is from Bailey, Ambitious Black Isolated Individualists] jabaileymd.com

SUBCONSCIOUS: variously called occulted, hidden, , unconscious, the spirit, psyche, the soul. See Underworld; Amenta; the Spirit

SUBJECTIVE: the aspect of reality in which Energy/Matter are undifferentiated, unformed, in a virtual state but not disorganized. In my dictionary of Medical-Legal terms (p91), "*Objective*" has a perceptive origin outside the mind—whether of a Tangible, Intangible, *Objective Minus* ("what is there but is not" and "what is not there but is"), and *Subjective Plus* (because it "fits" or "works" implies the truth seems valid in advance of Proof). An example of Objective Minus is acquiring Knowledge of the existence of all quantifiable events that cannot be perceived through the senses by using African Qualitative Algebraic derived Logic as well as by Quantitative Logic. By contrast, "*Subjective,*" as I use it, is based on psychological processes—i.e. dependent of any interpretations or likes/dislikes. Both Objective and Subjective are to be distinguished from "*Subjective Minus*"—it is untrue and not there because it is Contingent. See Concrete; Objective

SUBJECTIVE SCIENCE: Subjective Science skills of Observation, Reflection, "Pure" Feelings, Productive Imagination from an unbiased and unprejudiced position to see things as they are in reality. This requires observing things without an opinion and then having the Courage to assess and examine deeply and thoroughly all aspects of every belief--and particularly those clung to. Then, the resultant thought products are carried through the process of Contemplation (thoughtfully dissolving into and identifying with Universal Truths) so as to establish a platform for Inductive (Inferring general principles from particular facts) and Deductive (making inferences from general truths to particular truths) Reasoning. Out of those conclusions, even if based on Circumstantial Evidence, Inferences are made within the Common Sense that applies to the Spiritual Elements of Unconditional Love, Truth, Reality, and the Natural.

SUBJECTIVE SCIENCE: Observation, Reflection, "Pure" Feelings, Productive Imagination, Contemplation, Inductive and Deductive Inferences, and Common Sense

SUBJECTIVE SCIENCE TOOLS: Observation, Reflection, "Pure" Feelings, Productive Imagination, Contemplation, Inductive and Deductive Inferences, and Common Sense

SUBLIME MINDSETS: *Sublime* ("just under the lintel"--like the cross-piece of a door underneath which people walk) is an *Intangible* transitional plane between the Heavens (the Immaterial) In preparation to set up "Learning Temples," Very Ancient African Sages first determined what plane of Cosmic existence would be most desirable for a scholarship mindset. Those choices included: the Spiritual (known by Instincts), the Sublime (Felt), the Astral (Experienced), the Supernatural (Fantasized), and the Physical (Observed + Thought). They selected the "*Sublime*". By constituting the *Intangible Realm of the Cosmos*--i.e. the transition between Profound Peace (Hetep) of the Subjective Realm into that of Energy and Matter--its Ethereal space is filled with "Ether"--also called Universal Energy (Yogi), "Prana" (Buddhist), Chi (Chinese), and the "Lofty" (Europeans). Since the Sublime is located just below "the Heavens" and representing the region of the stars and planets, they inferred it is the most accessible of the Cosmic Spiritual planes of existence. Also, it possesses some of the following Scholarship mindset features: (1) it is without bounds or limits regarding time, space, quantity, number, or dimensions and whether in fact or in thought--an end or limit cannot be determined, not that there is no end or limit; (2) Its Pure Emotions wallows in the Wisdom of the Cosmic Organism; (3) Its *Spiritual* part gives the sense of being in the Spiritual Elements' midst of harmonious relationships—especially Unconditional Love; (4) Its *Intellectual* part opens doors to multiple realms of wonderful frontier explorations by providing understanding into the Essence; and (5) Its *Aesthetic* portion means one enjoys it without an inclination to possess it. Reasons for these were from inferences of Cosmic Forces being most heavily concentrated in Ethereal spaces, and hence conducive to learning Laws of Nature, so as to create a path to the Heaven Afterlife. Qualifications for entering and existing within the Sublime require (among others) a *Free Mind*. Concluding *"good"* people's minds and spirits ought to always stay in contact with the Sublime, African Sages built temples on the topmost place of a sacred mountain. Besides being a strategic position for defending against animal attacks, that special *"high place"* (root for "*Supreme*") was a sanctuary--a source of inspiration--and a sacred atmosphere for religious *Rites* (more about the "Why" giving rise to the social ceremony) and

Rituals (more about symbolic meanings expressed in physical drama and impacted in the performance of the ceremony). Ancient Africans Rites and Rituals--based upon Ancient African (Bible) Spiritual Literature Principles--were inside a sacred space, meaning its atmosphere surrounded any human participating in a communal event. Such was to signify a sort of "*Religious*" practice serving as a symbol to stay with or re-yoke to the Cosmic Creator as a way of life. That *Unity among Diversity* became African Tradition's theme. Each temple's location, presumed to be beyond the earth's normal atmosphere, was assumed to be filled with "Ether". Since this Sublime location contained the highest concentration of Love, Goodness, Truth, and Beauty, they reasoned Spiritual "*Thought Cloud*" atmospheres were present within it (Ramacharaka, Fourteen Lessons, p 77). Next introduced was the practice of *Meditation*—i.e. inducing experiences of altered and higher states of Consciousness for Spiritual Elements achievements—by means of *transcending* (i.e. by over-reaching human mental limitations) into the Sublime magnitudes exceeding life. Such happens by ones true self-identity dissolving into a unity with everything Real in the Cosmos, while yet retaining ones birth gift individuality. *Step I*: locate the entrance into the Sublime by being inside the atmosphere of Beauty. Helpful is to have a vivid mental picture of the Sublimity featured in a small pond, a creek, walking through a pleasant meadow, standing in a trickling stream, or other communions with Nature. *Step II:* Means of transcendence include: creating and living in lofty thoughts; focusing on Human Ideals; and giving Selfless Service to benefit Humanity and/or Nature. *Step III:* ease into Sublime flows via Meditation (formal and informal) and Contemplation. How long one stays in the Sublime can be temporary or relatively permanent. *Step IV:* to approach permanency requires Ma'at living with a "Pure Heart". From a "Pure Heart" ones Spiritual Feelings are connected to the Ultimate Power of Love by the "Silver Cord" (the spiritual equivalent to the mother's umbilical cord). jabaileymd.com

SUBLIMINAL: (1886, below Sensory Consciousness's threshold) is "Osmosis" messages readily absorbed, especially by children's naturally (in the sense of relatively pure) receptive minds. Its entrance is into the non-creative part of a child's Intuitive Natural Right brain as "second nature" or "*Sixth Sense*"--whether consciously or hiding in sub-awareness realms. By this Ancient Brain portion lacking any protective faculties, what is interpreted constitutes the child's reality.

SUBSTANCE: *In African Tradition,* the spirit of God

SUBSTANCE ORIGIN IN AFRICAN TRADITION: For one significant African Tradition word as, for example, Essence, not only will I go through 1000 books hoping to get some ideas about it, but I may spend weeks on it to see how it appears and what it does. A problem is that Europeans, having no concept of their Esoteric (hidden Spiritual) meanings, make a mess of it by giving different names and different hazy, confusing, and conflicting definitions to the same thing. Allow me to begin the story of Essence with Ancient Africans' use of "*Substance*" to indicate the true Divine Logos. The "One"—"The All"—the "Absolute" only Universal High God, Amen--living in "The Other World" or the Amenta ("Alaiye" in Sanskrit) is where True Reality originates and lies. The *Divine Logos--the Verbum-- "The Word"--is itself the power of the Divine Presence.* Its Germ Plasm (Androgynic Plast) or Substance is the Spiritual Elements—i.e. Unconditional Love, Truth, Reality, and the Natural—flowing through all of the Cosmic Organism's Creatures and Creations. Contained in the Substance of the Divine Logos is the primeval Feminine/Masculine duality which spills the Ocean of Nun into the Universe (or Cosmic Realm) so as to form the Subjective Realm (i.e. a sphere of Influential Power). Since the Cosmic Realm is a copy or Image out of the "Big Mind" of God, the Substance in it is called Divine Essence. Inside the Substance has been *Involuted* God's customized "what and why" for each of the Archetype Unrealized Realities residing in the Nun + the Spiritual Elements "Genetics" which form the Essence of all of God's Creatures and Creations + the Spirit (Energy) and Matter for each Entity that will be expressed in the Cosmos. Inside the Ocean of Nun are the Amenta's contents of the Divine Archetypes

("Seeds") in a Virtual state—meaning the unformed (formlessness without boundaries), and "non-ordered" (i.e. undifferentiated)--but *not "disordered"*. These Archetypes of all God's Creatures and Creations are the Unrealized Realities destined to form all aspects of the Cosmos. Every Cosmic aspect is connected to all others as if they were part of a big Spider's Web and with the Spiritual Elements "Genetics" comprising them and the Web. Just as the Spider's web has a central headquarters, so does the center of the Cosmic Organism have its orchestrating Cosmic Mind. That "Big Mind" Force imparts a Divine Disposition into the Spark of God Essence of which serves as the "Self" or core of each Creature and Creation. When time comes for, a human, to "descend into Matter," upon moving into the Sublime plane spurs the God Substance/Essence Spirit (Energy) and Matter contained in that human's customized Essence thereby activate its Involuted Essentials to emanate its Character, Characteristics, Traits, and Features. The "What and Why" Message of the Cosmic Mind that is contained in the Essence of that human then orchestrates those Essentials. All will follow a path that are within the Processes of Nature unless and until that human uses her/his Free Will to alter the course. From that point onward, all particular Things related to that human's Selfhood result from the varying degrees of composition of Spiritual Energy and Matter. These thing derive from the Pattern of the Essence, which has a Self-Image on the outside and its *Matrix* (womb which brings "nourishment" to the Pattern) on the inside. *Properties* (what a Thing has) of that human include customized Attributes of the Spiritual Elements within the Essence and Essentials called *Endowments* (i.e. natural Primary Qualities) + *Propensities* (in-born tendencies, e.g. a human's capacities, abilities, and language). Each will operate different processes of that human's Selfhood so as to make her/him "What it is," "what it does" and "how it appears." Ones *Spiritual Essence is* exhibited within ones Private Self as innermost patterns of certain types of mental activities which imparts an embryonic readiness way to think, feel, express, and/or behave in a certain Ma'at (God's messages) manner--Patterns emanates outward to fashion ones ones Public Self and, from there, corresponding Patterns into the External World. The Disposition's Private Self Patterns consists of: (a) the *Inclination* of the Disposition, analogized as a 'physical' "leaning toward" or "leaning" away from something; (b) the Intension driven by Spiritual Energy; (c) the Attitude; and (d) the *Temperament*. Both the Attitude and Temperament are physiological Sensory Consciousness systems fashioning the type of reaction the aroused person takes.

SUBTLE FALLACIES "SEEMS RIGHT" INFORMATION: The C14 English word SUBTLE--a weaving term (under, sub; a woven thing, like cloth, tela) literally means "*beneath the lengthwise threads in a loom.*" It originally referred to whatever is of a fine or delicate texture and so interwoven as to not be discerned. In this sense it concerned more the idea of crafty and artful. Then it expanded to be about the attributes of things, suggesting the tenuous and the elusive in contrast to the flagrant and the gross. Subtlety (Subtlety) deals chiefly with nicety of discernment, discrimination of taste, acuteness of judgment. "Discernment" is lesser subtlety, meaning derivatively ability to distinguish from. It is hard to seize unless one has done the prior preparation needed for discerning. But an additional aspect is not only the subtle being beneath the obvious, but also how far down does that "beneath" go -- like an iceberg. An analogy is a piece of ice floating in the ocean as opposed to an iceberg. With the floating piece of ice what one sees is almost all there is. With an *iceberg*, most of its ice (e.g. 6/8 to 7/8 of its mass) is hidden underneath the water. When a large iceberg is sighted from a ship, no one can tell how far the ice extends under the water. The ship may be rammed by hidden ice and, as a consequence, sunk. An example is a web under a leaf, known for being crafty, artful, tenuous, elusive, and in contrast to the flagrant and the gross. However, its effects contain categories of Mild, Slight, Moderate, and Extreme on a good or evil scale. Ancient Greek *Sophistry terms* are designed to subtly present "tainted" ideas, concepts, and thoughts about what is being done in a manner that is *just a shade off the Truth-Track*--called *Fallacies* (Greek, phelos, "deceitful"). This makes them plausible but misleading or fallacious presentations of information with the intent of deception. Where Subtle information works best is for people who are "Standing on the Chain" because of indecision; because of not having strong views of something; because of being naïve and gullible; and/or because of simply not caring. Before what "SEEMS right" can be properly assessed it requires a standard of Certainty against which it can be compared. That standard is selected based upon the philosophy of life (POL) one selects. For me, after studying all of the world's major POLs, there is absolutely no question that Ancient Africans had the ultimate in a POL, with the Spiritual Elements serving as a standard, filter, and guide of Certainty. Thus, anything that takes one away from the Spiritual Elements heads in the direction of Extremely evil but its beginnings may "SEEM" innocent or innocuous. So let us apply Critical Thinking (CT) subtly changes and Human Nature. Briefly, as background, *"Primary" Human Nature* constitutes the qualities and characteristics shared by all human beings -- independent of race, religion, creed, age, gender, time period, or culture. *"Second" Nature* consists of what is absorbed from socialization. *"Tertiary" Nature* is the same as what the public calls the *"Self-Made"* person. It consists of an "I'll do it my way" orientation—regardless of whether this relates to think, feel, say, and do ways of an individualistic decision. Ancient Africans said that human's nature is manifested by Instincts which reflect the mind of God and that *the most natural way to live is by what naturally flows out of ones Dignity (ones God image) and Divinity (from being a God drop)*. This occurs spontaneously (happening of itself) and therefore it is to be trusted. Following birth, for an individual to remain "natural" requires maintaining a direct connection between his/her Real Self and Higher Powers by means of Spiritual Energy. By so doing, Instincts are known by what is *intuited* (meditating to gain from ones inner Spirit insights above and beyond the realm of the mind's thought processes). It is important to understand that human nature's Passions are part of animal appetites (e.g. greed) but reasoning is not and those passions tend to overrule what has to be developed to achieve ones Highest Self. However, Reason is intended to govern them, particularly when passion eats up everything despite it needing to be spread out. Yet, for those not subscribing to African POL, rational words are used to say what Human Nature is, even though it cannot be defined or described in light of Truth. So by not seeing the Spiritual Aspect of Human Nature causes their focus to be on the passions and to say that uncontrolled passions cause one to be in chaos.

The resultant Selfhood Splintering means one is going in opposite directions concerning a significant issue which causes inner problems and problems for the society. This is because to be in conflict with ones Human Nature means one is going nowhere and is not able to do much. Such a concept might have arisen from European Supernatural Biblical scholars attributing "Original Sin" as justification for humans not relying on what comes out of their Human Nature. In order to keep freedom from getting out of control and since people are in conflict as to what constitutes personal freedom and its abuse, there are countless laws written up by lawyers to ensure there are no loopholes to allow for the abuse of freedom. This means that people are "encaged" from a distrust of their own Instincts and they lose sight of how to let it flow freely as part of the "Play" needed to enjoy life. Of course, such goes go against the very Human Nature freedom part designed for living the property type of life. "Tertiary" Nature thinkers are threatened, isolated, or punished by the Socialized majority.

SUCCESS: The fact that one is alive means one is living in Success. Additional Success categories can be about what one knows—about what one does, especially regarding ones Mission in life—and about who one is (living well with Integrity, Laughed much, and Unconditionally Loved "ME/WE" deeply). Any of these can be done by ones own Selfhood Greatness cultivation and/or by gaining insight from the folly of others. Success, as a result and not a goal, is just as likely to occur from the hard work involved in careful, systematic, thorough preparation as it is from ones Genius and Talents or to make oneself Necessary. These--by requiring constancy of Purpose and Courage with Presence of Mind when in Distress--are much harder to do than cheating but are longer lasting in self-pride and self-improvement. The gathering of personally meaningful ideas and converting them into masterpiece Things—whether Useful or Useless (e.g. for Play, Music, Dance, Art, Humor)—are ingredients for ones Private and Public Selfhood success. Then it takes Wisdom to know what to do with this Success. Perhaps the sweetest success is a thing of significant Worth from the mess one has made of something or the mess one was born into, for either are about climbing out of the bottom. That process also gives one insight in to how hard the unsuccessful find life and what it takes to help them. Such is motivating to ones self-confidence to keep on being about success adventures of increasingly higher magnitude. A minute of success is worth the thousands of hours it took to get to that point. That minute is greatly dependent on not knowing how long it will take to achieve "overnight" Success. Success is measured by distance travelled from where one was and the overcoming of "alligators" (losses, lacks, obstructions) one has overcome. Time, Energy, Effort, and difficulties in struggle are better measures of success than outcome. Everyone thinks they are above average in abilities to be successful but everybody cannot be since otherwise there would be no average.

SUMMARIZE: Picture this! Your airplane is out of control. The pilot has been shot and you need him to tell you how to regain control of the plane and land it. What you want him to give you is a Summary. The setting outline in writing or delivering a speech is the use of the Patterned Mental Skeleton Tool scope from start and finish that says: "*Tell them what you are going to tell them/Tell them/Then tell them what you told them.*" The C15 word "Summary" (highest, chief, main) is a compressed to the utmost, concise, brief, and comprehensive statement of the three chief points under the principle heads of a subject. Each of those 3 have been explained—analogized--illustrated by examples or tables or figures—and concluded with its "keystone impact" concepts saying its disadvantages and how its positive could benefit. The Summary itself at the end is a brief statement or restatement of the main points, especially as the conclusion of a work. It contains the spotlighted points in a concise, brief, comprehensive, and quick way. By providing only the bare outlines, with no details at all, its intent is to give a gist of the substance contained in the whole, focusing on the conclusion--"a minimum of sound [or space] to a maximum of sense" (Mark Twain). It is extremely helpful to get children to summarize the main 3 point that they learned since that "cements" it into their memories and listeners get the benefit of what they missed or forgot. An advertising summary is a *Synopsis* of the proposed presentation—i.e. a condensed statement giving a general view of a subject.

SUN: In African Tradition, the One God, Aten, is symbolized by the Sun--while the mythological God, Ra, is the Sun's rising attributes—i.e. as it transforms from the undifferentiated Subjective into an Objective Being. Upon the Sun's return ("sets") to its original unformed state in the Subjective, it is Temu. Such organized multiplicity of Unity is an unnamed One Being--a Cosmic Force conveniently called Sekhem. In short, the Supreme Being is ever coming into existence as Things in the Cosmos and returning to its essential undifferentiated state—i.e. *Reincarnations*. Each human's Spiritual "Soul Sunshine" aspect—i.e. a Spark of God--brightens ones Subconscious so as to guide ones ultimate Destiny to do the same. Ancient African Sages knew the Sun's Physics as the factory for creating all physical Matter and Energies—the forces and building blocks of all Things in the Cosmos—the nexus of transformation of unshaped ingredients into shaped Matter (Amen, Metu Neter II:65). African Groits (storytellers) represented ways to a human's "Soul Sunshine" source—the Divine Self—by the Sun and Moon (Asar who symbolizes the Mind) forming Ra's eyes to serve as passageways. Asar is Consciousness dwelling within an inert and dead body--a death-like cessation of all activities, except for ones Divine Consciousness—and experienced as great peace and relaxation. This realm of the Setting Sun—the Beautiful West—the Amenta—is returned to when one succeeds in cultivating an *intuitive Intellect which understands the nature of Creation and the Oneness of all things in the "One Hidden God"*—called *"Knowing Thyself."* Humans see moonlight because of the Sun shining light on the moon and then reflecting it onto

Earth. Similarly, the Mind shines with awareness because Universal Consciousness's (God) Light is reflecting in a human's Divine Consciousness. An analogy is water sustained in a glass because the glass is holding and supporting it. Thus, humans reflecting their Underlying Divine Consciousness supporting Light can exist, think, be aware, and stay awake. From the Sun, Aten extend rays that terminate with hands which bestow Ankhs (Life Force) to all Creation.

In its manifested aspect, the divine Universal Soul—the ever-burning light—the personified Sun—is a web of Associations. That Web-like system is each of all God's Creatures and Creations being interconnected. All independently act and interdependently interact in accordance with the God assigned identities of each. By being a "ME/WE" Web, what is done in any part of the Web affects the entire Web and its contents. That *Correspondence* is God's displayed manifestations, giving insight into the *Circumstantial* Unknown. Hence, on any plane of Cosmic existence or on any one plane--and regardless of the appearances or functions of whatever is being considered in a given God-made situation--it can be analogized to the Tree Concept. Whereas the Underground "Seed" is the *Essence*, the Underground "Roots" and All of the above ground aspects—Trunk, Branches, Leaves, and Fruit—are *Essence's Essentials*. Still, despite those above ground aspects—some seemingly having no relationship to each other--those *underlying possess a web of relationships that are a Unified realm of complexity and multiplicity Patterns.* Certain Patterns operate in Nature and thus throughout the Cosmos in the macro-Cosmic Solar System. Other Patterns operate in the micro-Cosmic Atom System. Yet, all of these large and small Patterns possess a *consistent, permanent, stationary, and unchanging state of Continuity (unity among apparent diversity).* But the shared-in-common *Home Base* Underlying these Underground Patterns consists of movingly displayed Spiritual Elements Essences. In short, the *Cosmic Web's Spiritual Elements' Essence of Unconditional Love, Truth, Reality, and the Natural manifest as independently working systems inside Cosmic Harmony.* This knowledge enabled Ancient Africans to apply Mathematics to the Metaphysical, mainly using Qualitative Algebra to gain Principles from all planes of Cosmic existence and their relationships. Understanding these Mathematical Principles is the way they developed dormant Divine Life Forces within, so as to be an Earthly embodiment of God's designing intelligence. To this end, they subjected their *"Self's"* (Spark of God Soul, constituting a human's divinity)--the Consciousness/Will--*to the Divine Spirit in order to command the Life-Force in harmony with the Laws of Nature.* Thereafter, whatever flowed out of the "ME" of a human, was of a Cosmic Organism Rhythm nature which, in turn, would similarly affect all "WE" Web strings--a "ME/WE" Concept of Unity by a human's Non-Self. A *"Non-Self"* has the obligation, duty, and responsibility to *discover and conform to underlying relationship webs* operating in all Patterns of the Cosmic Nature. As a result, its "ME" aspects can transcend into the Sublime's natural flowing part of Cosmic Knowledge—a flow where one recognizes ones own Being as vital to the All (i.e. "Oneness" within the Cosmic Mind). Here, in the "ME/WE" Sublime realm, Knowledge is known without proof. *Being in this infinity of Knowledge* allows one to discover new insights about any Spiritual Elements' attribute anywhere in the Web; compare old blind-nesses to the now obvious; and get new perspectives upon hearing old Wisdom over and over. Hence, even though each Entity is "Unique," *being part of the Cosmic Web gives each Correspondence* with every other part of the Cosmic Circle of Wholeness. From operating by Ma'at Principles and Laws, all Knowledges of them are very few in number. To see all of these aspects together in their web-like interrelationships enables one to become aware of links connecting and meshing the Uniqueness of each member into the inner nature Sameness that makes up the Cosmic Family. These Processes are designated *"Circumstantial"* because by Nature existing "all over" at once, some are hidden and no part can be reasoned from direct demonstrations. This entire process starts with the Spark from God's Sun symbol—and with its Halo constituting the Cosmos. That Spark is imparted into a human to display as a "Soul Sunshine" Halo. Just as with the macro-Cosmic Solar System, with its Sun at its center and the planets orbiting around it, so is each human an image of that. In both instances there is an identical Correspondence web pattern of Associations with all God's Creatures and Creations—even down to the microcosmic atom, with the nucleus at its core, orbited by protons, electrons, and neutrons. Everything from the greatest Sun to the tiniest atom is in vibration. Each has a unique vibration rate--as seen in the circling of the planets around the Sun; the rise and fall of the sea; or the ebb and flow of the tide. By following the above mentioned Sun and Moon avenues, energies of the mind and body may be channeled toward a higher, spiritual goal in life (Ashby, Book Of Dead p130, 139, 167, 234). Resultant Spiritual Enlightenment—freedom from ones Lower (animalistic) Self demons--leads to liberation while alive and after death. The "Prt m Hru" (epitaph)--a name for Humankind's original Bible and dating to 60,000 BC (Seleem p 59, xiii), the "Book of Life"—says: *righteousness leads to spiritual realization; purification is acting with righteousness; and by learning about the nature of the Divine—acting, feeling, and thinking as the Divine—it is finally possible to become one with the Divine.* Such is an abstract of the transcendental nature of the Divine as a Principle, as opposed to a Personality like that for Europeans. Here, the Sun's Rays equate to the Psycho-Spiritual Virtues Ancient Africans said must be cultivated in a 7 fold manner: (1) Righteousness; (2) Sex urge control; (3) Selfless Service; (4) Unconditional Love; (5) Silence, Introspectiveness, Self-Discipline; (6) Divine Vision; and (7) Transcendence into "Non-Self". Regardless of the aspect in life, one is to remain in the *moving Essences of the Spiritual Elements and develop all Think, Feel, Say, and Do aspects of life out of their Attributes.* These provide *the "5Ss"—Safety, Security, Sureness/Self-Confidence, Strength, and Stability—to a human's Private Self and Thriving life.* This has nothing to do with Materialism characterizing ones Lower Self or with the European Supernatural. See Ra

SUPER: The prefix "*Super*" originally meant 'balance left over' and "*Superior*" (C14, higher). But exploding in C19 its varied usages embraced above, beyond, over--superstructure; to extreme degrees--superabundance; extra large--super-continent; having greater influence of a higher kind/capacity--superpower, superbike--super-family.

SUPERIOR: The prefix "*Super*" originally meant 'balance left over' and "*Superior*" (C14, higher). But exploding in C19 were Supernaturals varied usages--embracing above, beyond, over--superstructure; to extreme degrees--superabundance; extra-large--super-continent; having greater influence of a higher kind/capacity--superpower, superbike--super-family. Today it means highest or greatest possible—Supreme.

SUPERNATURAL: Warren's Psychology defines "*Supernatural*" as belonging to a higher order or system than that of Nature, or transcending the ordinary course of Nature. Supernatural is Noumena—'things-in-themselves'—which remain forever unknowable. This means the Supernatural is not to be questioned for it is unconquerable, unmovable, undeniable, unexplainable, incomparable, unimaginable, immeasurable, and unthinkable. This supposed phenomena, prominent in Medieval times, of Contingent Beings (like the Bogeyman) agencies and their influences, were disproved with present-day European scientific methods (e.g. Bulletin of Atomic Scientists) and is now relegated to superstitions by Europeans. Today's Encyclopedia of [European] Philosophy (2-520) defines: "super" or "supranatural" as "the miracle, the revealed truths of religion. For the enlightened, all these are simply figments of the imagination, nonexistent, indeed at the bottom priestly inventions designed to keep men ignorant of the ways of Reason and Nature." To paraphrase, it continued by saying the corruptions of religion, social structure, convention, and indeed, beneath the often misleading impressions of sense experience not properly organized by Reason, has led to hypostatized conceptions of the beautiful and the Good. "*Hypostatize*" means to transform a conceptual entity—a Contingent Being—a phantom—into or construe as a self-subsistent substance. Cup A deals with God's Life/Love as Base for thought. Cup E is virtual and "larger than life". Cup E is outside Cup A's reality and lacking any sound Base for building a Thought Structure, except quicksand. The Supernatural, in order to be "superior," as its believers claim they are, necessarily has to be against the Spiritual Elements of Unconditional Love, Truth, Reality, and the Natural. That, by definition, makes Satanists of Supernatural believers. Although the Supernatural does not exist--except as Contingent Beings (e.g. Hell, the Devil, and a Supernatural God) with powerful payloads in what they represent--all are able to design *reality and unreality* into a surreal state of a human's or a group's internal ideas (reality). By accepting this Fantasy, they project their messages of Indifference/Hate/Evil/Sadism to make all of it mesh with their human-made external--i.e. an unreality projected externally and made to fuse with the corresponding human-made external world unrealities. For *one to accept delusions, hallucinations, and illusions that could result in* Superstitions and actual pain and suffering, *all that is required is that they do not clash with any of the Crowd's currently held Belief or threaten any ones System of Values that are "For me or my well-being; or against me."*

SUPERNATURAL DEFINITION OF EUROPEAN: The European Supernatural is what dominates the world today. It is extremely hard to find any information about it and even that is scattered among a variety of terms. Examples include: Numen, Vitalism, and Teleology—all spoken of as being about mysterious "vital" forces. Teleology started in ancient European times as the oldest mode of explanation of human conduct and evolved fantastic fantasy concepts. It postulated a hypothetical vital Supernatural directing agency or force which gives rise to and designs life products, their actions and purposes—but not by mechanical causes. It was countered by Mechanical causes of biological phenomena. Although this Vitalism has long ago been abandoned by experimental biologists, its aura and atmosphere remain in full force today, even to the point of continued beliefs by many Europeans. "*Numinous (Supernatural) Feelings*" consist of being filled up with a sensation of a Supernatural Numen presence pertaining to something which is both a value (e.g. the "excitement" of sort after Material "Things") and an objective reality (e.g. the indulging of a human's animalistic desires)—gained from visual experiences. *To understand the following will clear up many points of profound confusion and conflicts resulting from the "it doesn't seem quite right" one was socialized into and in keeping with what "everybody" believes.* A defining moment for the world's 37 billion peoples came when these Supernatural stories were cultivated for purposes of controlling the minds of undisciplined and uninformed peoples. To be convincing, these human creators generated a grand "fireworks" type of "Con-Artist" display by telling their followers that they were attacking all that was powerful in the Natural World because their Supernatural world was the supreme power and therefore that made them the superior people. By definition, this made Satanists (or its equivalent) of those who attacked the Spiritual Elements of Unconditional Love, Truth, Reality, and the Natural—i.e. the Essence of the Spiritual Cosmic Force, Sekhem. As part of the process of turning the followers' minds "Inside-Out," the Satanist leaders stated that the Supernatural—the Unnatural—was the true "Natural." That concept applied to whatever was deemed to be Right in the Natural World. Thus, in the Supernatural mind, it was "Right" to do Evil and wrong to do Good. This was made into a Satanist religion that wore a "Double Face".

Its true "Evil oriented Face" was a display that left no doubt about what Satanists thought, felt, said, and did. However, Satanism's "*Hypocritical Face*" has always appeared to be the Spiritual Force, Sekhem, but with some opposite additions so subtly presented as to make it SEEM like Natural World concepts and Natural World "Right Life Living." Although *Religion is a European invention situated within the Supernatural,* the failure to distinguish its "Double Face" has progressed throughout the millennia to the present. For example, the American Heritage College Dictionary defines "*Religion*" as: "a Belief in and reverence for a supernatural power or powers regarded as creator and governor of the universe." It defines "*god*" as "a being of supernatural powers or attributes, believed in and worshiped by a people, esp. a male deity." It defines "*Supernatural*" as "Of or relating to existence outside the natural world; Attributed to a power that seems to violate or go beyond natural forces." The Latin word "*Supernatural*" is defined as 'super-nature'--referring to the realm, with *Supernormal*

Beings, existing above and beyond the realm of sense experience. *Supernormal* is defined as belonging to an unknown but natural order or system. "*Super-nature*" is beyond the universe, beyond entities, beyond identity. These all contradict every, and anything, humans know about the identity of what Ancient African Sages proved to have Correspondence. The African *Law of Correspondence* says all Cosmic Phenomena are limited and serial--and that they appear as scales or series on separate planes. Such can be readily observed in various aspects of the physical world by any sane person. Warren's 'Psychology' defines "*Supernatural*" as belonging to a higher order or system than that of Nature, or transcending the ordinary course of Nature. Funk & Wagnalls (1930) dictionary says: "Existing or occurring through some agency above the forces of nature; lying outside the sphere of natural law, whether psychic or physical; caused miraculously or by the immediate exercise of divine power." The Winston Dictionary (1946) says: "being outside or exceeding the forces or laws of nature: above, or superior to, the sequences of cause and effect in natural law; miraculous--that which is superior to the recognized forces or laws of nature. Throughout European history there have been raging conflicts on what orchestrates the Universe. That ranges from the Supernatural as *Noumena*—'things-in-themselves'—which remain forever unknowable—all the way over to there being no orchestrator. Prominent in Medieval times, the supposed *Noumena* phenomena was anti-Spiritual. Its belief in Contingent Being agencies and their influences were in opposition to the European Church's focus on a Supernatural God of their making—a lesser anti-Spiritual stance under the "Double Face" guise of SEEMS right. Nevertheless, Nominalism was disproved with present-day European scientific methods (e.g. those of the Bulletin of Atomic Scientists) and is now relegated to superstitions by Europeans. But otherwise, European Supernatural concepts of a God, Devil, and Hell remain intact. This means the *Supernatural is not to be questioned for it is unconquerable, unmovable, undeniable, unexplainable, incomparable, unimaginable, immeasurable, and unthinkable.* Some Europeans want it both ways—i.e. one of their God's being Supernatural and Unknowable; another Supernatural God, Jesus, being part of the people—a supreme illustration of a religious "Double Face". The people involved are not confused even though they are confusing. And that is the nature of Non-Rational Supernatural thinking. But the Icon Images, being like a composite "Disaster Star," emanate Rays radiating in endless numbers, in IHES depths, in KTDDOC, and have, without let-up, been a source of pain, suffering, and death for billions of people.

SUPERNATURAL'S DELUSIONAL WORLD: In the Delusional World the rule is for Europeans to serve their ideology and not humanity. Delusion means believing what is not real and not believing or not believing in what is real. And this is the definition of the European Supernatural. By believing there are only the Physical and Supernatural Realms--which can be analogized to a cup of diluted and polluted water--they fit all of what is readily evident in the Spiritual and Metaphysical Realms into that cup and thereby cause Conflict and Confusion. Furthermore, they present themselves as knowing everything there is to know simply because they know what they made up inside the cup--and what they do not know does not exist. The Delusional World is non-rational, filled with Superstitions--oriented to Material Riches, Power, Status, Prestige, Pride, Possessions, Enslaving others, Conspiracy, Horror, Thrill, Dread, Excitement, Control of Everything and Everybody--having Military type Order--the ensuring of Sameness throughout their "Troops" and their victims--maintaining an atmosphere of Confusion and Conflict. This means, by their mindsets being centered in Emotions, their problems must necessarily be settled by Force. Such a mindset characterizes Brute followers. Brute Leaders also use their Left-Brains to fashion how to most effectively carry out anti-Spiritual Element forces. One feels as if one is "Larger than Life" and that everyone is to cater to their self-seeking greedy pursuits. One feels as if one knows everything about everything and is in charge of anyone who is doing anything. Yet, that same one has no concept of what anything is really about. This arrogance comes from two things. First is the power of the GUN, which one possesses now and that power is backed by past atrocities generated by the collective GUN of fellow in-group members who have benefitted from the GUN. The second is the GUN backed Network that provides the power to Kill/Take/Destroy on a whim impulse and have opposition because of the Network of support. Manners and considering others is not necessary and being ill-mannered is a display of power. So is being wasteful of what other people really need. Without these two things they cannot back up their self-claimed "Superiority" in any area and that--envy, deficit in the "5Ss," fear--is a major reason they must maintain oppression

SUPERNATURAL BULLIES: "Bully" (1500, Dutch, 'sweetheart') originally meant "a fine, splendid fellow" (Shakespeare's Midsummer Night's Dream). But then it transformed into "swashbuckler" (gallant, boon companion); "hired tough" to do violence; "Pimp" who lives on the earnings of a prostitute (American Revolution); and today, an "overbearing ruffian." All Bullies possess an Indifference/Hate/Evil/Sadism (IHES) mindset. *Type I* are the rich and powerful socialized into connecting with like-kind Networks, enabling them indulge in varied Kill/Take/Destroy/Dominate/Oppress/Control (KTDDOC) practices. Insecurities reign in competing against each other. *Type II*--though socialized to play roles of "Superiority" over others, become increasingly insecure with each challenge. *Type III*, developing sometime after birth an Inferiority Complex, desperately engage in ranging attempts to acquire a Superiority Complex—i.e. donning a mask of self-confidence and greatness with a reality of arrogance and aggression, so as to conceal a sense of deep inferiority and self-hate. Thus they, and Type II, for the sake of their own Bad self-image must degrade scapegoats. Both create fantasies about themselves and their Scapegoats using the motto: "How great we are, how bad they are". Type I does the same evils deeds for everybody not rich and powerful. All types are Selfhood-Unknown—meaning they are *disconnected from their birth gift of Spiritual Elements*—suppliers of ones Private Selfhood *"5Ss"*—i.e. Safety, Security, Sureness/Self-Confidence, Strength, and Stability. On one side of a Scale of Destruction is their Disconnections. They include discontinuity within ones "ME"; separation from their pre-birth "ME/WE" interrelationships; losing intimate contact with significant others; and lacking any concept of others' human existence. On the opposite Scale side are happenings from being *Selfhood Splintered*.

This means half of ones Selfhood becomes *Self-Absorbed* (viewing everything within ones world in relationship to oneself in a "me, me, me" manner) and the other half following dictates of External World influences and greedy pursuits of what is deemed to be "Scarce Desirable" Material things.

Type III, not feeling worthy or believing "I'm not good enough," may beam their disaster bully effects in a host of directions and involving a host of destruction of things. Most are "Street" type troublemakers—Evil humans who live by the "Law of Force", as in doing beatings, rapes, and killings. Type II males are likely to believe they have such flawed "man-hoods" as to make them grossly incompetent. By being part of a Evil humans Network cult, they demonstrate kakistocracy (defecating) type authority—i.e. rule by terrible self-made social laws—laws allowing lying, cheating, stealing, gossiping, and any form of KTDDOC as the norm. Type I are Shrewd in their greedy pursuits of riches and power. *Shrewd's* etymology began as an ingredient of "Evil"— originally an Old English word meaning "uppity"--then "Bad"--then extreme moral wickedness. In 1280 AD, "Shrewd" signified evil, malicious, and dangerous before its euphemistic sense changed in 1520 to astute and cunning--and then to cleverness, scheming, and deception. *Euphemisms* are socially accepted indirect expressions substituting for harsh meanings contained in bad thoughts. To deal with being Self-Unknown, all engage in *Phantasmagoria*—i.e. *"Make-Believe"* displays, *featuring seeing reality in ways other than they are* regarding themselves and those whom they most envy. After acquiring the GUN from the Arabs in 1304 and developing it over the next 150 years, their top selected "enemy" was Black People because of historical envying their 200,000 years of world-shaping, world-changing, and world-maintenance achievements--achievements in who they are and in what they do. Such was above Bullies to achieve.

Extreme Envy is the beginning of hell on earth. It deals with ones Left Brain calculating emotional reasoning concerning comparisons related "for me or against me" Desires, and that is like being in an infinite abyss. This comes from envy always spotlighting ones consciousness of being inferior. Envy is so much about cowardice, inadequacy, and incompetency as for those owning it vigorously deny having it. Just as iron is eaten away by rust, so are the envious consumed by their own passions—so overwhelming/energy draining as to prevent them from cultivating their Rational minds. This leaves them with no choice but to do Non-Rational thinking—that which makes no sense. jabaileymd.com

SUPERNATURAL "EXCITEMENT": The act of contending against another(s) or against normative standards to gain exclusive goals, goods, trophies, status, recognition, or control of minds is an inescapable trait which Western culture believes is essential for the development of a Group Emotional Personality. But by always being extreme, such competitiveness in the marketplace is pathological and counter to sound health. Their keystone category feature of the type that attracts attention because of appearances, thoughts, behaviors, and/or deeds beyond those of ordinary people is recognition as "Larger than Life". By standing out and being spotlighted, if not floodlighted, the Effect thereby makes them disproportionately important--the equivalent to "*Flamboyant*." Originally "Flamboyant," an architectural term applied to a C15 and C16 French Gothic style, was characterized by wavy flame-like forms with shapes of flames conforming to the wavy flame-like tracery of the stonework in the windows of many Gothic cathedrals. The presents of these forms around some human (or thing) make ones "Larger than Life." However, the nature of those wavy forms has different ranges of significance, intensity, duration, presentations, and Effects. An analogy is the Stars in the sky. For eons, humankind has looked to the heavens and wondered at the lights in the sky. Ancient people, believing they could see shapes among the stars, identified both animals and people--and each had its own story. In transferring this concept, Mild "Flamboyance" is like the misconception that *stars twinkle*. Instead, the perception of twinkling stars is a result of atmospheric interference--an effect similar to what takes place on a hot summer day when one looks across hot pavement or a parking lot. Just as this rising air causes images to waver, it is also what causes the twinkling effect in stars. The lower a star is in the sky, the more it will twinkle because its light must pass through more of the atmosphere. Whether there is Slight, Moderate, or Extreme degrees of flamboyance depends upon the intensity and type of dramatic exaggerations in characteristics and attributes appearing to be real on a grand or heroic scale as well as how it affects observers. To describe this style-fashioning faculty requires understanding the concepts behind two different words--flare and flair. "*Flare*" originally (1550) referred to a flame or blaze that darted up suddenly. And when the flame was against a dark background, its light shown so brightly as to dazzle or blind the viewer. In the C19, if that blaze was characterized by wavy flame-like forms, it represented Moderate or Extreme Flamboyance. On the other hand, "*Flair*" (Old German 1390) originally related to a keen perception of smell, as present in a dog that hunts game by scent. Since it took discernment or shrewdness to pick out the correct scent, the meaning of "flair" was extended into a sense of special ability, natural aptitude, or talent. Hence, "Flair" is like the Star and "Flare" is like the Halo--both present in those deemed to be "Larger than Life." jabaileymd.com

SUPERNATURAL AFRICAN vs. EUROPEAN: The prefix "*Super*" originally meant 'balance left over' and "*Superior*" (C14, higher). But exploding in C19 were Supernaturals varied usages--embracing above, beyond, over--superstructure; to extreme degrees--superabundance; extra-large--super-continent; having greater influence of a higher kind/capacity--superpower, superbike--super-family. Nevertheless, the denotation of the Supernatural is a make-believe world where nothing impossible cannot come into Fantasy existence. In a Fantasy realm, even one illusion can totally transform a zillion realities but its kaleidoscope of shapes, shadows, airy tongues--or by objects moving faster than light—or by powerless "Things" that fly—or by creatures becoming invisible—or by humans walking on water—or by animals talking—or by imagination abandoning Reasoning so as to produce impossible many headed monsters. All of this is useful for humor or for telling entertaining tales. But what is this Delusional World Europeans live in and call 'second nature'? Because its way of thinking dominates in those who control the world, it is intriguing to explore. Yet, it has been extremely difficult for me--after going through hundreds of books on a vast variety of its "ought to be present" subjects--to find more than mere bits and pieces of information. My intrigue is because of the damage of untold and ever increasing magnitude caused by Supernatural concepts. Their practices--for all categories of people in all races, creeds, and colors--account for pain and suffering, conflict and confusion, doubt and uncertainty, inferiority and superiority complexes. What is it about the religious content of the Supernatural and its Superstition partners that, as a lifestyle, inspire such widespread and deep inner Self-Turmoil and hatred of "Faceless" outsiders? Why do they produce such grandeur of mind about being "right" and thus superior concerning what is incomprehensible? What is the reason for such killing in the name of their God? What has been tattooed in the cradle of ones society's philosophy to justify a need to cultivate a fear of God while ascribing human attributes to God?--and Why? Yet, all of these primitive European concepts—all of their perceptions—all of their practices have were culturally transmitted into today's descendants.

SUPERNORMAL: defined as belonging to an unknown but natural order or system.

SUPPOSE: temporarily assume a thing as true

SYLLOGISM: *Syllogism* reasoning scheme formed of three categorical statements, consisting of three successive and interrelated propositions. The first is the Major Premiss/Premise; the second, the Minor Premiss/Premise; the third, the Conclusions. The 2 premises (major, minor) are so related that they logically imply the third proposition (the conclusion). An example is the deduced Syllogism of Aristotle: (1) "All men are mortal"--a major premise (a generalization of a known truth or a concept accepted as truth); (2) Socrates is a man -- a minor premise (a deduction from the major one); and (3) Socrates is mortal--a conclusion logically necessary from the premises which, in this case, are factual rather than probable. By applying the minor to the major premise, a valid conclusion is reached.

SYLLOGISM LOGIC IN AFRICAN TRADITION--TYPE III African Logic follows the Ma'at System of Thought Logic using the power to think Reasonably according to a predetermined plan and therefore in an orderly manner. In situations dealing with a human's function in the world inside the frame by her/his interrelationship with God, with God's creatures and creations, as well as with the environment/Nature, there may be no predetermined plan. Thus, when there may be insufficient knowledge to follow that Ma'at Pattern, *African Syllogisms are required and they feature Poetic Logic*—hence the meaning of Syllogism as "reasoning together" with one Pure Emotions and Intellect. A problem starting a Thought Structure with uncertainty is there is no notion of the sort and amount of evidence needed to prove the simplest matter of fact. For Africans, they still needed to follow the African Logic Plan, staying as close to its guidelines as possible while using Right and Left Brain Reasoning. In other words, African Logic is primarily a Right Brain function concerned with realities and Truth existing beyond the visible and if the Syllogistic faculty of ones mind is used, then *Poetic Reasoning* results. For example, when they had no idea of the starting point's validity, they did the next best thing of filling the gaps of their Knowledge from Analogy. To this end, the foundation for and frame within which African Logic Thoughts exist is mathematical—within the context of Pure Emotions as a "check and balance" on the intellect's use in Reasoning (Right and Left Brain usage) In order to get started, one proceeds to go down the ladder from Knowledge in order to see what is "Workable." Although the next best to Knowledge is the use of an Axiom, if that does not work, one resorts to Syllogism, but they are frought with problems. Syllogisms consist of Propositions; Propositions consist of words; words are Symbols of Notions. Therefore, if the Notions themselves—which is the root of the matter—are confused, misinterpreted, or over-hastily abstracted from the facts, there can be no firmness in the superstructure. This applies to even the most likely reasonable of *Assumptions* (taking something for granted without mention or without examination); *Postulates* (voluntarily accepted assumptions which, when agreed upon by the experts in a certain science, become its conventional basis); or *Presumptions* (implies some justification by way of practice or example or logical procedure). All three—Assume, Postulate, and Presume are in the family of "Guess," Think, Reckon, and Expect. However, African Premises are true by following the Ma'at system of thought whereby the Proposition to be used as a Premise is examined according to the Laws of intra-relationships and inter-relationships. Amen (Tree of Life p156) advises to took at human's functions in the world, framed by their interrelationships with God + the environment and other creatures which determine ones makeup (form/function relationship) in order to arrive at the proper Propositions to be used as the Premise in all logical thinking regarding humans. African Sages would use Postulates as *Assumptions* (taking a position in realms of uncertainty). When the Assumption or, more properly, the *Proposition*, was shown to be true by logical analysis, African Sages applied the term known in English as *Theorem*—and with the understanding that it would be replaced as soon as better information became available. This choice was based upon African Logic's distinguishing feature of starting a Thought Structure from the soundest base—meaning starting with something having an unblemished Base of Unconditional Love. The evolving Structure process always remains rooted in African Law. Off of that Base—consisting of a Proposition being used as a *Premise* (a statement *accepted as a basis for further reasoning*)--the Thought Structure would follow a Mathematical Process of Nature. As each building block was added to the Structure, it would be checked with the tools of Pure Emotions and Intellect for purposes of ensuring and then establishing the legitimacy (i.e. are parts of a pure Spiritual Elements nature) of and correspondence between all the ingredients used. An evolving sound unit of internal linkages, as indicated by there being an unchanging Unity as well as Coherence, Consistency, Compatibility, Balance, Enduring, Harmony, and unchanging Elements or Pattern. *Verification* would be added by examining all aspects of the process and the conclusion according to the Tree of Life Laws (Amen, Tree of Life) of intra-relationships and inter-relationships. Truth concerns the Spiritual Elements validation of the Premise operated on in Logical Thinking. To be included in African Logic Syllogistic Conclusion, there must be a Characteristic distinguishing mark concerning the Law of Identity as it applies so something corresponding to a Thing in the Divine, the Spiritual, and/or the Metaphysical planes. That distinction comes from what is involved in the Law of Correspondence. Then, using the Familiar to Circumstantially recognize the Unknown so as to have a non-contradictory identification and harmonious integration of all the available evidence, makes for a compatibility with ones Conscious. With Logic, contradictions are not part of the Elements involved. As an Atom is itself, and the Cosmos is itself, neither can contradict its own respective identity—nor can a part of each contradict the whole. No concept or conclusion is valid if all the ingredients are not harmoniously integrated into the total sum of Knowledge—and without contradiction. See Dialectic

SYLLOGISTIC LOGIC: *Wisdom* is the *direct perception of reality itself (instead of manipulating symbols)*. However, when *Implied* direct perception is through induction, deduction, and inference, it is called *Syllogistic Logic* (Cartesian, Analytical, Serial, Linear, Deductive, and Segregative). In Western science it tries to establish one-to-one cause and effect (Amen, Metu Neter I:216). But the difference is that what is man-made varies from time to time, and from place to place while maintaining "certain sameness" which allow for inferences to be made about humans. European Logic is mainly concerned with *Valid Inferred Judgments* and not True inferences or of any Beliefs. To elaborate, Logic is "*Valid*" when it justifies the evidence given in support of it. It is "True" in a Physical Knowledge World sense if it expresses the facts as they are. An inference may be both, one, or neither. For example, spectators who make inferences which turn out to be true may not be valid because what was said was not justified by available evidence. At the top of the competency ladder of Europeans Syllogistic Logic are candidates for Physical Knowledge which derive from General Premises, called *Axioms*--self-evident, indisputable, and generally accepted truths which, by absolute standards, are unproved. Examples: the shortest distance between two points is a straight line; two straight lines can cross only at one point. By it conforming to Mathematical Laws means it is accepted as *Physical Knowledge*. If not, it is High-Level Information with an element of doubt. Despite it SEEMING to be right, Critical Thinking (CT) challenges what is almost or not good enough. Axioms lack absoluteness if its creator is human. Ignorant and evil people, to cover up flaws, make what SEEMS right very attractive (videos, movies)--like a shiny penny that causes excitement. They widely advertise it and make SEEMS as if "everybody" believes it and is doing it. CT assesses whether or not what SEEMS right has Essence (i.e. what was it when it came into existence); who was its creator; the credibility of that creator; why there is agreement for it not needing to be proved; and its consequences.

The C14 English word "*Consequence*" (to follow closely)--the offspring of a Cause and Effect parents--carries such a peculiar birthing concept as to be placed in the "Kangaroo Pouch" category of words. It originally meant an inference or conclusion drawn from what possesses observable aspects for all or what was assumed to be so obvious and universally accepted as to need no proof (e.g. the beauty of flowers)--neither of which makes it "Right" or the truth. Yet, this beginning statement or proposition is a real, distorted, or false *Presupposition* (a thing taken for granted or assumed). In Logic, the first two syllogism propositions are called Premises. *Inferences determine the unknown from the already known by reasoning from circumstances and observations to draw conclusions from evidence or Premises.* Trained Right Brains pick up a clue of what is barely visible and generate inferences within the context of the Law of Correspondence so as to thereby complete the "big picture." For example, if the one clue is the corner of a table, from prior experiences one has a good idea that the highest percentages of tables have four legs. Thus, one has an impression of what the other three corners look like so as to arrive at the conclusion of the hazy object being a table. *Inference* goes beyond the evidence given or known and manipulates/maneuvers links between Cause and Effect so as to produce different types of Consequences. *Induction Inference* reasons from examining particular facts, individual cases, or specific things to the general--from the individual to the universal—from the known in the earth world to the unknown in realms above the earth world. In transferring this process of thinking, Inferences can uncover Patterns obscured by their context; find hidden relationships between seemingly unrelated pieces of Patterns; give clues to what is underlying a problem; and recognize a known principle in disguise so as to generate a match--as evidenced by the resultant Thing's coherent, enduring, balanced, harmonious, connectedness, and unchanging elements/pattern. Yet, to arrive at "*Esoteric Knowledge*"—i.e. understanding inner truths hidden within the core of fundamental concepts about foundational Realities--requires inference leaping by illogical, not logical thinking. Carried even further, this is a way to solve any seemingly "IMPOSSIBLE PROBLEM" (Bailey, Leadership Critical Thinking).

SYLLOGISMS ORIGIN: To repeat, when properly used within the flow of the Spiritual Elements Subjective Science, emphasizing Observation, becomes Poetic Logic which is able to explain the Divine, the Spiritual, and the Metaphysical. In this context, Subjective Science supersedes "Objective Science" for that is limited to the "Concrete" or Physical World. Very Ancient African priest-astronomers, after developing Algebra and Geometry--both Qualitative Logic--and trigonometry (Quantitative Logic) inferred the Universe (meaning a One or Uni Verse--i.e. one statement) to be Oneness whose Harmony is established and maintained by Cosmic Laws. By extracting Principles (unchanging realities) out of these Laws, they used an analogy—perhaps the equivalent to what is known today. For example, in the manner all humans derived from one ultimate African Ancestor parent 200,000 years ago, similarly from the ultimate Cosmic Creator (parent) have come all creatures and creations--making all Spiritually related (the Law of Sympathy). This means the Continuity is in the Spiritual Elements "Genetics"--i.e. uninterrupted existence of germ plasm called Androgynic Plast: God' creatures began out of Feminine/Masculine primeval Substance. The way this came about follows the Tree Concept of the "Seed" giving rise to Roots, Trunk, Branches, Leaves, and Fruit. Naturally, the whole is inside the Seed; the whole is contained in each of the Seed's manifested parts; and the Seed is found throughout the whole. This Law of Holonomy is the basis for Ancient Africans inferring the Law of Correspondence. Similar to the course of the "Seed", the evolution of Correspondence is that what first exists in the Spiritual Realm is later manifest on every plane of Material World existence--in accordance with God's "Genetics" of the Spiritual Element.

This Correspondence Law arose from the *Divine Logos--i.e. God's Universal Reason—Thought and Creative Utterance and Power—the Word.* This *Verbum* is the outward expression of the Ocean of Nun's essence before its Spiritual Elements' "Genetics" (SEG) reproduced itself in every later manifested plane of Cosmic existence in Mathematical Order. That expression was in the form of Vibrations and the Effect of Vibrations, for manifested creatures and creations, have Mathematical Order. The ever concealed God Source is beyond human knowledge or conception, whether in the ordinary or the clairvoyant states—thus making God Unknowable. Yet, God's manifestations through Cosmic creative works makes God known as the Logos. The Cosmos itself puts boundaries on the boundless God in order to enhance awareness of God's existence as Oneness of Will (what starts the evolutionary process), Wisdom (aggregated diffuse Matter into Form), and Activity (creating Matter). That "Oneness" is at the basis for Cosmic Correspondence as well as enabling the realization of a Sample of its Esoteric Creator. That Sample, called a Circumstance companion, enables the Esoteric Creator or its Esoteric realms to be known with Certainty because of the Law of Correspondence. Since *"The Word"* from the Cosmic Spiritual Force, Sekhem, is *itself the Divine Presence, its power, and its manifestation,* the term Divine Logos stands for itself contents--for its creatures and creation offspring throughout the Cosmos—and for designating the hidden aspects of how the work of the Cosmic Spiritual Force, Sekhem, is bound into Cosmic Correspondence Harmony. Thus, African logic, derived from astro-mathematically verified Cosmic Principles, stayed grounded in it while evolving out of that Spiritual Elements' "Genetics" flow. Since Spiritual Elements' "Genetics" Metaphysical Order (i.e. Natural Cosmic Knowledge) is the complementary opposite to and equal of the Metaphysical Disorder surrounding it, multiple problems in ones life would indicate one is in the flow of Metaphysical Disorder--the correction being to start using ones Intellectual and Poetic faculties (logical and artistic) to assess the "Seed" out of which it arose. In borrowing these concepts, ancient Greeks chose to disregard their Right Brain and its Spiritual Elements' "Genetics" influence over the Left Brain. After stepping out of African Tradition's Spiritual Elements' "Genetics" flow, the remainder of the African Logos concepts borrowed by ancient Greeks and renamed *Syllogism* ('a thinking out'). This (among others) designed ancient Greek Logic into a *Syllogism* reasoning scheme formed of three categorical statements, consisting of three successive and interrelated propositions--a scheme conveyed along two forms of mental processes. First, typical of Brutes, is into emotional and sensuous Patterned Thinking.

Second, Brute leaders apply *Syllogistic* (Cartesian) Logic (direct perception through induction, deduction, and inference) to create deception. Their Syllogisms redefine African terms; put boundaries on African Traditions' Spiritual and Metaphysical boundlessness concepts; convert Ancient Africans boundless Spiritual Principles into the Supernatural; and/or simply ignore African Traditions' Spiritual and Metaphysical realms. Next, their starting point for thinking is inside their make-believe Supernatural realm or often out of inappropriate Material World realms. Such faulty thinking is based on their Premises that could be true (i.e. in a purely

Physical knowledge sense)--and that starts thinking on the right path. Or, it is distorted or false--the wrong path. Yet, that wrong path does not prevent the "right" reasoned conclusion from being "*Valid.*" Valid is the result of what integrates all and contradicts none of the relevant data + exhibiting the property of being legitimately derived from premises by logical inference. The reason is that Validity is merely what is inferred from an antecedent premise and is independent of truth. In other words, in Supernatural Logical processes, Syllogisms are usually inside a realm of *Illusions* (seeing 'reality' where it is not and failing to see reality where it is). This is perfectly acceptable to European Logic's focus on the *correctness of the pattern* of thought. As assessed by only spotlighting (Left Brain) analysis, its mere concern is with valid systems of organized thinking in reasoning and language methodology. These Brute Brain/Left Brain patterns author illusions for self-deception as well as generate delusions for others. Converting African Knowledge into Information--a foundational separation from African Logic--means European Logic has devastating Consequences for all of the world's Peoples. Truth-seeking Critical Thinkers are alarmed at this acceptance of the correctness of this terrible reasoning pattern while knowingly being on the wrong path and then applying it to all life-shaping and life-changing things over which Europeans dominate. Such is highly deceptive because it SEEMS right to the naive. To illustrate, what ancient Greeks got from studying at the feet of Ancient African Sages in Africa was that God is benevolent, *Omnipotent* (unlimited and universal power), *Omnipresent* (present everywhere simultaneously), *Omniscient* (having total knowledge of everything), and *Immanent* (entirely a mind). However, Western Super-naturalists presented the major premise that, from its beginnings, the universe has contained not only good but evil. If God is omnipotent, it is within God's power to create a universe without evil--and since that is not true, God is responsible for the existence of Evil (minor premise), as of everything else--and thus is not benevolent (conclusion). Hence, they developed Satan to account for Evil. Yet, what these Greeks disregarded is that humans have *Free Wills*. African Sages taught that Evil is an imagined unreality--manifested as a delusional belief--and is expressed inside reality. Evil per se does not exist but rather it is a display of disharmonious Ignorance. Such Ignorance comes from humans using their Free Will to disconnect from the Ocean of Nuns flow throughout the Cosmos. This disconnection from the contents of the Spiritual Elements and the Cosmic Organism is simply the denial of God. That denial is deemed in African Tradition to be the greatest disease of the Soul and it puts people on anti-Ma'at paths that start with Indifference and progress to Hate, Evil deeds (those that deliberately destroy Harmony), and Sadism (boundless displays of Indifference, Hate, and Evilness). A human's Will--a faculty of the essential expression of who one is--exists apart from the functions it sanctions, initiates, suppresses, selects, and controls. It is shared with God and is the essence of a human's freedom (Amen, Tree of Life p9). This means there is no "un-free" Will and thus "Free Will" is a redundant term. Who ones Selfhood actually is comes from an orchestrating source—i.e. ones Real Self's Divine Consciousness—which, in favor of following God's Laws, naturally heads in the Ocean of Nun stream flow that transcends the Lower Self's blind impulses. *Ones Real Self is who one naturally is at birth.* But following birth, one is free to exercise freedom of choice using the process of Volition. *Volition* is ones mental activities which select ingredients from ones System of Values to determine which step to take at the cross-road of ones Lower Self path, ones Highest (Divinity) Self path, and *choose to do or to not do something while on the chosen path.* Yet, ones choices, as agencies/Causations, have Effects, and those Effects have layers of Consequences. These European beliefs and opinions illustrate how their terribly limited awareness of reality is "a destructive thing."

SYLLOGISMS--AFRICAN LOGIC: Logic implies the power to think Reasonably according to a pre-determined plan and therefore in an orderly manner. African Logic's distinguishing feature is the following of a Mathematical Process of Nature that starts upon a Base of Unconditional Love. Then it builds its structure along the Processes of Nature to establish the legitimacy (i.e. are parts of the Spiritual Elements) of and correspondence between ingredients and that the process is rooted in African Law. However, when there may be insufficient knowledge to follow the Ma'at Pattern and thus Syllogisms are required. The next best was the use of an Axiom and if it, or even a Postulate was available, African Sages would use them as *Assumptions* (taking a position in realms of uncertainty). When the Assumption or, more properly, the *Proposition*, was shown to be true by logical analysis, African Sages applied the term known in English as *Theorem*—and with the understanding that it would be replaced as soon as better information became available. The problem with starting a Thought Structure with a Proposition is that there is no notion of the sort and amount of evidence needed to prove the simplest matter of fact. For Africans, that Plan has guidelines whereby the intellect is used in Reasoning (Right and Left Brain usage) or by the Syllogistic faculty of ones mind. For example, when they had no idea of the starting point's validity, they did the next best thing of filling the gaps of their Knowledge from Analogy. Resultant insight would enable ones Vision to then see the Infinite in the finite. For European Logic the Plan is based upon the Syllogistic (Left Brain only) written rules they devised. Yet, without the context of African Laws, Reasoning is unable to discern the truth or falsehood of a Premise. Thus, Europeans' processes may be "Logical but not necessarily true." Hence, European Reasoning and their Scientific Method (which was borrowed from Ancient Africans and then modified) are unable to arrive at the truth because of lacking a Spiritual Elements Base and because of failing to reason within the context of the Processes of Nature. As a result Europeans must "Assume" a Premise to be true and then build an elaborate Thought Structure on top of that "quicksand" Base. But there are many problems with this process. First, a primary Unwritten Rule has as its aim to impress others that clearness of thought, soundness of reasoning, and freedom from bias underlie ones arguments, ones decisions, and ones policies. This is because it is safer to appeal to human's perceptions than to their Rational Logic. But Common Sense say no good ever comes from pretending to more precision than the Thing itself admits of. Second, a premature desire to generalize, an eagerness to arrive at conclusions, and a readiness to rest in them are serious hindrances to the right acquisition of Facts. What tends to be overlooked here is abstractions or opinions are not Facts. Third, the Propositions used consist of words and words are symbols of notions. Thus, if the notions themselves (which are the root of the matter) are confused and over-hastily abstracted from the facts, there can be no firmness in the super-structure. Fourth is to erroneously infer that things which are consecutive in order of time have necessarily the relation of Cause and Effect. The invariable antecedent of any event and/or the invariable consequence are not necessarily its Cause and Effect. This *arbitrarily "Assumed" true Premise + Logical Thinking = Opinions*. The well-known Syllogistic Formula: if A = B, and B = C, then A = C is stated: Socrates (A) is a man; men are mortal (A = B), then Socrates is mortal (A = C). This conclusion about the Specific entity Socrates (his mortality) from the General observation (mortality of men)—Deduction—is based on the Assumption that the physical entities known as Socrates and other humans represent the category "Human." While this Logical Deduction is true for the physical entities (humans), it is not true for the Entity "Human" which is the basis of the Premise. Acceptance of the above reasoning without examining the Premise will convey the false belief in the mortality of a human's true Self—which is the Spiritual. Many other European sayings are like this: "Man is a rational animal" (Amen, Tree of Life p155) or Descartes: "I think therefore I am." This logic, which is incapable of determining truth, is used to establish the Premise that is assumed to be true—called Circular Thinking.

SYLLOGISTIC OR CARTESIAN LOGIC. This is based upon the belief of Descartes that information of ones own mind or self is more direct and certain and basic than any other. This, itself, does not make sense because certain is absolute and there can be no "more certain. Despite being unable to have any path to the Truth or to establish any Knowledge, the conglomerates of their thinking within this context, is what they consider as "*Logic*"—or more specifically *Syllogistic or Cartesian Logic*. It pertains to the methods and doctrines of Rene Descartes, a French philosopher and mathematician. It is about the practice of drawing conclusions from Premises in arriving at beliefs. What the ancient Western world called Logic now embraces the additional term of European Critical Thinking (CT)--the process of using the rules of reasoning (the practice of drawing conclusions from premises) to arrive at conclusions. *General Premises are called Axioms* (e.g. the shortest distance between two points is a straight line; two straight lines can cross only at one point). More specific premises of mathematical type things are called *Postulates*. Induction is significant in these processes (Bailey, Critical Thinking; Bailey, Rational Thinking). To spotlight these points let us analyze the syllogism's soundness in the following European false and evil stereotype: For them, "right" reasoning is in Europeans engaging in a piece of *Deductive* reasoning in proceeding to follow the pattern of 3 categorical statements or Propositions. *Major Premise*: Blacks are ignorant and shiftless/ *Minor Premise*: Sam is a Black man/ *Conclusion*: Therefore, Sam is ignorant and shiftless. The conclusion is *valid* (meaning it integrates all and contradicts none of the relevant data) by following logically from the assumptions which precede it. Yet, when one is dealing with racism and bigotry the *major premise (or assumption or hypotheses)* must be challenged—not the "logic"--because it does not contain truth. To illustrate with a common racist argument: "surely, you don't want people like that as neighbors, do you? The "logical" answer: Of course not!—an answer now trapping you. But to flush out the real issue and to shift the burden of proof, ask: "people like what?"—what is your evidence that Blacks are invariably ignorant and shiftless? There can be no evidence because the overwhelming majority of Blacks are industrious.

Ones CT demands knowing the background leading to faulty reasoning. In their attempt to connect things in different worlds the slave owners shifted from talking about slavery by substituting cattle for the Enslaved but logically the world of cattle has no relationship to human Slaves. They said just as no "reasonable" person would free their cattle and then fight to abolish their ownership of their cattle it made sense to preserve slavery. They used biological justifications drawn from the assumption of the Slaves, like cattle, were a separate species (moving chattel). These assumptions came from eminent White physicians and sham scientists and White racists provided the two ethnocentric justifications for slavery--first, slavery was in accord with Whites' own group interests and second, because reason and logic showed clearly to the reasonable and intelligent (White) man that slavery was good. In other words, to Racist slavery was justified—even praised—on the basis of a complex ideology showing quite conclusively how useful slavery was to (White) society and how uplifting Whites thought it was for the Slaves. Based on the assumption of slavery being all for which Negroes were suited, nothing was illogical about slavery. Belief in correctness of slavery was wrong since the assumption (major premise) was wrong—not because it did not make sense--for it made perfect sense to the slave owners. A job of CT is to find the assumption lurking behind the (quite valid) conclusion.

SYLLOGISM--WESTERN'S "SEEMS RIGHT" DECEPTION: Ancient Africans' Law of Correspondence arose--in accordance with God's plan--from the Ocean of Nun's essence before its Spiritual Elements' "Genetics" (SEG) reproduced itself in every later manifested plane of Cosmic existence. Thus, African logic, derived from astro-mathematically verified Cosmic Principles, stayed grounded in it while evolving out of that SEG's flow. Since SEG's Metaphysical Order (i.e. Natural Cosmic Knowledge) is the complementary opposite to and equal of the Metaphysical Disorder surrounding it, multiple problems in ones life would indicate one is in the flow of Metaphysical Disorder--the correction being to start using ones intellectual faculties (logical and artistic) to assess the "Seed" out of which it arose. In borrowing these concepts, ancient Greeks chose to disregard their Right Brain and its SEG influence over the Left Brain--and thus stepped out of the SEG flow. This (among others) designed ancient Greek Logic into a *Syllogism* ('a thinking out') reasoning scheme--a scheme formed of three categorical statements, consisting of three successive and interrelated propositions--a scheme conveyed along two forms of mental processes. First, typical of Brutes, is into emotional and sensuous Patterned Thinking. Second, Brute leaders apply *Syllogistic* (Cartesian) Logic (direct perception through induction, deduction, and inference) to create deception. Their Syllogisms redefine African terms; put boundaries on African Traditions' Spiritual and Metaphysical boundlessness concepts; convert Ancient Africans boundless Spiritual Principles into the Supernatural; and/or simply ignore African Traditions' Spiritual and Metaphysical realms. Next, their starting point for thinking is inside their make-believe Supernatural realm or often out of inappropriate Material World realms. Such faulty thinking is based on their Premises that could be true (i.e. in a purely Physical knowledge sense)--and that starts thinking on the right path. Or, it is distorted or false--the wrong path. Yet, that wrong path does not prevent the "right" reasoned conclusion from being "*Valid.*" Valid is the result of what integrates all and contradicts none of the relevant data + exhibiting the property of being legitimately derived from premises by logical inference. The reason is that Validity is merely what is inferred from an antecedent premise and is independent of truth. In other words, in Supernatural Logical processes, Syllogisms are usually inside a realm of *Illusions* (seeing 'reality' where it is not and failing to see reality where it is). This is perfectly acceptable to European Logic's focus on the *correctness of the pattern* of thought. As assessed by only spotlighting (Left Brain) analysis, its mere concern is with valid systems of organized thinking in reasoning and language methodology. These Brute Brain/Left Brain patterns author illusions for self-deception as well as generate delusions for others. Converting African Knowledge into Information--a foundational separation from African Logic--means European Logic has devastating Consequences for all of the world's Peoples. Truth-seeking Critical Thinkers are alarmed at this acceptance of the correctness of this terrible reasoning pattern while knowingly being on the wrong path and then applying it to all life-shaping and life-changing things over which Europeans dominate. Such is highly deceptive because it SEEMS right to the naive. To illustrate, what ancient Greeks got from studying at the feet of Ancient African Sages in Africa was that God is benevolent, *Omnipotent* (unlimited and universal power), *Omnipresent* (present everywhere simultaneously), *Omniscient* (having total knowledge of everything), and *Immanent* (entirely a mind). However, Western Super-naturalists presented the major premise that, from its beginnings, the universe has contained not only good but evil. If God is omnipotent, it is within God's power to create a universe without evil--and since that is not true, God is responsible for the existence of Evil (minor premise), as of everything else--and thus is not benevolent (conclusion). Hence, they developed Satan to account for Evil. *But, Critical Thinking always challenges the Major Premise.* African Tradition says God's Cosmic Creation did not include evil--and Evil's presence is Virtual. However, Black Americans have only been taught the European concept of Evil and deliberately not exposed to the vastly different African Truth of Evil being a manifestation of Ignorance. These practices alone are powerful ways to confuse and adversely control the Black Mind.

SYMBOLS TERMINOLOGY: As background, one must be clear about what are an Icon and a Symbol. Symbols have been extensively discussed in Bailey, Mentoring Black Boys; Bailey, Post-Traumatic Distress Syndrome. *The C15 word "Symbol"* ("throwing them together" -- with "them" referring to two things, each with a story) and "*Parable*" ("throwing them side by side," referring to an Allegory-type deduced veiled story from an obvious story) were originally synonyms. Both were used in the comparative sense of *Identity* ("unchanging sameness") to prove (after scrutinizing for any contrasting features) the two parts of something matched. The principle which corresponds to this is discussed from "yoking" above. A variation concerned a coin applied when the bank vault contained half of a divide coin (the symbol) while the absent customer's half was not available to be seen (the mystery). When the Customer returned to claim her money, she proved her identity when her half of the coin matched the half in the bank vault. From this practice one concept of a Symbol was a concrete (touchable) object (the half coin in the bank) yoked to its absent near twin (the customer's half, the token). Like an Icon, a Symbol is *a microcosm* (a "little world") of the "Macrocosm" it represents (i.e. a great world). The interrelatedness of the two might be signified by the outward and visible appearances resembling and/or by the Symbol carrying a crystalized gist of the inward and hidden meaning of the "Thing" it symbolizes. The *Symbol* part of this Belief/Opinion System Schema is first a summary of everything contributing to the formation of the archetype Seed—i.e. the Essence--of a Belief/Opinion System. Second, since the System's matrix and Disposition contain rays of varied meanings, with each being able to connect to "Like-Kind" things and thereby influence the meanings of each of those Things, the Symbol is a summary of everything within the Roots, Trunk, Branches, Leaves, and Fruit potentially derivable from Belief/Opinion System. These make a Symbol a thing of power that, when used within the context of Affect Symbolic Imagery, is capable of elucidating by means of analogy (similar parts in dissimilar things) or allegory (a veiled meaning within a story) something belonging entirely to the domain of the unknown; something known; and/or something yet to be. Therefore, Symbols are a way of becoming aware of keystone meanings, either in simple things or within complex things. *By being the point where the Physical and the Metaphysical meet, Symbols can shape the infinite by making it finite or take away shape by making infinite the finite.* An Afrocentric Symbol -- something invested with such significance as to be carried beyond itself in meaning -- is either a shapeless cocoon designating an Abstract in Metaphysical realms or designating an Abstraction or a thing with physical form (a pattern of energy movement frozen in space) in Material realms. Special Symbols, whether entailing objects, situations, or concepts, have the capacity to draw upon 'social-psychological associations' (e.g. sensualities) which are heavily compressed in time and space and give the objects, situations, or concepts an air of 'transcendence'. To illustrate, a mythological story of the Ancient Egyptian Goddess *Matet* opens with her arising before daybreak; climbing onto a golden chariot drawn by white horses; and journeying across the heavens to announce mid-day and finally sunset. This Schema principle in life is illustrated by taking a path and doing what is required to transform from being a child over to being a mature adult. To elaborate, as stated in "Re-Yoking," *a human's Spark of God constituting the core of that human's Soul (the Eternal Immaterial aspect signifying ones Self-Identity) has a sheath around it. Although they are like two sides of one coin, the Sheath contains those lesser faculties that relate to the Earth World.* The Sheath enables newborn babies to operate out of their Lower (animalistic) Selves, complete with survival instincts and with passions oriented to: "I want what I want and I want it now." When the Sheath part is spotlighted as the baby develops, that child is inclined to embrace Socialization's "Trinkets and Trivia," Beliefs, and practices that initiate and enlarge into "balloonment" upon ones Acquired Emotions. Continuing on that course is what fashions a False Self. Yet, in spite of the effect of that sheath keeping the False Self person at some distance away from God, the "Spark" in ones Soul which is in the image of God is always within the core of ones Soul. The problem is that Clouds are placed over its "Soul Sunshine" and those Clouds cause one to draw ingredients for thinking from the External World. By External World ingredients being the source of Belief and Opinion Systems which generate Metaphysical Disorder and the Supernatural's Disharmony, what flows out of these Systems is what is self-defeating and destructive to the "ME/WE". *Metaphysical Disorder* per se is of a non-moral nature and yet implies to "go astray," become lost," stray from correct behavior by going outside the boundaries of Ma'at to enter "Badness." By Metaphysical Disorder being of the nature of the influence of a *"Disaster Star,"* one clings to its think, feel, say, and do ways. The *Supernatural's Disharmony* is about Delusions—believing what is not real and not believing what is real. Both Metaphysical Disorder and the Supernatural's Disharmony dissolve distinctions between Knowledge and information to thereby fashion Bad Information as its dominating sources for thought and actions. People who operate out of such Bad Belief/Opinion Systems are under the delusion that their identification as a person is determined by what they believe. Yet, by being disconnected from their Highest (divinity) Self, False Selves' delusions, illusions, integrity gaps, and excuses are formed by their Lower (animalistic) Selves. These Beliefs are equivalent to "Seeds" which fashion Tree components that are incorporated into the far ranging thoughts, emotions, expressions, and deeds that are ever branching and forming "Leaves" in ones daily life. As these Bad Branchings and Bad Leaves go, so goes the Bad Fruit that fashions ones destiny "meal" on earth. Bad Beliefs/Bad Opinions cause people to be slowed, stopped, or reversed in their wholesome progress and what they have no other choice of adopting is automatically made to "SEEM" right. To accept what "SEEMS" right frees people to follow their Wants and "go along to get along" with the Crowd. The Cloud over their "Soul Sunshines" makes them unable to see soon enough that being guided by their Acquired Emotions will make their lives increasingly more difficult and them more and more insecure, emotionally hypersensitive, and unhappy to the point of needing "Addicting Escapes." To complicate matters, all that threatens ones emotional inclinations or that are difficult, ambiguous, contradictory, boring or cause pain lead to layers of anger, shame, fear, and mental "funk." A major problem for those not on the "Spiritual Elements Track" is in that they rationalize their self-defeating displays according to their identification with their Lower Self. See Sign; Icon

SYMBOL--TOTIPOTENT: A *Totipotent Symbol* means: (1) *symbolic messages which disregard the limitations and boundaries of ordinary human thought in order to: (2)* make unsuspected and novel connections between seemingly unlike Things; (3) carry a payload in and of itself or in its offspring that is capable of producing *implicit ideas of the indescribable that touch the "Heart" or "Head"; (4)* cause an impact leading to what is like the technological concept called Rastrophiliopustrocity—i.e. a spontaneous combustion of a creative spark that is followed by actions in order to manifest and bring something into existence; *and/or* (5) take any ray out of an existing entity or out of a new entity so as to, by itself, reproduce itself, and become the thing it makes

SYMBOLS' "WHAT IT IS": *Metaphors* (equates unlike things by implication), *Simile (*the abstract or suggestive aspect is directly expressed), *Allegories* (a hidden story within an obvious story), *Fables* (animals impersonating humans to impart a moral), *Personification* (making a lifeless or abstract thing alive), *Analogies* (explaining something unfamiliar by comparing it to something familiar), *Legend* (a story, above mere fiction, combining fact and personified spiritual concepts), and *Symbols* (symbolic messages disregard the limitations and boundaries of human thought in order to impart ideas of the indescribable). The Pattern of the Essence of a "Seed" Symbol of a Belief or Opinion's may be based upon an Abstraction or an Abstract that is real, distorted, or fantasy. *Abstraction* and Abstract Messages one entertains in the mind are forms of frozen energy within a plane "State." Recall that the fully realized form of the Essence of a Thing, called its Pattern, has an Image on the outside of the Form. On the inside is a Matrix--womb bringing nourishment—e.g. memory, energy--to the contained ingredients and that enables it to grow and enlarge. That Image is a Symbol--a metaphoric device vehicle for the conception of what the Essence is *when it came into Being* and/or what is intended by the Disposition in the Belief or Opinion. The Image or Symbol's payload message summarizes the *"What it Is"* of that Belief or Opinion's Circle of Wholism System. Its matrix and Disposition contain rays of varied meanings with each being able to connect to "Like-Kind" things and thereby influence the meanings of each of those Things. Since the Image of that System derives from ones Sensory Experience, that Belief or Opinion's Circle of Wholism *System is flawed.* This is because: *(1) what ones Sensory Experience, that now serves as the Essence, consisted of at the time it was formed was not all there is to what was present in the situation; (2) because of flawed interpretations of all aspects of that reality; and (3) because of additions (e.g. by ones memory) or subtractions (e.g. by what one wanted it to be or not be) were designed from ones Imagination.*

SYMBOLS' "WHAT IT DOES": As mentioned above, the Image or Symbol's payload message of the Essence of a Belief/Opinion System summarizes the *"What it Is"* of that Belief or Opinion's Circle of Wholism

System. The System's matrix and Disposition contain rays of varied meanings, with each being able to connect to "Like-Kind" things and thereby influence the meanings of each of those Things. The *Symbol's "What it does"* provides details of how to connect with those *"Like-Kind" things and its* processes of completion. On a theater stage of ones mind, a beginning connection of the Symbol and the Mystery is for ones Imagination on one side of the stage to dematerialize the boundaries between the visible and the Effect (mysterious). To *"Dematerialize"* means to *disregard the limitations and boundaries of human thought so that the symbolic messages are able to transform themselves inside the Mystery into a schema Principle that may display as a Contingent Being or Entity.* By so doing, perhaps a "phantom" is generated on the theater stage of ones mind that is free flowing and carrying, in a mosaic manner, the essence features of the Symbol and the Mystery. The Symbol and the Mystery establish a connection in both directions so as to enable ones Selfhood to intuitively recognize the "Like-Kind" essences, even though they are not identical. But note that the "What the Symbol does" is in three parts: (1) on one side of the stage, the Symbol "stands apart" from the performers and their message; (2) the Symbol carries the essence performers and their message across the bridge ('a spanning road or structure') of the stage to enter the Mystery Atmosphere; and (3) The impact of the Visible with the Mystery on the far side of the bridge or stage makes meaningful connections that form a Schema.

SYMPATHY: Whereas emotional experiences involve awareness of widespread bodily commotion, to impart emotional "love" in degrees is to determine how much of what kind of "love" to give and to whom--both concepts implied in the Western word *Sympathy*. Black people lack a concept of "Sympathy" because of the absence of sharing a Spiritual Space, as there is with Compassion. Since the Eurocentric literature views "love" as an Earth World Emotion, it is not only man-made but changable for self-interest purposes *having nothing to do with Spirituality*. See Bounding Conditional Love

SYNTHESIS: out of, say, the egg and the sperm which join to produce a fetus, comes a new and novel "Seed" product *by means other than through a mere summation of the elements originally involved, of a new and original fetus, Entity, or Concept—a Mosaic unique picture from the "Genetic" pattern of the parents.* The African Hermes Trismegistus laid out principles that would give rise to the philosophical concepts behind Afrocentric synthesis. One of those, the *Principle of Polarity* (known today as the Yin/Yang concept) and other messages of Hermes imply that Synthesis is the *creation of unity, the making of something whole and therefore the establishing of a piece of reality*. To elaborate, the egg and sperm joining to begin a fetus is a Synthesis of the mother's and father's genes to produce this fetus is likened to shuffling a pack of cards. Although the Zygote (i.e. the new and novel "Seed" or fetus product) has the same genetic material of the parents, its genes are synthesized in different amounts, in different combinations, and different arrangements so as to create a new mosaic pattern that individualizes the new human into a unique individual. Though some feature/traits are dominant from the mother, some dominant from the father, and some are a blend, they will breed true in the resultant individual's off-spring. Thus, what Synthesis implies is that the new and novel Mosaic unique product results *by means other than through a mere summation of the elements (e.g. genes) originally involved*. This Principle applies whether referring to a new and original fetus, Entity, or Concept. This whole constitutes a Symbol. Because Synthesis is present on different planes of existence—whether physical, mental, or spiritual—each Synthesized Entity is represented by a Symbol. The Black African Imhotep (2600 BC)—the "Universal Father of Medicine"--effectively used Tehuti's synthesis message of Rebirth (to bring ones spiritual, mental, and physical self into alignment synthesis) in medicine so that patients could achieve maximum health experiences of security and adequacy. In short, the Aim of Synthesis is to be a reasonable connecting link between the problem and the solution. Whereas in Analysis, one descends from general cases to particulars or specific things (deductive), in Synthesis, one ascends from specific things to general ones (inductive) so as to generate a list of options for possible solution.

T

"T"-SCALE CONCEPT: An Imaged Thinking Pattern Tool--the *"T" Scale*—deals with Absolute/ Relative, Spiritual/Worldly, and Constant/Change differences. The horizontal line symbolizes the Spiritual; the Secular by the vertical line. For *Supernatural Inference types,* a parallel vertical line is represented by a fish, whose splayed tail embraces three common gross deceptions for mind control—i.e. the triad: *Allusions, "Almost Good Enough," and "Seems" Right*. First, *"SEEMS right"* means the Inference Conclusion is not actually right but one accepts it as so because one wants it to be that way or because one is too lazy to do the research. To be off by 0.0001 degree in going from Earth to the Moon means one will wind up on Mars. Second, most accept *"Almost Good Enough"* and then proceed as if it were truth, rather than using it simply as a vehicle to get started and then making alterations or replacements as new and better ideas come available. "Almost" will not get one into heaven. Third, *Allusions* (C16, playful reference) are roundabout, indirect, and suggestive indicators presented as: "by the way"; "or in passing"; "on second thought"; or "dropped in passing," as with little thought. Two main types of Allusions dominate. The *Imply Allusion* type refers to something in the speaker's words that led the listener into an unstated association that forms an unrealistic image of what is presented. Hence, any conclusion lacks evidence and is merely a guess, conjecture, or opinion. The *Suggest Allusion* type is something in the speaker's words that conveys an implicit quality with an entangling certain meaning within the context of a bias or prejudice and pointing to a Thing's identity. Both Imply and Suggest spur the listener to "Deduce" what is meant, by reasoning on a sample of the evidence or previously made false judgment or prior inadequate conclusion—not direct observation. That Deduced reasoning leads to an indirect *"Almost Good Enough" and/or "Seems" Right* conclusion. In short, deduced (i.e. reasoning drawn from evidence/premises) Inferences are not explicit conclusions or opinions, by failing to unfold into clarity the *"Identity"* in what is said. See Thinker's Scale

TAKE CHARGE: self-responsibility for ones own destiny"

TAKE CONTROL: directing ones lifestyle into providing and maintaining the "5Ss"

"TAKING WHOLE": Chinese Sun Tzu said *"Taking Whole"* is playing "rough" but without opponents necessarily losing. "Rough" is not the same as "dirty" (i.e. brute practices) but instead is doing things that are intimidating and respected, even though the opposition does not like them.

TALENTS: The 4 categories of Talents—Unconditional Love (a subdivision being Compassion), Truth, Reality, and the Natural contain a family of subdivisions sharing similar Correspondent vibration rates. For example, as a small boy I discovered my Talent was in the category of Unconditional Love and Compassion was my subdivision of Unconditional Love. Such was detected by my running to help a fallen classmate in the school yard rather than joining the other kids who stood around laughing. Being aware of the Subdivision can lead to deciding which particular one is most suitable at a given passage in life. Thus, one might be an opera singer until one gets married. Music is wholistic within itself and does not go anywhere and yet has waves of rhythms and feelings. Similarly, being a financial advisor shares the same Underlying features as Music despite being quite different in external aspects. An example is sharing the same wave type harmony vibration rate.

TASTE: The Spiritually Confident deals with spiritual matters, not by rules, but by applying the Spiritual Elements with "Subtleties" in the form of Guidelines. The "Taste" of that enhances the discernments leading towards establishing harmony, order, congruity, balance, movement, color, and texture throughout the whole--"Subtleties" which design Happiness. The art of making appearances (e.g. reflections in water and in solid, smooth and polished bodies). Each gives off its unique feature and that feature is reflected in mirrors inside the tube. Made by reflections of reflections, no two patterns are ever quite alike Rainbows are beautiful bands of colors in the form of a half circle. Each raindrop, acting like a tiny prism, reflects and refracts the white rays of sunlight into seven colors. As we look at the rainbow from the top down and with our backs to the sun, we see red, orange, yellow, green, blue, indigo, and violet merging into one another. Note that the edges of the hues blend into a mixture of two colors. These are the same as seen in masterpieces of Art, Music, or Poetry which cannot be procedurally taught. A confident person looks like he/she has something to teach. Art reflect sorrows, enjoyment, fears, and hopes. Such works of Art express these general "laws" and invite, not an emotional response, but a kind of insight into a universal understanding of human needs.

TEACHING: "*Education*" ("to lead out what is inside"); "*Teaching*" ("to show" so as to impart knowledge for learning); *Instructing* ("to build in or into"), or "*Training*" (active mind exercising in order to form habits)—in short, by study, reflection, and/or practice--depending upon the topic.

TEHUTI'S TWELVE TORMENTORS: Ignorance; Grief; Intemperance (excessive indulgence of a natural appetite or passion); Incontinence (lacking a restraint, especially over the sexual appetite); Injustice; Avarice (greed); Falsehood; Envy; Guile (cunning, deceit); Anger/Rage; Rashness (impulsive, acting without due consideration); and Malice (desire to inflict harm).

TELEOLOGY: Plato and Aristotle laid out the extremely complex ideas about *Teleology (Gr. Goal)*--the oldest mode of explanation of human conduct. A crude over-simplification is that just as orchestral instruments combine to make symphonic music, Aristotle said every separate thing has its purpose to make the world whole and serve one complete purpose. See Gods--European

TELL: In C14, "*Tell*" was designated as a general word meaning to make known by speech or writing. Inform then took on the compounded confusing sense of "to impart knowledge by communicating certain facts," separating it from "*Advise*"--an opinion suggesting a course of conduct be followed.

TEN COMMANDMENTS: growing discoveries within ones ones deeper Self would urge such spiritual aspirations as to seek an African Sage to assist in self-discovery by cultivating virtue. That is the reason Sages created the 42 Ma'at Philosophy injunctions--10 borrowed ones are called the Ten Commandments in the European Bible (Bailey, Ancient African Bible Messages).

TERMINOLOGY: C12 "*Term*" (limit, boundary) is a word, phrase, or a sense of a word or phrase that has a particular (often unusual) meaning because of the context in which it is used. It typically names something in a specialized field (e.g. hysterectomy). The C18 word "*Terminology*" (limit or boundary + study) may be about general words and the vocabulary of a specialized field. Common public words can have technical applications and specialty words are often for public usage. Whereas different segments of European wordsmith give hazy separation between these terms and categories, Ancient Africans did not because they viewed the Cosmos to be an *underling web of relationships operating in Nature* and thus independent things worked interdependently for the benefit of the whole. An example is them applying Mathematics to the Metaphysical and using Algebra on all planes of Cosmic existence. See Glossary

TESTS: Tested (C14, proves something) originally came from ancient times. One version was Alchemists trying things by heating them in a pot to see what they were like under those conditions. Another was from the tongue of a balance used for weighing as part of "trying the thing by weight," as a doctor weighing the patient's physical condition. From that came the ideas of ponder, consider, test. Third is a Trial (a trying out or processing in order to see whether the results of experiment are trustworthy). All of this are about determining the correctness or genuineness of a Thing by a thorough study of all details.

"THAT IT IS": The *"That it is"* is the Immaterial Image of what a Thing is when it came into Being-hood. The "that it is"-- a formless tool of action--a "Virtual" (boundless) entity contains the power of the Disposition. Its "Genetics" determines the capabilities for how the What it is will develop, for what it is to do, for how it is to grow, and for the type of 'payload' impact it will have. It identifies the Spiritual part (which is undifferentiated and unformed but not disorganized) of a "Thing" by pointing to its specificity, individuality, and 'here/now-ness'—its nature. Its natural qualities is the Essence's *Ground of Being*). This means the *"That it is"* refers to any Immaterial Primary Quality (e.g. Spiritual Emotion) in any category because that Thing's essence lacks a Form-Body and thus is itself a virtual body (lacking boundaries).

THIRD CANDLE CONCEPT: At a wedding, the bride and groom's candle (representing her and his character) lights a third candle to indicate a joining of their Spiritual Humanity to independently work inter-dependently toward a successful marriage. Hence, the *"Third Candle"* Concept implies that the marriage is more important than the bride's or the groom's different ways of thinking--of their moods/emotions--of their different ways of expressions—or doing selfish behaviors.

"T"-SCALE CONCEPT: An Imaged Thinking Pattern Tool--the *"T" Scale*—deals with Absolute/Relative, Spiritual/Worldly, and Constant/Change differences. The horizontal line symbolizes the Spiritual; the Secular by the vertical line. For *Supernatural Inference types,* a parallel vertical line is represented by a fish, whose splayed tail embraces three common gross deceptions for mind control—i.e. the triad: *Allusions, "Almost Good Enough," and "Seems" Right*. First, *"SEEMS right"* means the Inference Conclusion is not actually right but one accepts it as so because one wants it to be that way or because one is too lazy to do the research. To be off by 0.0001 degree in going from Earth to the Moon means one will wind up on Mars. Second, most accept *"Almost Good Enough"* and then proceed as if it were truth, rather than using it simply as a vehicle to get started and then making alterations or replacements as new and better ideas come available. "Almost" will not get one into heaven. Third, *Allusions* (C16, playful reference) are roundabout, indirect, and suggestive indicators pre-sented as: "by the way"; "or in passing"; "on second thought"; or "dropped in passing," as with little thought. Two main types of Allusions dominate. The *Imply Allusion* type refers to something in the speaker's words that led the listener into an unstated association that forms an unrealistic image of what is presented. Hence, any conclusion lacks evidence and is merely a guess, conjecture, or opinion. The *Suggest Allusion* type is something in the speaker's words that conveys an implicit quality with an entangling certain meaning within the context of a bias or prejudice and pointing to a Thing's identity. Both Imply and Suggest spur the listener to "Deduce" what is meant, by reasoning on a sample of the evidence or previously made false judgment or prior inadequate conclusion—not direct observation. That Deduced reasoning leads to an indirect *"Almost Good Enough" and/or "Seems" Right* conclusion. In short, deduced (i.e. reasoning drawn from evidence/premises) Inferences are not explicit conclusions/opinions by failing to unfold into clarity the *"Identity"* in what is said. See Allusions

"THE GAME" OF EUROPEAN "GENTLEMEN": The idea was to acquire the most "Adult Toys"--regardless of how--and thereby be the winner. "The Game" caused them to be overly-concerned with making a good appearance by displaying a hedonistic lifestyle and fads--a foundational stone of today's Europeans. Hence, starting in C15 and C16 Europe there was the compulsion to live up to accepted standards of "ideal-ism." This was carried over into Slavery in the Americas and displayed out of Fear and Envy of not being able to "keep up with the Jones"--i.e. their fellow slave owners. Hence, their primary obsession was to make money. Their compulsion was to do this by Slave labor carried out in sequences of acts and adhering rigidly to a cer-tain order of behavior. To exhibit a hedonistic lifestyle, most slave owners would take frequent trips to various places in the world and derive pleasure from drinking, gambling, eating, etc.--a distinguishing feature from the Obsessive-Compulsive Disorder. They had some element of schizophrenia by failing to see how absurd their compulsions were. The Renaissance "Gentlemen" in Europe were the immediate ancestors of the African American slave owners. Their insatiable appetites, as a result of being "filthy rich" from what they had robbed from the Colored Peoples of the World, quickly shaded into Obsessions and Compulsions. The agony of fear of losing "The Game" or not making a good showing caused slave owners to pay any price, defying logic, and bringing about sacrifices of their practical self-interests and those of their family--and, in fact, caused many to forfeit their lives. Note how the price paid was any but the one which could save them--i.e. failing to acknowledge and correct their fraudulent defenses and desires held in such high regard by European culture. To be seen as a winner or to be admired as an achiever was the European "gentleman's" means of cultural survival and the proof of his personal value within the context of his Self-Esteem. In C18 there was a compulsion among Whites to engage in sham scientific issues directed toward proving White Superiority so as to overcome their "without the GUN" sense of inadequacy and inferiority. Some denied their underlying destructive desires by going to the opposite extreme--the mechanism of *Reaction Formation*--as in speaking about being God-fearing. By so doing they hoped to deflect observation of their brute-ness and thereby deceive others into admiring their ill-gotten gains. Their limited ability to express sincerity to fellow slave owners (or anybody) gave the appearance of a stiff formality in relationships. In order to hide their loneliness and because they would need alliances in the future they then would do nice thing for and with fellow Whites. Those who netted fortunes would occasionally step out of "Brute-hood" because of feeling guilty over their evil and sadistic lifestyle and deeds by giving large sums to charitable organizations. One reason was for tax purposes and another was a self-appeasement by clinging to the "ideal" of altruism (under the belief that charity is a moral substitute for dishonorableness); by counteracting, expiating, or atoning for their evil deeds; being seen in church; and by forming a facade vision of himself as a humanitarian. Meanwhile, non-rich European males tended to follow rules and regulations of Brutes. This came from having been reared by authoritarian and obstinate parents into an overly-controlled state. Such might help explain European males' military orientation and willingness to follow their leader into death. They needed (and need) this personal identity so as to lose their inner emptiness. Still boosting their unhappy state and giving security in their narrow, predictable, unimaginative, and disharmonious lives is hiding behind the GUN. But they made feeble non-coward attempts to blot this out in the Old West by daily Bar Brawls and presently doing daredevil things (e.g. bungy-jumping) in hopes of appearing to be who they are not. Yet, for Victims adopted to be scapegoats, similar Forms of display are seen. European reward those in the Victim group who are so judgmental that any fellow victim who disagrees with the Satanist leaders is automatically declared wrong and needs to be beaten into submission until he/she agrees. Another way is their belief that: "I know and you don't"--regardless of something they know nothing about (e.g. in outsiders deciding what is best for Black People). A third is the stance of: "my way or the highway and if you don't agree with me let's go to war." The "stay-in-your-place" applied to their own Troops as much as to their Victims. And that is what was brainwashed into Enslaved Africans brought to the Americas and much has been culturally transmitted into many of today's Black Americans, causing "Inside-Out" thinking. **THEOREM**: African Sages would use Postulates as *Assumptions* (taking a position in realms of uncertainty). When the Assumption or, more properly, the *Proposition*, was shown to be true by logical analysis, African Sages applied the term known in English as *Theorem*—and with the understanding that it would be replaced as soon as better information became available. This choice was based upon African Logic's distinguishing feature of starting a Thought Structure from the soundest base—meaning starting with something having an unblemished Base of Unconditional Love. The evolving Structure process always remains rooted in African Law. Every conclusion obtained by Deduction may not be significant, but the result of 10 or 20 such arguments arrived at similarly could be. If so, it is a "Theorem" since it is a "Probable" explanation.

THEORY: An hypothesis which has been verified by continued Observation, Experiment, and Investigation is advanced in rank and known as a *Theory—best answers all the requirements and best explains the facts*. Still further advancement is called by Europeans a Law.

THESIS/ANTI-THESIS OF EUROPEANS: Two kinds of Inquiries or Questions are the Hypothesis (or Cause or Case involving definite persons, places, times, actions or affairs) and the general Question called a Thesis or Proposition (only part of a Case and entails only one or several of these factors). In African Logic, to clear up conflicts and get to the Truth, Complementary Opposites must be distinguished from *Contrary Opposites*. However, this admonition was ignored by Europeans when they borrowed and then modified African Logic Concepts. Such changes put European Logic into a Supernatural realm, with a name, objective, and process that SEEMS right but is far, far from Right. To elaborate, European *Thesis* has the special meaning of Proposition or Postulate or Affirmation stated explicitly at the beginning of a discourse as a challenge or provocation to proof. It may also constitute a declaration of policy or a series of steps in the policy but these are not dealt with here. Martin Luther's 95 theses against indulgences, which he nailed on the door of the church at Wittenberg were propositions that he was willing to champion against all opponents. In this sense, a thesis is a Proposition or a Question for debate—i.e. a subject to be discussed and argued affirmatively (believed in) or negatively (denied). *Propositions* are the organization of Concepts and depend upon the truth or falsehood of the Base upon which it rests; or the relation of the Concepts to the Truth; the proper internal linkages of one Concept with another; on the truth or falsehood of the definition of the Concepts—which rests upon having determined the right keystone Characteristic; but most of all on the *"what it is" of the keystone word of the topic* and designing the right Source and credibility of that Source. *Antithetical* denotes deliberate staging of Opposite or Contrary ideas, judgements, opinions for the sake of emphasis or clarification. In Hegel's Dialectic, the interaction or struggle between the Thesis and Antithesis ideally produces a new idea (thought or condition) that combines elements from others, known as the Synthesis (a mosaic). Once established, the Synthesis becomes the Thesis for a new cycle until everything is realized in the infinite Synthesis of Absolute Spirit. Each resulting level of consciousness includes its predecessors—like building a brick wall. But the first problem is with defining "Synthesis" and its ingredients.

THESIS FALLACIES: A thesis is a position one advances by means of an argument in which a particular view of a subject is set forth with supporting evidence (e.g. a master's thesis). In Logic, a thesis is equated with a conclusion. The Fallacy of Irrelevant Thesis is an argument in which an attempt is made to prove a conclusion that is not the one at issue. It assumes an argument that while seeming to refute another's argument, actually advances a conclusion different from the one at issue in the other's argument.

THEOLOGY: Europeans say the systematic exposition of humans' 'knowledge' of God is the science of *Theology* (Greek, 'god' or study of divine things) and is of two sorts: Group I is *Natural 'Knowledge*,' obtained by ordinary processes of observation and reasoning--the work of philosophers. Group II is *Supernatural 'Knowledge*.' Group I says religion has a purely natural origin, making it no different from philosophy and science as an element of culture. Perhaps a reason why European scientists and psychics tend to avoid the word "Supernatural" (above or beyond Nature) is it implies phenomena exists in which Nature's laws are broken. To deny psychic phenomena defy Nature's laws is to put this concept in *Paranormal* realms ('beside' or parallel to the familiar Natural laws), but not beyond or above them--the study of *Parapsychology*. They say the Supernatural is the domain of the miraculous, fantasizing the intervention of Supernatural Beings. Some accept a spiritual dimension to Reality, with laws of Nature applying to spiritual forces of which European physical science is unfamiliar. A reason for their confusion is by defining the "*Natural*" as that which is due or owed to the essence, requirements, powers, and merits of created Nature--which makes no sense. The more curious speculate that although the Supernatural is above and beyond the realm of sense experience, still behind the world of ordinary, everyday experience is the Spiritual realm transcending Nature's powers or what natural causes cannot produce. Otherwise, they continue, it is an illusion to suppose faith is God's gift rather than man's own will to believe. This means to the "faith" oriented that his critics lack the faith gift. Also, the Supernatural makes redemption possible. Group II's *Supernatural "Knowledge"* is in the sense of their religions having a Supernatural foundation derived from their own concepts of divine revelation, in God's authority, and on having Faith, as outlined by theologians seeking to understand this Faith. Such understanding concerns the deeper aspects of ones religious creed, acts of piety and worship, recourse to prayer, the partaking of sacraments, the observances of certain rituals, the performance of sacrifices and purifications, obeying God's commandments, and leading a life which shall seem worthy to God. They consider their religion, based on their faith, to have a Supernatural foundation in God's revelation and authority. In Christian theology the *Supernatural is the realm of the infinite, eternal Spirit, God* (??) who reveals his nature and purpose to humans in a special manner. Catholics say that while humans have no claim on Supernatural things and do not need them in order to exist and act on a natural level, they do need them in order to exist and act in the higher order or economy of grace established by God for their salvation. Group III, a combination of Groups I and II, opines the root of religion is man's immediate sense of the Supernatural, "an intuition of reality--an intercourse between a universe, present always in all its meaning, and a spirit, responding with all its understanding." This is about a larger environment, which has its own particular sanctions, through commerce with which man receives his characteristically human degree of independence within his natural environment. Intra-Group disputes over each of these issues has fashioned unimaginable conceptual chaos in Western tradition's plurality of religions + incredible numbers of varied religious foundation beliefs regarding revelations, miracles, and prophecies--stemming from the source (e.g. man-made, the Supernatural)--disagreeing on methods for "proof" and what rules apply to being right. There is great disagreement on the best way to worship, conform to rites, or be inspired. Amazingly, despite their own in-group religious confusion, conflicts, and chaos--and while knowing little about what they believe--Europeans stay on top of criticizing others without knowing anything about it. Any religion differing from theirs is labeled with such epithets as Idolatrous, Superstitious, Heretical, and Schismatic. Also, most foolishly join to condemn the superior African Tradition Spirituality as "Pagan." Critical Thinking needs to have the 'big picture' of all of these religious aspects for making sound assessments of opinions and for asking proponents: *How do you know that?*

"THE RACK: *"The Rack"*--an oblong wooden frame with rollers at each end. Such Ordeal practices applied to Enslaved African Americans "Seasoned" them into making them fearfully fit for use—with the aim being to fashion "Ideal Slaves." Any "spirited" Slaves had their ankles bound to one roller and the wrists to the other. The rollers were then turned by a windlass (similar to a fishing reel)—being terribly painfully twisted and stretched until victims' confessed or had their joints pulled from their sockets and died. It was essential for all of the plantation Slaves to witness this for purposes of "killing their Spirits"—and particularly Black males whom the captors so envied.

"THE WAY" FOR RE-YOKING: "The Way" of African Tradition concerns following the Divine Presence and its Ma'at powers of manifestation from Earth World living to the Heaven "Afterlife". The Ma'at System is the *Divine Logos--i.e. God's Universal Reason—i.e. God's Thought and Creative Utterance and Power—i.e. "The Word" of God* which consists of *Germ Plasm* called Androgynic Plast. "The Word" is a continuous flow of vibratory Unconditional Love, Truth, Reality, and the Natural. These four Spiritual Elements are moving Essences within a Living Force which pervades the whole universe—continuing in a Circle of Integrity forever. Situated inside this Wholistic Circle is the realization that all God's creatures and creations—despite the "Uniqueness" of each—possess a Spiritual "Sameness," regardless of how remote in time or space. The Synthesis of these aspects into "Wholism" happens because all of God's creatures and creations have a place--and each is in its proper place--and each is essential to the Integrity of the whole. Together they become elevated into the highest plane of existence of which the human mind is capable of perceiving. The Ancient African master of all Earthly masters, Tehuti, said: "God is a circle whose circumference is nowhere and whose center is everywhere." This is because the Substance of God is within every real Thing. Considering all things of the universe to be like "circles within circles," he said God creates eternity; eternity creates the cosmos; the cosmos, time; and time, generation. Also, everything within the Wholistic Circle has to be accounted for since every part is significant and works together (Asante, Egyptian Philosophy p1, 4). The Circle's *Metaphysics* (Spiritual Energy concepts) and Philosophy (i.e. interconnectedness, interdependence, interrelatedness, and synthesis) prevail in all human ideas and acts. That blending is part of the Law of Sympathy. Within the Wholism Circle and imparted by the Cosmic Force, the Amenta, the Nun (potential possibilities for unrealized reality objects), and *Spiritual Hope* (i.e. existing un-realized realities) possess *Immaterial Reality/Truths* pertaining to "the heavens." They are of a timeless, eternal, and unchanging reality nature—which, when adhered to, Ancient Africans called "The Way". This concept was borrowed by ancient Eastern cultures (e.g. Buddhists).

Africans living within the flow of "The Way" were deemed to be "Wise" because of them apparently "Knowing The Way." Otherwise, Ancient Africans said that people are born ignorant and thereafter learn *Illusions* (seeing what is not there and not seeing what is there), *Delusions* (believing what is not real and not believing what is real), and "Things" that take them further away from the Truth. They said that "As we believe, so we act. As we act, so goes our destiny and Ari (i.e. Karma)" (Amen, Metu Neter I:143). Thus, before being able to get on to the road to Wisdom ones Belief System must be refashioned so as to conform to the indwelling intelligence present with ones Real Self—i.e. reshaping in light of the identification with the indwelling "Soul Sunshine" Intelligence at the center of ones mental and bodily processes. Part of the process is about removing impediments of wrong beliefs rather than evolving into Knowledge. This Ancient African Concept is termed "*Opening of the Way*" (Egyptian, Ap-Uat of the Pyramid Text—Pyramid of Unas I. 187). The Up-uat is depicted in the form of a wolf, but Anubis and Up-uat are often confounded in funery scenes because of having some connection with the funereal world (Budge, Book of the Dead p 182).

Ways of removing barriers to ones Real Self have been discussed in my book on: Selfhood Mastery. Briefly, reclaiming "The Way" is through three stages: (1) undergoing a *Mystical Death* of ones False Self; (2) proceeding into a *Spiritual Transformation*-- e.g. recognizing the Dignity (God's image) within all beings and having compassion for their pain and suffering, even if you detest what they do because they are one of God's creatures to which you are spiritually related; and (3) emerging into a *Rebirth*-- into knowing what Love really is and how to spread it is in order to do the most good—for the most people—over the longest period of time. Such harmonious balance constitutes the *Inner Self Stability Platform* from which all choices, decisions, creations, and solutions spring forth. In short, the "Way" is a symbol for ones beliefs and ideas as conduits of the course of ones life. The Truth—The Way—is a living, ongoing experience that is above human's ability to put into words.

"**THE WORD**": *The Word*" from the Cosmic Spiritual Force, Sekhem, is *itself the Divine Presence, its power, and its manifestation expressed as Vibrations.*

THE "WORD'S"REVELATION: The concept for the C14 word "Reveal" (to unveil it) originated with Ancient African Sages saying that the reshaping of ones Belief System into the light of the identification with the Cosmic Intelligence and to ones own indwelling intelligence that are at the center of all Mental and Bodily processes is called the Opening of the Way. One does not learn how to grow spiritually but rather by removing the "Clouds" over ones Soul's Divine Spark, which I call "Soul Sunshine." Those impeding Clouds shut out ones full Divine Essence manifestations which characterized ones Highest (Divine) Self. The "Way" opens by stepping behind ones Beliefs, Assumptions, labels, definitions, Emotional Junk to have a direct experience of Reality—an experience called Knowledge in African Tradition. Humans can only be Receivers of Cosmological Revelations and Ancient African Sages did this by means of Intuiting the Will of God. Revelations are by means of Symbols and, in spite of not being authoritative on their own, the Symbols are sufficiently suggestive to *Symbols touch and awaken the Truths already present in a human's Soul*. If the mind is pre-occupied and antagonistic, the new Truth will not be aroused in ones mind. Of course, Cosmic Knowledge pre-existed humans but African Sages realized it was by means of Revelations of the Un-Seeable Cosmic Mind that manifestations of Knowledge can be known. Such is the way the African Sage Tehuti derived his wisdom. A specific recording (Freke, The Hermetica, p35; Chandler, Ancient Future p55) in the beginning of "Poimandres" (the Vision of Hermes) is that the African Sage Tehuti derived his Wisdom by intuiting God's Will from a dramatic mystical revelation while searching for Divine Truth. In seeking solitude and coming to a place of rest, he gave himself over to meditation. With an alert mind, yet still and empty, he hears God speaking to him. After asking to be shown the true nature of reality, suddenly everything begins to change before him—meaning that Tehuti witnesses the creation of the world. Revealed to Tehuti was that which embodied the Word of God and Natural Laws. An example is that the Physical world being temporal and what first exists in the Spiritual is later manifest in the Physical and both must be pursued together since they represent the Whole Unit of Cosmic *Circumstances-Correspondence*. By the Spiritual and the Material being interwoven, the underlying theme flowing throughout the Cosmos is that what is above parallels what is below—i.e. the *Law of Correspondence*. This vision was not meant to be understood intellectually but rather contemplated like images from a dream. Examples of other Revelations to Africans Sages are first, there are many planes of Cosmic Existence on which Truth exists, but all being in Correspondence. Second, the Esoteric "Secrets" concerned revelations to which Very Ancient African priests were exposed but, up to that point, had not fully realized—i.e. revelations about *the inner meaning of external appearances being the Same* of whatever was related to sacred aspects of the Cosmos. Third, the Cosmos originated from "the Other World" -- the Amenta -- the Ultimate plane of existence, Reality, and Truth. Out of it forms the *Subjective Plane* (i.e. the Ocean of Nun). The Amenta and the Nun (potential possibilities for unrealized Reality objects) possess *Immaterial Reality/Truths* pertaining to "The Heavens." They are of a timeless, eternal, and unchanging reality nature—which Ancient Africans called "The Way" of the Cosmos, a concept borrowed by ancient Eastern cultures (e.g. Buddhists). From compatible Direct Knowledge, Sages used astro-mathematical calculations to derived Circumstantial Knowledge. This means these *Circumstances-Correspondence* insights paved the way to explain Esoteric Un-Knowns in Un-Seeable realms. From these Revelations and derived Laws—each verifying the other--Ancient African Sages formulated the Spiritual Elements of Unconditional Love, Truth, Reality, and the Natural.

One of the revelations was that the Supreme Being had to establish Law as the foundation of creative acts and a plan that can be mathematically assessed. Resultant interpretations guided African Sages' Subjective Science tools and Astro-Mathematics into conclusions used to make *Spiritual Inferences to arrive at Circumstantial Evidence* and judgments. These, in turn, verified African Sages' Revelations so as to arrive at Circumstantial Truths about Laws of Natures and concepts of God. Also, they concluded that God--the only Life which exists entirely in itself, from itself, and by itself is an Unknowable Life—the Absolute--"The All". The Absolute equates to God by residing within itself—wholly without change or variation. The "One" is God's inner nature of Unconditional Love. The "All" represents God's outer nature of Life—that part of Divine Life which discloses itself—appears or becomes visible—through its manifestations in the Cosmos. From these Revelations and derived Laws—each verifying the other--Ancient African Sages formulated the Spiritual Elements of

Unconditional Love, Truth, Reality, and the Natural. Using their *Subjective Sciences* as well as their *Objective Science* (which Ancient Africans formalized, between 2000 and 1500 BCE, into today's recognized Scientific Method), African Mathematics led to the conclusion that the "Oneness" of Cosmic Origin in the Spiritual realm is the basis of *Order* throughout the Cosmos. According to Tehuti's Revelation, the Ocean of Nun is *to make all God's creatures and creations in a manner of each Involuting back into itself again*. The ultimate purpose is to return again by Evolution after having accomplished the Mission for which they existed. That Mission for every human is for the growth and exaltation of the myriad Souls of Humanity. So, in the beginning out of the "Other World"—the Amenta--flowed the Ocean of Nun, from which all designated for the Phenomenal Universe would evolve. From the Universal Principle of Mind—i.e. the Great Ocean of "Mind-Stuff"--there is a "raying out" of all the Laws of Nature, all Qualities, all Potencies, and all Prototypes required for the Cosmos. Meanwhile, there first proceeded the Universal Principle of Spiritual Energy or Force and from that Energy, came the Principle of Matter in its disorganized, motionless state. The Laws of Nature compelled the Causes of the Great Involution (to wrap up; to cover; to hide; rolled up on itself). This involved the Spirit instituting Evolution to allow expression of all that came out of the "Mind-Stuff". Hence, the Spirit activated Intangible flimsy matter which, in turn, became increasingly more and more gross—like a snowball rolling down a hill and getting bigger and bigger. At Involution's grossest point, a moment's pause occurred in its spiral curving. This was followed by a reversal into Cosmic *Evolution.* Thereafter, the grossest forms of Matter began pairing down into refined forms while entering outer space.

"THE WORD" & WORDS ASSESSMENTS: Because Tehuti's divine revelation, which embodied the Word of God and Natural Laws, was verified as true by Subjective and Objective Sciences as well as by Correspondence, African Sages deemed Tehuti interpreter of all that was divine and the conveyor of the *"Word of God"*--meaning related to processes of thought and speech and thereby to divine wisdom by means of a system of Symbols. This Ancient African sacred language is called the *Medu-Netru.* Tehuti has long been known as the 'teachers' teacher--the mediator, the one who sees the 'big picture' and finds a solution for every problem. The beginning of his teachings was centered on the *"love of truth and the hatred of abomination."* He crystallized the kernel of the true meaning of Wisdom by saying the will of humans must be directed by God (Amen, Metu Neter I:159). Put another way, although non-Africans thought of *"the Word"* in physical, concrete terms, the words of Tehuti were related to the process of thought and speech and thereby to divine Wisdom. Its origin and process of progress is through vibrations--the means by which ones mind creates thoughts compatible with the Cosmic Mind as well as the means by which the Cosmic Mind (God) brings into being and sustains Creation. Despite European religious authorities saying the "Word of God" was revealed to their writers, the history of their Bible does not bear this out. This is because a Revelation is Symbolic Communication from the Cosmic Mind to the human Soul which imparts Truths of the invisible Cosmic aspects. Revelations so not and cannot arise from a human because it is self-evident that humans are incapable of composing Revelations of Cosmical beginnings and their natures. The nonsense of the meddling scribes has come from them altering the Symbolic Language of their interpretations from the Ancient African Bible and then introducing interpolations of what is unalterable so as to be in accord with their own Ignorance. No Revelation can be adequately given by the address of one human to another—whether by writing or orally, even if the conveyor be put in possession of thoughtfully derived Truth itself. This is because the words used are merely like coins of an intellectual exchange. There is as little resemblance between the silver coin and the bread it purchases as between the words used and the things they stand for. Just as looking at the coin for the first time does not bring to mind the form of the bread, listening to the words do not give rise to the idea for which it stands, unless one is already in possession of it. The Truth of something must be felt.

Another example is the African Divine Logos concept is to be distinguished from *Logos* as defined by Europeans—i.e. the synergetic art involving the process of unifying ideas and forms within a single meaning. Pay careful attention to the vast difference Europeans have given this for it illustrates clearly why European definitions are never to be used for African concepts.

THINK: ("it seems"; "it appears") causing Images or Reflections to appear to oneself in ones brain.

THINKER'S SCALE/"T"-SCALE CONCEPT: A special creation of two Thought Pattern Tools are used here—i.e. The "T"-Scale with its vertical limb being the Thinker's Scale. The "T"-SCALE CONCEPT embraces Knowledge (on the Horizontal line) vs. Information (on the Vertical Line) by dealing respectively with the differences and relations of the Absolute/Relative, the Spiritual/Worldly, and the Constant/Change aspects. The *"T" Scale's* horizontal line also symbolizes the Divine (Absolute), Spiritual. The *"T" Scale's* vertical line represents the Secular—the best and worst of the Informational Relative, its Matter of the World orientation, its Judgments of what is and is not "Scarce Desirables," and that of Change. The *"T" Scale's* junction of the horizontal and the vertical line signifies the Metaphysical—Knowledge explained by Information. The "THINKER'S SCALE CONCEPT" is a positive and negative ruler separated by a Zero. It is useful for assessing pros/cons, advantages/disadvantages of anything and their degrees. Something constructive or destructive may be mildly, slightly, moderately, or extremely so. On the Positive Scale: Mild ranges from 1 to 24; Slight, from 25 to 49; Moderate, from 50 to 74; and Extreme, from 75 to 100. These numbers correspond on the negative scale but signify something bad, threatening, disturbing, or destructive. See T-Scale

THINKING COMPONENTS CATEGORIES: *"Think"* ("it seems"; "it appears") originates with *Mental Imagery* production since it is a first and natural display of the human mind before it develops the ability to do abstract thinking. When "like-kind" memories (*Apperceptions*) are called up, it is termed an *Image* (an Imagination form or figure with 'character' and power). *Image is a sort of pictorial representation in ones mind of a specific event or object which shows the 'highlights' of the original.* Some are *"Metaphysical Notions"* (about complex things)—called *Abstracts* if drawn out of the Metaphysical or *Abstractions* if drawn out of Physical Realms. Abstract or Abstraction vivid Images (like a bouquet of different colored flowers) spur sentiment reflections that strengthen/enlarge upon the intended meaning that can be Pre-Verbal (i.e. Emotions) or Verbal (statements). In other words, anything about which a notion (half-formed idea) could be formed around a meaning related to the Un-seeable, leads to the creation of "handles" called Idea or Thought Symbols and Images. Obviously, the notion would have no relation to Matter and no proper location in time and space. For example, one might have a notion of a good spirit in the Supernatural realm possessing an amorphous form and no features. The point is that Notions, Ideas, or Thought contain some percentage of Emotions. These *Emotions are invoked—not by the situations in which one is in or with which one is interacting—but by the Images associated with them.* Such Images are then *collected to form imagery; next, the imagery is extended into thought patterns; and finally, the thought patterns are extended into various types of activity. A Symbol is a more abstract unit of thought than Images* and may have a number of meanings.

THINKING CRITICALLY: In African Tradition, *Critical Thinking* (CT) applies both to the Process of Nature as well as Intellect devised processes of Reasoning for the purposes of: (1) determining what is and is not part of the Spiritual Elements; (2) helping to evolve what is in the Spiritual Elements flow; (3) quashing (to overthrow or make void) what is not real or is anti-Spiritual Elements oriented; (4) ever-looking to create, enhance, and maintain harmony; (5) protect and defend against any disharmony in preparation to go on the offense with the least amount of harm to all concerned; (6) detect whatever is preventing harmony; and (7) figure out ways to get around any losses, lacks, and/or obstructions keeping one from going "straight ahead." The Essences and Principles of gathered materials which qualitatively address the Spiritual and Metaphysical realms are then presented in a carefully organized flow of the Spiritual Elements. Scholars can make any subject great by steering CT into following pertinent natural processes of Nature. What this does is to show new ideas, information, or knowledge amid appearances as well as the way to become acquainted with patterns of the "impossible" by having insight into what has already happened in Nature's Processes.

THINKING INSIDE NATURE'S PROCESSES: Nature is imaged by the human mind to be configured into *an underlying web of relationships operating* throughout the Cosmos. Nature consists, *on all planes of existence,* of a *complexity and multiplicity of Patterns*—some reproducible; others being new creations from moment to moment, like foams in ocean waves. Yet, the *Unification of these relationships and patterns make for* an infinite *Continuity and Harmony.* Humans' *work of Spirituality is the subjection of their minds to the Divine Spirit so it can command the Life-Force in harmony with the Laws of Nature.* When that is done and maintained, then human's *most primitive unit of thought is the Virtual Image derived from their Divine Consciousness.* The subsequent development of that Virtual Image into a Thought means one has the Spiritual Elements attributes to draw on within the context of Ma'at Principles inside the Cosmic Wholism—those responsible for Nature's Patterns. Thus, to thoroughly understand one of Nature's Patterns—or a piece of one--gives insight into the Esoteric (Unknown) Cosmic Circle of Things.

Such occurs since they all possess the same Spiritual Elements "Genetic Harmony" wherever located within the Cosmic Organism Web. Hence, even though each Entity is "Unique," *being part of the Cosmic Web gives each Correspondence* with every other part of the Cosmic Circle of Wholeness. From operating by Ma'at Principles and Laws, all Knowledge of it is very few in number. To see all of these aspects together in their web-like interrelationships enables one to become aware of links connecting and meshing the Uniqueness of each member into the inner nature Sameness that makes up the Cosmic Family. *Seeing these links and arranging/rearranging and/or combining/recombining is Creativity.* These Correspondence Processes, designated "*Circumstantial,*" by being in Nature, they exist "all over" at once—in the Seeable and Un-seeable. Thus, no part can be reasoned by direct demonstrations.

THINKING COMPARTMENTALIZED: Eastern teachers, following the path of Ancient Africans, encourage students to find out things for themselves, no matter how long it takes or how hard or how boring. In the process, one learns to focus on a thing for prolonged periods. Because there is so much to know about an important subject, when students stop focusing on one aspect concerning that subject they shift to another compartment of that same subject. However, Western world authorities "spoon-feed" so as to control the people. Thus their information discourages independent or critical thought or creative actions; generates delusions; and its "flashing lights" nature makes it enchanting and keeps one in a passive or trivia oriented mindset. Thus, one skips from one compartment to another in a manner that conforms to multi-tasking. When overdone one "shuts off" thinking of what one is doing in the moment while engaging in "Automatic Pilot" talking. It is this situation of lacking awareness of the surroundings that accounts for why many females are easy to attack while walking down the street. As a boy, not knowing about *the unity of all Reality* caused me to see the problems of life as endless in variety and number. The resolution of being so overwhelmed came from realizing there are only a few problem categories which can be analogized to a six-pack of sodas. Names for the cans are losses, lacks, obstructions, opposition, personal difficulties, and relationship problems. Similarly, each way of thought for handling these problems can be analogized as compartmentalized slots in a case of water bottles. In the *Organized Slot Thinking* one divides and shifts ones attention among tasks while emphasizing focus on what is most important. An analogy for *Unorganized* types is a television station's Master Control room, the technical hub of a broadcast operation. If it has 20 television monitors, undisciplined minds may have the same program on the 20 television monitors in their brains when they should be paying attention to life challenging problems. This means they are not dividing and shifting their attention but rather staying focused on what is not the most important. By contrast, scattered attention occurs from their multi-tasking during times when Critical Thinking (CT) is required. Perhaps their CT focus is on only one monitor and the rest on the 19 monitors presenting Attractive Distractions. Such is illustrated by teenagers driving a car and managing electronic tasks. Teens may be good with those tasks but most are not good at separating them and keeping their eyes on the road. The reason is the human brain develops from back to front and the last region to be completed is the prefrontal cortex where important task decisions are made. Adults have the fore-sight and forethought to keep looking back at the road. Whereas all of the required brain "wiring" is not fully connected until one reaches the early 20s, the negative emotions associated with Traumatized Thinking (TT) simply overwhelm the reasoning part of the brain. Thus, TT fails to accept the personal mental powers they know they possess and even forget they have the power to take charge and control of their lives. TT adversely affects perception of how things really are and that causes poor judgment. *TT is continually involved in viewing all the separate "television" programs at once and that keeps their minds in a chaotic state* which, of course, prevents the managing of even any mildly complex problem. Thus, they are easily led by incompetent and often evil intentioned people. If self-help is not feasible, then outside help is needed in establishing rules to follow and ensuring those rules are followed. First, break the habit of "Switching off" thinking, emotional thinking, and doing things impulsively or out of habit. Second, practice focusing at every chance, as in counting ones breath. Third, *think about every little thing one does and determine why it is done.* Fourth, handle serious business with (guided) CT or the best CT one has available, for "practice makes perfect".

THINKING--SUPERNATURALS' NON-RATIONAL: Ancient Africans were masters in perfecting the use of their entire Brain, but having the Right Brain orchestrate all of it. This is because the Right Brain tends to see the "Big Picture" of a situation and search in what underlies the Obvious for the "What it is." When parts and phases are seen from the perspective of the whole, one is better able to see the complementary relationships of the ingredients involved, despite having different appearances otherwise. The resultant Understanding of the Primary Qualities that separate parts of the whole and maintain their individuality and yet are interdependent in making for wholism is why Ancient Africans focused on Principles of Essences. Such Principles because to see any shared aspects having Correspondence gave insight into what was part of the same Web but not visible. Verification comes from *Living in Truth*—and that can only be done by being consistent in the observance of the Spiritual Laws at each and every crossroad situation. By contrast, Supernaturals prefer their Left Brains as almost exclusive but within the setting of biased and prejudiced thoughts wrapped in acquired emotions so as to be directed to specific things. Instead of Cosmic Principles or even seeing the Secular "big picture," they prefer only "Examples" into which they see or fashion the differences that the Left Brain promotes. Those differences are converted into antagonistic relationships that are assessed by their Indifference/Hate/Evil/Sadism (IHES) complex and form compatible conclusions. But the reason why *Syllogistic or Cartesian logic cannot give insight into the Truth of premises is its inability to establish logical connections between parts and the whole* to which they belong (Amen, Metu Neter I:254-5). This is because it only deals with the outer form of things, as is evidenced by their spotlighting of different cultures' skin color. By being willfully ignorant of the Spiritual Elements, they do not know Truth, not know how to get to Truth, and uninterested in learning Truth. Besides, Truth is not appealing to Supernaturals because whereas they are geared to "Excitement"—like little children. This is profoundly important because the Crowds' mind has been programmed to believe that unless an idea has emotional or sensual force behind it, it should not, or cannot be carried out. When confronted with what they say that does not make sense, they immediately withdraw into the defense mechanism cliché: "what you don't know can't hurt you". The consequence of this position being one can never know the whole mystery of

Beauty or the sweetness of solitude or the profoundness of Thought is not an issue for them since they have no idea what the inner world realm of "ME/WE" mental activity is about. By choosing to be a Supernatural slides them into an alien False Self. The switch out of ones Divine Private "Self" and Conscience in order to live life out of ones External World Personality is like being in a mental cage. That new and independent Public Self Personality, now wrongly accepted as ones "Self-Identity," is "locked" into dealing with ones Lower (animalistic) Self. In that mindset of one failing to realize one is able to ignore all emotional and sensual impulses, one is a slave to them.

Others are so insecure and feel so inadequate as to seek to cultivate the Lower Self fetters oriented to "me, me, me." Either way, one is then unable to awaken, or even to transcend back to ones Real Self, in order to tap into ones Genius' infinite potential. Thus, Supernatural leaders stress that the *Principle way of living is by the "Good Life"—i.e. one of Convenience*—one of hedonistic pleasure-seeking, un-tempered by moral restraints or ethics which come from religion. Thus, corruption and greed degrades the moral structure of the people, as with Individualism, seeking the "high-living" self-gratification (Ashby, African p247). This shows as being irresponsible, having no Accountability, and attacking any who are "against a materialistic Good life". As a compromise with their religion, they apply "Flexible Morals"—being amoral when it is in their self-interest; showing pettiness to others not like time most of the time, and evolving into "*Righteous Indignation*" for those even rumored to do what they do. *When ones mind is in flexible morals' foundational chaos, one is self-absorbed and rationalize dishonorable acts.* An example of putting virtues aside is in promising to pay back a loan from a rich person and then not doing so because "the rich can afford it." Ensuring their mental activities stay superficial is a way to keep doing what *brings "Escapes."* These instabilities of mindset manifest as Inconsistencies in behaviors.

THOUGHT DEVELOPMENT: Thinking in African Tradition models the Processes of Nature. It begins with the Spiritual Elements. It expands by the Spiritual Elements forming an Interchange formation. That Interchange produces mosaic pieces which, according to the Divine Plan, go into various arrangements and combinations. All of this is powered by an unending Creativity and proceeds to produce Creatures and Creations according to Mathematical Order. The mosaic patterns are Virtual Images and those that descend from the Spiritual realm enter the Metaphysical where Matter is added. Such is the pattern of Thinking. The Spiritual Elements—the 4 Cosmic Essences originally formed out of God's Androgynic plast--constitute the "Genetics" for all of God' Creations and Creatures. Thus, each Cosmic Essence has Spiritual and Matter as well as Feminine/Masculine ingredients as part of its primeval Substance. Each of these ingredients is a Principle. Human Genetics are a microcosm of the Cosmic Genetics. To repeat, a human mother's egg is fertilized by the father's sperm so as to produce *Virtual Identical (monozygotic) Twins*. Although the sperm has 23 and the egg has 23 Chromosomes, note the important concept of both *twins having Uniqueness despite their "Sameness" Genetics*--the equivalent of the entire Cosmic Organism originating from God's Androgynic plast.

THOUGHT INGREDIENTS: To give a gist overview, the story of any Entity on any plane of existence begins when it comes into Being. It possesses God's Substance as its Essence. That Essence imparts a "what it is" Self-Identity (with its "What" and "Why" Message for humans) or "Thing-Identity" (with its Divine Plan assignments for non-humans). That Essence contains *Properties* (what a thing has) consisting of: (1) *Endowments* and *Propensities*; (2) a Character; (3) *Essentials of Characteristics, Traits, and Features*; and (4) a *Disposition* with its "What" and "Why" Message received from its Source + an Inclination + an Intention + a Temperament + an Attitude. The fully realized form of an Essence, called its *Pattern*, possesses an Image on the outside and a Matrix (womb bringing nourishment to the offspring) on the inside. The *Nature* of the Embryonic Entity consists of its Essence + Character. On the inside, the Character is controlled by the Genetics of which the Essence is composed and carries the "what it does" potential for *the proper acts or operations of its Earthly Substance or Essence when it came into Being.* The Activity Networks of that Character are in the pre-birth *Matrix* (or *Womb*--the nourisher of the Substance's creation) of the Entity's Essence Pattern. On the outside of the Pattern is a Virtual Image. That Image's *Shape* (a pattern of energy movement frozen in space) possesses a specific power given to it by its Nature. The Nature of the Essence's Endowments and Propensities are orchestrated by the Disposition. The Essentials *of Characteristics, Traits, and Features* give the Entity a "Trademarked" Individuality and its "how it appears" display is made known by and in the form of its Pattern's Image. The *Properties* (what an Entity's Essence has)—the Endowments and Propensities--are in an Interchange configuration. Since the Interchange is the core of the Essence—which Ancient Africans called the *"That" of the Thing*—what generates all of the Thing's active and passive Qualities is the "That's" underlying "Eye"—like the 'happenings' which occur within the "Eye" of a storm. Inside that Interchange *the proper acts or operations of its Substance or Essence when it came into Being* generate Mosaics out of the Endowments and Propensities. Next, what buds out of that Interchange is a new Quality Form. A given Form may be one or more *Characteristics, Traits, or Features* which highlights and enhances the Trademark Identity. Then, after birth, the Entity is modified by *"Nurture"*--something that nourishes in the act of its cultivation and rearing into maturity. The type of "Nurture" depends upon the Essence put into the Entity by its Source--whether Spiritual (by God), Metaphysical (e.g. by Sages or their equivalents), or Supernatural (by constructive or destructive human mindsets). This Nurture Source determines the kind and degree of alterations of the Entity' pre-birth "What it is," its pre-birth "What it Does," and/or its pre-birth "How it Appears." The mature organism is a combination of Nature (its Essence + Character) and varying degrees of Nurture (i.e. the sum Effects of environmental influences and conditions acting on an organism). The *Source* of the Cause, the Nature Causation aspects (its "what it is" Essence), and the Effects (the potential operations) arising out of the Cause can remain as is when it came into Being—can be distorted or might be modified beyond its natural Identity. Which of these occur and to what degree of distortion or modification by additions of Nurture are what fashion Consequences pertaining to deviations from its naturally developing "What it Does" and "How it Appears". While the Essence that generates the basic "What it Does" aspects of a Thing when it came into Being is part of Knowledge concerning its "What it is," the "Nurture" part is not. Thus, to see and comment on the Thing's over-all Result is Information because "Nurture" brings in variability and changeability. In personal practical application, over-time, my associated thoughts led me to discern things so numerous and important that they required "classifying." The resultant organization sharpened my focus and its penetration into "Impossible" problems. Gradually, I came to realize that the star of the hidden part of any "Impossible" problem is its Infra-structure, followed by its Foundational Base. This Base/ "Seed" Principle (the setting of the Tree concept) has *Holonomy* features -- i.e. the whole is inside the Seed; the whole is contained in each of the Seed's manifested parts; and the Seed is found throughout the whole. Thus, anything which comes out of a Spiritual Seed (i.e. composed of the Spiritual Elements) -- like Roots, Trunk (or Vines), Branches, Leaves, and Fruit will have Correspondence. This is fundamental to understand in dealing with *"Viable Impossible"* problems of an Organism nature. However, the concept is also applicable to Mechanical (Greek, machine) Structures or to "hybrids."

THOUGHT ORIGINAL FORMATION: With respect to any given Virtual human, that human's Soul Sunshine comes into being as a first and original happening prior to birth into the Earth World. This is a process of *Instructing* ("to build in or into") the human Cosmic Principles—called *First Knowledge or First Wisdom*—so as to assist in self-protective and thriving learning in the Earth World. When the Chromosomes meet to begin a zygote (yoking or joining together), the genes undergo a synthesis process, likened to shuffling a pack of cards. Despite having the same Spiritual Elements Essence, the "Genetics" dynamics inside each Cell differs in combination and arrangement. That explains why people's Talents and Individuality are "Unique" and yet they have the "Same" Human Nature aspects. Like the processes done with the pertinent material, the shuffled Genes are arranged in many different ways, dealing each brother and sister [or Option possibility] a different "hand". Note that the zygote has the same genetic material of the parents but it is synthesized in different amounts, different combinations, and different arrangements to creates a new Virtual individual [or Option possibility]. Many traits are even further synthesized by more than one pair of genes from each parent, as in designating body size and resistance to certain diseases. Like any Option, these ingredients inside the Virtual + certain dominant features of the mother + certain dominant features of the father are present in the newborn and will breed true in his/her off-spring. Before the Virtual human twins separate, they move to opposite poles within *the same egg*—a situation called *Meiosis*—the equivalent of the Subjective Realm in which all the Cosmic Organisms reside. The same Meiosis is featured in the Cosmic Organism's humans, Animals, Plants, and Minerals --residing in the same Cosmic "Cell" prior to being born. Hence, even though each Entity is "Unique," *being part of the Cosmic Web gives each Correspondence* with every other part of the Cosmic Circle of Wholeness. Next, the egg splits--called *Mitosis*—to separate the Twins so as for each to struggle to survive on their own. As with all of God's Creatures and Creations destined to descend into Matter, each virtual Image moves into the Metaphysical to have added varying degrees of Matter. Such Cosmic Organism processes are like a human faced with a Problem, Situation, or Circumstance needing to be handled. Such Thinking begins with Information Gathering to acquire ingredients for an Idea— separating the pertinent from the non-pertinent and then putting the pertinent into prioritized order to fashion a "mental Skeleton"—the equivalent of an "Idea-Form" called a Percept. Thereafter, each twin or Entity has a customized and unique existence leading to an individualized Character and Personality. These products are the result of their different experiences in their different existences within the same womb, and then after birth. Each Cell--while moving through a human's life, an African Group's Spirit, or the African Diaspora throughout the Ages--is orchestrated by a spirit force apart from its DNA Essence. Thus, all *Genes in each Cell have a memory of where they came from.*

THOUGHTS' EARTH WORLD BIRTH: The Thought equivalent of this pre-birth process is like a Virtual Image Percept with beginning Matter that is the parent of a Thought. One is born with First Wisdom, consisting of all the Laws of Nature within ones Selfhood. "*Survival*"—a Lower Self's "First Law of Nature"— is about self-protecting and self-preserving of all in the Animal and Plant Kingdoms, independent of any other Entity. That equates to human's Critical Thinking. *Step I: Source.* There is a Cosmic Divine Source which operates independently of all else. It imparts, in a given human, a Divine Consciousness (Soul, Spark of God). That Divine Consciousness fashions a disposition message *(the What and Why of what is to be manifest)*. The nature of the *Substance*—so-called when from the Cosmic Mind or called *Essence* when inside the Cosmos--is its *Character*. That Character--as the orchestrator of the Essential within the Essence--is the Essence's displayed *Nature in a Thing*—the "*It is*"--the how each of its properties' operations manifest. The *Properties* consist of a Thing's *Endowments* (i.e. natural qualities--the "*That it is*") and *Propensities* (in-born tendencies, like a given human's capacities, abilities, and language). The most consistent Pattern(s) of the Operations of the Essentials in action is its *Trait(s)*. The most outstanding Trait(s) operation is its *Feature(s)*. The most outstanding Featured Trait of the Character is the Essence "*Trademark*." The *Traits and Features constitute the Characteristics* of the Essence. A human's Divine *Will* takes the Disposition with its message *(the What and Why)* from ones Divine Consciousness; arranges it into a Spiritual Virtual Image; and directs its powers in keeping with the Source's Disposition inclination and intension. When carried to completion by going through steps leading to Thoughts, is what brings about a human's Ma'at change. *Step II: Percepts.* In a human's *Evolution of a Thought,* it is somewhat like a beginning flower bud evolving into a mature flower. Its beginning seed may be either from the Inner World or from the External World. If the Seed is from the External World, there is the acquiring of sensory input as "raw materials". The presenting of those Sensations to the mind starts the process of Image formation called a *Percept*--the mental entity of organized Sensations to constitute a "Thing" when it comes into Being-hood--sensations making one aware of something good or bad (like a threat, disturbance in harmony, or atmosphere of danger). *Percepts are* sensations, similar to the ingredients for a flower bud, making one very faintly aware of something good or bad. The Percept's evolution into a beginning *Conceptual state*—a maturing Identity--is heralded by the *Implicit* (understood though not directly expressed). It consists of vague, hazy, organized Sensations molding ones mind into a sort of better awareness of what is contained or included, though not expressed, in the Sensation of the Percept. However, the Implicit is capable of being implied by inference and without being stated. *Stage III: Notion*. Further advancement of the Implicit is into a *Notion* –a recognizable "what it is"--an "*Entity*" with a specific nature hinting at the "Thing's" Identity and its specific attributes. The newly forming flower bud itself is a *Notion*--joined ideas and/or images with vague, hazy, organized Sensations—an "Idea-Form". Notion is a newly created organism which begins a thought and needs to be nourished past a half-formed Idea stage in order to possess the capacity to maintain its separate existence. If there are no interferences, there is evolving and further development into an "Idea". *Stage IV: Ideas* ('a becoming') are flower-bud like, with Images or Reflections appearing in ones brain. Its formation is contributed to by the *Imagination* faculty. An Idea: 1) is an awareness of specific, particular aspects--e.g. properties, characteristics, traits, features; 2) represents an *explicit* ('unfolded' into clarity) concept of "*Identity*"; 3) a patterned quantity of "frozen" energy; and 4) forces shaped into a defined "Thing"--the shape that imparts power.

Stage V: Concept Units. The Right and Left Brains form relationships with these like-kind things in Ideas—things like shapes or color or weight or size or atomic structure—with respect to the ingredients in the Idea. This makes for a *Common Ingredient Factor,* called a "Unit". That "*Unit*" has a Disposition from its Essence Source containing a *'payload' message* of the Essentials, orchestrated by the influences of the Essence, as *shared properties of* an *Inclination*, a *Temperament*, and an *Attitude*. Such a matured idea which forms a "Unit" is a Concept—a mature Idea component. *Stage VI: Thoughts*. Concepts are the building blocks of Thoughts. A Thought results from blending and weaving together all bits and pieces of mental Things. In the process, they undergo arranging/rearranging, and/or combining/recombining in order to arrive at a conclusion. An example of how two ideas can be arranged, or combined to form a relation is: "Titan is good". Here, "Titan" and "Good" combine to form a meaning and together they cause Images or Reflections to appear to oneself in ones brain and containing the Disposition of the Source. At that point, a Thought may or may not lead to Deeds.

THOUGHT DEVELOPMENT OF THE NUANCE FAMILY: This family's members include: Nuance, Subtlety (Subtilety), and "Discernment". Broadly, *Subtlety* (Subtilety) deals chiefly with nicety of discernment, discrimination of taste, acuteness of judgment. "*Discernment*" is lesser subtlety, meaning derivatively the ability to distinguish from. Whereas an *Umbra* is a complete and fully formed dark shadow, *Penumbra* are partial shadows outside the complete shadow, as that formed by the sun or moon during an eclipse. The Penumbra characterizes the essence of the meaning of *Nuance*--to show variations (slight differences) of shade, like a cloud. Decreasing Shade is removing tiny differences of darkness while increasing Shade is adding more layers of darkness. The differences between light and dark—or white and black—is the amount of Ether. African Tradition's concepts for the words Nuances, "*Subtle*" (Subtile), and Discernment concerns different layers of Ether (i.e. Matter) in relation to light and dark—or white and black. This starts with a Spiritual or Secular Essence when it came into Being—the "That it is." Stage I of Subtle came from the concept of the "Ether" at a beginning appearance stage equated to a quanta of energy and matter that constitutes the minimum amount needed for any potential physical entity to become involved in an interaction. Ether is the purest, most highly concentrated form of a nature or essence, it is the shiny, pure, upper air. In other words, Stage I of Ether—the "This-ness" is in the form of a subtle fluid of pre-matter consisting of a fine, flimsy, vapor mist of which "the Heavens," the lintel's (i.e. the Sublime) stars and planets, Nature, and natural laws are made. In the "That it is" (i.e. the Essence when it came into existence) undergoing a descent toward the Physical World—which Ancient Africans referred to it as "to move a Phantom"--it *Involutes* (processes of getting involved). Stage II Ether has a few layers which have involuted inside the beginning Metaphysical realms as to become a "That it is". Stage III Ether occurs when a "That it is" gains a few more layers of Ether and thereby becomes so fine or tenuous in quality or consistency as to be hard to perceive, detect, or be recognized. These are transferrable to Thought evolution.

The equivalents of an evolving Idea is that Stage II Subtle Ether is like a Percept and Stage III is like a Notion—both eluding proof because there is nothing to which they can be compared as well as there not being enough of a "what it is" for opinions to be formed. Still, a *Notion* formation has a sufficient quantity of Ether as for one to have an awareness of its specific nature. That awareness hints at its Identity by means of its specific attributes. To elaborate, a potential "*Awareness*" is knowing the existence of the "That it is" of a "Thing" when it came into Being-hood—i.e. its Primary Quality--but not knowing its Ether laden Metaphysical or Physical "what it is," "what it does," "how it appears," "how it is," "how it came about," or "where it is going." For the highly skilled, an actual Awareness might occur at the Percept stage. A Notion is an abstract imaged and hazy perception of something so as to constitute the earliest stages of a developing idea. It consists of a vague and partially formed Image —an Image in keeping with the Disposition of the "That it is". An example is the Disposition's Image which contains the Principle of "Chair-ness," the parent of all "chairs". When Stage IV Ether occurs and enters the Physical World, the evolving and further internally developing Percept/Notion is like the beginning flowering of a flower bud. That arising out of a Notion is called an "*Idea*" ('a becoming'). An Idea is an awareness of specific, particular aspects--e.g. properties, characteristics, traits, or features--which represent an explicit concept of "*Identity*." An *Idea* ('model'; form) is a patterned quantity of "frozen" energy whose forces are shaped into a defined "Thing"--the shape that imparts power. Stage V is like the flower that blooms--meaning a matured idea is the formation of a Concept. This Concept is the beginning exposure to ones Sensory Consciousness whereby it attracts Apperceptions. *Apperceptions* are the result of bringing together a mass of ideas already in the mind's Memory, concerning stored ideas, thoughts, and interpretations of experiences. They become "The Unit" (joined together) as a result of ingredients in the similarities/differences within the interactions of the Concept and Apperceptions meshing into sensible relationships. Inside this process of joining the Concept and Apperceptions, ones mind engages in *erasing boundaries* and *disregarding limitations of human thought* normally separating them. The effect of this interaction is the startling juxtaposition of unexpected items or themes in an atmosphere in which all ingredients are fashioned into unnatural combinations and arrangements of mental activity. From "distilling" mosaic pieces out of all involved, a sort of synthesis thereby forms a new perception or perhaps an Insight. Stage VI is putting the new Perception or Insight into action. As background, the Essentials of the "That it is" Essence enables the identifying markings in that Concept to be a new Perception or an Insight. This is because those markings consist of Mosaic pieces derived from the Interchange of its Essence parent—pieces assembled into an Icon Image. The Endowments and Propensities of the Essence with its Disposition's Principle together are its nature. The operations of that nature stand for the Unique "what it is" of its Essentials family and that is highlighted by the Essence's inherent Characteristic(s) so much so as to give it a distinctive Feature. Featured is *the Icon Image of the Essence* + *the "how it appears" of its Nature* + the Disposition's Message in a Principle form. That combination of the *Essence's Icon Image, with its Essence Message, constitutes the "payload" effect of the "That it is."*

Stage VII is the Fruiting of the Flower or not. That "Payload" can be ignored; can be generated into ones hazy Ideas to stay as is, or fade away; or can be cultivated into a Vivid Image that leads to good or bad thoughts, emotions, sensations, and physical actions. An example of the "Payload" impact is that of the Disposition's Principle of "Chair-ness," the parent of all "chairs." The Principle manifested by that Icon Image serves as a Prototype with totipotency allowing for creativity in the manifestations of that Disposition's Principle. The plan might now be to bring first one type of chair into reality for marketing and then another type. The differences in the types of chairs created may be the subtle or nuanced moves in one thing stored in the mood, ideas, thoughts, or interpretations of experiences in ones Memory into another space, point, depth, or plane of thought so as to create a new Perception or Insight. In other words, it is changing the degree of Ether in the thoughts evolution.

This also explains why people cannot see another's point of view—not sharing the same experiences. Some put the mosaic pieces of the same experiences in different arrangements and combinations or operating in different planes of existences or in entirely different worlds (e.g. the Supernatural vs. the Spiritual). This also applies to not being able to appreciate the same things or see Beauty the same way. Thus, one who does not agree are deemed to be "weird" or wrong. Some come to the same point from different directions and/or different levels, complicated by not seeing all the angles and sides. Some people do not think mathematically or poetically; some do not see things as they are; some wear different colored lens; some only see one side of the coin or part of only one side; some have knowledge but most have information; there are degrees of bad information in different categories—confusion, conflict, evil, incomplete, broad-stroke some think outside the Spiritual Elements; some disregard integrity and honorableness; some keep doing the same thing hoping for a different result. Look at Box in a unique way for each new problem, instead of thinking the same problem repeats itself—instead of appreciating its nuances and subtleties. Atmospheres and auras have nuances. A thought atmosphere is different from a hostile or congenial or loving. People cling to a bad way and follow the same pattern without seeing what extends beyond. In making a cake, to substitute a tomato for an egg gives a nuanced difference

THOUGHT ATMOSPHERE: Thought is a system of symbols that stands apart from Reality. *Thoughts are things* and can be seen (like an aura) by the true psychic sight and felt by the Sensitives. There are a variety of theories of what produces thoughts. Evolutionists have claimed the animal ancestors of man had already been thinking to some degree and that the greater responsibilities of humans fashioned specialization of one aspect of Feelings. African and later Eastern philosophers speculated that thoughts resulted from certain vibratory activities in the brain/mind. Western scientists propose that thoughts were placed in the mind from the brains' neuro-chemical mechanisms. Just as "birds of a feather flock together," so do thoughts—and this creates a *Thought Atmosphere*. Thought Atmospheres can also contain Feeling Tones, as I have noticed while visiting places that were once emotionally charged (e.g. an empty prison). A Thought's power depends upon its ability to attract to itself other thoughts of a similar nature (and thus combine forces). The strength with which a Thought has been projected concerns the focus, and the amount of its Ether, Ch'I or Prana vitalizes the thought (Ramacharaka, Fourteen Lesson p78). See Aura; Atmosphere

THOUGHT STRUCTURE ASSESSINGS: African Logic says all life-shaping and life-changing decisions based upon Spiritual Elements can have its source "Known" and thus by-passing the need to have "faith" in what one is told to believe. Clearly note here that for Ancient Africans, CT understanding by Spiritual Proof was infinitely more important than the Secular Proof upon which Europeans fully rely. African Logic is Ma'at (Spiritual Elements in action) applied to thinking via laws that establish Spiritual Elements' correspondence and connections between Principles for purposes of making Inferences of a Circumstantial Knowledge nature.

Logic implies the power to think according to a predetermined plan and therefore in an orderly manner. For Africans, that Plan has guidelines whereby the intellect is used in Reasoning (Right and Left Brain usage). In other words, Logic is primarily a Right Brain function concerned with realities and Truth existing beyond the visible. To this end, the foundation for and frame within which African Logic Thoughts exist is mathematical. As a result, what arises out of a given mathematical Thought "Seed" is a thinking pattern which also follows *mathematical designs and in a layered manner (as do patterns of Nature)*. This necessarily means African Logic—determining legitimacy between ideas to prove/disprove Spiritual Elements conformity--starts with an Unconditional Love Base—and proceeds Mathematically when dealing with the Metaphysical or Physical or the Spiritual Elements, if it is Spiritual--to arrive at an evolved Truth. Very Ancient Africans fashioned the tool of Astro-Mathematics and then subdivided Mathematics into Numbers, Multitude, and Magnitude. In Astronomy, *Magnitude* is a number designating the apparent "Brightness" of a star (not its size) on a scale. The higher the number expressing the magnitude, the fainter the star. African Sages said *Multitude* consisted of two main subjects: the relation of a given part to itself (Arithmetic) and the relation of one part to other parts (Music). *Music (or Harmony)* means both the living practice of African *Philosophy* (i.e. the adjustment of human life into harmony with God) and the living practice of Mathematics (since African Philosophy is Mathematics put into words), out of which all African Logic is based. Based on the Law of Correspondence + being composed of the Laws of Nature + following the Harmonious patterns of Mathematics, African Logic's methods and tools are illustrated in things able to be seen in Nature for use to discover Un-Seeable and/or Unknown Things.

Scholars use this, not in a ritual but in a Circumspect manner to assess all the reality aspects of the subject so as to separate the "What it is," the "what it does," and the "how it appears from each aspect of what is involved. The Scholar's objective is to arrive at the Worth of the Thing—i.e. whatever expands ones "ME/WE" Consciousness. When a Thought Structure was formed whereby it had to be based upon a premise, the *Ma'at System of Thought* was used. This says the proposition as a premise is examined according to the laws of intra-relationships and inter-relationships -- i.e. look at human's function in the world, framed by their interrelationship with God, the environment, and other creatures which determines humans' makeup (form/function relationship). The most fundamental theme of African Logic is the Association of Truth, Justice, Compassion, Harmony, Balance, Reciprocity, and Order. Deduction conclusion about a certain thing is reached by drawing out facts from a knowledge of the class to which it belongs. A "seed" job of Critical Thinking is to *find the assumption lurking behind the (quite valid) conclusion*. Whatever argument anyone is making, focus carefully on the Assumption used to begin their argument. If the assumption (major premise) they use is wrong, then the essence of whatever else they say is wrong—and not because it does not make sense. In fact, it makes perfect sense to the naïve but it is simply not the Truth. Assumptions cannot be based on faith. What comes from "Supernatural Revelation" cannot be analyzed since faith does not involve or resolve reasoning. Thus, if someone's major premise starts with: "God says or God does or God thinks," nothing else they say is to be believed. Or, if European males claim "God is on our side!" Reasons why these cannot stand up to the test of Truth are that he/she has *no way of knowing that* and there is no answer for "How can that be?" Because the ancient Greeks were the model for presenting European information (roughly in Syllogism form), anytime a European writing is assessed, the first thing to challenge is its major premise. (Keep in mind about the starting job of CT is to *find the assumption lurking behind their (seemingly quite valid) conclusion*. Buying the wrong assumption takes one down a self-defeating path whereby one loses control over what happens and be at the mercy of evil forces. To properly assess information for the Truth requires an awareness of the Message items: (1) who or what is the Source of the message -- is it likely to be creditable or to have an evil self-interest agenda?; (2) is the translation and Interpretation of the message of that source creditable?; (3) is the message resulting from that interpretation translated creditably?; (4) was that message subsequently altered by the messenger or altered by the messenger's bosses?; and (5) did the receiver of the message alter it by misunderstanding the true meaning or by adding apperceptions from prior experiences or concepts? Wherever there are flaws in these five, their detection and proper corrections must be made before proceeding. A most useful tool for assessing any objective and subjective information is the Thinker's Scale -- a hierarchy Scale of Importance. For me, this is the single most important thinking tool for assessing any objective and subjective information. Interpretation of findings is as crucial as the finding themselves and methods employed to obtain them.

TOTIPOTENT: "Totipotent" is an example of a word having application on all planes of Cosmic existence. Similar to the macrocosmic ('boundless world') androgynic plast of God's Spiritual Elements to produce all of God's creatures and creations, the microcosm ('bounded little world') equivalent is the ability of an organism cell to differentiate into any type of cell needed at that time by the organism. The fertilized ovum is a totipotent cell capable of giving rise to every cell type in an adult body. The meaning in that shared "Seed" Principle has totipotency by being a qualitative Circumstantial Truth now operative in Metaphysical Realms as well as a Quantitative Reasoning Conclusion operational in the Physical Realm. Both enable the ASI prepared mind to have a great deal of flexibility for creativity within areas of realism, distortion, and/or fantasy--flexibility which does not violate the Spiritual Elements (as occurs in European generated Supernatural Realms). Essences and Virtual have totipotence. Totipotent is capable of giving an Entity existence out of any ray of which its Essence is capable of producing + the ability to make unsuspected and novel connections.

TOTIPOTENCY: cells that can give rise to cells of all types

TRADEMARK: Featured Trait of the Character is the Essence "*Trademark*"

TRAINING: "*Education*" ("to lead out what is inside"); "*Teaching*" ("to show" so as to impart knowledge for learning); *Instructing* ("to build in or into"), or "*Training*" (active mind exercising in order to form habits)—in short, by study, reflection, and/or practice--depending upon the topic. **TRAITS:** The Mosaic Image derived from the Interchange of its Essence parent whose operation is "what it does" of the Characteristics, Traits, and Features family of a given Essence. It consists of a Contingent Disposition, Tendency, and/or Behaviors

TRANSFORMATION: The three parts for going from ones Lower Self (animal nature) to ones Highest Self are: Mystical Dying of the mortal part of ones Soul (the Ka); Regeneration by "re-yoking" ones Selfhood to God; and Rebirth by living and spreading Ma'at Principles (Unconditional Love and Truth).

TRANSITION: In African Tradition a "*Transition*" is the process of going from one plane of existence to another. Examples are the switch from the pre-birth realm to enter the Earth World as a newborn; stepping from puberty to adulthood; or the process of going from life to death). Or, if related to public life, a Transition is a change in a person's social position (e.g. marriage; a business promotion or demotion). Transitions share features of an Interchange in that their internal ingredients are derived from what is on all side and are in an undefined, unformed, and undifferentiated state The C15 English word Transition" originated from ancient Romans relating the word "*Fundamentals*" to the ground for burial. This implied "Fundamental" consisted of three parts: the foundation of stability below ground; the rest of the structure resting on the fundamentals above ground; and the connection between the two, called its *transitional* aspect and carrying the sense of to go through (something like the stricture of an hour-glass), go underneath, go around, or go over in bridge-like fashion to change from one place, state, condition, or circumstance to another. See Archery Pad

TRANSLATION HISTORICAL FLAWS OF RELIGIOUS INFORMATION: People want to base ideas and actions on authority's standards. Scribes could not say anything unless someone had said it before. Certain way of life had to be authorized by God or laws of Nature or some successful group of people. Authority outside ones own will and judgment is an excuse to not be responsible for what one is going to do anyway. Using Hebrew, Greek, or Latin as a standard for definitions is a superficial source. Descriptions using colorful image get away from the Truth. These images are filled with imagination. Things are said never backed up with scripture--heaven's streets are paved with gold; pearly gates; Lucifer; morning star. It is assumed it is God's will to be poor but this is not in the Bible. It is a wrong premise for saying: "It's my fate!" which itself is a wrong assumption. Image premises are made--many of which are false and they lead one off the truth track while giving one the answer they want. The false ones are swallowed and establish credibility because they are old and because they are generally accepted. Once on this wrong path one can be even more easily misled. What happens in history is irrational but historians give it meaning. Religious History (or any history) is an art, is constructed, and is an opinion. The way it is written by someone is the way that someone is and how that someone evokes the world, which depends on how one is. Much of the information relied on by religious believers is not what Jesus and others like him said but rather what theologians put into his mouth. Oral tradition does not preserve certain historical landmarks such as the name at the time. Rather that name was changed each time the story was told and recorded. Points are put in numerical list so they can be remembered. However, some monks had added to what is handed down, not in a dishonest way back then but it would be dishonest today. Author were not allowed to put their names but to attribute it to the Source or the Spirit imparted to them. People use images and figures of speech to describe what they are trying to convey and the nature of those chosen depend upon what people believe. Thus a given description by different is typically completely different about the same shared experience -- a difference based only on what the people observed and their imagination and images chosen to describe it. Yet not are absolutely true. In the finite world the law of Opposites prevents from being a specific truth. Brutes get away with rewriting history because people believe there is a fixed truth. One who writes history is merely giving a point of view--why did he choose this way?

TRAPS: A physical trap is a device used to catch an animal and either hold it alive but so it cannot escape or injure and kill it. Types of traps are nets, fences, trapdoors, bait (e.g. with molasses), snares, steel traps (like a mouse trap) which causes the animal to suffer greatly, pitfalls--a deep hole in the ground covered with sticks and leaves to make it look like ground so that when the animal steps on it and falls, it lands on upward pointing spears. Other examples include: a trap door—a programming gap inserted intentionally as a means of bypassing security and gaining access to the program at a later date; a door in the stage floor through which performers may enter or exit; to double-team a player with the ball in an attempt to make a steal; any device or pitfall, usually baited, that snaps or falls on the slightest disturbance and thus captures or kills its victim. Even more varieties of traps are used by Supernatural people to trap Colored Peoples mentally, physically, and Spiritually—whether for exploiting, killing, to satisfy desires to cause pain and misery, or as a demonstration of what the power of "the Gun" allows them to do in support of their ridiculous claim of being "superior". Supernatural Traps shatter a human's "Soul Sunshine" and its Rays and thereby Enslave the Mind. So, Selfhood Traps are imposed or self-imposed "*Clutches*"--a C13 English word for a claw developed into a swift, eager, tenacious grasping movement of fingers seizing for the sake of saving a situation (1525) and thence into a "tight grasp" of the whole hand. The result of being Clutched is to "*Cling*"--Old English, implying hanging on a tow-rope for "dear life" because of a lack of Courage. Clinging is done for fear of abandonment and fear of being left on ones own while feeling worthless. Their mindsets are in a chronic self-absorbed state of neediness and anxiety from being empty of the "5Ss"—Safety, Security, Self-Confidence, Strength, and Stability. That *Tow-Rope* may be dependency on ones in-group or the Crowd—on technology and its "Flashing Light" gadgets (e.g. via cell phone) or other Trinkets—on Trivia and "Small Talk"—"Street Drugs, Alcohol, or other

Addictions--or Clinging to Beliefs that SEEM right or whatever else maintains the Status Quo. Then, to the Oppressors there is "*Cleaving*"--Old English meaning both to 'cut' (split, hollow out) as well as to 'adhere' (glue, cling). During slavery, Cleaving was formed by what I call the "*Evil Savior Syndrome*". Despite the horrendous Indifference/Hate/Evil/Sadism applied to the Enslaved and no matter how meager their provisions, anything provided or even promised to be provided to them resulted in a "Clinging Bonding" with the Oppressor. And that close attachment--entwining, clutching, or hanging on--has been culturally transmitted into many of today's descendants. *Clutching, Cleaving and Clinging are the roots of the background daily living problems of the Afflicted.* The major barrier is that they *resist any change and will not accept the Truth--both from them fearing no longer having anything to hold on to and nothing of which they are aware that would serve as a sound replacement Tow-Rope.* Besides, having been brainwashed causes them to do "*Inside-Out*" *thinking, as in disregarding what it takes for Survival, Self-Preservation, and Self-Protection.* "Inside-Out" thinking causes, among others, the afflicted to feel "*less than human*" and then accept that False Selfhood condition as: "It's my fate!"—itself displaying in its own unique ways of thinking, feeling, expressing, and behaving. The combination of being Clutched to the point of Cleaving and Clinging produces *Anxiety and Anguish*--words having self-strangulation (Latin, tightness, narrow) as its roots and which prevent one from having a free mind. Clutched/Cleaving/Clinging also designs *Selfhood Splintering*--meaning one part of ones Selfhood becomes Self-Absorbed (viewing everything within ones world in relationship to oneself); the other follows dictates of External World influences. Distortions and Fantasies make for *Uncertainty* which, in turn, brings defensiveness and Clinging and Clutching to whatever is available, as does a drowning person grabbing at straws. Clutched/Cleaving/Clinging causing Selfhood Splintering necessarily fashions flawed, irrational, and illogical mental activities. False Self supports (e.g. the Crowd) and False perspectives (e.g. seeing through Tainted glasses) distort mental and emotional assessments of people and things in daily life. These display as: *Self-Absorption*, which negates caring about others feelings; emotional outbursts; a personal sense of weakness from the absence of power to get things done; and procrastinating in taking self-improvement actions for rising above mental, physical, spiritual, and social poverty. Anxiety makes them envious of Real Self people to the point of doing what it takes to isolate them and throw stones at them--of various natures and with various impacts. Their "Inside-Out" thinking will cause some to cut off definite benefits to keep their Jegna Helpers from appearing more powerful.

    "TRAP" ETYMOLOGY: The word category for the countless ways of being "Trapped" is that of "*Maze*" (C13, a shortening of "*Amaze*") meaning "*Delusion*" (believing ideas opposed to reality) and "*Delirium*" (temporary mental disturbance)--as if one was in a *Daze*. Not until C14 did it begin to be used for a "structure of bewildering complexity" causing confusion, traps, entanglements, or complications of any sort. "*Bewildered*" is a state of *Irrationality and the Illogical resulting from an Idea-Form* Dissociation. This separation Substance/Essence and its Form generates a "*Non Sequitur*" ('it does not follow') mental state of activity. When all the parts are present, the Dissociation displays as a paradox or "impossible" to solve. *Bewitch* is a similar state of *Irrationality and the Illogical* resulting from an essential part concerning the inner workings or the obvious or the foundation is overlooked or a part is suppressed by some covering (as occurs with the esoteric meanings in allegories) so as to give the sense of a Superstition. The 1330 English word "*Confuse*" (pour together; mix together; fail to distinguish) meant to defeat, frustrate; then throwing into disorder; and later bewilder. The '-con' means *with* and the 'fusion,' says Sharon Bingaman, is like things melted together—like gold rings, bracelets, and earrings together so the distinctions among the pieces are not visible.

    Despite all the pieces being there, each is hidden in another form. When all the parts are present but an essential part concerning the inner workings or the obvious or the foundation is overlooked or a part is suppressed by some covering (as occurs with the esoteric meanings in allegories) or that which was already present in a disguised form, then confusion is present. This confusion may also display as a paradox or "impossible" to solve. Confusion stirs up so much disharmony, fear, and difficulty as to cause *Illusions* (seeing what is not there and not seeing what is there); *Hallucinations*--a false image or belief which has nothing, outside a disordered mind, to suggest it. *Delusions* (believing what is not real and not believing what is real); and *Misinterpretations* as to prevent one from no longer being sure of anything they previously thought they knew.

TRAPS--MIND CONTROL: Inside Confusion, Illusions, Hallucinations, Delusions, Bewitchment, and Bewilderment are such inconsistencies as to put one into a state of such Frustration. Those Frustrations are an association of so many ridiculous contradictions that one has no idea at what place to start unraveling the mess. The confused will then either say: "I don't want to think about it" and that opens the door for there to be a shift of power over to being the Victim of the human source. That mindset of being overwhelmed and in despair eases one into looking for and readily acceptance guidance from anyone. In a Supernatural setting, that "someone" takes charge of the Frustrated minds and thereafter controls them and leads them into "the lion's den" to be "eaten" or into a Zombie mindset to thereafter be enslaved. What mind controllers then do is to present such reconciling ambivalent attitudes with highly abstracted (what is taken out of physical aspects) formulations—wrapped in "Big Words" that are undefinable--that opponents simply find it best to "give-in." Thus, Victims figure out an "okay" something that "SEEMs" right so as to get satisfaction from their confusion that is compatible with "going along to get along" with the Crowd. Onto that "mental skeleton" of what "SEEMs" right is added the various layers fellow cult members say about it. This had/has practical application for savage Satanists--self-worshippers with "Toxic Masculinity--who attack the Spiritual Elements of Unconditional Love, Truth, Reality, and the Natural) in order to fool themselves into being "superior" to these. But equally as important is that they have always wanted what Black Africans of World history had as well as envying the African Intellectual, Civilization, and Cultural achievements they were incapable of accomplishing on their own. So they instituted a chain of traps within the "Take-Down" setting of methods: *penetration, conquest, occupation, and colonization.* To Black People, the importance of Confusion and its associates which generate Conflict is in how it was used by Europeans to substitute their "Trinket and Trivia" information for the "Treasure" Knowledge and Wisdom of Ancient Africans. This "flip-flop" has been so subtle that most Black People, to this day, have been unaware of it and that it has turned their minds "Inside-Out"—meaning they advocate for what is self-destructive. To show that they have no idea of what religious Faith/Belief/Trust mean, note in the following discussion of these words how Europeans only deal with what they do and how they appear--both of which are mere opinions. I daresay that every adult Black person, and that is true of me, can give several form of traps they have been victims of as a result of Europeans deceptions. For example, during my Orthopaedic residency training, I was under a microscope by those wanting me out to do anything short of excellent but without giving me any information. I heard stories about Black People's traps as a book vendor.

TRAPS--SUPERNATURALS' ACADEMIC FOR MIND CONTROL: Without exception, I have never seen a bully capable of doing Rational—i.e. mathematic processes—thinking. This is because the Brute Brain for dealing with things of daily living—i.e. their Left Brain admixed with Acquired Emotions of a Fettered nature. The Brute Brain embraces animalistic sensuality/lust, hate of even the "faceless," attachments to Things, lies, greed, extreme selfishness, Indifference, arrogance, and false pride. This is because this Delusional World is powered by arrogant "Me, Me, Me" Individualistic "little gods" with a sense of inferiority, self-hatred, insecurities, shame from self-image problems, chronic anger/rage, egoism, envy, jealousy, frustration, fear, violence, and whose "manhood" is solely dependent on control by the GUN (whatever kills). Brutes do Non-Rational thinking—i.e. what they claim to be above the ultimate (beyond which there is no other) Thought Base in the Natural World—i.e. Unconditional Love. Unconditional Love is the Base from which all Ancient African Philosophy springs and since it is in all God's Creatures and Creations, its natural patterns enable mathematics to determine the workings of the processes of Nature. This means that Non-Rational must either use the "Air" as their Base for thinking or whatever they make up to be their Base and thereby cause fellow Supernatural members and those who imitate them to completely rely on Belief and Faith. Non-Rational thinking is in the setting of a surreal fantasy and that means what comes out of it is Illogical (not mathematical and thus not reproducible) and Irrational (no pattern because of its infinite variability). That orientation validates and justifies their Fear reactions; openly deny reason; dispense with multi-culture agreed upon definitions; deal only with the "how it Appears" or "what it does" rather than the "What it is"; and dispense with Evidence or Proof since there is no way to arrive at either. Hence, Non-Rational thinking can never arrive at Truth, Knowledge, or Wisdom. Thus, any conclusion for their arguments are unacceptable because these conclusions have derived from Invalid reasoning. So, to by-pass their inability to determine the "What it is" and thereby know its essence (what it is when it came into Being), they maneuver and manipulate the context of "how it Appears" or "what it does". The intent is to appeal the pleasure of, to confuse, or to generate fear and create unfair advantages for them and unfair disadvantages for the opponent.

A consequence of Non-Rational thinking is that there can be no concepts of Worth (i.e. the Spiritual Beautiful) and therefore no Base from which can arise an *Underground Foundation*, from which only can emerge ones System of Values. For this reason the Supernatural "Air Castle" determines its own versions of success, as with status, riches, and possessions. By the Supernatural operating out of the fantasy of human's Brute Brains, their unstable "Air" Base and "Air" Underground Foundation consists of Indifference/Hate/Evil/Sadism (IHES). Out of this Complex is fashioned the *above ground foundation* portion of their "Air Castle" and consists of an Aggressive Power Approach to dealing with life's issues. The Castle's Air *Frame* is a Supernatural Fettered Attitude serve as models for them to determine the nature of cult members' thoughts and emotions for carrying out the *Seven Deadly Sins*.

Maintenance of the "Air Castle" is by Kill/Take/Destroy/Dominate/Oppress/Control Approaches to life. Cult members eagerness to use these approaches in the most inhumane methods and techniques is what is persuasive for them getting their way in life. However, since they can trust no one, they do not even like each other—and seeing who can win from applying what they normally due is what will eventually destroy all of them. Yet, short of that, Non-Rational thinking has its focus on "Scarce Desirable" Objects--measurable Tangible things inside the material world to which Value (e.g. money) is given. *Children's senses are always searching for Objects that are of interest to the desires of the body.* When this normal way of being persists into adulthood, it is the ignorant, superficial, or Supernatural mind that does not understand Object's inability to satisfy any desire of the body—but only to multiply them into infinity. But "Scarce Desirable" Objects are of prime importance to Supernaturals and their victims have been brainwashed to believe are the ultimate things for having a "Good Life." This traps them so that they become pawns (of lowest rank) in "The Game" of acquiring the most "Adult Toys" (e.g. money, power)—a Game in which the Supernaturals are trapped.

TRAPPERS--"ALLIGATOR" POVERTY-MINDED: The Predator Supernaturals show a wide variety of acts involving aggression motivated by *Delusional Fears*—i.e. false problems created as justification for doing harm to "feigned enemies" for purposes of acquiring unfair advantages, benefits, and Things. To this end, Victims are imaged in the Predators imaginations as "Phantasmagoric" Contingent Beings and labeled with imagined, false, dangerous characters, characteristics, traits, and features who cause facade problems. Those problems are "colored" with Essence-less Secondary and Tertiary Qualities and presented as so intimidating as for "all of us" to fear. Delusional Fears are maintained so that the military and civilian members of the cult will continued to keep Victims down, fearful, in flight and by ensuring they have no power, no voice, and no status as humans or ever being visible for humanity considerations. Whatever is amoral, illegal for others, or dishonorable are normal parts of their system. They are *Obsessive* (persistent uncontrollable impulses to think certain thoughts). Their *Monomania* nature—i.e. a philosophical-pathological obsession with one idea or subject, as "he thought of it constantly"—displays as *Compulsions* or uncontrollable impulses to be a certain way or carry out certain actions irresistibly and contrary to the inclination or will. Both are reflections of *Engrams* (permanent memories) powering imagination dominating their Non-Rational thinking—i.e. a Chimerical faculty responsible for visionary imaginativeness (e.g. monster, or hybrid, or bogy—an evil or mischievous spirit, hobgoblin) to an excessive degree. The Greek "*Chimaira*" means she-goat with the head of a lion, body of a goat, tail of a dragon, and capable of spitting fire. Those Chimera images are based upon some minor degree of reality--for obsessive-compulsive fulfillment. Since Chimera images are normal in children, this greatly enhances their abilities to absorb all aspects of Supernatural Predatory practices than most realize. Perhaps starting as teen bullies, they exploit, in word and deed, whomever and whenever they can—and without any inner or outer accountability. The same applies in adulthood and they are above the law. They ignore inconvenient truths; and never are on the defensive; are disconnected from human emotions, human dignity + as from the lives normal people lead. By being rich, from amoral practices, they can get away with having a "toxic masculinity." They roam the earth, objectifying themselves into a "*Brand*"—i.e. to mark into a "sign" or "trademark"—as in branding cattle with a hot iron—to designate, in merchandizing oneself, as "I am the greatest!" in front of the cameras. To try to get them to be humane is like planting water-lilies on dry land or trying to get "blood out of a turnip". Those who apply opposing Humane Forces in attempting to "call out" the evil and sadistic things done by these Social Institutions are ignored, drowned out, disabled in any number of ways, or killed off. Otherwise, if there is no way to avoid the issues on which one is "called out," *Deflections* (C16, bend away from a fixed direction) are automatic, as illustrated by *Reaction Formation* (a reality/fantasy reversal)--e.g. saying about and to the victim: "you are the one causing the problem, not me!". Deflections are what the guilty use to defend themselves against their own unconscious negative impulses or qualities by denying their existence in themselves while attributing them to others. These are the greatest cozenage (deceitful) things a predator does to his/her mind to break down any remote sense of moral "Right." *Deflection* method alterations include: diverting ones "Dark Side" deeds to someone else as being the responsible party; swerving their "Dark Side" into something honorable; causing to run aside something that is worse done by the accuser; and Projection.

Projection is a façade of accusing the other side of what the guilty did--accusations derived from fantasies which design feigned necessities—i.e. imaginary necessities. They will never change!—and will always lie, cheat, steal, add their "wild" imaginations in setting out to disprove the deeds of what is on record (e.g. writings, television, videos); take no responsibility for any IHES actions. When "Called Out" they immediately jump on another track having nothing to do with the issue. Or, they go on the attack when caught--invariably blaming, criticizing, and finding fault with attackers and Scapegoats—even by attacking them for their associations or "attacking her by what he said". This implies they are above the Rules and are not fair game for having flaws.

TRAPS--"ALLIGATORS" FOR COLORED PEOPLES: "Trapped" is the 'umbrella term' for being caged in countless mental, physical, and Spiritual ways—whether for exploiting, for pleasure in causing pain and misery, for intimidation, or for killing. All Traps by Supernaturals are demonstrations of what "the GUN"—not intellect--allows them to do in support of their ridiculous claim of being "superior". On any mental and spiritual planes of existence, the word "Trap" conveys "*Maze*" (C13, a shortening of "*Amaze*") meaning

"Delusion," "Delirium," Daze, Illusion, and Hallucination. Not until C14 did it begin to be used for a "structure of bewildering complexity" causing confusion, entanglements, or complications of any sort. *"Bewildered"* is a state of *Irrationality and the Illogical resulting from an Idea-Form* Dissociation. Such occurred from African American Enslaved having the formlessness of the Spiritual Force replaced with the slavers Supernatural God. This separation and switch of Spiritual Substance/Essence over to a Fantasy generated a *"Non Sequitur"* ('it does not follow') mental state of activity which profoundly trapped Black People. By not having recovered means they built a self-defeating lifestyle around it. Inside Confusion, Illusions, Hallucinations, Delusions, Bewitchment, and Bewilderment are such inconsistencies as for ones daily living with a host of them to be put in a chronic state of Frustration. Entangle in these Frustrations are so many ridiculous contradictions and confusion that one is overwhelmed. The confused will then either say: "I don't want to think about it". That opens doors for Supernaturals to give "SEEMs" right explanations that start controlling the Seekers mind as they are led into "the lion's den" to be "eaten" or into a Zombie mindset to thereafter be enslaved. What mind controllers then do is to present such reconciling ambivalent attitudes with highly abstracted (what is taken out of physical aspects) formulations—wrapped in "Big Words" that are undefinable--that opponents simply find it best to "give-in." Thus, Victims figure out an "okay" something that "SEEMs" right so as to get satisfaction from their confusion. The result is what is compatible with "going along to get along" with the Crowd. Onto that "mental skeleton" of what "SEEMs" right is added the various layers fellow cult members say about it. This had/has practical application for savage Satanists--self-worshippers with *"Toxic Masculinity*--who attack the Spiritual Elements of Unconditional Love, Truth, Reality, and the Natural) in order to fool themselves into being "superior" to these. But equally as important is that Supernaturals have always wanted what Black Africans of World history had/have. They also envy African Intellectual, Civilization, and Cultural achievements since they were/are incapable of accomplishing any of it on their own. So they instituted a chain of traps within the "Take-Down" setting of methods: *penetration, conquest, occupation, and colonization* of Africans, the African continent, and African Intellectual property. To elaborate, for Black People, the importance of Confusion and its Conflict associates are what Europeans used to substitute their "Trinket and Trivia" information to "take over" the "Treasure" Knowledge, Things of Worth and Value, and Wisdom of Ancient Africans, while destroying the rest.

This "flip-flop" has been so subtle that most Black People, to this day, have been unaware of it and that it has turned their minds "Inside-Out"—meaning they advocate for what is self-destructive. To show they have no idea of what religious Faith/Belief/Trust mean, is to be aware of all the Traps almost all Colored Peoples are in. A place to start the unraveling of the entangled mess is to stop the false foundational belief Black People have for thinking White Supermacists are "Normal Varients" inside the Spiritual World. The reality is that they are from an alien realm and attack all Spiritual Elements and their attributes "head-on"—in attempts to convince themselves and others that they are "superior"—the most ridiculous concept ever invented by humans. Next is to completely shed the delusion that Europeans are needed by Black People for anything. Since the Spiritual deals with things of Worth, opposed to the Material things of Value, as is the focus of Europeans, they Black People's spotlight is to be on the same things as those of their super-brilliant Ancient African Ancestors. When those are thoroughly known, Black People will resort to their Creativity and Industry to make money and devise creature comforts that make for a thriving life and sense of well-being.

TRAPPED BLACK PEOPLE BY EUROPEANS: Since their beginnings 45,000 years ago, Europeans have used their own warrior self-image to create a Supernatural realm of Fantasy out of their Pattern of Indifference/Hate/Evil/Sadism (IHES) Complex mindsets. This is done within military context in order to control the minds of their Troops and their Victims using the anti-Spiritual Elements Aggressiveness behaviors of Kill/Take/Destroy/Dominate/Oppress (KTDDO). For Victims not killed, they were so beaten down and then continually brainwashed in their state of desperation as to become instruments of their own destruction by an "Inside-Out" mindset. That mindset attacks their own First Law of Nature—i.e. Survival, Self-Protection, and Self-Preservation. This has been associated with assuming the role of their oppressors to oppress each other like "crabs-in-a-barrel" pulling each other down from progressing; to engaging in self-oppression; and to protecting and defending their real European oppressors. European warriors have made a two-sided Supernatural God—with one side being Satan (made in their own warrior self-image) in control of a fantasy Hell—and the other side being a kaleidoscope God that SEEMS right to their Troops and to their Victims. They use this Supernatual God in various ways to control the minds of their Troops and their Victims. By not believing in anything in the Natural World, including its Spiritual God, they attack the Spiritual Elements. Thus, they have no belief in an Afterlife and that "when you're dead, you're dead." This means they want to be in the Hall of Infamy. Its qualifications are to win the "Game" by any means necessary. The "Game" is to acquire the most "Adult Toys"--e.g. money and possessions; killing and ruining the lives of the most people; being an "Individualist"; having the highest status; controlling the most people by creating rules for them to follow but being exempt from those rules; being a "little god" who is treated like a king. But in order for all this to happen, they must join forces with each other in alliances and liaisons in order to engage in KTDDO. To motivate their Troops requires making the most of Fears of every type so as to spur a rage reaction in them to destroy their assigned feigned Victims. By being against all morals, they intimidate all by their eagerness to kill "for no reason" anybody who does not agree with them or who gets in the way or just for excitement. If the Satanist leaders are thought of as the bull's eye on an Archery Pad, as the rings surrounding the bull's eye ripples outward, all on the Archery Pad possess mosaic pieces of the leaders' propaganda and bathe in the aura and atmosphere Satanism gives off. This means that every European Institution has the same warrior pattern but with unique ways. A "Sameness" shows as none being honorable and thus they lie, cheat, and steal at every opportunity. They all express various aspects of the "Game" and get away with it, including KTDDO, because of their Network—i.e. being in charge of all institutions involving the World Crowd. Such power came about by means of the GUN (discussed elsewhere). Another "Sameness" is the entire cults' focus on any outsider who has what the cult wants—and those outsiders become feigned enemies. Another reason those scapegoats are feigned is because the cult needs them so as to project their "Dark Side" thoughts, feelings, expressions, and deeds. Then, to now see their "Dark Side" in the scapegoats enables that Projection to be fantasized as being a real switch—and that serves as a justification for doing KTDDO and/or using IHES mindsets to generate hardships for the scapegoats. Segregation is essential for otherwise the aggressors and victims may get to like each other. Since such would keep the generals from having power over all Troops and Victims and "little god" privileges, the generals are forced to use mind control and punish violators or reluctant Troops by isolation; keep the Troops stupid; devise all types of means (e.g. Trinkets and Trivia) to ensure the Troops are incompetent in all non-military areas—for that breeds the insecurities which cause the inadequate to look for direction; segregate the cult from scapegoats to spotlight differences. Scapegoats are needed for six main reasons. First, the Brute Mind, the lowest of any humans, is in an abyss a bottomless gulf—immeasurable and unfathomable; a symbolized realm of being out of the cycle of life featuring the fantasy of being Supreme. Its feature is an IHES orientation where there is a need to kill the scapegoats they designated to carry their projected "Dark Side". Second, since IHES mindsets are filled with devising KTDDO daily living behaviors, they are incapable of developing Rational (i.e. Mathematical) Intellect. Thus, they must steal the Intellectual Property from the scapegoats. Since they know nothing but Fear and Hatred, they must rely on scapegoats to provide entertainment and fashions. Fourth, since "misery loves company," the cult reproduce their ways of think, feel, say, and do in the scapegoats by what is superficial and "Exciting"—both being self-destructive. Fifth, the cult leaves scapegoats in such poverty that they have to rely on the cult for "crumbs off the dinner table". Six, scapegoats are the source of *Delusional Fears*—the false creation of a "Scarcity Survival" reaction that has to be publicized so as to present an abstract Righteous Indignation Cause. Delusional Fears demand protection from those "who are after taking everything we claim" and to get support from observing fellows. Yet the real reason is the cult leaders are dedicated to acquiring Power, Property, Profit, and Control. So, Satanist leaders stir up non-existent causes for conflict in both the Victims and the Troops. They always stir Victims to fight each other by Europeans attacking one Black group and claiming another Black group did it. Meanwhile, they choose out of the Troops those who feel profoundly insecure about their thinking limitations and separate themselves from those they envy by claiming themselves to be superior. Generating fear to motivate their Troop Bullies is done by creating bad stories about those scapegoats they envy—stories having absolutely no basis in fact since they reflect the "Dark Side" of what the cult wrestles with in their own minds. Yet, these are stories, coupled with the generating of Delusional Fears, that are so effective as for the Troops to blame, criticize, and punish the scapegoats for them. The call to action by the generals generating Delusional Fear is done for the Troops. There is such "faceless hatred" reactions as to rouse them to KTDDO the scapegoats. Such an *IHES mindset and their associated philosophies* of life *are at the root and is the source of all natural and moral evils.* Since all cult members remain tremendously Needy for support from like-kind bullies or from those who agree or admire them, they have the need to publicly justify their IHES mindsets and KTDDO behaviors by means of those fantasy stories. Like a tape recording, the stories presented to the public by the evil doers and the Media is that these KTDDO actions were done to protect the public from evil forces created by the feigned scapegoats. The implied threat is that "if we are not allowed to KTDDO on a whim and when we so desire, then you will have no protection from the scapegoats waiting to come take everything back that you took from them. The rule for the Troops is to routinely respond with abstract "Righteous Indignation" to what the scapegoats were said to have done—even in the face of documented contrary evidence. This is why no "Killer" policeman is prosecuted for killing unarmed Black People. All of this is to prevent the Troops from realizing they were not getting the benefit of the generals and so would not figure out the scapegoats had done nothing bad to them. Julian Jarvis put it well pertaining to the European Network: The arresting officer is cool with the sergeant; the sergeant rides motorcycles with the chief; the chief of police is cool with the prosecutor; the prosecutor plays golf with the district attorney; the district attorney was in the same fraternity as the judge; the judge endorsed the mayor; the mayor went to the same college as the governor; the governor has stock in private prisons; and prisons are filled with Black and Brown in-mates.

 "**TRAUMA**": means wound or hurt occurring as a result of injury, accident, or violence.

 '**TREE CONCEPT**' for assessment into some order. The natural "Tree Concept" consists of a Seed, Sprouts, Roots, Trunk/Vines, Branches, Leaves, Flowers, and Fruit

 TRIANGLE: Mathematically, this was like a triangle with three equal sides—called an Equilateral or Equiangular Triangle whereby the sides and angles are equivalent and thus have Correspondence. This would be true even if a portion of that triangle could not be seen—and yet mathematically figured out. The "figured out" would be called Circumstantial but still have Certainty. See Certainty

 TRICKERY: *Fraud* (gaining an unfair advantage over bodies of people) involved those aspects of "*Trickery*" (deliberately giving the wrong impression) that includes "*Deceit*" (the pursuit of personal gain at the expense of victims) and "*Manipulation*" (here meaning hypocritical dishonorableness).

 TRUTH: *Truth is both Evidence and Proof when it has Correspondence with established Laws of Nature.* An African Saying defines "Truth" as *anything having Unconditional Love at its core while displaying its attributes*

(e.g. Harmony, Unity, Peace, Compassion, and Affection). In other words, Truth is anything containing the Spiritual Elements throughout. Truth is both Evidence and Proof when it has Correspondence with established Laws of Nature. *Anything deviating from "Truth" is Deception brought about by the Weak, the Ignorant, Brutes, or Satanists. So, Deception is a lie displayed in applications, especially of appearances, which alter the course of Right Life Living—each falsehood having Insincerity as its keystone.* Such is an issue of Trust. There are Spiritual Truths and Earth Worth truths and they are simply Principles of the same Essence Spiritual Elements Truth. No one knows for sure what the definition is for Truth but my concepts are that anything having Unconditional Love, Reality, and the Natural as the sole ingredients is the Truth. Unless it can be verified, anything said about the definition proposed to be truth is merely an opinion. However, some opinions are better than others and can be ranked on the Truth Ladder. My thought is what exhibits the Law of Correspondence as well as anything containing African type Unconditional Love (i.e. the Essence of God, as agreed upon by all the Sages of all cultures and throughout the ages) is Truth. Thus, the highest ranking Truth is what does the most good, for the most people, over the longest period of time. *To Know Truth You Must Live It.*

TRUTH—CIRCUMSTANTIAL: Circumstance, an indivisible Spiritual/Matter state of affairs, implies there is the exercising the pressure in which a thing acts. Since what is round a Thing means the situation is in the Circumstance—whether in vertical/ horizontal relations, in outside/inside relations, and/or in Seeable/ Un-seeable relations. Resultant actions affected are performed under those Circumstances. In any of those relations, if there is shared Correspondence—as in strings of a tennis racket or in a fishnet—then Circumstance is in intimate and "sameness" association with Correspondence. Because African Sages knew God is Unknowable directly they believed God could be known indirectly by a system within ones brain which they perfected. However, for the people, they taught that an entrance to the subject was by explaining keystone concepts -- like first cleaning up a room before being able to find thing using a system. That entrance is by means of Circumstantial Truths. Since this is a difficult concept to understand, allow me to assist. To Ancient Africans "Evidence" -- direct and circumstantial pieces of the Truth puzzle forming the "big picture" of Proof -- was intuited in the flow of reality, enabling the mind to see the Truth. Evidence for them was considering and weighing the facts on the way to arriving at the Truth—i.e. what corresponds with Reality. In the early Western world, *"Evidence"*—an offspring of *"Evident"*—meant a distinction so clear to the eye that it impressed the mind with its luster or splendor. Such brilliantly shiny things -- whether concerned what was seen, heard, smelled, tasted, and/or touched -- applied to deciding disputes. When present, they were deemed to be "Proof" under the belief that how something appeared was the same as saying what it was. Note that this European way is a feature seen in children and immature thinkers. Both will select shiny trinkets over a dull appearing treasure. As a result, European Evidence has come to mean all the ways information can be presented to prove or disprove disputes. Yet, such Evidence cannot be relied upon to be true. One reason in the Western world is Proof and Evidence are supposed to relate to the objective but both are actually checkered with the subjective (e.g. opinions, tastes, bias, and prejudices) while ignoring the spiritual. Regardless of the type of Evidence— whether good, bad, or indifferent—most people are willing to accept what does not harmoniously fit because they want or do not want things to be a certain way or because they intensely desire to conform or because they are gullible and naïve or because of biases and prejudices. The problem is complicated when the dispute or issue involves more than one plane of existence. The story of "Circumstantial Truth" began with Very Ancient Africans standing inside a *Ring Shout* circle -- the Primary Event. Surrounding the outside of this circle were "Secondary Events" going on at the same time. The same idea is present in a "three-ring" circus performance. The ritual aspects of the entire Ring Shout ceremony alone was sufficient to indicate what the religious happening was about, even if people only saw the ceremony from a distance and could not see the people doing the Ring Shout dance. This practice conveyed the idea of a *"circumstance" being positioned around a circle as an offspring and containing a bit of the atmosphere of whatever is inside the circle (e.g. a symbol, object, figure, or event)*. Thus, to have a sense of the mathematical components (primary and secondary seen as a unit) and what is going on inside each component, then an awareness of just a few of those is sufficient to convey a picture of the entire happening. Suppose the primary (inner) circle is a liberation enactment (Fanon, The Wretched of the Earth) where there is protection and permission for men and women to engage in pantomime actions as, for example, of shaking their heads and throwing their bodies backward. Though seemingly disorganized, it is extremely systematic in representing the community's purpose of exorcising itself or liberating itself or explaining itself. Now suppose there are groups of people in different circles -- secondary events -- situated around the primary circle -- which are engaged in movements honoring the Ancestors (Stuckey, Slave Culture). By clearly understanding all aspects of this Ritual enables one to recognize it even if only a piece of it is seen in another country. This recognition of a Circumstance helps explain aspects of the Shout in the Americas that are otherwise difficult to understand. Most learning of human truth is circumstantial.

TURBULENCE: (troubled, tumbling, erratic, chaotic, confused). Features of such minds would be chronic anger at oneself and fear; a sense of inadequacy and "I'm not good enough" from being flawed and weak; a feeling of disconnection from others and therefore alone; the emotions of sadness, terror, and bereavement from no longer having the "5Ss"; and the belief of being unworthy, powerless, unimportant, inferior, disgusting, and diminished in human nature. *"Turbulence"* is the driving force of human generated violence is a whirl of uncontrolled and unnatural emotions which, of course, is a reflection of the state of that human's mindset.

TWA AFRICANS: Perhaps humans first Qualities were sounds of Languages arising like springs among the far-hidden heart of Ethiopia's Afar beautiful, snow-capped Rwenzori ("rainmaker") mighty Mountains 200,000 years ago. Those humans, according to Shahar Harari, discovered in Tanzania, at Lake Victoria's Ngorongoro Crater and the Olduvai Gorge in Kenya, Uganda, and Tanzania, are the oldest known remains of human species. These first "small stature" people, the "Ba-Twa", worshipped the God Bes (who, incidentally, dons the cover of my book: Disproportionate Short Stature, Diagnosis and Management). Egyptian texts of c2500 BC refer to the Twa as little men from the land of trees and spirits at the foot of the Mountains of the Moon. Bes was a primitive human forerunner form of Horus I who, in turn, was the earliest form of the Black Ptah, the God of Gods, as symbolized in the Egyptian Mystery System. The Twa, modern humans or Homo sapiens sapiens, are a diminutive Africoid people residing in the rain forests of Central Africa, with related groups in South and Southeast Asia. The Twa are said to have migrated the 4100 miles of the Nile river, contributing to the establishment of the later Egyptian civilization. The north-south line of lakes, Albert, Ruranzige, Kivu, and Tanganyika, make the eastern edge of the Ituri Forest in Congo where the Efe Twa lived. It was called the Towering massif of Ruwenzori Baba Tiba, the Mountains of the Moon. In Efe theology, the first man ascended to the heavens after serving as a benevolent governor of the primordial Twa nation. He then established residence on the moon where he still assists God by serving as the angel-of-the-moon. For tropical Black Africans, the Moon--not the Sun--was, and remains, the favorite object of veneration. Egyptian king Nefrikare sent an expedition into central Africa and it returned with a dancing dwarf known as Akka. In the Pyramid Text of the sixth-dynasty, monarch Pepi I declared: "He who is between the thighs of Nut is the Twa who danceth like the god and who pleaseth the heart of the god before his great throne." Nut was the goddess of heaven and the mother of Osiris. This Twa, called Bes, was a guardian god—foreign born import from the land of Nubia--jolly, fond of music, and dancing--and so popular as to be adopted by the middle classes as a tutelary god of childbirth and, oddly, of cosmetics and female adornments. As the protective deity of the royal house of Egypt as well as the household deity throughout Egypt, Bes was said to chase away demons of the night and guard humans from dangerous animals. He eventually became a protector of the Dead, symbolized by his image being carved on bedposts--and, competed with even the refined and magnificent god Osiris for the attentions of humans. Because animals were readily available, the Twa taught their youth to use their senses to communicate directly with animals by means of imitative unspoken voice sounds (e.g. the bird's "cau, cau, cau"). Out of such communications with animals, descendants of the Ba-Twa Primitive Africans--the Sans (Bushman as called by Europeans) of Kalahari--to this day engage in the Click, Whistle, and similar imitative language practices of animals. Thereafter, a series of Quality aspects of life appeared, starting with the Twa--derogatively called Pygmies by Europeans. At least as early as 77,000 years ago the Twa wore the "Cross" around their necks as jewelry and as amulets for protection. Sometime thereafter, Very Ancient African Sages said their "Life Force"—the beginning of concepts of Divine Cosmic Essence--was contemplated (assumed Circumstantial Truths) to be the spirit of God. The resultant Essentials (or Primary Quality) imparted was that of the personal "Aliveness" needed for acquiring a pure Spiritual Essence as well as for communicating with Higher Powers. They fashioned to the modified Cross of Primitive Africans a Circular Cross which originally may have been a knot with mythical, practical, and/or religious significance. The Circle represented the immortal and eternal part (absolute reality) while the Cross represented what is mortal and transient (illusionmatter). This, the origin of the Idea-Form concept so vital to African Tradition, consisted of a looped Cross symbolizing "Life"-- both in the "here and now" as well as in the "hereafter". It included within itself the three elementary powers of creation: Emen-Ra; Reh, the sound which caused creation; and Waters of Nu (Waters of Chaos) (Saleem, Book of Dead, p41). Later, this esoterically symbolized the Annu Khet or "Stream of Cosmic Life Energy" animating all Life, emanating from the Godhead Annu (personified as Sun Goddesses). The Loop was called the *Shen*. The boomerang, an instrument developed by Twa people, is an object resembling a bird or airplane, with a bend near the middle of its wings. As a young boy, I was taught the Quality lesson of never saying bad things to other people about themselves or wish them bad luck because of the "*boomerang*" effect. The point of my teachers was that to throw out bad stuff in the world means it will come back just that way. This is known today as: "*what goes around comes around*" in the sense of whatever one sends into ones Internal World and/or the External World will come back with the same type of nature. Black People have said, if "you throw mud, some will spill on you." These Ba-Twa or Twa, from the boomerang aerodynamics, figured out reasons for an Echo—repetitive Qualities from the same source. Sound waves, upon striking a solid object, would bounce back through the air in a conduit or channel fashion in order to return to the source of what produced it. Therefore, the echo and its source, no matter how far apart, were never isolated or separated from the other. Meanwhile, Primitive Africans' Rock Art of Shamanic figures were often painted with them in strange 'bending forward' postures. This posture was adopted, say modern day Shaman, during their trance dances because they experienced a great deal of varying Quality pains when the 'potency' starts boiling in their stomachs with associated spontaneous nosebleeds (Bailey, Ancient African Bible Messages). There are indications the Twa people envisioned this pattern as a shaft (the spine) intertwined by the serpent's two aspects--its poison (with its heat and pain going up the spine) and its blood providing cooling nourishment—the origin of the *African Caduceus* indicating the power of transcendence. Since the "elixir" of the serpent (or totem) was thought to be a specific force of Nature, its image, called *Ka* by later Ancient Africans, was deemed sacred with the meaning of "the one great spirit." When this concept was passed into the setting of Ancient Africans' Kundalini Yoga (c10,000 BC) is was said to be the Serpent Power (internal life force) within all living Beings. The *African Caduceus* symbolized the three main channels of Life Force energy of the Serpent Power (Ashby, Book of Dead p124, 128)--the positive solar and negative lunar (the opposites of creation) from the external + the internal life forces which sustain the human body. If it operates in its higher energy-consciousness centers, one will have access to Cosmic Consciousness, Peace or bliss in ordinary human life. If its power were to be harnessed and transformed into spirit it would bring about ones spiritual evolution by "awakening" one to the deeper spiritual life existing in the unconscious depths of ones experience. Such is to "re-member"—i.e. put back together the consciousness of finite material aspect of ones life with the infinite collective and luminous life of the great Spiritual Being. The Serpent in the Ancient African Bible represents not evil—as in the European Bible, but instead the life force. Such is illustrated in the original medical caduceus of Africans. Historically, the root and framework of today's Essences for Africology Human Ideals is also from the Bantu—now called "Negroes, Pygmies, Twa, Nilotes," and others by Europeans. The concept of NTU (pronounced "*in*-to")--a universal, unifying force touching all aspects of existence--is a universal energy comprising the "Essence" of all that exists. Ancient Africans said this came from the Cosmic-Spirit--the Life-Force energy (Universal Energy or Ch'i, Ether, Prana) that penetrates, pervades, and enlivens all things. By being essential to life, it conveys the idea of freshness in whatever is full of life inside or outside the mind. For example, good emotions, self-protective emotions, or "bad" emotions which evoke life-like mental images, bubble with the vigor and freshness contained in the immediate sense experience. NTU highlights the interrelatedness between the intrinsic and the extrinsic factors involved in ones ability to respond to the problems of daily living. *Harmony, interconnectedness, authenticity*, and *balance* are NTU's four principles. *Harmony* has always carried the concept that Spiritual forces connect all forms of life. Through these forces, Spirituality, direction, and purpose arise for daily functioning. With a focus on communal systems, interconnectedness is a primary feature of the NTU philosophy. The individual, family, group, and community are all integral parts of a larger, interdependent system with a shared desire for systemic harmony. According to the African Tradition *Doctrine of Authenticity*, the highest significance is placed on interactions and interpersonal relationships. The key to fulfillment in interactions is through Real Self genuineness and authentic behavior. Finally, *Balance* is a state of equilibrium achieved through mediating opposing forces within and between individuals. These principles guide daily experiences and affect an individual's view of the world. Affect Symbolic Imagery provides NTU philosophical and operational descriptions in a manner acceptable for young minds undergoing a maturity process.

U

****ULTIMATE STANDARD FOR AFRICAN RIGHT LIFE LIVING: The Disposition in all human newborns Divine Consciousness (their Spark of God) contains a Right Life Living Plan. This Ultimate Standard Plan consists of Spiritual Elements' attributes of Unconditional Love, Truth, Reality, and the Natural flowing into all aspects of the Real Cosmos. That Standard is against which all comparisons of what one thinks, feels, says, and does are to be made. Even the tiniest degree of variation from that Standard is not acceptable because it is Spiritual and therefore of an "All-or-None" nature. The Divine Consciousness also provides Genius and Wisdom to enable one to follow "*The Way*"—also called the Middle Way; Middle Path, Mean Doctrine, or "*Keeping the Balance*". In African Tradition, "The Way" concerns following the Divine Presence and manifesting its Ma'at Earth World living power patterns throughout life and on into the Heaven "Afterlife". Illustrated to Ancient African people in how these contents play out was in the *Judgment Day (Psychostasis)* metaphorical context. In order to conform to the Standard, "*Keeping the Balance*" concerns rendering no favorites on either side of a Balance Scale. That Balance Scale is not about a mid-point in a straight line joining two extremes represented by points. Instead, being Metaphysical, it is analogized to the Sun (symbolizing the Ultimate Standard) and its rays (concerning Right Life Living)—all being Spiritual Elements attributes featured in an spider-like network. So, the Sun guides all God's Creatures (including any given human) and Creations. In this web, despite individualized "Uniqueness" in the "what it does" and "how it appears" of each Entity, all are part of an integrated Cosmic System—with the orchestrating Sun at its center. This *"Oneness" is the basis for Cosmic Correspondence, meaning all members of the Cosmic Organism Family possess "Equivalence"* (i.e. the Sun's "what it is" Essence). Hence, each of the Unique others shares a Spiritual Elements "Genetics" "Sameness". The Essence Pattern of that "Oneness" possesses: (1) Coherence (its hidden internal links and components being consistent with one another); (2) Consistency (standing firmly together within a state of harmony and balance with what makes sense); (3) Compatibility with Reality (practical); (4) Interconnectedness (everything real depends on every other real thing); (5) Order (sharing the "Oneness" of the Cosmic Primordial Substance center); (6) Regularity (conforming to the prescribed standard or the established pattern for it kind); (7) Balance (rendering no favorites on either side but conforming to the Ultimate Standard); (8) Harmony (complete adaptation of each part to the Wholistic Circle); (9) Endurance (progressing inside/in tune with the Spiritual Elements); and (10) Predictability. This means there is "ME/WE" *Continuity* (Unity running through Multiplicity) from each Entity interdependently doing its independent things for the benefit of the whole. Meanwhile, this Continuity is within the *course* of the Processes of Nature. Such is what *represents the Ultimate Cosmic Standard*. This Standard is to be modelled by each human for "ME/WE" Ma'at displays in all of its Life Living activities. While corresponding with the Sun's Substance, rays of this Cosmic Sun flow into ones Selfhood, ones Family, ones Career, ones social life, and ones leisure—all in a human's own integrated web-like system. Hence, when a human lives within the Ultimate Standard, ones life is organized and systematized. Anything short of that represents disassociation, disorganization, and maybe chaos. Humans can "know" the Ultimate Standard via their Cosmic Mind connected Divine Consciousness (their Highest or Divinity Self)—which Ancient Africans called "*Knowing Thyself*". That powers a process of striving for *Human Ideal Perfection,* using lifestyle patterns in each aspect of the Spiritual Elements' overall Goodness. Spontaneous striving is associated with natural inclinations of ones Highest Self. Both are generated by ones Divine Self, becoming increasingly impactful as they develop their fullest potential. *Spiritual Success is not the same as people view any of the Secular successes.* Spiritual Success embraces ones selections, particularly those based upon ones *intentions for ones deeds.* Of lesser or of no importance are Judgments based upon the degree of impact of ones deeds on resultant Effects and Consequences. Yet, ones cultivated Pre-birth Emotions and Pure Intellect are the best guides for the "Selection of the Superior," instead of one being guided by following any established Earth World pattern. *When ones Intent, Deeds, Effects, Consequences, and Results all give "ME/WE" Harmonious benefits that make a piece of the world a little better, this is the fullest display of Wisdom.* Still, operating out of any Spiritual Elements flow in some way carries the "ME/WE" consequence of the continual "Lifting of WE while there is striving for "ME to be consistently Climbing". *Ones Success,* rather than being in acts themselves, *is in the Intent of an action. The Material Values (e.g. riches, power over people) have no place.* To elaborate, the experience of mystical "ME/WE" Compassion (sharing the same Spiritual Space) occurs when the 'ME'—which has risen to the status of a "Non-Self"--sends a Cosmic enhancing Intent towards the 'WE'. That causes ones Personal Power to encounter and interfuse with the 'WE' at a Primordial Substance (Ocean of Nun) plane of existence--an experience of Human Perfection called *Compassion.* Such harmonious balance constitutes the *Inner Self Stability Platform* from which all choices, decisions, creations, and solutions spring forth—and without being "perfect" in everything—a human impossibility. So, "Weighing of Ma'at's feather" on Judgment Day is to merely "balance" it, not be lighter than it (Bailey, Ancient African Bible Messages). In other words, a Disharmonious result is overruled by a Harmonious Intent to "Be Right," "Recognize Right," "Do Right," "Make Things Right," & "Defend the Right". To these desired Heaven Afterlife ends, Jegna leaders are African Tradition educators who draw "First Wisdom" out of youth. jabaileymd.com

UNCONDITIONAL LOVE PLATTER: the instinct to Love themselves or others; to spread Love; to be Loved; and to be Lovable.

UNDERLYING: the innate core of a (Thought) Structure containing an Essence/Essentials—i.e. what is born to be its underground "seed" from which can spring all of its above-ground aspects.

UNDERTONES/OVERTONES: For whatever reason, people can be on the wrong track or in the wrong place, despite going in the right direction; or be on the right track or in the right place but going in the wrong direction. Those so Socialized or so choosing view their wrong way as being right and the right way as being wrong. They are as resistant to change. So are those too lazy to put forth time/energy/effort; or those nursing such significant psychic traumas as to have generated a "Raw Nerve" and needing to hide the shame of it from themselves and from others. *Step I* is to engage in the *Overtone called Wooing.* Its story began with the C11 concept of Courtly love. Its background came from works of the colorful Black Arab lover-warrior-poet *Antar* (Antarah Ibn Shaddad). His writings of "The Antar Romance" (580 AD)--a celebrated epic pertaining to the Arabic romance of chivalry--was the prototype for the development of European "Chivalry." His ideas were basic to European kings' 'court yard' castles in order for justice to be dispensed by to the king's subjects. Typical of that time and continuing thereafter was that those seeking justice would "Court" (used in the non-love sense of "to seek favor") members of the king's entourage in hopes they would convey to the king a good impression. The keystone point was that in discussions with the entourage, the guilty would embellish themselves into an overtone of being honorable. Their pitch was to incline their overtones so that the entourage's full attention was given having the best intentions in doing their evil acts. To "butter-up" the entourage so as to attract them to the message, they engaged in lavish flattery and allurements. The sense of '*Attract*' in its ancient context embraces '*Alluring*' into something harmful by means of an enticing (exciting hope or desire) decoy possessing energetic twisting and squirming pleasurable motives or ideas of a fantasy nature. Alluring also conveys the idea of charm providing some prospect of pleasure or advantage done by purpose and endeavor. The feature of "Attract" is the drawing of "Like to Like." Similarly, to woo those needing to improve but are resistant to change is to observe who they are, what they do, how they appear, or what they have—overtone what they pride themselves on--and lavishly compliment that. This immediately soothes their desire to be Important, to Matter, and to be shown Respect. *Step II*, Appreciate the Undertone positives they do inside all of their negatives—e.g. not doing as many negatives as usual; or what they did was "less bad"; or they finally did one thing of a Ma'at nature, even if by accident. These deserve compliments: "I am proud of that! See how you are improving?" "I admire what you are doing in this and in other areas." Any given area spotlights a place on which they can focus. *Step III*, meaningful discussions give them a chance to be heard so that they can learn more about undertones they think about in private. Rather than having the idea of trying to "save them," or pound in narrow-minded values, or exert authority, like "do it because I said so," let them be the teacher of who they are. In my daily Family Talks, all of us would decide on the "Rules," the "why's," and the punishments. Whenever possible, all of this was kept in an overtone humorous vain and with the "let's make this a game" atmosphere. *Step IV* focuses on their self-appreciation. Drive home their *Selfhood Greatness* from having a Spark of God orchestrating their lives—and carrying the same Genetics of their Ancient African Ancestors, the most brilliant people that ever lived—and possessing a Unique Talent no one has, or ever has had, or will ever have. Show how each is connected to all God's creatures—i.e. sharing Correspondence with their brothers and sisters, since all have the same Genetics but each is unique--correspondence between them and animals—e.g. the "Sameness" of needing to eat, sleep, self-protect; between them—correspondence with plants—both need the Sun for Vitamin D. Taking them into Nature, like the ocean, helps them gets the familiar with parts of their Selfhood and the power of each part. *Step V*, give them individual and group work projects; make it a game to see how Perfect they can make the results. This fashions *self-reliance and self-pride* while also getting them familiar with the necessity for struggles that must be overcome. *Step VI* is to get rid of all bad Emotions—e.g. anger, hate—by discussions and having them draw pictures of their pain. *Step VII*, keep stressing the importance of them *Keeping Their Word*—always doing what they say they are going to do for that builds Self-Trust. *Step VIII* is to daily practice *Manners*. jabaileymd.com

UNCONDITIONAL LOVE: My definition of Unconditional Love displays is: "paying a high price to provide Selfless Service of my very best to what is the greatest need for a given individual." It is up to the Receiver to do with it however they see fit, if at all—or even if abused for doing it. It is Ideal (i.e. perfect, permanent, stationary, enduring, eternal, and an all powerful force). When internalized by humans it imparts the "5Ss"—Safety, Security, Sureness/Self-Confidence, Strength, and Stability. Knowing ones Unconditional Love is spontaneous, said Ancient Africans, occur "when you can feel yourself related to another, to Nature, and to the Universe in the same complete and natural way as the child to the mother. Then you are aware of being in complete harmony with the Unconditional Love inside humanity and in tune with the natural rhythms of the universe" (Bailey, Common Sense p123). Unconditional Love, said Ancient Africans, represents God's inner nature—and serves as the Force of "Oneness" with all God's Creatures and Creations. Unconditional Love is what African Sages said is, of itself is beyond the ability of the human mind to grasp—making it Unknowable. In its *Cosmic Ideal,* Unconditional Love is the perfect, permanent, stationary, enduring, eternal, and an all-powerful force. When its Fire of Flame is implanted in each human as the Spark of God, it imparts the "5Ss" (safety, security, self-confidence, strength, and stability). There are not different types of Unconditional Love, as with Europeans. Yet, its attribute expressions vary on different planes of existence in both Spiritual and Material ways. In the *Earth World*, many attributes of Unconditional Love—like rays of the Sun—can be known based upon their manifestations—rays that can be modeled. An example is "Mother's Love" shown throughout the Animal Kingdom. Ancient Africans said such occurs "when you can feel yourself related to another, to Nature, and to the Universe in the same complete and natural way as the child to the mother. Then you are aware of being in complete harmony with the Unconditional Love inside humanity and in tune with the natural rhythms of the universe. Any Unconditional Love anywhere: has no consideration for what the Giver might get; possesses. Aliveness which is totally independent of external circumstances or situations; and is given—not asking if one deserves but, instead to fulfill a genuine need--and "That's the way it is!" With the maturing humans come ever widening of different levels in human expressions, depending on the mindset and interpreted experiences one gets in coming to a Greater Awareness of Self. It leads one to the instinctual designing of ones lifestyle to model the guiding manifestations of the work the God spirit does in Nature. Such is best known by spending all spare time listening to Nature's attractive sounds—e.g. the chirping of birds, the babbling brooks, the patter of rain, the rumbling of waterfalls, the wind rustling leaves of trees, and the whoosh of waves breaking on the seashore. A way for humans to become aware of Natures manifestations of Unconditional Love is by getting inside the flow of Nature's Processes. The process for direct perceiving is cultivation of ones potential capacity to *Intuit* (i.e. learn from within) the *Will of God in order to form "ME/WE" Order, Unity, and Harmony as expressions of "Life Living."* Being able to arrive at Right conclusions or judgments by direct perception of Reality results from having connected with God's *Omnipotence* (Unlimited and universal power); *Omnipresent* (everywhere simultaneously), and *Omniscient*--total knowledge of everything which characterizes God's Being. That connection puts one into the realm of the ultimate in human Wisdom. Fundamental to entering into this process is to maintain a deep state of Peace within ones Selfhood—and it is critically important to be calm during the worst of life's problems. Ancient Africans said deep Peace—Hetep—represents each human's original and natural state inside the Cosmic Organism. This is the Unconditional Love experience—done through time and space and not instantly--of *Omnipresence*—as in a "ME/WE" feeling of Oneness as a "Non-Self" with all of God's Creatures and Creations; *Omniscience*—intuiting (Spiritual Elements awareness without thinking) that lead to Knowledge and Wisdom; and *Omnipotence* which comes from sharing with God the same quality of powers, though not the same Quantity or Capacity at any given time. Amen (Metu Neter II: 17) says a classical though not exact analogy is that of a drop of water having the same life giving properties of as its ocean parent but not the capacity to hold the numberless things that can be fitted in the ocean. As one approaches the ultimate in self-discipline of both sides of ones brain, with the Right Brain orchestrating—as did Ancient Africans—nothing within the realm of a given human's potential will be impossible to achieve. Armed with this Omnipresence, Omniscience, and Omnipotence one possesses a near human-god ability to organize Immaterial Ideas into its complementary Form to thus fashion Idea-Forms which reproduce itself in solving problems. One is on the path to being a "Human-God" when ones "ME/WE" is a "specific-less" user of the *Unconditional Love Platter*—i.e. the instinct to Love; to spread Love; to be Loved; and to be Lovable. In turn, the Spiritual Energy in which these flow give rise to an "Aliveness"—i.e. the ever expanding Spiritual Beauty called *Happiness*.

UNDEFINABLE: Spiritual and Metaphysical happens cannot be defined and there is no possibility of having adequate Descriptions or Explanations or realistic Translations or Interpretations. To "*Describe*" (C13 'to give an account of') is to convey a pictorial impression or image in words of some of the general features and particularly regarding the appearance and the nature of the Thing. To "*Explain*" (C15 'make it plain' by flattening it out and making it smooth) means to give details of a matter so as to make it intelligible by clarification. In short, an *Explanation* give a general translation of the "gist" history of something about Love and Life or of what happened concerning either so as to throw light upon some point of special difficulty. To elaborate, both Describe and Explain require "*Interpretations*" (translation) which give the meaning of something by paraphrase, with emphasis on a doubtful or hidden meanings of that which is perplexing. This "*Translation*" is a rendering of how the Thing seems to be of what the mind can grasp by implication into another form, as do Figures of Communication (including Figures of Speech and Figures of Thought).

UNDERSTAND: the inner truth lying hidden; exposing intricacies of what defys fundamental thoughts/ beliefs --a mindset resulting from systematic mental discipline in general and self-control in particular. That *Knowledge*, according to African Sages, is defined as the direct perception of Reality -- an act of understanding without the use of thoughts. African Sages used much time, energy, and effort to understand the smallest of details. As a result of understanding in the flow of the Divine Logos, when additional work is done to master it, one has at the same time insight into and understanding of many things. That is a reason those interested only in the Practical lose out on much. Higher and larger views mainly come from struggles being forced upon one to completely handle—those one would have avoided if one could have. Understanding can only occur when the mind listens completely from beginning to end and without the mind wandering in between. People who do not understand themselves have a craving for understanding—and that only comes when they say every-thing they have to say. A key to understanding others is to accompany them in their mind's experiences—but this requires being non-judgmental. People feel comforted once they are understood, and that begins with validating them—"I see what you mean"—which not about approving. The more one understands how one got to be the way one is, the less inclined one is to blame, find fault, and criticize. *Understanding* means see-ing *Inner Similarities* in dissimilar things: fashioning interrelationships; distinguishing the superficial from the profound; separating the Truth from its look-alikes; selecting what to analyze; and determining what to ma-nipulate and maneuver into Options to connect Cause/Effect. They understood *knowledge advances by finding how similarities and differences are related, harmonized, and synthesized*. The objective was to arrive at the Truth of Thought by Synthesis. Then they positioned evidence and proof on the proper rungs of the Cosmic Ladder and maneuvered them according to the unique Cosmic Guidelines operating on a given rung. Principles on a given plane of existence were harmoniously fit to form Knowledge. African Sages learned that the ability to distinguish truth from falsehood can only be determined by the knowledge of the relations between parts with each other and the whole (Amen Metu Neter I: 107). Basic to the subject at hand (e.g. on a given plane of existence in scientific and esoteric realms), Principles were harmoniously fit to form applicable Circumstantial Rational/Logical knowledge.

"UNIQUENESS/SAMENESS" CONCEPT: A Salad (to salt) consist of like-kind but unrelated raw green leafy vegetables, often with other raw vegetables and/or chopped fruit, meat, fish, eggs, and the like. Each of these ingredients has a different external appearance, internal ingredients that have similarity in some aspects but not in others; and what underlies their internal ingredients—whether the same, alike, or different—are identical or "Sameness" elements formed by a preexistence of a bodiless intelligence responsible for what gives rise to the atoms in the identical elements. The "Sameness" elements in the internal ingredients produce in-ternal ingredients that are the same, alike, or different because of the way their atoms are arranged/rearranged and combined/recombined to create new and unique forms and unique structures. The power carrying out all of these processes is a bodiless system of energy—each pattern following the Plan of the bodiless intelligence. Hence the "creation" of physical matter or Metaphysical products is executed by a bodiless Entity using its intelligence and power. There can be many ways to shared "Sameness" apart from their "Unique" features. Human pre-birth Emotions and Intellect have a similar access to Cosmic Intelligence and are able to tap into it upon the process to do so. Similar "Things" having unlike outward appearances may have like-kind inner aspects ingredients—as with siblings sharing the same Genetics; or like-kind outer aspects sharing inner mean-ings, as in being "brothers from different mothers"; or from having harmonious interrelationships in parts, in similarities of *the inner meaning of external appearances* and/or characters of the *Same type*--despite their other dissimilarities. Sameness is an Abstract or Abstraction of the inner nature of the "Genetics" of all that make up a given Family. Furthermore, one can then use this bodiless energy system to affect physical events, matter, and Metaphysical Things through a Metaphysical force called Telepathy (direct communication from one mind to another; Telekinesis (the ability to alter the shape or position of physical matter through "mental" means) and Clairvoyance (the ability to see into the past, future, and present since they are all same above time or space as well as see into distant physical locations in the present) (Amen, MAAT p64-5).

UNKNOWNS/KNOWNS: Human-made Inferences best follow Nature's Processes—and those are roughly Algebraic. Thus, there are four situations: Type 1-- Earth World Known; Type 2 -- Earth World Unknown; Type 3 -- Spiritual Unknown; and Type 4 -- Circumstantial Known. From Very Ancient African's invention of Algebra, they could apply the Algebraic Known, using a number, to what is Unknown, denoting it by an "X". The original Mathematical problem is now reduced to an equation involving an Unknown number. Since Algebra was the mathematical tool initiating the acquisition of knowledge, in considering Types I-IV, it was vital to recognize Continuity (Unity running through Multiplicity) on the Known side that into and throughout the Unknown or Hidden side of the equation. For the Unknown to be deemed a Circumstantial Truth it was necessary that these "big four" components stayed within Nature's Processes and that each followed the course of those *Natural Processes. This meant that while each was* doing its independent things, all of the "big four" were interdependently working for the benefit of the whole Cosmic Organism. That *Continuity* (unity among diversity) in the *course* of the Known/Unknown *Natural Processes* could be about: (a) possessing the same "Genetics" or Essence; (b) being a member of a given Archetype Family; (c) having *Inner Similarities despite their* dissimilar appearances; (d) manifest interrelationships between dissimilar and similar things; or (e) sharing common points—as where "A" in the Known (Type 1 and/or 4) touches "X" in the Unknown (Type 2 and/or 3) and appropriately belongs with it, even though the relationships or ingredients of the rest are undetermined. Within this context, one could have a sense of remaining on the path leading to Circumstantial Human-made Truths. Thus, the adequacy of Inferences could be determined by staying within the Type 1 and/or 4 flow of their Knowledge of the Correspondence relation between parts with each other and the whole. This could be between two Knowns or between what is Known and the Unknown.

USELESS BENEFITS: The 1200 AD English word "Use" meant to employ for a purpose or the act of putting into service, as in exercising to acquire a skill or for performances. The first English record of "Useless" was in Shakespeare's "The Rape of Lucrece" (1595) in the sense of lacking actual fitness for a purpose. Later, it was part of the family of futile or vain (lacks imaginable fitness) deemed to be inherently incapable of accomplishing a specified result. Useless, in the widest sense, signifies not of use for any valuable purpose and is thus closely similar to valueless and worthless. More specifically, dictionaries define it as having or being of no beneficial use; ineffective (having no means to accomplish a purpose or having no effect); incapable of functioning or assisting. But Critical Thinking (CT) does not look at the useless that way--as a thing having no benefit. First, with sufficient creativity everything has usefulness of some sort. Rather, CT looks at the "Big Picture" to decide if the situation is/is not worth getting involved with this thing and under these circumstances (which brings to mind ones top priorities and standards)--or, if it is worth it, it is/is not in ones best interest to do so after considering the consequences to oneself and to others. Something may be interesting (e.g. trivia) and important but are useless when chosen over something that necessarily needs to be done immediately. First, CT may retry the "Useless" for a difficult problem when study indicates the thing deemed to be a failure inside a given channel has possibilities. Perhaps others misapplied it (e.g. in the wrong direction or on the wrong plane of existence); or applied at the improper time; or it was defective; or it needing updating.

Yet, its "home" may be in another channel or awaiting the proper channel to be discovered. For this reason, CT never discards the "useless" but rather puts it aside awaiting the proper place for it. This requires a storage system that is available with only second of research to find it. Second, CT may spend idle time playing with the "Useless," for this is an excellent way to develop skills for designing Options, creativity, and inventions. Third, "Useless" simply means there is no goal to achieve in the activity because the benefit is in the doing. Such beneficial useless things, simply because they exist, are intended to be enjoyed as they are. Play creates order and in fact is order. Into an imperfect world and into the confusion of life and the maze through which one goes through life, Play brings a temporary and a limited perfection. Games are played for their own sake-- and that is perfection of a simple design. Music and dance benefits are in the doing and that is the destination. Mountain climbing is done because it is there. Fourth, Things done playfully, whimsically, for its own sake or with abandon is an expression of that person's autonomy. This means it has its own realm of Being--and that is perfection. Nothing about it per se will contribute to achieving immortality. Yet, it is *Spontaneous* (that which happens of itself) and in spontaneity alone lies the true spirit of play--done for no reason--and containing no reason--and present independent of the struggle of existence. This is a Free Mind state. Besides, spontaneity has no commercial value and it never should since that would injure the spirit of the creation. Play is its own good reason --a reason free and unhampered and existing for its own sake--a reason resulting from the overflow of spiritual, mental, and physical energy (called the Creative Play impulse). Freedom is the very key of Spiritual Play--and it comes from ones Dignity (representing the image of God in African Tradition). Being into African tribal dancing—with movement of the entire body to syncopated rhythms checkered with asymmetrical fluidity; angular bending of the arms, legs, and torso; shoulder and hip movement; and scuffing, stamping, and hopping--and doing so with a free spirit of improvisation indicates the participants are using that as a means of connecting with their Dignity.

V

VALID: Valid is the result of what integrates all and contradicts none of the relevant data + exhibiting the property of being legitimately derived from premises by logical inference. The reason is that Validity is merely what is inferred from an antecedent premise and is independent of truth.

VALIDITY: *the entire process remain within and evolve out of the Spiritual Elements.*

VALUES: Values refer to central aspects of people's self-identities and self-perceptions differ from related constructs such as moral attitudes, which refer to specific issues and do not necessarily reflect broader values. As opposed to using *Measurements* for quantitative items (e.g. things one can see), Qualities undergo assessments, grading, prioritizing, and category rankings by *Estimates* of it qualitative aspects (i.e. things one cannot see) into Mild, Slight, Moderate, and Extreme degrees. The word "Estimate" means to estimated measured Values. Values are what "touch" a part of ones Selfhood regarding what the "Thing" is, what it does, and/or how it appears. Estimated assessments of the significance of the proposed given and received "Thing" to ones Selfhood gave rise to the displaying of one or more whole numbers"take aim" by locking on to something in ones sights or fix on a particular figure without exact calculation. That is special which receives or which, in someone's estimation, ought to receive unusual attention or treatment because it is uncommon. See Estimate

VERIFICATION: Verification results from extended and continued Observation and Testing. Europeans say it accounts for all the facts which are properly related to it and there must not be any other possible hypothesis to account for the same facts.

VIABLE: "*Vital*" (C14; 'life' and 'living') birthed "*Viable*" (C19; capable of life) and its wide range

"VIBRATIONS" FOR ANCIENT AFRICAN SCHOLARS: "Alkebu-Lan" or Egyptian "Afru-ika" (Mother Land)--c50,509 BC: "Nothing rests; everything moves; everything vibrates and moves in circles" (The Kybalion p137). When in the fourth grade, my teacher told us students that everything has a vibrating rhythm, even the desk we were sitting in. That stunned me and, since I could not see any desk actions, I felt it all over without detecting any movements. Such is an example of how things can be present beyond ones ability to detect them. The word "*Vibration*," the basic element of "The Natural," means 'to move quickly to and fro'; 'to shake or brandish.' It involves the idea of a motion, not always in the same direction, but in which the moving Thing goes back and forth. Very Ancient Africans' Vibration rhythm and pattern recognition led them to an awareness of cycles in Nature, to the earliest forms of codified Mathematics, and to the perception of distant rhythms in the solar abyss—from which they derived the "*Music of the Spheres*". Ancient Africans linked these to their accurate calendar (4236 BC), to the rhythms of the stars and Nile River, to the rhythms within a human's body, and to stimulations of Kundalini via neuro-melanin nerve currents, then moving through the body like a living energy current (Bynum, African Unconscious p141-4; Diop, African Origin). Tehuti, the African master of all the world's masters, said varying rates and modes of vibration account for the "differences" between various manifestations of Cosmic Powers/Displays. Even THE ALL, in itself, manifests a constant vibration of such an infinite degree of intensity and rapid motion as to seem to be at rest, like one sees in a highly revolving wheel. Tehuti's *Principle (4) of Polarity* says: "Everything is dual; everything has poles; everything has its pair of opposites; like and unlike are the same; opposites are identical in nature, but different in degree…" This is the basis for the profound *Principle (2) of Correspondence*—"Uniqueness in Sameness" (my summary). The *Vibration Principle* (3) was from what African Sages fashioned original concepts of "*The Way*"--the *Divine*

Logos—i.e. "The Word"--written in the Egyptian "Book of Coming Forth by Day," the oldest written text in the world (60,000 BC, Seleem, p 59, xiii). Europeans mislabeled it "The Book of the Dead"; St. John plagiarized "The Word" and put it into The Gospel of the European Bible. Tehuti continued by saying that the God Spirit is at one end of the Pole of Vibration—and at the other end are extremely gross forms of Matter—while in-between are millions upon millions of different rates and modes of vibrations--e.g. Matter, Energy, the phenomena of Mind and of the Soul. A "*Soul Trademark*" is my symbolic term for what is "stamped" on the "Virtual" Soul of a given human while inside and joined to the Cosmic Organism prior to Earth birth. A human's "Trademark" (standing for the Spark of God's Essence) has the *highest of a Cosmic vibratory rate--i.e. the Spiritual Elements* of Unconditional Love, Truth, Reality, and the Natural. A Soul Trademark's Interchange is like a Radar Beacon looking for "Soul Mates." Its transmitter part send out extremely high vibrating wave pulses (a short bundle of waves) capable of penetrating through even dark "Clouds" over another human's "Soul Sunshine". After depositing a *payload impact,* its rays simultaneously move out in all directions. The transmitter rhythmically radiates energy into space as electromagnetic waves, alternating between off and on. This is similar to vibrations set up when energy is applied to a violin string—and using stringed instruments was how Very Ancient African Sages learned about Harmony. When "off," its receiver is "on" for the purpose of picking up any returning waves caused by the transmitter's payload impact. A Correspondence match then stimulates the Thing with a like-kind vibratory rate to harmonize with its ever-waiting Complementary Equal "Soul Mates." The resultant Tone and Spirits meshing into Unity are like what the baby has for its mother before acquiring the ability to discern who she is--the magical power of an Unconditional Love experience. *By having the Spiritual Elements "stamped" onto every human's Soul before birth, each and all of their full or partial manifestations can be known to humans by being "Felt"--even if one has never experienced them, seen them, or heard of them before.* So, even if one hears anything about any part of any of the Spiritual Elements for the first time, one can recognize it by its high vibration rate. This accounts for many Black People being exposed to Ancient African Bible teachings for the first time and having the reaction: "I know that's right!" jabaileymd.com

VIBRATIONS IN THE NUANCE FAMILY: Ancient African Sages realized everything in the Cosmos (including the stars and planets) is based upon a specific pattern, for each has a different and specific vibration rate. What is *below the human mind's ability to conceive or beyond the scope of the most powerful pertinent technology is the Cosmic Mind's vibrations at such an infinite degree* of intensity and rapid motion as to seem to be at rest, like one sees in a highly revolving wheel. Otherwise, Tehuti, the African master of all the world's masters, said varying rates and modes of vibration account for the "differences" between various manifestations of Cosmic Powers/Displays. For convenience, these can be divided into Mild, Slight, Moderate, and Extreme degrees. At the *Mild*est—i.e. at the bottom--is Evil's very slow vibrating Things. The *Slight* Vibration Category embrace Gross Matter of the Physical Realm and on up to non-evil Spirits which have higher vibrations than gross matter. At the top is the is *Extreme* Vibrations Category, manifesting as Spiritual Principles based on Vibration rates that conformed into patterns of Universal Rhythms—Principles African Sages inferred to be *Idea-Forms*—i.e. self-realizable Divine idea-patterns fixed in Nature and with the capability to reproduce themselves in their own Essence Virtual Image (what it was when it came into Being-hood) so as to become the Thing it makes. It was the Ether (the primary life-force) which fashioned the Virtual Image into a beginning physical Form. This began the *Moderate Vibratory Category of Things*—the realm of the family of Spiritual Nuances, Subtlety, and Discernments. Since Ancient Africans considered Ether to be spiritual and equivalent to the Cosmic Psyche or "Soul," it was called *Quality* so as to avoid confusing it with the Soul and Mind of humans. When Ether was the *Cause* of the mental conception of a Thing (because the Thing is invested in at least flimsy Matter, like an idea in ones mind) and/or when

Ether was the *Cause* of the existence of a Thing (like a Halo in the Spiritual Realm—or like taste, smell, hearing, and touch feeling in Secular realms) it was termed a *Primary Quality*. But when Ether simply played a *supporting* part for the conception or existence of something (e.g. color) already in "Being-hood," it was a *Secondary Quality*. Broadly, *Subtlety* (Subtlety) deals chiefly with nicety of discernment, discrimination of taste, and acuteness of judgment. "*Discernment*", meaning derivatively the ability to distinguish from, is lesser subtlety. The foundational meaning of *Nuance* is to show variations (slight differences) of shade, like a cloud, is characterized by Penumbra. Whereas an *Umbra* is a complete and fully formed dark shadow, *Penumbra* are partial shadows outside the complete shadow, as that formed by the sun or moon during an eclipse. Decreasing Shade is removing tiny differences of darkness while increasing Shade is adding more layers of darkness. The differences between light and dark—or white and black—is the amount of Ether (i.e. Matter). The African word "*Subtle*", in relation to Nuance and Discernment concerns different layers of Ether on an Essence when it came into Being—the dark "That it is." Thus, the dark Ether dampens the dark Divine's so dazzling illuminated Essence so it can appear light. Stage I of Subtle came from the concept of the "Ether"--the shiny, pure, upper air--at its *Moderate Vibratory Category* beginning appearance form. Ether is the purest, most highly concentrated form of a nature or essence of a Thing. Here, the form is called the "*This-ness*" since it is a subtle fluid of pre-matter consisting of a fine, flimsy, vapor mist of which "the Heavens," the lintel's (i.e. the Sublime) stars and planets, Nature, and natural laws are made. "This-ness" means it equates to a quanta of energy and matter that constitutes the minimum amount needed for any potential physical entity to become involved in an interaction. Ether is first added in the Sublime Plane. Next, as the "That it is" undergoes a descent toward the Physical World—which Ancient Africans referred to it as "to move a Phantom"--it *Involutes* (the process of getting involved). Stage II Ether implies a few more layers of Ether are added to the "That it is" upon entering Metaphysical realms. Stage III Ether occurs when a "That it is" gains a few more layers of Ether. At each Stage from top to bottom, where they overlap constitutes a Nuanced Interchange where mosaic pieces from each overlapping contributor is reassembled into a unique Identity Image, complete with its own Disposition primed to deliver its "what and why" message and carry out its Mission according to the Divine Plan.

VICTIMS OF BULLIES: "Victim" and Victimize" (sacrificial animal) come from early Romans belief that animal sacrifice had magical overtones. "Victima" related to the English word "Witch" and "Wile" (which originally meant Sorcery and Divination). In C15, Victim referred to a creature killed as a religious sacrifice; in C17, a person harmed by another; and C18, to fall a victim by causing someone to suffer or killed by something. As to the moral or just aspects of how one becomes a Victim is that the victor will always be the judge, and the vanquished will always be the accused. An example is 100,000 babies were annually added to the Victims of slavery while 20,000 lives were annually sacrificed on the plantations. This was seen as it should be by Christian slave owners. Hence, victory has nothing to do with what is right but instead has the power to devastate by destruction. Too many of today's Victims of the Supernatural cling to the cloak of passivity to cover their sense of impotence. They have "Inside-Out" mindsets that tell them they are powerless and that nothing they do will ever hurt anyone and any thing they can do will not benefit anyone. Furthermore, many are apologetic to the oppressors for being Victims of the oppressors' mistakes of making themselves homemade monsters, and not their own from choosing to remain Victims. The mass of the public fall victim a little more easily to a big lie than to continuous small ones. Public support for predators comes from leaders marking victims most beneficial to control or destroy; denouncing those Victims; exciting the public odium and the public hatred—and keeping the public excited with addicting Trinkets—all to conceal the leaders own abuses and encroachments. The way such a Cult Network is formed has been well put by Julian Jarvis: "The arresting officer is cool with the sergeant; the sergeant rides motorcycles with the chief; the chief of police is cool with the prosecutor; the prosecutor plays golf with the district attorney; the district attorney was in the same fraternity as the judge; the judge endorsed the mayor; the mayor went to the same college as the governor; the governor has stock in private prisons; and prisons are filled with Black and Brown in-mates"—to which I add who allow all of this to happen without accountability. By victims being daily controlled by the perpetrators, they adopt their personalities and ways—as if they are Halos of a "Disaster Star". But the displays of Victims' adoptions go in the opposite direction of the oppressors unless they have been selected to be representatives for the oppressors. Fredrick Douglass (p. 61) said: "A man's character greatly takes its hue and shape from the form and color of things about him. Under the whole heavens there is no relation more unfavorable to the development of honorable character than that sustained by the slaveholder to the slave. Reason is imprisoned here, and passions run wild. Like the fires of the prairie, once lighted, they are at the mercy of every wind, and must burn till they have consumed all that is combustible within their remorseless grasp." For example, the oppressors devise evil Supernatural justifications for doing inhumane acts to their victims--and without any compassion. Such is imitated by their hand-picked Victim-Puppets, as amply displayed by Douglass: In speaking of a "Negro breaker" who succeeded in crushing his spirit, Fredrick Douglass said: "We were worked in all weathers.... The longest days were too short for him, and the shortest nights were too long for him... until I was broken in body, soul and spirit ... a man transformed into a brute!" Douglass mentioned at length the inadequate amounts of food, the inappropriate and limited supply of clothing, and the ever-present floggings -- often for no reason. "There were no wages for slave work, no praise for well doing, no motive for toil but the lash" -- all translating into a reduced incentive to work any more than necessary to escape punishment. The result is that Victims mindsets, like those of the oppressors, undergo *Selfhood Splintering--with* half of ones Selfhood becomes *Self-Absorbed* (viewing everything within ones world in relationship to oneself in a "me, me, me" manner) and the other half following dictates of External World influences designated by the oppressors. Because Victims see themselves as dependent on the oppressors for their very survival—in a manner similar to the child to its parents—they become bonded to them—complete with protecting the oppressors from fellow Victims. So afflicted Victims with do all they can to reject or even fight the ones trying to help them—thus acting as oppressors do.

VIGNETTE: Middle English originally used as an architectural term for a carved representation of a vine. In C18 it described any decorative design in the midst of printed matter and later for the printed matter itself.

VIRTUAL: (a boundless 'Becoming Being')

VISION: *art of seeing invisible essences others are unable to see.* enables one to fashion Options of how to best handle problems by establishing connections of Cause to the Effects and then devising Solutions to handle the Effects A "This-ness" can be apprehended as a "*Vision*"—*equating to a Prophetic Percept.*

VIOLENCE: Any threat to--or disturbance caused by an attack on—or the destruction of the Spiritual Elements—whether in the form of the spiritual, emotional, mental, physical, social, financial, or what is materially meaningful

VIRTURES—CARDINAL OF AFRICAN TRADITION: symbolizing human excellence—are: Propriety (be in accordance with the fitting and appropriate), Balance, Order, Truth, Harmony, Peace and Tranquility, Fellowship, Justice, Rightness, Straightness or Righteousness, and Reciprocity ("the reward of one whose acts consist in the fact that one will act for her/him" in doing good).

VISION: The art of being aware of invisible essences others are unable to see--enables Intuiting, seeing similarities in the dissimilar and discerning uniqueness in similarities. *Vision leads one to see the infinite in the finite* and thereby fashion Options of how to best handle problems.

VITAL: "*Vital*" (C14; 'life' and 'living') birthed "*Viable*" (C19; capable of life) and its wide range

VOICE OF THE SILENCE: says everything by not saying anything at all while it retains everything by giving away everything—each are tonics to quiet disturbed minds.

VOLITION: ones mental activities which select ingredients from ones System of Values to determine which step to take at the cross-road of ones Lower Self path and ones Highest (Divinity) Self path. It also is the *choice to do or to not do something while on the chosen path*. Yet, ones choices, as agencies/Causations, have Effects, and those Effects have layers of Consequences.

VOLITIONAL LIFE-SHAPING DECISIONS: To be distinguished from the Brain/Mind's Cognition (concerning intelligence) and the Affective (Emotional) aspects are the *Conative*--the power driving how one acts on those thoughts and Emotions--the power for any natural tendency related to purposive behavior directed toward action or change--the power for impulse, desiring, striving, and resolving. Conative power is in Mild, Slight, Moderate, and Extreme degrees—driven, said the ancients, by "animal spirits." Whereas Extreme is conviction, *Velleity* implies a Mild or weak desire or inclination so insignificant that one makes little or no attempt to realize it by actions. The state of mind which generates the pertinent mental activity for these to occur as well as the choice to do/not do is called *Volition*. The Effect is the initiation of action, called an act of volition, or the act of Willing. Volition and the act of Willing constitute the action. The moving of ones hand is what one does or makes to happen and this is not the same as "the hand is in motion" (something that happens as, for example, a reflex, as from a muscle spasm) or someone lifting ones hand. A movement action, as distinct from a motion, is two things causally connected--like the two sides of a coin engaged in a dualistic action of differences for a common purpose. This is called a "*Such-ness*" action whereby Metaphysical aspects of different things are participating in a given interaction's '*what it is doing*' or "what is happening." To elaborate, a "movement" happens from: (1) a mental activity and (2) its effect, a bodily motion. The process starts with a Disposition, whose contents are supplied by a Source. The impetus or underlying motivation powering the Disposition is called the *Conative Element*. With adequate power to activate the faculty of the Will or the Will's functional set of abilities that yield the mental events involved in initiation action, the Will must first accept the message from the Disposition directing the mental activity. That acceptance is a choice, called Volition. Second, the Will must integrate the message into a meaning and compatible abstract. Third, the Will supplies the Ether--a quanta of energy constituting the minimum amount needed for any physical entity to become involved in an interaction. In other words, the Will is the initiator of the intensions of all that happens in ones life by means of Images. Self-made Life-shaping decisions focus on Volition--imaged in the Tree Concept. To elaborate, a human's Soul has its origin in the Cosmic Intelligence and thus consists of *Divine Consciousness* as its state of Being--i.e. the background of what a human generates as manifestations in the foreground of that human's life. The background *Consciousness* part of ones Soul is ones Selfhood-Awareness. The Divine aspect of that Divine Consciousness is God's Spirit of Unconditional Love which is eternal and independent of and uninfluenced by anything, including whatever evil a human does. There is a natural tendency for one to make foreground choices derived from ones Divine Consciousness. However, its Unconditional Love aspect means each human is free to choose to stay inside the Cosmic Circle of Wholism or step out of it. The state of mind which generates that "Choice" for the foreground, called ones Sensory Consciousness, is its volitional aspect, meaning a selection from two or more alternatives. Its "Seed" or supreme life-shaping decision is to step out of the Circle. Its "Roots" are the choice to Think or not to Think--a decision determining the System of Values that will be ones Standards, Guides, and Filter through life. Whether the "raw" materials for Perceptions come from Sensations or Metaphysical entities, those Perceptions are integrated into Concepts as *Abstracts*-- i.e. the Virtual (an inactive boundary-less 'Becoming Being') in Metaphysical or Supernatural realms as well as *Abstraction* (the same but in Physical realms). This integration is done by Choice--a process of Reason, of Thought that has to be initiated, sustained, defended, and protected. This choice is to maintain a state of full awareness or to drift aimlessly, as if one is a robot or zombie--being at the mercy of ones animalistic or outside forces. To not Think is to not Focus and thus whatever one assesses is "Broad-Stroked" in the sense of stereo-typing uniqueness in things or people--unable to distinguish what is real, distortions, or fantasy--unable to correct ones flaws and errors--unable to separate Certainty, information, beliefs, and opinions--unable to be self-sufficient and thrive. jabaileymd.com

WADING: African metaphor for the intuited spiritual learning required to walk into and on through whatever offers resistance, impedes, or makes movement difficult.

WARRIORS—PRIMITIVE/ANCIENT EUROPEAN: C14 Old French "Warrior" (one who wages war) means an experienced fighting soldier. For those who make war, better things do not exist for them--for this is where they show the "primitive" masculinities of courage, strength, and virility. Each battle is an opportunity to reclaim and prize these. Primitive European warriors' battles were initially oriented to overcoming their human nature Scarcity needs. Eventually, they expanded to embrace their concept of happenings in those Unseen Realms influencing their existence--concepts manifesting in a mainly religious to a mainly violence range. Varied subdivisions were involved in local battles or in 'shamanism' (those thought to have visions and to perform healing) or in hierarchical organizations. But common to each form, regardless of its nature, was the '*Charismatic*' (Greek, favor or grace) leader—spotlighting powers demonstrated to be an irresistible self-interest force in human affairs. One form was "*Religious Warriors*" who engaged in sacrifices as the root of their religious rituals. Overtime, Sacrifice was a collective celebration that ritually undermined the prohibition or taboo on murder, especially of relatives and kinfolk. However, in the big picture, sacrifice as a collective ritual, obscured the origins of religious practices by resorting to actual murder and physical violence. Another form, "*Battle Warriors*," turned their individuality completely over to the leadership and lived by the code: "I will always place my mission first; I will never accept defeat; I will never quit; I will never leave a fallen comrade" (Samet, *Armed Forces & Society, 2005*). Honor, the first of their two obsessive concerns, was deemed insepa-rable from external measures and spoils. For example, there was no grander or nobler prospect for exhibiting an "honorific trophy" than to carry home the bloody armor stripped from an enemy's back. Yet, generating an even greater share of honor was being able to display enemies' heads. Failure to obtain, or retain, such treasures following battle brought with it a corresponding shame. A second obsession was with each fellow fallen soldier thereby becoming the momentary object of a new frenzy from the rest of the Troops. Fellow warriors would strip off his armor before starting to drag the corpse back into their lines. Often this was done at the expense of losing sight of both tactical and larger strategic aims, thereby allowing the enemy to regroup and charge again. Primitive/Ancient codes of loyalty and honor manifested themselves nowhere more clearly than in a steadfast determination to protect the body from the enemy, even at the loss of ones own life. Homer put this into words by indicating the corpse acquires a value independent of its armor--becoming a tactical objective on the battlefield—the vehicle through which one retains nobility. The imperative to retrieve a fallen comrade's body from the field regardless of tactical cost also suggested the preeminence of the dead over the living. Warriors of the Classical period somewhat altered these patterns. While fighting for countless reasons, they continued to emphasize primitive warfare's centrality of the dead body by taking honor in its possession and returning home with it. This satisfied many things for fellow warriors to see and admire: loyalty, fear, vengeance, and honor. By contrast, whereas the body is real, the principles behind humanitarian intervention, peacekeeping, and pursuing terror seemed far more elusive. Nevertheless, there was an expansion of their actions in two parts. One is that rather than being a mere reflection of the customary practice regarding retrieval and identification of battlefield dead, the return of corpses in itself was tantamount to an acknowledgment of victory, defeat, or stalemate. Another was that they fought most frequently and most desperately to preserve the honor of the living. In Biblical times, a central OT Icon Image for the nature and activity of the Jewish God is that of being the divine warrior (Exod. 15:3; Isa. 42:13; Psalm 24:8). Although this "man of war" image did not conform to European Christianity's dogma about God as love, there has been the ever presence of a fusion in Christianity of violence and the sacred in institutional forms. Examples are plentiful in history—e.g. the C11-C13 AD Crusades; the C13-C19 *Inquisition* (gaining confessions through torture for unjust trials); and Middle Ages Feudalism, where religion provided an institutional check on interpersonal violence by integrating warriors into society.

WATER QUALITY TOOLS: "Water's Qualities" tools are first illustrated by Water unresistingly accepting the lowest level and settling into the lowest places, rather than seeking the highest levels. Second, water demonstrates *getting its way by yielding*--avoiding confrontation by going around whatever gets in its way, taking the path of least resistance, and, in the process, wearing down everything of resistance in its path while eroding the hardest substance. Third, flowing water always penetrates crevices, slows to fill deep places, and is persistent in continuing to flow onward. Fourth, water maintains integrity by holding to its true nature and by following the natural forces in the Cosmos. Fifth, water has great flexibility, as seen in its liquid, gas, solid, cold, and moist states.

WEAK PEOPLE: C13, "Weak" means something bendable, from prehistoric German "soft"; give way; and yield. The term "Weak People" refers, not to their physical being, but to their mental faculties as a result of an undisciplined Right Brain (allowing ones thoughts to drift without order) which prevents one from possessing emotional control or causes one to get out of emotional control. This means that Left Brain skills have either been inadequately developed or its skills have been over-ruled by emotional impulsiveness. Weakness has nothing to do intellectual potential as evidenced by the fact that many Weak People have intellectual skills in certain areas of their lives. Otherwise, when in an out of control emotional state these individuals have a low level of functioning intellectual competence. Weak people can be separated into two main categories. First are those with a *Problematic Self-Esteem* who allow themselves to be led by others. Their outstanding feature is being a follower of the crowd. Of course, this makes them "Be-ers" (a life centered on doing what others do and who judge themselves by how others judge them). As a result of this lack of a healthy Self-Esteem, these individuals become Self-Absorbed and their efforts are focused on trying to hide or deny perceived flaws, limitations, or incompleteness in some area of their Selfhood and lives. They are not the subject of this discussion. Second are those with a *Manifest "Dark Side"* with features including Indifference, Envy, Hateful thoughts, and doing Evil and Sadistic deeds. The Emotional Energy based aggressiveness which generates the "Dark Side" causes these individuals to assume the role of a superiority complex (donning a mask of self-confidence and greatness with a reality of arrogance and aggression to conceal a sense of deep inferiority). There is a Certain Sameness about this because these individuals are operating out of their Brute Brains and model themselves after their like-kind "Dark Side" leaders. Their focus is on relieving their overwhelming Spiritual Pain (which automatically comes from being disconnected from their Creator and their Human Organism consisting of all God's creatures and creations). To hopefully get even a moment of the lessening of their Spiritual Pain they do two general things. One is to go after the "shiny penny" (as babies do) instead of things of Worth (e.g. Love, Peace, Harmony) infinitely more powerful and enduring and unchanging. The other is to engage in destruction--either for its own sake if it is of no benefit to them or destroy anyone they envy. The barbaric see no need for justification. However, those who are a step up from the barbaric engage in "Civility" and therefore manufacture façade justifications. At the core of those fantasy justifications is Delusional Fears and they tell their fellows these fears so as to have support for their evil and sadistic deeds. When histrionics, self-righteousness, and "Righteous-Indignation" (how dare you do the evil things we do) are added to this mix even higher degrees of fearfulness serve as a call to action to attack the innocent. "Delusional Fear" is that which is present in individuals who are actually afraid of unreal dangers as a result of operating out of their Brute Brain and not because of a reality and not because of a psychiatric disorder. It is this Brute Brain "Delusional Fear" that is at the base of ones Dark Side. "Delusional Fear(s)" generate behaviors constituting the Brute Syndrome and when chronic they become an addiction--and possessing all the features of the Brute Brain. At the core of mental "weakness" is a philosophy of life (POL) which either fails to embrace Unconditional Love or one which is disconnected from it so that the individual lacks the "5Ss"--safety, security, self-confidence, strength, and stability. All of these points are abundantly clear in European literature written by and about Europeans. However, that literature is not available in schools or the media but its realization can be life-changing for seeing Europeans for who they really are.

WEIGHING OF THE HEART: this Scale is the origin of the *Symbol for Justice* in today's legal community. Throughout the "*Weighing of the Scales of Justice*" the "Heart" of the Deceased would be examined by Anubis and the deities. Standing nearby the scale would be a monster Devourer of the Dead--a beast with the head of a crocodile, the chest and forelegs of a leopard, and hind legs of a hippopotamus—a symbol for destroying records of the "Heart's" earthly bad emotional experiences (the Sahu)—i.e. the sinful part of the "Heart" (not the Soul). The weighed "Heart" passed the test by Living a Ma'at life (by the Spiritual Elements) which provided a "Light Heart"; it failed (i.e. too heavy to pass from being a bundle of ill-programmed behavioral responses) if its life's actions had been motivated by emotional (animal), rather than divinity Soul parts of ones spirit. It also failed by it having been so overly religious as to live by rules outside what it takes to be human. See Nothing

"WHAT'S BEHIND THAT?" QUERY PROCESS: Observing animals (e.g. rabbits, snakes, cattle) remain motionless for prolonged periods and then asking: What's behind that sameness feature"? is a type of thinking needed for self-improvement. "Why" leads to discovering the "Seed" giving rise to the bad "Fruit" within ones life experiences. If a "Leaf" problem is from not having enough money and another "Leaf" problem is seeming to be showered with bad luck, then by realizing those "Leaves" come off branches attached to a "Vine or Trunk" which in turn arose from "Roots" is to understand the "What's Behind That? Query Process." After tracing "Leaf" problems back to their "Roots," one finally looks for the "Seed" underlying all of ones bad "Fruit." In spite of how bad ones poverty is or how bad are ones problems or the number of people "who have done me wrong" or the bad environment in which one lives, what is the most important is how one thinks. Thinking is the "Seed" underlying ones Earth World Fate. To detect how one thinks and relate that to how ones life is going can be explored by the following.

Step I is to every day (for weeks and months) conscientiously write out *everything* on ones mind about all of ones problems. This requires asking the right questions and with honesty. Do not blame oneself or others. Do not be concerned about spelling or grammar. Write in some code so others, if they discover it, cannot make sense of it. Hide the journal in between writings. It may take 10 pages to come up with one meaningful thought. But the key question at that point is to ask oneself: "What is Behind That?" When that question is answered keep writing to answer what caused the answer given for the previous "What is Behind That?" Step II is to write out everything about how one acted and reacted. One of those set up certain patterns of self-defeating problems around which one has built a lifestyle--a lifestyle now serving as a barrier to ones Real Self. Keep doing this same process and eventually one will get to a place where there is nothing "Behind That?" One knows that point is reached because one is brought to tears or has the urge to immediately do something else. If one pushes past either reaction one feels a sense of accomplishment and relief--like scratching the bump that itches. My reaction is: "That's it!" What is discovered is something that may have been pushed into ones subconscious or something considered insignificant at the time. The more you think about it the more memories unfold. It may take days to exhaust all the questions and answers. Step III is to clear your system completely and permanently by writing out all of those aspects involved and what you think and feel about each. Get out all the nastiness, including those about oneself. Avoid taking personally what does not make one look good by feeling bad about not being perfect. Self-blame has absolutely no place because the bigger issue is to lead to a life of thriving. Self-blame removes ones personal power and makes one vulnerable to outsiders known to be controlling. The associated self-judgments simply generate more tension and push one closer to giving up. Acknowledge and embrace any self-traits that have been denied. Step IV, look through the list of self-defeating traits and determine if they came out of a common small trauma early in life. Step V, determine which is the most important problem, the key-stone one, and spend much time writing about how it came about and where it applies in every aspect of ones life. This will take many weeks and will pop up unexpectedly--often causing disappointment in oneself. Step VI is to determine what is the flaw inside the "Seed." CT will show if it is something absent, weak, incomplete, of a "wrong" standard, or bad cherished values. Step VII: correct the flaw going in the wrong direction; doing relatively unimportant things; or being on the wrong plane of existence. Replace these with the Philosophy of life of African Tradition (Unconditional Love as the Standard and Ma'at (Love in action) as the guide.

"WHAT IT IS": The "What it is"—part of the Essence of a Thing--gives the "That it is" a beginning "what it does" Identity, called a *Notion* –a recognizable "what it is"--an "*Entity*" or Thing with a specific nature. The Cause (its "what it is" Essence) of the "That it is" Power gives the potential for an Effect (its operations based upon its nature when it came into Being) that displays Consequences (from the addition of Nurture") to give an over-all Life Living Result.

WILE: originally meant Sorcery and Divination)

WILLFUL IGNORANCE: Generating a Sensory Consciousness Background of "SEEMs" right and its Foreground companion of "Being Blind to the Elephant" in the room are vital to the Willful Ignorance that leads to Mind Control of the Crowd. Whereas *Total Ignorance* is not knowing one does not know something at hand, *Willful Ignorance* is choosing a refusal to know—issuing from cowardice, pride, crowd addiction, laziness of mind, or "Me, Me, Me" self-interest. A *Mystery* is incomplete Ignorance in that one is aware of a "that it is" of a "Thing," but does not know its "what it is," "what it does," "how it appears," "how it is," "how it came about," or "where it is going." An example of all 3 is the Supernatural Crowd being totally ignorant of what Black Peoples have historically done; are willfully ignorant and deny the poverty conditions Supernatural people have put them in; and are Mystery ignorant of anything pertaining to Black People that does not ben-efit them—as to confiscate or to denigrate for Projection scapegoat purposes. So as to permit the Crowd to al-ways appear to be the hero who defeated the lion, these 3 allow for mis-interpretations, mis-characterizations, and mis-presentations that are presented as for the good of all concerned. The Crowd is too Selfhood weak to face the Truth. Perhaps such Conditioned Reflexes began with Step I: cross-cultural separations as part of "divide and conquer" measures. Step II has been to keep people ignorant by not teaching Truth to ensuring their thinking stays superficial. This means people's Left Brains are incapable of seeing beneath the surface so as to lack in understanding the Essence of things. Such is achieved by having people never focus on the "what it is" of a Thing as opposed to seeing it simply as it is. This is a main reason making "Exciting" the exchanges or lack of exchanges about affections, the sensual pleasures, and the sharing of responsibilities. Such is why Supernaturals define "love" as an emotion—Step III—and thereby make the public blind to the obvious fact of Spiritual or Unconditional Love.

On the one hand, *Conditional Love* is superficial ("I won't love you if you do...") in that the Left Brain is interpreting all aspects of this within the setting of concrete terms, which includes the returns the Giver might receive. That implies the absence of *Spiritual Aliveness* which is totally independent of external circumstances or situations. On the other hand, *Unconditional Love* is known to practically all throughout the Animal Kingdom via "Mother's Love" as "That's the way it is!" Its "Just Because" doings fulfill a genuine Spiritual need, absent any receiving in return intent and not asking if the Receiver deserves it. Ancient Africans put Spirituality this way: "when you can feel yourself related to another, to Nature, and to the Universe in the same complete and natural way as the child to the mother, then you are aware of being in complete harmony with the Unconditional Love—in being inside Humanity--and in tune with Nature's natural rhythms. A feature of Unconditional Love is that it is *Selfless*—"giving and expecting nothing in return." One cannot be Selfless and hate and vent anger on the one who is loved Unconditionally. Such a rejection of Knowledge comes from humans using their Free Will to disconnect from the Ocean of Nun's flow throughout the Cosmos, with its contents of the Spiritual Elements and the Cosmic Organism. This disconnection--i.e. the denial of God--is deemed in African Tradition to be the greatest disease of the Soul and puts people on anti-Ma'at paths.

The unwritten "Crowd Code" is to be willfully ignorant of the Spiritual Elements in order to emphasize the wisdom of its various categories of Ignorance. Its judgment—a mere lottery of useful (for them) understanding of Trinkets and Trivia--is how to make Ignorance flow comfortably for their Earth World living. To be in the flow of Ignorance means one embraces the "SEEMs" right pseudo- truisms that Ignorance is the mother of admiration, impudence, devotion, beneficial superstitions, satisfaction with ones opinions and beliefs—and thereby promotes companionship. It implies one must not know too much, or doubt anything ('anything's possible'); or be too precise or scientific (like a nerd) about activities of daily living. By contrast, one must know things not necessary and being "human" makes errors okay (e.g. knowing things falsely). These provide free margins to operate with some degree of vagueness, impulsiveness, and naïvete so as to ensure Crowd pleasure experiences. The "in-Crowd" is riveted to Technology, a compounder of Ignorance.

WISDOM: *Wisdom comes from the cumulative effects of a series of small lessons concerning successes, set-backs, and failures causing the uplifting of ones Consciousness. Unconditional Love displays are the highest Wisdom.* There are many types of Wisdom. However, while on ones Death Bed, living a Wise life is based upon what one would desire one would have done to live the "Good Life". *Wisdom is the making of consistent right choices on things of significance that are free from error.* Ones synthesized life and knowledge experiences to make natural principles for living. There is no other door to Knowledge than the door Nature opens into the realm of Wealth (that which is beautiful, calm, and imparts happiness). Such "Wealth" is *Wisdom*--the actualized intuition (learning from within)—i.e. providing direct perceptions of reality so that its ingredients can be maneuvered and manipulated into Spiritual Elements packages of Ma'at Principles that form options for what is appropriate and most workable for solving the issue.

WISDOM IN AFRICAN TRADITION: Wisdom is a vital part of the Essence of: "All is in One, and One is in All"—i.e. the Essence of the philosophy concerning all God's creatures and creations in the Cosmic Organism. But to put Wisdom into context starts with understanding that "The All" is an Ancient African term for God. The "One" and The "All" both equate to God because of the Interchange formed by the Subjective realm's Ocean of Nu. In it the Cosmic Organism, produced and orchestrated by the Cosmic Mind, is "All in One," the "All" equating to God being manifest by the collection of God's creatures and creations coming out of the One God. The same "All is in One" pertains to God's creatures and creations being a manifestation of God in the physical world. This is despite each Entity manifesting uniquely in the Physical World because they maintain the same Spiritual Elements "Genetics". Thus, in both the Subjective and Physical realms, there remains a Unity but in different forms. In both instances, separate Unique Entities, each having independent duties, have come together as an interdependent team—and stay Spiritually connected regardless of the plane of existence upon which they are individually located. Implied in the Spiritual connection is that each shares the same Spiritual Space where Compassion occurs and because of shared Spiritual Elements Genetics. These make for Unity, Harmony, and Balance throughout the scope of the Cosmic Web in which all reside. In African Tradition, one with Wisdom first identifies oneself in relationship with the Cosmic Organism of God's creatures and creations as well as by Selfless Service. Thus, one knows oneself, not in isolation, but in a "Non-Self" communal relationship identity of: "I am because we are and since we are, therefore I am". To elaborate, African Tradition says: *Nature's Processes embrace the independent workings of each pair of its Complementary Natural Opposites*—e.g. heat/cold, light/dark, black/white, as well as each and every communal relationship. Cosmic Harmony is achieved through balance of complementary forces--and it is impossible to have a functioning whole without harmonious interaction and the existence of balancing pairs. Meanwhile, the Cosmic Mind imparts its Intelligence as a Disposition into each entity within the entire Cosmic Web. That Disposition carries the "Trademark" Message of its parent Essence so as to reflect its identity and express its individuality within the context of its Mission in life. So, this is the Cosmic Circle of Wholism's "What it is".

WISDOM'S REALM: All things in Nature that are an intimate part of the Cosmic Organism are harmoniously made and are connected to each other in a Spider Web fashion. A Spider makes this web by first laying down an irregular rectangle of silk, known as the scaffolding. Next is putting in the Spokes, which run from the center to the edge. Over the spokes is laid circular threads. Finally, in the center, it makes the sticky, closely spaced snare. This is roughly similar to how Ancient Africans described the formation of the Cosmos. For example, just as the Spider that spins the web, itself lives in a leaf at the side of the web, so does the one Universal High God, Amen, live in "The Other World" or the Amenta ("Alaiye" in Sanskrit) where True Reality lies. Just as silk spills out of the Spider's abdomen in making its web, spilling of Feminine/Masculine primeval Substance, called God's Androgynic plast, occurs from the Amenta into the Universe (or Cosmic Realm) so as to form the Subjective Realm. What is spilled is the primal waters, called the Ocean of Nun. The Androgynic plast consists of the Spiritual Elements "Genetics" of Unconditional Love, Truth, Reality, and the Natural which form the Essence of all of God's Creatures and Creations. Inside the Ocean of Nun are the Amenta's contents of the Divine Archetypes ("Seeds") in a Virtual state—meaning the unformed (formlessness without boundaries), and "non-ordered" (i.e. undifferentiated)--but *not "disordered"*. These Archetypes of all God's Creatures and Creations are Unrealized Realities destined to form all aspects of the Cosmos. Just as the Spider's web has a central headquarters, so does the center of the Cosmic Organism have its orchestrating Cosmic Mind that imparts a Divine Disposition into each Creature and Creation. The results of a Cosmic Organism Web of Associations is of independent items working interdependently in accordance with God's plan. In short, each Web strand's interrelationships is like a link connecting each member's "*Uniqueness*" into God's plan. All of these aspects constitute the Realm of Wisdom. Realm means a sphere of Influencial Power. Whereas *African Logic is about the manipulation and maneuvering of Form-Realities in Metaphysical and Physical Realms, Wisdom is what results from participating in the influential Powers of the Cosmic Organism manifestations in the Sublime Realm.* It is here that manifesting Totipotency of the Archetypes transitioning into Prototypes occurs. In this Sublime Realm there are Divine Dispositions with their "What and Why" messages in preparation to manifest in the Cosmos as Realized Realities. Yet, while in a Potential Reality state, a human's Wisdom is able to: (1) recognize them; *(2)* manipulate and maneuver aspects of them in order to make unsuspected and novel connections between seemingly unlike Things; (3) direct the payload of the resultant product so as to generate an impact leading to *implicit ideas of the indescribable Divine Disposition that then touch the "Heart" or "Head".* The result is always in keeping with what is in the best interest of "ME/WE". This is because all of what is done is interconnected like strings in a spider web. In this manifested way of Correspondence, all

African derived Plain Geometry, Sacred Geometry, Cosmology, Astrology, Harmonics, Music, and the like are Spiritually related. They are all connected in a Cause, Effect, Consequence, and Result fashion.

WISDOM--AFRICAN HISTORY: An Ancient Egyptian word for "Wisdom" is "Seba"—which gives rise to the word "Philosophy". The "Philosophy" part of a philosophy of life originated by Ancient Africans came from that part of Africa's Creation Mythology called the Nun (Nu)—the Subjective Realm of the Cosmos. This undifferentiated—but not disordered--material basis of the Cosmos was personified and called Soph or Seba from the Kamitic Sofik, the Goddess of Wisdom (Asante, African Intellectual Heritage, p. 285). Such Wisdom came from using Vision to see and distinguish Good from Evil. This African Goddess Sofik--the Matron of Scribes and the female counterpart of Tehuti (Thoth, Hermes Trismegistus, Tout, Tehuty or Djehwty), the God of Wisdom. I suspect Sofik was related to the goddess Ma'at crystallized the "Big Picture" Seed, Pattern, and Vision of Divine Cosmic Order. Besides being a model on how to Live Life, Ma'at was next designated as the feminine counterpart of Tehuti (god-man of Wisdom)--and was viewed as a correspondent between the Earth and Celestial realms. In the Book of Ptah-hotep (?4599-4402 BC)—the oldest complete Sebait (probably another name for Seba), also called the Books of Wise Instruction which also contained Ancient African Moral Philosophy)—the concept of Ma'at is introduced as an intimate link with the Ultimate Divine Plan Ideal. Thus, Ma'at's name was associated with Truth, Righteousness, and Order—with what concerns respect, levelness, genuineness, uprightness, and with the world steadfast and in equilibrium. This meant Ma'at became an unalterable connection of measurement for Social and Spiritual order—by the relationship between one human being and another—between humankind and the gods—and serving to bridge humankind and the Living Dead. African Sages deemed *Nature to be the home of God's Laws; Nature to be the source of humans' wisdom;* and Nature and humans to be an indivisible unity, like two sides of a coin. Hence, all of the Wisdom one needs to thrive in Earth World (Secular) life comes from ones nature which is already within. This implies *all the Truths one needs in life,* powered by ones Spiritual Elements, *are already present in ones Selfhood,* simply awaiting one to cultivate them into their manifestations. Sofik was borrowed by the ancient Greeks who translated it into "Sophia," meaning "loving wisdom" (Amen, Vol II: 31). The Greek "Sophia" was compounded with "philos" (love) to form "Philosophy." Seba was translated into ancient Greek as "Sophia," meaning "loving wisdom." From there, it went into Old English c725, Beowulf—in the sense of full of knowledge with judgment—i.e. the Way or mode of doing a thing.

WISDOM PHILOSOPHY OF LIFE IN AFRICAN TRADITION: Ancient Africans said humans derive Wisdom from the Cosmic Mind placing a "Spark" of its Cosmic Force "Flame" in the Soul of each Virtual human prior to birth. At birth, this "First Wisdom," called Ma'at, possesses all of Laws of the Cosmos + an intimate link with the Mission imparted the by Divine Plan. It serves as a source for Right Life Living based upon attributes of the Spiritual Elements—e.g. Ma'at. African Sages introduced Ma'at as an intimate link with the Ultimate Divine Plan Ideal. Thus, *Ma'at Wisdom* lays out pathways symbolizing the highest of human excellence—Propriety (be in accordance with the fitting and appropriate), Balance, Order, Truth, Harmony, Peace and Tranquility, Fellowship, Justice, Rightness, Straightness or Righteousness, and Reciprocity ("the reward of one whose acts consist in the fact that one will act for her/him" in doing Good). These combine to emanate what is known as Respect, Levelness, Genuineness, Uprightness, and Equilibrium in decision making and problem solving. However, Ma'at Wisdom is part of a human's mind Background structure called the "Self" or Divine Consciousness. It resembles a skyscraper building resting on the *Base of Unconditional Love*--the only thing in existence that is permanent, stationary, unchanging, eternal, and of absolute strength. Out of that Base arises an *Underground Foundation* (likened to Truth), from which arises an *Above Ground Foundation* (like the Foreground of a human's mind, consisting of Reality). Situated on the Above Ground Foundation is the visible skyscraper building (likened to what is Natural). The concept of "Truth" belongs to the Base upon which the POL of African Tradition rests. Thus, it manifests throughout ones entire Private and Public Self Thought Structure, powered by Pure Emotions (Feelings) and its Pure born Intellect partner. That POL and its "Truth" are what give rise to an individual or a culture's Thought Structure, System of Values, and Lifestyle. Inside that structure a human's Character is born to fashion her/his Philosophy of Life (POL) into three parts: (1) a Standard (like the Base of the skyscraper); (2) the Cherished Values (which emanates or issues forth out of the Standard, as does the Underground Foundation of the skyscraper), and (3) the Power Approach (the vehicle for carrying out ones Cherished Values throughout life and equivalent to the above ground part of the skyscraper). The Standard and the Cherished Values are "Un-seeable" Infra-structures (underlying). By being the essential elements of ones POL, together they constitute ones "Philosophy." Since mosaic pieces of the Spiritual Elements are the ingredients of Wisdom, its distinctive mark is that it cannot be misused because Wise humans act well as a result of being powered by Wisdom. This is because Wisdom, unlike Knowledge, comes from using Inner Vision to see and distinguishes Good from Evil. This was elaborated on in Africa by the Books of Wise Instruction—i.e. the Book of Ptah-hotep (?4599-4402 BC)—the oldest complete Sebait (probably another name for Seba). It contains Ancient African Moral Philosophy--a work on the conduct of life—and teaching about the glory of Cosmic Order and Ma'at while infusing a spiritual consciousness into the social and political areas of society. Rather than being arbitrary and about opinions, African Sages entire POL, Thought Structures, System of Values, and principles for living were mathematically based and operate inside Nature's Processes—thus adopted as African Tradition's Icon Frame. By this POL only being able to manifest in ones Real Self, it is of a "ME/WE" nature in a "Non-Self" sense—referring to a Cosmic Organism "Sameness" and an individualized "Uniqueness". Concomitances of ones POL are first a *Philosophical Warehouse* where ones Wisdom is stored for making emergency or urgent decisions, without one having to think or know more before acting. A second is "*Information Waiting Compartment*" where "SEEMs" right information is put "on-hold"—like call-waiting—until its credibility is "checked out". Adhering to an African Tradition POL is what makes Black People a Metaphysical people.

WISDOM--AFRICAN TRADITION CONCEPTS: The Blueprint, Pattern, and Exemplar (model) of Wisdom is that of our Ancient African Ancestors. Wisdom's core is the Truth based upon Understanding. Understanding is to become "One" with the Thing. Hence, Wisdom implies, whether in God or in humans, both Power and Knowledge as attributes to be employed in the interest of what is morally of the highest and supremely valuable Good. This *Good*, by African Tradition standards, includes the Good of Happiness, the Good of Beauty, and the Good of Morality—all in one Ideal in everything that has Worth. Hence, African Sages conveyed to the people that Wisdom is the Good, the Right, and the Descent thing within the context of Ma'at (Spiritual Elements in action). Therefore, it is *both an intellectual and a moral virtue.* Ancient Africans viewed these virtues as the same aspects needed for living life (Karenga, p238), since they combine the Spiritual with the Material. This Practical Wisdom is based upon certain knowledge of the Spiritual (as Ancient African Sages obtained by means of Circumstantial Truths) and Matter--and not faith, beliefs, or mysticism. *Worth* is concerned with those qualities which deal with Spiritual Enlightenment (the highest level of spiritual awakening) and Immortality--both deemed to be more significant than Harmony and Peace by Ancient Africans. A reason is that it is within these realms that the Self (Divine Consciousness) of humans can realize its Divine Source and itself. Both realizations are the sense of experiencing "Oneness" with all other creatures--an experience of Reality--not the mere intellectual notion of, or belief in ones "Oneness"—an experience of *Wholistic Knowledge Integrity*--i.e. Omniscience (having total knowledge of everything).

Worth is concerned with those qualities which deal with Spiritual Enlightenment (the highest level of spiritual awakening) and Immortality--both deemed to be more significant than Harmony and Peace by Ancient

Africans. A reason is that it is within these realms that the Self (Divine Consciousness) of humans can realize its Divine Source and itself. Both realizations are the sense of experiencing "Oneness" with all other creatures--an experience of Reality and not the mere intellectual notion of, or belief in ones "Oneness"—an experience of *Wholistic Knowledge Integrity*--i.e. Omniscience (having total knowledge of everything). By being God-based, African Wisdom's Disposition message is for humans to focus on reaching the Afterlife. Putting this Inclination and Intention into action requires the awakening and functioning of the Wisdom faculty. That depends on the perfection of the ability to shut down ones thinking processes in the higher stages of Meditation (Amen, Metu Neter II:117-118) so as to allow ones Free Mind to be open to Critical Thinking awareness of the mathematical properties of Natural events. Inside this realm, one is able to locate what to appreciate as priority by means of the Spiritual Elements being a radar-like "Trademark" expressed out of the Spark of God present in each human's Soul prior to birth. This is about the *Law of Vibration*. Vibrations of the Same frequency resonate with each other. Specifically, that radar frequency vibrates at the same high rate as Spiritual Things of Worth in the Cosmos—e.g. Unconditional Love, Goodness, Wellness, Natural Order, Perfection, Universal Truth, and the Reality—whether viewed in Nature or in Real Self people or in acts of helping those in true need from no deliberate causes of their own making. These lead to Beauty and Happiness. So, "like-kind" attracts "like-kind" Spiritual Energy. Every Real (God-made) Entity is Spiritual, including Thoughts coming out of ones Real Self (e.g. human newborns). Focusing on a particular "like-kind" Entity attracts its Vibrational match. A human newborn's cooing is a Spiritual Elements display which has a "like-kind" attraction on its mother's Soul "Trademark"—and that match causes the mother to respond. By being God-based, African Wisdom's Disposition message is for humans to focus on reaching the Afterlife. Putting this Inclination and Intention into action requires the awakening and functioning of the Wisdom faculty. That depends on perfecting the ability to shut down ones thinking processes in higher stages of Meditation (Amen, Metu Neter II:117-118) so as to allow ones Free Mind to be open to Critical Thinking awareness of the mathematical properties of Natural events. In order for Meditation to be effective requires ones Inner Selfhood be purified and renewed to the point of allowing ones enlightened Conscious—ones "Soul Sunshine"—derived from ones Soul to be the Selfhood orchestrator. Next comes *Spiritual cultivation* as a specific way of handling ones Thoughts, Emotions, Divine Consciousness, and Spiritual Energy. Ones mind must be impartial to ('be one with') all things and events--the criteria for *Selfhood Peace*. This induces in the mind a free flow of ideas and intuition revealing all possibilities in a situation (Amen, Maat p55).

WISDOM IN ANCIENT AFRICAN BIBLE: For the knowledge placed in the Ancient African Bible—the one from which all other of the world's Bibles derive--African Sages used the term "*Ultimate Wisdom*" because they dealt with "Certainty." For example, their certainty of God came from what was revealed to them and then verified by Circumstantial Truths drawn from the Correspondences of Nature and placed in the pattern of astro-mathematics. Thus, in contrast to the European Bible being wrongly put together and wrongly interpreted as a book of Religious history, the Ancient African Bible (also called Ancient African Spiritual Literature) is simply a book of Theology. It describes *the ultimate and transcendental Reality and Wisdom which puts a given human being in touch with the ground of his/her own Being*. Ancient African Sages determined truly metaphysical forces are life-shaping or life-altering and operate in mental and divine planes of existence. However, Reason, with varying degrees of Emotions, operates directly on physical matter and events. To help others understand the spiritual significance of "Ultimate Reality and Wisdom," African Sages resorted to Metaphors. It explains certain *fundamental aspects of human nature and conveys abstract or lifeless things* of great significance by means of Metaphors and Personifications (giving life to some non-feeling and unreal Being). They are selected to indicate the Kingdom of God is within each individual. This Primitive (the first) African method enables people to become aware of spiritual powers and unity through the use of the "atmosphere" generated in metaphorical language and meanings. Metaphors thus convey understanding beyond the ability of words to do or describe. For example, when a metaphor speaks of gods, its symbolic "atmosphere" concerns entities actually within the person touched by them, and not referring to some invisible Being. But grave errors occurred from foreigners who did not understand that African Sages built all theological structures for African tradition upon "*Ultimate Wisdom*" metaphors. What they foolishly did was to switch African metaphors into "Delusional Facts" -- the act of making non-truths for the European Bible out of the African Bible's God-revealed Truths. In people's Secular Faith use of these non-truths in life-shaping/life-changing decisions, billions have been taken far away from Love, Truth, and Reality. Still, lurking in the back of their minds is an aura of uncertainty. That slightest doubt about ones Religion can cause one to lose faith/trust in all of it.

WISDOM'S CHAIN OF COMMAND: The mental activities of Real Self people embrace all planes of existence—the Spiritual, Sublime, the Metaphysical, the Physical, and the Supernatural (in the context of Metaphorically explaining the other planes). In a sense, their harmonious operations can be thought of as a Chain-of-Command Ladder. Here, Messages start with the high ranking and progressively descend a ladder to the lowest ranking. Note that on the Spiritual Chain of Command Ladder—the Ladder itself is made of the same ingredients throughout. But there are different and unique changes at each rung. On a given rung different things happen in its unique environment—an environment consisting of an Interchange because of the rung immediately above and immediately below the rung in question. This is like what happens on different planes of Cosmic existence. The *Principle of* these happenings is there is throughout the Ladder a *"Sameness" from being composed of vibrations. Yet, on each rung, those same vibrations are "Uniquely" changed while remaining in place + conforming to the different vibratory rates which characterize each rung.* Each rung is like an Entity, as an independent worker—an Entity that interdependently works harmoniously with all the other rungs (Entities) to maintain a "seemingly" normal whole Ladder. But still, in going from one rung to the next there are nuances in the up or down progression as well as constant nuance changes on each rung. *Each independent activity is a tiny, multiple, ongoing series of changes.* However, that Ladder has its bottom resting in scooped out areas just below the ground's surface to serve as its Foundation. In turn, the ground is resting on a Base. Despite all the activities going on with the rungs, what remains the same is the Foundation and Base. When the nuances of each independent thing are accumulated off each rung, their harmonious meshing is in a completely new form--a form that goes off on a different course, with different requirements, and to do a different purpose, as dictated by the Base and orchestrated by the Foundation. Examples of these Principles are present in many forms. One form, in the Physical World of a *Chain of Command*, is defined in the dictionary as a series of executive positions or of officers and subordinates in order of authority, especially with respect to the passing on of orders, responsibilities, reports, or requests from higher to lower or lower to higher. Example: the President of the USA gives the ultimate command to the Generals and Admirals in charge. That command then trickles down to lower ranking Generals and Admirals who, in turn, pass the orders to Colonels, Captains, and so on down to those of the lowest ranks. Second is the *Stream of Flow* pertaining to the Metaphorical boundless ocean representing God's "Big Mind". Out of that Ocean is taken a drop and implanted into each human to signify that human's Genius. From that Ocean comes rivers, rivelets, streams, brooks, and creeks. Third is the abstract explanation for how Real Self humans *subject their minds to the Divine Cosmic Spirit so it can command the Life-Force in harmony with the Laws of Nature.* In this way there is a connection of ones Highest Self with Living on different planes of existence that involves proceeding through an Ordered Chain of Command carried out by a given human's Divine Will. Fourth, if ones Genius is an Interchange, then Wisdom is a Mosaic Pattern reflecting of the ingredients of Genius. Then Logic, Reasoning, and Common Sense are Mosaic pieces of that Genius. Now, allow me to use a skyscraper building above and below ground parts to illustrate the various thinking methods a Real Self person uses in successfully going through life. COMMON SENSE: Inside the above ground portion of the skyscraper building are all the workers—janitors, cooks, clerks, messengers—who do their work in a Common Sense manner based upon *Information* received from their boss.

REASONING: Their bosses do the *Reasoning* that indicates the best *Approaches* (the way a goal is reached), *Methods* (how to do the job), *Techniques* (how tools are used in the approach and method) and *Manner* (the different ways a technique can be handled). KNOWLEDGE: The department head is Logic who uses *Knowledge* to elaborate on the different aspects for how the bosses in the department are to base their Reasoning. They bring order by determining: (1 and 2) *Who* and *Which* -- to bring out and establish the identity of the thing, (3) *What* -- to show the action to or by the thing, (4) *When* -- to tell the time, (5) *Where* -- to locate a place, (6) *Why* -- to give the reason or purpose; and (7) *How* -- to describe the manner of the action (e.g. approaches, methods, techniques, and manner).

WISDOM: The department heads get their "Orders" from *Wisdom,* whose Underground "office" is in the Foundational aspect of the skyscraper. Wisdom features a Nuance shift *from Human-Made Patterns of Thinking* (e.g. in *Linear* fashion, which is one-dimensional) *over to Processes inside the Flowing Patterns that conform to Laws of Nature.* The "big picture" is that *Reality is composed of multiple variables,* each on different *Planes* of activity, but occupying the same space. Also, everything in each Plane of the Cosmos is happening at once (which makes them non-linear). Wisdom deals with the infinite order of Nature and its Processes, meaning those configured into *an underlying web of relationships operating in Nature* throughout the Cosmos. The keystones allowing the recognition of a Cosmic Web are Carbon atoms present in all ingredients from the Sublime, the Metaphysical, and the Physical as well as Melanin, which also includes the Spiritual and the Divine planes, as determined by Circumstance Correspondence. Throughout this Cosmic Web of Nature there are *consistent, permanent, stationary, and unchanging patterns (matured Spiritual Elements Essences) and Elements (moving Essences).* Despite *its realm of complexity and multiplicity Patterns on all planes of existence*—some being reproducible while others are new creations from moment to moment, like foams in ocean waves—*its Unification makes for* an infinite *Continuity.* These Patterns of Nature can only be known by Wisdom because of its ability to discern and apprehend various nuances—i.e. *tiny, multiple, ongoing series of changes*--present in *each independent activity.* Such tiny, multiple, ongoing series of changes escape perception by those in the publicly displayed skyscraper because of interferences from the outside world.

GENIUS: the experiences of Wisdom, which provide an awareness of Nature's Continuity, leads Wisdom to apprehend there is a Base upon which the Underground foundation rests—a realm of the highest of all Orders—the total Pattern of the Cosmos orchestrated by the boundless Force which Ancient Africans called Sekhem.

WISDOM OPERATES WITH THE UNDERLYING: A prominent Ma'atian concept during Ancient Egypt's Old Kingdom (5660-4188 BC) was of humans modeling the image of God. This means that a Spark of the Cosmic Force, Sekhem, constitutes the center of a human's Soul—the highest faculty because in it is the presence of the Divine Logos. By being the "Spark" makes it unlike any of the other lesser faculties which are among each other. Yet, the Soul is served by all the other faculties which assist it to reach the Source of the Soul by raising the Soul out of the sphere of the Lower (animalistic) Self. The Spark aspires to the Absolute—to a unity with the Cosmic Mind Force. Features of the Soul's Spark are that by being imbued with Free Will—the same that is in God—it is free from laws and all activity. Such is not true with the other faculties of the Soul—e.g. desires, feelings, pre-birth Emotions, and actions. Hence, the Spark of the Soul is at all times yoked to God which, in turn, determines the nature of the Soul's other faculties as long as there is no Cloud covering the Spark that conveys the Soul's Sunshine. What arises from the Spark is the Principle of all the Principles, called the Mysterious Wisdom, the Primordial crown of all that which there is of the most High—meaning it is above Wisdom itself. It operates through a human's higher mind and upon that human's Lower (animalistic) Self nature through Truth, Unconditional Love, and action. The highest Wisdom has but one science—the science of Whole—the Science explaining the whole creation and human's place in it—the Science that begins with the Spiritual Elements. Wisdom unites this Knowledge when engaging in Actions. As a result of Wisdom being a Mosaic Pattern of ones Genius, it is able to transcend into the Sublime's reality flow—a natural flowing part of the Cosmic Mind—a flow in which Wisdom recognizes itself as vital to being integrated into the All--i.e. the "Oneness" within the Cosmic Mind with all of its associated Entities, as discussed above. Here, in the "ME/WE" Sublime realm, Knowledge is known without proof. Benefits from that Knowledge have nothing to do with Materialism characterizing ones Lower Self or with the European Supernatural. As the mindset of ones "Non-Self," Wisdom—which is incorporated into all planes of existence—means its Higher striving assets enter paths enabling one to now *Perceive* in the sense of deeper understandings, more pointed meanings, and a wider variety of implications; seeing the common in the uncommon; the uncommon in the common; *Inner Similarities in things with* dissimilar appearances; discern uniqueness in similarities; and interrelationships between dissimilar and similar things. The resultant new meanings increase ones insights for determining the *Order and consistent Patterns underlying natural events; and that enables arriving at the Mystery's answer.* Every advancement expands ones Consciousness from the inside out and toward the Eternal. Thereafter, layers of coverings are removed from Esoteric Knowledge (i.e. "ME/WE" secrets) on the way to apprehending richer meanings in each new insight concerning ones Selfhood within the sum of the Cosmic Whole. Each new meaning gives more in-depth understanding of Spiritual Elements Principles (pieces of Truth and its Unchanging Reality) which, in turn, peels away another top covering layer so as to get to the core.

WISDOM IN ACTION: Wisdom is born of Hetep (Peace) coming from Reason harmonizing with Unconditional Love to produce "ME/WE" Knowledge and Power. Dealing with and orchestrating these complexities and multiplicity Patterns as they relate to ones lifestyle is the realm of operation of a human's Wisdom. The Wise have the obligation/duty/responsibility to *discover and conform to the underlying web of relationships operating in Nature* throughout the Cosmos. As a result, its "ME" aspects are then able to transcend into the Sublime's reality flow as a "Non-Self"—a natural flowing part of Cosmic Knowledge—a flow in which one recognizes ones own Being as vital to the All (i.e. "Oneness" within the Cosmic Mind). *Being in this infinity of Genius and Wisdom* allows one to discover new insights about any Spiritual Elements' attribute; see ones old blind-nesses to the obvious; and acquire new perspectives upon hearing old Wisdom over and over. These create, enhance, or maintain ones Knowledge, Logic, Rationality, and Common Sense skills. This entire process is one of *Synthesis whereby the "ME/WE" whole is greater than the sum of its parts.* Such is illustrated each time I repeat the study of a difficult topic by drawing on new sources for new ideas. Then, repeated reflections on the acquired ingredients + the new insights gained from the re-read pieces + manipulating and maneuvering them into different arrangements and combinations give wider scopes of understanding of the topic and asides associated with the topic. Most of these improve my insights into like-kind things—into Options—and into Creative handlings of problems never seen nor heard of before. The results simply "Feel" right in ones Selfhood Center--a "Feeling" known to be from ones Pure Emotions because it spurs "Aliveness"—a Spiritual Energy continually urging one to Self-Improve for "ME/WE" purposes and to develop "ME/WE" Harmonious products out of it.

WISDOM CLASSIFICATION: The Selfhood components of Wisdom are ones Pure Emotions (called "First Wisdom") and ones Spiritual Elements derived Intellect. Together, when at their best, they are "One" with the *web of relationships operating in Nature* throughout the Cosmos—the web underlying problems with Opposites. Otherwise, Wisdom may be about "bits and pieces" or imitations. The personal benefits of a classification is that it allows me to find a "home" of thoughts and practices that have floated aimlessly around in my life. *Class I* is ones in-born *"First Wisdom"*—which is ever present, whether it put into consistent or inconsistent practice. By being part of the Soul, it is its own proof and is above being susceptible of proof. It embraces explanations for the Whole creation and all of God's creatures and creation's place in the Cosmic Whole. "First Wisdom" is the "Black Light" of the Amenta, dealing with Wealth, Worth, and Necessity. This is about Certainty Truth and Rightness applied to all stages, ages, objects, and qualities and thus is immortal—a "Classic". It displays a Pure Emotion type Common Sense. There is no doctrine and no scheme but, instead, simply playing the hand one is dealt at that moment. Though taking things apart is essential for Knowledge, what is necessary for the Common Sense/Wisdom link is to put things back together. It sees the infinite in the finite; models Nature's Laws; judges Good by what lasts forever; does "ME/WE" benefits that out-rank all bad consequences. *Class II: Self-Made Practical Wisdom is deliberation Prudence,* derived from the *Selfhood Wisdom of "Knowing Thyself"* and the subjection of ones mind to the Cosmic Mind that deals with "ME/WE". Here, Wisdom and Prudence are qualities of the mind, not of ones Character—meaning these Contemplate Truth and directs conduct for "ME/WE" Harmonious interests—both concerning sound Judgment pertaining to the hazy, confusing, and conflicting; the conduct of life (the ability to discern modes of action with a view to their results); 'that which preserves by conformity to the guidelines (in African Tradition), as opposed to the rules in European Tradition, of reason, truth, and decency at all times—but always putting the proper use of Courage in all circumstances. They select the keystone task, finish the moment pertaining to it, stay on point in every step of the journey; get the most of every part of a second. It reaches its potential without attempting to stretch into what is gigantic and out of the realm of its capabilities, but never being deterred by it being too hard or has never been done before. Its doors for learning are never shut. Their cultivation of Foresight and Forethought enables them to see the storm coming before the clouds appear. They prefer Principle and applicable General Statements to specific examples—for to understand one Principle gives insight into two more. They learn from everyone. Extract from every situation the lesson it teaches so as not to avoid ever doing anything in that situation again. There is self-pride in achieving Human Ideals and appreciates the Beauty in who one is, what one does, and how one appears. It never does desperate things and, if desperation occurs, its Intellect resolves the problem or "Buys its Peace." Prudent Wisdom spends much time, energy, and effort in preventing the desperate from happening. That involves the practical knowledge of things to stop doing—i.e. whatever gets you into and keeps you in trouble. Prudence deals with the "Thinker's Scale". The positive features understanding of the practical knowledge of things to be sought. The negative scale is mainly about self-restraint: the "Thou shalt nots". By prudence "Never" going to the opposite extremes of the scale means it is the keystone of all of ones virtues. There is a time and place for everything and prudence and discretion are knowing answers to the *Seven Questions of Inquiry*--who, which, what, when, where, why, and how—promptly applied to 'right' situations. It is from properly answering these questions that give one a lead to explore more paths into the subject and perhaps arrive at the "bull's eye" of the subject. They know that almost every wise saying has its opposite, no less wise, to balance it. When they do not know—and that is with every new situation—they are methodical. They work around the fact that Wisdom and Goodness to vile seem vile, for they only savoir themselves. *Class III, Humanity Wisdom*--for non-evil people--is the application of Pure Emotions and Intellect within the context of Integrity in dealings with all people as if they are family members—i.e. *Moral values arising from human fellowship fashion ideas of Humanity*. Most situations concern Pure Emotions in settings of Compassion (sharing the same Spiritual Space). In relationship situations they use Intellect to get through the obstacles to get to the right course and then Reason ceases. There is a shift to Pure Emotions which draws on the Soul's Beauty to direct outcomes, which I call the "Soul's Sunshine." *Class IV, Humanity Wisdom applied to dealing with evil people* is about Survival, Self-Protection, and Self-Preservation—first in a "ME" sense and, when possible in a "ME/WE" sense. It is Defense, Protection, and Offense in application to Evil people is best done by the method of Sun Tzu called "Taking Whole." Its infallible criterion for Success is about doing intimidating but respectable things, even though the opposition does not like them (Bailey, Marketplace p200).

Class V is the specialty of ones Wisdom applied to daily living from proper motivation, from being in the proper setting, or from situations offering favorable conditions and circumstances. They may be wise with the wisdom of their time only without having any Ancient wisdom awareness. They have an uncommon degree of Common Sense. *Class VI* concerns those Wise in their own eyes and prudent in their own sight, with or without the help of the Crowd. Here reigns the SEEMS right of being wise for others but not for oneself. Such is in the category of Conventional Wisdom--what it is as the result of human intervention by conformity. Thus, much of what this Crowd claims to be Wisdom are simply Supernatural concepts derived from the mythical minds of its leaders. *Class VII* is *Situational Wisdom*, as in knowing when to stay silent. They do not concern themselves with disagreeing with "Things that Are" and avoid getting in a position whereby they have to do desperate things. To accomplish their ends, they may carry enemies on their shoulders. *Class VIII* are the diluted and polluted Potential Wise—those who might have arrived at Wisdom had they not believed themselves to have arrived there already.

WISDOM AFRICAN THINKING: *African Wisdom* is the expert use of Common Sense, Rational Thinking, and Critical Thinking within the context of Knowledge and its genius is to perceive, maneuver, and manipulate Spiritual Elements ingredient in un-habitual ways. It generates the three "Goods": The Good of Morality, of Beauty, and of Happiness in all that has Worth in a manner that gives an Archetype Form comprising all of its Prototype Quality Forms on all planes of existence. These are models which serve as Thinking Tools for making choices, decisions, and solutions. Wisdom's personal benefits are to evolve itself upon the lower planes and thereby perfect its lower nature to point of realizing its higher nature. In the External World, Wisdom's focus depends upon the degree to which similarity of models of the Good have to the situation at hand. Reconciling Opposites starts with Appreciation of seeing the infinite in the finite and what calls attention to specific parallels or relations between things that are unlike that can be harmonized. The proper application of Wisdom is analogized to a good map of Arkansas which similates the territory it represents in order to allow for prediction of what is ahead. By contrast, a poor map is worthless to the traveler. More specifically, Wisdom processes concern mainly *Circumstantial Equivalents as,* for example, "Knowledge is to the mind what light is to the eye". Whereas Knowledge is more often about things in the Material World, Wisdom's focus is on creating, enhancing, maintaining, defending, and protecting harmonious Spiritual situations and discoveries. Wisdom, in discerning between the Spiritual Element and the anti-Spiritual Elements, processes are an advancement over Reasoning by Analogy (the comparing of two or more systems similar in structure and then taking the familiar in one to explain the unknown in the other). Examples may include: (1) *Induction Analogy*--reasoning from one particular instance to another particular instance, implying if two things are alike in a number of important points, they will be alike in the point in question; (2) *Complex Comparisons* involving two or more systems, based upon two or more things (e.g. analogous events), leading to the inference they are similar in structure; (3) comparing two or more systems similar in structure and then taking the familiar in one to explain the unknown in the other; and (4) "*Anomaly*" ("irregular")--referring to the resemblance of function between organs which are essentially different. In biology, Analogies denote the physiological similarities

---

independent of morphological resemblance. Organs are analogous to one another, or are analogs, when they perform the same function, though being altogether different in structure. Examples are wings of a bird and the wings of an insect. Organs are *Homologous*, or Homologs, when they are constructed on the same plan; undergo a similar development; and bear the same relative position. And this is independent of either form or function. Whereas Knowledge is for the present, Wisdom is for the ages.

WISDOM-KNOWLEDGE CERTAINTY COIN: *The Essence out of the Whole—out of the "Big Picture"— is what African Sages always looked for in order to acquire the Seed for the entire perspective on a situation or issue.* The reason is explained by the *African Law of Holonomy*: the whole is inside the Seed; the whole is contained in each of the Seed's manifested parts; and the Seed is found throughout the whole. The top of a human's mental achievements is to possess a mindset analogized to a Coin whereby Knowledge is on one side, Wisdom is on the other side, Certainty connects the two. For African Sages, whatever has Certainty is *Metaphysical Knowledge*. Ancient Africans said *Divine Certainty* and *Spiritual Certainty* are absolutes that refer to the "Being-hood" of the Creator of the Cosmos and all of its creatures and creations. By means of astro-Mathematics devised in 20,000 BC, African Sages inferred that out of the Creator emanates the Spiritual Elements--i.e. Unconditional Love, Truth, Reality, and the Natural. These--the Base for all Cosmic Organism creatures and creations--possess Cosmic Certainty. Thus, everything that grows out of Cosmic Certainty has the same "Genetics" and thus the essence of Reality Knowledge and Wisdom is Certainty. That is the reason each Entity is part of the *Law of Correspondence*. Certainty embraces all planes of existence but its Cosmic Entity form may have a different appearance on each. Certainty is present because each Cosmic Entity is composed of the Spiritual Elements--and out of them are fashioned shapes and patterns--each being a unique entity with Cosmic "Genetic" content and appearance. That entity's *Certainty is what it was when it came into Being--and its "What it is" persists without change, above any human's ability to grasp its full meaning or to express meaningful contrary opinions about.* Thus, for example, no insults can lessen who one is without ones permission for it to be "Clouded" out. In the way a tree evolves out of its Seed which, in turn produces Roots, a Trunk, Branches, Leaves, and Fruit, Nature's Certainty can be seen in all parts of its fruitful tree products. As a result, all judgments made by rational minds are in conformity with the Cosmic Womb Rhythm—i.e. those of and within the Spiritual Elements—and have Certainty upon which everyone can rely. Anything outside Certainty and *Physical Knowledge* (dealing with mathematically proven "Facts"), no matter how tiny the flaw, is a false representation, making it Information. So, when one "Knows" something, the something happening is out of its Certainty. But how can one be Certain that one Knows?" Step I is to determine the Thing's Essence state of Being—that it has existence, not merely in thought, but in fact. Step II is to discover the Source of that Being. If it is from a Spiritual Elements source, then it has Certainty; is nourishment for the Spiritual Human Nature Needs (SHNN) of all who accept it; it has no degrees; is not subject to human opinions; and it provides the "5Ss" (safety, security, self-confidence, strength, and stability). One feels no doubt about its Certainty because it has happened or it is happening in a manner that harmoniously expands ones Consciousness. The happening, by serving as "Food of Knowledge" to nourish ones SHNN, leads to the Natural growth of the Spiritual Elements within ones Selfhood, as seen by an increase in ones Private and Public Self expansion from the inside out—all at once. The result is the moving further towards ones Highest (Divinity) Self and further away from ones Lower (animalistic) Self. This movement is determined by ones increased attraction to do "ME/WE" beneficial work products. The Certainty of such knowledge conveys the "5Ss"—Safety, Security, Sureness/Self-Confidence, Strength, and Stability—within ones Private Selfhood as well as Mental Toughness in a crisis or during trials and tribulations. Both enable one to continue to produce "Human Ideals" while handling the difficulties. Step III, the Certainty/Knowledge Coin begets itself in all types of areas. First is for one to see that what is considered "bad" by the Crowd may be quite valuable when viewed on its opposite side. Examples are Self-Love, Selfishness, Selfhood Greatness, and Obssessive-Compulsive acts--all are degraded by the Crowd and yet they are important tools for Thriving leading to a Happy life. To illustrate, *Self-Love* means one will not allow oneself to do what is harmful to oneself nor to willingly accept harm from others. *Selfishness* is the first Law of Nature and is essential for Survival, Self-Protection, and Self-Preservation. *Selfhood Greatness* is what gives one the Courage to be who one is and to follow ones birth-gift Mission via discovering and developing ones Talent in order to carry out that Mission. To be *Obsessive-Compulsive* about seeking the Truth removes being "Blind to the Obvious"—removes being "Deaf to the Sounds" of what is of life-shaping importance--and causes one to start detecting nuances that enable seeing the common in the uncommon and seeing the uncommon in the common. These new insights generate endless Curiosity and Creativity.

WISDOM'S AFRICAN CIRCUMSTANTIAL EQUIVALENCES REASONING: *Wisdom* is the *direct perception of reality itself (instead of manipulating symbols)*. To return to the scenario of rivers, lakes, ponds, streams, and and the ocean from which they arise. Despite each having a different name, they are all "equivalent" because each and all contain water from the same Ocean source—water in each that varies in amount, in "what it does" and in "how it appears". Let us say that out of view and hidden from sight are the rivers that are outshoots of the ocean and the ocean itself. Yet, it is evident that the ocean and rivers are in existence, in the same way that one does not see a skyscraper's underground foundation and Base upon which it rests or in the way one does not see the gravity responsible for keeping Earth things from floating away. This is how Unseeable things of Worth are in relation to seeable things of Value. Still, the *consistent Patterns of the* Unseeable is what gives the *Order to the underlying natural events of what is* the Seeable. These Unseeables are Circumstantial because they have Correspondence with what is Seeable. Once the Circumstantial ("X") is established by the Seeable, although it is Unseeable it can be used to establish Correspondence with other Circumstantial Things ("Y") that are also established to exist and yet remain Unseeable. Estimates about ("X") and ("Y") can be made via Algebraic Qualitative Mathematical manipulations and maneuverings, as in the way Bartering is done. Also, going deeper into the Esoteric Unknows of both ("X") and ("Y") in using Reasoning by Analogy of whatever is known in either ("X") or ("Y"), as in using the known in ("X") to explore the unknown in ("Y"). Algebraic Qualitative Mathematics opens mental allows ones in-born Pre-Birth Emotions and Intellect to generate assessments which give rise to Thoughts which are beyond comparison.. The prioritization of those Thoughts provides the clearness and the Order to lay out paths for the "Rightness" of choices, decisions, and solutions. It was from such insights into Cosmic Rhythms discovered by Very Ancient Africans that laid the path leading to the exact science of Mathematics. Close observation of the Rhythms of the stars and planets was tightly woven into the internal structure of the Great Pyramid. And this was not confined to the Quantitative Mathematical aspects of the Earth, the cycles of Nature, or to the systems of the body. Included were the stars, the planets, and the Constellations in such Qualitative Mathematical manners as the cycles of the Nile River reflected in the celestial river overhead—i.e. the Milky Way—being integrated into their Cosmic Religion. The reflection of the heavens on Earth gave rise to Tehuti's axiom: "as above, so below," as encoded in the sacred book of "What is in the Duat The Pharaoh, at death, would make the great journey in his solar boat, becoming one with the immortals who had preceded him. Another example is that the three great Giza pyramids and the Sphinx are in exact alignment with the three stars of Orion Belt, known as the Duat, the Coffin Texts, Book of Coming Forth by Day, the Book of Gates, and the oldest of them all, the Pyramid Texts (Bynum, African Unconscious p109). Ancient Africans' Qualitative Knowledge of the Good came from seeking the ultimate Principle on which all within their area of concern depended--examining the premises themselves—and deducing conclusions from premises through movement from the Physical or Metaphysical ("X") upward tow the Spiritual ("Y"). By being in the flow of the Spiritual Elements Patterns, one is able to gain Knowledge by "*Connaturality*" (connected by Nature)--referring to what can be intuited in other persons or creatures because all are co-natured with each other—to know other's Human Nature from ones own Human Nature. This—called *Poetic Knowledge*—is acquired by union with and attachment to the Thing by a "Oneness" in the Cosmic Organism Emotions—being imbedded into a fusion that cannot be reduced to anything more basic (Hodge p100, 208, 221). An example might be the bonding occurring between the mother and her newborn. The same principles applies by using Algebraic Qualitative Mathematics. Conceptual relationships, as in Mathematics and Logic, are permanent and unchanging. For example 2 + 2 = 4 which no amount of experience can ever change. The same holds for proofs in Mathematics and Logic. Thus, if the Good, which is unchanging and permanent, is to be known, it must be known by means of these unchanging and permanent conceptual relationships. The conceptualizing part is called the Mind.

WISDOM REASONING BY CORRESPONDENCE: When Very Ancient Africans determined that Melanin and Carbon are in all God's creatures and creations, this was imaged as the Cosmos being like a Spider Web. Hence, every real thing shares a "Sameness" in spite of its Uniqueness. The profoundness of this concept is that on the way to inferred Wisdom, the most powerful tool created by Ancient African Sages for arriving at Knowledge is the Law of Correspondence. Thus, the types of Correspondences can be: Type I--involving a Known Physical and an Unknown Physical; Type II--a Known Physical and an Unknown Metaphysical; or Type III--a Known Metaphysical and an Unknown Metaphysical. Cosmic "Oneness" is at the basis for Cosmic Correspondence as well as enabling the realization of a Sample of its Esoteric Creator. That Sample, called a *Circumstance Companion*, enables the Esoteric Creator or its Esoteric realms to be known with Certainty because of the Law of Correspondence. So, the key to Reasoning by Correspondence is to stay within and evolve concepts out of the Spiritual Elements—those in the flow of Nature's Processes. This leads one into "*Esoteric Knowledge*"—i.e. *understanding the inner truth lying hidden within the core of fundamental concepts about foundational Realities*. This is because Correspondence is based on Ancient Africans determining Cosmic Laws which refer to the foundation of all Cosmic manifestations—Laws which denote a sequence of inherently related events that occur with unvarying uniformity under the same conditions—Laws whose nature is that of Vibrations and thereby lend themselves to being *Mathematically* determined. So, in African Tradition, "*Correspondence*" is demonstrated everywhere and with everything inside the Cosmic Circle of Wholeness. Out of this *Correspondence* and by *following Nature's Processes along paths leading into Unperceivable realms*, African Sages gained insight into the Esoteric from which they inferred Philosophical Principles called Ma'at. To clearly understand the words Correspondence, Circumstance, Essence, and Essentials is to step inside the Ancient African Mystical fundamental flow pertaining to the Seeable, the Known but Unseeable, and the Unknown and Unseeable Realms of Knowledge and Certainty in African Tradition. To give a gist overview, the story of any God-made *Entity*--a Thing having a separate innate Essence existence with "Sameness/ Uniqueness" displays--on any plane of existence begins when it comes into Being. By being Spiritually related to all God's creatures and creations, it possesses as shared "Sameness" of God's Substance—the Spiritual Elements of Unconditional Love as its inner nature and Truth, Reality, and the Natural for its outer nature. Humans put these together in varying combinations and with varying results by means of mental inner working Interchanges and Mosaic patterns. Another application is that when Ancient African Sages discovered *all God's creatures and creations demonstrate similarities, those alone imply Circumstantial Evidence of Correspondence. Then various means such as the Subjective Sciences was able to* arrive at additional Evidence which leads to Proofs and on to Circumstantial Truths. A way this came about was by Very Ancient African Sages saying God revealed to them the Truth and Reality of Nature by means of its Circumstantial Laws (note they did not say God said this). An elaboration on those Laws came from Very Ancient priest-astronomers (c20,000 BC) studying the sky; then, fashioning derived Principles into a structure of universal rhythms. As a result of contemplating on their insights (internalizing the Truth) + using *Intuitive Inductions* (inferring general principles from particular facts present in the Cosmic Order), a Celestial Order ("course" or "way") path was opened which enabled them to generate organizing principles of harmony, situations for facts, laws, themes, and correspondences. Out of this broad scope of knowledge were extracted Principles which were then organized into Truths and Order called Ma'at (Love in action). By recognizing different planes of Cosmic existence, they devised Standards specific to each plane. This was based on their belief that Human Truths require living by a standard imposed by ones essential divine nature, which implied there would be a "certain sameness" of good character imparted by the Law of Sympathy. Their five basic Standards can be featured by using the *"T" Concept*. On the horizontal crossbar are Absolute Standards of a Divine nature (ones studied conception of God's Circumstantial Truths). Divine Standards are based upon things of Worth (i.e. the Love Platter, peace, harmony, order, balance, and unity). These standards have a Philosophical Base of Unconditional Love and a Philosophical Frame of God's Circumstantial Truths--both serving as the eternally fixed anchor around which they built their entire philosophy of life--both serving as guides by which everything in the universe is judged.

On the vertical part of the *"T" Concept* a "Root" Standard for the Intangible plane is the Beauty, Goodness, and Reality which derives from ones Real Self. For the Unbounded Tangible Plane of a Feeling nature (reflecting the Will of God), the Standard is harmony and unity naturally springing out of Unconditional Love; for the Partially Bounded Plane it is Health; and for the Concrete Tangible planes, proper Truth measurements derive from mathematics and honorable educated estimates applied to such things as "How much is enough money to thrive in my life" and then figuring out how to honorably acquire it. Despite differences, these standards are all related to and are part of the big picture of Good Living and Humaneness. Each represents the frame in which right decisions and right actions are made. Thus, they symbolize points of stability. After going through all these steps, what is most likely to be the Truth is that truthful building materials have *Coherence* (its internal components are consistent with one another); *Consistency* (standing firmly together in a state of harmony with what makes sense); and *Compatibility* with Reality (practice). If it is Real it will expand ones entire Selfhood all at the same time. All of this (among others) went into the concepts of Archetypes ("Seeds" for a Class of things in the Cosmos, like Animal and Plant Kingdoms). From this, Very Ancient Africans inferred *Idea-Forms* to be patterns fixed in Nature which reproduce themselves in their own image so as to become the Thing it makes. Such is mathematical pattern of Ma'at. Out of Ma'at came African Traditions. For example, based upon Correspondence, self-realizable Divine ideas can be had because they are patterns fixed in Nature. Out of these patterns pertaining to God-created Divine Forms, they applied these aspects to assessing such things as Music, Mathematics, Beauty, Goodness, and Thought--each containing an Archetype Seed with its Archetype Essence pattern.

"WISE" AFRICAN HISTORY: "Wise" is a word originally used by Primitive Africans for those who had success with Magic. Then, throughout the ancient world, the terms "Wisdom" or "Wise" were placed on very shrewd or knowledgable persons, especially in their relation to Magic. By assuming these Wise men were somehow connected to a source of unlimited Wisdom—and thereby likely to *"know the way"*-- they were called Shamen Seers, Prophets, and Sages. Those who did "know "The Way" used the Spiritual Elements of Unconditional Love, Truth, Reality, and the Natural as the anchor for how to live life--meaning ones Real (Highest) Self orchestrated the Chain of Command for all think, feel, say, and do aspects. Similarly, Primitive and Very Ancient African gathered Knowledge that enabled them to infer the Spiritual Elements. These were the Essences of Wisdom and nothing outside them, even to the tiniest degree, qualified to be Wisdom. Although such was considered the ultimate by being of God's Essence, Ancient Africans used the Spiritual Elements as a springboard and the means to be better and better, everyday and in every way. *Virtue* was the application of such Wisdom by: (1) using the truth distillate of experience as the Principle of doing things in the correct way, in the right system, and at the appropriate time; (2) the Principle of Justice--doing things equally in public and private; (3) Fortitude— synonymous with Courage--the Principle of not flying from danger, but meeting it with a display of strength to sustain action, even when the flesh and blood can carry on no further; and (4) Temperance—the Principle of subduing desires and living moderately. The qualifying test for these applications was in making decisions and solving problems without causing harm in the final analysis. These aspects of Wisdom, under the term "*Seboyet*"--normally translated as "Instruction" or "Wisdom"--constituted the teaching theme within Ancient Egyptians' Houses of Life (prior to 12,000 BC). It was symbolized in the *Mdu Ntr (Divine Words)* carrying a star as one of its glyphs to indicate perception, insight, and light (i.e. Wisdom)--the result of ones Common Sense perfection of ones own pre-birth Emotions and ones Rational Intellect. Two signs these are harmonious and properly put together is when one can see the infinite in the finite or the miraculous in the common—the Visionary process of *tracing Effects to their Causes*—a form of A-Posteriori Reasoning. When Wise minds are functioning properly, one is in a perpetual state of inner peace (Happiness, Hetep, and Nirvana), a requirement for thoughts of a Wisdom nature--thoughts as actualized intuitions from ones Divine Consciousness (Wisdom). If one remains open to them through ones Real Self, what one wills is not based upon personal desires but instead gives oneself over to what is in harmony with ones Divine Consciousness. This implies the *subjection of ones mind to the Divine Spirit so it can command the Life-Force in harmony with the Laws of Nature.* Such knowledge comes only with experiencing Reality itself. *Proper dealings with Reality is by conforming to the Spiritual Elements.* Those striving to be Wise are aware of their own ignorance so as to use this spur to keep their eyes glued on Wisdom type patterns—seeing the "what it is" of a Thing and distinguishing that from "what it does" and "how it appears"--talking less and saying more—seeking what is profound of only a few significant things--learning from fools and tragedy what not to do—extracting the lessons of disillusionments and sufferings—to bear with the stupidity of the ignorant and the psychically traumatized—learning that some things do not have answers but, instead, "Just Are"—knowing what to overlook and what not to know. The wise look foolish among fools. With difficulty they learn to be generous and when to exhibit "Tough Love." They do those things in the living which they would wish they had done on their Death Bed. For me, I get far more usefulness out of talking with those on the low end of the Social Ladder than from those higher up. I also draw more from enemies than from acquaintances.

WISE'S MENTAL TOOLS: First is the cultivation of the enjoyment of learning. Curiosity is the hallmark of scholarship. To yield to every whim of curiosity—to allow ones passion for inquiry be unrestrained shows an eagerness of the mind. But it is Wisdom that selects from among the innumerable problems which present and engages in solutions of significance to humankind. In my Orthopaedic Surgical practice, following an extensive evaluation of my patients, I would ask them to tell any question they had about any medical problem. Then, at home, I would spend up to 40 hours doing research to find answers—studying books out of my field like obstetrics, gynecology, chest, dermatology. What was amazing was the discovery of orthopaedic information in these text I had never seen before. These discoveries were transferred into my own domain style. To go through the struggle to locate, gather, and understand Classic Knowledge, as written in the Ancient African Bible, is the best way to spend ones free time. The very best place to learn Knowledge is in Nature—using ones own observations, ratified by ones own proofs, and matured by ones own thoughts. Embraced here is noticing correspondences—i.e. "equivalents," resemblances, and recurrences in the application of Principles (unchanging realities) and Events (changing realities) that are happening within ones view. The Effect is that Knowledge imparts serenity of mind. This pursuit of Truth will require separating it from Established Information—expecially conceptions from the past that blind one to those Spiritual Elements Principles slapping one in the face. A place to start here is with those which for the longest period have remained unquestioned. Then, a daily process is to apply that Knowledge with Compassion born of understanding in a simplified manner—so as to develop Wisdom practices.

WISE DISPLAYS: The Wise are Just, Upright, lives by Truth; do things while living which are to be desired when dying; and know how to take advantage of Thought Atmospheres—e.g. do all deep thinking in the same spot without leaving until a conclusion is reached.. One is the ready and accurate perception of Figures of Communications, like Analogies. The Wise welcome criticisms of their work because that is how they learn. The Wise constantly seek how to use their time, energy, and effort to greatest advantage—focusing on the best goal that causes "stretching" to reach, in the best way that benefits the most, over the longest period of time. The Wise seek perfection in what they do, more on the order of a game, for that is how they build self-pride. Great self-pride comes from achievements like no others in being in charge and control of oneself, what one does, and ones situations.

WOMANHOOD: To be a perfect unity Image of God, Ancient Africans said humans were created male and female (thus God is not "He")—a duality "Oneness" for purposes of unfolding the divine likeness Males and females are complementary equals who each do different things for the benefit of all. If there are disagreements they are to be worked out immediately, while respecting each other and realizing each gender is only half right. *The true worth of a race must be measured by the character of its womanhood" (Mary McLeod Bethune).* Today, "Womanhood" is defined as: (1) The state or time of being a woman; (2) The composite of qualities thought to be appropriate to or representative of women; (3) Women considered as a group. Part of Womanhood has taking care of her man and children as major aspects of family duties. Smart woman prepare early in how to get along with professional men for each is an Isolated Individualists.

WOO: *Woo the reluctant by developing their Curiosity to increase their insight, for both, by getting them wrapped up in the "here and now," conquers fear faster than anything because of them forgetting to be afraid.* Vanity—i.e. whatever is not honest but that the leader is into as an adopted personal trait; what gives undue and undeserved pride in ones self-chosen identity, with ones appearance.

WORDS: By studying the stories of Words as my hobby—perhaps over 30,000—I have a wide variety of sources to draw on when putting together a complex subject. What I have discovered is that seemingly unrelated words, when looking at their underlying sources, have inner similarities. Ultimately, their source is from Ancient African "Seeds" that have subsequently been diluted and polluted by each of the foreign cultures.

WORD ASSESSMENTS: African words like Essence have very specific meanings which are not recognized by Europeans and even most Black scholars. Europeans present African concepts that they stole, made facts out of the African metaphors, and then changed their meanings. Since that may be the only source of that African knowledge, the European process must be returned through each of those faulty steps. In Alchemy, Europeans speak of Gold when its African origin pertained to the Higher Self while the other "base metals" of Europeans refers to Africans' reference to the Lower Self. I am able to go back into definitions I formulated 10 years ago and get new meanings or meanings from them that I did not know then that they existed. My evolution in definitions of the same word is now more expansive in scope and in depth as well as deeper in depth. So any reading my works would best start from the most recent and work backward. But to learn history, start at the beginning of my writings and go forward. What Europeans write about Black history is typically wrong. Pythagorus added Ether to the 4 Matter elements of Africans—Fire, Water, Earth, Air and called it Quintessence. However, Ether is not an element because it is a mixture of Spiritual Energy made into the finest of Matter. So, Do Not Believe What Authority Say with checking it out.

WORD CHANNELLING: the language of the Enslaved selected and "channeled" into restraints by determining the names for things; by determining the meanings and values of those things; and by determining the rules shaping and influencing how the Enslaved related to those things.

WORD DEPREVIATION: selecting and restricting the number of words for victims. Being victims of "Word Channeling" and "Word deprivation" began a continuous episode of "brain-washing" (i.e. coercive persuasion or re-socialization).

WORD DETAILS: What is most important about Words is what each stands for—and is it good or bad. Or, if it stands for anything, is it significant by enabling one to examine or identity certain specific Essentials (e.g. characteristics) which can be distinguished from any other set of Essentials (e.g. character) in a manner that is publicly intelligible. This means communicating meaning without ambiguity—and that is best done by focusing on the Denotation of the word. But in speaking to people, their Connotation best aids their understanding while introducing many entries for mis-interpretation and leaving the realm of Common Ground. Nevertheless, the Words used for oneself are those springing out of the Spiritual Elements because they leave no doubt in the minds who understand those meanings. Besides, they provide a beginning Mental Skeleton start a Thought Structure on a Sound (i.e. Real) Base and then following a Mathematical (reproducible results) pattern. Besides, when people used those words (e.g. "love") one can determine a great deal about those people by how they elaborate on it—as in Unconditional Love (African Tradition) vs. "Love" defined as an emotion and kept within the confines of "Conditional" ("I won't love you if..."). *Postulates* are voluntarily accepted assumptions which, when agreed upon by the experts in a certain science, become its conventional basis. If a Postulate is in the Physical realm, it may or may not start from Truth. Still, it cannot start from Truth or Reality if it derives out of the Supernatural. *Presume* implies some justification by way of practice or example or logical procedure. A "*Premise*" is a statement accepted as a fact--making no further inquiry concerning the truth of the same; as a basis for further reasoning; and yet it may be true, distorted, or fantasy. CONJECTUREs (to put together the nearest available materials for a provisional opinion based upon insufficient evidence) are put in the category of Hypothesis (a statement of what is deemed possible true, assumed, and reasoned upon as if certainly true, with a view of reaching truth not yet surely known); Suppose (temporarily assume a thing as true); and Likely. Nevertheless, Causes, Effects, and Conjuncts are best suited to Conjecture. *Propositions* set forth what is claimed to be truth in formal statements. Concepts are building blocks for propositions--definitive declarative statements about the subject. In European logic's practical application, Premises, like a *Postulate* or Proposition, it may or may not start from Truth if it is in the Physical realm and cannot start from Truth or Reality if it derives out of the Supernatural, the Divine, the Spiritual, or the Metaphysical. *Presuppositions,* under which these terms are encompassed, is a thing taken for granted or assumed. It is always best to assume that a Proposition, Postulate, Premise, Assumption, or Presumption is distorted, or false—based upon unexamined Assumptions and doubt.

From logical or non-rational evolutions of Presuppositions come Effects from being used in Creativity, Conclusions, Inferences, Actions, Consequences, and Results. How good are ones Presuppositions Bases depends upon the Source of the ingredients involved + the proper selection of the ingredients + the nature and soundness of the ingredients + the skill and method used to make up a workable definition from the Ingredient + how properly were the Units in each Concept maneuvered and manipulated to arrive at the resultant Presuppositions. The "Big Picture" Result either generates harmony or the chaos of mental disinte-gration. Invalid Concepts have integrated errors, contradictions, or false propositions and that makes for bad Effects and Consequences. All of this is flawed thinking in African Tradition for all thinking processes must stay within and evolve out of the Spiritual Element—and not be off to the tiniest of a degree. Doubt at the core of "Guesses" blocks entering the African Divine Logos Path. See Denotations vs. Connotations; Definitions

WORD ORIGINS--UNEXAMINED ASSUMPTIONS: What can make European dictionaries so Spiritual Elements devastating is the way they change, by translation, African Philosophical words into a "SEEMs" right context that is actually "off- track." Then that "off-track" meaning is carried far, far, away from the Truth. To elaborate, any Afrocentric person knows the significance of Nature to everything having to do with the Spiritual Force God—also termed Sekhem, Amen, and others + all of God's Creatures and Creations. For example, even though God is Unknowable, God is known by Sekhem's manifestations in Nature. As a result of Very Ancient Africans devising African Tradition Thought Structure ingredients from amazing Astro-Mathematically determined research, from those conclusions came Inferences of there being *an underlying web of relationships operating in Nature* throughout the Cosmos. This Web of Nature has *consistent, permanent, sta-tionary, and unchanging patterns (matured Spiritual Elements Essences) and Elements (moving Essences)*. This pro-cess, called the Law of Correspondence, means that what goes on in Nature is also going on in the mind, body, and spirit of each Real Self individual. This is because *Nature* is *the God Substance* the Cosmic Spirit impregnates into the essence of God's creatures and creations; the home of God's Laws; the source of humans' wisdom--and that Nature and humans are an indivisible unity, like two sides of a coin. Also, to be found in Nature is the model for the cultivation of ones in-born Genius, in general, and any life-shaping or life-changing esoteric (hidden) subject, in particular. Both the English words "Nature" and "Natural" derive from the ancient Latin term "natural," neutral, and eternity. In turn, those words derive from the Egyptian words "*Neter*" (God) and "*Neteru*" (God's manifestations). Natural means resulting from Nature, implying what is inborn or inherent. However, in the translations pertaining to "God," Europeans first substituted their Supernatural God (and, at that time, which particular one is uncertain) for the Spiritual God, Sekhem; second, invented the word "God" whose etymology comes from a wide variety of sources; third and then went on to discuss the Supernatural God as if it was the Spiritual God. Examples include the *Heathen Gods*, as with those of Brutes, whose ideas embraced a Being more powerful than humans but not necessarily better. They had no redeeming virtue, were more like devils who were especially those strong, very jealous, and believed to be extremely harsh punishers if they faltered in their worship. When one tribe conquered another that was proof of the superiority of their gods. These, as many forms, were carried into ancient Greek gods, displayed in myths as cruel, vengeful, and/or amoral—but without shaking the faith or allegiance of worshipers—a form of "Flexible Morals" and/or Virtues seen today. Early *Hebrew* Ideas of God concerned a tribal deity who had no concern with the welfare of any people but the Hebrews and who care more for formal rites of worship than for any moral purity. Gradually, the conception broadened until God became the strong moral force and was deemed to control other nations as well as Israel. After *European Christianity* formed, both they and the Hebrew God was said to care for all peoples alike. All sorts of concepts developed about Europeans' Supernatural God involving such things as being a personality or a mere Force; made in European men's own image or of something else; with whom humans could communicate or was remote; whether existing or not. But this God, in contrast to Africans' Spiritual God, was and remote. Athetists fall back on their own inner convictions and reject a God who could be completely comprehended by a finite mind cannot exist. Satanists simply attack the Spiritual Elements of Sekhem. Colored Peoples who have been brainwashed into absorbing by osmosis (socialization) this religious chaotic atmosphere see it as ranging among all of those just mentioned. They accept the dictionary definitions of "God" as "a being of supernatural powers or attributes, believed in and worshiped by a people, esp. a male deity." This powerful "SEEMs" right switch remains in their mental Foreground! The Collective Unconscious Spirituality of early Africans remains so deeply embedded in the inner recesses of their descendants' mind, as to not change this established spirituality by converting to another Religion/Spirituality system. Instead, their Spiritual God Spirituality stays the same and the only changes are the rituals in which it is packaged so as to make it an expressed hybrid.

WORK IN AFRICAN TRADITION: The single most important preparatory tool for Critical Thinking (CT) is African Tradition's work practices. Africans philosophically viewed it *as an intensification of the work the God Spirit* does in Nature, but on a tiny scale. This necessarily involves working out of Spiritual Energy, as opposed to Emotional Energy. Ancient Africans explained this by saying "a kind of individualized fragment of the Supreme Being" present in the very beginning of each human provides inner spiritual illumination that embraces the Spiritual Elements of Unconditional Love, Truth, Reality, and the Natural. Like blood in the human body, the "blood" of Spiritual Elements is Spiritual Energy which, when working naturally, flows into, around inside, and then, starting with an aura, ripples outside ones physical self. Its "blood vessels" are "Pure" Feelings which spring out of God's Will to supply ones entire Selfhood. Being an aspect of Spiritual Elements and sharing its features, by itself Spiritual Energy reproduces itself and thereby becomes the thing it reproduces, regardless on what plane of existence. A human's *Self-Love*, deriving from the Spiritual Element's Unconditional Love, reproduces itself while *providing the Spiritual Energy/Knowledge to Thrive; to help others while Thriving; and to prevent any harm to oneself or to others.* Within this context Spiritual Energy is like "Soul Music's" symbolizing a love of life because it produces within oneself a sort of individualized celebration of well-being. Spiritual Energy is a builder of ones Character and Self-Esteem by elevating ones Self-Identity, Self-Meaning, and Self-Respect; by recognizing ones Dignity and Divinity; and by imparting a sense of ones connectedness to the Cosmic Organism. Spiritual Energy motivates and powers each human's *Energy Package* (dedication, commitment, loyalty, determination, persistence, and perseverance) which will get any job done that is conveyed by Higher Powers through ones Feelings. Spiritual Energy manifests in the experience of being so engrossed in a task as to lose track of time; as being so excited that one would rather do the task than to do a favorite past-time; as getting up early and staying up late to work on the task; and as a willingness to do the "dirty," the difficult, the boring, and the tedious (as with research) to gain insights. One realizes that although the task is so huge and overwhelming as to cause one to feel like an ant trying to eat an elephant, ones "Spirit" urges the "ant" to proceed to eat one bite at a time. There is no "giving up" when set-backs or personal defeats occur. Instead, one uses these as opportunities to troubleshoot areas where there was improper or inadequate preparation or to find where one got off course. Then one is eager to resume the destination task with an updated perspective. This is how humans model the work the God Spirit does in Nature. It is enjoyable contentment. However, this African work ethic was shattered when Africans were brought to the Americas as Slaves. One effect on the Slaves was that, instead of working for God, they bitterly resented working for the extremely evil and sadistic European captors. As a result, their attitudes about work headed in all sorts of directions. One prominent display of this seen in today's descendants stuck in the status quo is the: "I'm too busy" excuse (anything but the Truth). In contrast to having no trouble clearing time to party, watch television, talk on the phone, "I'm too busy" is a declaration of ones unwillingness to prioritize, focus on the important, and do very hard work needed to Thrive. One must make space in ones life to do tedious planning, in-depth research, perfect required skills, and accept performing "a mile of work just to make an inch of progress." The "I'm too busy" approach ensures one will never engage in meaningful CT. To prevent this, the very best thing parents can do is to teach their children how to work somewhat like *the God Spirit* does in Nature. The work is done for free at home; free for the disabled; and otherwise for pay.

WORKABLENESS FOR AFRICAN CRITICAL THINKING: Avoid having fixed ideas about and fixed reactions to anything that is uncertain. Second, having a 'big picture' of the situation, followed by careful planning by means of the Box Concept that leads to a Human Ideal Goal, take only one step at a time. After arranging/rearranging and combining/recombining them into workable options, the best option becomes Plan A, and the next two best are Plans B and C. However, if no piece of the puzzle is found or if any of the Options do not give a workable connection, something has to be created to arrive at a workable solution. Critical Thinking then looks at what is available in a new way, for the purpose of seeing the common in the uncommon or seeing the uncommon in the common. The struggle that it takes to come up with options is the key to ones Judgments/Success about anything. I define the most *"Workable"* done right manner in what is situationally practical in action—and that is *Efficient* (doing more with less effort and/or time than with any other option)—and that is *Effective* (the desired effect satisfies the solution better than any alternative) is as hard of a task as one will face in life. It requires making whatever is available fit for use to discover Truth and/or to build all decisions around Truth so as to have a Beautiful Effect. The aim is to have realistic Human Ideals—i.e. decisions and solutions workable for the situation and the people at issue. For each of these steps, the only way to gain a workable definition, new ideas or workable options for the solution is to use the Box Concept.

    A. *look at things as they really are*
    B. *avoid seeing only what is liked*
    C. *do not be blind to the obvious of what one does not want to see*
    D *avoid a like/dislike opinion* about what has to be done
    E. Never avoid what is disliked if it has to be done

Creative Thinking takes any of those new views as well as takes some of this from Option I and some of that from Option IV and arranges/rearranges and combines/ recombines them into new forms. It is essential to considering different planes of existence so as to do Creative maneuvers and manipulations, like doing acrobatics. By so doing, one realizes that things can be the opposite of how they are customarily thought to be. Or you go in instead of out; up instead of down; right to left instead of left to right; the top instead of the bottom; accident with a purpose (Serendipity); look for the common in the uncommon and the uncommon in the common. Consider what seems impossible, as the present can give rise to the past, as when a water wake is created by a ship. Then various situations of a Trial-and-Error nature are set up to see if any of the new forms is satisfactorily workable. If that does not work then the most pertinent components in the situation at hand are blended, molded, or synthesized into new Options. The three Options which seem to be the most workable solutions are selected -- and that selection process into Plans A, B, and C is the Judgment phase of CT. Although this Judgment is made largely on figuring it out (like a math problem), how things "Feel" plays a part -- and this has nothing to do with being impulsive. Options are workable answers offered for choice during problem-solving. The solution is no better than the best Option chosen--but it must serve as a connecting link between the Cause or the problem and the Solution and/or the desired Effect. Then one considers each Option in detail to evaluate how well that Option works to explain the conclusion or to be the best workable solution. Much of the time this comes about by making individual changes in a pattern, one at a time. In turn, Options can be prioritized to enable one to determine what is the most important. Dealing with the most important (or the simplest) first puts one on the path to correct Diagnoses and Management--a path that eliminates impulsiveness. Once started on this path there will be insights to open further the difficult subject.

WORKABLE PREPARATIONS: the most *"Workable"* as getting what one really, really wants and avoids getting what one really, really does not want. This is about being Creative, Inventive, and Innovative—with absolutely Focused Attention--in doing *What is Situationally Practical* within the settling of *What is Available* (the reserves, the time, the people to carry some of the load, the lack of overwhelming odds), *What is Reasonable* (is it best for "ME/WE"), and *What is Honorable* (no lying, cheating, or stealing). This is achieved within the context of doing the task "*Right*" (so superbly as to impart Self-Pride); *Efficiently* (done quickly without wasted time, energy, and effort compared with any other option); and *Effective* (the desired effect satisfies the solution better than any alternative). These are what bring about *Efficacy*—the ongoing *Self-Empowerment* urging one to fashion an intended result that is headed towards ones ultimate Human Ideal goal. *Prioritized Order* for doing what has to be done is essential. The first law of Nature is Survival. Not only does one have to first take care of oneself but one cannot properly help others climb until one becomes an expert in what it has taken to rise above where they are. Until that point is reached, the best one can do is to simply "be with them" where they are, while being Compassionate, Supportive, and Social. Essential preparation for this is by face-to-face interactions—and not through Social Media. Critical Thinking (CT) is required to determine the *Seven Questions of Inquiry--who, which, what, when, where, why, and how much?* For example, who that shall be?—and when?—and which way? And where?—and why?—and how long?—and to what degree? CT requires having a workable idea about what is "normal." When we Orthopaedic residents at the Hospital for Joint Diseases were learning the finer points of how to read x-ray films, every morning before breakfast we visited the radiologist to study normal radiographs (x-ray films). Once we had a clear picture of "normal" and "normal variants" (those not quite normal but were ordinarily not a problem), we could more quickly pick up what is abnormal. "Normal" refers to those traits or features or characteristics clustered closely around the average of whatever has a range.

WORTH: Things of *Worth* are originally determined by a human's Spark of God Essences, with their attributes being the Essentials of Cosmic Organism oriented Beauty, Goodness, Happiness, Wellness, and Natural Order. Worth, measured by estimates, is concerned with the underlying consistent, permanent, stationary, and unchanging *Pattern* (imparting a significant meaning) and *Shape* (emitting a certain power) of a given person, place, or thing. Things of Worth/Value are seen in how one spends ones time. *Values* are what one sees in a "Thing" in more ways than just itself—ways termed Worth and Value—each parsed into Mild, Slight, Moderate, or Extreme Classes. Manners are about dealing with things of Worth—i.e. the Spiritual Elements and their attributes (which are like the Sun and its rays" all being "involved" (i.e. its mosaics wrapped up together) when approaching others so as to become "evolved" (unwrapped in manifesting) in a harmonious manner. That harmony makes for *complete adaptation of each part to the whole, implying perfect adjustment of all conditions*—and this experience of Worth, which gives one an inner sense of Order and Balance, is true on all planes, mental, physical, and spiritual. By being about the Implicit Beauty of a Thing or what is significant for its own sake as a result of simply having come into Being within the Cosmic Organism is what expands ones "ME/WE" Consciousness.

WRITING: Writing had been invented by Interior Africans at least by 77,000 BC and the Nubians had developed an alphabet consisting of 24 alphabetic symbols (representing vowels and consonants). Then, Ancient Egyptians increase the flexibility the alphabet, applications of ASI, and creative thinking by modifying the original Nubian alphabet into a sophisticated hieroglyphic system. See Affect Symbolic Imagery

Y

YIN/YANG: The Chinese Symbols for the African Law of Opposites are Yin (negative principles of the Cosmos) and Yang (positive Principles) fishes positioned in oppositions to each other and go round and round, like night and day. Complementary (Yin/Yang) opposites mean both components are real; are identical in nature; and with both being equally significant but in different ways--like ocean waves. These criteria are the essentials to qualify as *Polar Opposites'* two natures are like two sides of a coin--each side joined to the other--for one is void without the other. Examples include: black/white, hot/cold, yes/no, inside/outside, light/dark, chicken/egg, bees/flowers. Each behaves independently while in the process of working together interdependently in a connected net to bring self-regulating Order, Truth, Justice. *Yin/Yang* are not in conflict, as in trying to eat each other, but each can only be there because of the other. So, see these differences as a "Oneness"--an Awakening intimately a part of "Knowing Thyself"--meaning everything in the external world is part of oneself. Seeing life and the Cosmos as a "Unified Dance" of opposites is key to a Free Mind. A *Binary Number* system represents numbers having two as its base and using the digits 0 and 1. Yes/no, on/off, and positive/negative are all encounters of a binary nature. This System--persisting in what the Chinese called the *I-Ching* (Bynum, African Unconscious p182)--contains symbols dating to 20,000 BC--symbols used for forecasting--symbols subsequently becoming the basis of the machine language of today's complex computers. When Duality is integrated within a higher context, its Binary System is based on the counterbalanced forces of two opposite poles--forces either symmetrical (i.e. identical in extent and intensity) or asymmetrical--either successive (day/night) or simultaneous (e.g. masculine/feminine in each human). See Dance—Metaphysical

YOKING TO AFRICAN TRADITION SCHOLARSHIP: Private Self "yoking" in African Tradition means humans' mind make notches into their inner Divine Logos by means of their first *work of Spirituality being subjecting their minds to the Divine Spirit so it can command the Life-Force in harmony with the Laws of Nature.* Such "yoking" thereby allow ones mind to Metaphysically express "The Word" or Verbum Patterns of the ever concealed Logos. That is what Ancient African Sages called *Logic.* Broadly, "Yoke," in African Tradition, is to "Bond" (so as to be 'fed') for the purpose of working together as a unit by means of Unconditional Love. Such a "Bonding" is in the form of a "Virtual" experience with all of God's creatures and creations prior to each being born into the Material World. In that Bonded state, all are "fed" with Unconditional Love emanating out of the Cosmic Mind. This awareness was symbolized in two practical ways. First was the interior African invention of agriculture with its plow pulled by two oxen connected by a crossbar (c20,000 BC). Second was Ancient Africans' invention of Yoga practices (c10,000 BC)—certain physical, mental, and spiritual disciplines for well-being with the Cosmic Mind while meditatively withdrawn from the sensible world. The intent was/ is fashion a *"Non-Self" wholistic "ME/WE"* mental Image that symbolically and virtually reconnects one with original Cosmic Organism. In this way, one is "fed" attributes of the Spiritual Elements, like the "5Ss" of Safety, Security, Sureness/Self-Confidence, Strength, and Stability to ones Private Selfhood.

This image perhaps derived from the plowing oxen, for it conveyed many other concepts: (1) the Seeable yoked ox was definitely present; (2) if an ox was absent (the mystery), it could be inferred that the empty space of the crossbar had a meaning; (3) the absent yoke space should have another ox in it instead of some other type of animal and that absent ox resembled the Seeable ox (the symbol); (4) the absent ox was a vital bonding part of the same unit; and (5) the Seeable ox could not nearly work as Efficiently (as in doing the job more quickly with much less wasted time, energy, and effort) and Effectively (the desired job is done right and has the best effect in satisfying the solution). Thus, by understanding the known (the "Seeable" ox), African Sages could infer (by Deductive and Inductive reasoning) much that would otherwise be unknowable (the Missing ox). Note: the *Cause* (the visible ox "standing for" the mystery ox) gives rise to an *Effect* (the inferring of what the Missing ox could be like). That Effect is pregnant with the *Consequence*--an organized completion into a gestalt or whole idea or a memory that completes a present sensory experience of what it is like to have both oxen side-by-side--even though the visible ox and the mystery ox are not identical.

A modified form of this type of situation is what was experienced by Enslaved Africans being brought to the Americas by Sadistic Satanist Europeans. To repeat Howard Thurman: "When the slaves were taken from their homeland, the primary social unit was destroyed, and all immediate tribal and family ties were ruthlessly broken. This meant the severing of the link that gave the individual African a sense of persona. There is no more hapless victim than one who is cut off from family, from language, from one's roots. He is completely at the mercy of his environment, to be cowed, shaped, and molded by it at will . . ." In addition, the Enslaved felt disserted by their Living-Dead Ancestors and even by God. Although some eventually reconnected, others only partially reconnected, while still others were swept along in the flow of the Satanist Europeans, even to this day. So, what is now required is: (a) for the handling of their Physical Human Nature Needs; (b) removing the mental and physical barriers to returning to possessing a Free Mind needed for re-yoking; (c) re-ordering their Private Selfhood with an updated or Human Ideal Philosophy of Life (POL) replacement; (d) prepare ones Public Self to get on the path to a thriving future; (e) take care of family and loved ones; and (f) begin preparation for satisfying their Mission in life.

These are the Necessities and Important things that require prioritizing so that each can be handled by the *"9Ps"--Preparing to Prepare; Purpose; Plan; Planes of Existence; Preparation; Practice; Performance; Platform; and Post-Action Judgments* (Bailey, Metaphysical Glossary, Vol. 5). Individual and full attention is to be given to the top 75 while the rest as well as ones Desires can be done while multitasking (as in socializing). To do these well and in good order is the process that brings about Self-*Efficacy* (i.e. self-empowerment leading to an eagerness to take on bigger challenges) and Self-Pride. To return to the statement of by understanding the known (the "Seeable" ox), African Sages could infer (by Deductive and Inductive reasoning) much that would otherwise be unknowable (the Missing ox). Such Reasoning by Analogy is the basic Principle of Correspondence. So, *to get into the flow of Spiritual Elements are making all decisions and solutions out of it is the way to plan for the present and the future.* Each of the Necessities have been addressed in my other books.

Z

"ZOMBIES": Haitian Creole term for those in a "walking coma" state--a state generated by a group called the Power Elite or the Illuminati. They are a small group of corporate, banking and political leaders who declare themselves as "little gods" and the world's highest power. Their intent is to rob the world of its riches, humanity, and dignity so as to enslave the people's minds. Their success is dependent upon the optimal consent and minimal resistance from the majority of the world's people, as by those who do not vote and those who only think about "Trinkets and Trivia." They have quashed (made to disappear) the super-brilliant Ancient African intellectual property because it is so powerful as to prevent people who are aware of it from being controlled. This is why people of the world are not taught such African Tradition tools as Critical Thinking, Dialectic, Philosophy, Spirituality, and Subjective and Objective Sciences. Instead these subjects are so confusing and taught in ways that make no sense as for almost everybody to give up trying to learn them.

ZOMBIE HABITS: Culturally transmitted out of slavery via the Enslaved who proceeded through the Struggling Tunnel (connecting the quarters of the Enslaved with today's inner cities) were the "Tape Recorded" messages of "Stay-in-your-place" which, in turn, became part of the Family tradition + the various poverties that had been fashioned during slavery + a relative lack of skilled thinking abilities because of using their Omnibus Brains + the absence of constructive role models + the "Rolling Stone" natures of many Black males + countless other practices. Together they constitute *Slave Survivals*--meaning that though they worked "okay" for the Enslaved, out of slavery they are now self-defeating when applied to today's marketplace. Slave Survivals manifest as "*Zombie Habits*" (i.e. the reasons for the practices faded away but the practices continued). Such "Zombie Habits" cloud over ones Self-Greatness + cause a loss of the "5Ss" + lead one to question ones SELF-WORTH = putting one on a self-fulfilling adverse course. An Indian female USA judge, in speaking of the "Historical Trauma" of Amerindians, said: "Wounds passed wordlessly through generations with an accumulating grief and the urge to salve it with alcohol and drugs. This is the sickness of this land."

ZONE: Any region or areas set off from adjacent regions.

ZONE OF REALITY: The way Figures of Communication or Vivid Imaging or Visualization work is by ones mind blending into the thing and thereby switches from Thought to Feelings. Now one has eased into "the Zone" of Reality so that everything happening inside and outside ones Selfhood is experienced as a flowing harmony of which one is a part. At that point focusing gets easier and one gains a **sense of control over what is being viewed.**

ZYGOTE: "Genetics" (to beget, related to birth and creation) explain why one person looks at least a little different from his/her parents and brothers and sisters. ""*Gender Cells*" contained in the father's sperm (with its 23 Chromosomes) and in the mother's egg (with its 23 Chromosomes) meet to produce a Zygote (yoking or joining together). Within the nucleus (the core of the cell) *Chromosomes* line up in the shape of rods just before the original cell divides. Genetic factors within the cell of a *Zygote* (the first stage of development of a human yet to be born) are called Chromosomes (thread-like objects). Genes are what cause resemblances and variations in how one appears in relation to ones family members.

BOOKS BY DR. BAILEY

I Am a Special Somebody is for anyone having strayed away from his/her destination in life and yet still possesses the intense desire to get back on the path and then head toward happiness.

Self-Esteem in Black Americans presented from a historical perspective, is extensively discussed from the dawn of mankind to the present. Nine major syndromes prominently found in Black people are featured—and with suggestions on how to improve each.

Echoes of Ancient African Values discusses who Ancient Africans were as a people; their genius and creative ways of thinking; their philosophical and spiritual foundations; their world shaping achievements; and how these echo into today's Black Americans.-- $30.00

Preparing to Prepare (iUniverse.com) is about implanting seed ideas of a good character nature. Lesson plans are plentiful to serve as a guideline for stimulating ideas and methods to help youth achieve their dreams and talents for a balanced, mature, and wealthy life.-- $28.00

Good Character explains the history of 50 traits and discusses in practical terms the skills needed to instill or develop good character--traits are fundamental for achieving a successful, happy life.--$30.00

Becoming a Champion Somebody provides the "nuts & bolts" of choosing ones legacy dream, discovering ones talent, and becoming a successful person. The approach a systematic 9 step process-- called the 9Ps—is based on practical experiences of many people. It is designed to help youth in identifying and pursing their goal in a way that applies to any career or for adults keen on achieving even greater success.

American Crime From A Black American Perspective points out the USA conspiracy against Black males; exposes who the real (non- Black) criminals are; and explores in detail the course of Black males likely to be pushed into and then be destroyed as they go through the unfair prison system.

Manhood in Black Americans classifies the nine broad types of manhood and gives approaches and methods to structuring male children and restructuring the orientation of youth who are off the path that is best for them. Both are mainly directed toward single mothers.

Afrocentric English and Critical Thinking is a book designed for making these subjects more interesting for Black youth from a Yin/Yang perspective. This traces the history of African languages through Europe and on into the Americas up to the present. A full discussion is given on Black English, Ebonics, and the special ways Black Americans use both. The stories of 25 key words required for formal English are given.

Enslaved Minds in Black Americans starts with their origin in slavery and with contributions from "bad" African retentions. Numerous patterns of enslaved minds are then given (e.g. procrastination), with extensive comments on their diagnoses and management.

Common Sense inside African Tradition centers on how it developed and was used by Ancient Africans and how it can be developed and used in Black American children. For this to happen requires the cultivation of pure feelings and poetic thinking of African Tradition. The approaches for teaching are out of mathematics, art, literature, and games.

Anger in Black Americans is the primary emotion related to racism. Though entirely justified, it is self-destructive for daily living. This book points out why and offers a variety of detailed management approaches for a variety of chronic anger types--approach which have a track record of effectiveness.

Creativity, Invention, and Discoveries emphasizes ways to cultivate each in children, reactivate them in those who have fallen into a rigid predictable pattern of living, and remove limitations on those desiring to explore new worlds. Methods are presented for practical application on how to see the uncommon in the common and the common in the uncommon.

Rising above Poverty is about changing the belief system of those who chronically struggle in life. For Black Americans this means switching from an Enslaved Mind belief system to that laid out in African Tradition because its brilliance has stood the test of time. This switch is followed by correcting self-defeating bad habits which are spin-offs from bad beliefs.

Selfhood Mastery inside African Tradition is a guide for creating, enhancing, and maintaining the Inner Strength and Inner Peace that leads to contentment and happiness. It emphasizes stabilizing your inner self and maintaining it by Mental Toughness in order to remain in control and be alert while dealing with life's most difficult problems.

Managing Emotions is a work that has arisen out of experiences from patients in my Orthopaedic Surgical practice, from personal happenings, and from a lifetime involvement with the struggling poor (whose bad emotional contents differ from the population at large). There are long discussions on Good and Pleasure Emotions. To aid ones understanding of Good and Bad Emotions and to make easier customized management, stories of 116 emotions are presented.

Supreme Thinking of Ancient Africans is presented for the first time and is the result of 25 years of research. It tells how Ancient Africans taught their students; explores the details of the ten steps of Rational Thinking; and gives the steps for becoming a Visionary by means of Poetic Thinking.

Rational Thinking is the result of how the author learned to think over a 40 year period, particularly in the Medical/Legal arena, but is applicable to every aspect of life. It is geared to teenagers and emphasizes pictures helpful for thinking about personal problem solving. It is the author's signature book.

Afrocentric Critical Thinking is any form of Productive Thinking consisting of a collection of mental disciplines that draw on wise and pertinent lessons of the past to achieve a goal in the present and/or the future. The uniqueness of this book is that it mentally guides Black people in maneuvering through the Eurocentric marketplace for offensive and defensive purpose.

Special Minds among Struggling Black Americans discusses what the struggling Blacks need in order to break up their vicious cycles. For them to rise above poverty requires shedding delusions and stubbornness; establishing a sound Ancient African philosophy of life and worldview; and perfecting Left and Right Brain thinking skills (e.g. foresight, forethought) by critical and rational thinking.

From Africa to Black Power by Joseph A. Bailey Sr. traces the history of Black Americans through African American slavery from 1433 to 1964. Emphasized is that of the economic, political, human aspects. It is the best work I have ever read on the subject.

Word Stories Originated By Ancient Africans contains 1000+ life-changing and life-shaping words that are now prominent in the English Language. They give an overview of African Tradition, philosophy, and practices.--$50.00

Word Stories Surrounding African American Slavery contains 2000+ words related to and spoken by Black Americans throughout USA History.--$50.00

Self Protection Syndrome is self-defeating Slave Survivals characterized by "Too Much," "Too Little," or "Just Right" but somehow inappropriate behaviors. Suggestions include helping afflicted Black Americans switch back to using their Thriving Minds; reducing or preventing the need for improper self-protection; and how to feel safe, secure, confident, strong, and stable.

Black Americans Entering the Marketplace speaks to preparing for marketplace success, including essential offensive and defensive practices.--$30.00

Unlocking Minds of Black Boys concerns what it takes to remove the Enslaved Minds of Black boys from their Mental Vaults so as to be mentally free to receive constructive information.$30.00

Mentoring Minds of Black Boys discusses building blocks of Ancient African Philosophy; how to change Belief Systems with Symbols; Art and Music as mind stimulants; Abstract Thinking; Self-Esteem; Ancient African Mathematics; and Diagnosing and Managing Chronic Juggling.--$30.00

Word Stories Encyclopaedia (Afrocentric Vol. III) has 2300 words for teaching youth Word Stories in the easiest, fastest, and most pleasant way in order to learn well-rounded information. These stories generate curiosity, imagination, and an eagerness to learn -- $50.00.

Ancient African Bible Messages spotlights the Spiritual Elements of Unconditional Love, Truth, Reality and the Natural as the standard and filter for "How Shall I live." It gives in-depth African history starting 200,000 years ago; charts the evolution of the world's first Bible; and points out how all the other Bibles of the world evolved out of the African Bible -- $30.00.

Leadership Critical Thinking in African Tradition elaborates on how to orchestrate survival, protection, and preservation under physical, emotional, thoughtful, social, financial, and relationship conditions; on spotlighting standards, filters, and guiding thriving ways for self-help and/or helping others; and on providing mental fun as play, a sport, a dance--$25.00.

Private Selfhood Greatness in Black Americans: The Certainty upon which a human's Base and Foundation rests is their Selfhood Greatness consisting of a "Drop of God," super-brilliant Ancient African Ancestors' Genetics, and one unique Talent. Personal Integrity is maintained by cultivating these three to their greatest potential while remaining inside the context of the Spiritual Elements of Unconditional Love, Truth, Reality, and the Natural--as discussed in this book--$30.00

Post-Traumatic Distress Syndrome in Black People: Those afflicted have allowed a Cloud to cover their birth gift of Selfhood Greatness as a result of deficiencies in their Spiritual Human Nature Needs (e.g. to be loved, to belong). This book gives the diagnosis and management of both in the setting of the Metaphysical aspects which characterized Black People--$30.00.

Teaching Black Youth—Affect Symbolic Imagery & African Dialectic: ASI is Ma'at Supernatural stories for Right living while Dialectic is a means to bring out the Divine Knowledge already in each human. This is designed for teachers and mentors who deal with all Black youth, including those of "the Streets."--$30.00

Bailey II, JA: African Tradition For Black Youth—Pursuit of a Free Mind. North Charleston, South Carolina: CreateSpace Independent Publishing Platform 2015. Humans are born with all they need to have a thriving and happy life. Success is guaranteed by staying within and evolving out of the Spiritual Elements for they provide ones Private Self with the "5Ss" of Safety, Security, Self-Confidence, Strength, and Stability. The "5Ss" underlie what all are searching for in life and their absence causes people to "act ugly." This books discusses ways to make happen the "5Ss"--$30.00

Bailey II, JA: STOPPING THE VIOLENCE. Persistent European male violence, driven by Ice Age "Scarcity Survival," graduated into Greed, Mind Control of the World Crowd, and Satanist practices featuring Kill/Take/Destroy/Dominate methods on the world's Colored nations. Resultant Poverty Devastation constituted the "Seed" for violence everywhere (e.g. the "Killer" police). This 630 page book's focus is on Diagnosing all Violence patterns and presenting a Management Plan.

North Charleston, South Carolina: CreateSpace Independent Publishing Platform 2015: $30.00

Bailey II, JA: REKINDLING BLACK PEOPLE'S GENIUS. This book's purpose aims to: (1) start giving Black People back their Ancestors' super-brilliant history; (2) point out the "who, which, what, when, where, why, and how much" Causes of their "take down" victimization and "keep down" oppression; (3) spotlight the absolute necessity of converting back to our Ancient Ancestor's "Sun" philosophies to progress out of all African American slavery fashioned poverties; (4) impart suggestions for "How To" Rekindle Black People's historical birth-gift Genius and Selfhood Greatness; and (5) lay out lifestyle Thriving paths by modeling Ancient Africans' Supreme Critical Thinking Skills, Talents, and Creativity for Defense, Protection, Offense, and Thriving.

North Charleston, South Carolina: CreateSpace Independent Publishing Platform 2016: $30.00

Bailey II, JA: Bailey's Ancient African Metaphysical Glossary, Vol. 5. This is the first known glossary to have all researched Ancient African Definitions for 2300 words they devised. Using such words are the only way to make progress in understanding African Tradition Philosophy and its Principles. To pick and choose between these and European concepts will only cause great confusion. One will find there are only a few Principles compared with infinite amounts of information used by Europeans. To know those Principles aids Critical Thinking, Creativity, the development of Self-Confidence. North Charleston, South Carolina: CreateSpace Independent Publishing Platform 2016: $50.00

Bailey II, JA: AFRICAN TRADITION WISDOM vs. EUROPEAN INFORMATION. African Tradition builds all Thought Structures on the "What it is" of a person, place, or thing when it comes into existence out of the Spiritual Elements of Unconditional Love, Truth, Reality, and the Natural. To stay within that and develop all thoughts, feelings, expressions, and action out of that is to have Harmony. This is the essence of African Wisdom. Anything varying from that is Information. The intracacies of both thought Harmony and Disharmony are discussed in this book. North Charleston, South Carolina: CreateSpace Independent Publishing Platform 2016: $35.00

Bailey II, JA: AMBITIOUS BLACK ISOLATED INDIVIDUALISTS. Cultivating ones in-born Selfhood Greatness guides Thriving + Survival, Self-Protection, Self-Preservation from "Alligators." Emphasized is following African Tradition's Practices to become Private Selfhood Sound and Knowledgeable—fundamentals for calmly/confidently handling Necessities in the face of overwhelming losses, lacks, obstructions, resistance, criticism, and/or persecution. Self-Reliance on this "Hard" journey, being Self-Reliant progresses into Senior years with Wisdom and Contentment.

North Charleston, South Carolina: CreateSpace Independent Publishing Platform 2016: $35.00

All books can be reviewed and ordered at http://jabaileymd.com
THE PRICES OF THE BOOKS ARE $20.00 EXCEPT THOSE LABELED OTHERWISE

REFERENCES

Adler, MJ. The Great Ideas. Chicago: William Benton: Encylopaedia Britannica, Inc. 1952

Alderman LA. *Rum, Slaves and Molasses.* New York: Crowell-Collier Press, 1972.

Amen, RUN. Metu Neter vol. 1, Bronx N.Y.: Khamit Corp., 1990.

Amen, RUN. Metu Neter vol. 2, Brooklyn: Khamit Media Trans Visions, Inc., 1994.

Amen, RUN. Metu Neter vol. 3, Brooklyn: Khamit Media Trans Visions, Inc., 1100 Albemarie Road, Brooklyn, NY 11218:2003

Amen, RUN. Metu Neter vol. 7, Brooklyn: Khamit Media Trans Visions, Inc., 1100 Albemarie Road, Brooklyn, NY 11218: 2012

Amen, RUN. Tree of Life Meditation System, Brooklyn: Khamit Media Trans Visions, Inc. 1996

Amen, RUN. Maat, THE 11 LAWS OF GOD Brooklyn: Khamit Media Trans Visions, Inc., 2003

Amen RUN. Not Out of Greece. Brooklyn: Khamit Publications 2002

Amen RUN. An Afrocentric Guide To A Spiritual Union. Brooklyn: Khamit Publications 1992

Amen, RUN. Maat, Nuk Au Neter, Brooklyn: Khamit Media Trans Visions, Inc., 2008

Amen, RUN. Metu Neter vol. 4, Brooklyn: Khamit Media Trans Visions, Inc., 1100 Albemarie Road, Brooklyn, NY 11218: 2010

Ani M. *Yurugu*, Trenton, NJ: Africa World Press, Inc., 1994.

Arieti S. *Creativity, The Magic Synthesis.* New York: Basic Books, Inc., Publishers, 1976.

Ashby MA. *Egyptian Yoga*, Miami: Cruzian Mystic Books, 1995

Ashby, MA: The Mystical Journey From Jesus to Christ: Miami: Selma Institute/Cruzian Mystic Books. 1998

Ashby, SM: Egyptian Mysteries Vol. 3 The Priests and Priestesses of Ancient Egypt; Cruzian Mystic Books/ Sema Institute of Yoga; Miami, Florida 2004

Ashby MA. *Egyptian Yoga*, Miami: Cruzian Mystic Books, 1995

Ashby, MA. The Egyptian Book of the Dead. Miami: Cruzian Mystic Books, 2006

Ashby MA: The African Origins of Civilization, Religion, Yoga, Mystical Spirituality and Ethics Philosophy, Book III. Part 3. Miami: Cruzian Mystic Books, 2002.

Bailey Sr., JA. From Africa to Black Power. Livermore, California: 2008.

Bailey II, JA: African Tradition Wisdom vs. European Information North Charleston, South Carolina: CreateSpace Independent Publishing Platform 2016

Bailey II, JA: Bailey's Ancient African Metaphysical Glossary, Vol. 5. North Charleston, South Carolina: CreateSpace Independent Publishing Platform 2016

Bailey II, JA: Rekindling Black People's Genius. North Charleston, South Carolina: CreateSpace Independent Publishing Platform 2016

Bailey II, JA: Stopping The Violence. North Charleston, South Carolina: CreateSpace Independent Publishing Platform 2015

Bailey II, JA: African Tradition For Black Youth—Pursuit of a Free Mind. North Charleston, South Carolina: CreateSpace Independent Publishing Platform 2015

Bailey II, JA: Teaching Black Youth—Affect Symbolic Imagery & African Dialectic. North Charleston, South Carolina: CreateSpace Independent Publishing Platform 2014

Bailey II, JA: Post Traumatic Distress Syndrome in Black People. North Charleston, South Carolina: CreateSpace Independent Publishing Platform 2014

Bailey II, JA: Private Selfhood Greatness in Black Americans. North Charleston, South Carolina: CreateSpace Independent Publishing Platform 2013

Bailey II, J.A. (2013): Leadership Critical Thinking in African Tradition. Mira Loma, California: Parker Publishing Inc.

Bailey II, JA. Ancient African Bible Messages. Inglewood, Ca.: Reflections Publishing House 2013

Bailey II, JA. Word Stories Encyclopaedia. Livermore, California: Wing Span Press, 2012.

Bailey II, JA. Mentoring Minds of Black Boys. Livermore, California: Wing Span Press, 2011.

Bailey II, JA. Unlocking Minds of Black Boys. Livermore, California: Wing Span Press, 2011.

Bailey II, JA. Black Americans Entering the Marketplace. Livermore, California: Wing Span Press, 2010.

Bailey II, JA. Self-Protection Syndrome In Black Americans. Livermore, California: Wing Span Press, 2010.

Bailey II, JA. Word Stories Surrounding African American Slavery. Livermore, California: Wing Span Press, 2010.

Bailey II, JA. Word Stories Originated by Ancient Africans. Livermore, California: Wing Span Press, 2009.

Bailey, II, JA. Offensive Language Afflicts Black Youth's Psyche. The Western Journal of Black Studies, Vol. 30, No. 3, 2006 p142-154

Bailey II, JA. Afrocentric Critical Thinking, Livermore, California: Wing Span Press 2008.

Bailey II, JA. Freeing Enslaved Minds in Black Americans, Livermore, California: Wing Span 2006.

Bailey II, JA. The Foundation Of Self-Esteem. J. Natl. Med. Assoc. 2003; 95: 388-393.

Bailey II, JA. A Classification of Black-American Self-Esteem; J. Natl. Med. Assoc. 2004; 96: 23-28.

Bailey II JA. Echoes of Ancient African Values, Bloomington, Indiana: Authorhouse, 2005.

Bailey II JA. Good Character, Canada: Trafford, 2004.

Bailey II JA. The Handbook for Worker's Compensation Doctors. California: I.C.E. Publishers, 1994.

Bailey II, JA. Afrocentric English and Critical Thinking, Livermore, California: Wing Span 2006.

Bailey II, JA. American Crime From A Black American Perspective, Livermore, CA: Wing Span Press, 2006.

Bailey II, JA. Anger In Black Americans. Livermore, California: Wing Span Press, 2006.

Bailey II, JA. Becoming a Champion Somebody, Livermore, CA: Wing Span Press, 2006.

Bailey II, JA. Black Voice News, Riverside, California: (blackvoicenews.com).

Bailey II, JA. Common Sense Inside African Tradition, Livermore, California: Wing Span Press, 2006.

Bailey II, JA. Creativity, Invention & Discovery, Livermore, California: 2007.

Bailey II, JA. Deceptive Orthopaedic Patients. Unpublished, 1995.

Bailey II, JA. Disproportionate Short Stature -- Diagnosis and Management, Philadelphia: W.B. Sanders Co., 1973.

Bailey II, JA. I Am A Special Somebody, California: wingspanpress.com, 2005.

Bailey II, JA. Manhood in Black Americans; Livermore, CA: Wing Span Press, 2006.

Bailey II, JA. Preparing to Prepare, Teacher's Guide, Lincoln, Ne: iUniverse, 2005.

Bailey II, JA. Rising Above Poverty. Livermore, CA: Wing Span Press, 2007

Bailey II, JA. Managing Emotions. Livermore, CA: Wing Span Press, 2007

Bailey II, JA. Selfhood Mastery. Livermore, CA: Wing Span Press, 2007

Bailey II, JA. Self-Esteem in Black Americans, Livermore, CA: Wing Span Press, 2005.

Bailey II, JA. Self-Esteem Masqueraders in Struggling Black Americans; Accepted for publication in the Journal of Black Studies in the Fall of 2005.

Bailey II, JA. Self-Image, Self-Concept, and Self-Identity Revisited. J. Natl. Med. Assoc. 2003; 95: 383-386.

Bailey II, JA. The Concise Dictionary of Medical-Legal Terms; London: The Parthenon Publishing Group, 1998.

Bailey II, JA. Supreme Thinking—Rational, Poetic, & Visionary—of Ancient Africans, Livermore, California: Wing Span Press, 2008. (Wingspanpress.com)

Bailey II, JA. Rational Thinking. Livermore, CA: Wing Span Press, 2008

Bailey II, JA. Special Minds Among Struggling Black Americans. Livermore, CA: Wing Span Press, 2009

Bailey II, JA. The Purpose of Education: in Smylie MA. Why Do We Educate? Voices From The Conversation. Volume 107, Issue 2 Malden, Massachusetts: Wiley-Blackwell 2008

Bartmanski J. Sociology, 2014

Beckman, K. in Asante, Encyclopedia of Black Studies. London: Sage Publications, 2005

Ben-jochannan YAA. Africa Mother of Western Civilization. Baltimore: Black Classic Press 1988

Bingaman, Sharon: Personal Communications

Bynum EB. The African Unconscious. New York: Teachers College Press, 1999.

Campbell J. The Inner Reaches of Outer Space. Novato, California: New World Library 1986

Campbell J. *An Open Life*, New York: Harper and row, 1989.

Bynum, EB: Dark Light Consciousness. Rochester, Vermont: Inner Traditions 2012

Chandler WB. Ancient Future, Atlanta: Black Classic Press, 1999

Claiborne R: *Our Marvelous Native Tongue*, New York Times Books, 1983, 249.

Diop CA: Civilization or Barbarism. Brooklyn, Lawrence Hall Books; 1991.

Diop CA. The African Origin of Civilization. Chicago: Lawrence Hill & Co., 1974.

Diop CA: Great African Thinkers. New Brunswick, New Jersey: Transaction Books, Rutgers—The State University 1986

Donkor AE. *African Spirituality.* Trenton, NJ. Africa World Press, Inc., 1997.

Douglass F: My Bondage and My Freedom. New York: Penguin Books 1855: 53

DuBois WEB. *The Souls of Black*. New York: Gramercy Books, 1994.

Edwards, P. The Encyclopedia of Philosophy, Vol 2. New York: Macmillan Publishing Co., Inc. 1967

Freke T, Candy P. *The Hermetica*, New York, J, P. Tarcher/Putman; 1997.

Gadalla, Moustafa: The Ancient Egyptian Roots of Christianity; Tehuti Research Foundation/ PO Box 39406/ Greensboro, NC 27438-9406

Gaskell GA. *Dictionary of All Scriptures and Myths.* New York: Arenel Books, 1960.

Hodge JL, Struckmann DK, Trost LD. *Cultural Bases of Racism.* Berkeley: Two Riders Press, 1975.

Huggins NI. *Black Odyssey* New York: First Vintage Books Edition 1977.

James GGM. *Stolen Legacy*, Trenton, N.J., Africa World Press, Inc., 1954; 88.

Karenga M: Ma'at. Los Angeles: University of Sankore Press, 2006.

King R. *African Origin of Biological Psychiatry*, Hampton, Virginia: U.B. and U.S. Communications Systems, Inc., 1984.

McPherson JM, Holland LB, Banner, Jr., Weiss NJ, Bell MD. Blacks In America Garden City, New York: Anchor Books 1971.

Moore, T. Owens: **Revisited Affect-Symbolic Imagery,** *Journal of Black Psychology* 1996 22: 443).

Nobles in Jones, RL. *Black Psychology,* 2nd ed. New York: Harper and Row Publishers, 1980.

Poe R. Black Spark White Fire. Rocklin, Ca: Prima Publishing 1997

Ramacharaka Y. Raja Yoga, Chicago: The Yogi Publication Society, 1934

Ramacharaka Y. Fourteen Lessons in Yogi Philosophy, Chicago: Yogi Publication Society, 1904: 77.

Ramacharaka Y: Lessons in Gnani Yoga. Chicago: The Yogi Publication Society 1934.

Rand Ayn: *The Ayn Rand Lexicon.* New York: A Meridian Book; 1986

Seleem R. Egyptian Book of the Dead. New York: Sterling Publishing Company 2001

Stockhammer M. Plato Dictionary. New York: Philosophical Library 1963

Three Initiates. The Kybalion. Chicago: The Yogi Publishing Society, 1940.

Tyson ND, Goldsmith D: Origins. New York: W.W. Newton and Company, 2004.

Walker BG: The Woman's Dictionary, New York: Harper Collins Publishers, 1988.

Wells-Wilbon R, Jackson ND, and Schiele JH. Lessons From the Maafa: Rethinking the Legacy of Slain Hip-Hop Icon Tupac Amaru Shakur J. Black Studies March 2010 40: 509-526

Williams C. The Destruction of Black Civilization, Chicago, Third World Press; 1987; 175.

ABOUT THE AUTHOR

If you are truly interested in researching and studying Ancient African Traditions, then you will need to be educated into the true meanings of the words and especially those used by Ancient Africans. To attempt to understand the knowledge from the Ancient Africans using European definitions would be to dilute, pollute and thoroughly misinterpret their messages. To find the essences of their words has been the life-long pursuit of the author, Joseph A. Bailey II, MD. He has quite a list of credentials which include, physician, surgeon, inventor, author, business man, scholar, mentor, educator, lecturer and philanthropist. We can add to his very long list of life achievements, the title of *Lexicographer*—a title well-earned as this is his sixth volume of Lexicons. A lexicographer is defined, in *Webster's New Dictionary*, as "a person who compiles dictionaries". Dr. Bailey's definition is even more specific as to say a lexicographer is "a person who compiles dictionaries of words on a specific subject". The word lexicographer is a 17th century word meaning "about writing words". Dr. Bailey gives us the "big picture" of words to the best of his ability and he does it in the most interesting and educational of ways—he uses Word Stories. His particular interest is in the "Detour" concepts occurring in the course of the history of a word. Dr. Bailey has credited his Mother with the start of his life-long pursuit of bringing clarity to the meaning of words. As he tells the story, his Mother was very interested in Greek Mythology which he, at first, was not. But then something told him to look again at the stories of the mythological Greek gods and their names. With much research, skill, time and patience, Dr. Bailey began to back-track until he found that these were the gods stolen by the Greeks from the Egyptians with the names being changed. Here then began a foundation on which to build. It started him on a path to collect books on words, their meanings now and meanings when they first came into being along with the discussions of how and why they changed over the centuries.

Dr. Bailey now works among his collection of 46 sets of encyclopedias and thousands of books on Etymology, street language, slang, language of Black culture, Art, Music, Sociology, Psychology, Psychiatry and many more. With Dr. Bailey's special mix of knowledge, skill and creativity, his presentation of words makes it possible for those words and meanings to stay with us. The word "legacy" is a good example. The Doctor proposes that "perhaps the word came from the idea of a limb of a tree being separated from the tree yet joined to it. Another name for a limb is a leg and a leg is something to stand on. Whenever a senior citizen hands "legs over to the youth, this will ensure those "legs" will continue to "walk" into the future. In transposing this idea, a legacy is a gift to be delivered from generation to generation, even to those yet unborn. A legacy work is much like transplanting the limb of an apple tree so the new tree can grow to produce its own apples. In the case of human beings, "the limb" or "leg" we leave to the world may be good thoughts, good feelings, good approaches, good methods, good techniques, a good piece of work, a good set of values or insightful visions…. What matters most is that it is beneficial, good and beautiful". How fortunate we are to have this master with us in this life time so we can witness his "legacy" in the making. Part of that legacy includes word stories that pertain to the Ancient Africans and to the Enslaved so that we may get a fuller, deeper understanding of the words we use. Dr. Bailey has brought the same precision and Integrity to the study of words as he did to his Orthopaedic Surgery practice, his teaching youth, mentorship and love for people truly in need. His body of work product, his "legacy" for future generations, stretches out to reach so many in so many different ways. This Lexicographer's articles appear in a local Black newspaper three times a week as they have for more than 25 tears. He continues to write and publish books aimed at the betterment of Black People which are available on line, at the Schomburg Library in New York City, the library at Meharry Medical college in Nashvillle, Tennessee and on his website @ jabaileymd.com. Please come join him as he shares his love of words with the world and makes clear for us the messages of Ancient Africans.

Sharon Bingaman R.N.

Made in United States
Orlando, FL
23 September 2023

37206634R00343